Principles of Marketing

Global Edition

Principles of Marketing 16e

Global Edition

Philip Kotler
Northwestern University

Gary Armstrong
University of North Carolina

PEARSON

Boston Columbus Indianapolis New York San Francisco Amsterdam Cape Town
Dubai London Madrid Milan Munich Paris Montréal Toronto
Delhi Mexico City São Paulo Sydney Hong Kong Seoul Singapore Taipei Tokyo

Editor-in-Chief: Stephanie Wall
Acquisitions Editor: Mark Gaffney
Program Manager Team Lead: Ashley Santora
Program Manager: Jennifer M. Collins
Editorial Assistant: Daniel Petrino
Vice President, Product Marketing: Maggie Moylan
Director of Marketing, Digital Services and Products: Jeanette Koskinas
Executive Product Marketing Manager: Anne Fahlgren
Field Marketing Manager: Lenny Ann Raper
Senior Strategic Marketing Manager: Erin Gardner
Project Manager Team Lead: Judy Leale
Senior Project Manager: Jacqueline A. Martin
Operations Specialist: Carol Melville
Cover Designer: Lumina Datamatics Ltd.
Cover Image: Vasya Kobelev/Shutterstock
Vice President, Director of Digital Strategy & Assessment: Paul Gentile
Senior Manufacturing Controller, Global Edition: Trudy Kimber
Manager, Media Production, Global Edition: M. Vikram Kumar
Acquisitions Editor, Global Edition: Steven Jackson
Assistant Project Editor, Global Edition: Priyanka Shivadas
Manager of Learning Applications: Paul Deluca
Digital Editor: Brian Surette
Digital Studio Manager: Diane Lombardo
Digital Studio Project Manager: Robin Lazrus
Digital Studio Project Manager: Alana Coles
Digital Studio Project Manager: Monique Lawrence
Digital Studio Project Manager: Regina DaSilva
Full-Service Project Management and Composition: S4Carlisle Publishing Services
Printer/Binder: Courier Kendallville
Cover Printer: Courier Kendallville
Text Font: Palatino 9/11.5

Pearson Education Limited
Edinburgh Gate
Harlow
Essex CM20 2JE
England

and Associated Companies throughout the world

Visit us on the World Wide Web at:
www.pearsonglobaleditions.com

Authorized adaptation from the United States edition, entitled Principles of Marketing, 16/e, ISBN 978-0-133-79502-8, by Philip Kotler and Gary Armstrong, published by Pearson Education © 2016.

ISBN 10: 1-292-09248-3
ISBN 13: 978-1-292-09248-5
British Library Cataloguing-in-Publication Data
A catalogue record for this book is available from the British Library

18 17 16
14 13 12 11 10 9 8 7 6 5 4

Typeset by S4Carlisle Publishing Services in Palatino 9/11.5 pt.
Printed and bound in Malaysia (CTP-VVP)

Dedication

To Kathy, Betty, Mandy, Matt, KC, Keri, Delaney, Molly, Macy, and Ben;
and Nancy, Amy, Melissa, and Jessica

Dedication

To Kathy, Betty, Mandy, Matt, K.C., Keri, Delaney, Molly, Macy, and Ben;
and Nancy, Amy, Melissa, and Jessica

ABOUT THE AUTHORS

As a team, Philip Kotler and Gary Armstrong provide a blend of skills uniquely suited to writing an introductory marketing text. Professor Kotler is one of the world's leading authorities on marketing. Professor Armstrong is an award-winning teacher of undergraduate business students. Together, they make the complex world of marketing practical, approachable, and enjoyable.

Philip Kotler is S.C. Johnson & Son Distinguished Professor of International Marketing at the Kellogg School of Management, Northwestern University. He received his master's degree at the University of Chicago and his PhD at M.I.T., both in economics. Dr. Kotler is the author of *Marketing Management* (Pearson), now in its fifteenth edition and the most widely used marketing textbook in graduate schools of business worldwide. He has authored dozens of other successful books and has written more than 100 articles in leading journals. He is the only three-time winner of the coveted Alpha Kappa Psi award for the best annual article in the *Journal of Marketing*.

Professor Kotler was named the first recipient of four major awards: the *Distinguished Marketing Educator of the Year Award* and the *William L. Wilkie "Marketing for a Better World" Award*, both given by the American Marketing Association; the *Philip Kotler Award for Excellence in Health Care Marketing* presented by the Academy for Health Care Services Marketing; and the *Sheth Foundation Medal for Exceptional Contribution to Marketing Scholarship and Practice*. His numerous other major honors include the Sales and Marketing Executives International *Marketing Educator of the Year Award*; The European Association of Marketing Consultants and Trainers *Marketing Excellence Award*; the *Charles Coolidge Parlin Marketing Research Award*; and the *Paul D. Converse Award*, given by the American Marketing Association to honor "outstanding contributions to science in marketing." A recent *Forbes* survey ranks Professor Kotler in the top 10 of the world's most influential business thinkers. And in a recent *Financial Times* poll of 1,000 senior executives across the world, Professor Kotler was ranked as the fourth "most influential business writer/guru" of the twenty-first century.

Dr. Kotler has served as chairman of the College on Marketing of the Institute of Management Sciences, a director of the American Marketing Association, and a trustee of the Marketing Science Institute. He has consulted with many major U.S. and international companies in the areas of marketing strategy and planning, marketing organization, and international marketing. He has traveled and lectured extensively throughout Europe, Asia, and South America, advising companies and governments about global marketing practices and opportunities.

Gary Armstrong is Crist W. Blackwell Distinguished Professor Emeritus of Undergraduate Education in the Kenan-Flagler Business School at the University of North Carolina at Chapel Hill. He holds undergraduate and master's degrees in business from Wayne State University in Detroit, and he received his PhD in marketing from Northwestern University. Dr. Armstrong has contributed numerous articles to leading business journals. As a consultant and researcher, he has worked with many companies on marketing research, sales management, and marketing strategy.

But Professor Armstrong's first love has always been teaching. His long-held Blackwell Distinguished Professorship is the only permanent endowed professorship for distinguished undergraduate teaching at the University of North Carolina at Chapel Hill. He has been very active in the teaching and administration of Kenan-Flagler's undergraduate program. His administrative posts have included Chair of Marketing, Associate Director of the Undergraduate Business Program, Director of the Business Honors Program, and many others. Through the years, he has worked closely with business student groups and has received several UNC campuswide and Business School teaching awards. He is the only repeat recipient of the school's highly regarded Award for Excellence in Undergraduate Teaching, which he received three times. Most recently, Professor Armstrong received the UNC Board of Governors Award for Excellence in Teaching, the highest teaching honor bestowed by the 16-campus University of North Carolina system.

BRIEF CONTENTS

CONTENTS

16 Personal Selling and Sales Promotion 500

17 Direct, Online, Social Media, and Mobile Marketing 532

Part 4: Extending Marketing 566

18 Creating Competitive Advantage 566

19 The Global Marketplace 592

PREFACE

The Sixteenth Edition of Kotler/Armstrong's *Principles of Marketing!* The World Standard in Undergraduate Marketing Education

Across five continents, in more than 40 countries, and in 24 languages, students and professors rely on Kotler/Armstrong's *Principles of Marketing* as the most-trusted source for teaching and learning basic marketing concepts and practices. More than ever, the sixteenth edition introduces new marketing students to the fascinating world of modern marketing in an innovative, complete, and authoritative yet fresh, practical, and enjoyable way. In this sixteenth edition, we've once again added substantial new content and poured over every page, table, figure, fact, and example in order to keep this the best text from which to learn about and teach marketing. Enhanced by MyMarketingLab, our online homework and personalized study tool, the sixteenth edition of *Principles of Marketing* remains the world standard in introductory marketing education.

Marketing: Creating Customer Value and Engagement in the Digital and Social Age

Top marketers share a common goal: putting the consumer at the heart of marketing. Today's marketing is all about creating customer value and engagement in a fast-changing, increasingly digital and social marketplace.

Marketing starts with understanding consumer needs and wants, determining which target markets the organization can serve best, and developing a compelling value proposition by which the organization can attract and grow valued consumers. Then, more than just making a sale, today's marketers want to *engage* customers and build deep customer relationships that make their brands a meaningful part of consumers' conversations and lives. In this digital age, to go along with their tried-and-true traditional marketing methods, marketers have a dazzling set of new customer relationship-building tools—from the Internet, smartphones, and tablets to online, mobile, and social media—for engaging customers anytime, anyplace to shape brand conversations, experiences, and community. If marketers do these things well, they will reap the rewards in terms of market share, profits, and customer equity. In the sixteenth edition of *Principles of Marketing*, you'll learn how *customer value* and *customer engagement* drive every good marketing strategy.

What's New in the Sixteenth Edition?

We've thoroughly revised the sixteenth edition of *Principles of Marketing* to reflect the major trends and forces impacting marketing in this digital age of customer value, engagement, and relationships. Here are just some of the major and continuing changes you'll find in this edition.

- More than any other developments, sweeping new **online, social media, mobile, and other digital technologies** are now affecting how marketers, brands, and customers engage each other. The sixteenth edition features new and revised discussions and examples of the explosive impact of exciting *new digital marketing technologies* shaping marketing strategy and practice—from online, mobile, and social media engagement technologies discussed in Chapters 1, 5, 13, 14, 15, and 17; to "real-time listening" and "big data" research tools in Chapter 4, online influence and brand communities in Chapter 5, and location-based marketing in Chapter 7; to the use of social media and social selling in business-to-business marketing in Chapters 6 and 16; to consumer Web, social media, mobile marketing, and other new communications technologies in Chapters 1, 5, 14, 15, 17, and throughout the text.

A new Chapter 1 section on *The Digital Age: Online, Mobile, and Social Media Marketing* introduces the exciting new developments in digital and social media marketing. A completely revised Chapter 17 on *Direct, Online, Social Media, and Mobile Marketing* digs deeply into digital marketing tools such as online sites, social media, mobile ads and apps, online video, e-mail, blogs, and other digital platforms that engage consumers anywhere, anytime via their computers, smartphones, tablets, Internet-ready TVs, and other digital devices. The sixteenth edition is packed with new stories and examples illustrating how companies employ digital technology to gain competitive advantage—from traditional marketing all-stars such as Nike, P&G, Coca-Cola, Walmart, IBM, and McDonald's to new-age digital competitors such as Google, Amazon, Apple, Netflix, Pinterest, and Facebook.

- The sixteenth edition features completely new and revised coverage of the emerging trend toward **customer engagement marketing**—building direct and continuous customer involvement in shaping brands, brand conversations, brand experiences, and brand community. The burgeoning Internet and social media have created better informed, more connected, and more empowered consumers. Thus, today's marketers must now *engage* consumers rather than interrupt them. Marketers are augmenting their mass-media marketing efforts with a rich mix of online, mobile, and social media marketing that promote deep consumer involvement and a sense of customer community surrounding their brands. Today's **new customer engagement-building tools** include everything from online sites, blogs, in-person events, and video sharing to online communities and social media such as Facebook, YouTube, Pinterest, Vine, Twitter, or a company's own social networking sites.

  In all, today's more engaged consumers are giving as much as they get in the form of two-way brand relationships. The sixteenth edition contains substantial new material on **customer engagement** and related developments such as **consumer empowerment, crowdsourcing, customer co-creation, consumer-generated marketing**, and **real-time marketing**. A new Chapter 1 section—*Engaging Customers*—introduces customer engagement marketing. This and other related customer engagement topics are presented in Chapter 1 (new or revised sections on *Customer Engagement and Today's Digital and Social Media* and *Consumer-Generated Marketing*); Chapter 4 (big data and real-time research to gain deeper customer insights); Chapter 5 (managing online influence and customer community through digital and social media marketing); Chapter 13 (online, social media, and digitized retailing); Chapter 9 (crowdsourcing and customer-driven new-product development); Chapters 14 and 15 (the new, more engaging marketing communications model and *content marketing*); and Chapter 17 (direct digital, online, social media, and mobile marketing).
- The sixteenth edition continues to build on and extend the innovative **customer-value framework** from previous editions. The customer value and engagement model presented in the first chapter is fully integrated throughout the remainder of the book. No other marketing text presents such a clear and compelling customer-value approach.
- The sixteenth edition provides revised and expanded coverage of developments in the fast-changing area of **integrated marketing communications**. It tells how marketers are **blending traditional media with new digital and social media** tools—everything from Internet and mobile marketing to blogs, viral videos, and social media—to create more targeted, personal, and engaging customer relationships. Marketers are no longer simply creating integrated promotion programs; they are practicing **content marketing** in paid, owned, earned, and shared media. No other text provides more current or encompassing coverage of these exciting developments.
- New material throughout the sixteenth edition highlights the increasing importance of **sustainable marketing**. The discussion begins in Chapter 1 and ends in Chapter 20, which pulls marketing together under a sustainable marketing framework. In between, frequent discussions and examples show how sustainable marketing calls for socially and environmentally responsible actions that meet both the immediate and the future needs of customers, companies, and society as a whole.

- The sixteenth edition provides new discussions and examples of the growth in **global marketing**. As the world becomes a smaller, more competitive place, marketers face new global marketing challenges and opportunities, especially in fast-growing emerging markets such as China, India, Brazil, Africa, and others. You'll find much new coverage of global marketing throughout the text, starting in Chapter 1; the topic is discussed fully in Chapter 19.
- The sixteenth edition continues its emphasis on **measuring and managing return on marketing**, including many new end-of-chapter financial and quantitative marketing exercises that let students apply analytical thinking to relevant concepts in each chapter and link chapter concepts to the text's innovative and comprehensive Appendix 2: *Marketing by the Numbers*.
- The sixteenth edition continues to improve on its **innovative learning design**. The text's active and integrative presentation includes learning enhancements such as annotated chapter-opening stories, a chapter-opening objective outline, and explanatory author comments on major chapter sections and figures. The chapter-opening layout helps to preview and position the chapter and its key concepts. Figures annotated with author comments help students to simplify and organize chapter material. End-of-chapter features help to summarize important chapter concepts and highlight important themes, such as **digital and social media marketing**, **marketing ethics**, and **financial marketing analysis**. This innovative learning design facilitates student understanding and eases learning.
- The sixteenth edition provides 20 new or revised end-of-chapter company cases by which students can apply what they learn to actual company situations. The sixteenth edition also features 20 video cases, with brief end-of-chapter summaries and discussion questions. Finally, all of the chapter-opening stories and Real Marketing highlights in the sixteenth edition are either new or revised to maintain currency.

Five Major Customer Value and Engagement Themes

The sixteenth edition of *Principles of Marketing* builds on five major value and customer engagement themes:

1. *Creating value for customers in order to capture value from customers in return.* Today's marketers must be good at *creating customer value, engaging customers,* and *managing customer relationships*. Outstanding marketing companies understand the marketplace and customer needs, design value-creating marketing strategies, develop integrated marketing programs that engage customers and deliver value and satisfaction, and build strong customer relationships and brand community. In return, they capture value from customers in the form of sales, profits, and customer equity.

   This innovative *customer-value and engagement framework* is introduced at the start of Chapter 1 in a five-step marketing process model, which details how marketing *creates* customer value and *captures* value in return. The framework is carefully developed in the first two chapters and then fully integrated throughout the remainder of the text.
2. *Customer engagement and today's digital and social media.* New digital and social media have taken today's marketing by storm, dramatically changing how companies and brands engage consumers, as well as how consumers connect and influence each other's brand behaviors. The sixteenth edition introduces and thoroughly explores the contemporary concept of *customer engagement marketing* and the exciting new digital and social media technologies that help brands to engage customers more deeply and interactively. It starts with two major new Chapter 1 sections: *Customer Engagement and Today's Digital and Social Media* and *The Digital Age: Online, Mobile, and Social Media Marketing*. A completely revised Chapter 17 on *Direct, Online, Social Media, and Mobile Marketing* summarizes the latest developments in digital engagement and relationship-building tools. Everywhere in-between, you'll find revised and expanded coverage of the exploding use of digital and social tools to create customer engagement and build brand community.
3. *Building and managing strong, value-creating brands.* Well-positioned brands with strong brand equity provide the basis upon which to build customer value and profitable customer relationships. Today's marketers must position their brands powerfully and

manage them well to create valued brand experiences. The sixteenth edition provides a deep focus on brands, anchored by a Chapter 8 section on *Branding Strategy: Building Strong Brands*.

4. *Measuring and managing return on marketing.* Especially in uneven economic times, marketing managers must ensure that their marketing dollars are being well spent. In the past, many marketers spent freely on big, expensive marketing programs, often without thinking carefully about the financial returns on their spending. But all that has changed rapidly. "Marketing accountability"—measuring and managing marketing return on investment—has now become an important part of strategic marketing decision making. This emphasis on marketing accountability is addressed in Chapter 2, Appendix 2: *Marketing by the Numbers*, and throughout the sixteenth edition.
5. *Sustainable marketing around the globe.* As technological developments make the world an increasingly smaller and more fragile place, marketers must be good at marketing their brands globally and in sustainable ways. New material throughout the sixteenth edition emphasizes the concepts of global marketing and sustainable marketing—meeting the present needs of consumers and businesses while also preserving or enhancing the ability of future generations to meet their needs. The sixteenth edition integrates global marketing and sustainability topics throughout the text. It then provides focused coverage on each topic in Chapters 19 and 20, respectively.

An Emphasis on Real Marketing and Bringing Marketing to Life

Principles of Marketing, sixteenth edition, takes a practical marketing-management approach, providing countless in-depth, real-life examples and stories that engage students with marketing concepts and bring modern marketing to life. In the sixteenth edition, every chapter includes an engaging opening story plus *Real Marketing* highlights that provide fresh insights into real marketing practices. Learn how:

- Nike's outstanding success results from more than just making and selling good sports gear. It's based on a customer-focused strategy through which Nike creates brand engagement and close brand community with and among its customers.
- At T-shirt and apparel maker Life is good, engagement and social media are about building meaningful customer engagement, measured by the depth of consumer commenting and community that surround the brand.
- Chipotle's sustainability mission isn't an add-on, created just to position the company as "socially responsible"—doing good is ingrained in everything the company does.
- Sony's dizzying fall from market leadership provides a cautionary tale of what can happen when a company—even a dominant marketing leader—fails to adapt to its changing environment.
- Netflix uses "big data" to personalize each customer's viewing experience; while Netflix subscribers are busy watching videos, Netflix is busy watching *them*—very, very closely.
- Giant social network Facebook promises to become one of the world's most powerful and profitable digital marketers—but it's just getting started.
- Wildly innovative Google has become an incredibly successful new product "moonshot factory," unleashing a seemingly unending flurry of diverse products, most of which are market leaders in their categories.
- Retail giants Walmart and Amazon are fighting it out in a pitched price war for online supremacy.
- Direct marketing insurance giant GEICO has gone from bit player to behemoth thanks to a big-budget advertising campaign featuring a smooth-talking gecko and an enduring "15 minutes could save you 15 percent" tagline.
- The explosion of the Internet, social media, mobile devices, and other technologies has some marketers asking: "Who needs face-to-face selling anymore?"
- Under its "Conscious Consumption" mission, outdoor apparel and gear maker Patagonia takes sustainability to new extremes by telling consumers to buy *less*.

Beyond such features, each chapter is packed with countless real, engaging, and timely examples that reinforce key concepts. No other text brings marketing to life like the sixteenth edition of *Principles of Marketing*.

Learning Aids That Create Value and Engagement

A wealth of chapter-opening, within-chapter, and end-of-chapter learning devices help students to learn, link, and apply major concepts:

- *Integrated chapter-opening preview sections.* The active and integrative chapter-opening spread in each chapter starts with a *Chapter Preview,* which briefly previews chapter concepts, links them with previous chapter concepts, and introduces the chapter-opening story. This leads to a chapter-opening vignette—an engaging, deeply developed, illustrated, and annotated marketing story that introduces the chapter material and sparks student interest. Finally, an *Objective Outline* provides a helpful preview of chapter contents and learning objectives, complete with page numbers.
- *Real Marketing highlights.* Each chapter contains two carefully developed highlight features that provide an in-depth look at real marketing practices of large and small companies.
- *Author comments and figure annotations.* Throughout each chapter, author comments ease and enhance student learning by introducing and explaining major text sections and organizing figures.
- *Objectives Review and Key Terms.* A summary at the end of each chapter reviews major chapter concepts, chapter objectives, and key terms.
- *Discussion Questions and Critical Thinking Exercises.* Sections at the end of each chapter help students to keep track of and apply what they've learned in the chapter.
- *Applications and Cases.* Brief *Online, Mobile, and Social Media Marketing; Marketing Ethics;* and *Marketing by the Numbers* sections at the end of each chapter provide short application cases that facilitate discussion of current issues and company situations in areas such as mobile and social marketing, ethics, and financial marketing analysis. A *Video Case* section contains short vignettes with discussion questions to be used with a set of 4- to 7-minute videos that accompany the sixteenth edition. End-of-chapter *Company Case* sections provide all-new or revised company cases that help students to apply major marketing concepts to real company and brand situations.
- *Marketing Plan appendix.* Appendix 1 contains a sample marketing plan that helps students to apply important marketing planning concepts.
- *Marketing by the Numbers appendix.* The innovative Appendix 2 provides students with a comprehensive introduction to the marketing financial analysis that helps to guide, assess, and support marketing decisions. An exercise at the end of each chapter lets students apply analytical and financial thinking to relevant chapter concepts and links the chapter to the *Marketing by the Numbers* appendix.

More than ever before, the sixteenth edition of *Principles of Marketing* creates value and engagement for you—it gives you all you need to know about marketing in an effective and enjoyable total learning package!

A Total Teaching and Learning Package

A successful marketing course requires more than a well-written book. Today's classroom requires a dedicated teacher, well-prepared students, and a fully integrated teaching system. A total package of teaching and learning supplements extends this edition's emphasis on creating value and engagement for both the student and instructor. The following aids support *Principles of Marketing,* sixteenth edition.

Instructor Resources

At the Instructor Resource Center, www.pearsonglobaleditions.com/Kotler, instructors can easily register to gain access to a variety of instructor resources available with this text in downloadable format. If assistance is needed, a dedicated technical support team is ready to help with the media supplements that accompany the text. Visit http://247.pearsoned.com for answers to frequently asked questions and toll-free user support phone numbers.

The following supplements are available with this text:

- **Instructor's Resource Manual**
- **Test Bank**
- **TestGen® Computerized Test Bank**
- **PowerPoint Presentation**

Learning Aids That Create Value and Engagement

A wealth of chapter-opening, within-chapter, and end-of-chapter learning devices help students to learn, link, and apply major concepts:

- *Integrated chapter-opening preview sections.* The active and integrative chapter-opening spread in each chapter starts with a *Chapter Preview*, which briefly previews chapter concepts, links them with previous chapter concepts, and introduces the chapter-opening story. This leads to a chapter-opening vignette—an engaging, deeply developed, illustrated, and annotated marketing story that introduces the chapter material and sparks student interest. Finally, an *Objective Outline* provides a helpful preview of chapter contents and learning objectives, complete with page numbers.
- *Real Marketing highlights.* Each chapter contains two carefully developed highlight features that provide an in-depth look at real marketing practices of large and small companies.
- *Author comments and figure annotations.* Throughout each chapter, author comments ease and enhance student learning by introducing and explaining major text sections and organizing figures.
- *Objectives Review and Key Terms.* A summary at the end of each chapter reviews major chapter concepts, chapter objectives, and key terms.
- *Discussion Questions and Critical Thinking Exercises.* Sections at the end of each chapter help students to keep track of and apply what they've learned in the chapter.
- *Applications and Cases.* Brief *Online, Mobile, and Social Media Marketing*, *Marketing Ethics*, and *Marketing by the Numbers* sections at the end of each chapter provide short application cases that facilitate discussion of current issues and company situations in areas such as mobile and social marketing, ethics, and financial marketing analysis. A *Video Case* section contains short vignettes with discussion questions to be used with a set of 4- to 7-minute videos that accompany the sixteenth edition. End-of-chapter *Company Case* sections provide all-new or revised company cases that help students to apply major marketing concepts to real company and brand situations.
- *Marketing Plan appendix.* Appendix 1 contains a sample marketing plan that helps students to apply important marketing planning concepts.
- *Marketing by the Numbers appendix.* The innovative Appendix 2 provides students with a comprehensive introduction to the marketing financial analysis that helps to guide, assess, and support marketing decisions. An exercise at the end of each chapter lets students apply analytical and financial thinking to relevant chapter concepts and links the chapter to the *Marketing by the Numbers* appendix.

More than ever before, the sixteenth edition of *Principles of Marketing* creates value and engagement for you—it gives you all you need to know about marketing in an effective and enjoyable total learning package!

A Total Teaching and Learning Package

A successful marketing course requires more than a well-written book. Today's classroom requires a dedicated teacher, well-prepared students, and a fully integrated teaching system. A total package of teaching and learning supplements extends this edition's emphasis on creating value and engagement for both the student and instructor. The following aids support *Principles of Marketing*, sixteenth edition.

Instructor Resources

At the Instructor Resource Center, www.pearsonglobaleditions.com/Kotler, instructors can easily register to gain access to a variety of instructor resources available with this text in downloadable format. If assistance is needed, a dedicated technical support team is ready to help with the media supplements that accompany the text. Visit http://247.pearsoned.com for answers to frequently asked questions and toll-free user support phone numbers.

The following supplements are available with this text:

- Instructor's Resource Manual
- Test Bank
- TestGen® Computerized Test Bank
- PowerPoint Presentation

ACKNOWLEDGMENTS

No book is the work only of its authors. We greatly appreciate the valuable contributions of several people who helped make this new edition possible. As always, we owe very special thanks to Keri Jean Miksza for her dedicated and valuable help in *all* phases of the project, and to her husband Pete and daughters Lucy and Mary for all the support they provided Keri during this very absorbing project.

We owe substantial thanks to Andy Norman of Drake University for his skillful help in developing chapter vignettes and highlights, company and video cases, and the Marketing Plan appendix. This edition, as well as the previous editions, have benefited greatly from Andy's assistance. We also thank Laurie Babin of the University of Louisiana at Monroe for her dedicated efforts in preparing end-of-chapter materials and for keeping our Marketing by the Numbers appendix fresh. Additional thanks go to Carol Davis at California State University Monterey Bay for her work in updating the Instructor's Manual and Test Item File, and to Douglas Martin at Forsyth Technical Community College for updating the PowerPoint slides. Finally, we'd like to thank the professors who assisted with our work on MyMarketingLab: George D. Deitz, The University of Memphis; Barbara S. Faries, Mission College, Santa Clara; Todd Korol, Monroe Community College; Lori Olson, San Diego State University; and Julia Wells, University of San Diego. All of these contributors are greatly appreciated in making the sixteenth edition of *Principles of Marketing* a robust teaching and learning system.

Many reviewers at other colleges and universities provided valuable comments and suggestions for this and previous editions. We are indebted to the following colleagues for their thoughtful input:

Sixteenth Edition Reviewers

Sucheta Ahlawat, Kean University
Darrell E. Bartholomew, Rider University
Leta Beard, University of Washington
Christopher P. Blocker, Colorado State University
Kathryn Boys, Virginia Tech
Christina Chung, Ramapo College of New Jersey
Ed Chung, Elizabethtown College
Marianne Collins, Winona State University
Deborah L. Cowles, Virginia Commonwealth University
Patti Diggin, West Chester University of Pennsylvania
Frank Franzak, Virginia Commonwealth University
George J. Gannage Jr., Embry Riddle Aeronautical University
David A. Gilliam, University of Arkansas at Little Rock
Deborah M. Gray, Central Michigan University
Amy Handlin, Monmouth University
James Heyman, University of St. Thomas
Ken Knox, Eastern Gateway Community College
Ann T. Kuzma, Minnesota State University, Mankato
Geoffrey P. Lantos, Stonehill College
Yun Jung Lee, Adelphi University
Carolyn A. Massiah, University of Central Florida
Ed Petkus Jr., Ramapo College of New Jersey
James Sawhill, Washington University–Missouri
Mid Semple, SUNY Broome
Shweta Singh, Kean University
Michaeline Skiba, Monmouth University
Joseph G. Slifko Jr., Pennsylvania Highlands Community College
Susan D. Williams, New Jersey City University
Poh-Lin Yeoh, Bentley University

Fifteenth Edition Reviewers

Greg Black, Metropolitan State University of Denver
Rod Carveth, Naugatuck Valley Community College
Linda Morable, Richland College
Randy Moser, Elon University
David Murphy, Madisonville Community College
Donna Waldron, Manchester Community College
Douglas Witt, Brigham Young University

Fourteenth Edition Reviewers

Rod Carveth, Naugatuck Valley Community College
Anindja Chatterjee, Slippery Rock University of Pennsylvania
Mary Conran, Temple University
Eloise Coupey, Virginia Tech
Alan Dick, University of Buffalo
Karen Gore, Ivy Tech Community College, Evansville Campus
Charles Lee, Chestnut Hill College
Samuel McNeely, Murray State University
Chip Miller, Drake University
David Murphy, Madisonville Community College
Esther Page-Wood, Western Michigan University
Tim Reisenwitz, Valdosta State University
Mary Ellen Rosetti, Hudson Valley Community College
William Ryan, University of Connecticut
Roberta Schultz, Western Michigan University
J. Alexander Smith, Oklahoma City University
Deb Utter, Boston University
Donna Waldron, Manchester Community College
Wendel Weaver, Oklahoma Wesleyan University

We also owe a great deal to the people at Pearson Education who helped develop this book. Senior Acquisitions Editor Mark Gaffney provided fresh ideas and support during the revision. Senior Project Manager Jacqueline Martin and Program Manager Jennifer Collins provided valuable assistance and advice in guiding this complex revision project through development, design, and production. We'd also like to thank Stephanie Wall, Judy Leale, Anne Fahlgren, Erin Gardner, Lenny Ann Raper, and Daniel Petrino for their able assistance along the way. We are proud to be associated with the fine professionals at Pearson. We also owe a mighty debt of gratitude to Project Manager Roxanne Klaas and the fine team at S4Carlisle Publishing Services.

Finally, we owe many thanks to our families for all of their support and encouragement—Kathy, Betty, Mandy, Matt, KC, Keri, Delaney, Molly, Macy, and Ben from the Armstrong clan and Nancy, Amy, Melissa, and Jessica from the Kotler family. We dedicate this book to them.

Gary Armstrong
Philip Kotler

Pearson gratefully acknowledges and thanks the following people for their work on the Global Edition:

Sixteen Edition Contributors

Jon Sutherland, writer, UK
Diane Sutherland, writer, UK
Geoff Fripp, University of Sydney
Hamed M. Shamma, The American University in Cairo
Dimple Mirpuri, CCCU City University of Hong Kong
Serdar Sayman, Koç University
Gert-Jan Hospers, University of Twente & Radboud University
Sophie Yang, Coventry University
Aykan Candemir, Ege University

Sixteen Edition Reviewers

Ronan Jouan de Kervenoael, Aston Business School
Johnny Chiu Sik Leung, Hong Kong Institute of Vocational Education (Tsing Yi)
Patrick Poon, Lingnan University
Jie Liu, Manchester Metropolitan University
Ayantunji Gbadamosi, University of East London
Yim Frederick H K, Hong Kong Baptist University
Lailani L. Alcantara, Ritsumeikan Asia Pacific University

Principles of Marketing

Global Edition

1 Marketing
Creating Customer Value and Engagement

Chapter Preview This chapter introduces you to the basic concepts of marketing. We start with the question: What is marketing? Simply put, marketing is engaging customers and managing profitable customer relationships. The aim of marketing is to create value for customers in order to capture value from customers in return. Next we discuss the five steps in the marketing process—from understanding customer needs, to designing customer value-driven marketing strategies and integrated marketing programs, to building customer relationships and capturing value for the firm. Finally, we discuss the major trends and forces affecting marketing in this new age of digital, mobile, and social media. Understanding these basic concepts and forming your own ideas about what they really mean to you will provide a solid foundation for all that follows.

Let's start with a good story about marketing in action at Amazon.com, by far the world's leading online and digital marketer. The secret to Amazon's success? It's really no secret at all. Amazon is flat-out customer obsessed. It has a deep-down passion for creating customer engagement, value, and relationships. In return, customers reward Amazon with their buying dollars and loyalty. You'll see this theme of creating customer value in order to capture value in return repeated throughout this chapter and the remainder of the text.

AMAZON.COM: Obsessed with Creating Customer Value and Relationships

When you think of shopping online, chances are good that you think first of Amazon. The online pioneer first opened its virtual doors in 1995, selling books out of founder Jeff Bezos's garage in suburban Seattle. Amazon still sells books—lots and lots of books. But it now sells just about everything else as well, from music, electronics, tools, housewares, apparel, and groceries to fashions, loose diamonds, and Maine lobsters.

From the start, Amazon has grown explosively. Its annual sales have rocketed from a modest $150 million in 1997 to more than $74 billion today. During just the past three years, Amazon's revenues have more than doubled. This past Cyber Monday alone, Amazon.com sold 37 million items to its 237 million active customers worldwide—that's 428 items per second. Amazon's revenues will likely reach $100 billion within the next year, faster to that mark than any other company in history (it took Walmart 34 years). That would make it the nation's second-largest retailer, trailing only Walmart.

What has made Amazon such an amazing success story? Founder and CEO Bezos puts it in three simple words: "Obsess over customers." To its core, the company is relentlessly customer driven. "The thing that drives everything is creating genuine value for customers," says Bezos. Amazon believes that if it does what's good for customers, profits will follow. So the company starts with the customer and works backward. Rather than asking what it can do with its current capabilities, Amazon first asks: Who are our customers? What do they need? Then, it develops whatever capabilities are required to meet those customer needs.

At Amazon, every decision is made with an eye toward improving the Amazon.com customer experience. In fact, at many Amazon meetings, the most influential figure in the room is "the empty chair"—literally an empty chair at the table that represents the all-important customer. At times, the empty chair isn't empty, but is occupied by a "Customer Experience Bar Raiser,"

Amazon.com's deep-down passion for creating customer engagement, value, and relationships has made it the world's leading online retailer. Amazon has become the model for companies that are obsessively and successfully focused on delivering customer value.

an employee who is specially trained to represent customers' interests. To give the empty chair a loud, clear voice, Amazon relentlessly tracks performance against nearly 400 measurable customer-related goals.

Amazon's obsession with serving the needs of its customers drives the company to take risks and innovate in ways that other companies don't. For example, when it noted that its book-buying customers needed better access to e-books and other digital content, Amazon developed the Kindle e-reader, its first-ever original product. The Kindle took more than four years and a whole new set of skills to develop. But Amazon's start-with-the-customer thinking paid off handsomely. The Kindle is one of the company's best-selling products, and Amazon.com now sells more e-books than hardcovers and paperbacks combined. What's more, the company's growing line of Kindle Fire tablets now leads the market for low-priced tablet computers. Thus, what started as an effort to improve the customer experience now gives Amazon a powerful presence in the burgeoning world of digital, mobile, and social media. Not only does the Kindle allow access to e-books, music, videos, and apps sold by Amazon, it makes interacting with the online giant easier than ever. Customers use their Kindles to shop at Amazon.com and interact with the company on its blogs and social media pages.

Perhaps more important than *what* Amazon sells is *how* it sells. Amazon wants to deliver a special experience to every customer. Most Amazon.com regulars feel a surprisingly strong relationship with the company, especially given the almost complete lack of actual human interaction. Amazon obsesses over making each customer's experience uniquely personal. For example, the Amazon.com site greets customers with their very own home pages, complete with personalized recommendations. Amazon was the first company to sift through each customer's past purchases and browsing histories and the purchasing patterns of customers with similar profiles to come up with personalized site content. Amazon wants to personalize the shopping experience for each individual customer. If it has 237 million customers, it reasons, it should have 237 million stores.

Visitors to Amazon.com receive a unique blend of benefits: huge selection, good value, low prices, and convenience. But it's the "discovery" factor that makes the buying experience really special. Once on the Amazon.com site, you're compelled to stay for a while—looking, learning, and discovering. Amazon.com has become a kind of online community in which customers can browse for products, research purchase alternatives, share opinions and reviews with other visitors, and chat online with authors and experts. In this way, Amazon does much more than just sell goods online. It engages customers and creates direct, personalized customer relationships and satisfying online experiences. Year after year, Amazon places at or near the top of almost every customer satisfaction ranking, regardless of industry.

Based on its powerful growth, many analysts have speculated that Amazon will become the Walmart of the Web. In fact, some argue, it already is. Although Walmart's total sales of $469 billion dwarf Amazon's $74 billion in sales, Amazon's online sales are more than seven times greater than Walmart's. So online, it's Walmart that's chasing Amazon. Put another way, Walmart wants to become the Amazon of the Web, not the other way around. However, despite its mammoth proportions, to catch Amazon online, Walmart will have to match the superb Amazon.com customer experience, and that won't be easy.

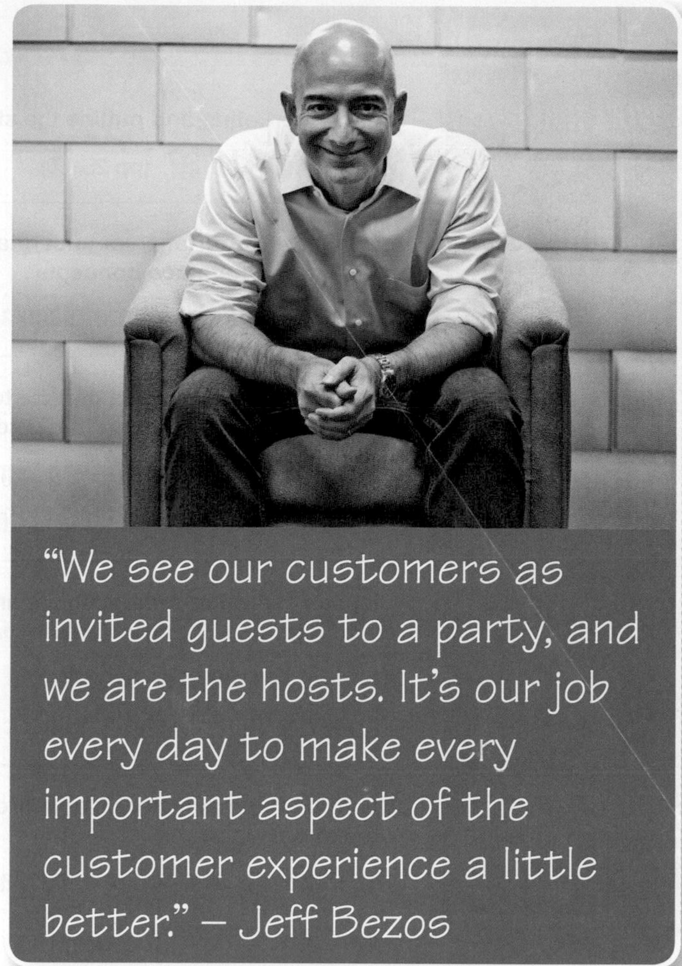

"We see our customers as invited guests to a party, and we are the hosts. It's our job every day to make every important aspect of the customer experience a little better." – Jeff Bezos

Amazon.com does much more than just sell goods online. It creates satisfying online customer experiences. "The thing that drives everything is creating genuine value for customers," says Amazon founder and CEO Jeff Bezos, shown above.
Contour by Getty Images

Whatever the eventual outcome, Amazon has become the poster child for companies that are obsessively and successfully focused on delivering customer value. Jeff Bezos has known from the very start that if Amazon creates superior value for customers, it will earn their business and loyalty, and success will follow in terms of company sales and returns. As Bezos puts it, "When things get complicated, we simplify them by asking, 'What's best for the customer?' We believe that if we do that, things will work out in the long term."[1]

Objective Outline

Today's successful companies have one thing in common: Like Amazon, they are strongly customer focused and heavily committed to marketing. These companies share a passion for understanding and satisfying customer needs in well-defined target markets. They motivate everyone in the organization to help build lasting customer relationships based on creating value.

Customer relationships and value are especially important today. Facing dramatic technological advances and deep economic, social, and environmental challenges, today's customers are relating digitally with companies and each other, spending more carefully, and reassessing how they engage with brands. New digital, mobile, and social media developments have revolutionized how consumers shop and interact, in turn calling for new marketing strategies and tactics. In these fast-changing times, it's now more important than ever to build strong customer relationships based on real and enduring customer value.

We'll discuss the exciting new challenges facing both customers and marketers later in the chapter. But first, let's introduce the basics of marketing.

Author Comment | Pause here and think about how you'd answer this question before studying marketing. Then see how your answer changes as you read the chapter.

What Is Marketing?

Marketing, more than any other business function, deals with customers. Although we will soon explore more-detailed definitions of marketing, perhaps the simplest definition is this one: *Marketing is engaging customers and managing profitable customer relationships.* The two-fold goal of marketing is to attract new customers by promising superior value and to keep and grow current customers by delivering satisfaction.

For example, McDonald's fulfills its "i'm lovin' it" motto by being "our customers' favorite place and way to eat" the world over, giving it nearly as much market share as its nearest four competitors combined. Walmart has become the world's largest retailer—and the world's largest *company*—by delivering on its promise, "Save Money. Live Better." Facebook has attracted more than a billion active Web and mobile users worldwide by helping them to "connect and share with the people in their lives."

Sound marketing is critical to the success of every organization. Large for-profit firms, such as Google, Target, Procter & Gamble, Coca-Cola, and Microsoft, use marketing. But so do not-for-profit organizations, such as colleges, hospitals, museums, symphony orchestras, and even churches.

Marketing is all around you, in good old traditional forms and in a host of new forms, from Web sites and mobile phone apps to videos and online social media.

Justin Lewis

You already know a lot about marketing—it's all around you. Marketing comes to you in the good old traditional forms: You see it in the abundance of products at your nearby shopping mall and the ads that fill your TV screen, spice up your magazines, or stuff your mailbox. But in recent years, marketers have assembled a host of new marketing approaches, everything from imaginative Web sites and mobile phone apps to blogs, online videos, and social media. These new approaches do more than just blast out messages to the masses. They reach you directly, personally, and interactively. Today's marketers want to become a part of your life and enrich your experiences with their brands—to help you *live* their brands.

At home, at school, where you work, and where you play, you see marketing in almost everything you do. Yet, there is much more to marketing than meets the consumer's casual eye. Behind it all is a massive network of people, technologies, and activities competing for your attention and purchases. This book will give you a complete introduction to the basic concepts and practices of today's marketing. In this chapter, we begin by defining marketing and the marketing process.

Marketing Defined

What *is* marketing? Many people think of marketing as only selling and advertising. We are bombarded every day with TV commercials, catalogs, spiels from salespeople, and online pitches. However, selling and advertising are only the tip of the marketing iceberg.

Today, marketing must be understood not in the old sense of making a sale—"telling and selling"—but in the new sense of *satisfying customer needs.* If the marketer engages consumers effectively, understands their needs, develops products that provide superior customer value, and prices, distributes, and promotes them well, these products will sell easily. In fact, according to management guru Peter Drucker, "The aim of marketing is to make selling unnecessary."[2] Selling and advertising are only part of a larger *marketing mix*—a set of marketing tools that work together to engage customers, satisfy customer needs, and build customer relationships.

Marketing
The process by which companies create value for customers and build strong customer relationships in order to capture value from customers in return.

Broadly defined, marketing is a social and managerial process by which individuals and organizations obtain what they need and want through creating and exchanging value with others. In a narrower business context, marketing involves building profitable, value-laden exchange relationships with customers. Hence, we define **marketing** as the process by which companies create value for customers and build strong customer relationships in order to capture value from customers in return.[3]

The Marketing Process

Figure 1.1 presents a simple, five-step model of the marketing process for creating and capturing customer value. In the first four steps, companies work to understand consumers, create customer value, and build strong customer relationships. In the final step, companies reap the rewards of creating superior customer value. By creating value *for* consumers, they in turn capture value *from* consumers in the form of sales, profits, and long-term customer equity.

In this chapter and the next, we will examine the steps of this simple model of marketing. In this chapter, we review each step but focus more on the customer relationship steps—understanding customers, engaging and building relationships with customers, and capturing value from customers. In Chapter 2, we look more deeply into the second and third steps—designing value-creating marketing strategies and constructing marketing programs.

Author Comment | Marketing is all about creating value for customers. So, as the first step in the marketing process, the company must fully understand consumers and the marketplace in which it operates.

Understanding the Marketplace and Customer Needs

As a first step, marketers need to understand customer needs and wants and the marketplace in which they operate. We examine five core customer and marketplace concepts: (1) *needs, wants, and demands*; (2) *market offerings (products, services, and experiences)*; (3) *value and satisfaction*; (4) *exchanges and relationships*; and (5) *markets.*

Customer Needs, Wants, and Demands

Needs
States of felt deprivation.

Wants
The form human needs take as they are shaped by culture and individual personality.

Demands
Human wants that are backed by buying power.

The most basic concept underlying marketing is that of human needs. Human **needs** are states of felt deprivation. They include basic *physical* needs for food, clothing, warmth, and safety; *social* needs for belonging and affection; and *individual* needs for knowledge and self-expression. Marketers did not create these needs; they are a basic part of the human makeup.

Wants are the form human needs take as they are shaped by culture and individual personality. An American *needs* food but *wants* a Big Mac, french fries, and a soft drink. A person in Papua, New Guinea, *needs* food but *wants* taro, rice, yams, and pork. Wants are shaped by one's society and are described in terms of objects that will satisfy those needs. When backed by buying power, wants become **demands**. Given their wants and resources, people demand products and services with benefits that add up to the most value and satisfaction.

Outstanding marketing companies go to great lengths to learn about and understand their customers' needs, wants, and demands. They conduct consumer research, analyze mountains of customer data, and observe customers as they shop and interact, offline and online. People at all levels of the company—including top management—stay close to customers:[4]

Walmart president and CEO Michael Duke and his entire executive team make regular store and in-home visits with customers to get to know them and understand their needs. Top McDonald's marketers hold frequent Twitter chats, connecting directly with McDonald's Twitter followers, both fans and critics, to learn their thoughts about topics ranging from nutrition and sustainability to products and brand promotions. And Boston Market CEO George Michel makes frequent visits to company restaurants, working in the dining room and engaging customers to learn about "the good, the bad, and the ugly." He also stays connected by reading customer messages on the Boston Market Web site and has even cold-called customers for insights. "Being close to the customer is critically important," says Michel. "I get to learn what they value, what they appreciate."

Staying close to customers: Boston Market CEO George Michel frequently visits the company's restaurants, working in the dining room and engaging customers to learn about "the good, the bad, and the ugly."
Invision for Boston Market

Market Offerings—Products, Services, and Experiences

Consumers' needs and wants are fulfilled through **market offerings**—some combination of products, services, information, or experiences offered to a market to satisfy a need or a want. Market offerings are not limited to physical *products.* They also include *services*—activities or benefits offered for

FIGURE | 1.1
The Marketing Process: Creating and Capturing Customer Value

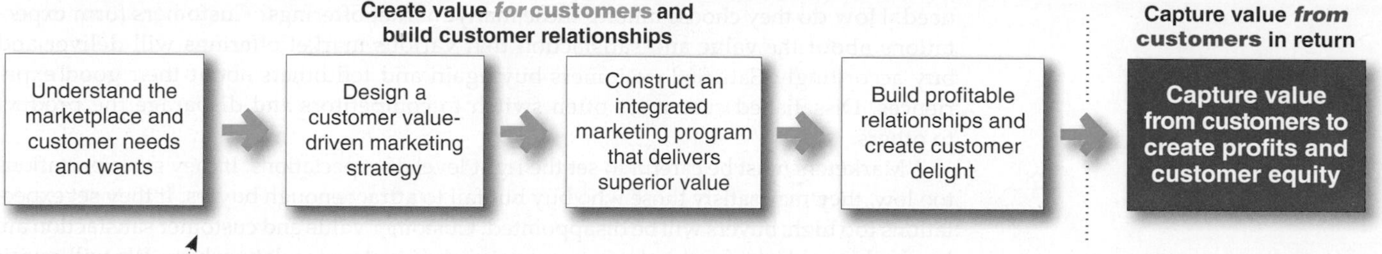
Create value *for* customers and build customer relationships
Understand the marketplace and customer needs and wants
Design a customer value-driven marketing strategy
Construct an integrated marketing program that delivers superior value
Build profitable relationships and create customer delight
Capture value *from* customers in return
Capture value from customers to create profits and customer equity

This important figure shows marketing in a nutshell. By creating value *for* customers, marketers capture value *from* customers in return. This five-step process forms the marketing framework for the rest of the chapter and the remainder of the text.

sale that are essentially intangible and do not result in the ownership of anything. Examples include banking, airline, hotel, retailing, and home repair services.

More broadly, market offerings also include other entities, such as *persons, places, organizations, information*, and *ideas*. For example, the "Pure Michigan" campaign markets the state of Michigan as a tourism destination that "lets unspoiled nature and authentic character revive your spirits." And the Ad Council and the National Highway Traffic Safety Administration created a "Stop the Texts. Stop the Wrecks." campaign that markets the idea of eliminating texting while driving. The campaign points out that a texting driver is 23 times more likely to get into a crash than a non-texting driver.[5]

Market offerings
Some combination of products, services, information, or experiences offered to a market to satisfy a need or want.

Marketing myopia
The mistake of paying more attention to the specific products a company offers than to the benefits and experiences produced by these products.

Many sellers make the mistake of paying more attention to the specific products they offer than to the benefits and experiences produced by these products. These sellers suffer from **marketing myopia**. They are so taken with their products that they focus only on existing wants and lose sight of underlying customer needs.[6] They forget that a product is only a tool to solve a consumer problem. A manufacturer of quarter-inch drill bits may think that the customer needs a drill bit. But what the customer *really* needs is a quarter-inch hole. These sellers will have trouble if a new product comes along that serves the customer's need better or less expensively. The customer will have the same *need* but will *want* the new product.

Smart marketers look beyond the attributes of the products and services they sell. By orchestrating several services and products, they create *brand experiences* for consumers. For example, you don't just visit Walt Disney World Resort; you immerse yourself and your family in a world of wonder, a world where dreams come true and things still work the way they should. "Let the magic begin!" says Disney.

Similarly, Angry Birds is much more than just a mobile game app. To more than 200 million fans a month in 116 countries, it's a deeply involving experience. As one observer puts it: "Angry Birds land is a state of mind—a digital immersion in addictively cheerful destruction, a refuge from the boredom of subway commutes and doctors' waiting rooms, where the fine art of sling-shotting tiny brightly hued birds at wooden fortresses to vanquish pigs taking shelter inside makes eminent sense and is immensely satisfying." So far, in all its forms, Angry Birds has been downloaded more than two billion times. The game's creator, Rovio, plans to expand the Angry Birds experience through everything from animated short videos (called *Angry Birds Toons*) and three-dimensional animated movies to a growing list of new games, licensed toys, apparel, yard art, and even Angry Birds–branded playgrounds, activity parks, and theme parks.[7]

ANGRY BIRDS

Marketing experiences: More than just a mobile game app, Angry Birds is "a digital immersion in addictively cheerful destruction." Creator Rovio plans to expand the Angry Birds experience through animated videos, licensed products, and even Angry Birds-branded playgrounds and activity parks.
Archivo CEET GDA Photo Service/Newscom

Customer Value and Satisfaction

Consumers usually face a broad array of products and services that might satisfy a given need. How do they choose among these many market offerings? Customers form expectations about the value and satisfaction that various market offerings will deliver and buy accordingly. Satisfied customers buy again and tell others about their good experiences. Dissatisfied customers often switch to competitors and disparage the product to others.

Marketers must be careful to set the right level of expectations. If they set expectations too low, they may satisfy those who buy but fail to attract enough buyers. If they set expectations too high, buyers will be disappointed. Customer value and customer satisfaction are key building blocks for developing and managing customer relationships. We will revisit these core concepts later in the chapter.

Exchanges and Relationships

Exchange
The act of obtaining a desired object from someone by offering something in return.

Marketing occurs when people decide to satisfy their needs and wants through exchange relationships. **Exchange** is the act of obtaining a desired object from someone by offering something in return. In the broadest sense, the marketer tries to bring about a response to some market offering. The response may be more than simply buying or trading products and services. A political candidate, for instance, wants votes; a church wants membership; an orchestra wants an audience; and a social action group wants idea acceptance.

Marketing consists of actions taken to create, maintain, and grow desirable exchange *relationships* with target audiences involving a product, service, idea, or other object. Companies want to build strong relationships by consistently delivering superior customer value. We will expand on the important concept of managing customer relationships later in the chapter.

Markets

Market
The set of all actual and potential buyers of a product or service.

The concepts of exchange and relationships lead to the concept of a market. A **market** is the set of actual and potential buyers of a product or service. These buyers share a particular need or want that can be satisfied through exchange relationships.

Marketing means managing markets to bring about profitable customer relationships. However, creating these relationships takes work. Sellers must search for and engage buyers, identify their needs, design good market offerings, set prices for them, promote them, and store and deliver them. Activities such as consumer research, product development, communication, distribution, pricing, and service are core marketing activities.

Although we normally think of marketing as being carried out by sellers, buyers also carry out marketing. Consumers market when they search for products, interact with companies to obtain information, and make their purchases. In fact, today's digital technologies, from online sites and smartphone apps to the explosion of social media, have empowered consumers and made marketing a truly two-way affair. Thus, in addition to customer relationship management, today's marketers must also deal effectively with *customer-managed relationships*. Marketers are no longer asking only "How can we influence our customers?" but also "How can our customers influence us?" and even "How can our customers influence each other?"

Figure 1.2 shows the main elements in a marketing system. Marketing involves serving a market of final consumers in the face of competitors. The company and competitors research the market and interact with consumers to understand their needs. Then they create and exchange market offerings, messages, and other marketing content with consumers, either directly or through marketing intermediaries. Each party in the system is affected by major environmental forces (demographic, economic, natural, technological, political, and social/cultural).

Each party in the system adds value for the next level. The arrows represent relationships that must be developed and managed. Thus, a company's success at engaging customers and building profitable relationships depends not only on its own actions but also on how well the entire system serves the needs of final consumers. Walmart cannot fulfill its promise of low prices unless its suppliers provide merchandise at low costs. And Ford cannot deliver a high-quality car-ownership experience unless its dealers provide outstanding sales and service.

FIGURE | 1.2
A Modern Marketing System

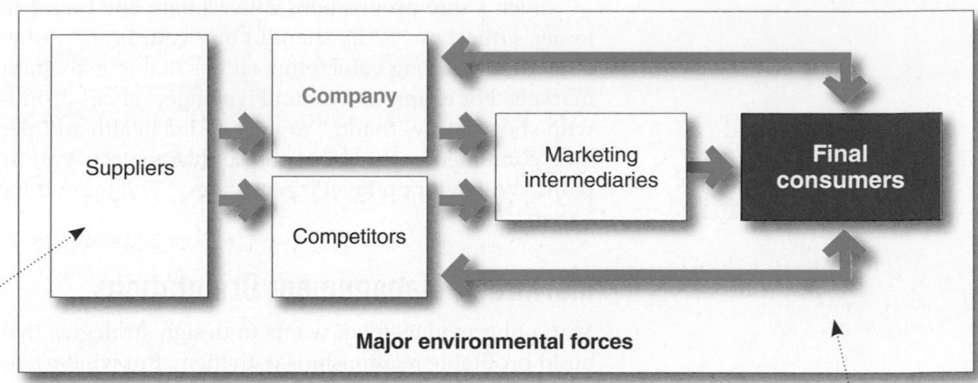

Each party in the system adds value. Walmart cannot fulfill its promise of low prices unless its suppliers provide low costs. Ford cannot deliver a high-quality car-ownership experience unless its dealers provide outstanding service.

Arrows represent relationships that must be developed and managed to create customer value and profitable customer relationships.

Author Comment | Once a company fully understands its consumers and the marketplace, it must decide which customers it will serve and how it will bring them value.

Designing a Customer Value-Driven Marketing Strategy

Once it fully understands consumers and the marketplace, marketing management can design a customer value-driven marketing strategy. We define **marketing management** as the art and science of choosing target markets and building profitable relationships with them. The marketing manager's aim is to find, engage, keep, and grow target customers by creating, delivering, and communicating superior customer value.

Marketing management
The art and science of choosing target markets and building profitable relationships with them.

To design a winning marketing strategy, the marketing manager must answer two important questions: *What customers will we serve (what's our target market)?* and *How can we serve these customers best (what's our value proposition)?* We will discuss these marketing strategy concepts briefly here and then look at them in more detail in Chapters 2 and 6.

Selecting Customers to Serve

The company must first decide *whom* it will serve. It does this by dividing the market into segments of customers (*market segmentation*) and selecting which segments it will go after (*target marketing*). Some people think of marketing management as finding as many customers as possible and increasing demand. But marketing managers know that they cannot serve all customers in every way. By trying to serve all customers, they may not serve any customers well. Instead, the company wants to select only customers that it can serve well and profitably. For example, Nordstrom profitably targets affluent professionals; Dollar General profitably targets families with more modest means.

Ultimately, marketing managers must decide which customers they want to target and on the level, timing, and nature of their demand. Simply put, marketing management is *customer management* and *demand management.*

Value propositions: Vine gives you "the best way to see and share life in motion" through "short, beautiful, looping videos in a simple and fun way for your friends and family to see."
Twitter, Inc.

Choosing a Value Proposition

The company must also decide how it will serve targeted customers—how it will *differentiate and position* itself in the marketplace. A brand's *value proposition* is the set of benefits or values it promises to deliver to consumers to satisfy their needs. BMW promises "the ultimate driving machine," whereas the Nissan Leaf electric car is "100% electric. Zero gas. Zero tailpipe." New Balance's Minimus shoes are "like barefoot only better"; and with Vibram FiveFingers shoes, "You are the technology." Facebook helps you "connect and share with the people in your life," whereas YouTube "provides a place for people to connect, inform, and inspire others across the globe." And Twitter's Vine app gives you "the best way to see and share life in motion" through "short, beautiful, looping videos in a simple and fun way for your friends and family to see."[8]

Such value propositions differentiate one brand from another. They answer the customer's question, "Why should I buy your brand rather than a competitor's?" Companies must design strong value propositions that give them the greatest advantage in their target markets. For example, Vibram FiveFingers shoes promise the best of two worlds—running with shoes and without. "You get all the health and performance benefits of barefoot running combined with a Vibram sole that protects you from elements and obstacles in your path." With Vibram FiveFingers shoes, "The more it looks like a foot, the more it acts like a foot."

Marketing Management Orientations

Marketing management wants to design strategies that will engage target customers and build profitable relationships with them. But what *philosophy* should guide these marketing strategies? What weight should be given to the interests of customers, the organization, and society? Very often, these interests conflict.

There are five alternative concepts under which organizations design and carry out their marketing strategies: the *production*, *product*, *selling*, *marketing*, and *societal marketing concepts*.

The Production Concept

Production concept
The idea that consumers will favor products that are available and highly affordable; therefore, the organization should focus on improving production and distribution efficiency.

The **production concept** holds that consumers will favor products that are available and highly affordable. Therefore, management should focus on improving production and distribution efficiency. This concept is one of the oldest orientations that guides sellers.

The production concept is still a useful philosophy in some situations. For example, both personal computer maker Lenovo and home appliance maker Haier dominate the highly competitive, price-sensitive Chinese market through low labor costs, high production efficiency, and mass distribution. However, although useful in some situations, the production concept can lead to marketing myopia. Companies adopting this orientation run a major risk of focusing too narrowly on their own operations and losing sight of the real objective—satisfying customer needs and building customer relationships.

The Product Concept

Product concept
The idea that consumers will favor products that offer the most quality, performance, and features; therefore, the organization should devote its energy to making continuous product improvements.

The **product concept** holds that consumers will favor products that offer the most in quality, performance, and innovative features. Under this concept, marketing strategy focuses on making continuous product improvements.

Product quality and improvement are important parts of most marketing strategies. However, focusing *only* on the company's products can also lead to marketing myopia. For example, some manufacturers believe that if they can "build a better mousetrap, the world will beat a path to their doors." But they are often rudely shocked. Buyers may be looking for a better solution to a mouse problem but not necessarily for a better mousetrap. The better solution might be a chemical spray, an exterminating service, a housecat, or something else that suits their needs even better than a mousetrap. Furthermore, a better mousetrap will not sell unless the manufacturer designs, packages, and prices it attractively; places it in convenient distribution channels; brings it to the attention of people who need it; and convinces buyers that it is a better product.

The Selling Concept

Selling concept
The idea that consumers will not buy enough of the firm's products unless the firm undertakes a large-scale selling and promotion effort.

Many companies follow the **selling concept**, which holds that consumers will not buy enough of the firm's products unless it undertakes a large-scale selling and promotion effort. The selling concept is typically practiced with unsought goods—those that buyers do not normally think of buying, such as life insurance or blood donations. These industries must be good at tracking down prospects and selling them on a product's benefits.

Such aggressive selling, however, carries high risks. It focuses on creating sales transactions rather than on building long-term, profitable customer relationships. The aim often is to sell what the company makes rather than making what the market wants. It assumes that customers who are coaxed into buying the product will like it. Or, if they don't like it, they will possibly forget their disappointment and buy it again later. These are usually poor assumptions.

FIGURE | 1.3
Selling and Marketing Concepts Contrasted

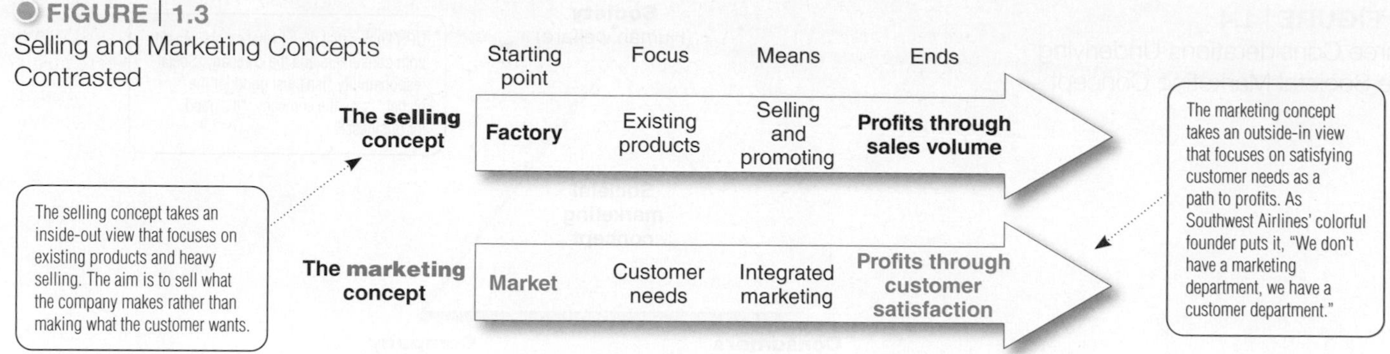
Starting point
Focus
Means
Ends
The selling concept
Factory
Existing products
Selling and promoting
Profits through sales volume
The marketing concept
Market
Customer needs
Integrated marketing
Profits through customer satisfaction
The selling concept takes an inside-out view that focuses on existing products and heavy selling. The aim is to sell what the company makes rather than making what the customer wants.
The marketing concept takes an outside-in view that focuses on satisfying customer needs as a path to profits. As Southwest Airlines' colorful founder puts it, "We don't have a marketing department, we have a customer department."

The Marketing Concept

Marketing concept
A philosophy in which achieving organizational goals depends on knowing the needs and wants of target markets and delivering the desired satisfactions better than competitors do.

The **marketing concept** holds that achieving organizational goals depends on knowing the needs and wants of target markets and delivering the desired satisfactions better than competitors do. Under the marketing concept, customer focus and value are the *paths* to sales and profits. Instead of a product-centered *make-and-sell* philosophy, the marketing concept is a customer-centered *sense-and-respond* philosophy. The job is not to find the right customers for your product but to find the right products for your customers.

Figure 1.3 contrasts the selling concept and the marketing concept. The selling concept takes an *inside-out* perspective. It starts with the factory, focuses on the company's existing products, and calls for heavy selling and promotion to obtain profitable sales. It focuses primarily on customer conquest—getting short-term sales with little concern about who buys or why.

In contrast, the marketing concept takes an *outside-in* perspective. As Herb Kelleher, the colorful founder of Southwest Airlines, once put it, "We don't have a marketing department; we have a customer department." The marketing concept starts with a well-defined market, focuses on customer needs, and integrates all the marketing activities that affect customers. In turn, it yields profits by creating relationships with the right customers based on customer value and satisfaction.

Implementing the marketing concept often means more than simply responding to customers' stated desires and obvious needs. *Customer-driven* companies research customers deeply to learn about their desires, gather new product ideas, and test product improvements. Such customer-driven marketing usually works well when a clear need exists and when customers know what they want.

In many cases, however, customers *don't* know what they want or even what is possible. As Henry Ford once remarked, "If I'd asked people what they wanted, they would have said faster horses."[9] For example, even 20 years ago, how many consumers would have thought to ask for now-commonplace products such as tablet computers, smartphones, digital cameras, 24-hour online buying, video sharing services, and GPS systems in their cars and phones? Such situations call for *customer-driving* marketing—understanding customer needs even better than customers themselves do and creating products and services that meet both existing and latent needs, now and in the future. As an executive at 3M put it, "Our goal is to lead customers where they want to go before *they* know where they want to go."

The Societal Marketing Concept

Societal marketing concept
The idea that a company's marketing decisions should consider consumers' wants, the company's requirements, consumers' long-run interests, and society's long-run interests.

The **societal marketing concept** questions whether the pure marketing concept overlooks possible conflicts between consumer *short-run wants* and consumer *long-run welfare.* Is a firm that satisfies the immediate needs and wants of target markets always doing what's best for its consumers in the long run? The societal marketing concept holds that marketing strategy should deliver value to customers in a way that maintains or improves both the consumer's *and society's* well-being. It calls for *sustainable marketing*, socially and environmentally responsible marketing that meets the present needs of consumers and businesses while also preserving or enhancing the ability of future generations to meet their needs.

FIGURE | 1.4
Three Considerations Underlying the Societal Marketing Concept

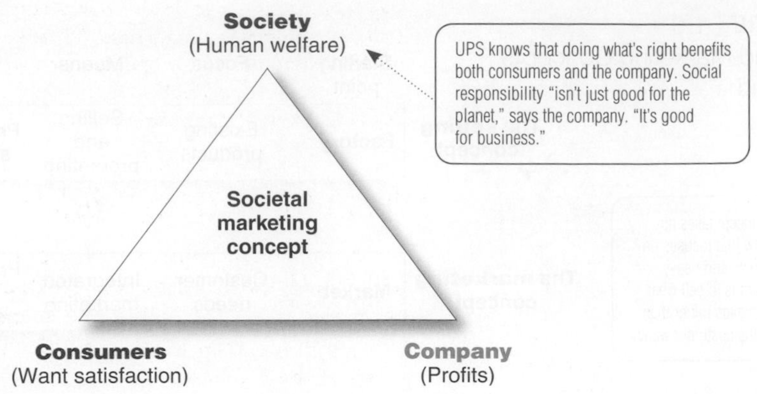

(Human welfare)

UPS knows that doing what's right benefits both consumers and the company. Social responsibility "isn't just good for the planet," says the company. "It's good for business."

Even more broadly, many leading business and marketing thinkers are now preaching the concept of *shared value,* which recognizes that societal needs, not just economic needs, define markets.[10] The concept of shared value focuses on creating economic value in a way that also creates value for society. A growing number of companies known for their hard-nosed approaches to business—such as GE, Dow, Google, IBM, Intel, Johnson & Johnson, Nestlé, Unilever, and Walmart—are rethinking the interactions between society and corporate performance. They are concerned not just with short-term economic gains, but with the well-being of their customers, the depletion of natural resources vital to their businesses, the viability of key suppliers, and the economic well-being of the communities in which they produce and sell.

One prominent marketer calls this *Marketing 3.0*. "Marketing 3.0 organizations are values-driven," he says. "I'm not talking about being value-driven. I'm talking about 'values' plural, where values amount to caring about the state of the world." Another marketer calls it purpose-driven marketing. "The future of profit is purpose," he says.[11]

As **Figure 1.4** shows, companies should balance three considerations in setting their marketing strategies: company profits, consumer wants, *and* society's interests. British-based cosmetics retailer Lush operates this way:[12]

A LUSH LIFE
WE BELIEVE
... in making effective products from fresh organic* fruit and vegetables, the finest essential oils and safe synthetics.
We believe in buying ingredients only from companies that do not conduct or commission tests on animals and in testing our products on humans.
We invent our own products and fragrances, we make them fresh* by hand using little or no preservative or packaging, using only vegetarian ingredients and tell you when they were made.
We believe in happy people making happy soap, putting our faces on our products and making our mums proud.
We believe in long candlelit baths, sharing showers, massage, filling the world with perfume and in the right to make mistakes, lose everything and start again.
We believe our products are good value, that we should make a profit and that the customer is always right.
*We also believe words like 'Fresh' and 'Organic' have an honest meaning beyond marketing.
REHAB
BIG
CHARITY POT
CURLY WURLY

The societal marketing concept: Cosmetics retailer Lush does more than just make and sell premium body care products for profit. It also dedicates itself to doing right by customers, employees, the environment, and society.
Lush Fresh Handmade Cosmetics

Lush is known for "Fresh Handmade Cosmetics"—premium beauty products made by hand from the freshest possible natural ingredients. It sells products with evocative names such as Flying Fox shower gel, Angels on Bareskin cleanser, and Honey I Washed the Kids soap. But Lush does much more than just make and sell body care products for profit. It also dedicates itself to doing right by customers, employees, the environment, and society. Its do-good mission is spelled out in a seven-point statement titled, "A Lush Life: We Believe. . . ." For example, the company believes in inventing and making its own products from fresh organic fruits and vegetables using little or no preservatives or packaging. Lush has strict policy against animal testing and supports Fair Trade and Community Trade efforts. Each year, the company invests heavily in sustainable initiatives and support of grassroots charities. Lush takes care of its employees—"We believe in happy people making happy soap . . . " In fact, Lush seems to wish well to everyone, everywhere—"We believe in long candlelit baths, sharing showers, massage, filling the world with perfume, and the right to make mistakes, lose everything, and start again." Only in its final belief does Lush mention profits—"We believe our products are good value, that we should make a profit, and that the customer is always right." Thanks to its societal mission, Lush is thriving like fresh flowers in springtime. It now operates stores in 50 countries, with e-commerce sites in 27 countries. Its sales have nearly doubled in just the past three years, suggesting that doing good can benefit both the planet and the company.

Author Comment The customer value-driven marketing strategy discussed in the previous section outlines which customers the company will serve (the target market) and how it will serve them (positioning and the value proposition). Now, the company develops marketing plans and programs—a marketing mix—that will actually deliver the intended customer value.

Preparing an Integrated Marketing Plan and Program

The company's marketing strategy outlines which customers it will serve and how it will create value for these customers. Next, the marketer develops an integrated marketing program that will actually deliver the intended value to target customers. The marketing program builds customer relationships by transforming the marketing strategy into action. It consists of the firm's *marketing mix*, the set of marketing tools the firm uses to implement its marketing strategy.

The major marketing mix tools are classified into four broad groups, called the *four Ps* of marketing: product, price, place, and promotion. To deliver on its value proposition, the firm must first create a need-satisfying market offering (product). It must then decide how much it will charge for the offering (price) and how it will make the offering available to target consumers (place). Finally, it must engage target consumers, communicate about the offering, and persuade consumers of the offer's merits (promotion). The firm must blend each marketing mix tool into a comprehensive integrated marketing program that communicates and delivers the intended value to chosen customers. We will explore marketing programs and the marketing mix in much more detail in later chapters.

Author Comment Doing a good job with the first three steps in the marketing process sets the stage for step four, building and managing customer relationships.

Building Customer Relationships

The first three steps in the marketing process—understanding the marketplace and customer needs, designing a customer value-driven marketing strategy, and constructing a marketing program—all lead up to the fourth and most important step: building and managing profitable customer relationships. We first discuss the basics of customer relationship management. Then, we examine how companies go about engaging customers on a deeper level in this age of digital and social marketing.

Customer Relationship Management

Customer relationship management is perhaps the most important concept of modern marketing. In the broadest sense, **customer relationship management** is the overall process of building and maintaining profitable customer relationships by delivering superior customer value and satisfaction. It deals with all aspects of acquiring, engaging, and growing customers.

Customer relationship management
The overall process of building and maintaining profitable customer relationships by delivering superior customer value and satisfaction.

Relationship Building Blocks: Customer Value and Satisfaction

The key to building lasting customer relationships is to create superior customer value and satisfaction. Satisfied customers are more likely to be loyal customers and give the company a larger share of their business.

Customer Value. Attracting and retaining customers can be a difficult task. Customers often face a bewildering array of products and services from which to choose. A customer buys from the firm that offers the highest **customer-perceived value**—the customer's evaluation of the difference between all the benefits and all the costs of a market offering relative to those of competing offers. Importantly, customers often do not judge values and costs "accurately" or "objectively." They act on *perceived* value.

Customer-perceived value
The customer's evaluation of the difference between all the benefits and all the costs of a marketing offer relative to those of competing offers.

To some consumers, value might mean sensible products at affordable prices. To other consumers, however, value might mean paying more to get more. For example, what's a cooler worth—one of those insulated containers you take camping or haul to a picnic or tailgate party? If it's a YETI cooler, you can expect to pay from $229 to as much as $1,300 for the top-of-the-line Tundra model. However, despite their high prices and spare, boxy designs, YETI coolers have achieved an almost cult status among the field-and-stream set, or on construction sites, ranches, or even military bases. The company's slogan: "YETI Coolers—Wildly Stronger. Keeps Ice Longer!" suggests the reasons why. Devoted users will tell you that a YETI

Perceived value: Is a YETI cooler worth its premium price? To devoted YETI users, the answer is a resounding "yes." The "Wildly Stronger. Keeps Ice Longer!" coolers are even certified as Grizzly bear-resistant by the Interagency Grizzly Bear Committee.

YETI Coolers and the Interagency Grizzly Bear Committee (IGBC)

does keep things cooler—with a FatWall design (with twice the insulation of competitors) and an interlocking lid system with a gasket that keeps the cold in. And rugged YETI coolers are made to last—no more busted hinges, failed latches, or caved in lids. They're even certified as Grizzly bear-resistant by the Interagency Grizzly Bear Committee. One reporter describes a YETI as "a cooler fit for the apocalypse," and the company claims it's "The cooler you've always wanted. The last cooler you'll ever need." So, is a YETI cooler worth the premium price compared to less expensive coolers made by Igloo or Rubbermaid? To many consumers, the answer is no. But to YETI's target buyers, the answer is a resounding yes.[13]

Customer Satisfaction. **Customer satisfaction** depends on the product's perceived performance relative to a buyer's expectations. If the product's performance falls short of expectations, the customer is dissatisfied. If performance matches expectations, the customer is satisfied. If performance exceeds expectations, the customer is highly satisfied or delighted.

Outstanding marketing companies go out of their way to keep important customers satisfied. Most studies show that higher levels of customer satisfaction lead to greater customer loyalty, which in turn results in better company performance. Smart companies aim to delight customers by promising only what they can deliver and then delivering more than they promise. Delighted customers not only make repeat purchases but also become willing marketing partners and "customer evangelists" who spread the word about their good experiences to others.

For companies interested in delighting customers, exceptional value and service become part of the overall company culture. For example, year after year, Ritz-Carlton ranks at or near the top of the hospitality industry in terms of customer satisfaction. Its passion for satisfying customers is summed up in the company's credo, which promises that its luxury hotels will deliver a truly memorable experience—one that "enlivens the senses, instills well-being, and fulfills even the unexpressed wishes and needs of our guests."[14]

Customer satisfaction: Ritz-Carlton hotels deliver a truly memorable experience that fulfills even the unexpressed wishes and needs of its guests.

Toronto Star via Getty Images

> Check into any Ritz-Carlton hotel around the world, and you'll be amazed by the company's fervent dedication to anticipating even your slightest need. Without ever asking, they seem to know that you're allergic to peanuts and want a king-size bed, a nonallergenic pillow, extra body gel, the blinds open when you arrive, and breakfast with decaffeinated coffee in your room. Each day, hotel staffers—from those at the front desk to those in maintenance and housekeeping—discreetly observe and record even the smallest guest preferences. Then, every morning, each hotel reviews the files of all new arrivals who have previously stayed at a Ritz-Carlton and prepares a list of suggested extra touches that might delight each guest. For example, according to one Ritz-Carlton manager, if the chain gets hold of a picture of a guest's pet, it will make a copy, have it framed, and display it in the guest's room in whatever Ritz-Carlton the guest visits.
>
> Once they identify a special customer need, Ritz-Carlton employees go to legendary extremes to meet it. For instance, to serve the needs of a guest whose son had food allergies, a Ritz-Carlton chef in Bali located special eggs and milk in a small grocery store in another country and had them delivered to the hotel. In another case, when a businessman attending a conference at the Ritz-Carlton Orlando ordered his favorite soda during a dinner in a hotel ballroom, his banquet server told him that the hotel didn't serve that beverage but he would see what he could do. To no one's surprise, the server quickly returned with the requested beverage, and for the rest of the week he had the drink waiting for the guest. But here's the best part. A year later when the guest returned for the conference, as he sat in the ballroom waiting for dinner the first night, the same server walked up with his favorite drink in hand. As a result of such customer service heroics, an amazing 95 percent of departing guests report that their stay has been a truly memorable experience. More than 90 percent of Ritz-Carlton's delighted customers return.

Other companies that have become legendary for customer delight and their service heroics include Zappos.com, Amazon.com, Nordstrom department stores, and

Customer satisfaction
The extent to which a product's perceived performance matches a buyer's expectations.

JetBlue Airways (see Real Marketing 1.1). However, a company doesn't need to have over-the-top service to create customer delight. For example, no-frills grocery chain ALDI has highly satisfied customers, even though they have to bag their own groceries and can't use credit cards. ALDI's everyday very low pricing on good-quality products delights customers and keeps them coming back. Thus, customer satisfaction comes not just from service heroics, but from how well a company delivers on its basic value proposition and helps customers solve their buying problems. "Most customers don't want to be 'wowed,'" says one marketing consultant. "They [just] want an effortless experience."[15]

Although a customer-centered firm seeks to deliver high customer satisfaction relative to competitors, it does not attempt to *maximize* customer satisfaction. A company can always increase customer satisfaction by lowering its prices or increasing its services. But this may result in lower profits. Thus, the purpose of marketing is to generate customer value profitably. This requires a very delicate balance: The marketer must continue to generate more customer value and satisfaction but not "give away the house."

Customer Relationship Levels and Tools

Companies can build customer relationships at many levels, depending on the nature of the target market. At one extreme, a company with many low-margin customers may seek to develop *basic relationships* with them. For example, Procter & Gamble's Tide detergent does not phone or call on all of its consumers to get to know them personally. Instead, Tide creates engagement and relationships through brand-building advertising, Web sites, and social media presence. At the other extreme, in markets with few customers and high margins, sellers want to create *full partnerships* with key customers. For example, P&G sales representatives work closely with Walmart, Kroger, and other large retailers that sell Tide. In between these two extremes, other levels of customer relationships are appropriate.

Beyond offering consistently high value and satisfaction, marketers can use specific marketing tools to develop stronger bonds with customers. For example, many companies offer *frequency marketing programs* that reward customers who buy frequently or in large amounts. Airlines offer frequent-flyer programs, hotels give room upgrades to frequent guests, and supermarkets give patronage discounts to "very important customers." These days almost every brand has a loyalty rewards program. However, some innovative loyalty programs go a step beyond the usual. ● Consider Walgreens:[16]

Members of Walgreens' Balance Rewards program earn points for in-store or online product purchases, redeemable for purchases in Walgreens stores or online. And members receive surprise offers and giveaways, everything from free movie passes to gift cards. But in line with the chain's mission "to keep our community happy and healthy," the unique Walgreens Balance Rewards program goes beyond just points for purchases. It also includes programs that reward customers for taking steps toward a happy, healthy, well-balanced life. The program has included giving members points for every mile they walk or run, every daily weigh-in as they track their weight, and every prescription and immunization. Walgreens even provides online and mobile tools that help members set healthy goals and track their progress, celebrating their achievements with milestone badges. Thus, the Walgreens Balance Rewards program builds stronger customer relationships and helps the brand by helping customers, befitting the chain's slogan: "Walgreens: At the corner of happy & healthy."

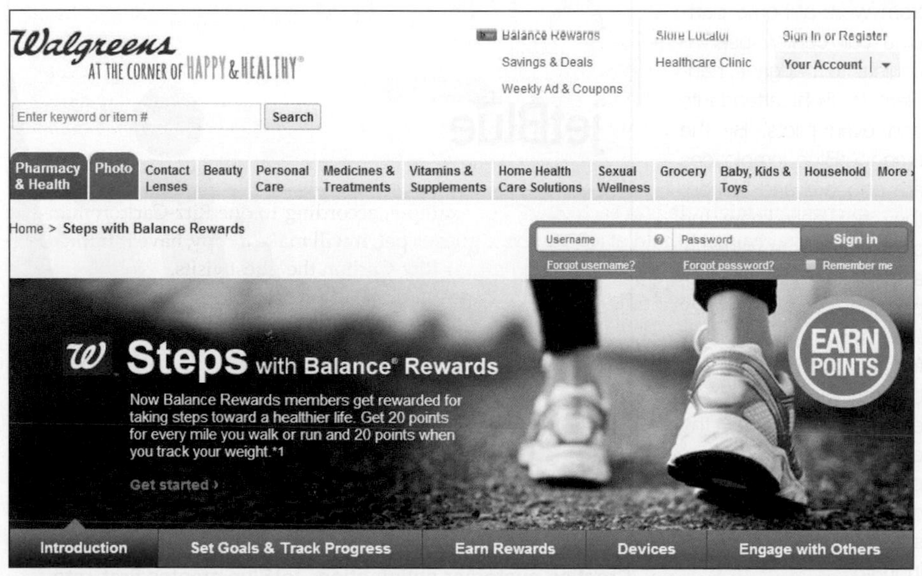

● **Relationship marketing tools: The innovative Walgreens Balance Rewards program builds stronger customer relationships and helps the brand by helping customers, befitting the chain's slogan: "Walgreens: At the corner of happy & healthy."**

Real Marketing 1.1

JetBlue: Delighting Customers and Bringing Humanity Back to Air Travel

There's an old adage in the airline industry: "You're not flying planes, you're flying people." These days, however, it seems that many big airlines overlook the people factor. Instead, they focus on moving their human cargo as efficiently as possible while charging as much as the traffic will bear. The American Customer Satisfaction Index rates the airline industry near the bottom among 47 industries in customer satisfaction, barely ahead of perennial cellar-dwellers subscription TV and Internet service providers.

Not so at JetBlue Airways. From the very beginning, young JetBlue (little more than 15 years old) has built a reputation for creating first-rate, customer-satisfying experiences. Its slogan—YOU ABOVE ALL—tells the JetBlue faithful that they are at the very heart of the company's strategy and culture. JetBlue is on a heartfelt mission to bring humanity back to air travel.

At JetBlue, customer care starts with basic amenities that exceed customer expectations, especially for a low-cost carrier. JetBlue's well-padded, leather-covered coach seats allow three inches more legroom than the average airline seat. Although the airline doesn't serve meals, it offers the best selection of free beverages and snacks to be found at 30,000 feet (including unexpected treats such as Terra Blues chips, Linden's chocolate chip cookies, and Dunkin' Donuts coffee). Every JetBlue seat has its own LCD entertainment system, complete with free 36-channel DirectTV and 100+ channels of SiriusXM Radio. JetBlue rounds out the amenities with a recently launched industry first—Fly-Fi, an in-flight high-speed Internet service with free basic browsing on all equipped planes.

JetBlue continuously innovates to find new ways to delight customers. Its "Even More Space" seats give customers the option of going from "roomy to roomier," allow early boarding, and give early access to overhead bins. Its "Even More Speed" service provides VIP passage through airport security screening. And JetBlue's Mint service puts a new spin on first-class air travel, offering front-of-the-plane, lie-flat "sweet seats," some of them in enclosed suites with their own doors. According to JetBlue, Mint services deliver "unexpected, individualized 'mo-mints' that revive and engage, keeping you in mint condition during your travels."

Such tangibles help keep JetBlue travelers satisfied. But JetBlue CEO David Barger knows that the tangibles are only a small part of what really makes JetBlue special. "The hard product—airplanes, leather seats, satellite TVs—as long as you have a checkbook, . . . can be replicated," says Barger. "It's the JetBlue *culture* that can't be replicated. The *human* side of the equation is the most important part of what we're doing." It's that JetBlue culture—the near-obsessive focus on the customer flying experience—that creates not just satisfied JetBlue customers, but *delighted* ones.

At JetBlue, developing a customer-centered corporate culture starts with hiring quality people whose personal values match JetBlue's values—from work-at-home part-time call center reservationists to baggage handlers to flight attendants and even pilots. By the time JetBlue employees are onboard and trained, they not only *know* the company's core values—safety, integrity, caring, passion, and fun—they *live* them. It's those heartfelt values that result in outstanding customer experiences. And the outstanding customer experiences make JetBlue's customers the most satisfied and loyal in the industry.

Whereas passengers on most competing airlines regard flying as an experience just to be tolerated, many JetBlue customers actually look forward to flying. And customers themselves spread the good word about JetBlue with evangelistic zeal. Recently crowned a "social media all-star" by *Fortune* magazine, JetBlue has been a leader in using a full range of social media to engage customers and get them talking with each other about the brand. And whereas other airlines are just now discovering the power of customer dialogue, throughout its history, in ads and promotions, JetBlue has often let its customers do the talking.

For example, its "Experience JetBlue" Web site features authentic testimonials from some of the airline's most devoted fans, who were found through Twitter and Facebook. The

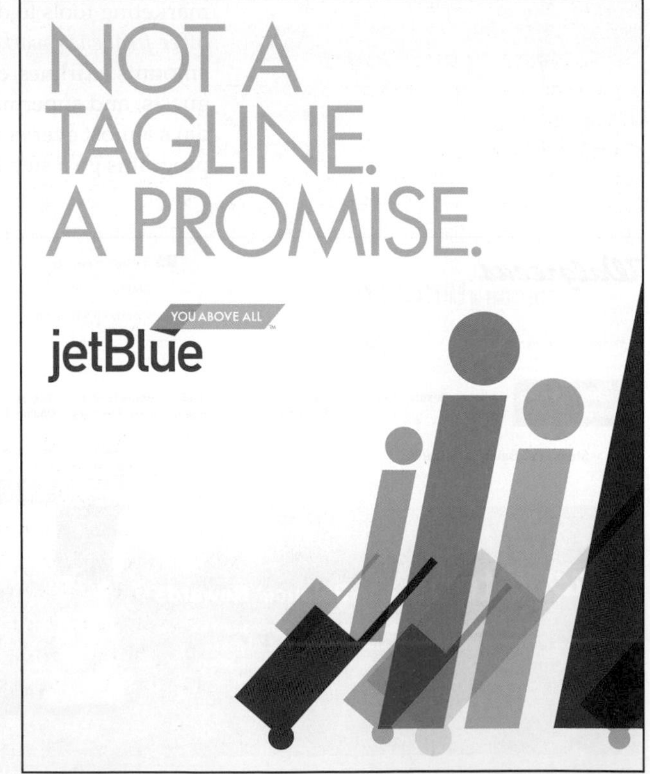

Creating customer satisfaction: JetBlue creates first-rate, customer-satisfying experiences. Its slogan—JetBlue: YOU ABOVE ALL—tells customers that they are at the very heart of JetBlue's strategy and culture.

JetBlue Airways

customers give glowing first-person accounts about why they like flying JetBlue. "It's like an open bar for snacks," says one customer. "They're constantly walking around offering it, so I'm never thirsty or hungry." Another JetBlue fan, a 6'3" woman from Portland, Oregon, likes the seating: "I can stretch and sit crosslegged—no black-and-blue knees," she says. "The customer service is above and beyond," declares a third customer, a small business owner from Boston. "[Coach on] JetBlue is very similar to flying first class."

In a former advertising campaign called "Sincerely, JetBlue," actual customers gave voice to even deeper JetBlue experiences. In one ad, for example, customer Melissa confided, "Let me tell you, I wanted not to like you, if only because everyone seems to love you. I got on a flight with a pen and paper, waiting to take down every irritating detail." But, she continued, "two flights later, I was staring at the same blank piece of paper. You've done nothing wrong and everything more than right, if that's possible." After detailing all the right things the airline does, she mock-lamented, "JetBlue, I wanted not to like you but it can't be done—at all. Sincerely, Melissa, Portland, Oregon."

In other Sincerely, JetBlue ads, customers recounted specific service heroics by dedicated JetBlue employees. For example, customer Ann recounted how, when her JetBlue flight was delayed by a snowstorm, the airline eased the long wait by providing pizza and even a live band. "My [three-year-old] son was dancing. I was dancing," she remembers. "It made a horrible experience really nice." And the Steins from Darien, Connecticut, told how they arrived late at night for a family vacation in Florida with their three very tired small children only to learn that their hotel wouldn't take them in. "Out of nowhere we heard a voice from behind us, go ahead, take my room," the Steins recalled. "A superhero in a JetBlue pilot's uniform, who sacrificed his room graciously, saved our night. And we slept like babies. Thank you, JetBlue."

Delighting customers has been good for JetBlue. Last year, the airline reported record revenues of $5.4 billion, up 90 percent in just the past four years. Even during recent hard economic times, as many competing airlines were cutting routes, retiring aircraft, laying off employees, and losing money, JetBlue was adding planes, expanding into new cities, hiring thousands of new employees, and turning profits.

Perhaps even more important to future success, customers continue to adore their JetBlue. For nine straight years, the customer-centered company has topped the J.D. Power and Associates customer satisfaction rankings among major U.S. airlines. For the past five years, JetBlue has flip-flopped with fellow customer-service champ Southwest Airlines for the airline industry's highest customer loyalty scores in the respected Satmetrix Net Promoter rankings. Every year, more than 60 percent of customers have rated JetBlue 9 or 10 on a 0-to-10 point scale indicating the likelihood that they would recommend JetBlue to others.

So, JetBlue really means it when it tells customers YOU ABOVE ALL. "Above all else," says JetBlue's Customer Bill of Rights, "JetBlue Airways is dedicated to bringing humanity back to air travel. We strive to make every part of your experience as simple and as pleasant as possible." Adds JetBlue's senior VP of marketing: "[YOU ABOVE ALL] gets us back to our DNA, to our original mission."

Sources: Iris Mansour, "Best in Customer Service," *Fortune*, August 29, 2013, http://money.cnn.com/gallery/technology/2013/08/29/social-media-all-stars.fortune/2.html; "JetBlue and Southwest's Net Rises on Gains From Capacity Expansion," *Forbes*, February 4, 2014, www.forbes.com/sites/greatspeculations/2014/02/04/jetblue-southwests-net-rises-on-gains-from-capacity-expansion/; Kevin Randall, "Red, Hot, and Blue: The Hottest American Brand Is Not Apple," *Fast Company*, June 3, 2010, http://www.fastcompany.com/1656066/red-hot-and-blue-hottest-american-brand-not-apple; "The American Customer Satisfaction Index: Benchmarks by Industry," www.theacsi.org/customer-satisfaction-benchmarks/benchmarks-by-industry, accessed June 2014; Rupal Parekh, "The Newest Marketing Buzzword? Human," *Advertising Age*, September 20, 2013, http://adage.com/print/244261/; and http://experience.jetblue.com/ and www.jetblue.com/about/, accessed September 2014.

Other companies sponsor *club marketing programs* that offer members special benefits and create member communities. For example, Apple encourages customers to form local Apple user groups. More than 800 registered Apple user groups worldwide offer monthly meetings, a newsletter, advice on technical issues, training classes, product discounts, and a forum for swapping ideas and stories with like-minded Apple fans. Similarly, buy one of those Weber grills and you can join the Weber Nation—"the site for real people who love their Weber grills." Membership gets you exclusive access to online grilling classes, an interactive recipe box, grilling tips and 24/7 telephone support, audio and video podcasts, straight-talk forums for interacting with other grilling fanatics, and even a chance to star in a Weber TV commercial. "Become a spatula-carrying member today," says Weber.[17]

Engaging Customers

Significant changes are occurring in the nature of customer brand relationships. Today's digital technologies—the Internet and the surge in online, mobile, and social media—have profoundly changed the ways that people on the planet relate to one another. In turn, these events have had a huge impact on how companies and brands connect with customers, and how customers connect with and influence each other's brand behaviors.

Customer Engagement and Today's Digital and Social Media

The digital age has spawned a dazzling set of new customer relationship-building tools, from Web sites, online ads and videos, mobile ads and apps, and blogs to online communities and the major social media, such as Twitter, Facebook, YouTube, Instagram, and Pinterest.

Yesterday's companies focused mostly on mass marketing to broad segments of customers at arm's length. By contrast, today's companies are using online, mobile, and social media to refine their targeting and to engage customers more deeply and interactively. The *old marketing* involved marketing brands *to* consumers. The *new marketing* is **customer-engagement marketing**—fostering direct and continuous customer involvement in shaping brand conversations, brand experiences, and brand community. Customer-engagement marketing goes beyond just selling a brand to consumers. Its goal is to make the brand a meaningful part of consumers' conversations and lives.

Customer-engagement marketing
Making the brand a meaningful part of consumers' conversations and lives by fostering direct and continuous customer involvement in shaping brand conversations, experiences, and community.

The burgeoning Internet and social media have given a huge boost to customer-engagement marketing. Today's consumers are better informed, more connected, and more empowered than ever before. Newly empowered consumers have more information about brands, and they have a wealth of digital platforms for airing and sharing their brand views with others. Thus, marketers are now embracing not only customer relationship management, but also *customer-managed relationships,* in which customers connect with companies and with each other to help forge their own brand experiences.

Greater consumer empowerment means that companies can no longer rely on marketing by *intrusion*. Instead, they must practice marketing by *attraction*—creating market offerings and messages that engage consumers rather than interrupt them. Hence, most marketers now augment their mass-media marketing efforts with a rich mix of online, mobile, and social media marketing that promotes brand–consumer engagement and conversation.

For example, companies post their latest ads and videos on social media sites, hoping they'll go viral. They maintain an extensive presence on Twitter, YouTube, Facebook, Google+, Pinterest, Vine, and other social media to create brand buzz. They launch their own blogs, mobile apps, online microsites, and consumer-generated review systems, all with the aim of engaging customers on a more personal, interactive level.

Take Twitter, for example. Organizations ranging from Dell, JetBlue, and Dunkin' Donuts to the Chicago Bulls, NASCAR, and the Los Angeles Fire Department have created Twitter pages and promotions. They use "tweets" to start conversations with and between Twitter's more than 645 million registered users, address customer service issues, research customer reactions, and drive traffic to relevant articles, Web and mobile marketing sites, contests, videos, and other brand activities.

Similarly, almost every company has something going on Facebook these days. Starbucks has more than 36 million Facebook "fans"; Coca-Cola has more than 80 million. And every major marketer has a YouTube channel where the brand and its fans post current ads and other entertaining or informative videos. Artful use of social media can get consumers involved with and talking about a brand.

Rental car company Hertz uses a broad range of digital and social media to engage its customers and boost sales:[18]

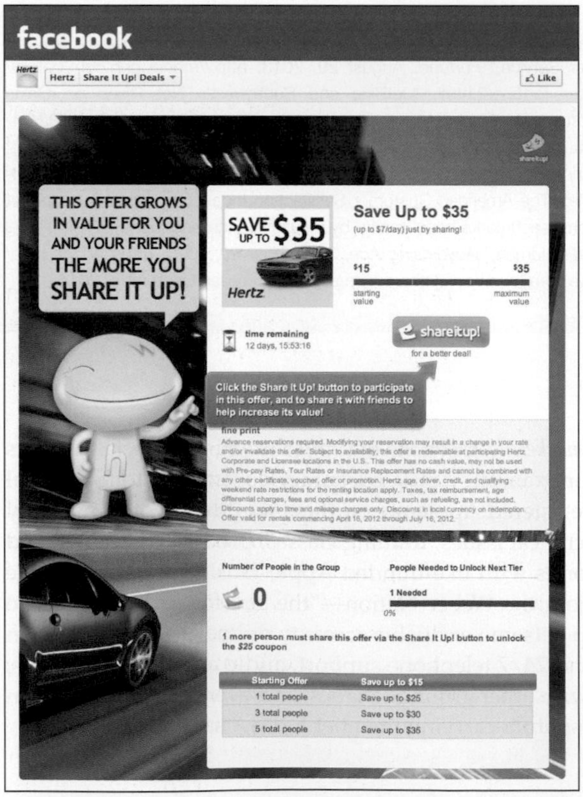

> A recent Hertz study found that consumers who engage in social conversations about the brand are 30 percent more likely to make a purchase than those who don't. And customers who engage in Hertz-related social activity in early stages of the rental process are four times more likely to visit Hertz's Web site. So, Hertz now incorporates social media in almost all of its marketing, such as Twitter hashtags, links to major social media, and sharing features. For example, Hertz's Twitter feed is a 140-character customer-service line that tends to each problem and question posted by members. On the brand's Facebook and Google+ pages, Hertz posts specials, such as waiving the young driver fee for car rentals during the spring break season. On its "Traveling at the Speed of Hertz" YouTube channel, Hertz posts

Customer engagement and the social media: Hertz's "Share It Up" social media campaign gave larger discounts to customers who shared Hertz coupons with social network friends. At least 45 percent of users who saw the coupons ended up sharing them.

Hertz System, Inc.

its latest commercials as well as videos about new features such as its ExpressRent Interactive Kiosks. More than just creating conversations, Hertz also uses the social media to help build sales. ● Last year, the brand ran a "Share It Up" campaign on Facebook using social coupons to increase visibility. Users who shared the coupons with friends on Facebook and other social networks earned larger discounts based on how often they shared the coupon with friends. At least 45 percent of users who saw the coupon ended up sharing it.

The key to engagement marketing is to find ways to enter consumers' conversations with engaging and relevant brand messages. Simply posting a humorous video, creating a social media page, or hosting a blog isn't enough. Successful engagement marketing means making relevant and genuine contributions to consumers' lives and conversations. According to David Oksman, chief marketer for T-shirt and apparel maker Life is good, engagement and social media are "about deep meaningful relationships that go beyond the product you are selling. The real depth of engagement is in the commenting and community that go on [around the brand]" (see Real Marketing 1.2).[19]

Consumer-Generated Marketing

Consumer-generated marketing
Brand exchanges created by consumers themselves—both invited and uninvited—by which consumers are playing an increasing role in shaping their own brand experiences and those of other consumers.

A growing form of customer-engagement marketing is **consumer-generated marketing**, by which consumers themselves are playing a bigger role in shaping their own brand experiences and those of others. This might happen through uninvited consumer-to-consumer exchanges in blogs, video-sharing sites, social media, and other digital forums. But increasingly, companies themselves are inviting consumers to play a more active role in shaping products and brand content.

Some companies ask consumers for new product and service ideas. For example, at its My Starbucks Idea site, Starbucks collects ideas from customers on new products, store changes, and just about anything else that might make their Starbucks experience better. "You know better than anyone else what you want from Starbucks," says the company at the Web site. "So tell us. What's your Starbucks idea? Revolutionary or simple—we want to hear it." The site invites customers to share their ideas, vote on and discuss the ideas of others, and see which ideas Starbucks has implemented.[20]

Other companies invite customers to play an active role in shaping ads. For example, for the past eight years, PepsiCo's Doritos brand has held a "Crash the Super Bowl" contest in which it invites 30-second ads from consumers and runs the best ones during the game. The consumer-generated ads have been a huge success. Last year, Doritos opened up the contest to people in all 46 countries where Doritos are sold. From more than 5,400 entries, Doritos aired two fan-produced ads during the Super Bowl. Past campaigns have produced numerous top-place finishers in *USA Today's* AdMeter rankings, earning their creators $1 million in cash prizes from PepsiCo's Frito-Lay division. In the recent campaign, the prizes were instead awarded based on fan votes at Doritos.com. The winner, "Time Machine"—a witty ad about a man who humors a small kid by taking a ride in his cardboard box time machine, only to be hoodwinked out of his bag of Doritos—earned its amateur creators the $1 million in cash. The homemade commercial cost $200 to make and took just eight hours to shoot.[21]

● Consumer-generated advertising difficulties: McDonald's now-infamous #McDStories Twitter campaign backfired when Twitter users turned the hashtag into a "bashtag."

© PSL Images / Alamy (logo) and © John Schwegel / Alamy (bird)

Despite the successes, however, harnessing consumer-generated content can be a time-consuming and costly process, and companies may find it difficult to glean even a little gold from all the garbage. For example, when Heinz invited consumers to submit homemade ads for its ketchup on its YouTube page, it ended up sifting through more than 8,000 entries, of which it posted nearly 4,000. Some of the amateur ads were very good—entertaining and potentially effective. Most, however, were so-so at best, and others were downright dreadful. In one ad, a contestant chugged ketchup straight from the bottle. In another, the would-be filmmaker brushed his teeth, washed his hair, and shaved his face with Heinz's product.[22]

Moreover, because consumers have so much control over social media content, inviting their input can sometimes backfire. ● For example, McDonald's famously launched a Twitter campaign using the hashtag #McDStories, hoping that it would inspire heartwarming stories about Happy Meals. Instead, the effort was hijacked by Twitter users, who turned the hashtag into a "bashtag" by posting less-than-appetizing messages about their bad experiences with the fast-food chain. McDonald's pulled the campaign within only two hours, but the hashtag was still churning weeks, even months later.[23]

As consumers become more connected and empowered, and as the boom in digital and social media technologies continues, consumer brand engagement—whether invited

Real Marketing 1.2

Life is good: Engaging Customers and Spreading Optimism

Building customer engagement may sound simple at first. But meaningful engagement involves much more than just tacking a buzzword onto a mission statement or setting up social media pages. The fibers of true customer engagement are woven deeply into the company and brand culture.

For starters, a brand must have a story to tell—an authentic, engagement-worthy sense of purpose that goes beyond the product. Then, rather than force-feeding the brand to customers, the company must engage them on their own terms, letting them help shape and share their own brand experiences. Finally, weaving the brand into customers' lives requires going where customers congregate. Increasingly, that means meeting up with customers in the digital world with online and social media.

All of these customer-engagement essentials seem to come naturally to T-shirt and apparel maker Life is good. The brand was founded with a deeply felt sense of purpose: spreading the power of optimism. Optimism is where everything begins for us. Life is good. It's not a strategy; it's ingrained in who the company is.

In fact, Life is good doesn't even consider itself a clothing company. Instead, it's a lifestyle brand that spreads the power of optimism. More than just making T-shirts with fun sayings on them, the brand rallies people around the belief the power of optimism, and everything spirals out from there. The company backs its optimism philosophy with good deeds. For example, it donates 10 percent of its net profits each year to the Life is good Foundation to help kids in need.

It all started with founders Bert and John Jacobs selling T-shirts out of an old van at colleges and street fairs. After five years, with little to show for their efforts and on the verge of closing up shop, the brothers gathered friends at their apartment to get feedback on a new set of designs. The friends overwhelmingly chose Jake—the now-familiar beret-wearing, happy-go-lucky stick figure—and the slogan, "Life is good." Jake has now become a pop-culture icon. And the company's apparel has become a canvas for the optimistic Life is good message.

Life is good's infectious philosophy is a powerfully engaging one that people want to embrace and pass along to others. "The brand is about helping people to open up, create relationships, and connect with other people. Engagement . . . spreading optimism . . . is what Life is good does."

Such fundamental Life is good concepts—connecting, sharing, spreading optimism—don't lend themselves well to traditional apparel marketing that pushes products and messages out to the masses. Instead, the Jacobs brothers understood that nurturing the Life is good brand would require letting customers interact with and share the brand on their own terms. For example, every year the brand holds a Life is good Festival that draws tens of thousands of fans with family-friendly activities and an all-star entertainment lineup.

More recently, as all things digital have exploded onto the marketing scene, online and social media have become a perfect fit for sharing the Life is good mission with customers. Today, the company fosters a community of Optimists with more than 2.5 million Facebook fans, 250,000 Twitter followers, 25,300 followers on Pinterest, and an active YouTube channel. Life is good Radio provides a 24/7 playlist, because—as the site tells us—"Good tunes and good vibes go hand in hand."

But the strongest engagement platform is the brand's own Web site, Lifeisgood.com, one of the most active customer-engagement sites found anywhere online. The site's "Live It" section gives brand fans a breath of "fresh share." It's a place where they share photos, videos, and stories showing the brand's role in their trials, triumphs, and optimism. The postings illustrate the depth of engagement and inspiration the Life is good brand engenders. Here are just a few examples from the hundreds, even thousands, of user-generated postings you'll find at the Lifeisgood.com:

- *Jake and Jackie.* A photo of a couple's forearms, one featuring a colorful tattoo of Jake, the other a tattoo of his female counterpart Jackie, each with the Life is good tagline. "Here are pictures of our tattoos," says the couple. "Life is truly good!"
- *Love Is in the Air.* A couple holding up a Life is good banner, proclaiming "We used this pic [to spread] news of our engagement!!"
- *Thanks from Sebeta!* A picture of two young boys with the caption, "A couple of the blind students at the Sebeta School

Engaging customers: Life is good starts with a deeply felt, engagement-worthy sense of purpose: spreading the power of optimism. Then, "the real depth of engagement is in the commenting and community that go on around the brand."

for the Blind in Sebeta, Ethiopia, rocking in their new Life is good shirts!"

- *Snow Shoeing the Winter Away.* A picture posted by a registered nurse from northeast Washington of herself in a wintery forest. "At age 54 I learned to downhill ski," she says, "and this year, at age 59, I put on my first pair of snowshoes. As an RN for 40 years, I have seen way too many lives end early. So to honor those [whose] years were short, I am living my life to the fullest and it is good!"
- *All the Way Full.* A photo of a family of four on the beach accompanied by this story: "Throughout my Grace's treatment for a malignant brain tumor, we looked for silver linings. A friend gave me one of your shirts—HALF FULL—and it entered heavy rotation in my wardrobe. Grace loves the softness of the shirt, which was particularly nice against chemo-sore skin. Though only five at the time of her diagnosis, Grace understood fully the meaning of the shirt, and declared, "But Mommy, you're not HALF FULL, you're ALL THE WAY FULL!" And so ALL THE WAY FULL is how we're getting through cancer. This June, Grace will be two years beyond the end of treatment. We wanted to make sure you knew the significance your positivity has played in our lives."

These kinds of interactions from brand lovers are customer engagement at its best. In the end, the brand belongs to those who use and share it. Life is good doesn't solicit the stories at all. It knows that it doesn't own optimism—its community does. So it creates tools that let its consumers engage. To Life is good, true engagement is about deep meaningful relationships that go beyond the products it is selling. The real depth of engagement is in the commenting and community that go on around the brand. According to CEO Bert Jacobs: "You can't build a brand on your own; we have entered a world where customers co-author your story." The brand and its customers, Life is good.

Sources: Based on information from Gordon Wyner, "Getting Engaged," *Marketing Management*, Fall 2012, pp. 4–9; Bob Garfield and Doug Levy, "The Dawn of the Relationship Era," *Advertising Age*, January 2, 2012, pp. 1, 8–11; David Aponovich, "Powered by People, Fueled by Optimism," *Fast Company*, July 18, 2012, www.fastcompany.com/1842834/life-good-powered-people-fueled-optimism; "Bert and John Jacobs Deliver Commencement Address at 94th Annual Bentley University Ceremony," *Wall Street Journal*, March 18, 2012, http://online.wsj.com/article/PR-CO-20130318-909680.html?mod=crnews; Celia Brown, "Life is good Redefines Retailing Through Joy," *Forbes*, January 17, 2014, www.forbes.com/sites/sap/2014/01/17/life-is-good-redefines-retail-through-joy/; and www.lifeisgood.com and www.lifeisgood.com/good-vibes/, accessed September 2014.

by marketers or not—will be an increasingly important marketing force. Through a profusion of consumer-generated videos, shared reviews, blogs, mobile apps, and Web sites, consumers are playing a growing role in shaping their own and other consumers' brand experiences. Engaged consumers are now having a say in everything from product design, usage, and packaging to brand messaging, pricing, and distribution. Brands must embrace this new consumer empowerment and master the new digital and social media relationship tools or risk being left behind.

Partner Relationship Management

When it comes to creating customer value and building strong customer relationships, today's marketers know that they can't go it alone. They must work closely with a variety of marketing partners. In addition to being good at *customer relationship management*, marketers must also be good at **partner relationship management**—working closely with others inside and outside the company to jointly engage and bring more value to customers.

Partner relationship management
Working closely with partners in other company departments and outside the company to jointly bring greater value to customers.

Traditionally, marketers have been charged with understanding customers and representing customer needs to different company departments. However, in today's more connected world, every functional area in the organization can interact with customers. The new thinking is that—no matter what your job is in a company—you must understand marketing and be customer focused. Rather than letting each department go its own way, firms must link all departments in the cause of creating customer value.

Marketers must also partner with suppliers, channel partners, and others outside the company. Marketing channels consist of distributors, retailers, and others who connect the company to its buyers. The *supply chain* describes a longer channel, stretching from raw materials to components to final products that are carried to final buyers. Through *supply chain management*, companies today are strengthening their connections with partners all along the supply chain. They know that their fortunes rest on more than just how well they perform. Success at delivering customer value rests on how well their entire supply chain performs against competitors' supply chains.

Author Comment | Look back at Figure 1.1. In the first four steps of the marketing process, the company creates value *for* target customers and builds strong relationships with them. If it does that well, it can capture value *from* customers in return, in the form of loyal customers who buy and continue to buy the company's brands.

Capturing Value from Customers

The first four steps in the marketing process outlined in Figure 1.1 involve building customer relationships by creating and delivering superior customer value. The final step involves capturing value in return in the form of sales, market share, and profits. By creating superior customer value, the firm creates highly satisfied customers who stay loyal and buy more. This, in turn, means greater long-run returns for the firm. Here, we discuss the outcomes of creating customer value: customer loyalty and retention, share of market and share of customer, and customer equity.

Creating Customer Loyalty and Retention

Good customer relationship management creates customer satisfaction. In turn, satisfied customers remain loyal and talk favorably to others about the company and its products. Studies show big differences in the loyalty of customers who are less satisfied, somewhat satisfied, and completely satisfied. Even a slight drop from complete satisfaction can create an enormous drop in loyalty. Thus, the aim of customer relationship management is to create not only customer satisfaction but also customer delight.

Keeping customers loyal makes good economic sense. Loyal customers spend more and stay around longer. Research also shows that it's five times cheaper to keep an old customer than acquire a new one. Conversely, customer defections can be costly. Losing a customer means losing more than a single sale. It means losing the entire stream of purchases that the customer would make over a lifetime of patronage. For example, here is a classic illustration of **customer lifetime value**:[24]

Customer lifetime value
The value of the entire stream of purchases a customer makes over a lifetime of patronage.

Stew Leonard, who operates a highly profitable four-store supermarket in Connecticut and New York, once said that he sees $50,000 flying out of his store every time he sees a sulking customer. Why? Because his average customer spends about $100 a week, shops 50 weeks a year, and remains in the area for about 10 years. If this customer has an unhappy experience and switches to another supermarket, Stew Leonard's has lost $50,000 in lifetime revenue. The loss can be much greater if the disappointed customer shares the bad experience with other customers and causes them to defect.

To keep customers coming back, Stew Leonard's has created what the *New York Times* has dubbed the "Disneyland of Dairy Stores," complete with costumed characters, scheduled entertainment, a petting zoo, and animatronics throughout the store. From its humble beginnings as a small dairy store in 1969, Stew Leonard's has grown at an amazing pace. It's built 29 additions onto the original store, which now serves more than 300,000 customers each week. ● This legion of loyal shoppers is largely a result of the store's passionate approach to customer service. "Rule #1: The customer is always right. Rule #2: If the customer is ever wrong, reread rule #1."

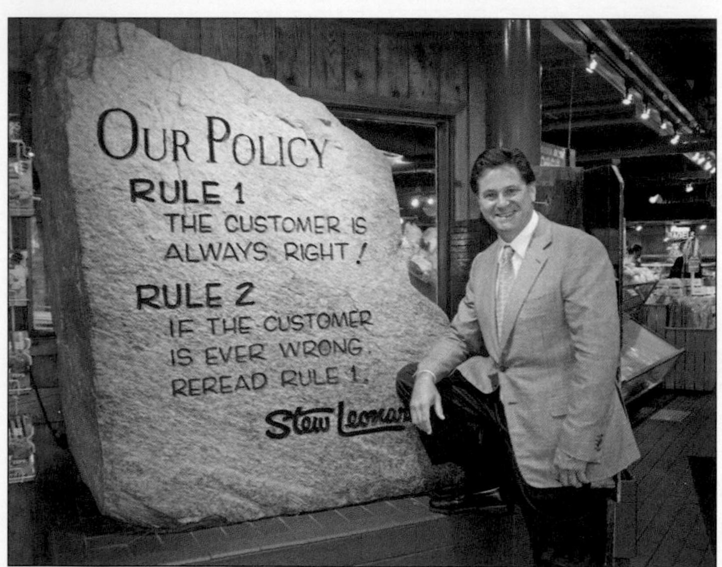

● **Customer lifetime value: To keep customers coming back, Stew Leonard's has created the "Disneyland of dairy stores." Rule #1—The customer is always right. Rule #2—If the customer is ever wrong, reread rule #1.**

Courtesy of Stew Leonard's

Stew Leonard is not alone in assessing customer lifetime value. Lexus, for example, estimates that a single satisfied and loyal customer is worth more than $600,000 in lifetime sales, and the estimated lifetime value of a Starbucks customer is more than $14,000.[25] In fact, a company can lose money on a specific transaction but still benefit greatly from a long-term relationship. This means that companies must aim high in building customer relationships. Customer delight creates an emotional relationship with a brand, not just a rational preference. And that relationship keeps customers coming back.

Growing Share of Customer

Beyond simply retaining good customers to capture customer lifetime value, good customer relationship management can help marketers increase their **share of customer**—the share they get of the customer's purchasing in their product categories. Thus, banks want to increase "share of wallet." Supermarkets and restaurants want to get more "share of stomach." Car companies want to increase "share of garage," and airlines want greater "share of travel."

Share of customer
The portion of the customer's purchasing that a company gets in its product categories.

To increase share of customer, firms can offer greater variety to current customers. Or they can create programs to cross-sell and up-sell to market more products and services to existing customers. For example, Amazon is highly skilled at leveraging relationships with its 237 million customers to increase its share of each customer's spending budget:[26]

Once they log onto Amazon.com, customers often buy more than they intend, and Amazon does all it can to help make that happen. The online giant continues to broaden its merchandise assortment, creating an ideal spot for one-stop shopping. And based on each customer's purchase and search history, the company recommends related products that might be of interest. This recommendation system influences up to 30 percent of all sales. Amazon's ingenious Amazon Prime two-day shipping program has also helped boost its share of customers' wallets. For an annual fee of $99, Prime members receive delivery of all their purchases within two days, whether it's a single paperback book or a 60-inch HDTV. According to one analyst, the ingenious Amazon Prime program "converts casual shoppers, who gorge on the gratification of having purchases reliably appear two days after the order, into Amazon addicts." As a result, Amazon's 16.7 million Prime customers now account for 56 percent of its U.S. sales. A Prime member is about six times more valuable to Amazon that a non-Prime member.

Building Customer Equity

We can now see the importance of not only acquiring customers but also keeping and growing them. The value of a company comes from the value of its current and future customers. Customer relationship management takes a long-term view. Companies want not only to create profitable customers but also "own" them for life, earn a greater share of their purchases, and capture their customer lifetime value.

What Is Customer Equity?

Customer equity
The total combined customer lifetime values of all of the company's customers.

The ultimate aim of customer relationship management is to produce high *customer equity*.[27] **Customer equity** is the total combined customer lifetime values of all of the company's current and potential customers. As such, it's a measure of the future value of the company's customer base. Clearly, the more loyal the firm's profitable customers, the higher its customer equity. Customer equity may be a better measure of a firm's performance than current sales or market share. Whereas sales and market share reflect the past, customer equity suggests the future. ● Consider Cadillac:[28]

In the 1970s and 1980s, Cadillac had some of the most loyal customers in the industry. To an entire generation of car buyers, the name *Cadillac* defined "The Standard of the World." Cadillac's share of the luxury car market reached a whopping 51 percent in 1976, and based on market share and sales, the brand's future looked rosy. However, measures of customer equity would have painted a bleaker picture. Cadillac customers were getting older (average age 60) and average customer lifetime value was falling. Many Cadillac buyers were on their last cars. Thus, although Cadillac's market share was good, its customer equity was not.

Compare this with BMW. Its more youthful and vigorous image didn't win BMW the early market share war. However, it did win BMW younger customers (average age about 40) with higher customer lifetime values. The result: In the years that followed, BMW's market share and profits soared while Cadillac's fortunes eroded badly. BMW overtook Cadillac in the 1980s. In recent years, Cadillac has struggled to make the Caddy cool again with edgier, high-performance designs that target a younger generation of consumers. The brand now bills itself as "The New Standard of the World" with marketing pitches based on "power, performance, and design," attributes that position it more effectively against the likes of BMW and Audi. However, for the past decade, Cadillac's share of the luxury car market has stagnated. The moral: Marketers should care not just about current sales and market share. Customer lifetime value and customer equity are the name of the game.

● Managing customer equity: To increase customer lifetime value, Cadillac is trying to make the Caddy cool again with edgier, high-performance designs that target a younger generation of consumers.
Toronto Star via Getty Images

Building the Right Relationships with the Right Customers

Companies should manage customer equity carefully. They should view customers as assets that need to be managed and maximized. But not all customers, not even all loyal customers, are good investments. Surprisingly, some loyal customers can be unprofitable, and some disloyal customers can be profitable. Which customers should the company acquire and retain?

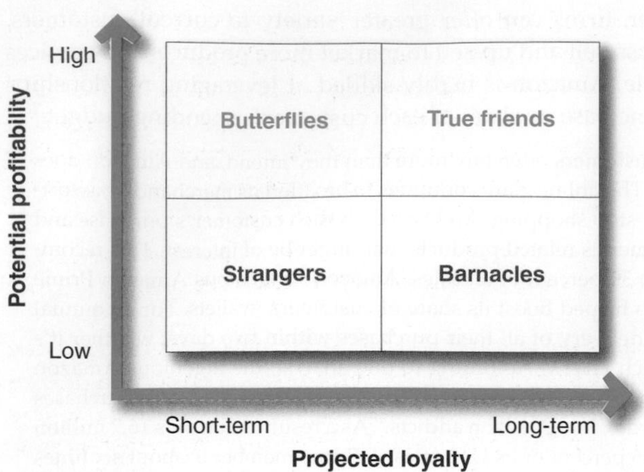

FIGURE | 1.5
Customer Relationship Groups

The company can classify customers according to their potential profitability and manage its relationships with them accordingly. **Figure 1.5** classifies customers into one of four relationship groups, according to their profitability and projected loyalty.[29] Each group requires a different relationship management strategy. *Strangers* show low potential profitability and little projected loyalty. There is little fit between the company's offerings and their needs. The relationship management strategy for these customers is simple: Don't invest anything in them; make money on every transaction.

Butterflies are potentially profitable but not loyal. There is a good fit between the company's offerings and their needs. However, like real butterflies, we can enjoy them for only a short while and then they're gone. An example is stock market investors who trade shares often and in large amounts but who enjoy hunting out the best deals without building a regular relationship with any single brokerage company. Efforts to convert butterflies into loyal customers are rarely successful. Instead, the company should enjoy the butterflies for the moment. It should create satisfying and profitable transactions with them, capturing as much of their business as possible in the short time during which they buy from the company. Then, it should move on and cease investing in them until the next time around.

True friends are both profitable and loyal. There is a strong fit between their needs and the company's offerings. The firm wants to make continuous relationship investments to delight these customers and nurture, retain, and grow them. It wants to turn true friends into *true believers*, who come back regularly and tell others about their good experiences with the company.

Barnacles are highly loyal but not very profitable. There is a limited fit between their needs and the company's offerings. An example is smaller bank customers who bank regularly but do not generate enough returns to cover the costs of maintaining their accounts. Like barnacles on the hull of a ship, they create drag. Barnacles are perhaps the most problematic customers. The company might be able to improve their profitability by selling them more, raising their fees, or reducing service to them. However, if they cannot be made profitable, they should be "fired."

The point here is an important one: Different types of customers require different engagement and relationship management strategies. The goal is to build the *right relationships* with the *right customers*.

Author Comment | Marketing doesn't take place in a vacuum. Now that we've discussed the five steps in the marketing process, let's look at how the ever-changing marketplace affects both consumers and the marketers who serve them. We'll look more deeply into these and other marketing environment factors in Chapter 3.

The Changing Marketing Landscape

Every day, dramatic changes are occurring in the marketplace. Richard Love of HP observed, "The pace of change is so rapid that the ability to change has now become a competitive advantage." Yogi Berra, the legendary New York Yankees catcher and manager, summed it up more simply when he said, "The future ain't what it used to be." As the marketplace changes, so must those who serve it.

In this section, we examine the major trends and forces that are changing the marketing landscape and challenging marketing strategy. We look at five major developments: the digital age, the changing economic environment, the growth of not-for-profit marketing, rapid globalization, and the call for more ethics and social responsibility.

The Digital Age: Online, Mobile, and Social Media Marketing

The explosive growth in digital technology has fundamentally changed the way we live—how we communicate, share information, access entertainment, and shop. An estimated 3 billion people—40 percent of the world's population—are now online. Nearly half of all American adults now own smartphones; 50 percent of those adults use their smartphones and other mobile devices to access social media sites. These numbers will only grow as digital technology rockets into the future.[30]

Most consumers are totally smitten with all things digital. For example, according to one study, more than half of Americans keep their mobile phone next to them when they sleep—they say it's the first thing they touch when they get up in the morning and the last thing they touch at night. Favorite online and mobile destinations include the profusion of Web sites and social media that have sprung up. Last year for the first time, people in the United States averaged more time per day with digital media (5.25 hours) than viewing TV (4.5 hours).[31]

Digital and social media marketing
Using digital marketing tools such as Web sites, social media, mobile apps and ads, online video, e-mail, and blogs that engage consumers anywhere, at any time, via their digital devices.

The consumer love affair with digital and mobile technology makes it fertile ground for marketers trying to engage customers. So it's no surprise that the Internet and rapid advances in digital and social media have taken the marketing world by storm. **Digital and social media marketing** involves using digital marketing tools such as Web sites, social media, mobile ads and apps, online video, e-mail, blogs, and other digital platforms that engage consumers anywhere, anytime via their computers, smartphones, tablets, Internet-ready TVs, and other digital devices. These days, it seems that every company is reaching out to customers with multiple Web sites, newsy Tweets and Facebook pages, viral ads and videos posted on YouTube, rich-media e-mails, and mobile apps that solve consumer problems and help them shop.

At the most basic level, marketers set up company and brand Web sites that provide information and promote the company's products. Many of these sites also serve as online brand communities, where customers can congregate and exchange brand-related interests and information. For example, Mountain Dew's "This Is How We Dew" Web site serves as a lifestyle hub where the brand's super-passionate fans can check out the latest Mountain Dew ads and videos, vote on new flavors, follow the adventures of Mountain Dew's amateur skateboarding team, "chase the taste" with NASCAR driver Dale Earnhardt, Jr., or just check out the Mountain Dew product lineup.[32]

Beyond brand Web sites, most companies are also integrating social and mobile media into their marketing mixes.

Social Media Marketing

It's hard to find a brand Web site, or even a traditional media ad, that doesn't feature links to the brand's Facebook, Twitter, Google+, LinkedIn, YouTube, Pinterest, Instagram, or other social media sites. Social media provide exciting opportunities to extend customer engagement and get people talking about a brand. ● Nearly 90 percent of all U.S. companies now use social media as part of their marketing mixes, and 78 percent have dedicated social marketing teams. By various estimates, social media spending accounts for about 10 percent of marketing budgets and will rise to an estimated nearly 20 percent within the next five years.[33]

● **Social media marketing: 90 percent of all U.S. companies now use social media. It's hard to find a brand that doesn't feature Facebook, Twitter, Google+, Pinterest, Instagram, YouTube, and other social media sites.**

© Anatolii Babii / Alamy

Some social media are huge—Facebook has more than 1.1 billion members; Twitter has more than 500 million; and Pinterest draws in 70 million. Instagram racks up an estimated 85 million unique monthly visitors. And Reddit, the online social news community, has nearly 70 million unique visitors a month from 174 countries. But more focused social media sites are also thriving, such as CafeMom, an online community of 20 million moms who exchange advice, entertainment, and commiseration at the community's online, Facebook, Twitter, Pinterest, YouTube, Google+, and mobile sites. Online social networks provide a digital home where people can connect and share important information and moments in their lives.

Using social media might involve something as simple as a contest or promotion to garner Facebook Likes, Tweets, or YouTube postings. For example, when Boylan Bottling Company ran Facebook promotions giving free bottles of its Shirley Temple soda to consumers who shared the promotion with others, Facebook chatter about the brand jumped to five times normal. But more than just "Likes," "tweets," or video posts, the goal of most social media campaigns is *social sharing*, getting people to talk with others and pass along their positive brand experiences. As Boylan Bottling's CEO puts it: "We've done some advertising to get Facebook likes, . . . but we've found that Facebook is a better place to percolate a frenzy around our brand."[34]

Method, maker of eco-friendly household cleaning and personal care products, relies *exclusively* on social media to promote its products and engage customers. Its quirky, zero-dollar global brand campaign—Clean Happy—is built entirely around 90-second brand videos posted on YouTube, Facebook, Twitter, and Method's blogger network. "We are the people against dirty," the videos proclaim. "Join us and clean happy." The social media work well for smaller brands like Method, which has an engaging eco-based story to tell. "The brands we compete against thrive in a 30-second spot world, . . . but we can't afford to go there yet," says Method's cofounder Eric Ryan. However, "brands [like ours] that have stories to tell have an advantage [in social media]."[35]

Mobile Marketing

Mobile marketing is perhaps the fastest-growing digital marketing platform. Twenty-nine percent of smartphone owners use their phones for shopping-related activities—browsing product information through apps or the mobile Web, making in-store price comparisons, reading online product reviews, finding and redeeming coupons, and more.[36] Smartphones are ever-present, always on, finely targeted, and highly personal. This makes them ideal for engaging customers anytime, anywhere as they move through the buying process. ● For example, Starbucks customers can use their mobile devices for everything from finding the nearest Starbucks and learning about new products to placing and paying for orders.

● **Mobile marketing: Starbucks customers can use their mobile devices for everything from finding the nearest Starbucks to placing and paying for orders.**
Associated Press

Marketers use mobile channels to stimulate immediate buying, make shopping easier, enrich the brand experience, or all of these. For example, P&G recently used mobile marketing to boost sampling through vending machines—called Freebies—that it placed in Walmart stores. To get a sample of, say, Tide Pods, customers first used their mobile phones in the store to check into the Tide Pods Facebook site, where they received product information and marketing.

Walmart and PEDIGREE joined forces to run a mobile-based "Pets Love Walmart" campaign to promote the retailer as a place to shop for pet food while also improving the brand's sales:[37]

> Prior to the "Pets Love Walmart" campaign, of the 90 million pet owners who shop weekly at Walmart, fewer than 60 percent were buying pet food from the retailer. That left plenty of opportunity to capture more sales. When shoppers used their phones in stores to scan QR codes on PEDIGREE pet food packages, a "bowl of food" was donated directly to a pet shelter. The code also sent shoppers to a mobile Web site within Walmart.com, where they found promotional offers, information about pet care and Walmart's in-store pet education events, and a link to make additional charitable donations to local pet shelters. The award-winning mobile campaign boosted PEDIGREE brand sales in Walmart stores by 25 percent and caused a 15-point jump in customer agreement with the statement "Walmart is the first place I think of for pet supplies."

Although online, social media, and mobile marketing offer huge potential, most marketers are still learning how to use them effectively. The key is to blend the new digital approaches with traditional marketing to create a smoothly integrated marketing strategy and mix. We will examine digital, mobile, and social media marketing throughout the text—they touch almost every area of marketing strategy and tactics. Then, after we've covered the marketing basics, we'll look more deeply into digital and direct marketing in Chapter 17.

The Changing Economic Environment

The Great Recession of 2008 to 2009 and its aftermath hit American consumers hard. After two decades of overspending, new economic realities forced consumers to bring their consumption back in line with their incomes and rethink their buying priorities.

In today's post-recession era, consumer incomes and spending are again on the rise. However, even as the economy has strengthened, rather than reverting to their old free-spending ways, Americans are now showing an enthusiasm for frugality not seen in decades. Sensible consumption has made a comeback, and it appears to be here to stay. The new consumer spending values emphasize simpler living and more value for the dollar. Despite their rebounding means, consumers continue to buy less, clip more coupons, swipe their credit cards less, and put more in the bank.

Many consumers are reconsidering their very definition of the good life. "People are finding happiness in old-fashioned virtues—thrift, savings, do-it-yourself projects, self-improvement, hard work, faith, and community," says one consumer behavior expert. "We are moving from mindless to mindful consumption." The new, more frugal spending values don't mean that people have resigned themselves to lives of deprivation. As the economy has improved, consumers are indulging in luxuries and bigger-ticket purchases again, just more sensibly.

In response, companies in all industries—from discounters such as Target to luxury brands such as Lexus—have realigned their marketing strategies with the new economic realities. More than ever, marketers are emphasizing the *value* in their value propositions. They are focusing on value-for-the-money, practicality, and durability in their product offerings and marketing pitches.

For example, for years discount retailer Target focused increasingly on the "Expect More" side of its "Expect More. Pay Less." value proposition. Its carefully cultivated "upscale-discounter" image successfully differentiated it from Walmart's more hard-nosed "lowest-price" position. But when the economy soured, many consumers worried that Target's trendier assortments and hip marketing also meant higher prices. So Target has shifted its balance more toward the "Pay Less" half of the slogan, making certain that its prices are in line with Walmart's and that customers know it. Although still trendy, Target's marketing now emphasizes more practical price and savings appeals. Offering "more for your money" holds a prominent place in the Target mission. "We think a lot about your budget and how to give you the best value every time you shop with us," says the company.[38]

In adjusting to the new economy, companies may be tempted to cut their marketing budgets and slash prices in an effort to coax more frugal customers into opening their wallets. However, although cutting costs and offering selected discounts can be important marketing tactics, smart marketers understand that making cuts in the wrong places can damage long-term brand images and customer relationships. The challenge is to balance the brand's value proposition with the current times while also enhancing its long-term equity. Thus, rather than slashing prices in uncertain economic times, many marketers hold the line on prices and instead explain why their brands are worth it.

The Growth of Not-for-Profit Marketing

In recent years, marketing has also become a major part of the strategies of many not-for-profit organizations, such as colleges, hospitals, museums, zoos, symphony orchestras, foundations, and even churches. The nation's not-for-profits face stiff competition for support and membership. Sound marketing can help them attract membership, funds, and support.

For example, Alex's Lemonade Stand Foundation is a not-for-profit organization with a special mission: "Fighting childhood cancer, one cup at a time." It all started with a simple lemonade stand, run by 4-year-old Alexandra "Alex" Scott, who was battling cancer. Alex wanted to raise money for doctors so that they could "help other kids, like they helped me." In its first summer, little Alex's lemonade stand raised $2,000. By age 8, with the help of founding sponsor Volvo and a nationwide network of volunteer-held lemonade stands, Alex had raised one million dollars for pediatric cancer research. ● Although Alex has passed away, the Alex's Lemonade Stand Foundation (ALSF) keeps her dream alive through a comprehensive marketing effort:[39]

> The Alex's Lemonade Stand Foundation's marketing revolves around a well-designed Web site (*AlexsLemonade.org*), which details the organization, its mission, sponsored research, a logo gifts and gear store, and special events such as National Lemonade Days, the Great Chefs Event, and Alex's Million Mile—Run, Walk, Ride. The site also gives detailed instructions for holding a successful local lemonade stand, backed by a fund-raising kit containing ALSF-branded banners, signs, posters, and flyers. ALSF makes good use of social media. Its blog discusses issues of childhood cancer and shares stories about ALSF "heroes and amazing supporters." And its well-curated Facebook, Instagram, Twitter, YouTube, Pinterest, and LinkedIn sites have created an active community of dedicated fans.

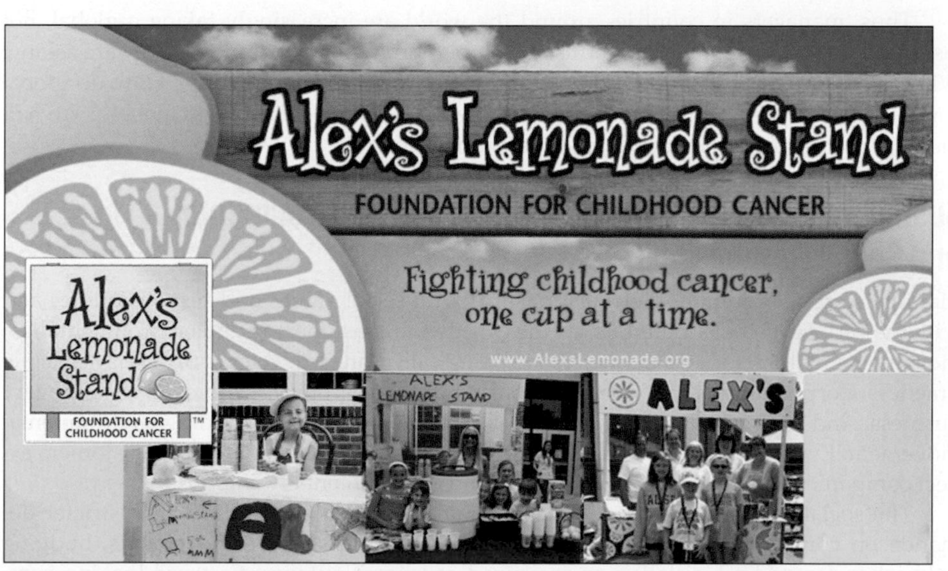

● **Not-for-profit marketing: Alex's Lemonade Stand Foundation effectively markets its mission of "Fighting childhood cancer, one cup at a time." ALSF has raised more than $75 million for pediatric cancer research.**

Alex's Lemonade Stand Foundation for Childhood Cancer

Finally, ALSF has assembled a network of corporate marketing partners—from Volvo, Northwestern Mutual, and Toys "R" Us to Applebee's, Rita's Italian Ice, and A&P. For example, at Applebee's, if you donate to ALSF, you get a coupon for a free kid's meal or frozen lemonade. At Rita's, you can buy a paper lemon for $1 or text to a number to donate $5. Volvo holds raffles for new cars, with all proceeds going to ALSF. Northwestern Mutual supports the ALSF's Family Travel Fund, which pays for gasoline and other expenses to help families get their children to and from treatment. Thus, Alex's one lemonade stand sparked a foundation that effectively markets her cause to raise funds to fight childhood cancer. Since 2005, the Alex's Lemonade Stand Foundation has raised more than $75 million and funded over 375 medical research projects.

Government agencies have also shown an increased interest in marketing. For example, the U.S. military has a marketing plan to attract recruits to its different services, and various government agencies are now designing social marketing campaigns to encourage energy conservation and concern for the environment or discourage smoking, illegal drug use, and obesity. Even the once-stodgy U.S. Postal Service has developed innovative marketing to sell commemorative stamps, promote its Priority Mail services, and lift its image as a contemporary and competitive organization. In all, the U.S. government is the nation's 50th largest advertiser, with an annual advertising budget of more than $827 million.[40]

Rapid Globalization

As they are redefining their customer relationships, marketers are also taking a fresh look at the ways in which they relate with the broader world around them. Today, almost every company, large or small, is touched in some way by global competition. A neighborhood florist buys its flowers from Mexican nurseries, and a large U.S. electronics manufacturer competes in its home markets with giant Korean rivals. A fledgling Internet retailer finds itself receiving orders from all over the world at the same time that an American consumer goods producer introduces new products into emerging markets abroad.

American firms have been challenged at home by the skillful marketing of European and Asian multinationals. Companies such as Toyota, Nestlé, and Samsung have often outperformed their U.S. competitors in American markets. Similarly, U.S. companies in a wide range of industries have developed truly global operations, making and selling their products worldwide. Quintessentially American McDonald's now serves 69 million customers daily in more than 34,000 local restaurants in 118 countries worldwide—71 percent of its corporate revenues come from outside the United States. Similarly, Nike markets in 190 countries, with non-U.S. sales accounting for 55 percent of its worldwide sales.[41] Today, companies are not just selling more of their locally produced goods in international markets; they are also sourcing more supplies and components abroad and developing new products for specific markets around the world.

Thus, managers in countries around the world are increasingly taking a global, not just local, view of the company's industry, competitors, and opportunities. They are asking: What is global marketing? How does it differ from domestic marketing? How do global competitors and forces affect our business? To what extent should we "go global"? We will discuss the global marketplace in more detail in Chapter 19.

Sustainable Marketing—The Call for More Environmental and Social Responsibility

Marketers are reexamining their relationships with social values and responsibilities and with the very Earth that sustains us. As the worldwide consumerism and environmentalism movements mature, today's marketers are being called on to develop *sustainable marketing* practices. Corporate ethics and social responsibility have become hot topics for almost every business. And few companies can ignore the renewed and very demanding environmental movement. Every company action can affect customer relationships. Today's customers expect companies to deliver value in a socially and environmentally responsible way.

The social responsibility and environmental movements will place even stricter demands on companies in the future. Some companies resist these movements, budging only when forced by legislation or organized consumer outcries. Forward-looking companies, however, readily accept their responsibilities to the world around them. They view sustainable marketing as an opportunity to do well by doing good. They seek ways to profit by serving immediate needs and the best long-run interests of their customers and communities.

Sustainable marketing: Ben & Jerry's three-part "linked prosperity" mission drives it to make fantastic ice cream (product mission), manage the company for sustainable financial growth (economic mission), and use the company "in innovative ways to make the world a better place" (social mission).

Some companies, such as Patagonia, Timberland, Method, Ben & Jerry's, and others, practice *caring capitalism*, setting themselves apart by being civic minded and responsible. They build social and environmental responsibility into their company value and mission statements. For example, Ben & Jerry's, a division of Unilever, has long prided itself on being a "values-led business," one that creates "linked prosperity" for everyone connected to the brand—from suppliers to employees to customers and communities:[42]

> Under its three-part mission, Ben & Jerry's wants to make fantastic ice cream (product mission), manage the company for sustainable financial growth (economic mission), and use the company "in innovative ways to make the world a better place" (social mission). Ben & Jerry's backs its mission with actions. For example, the company is committed to using wholesome, natural, non-GMO, Fairtrade-certified ingredients and buys from local farms. It employs business practices "that respect the earth and the environment," investing in wind energy, solar usage, travel offsets, and carbon neutrality. Its Caring Dairy program helps farmers develop more sustainable practices on the farm ("Caring Dairy means happy cows, happy farmers, and a happy planet"). The Ben & Jerry's Foundation awards nearly $2 million annually in grassroots grants to community service organizations and projects in communities across the nation. Ben & Jerry's also operates 14 PartnerShops, scoop shops that are independently owned and operated by community-based not-for-profit organizations. The company waives standard franchise fees for these shops.

Sustainable marketing presents both opportunities and challenges for marketers. We will revisit the topic of sustainable marketing in greater detail in Chapter 20.

Author Comment Remember Figure 1.1 outlining the marketing process? Now, based on everything we've discussed in this chapter, we'll expand that figure to provide a roadmap for learning marketing throughout the remainder of the text.

So, What Is Marketing? Pulling It All Together

At the start of this chapter, Figure 1.1 presented a simple model of the marketing process. Now that we've discussed all the steps in the process, **Figure 1.6** presents an expanded model that will help you pull it all together. What is marketing? Simply put, marketing is the process of engaging customers and building profitable customer relationships by creating value for customers and capturing value in return.

The first four steps of the marketing process focus on creating value for customers. The company first gains a full understanding of the marketplace by researching customer needs and managing marketing information. It then designs a customer-driven marketing strategy based on the answers to two simple questions. The first question is "What consumers will we serve?" (market segmentation and targeting). Good marketing companies know that they cannot serve all customers in every way. Instead, they need to focus their resources on the customers they can serve best and most profitably. The second marketing strategy question is "How can we best serve targeted customers?" (differentiation and positioning). Here, the marketer outlines a value proposition that spells out what values the company will deliver to win target customers.

With its marketing strategy chosen, the company now constructs an integrated marketing program—consisting of a blend of the four marketing mix elements, the four Ps—that transforms the marketing strategy into real value for customers. The company develops product offers and creates strong brand identities for them. It prices these offers to create real customer value and distributes the offers to make them available to target consumers. Finally, the company designs promotion programs that engage target customers, communicate the value proposition, and persuade customers to act on the market offering.

Perhaps the most important step in the marketing process involves building value-laden, profitable relationships with target customers. Throughout the process, marketers practice customer relationship management to create customer satisfaction and delight. They engage customers in the process of creating brand conversations, experiences, and community. In creating customer value and relationships, however, the company cannot go it alone. It must work closely with marketing partners both inside the company and

FIGURE | 1.6
An Expanded Model of the Marketing Process

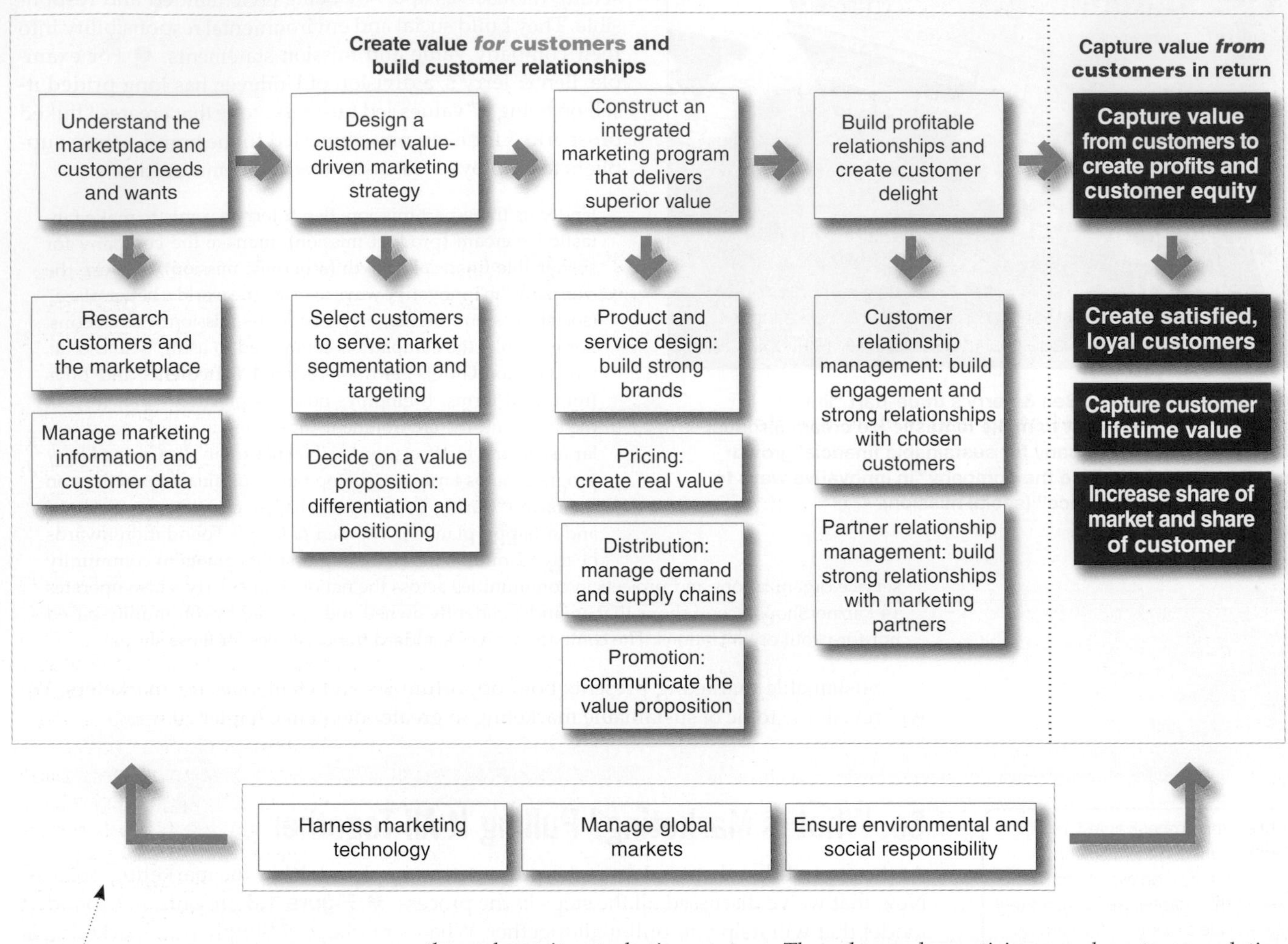

Create value for customers and build customer relationships
Capture value from customers in return
Understand the marketplace and customer needs and wants
Design a customer value-driven marketing strategy
Construct an integrated marketing program that delivers superior value
Build profitable relationships and create customer delight
Capture value from customers to create profits and customer equity
Research customers and the marketplace
Manage marketing information and customer data
Select customers to serve: market segmentation and targeting
Decide on a value proposition: differentiation and positioning
Product and service design: build strong brands
Pricing: create real value
Distribution: manage demand and supply chains
Promotion: communicate the value proposition
Customer relationship management: build engagement and strong relationships with chosen customers
Partner relationship management: build strong relationships with marketing partners
Create satisfied, loyal customers
Capture customer lifetime value
Increase share of market and share of customer
Harness marketing technology
Manage global markets
Ensure environmental and social responsibility

This expanded version of Figure 1.1 at the beginning of the chapter provides a good road map for the rest of the text. The underlying concept of the entire text is that marketing creates value for customers in order to capture value from customers in return.

throughout its marketing system. Thus, beyond practicing good customer relationship management and customer-engagement marketing, firms must also practice good partner relationship management.

The first four steps in the marketing process create value *for* customers. In the final step, the company reaps the rewards of its strong customer relationships by capturing value *from* customers. Delivering superior customer value creates highly satisfied customers who will buy more and buy again. This helps the company capture customer lifetime value and greater share of customer. The result is increased long-term customer equity for the firm.

Finally, in the face of today's changing marketing landscape, companies must take into account three additional factors. In building customer and partner relationships, they must harness marketing technologies in the new digital age, take advantage of global opportunities, and ensure that they act sustainably in an environmentally and socially responsible way.

Figure 1.6 provides a good road map to future chapters of this text. Chapters 1 and 2 introduce the marketing process, with a focus on building customer relationships and capturing value from customers. Chapters 3 through 6 address the first step of the marketing process—understanding the marketing environment, managing marketing information, and understanding consumer and business buyer behavior. In Chapter 7, we look more deeply into the two major marketing strategy decisions: selecting which customers to serve (segmentation and targeting) and determining a value proposition (differentiation and positioning). Chapters 8 through 17 discuss the marketing mix variables, one by one. Chapter 18 sums up customer-driven marketing strategy and creating competitive advantage in the marketplace. The final two chapters examine special marketing considerations: global marketing and sustainable marketing.

1 Reviewing the Concepts

OBJECTIVES REVIEW AND KEY TERMS

Objectives Review

Today's successful companies—whether large or small, for-profit or not-for-profit, domestic or global—share a strong customer focus and a heavy commitment to marketing. The goal of marketing is to engage customers and manage profitable customer relationships.

OBJECTIVE 1 Define marketing and outline the steps in the marketing process. *(pp 29–30)*

Marketing is the process by which companies create value for customers and build strong customer relationships in order to capture value from customers in return. The marketing process involves five steps. The first four steps create value *for* customers. First, marketers need to understand the marketplace and customer needs and wants. Next, marketers design a customer-driven marketing strategy with the goal of getting, keeping, and growing target customers. In the third step, marketers construct a marketing program that actually delivers superior value. All of these steps form the basis for the fourth step, building profitable customer relationships and creating customer delight. In the final step, the company reaps the rewards of strong customer relationships by capturing value *from* customers.

OBJECTIVE 2 Explain the importance of understanding the marketplace and customers and identify the five core marketplace concepts. *(pp 30–33)*

Outstanding marketing companies go to great lengths to learn about and understand their customers' *needs*, *wants*, and *demands*. This understanding helps them to design want-satisfying market offerings and build value-laden customer relationships by which they can capture *customer lifetime value* and greater *share of customer*. The result is increased long-term *customer equity* for the firm.

The core marketplace concepts are needs, wants, and demands; market offerings (products, services, and experiences); value and satisfaction; exchange and relationships; and markets. Wants are the form taken by human needs when shaped by culture and individual personality. When backed by buying power, wants become demands. Companies address needs by putting forth a value proposition, a set of benefits that they promise to consumers to satisfy their needs. The value proposition is fulfilled through a market offering, which delivers customer value and satisfaction, resulting in long-term exchange relationships with customers.

OBJECTIVE 3 Identify the key elements of a customer-driven marketing strategy and discuss the marketing management orientations that guide marketing strategy. *(pp 33–37)*

To design a winning marketing strategy, the company must first decide whom it will serve. It does this by dividing the market into segments of customers (*market segmentation*) and selecting which segments it will cultivate (*target marketing*). Next, the company must decide *how* it will serve targeted customers (how it will *differentiate and position* itself in the marketplace).

Marketing management can adopt one of five competing market orientations. The *production concept* holds that management's task is to improve production efficiency and bring down prices. The *product concept* holds that consumers favor products that offer the most in quality, performance, and innovative features; thus, little promotional effort is required. The *selling concept* holds that consumers will not buy enough of an organization's products unless it undertakes a large-scale selling and promotion effort. The *marketing concept* holds that achieving organizational goals depends on determining the needs and wants of target markets and delivering the desired satisfactions more effectively and efficiently than competitors do. The *societal marketing concept* holds that generating customer satisfaction *and* long-run societal well-being through sustainable marketing strategies is key to both achieving the company's goals and fulfilling its responsibilities.

OBJECTIVE 4 Discuss customer relationship management and identify strategies for creating value *for* customers and capturing value *from* customers in return. *(pp 37–48)*

Broadly defined, *customer relationship management* is the process of building and maintaining profitable customer relationships by delivering superior customer value and satisfaction. *Customer-engagement marketing* aims to make a brand a meaningful part of consumers' conversations and lives through direct and continuous customer involvement in shaping brand conversations, experiences, and community. The aim of customer relationship management and customer engagement is to produce high *customer equity,* the total combined customer lifetime values of all of the company's customers. The key to building lasting relationships is the creation of superior *customer value* and *satisfaction.*

Companies want to not only acquire profitable customers but also build relationships that will keep them and grow "share of customer." Different types of customers require different customer relationship management strategies. The marketer's aim is to build the *right relationships* with the *right customers.* In return for creating value *for* targeted customers, the company captures value *from* customers in the form of profits and customer equity.

In building customer relationships, good marketers realize that they cannot go it alone. They must work closely with marketing partners inside and outside the company. In addition to being good at customer relationship management, they must also be good at *partner relationship management.*

OBJECTIVE 5 **Describe the major trends and forces that are changing the marketing landscape in this age of relationships.** *(pp 48–53)*

Dramatic changes are occurring in the marketing arena. The digital age has created exciting new ways to learn about and relate to individual customers. As a result, advances in digital and social media have taken the marketing world by storm. Online, mobile, and social media marketing offer exciting new opportunities to target customers more selectively and engage them more deeply. Although the new digital and social media offer huge potential, most marketers are still learning how to use them effectively. The key is to blend the new digital approaches with traditional marketing to create a smoothly integrated marketing strategy and mix.

The Great Recession hit American consumers hard, causing them to rethink their buying priorities and bring their consumption back in line with their incomes. Even as the post-recession economy has strengthened, Americans are now showing an enthusiasm for frugality not seen in decades. Sensible consumption has made a comeback, and it appears to be here to stay. More than ever, marketers must now emphasize the *value* in their value propositions. The challenge is to balance a brand's value proposition with current times while also enhancing its long-term equity.

In recent years, marketing has become a major part of the strategies for many not-for-profit organizations, such as colleges, hospitals, museums, zoos, symphony orchestras, foundations, and even churches. Also, in an increasingly smaller world, many marketers are now connected *globally* with their customers and marketing partners. Today, almost every company, large or small, is touched in some way by global competition. Finally, today's marketers are also reexamining their ethical and societal responsibilities. Marketers are being called on to take greater responsibility for the social and environmental impacts of their actions.

Pulling it all together, as discussed throughout the chapter, the major new developments in marketing can be summed up in a single concept: *creating and capturing customer value*. Today, marketers of all kinds are taking advantage of new opportunities for building value-laden relationships with their customers, their marketing partners, and the world around them.

MyMarketingLab

Go to **mymktlab.com** to complete the problems marked with this icon .

Key Terms

OBJECTIVE 1

Marketing (p 29)

OBJECTIVE 2

Needs (p 30)
Wants (p 30)
Demands (p 30)
Market offerings (p 31)
Marketing myopia (p 31)
Exchange (p 32)
Market (p 32)

OBJECTIVE 3

Marketing management (p 33)
Production concept (p 34)
Product concept (p 34)
Selling concept (p 34)
Marketing concept (p 35)
Societal marketing concept (p 35)

OBJECTIVE 4

Customer relationship management (p 37)
Customer-perceived value (p 37)
Customer satisfaction (p 38)
Customer-engagement marketing (p 42)
Consumer-generated marketing (p 43)
Partner relationship management (p 45)
Customer lifetime value (p 46)
Share of customer (p 46)
Customer equity (p 47)

OBJECTIVE 5

Digital and social media marketing (p 49)

DISCUSSION AND CRITICAL THINKING

Discussion Questions

1-1 Define marketing. What is marketing myopia and how can it be avoided? (AACSB: Communication; Reflective Thinking)

1-2 Explain the importance of needs, wants, and demands and how these frame marketing activities. (AACSB: Communication)

1-3 Describe the five different competing marketing orientations that a company can adopt to drive its marketing strategy. (AACSB: Communication; Reflective Thinking)

1-4 Companies want to acquire profitable customers. Describe how marketers build relationships with customers. (AACSB: Communication; Reflective Thinking)

1-5 When implementing customer relationship management, why might a business desire fewer customers over more customers? Shouldn't the focus of marketing be to acquire as many customers as possible? (AACSB: Communication; Reflective Thinking)

Critical Thinking Exercises

1-6 Select an FTSE 100 company. How much did the company spend on marketing activities in the most recent year for which data are available? What percentage of sales do marketing expenditures represent for the company? Have these expenditures increased or decreased over the past five years? Write a brief report of your findings. (AACSB: Communication; Analytic Reasoning)

1-7 Some believe that social marketing is primarily effective only for bigger companies with the time and capacity to manage and update their media content. Choose a local business and evaluate its effectiveness in creating customer engagement. Is the content up to date and relevant? How does it manage its content? (AACSB: Communication; Use of IT; Reflective Thinking)

1-8 Use the Internet to search for salary information regarding jobs in marketing in your country or region. What is the national average salary for five different jobs in marketing? How do the averages compare in different areas of the country? Write a brief report on your findings. (AACSB: Communication; Use of IT; Reflective Thinking)

MINICASES AND APPLICATIONS

Online, Mobile, and Social Media Marketing Retro Console

The ZX Spectrum was an 8-bit personal home computer released in the UK in 1982 by Sinclair Research Ltd. Scroll forward 23 years and the Spectrum is back! Not exactly as the same device; for one thing, you cannot program with it. And there is no need for it, as the new version comes already loaded with over 1,400 games. Since the launch of the machine, over 24,000 compatible software titles have been released, and even today about 100 are released every year. Behind the original computer was Sir Clive Sinclair, who was also the inventor of the first pocket TV in 1966 and the first pocket calculator in 1972. It has been estimated that over 5 million Spectrum units were sold. The original buyers, now in their late 40s or early 50s, have flocked to the Indiegogo crowd-funding campaign for the Sinclair Spectrum Vega, which is based on the original Spectrum, and has a simple and elegant design with five buttons and a control pad. The plan for the new Vega is that oncethe first 1,000 limited-edition versions have been manufactured and shipped by Retro Computers Ltd, the company will make the next 3,000 units and then move on to batches of 10,000. As production scales up, the price will drop. Even at the launch price, with the games included, the Vega costs about 1 percent of the total cost of the computer and the games when they were launched.

1-9 Debate whether there is still a market for this sort of product beyond a relatively small market consisting of fans with an interest in retro products. (AACSB: Communication; Reflective Thinking)

1-10 Brainstorm three similar technology-based products that could be reinvented for today's market. Again, speculate on whether there is just a small market of enthusiasts for such products or whether a broader market potential could be discovered. (AACSB: Communication; Reflective Thinking)

Marketing Ethics Extreme Baby Monitoring

Every parents' fear when they put an infant to sleep is Sudden Infant Death Syndrome (SIDS)—the sudden unexplainable death of an otherwise healthy baby. In the United States, about 2,000 infants die each year of SIDS, the third leading cause of infant death. For $199, parents can buy monitors that track babies' vital signs, such as respiration, heart rate, skin temperature, sleeping position, and quality of sleep. The Mimo Smart Baby Monitor is a cute clip-on turtle that attaches to a special organic cotton onesie, and the Owlet Baby Monitor is a smart sock that looks like a little toeless boot. If parents don't want to attach these devices on their little ones, they can opt for the SafeToSleep Breathing Monitor sheet with a built in monitor. All of these devices stream data to parents' smartphones. Manufacturers of these devices promote them to parents for "your baby's health" or "gives you that extra assurance" to protect against SIDS. However, several government agencies such as the Food and Drug Administration, the Consumer Product Safety Commission, the Center for Disease Control, and the National Institute of Health, as well as the American Academy of Pediatrics, all agree that these devices cannot protect a baby from SIDS. But fear sells, and most of these manufacturers cannot keep up with the demand for their products.

1-11 Is it right for marketers to play on parents' fear to sell products that experts conclude are not necessary or effective? (AACSB: Communication; Ethical Reasoning; Reflective Thinking)

1-12 Discuss other examples of marketers using emotion to sell products. Are they ethical? (AACSB: Communication; Ethical Reasoning)

Marketing by the Numbers Consumers Rule!

Private consumption makes up a large portion of the UK gross domestic product (GDP). The UK Customer Satisfaction Index (UKCSI) is the national measure of customer satisfaction. Published every six months, the index is based on an online survey of consumers that has been designed to be demographically representative of the UK population. The July 2013 UKCSI incorporated over 30,000 responses from approximately 9,000 individual customers. The UKCSI rates organizations in 13 sectors of the economy. It provides satisfaction ratings for each of the 13 sectors and an overall UK rating. It is published bi-annually and is used to track trends over time as well as to provide a snapshot of ratings. The UKCSI is based on real consumers' actual (and recent) experiences with specific organizations.

1-13 Visit www.instituteofcustomerservice.com and learn about the UKCSI. Write a report explaining the index and comparing the ratings for five different industries along with the national average. Are there differences in customer satisfaction across industries? Explain why or why not. (AACSB: Communication; Use of IT; Reflective Thinking)

1-14 The Customer Satisfaction Index (CSI), similar to the UKCSI, is used in many countries. Find another country's CSI and compare these results to those in the UKCSI. Are UK consumers more or less satisfied than consumers in the other country? Are trends in the national score similar? (AACSB: Communication; Use of IT; Reflective Thinking)

Video Case Zappos

These days, online retailers are a dime a dozen. But in a short period of time, Zappos has become a billion-dollar e-tailer. How did it hit the dot-com jackpot? By providing some of the best service available anywhere. Zappos customers are showered with such perks as free shipping both ways, surprise upgrades to overnight service, a 365-day return policy, and a call center that is always open. Customers are also delighted by employees who are empowered to spontaneously hand out rewards based on unique needs.

With such attention to customer service, it's no surprise that Zappos has an almost cultlike following of repeat customers. But remaining committed to the philosophy that the customer is always right can be challenging. This video highlights some of the dilemmas that can arise from operating within a highly customer-centric strategy. Zappos also demonstrates the ultimate rewards it receives from keeping that commitment.

After viewing the video featuring Zappos, answer the following questions:

1-15 Describe Zappos' market offering.

1-16 What is Zappos' value proposition? How does it relate to its market offering?

1-17 How does Zappos build long-term customer relationships?

Company Case Abou Shakra Restaurant: Creating Customer Value the Old-Fashioned Way

Abou Shakra is a chain of restaurants in Egypt well known for charcoal cooking—grilled meat, kebabs, and kofta. In 1947 Ahmed Abou Shakra opened his first Abou Shakra restaurant in El Kasr El Einy, a famous central district in Cairo. The first restaurant was not in a consumer-attractive neighborhood, but that did not stop Abou Shakra, who believed that offering healthy, tasty, and well-marinated food was more important than location in attracting customers and having them return time and again—if they received a good meal, the location of the restaurant would not have much bearing on their future dining decisions. Initially the restaurant's menu was very simple; it mainly consisted of basic traditional Egyptian dishes, which was the standard menu offered in similar establishments at the time. Abou Shakra decided to keep his menu simple and traditional to avoid the risks associated with offering unfamiliar dishes to consumers. As a result, he focused on providing well-known traditional dishes of exceptional quality.

Succeeding in a Competitive Market

When the first Abou Shakra restaurant was established, there was not a wide variety of cuisines featured at restaurants, such as Indian, Chinese, and Italian, which are widely available today. As noted, Abou Shakra's competitors at the time also offered traditional oriental Egyptian food, and due to a lack of other cuisines, he was essentially competing with the whole market. It was thus very challenging to start up a business in a highly competitive market, and it was necessary for Abou Shakra to ensure that he could offer something that would give him an advantage over his competitors. This advantage turned out to be the great customer value offered by Abou Shakra, which was not offered by the majority of his competitors.

Abou Shakra restaurants have maintained the persistent focus on customer well-being and satisfaction that originally gave them an advantage over their competitors, and this is one of the reasons for their success. The importance that the company places on elegant dishes, prepared with passion, and providing a memorable experience to their guests has endured right from Abou Shakra's establishment. We will now take a closer look at how Abou Shakra applies the philosophy of offering customer value.

Abou Shakra owns its own factory, which supplies all branches and outlets with their daily requirements of fresh meat and poultry. The meat is of high quality—only the best beef and lamb. Meat is delivered to the factory daily, and a governmental veterinary inspection is performed to ensure that the meat is fresh and of good quality. The factory is equipped with the latest technology to guarantee that the meat is stored at the correct temperature to ensure its freshness.

The fruits and vegetables are also delivered daily and are specially stored to maintain freshness up to the time of serving. Abou Shakra's quality control department ensures that all finished products are of outstanding quality, and oversees practices that prevent any of the ingredients from being contaminated. The company has signed a contract with SGS Egypt to supervise its health, safety, and hygiene practices, ensuring that they are of the highest standard.

The Abou Shakra menu has changed very little over the past 60 years, maintaining the simple offering of traditional Egyptian dishes with a particular focus on grilled dishes, which is now Abou Shakra's speciality. The primary aim of Abou Shakra is to keep the menu simple so as to wholly master the dishes offered. This has encouraged customer loyalty, as customers often choose their favorite dishes every time they eat at Abou Shakra. This has also led to Abou Shakra being one of the most popular places for oriental food in Egypt.

Keeping the menu simple also limits the costs of purchasing different ingredients from several suppliers. If this was not the case, the recruitment of more managers would be required to contact the suppliers and follow up on the orders. There would also be more supervisors needed to ensure that the delivery and storage processes take place smoothly and that each outlet receives its supplies on time. In addition, more chefs who are specialized in the new dishes added to the menu would be necessary as well.

Abou Shakra's managers pay attention to every small detail; they ensure that each restaurant is spotless and that the kitchen is held to the highest cleanliness standard. All utensils and cutlery go through a sterilization process to ensure their sanitation and safety. The tables are wiped with a special detergent so that customers feel they are eating in a hygienic environment.

Focusing on Customer Service

Abou Shakra restaurants do not rely solely on their food to please their customers, but also on well-trained employees who deliver extraordinary customer service. They hire energetic, friendly, and passionate employees. Abou Shakra restaurants realized the significance of educating their workers as to the importance of customer satisfaction, and this led to the establishment of their own training center. The center has a proficient team of trainers who ensure that employees will have the necessary skills to provide the guests with the best kind of service. Abou Shakra relies on continuous training to provide employees with the necessary confidence and skills to provide the utmost customer satisfaction. The company believes that its greatest asset is its employees, and Abou Shakra thus invests heavily in recruiting and training them in order to maintain the company's reputation in the competitive market. One of the core principles of the company is that by taking good care of the employees, the employees will take good care of the customers.

International Expansion

Abou Shakra's solid customer base is not only due to the quality of the food and the service offered, but also its slow-growth expansion strategy. Abou Shakra restaurants cannot be found on every corner; even after 65 years only 13 outlets are operating throughout Egypt. Abou Shakra decided to stay small and focus on having a few outlets that provide outstanding service rather than have many outlets with average service. A new outlet is only opened when the required employees have been trained and are prepared to offer the outstanding service that is associated with Abou Shakra. It took the company 56 years to open its first branch outside Cairo, which debuted in Alexandria in 2003.

The popularity of Abou Shakra has extended far beyond Egypt, with the company receiving many requests to open international branches from customers living abroad who had tasted Abou Shakra while on a holiday. The opening of a branch in Saudi Arabia in 2005 and another in Kuwait in 2007 are great milestones in the history of Abou Shakra.

This expansion was not an easy step for the company, and a great deal of research was undertaken beforehand to find the correct locations for the restaurants. First, Abou Shakra needed to find suppliers that could deliver fresh ingredients on a daily basis; this was an important factor for Abou Shakra to succeed; it had to be ensured that the quality of food provided in any new outlets would equal that of the Egyptian branches. Employees also needed to be recruited and trained in the same manner as the employees in Egypt, to make sure that they provide their customers with the same outstanding service.

Along with other aspects of its simple but focused strategy, Abou Shakra does not spend a great deal on advertising. Only a small proportion of its budget is set aside for advertising in newspapers and on television, as the company relies heavily on word-of-mouth recommendations between customers and their friends and families. Abou Shakra believes that the main objective is to take care of customers, and to provide them with high-quality food and service is better than spending money on advertising, as satisfied customers will be the best advertising tool. They will tell their friends and family members about their positive experiences at Abou Shakra, and consumers are more likely to follow the advice of people close to them than promotional ads. This is also a strategy the company uses to reduce expenses. Instead of spending a large amount of money on advertising, which may not generate profitable returns, more money is spent on increasing the quality of food and service provided.

Many have questioned whether Abou Shakra's 65-year legacy can be sustained. Its restaurants are run by co-founders and owners Ahmed and Hussein Abou Shakra, who have drawn up an efficient blueprint for all of their employees to follow. They believe that if desirable employees are recruited and trained correctly and provided with the appropriate working environment, then success is inevitable. Ahmed Abou Shakra, the company's chairman, played a critical role in the formation of the strategy that the company would follow. He detailed the long- and short-term goals in a manner that is easy for all involved to comprehend. The daily operations are organized and controlled by him, and he has developed an efficient system to ensure that managers report to him. This system was developed when the business began to grow, as one person could not manage the daily operations of every restaurant efficiently.

Hussein Abou Shakra is the vice-chairman of the company, and he ensures that the financial goals and objectives of the company are being met. He supervises the preparation of the financial statements and the budgets of the company. In the same manner as the chairman, he has set up a structure by which all the finance managers report to him with daily updates.

The legacy of Abou Shakra is expected to continue with or without its founders. This is because Abou Shakra has become a corporation that was established with strategies and objectives that, if managed correctly, will lead to a successful business. This business legacy, so long as the business objectives are met and customers are continued to be placed first, is expected to last.

Questions for Discussion

1-18 Describe Abou Shakra in terms of the value it provides for customers.

1-19 Do you think Abou Shakra should develop a high-growth strategy? Why or why not?

1-20 Should Abou Shakra spend more on advertising than what is currently expended?

1-21 Do you think the legacy of Abou Shakra will continue with an increasing number of consumers disposed toward nontraditional cuisine? Why or why not?

1-22 Suggest other methods by which Abou Shakra can provide value to its customers.

Sources: "Abou Shakra, Cairo—Restaurant Review," Reviews of Hotels, Flights and Vacation Rentals, TripAdvisor, www.tripadvisor.com/Restaurant_Review-g294201-d1201482-Reviews-Abou_Shakra-Cairo.html, accessed November 5, 2012; and "Abou Shakra," www.aboushakra.net/main.htm, accessed November 5, 2012.

MyMarketingLab

Go to **mymktlab.com** for the following Assisted-graded writing questions:

1-23 Discuss trends impacting marketing and the implications of these trends on how marketers deliver value to customers. (AACSB: Communication)

1-24 When implementing customer relationship management, why might a business desire fewer customers over more customers? Shouldn't the focus of marketing be to acquire as many customers as possible? (AACSB: Communication; Reflective Thinking)

References

1. See Brad Stone, "Amazon Reveals Holiday Sales: Cyber Monday Orders Rose 39%," *Bloomberg Businessweek*, December 26, 2013, www.businessweek.com/articles/2013-12-26/amazon-reveals-holiday-sales-facts-cyber-monday-orders-rose-39-percent-and-other-fun-facts; Morten T. Hansen, Herminia Ibarra, and Urs Peyer, "The Best-Performing CEOs in the World," *Harvard Business Review*, January–February 2013, pp. 81–86; George Anders, "Jeff Bezos's Top 10 Leadership Lessons," *Forbes*, April 4, 2012, www.forbes.com/sites/georgeanders/2012/04/04/bezos-tips/; "Q4 2013 Earnings Call Transcript," *Morningstar*, January 30, 2014, www.morningstar.com/earnings/earnings-call-transcript.aspx?t=amzn®ion=usa&pindex=1; "Benchmarks by Company: Amazon," ACSI, www.theacsi.org/?option=com_content&view=article&id=149&catid=&Itemid=214&c=Amazon, accessed June 2014; and annual reports and other information found at www.amazon.com, accessed September 2014.

2. See Philip Kotler and Kevin Lane Keller, *Marketing Management*, 14th ed. (Upper Saddle River, NJ: Prentice Hall, 2012), p. 5.

3. The American Marketing Association offers the following definition: "Marketing is the activity, set of institutions, and processes for creating, communicating, delivering, and exchanging offerings that have value for customers, clients, partners, and society at large." See www.marketingpower.com/_layouts/Dictionary.aspx?dLetter=M, accessed September 2014.

4. See "50 Years of Helping Customers Save Money and Live Better," Walmart Annual Report, March 2013, www.walmartstores.com/sites/annual-report/2012/WalMart_AR.pdf, p. 5; Christine Birkner, "10 Minutes with Ashlee Yingling," *Marketing News*, May 31, 2012, pp. 24–28; and Daniel P. Smith, "Keep in Touch," *QSR Magazine*, July 2013, www.qsrmagazine.com/executive-insights/keep-touch.

5. See www.michigan.org and http://stoptextsstopwrecks.org/#home, accessed September 2014.

6. See Theodore Levitt's classic article, "Marketing Myopia," *Harvard Business Review*, July–August 1960, pp. 45–56. For more recent discussions, see Minette E. Drumright and Mary C. Gentile, "The New Marketing Myopia," *Journal of Public Policy & Marketing*, Spring 2010, pp. 4–11; Roberto Friedmann, "What Business Are You In?" *Marketing Management*, Summer 2011, pp. 18–23; and Al Ries, "'Marketing Myopia' Revisited: Perhaps a Narrow Vision Is Better Business," *Advertising Age*, December 4, 2013, http://adage.com/print/245511.

7. See J. J. McCorvey, "Bird of Play," *Fast Company*, December 2012/January 2013, pp. 100–107+; Neil Long, "Two Billion Downloads? We're Just Getting Started, Says Angry Birds Creator Rovio," *Edge*, January 23, 2014, www.edge-online.com/features/two-billion-downloads-were-just-getting-started-says-angry-birds-creator-rovio/; and www.angrybirds.com, accessed September 2014.

8. See https://play.google.com/store/apps/details?id=co.vine.androidm, accessed September 2014.

9. "The Difference in Creating Companies and Categories," *happycustomer*, March 4, 2014, http://happycustomer.stellaservice.com/2014/03/04/column-the-difference-in-creating-companies-and-categories/.

10. See Michael E. Porter and Mark R. Kramer, "Creating Shared Value, "*Harvard Business Review*, January–February 2011, pp. 63–77; Marc Pfitzer, Valerie Bockstette, and Mike Stamp, "Innovating for Shared Value," *Harvard Business Review*, September 2013, pp. 100–107; "About Shared Value," *Shared Value Initiative*, http://sharedvalue.org/about-shared-value, accessed September 2014; and "Shared Value," www.fsg.org, accessed September 2014.

11. Michael Krauss, "Evolution of an Academic: Kotler on Marketing 3.0, "*Marketing News*, January 30, 2011, p. 12; and Simon Mainwaring, "Marketing 3.0 Will Be Won by Purpose-Driven, Social Brands," *Forbes*, July 16, 2013, www.forbes.com/sites/simonmainwaring/2013/07/16/marketing-3-0-will-be-won-by-purpose-driven-social-brands-infographic/.

12. See Scott Campbell, "Lush Defies the Christmas Retail Slump," *The Telegraph*, January 6, 2014, www.telegraph.co.uk/finance/newsbysector/retailandconsumer/10554068/Lush-defies-the-Christmas-retail-slump.html; and "Lush Life: We Believe," www.lushusa.com/on/demandware.store/Sites-Lush-Site/en_US/AboutUs-OurStoryShow?cid=we-believe, accessed June 2014.

13. Based on information from Keenan Mayo, "A Cooler Fit for the Apocalypse," *Bloomberg Businessweek*, October 28–November 3, 2013, p. 62, and http://store.yeticoolers.com/, accessed September 2014.

14. Based on information from Michael Bush, "Why You Should Be Putting on the Ritz," *Advertising Age*, June 21, 2010, p. 1; Julie Barker, "Power to the People," *Incentive*, February 2008, p. 34; Philip Kotler and Kevin Lane Keller, *Marketing Management*, 14th ed. (Upper Saddle River, NJ: Prentice Hall, 2012), p. 381; http://corporate.ritzcarlton.com/en/About/Awards.htm, accessed June 2014; and "Stories That Stay with You," www.ritzcarlton.com/en/StoriesThatStay.htm, accessed June 2014.

15. "Delighting the Customer Doesn't Pay," *Sales & Marketing Management*, November 11, 2013, http://salesandmarketing.com/content/delighting-customers-doesnt-pay.

16. See www.walgreens.com/Balance, accessed September 2014.

17. For more information, see www.apple.com/usergroups/ and www.webernation.com, accessed September 2014.

18. Based on information from Noreen O'Leary, "Hertz Learns Value of Sharing in Purchase Cycle," *Adweek*, May 30, 2012; "Hertz Fans Share It Up! on Facebook," *PRNewswire*, April 11, 2012, www.prnewswire.com/news-releases/hertz-fans-share-it-up-on-facebook-146987185.html; "The Top 10 Social Media Success Stories of 2012 & What We Can Learn from Them," *Social Media Strategies Summit Blog*, November 28, 2012, http://socialmediastrategiessummit.com/blog/the-top-10-social-media-success-stories-of-2012-what-we-can-learn-from-them; "Hertz Moves with the High-Tech Times to Breathe New Life into the Brand," *Eye for Travel*, January 16, 2014, www.eyefortravel.com/social-media-and-marketing/hertz-moves-high-tech-times-breathe-new-life-brand; and www.Hertz.com, accessed September 2014.

19. Gordon Wyner, "Getting Engaged," *Marketing Management*, Fall 2012, pp. 4–10. For more discussion on customer engagement, see Don E. Schultz, "Social Media's Slippery Slope," *Marketing Management*, February 2013, pp. 20–21; and "The Engagement Project," *Google Think Insights*, www.thinkwithgoogle.com/collections/engagement-project.html, accessed September 2014.

20. See http://mystarbucksidea.force.com, accessed September 2014.

21. "2014 USA Today Ad Meter," http://admeter.usatoday.com/, accessed February 2014; and www.doritos.com/, accessed February 2014.

22. See Gavin O'Malley, "Entries Pour in for Heinz Ketchup Commercial Contest," August 13, 2007, http://publications.mediapost.com; and www.youtube.com/watch?v=JGY-ubAJSyl, accessed November 2013.

23. See "#Bashtag: Avoiding User Outcry in Social Media," *WordStream*, March 8, 2013, www.wordstream.com/blog/ws/2013/03/07/bashtag-avoiding-social-media-backlash; and "What Is Hashtag Hijacking?" *Small Business Trends*, August 18, 2013, http://smallbiztrends.com/2013/08/what-is-hashtag-hijacking-2.html.

24. "Stew Leonard's," *Hoover's Company Records*, July 15, 2012, www.hoovers.com; and www.stew-leonards.com/html/about.cfm, accessed September 2014.

25. See Mai Erne, "Calculating Customer Lifetime Value," HaraPartners, www.harapartners.com/blog/calculating-lifetime-value/, accessed September 2014.

26. Based on quotes and information from Brad Stone, "What's in the Box? Instant Gratification, "*Bloomberg Businessweek*, November 29–December 5, 2010, pp. 39–40; Patrick Seitz, "Amazon Prime Is a Growing Threat to Netflix," *Investor's Business Daily*, December 9, 2013; and www.amazon.com/gp/prime/ref=footer_prime, accessed September 2014.

27. For more discussions on customer equity, see Roland T. Rust, Valerie A. Zeithaml, and Katherine N. Lemon, *Driving Customer Equity* (New York: Free Press, 2000); Rust, Lemon, and Zeithaml, "Return on Marketing: Using Customer Equity to Focus Marketing Strategy," *Journal of Marketing*, January 2004, pp. 109–127; Christian Gronroos and Pekka Helle, "Return on Relationships: Conceptual Understanding and Measurement of Mutual Gains from Relational Business Engagements," *Journal of Business & Industrial Marketing*, Vol. 27, No. 5, 2012, pp. 344–359; and Peter C. Verhoef and Katherine N. Lemon, "Successful Customer Value Management: Key Lessons and Emerging Trends," *European Management Journal*, February 2013, p. 1.

28. This example is adapted from information found in Rust, Lemon, and Zeithaml, "Where Should the Next Marketing Dollar Go?" *Marketing Management*, September–October 2001, pp. 24–28; with information from Jeff Bennett and Joseph B. White, "New Cadillac, Old Dilemma," *Wall Street Journal*, March 27, 2013, p. B1; and Grant McCracken, "Provocative Cadillac, Rescuing the Brand from Bland," *Harvard Business Review*, March 4, 2014, http://blogs.hbr.org/2014/03/provocative-cadillac-rescuing-the-brand-from-bland/.

29. Based on Werner Reinartz and V. Kumar, "The Mismanagement of Customer Loyalty," *Harvard Business Review*, July 2002, pp. 86–94. Also see Stanley F. Slater, Jakki J. Mohr, and Sanjit Sengupta, "Know Your Customer," *Marketing Management*, February 2009, pp. 37–44; Crina O. Tarasi et al., "Balancing Risk and Return in a Customer Portfolio," *Journal of Marketing*, May 2011, pp. 1–17; and Chris Lema, "Not All Customers Are Equal—Butterflies & Barnacles," April 18, 2013, http://chrislema.com/not-all-customers-are-equal-butterflies-barnacles/.

30. See Stuart Feil, "Mobile on the Cusp (Again)," *Adweek*, February 11, 2013, pp. M1–M3+, "ITU Release Latest Tech Figures & Global Rankings," October 7, 2013, www.itu.int/net/pressoffice/press_releases/2013/41.aspx#.Uumujvad6cC; and John Heggestuen, "One in Every 5 People in the World Own a Smartphone, One in Every 17 Own a Tablet," *Business Insider*, December 15, 2013, www.businessinsider.com/smartphone-and-tablet-penetration-2013-10.

31. "Digital Set to Surpass TV in Time Spent with US Media," *eMarketer*, August 1, 2013, www.emarketer.com/Article/Digital-Set-Surpass-TV-Time-Spent-with-US-Media/1010096.

32. For these and other examples, see "The State of Online Branded Communities," *Comblu*, November 2012, p. 17, http://comblu.com/thoughtleadership/the-state-of-online-branded-communities-2012; and www.mountaindew.com, accessed September 2014.

33. See Stuart Feil, "How to Win Friends and Influence People," *Adweek*, September 12, 2013, pp. S1–S7; Joe Mandese, "Carat Projects Digital at One-Fifth of All Ad Spend, Beginning to Dominate Key Markets," *MediaPost News*, March 20, 2013, www.mediapost.com/publications/article/196238/carat-projects-digital-at-one-fifth-of-all-ad-spen.html#axzz2PsYL9uFf; and Julia McCoy, "A 2014 Social Media Guide: New Trends and Solutions to Live By," *socialmediatoday*, January 15, 2014, http://socialmediatoday.com/expresswriters/2066416/2014-social-media-guide-new-trends-and-solutions-live.

34. Christopher Heine, "Brands Favor Social Shares Over Likes: Chatter Is the Key," *Adweek*, April 1, 2013, www.adweek.com/print/148256.

35. See Feil, "How to Win Friends and Influence People," pp. S1–S7; and www.youtube.com/watch?v=4P6Qwppw-3U and method-home.com/cleanhappy/, accessed September 2014.

36. Michael Applebaum, "Mobile Magnetism," *Adweek*, June 25, 2012, pp. S1–S9; and Bill Briggs, "M-Commerce Is Saturating the Globe," *Internet Retailer*, February 20, 2014, www.internetretailer.com/2014/02/20/m-commerce-saturating-globe.

37. See Applebaum, "Mobile Magnetism," p. S7; and Brian Quintion, "2012 PRO Award Winner: Catapult Action Biased Marketing for Mars Petcare," *Chief Marketer*, August 3, 2012, www.chiefmarketer.com/agencies/2012-pro-award-winner-catapult-action-biased-marketing-for-mars-petcare-03082012.

38. See "Our Mission," https://corporate.target.com/about/mission-values, accessed September 2014.

39. See Lisa Wirthman, "How a Lemonade Stand Sparked a Movement to Cure Pediatric Cancer," *Forbes*, January 15, 2014; Jennifer Aaker and Andy Smith, "The Dragonfly Effect," *Stanford Social Innovation Review*," Winter 2011, pp. 31–35; and www.alexslemonade.org, accessed September 2014.

40. "100 Leading National Advertisers," *Advertising Age*, June 24, 2013, p. 18.

41. www.aboutmcdonalds.com/mcd and www.nikeinc.com, accessed June 2014.

42. See www.benjerry.com/values, www.benandjerrysfoundation.org/, and www.unilever.com/brands-in-action/detail/ben-and-jerrys/291995/, accessed September 2014.

2 Company and Marketing Strategy

Partnering to Build Customer Engagement, Value, and Relationships

Chapter Preview In the first chapter, we explored the marketing process by which companies create value for customers to capture value from them in return. In this chapter, we dig deeper into steps two and three of that process: designing customer value-driven marketing strategies and constructing marketing programs. First, we look at the organization's overall strategic planning, which guides marketing strategy and planning. Next, we discuss how, guided by the strategic plan, marketers partner closely with others inside and outside the firm to engage customers and create value for them. We then examine marketing strategy and planning—how marketers choose target markets, position their market offerings, develop a marketing mix, and manage their marketing programs. Finally, we look at the important step of measuring and managing marketing return on investment (marketing ROI).

First, let's look at Nike, a good company and a good marketing strategy story. During the past several decades, Nike has built the Nike swoosh into one of the world's best-known brand symbols. Nike's outstanding success results from much more than just making and selling good sports gear. It's based on a customer-focused marketing strategy through which Nike creates valued brand engagement and close brand community with and among its customers.

NIKE'S CUSTOMER-DRIVEN MARKETING: Building Brand Engagement and Community

The Nike "swoosh"—it's everywhere! Just for fun, try counting the swooshes whenever you pick up the sports pages or watch a basketball game or tune into a televised soccer match. Over the past nearly 50 years, through innovative marketing, Nike has built the ever-present swoosh into one of the best-known brand symbols on the planet.

Early on, a brash, young Nike revolutionized sports marketing. To build image and market share, the brand lavishly outspent competitors on big-name endorsements, splashy promotional events, and big-budget, in-your-face "Just Do It" ads. Whereas competitors stressed technical performance, Nike built customer engagement and relationships. Beyond shoes, apparel, and equipment, Nike marketed a way of life, a genuine passion for sports, a "just-do-it" attitude. Customers didn't just wear their Nikes, they *experienced* them. As the company stated on its Web page, "Nike has always known the truth—it's not so much the shoes but where they take you."

Nike powered its way through the early years, aggressively adding products in a dozen new sports, including baseball, golf, skateboarding, wall climbing, bicycling, and hiking. It seemed that things just couldn't be going any better. In the late 1990s, however, Nike stumbled and its sales slipped. As the company grew larger, its creative juices seemed to run a bit dry and buyers seeking a new look switched to competing brands. Looking back, Nike's biggest obstacle may have been its own incredible success. As sales grew, the swoosh may have become too common to be cool. Instead of being *anti*establishment, Nike *was* the establishment, and its hip, once-hot relationship with customers cooled. Nike needed to rekindle the brand's meaning to consumers.

To turn things around, Nike returned to its roots: new product innovation and a focus on customer relationships. But it set out to forge a new kind of brand–customer connection—a deeper, more personal, more engaging one. This time around, rather than simply outspending competitors on big media ads and celebrity endorsers that talk *at* customers, Nike shifted toward cutting-edge digital and social media marketing tools that interact *with* customers to build brand connections and community. According to one industry analyst, "the legendary brand blew up its single-slogan approach and drafted a whole new playbook for the digital era."

Nike's outstanding success results from much more than just making good sports gear. The iconic company's strategy is to build engagement and a sense of community with and between the Nike brand and its customers.

Nike still invests heavily in traditional advertising. But its spending on TV and print media has dropped by a whopping 30 percent in only three years, even as its global marketing budget has increased steadily. Traditional media now account for only about 20 percent of the brand's $1 billion U.S. promotion budget. Instead, Nike spends the lion's share of its marketing budget on nontraditional media. Using community-oriented, digital-based social networking tools, Nike is now building communities of customers who talk not just with the company about the brand, but with each other as well.

Nike has mastered social networking, both online and off. Whether customers come to know Nike through ads, in-person events at Niketown stores, a local Nike running club, or at one of the company's profusion of community Web and social media sites, more and more people are bonding closely with the Nike brand.

Nike has mastered social networking, both online and off, creating deep engagement and community among customers. Its Nike+ and FuelBand apps and technologies have made Nike a part of the daily fitness routines of millions of customers around the world.

Stefano Dal Pozzolo/Contrasto/Redux

Nike has raced ahead of its industry in the use of today's new social networking tools. In a recent ranking of 42 sportswear companies, digital consultancy L2 crowned Nike "top genius" in "digital IQ" for its innovative use of online, mobile, and social media. L2 also placed Nike first in creating brand "tribes"—large groups of highly engaged users—with the help of social media platforms such as Facebook, Twitter, Instagram, and Pinterest. For example, the main Nike Facebook page has more than 16.4 million Likes. The Nike Soccer page adds another 21.6 million, Nike Basketball page 5.4 million more, and Nike Running another 1.8 million. More than just numbers, Nike's social media presence engages customers at a high level and gets them talking with each other about the brand.

Nike excels at cross-media campaigns that integrate the new media with traditional tools to build brand community. For example, Nike's "Find Your Greatness" campaign for the 2012 Olympics launched two days before the opening ceremonies—not with splashy media ads but with a video posted on YouTube, Nike Web sites, and other digital platforms. The compelling video featured people getting in touch with their inner athlete. Then, on opening day, Nike followed up with big-budget TV ads in 25 countries based on the video. But rather than just running the ads in isolation, the campaign urged customers to share their feelings about the "Find Your Greatness" message via Twitter and other digital media using a "#findgreatness" hashtag. Within a month, the video had been viewed more than 5 million times on Nike's YouTube channel alone.

Nike has also built brand community through groundbreaking mobile apps and technologies. For example, its Nike+ apps have helped Nike become a part of the daily fitness routines of millions of customers around the world. The Nike+ FuelBand, for instance, is an ergonomic work of art. Worn on the wrist, FuelBand converts just about every imaginable physical movement into NikeFuel, Nike's own universal activity metric. According to a recent Nike video called "Counts," whether your activity is running, jumping, baseball, skating, dancing, stacking sports cups, or chasing chickens, it counts for NikeFuel points. "Life is a sport," the video concludes. "Make it count." Everyday athletes can use NikeFuel to track their personal performance, then share and compare it across sports and geographic locations with others in the global Nike community. The Nike+ FuelBand mobile app lets users watch their progress, get extra motivation on the go, and stay connected with friends.

Nike+ has engaged a huge global brand community. The tickers on nikeplus.com update continuously with numbers in the billions: 85,566,409,830 steps taken, 50,841,842,647 calories burned, and 36,364,639,579 NikeFuel points earned. The site also tracks personal achievements earned and daily goals hit by individuals in the Nike+ community. To date, the millions of Nike+ users worldwide have logged 1,118,434,247 miles. That's 44,914 trips around the world or 4,682 journeys to the moon and back.

Thus, Nike has built a new kinship and sense of community with and between the brand and its customers. Nike's marketing strategy is no longer only about big-budget ads at arm's length and aloof celebrity endorsers. Instead, the brand is connecting directly with customers, whether it's through local running clubs, a performance-tracking wristband, a 30-story billboard that posts fan headlines from Twitter, or videos that debut on YouTube rather than primetime TV. More than just something to buy, the Nike brand has once again become a part of customers' lives and times.

As a result, Nike remains the world's largest sports apparel company, an impressive 26 percent larger than closest rival Adidas. During the past seven years, even as the faltering economy left most sports apparel and footwear competitors gasping for breath, Nike's global sales and income sprinted ahead nearly 70 percent.

As in sports competition, the strongest and best-prepared brand has the best chance of winning. With engagement and deep brand–customer relationships comes powerful competitive advantage. And Nike is once again very close to its customers. Notes Nike CEO Mark Parker, "Connecting used to be, 'Here's some product, and here's some advertising. We hope you like it.' Connecting today is a dialogue."[1]

Objective Outline

Author Comment | Company-wide strategic planning guides marketing strategy and planning. Like marketing strategy, the company's broader strategy must also be customer focused.

Company-Wide Strategic Planning: Defining Marketing's Role

Each company must find the game plan for long-run survival and growth that makes the most sense given its specific situation, opportunities, objectives, and resources. This is the focus of **strategic planning**—the process of developing and maintaining a strategic fit between the organization's goals and capabilities and its changing marketing opportunities.

Strategic planning
The process of developing and maintaining a strategic fit between the organization's goals and capabilities and its changing marketing opportunities.

Strategic planning sets the stage for the rest of planning in the firm. Companies usually prepare annual plans, long-range plans, and strategic plans. The annual and long-range plans deal with the company's current businesses and how to keep them going. In contrast, the strategic plan involves adapting the firm to take advantage of opportunities in its constantly changing environment.

At the corporate level, the company starts the strategic planning process by defining its overall purpose and mission (see **Figure 2.1**). This mission is then turned into detailed supporting objectives that guide the entire company. Next, headquarters decides what portfolio of businesses and products is best for the company and how much support to give each one. In turn, each business and product develops detailed marketing and other departmental plans that support the company-wide plan. Thus, marketing planning occurs at the business-unit, product, and market levels. It supports company strategic planning with more detailed plans for specific marketing opportunities.

Defining a Market-Oriented Mission

An organization exists to accomplish something, and this purpose should be clearly stated. Forging a sound mission begins with the following questions: What *is* our business? Who is the

FIGURE | 2.1
Steps in Strategic Planning

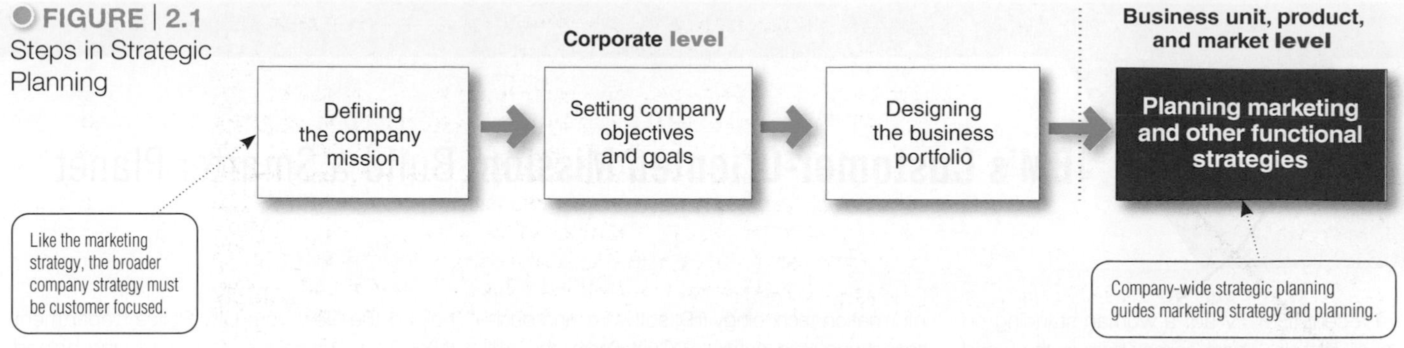

customer? What do consumers value? What *should* our business be? These simple-sounding questions are among the most difficult the company will ever have to answer. Successful companies continuously raise these questions and answer them carefully and completely.

Mission statement
A statement of the organization's purpose—what it wants to accomplish in the larger environment.

Many organizations develop formal mission statements that answer these questions. A **mission statement** is a statement of the organization's purpose—what it wants to accomplish in the larger environment. A clear mission statement acts as an "invisible hand" that guides people in the organization.

Some companies define their missions myopically in product or technology terms ("We make and sell furniture" or "We are a chemical-processing firm"). But mission statements should be *market oriented* and defined in terms of satisfying basic customer needs. Products and technologies eventually become outdated, but basic market needs may last forever. For example, IBM doesn't define itself as just a computer hardware and software company. It wants to provide data and information technology solutions that help customers "build a smarter planet" (see Real Marketing 2.1). Likewise, social scrapbooking site Pinterest doesn't define itself as just an online place to post pictures. Its mission is to give people a social media platform for collecting, organizing, and sharing things they love. And Chipotle's mission isn't to sell burritos. Instead, the restaurant promises "Food with Integrity," highlighting its commitment to the immediate and long-term welfare of customers and the environment. To back its mission, Chipotle's serves only the very best natural, sustainable, local ingredients. **Table 2.1** provides several examples of product-oriented versus market-oriented business definitions.[2]

Table 2.1 | Product- versus Market-Oriented Business Definitions

Company	Product-Oriented Definition	Market-Oriented Definition
Chipotle	We sell burritos and other Mexican food.	We give customers "Food With Integrity," served with a commitment toward the long-term welfare of customers and the environment.
Facebook	We are an online social network.	We connect people around the world and help them share important moments in their lives.
Home Depot	We sell tools and home repair and improvement items.	We empower consumers to achieve the homes of their dreams.
IBM	We make computer hardware and software.	We provide technology solutions that help customers "build a smarter planet."
NASA	We explore outer space.	We reach for new heights and reveal the unknown so that what we do and learn will benefit all humankind.
Revlon	We make cosmetics.	We sell lifestyle and self-expression; success and status; memories, hopes, and dreams.
Ritz-Carlton Hotels & Resorts	We rent rooms.	We create the Ritz-Carlton experience—a memorable stay that far exceeds guests' already high expectations.
Walmart	We run discount stores.	We deliver low prices every day and give ordinary folks the chance to buy the same things as rich people. "Save Money. Live Better."

Real Marketing 2.1

IBM's Customer-Oriented Mission: Build a Smarter Planet

In a recent IBM TV ad, a woman standing on a busy big-city street somewhere in the world proclaims, "All over the world, cities are learning from other cities." As she narrates, the ad shows how shared solutions helped Washington, DC, improve its sewer systems based on analytics that had helped Rio de Janeiro prepare for flooding emergencies and helped Singapore make traffic flow more efficiently. What connects these seemingly separate activities in cities around the world? The woman explains: "With two thousand projects underway, IBM is helping to make cities smarter. I'm an IBMer. Let's build a smarter planet, city by city."

That's IBM today—a full-service supplier of digital-age data technologies and services. But not that many years ago, IBM was known mostly for peddling mainframe computers, PCs, and other basic computer system components. Back then, if you'd asked top managers at "Big Blue" what their mission was, they'd have answered, "to sell computer hardware and software." IBM had dominated the computer market for decades, achieving astounding success. By the early 1990s, however, a heavily product-focused IBM had lost sight of its customers' needs. Sales and profits tumbled, and IBM was rapidly becoming a big blue dinosaur.

Since those sadly blue days, however, IBM has undergone a remarkable transformation. The turnaround started with top IBM managers meeting face to face with important customers—what they called "bear-hugging customers"—to learn about their problems and priorities. The managers learned that in this connected digital age, companies face a perplexing array of data and information technologies. Today's customers don't need just computers and software. Instead, they need total solutions to ever-more-bewildering data and information problems. Such solutions often involve a complex, integrated mix of hardware, software, services, and advice across collaborative online, mobile, and social networks.

This realization led to a fundamental redefinition of IBM's business. Now, if you ask IBM managers to define the mission, they'll tell you, "We deliver *smart solutions* to customers' data and information technology problems." Under this new customer-solutions mission, IBM began shifting emphasis away from computer hardware. Instead, it added a full slate of integrated information technology (IT), software, and business consulting services. Customers can still buy mainframe computers from IBM, but they are more likely to buy services, systems, and advice. The transformed IBM now works arm-in-arm with customers on everything from assessing, planning, designing, and implementing their data analytics and IT systems to actually running those systems for them.

IBM's customer-focused mission is summed up by the company's five-year-old marketing and positioning campaign: "Let's Build a Smarter Planet." The campaign markets IBM as a company that helps customers turn today's data and technology explosion into smart solutions that will transform their businesses and improve the world's data IQ. "What is a smarter planet?" asks the company. It's one that uses data in an "instrumented, intelligent, and interconnected" way. IBM's services now include everything from data analytics to mobile, social business, and cloud-computing technologies.

IBM smart solutions span an incredible breadth of industries and processes—from commerce and digital communications to health care, education, and sustainability. For example, one Smarter Planet ad tells how IBM is helping to "track food from farm to fork" in an effort to reduce the 25 percent of the world's food currently lost to spoilage. At the other extreme, ads tell how IBM analytics helped the New York City Police Department (NYPD) cut crime by 35 percent and helped New York State save $889 million by catching tax dodgers.

Here are just a few more examples showing how IBM has applied its "Smarter Planet" mission to finding solutions across its diverse customer base:

- IBM's MobileFirst group helped Air Canada design, implement, and manage a self-service customer check-in and travel information system that lets customers travel smarter, and helps Air Canada keep better track of how these services are used and valued. The system—a blend of sophisticated IBM hardware, software, and services—lets customers conveniently access a broad array of check-in and information services through Web, kiosk, and mobile devices. It then provides Air Canada with the analytics needed to improve the design, costs, and customer value of the system.
- IBM's SmartCloud group helped Russell's Convenience—a 25-store convenience store chain in the western United States—set up a system by which employees can collaborate across stores and with suppliers to improve service to customers. Before working with IBM, Russell's management relied on scattered phone calls, e-mail, and travel to keep track of planning

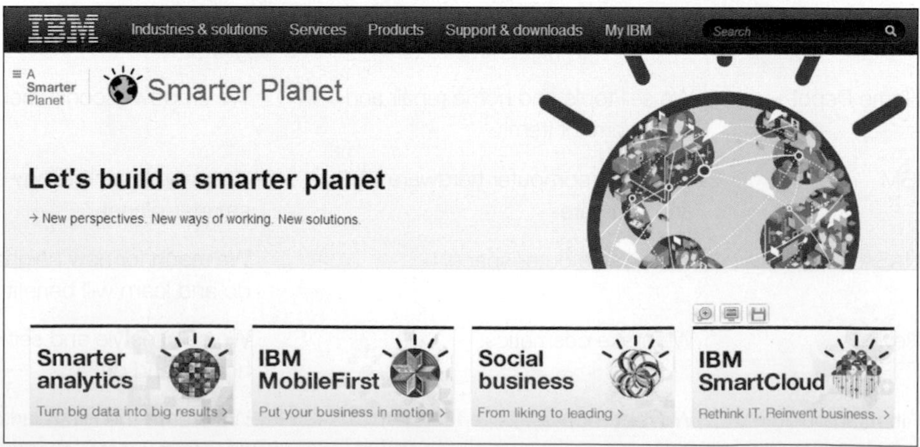

IBM's customer-focused mission is summed up by the company's marketing and positioning campaign: "Let's Build a Smarter Planet."

and day-to-day business issues, and many tasks fell through the cracks. Now, using IBM's SmartCloud Engage services, employees and selected suppliers have instant access to cloud-based social networking and collaboration tools. Instead of searching through e-mails or making multiple phone calls, employees can now interact systematically online in real time. "IBM is helping our [stores] to operate as one business—one that is connected, informed, and cohesive," says the company's president.

- Vestas Wind Systems, the world's largest wind energy company, needed to find good wind turbine locations that would optimize energy output and maximize return on investment. IBM's Smart Analytics groups found the solution in its BigInsights software and "Firestorm" supercomputer (capable of 150 trillion calculations per second). The IBM system pinpoints the best turbine placements by analyzing massive amounts of data, such as weather reports, tidal phases, geospatial and sensor data, satellite images, deforestation maps, and weather modeling research. Such analysis used to take weeks. But thanks to IBM's smart solution, it can now be done in less than one hour. Once a turbine is operational, engineers at Vestas use the analytics system to predict its performance, analyze how each blade reacts to weather changes, and determine the best times to schedule maintenance.

Thus, IBM doesn't just sell computers anymore. Under its broader, customer-oriented mission, today's IBM provides cutting-edge data analytics and solutions-based services that make customers and the world better and smarter. In fact, more than 90 percent of IBM's profits now come from software, services, financing, and business-consulting solutions.

Whether it's smarter business operations, smarter city management, smarter health care, or smarter anything else, what's smart for IBM's customers is also smart for IBM. In the five years since the start of the "Building a Smarter Planet" campaign, IBM's stock price has spurted from around $70 per share to around $200. By defining itself in terms of the customer needs it solves rather that the products it sells, IBM has transformed itself from a big blue dinosaur to the blue horizons of tomorrow's smarter planet.

Sources: Based on information and examples from Ashlee Vance, "IBM on a Mission to Save the Planet," *Bloomberg Businessweek*, March 15, 2012, pp. 51–52; Natalie Zmuda, "How Purpose Affects the Bottom Line," *Advertising Age*, October 8, 2012, http://adage.com/article/print/237597/; "Vestas Wind Systems Turns to IBM Big Data Analytics for Smarter Wind Energy," October 24, 2011, www-03.ibm.com/press/us/en/pressrelease/35737.wss; "Russell's Convenience Chooses IBM for Cloud Collaboration," *CSPnet.com*, August 16, 2011, www.cspnet.com/news/technology/articles/russells-convenience-chooses-ibm-cloud-collaboration; "Air Canada: On a Never-Ending Push to Make Life Simpler for the Customer," www.ibm.com/smarterplanet/us/en/leadership/aircanada/assets/pdf/AirCanada_Paper.pdf, accessed September 2014; "IBM Smarter Cities: The Future City Is a Smarter City," http://www.youtube.com/watch?v=3yVe1DL2qjs, accessed September 2014; and "What Is a Smarter Planet?" www.ibm.com/smarterplanet/us/en/overview/ideas/index.html?re=sph, accessed September 2014.

Mission statements should be meaningful and specific yet motivating. Too often, mission statements are written for public relations purposes and lack specific, workable guidelines. Instead, they should emphasize the company's strengths and tell forcefully how it intends to win in the marketplace. For example, Google's mission isn't to be the world's best search engine. It's to give people a window into the world's information, wherever it might be found.[3]

Customer-focused mission: The fast-growing Buffalo Wild Wings chain's mission is to provide a total eating and social environment that "fuels the sports fan experience." As a result, it creates in-store and online experiences that promote brand fan engagement.

Jeffery A. Salter/Redux

Finally, a company's mission should not be stated as making more sales or profits; profits are only a reward for creating value for customers. Instead, the mission should focus on customers and the customer experience the company seeks to create. Thus, the fast-growing Buffalo Wild Wings restaurant chain's mission isn't just to sell the most wings at a profit:[4]

> Customers do, in fact, come to Buffalo Wild Wings to eat wings and drink beer, but also to watch sports, trash talk, cheer on their sports teams, and meet old friends and make new ones—that is, a total eating and social experience. "We realize that we're not just in the business of selling wings," says the company. "We're something much bigger. We're in the business of fueling the sports fan experience." Each table has two types of servers, a food-order waiter and a "guest experience captain," whose job is to make sure that customers can see whatever game they came to watch on one of the 40 to 60 screens lining the walls, over the bar, and about everywhere else. True to that broader mission, Buffalo Wild Wings creates in-store and online promotions that inspire camaraderie. "It's about giving them tools to

not just be spectators but advocates of the brand," says the chain. For example, the brand's very active Web site draws 2 million visitors per month; its Facebook page has more than 12 million fans. Pursuing a customer-focused mission has paid big dividends for Buffalo Wild Wings. The wing joint's sales have quadrupled in the past eight years and the company brags that it's the number one brand in its industry for fan engagement.

Setting Company Objectives and Goals

The company needs to turn its mission into detailed supporting objectives for each level of management. Each manager should have objectives and be responsible for reaching them.

For example, most Americans know H. J. Heinz for its ketchup—it sells billions of bottles of ketchup each year. But Heinz owns a breadth of other food products under a variety of brands, ranging from Heinz and Ore-Ida to Classico. Heinz ties this diverse product portfolio together under this mission: "As the trusted leader in nutrition and wellness, Heinz—the original Pure Food Company—is dedicated to the sustainable health of people, the planet, and our company." The company's vision is "To be the best food company, growing a better world," based on values of putting customers first, quality, and innovation.[5]

Heinz's overall vision is "To be the best food company, growing a better world." Its marketing strategies and programs must support this vision.

H.J. Heinz Company

This broad mission and vision leads to a hierarchy of objectives, including business objectives and marketing objectives. Heinz's overall objective is to build profitable customer relationships by developing foods "superior in quality, taste, nutrition, and convenience" that embrace its nutrition and wellness mission. It does this by investing heavily in research. However, research is expensive and must be funded through improved profit, so improving profits becomes another major objective for Heinz. Profits can be improved by increasing sales or reducing costs. Sales can be increased by improving the company's share of domestic and international markets. These goals then become the company's current marketing objectives.

Marketing strategies and programs must be developed to support these marketing objectives. To increase its market share, Heinz might broaden its product lines, increase product availability and promotion in existing markets, and expand into new markets. For example, Heinz recently added "Grillers" potatoes, which are ready for outdoor grilling, to its Ore-Ida product line to keep demand for its potatoes strong during the summer season. And it purchased an 80 percent stake in Quero, a Brazilian brand of tomato-based sauces, ketchup, condiments, and vegetables. Quero is expected to double Heinz's sales in Latin America this year and to serve as a platform to market Heinz in Brazil.

These are Heinz's broad marketing strategies. Each broad marketing strategy must then be defined in greater detail. For example, increasing the product's promotion may require more advertising and public relations efforts; if so, both requirements will need to be spelled out. In this way, the firm's mission is translated into a set of objectives for the current period.

Designing the Business Portfolio

Guided by the company's mission statement and objectives, management now must plan its business portfolio—the collection of businesses and products that make up the company. The best **business portfolio** is the one that best fits the company's strengths and weaknesses to opportunities in the environment.

Business portfolio
The collection of businesses and products that make up the company.

Most large companies have complex portfolios of businesses and brands. Strategic and marketing planning for such business portfolios can be a daunting but critical task. For example, GE is a giant $146 billion conglomerate operating in dozens of consumer and business markets, with a broad portfolio of products that "move, power, build, and cure the world." Most consumers know GE for its home appliance and lighting products, part of the company's GE Home & Business Solutions unit. But that's just the beginning for GE. Other company units—such as GE Transportation, GE Aviation, GE Energy Management, GE Power & Water, GE Gas & Oil, GE Healthcare, and others—offer products and services ranging from jet engines, diesel-electric locomotives, wind turbines, and off-shore drilling solutions to aerospace systems and medical imaging equipment. GE Capital, which accounts for about a third of

GE's total revenues, offers a breadth of business and consumer financial products and services. Successfully managing such a broad portfolio takes plenty of management skill and—as GE's long-running corporate slogan suggests—lots of "Imagination at work."[6]

Business portfolio planning involves two steps. First, the company must analyze its *current* business portfolio and determine which businesses should receive more, less, or no investment. Second, it must shape the *future* portfolio by developing strategies for growth and downsizing.

Analyzing the Current Business Portfolio

Portfolio analysis
The process by which management evaluates the products and businesses that make up the company.

The major activity in strategic planning is business **portfolio analysis**, whereby management evaluates the products and businesses that make up the company. The company will want to put strong resources into its more profitable businesses and phase down or drop its weaker ones.

Management's first step is to identify the key businesses that make up the company, called *strategic business units* (SBUs). An SBU can be a company division, a product line within a division, or sometimes a single product or brand. The company next assesses the attractiveness of its various SBUs and decides how much support each deserves. When designing a business portfolio, it's a good idea to add and support products and businesses that fit closely with the firm's core philosophy and competencies.

The purpose of strategic planning is to find ways in which the company can best use its strengths to take advantage of attractive opportunities in the environment. For this reason, most standard portfolio analysis methods evaluate SBUs on two important dimensions: the attractiveness of the SBU's market or industry and the strength of the SBU's position in that market or industry. The best-known portfolio-planning method was developed by the Boston Consulting Group, a leading management consulting firm.[7]

Growth-share matrix
A portfolio-planning method that evaluates a company's SBUs in terms of market growth rate and relative market share.

The Boston Consulting Group Approach. Using the now-classic Boston Consulting Group (BCG) approach, a company classifies all its SBUs according to the **growth-share matrix**, as shown in **Figure 2.2**. On the vertical axis, *market growth rate* provides a measure of market attractiveness. On the horizontal axis, *relative market share* serves as a measure of company strength in the market. The growth-share matrix defines four types of SBUs:

1. *Stars.* Stars are high-growth, high-share businesses or products. They often need heavy investments to finance their rapid growth. Eventually their growth will slow down, and they will turn into cash cows.
2. *Cash cows.* Cash cows are low-growth, high-share businesses or products. These established and successful SBUs need less investment to hold their market share. Thus, they produce a lot of the cash that the company uses to pay its bills and support other SBUs that need investment.
3. *Question marks.* Question marks are low-share business units in high-growth markets. They require a lot of cash to hold their share, let alone increase it. Management has to think hard about which question marks it should try to build into stars and which should be phased out.
4. *Dogs.* Dogs are low-growth, low-share businesses and products. They may generate enough cash to maintain themselves but do not promise to be large sources of cash.

FIGURE | 2.2
The BCG Growth-Share Matrix

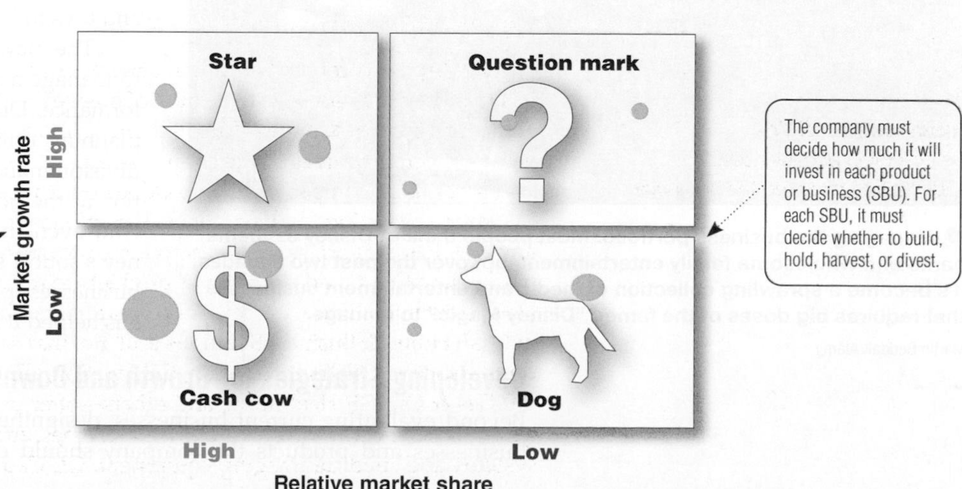
Star
Question mark
Cash cow
Dog
Market growth rate
High
Low
Relative market share
High
Low
The company must decide how much it will invest in each product or business (SBU). For each SBU, it must decide whether to build, hold, harvest, or divest.

Under the classic BCG portfolio planning approach, the company invests funds from mature, successful products and businesses (cash cows) to support promising products and businesses in faster-growing markets (stars and question marks), hoping to turn them into future cash cows.

The 10 circles in the growth-share matrix represent the company's 10 current SBUs. The company has two stars, two cash cows, three question marks, and three dogs. The areas of the circles are proportional to the SBU's dollar sales. This company is in fair shape, although not in good shape. It wants to invest in the more promising question marks to make them stars and maintain the stars so that they will become cash cows as their markets mature. Fortunately, it has two good-sized cash cows. Income from these cash cows will help finance the company's question marks, stars, and dogs. The company should take some decisive action concerning its dogs and its question marks.

Once it has classified its SBUs, the company must determine what role each will play in the future. It can pursue one of four strategies for each SBU. It can invest more in the business unit to *build* its share. Or it can invest just enough to *hold* the SBU's share at the current level. It can *harvest* the SBU, milking its short-term cash flow regardless of the long-term effect. Finally, it can *divest* the SBU by selling it or phasing it out and using the resources elsewhere.

As time passes, SBUs change their positions in the growth-share matrix. Many SBUs start out as question marks and move into the star category if they succeed. They later become cash cows as market growth falls, and then finally die off or turn into dogs toward the end of the life cycle. The company needs to add new products and units continuously so that some of them will become stars and, eventually, cash cows that will help finance other SBUs.

Problems with Matrix Approaches. The BCG and other formal methods revolutionized strategic planning. However, such centralized approaches have limitations: They can be difficult, time consuming, and costly to implement. Management may find it difficult to define SBUs and measure market share and growth. In addition, these approaches focus on classifying current businesses but provide little advice for future planning.

Because of such problems, many companies have dropped formal matrix methods in favor of more customized approaches that better suit their specific situations. Moreover, unlike former strategic planning efforts that rested mostly in the hands of senior managers at company headquarters, today's strategic planning has been decentralized. Increasingly, companies are placing responsibility for strategic planning in the hands of cross-functional teams of divisional managers who are close to their markets.

For example, think about The Walt Disney Company. ● Most people think of Disney as theme parks and wholesome family entertainment. But in the mid-1980s, Disney set up a powerful, centralized strategic planning group to guide its direction and growth. Over the next two decades, the strategic planning group turned The Walt Disney Company into a huge and diverse collection of media and entertainment businesses. The sprawling company grew to include everything from theme resorts and film studios (Walt Disney Pictures, Touchstone Pictures, Pixar Animation, and Marvel Studios) to media networks (ABC Television plus ESPN, Disney Channel, parts of A&E and the History Channel, and a half dozen others) to consumer products (from apparel and toys to interactive games) and a cruise line.

● Managing the business portfolio: Most people think of Disney as theme parks and wholesome family entertainment, but over the past two decades, it's become a sprawling collection of media and entertainment businesses that requires big doses of the famed "Disney Magic" to manage.

Martin Beddall/Alamy

The newly transformed company proved hard to manage and performed unevenly. To improve performance, Disney disbanded the centralized strategic planning unit, decentralizing its functions to Disney division managers. As a result, Disney retains its position at the head of the world's media conglomerates. And even through the recently weak economy, Disney's sound strategic management of its broad mix of businesses, plus a touch of the famed Disney magic, has helped it fare better than rival media companies.[8]

Developing Strategies for Growth and Downsizing

Beyond evaluating current businesses, designing the business portfolio involves finding businesses and products the company should consider in the future. Companies need

Product/market expansion grid
A portfolio-planning tool for identifying company growth opportunities through market penetration, market development, product development, or diversification.

growth if they are to compete more effectively, satisfy their stakeholders, and attract top talent. At the same time, a firm must be careful not to make growth itself an objective. The company's objective must be to manage "profitable growth."

Marketing has the main responsibility for achieving profitable growth for the company. Marketing needs to identify, evaluate, and select market opportunities and establish strategies for capturing them. One useful device for identifying growth opportunities is the **product/market expansion grid**, shown in Figure 2.3.[9] We apply it here to Starbucks:[10]

STARBUCKS
STARBUCKS
STARBUCKS
Strategies for growth: To maintain its incredible growth, Starbucks has brewed up an ambitious, multipronged growth strategy.
© STEFAN WERMUTH/Reuters/Corbis

> In only three decades, Starbucks has grown at an astonishing pace, from a small Seattle coffee shop to an over $14.9 billion powerhouse with more than 20,000 retail stores in over 64 countries. In the United States alone, Starbucks serves more than 70 million espresso-dependent customers each week. Starbucks gives customers what it calls a "third place"—away from home and away from work. Growth is the engine that keeps Starbucks perking. However, in recent years, the company's remarkable success has drawn a full litter of copycats, ranging from direct competitors such as Caribou Coffee to fast-food merchants such as McDonald's McCafe. Almost every eatery, it seems, now serves its own special premium brew. To maintain its incredible growth in an increasingly overcaffeinated marketplace, Starbucks must brew up an ambitious, multipronged growth strategy.

Market penetration
Company growth by increasing sales of current products to current market segments without changing the product.

First, Starbucks' management might consider whether the company can achieve deeper **market penetration**—making more sales to current customers without changing its original products. It might add new stores in current market areas to make it easier for customers to visit. In fact, Starbucks plans to add 3,000 new U.S. stores over the next five years. Improvements in advertising, prices, service, menu selection, or store design might encourage customers to stop by more often, stay longer, or buy more during each visit. For example, Starbucks is remodeling many of its stores to give them more of a neighborhood feel. The chain is also adding more food and beverage offerings, such as new Starbucks handcrafted sodas and pastries under its newly acquired La Boulange brand. And to boost business beyond the breakfast rush, which still constitutes the bulk of the company's revenue, Starbucks has added an evening menu in a quickly expanding number of markets featuring wine, beer, and tapas such as "Truffle Mac & Cheese" and "Bacon Wrapped Dates with Balsamic Glaze."

Market development
Company growth by identifying and developing new market segments for current company products.

Second, Starbucks might consider possibilities for **market development**—identifying and developing new markets for its current products. For instance, managers could review new demographic markets. Perhaps new groups—such as seniors—could be encouraged to visit Starbucks coffee shops for the first time or to buy more from them. Managers could also review new geographic markets. Starbucks is now expanding swiftly in non-U.S. markets, especially Asia. The company operates more than 1,000 stores in China, now its second-largest market behind the United States, and is moving rapidly into India.

Product development
Company growth by offering modified or new products to current market segments.

Third, Starbucks could consider **product development**—offering modified or new products to current markets. For example, to capture a piece of the $2 billion single-serve market, Starbucks developed Via instant coffee, and sells its coffees and Tazo teas in K-Cup packs that fit Keurig at-home brewers. Starbucks recently introduced a lighter-roast coffee

FIGURE | 2.3
The Product/Market Expansion Grid

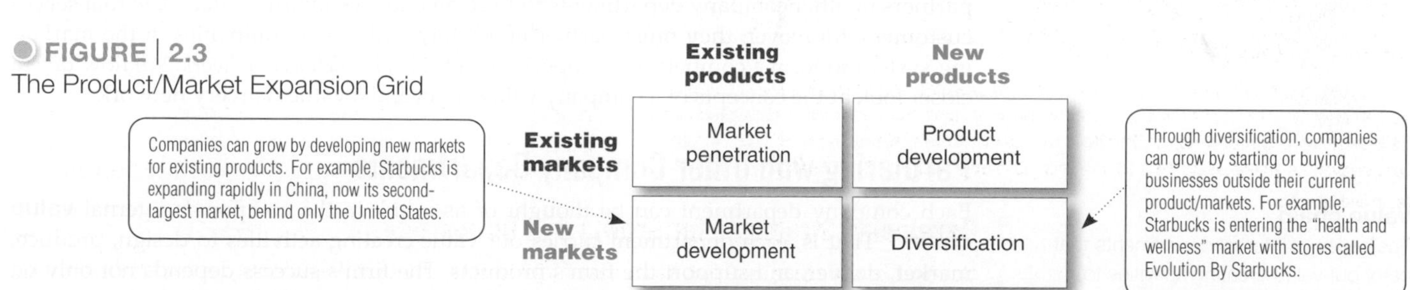
Existing products
New products
Existing markets
New markets
Market penetration
Product development
Market development
Diversification
Companies can grow by developing new markets for existing products. For example, Starbucks is expanding rapidly in China, now its second-largest market, behind only the United States.
Through diversification, companies can grow by starting or buying businesses outside their current product/markets. For example, Starbucks is entering the "health and wellness" market with stores called Evolution By Starbucks.

called Blonde, developed to meet the tastes of the 40 percent of U.S. coffee drinkers who prefer lighter, milder roasts. Starbucks is also forging ahead into new product categories. For instance, it recently entered the $8 billion energy drink market with Starbucks Refreshers, a beverage that combines fruit juice and green coffee extract.

Diversification
Company growth through starting up or acquiring businesses outside the company's current products and markets.

Finally, Starbucks might consider **diversification**—starting up or buying businesses beyond its current products and markets. For example, the company acquired Evolution Fresh, a boutique provider of super-premium fresh-squeezed juices. Starbucks intends to use Evolution as its entry into the "health and wellness" category, including standalone stores called Evolution By Starbucks. The company also recently acquired tea emporium operator Teavana. Recognizing that tea is the second-most consumed drink after water, Starbucks plans to open 1,000 Teavana Fine Teas + Tea Bar stores over the next 10 years.

Companies must not only develop strategies for growing their business portfolios but also strategies for *downsizing* them. There are many reasons that a firm might want to abandon products or markets. The firm may have grown too fast or entered areas where it lacks experience. The market environment might change, making some products or markets less profitable. For example, in difficult economic times, many firms prune out weaker, less-profitable products and markets to focus their more limited resources on the strongest ones. Finally, some products or business units simply age and die.

When a firm finds brands or businesses that are unprofitable or that no longer fit its overall strategy, it must carefully prune, harvest, or divest them. For example, over the past several years, P&G has sold off all of its big food brands—such as Crisco, Folgers, Jif, Sunny Delight, and Pringles—allowing the company to focus on household care and beauty and grooming products. And in recent years, GM has pruned several underperforming brands from its portfolio, including Oldsmobile, Pontiac, Saturn, Hummer, and Saab. Weak businesses usually require a disproportionate amount of management attention. Managers should focus on promising growth opportunities, not fritter away energy trying to salvage fading ones.

Author Comment | Marketing can't go it alone in creating customer value. Under the company-wide strategic plan, marketing must work closely with other departments to form an effective internal company value chain and with other companies in the marketing system to create an external value delivery network that jointly serves customers.

Planning Marketing: Partnering to Build Customer Relationships

The company's strategic plan establishes what kinds of businesses the company will operate and its objectives for each. Then, within each business unit, more detailed planning takes place. The major functional departments in each unit—marketing, finance, accounting, purchasing, operations, information systems, human resources, and others—must work together to accomplish strategic objectives.

Marketing plays a key role in the company's strategic planning in several ways. First, marketing provides a guiding *philosophy*—the marketing concept—that suggests the company strategy should revolve around creating customer value and building profitable relationships with important consumer groups. Second, marketing provides *inputs* to strategic planners by helping to identify attractive market opportunities and assessing the firm's potential to take advantage of them. Finally, within individual business units, marketing designs *strategies* for reaching the unit's objectives. Once the unit's objectives are set, marketing's task is to help carry them out profitably.

Customer engagement and value are the key ingredients in the marketer's formula for success. However, as noted in Chapter 1, although marketing plays a leading role, it alone cannot produce engagement and superior value for customers. It can be only a partner in attracting, engaging, and growing customers. In addition to *customer relationship management*, marketers must also practice *partner relationship management*. They must work closely with partners in other company departments to form an effective internal *value chain* that serves customers. Moreover, they must partner effectively with other companies in the marketing system to form a competitively superior external *value delivery network*. We now take a closer look at the concepts of a company value chain and a value delivery network.

Partnering with Other Company Departments

Value chain
The series of internal departments that carry out value-creating activities to design, produce, market, deliver, and support a firm's products.

Each company department can be thought of as a link in the company's internal **value chain**.[11] That is, each department carries out value-creating activities to design, produce, market, deliver, and support the firm's products. The firm's success depends not only on how well each department performs its work but also on how well the various departments coordinate their activities.

For example, True Value Hardware's goal is to create customer value and satisfaction by providing shoppers with the hardware and home improvement products they need at affordable prices along with top-notch customer service. Marketers at the retail-owned cooperative play an important role. They learn what customers need and help the 3,500 independent True Value retailers stock their store shelves with the desired products at competitive prices. They prepare advertising and merchandising programs and assist shoppers with customer service. Through these and other activities, True Value marketers help deliver value to customers.

However, True Value's marketers, both at the home office and in stores, need help from the company's other functions. True Value's ability to help you "Start Right. Start Here." depends on purchasing's skill in developing the needed suppliers and buying from them at low cost. True Value's information technology people must provide fast and accurate information about which products are selling in each store. And its operations people must provide effective, low-cost merchandise handling and delivery.

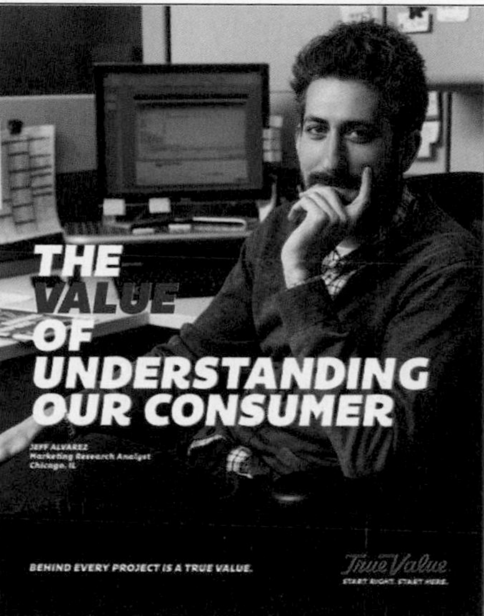

The value chain: These True Value ads recognize that everyone in the organization—from operations manager Tom Statham (left) to marketing research analyst Jeff Alvarez (right)—must contribute to helping the chain's customers handle their home improvement projects. They form the foundation for the brand's "Behind Every Project Is a True Value" positioning.

A company's value chain is only as strong as its weakest link. Success depends on how well each group performs its work of adding customer value and on how the company coordinates the activities of various functions. True Value's recent marketing campaign—"Behind Every Project Is a True Value"—recognizes the importance of having everyone in the organization—from in-store managers and employees to home-office operations managers and marketing research analysts—understand the needs and aspirations of the chain's do-it-yourself customers and help them handle home improvement projects.

Ideally, then, a company's different functions should work in harmony to produce value for consumers. But, in practice, interdepartmental relations are full of conflicts and misunderstandings. The marketing department takes the consumer's point of view. But when marketing tries to improve customer satisfaction, it can cause other departments to do a poorer job *in their terms*. Marketing department actions can increase purchasing costs, disrupt production schedules, increase inventories, and create budget headaches. Thus, other departments may resist the marketing department's efforts.

Yet marketers must find ways to get all departments to "think consumer" and develop a smoothly functioning value chain. One marketing expert puts it this way: "True market orientation . . . means that the entire company obsesses over creating value for the customer and views itself as a bundle of processes that profitably define, create, communicate, and deliver value to its target customers. . . . Everyone must do marketing regardless of function or department." Says another, "Engaging customers today requires commitment from the entire company. We're all marketers now."[12] Thus, whether you're an accountant, an operations manager, a financial analyst, an IT specialist, or a human resources manager, you need to understand marketing and your role in creating customer value.

Partnering with Others in the Marketing System

In its quest to create customer value, the firm needs to look beyond its own internal value chain and into the value chains of its suppliers, distributors, and, ultimately, its customers. Consider McDonald's. People do not swarm to McDonald's only because they love the chain's hamburgers. Consumers flock to the McDonald's *system*, not only to its food products. Throughout the world, McDonald's finely tuned value delivery system delivers a high standard of QSCV—quality, service, cleanliness, and value. McDonald's is effective only to the extent that it successfully partners with its franchisees, suppliers, and others to jointly create "our customers' favorite place and way to eat."

Value delivery network
The network made up of the company, its suppliers, its distributors, and, ultimately, its customers who partner with each other to improve the performance of the entire system.

More companies today are partnering with other members of the supply chain—suppliers, distributors, and, ultimately, customers—to improve the performance of the customer **value delivery network**. Competition no longer takes place only between individual competitors. Rather, it takes place between the entire value delivery network created by these competitors. Thus, Ford's performance against Toyota depends on the quality of Ford's overall value delivery network versus Toyota's. Even if Ford makes the best cars, it might lose in the marketplace if Toyota's dealer network provides more customer satisfying sales and service.

Author Comment | Now that we've set the context in terms of company-wide strategy, it's time to discuss customer-driven marketing strategies and programs.

Marketing Strategy and the Marketing Mix

The strategic plan defines the company's overall mission and objectives. Marketing's role is shown in **Figure 2.4**, which summarizes the major activities involved in managing a customer-driven marketing strategy and the marketing mix.

Consumers are in the center. The goal is to create value for customers and build profitable customer relationships. Next comes **marketing strategy**—the marketing logic by which the company hopes to create this customer value and achieve these profitable relationships. The company decides which customers it will serve (segmentation and targeting) and how (differentiation and positioning). It identifies the total market and then divides it into smaller segments, selects the most promising segments, and focuses on serving and satisfying the customers in these segments.

Marketing strategy
The marketing logic by which the company hopes to create customer value and achieve profitable customer relationships.

Guided by marketing strategy, the company designs an integrated *marketing mix* made up of factors under its control—product, price, place, and promotion (the four Ps). To find the best marketing strategy and mix, the company engages in marketing analysis, planning, implementation, and control. Through these activities, the company watches and adapts to the actors and forces in the marketing environment. We will now look briefly at each activity. In later chapters, we will discuss each one in more depth.

Customer Value-Driven Marketing Strategy

To succeed in today's competitive marketplace, companies must be customer centered. They must win customers from competitors and then engage and grow them by delivering greater value. But before it can satisfy customers, a company must first understand customer needs and wants. Thus, sound marketing requires careful customer analysis.

Companies know that they cannot profitably serve all consumers in a given market—at least not all consumers in the same way. There are too many different kinds of consumers

FIGURE | 2.4
Managing Marketing Strategies and the Marketing Mix

Marketing intermediaries
Competitors
Suppliers
Publics
Marketing analysis
Marketing planning
Marketing implementation
Marketing control
Product
Price
Place
Promotion
Segmentation
Targeting
Differentiation
Positioning
Customer value and relationships
At its core, marketing is all about creating customer value and profitable customer relationships.
Marketing strategy involves two key questions: Which customers will we serve (segmentation and targeting)? and How will we create value for them (differentiation and positioning)? Then, the company designs a marketing program—the four Ps—that delivers the intended value to targeted consumers.

with too many different kinds of needs. Most companies are in a position to serve some segments better than others. Thus, each company must divide up the total market, choose the best segments, and design strategies for profitably serving chosen segments. This process involves *market segmentation*, *market targeting*, *differentiation*, and *positioning*.

Market Segmentation

The market consists of many types of customers, products, and needs. The marketer must determine which segments offer the best opportunities. Consumers can be grouped and served in various ways based on geographic, demographic, psychographic, and behavioral factors. The process of dividing a market into distinct groups of buyers who have different needs, characteristics, or behaviors, and who might require separate products or marketing programs, is called **market segmentation**.

Market segmentation
Dividing a market into distinct groups of buyers who have different needs, characteristics, or behaviors, and who might require separate products or marketing programs.

Every market has segments, but not all ways of segmenting a market are equally useful. For example, Tylenol would gain little by distinguishing between low-income and high-income pain-relief users if both respond the same way to marketing efforts. A **market segment** consists of consumers who respond in a similar way to a given set of marketing efforts. In the car market, for example, consumers who want the biggest, most comfortable car regardless of price make up one market segment. Consumers who care mainly about price and operating economy make up another segment. It would be difficult to make one car model that was the first choice of consumers in both segments. Companies are wise to focus their efforts on meeting the distinct needs of individual market segments.

Market segment
A group of consumers who respond in a similar way to a given set of marketing efforts.

Market Targeting

After a company has defined its market segments, it can enter one or many of these segments. **Market targeting** involves evaluating each market segment's attractiveness and selecting one or more segments to enter. A company should target segments in which it can profitably generate the greatest customer value and sustain it over time.

Market targeting
The process of evaluating each market segment's attractiveness and selecting one or more segments to enter.

A company with limited resources might decide to serve only one or a few special segments or market niches. Such nichers specialize in serving customer segments that major competitors overlook or ignore. For example, Ferrari sells only 2,200 of its very-high-performance cars in North America each year but at very high prices—such as its Ferrari California model at $198,000 or the 740-horsepower F-12 Berlinetta at an eye-opening $312,000. Most nichers aren't quite so exotic. Profitable low-cost airline Allegiant Air avoids direct competition with larger major airline rivals by targeting smaller, neglected markets and new flyers. Nicher Allegiant "goes where they ain't." Abu Dhabi's Etihad Airways has also differentiated itself from fierce competition by focusing on a niche in the luxury air travel market and through high-quality customer service (see Real Marketing 2.2).

Alternatively, a company might choose to serve several related segments—perhaps those with different kinds of customers but with the same basic wants. Gap Inc., for example, targets different age, income, and lifestyle clothing and accessory segments with six different store and online brands: Gap, Banana Republic, Old Navy, Piperlime, Athleta, and INTERMIX. The Gap store brand breaks its segment down into even smaller niches, including Gap, GapKids, babyGap, GapMaternity, and GapBody.[13] Or a large company (for example, car companies like Honda and Ford) might decide to offer a complete range of products to serve all market segments.

Most companies enter a new market by serving a single segment; if this proves successful, they add more segments. For example, Nike started with innovative running shoes for serious runners. Large companies eventually seek full market coverage. Nike now makes and sells a broad range of sports products for just about anyone and everyone, in about every sport. It designs different products to meet the special needs of each segment it serves.

Market Differentiation and Positioning

After a company has decided which market segments to enter, it must determine how to differentiate its market offering for each targeted segment and what positions it wants to occupy in those segments. A product's *position* is the place it occupies relative to competitors' products in consumers' minds. Marketers want to develop unique market positions for their products. If a product is perceived to be exactly like others on the market, consumers would have no reason to buy it.

Positioning
Arranging for a product to occupy a clear, distinctive, and desirable place relative to competing products in the minds of target consumers.

Differentiation
Actually differentiating the market offering to create superior customer value.

Positioning is arranging for a product to occupy a clear, distinctive, and desirable place relative to competing products in the minds of target consumers. Marketers plan

Real Marketing 2.2

Etihad Airways: Connecting Abu Dhabi to the World

Etihad Airways is considered to be one of the youngest, yet most successful airlines in the aviation industry. It was established by Royal (Amiri) Decree of Abu Dhabi in July 2003 as the national carrier of the United Arab Emirates, and became commercial in November 2003, from Abu Dhabi to the rest of the world. Etihad (which is an Arabic word for "United") was strategically chosen as its brand name, as the airline unites Abu Dhabi with the West and East, and it connects with the airline's tagline: "Connecting Abu Dhabi to the World." The company's unique vision of reflecting Arabian hospitality within the flights, consisting of warm, generous, and considerate treatment, as well as enhancing the prestige of the Abu Dhabi culture is what helps stand the company out from the competition. Etihad has received several awards that reflect its status as the leading premium airline, including Middle East's Leading Airline at the World Travel Awards in 2012, 2013, and 2014. Its wide variety of awards emphasizes its high-quality services and provides recognition for the constant effort to remain at the top of the industry. As this acclaim progresses, the Etihad Airways brand name strengthens and spreads within the region, increasing and building on its already-existing popularity.

Etihad has a fleet of 102 aircraft that serve the international network with more than 1,000 flights per week to 120 destinations in 63 countries. Its cargo destinations range from the Middle East and Africa to Europe, Australia, Asia, and North America. It also owns 40 percent of Air Seychelles, nearly 30 percent of Air Berlin, 21 percent of Virgin Australia, and almost 5 percent of Aer Lingus.

Etihad's goal is to differentiate itself as a global airline that is challenging and changing the conventional notion of airline hospitality—besides providing a relaxing experience, the airline strives to make travel as safe and environment-friendly as possible by adhering to the highest global standards. Etihad is planning new route launches and introducing new aircraft to further its success, and offers lower prices than its main competitors in the region. Its diversification through cargo, holiday, and air transportation services has resulted in total revenue of 7 billion dollars. Innovative cabins also attract technology-loving customers and offer promising potential opportunities for future advances.

What helps this business differentiate itself within the market is its unique "Diamond Class" service, which targets the business travelers segment by introducing a luxurious class with complete complementary offerings, taking into consideration their need for personal space and to maintain their elite lifestyle, on the ground and up in the air. The airline empowers its passengers by giving them access to their own lounges—which includes spas, showers and cigar lounges, while also considering family entertainment aspects by offering a wide range of television shows and Internet access.

The Diamond Class service also exclusively includes private suites with sliding Arabian style doors, luxurious extended "Poltrona Frau" seats, built-in socket power for any electronic device, wardrobe space, and an exclusive marble bathroom. In addition, a wide variety of food and beverages is available, as well as special-request meals and catering inspired by industries outside the airline industry. These special services led to four global awards, including World's Best First Class, Best First Class Seat, and Best First Class Onboard Catering, as well as the Passenger Choice Award voted by 17.9 million travelers around the world.

Etihad also created a loyalty program to help increase long-term customer loyalty to the brand, as well as to increase customer relationship management interactions, to create a sense of belonging between the customers and the brand. The collection of guest mile points that can be redeemed with the airline furthers these goals, and also enables the company to collect information on its customers for free, such as keeping track of customer needs, demographic changes, and travelling patterns through feedback and supporting statistics. Thus, the Etihad loyalty program plays a large role in the company's growth by allowing it to be more consumer-centric and by providing an in-depth understanding of customer wants and needs.

In 2013, Etihad Airways decided to spin off Etihad Guest, its 2.3 million member

Niche marketing: Award-winning Etihad Airways prides itself on its high-quality customer service and luxury in-flight experience. This differentiation also allows Etihad to avoid direct competition with major rivals.

loyalty program. The airline had recognized the fact that loyalty programs are not just about selling flights but they could be used as a tool to gather information about the habits and tastes of people. The data is used by commercial partners to help them market their products to Etihad customers. In 2012, the Etihad CEO had admitted that the loyalty program section was growing quickly. In the same year, Etihad had acquired a stake in Air Berlin's frequent flyer program – Top Bonus. They added this data to their own network data. It also meant that Etihad customers could earn Etihad Guest Miles on airlines Etihad had a stake in, including Virgin Australia and Air Seychelles. The idea was that the loyalty program would become self-funding and would be floated off as a separate entity from the airline business. Guest Miles can be earned on all routes, with 6,000 products being offered through the online shop.

All in all, Etihad Airways has proven in merely 11 years to be a strong standing competitor, with its plan to "Connect Abu Dhabi to the World," and has won a large range of awards, reflecting its position as one of the leading premium global airline brands. By maintaining its image, constantly innovating, and keeping up with consumer needs, Etihad Airways will continue to grow in the region and add on to its existing awards. Its current earnings and expected growth surpass those of its competitors, and it is becoming one of the fastest growing airlines in the history of commercial aviation.

Sources: Based on information from Abu Shahout, Abdel Razzq, Fain Abraham Punnose, and Khalil Khalifa, "Etihad Airways Marketing Strategy," *Scribd*, March 18, 2011, www.scribd.com/doc/54943204/Etihad-Airways-Marketing-Strategy; Etihad Airways, "Our Story," www.etihadairways.com/sites/etihad/eg/en/aboutetihad/Pages/etihadstoryposting.aspx, accessed October 30, 2012; Joyner Rodrigues, "Etihad Airways—Marketing Plan," *Scribd*, August 23, 2010, www.scribd.com/doc/42673475/Etihad-Airways-Marketing-Plan; and Etihad Airways, "Vision," n.d., www.etihadairways.com/sites/Etihad/eg/en/aboutetihad/etihadstory/pages/etihadvsion.asp&xgt, accessed October 30, 2012, http://www.thenational.ae/business/industry-insights/aviation/etihad-airways-goes-the-extra-mile-with-loyalty-programme-spin-off, accessed November, 2014.

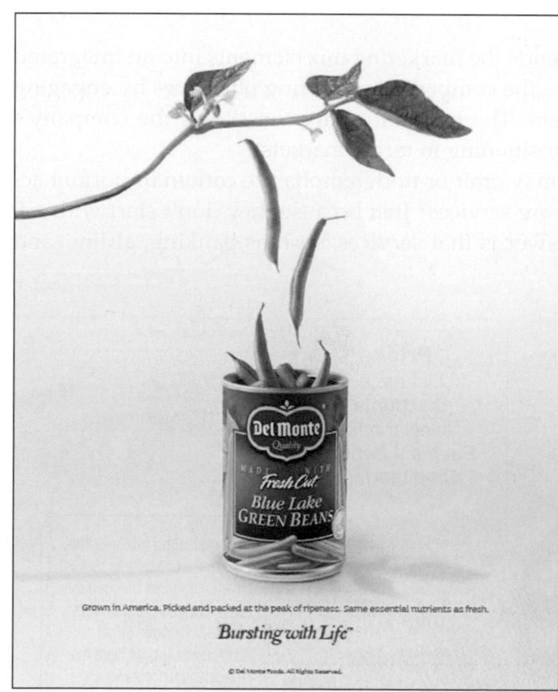

Positioning: The 100-year-old Del Monte brand positions itself as "Bursting with Life: Made in America. Picked and packed at the peak of ripeness. Same essential ingredients as fresh."

Del Monte Foods, Inc.

positions that distinguish their products from competing brands and give them the greatest advantage in their target markets.

Audi promises "Truth in Engineering"; Subaru is "Confidence in Motion." Coke is all about "open happiness"; Pepsi says "live for now." Del Monte is "Bursting with Life"; Cascadian Farm products are "Certified Organic. Guaranteed Delicious." At Panera, you can "Live Consciously. Eat Deliciously." At Wendy's, "Quality Is Our Recipe." Such deceptively simple statements form the backbone of a product's marketing strategy. For example, the iconic 100-year-old Del Monte brand designed its entire integrated marketing campaign—from television and print ads to its online, mobile, and social media content—around the "Bursting with Life" positioning. More than just words, the campaign slogan positions Del Monte's canned fruits and vegetables as quality ingredients that contribute to a healthy lifestyle. They are "grown in America, picked and packed at the peak of ripeness, [and contain the] same essential nutrients as fresh."

In positioning its brand, a company first identifies possible customer value differences that provide competitive advantages on which to build the position. A company can offer greater customer value by either charging lower prices than competitors or offering more benefits to justify higher prices. But if the company *promises* greater value, it must then *deliver* that greater value. Thus, effective positioning begins with **differentiation**—actually *differentiating* the company's market offering so that it gives consumers more value. Once the company has chosen a desired position, it must take strong steps to deliver and communicate that position to target consumers. The company's entire marketing program should support the chosen positioning strategy.

Developing an Integrated Marketing Mix

Marketing mix
The set of tactical marketing tools—product, price, place, and promotion—that the firm blends to produce the response it wants in the target market.

After determining its overall marketing strategy, the company is ready to begin planning the details of the **marketing mix**, one of the major concepts in modern marketing. The marketing mix is the set of tactical marketing tools that the firm blends to produce the response it wants in the target market. The marketing mix consists of everything the firm can do to influence the demand for its product. The many possibilities can be collected into four groups of variables—the four Ps. **Figure 2.5** shows the marketing tools under each P.

- *Product* means the goods-and-services combination the company offers to the target market. Thus, a Ford Escape consists of nuts and bolts, spark plugs, pistons, headlights, and thousands of other parts. Ford offers several Escape models and dozens of optional features. The car comes fully serviced and with a comprehensive warranty that is as much a part of the product as the tailpipe.
- *Price* is the amount of money customers must pay to obtain the product. For example, Ford calculates suggested retail prices that its dealers might charge for each Escape. But Ford dealers rarely charge the full sticker price. Instead, they negotiate the price with each customer, offering discounts, trade-in allowances, and credit terms. These actions adjust prices for the current competitive and economic situations and bring them into line with the buyer's perception of the car's value.
- *Place* includes company activities that make the product available to target consumers. Ford partners with a large body of independently owned dealerships that sell the company's many different models. Ford selects its dealers carefully and strongly supports them. The dealers keep an inventory of Ford automobiles, demonstrate them to potential buyers, negotiate prices, close sales, and service the cars after the sale.
- *Promotion* refers to activities that communicate the merits of the product and persuade target customers to buy it. Ford spends more than $2.3 billion each year on U.S. advertising to tell consumers about the company and its many products.[14] Dealership salespeople assist potential buyers and persuade them that Ford is the best car for them. Ford and its dealers offer special promotions—sales, cash rebates, and low financing rates—as added purchase incentives. And Ford's Facebook, Twitter, YouTube, and other social media platforms engage consumers with the brand and with other brand fans.

An effective marketing program blends the marketing mix elements into an integrated marketing program designed to achieve the company's marketing objectives by engaging consumers and delivering value to them. The marketing mix constitutes the company's tactical tool kit for establishing strong positioning in target markets.

Some critics think that the four Ps may omit or underemphasize certain important activities. For example, they ask, "Where are services? Just because they don't start with a *P* doesn't justify omitting them." The answer is that services, such as banking, airline, and

FIGURE | 2.5
The Four Ps of the Marketing Mix

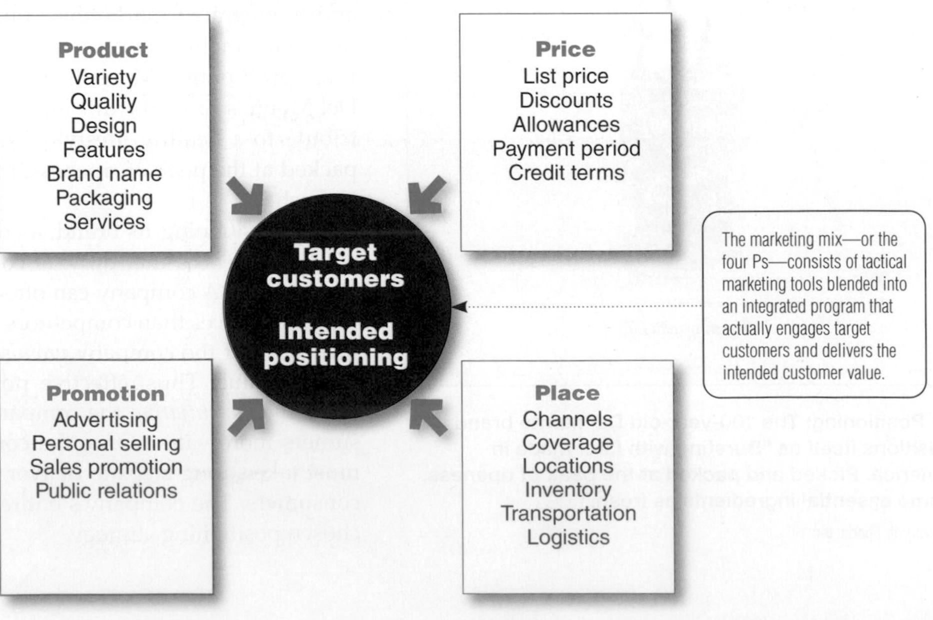

retailing services, are products too. We might call them *service products*. "Where is packaging?" the critics might ask. Marketers would answer that they include packaging as one of many product decisions. All said, as Figure 2.5 suggests, many marketing activities that might appear to be left out of the marketing mix are included under one of the four Ps. The issue is not whether there should be four, six, or ten Ps so much as what framework is most helpful in designing integrated marketing programs.

There is another concern, however, that is valid. It holds that the four Ps concept takes the seller's view of the market, not the buyer's view. From the buyer's viewpoint, in this age of customer value and relationships, the four Ps might be better described as the four Cs:[15]

Four Ps	**Four Cs**
Product	Customer solution
Price	Customer cost
Place	Convenience
Promotion	Communication

Thus, whereas marketers see themselves as selling products, customers see themselves as buying value or solutions to their problems. And customers are interested in more than just the price; they are interested in the total costs of obtaining, using, and disposing of a product. Customers want the product and service to be as conveniently available as possible. Finally, they want two-way communication. Marketers would do well to think through the four Cs first and then build the four Ps on that platform.

Author Comment | So far we've focused on the *marketing* in marketing management. Now, let's turn to the *management*.

Managing the Marketing Effort

In addition to being good at the *marketing* in marketing management, companies also need to pay attention to the *management*. Managing the marketing process requires the five marketing management functions shown in **Figure 2.6**—*analysis, planning, implementation, organization,* and *control*. The company first develops company-wide strategic plans and then translates them into marketing and other plans for each division, product, and brand. Through implementation and organization, the company turns the plans into actions. Control consists of measuring and evaluating the results of marketing activities and taking corrective action where needed. Finally, marketing analysis provides the information and evaluations needed for all the other marketing activities.

SWOT analysis
An overall evaluation of the company's strengths (S), weaknesses (W), opportunities (O), and threats (T).

Marketing Analysis

Managing the marketing function begins with a complete analysis of the company's situation. The marketer should conduct a **SWOT analysis** (pronounced "swat" analysis), by which it evaluates the company's overall strengths (S), weaknesses (W), opportunities (O),

FIGURE | 2.6
Managing Marketing: Analysis, Planning, Implementation, and Control

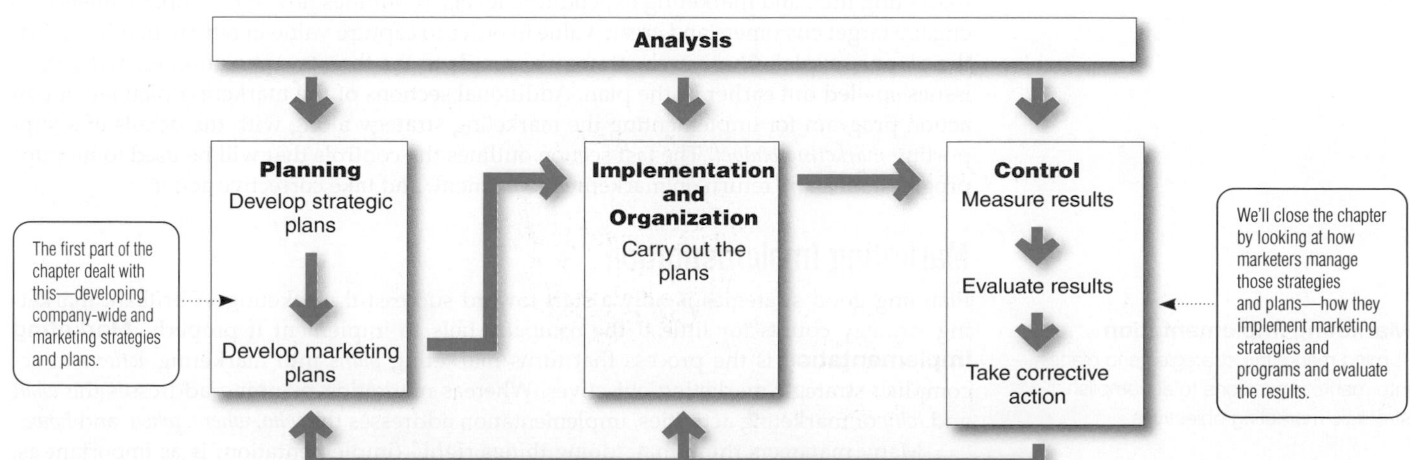

FIGURE | 2.7
SWOT Analysis: Strengths (S), Weaknesses (W), Opportunities (O), and Threats (T)

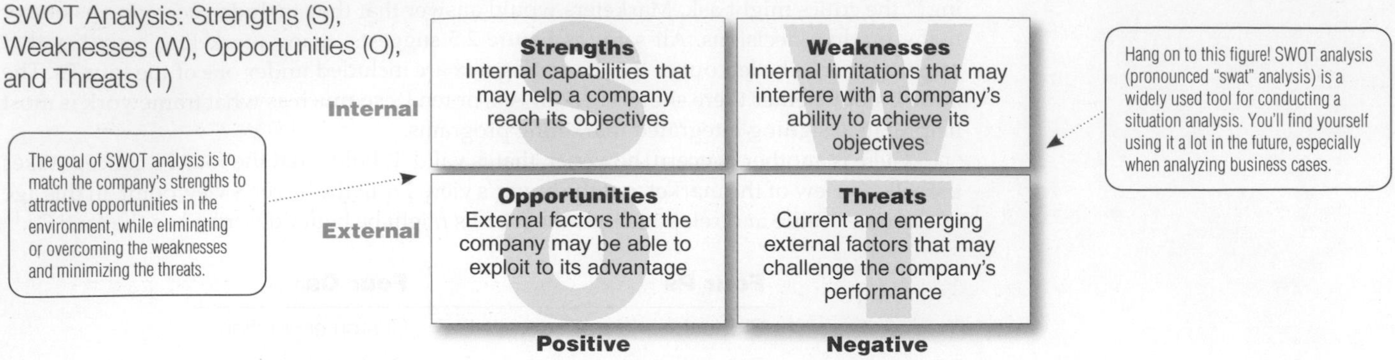

	Positive	Negative
Internal	**Strengths** Internal capabilities that may help a company reach its objectives	**Weaknesses** Internal limitations that may interfere with a company's ability to achieve its objectives
External	**Opportunities** External factors that the company may be able to exploit to its advantage	**Threats** Current and emerging external factors that may challenge the company's performance

The goal of SWOT analysis is to match the company's strengths to attractive opportunities in the environment, while eliminating or overcoming the weaknesses and minimizing the threats.

Hang on to this figure! SWOT analysis (pronounced "swat" analysis) is a widely used tool for conducting a situation analysis. You'll find yourself using it a lot in the future, especially when analyzing business cases.

and threats (T) (see **Figure 2.7**). Strengths include internal capabilities, resources, and positive situational factors that may help the company serve its customers and achieve its objectives. Weaknesses include internal limitations and negative situational factors that may interfere with the company's performance. Opportunities are favorable factors or trends in the external environment that the company may be able to exploit to its advantage. And threats are unfavorable external factors or trends that may present challenges to performance.

The company should analyze its markets and marketing environment to find attractive opportunities and identify threats. It should analyze company strengths and weaknesses as well as current and possible marketing actions to determine which opportunities it can best pursue. The goal is to match the company's strengths to attractive opportunities in the environment, while simultaneously eliminating or overcoming the weaknesses and minimizing the threats. Marketing analysis provides inputs to each of the other marketing management functions. We discuss marketing analysis more fully in Chapter 3.

Marketing Planning

Through strategic planning, the company decides what it wants to do with each business unit. Marketing planning involves choosing marketing strategies that will help the company attain its overall strategic objectives. A detailed marketing plan is needed for each business, product, or brand. What does a marketing plan look like? Our discussion focuses on product or brand marketing plans.

Table 2.2 outlines the major sections of a typical product or brand marketing plan. (See Appendix 2 for a sample marketing plan.) The plan begins with an executive summary that quickly reviews major assessments, goals, and recommendations. The main section of the plan presents a detailed SWOT analysis of the current marketing situation as well as potential threats and opportunities. The plan next states major objectives for the brand and outlines the specifics of a marketing strategy for achieving them.

A *marketing strategy* consists of specific strategies for target markets, positioning, the marketing mix, and marketing expenditure levels. It outlines how the company intends to engage target customers and create value in order to capture value in return. In this section, the planner explains how each strategy responds to the threats, opportunities, and critical issues spelled out earlier in the plan. Additional sections of the marketing plan lay out an action program for implementing the marketing strategy along with the details of a supporting *marketing budget*. The last section outlines the controls that will be used to monitor progress, measure return on marketing investment, and take corrective action.

Marketing Implementation

Marketing implementation
Turning marketing strategies and plans into marketing actions to accomplish strategic marketing objectives.

Planning good strategies is only a start toward successful marketing. A brilliant marketing strategy counts for little if the company fails to implement it properly. **Marketing implementation** is the process that turns marketing *plans* into marketing *actions* to accomplish strategic marketing objectives. Whereas marketing planning addresses the *what* and *why* of marketing activities, implementation addresses the *who, where, when*, and *how*.

Many managers think that "doing things right" (implementation) is as important as, or even more important than, "doing the right things" (strategy). The fact is that both are

Table 2.2 | Contents of a Marketing Plan

Section	Purpose
Executive summary	Presents a brief summary of the main goals and recommendations of the plan for management review, helping top management find the plan's major points quickly.
Current marketing situation	Describes the target market and the company's position in it, including information about the market, product performance, competition, and distribution. This section includes the following: • A *market description* that defines the market and major segments and then reviews customer needs and factors in the marketing environment that may affect customer purchasing. • A *product review* that shows sales, prices, and gross margins of the major products in the product line. • A review of *competition* that identifies major competitors and assesses their market positions and strategies for product quality, pricing, distribution, and promotion. • A review of *distribution* that evaluates recent sales trends and other developments in major distribution channels.
Threats and opportunities analysis	Assesses major threats and opportunities that the product might face, helping management to anticipate important positive or negative developments that might have an impact on the firm and its strategies.
Objectives and issues	States the marketing objectives that the company would like to attain during the plan's term and discusses key issues that will affect their attainment.
Marketing strategy	Outlines the broad marketing logic by which the business unit hopes to engage customers, create customer value, and build customer relationships, plus the specifics of target markets, positioning, and marketing expenditure levels. How will the company create value for customers in order to capture value from customers in return? This section also outlines specific strategies for each marketing mix element and explains how each responds to the threats, opportunities, and critical issues spelled out earlier in the plan.
Action programs	Spells out how marketing strategies will be turned into specific action programs that answer the following questions: *What* will be done? *When* will it be done? *Who* will do it? *How* much will it cost?
Budgets	Details a supporting marketing budget that is essentially a projected profit-and-loss statement. It shows expected revenues and expected costs of production, distribution, and marketing. The difference is the projected profit. The budget becomes the basis for materials buying, production scheduling, personnel planning, and marketing operations.
Controls	Outlines the controls that will be used to monitor progress, allow management to review implementation results, and spot products that are not meeting their goals. It includes measures of return on marketing investment.

critical to success, and companies can gain competitive advantages through effective implementation. One firm can have essentially the same strategy as another, yet win in the marketplace through faster or better execution. Still, implementation is difficult—it is often easier to think up good marketing strategies than it is to carry them out.

In an increasingly connected world, people at all levels of the marketing system must work together to implement marketing strategies and plans. At John Deere, for example, marketing implementation for the company's residential, commercial, agricultural, and industrial equipment requires day-to-day decisions and actions by thousands of people both inside and outside the organization. Marketing managers make decisions about target segments, branding, product development, pricing, promotion, and distribution. They talk with engineering about product design, with manufacturing about production and inventory levels, and with finance about funding and cash flows. They also connect with outside people, such as advertising agencies to plan ad campaigns and the news media to obtain publicity support. The sales force urges and supports independent John Deere dealers and large retailers like Lowe's in their efforts to convince residential, agricultural, and industrial customers that "Nothing Runs Like a Deere."

Marketing Department Organization

The company must design a marketing organization that can carry out marketing strategies and plans. If the company is very small, one person might do all the research, selling, advertising, customer service, and other marketing work. As the company expands, however, a marketing department emerges to plan and carry out marketing activities. In large companies, this department contains many specialists—product and market managers, sales managers and salespeople, market researchers, and advertising and social media experts, among others.

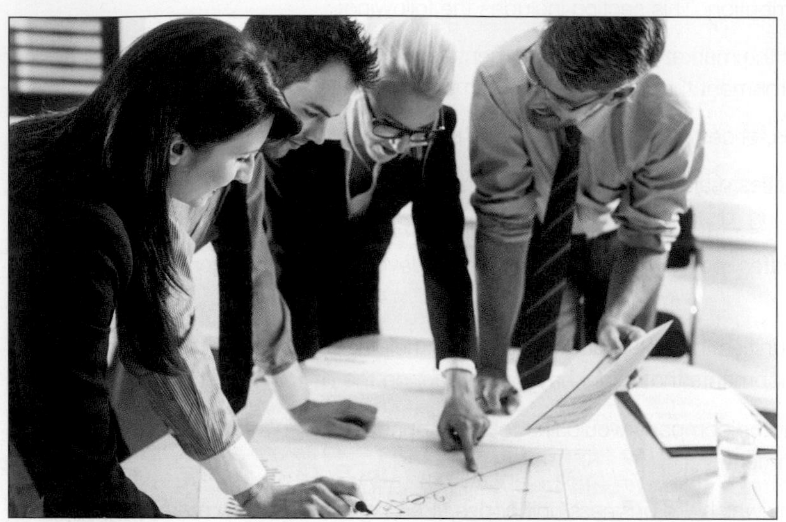

● **Marketers must continually plan their analysis, implementation, and control activities.**
Kzenon/Shutterstock

To head up such large marketing organizations, many companies have now created a *chief marketing officer* (or CMO) position. This person heads up the company's entire marketing operation and represents marketing on the company's top management team. The CMO position puts marketing on equal footing with other "C-level" executives, such as the chief operating officer (COO) and the chief financial officer (CFO). As a member of top management, the CMO's role is to champion the customer's cause—to be the "chief customer officer."

Modern marketing departments can be arranged in several ways. The most common form of marketing organization is the *functional organization*. Under this organization, different marketing activities are headed by a functional specialist—a sales manager, an advertising manager, a marketing research manager, a customer service manager, or a new product manager. A company that sells across the country or internationally often uses a *geographic organization*. Its sales and marketing people are assigned to specific countries, regions, and districts. Geographic organization allows salespeople to settle into a territory, get to know their customers, and work with a minimum of travel time and cost. Companies with many very different products or brands often create a *product management organization*. Using this approach, a product manager develops and implements a complete strategy and marketing program for a specific product or brand.

For companies that sell one product line to many different types of markets and customers who have different needs and preferences, a *market* or *customer management organization* might be best. A market management organization is similar to the product management organization. Market managers are responsible for developing marketing strategies and plans for their specific markets or customers. This system's main advantage is that the company is organized around the needs of specific customer segments. Many companies develop special organizations to manage their relationships with large customers. For example, companies such as P&G and Stanley Black & Decker have created large teams, or even whole divisions, to serve large customers, such as Walmart, Target, Kroger, or Home Depot.

Large companies that produce many different products flowing into many different geographic and customer markets usually employ some *combination* of the functional, geographic, product, and market organization forms.

Marketing organization has become an increasingly important issue in recent years. More and more, companies are shifting their brand management focus toward *customer management*—moving away from managing only product or brand profitability and toward managing customer profitability and customer equity. They think of themselves not as managing portfolios of brands but as managing portfolios of customers. And rather than managing the fortunes of a brand, they see themselves as managing customer-brand engagement, experiences, and relationships.

Marketing Control

Marketing control
Measuring and evaluating the results of marketing strategies and plans and taking corrective action to ensure that the objectives are achieved.

Because many surprises occur during the implementation of marketing plans, marketers must practice constant **marketing control**—evaluating the results of marketing strategies and plans and taking corrective action to ensure that the objectives are attained. Marketing control involves four steps. Management first sets specific marketing goals. It then measures its performance in the marketplace and evaluates the causes of any differences between expected and actual performance. Finally, management takes corrective action to close the gaps between goals and performance. This may require changing the action programs or even changing the goals.

Operating control involves checking ongoing performance against the annual plan and taking corrective action when necessary. Its purpose is to ensure that the company achieves the sales, profits, and other goals set out in its annual plan. It also involves determining the profitability of different products, territories, markets, and channels. *Strategic control* involves looking at whether the company's basic strategies are well matched to its opportunities. Marketing strategies and programs can quickly become outdated, and each company should periodically reassess its overall approach to the marketplace.

Author Comment | Measuring marketing return on investment has become a major emphasis. But it can be difficult. For example, a Super Bowl ad reaches more than 100 million consumers but may cost more than $4 million for 30 seconds of airtime. How do you measure the return on such an investment in terms of sales, profits, and building customer engagement and relationships? We'll look at this question again in Chapter 15.

Measuring and Managing Marketing Return on Investment

Marketing managers must ensure that their marketing dollars are being well spent. In the past, many marketers spent freely on big, expensive marketing programs and flashy advertising campaigns, often without thinking carefully about the financial returns on their spending. Their goal was often a general one—to "build brands and consumer preference." They believed that marketing produces intangible creative outcomes, which do not lend themselves readily to measures of productivity or return.

In today's leaner economic times, however, all that has changed. The free-spending days have been replaced by a new era of marketing measurement and accountability. More than ever, today's marketers are being held accountable for linking their strategies and tactics to measurable marketing performance outcomes. One important marketing performance measure is **marketing return on investment** (or **marketing ROI**). *Marketing ROI* is the net return from a marketing investment divided by the costs of the marketing investment. It measures the profits generated by investments in marketing activities.

Marketing return on investment (or marketing ROI)
The net return from a marketing investment divided by the costs of the marketing investment.

In one recent survey, 64 percent of senior marketers rated accountability as a top three concern, well ahead of the 50 percent rating the hot topic of integrated marketing communications as a top concern. However, another survey found that only about a third of chief marketing officers felt able to quantitatively measure the short- or long-term return on their marketing spending. A startling 57 percent of CMOs don't take ROI measures into account when setting their marketing budgets, and an even more startling 28 percent said they base their marketing budgets on "gut instinct." Clearly, marketers must think more strategically about the marketing performance returns of their marketing spending.[16]

Marketing ROI can be difficult to measure. In measuring financial ROI, both the *R* and the *I* are uniformly measured in dollars. For example, when buying a piece of equipment, the productivity gains resulting from the purchase are fairly straightforward. As of yet, however, there is no consistent definition of marketing ROI. For instance, returns such as engagement, advertising, and brand-building impact aren't easily put into dollar returns.

A company can assess marketing ROI in terms of standard marketing performance measures, such as brand awareness, sales, or market share. Many companies are assembling such measures into *marketing dashboards*—meaningful sets of marketing performance measures in a single display used to monitor strategic marketing performance. Just as automobile dashboards present drivers with details on how their cars are performing, the marketing dashboard gives marketers the detailed measures they need to assess and adjust their marketing strategies. For example, VF Corporation uses a marketing dashboard to track the performance of its more than 30 lifestyle apparel brands—including Wrangler, Lee, The North Face, Vans, Nautica, 7 For All Mankind, Timberland, and others. VF's marketing dashboard tracks brand equity and trends, share of voice, market share, online sentiment, and marketing ROI in key markets worldwide, not only for VF brands but also for competing brands.[17]

Increasingly, however, beyond standard performance measures, marketers are using customer-centered measures of marketing impact, such as customer acquisition, customer engagement, customer retention, customer lifetime value, and customer equity. These measures capture not only current marketing performance but also future performance resulting from stronger customer relationships. **Figure 2.8** views marketing expenditures as investments that produce returns in the form of more profitable customer relationships.[18] Marketing investments result in improved customer value, engagement, and satisfaction,

FIGURE | 2.8
Marketing Return on Investment
Source: Adapted from Roland T. Rust, Katherine N. Lemon, and Valerie A. Zeithaml, "Return on Marketing: Using Consumer Equity to Focus Marketing Strategy," *Journal of Marketing*, January 2004, p.112. Used with permission.

Beyond measuring marketing return on investment in terms of standard performance measures such as sales or market share, many companies are using customer relationship measures, such as customer satisfaction, engagement, retention, and equity. These are more difficult to measure but capture both current and future performance.

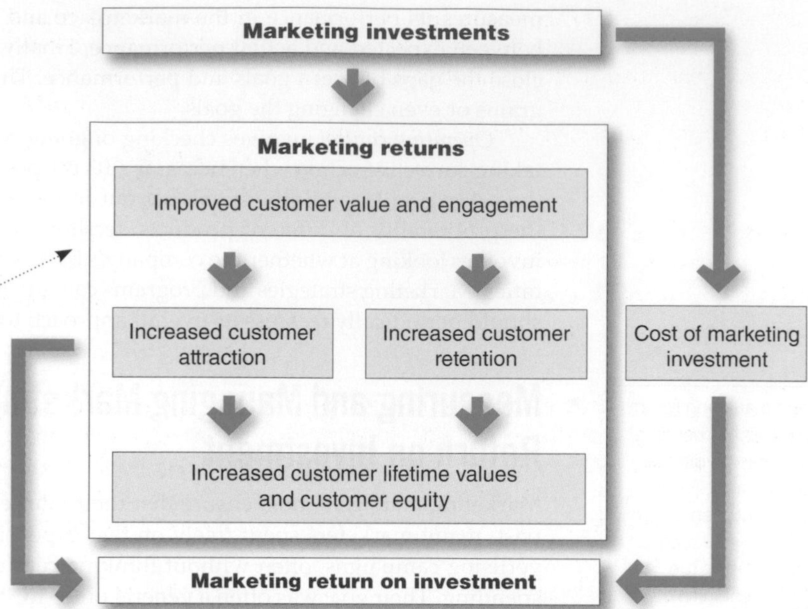

which in turn increases customer attraction and retention. This increases individual customer lifetime values and the firm's overall customer equity. Increased customer equity, in relation to the cost of the marketing investments, determines return on marketing investment.

Regardless of how it's defined or measured, the marketing ROI concept is here to stay. In good times or bad, marketers will be increasingly accountable for the performance outcomes of their activities. As one marketer puts it, marketers "have got to know how to count."[19]

2 Reviewing the Concepts

OBJECTIVES REVIEW AND KEY TERMS

Objectives Review

In Chapter 1, we defined marketing and outlined the steps in the marketing process. In this chapter, we examined company-wide strategic planning and marketing's role in the organization. Then we looked more deeply into marketing strategy and the marketing mix and reviewed the major marketing management functions. So you've now had a pretty good overview of the fundamentals of modern marketing.

OBJECTIVE 1 Explain company-wide strategic planning and its four steps. *(pp 64–68)*

Strategic planning sets the stage for the rest of the company's planning. Marketing contributes to strategic planning, and the overall plan defines marketing's role in the company.

Strategic planning involves developing a strategy for long-run survival and growth. It consists of four steps: (1) defining the company's mission, (2) setting objectives and goals, (3) designing a business portfolio, and (4) developing functional plans. The company's *mission* should be market oriented, realistic, specific, motivating, and consistent with the market environment. The mission is then transformed into detailed *supporting goals and objectives*, which in turn guide decisions about the business portfolio. Then each business and product unit must develop *detailed marketing plans* in line with the company-wide plan.

OBJECTIVE 2 Discuss how to design business portfolios and develop growth strategies. *(pp 68–72)*

Guided by the company's mission statement and objectives, management plans its *business portfolio*, or the collection of businesses and products that make up the company. The firm wants to produce a business portfolio that best fits its strengths and weaknesses to opportunities in the environment. To do this, it must analyze and adjust its *current* business portfolio and develop *growth* and *downsizing* strategies for adjusting the *future* portfolio. The company might use a formal portfolio-planning method. But many companies are now designing more-customized portfolio-planning approaches that better suit their unique situations.

OBJECTIVE 3 **Explain marketing's role in strategic planning and how marketing works with its partners to create and deliver customer value.** *(pp 72–74)*

Under the strategic plan, the major functional departments—marketing, finance, accounting, purchasing, operations, information systems, human resources, and others—must work together to accomplish strategic objectives. Marketing plays a key role in the company's strategic planning by providing a *marketing concept philosophy* and *inputs* regarding attractive market opportunities. Within individual business units, marketing designs *strategies* for reaching the unit's objectives and helps to carry them out profitably.

Marketers alone cannot produce superior value for customers. Marketers must practice *partner relationship management*, working closely with partners in other departments to form an effective *value chain* that serves the customer. And they must also partner effectively with other companies in the marketing system to form a competitively superior *value delivery network*.

OBJECTIVE 4 **Describe the elements of a customer value-driven marketing strategy and mix and the forces that influence it.** *(pp 74–79)*

Customer value and relationships are at the center of marketing strategy and programs. Through market segmentation, targeting, differentiation, and positioning, the company divides the total market into smaller segments, selects segments it can best serve, and decides how it wants to bring value to target consumers in the selected segments. It then designs an *integrated marketing mix* to produce the response it wants in the target market. The marketing mix consists of product, price, place, and promotion decisions (the four Ps).

OBJECTIVE 5 **List the marketing management functions, including the elements of a marketing plan, and discuss the importance of measuring and managing marketing return on investment.** *(pp 79–84)*

To find the best strategy and mix and to put them into action, the company engages in marketing analysis, planning, implementation, and control. The main components of a *marketing plan* are the executive summary, the current marketing situation, threats and opportunities, objectives and issues, marketing strategies, action programs, budgets, and controls. Planning good strategies is often easier than carrying them out. To be successful, companies must also be effective at *implementation*—turning marketing strategies into marketing actions.

Marketing departments can be organized in one way or a combination of ways: *functional marketing organization*, *geographic organization, product management organization*, or *market management organization*. In this age of customer relationships, more and more companies are now changing their organizational focus from product or territory management to customer relationship management. Marketing organizations carry out *marketing control*, both operating control and strategic control.

More than ever, marketing accountability is the top marketing concern. Marketing managers must ensure that their marketing dollars are being well spent. In a tighter economy, today's marketers face growing pressures to show that they are adding value in line with their costs. In response, marketers are developing better measures of *marketing return on investment*. Increasingly, they are using customer-centered measures of marketing impact as a key input into their strategic decision making.

MyMarketingLab

Go to **mymktlab.com** to complete the problems marked with this icon .

Key Terms

OBJECTIVE 1

Strategic planning (p 64)
Mission statement (p 65)

OBJECTIVE 2

Business portfolio (p 68)
Portfolio analysis (p 69)
Growth-share matrix (p 69)
Product/market expansion grid (p 71)
Market penetration (p 71)
Market development (p 71)
Product development (p 71)
Diversification (p 72)

OBJECTIVE 3

Value chain (p 72)
Value delivery network (p 74)

OBJECTIVE 4

Marketing strategy (p 74)
Market segmentation (p 75)
Market segment (p 75)
Market targeting (p 75)
Positioning (p 75)
Differentiation (p 77)
Marketing mix (p 78)

OBJECTIVE 5

SWOT analysis (p 79)
Marketing implementation (p 80)
Marketing control (p 82)
Marketing return on investment (marketing ROI) (p 83)

DISCUSSION AND CRITICAL THINKING

Discussion Questions

2-1 Explain how a company's mission needs to be oriented and written in order to be successful. (AACSB: Communication)

2-2 Describe how a company's mission statement and objectives affect the way management plans its business portfolio. (AACSB: Communication; Reflective Thinking)

2-3 Why is just marketing not enough to produce superior value for customers? (AACSB: Communication)

2-4 What are the four Ps of marketing? What insights might a firm gain by considering the four Cs rather than the four Ps? (AACSB: Communication; Reflective Thinking)

2-5 What is a marketing dashboard and how is it useful to marketers? What types of performance measures do marketers use to assess marketing performance? (AACSB: Communication)

Critical Thinking Exercises

2-6 Form a small group and conduct a SWOT analysis for your school, a group that you are a member of, a publicly traded company, a local business, or a nonprofit organization. Based on your analysis, suggest a strategy from the product/market expansion grid and an appropriate marketing mix to implement that strategy. (AACSB: Communication; Reflective Thinking)

2-7 The Boston Consulting Group (BCG) Matrix is a useful strategic tool. Another classic portfolio planning method useful to marketers is the GE/McKinsey Matrix (see www.quickmba.com/strategy/matrix/ge-mckinsey/). How is the GE/McKinsey Matrix similar to and different from the BCG Matrix? (AACSB: Communication; Reflective Thinking)

2-8 Create a mission statement for a nonprofit organization you would be interested in starting. Have another student evaluate your mission statement while you evaluate the other student's statement, suggesting areas of improvement. (AACSB: Communication; Reflective Thinking)

MINICASES AND APPLICATIONS

Online, Mobile, and Social Media Marketing **Twitter Peaked?**

In 2014, Twitter, the online messaging platform, was face to face with some difficult choices. Share value had halved in the past year and many believed that the social network had peaked at around 20 percent of the size of Facebook. Twitter has been trying to find ways to boost the amount of time that users spend on the platform. It was actively looking to acquire online music services and, according to many, had set its sights on both SoundCloud, valued at $700 million, and Spotify, valued at $4 billion. In acquiring new and successful businesses such as those that offer music streaming services, Twitter would not only be enjoying its largest acquisition to date, but would also be securing new areas for growth. Acquisitions are, however, not new for Twitter. It bought the start-up Vine, a video-clip sharing service, in 2012, and recently acquired Gnip, a provider of social data. The problem is that Twitter is not profitable and may not have large sums of cash to acquire a music service.

2-9 Explain which product/market expansion grid strategy Twitter is using in order to keep up with competitors like Apple and Facebook. (AACSB: Communication; Reflective Thinking)

2-10 Discuss whether organic growth is more sustainable or whether companies should keep pushing their growth by acquiring other companies. (AACSB: Communication; Reflective Thinking)

Marketing Ethics **Predicting the Future**

In 1966, *Time* magazine made a prediction of the retail world in 2000. It confidently predicted that remote shopping, although feasible, would never be likely to catch on. *Time* made this prediction based on the reasoning that women, in particular, like to handle merchandise before they purchase it. Not only was the prediction hugely inaccurate, it was chauvinistic as well. Global online sales are now in excess of $500 billion. It is not only men who spend massive sums online, but also women, in direct contradiction of *Time*'s prediction. In contrast to this poor prediction, there are cases of articles in the press correctly predicting digital trends in the future, but many predictions still fall short of reality. For example, Robert Metcalf, the inventor of Ethernet, made a prediction in 1995 that, within a year, the Internet would spectacularly collapse. In 2007, *The New York Times* predicted that Twitter would never be any more relevant to modern-day communication than an old-fashioned short-wave radio. Tuning into predictions can be dangerous, but should they really be ignored?

2-11 In some cases, short-term predictions are far more reliable than long-term ones. To what extent should businesses base their long-term planning on the views of "experts"? (AACSB: Communication; Analytic Thinking)

2-12 Business Monitor International is one of the several organizations that seek to predict future trends in sectors, countries, and financial markets. How are these services sold to businesses as legitimate business planning tools? (AACSB: Communication; Reflective Thinking)

Marketing by the Numbers McDonald's vs. Burger King

In 2013, McDonald's reported profits of almost $6 billion on sales of $28 billion. For that same period, Burger King posted a profit of almost $234 million on sales of $1.1 billion. So McDonald's is a better marketer, right? Sales and profits provide information to compare the profitability of these two competitors, but between these numbers is information regarding the efficiency of marketing efforts in creating those sales and profits. Appendix 2, Marketing by the Numbers, discusses other marketing profitability measures beyond the return on marketing investment (marketing ROI) measure described in this chapter. Review the Appendix to answer the questions using the following information from McDonald's and Burger King's incomes statements (all numbers are in thousands):

	McDonald's	Burger King
Sales	$28,105,700	$1,146,300
Gross Profit	$10,902,700	$ 951,000
Marketing Expenses	$ 1,600,500	$ 321,600
Net Income (Profit)	$ 5,585,900	$ 233,700

2-13 Calculate profit margin, net marketing contribution, marketing return on sales (or marketing ROS), and marketing return on investment (or marketing ROI) for both companies. Which company is performing better? (AACSB: Communication; Use of IT; Analytic Thinking)

2-14 Go to Yahoo! Finance (http://finance.yahoo.com/) and find the income statements for two other competing companies. Perform the same analysis for these companies that you performed in the previous question. Which company is doing better overall and with respect to marketing? For marketing expenses, use 75 percent of the company's reported "Selling General and Administrative" expenses, as not all of the expenses in that category are marketing expenses. (AACSB: Communication; Analytic Reasoning; Reflective Thinking)

Video Case OXO

You might know OXO for its well-designed, ergonomic kitchen gadgets. But OXO's expertise at creating handheld tools that look great *and* work well has led it to expand into products for bathrooms, garages, offices, babies' rooms, and even medicine cabinets. In the past, this award-winning manufacturer has managed to move its products into almost every home in the United States by relying on a consistent and in some cases nontraditional marketing strategy.

But in a highly competitive and turbulent market, OXO has focused on evaluating and modifying its marketing strategy in order to grow the brand. This video demonstrates how OXO is using strategic planning to ensure that its marketing strategy results in the best marketing mix for the best and most profitable customers.

After viewing the video featuring OXO, answer the following questions:

2-15 What is OXO's mission?

2-16 What are some of the market conditions that have led OXO to reevaluate its marketing strategy?

2-17 How has OXO modified its marketing mix? Are these changes in line with its mission?

Company Case Dyson: Solving Customer Problems in Ways They Never Imagined

From a head-on perspective, it has a sleek, stunning stainless steel design. With wings that extend downward at a 15-degree angle from its center, it appears ready for takeoff. The latest aeronautic design from Boeing? No. It's the most innovative sink faucet to hit the market in decades. Dyson Ltd.—the company famous for vacuum cleaners, hand dryers, and fans unlike anything else on the market—is about to revolutionize the traditional faucet.

The Airblade Tap—a faucet that washes *and* dries hands with completely touch-free operation—is the latest in a line of revolutionary Dyson products that have reinvented their categories. In fact, Dyson was founded on a few very simple principles. First, every Dyson product must provide real consumer benefits that make life easier. Second, each product must take a totally unique approach to accomplishing common, everyday tasks. Finally, each Dyson product must infuse excitement into products that are so mundane, most people never think much about them.

The Man behind the Name

James Dyson was born and raised in the United Kingdom. After studying design at the Royal College of Art, he had initially planned to design and build geodesic structures for use as commercial space. But with no money to get his venture started, he took a job working for an acquaintance who handed him a blow torch and challenged him to create a prototype for an amphibious landing craft. With no welding experience, he figured things out on his own. Before long, the company was selling 200 boats a year based on his design.

That trial-and-error approach came naturally to Dyson, who applied it to create Dyson Inc.'s first product. In 1979, he purchased what its maker claimed was the most powerful vacuum cleaner on the market. He found it to be anything but. Instead, it seemed simply to move dirt around the room. This left Dyson wondering why no one had yet invented a decent vacuum cleaner. At that point, he remembered something he'd seen in an industrial sawmill—a cyclonic separator that removed dust from the air. Why wouldn't that approach work well in vacuum cleaners? "I thought no one was bothering to use technology in vacuum cleaners," said Dyson. Indeed, the core technology of vacuum motors at the time was more than 150 years old. "I saw a great opportunity to improve."

Dyson then did something that very few people would have the patience or the vision to do. He spent 15 years and made 5,127 vacuum prototypes—all based on a bagless cyclonic separator—before he had the one that went to market. In his own words, "There were 5,126 failures. But I learned from each one. That's how I came up with a solution."

Dyson's all-new vacuum was far more than techno-gadgetry. Dyson had developed a completely new motor that ran at 110,000 revolutions per minute—three times faster than any other vacuum on the market. It provided tremendous suction that other brands simply couldn't match. The bagless design was very effective at removing dirt and particles from the air, and the machine was much easier to clean out than vacuums requiring the messy process of changing bags. The vacuum also maneuvered more easily and could reach places other vacuums could not. Dyson's vacuum really worked.

With a finished product in hand, Dyson pitched it to all the appliance makers. None of them wanted it. So Dyson borrowed $900,000 and began manufacturing the vacuum himself. He then convinced a mail-order catalog to carry the Dyson instead of Hoover or Electrolux because, as he told them, "your catalog is boring." Dyson vacuums were soon picked up by other mail order catalogs, then by small appliance chains, and then by large department stores. By the late 1990s, Dyson's full line of vacuums was being distributed in multiple global markets. At that point, Dyson, the company that had quickly become known for vacuum cleaners, was already moving on to its next big thing.

The Dyson Method

During the development of Dyson's vacuums, a development model began to take shape. Take everyday products, focus on their shortcomings, and improve them to the point of reinvention. "I like going for unglamorous products and making them a pleasure to use," Dyson told *Fortune* magazine. By taking this route, the company finds solutions to the problems it is trying to solve. At the same time, it sometimes finds solutions for other problems.

For example, the vacuum motor Dyson developed sucked air with unprecedented strength. But the flipside of vacuum suction is exhaust. Why couldn't such a motor blow air at wet hands so fast that the water would be pressed off in a squeegee-like manner, rather than the slow, evaporative approach employed by commercial hand dryers?

With that realization, Dyson created and launched the Airblade, a hand dryer that blows air through a 0.2-millimeter slot at 420 miles per hour. It dries hands in 12 seconds, rather than the more typical 40 seconds required by other hand dryers. It also uses cold air—a huge departure from the standard warm air approach of existing commercial dryers. This not only reduced energy consumption by 75 percent—a major bonus for commercial enterprises that pay the electric bills—but customers were much more likely to use a product that worked fast and did the job right.

With very observable benefits, the Airblade was rapidly adopted by commercial customers. For example, as part of a comprehensive plan to improve its environmental impact, Los Angeles International Airport (LAX) was looking for a solution to the financial and environmental costs of manufacturing, distributing, and servicing the paper towel dispensers in more than 100 restrooms throughout its terminals. Switching to recycled paper towels helped, but only minimally. The energy used by conventional hand dryers made them an unattractive alternative. But when LAX management saw a demonstration of the Dyson Airblade, it was a no-brainer. With Airblades installed throughout its terminals, LAX was able to significantly reduce landfill waste as well as costs. The overwhelmingly positive feedback from travelers was icing on the cake.

Today's Airblades have evolved, guided by Dyson's customer-centric approach to developing products. With the first Airblade, it was apparent that all that high-powered air is noisy. So Dyson spent seven years and a staggering $42 million to develop the V4 motor, one of the smallest and quietest commercial motors available. The new Airblade is quieter and almost six pounds lighter than the original. But even more advanced is Dyson's new Blade V, a sleeker design that is 60 percent thinner than the Airblade, protruding only four inches from the wall.

Assessing Real Customer Needs

Although Dyson sees itself as a technology-driven company, it develops products with the end-user in mind. But rather than using traditional market research methods, Dyson takes a different approach. "Dyson avoids the kind of focus group techniques that are, frankly, completely averaging," says Adam Rostrom, group marketing director for Dyson. "Most companies start with the consumer and say, 'Hey Mr. or Mrs. X, what do you want from your toothbrush tomorrow or what do you want from your shampoo tomorrow?' The depressing reality is that you often won't get many inspiring answers."

Rather, Dyson uses an approach it calls "interrogating products" to develop new products that produce real solutions to customer problems. After identifying the most obvious shortcomings for everyday products, it finds ways to improve them. Dyson's philosophy is so focused on solving customer problems, he even developed the James Dyson Award—the top prize at an annual contest that challenges college students to design something that solves a problem. Once a problem-centered design is in place, the company then tests prototypes with real consumers under heavy nondisclosure agreements. In this manner, Dyson can observe consumer reactions in the context of real people using products in their real lives.

This approach enables Dyson to develop revolutionary products like the Air Multiplier, a fan that moves large volumes of air around a room with no blades. In fact, the Air Multiplier looks nothing like a fan. By using technology similar to that found in turbochargers and jet engines, the Air Multiplier draws air in, amplifies it 18 times, and spits it back out in an uninterrupted stream that eliminates the buffeting and direct air pressure of conventional fans. Referring to the standard methods of assessing customer needs and wants, Rostrom explains, "If you . . . asked people what they wanted from their fan tomorrow, they wouldn't say 'get rid of the blades.' Our approach is about product breakthroughs rather than the approach of just running a focus group and testing a concept."

No-Nonsense Promotion

In yet another departure from conventional marketing, Dyson claims to shun one of the core concepts of marketing. "There is only one word that's banned in our company: brand," Mr. Dyson proclaimed at *Wired* magazine's *Disruption By Design* conference. What Dyson seems to mean is that the company is not about creating images and associations that do not originate with the quality and function of the product itself. "We're only as good as our latest product."

With its rigid focus on product quality and its innovative approaches to common problems, Dyson's approach to brand building centers on simply letting its products speak for themselves. Indeed, from the mid-1990s when it started promoting its bagless vacuums, Dyson invested heavily in television advertising. But unlike most creative approaches, Dyson's ads are simple and straightforward, explaining to viewers immediately what the product is, what it does, and why they need one.

"It's a really rational subject matter that we work on, so we don't need to use white horses on beaches or anything like that," Rostrom says, referring to Dyson's no-nonsense approach to advertising. "We need only to explain the products. One thing we're careful to avoid is resorting to industry-standard ways of communicating—fluffy dogs and sleeping babies and so on. We don't want to blend in that way."

Today, Dyson complements traditional advertising with digital efforts. Like its TV advertising, such methods are simple, straightforward, and right to the point. For example, e-mail communications are used sparingly, targeted to existing customers, and timed for maximum impact. And beyond the media it buys, Dyson considers public relations as the promotional medium that carries most of the weight. From product reviews in the mainstream media to online reviews and tweets about its products, word of Dyson's products gets around fast.

The Airblade Tap sink faucet, Dyson's most recent expansion into a new industry, is a microcosm of Dyson's marketing strategy. It took 125 engineers three years and 3,300 prototypes to develop the final product. The Airblade Tap provides clearly communicated solutions to everyday problems—solutions that make life easier. It solves those problems in ways that no other product has ever attempted, claiming to "reinvent the way we wash our hands." And it injects style into an otherwise boring product. Dyson sums it up this way: "Washing and drying your hands tends not to be a very pleasant experience. Water splashes, paper is wasted, and germs are passed along. The Tap is a totally different experience. You have your own sink, your own dryer." And at $1,500, it illustrates another element of the Dyson marketing mix—a high price point that communicates quality and benefits that are worth it. And if the Airblade Tap is a hit, it will serve to forward Dyson's goal of doubling its annual revenues of $1.8 billion "quite quickly."

At Dyson Ltd., innovation never ends. On a daily basis, James Dyson collaborates on top secret projects—many of them 5 to 10 years away from completion—with a sample of the company's army of designers and engineers. Its newest vacuum cleaner—the DC59 Animal—is yet another example of how Dyson's innovation cycle continues. It's cordless, weighs less than five pounds, is designed to be handheld, and boasts three times the suction of any other handheld vacuum on the market—cordless or not.

The company is not only continuing to demonstrate that it can come up with winning products again and again, it is expanding throughout the world at a rapid pace. Dyson products are sold in over 50 global markets, selling well in emerging economies as well as developed first-world nations. Dyson does well in both economic good times and recessionary periods. From a single vacuum cleaner to what Dyson is today in less than 20 years—that's quite an evolution.

Questions for Discussion

2-18 Write a market-oriented mission statement for Dyson.

2-19 What are Dyson's goals and objectives?

2-20 Does Dyson have a business portfolio? Explain.

2-21 Discuss Dyson's marketing mix techniques and how they fit within the context of its business and marketing strategy.

2-22 Is Dyson a customer-centered company? Explain.

Sources: Mary O'Neill, "James Dyson Revolutionizes Vacuum Cleaner Industry," *Investors.com*, February 5, 2014, www.news.investors.com/print/management-leaders-in-success/020514-688937-james-dyson-built-a-fortune-solving-everyday-problems-with-good-design.aspx; Darrell Etherington, "Dyson DC59 Review," *Techcrunch*, February 7, 2014, www.techcrunch.com/2014/02/07/dyson-dc59-review-a-portable-powerhouse-to-help-you-ditch-corded-vacuums-entirely/; Jonathan Bacon, "Cleaning Up All Over the World," *Marketing Week*, November 22, 2012, www.marketingweek.co.uk/trends/cleaning-up-all-over-the-world/4004751.article; Matthew Creamer, "Mr. Dyson: 'I Don't Believe in Brand'," *Advertising Age*, May 2, 2012, www.adage.com/print/234494; Kelsey Campbell-Dollaghan, "Dyson's Latest Coup: A $1,500 Sink Faucet That Dries Hands, Too," *Fastco Design*, February 5, 2013, www.fastcodesign.com/1671788/dyson-s-latest-coup-a-1500-sink-faucet-that-dries-hands-too; Alicia Kirby, "A Day in the Life of James Dyson," *Wall Street Journal*, December 5, 2013, www.online.wsj.com/news/articles/SB10001424052702303914304579192123334228460; and information found at www.dyson.com, accessed June 2014.

MyMarketingLab

Go to **mymktlab.com** for the following Assisted-graded writing questions:

2-23 How are marketing departments organized? Which organization is best? (AACSB: Communication, Reflective Thinking)

2-24 Marketers are increasingly held accountable for demonstrating marketing success. Research the various marketing metrics, in addition to those described in the chapter and appendix 2, used by marketers to measure marketing performance. Write a brief report of your findings. (AACSB: Communication; Reflective Thinking)

References

1. Based on information from Austin Carr, "Nike: The No. 1 Most Innovative Company of 2013," *Fast Company*, March 2013, pp. 89–93+; Mary Lisbeth D'Amico, "Report Sends Nike and Adidas to Head of Digital Marketing Class," *Clickz*, September 25, 2012, www.clickz.com/clickz/news/2208172/report-sends-nike-and-adidas-to-head-of-digital-marketing-class; Sebastian Joseph, "Nike Takes Social Media In-House," *Marketing Week*, January 3, 2013, www.marketingweek.co.uk/sectors/sport/nike-takes-social-media-in-house/4005240.article; John Cashman, "How Nike Is Killing It in Social Media Marketing," *Digital Firefly*, October 19, 2013, https://digitalfireflymarketing.com/how-nike-killing-it-social-media-marketing; and http://investors.nikeinc.com/Investors and https://secure-nikeplus.nike.com/plus/, accessed September 2014.
2. The NASA mission statement is from www.nasa.gov/about/highlights/what_does_nasa_do.html, accessed September 2014.
3. For more discussion of mission statements and examples, both good and bad, see Jack and Suzy Welch, "State Your Business; Too Many Mission Statements Are Loaded with Fatheaded Jargon. Play It Straight," *BusinessWeek*, January 14, 2008, p. 80; Piet Levy, "Mission vs. Vision," *Marketing News,* February 28, 2011, p. 10; Setayesh Sattari et al., "How Readable Are Mission Statements? An Exploratory Study," *Corporate Communications*," 2011, p. 4; and www.missionstatements.com/fortune_500_mission_statements.html, accessed September 2014.
4. Based on information from "Buffalo Wild Wings," a 22SQUARED case study, September 5, 2012, http://22squared.com/work/project/buffalo-wild-wings-flavor-fanatics-case-study; Lauren Johnson, "Buffalo Wild Wings Mobile Campaign Increased Purchase Intent by 45pc," *Mobile Commerce Daily*, April 15, 2013, www.mobilecommercedaily.com/buffalo-wild-wings-mobile-campaign-increases-purchase-intent-by-45pc; Brandon Southward, "The Crowd Goes Wild," *Fortune,* July 22, 2013, p. 18; and www.buffalowildwings.com/about/, accessed September 2014. Buffalo Wild Wings® is a registered trademark of Buffalo Wild Wings, Inc.
5. Information about Heinz and its mission and vision from www.heinz.com/our-company/about-heinz/vision-and-values.aspx, and www.heinz.com, accessed September 2014.
6. See "General Electric Co.," *Reuters,* www.reuters.com/finance/stocks/companyProfile?symbol=GE.N, accessed June 2014; and www.ge.com/ar2013/pdf/GE_AR13.pdf and www.ge.com/products, accessed September 2014.
7. The following discussion is based in part on information found at www.bcg.com/documents/file13904.pdf, accessed September 2014.
8. See http://corporate.disney.go.com/investors/annual_reports.html, accessed September 2014.
9. H. Igor Ansoff, "Strategies for Diversification," *Harvard Business Review*, September–October 1957, pp. 113–124.
10. Facts in this and the following paragraphs are based on information found in "Starbucks CEO Howard Schultz Opens Annual Meeting of Shareholders," *Wireless News,* March 25, 2013; Bruce Horovitz, "China to Become No. 2 Market for Starbucks," *USA Today,* September 16, 2013; Cherryh Butler, "Starbucks Reports Record-High EPS; Big Growth Plans for 2014," *FastCasual.com,* November 4, 2013, www.fastcasual.com/article/222377; Nat Rudarakanchana, "Starbucks Bets on Food, China and Innovation for 2014," *International Business Times,* March 12, 2014, www.ibtimes.com/starbucks-sbux-bets-food-china-innovation-2014-1560844; Bruce Horovitz, "Starbucks Serving Alcohol at More Locations," *USA Today,* March 20, 2014; and www.starbucks.com, accessed September 2014.
11. See Michael E. Porter, *Competitive Advantage: Creating and Sustaining Superior Performance* (New York: Free Press, 1985); and Michael E. Porter, "What Is Strategy?" *Harvard Business Review*, November–December 1996, pp. 61–78. Also see "The Value Chain," www.quickmba.com/strategy/value-chain, accessed July 2013; and Philip Kotler and Kevin Lane Keller, *Marketing Management*, 14th ed. (Upper Saddle River, NJ: Prentice Hall, 2012), pp. 34–35 and pp. 203–204.
12. Nirmalya Kumar, "The CEO's Marketing Manifesto," *Marketing Management*, November–December 2008, pp. 24–29; and Tom French and others, "We're All Marketers Now," *McKinsey Quarterly*, July 2011, www.mckinseyquarterly.com/Were_all_marketers_now_2834.
13. See www.gapinc.com/content/gapinc/html/aboutus/ourbrands/gap.html, accessed September 2014.
14. "100 Leading National Advertisers," *Advertising Age*, June 24, 2013, p. 16.
15. The four Ps classification was first suggested by E. Jerome McCarthy, *Basic Marketing: A Managerial Approach* (Homewood, IL: Irwin, 1960). For the four Cs, other proposed classifications, and more discussion, see Robert Lauterborn, "New Marketing Litany: 4P's Passé C-Words Take Over," *Advertising Age*, October 1, 1990, p. 26; Richard Ettenson and others, "Rethinking the 4 Ps," *Harvard Business Review,* January–February 2013, p. 26; and Roy McClean, "Marketing 101—4 C's versus the 4 P's of Marketing," www.customfitfocus.com/marketing-1.htm, accessed September 2014.
16. "Study Finds Marketers Don't Practice ROI They Preach," *Advertising Age*, March 11, 2012, http://adage.com/article/233243/; "Accountability Remains Senior Marketers' Top Concern," *Marketing Charts,* March 7, 2013, www.marketingcharts.com/wp/topics/branding/accountability-remains-senior-marketers-top-concern-27565/; and "Quantitative Proof of Marketing Spend's ROI Still Eludes CMOs," *Marketing Charts,* February 21, 2014, www.marketingcharts.com/wp/traditional/quantitative-proof-of-marketing-spends-impact-still-eludes-cmos-40005/.

17. For more on marketing dashboards and financial measures of marketing performance, see Ofer Mintz and Imran S. Currim, "What Drives Managerial Use of Marketing Financial Metrics and Does Metric Use Affect Performance of Marketing-Mix Activities?" *Journal of Marketing,* March 2013, pp. 17–40; and http://marketingnpv.com/dashboard-platform, accessed June 2013.

18. For a full discussion of this model and details on customer-centered measures of return on marketing investment, see Roland T. Rust, Katherine N. Lemon, and Valerie A. Zeithaml, "Return on Marketing: Using Customer Equity to Focus Marketing Strategy," *Journal of Marketing*, January 2004, pp. 109–127; Roland T. Rust, Katherine N. Lemon, and Das Narayandas, *Customer Equity Management* (Upper Saddle River, NJ: Prentice Hall, 2005); Roland T. Rust, "Seeking Higher ROI? Base Strategy on Customer Equity," *Advertising Age,* September 10, 2007, pp. 26–27; Andreas Persson and Lynette Ryals, "Customer Assets and Customer Equity: Management and Measurement Issues," *Marketing Theory*, December 2010, pp. 417–436; and Kirsten Korosec, "'Tomāto, Tomäto'? Not Exactly," *Marketing News*, January 13, 2012, p. 8.

19. "Marketing Strategy: Diageo CMO: 'Workers Must Be Able to Count,'" *Marketing Week*, June 3, 2010, p. 5. Also see Art Weinstein and Shane Smith, "Game Plan: How Can Marketers Face the Challenge of Managing Customer Metrics?" *Marketing Management,* Fall 2012, pp. 24–32; and Francis Yu, "Why Is It So Hard to Prove ROI When Data and Metrics Are So Abundant?" *Advertising Age,* October 15, 2012, p. 27.

3 Analyzing the Marketing Environment

Chapter Preview

So far, you've learned about the basic concepts of marketing and the steps in the marketing process for engaging and building profitable relationships with targeted consumers. Next, we'll begin digging deeper into the first step of the marketing process—understanding the marketplace and customer needs and wants. In this chapter, you'll see that marketing operates in a complex and changing environment. Other actors in this environment—suppliers, intermediaries, customers, competitors, publics, and others—may work with or against the company. Major environmental forces—demographic, economic, natural, technological, political, and cultural—shape marketing opportunities, pose threats, and affect the company's ability to engage customers and build customer relationships. To develop effective marketing strategies, a company must first understand the environment in which marketing operates.

To start, let's look at Microsoft, the technology giant that dominated the computer software world throughout the 1990s and much of the 2000s. With the recent decline in standalone personal computers and the surge in digitally connected devices—everything from smartphones and tablets to Internet-connected TVs—mighty Microsoft has struggled a bit recently to find its place in a fast-changing digital marketing environment. Now, however, the tech giant is making fresh moves to reestablish itself as a relevant brand that consumers can't live without in the post-PC world.

MICROSOFT: Adapting to the Fast-Changing Digital Marketing Environment

Little more than a dozen years ago, talking high tech meant talking about the almighty personal computer. Intel provided the PC microprocessors, and manufacturers such as Dell and HP built and marketed the machines. But it was Microsoft that really drove the PC industry—it made the operating systems that made most PCs go. As the dominant software developer, Microsoft put its Windows operating system and Office productivity suite on almost every computer sold.

The huge success of Windows drove Microsoft's revenues, profits, and stock price to dizzying heights. By the start of 2000, the total value of Microsoft's stock had hit a record \$618.9 billion, making it the most valuable company in history. In those heady days, no company was more relevant than Microsoft.

But moving into the new millennium, the high-tech marketing environment took a turn. PC sales growth flattened as the world fell in love with a rush of alluring new digital devices and technologies. It started with iPods and smartphones, and evolved rapidly into a full complement of digital devices—from e-readers, tablets, and sleek new laptops to Internet-connected TVs and game consoles. These devices are connected and mobile, not stationary standalones like the old PCs. They link users to an ever-on, head-spinning new world of information, entertainment, and socialization options. And, for the most part, these new devices don't use the old Microsoft products. Increasingly, even the trusty old PC has become a digital-connection device—a gateway to the Web, social media, and cloud computing. And these days, much of that can be done without once-indispensable Microsoft software.

In this new digitally connected world, Microsoft found itself lagging behind more-glamorous competitors such as Google, Apple, Samsung, and even Amazon and Facebook, which seemed to provide all things digital—the smart devices, the connecting technologies, and even the digital destinations. Over the past decade, although still financially strong and still the world's dominant PC software provider with 1.3 billion Windows users around the world,

Microsoft is undergoing a dramatic transformation to better align itself with the new digital world order in the post-PC era. More than just making the software that makes PCs run, Microsoft wants to be a full digital devices and services company that connects people to communication, productivity, entertainment, and one another.

Microsoft has lost some of its luster. In the year 2000—due largely to the collapse of the stock market technology bubble—Microsoft's value plummeted by 60 percent. And whereas other tech stocks recovered, Microsoft's share price and profits languished at 2000's levels for a dozen years or more.

But recently, Microsoft has begun a dramatic transformation in its vision and direction to better align itself with the new digital world order. Today, rather than just creating the software that makes PCs run, Microsoft wants to be a full-line digital devices and services company that delivers "delightful, seamless technology experiences" that connect people to communication, productivity, entertainment, and one another. Its mission is to help people and businesses realize their full professional and personal potential.

In the fast-changing digital marketing environment, mighty Microsoft is making fresh moves to reestablish itself as a brand that consumers can't live without in the post-PC world.
Getty Images

To make this mission a reality, over the past few years, Microsoft has unleashed a flurry of new, improved, or acquired digital products and services. Over one short span, it introduced a new version of Windows that serves not just computers but also tablets and smartphones; a next-generation Xbox console; a music and movie service to rival iTunes and Google Play; an upgraded version of Skype (acquired in 2011); a SkyDrive cloud storage solution; and even an innovative new tablet—the Microsoft Surface—that it hopes will give it a firmer footing in digital devices. Also rumored to be in the works is an Xbox TV device for TV streaming. And the company recently acquired Yammer, a Web-services provider and hip maker of business social networking tools—a sort of Facebook for businesses. In its boldest expansion move yet, Microsoft recently paid more than $7 billion to acquire Nokia's smartphone business.

More important than the individual new devices, software, and services is the way that they all work together to deliver a full digital experience. It all starts with Windows 8, a dramatic digital-age metamorphosis from previous Windows versions. Windows 8 employs large, colorful, interactive tiles and touchscreen navigation, making it feel lively and interactive. It works seamlessly across desktops and laptops, tablets, phones, and even Xbox, providing the cloud-based connectivity that today's users crave.

Using Windows 8 software and apps with Windows-based devices and cloud computing services, you can select a movie from a tablet, start playing it on the TV, and finish watching it on your phone, pausing to call or text a friend using Skype. What you do on one Windows device is automatically updated on other devices. Playlists created or songs and TV programs purchased from a mobile device will be waiting for you on your home PC. And Windows 8 is a social creature; for example, it updates contacts automatically with tweets and photos from friends.

The latest version of Microsoft Office, Office 365, has also been transformed for the connected age. Using touchscreen interfaces, you can use an Office app and share files across PCs, Windows tablets, Windows phones, and even Macs via the SkyDrive cloud. Or you can tap into a continuously updated, online-only version of Office from almost any device. In fact, Microsoft views Office as a service, not software. It sells the service by subscription: $99 per year will get you Office 365, 20 gigabytes of SkyDrive storage, and 60 minutes of Skype calls per month. "It embraces the notion of social," says Microsoft's recently departed CEO Steve Ballmer. "You stay connected and share information with the people you care about."

Perhaps Microsoft's biggest about-face is the development of its own hardware devices. In the past, the company has relied on partners like Dell, HP, and Nokia to develop the PCs, tablets, and phones that run its software. But to gain better control in today's superheated digital and mobile markets, Microsoft is now doing its own hardware development. For starters, it developed the cutting-edge Surface tablet. The Surface not only employs the Windows 8 interface and connectivity, it sports a nifty kickstand and thin detachable keyboard that also serves as a cover, making the Surface a unique combination of tablet and mini-laptop. The Surface, plus Xbox and the Nokia smartphone acquisition, will give Microsoft better control of access to three important new digital screens beyond the PC—tablets, TVs, and phones.

Thus, Microsoft's sweeping transformation is well under way. The company is putting a whopping $1.5 billion of marketing support behind its revamped mission and all its new software, hardware, and services. Still, Microsoft has a long way to go. Windows 8 and the Surface tablet are off to slow starts, and many tentative customers are still playing wait-and-see. Many still see Microsoft as mostly a PC software company. It will take a sustained effort to change both customer and company thinking. Some skeptics think that Microsoft may still be too tightly wedded to the olds ways. "Just having the Windows name still around captures the problems of this company," says one technology forecaster. "In their heads, they know the personal

Objective Outline

OBJECTIVE 1	**Describe the environmental forces that affect the company's ability to serve its customers.** The Microenvironment (pp 95–98) The Macroenvironment (p 98)
OBJECTIVE 2	**Explain how changes in the demographic and economic environments affect marketing decisions.** The Demographic Environment (pp 99–105) The Economic Environment (pp 106–107)
OBJECTIVE 3	**Identify the major trends in the firm's natural and technological environments.** The Natural Environment (pp 107–108) The Technological Environment (pp 108–111)
OBJECTIVE 4	**Explain the key changes in the political and cultural environments.** The Political and Social Environment (pp 111–114) The Cultural Environment (pp 114–117)
OBJECTIVE 5	**Discuss how companies can react to the marketing environment.** Responding to the Marketing Environment (pp 117–119)

computer revolution is over and that they have to move on, but in their hearts they can't do it. If Microsoft is around in 100 years, they will try and sell us a Windows teleporter."

But Microsoft seems to be making all the right moves to stay with or ahead of the times. Microsoft's sales have trended strongly upward over the past few years, and the company is confident that it's now on the right track. Still, continued success will depend on the company's ability to effectively adapt to—or even lead—the lightning-quick changes occurring in the marketing environment. "The opportunity ahead for Microsoft is vast," says new CEO Satya Nadella, "but to seize it, we must focus clearly, move faster, and continue to transform."[1]

Marketing environment
The actors and forces outside marketing that affect marketing management's ability to build and maintain successful relationships with target customers.

A company's marketing environment consists of the actors and forces outside marketing that affect marketing management's ability to build and maintain successful relationships with target customers. Like Microsoft, companies constantly watch and adapt to the changing environment—or, in many cases, lead those changes.

More than any other group in the company, marketers must be environmental trend trackers and opportunity seekers. Although every manager in an organization should watch the outside environment, marketers have two special aptitudes. They have disciplined methods—marketing research and marketing intelligence—for collecting information about the marketing environment. They also spend more time in customer and competitor environments. By carefully studying the environment, marketers can adapt their strategies to meet new marketplace challenges and opportunities.

The marketing environment consists of a *microenvironment* and a *macroenvironment*. The **microenvironment** consists of the actors close to the company that affect its ability to engage and serve its customers—the company, suppliers, marketing intermediaries, customer markets, competitors, and publics. The **macroenvironment** consists of the larger societal forces that affect the microenvironment—demographic, economic, natural, technological, political, and cultural forces. We look first at the company's microenvironment.

Author Comment The microenvironment includes all the actors close to the company that affect, positively or negatively, its ability to create value for and relationships with customers.

The Microenvironment

Marketing management's job is to build relationships with customers by creating customer value and satisfaction. However, marketing managers cannot do this alone. **Figure 3.1** shows the major actors in the marketer's microenvironment. Marketing success requires building relationships with other company departments, suppliers, marketing intermediaries, competitors, various publics, and customers, which combine to make up the company's value delivery network.

Microenvironment
The actors close to the company that affect its ability to serve its customers—the company, suppliers, marketing intermediaries, customer markets, competitors, and publics.

Macroenvironment
The larger societal forces that affect the microenvironment—demographic, economic, natural, technological, political, and cultural forces.

The Company

In designing marketing plans, marketing management takes other company groups into account—groups such as top management, finance, research and development (R&D), purchasing, operations, human resources, and accounting. All of these interrelated groups form the internal environment. Top management sets the company's mission, objectives, broad strategies, and policies. Marketing managers make decisions within these broader strategies and plans. Then, as we discussed in Chapter 2, marketing managers must work closely with other company departments. With marketing taking the lead, all departments—from manufacturing and finance to legal and human resources—share the responsibility for understanding customer needs and creating customer value.

Suppliers

Suppliers form an important link in the company's overall customer value delivery network. They provide the resources needed by the company to produce its goods and services. Supplier problems can seriously affect marketing. Marketing managers must watch supply availability and costs. Supply shortages or delays, natural disasters, and other events can cost sales in the short run and damage customer satisfaction in the long run. Rising supply costs may force price increases that can harm the company's sales volume.

Most marketers today treat their suppliers as partners in creating and delivering customer value. For example, cosmetics maker L'Oréal knows the importance of building close relationships with its extensive network of suppliers, who supply

FIGURE | 3.1
Actors in the Microenvironment

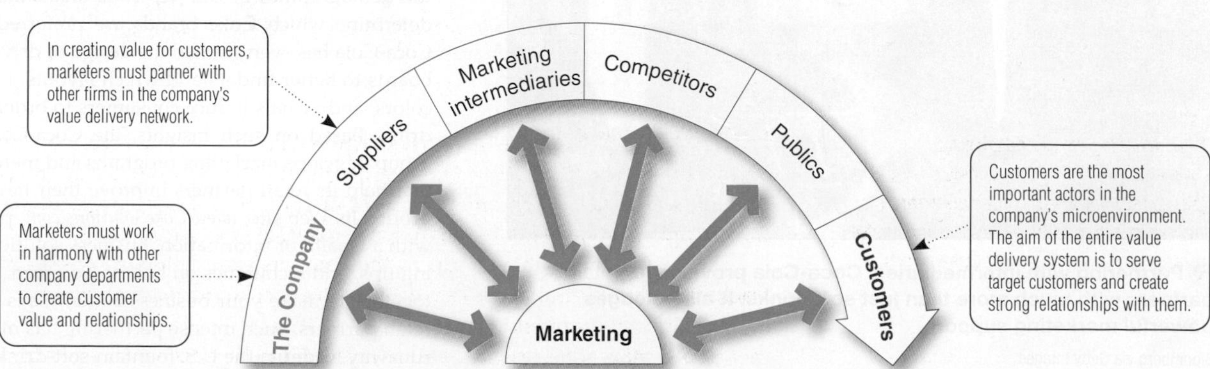

everything from polymers and fats to spray cans and packaging to production equipment and office supplies:[2]

> L'Oréal is the world's largest cosmetics maker, with 34 global brands ranging from Maybelline and Kiehl's to Lancôme and The Body Shop. The company's supplier network is crucial to its success. As a result, L'Oréal treats suppliers as respected partners. On the one hand, it expects a lot from suppliers in terms of design innovation, quality, and sustainability. On the other hand, L'Oréal works closely with suppliers to help them meet its exacting standards. According to the company's supplier Web site, L'Oréal treats suppliers with "fundamental respect for their business, their culture, their growth, and the individuals who work there." Each relationship is based on "dialogue and joint efforts. L'Oréal seeks not only to help its suppliers meet its expectations but also to contribute to their growth, through opportunities for innovation and competitiveness." As a result, more than 75 percent of L'Oréal's supplier partners have been working with the company for 10 years or more, and the majority of them for several decades. Says the company's head of purchasing, "The CEO wants to make L'Oréal a top performer and one of the world's most respected companies. Being respected also means being respected by our suppliers."

Marketing Intermediaries

Marketing intermediaries
Firms that help the company to promote, sell, and distribute its goods to final buyers.

Marketing intermediaries help the company promote, sell, and distribute its products to final buyers. They include resellers, physical distribution firms, marketing services agencies, and financial intermediaries. *Resellers* are distribution channel firms that help the company find customers or make sales to them. These include wholesalers and retailers that buy and resell merchandise. Selecting and partnering with resellers is not easy. No longer do manufacturers have many small, independent resellers from which to choose. They now face large and growing reseller organizations, such as Walmart, Target, Home Depot, Costco, and Best Buy. These organizations frequently have enough power to dictate terms or even shut smaller manufacturers out of large markets.

Physical distribution firms help the company stock and move goods from their points of origin to their destinations. *Marketing services agencies* are the marketing research firms, advertising agencies, media firms, and marketing consulting firms that help the company target and promote its products to the right markets. *Financial intermediaries* include banks, credit companies, insurance companies, and other businesses that help finance transactions or insure against the risks associated with the buying and selling of goods.

Like suppliers, marketing intermediaries form an important component of the company's overall value delivery network. In its quest to create satisfying customer relationships, the company must do more than just optimize its own performance. It must partner effectively with marketing intermediaries to optimize the performance of the entire system.

Thus, today's marketers recognize the importance of working with their intermediaries as partners rather than simply as channels through which they sell their products. For example, when Coca-Cola signs on as the exclusive beverage provider for a fast-food chain, such as McDonald's, Wendy's, or Subway, it provides much more than just soft drinks. ● It also pledges powerful marketing support:[3]

> Coca-Cola assigns cross-functional teams dedicated to understanding the finer points of each retail partner's business. It conducts a staggering amount of research on beverage consumers and shares these insights with its partners. It analyzes the demographics of U.S. zip code areas and helps partners determine which Coke brands are preferred in their areas. Coca-Cola has even studied the design of drive-through menu boards to better understand which layouts, fonts, letter sizes, colors, and visuals induce consumers to order more food and drink. Based on such insights, the Coca-Cola Food Service group develops marketing programs and merchandising tools that help its retail partners improve their beverage sales and profits. Its Web site, *www.CokeSolutions.com*, provides retailers with a wealth of information, business solutions, merchandising tips, and techniques on how to go green. We're "working together to make your business better," says Coca-Cola to its retail partners. Such intense partnering has made Coca-Cola a runaway leader in the U.S. fountain-soft-drink market.

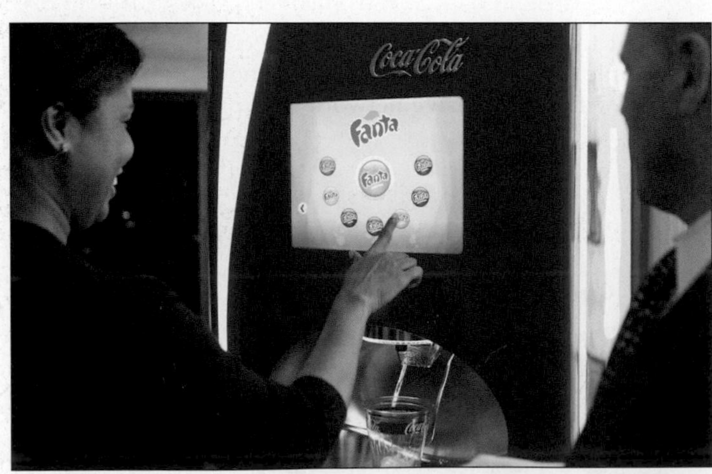

● **Partnering with intermediaries: Coca-Cola provides its retail partners with much more than just soft drinks. It also pledges powerful marketing support.**
Bloomberg via Getty Images

Competitors

The marketing concept states that, to be successful, a company must provide greater customer value and satisfaction than its competitors do. Thus, marketers must do more than simply adapt to the needs of target consumers. They also must gain strategic advantage by positioning their offerings strongly against competitors' offerings in the minds of consumers.

No single competitive marketing strategy is best for all companies. Each firm should consider its own size and industry position compared to those of its competitors. Large firms with dominant positions in an industry can use certain strategies that smaller firms cannot afford. But being large is not enough. There are winning strategies for large firms, but there are also losing ones. And small firms can develop strategies that give them better rates of return than large firms enjoy.

Publics

Public
Any group that has an actual or potential interest in or impact on an organization's ability to achieve its objectives.

The company's marketing environment also includes various publics. A **public** is any group that has an actual or potential interest in or impact on an organization's ability to achieve its objectives. We can identify seven types of publics:

- *Financial publics.* This group influences the company's ability to obtain funds. Banks, investment analysts, and stockholders are the major financial publics.
- *Media publics.* This group carries news, features, editorial opinions, and other content. It includes television stations, newspapers, magazines, and blogs and other social media.
- *Government publics.* Management must take government developments into account. Marketers must often consult the company's lawyers on issues of product safety, truth in advertising, and other matters.
- *Citizen-action publics.* A company's marketing decisions may be questioned by consumer organizations, environmental groups, minority groups, and others. Its public relations department can help it stay in touch with consumer and citizen groups.
- *Local publics.* This group includes neighborhood residents and community organizations. Large companies usually work to become responsible members of the local communities in which they operate. For example, Office Depot serves its communities through the Office Depot Foundation, an independent, nonprofit foundation that serves as Office Depot's primary charitable giving arm. The Foundation supports a variety of programs that give children tools to succeed in school and in life; build the capacity of nonprofit organizations; and help communities prepare for and overcome disasters. The company backs its "Listen Learn Care" mission with several key community programs supporting children, parents, and teachers. Since 2001, the Foundation's National Backpack Program has donated new backpacks containing essential school supplies to more than 3.3 million deserving children. The Office Depot Foundation works with the Kids In Need Foundation to fund Ready, Steady, GO! Teacher Grants that inspire innovative hands-on learning projects in primary and secondary classrooms. And the company's Be The Difference: Speak Up Against Bullying initiative sponsors school assemblies for students,

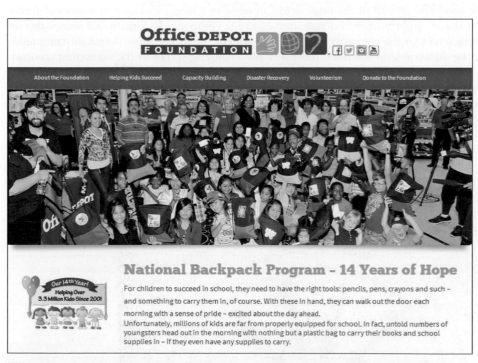

Publics: The Office Depot Foundation's "Listen Learn Care" mission calls for giving children tools to succeed in school . . . and in life. Its National Backpack Program has donated new backpacks containing essential school supplies to more than 3.3 million deserving children.
Office Depot Foundation

along with anti-bullying education sessions for parents, teachers, and administrators conducted by nationally known experts.[4]

- *General public.* A company needs to be concerned about the general public's attitude toward its products and activities. The public's image of the company affects its buying behavior.
- *Internal publics.* This group includes workers, managers, volunteers, and the board of directors. Large companies use newsletters and other means to inform and motivate their internal publics. When employees feel good about the companies they work for, this positive attitude spills over to the external publics.

A company can prepare marketing plans for these major publics as well as for its customer markets. Suppose the company wants a specific response from a particular public, such as goodwill, favorable word of mouth and social sharing, or donations of time or money. The company would have to design an offer to this public that is attractive enough to produce the desired response.

Customers

Customers are the most important actors in the company's microenvironment. The aim of the entire value delivery network is to engage target customers and create strong relationships with them. The company might target any or all of five types of customer markets. *Consumer markets* consist of individuals and households that buy goods and services for personal consumption. *Business markets* buy goods and services for further processing or use in their production processes, whereas *reseller markets* buy goods and services to resell at a profit. *Government markets* consist of government agencies that buy goods and services to produce public services or transfer the goods and services to others who need them. Finally, *international markets* consist of these buyers in other countries, including consumers, producers, resellers, and governments. Each market type has special characteristics that call for careful study by the seller.

Author Comment The macroenvironment consists of broader forces that affect the actors in the microenvironment.

The Macroenvironment

The company and all of the other actors operate in a larger macroenvironment of forces that shape opportunities and pose threats to the company. **Figure 3.2** shows the six major forces in the company's macroenvironment. Even the most dominant companies can be vulnerable to the often turbulent and changing forces in the marketing environment. Some of these forces are unforeseeable and uncontrollable. Others can be predicted and handled through skillful management. Companies that understand and adapt well to their environments can thrive. Those that don't can face difficult times. One-time dominant market leaders such as Xerox, Sears, and Sony have learned this lesson the hard way. In the remaining sections of this chapter, we examine these forces and show how they affect marketing plans.

FIGURE | 3.2
Major Forces in the Company's Macroenvironment

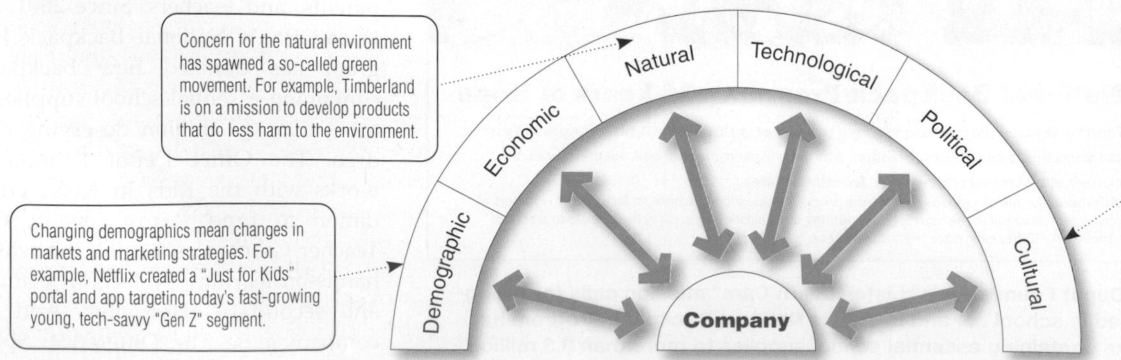
Concern for the natural environment has spawned a so-called green movement. For example, Timberland is on a mission to develop products that do less harm to the environment.
Changing demographics mean changes in markets and marketing strategies. For example, Netflix created a "Just for Kids" portal and app targeting today's fast-growing young, tech-savvy "Gen Z" segment.
Demographic
Economic
Natural
Technological
Political
Cultural
Company
Marketers also want to be socially responsible citizens in their markets and communities. For example, online eyeware seller Warby Parker was founded on a cause: For every pair of glasses Warby Parker sells, it distributes a free pair to someone in need.

Author Comment | Changes in demographics mean changes in markets, so they are very important to marketers. We first look at the biggest demographic trend—the changing age structure of the population.

The Demographic Environment

Demography
The study of human populations in terms of size, density, location, age, gender, race, occupation, and other statistics.

Demography is the study of human populations in terms of size, density, location, age, gender, race, occupation, and other statistics. The demographic environment is of major interest to marketers because it involves people, and people make up markets. The world population is growing at an explosive rate. It now exceeds 7.1 billion people and is expected to grow to more than 8 billion by the year 2030.[5] The world's large and highly diverse population poses both opportunities and challenges.

Changes in the world demographic environment have major implications for business. Thus, marketers keep a close eye on demographic trends and developments in their markets. They analyze changing age and family structures, geographic population shifts, educational characteristics, and population diversity. Here, we discuss the most important demographic trends in the United States.

The Changing Age Structure of the Population

The U.S. population currently stands at nearly 320 million and may reach almost 364 million by 2030.[6] The single most important demographic trend in the United States is the changing age structure of the population. Primarily because of falling birthrates and longer life expectancies, the U.S. population is rapidly getting older. In 1980, the median age was 23; by 2050, it is estimated to be 38.[7] This aging of the population will have a significant impact on markets and those who service them.

The U.S. population contains several generational groups. Here, we discuss the four largest groups—the baby boomers, Generation X, the Millennials, and Generation Z—and their impact on today's marketing strategies.

Baby boomers
The 78 million people born during the years following World War II and lasting until 1964.

The Baby Boomers. The post–World War II baby boom produced 78 million **baby boomers**, who were born between 1946 and 1964. Over the years, the baby boomers have been one of the most powerful forces shaping the marketing environment. Since being in diapers, "baby boomers have changed every stage of life through which they migrate," says one expert.[8] The youngest boomers are now in their fifties; the oldest are in their late sixties and well into retirement.

After years of prosperity, free spending, and saving little, the Great Recession hit many baby boomers hard, especially the preretirement boomers. A sharp decline in stock prices and home values ate into their nest eggs and retirement prospects. As a result, many boomers began spending more carefully and rethinking the purpose and value of their work, responsibilities, and relationships.

Although some might still be feeling a postrecession pinch, the baby boomers remain the wealthiest generation in U.S. history, what one analyst calls "a marketer's dream." Today's baby boomers account for about 35 percent of the U.S. population but control an estimated 70 percent of the nation's disposable income.[9] As they reach their peak earning and spending years, the boomers will continue to constitute a lucrative market for financial services, new housing and home remodeling, new cars, travel and entertainment, eating out, health and fitness products, and just about everything else.

In a recent campaign aimed at convincing companies to advertise in its magazine, the AARP (formerly the American Association of Retired Persons) advises that brands focusing on younger demographics groups are missing a big opportunity. The AARP ads feature people in their 50s and 60s, with headlines such as "I may be creased, but my money is crisp," and "I may be gray, but my money is as green as it gets." The ads continue: "Why is it all about 18–34, when they barely have a dime of their own? The story is simple, AARP . . . reaches the best boomers, and 68 percent of those over 50 give money to their adult kids."

Targeting baby boomers: *BOOM! Magazine* targets active 50+ consumers, urging them to "Live Smart—Live Well—Live Large."

It would be a mistake to think of the older boomers as phasing out or slowing down. Rather than viewing themselves that way, many of today's boomers see themselves as entering new life phases. The more active boomers—sometimes called zoomers—have no intention of abandoning their youthful lifestyles as they age. One recent study found that 65 percent of boomers near age 65 report feeling much younger than their actual age. Thus, although the boomers buy lots of products that help them deal with issues of aging—from vitamins to blood pressure monitors to Good Grips kitchen tools—they also constitute a lucrative market for products and services that help them live life to the fullest.

For example, Amazon created a site dedicated to customers over 50—called "50+ Active & Healthy Living." The site features four sections catering to healthcare, medical, and dietary needs, but five sections focused on products for travel and leisure, exercise and fitness, personal care, beauty, and entertainment. Similarly, the titles of many magazines targeting boomers suggest that these consumers are anything but the stereotypical faded, poverty-struck shut-ins. ● With titles such as *Everything Zoomer, WatchBoom,* and *BOOM! Magazine,* they appeal to an active boomer generation that is redefining the meaning of growing older:[10]

> *BOOM! Magazine* targets active 50+ consumers, with an appeal to "Live Smart—Live Well—Live Large." The magazine bills itself as "a lifestyle resource for active adults [that] inspires, educates, motivates, and delights readers with a vigorous new image of phase-two living." Monthly topics include financial news for living smart, health and wellness articles for living well, and travel and leisure information for living large. Regular columns cover topics ranging from home improvement, car reviews, computer advice, and second careers to sports, fitness, style tips, wine and food, and visual and performing art reviews. Each issue features local personalities in a *Fifty & Fabulous* spotlight. Fodder for old folks? You won't find much of that in *BOOM! Magazine* or its online newsletter *Boom! Blast*.

Generation X. The baby boom was followed by a "birth dearth," creating another generation of 49 million people born between 1965 and 1976. Author Douglas Coupland calls them **Generation X** because they lie in the shadow of the boomers.

Generation X
The 49 million people born between 1965 and 1976 in the "birth dearth" following the baby boom.

Considerably smaller than the boomer generation that precedes them and the Millennials who follow, the Generation Xers are a sometimes overlooked consumer group. Although they seek success, they are less materialistic than the other groups; they prize experience, not acquisition. For many of the Gen Xers who are parents, family comes first—both children and their aging parents—and career second. From a marketing standpoint, the Gen Xers are a more skeptical bunch. They tend to research products before they consider a purchase, prefer quality to quantity, and tend to be less receptive to overt marketing pitches. They are more likely to be receptive to irreverent ad pitches that make fun of convention and tradition.

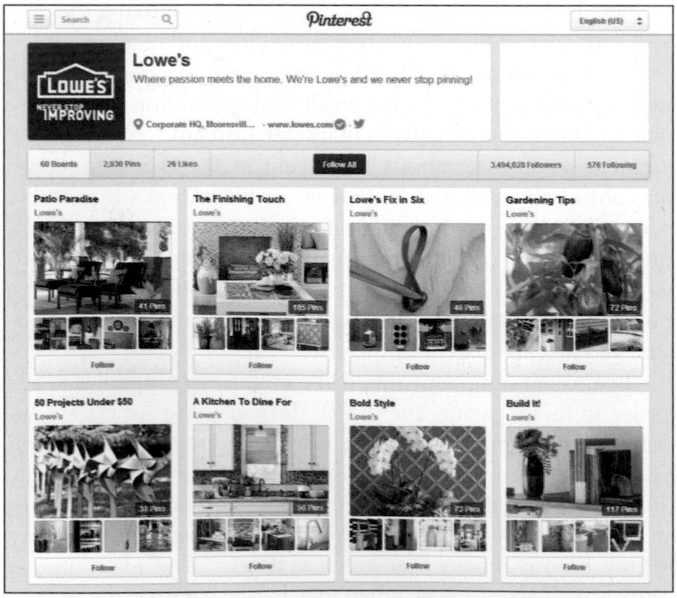

The first to grow up in the Internet era, Generation X is a connected generation that embraces the benefits of new technology. Some 49 percent own smartphones and 11 percent own tablets. Of the Xers on the Internet, 74 percent use the Internet for banking, 72 percent use it for researching companies or products, and 81 percent have made purchases online. Ninety-five percent have an active Facebook page.[11]

The Gen Xers, now approaching or in middle age, have grown up and are taking over. They are increasingly displacing the lifestyles, culture, and values of the baby boomers. They are moving up in their careers, and many are proud homeowners with growing families. They are the most educated generation to date, and they possess hefty annual purchasing power. However, like the baby boomers, the Gen Xers now face lingering economic pressures. Like almost everyone else these days, they are spending more carefully.

Still, with so much potential, many brands and organizations focus on Gen Xers as a prime target segment. For example, a full 82 percent of Gen Xers own their own homes, making them an important segment for home-and-hearth marketers. ● Home improvement retailer Lowe's markets heavily to Gen X homeowners, urging them to "Never Stop Improving." Through ads, online videos, and a substantial social media presence, Lowe's provides ideas and advice on a wide range of indoor and outdoor home improvement projects and problems, providing solutions that make life simpler for busy

● Targeting Gen Xers: Lowe's markets heavily to Gen X homeowners with ideas and advice on home improvement projects and problems, urging them to "Never Stop Improving." The Lowe's Pinterest page is loaded with tips for Gen Xers.

Gen X homeowners and their families. Its myLowe's app is like a 24/7 home improvement concierge that lets customers build room-by-room profiles of their homes, archive their Lowe's purchases, build product lists with photos, receive reminders for things like changing furnace filters, and even consult with store employees online as they plan out home improvement projects.[12]

Millennials (or Generation Y)
The 83 million children of the baby boomers born between 1977 and 2000.

Millennials. Both the baby boomers and Gen Xers will one day be passing the reins to the **Millennials** (also called **Generation Y** or the echo boomers). Born between 1977 and 2000, these children of the baby boomers number 83 million or more, dwarfing the Gen Xers and becoming larger even than the baby boomer segment. In the postrecession era, the Millennials are the most financially strapped generation. Facing higher unemployment and saddled with more debt, many of these young consumers have near-empty piggy banks. Still, because of their numbers, the Millennials make up a huge and attractive market, both now and in the future.

One thing that all Millennials have in common is their comfort with digital technology. They don't just embrace technology; it's a way of life. The Millennials were the first generation to grow up in a world filled with computers, mobile phones, satellite TV, iPods and iPads, and online social media. As a result, they engage with brands in an entirely new way, such as with mobile or social media. More than sales pitches from marketers, Millennials seek opportunities to shape their own brand experiences and share them with others.[13]

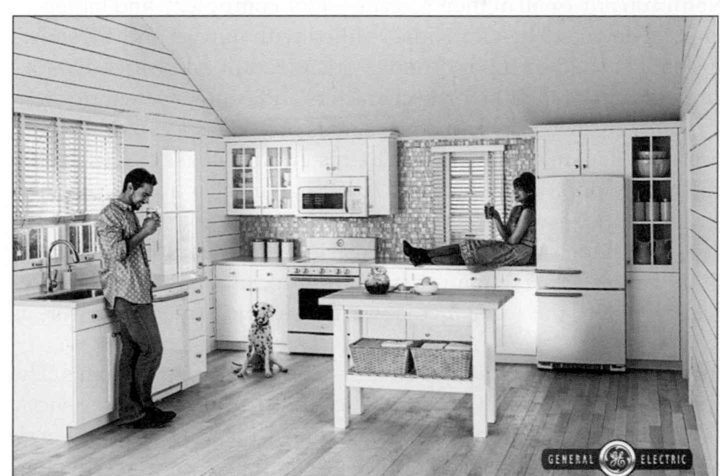

Targeting Millennials: GE's Artistry appliance line is designed to capture the fast-growing segment of tech-design savvy but price conscious Millennials who are buying and equipping their first homes.
GE

Many brands are now fielding specific products and marketing campaigns aimed at Millennial needs and lifestyles. For example, GE has created a new entry-level line of stylish but affordable home appliances called GE Artistry. GE has traditionally focused its marketing and design on consumers ages 45 to 60, who boast fatter wallets and fancier kitchens. However, the GE Artistry line is designed to capture the fast-growing segment of tech-design savvy but price conscious Millennials who are buying and equipping their first homes.[14]

Similarly, Marriott and IKEA recently joined forces to launch a new European hotel chain called Moxy Hotels. The innovative lifestyle hotel chain targets the fast-emerging market of young Millennial travelers by combining contemporary design, approachable service, high-tech features, and—perhaps most important—reasonable prices. Moxy hotels will offer stylish, no-frills accommodations to keep prices down. But they will feature plenty of the technologies that young Millennials favor, such as checking in via mobile devices, big screen TVs, plenty of built-in USB ports in rooms, free Wi-Fi, and "Plug and Meet" common areas furnished with state-of-the-art computers, writing walls, and large TV screens for presentations.[15]

Generation Z
People born after 2000 (although many analysts include people born after 1995) who make up the kids, tweens, and teens markets.

Generation Z. Hard on the heels of the Millennials is **Generation Z**, young people born after 2000 (although many analysts include people born after 1995 in this group). The Gen Zers make up important kids, tweens, and teens markets. For example, by themselves, U.S. "tweens" (ages 8 to 12) number 20 million girls and boys who spend an estimated $43 billion annually of their own money and influence a total of almost $200 billion of their own and parents' spending.[16] These young consumers also represent tomorrow's markets—they are now forming brand relationships that will affect their buying well into the future.

Even more than the Millennials, the defining characteristic of Gen Zers is their utter fluency and comfort with digital technologies. Generation Z take smartphones, tablets, iPods, Internet-connected game consoles, wireless Internet, and digital and social media for granted—they've always had them—making this group highly mobile, connected, and social. "If they're awake, they're online," quips one analyst. They have "digital in their DNA," says another.[17]

Gen Zers blend the online and offline worlds seamlessly as they socialize and shop. According to recent studies, despite their youth, more than half of all Generation Z tweens and teens do product research before buying a product, or having their parents buy it for

Targeting Generation Z: By themselves, U.S. "tweens" number 20 million girls and boys who spend billions of dollars annually of their own money and influence billions more of their parents' spending.

© Blend Images / Alamy

them. Of those who shop online, more than half *prefer* shopping online in categories ranging from electronics, books, music, sports equipment, and beauty products to clothes, shoes, and fashion accessories.

Companies in almost all industries market products and services aimed at Generation Z. For example, many retailers have created special lines or even entire stores appealing to Gen Z buyers and their parents—consider Abercrombie Kids, Gap Kids, Old Navy Kids, and Pottery Barn Kids. The Justice chain targets tween girls, with apparel and accessories laser-focused on their special preferences and lifestyles. Although these young buyers often have their mothers in tow, "the *last* thing a 10- or 12-year-old girl wants is to look like her mom," says Justice's CEO. Justice's stores, Web site, and social media pages are designed with tweens in mind. "You have to appeal to their senses," says the CEO. "They love sensory overload—bright colors, music videos, a variety of merchandise, the tumult of all of that." Fast-growing Justice now outsells even Walmart and Target in girl's apparel (that's impressive considering that Walmart has almost 4,000 U.S. stores compared to Justice's 920).[18]

Media companies and publishers are also targeting today's connected, tech-savvy Gen Zers and their parents. For example, Netflix has created a "Just for Kids" portal and app, by which children can experience Netflix on any or all of their screens—TVs, computers, and tablets or other mobile devices. "Just for Kids" is filled with movies and TV shows appropriate for children 12 and under, organized in a kid-friendly way with large images of their favorite characters and content categories.

Marketing to Gen Zers and their parents presents special challenges. Traditional media are still important to this group. Magazines such as *J-14* and *Twist* are popular with some Gen Z segments, as are TV channels such as Nickelodeon and the Disney Channel. But marketers know they must meet Gen Zers where they hang out and shop. Increasingly, that's in the online and mobile worlds. Although the under-13 set remains barred from social media such as Facebook and Instagram, at least officially, the social media will play a crucial marketing role as the kids and tweens grow into teens.

Today's kids are notoriously hard to pin down, and they have short attention spans. The key is to engage these young consumers and let them help to define their brand experiences. Says one expert, "Today's tweens demand a more personal, more tactile, truly up-close-and-in-person connection to their favorite brands."[19] Another Generation Z concern involves children's privacy and their vulnerability to marketing pitches. Companies marketing to this group must do so responsibly or risk the wrath of parents and public policy makers.

Generational Marketing. Do marketers need to create separate products and marketing programs for each generation? Some experts warn that marketers need to be careful about turning off one generation each time they craft a product or message that appeals effectively to another. Others caution that each generation spans decades of time and many socioeconomic levels. For example, marketers often split the baby boomers into three smaller groups—leading-edge boomers, core boomers, and trailing-edge boomers—each with its own beliefs and behaviors. Similarly, they split Generaton Z into kids, tweens, and teens.

Thus, marketers need to form more precise age-specific segments within each group. More important, defining people by their birth date may be less effective than segmenting them by lifestyle, life stage, or the common values they seek in the products they buy. We will discuss many other ways to segment markets in Chapters 5 and 7.

The Changing American Family

The traditional household consists of a husband, wife, and children (and sometimes grandparents). Yet, the historic American ideal of the two-child, two-car suburban family has lately been losing some of its luster.

In the United States today, married couples with children represent only 19 percent of the nation's 122 million households, less than half that of 1970. Married couples without children represent 28 percent, and single parents are another 18 percent. A full 34 percent are nonfamily households—singles living alone or unrelated adults of one or both sexes living

The American family: The changing composition of American families is increasingly reflected in popular movies and television shows, such as *Modern Family*, the award-winning TV sitcom about an extended nontraditional family.

ABC via Getty Images

together.[20] More people are divorcing or separating, choosing not to marry, marrying later, remarrying, or marrying without intending to have children. One in 12 married couples is interracial. The number of same-sex couples raising children has increased 75 percent since 2000. The changing composition of today's modern American families is increasingly reflected in popular movies and televisions shows, such as *Modern Family*, the award-winning TV sitcom about an extended nontraditional family. Marketers must consider the special needs of nontraditional households because they are now growing more rapidly than traditional households. Each group has distinctive needs and buying habits.

The number of working women has also increased greatly, growing from under 40 percent of the U.S. workforce in the late 1950s to 58 percent today. American women now make up 40 percent of primary family breadwinners. Among households made up of married couples with children, 58 percent are dual-income households; only the husband works in 28 percent. Meanwhile, more men are staying home with their children and managing the household while their wives go to work. Four percent of married couples with children in the United States have a full-time stay-at-home dad.[21]

Companies are now adapting their marketing to reflect the changing dynamics of American families. For example, a Samsung Galaxy phone ad features a dad swaddling and calming his newborn son while Mom runs errands. When the anxious mom calls home to check in, the newly minted swaddle master replies "We're having a dude's day here. We're fiiiiine. You take the *weekend* if you want to." Other ads reflect the evolving diversity in modern American households. For instance, one ad for Honey Maid graham crackers takes family diversity to a whole new level:[22]

> A single 30-second Honey Maid commercial features everything from a same-sex couple bottle-feeding their son, to an interracial couple and their three kids holding hands, to a Hispanic mother and an African-American father with their three mixed-race children. There's even a father covered in body tattoos. The century-old Honey Maid brand—owned by Mondelez, which also makes Oreos, Ritz, and Chips Ahoy—is reinventing itself as a wholesome but relevant snack for today's families. "No matter how things change," says the narrator in the ad, "what makes wholesome never will." The ad concludes: "Honey Maid everyday wholesome snacks. For every wholesome family." Says a Mondelez marketer, no matter what their skin color or sexual orientation, "these families that we portray all have wonderful parent and child connections. This is a recognition that the family dynamic in America is evolving . . . and we've evolved, too."

Geographic Shifts in Population

This is a period of great migratory movements between and within countries. Americans, for example, are a mobile people, with about 12 percent of all U.S. residents moving each year and 35 percent or more moving every five years. Over the past two decades, the U.S. population has shifted toward the Sunbelt states. The West and South have grown, whereas the Midwest and Northeast states have lost population.[23] Such population shifts interest marketers because people in different regions buy differently. For example, people in the Midwest buy more winter clothing than people in the Southeast.

Also, for more than a century, Americans have been moving from rural to metropolitan areas. In the 1950s, they made a massive exit from the cities to the suburbs. Today, the migration to the suburbs continues. And more and more Americans are moving to "micropolitan areas," small cities located beyond congested metropolitan areas, such as Bozeman, Montana; Natchez, Mississippi; Traverse City, Michigan; and Torrington, Connecticut. These smaller micros offer many of the advantages of metro areas—jobs, restaurants, diversions, community organizations—but without the population crush, traffic jams, high crime rates, and high property taxes often associated with heavily urbanized areas. Ten percent of the U.S. population now resides in micropolitan areas.[24]

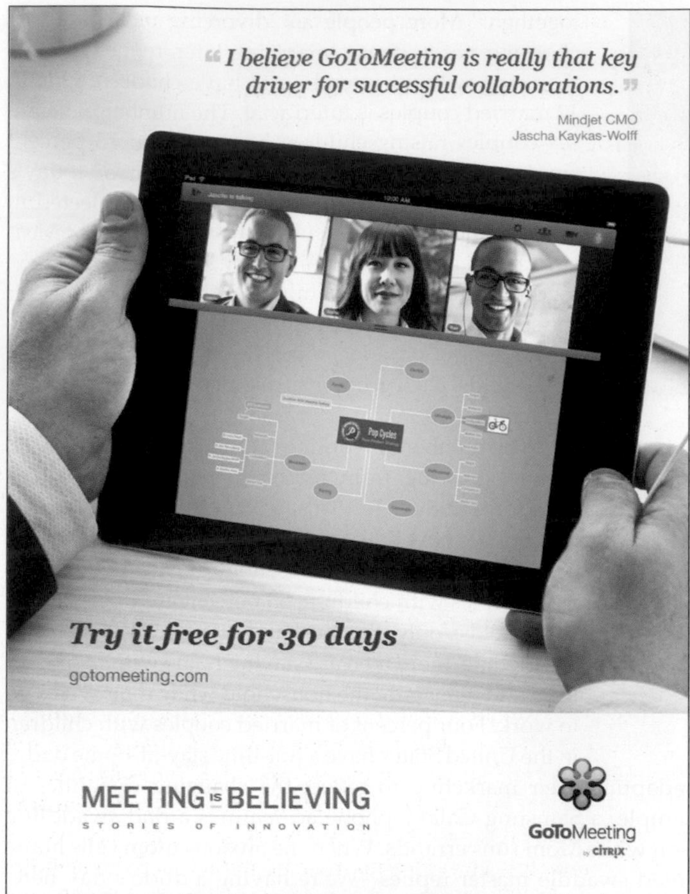

"I believe GoToMeeting is really that key driver for successful collaborations."
Mindjet CMO
Jascha Kaykas-Wolff
Try it free for 30 days
gotomeeting.com
MEETING IS BELIEVING
STORIES OF INNOVATION
GoToMeeting by citrix

Telecommuting: Applications like Citrix's GoToMeeting help people meet and collaborate online via computer, tablet, or smartphone, no matter what their work location.

Citrix Systems, Inc.

The shift in where people live has also caused a shift in where they work. For example, the migration toward micropolitan and suburban areas has resulted in a rapid increase in the number of people who "telecommute"—work at home or in a remote office and conduct business by phone or the Internet. This trend, in turn, has created a booming SOHO (small office/home office) market. Increasing numbers of people are working from home with the help of electronic conveniences such as PCs, smartphones, and broadband Internet access. One recent study estimates that 24 percent of employed individuals do some or all of their work at home.[25]

Many marketers are actively courting the lucrative telecommuting market. For example, online applications such as Citrix's GoToMeeting and Cisco's WebEx help connect people who telecommute or work remotely. With such applications, people can meet and collaborate online via computer, tablet, or smartphone, no matter what their work location. And companies ranging from *Salesforce.com* to Google and IBM offer cloud computing applications that let people collaborate anywhere and everywhere through the Internet and mobile devices. Additionally, companies such as NextSpace or Grind rent out fully equipped shared office space by the day or month for telecommuters and others who work away from the main office.[26]

A Better-Educated, More White-Collar, More Professional Population

The U.S. population is becoming better educated. For example, in 2012, 88 percent of the U.S. population over age 25 had completed high school and 32 percent had a bachelor's degree, compared with 66 percent and 16 percent, respectively, in 1980.[27] The workforce also is becoming more white collar. Job growth is now strongest for professional workers and weakest for manufacturing workers. Between 2010 and 2020, of 30 detailed occupations projected to have the fastest employment growth, 17 require some type of postsecondary education.[28] The rising number of educated professionals will affect not just what people buy but also how they buy.

Increasing Diversity

Countries vary in their ethnic and racial makeup. At one extreme is Japan, where almost everyone is Japanese. At the other extreme is the United States, with people from virtually all national origins. The United States has often been called a melting pot, where diverse groups from many nations and cultures have melted into a single, more homogenous whole. Instead, the United States seems to have become more of a "salad bowl" in which various groups have mixed together but have maintained their diversity by retaining and valuing important ethnic and cultural differences.

Marketers now face increasingly diverse markets, both at home and abroad, as their operations become more international in scope. The U.S. population is about 64 percent white, with Hispanics at almost 17 percent and African Americans at just over 13 percent. The U.S. Asian American population now totals more than 5 percent of the total U.S. population, with the remaining 1 percent being Native Hawaiian, Pacific Islander, American Indian, Eskimo, or Aleut. Moreover, one in eight people living in the United States—about 13 percent of the population—was born in another country. The nation's ethnic populations are expected to explode in coming decades. By 2050, Hispanics will be more than 30 percent of the population, African Americans will be almost 15 percent, and Asian Americans will increase to 8 percent.[29]

Most large companies, from P&G, Walmart, Allstate, and Wells Fargo to McDonald's and Levi Strauss, now target specially designed products, ads, and promotions to one or more of these groups. For example, Wells Fargo prepares separate advertising campaigns targeting Hispanic, African American, and Asian American segments. An example is the company's "With you when . . ." marketing campaign, designed to serve the specific needs of Asian American consumers:[30]

> Wells Fargo's research showed that Asian Americans are consistently more confident about their financial situations than other segments and are more likely to live within their means. They tend to avoid credit card debt and save more for future eventualities, such as having a family, buying a home, or entering retirement. So Wells Fargo's "With you when . . ." campaign targeting Asian Americans focuses on how the bank can help them plan, save, and invest for the future. One ad shows a young Chinese American father helping his son decorate a bedroom ceiling with stars and suggests that Wells Fargo is "With you when you look forward to tomorrow's opportunities." Another ad shows a young expectant Filipino couple examining an ultrasound image of their yet-to-be-born baby: Wells Fargo is "With you when life starts at this very moment." Still another ad shows South Asian men exercising on a beach, assuring them that Wells Fargo is "With you when your nest egg needs to get back in shape." Thus, the successful "With you when . . ." campaign relates well to Asian American attitudes toward saving and investing and positions Wells Fargo as a partner that can help Asian Americans create "a roadmap of where they'd like to go and how to get there," says a Wells Fargo marketer.

Diversity goes beyond ethnic heritage. For example, many major companies explicitly target gay and lesbian consumers. According to one estimate, the 6 to 7 percent of U.S. adults who identify themselves as lesbian, gay, bisexual, or transgender (LGBT) have buying power of more than $830 billion.[31] As a result of TV shows such as *Modern Family* and *Glee,* movies like *Brokeback Mountain* and *The Perks of Being a Wallflower,* and openly gay celebrities and public figures such as Neil Patrick Harris, Ellen DeGeneres, David Sedaris, and Apple CEO Tim Cook, the LGBT community has increasingly emerged in the public eye.

Numerous media now provide companies with access to this market. For example, Planet Out Inc., a leading global media and entertainment company that exclusively serves the LGBT community, offers several successful magazines (*Out*, *The Advocate*, *Out Traveler*) and Web sites (*Gay.com* and *PlanetOut.com*). In addition, media giant Viacom's MTV Networks offers LOGO, a cable television network aimed at gays and lesbians and their friends and family. LOGO is now available in more than 50 million U.S. households and its Web site is number one in the LGBT category of digital, mobile, and video streaming. More than 100 mainstream marketers have advertised on LOGO, including Ameriprise Financial, Toyota, Anheuser-Busch, Dell, Levi Strauss, eBay, J&J, Orbitz, Sears, Sony, and Subaru.

Companies in a wide range of industries are now targeting the LGBT community with gay-specific ads and marketing efforts—from Amazon, Chevrolet, and Apple to household goods retailer Crate & Barrel. American Airlines has a dedicated LGBT "Rainbow Team," sponsors gay and lesbian community events, and offers a special Web site (*www.aa.com/rainbow*), Facebook pages, and Twitter feed featuring LGBT-oriented travel deals, information, and discussion. The airline's focus on gay consumers has earned it double-digit revenue growth from the LGBT community each year for more than a decade.[32]

Another attractive diversity segment is the 57 million U.S. adults with disabilities—a market larger than African Americans or Hispanics—representing anywhere from $200 to $500 billion in annual spending power. Most individuals with disabilities are active consumers. For example, one study found that the segment spends $13.6 billion on 31.7 million business or leisure trips every year. And if certain needs were met, the amount spent on travel could double to $27 billion annually.[33]

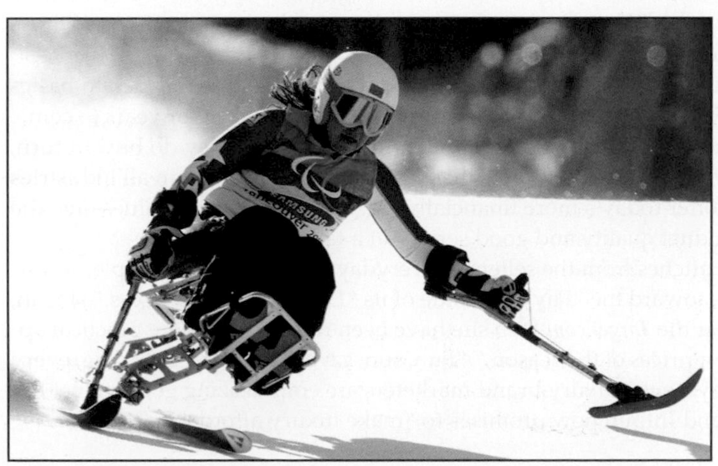

Targeting consumers with disabilities: Samsung features people with disabilities in its mainstream advertising and signs endorsement deals with Paralympic athletes.

GEPA/Imago/Icon SMI/Newscom

How are companies trying to reach consumers with disabilities? Many marketers now recognize that the worlds of people with disabilities and those without disabilities are one in the same. Marketers such as McDonald's, Verizon Wireless, Nike, Samsung, and Honda have featured people with disabilities in their mainstream marketing. For instance, Samsung and Nike sign endorsement deals with Paralympic athletes and feature them in advertising.

As the population in the United States grows more diverse, successful marketers will continue to diversify their marketing programs to take advantage of opportunities in fast-growing segments.

Author Comment The economic environment can offer both opportunities and threats. For example, in the postrecession era of more sensible consumer spending, "value" has become the marketing watchword.

The Economic Environment

Markets require buying power as well as people. The **economic environment** consists of economic factors that affect consumer purchasing power and spending patterns. Marketers must pay close attention to major trends and consumer spending patterns both across and within their world markets.

Nations vary greatly in their levels and distribution of income. Some countries have *industrial economies*, which constitute rich markets for many different kinds of goods. At the other extreme are *subsistence economies*; they consume most of their own agricultural and industrial output and offer few market opportunities. In between are *developing economies* that can offer outstanding marketing opportunities for the right kinds of products.

Consider Brazil with its population of more than 196 million people. Until recently, only well-heeled Brazilians could afford to travel by air. ● Azul Brazilian Airlines has changed that:[34]

> For decades, Brazilians with lesser means traveled the sprawling country—which is about the size of the continental United States but with less-well-developed roads—mostly by bus. However, David Neeleman, founder and former CEO of JetBlue Airways and himself native Brazilian, saw a real opportunity in serving Brazil's fast-growing middle class of more than 100 million people. He founded Azul Brazilian Airlines, a low-fare airline modeled after JetBlue ("azul" is Portuguese for "blue"). Azul provides a good-quality but affordable alternative to long bus rides—a trip that used to take 34 hours by bus now takes only 2 via Azul. And with many Azul flights costing the same or less than a bus trip, the thrifty airline has converted millions of Brazilians to air travel. Azul even provides free buses to the airport for its many passengers who don't have cars or access to public transportation. Customers with no or low credit can pay for tickets with bank withdrawals or by installment. After only five years, Azul has grown rapidly to become Brazil's third-largest air carrier, with a more than 16.5 percent domestic travel market share.

● **Economic environment: To tap Brazil's large and fast-growing middle class, former JetBlue founder David Neeleman, shown here, started low-fare Azul Brazilian Airlines, which provides a good-quality but affordable alternative to long bus rides across the sprawling country.**

Associated Press

Changes in Consumer Spending

Economic factors can have a dramatic effect on consumer spending and buying behavior. For example, until fairly recently, American consumers spent freely, fueled by income growth, a boom in the stock market, rapid increases in housing values, and other economic good fortunes. They bought and bought, seemingly without caution, amassing record levels of debt. However, the free spending and high expectations of those days were dashed by the Great Recession of 2008/2009.

Economic environment
Economic factors that affect consumer purchasing power and spending patterns.

As a result, as discussed in Chapter 1, consumers have now adopted a back-to-basics sensibility in their lifestyles and spending patterns that will likely persist for years to come. They are buying less and looking for greater value in the things that they do buy. In turn, *value marketing* has become the watchword for many marketers. Marketers in all industries are looking for ways to offer today's more financially frugal buyers greater value—just the right combination of product quality and good service at a fair price.

You'd expect value pitches from the sellers of everyday products. For example, as Target has shifted emphasis toward the "Pay Less" side of its "Expect More. Pay Less." slogan, the once-chic headlines at the *Target.com* Web site have been replaced by more practical appeals such as "Our lowest prices of the season," "Fun, sun, save," and "Free shipping, every day." However, these days, even luxury-brand marketers are emphasizing good value. For instance, upscale car brand Infiniti now promises to "make luxury affordable."

Income Distribution

Marketers should pay attention to *income distribution* as well as income levels. Over the past several decades, the rich have grown richer, the middle class has shrunk, and the poor have remained poor. The top 5 percent of American earners get over 22 percent of the country's adjusted gross income, and the top 20 percent of earners capture 51 percent of all income. In contrast, the bottom 40 percent of American earners get just 11.5 percent of the total income.[35]

This distribution of income has created a tiered market. Many companies—such as Nordstrom and Neiman Marcus—aggressively target the affluent. Others—such as Dollar General and Family Dollar—target those with more modest means. In fact, dollar stores are now the fastest-growing retailers in the nation. Still other companies tailor their marketing offers across a range of markets, from the affluent to the less affluent. For example, Ford offers cars ranging from the low-priced Ford Fiesta, starting at $14,100, to the luxury Lincoln Navigator SUV, starting at $56,165.

Changes in major economic variables, such as income, cost of living, interest rates, and savings and borrowing patterns, have a large impact on the marketplace. Companies watch these variables by using economic forecasting. Businesses do not have to be wiped out by an economic downturn or caught short in a boom. With adequate warning, they can take advantage of changes in the economic environment.

Author Comment | Today's enlightened companies are developing *environmentally sustainable* strategies in an effort to create a world economy that the planet can support indefinitely.

The Natural Environment

Natural environment
The physical environment and the natural resources that are needed as inputs by marketers or that are affected by marketing activities.

The **natural environment** involves the physical environment and the natural resources that are needed as inputs by marketers or that are affected by marketing activities. At the most basic level, unexpected happenings in the physical environment—anything from weather to natural disasters—can affect companies and their marketing strategies. For example, during a recent cold winter—in which the term "polar vortex" gusted into the American vocabulary—sales suffered across a wide range of businesses, from florists and auto dealers to restaurants, airlines, and tourist destinations. In contrast, the severe weather boosted demand for products such as salt, snow blowers, winter clothing, and auto repair centers.[36] Similarly, the damage caused by the recent earthquake and tsunami in Japan had a devastating effect on the ability of Japanese companies such as Sony and Toyota to meet worldwide demand for their products. Although companies can't prevent such natural occurrences, they should prepare contingency plans for dealing with them.

At a broader level, environmental sustainability concerns have grown steadily over the past three decades. In many cities around the world, air and water pollution have reached dangerous levels. World concern continues to mount about the possibilities of global warming, and many environmentalists fear that we soon will be buried in our own trash.

Marketers should be aware of several trends in the natural environment. The first involves growing shortages of raw materials. Air and water may seem to be infinite resources, but some groups see long-run dangers. Air pollution chokes many of the world's large cities, and water shortages are already a big problem in some parts of the United States and the world. By 2030, more than one in three people in the world will not have enough water to drink.[37] Renewable resources, such as forests and food, also have to be used wisely. Nonrenewable resources, such as oil, coal, and various minerals, pose a serious problem. Firms making products that require these scarce resources face large cost increases, even if the materials remain available.

A second environmental trend is *increased pollution*. Industry will almost always damage the quality of the natural environment. Consider the disposal of chemical and nuclear wastes; the dangerous mercury levels in the ocean; the quantity of chemical pollutants in the soil and food supply; and the littering of the environment with nonbiodegradable bottles, plastics, and other packaging materials.

A third trend is *increased government intervention* in natural resource management. The governments of different countries vary in their concern and efforts to promote a clean environment. Some, such as the German government, vigorously pursue environmental quality. Others, especially many poorer nations, do little about pollution, largely because they lack the needed funds or political will. Even richer nations lack the vast funds and political accord needed to mount a worldwide environmental effort. The general hope is that companies around the world will accept more social responsibility and that less expensive devices can be found to control and reduce pollution.

In the United States, the Environmental Protection Agency (EPA) was created in 1970 to create and enforce pollution standards and conduct pollution research. In the future, companies doing business in the United States can expect continued strong controls from

Environmental sustainability
Developing strategies and practices that create a world economy that the planet can support indefinitely.

government and pressure groups. Instead of opposing regulation, marketers should help develop solutions to the materials and energy problems facing the world.

Concern for the natural environment has spawned the so-called green movement. Today, enlightened companies go beyond what government regulations dictate. They are developing strategies and practices that support **environmental sustainability**—an effort to create a world economy that the planet can support indefinitely. Environmental sustainability means meeting present needs without compromising the ability of future generations to meet their needs.

Many companies are responding to consumer demands with more environmentally responsible products. Others are developing recyclable or biodegradable packaging, recycled materials and components, better pollution controls, and more energy-efficient operations. For example, Timberland's mission is about more than just making rugged, high-quality boots, shoes, clothes, and other outdoor gear. The VF brand is about doing everything it can to reduce the environmental footprint of its products and processes:[38]

> Timberland is on a mission to develop processes and products that cause less harm to the environment and to enlist consumers in the cause. For example, it has a solar-powered distribution center in California and a wind-powered factory in the Dominican Republic. It has installed energy-efficient lighting and equipment retrofits in its facilities and is educating workers about production efficiency. Timberland is constantly looking for and inventing innovative materials that allow it to reduce its impact on the planet while at the same time making better gear. Its Earthkeepers line of boots is made from recycled and organic materials, and the brand has launched footwear collections featuring outsoles made from recycled car tires. Plastic from recycled soda bottles goes into its breathable linings and durable shoe laces. Coffee grounds find a place in its odor-resistant jackets. Organic cotton without toxins makes it into its rugged canvas. To inspire consumers to make more sustainable decisions, Timberland puts Green Index tags on its products that rate each item's ecological footprint in terms of climate impact, chemicals used, and resources consumed. To pull it all together, Timberland launched an Earthkeeper's campaign, an online social media effort that seeks to inspire people to take actions to lighten their environmental footprints.

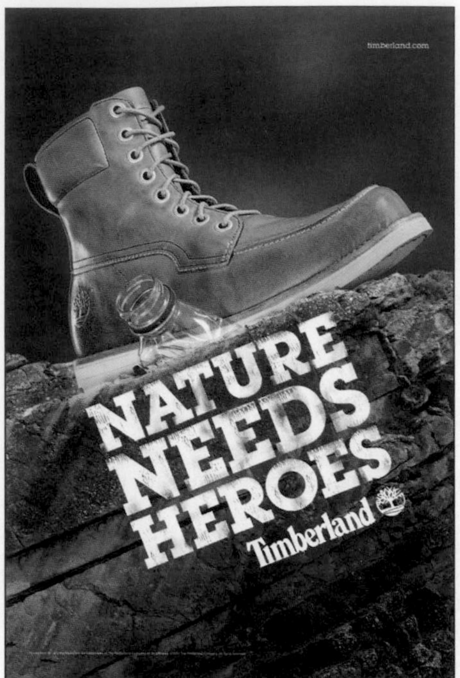

Environmental sustainability: Timberland is on a mission to do everything it can to reduce its impact on the planet while at the same time making better outdoor gear.
The Timberland Company

Companies today are looking to do more than just good deeds. More and more, companies are making environmental sustainability a part of their core missions. And they are learning that what's good for customer well-being and the planet can also be good business. For example, Chipotle Mexican Grill has built a thriving business around an environmentally responsible mission of providing "Food With Integrity" (see Real Marketing 3.1).

Author Comment | Technological advances are perhaps the most dramatic forces affecting today's marketing strategies. Just think about the tremendous impact on marketing of digital technologies—which have exploded in years. You'll see examples of the fast-growing world of online, mobile, and social media marketing throughout every chapter, and we'll discuss them in detail in Chapter 17.

The Technological Environment

Technological environment
Forces that create new technologies, creating new product and market opportunities.

The **technological environment** is perhaps the most dramatic force now shaping our destiny. Technology has released such wonders as antibiotics, robotic surgery, miniaturized electronics, smartphones, and the Internet. It also has released such horrors as nuclear missiles, chemical weapons, and assault rifles. It has released such mixed blessings as the automobile, television, and credit cards. Our attitude toward technology depends on whether we are more impressed with its wonders or its blunders.

New technologies can offer exciting opportunities for marketers. For example, what would you think about having tiny little transmitters implanted in all the products you buy, which would allow tracking of the products from their point of production through use and disposal? Or how about a bracelet with a chip inserted that would let you make and pay for purchases, receive personalized specials at retail locations, or even track your whereabouts or those of friends? On the one hand, such technology would provide many advantages to both buyers and sellers. On the other hand, it could be a bit scary. Either way, with the advent of radio-frequency identification (RFID) transmitters, it's already happening.

Many firms are already using RFID technology to track products through various points in the distribution channel. For example, Walmart has strongly encouraged suppliers shipping products to its distribution centers to apply RFID tags to their pallets. So far, more than 600 Walmart suppliers are doing so. And retailers such as American Apparel, Macy's, and Bloomingdales are now installing item-level RFID systems in their stores. Fashion and accessories maker Burberry even uses chips imbedded in items and linked to smartphones to provide personalized, interactive experiences for customers in its stores and at runway shows.[39]

Real Marketing 3.1 Chipotle's Environmental Sustainability Mission: Food With Integrity

Envision this. You're sitting in a restaurant where the people—from the CEO on down to the kitchen crew—obsess over using only the finest ingredients. They come to work each morning inspired by all the "fresh produce and meats they have to marinate, rice they have to cook, and fresh herbs they have to chop," says the CEO. The restaurant prefers to use sustainable, naturally raised ingredients sourced from local family farms. It's on a mission not just to serve its customers good food but to change the way its entire industry produces food. This sounds like one of those high-falutin', gourmet specialty restaurants, right? Wrong. It's your neighborhood Chipotle Mexican Grill. That's right, it's a fast-food restaurant.

In an age when many fast-feeders seem to be using ever-cheaper ingredients and centralization of food preparation to cut costs and keep prices low, Chipotle is doing just the opposite. The chain's core sustainable mission is to serve "Food With Integrity." What does that mean? The company explains it this way:

> Chipotle is committed to finding the very best ingredients raised with respect for animals, the environment, and farmers. It means serving the very best sustainably raised food possible with an eye to great taste, great nutrition, and great value. It means that we support and sustain family farmers who respect the land and the animals in their care. It means that whenever possible we use meat from animals raised without the use of antibiotics or added hormones. And it means that we source organic and local produce when practical, and that we use dairy from cows raised without the use of synthetic hormones. In other words, "integrity" is kind of a funny word for "good."

When founder and CEO Steve Ells opened the first Chipotle in Denver in 1993, his primary goal was to make the best gourmet burrito around. However, as the chain grew, Ells found that he didn't like the way the ingredients Chipotle used were raised and processed. So in 2000, Chipotle began developing a supply chain with the goal of producing and using naturally raised, organic, hormone-free, non-genetically-modified ingredients. Pursuing this healthy-food mission was no easy task. As the fast-food industry increasingly moved toward low-cost, efficient food processing, factory farms were booming, whereas independent farms producing naturally raised and organic foods were in decline.

To obtain the ingredients it needed, Chipotle had to develop many new sources. To help that cause, the company founded the Chipotle Cultivate Foundation, which supports family farming and encourages sustainable farming methods. Such efforts have paid off. For example, when Chipotle first started serving naturally raised pork in 2000, there were only 60 to 70 farms producing meat for the Niman Ranch pork cooperative, an important Chipotle supplier. Now, there are over 700. And as an added bonus, the more the supply chain of sustainable farmers grows, the more the cost comes down.

Today, 100 percent of Chipotle's pork and beef comes from producers that meet or exceed its "naturally raised" standards (the animals are raised in a humane way, fed a vegetarian diet, are never given hormones, and are allowed to display their natural tendencies). Chipotle's goal is to meet that same 100 percent mark for its chicken, dairy, and even its produce. It then plans to tighten its standards even more.

Sourcing such natural and organic ingredients not only serves Chipotle's sustainability mission, it results in one of the most nutritious, best-tasting fast-food burritos on the market—something the company can brag about to customers. Whereas some fast-food companies intentionally obscure the sometimes less-than-appetizing truths about their ingredients, Chipotle doesn't play that game. Instead, it commits fast-food heresy: Proudly telling customers what's really inside its burritos.

Chipotle chose the "Food With Integrity" slogan because it sends the right message in an appetizing way. "Saying that we don't buy dairy from cows that are given the hormone rBGH is not an appetizing message," says Ells. So the company is building its marketing campaign around the more positive message that food production should be healthier and more ethical. Chipotle communicates this positioning via an integrated mix of traditional and digital promotion venues, ranging from its Farm Team invitation-only loyalty program—by which customers earn rewards based not on frequent buying but on knowledge about food and how it is produced—to its Pasture Pandemonium smartphone app, where players try to get their pig across a pasture without getting trapped in pens or pricked by antibiotic needles.

While Chipotle doesn't spend much on traditional media advertising, the company uses both traditional and nontraditional promotional methods to broadcast its message. Chipotle made a big splash a few years ago during the broadcast for the Grammy Awards with its first-ever national television ad, "Back to the Start"—a two-and-a-half-minute stop-motion animation film showing the negative effects of industrialized farming. The ad received critical acclaim and racked up millions of views online.

As a follow-up, Chipotle released "The Scarecrow," another animated video indicting the industrial food industry. Accompanied by

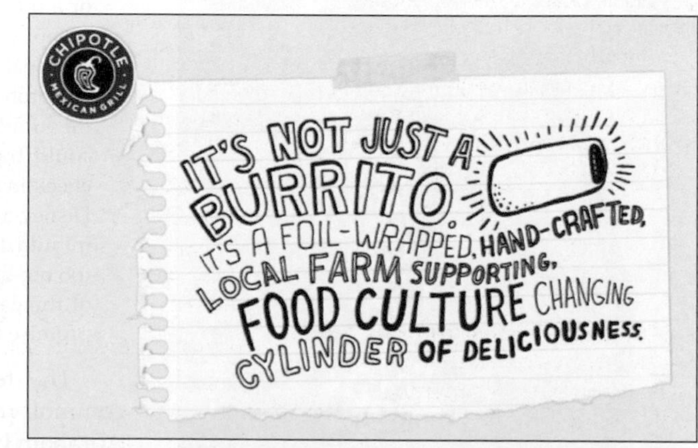

Environmental sustainability: What's good for customer well-being and the planet can also be good for business. Chipotle is thriving under its environmentally responsible mission of providing "Food With Integrity."

Fiona Apple's cover of "Pure Imagination," the star character leaves his job at a factory farm and opens his own little shop selling freshly prepared food under the banner, "Cultivate a better world." The online ad directed people to the campaign's centerpiece—an arcade-style game app. So far, the video has racked up more than 12 million views on YouTube and more than 9 million people have downloaded the app. Today, Chipotle has moved well beyond ads. The eco-conscious burrito maker is now producing sitcoms with a message. For example, it partnered with Hulu for the original comedy series, *Farmed and Dangerous,* attacking the sins of big agriculture and promoting the company's commitment to Food With Integrity.

Companies with a socially responsible business model often struggle to grow and make profits. But Chipotle is proving that a company can do both. Last year, its 37,000 employees chopped, sliced, diced, and grilled their way to $3.2 billion in revenues and $327 million in profits at Chipotle's 1,600 restaurants in 44 states. And the chain is growing fast, opening a new restaurant about every two days. In the past five years, Chipotle's stock price has quintupled, suggesting that the company's investors are as pleased as its fast-growing corps of customers.

Founder and CEO Ells wants Chipotle to grow and make money. But ultimately, on a larger stage, he wants to change the way fast food is produced and sold—not just by Chipotle but by the entire industry. "We think the more people understand where their food comes from and the impact that has on independent family farmers [and] animal welfare, the more they're going to ask for better ingredients," says Ells. Whether customers stop by Chipotle's restaurants to support the cause, gobble down the tasty food, or both, it all suits Ells just fine. Chipotle's sustainability mission isn't an add-on, created just to position the company as "socially responsible." Doing good "is the company's ethos and ingrained in everything we do," says Chipotle's director of communications. "Chipotle is a very different kind of company where the deeper you dig into what's happening, the more there is to like and feel good about."

Sources: Based on information and quotes from Denise Lee Yohn, "How Chipotle Changed American Fast Food Forever," *Fast Company*, March 14, 2014, www.fastcompany.com/3027647/lessons-learned/how-chipotle-changed-american-fast-food-forever; Tim Nudd, "Chipotle Makes Magic Yet Again with Fiona Apple and a Dark Animated Film," *Adweek*, September 12, 2013, www.adweek.com/print/152380; Danielle Sacks, "Chipotle: For Exploding All the Rules of Fast Food," *Fast Company,* March 2012, pp. 125–126; John Trybus, "Chipotle's Chris Arnold and the Food With Integrity Approach to Corporate Social Responsibility," *The Social Strategist,* March 22, 2012, https://blogs.commons.georgetown.edu/socialimpact/2012/03/22/the-social-strategist-part-xvi-chipotle%E2%80%99s-chris-arnold-and-the-food-with-integrity-approach-to-corporate-social-responsibility/; Emily Bryson York, "Chipotle Ups the Ante on Its Marketing," *Chicago Tribune,* September 30, 2011; Dan Mitchell, "Chipotle's Hilariously Scare Take on the Industrial Food System," *Fortune*, February 13, 2014, http://http://fortune.com/2014/02/13/chipotles-hilariously-scary-take-on-the-industrial-food-system/; and information from www.chipotle.com and www.chipotle.com/en-US/fwi/fwi.aspx, accessed September 2014.

Marketing technology: Disney is taking RFID technology to new levels with its cool new MagicBand RFID wristband.

Shelley Caran, *OntheGoInMCO.com*

Disney is taking RFID technology to new levels with its cool new MagicBand RFID wristband:[40]

> Wearing a MagicBand at The Walt Disney World Resort opens up a whole new level of Disney's famed magic. After registering for cloud-based MyMagic+ services, with the flick of your wrist you can enter a park or attraction, buy dinner or souvenirs, or even unlock your hotel room. But Disney has only begun to tap the MagicBand's potential for personalizing guest experiences. Future applications could be truly magical. Imagine, for example, the wonder of a child who receives a warm hug from Mickey Mouse, or a bow from Prince Charming, who then greets the child by name and wishes her a happy birthday. Imagine animatronics that interact with nearby guests based on personal information supplied in advance. You get separated from family or friends? No problem. A quick scan of your MagicBand at a nearby directory could pinpoint the locations of your entire party. Linked to your Disney phone app, the MagicBand could trigger in-depth information about park features, ride wait times, FastPass check-in alerts, and your reservations schedule. Of course, the MagicBand also offers Disney a potential motherload of digital data on guest activities and movements in minute detail, helping to improve guest logistics, services, and sales. If all this seems too big-brotherish, there will be privacy options—for example, letting parents opt out of things like characters knowing children's names. In all, such digital technologies promise to enrich the Disney experience for both guests and the company.

The technological environment changes rapidly. Think of all of today's common products that were not available 100 years ago—or even 30 years ago. Abraham Lincoln did not know about automobiles, airplanes, radios, or the electric light. Woodrow Wilson did not know about television, aerosol cans, automatic dishwashers, air conditioners, antibiotics, or computers. Franklin Delano Roosevelt did not know about xerography, synthetic detergents, birth control pills, jet engines, or Earth satellites. John F. Kennedy did not know about PCs, the Internet, or Google, and Ronald Reagan knew nothing about smartphones or social media.

New technologies create new markets and opportunities. However, every new technology replaces an older technology. Transistors hurt the vacuum-tube industry, digital photography hurt the film business, and digital downloads and streaming are hurting the CD and DVD businesses. When old industries fought or ignored new technologies, their businesses declined. Thus, marketers should watch the technological environment closely. Companies that do not keep up will soon find their products outdated. If that happens, they will miss new product and market opportunities.

As products and technology become more complex, the public needs to know that these items are safe. Thus, government agencies investigate and ban potentially unsafe products. In the United States, the Food and Drug Administration (FDA) has created complex regulations for testing new drugs. The Consumer Product Safety Commission (CPSC) establishes safety standards for consumer products and penalizes companies that fail to meet them. Such regulations have resulted in much higher research costs and longer times between new product ideas and their introduction. Marketers should be aware of these regulations when applying new technologies and developing new products.

Author Comment Even the strongest free-market advocates agree that the system works best with at least some regulation. But beyond regulation, most companies *want* to be socially responsible. We'll dig deeper into marketing and social responsibility in Chapter 20.

The Political and Social Environment

Marketing decisions are strongly affected by developments in the political environment. The **political environment** consists of laws, government agencies, and pressure groups that influence or limit various organizations and individuals in a given society.

Political environment
Laws, government agencies, and pressure groups that influence and limit various organizations and individuals in a given society.

Legislation Regulating Business

Even the strongest advocates of free-market economies agree that the system works best with at least some regulation. Well-conceived regulation can encourage competition and ensure fair markets for goods and services. Thus, governments develop *public policy* to guide commerce—sets of laws and regulations that limit business for the good of society as a whole. Almost every marketing activity is subject to a wide range of laws and regulations.

Legislation affecting business around the world has increased steadily over the years. The United States and many other countries have many laws covering issues such as competition, fair-trade practices, environmental protection, product safety, truth in advertising, consumer privacy, packaging and labeling, pricing, and other important areas (see **Table 3.1**).

Understanding the public policy implications of a particular marketing activity is not a simple matter. In the United States, there are many laws created at the national, state, and local levels, and these regulations often overlap. For example, aspirin products sold in Dallas are governed by both federal labeling laws and Texas state advertising laws. Moreover, regulations are constantly changing; what was allowed last year may now be prohibited, and what was prohibited may now be allowed. Marketers must work hard to keep up with changes in regulations and their interpretations.

Business legislation has been enacted for a number of reasons. The first is to *protect companies* from each other. Although business executives may praise competition, they sometimes try to neutralize it when it threatens them. Therefore, laws are passed to define and prevent unfair competition. In the United States, such laws are enforced by the Federal Trade Commission (FTC) and the Antitrust Division of the Attorney General's office.

The second purpose of government regulation is to *protect consumers* from unfair business practices. Some firms, if left alone, would make shoddy products, invade consumer privacy, mislead consumers in their advertising, and deceive consumers through their packaging and pricing. Rules defining and regulating unfair business practices are enforced by various agencies.

The third purpose of government regulation is to *protect the interests of society* against unrestrained business behavior. Profitable business activity does not always create a better quality of life. Regulation arises to ensure that firms take responsibility for the social costs of their production or products.

International marketers will encounter dozens, or even hundreds, of agencies set up to enforce trade policies and regulations. In the United States, Congress has established federal regulatory agencies, such as the FTC, the FDA, the Federal Communications Commission, the Federal Energy Regulatory Commission, the Federal Aviation Administration, the Consumer Product Safety Commission, the Environmental Protection Agency, and hundreds of others. Because such government agencies have some discretion in enforcing the laws, they can have a major impact on a company's marketing performance.

Table 3.1 | Major U.S. Legislation Affecting Marketing

Legislation	Purpose
Sherman Antitrust Act (1890)	Prohibits monopolies and activities (price-fixing, predatory pricing) that restrain trade or competition in interstate commerce.
Federal Food and Drug Act (1906)	Created the Food and Drug Administration (FDA). It forbids the manufacture or sale of adulterated or fraudulently labeled foods and drugs.
Clayton Act (1914)	Supplements the Sherman Act by prohibiting certain types of price discrimination, exclusive dealing, and tying clauses (which require a dealer to take additional products in a seller's line).
Federal Trade Commission Act (1914)	Established the Federal Trade Commission (FTC), which monitors and remedies unfair trade methods.
Robinson-Patman Act (1936)	Amends the Clayton Act to define price discrimination as unlawful. Empowers the FTC to establish limits on quantity discounts, forbid some brokerage allowances, and prohibit promotional allowances except when made available on proportionately equal terms.
Wheeler-Lea Act (1938)	Makes deceptive, misleading, and unfair practices illegal regardless of injury to competition. Places advertising of food and drugs under FTC jurisdiction.
Lanham Trademark Act (1946)	Protects and regulates distinctive brand names and trademarks.
National Traffic and Safety Act (1958)	Provides for the creation of compulsory safety standards for automobiles and tires.
Fair Packaging and Labeling Act (1966)	Provides for the regulation of the packaging and labeling of consumer goods. Requires that manufacturers state what the package contains, who made it, and how much it contains.
Child Protection Act (1966)	Bans the sale of hazardous toys and articles. Sets standards for child-resistant packaging.
Federal Cigarette Labeling and Advertising Act (1967)	Requires that cigarette packages contain the following statement: "Warning: The Surgeon General Has Determined That Cigarette Smoking Is Dangerous to Your Health."
National Environmental Policy Act (1969)	Establishes a national policy on the environment. The 1970 Reorganization Plan established the Environmental Protection Agency (EPA).
Consumer Product Safety Act (1972)	Establishes the Consumer Product Safety Commission (CPSC) and authorizes it to set safety standards for consumer products as well as exact penalties for failing to uphold those standards.
Magnuson-Moss Warranty Act (1975)	Authorizes the FTC to determine rules and regulations for consumer warranties and provides consumer access to redress, such as the class-action suit.
Children's Television Act (1990)	Limits the number of commercials aired during children's programs.
Nutrition Labeling and Education Act (1990)	Requires that food product labels provide detailed nutritional information.
Telephone Consumer Protection Act (1991)	Establishes procedures to avoid unwanted telephone solicitations. Limits marketers' use of automatic telephone dialing systems and artificial or prerecorded voices.
Americans with Disabilities Act (1991)	Makes discrimination against people with disabilities illegal in public accommodations, transportation, and telecommunications.
Children's Online Privacy Protection Act (2000)	Prohibits Web sites or online services operators from collecting personal information from children without obtaining consent from a parent and allowing parents to review information collected from their children.
Do-Not-Call Implementation Act (2003)	Authorizes the FTC to collect fees from sellers and telemarketers for the implementation and enforcement of a national Do-Not-Call Registry.
CAN-SPAM Act (2003)	Regulates the distribution and content of unsolicited commercial e-mail.
Financial Reform Law (2010)	Created the Bureau of Consumer Financial Protection, which writes and enforces rules for the marketing of financial products to consumers. It is also responsible for enforcement of the Truth-in-Lending Act, the Home Mortgage Disclosure Act, and other laws designed to protect consumers.

New laws and their enforcement will continue to increase. Business executives must watch these developments when planning their products and marketing programs. Marketers need to know about the major laws protecting competition, consumers, and society. They need to understand these laws at the local, state, national, and international levels.

Increased Emphasis on Ethics and Socially Responsible Actions

Written regulations cannot possibly cover all potential marketing abuses, and existing laws are often difficult to enforce. However, beyond written laws and regulations, business is also governed by social codes and rules of professional ethics.

Socially Responsible Behavior. Enlightened companies encourage their managers to look beyond what the regulatory system allows and simply "do the right thing." These socially responsible firms actively seek out ways to protect the long-run interests of their consumers and the environment.

Almost every aspect of marketing involves ethics and social responsibility issues. Unfortunately, because these issues usually involve conflicting interests, well-meaning people can honestly disagree about the right course of action in a given situation. Thus, many industrial and professional trade associations have suggested codes of ethics. And more companies are now developing policies, guidelines, and other responses to complex social responsibility issues.

The boom in online, mobile, and social media marketing has created a new set of social and ethical issues. Critics worry most about online privacy issues. There has been an explosion in the amount of personal digital data available. Users, themselves, supply some of it. They voluntarily place highly private information on social media sites, such as Facebook or LinkedIn, or on genealogy sites that are easily searched by anyone with a computer or a smartphone.

However, much of the information is systematically developed by businesses seeking to learn more about their customers, often without consumers realizing that they are under the microscope. Legitimate businesses track consumers' online browsing and buying behavior and collect, analyze, and share digital data from every move consumers make at their online sites. Critics worry that these companies may now know *too* much and might use digital data to take unfair advantage of consumers. Although most companies fully disclose their Internet privacy policies and most try to use data to benefit their customers, abuses do occur. As a result, consumer advocates and policy makers are taking action to protect consumer privacy. In Chapters 4 and 20, we discuss these and other societal marketing issues in greater depth.

Cause-Related Marketing. To exercise their social responsibility and build more positive images, many companies are now linking themselves to worthwhile causes. These days, every product seems to be tied to some cause. For example, the P&G "Tide Loads of Hope" program provides mobile laundromats and loads of clean laundry to families in disaster-stricken areas—P&G washes, dries, and folds clothes for these families for free. Walgreens sponsors a "Walk with Walgreens" program—do simple things like walk and log your steps, hit your goals, or just comment on other walkers' posts at the Web site, and you'll be rewarded with coupons and exclusive offers from Bayer, Vaseline, Degree, Slimfast, Dr. Scholls, or another program partner. And competitors AT&T, Verizon, Sprint, and T-Mobile have joined forces to spearhead the "It Can Wait" campaign, which addresses the texting-while-driving epidemic by urging people of all ages to take the pledge to never text and drive. The campaign's cause-related message: "No text is worth the risk. It can wait."[41]

WARBY PARKER
BUY A PAIR, GIVE A PAIR
For every pair purchased, a pair is distributed to someone in need.

Cause-related marketing: Eyewear company Warby Parker offers designer glasses at a revolutionary low price while also leading the way for socially conscious businesses. For every pair of glasses sold, Warby Parker distributes a pair to someone in need.

Warby Parker; Photographer: Esther Havens

Some companies are founded on cause-related missions. Under the concept of "values-led business" or "caring capitalism," their mission is to use business to make the world a better place. For example, Warby Parker—the online marketer of low-priced prescription eyewear—was founded with the hope of bringing affordable eyewear to the masses. The company sells "eyewear with a purpose." For every pair of glasses Warby Parker sells, it distributes a free pair to someone in need. The company also works with not-for-profit organizations that train low-income entrepreneurs to sell affordable glasses. "We believe that everyone has the right to see," says the company.[42]

Cause-related marketing has become a primary form of corporate giving. It lets companies "do well by doing good" by linking purchases of the company's products or services with benefiting worthwhile causes or charitable organizations. Beyond being socially admirable, Warby Parker's Buy a Pair, Give a Pair program also makes good economic sense, for both the company and its customers. "Companies can do good in the world while still being profitable," says Warby Parker co-founder Neil Blumenthal. "A single pair of reading glasses causes, on average, a 20 percent increase in income. Glasses are one of the most effective poverty alleviation tools in the world."[43]

Cause-related marketing has also stirred some controversy. Critics worry that cause-related marketing is more a strategy for selling than a strategy for giving—that "cause-related" marketing is really "cause-exploitative" marketing. Thus, companies using cause-related marketing might find themselves walking a fine line between increased sales and an improved image and facing charges of exploitation. However, if handled well, cause-related marketing can greatly benefit both the company and the cause. The company gains an effective marketing tool while building a more positive public image. The charitable organization or cause gains greater visibility and important new sources of funding and support. Spending on cause-related marketing in the United States skyrocketed from only $120 million in 1990 to $1.84 billion in 2014.[44]

Author Comment | Cultural factors strongly affect how people think and how they consume. So marketers are keenly interested in the cultural environment.

The Cultural Environment

The **cultural environment** consists of institutions and other forces that affect a society's basic values, perceptions, preferences, and behaviors. People grow up in a particular society that shapes their basic beliefs and values. They absorb a worldview that defines their relationships with others. The following cultural characteristics can affect marketing decision making.

Cultural environment
Institutions and other forces that affect society's basic values, perceptions, preferences, and behaviors.

The Persistence of Cultural Values

People in a given society hold many beliefs and values. Their core beliefs and values have a high degree of persistence. For example, most Americans believe in individual freedom, hard work, getting married, and achievement and success. These beliefs shape more specific attitudes and behaviors found in everyday life. *Core* beliefs and values are passed on from parents to children and are reinforced by schools, businesses, religious institutions, and government.

Secondary beliefs and values are more open to change. Believing in marriage is a core belief; believing that people should get married early in life is a secondary belief. Marketers have some chance of changing secondary values but little chance of changing core values. For example, family-planning marketers could argue more effectively that people should get married later than not get married at all.

Shifts in Secondary Cultural Values

Although core values are fairly persistent, cultural swings do take place. Consider the impact of popular music groups, movie personalities, and other celebrities on young people's hairstyle and clothing norms. Marketers want to predict cultural shifts to spot new opportunities or threats. The major cultural values of a society are expressed in people's views of themselves and others, as well as in their views of organizations, society, nature, and the universe.

People's Views of Themselves. People vary in their emphasis on serving themselves versus serving others. Some people seek personal pleasure, wanting fun, change, and escape. Others seek self-realization through religion, recreation, or the avid pursuit of careers or other life goals. Some people see themselves as sharers and joiners; others see themselves as individualists. People use products, brands, and services as a means of self-expression, and they buy products and services that match their views of themselves.

● **People's self-views: Yogi appeals to tea drinkers with a more spiritual view of themselves, their lives, and their teas. Yogi Sweet Tangerine Positive Energy tea "energizes and elevates mood." "How good can you feel?"**

Courtesy Yogi Tea. Photo in ad: Mark Laita, Absodels/Getty Images

For example, ads for Tetley tea focus on taste, appealing to tea drinkers with a more practical view and telling them to "Brew Up Something Brilliant." Its Classic Blend black tea offers "a deep amber color and delicious tea flavor." By contrast, Yogi Tea Company appeals to tea drinkers with a more transcendent, holistic view of themselves, their lives, and their teas. The brand offers more than 100 herbs and botanicals, blended "for both flavor and purpose." ● Yogi's slogan, "How Good Can You Feel?", suggests that its teas not only taste good but also make your body feel well, both physically and mentally. For example, Yogi Stress Relief tea is "a delicious, all-natural blend that helps soothe your body and mind." Yogi Sweet Tangerine Positive Energy tea "is a harmonizing and aromatic blend that energizes and elevates mood." A recent post at the Yogi Community online site invited everyone to have a "Happy Feel-Good Friday and a Happy Spring!"[45]

People's Views of Others. People's attitudes toward and interactions with others shift over time. In recent years, some analysts have voiced concerns that the Internet age would result in diminished human interaction, as people buried themselves in social media pages or e-mailed and texted rather than interacting personally. Instead, today's digital technologies seem to have launched an era of what one trend watcher calls "mass mingling." Rather than interacting less, people are using online social media and mobile communications to connect more than ever. Basically, the more people meet, network, tweet, and socialize online, the more likely they are to eventually meet up with friends and followers in the real world.

However, these days, even when people are together, they are often "alone together." Groups of people may sit or walk in their own little bubbles, intensely connected to tiny screens and keyboards. One expert describes the latest communication skill as "maintaining eye contact with someone while you text someone else; it's hard but it can be done," she says. "Technology-enabled, we are able to be with one another, and also elsewhere, connected to wherever we want to be."[46] Thus, whether the new technology-driven communication is a blessing or a curse is a matter of much debate.

This new way of interacting strongly affects how companies market their brands and communicate with customers. Consumers increasingly tap digitally into networks of friends and online brand communities to learn about and buy products, and to shape and share brand experiences. As a result, it is important for brands to participate in these networks too.

People's Views of Organizations. People vary in their attitudes toward corporations, government agencies, trade unions, universities, and other organizations. By and large, people are willing to work for major organizations and expect them, in turn, to carry out society's work.

The past two decades have seen a sharp decrease in confidence in and loyalty toward America's business and political organizations and institutions. In the workplace, there has been an overall decline in organizational loyalty. Waves of company downsizings bred cynicism and distrust. In just the last decade, major corporate scandals, rounds of layoffs resulting from the Great Recession, the financial meltdown triggered by Wall Street bankers' greed and incompetence, and other unsettling activities have resulted in a further loss of confidence in big business. Many people today see work not as a source of satisfaction but as a required chore to earn money to enjoy their nonwork hours. This trend suggests that organizations need to find new ways to win consumer and employee confidence.

People's Views of Society. People vary in their attitudes toward their society—patriots defend it, reformers want to change it, and malcontents want to leave it. People's orientation to their society influences their consumption patterns and attitudes toward the marketplace.

American patriotism has been increasing gradually for the past two decades. Marketers respond with renewed "Made in America" pitches and patriotic products and promotions, offering everything from orange juice to computers to cars with patriotic themes. For example, ads for PepsiCo's Tropicana Pure Premium orange juice proclaim that the brand is "100% pure Florida orange juice—made from oranges grown, picked, and squeezed in Florida." Chrysler's "Imported from Detroit" campaign, which declared that "the world's going to hear the roar of our engines," resonated strongly with Americans consumers. And Apple recently kicked off a $100 million "Made in America" push with the introduction of a new high-end Mac Pro personal computer. The Mac Pro, "the most powerful Mac ever," is built in Austin, Texas, with components made domestically.[47]

Although most such marketing efforts are tasteful and well received, waving the red, white, and blue can sometimes prove tricky. Flag-waving promotions can be viewed as corny, or as token attempts to cash in on the nation's emotions. For example, some critics note that, so far, Apple's "Made in America" push hasn't had much real impact. The Mac Pro contributes less than 1 percent of Apple's total revenues. More than 70 percent of the company's revenues come from its iPhone and iPad products, both built in China. Marketers must take care when appealing to patriotism and other strong national emotions.

People's Views of Nature. People vary in their attitudes toward the natural world—some feel ruled by it, others feel in harmony with it, and still others seek to master it. A long-term trend has been people's growing mastery over nature through technology and the belief that nature is bountiful. More recently, however, people have recognized that nature is finite and fragile; it can be destroyed or spoiled by human activities.

Riding the trend toward all things natural: Tom's of Maine "makes uncommonly good products that serve the common good."

Tom's of Maine

This renewed love of things natural has created a 41-million-person "lifestyles of health and sustainability" (LOHAS) market, consumers who seek out everything from natural, organic, and nutritional products to fuel-efficient cars and alternative medicine. This segment spends an estimated $290 billion annually on such products.[48]

Tom's of Maine caters to such consumers with sustainable, all-natural personal care products—toothpaste, deodorant, mouthwash, and soap—made with no artificial colors, flavors, fragrances, or preservatives.[49] The products are also "cruelty-free" (no animal testing or animal ingredients). Tom's makes sustainable practices a priority in every aspect of its business and strives to maximize the recycled content and recyclability of its packaging. Finally, Tom's donates 10 percent of its pretax profits to charitable organizations. In all, Tom's "makes uncommonly good products that serve the common good."

Food producers have also found fast-growing markets for natural and organic products. In total, the U.S. organic/natural food market generated $81.3 billion in retail sales last year, more than doubling over the past five years. Niche marketers, such as Whole Foods Market, have grown rapidly serving this market, and traditional food chains, such as Kroger and Safeway, have added separate natural and organic food sections. Even pet owners are joining the movement as they become more aware of what goes into Fido's food. Almost every major pet food brand now offers several types of natural foods.[50]

People's Views of the Universe. Finally, people vary in their beliefs about the origin of the universe and their place in it.

Although most Americans practice religion, religious conviction and practice have been dropping off gradually through the years. According to a recent poll, one-fifth of Americans now say they are not affiliated with any particular faith, double the percentage in 1990. Among Americans ages 18 to 29, one-third say they are not currently affiliated with any particular religion.[51]

However, the fact that people are dropping out of organized religion doesn't mean that they are abandoning their faith. Some futurists have noted a renewed interest in spirituality, perhaps as a part of a broader search for a new inner purpose. People have been moving away from materialism and dog-eat-dog ambition to seek more permanent values—family, community, earth, faith—and a more certain grasp of right and wrong. Rather than calling it "religion," they call it "spirituality."[52] This changing spiritualism affects consumers in everything from the television shows they watch and the books they read to the products and services they buy.

Author Comment | Rather than simply watching and reacting to the marketing environment, companies should take proactive steps.

Responding to the Marketing Environment

Someone once observed, "There are three kinds of companies: those who make things happen, those who watch things happen, and those who wonder what's happened." Many companies view the marketing environment as an uncontrollable element to which they must react and adapt. They passively accept the marketing environment and do not try to change it. They analyze environmental forces and design strategies that will help the company avoid the threats and take advantage of the opportunities the environment provides.

Other companies take a *proactive* stance toward the marketing environment. Rather than assuming that strategic options are bounded by the current environment, these firms develop strategies to change the environment. Companies and their products often create and shape new industries and their structures, products such as Ford's Model T car, Apple's iPod and iPhone, and Google's search engine.

Even more, rather than simply watching and reacting to environmental events, proactive firms take aggressive actions to affect the publics and forces in their marketing environment. Such companies hire lobbyists to influence legislation affecting their industries and stage media events to gain favorable press coverage. They run "advertorials" (ads expressing editorial points of view) and blogs to shape public opinion. They press lawsuits and file complaints with regulators to keep competitors in line, and they form contractual agreements to better control their distribution channels.

By taking action, companies can often overcome seemingly uncontrollable environmental events. For example, whereas some companies try to hush up negative talk about their products, others proactively counter false information. McDonald's did this when a photo went viral showing unappetizing "mechanically separated chicken" (also known as "pink goop") and associating it with the company's Chicken McNuggets:[53]

> McDonald's quickly issued statements disclaiming the pink goop photo as a hoax and noting that McNuggets are made using only boneless white breast meat chicken in a process that never produces anything remotely resembling the weird pink substance. But McDonald's took its response an important step further. To dispel the viral myths about what goes into Chicken McNuggets, McDonald's created its own nearly three-minute social media video. The video gave a tour of a company processing plant in Canada, showing the step-by-step process by which McNuggets are made. In the process, fresh chicken breasts are ground and seasoned, stamped into four nugget shapes (balls, bells, boots, and bow ties), battered, flash-fried, frozen, packaged, and shipped out to local McDonald's restaurants where they are fully cooked. There's not a trace of the gross pink goop anywhere in the process. The proactive video itself went viral, garnering more than 3.5 million YouTube views in less than six weeks.

Marketing management cannot always control environmental forces. In many cases, it must settle for simply watching and reacting to the environment. For example, a company would have little success trying to influence geographic population shifts, the economic environment, or major cultural values. But whenever possible, smart marketing managers take a *proactive* rather than *reactive* approach to the marketing environment (see Real Marketing 3.2).

Real Marketing 3.2

In the Social Media Age: When the Dialog Gets Nasty

Marketers have hailed the Internet and social media as the great new way to engage customers and nurture customer relationships. In turn, today's more-empowered consumers use the new digital media to share their brand experiences with companies and with each other. All of this back-and-forth helps both the company and its customers. But sometimes, the dialog can get nasty. Consider the following examples:

- Upon receiving a severely damaged computer monitor via FedEx, YouTube user goobie55 posts footage from his security camera. The video clearly shows a FedEx delivery man hoisting the monitor package over his head and tossing it over goobie55's front gate, without ever attempting to ring the bell, open the gate, or walk the package to the door. The video—with FedEx's familiar purple and orange logo prominently displayed on everything from the driver's shirt to the package and the truck—goes viral, with 5 million hits in just five days. TV news and talk shows go crazy discussing the clip.
- A young creative team at Ford's ad agency in India produces a Ford Figo print ad and releases it to the Internet without approval. The ad features three women—bound, gagged, and scantily clad—in the hatch of a Figo, with a caricature of a grinning Silvio Berlusconi (Italy's sex-scandal-plagued ex-prime minister) at the wheel. The ad's tagline: "Leave your worries behind with Figo's extra-large boot (trunk)." Ford quickly pulls the ad, but not before it goes viral. Within days, millions of people around the world have viewed the ad, causing an online uproar and giving Ford a global black eye.
- When 8-year-old Harry Winsor sends a crayon drawing of an airplane he's designed to Boeing with a suggestion that the company might want to manufacture it, the company responds with a stern, legal-form letter. "We do not accept unsolicited ideas," the letter states. "We regret to inform you that we have disposed of your message and retain no copies." The embarrassing blunder would probably go unnoticed were it not for the fact that Harry's father—John Winsor, a prominent ad exec—blogs and tweets about the incident, making it instant national news.

Extreme events? Not anymore. The Internet and social media have turned the traditional power relationship between businesses and consumers upside down. In the good old days, disgruntled consumers could do little more than bellow at a company service rep or shout out their complaints from a street corner. Now, armed with only a laptop or smartphone, they can take it public, airing their gripes to millions on blogs, social media sites, or even hate sites devoted exclusively to their least favorite corporations. "A consumer's megaphone is now [sometimes] more powerful than a brand's," says one ad agency executive. "Individuals can bring a huge company to its knees . . . simply by sharing their experiences and opinions on Facebook, Yelp, Twitter, Instagram, or other social forums."

"I hate" and "sucks" sites are almost commonplace. These sites target some highly resp-ected companies with some highly disrespectful labels: Walmartblows.com, PayPalSucks.com (aka NoPayPal), IHateStarbucks.com, DeltaREALLYsucks.com, and UnitedPackageSmashers.com (UPS), to name only a few. "Sucks" videos on YouTube and other video sites also abound. For example, a search of "Apple sucks" on YouTube turns up more than 600,000 videos; a search for Microsoft finds 143,000 videos. An "Apple sucks" search on Facebook links to hundreds of groups. If you don't find one you like, try "Apple suks" or "Apple sux" for hundreds more.

Some of these sites, videos, and other online attacks air legitimate complaints that should be addressed. Others, however, are little more than anonymous, vindictive slurs that unfairly ransack brands and corporate reputations. Some of the attacks are only a passing nuisance; others can draw serious attention and create real headaches.

How should companies react to online attacks? The real quandary for targeted companies is figuring out how far they can go to protect their images without fueling the already raging fire. One point on which all experts seem to agree: Don't try to retaliate in kind. "It's rarely a good idea to lob bombs at the fire starters," says one analyst. "Preemption, engagement, and diplomacy are saner tools." Such criticisms are often based on real consumer concerns and unresolved anger. Hence, the best strategy might be to proactively monitor these sites and respond honestly to the concerns they express.

For example, Boeing quickly took responsibility for mishandling aspiring Harry Winsor's designs, turning a potential PR disaster into a positive. It called and invited young Harry to visit Boeing's facilities. On its corporate Twitter site, it confessed "We're experts at airplanes but novices in social media. We're learning as we go." In response to its Figo ad fiasco, Ford's chief marketing officer issued a deep

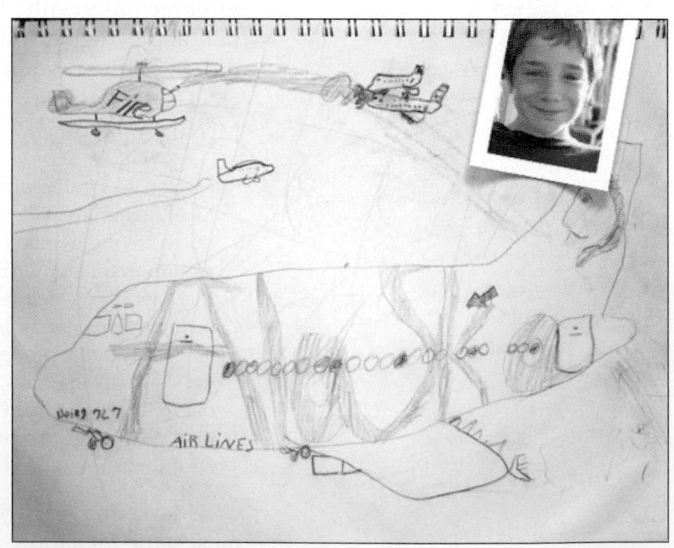

Today's empowered consumers: Boeing's embarrassing blunder over young Harry Winsor's airplane design made instant national news. However, Boeing quickly took responsibility and turned the potential PR disaster into a positive.

John Winsor

public apology, citing that Ford had not approved the ads and that it had since modified its ad review process. Ford's ad agency promptly fired the guilty creatives.

Similarly, FedEx drew praise by immediately posting its own YouTube video addressing the monitor-smashing incident. In the video, FedEx Senior Vice President of Operations Matthew Thornton stated that he had personally met with the aggrieved customer, who had accepted the company's apology. "This goes directly against all FedEx values," declared Thornton. The FedEx video struck a responsive chord. Numerous journalists and bloggers responded with stories about FedEx's outstanding package handling and delivering record.

Many companies have now created teams of specialists that monitor online conversations and engage unhappy consumers. For example, the social media team at Southwest Airlines includes a chief Twitter officer who tracks Twitter comments and monitors Facebook groups, an online representative who checks facts and interacts with bloggers, and another person who takes charge of the company's presence on sites such as YouTube, Instagram, Flickr, and LinkedIn. So if someone posts an online comment, the company can respond promptly in a personal way.

Not long ago, Southwest's team averted what could have been a major PR catastrophe when a hole popped open in a plane's fuselage on a flight from Phoenix to Sacramento. The flight had Wi-Fi, and the first passenger tweet about the incident, complete with a photo, was online in only 9 minutes—11 minutes before Southwest's official dispatch channel report. But Southwest's monitoring team picked up the social media chatter and was able to craft a blog post and other social media responses shortly after the plane made an emergency landing in Yuma, Arizona. By the time the story hit the major media, the passenger who had tweeted initially was back on Twitter praising the Southwest crew for its professional handling of the situation.

Thus, by monitoring and proactively responding to seemingly uncontrollable events in the environment, companies can prevent the negatives from spiraling out of control or even turn them into positives. Who knows? With the right responses, Walmartblows.com might even become Walmartrules.com. Then again, probably not.

Sources: Quotes, excerpts, and other information based on Matt Wilson, "How Southwest Airlines Wrangled Four Social Media Crises," *Ragan.com*, February 20, 2013, www.ragan.com/Main/Articles/How_Southwest_Airlines_wrangled_four_social_media_46254.aspx#; Vanessa Ko, "FedEx Apologizes after Video of Driver Throwing Fragile Package Goes Viral," *Time*, December 23, 2011, http://newsfeed.time.com/2011/12/23/fedex-apologizes-after-video-of-driver-throwing-fragile-package-goes-viral/; Michelle Conlin, "Web Attack," *BusinessWeek*, April 16, 2007, pp. 54–56; "Boeing's Social Media Lesson," May 3, 2010, http://mediadecoder.blogs.nytimes.com/2010/05/03/boeings-social-media-lesson/; Brent Snavely, "Ford Marketing Chief Apologizes for Ads," *USA Today*, March 27, 2013; David Angelo, "CMOs, Agencies: It's Time to Live Your Brands," *Advertising Age*, October 2, 2013, http://adage.com/print/244524; and www.youtube.com/watch?v=C5uIH0VTg_o, accessed September 2014.

3 Reviewing the Concepts

OBJECTIVES REVIEW AND KEY TERMS

Objectives Review

In this and the next two chapters, you'll examine the environments of marketing and how companies analyze these environments to better understand the marketplace and consumers. Companies must constantly watch and manage the *marketing environment* to seek opportunities and ward off threats. The marketing environment consists of all the actors and forces influencing the company's ability to transact business effectively with its target market.

OBJECTIVE 1 **Describe the environmental forces that affect the company's ability to serve its customers.** *(pp 95–98)*

The company's *microenvironment* consists of actors close to the company that combine to form its value delivery network or that affect its ability to serve its customers. It includes the company's *internal environment*—its several departments and management levels—as it influences marketing decision making. *Marketing channel firms*—suppliers, marketing intermediaries, physical distribution firms, marketing services agencies, and financial intermediaries—cooperate to create customer value. *Competitors* vie with the company in an effort to serve customers better. Various *publics* have an actual or potential interest in or impact on the company's ability to meet its objectives. Finally, five types of customer *markets* exist: consumer, business, reseller, government, and international markets.

The *macroenvironment* consists of larger societal forces that affect the entire microenvironment. The six forces making up the company's macroenvironment are demographic, economic, natural, technological, political/social, and cultural forces. These forces shape opportunities and pose threats to the company.

OBJECTIVE 2 Explain how changes in the demographic and economic environments affect marketing decisions. *(pp 99–107)*

Demography is the study of the characteristics of human populations. Today's *demographic environment* shows a changing age structure, shifting family profiles, geographic population shifts, a better-educated and more white-collar population, and increasing diversity. The *economic environment* consists of factors that affect buying power and patterns. The economic environment is characterized by more frugal consumers who are seeking greater value—the right combination of good quality and service at a fair price. The distribution of income also is shifting. The rich have grown richer, the middle class has shrunk, and the poor have remained poor, leading to a two-tiered market.

OBJECTIVE 3 Identify the major trends in the firm's natural and technological environments. *(pp 107–111)*

The *natural environment* shows three major trends: shortages of certain raw materials, higher pollution levels, and more government intervention in natural resource management. Environmental concerns create marketing opportunities for alert companies. The *technological environment* creates both opportunities and challenges. Companies that fail to keep up with technological change will miss out on new product and marketing opportunities.

OBJECTIVE 4 Explain the key changes in the political and cultural environments. *(pp 111–117)*

The *political environment* consists of laws, agencies, and groups that influence or limit marketing actions. The political environment has undergone changes that affect marketing worldwide: increasing legislation regulating business, strong government agency enforcement, and greater emphasis on ethics and socially responsible actions. The *cultural environment* consists of institutions and forces that affect a society's values, perceptions, preferences, and behaviors. The environment shows trends toward new technology-enabled communication, a lessening trust of institutions, increasing patriotism, greater appreciation for nature, a changing spiritualism, and the search for more meaningful and enduring values.

OBJECTIVE 5 Discuss how companies can react to the marketing environment. *(pp 117–119)*

Companies can passively accept the marketing environment as an uncontrollable element to which they must adapt, avoiding threats and taking advantage of opportunities as they arise. Or they can take a *proactive* stance, working to change the environment rather than simply reacting to it. Whenever possible, companies should try to be proactive rather than reactive.

MyMarketingLab

Go to **mymktlab.com** to complete the problems marked with this icon .

Key Terms

OBJECTIVE 1

Marketing environment (p 94)
Microenvironment (p 95)
Macroenvironment (p 95)
Marketing intermediaries (p 96)
Public (p 97)

OBJECTIVE 2

Demography (p 99)
Baby boomers (p 99)
Generation X (p 100)
Millennials (Generation Y) (p 101)
Generation Z (p 101)
Economic environment (p 106)

OBJECTIVE 3

Natural environment (p 107)
Environmental sustainability (p 108)
Technological environment (p 108)

OBJECTIVE 4

Political environment (p 111)
Cultural environment (p 114)

DISCUSSION AND CRITICAL THINKING

Discussion Questions

3-1 Name and briefly describe the elements of an organization's macroenvironment and discuss how they affect marketing. (AACSB: Communication)

✪ **3-2** What does the economic environment consist of as far as marketers are concerned, and why is it so important for them? (AACSB: Communication; Reflective Thinking)

3-3 Who are the Gen Zers, and why will they become interesting to marketers in the future? (AACSB: Communication; Reflective Thinking)

3-4 Compare and contrast core beliefs/values and secondary beliefs/values. Provide an example of each and discuss the potential impact marketers have on each. (AACSB: Communication; Reflective Thinking)

✪ **3-5** How should marketers respond to the changing environment? (AACSB: Communication)

Critical Thinking Exercises

3-6 The legal or regulatory frameworks affecting marketing are at different stages around the world; different priorities and influences are at work. Explain their impact on marketing in your country and how companies are reacting to the laws or regulations. (AACSB: Communication; Reflective Thinking)

3-7 Cause-related marketing has grown considerably over the past 10 years. Learn about companies in your country or region that have relied on cause-related marketing programs. Present a case study of a cause-related marketing campaign to your class. (AACSB: Communication; Use of IT)

3-8 Discuss a recent change in the technological environment that impacts marketing. How has it affected buyer behavior and how has it changed marketing? (AACSB: Communication; Reflective Thinking)

MINICASES AND APPLICATIONS

Online, Mobile, and Social Media Marketing **Social Data**

People have been using Twitter's social media platform to tweet short bursts of information in 140 characters or less since 2006 and now average 500 million tweets a day. The full stream of tweets is referred to as Twitter's fire hose. Data from the fire hose is analyzed and the information gleaned from that analysis is sold to other companies. Twitter recently purchased Gnip, the world's largest social data provider and one of the few companies that had access to the fire hose. Gnip also mines public data from Facebook, Google+, Tumblr, and other social media platforms. Analyzing social data has become a big business because companies such as PepsiCo, Warner Brothers, and General Motors pay to learn consumers' sentiments toward them. According to the CEO of social-media analysis company BrandWatch, "We're at the bottom of the foothills in terms of the kind of global demand for social data." Twitter alone earned more than $70 million last year from licensing its data. Perhaps Mark Twain's character, Mulberry Sellers, summed it up nicely—"There's gold in them thar hills"—and Twitter and other social media platforms and data analytic companies are mining that gold.

3-9 Discuss the value of social data for marketers. (AACSB: Communication; Reflective Thinking)

3-10 A "dark social channel" refers to a private channel or a channel difficult to match with other digital channels. An example of a dark channel is e-mail. However, Google routinely mines its roughly half a billion Gmail users' e-mails. Research how Google scans e-mail data and the fallout from those actions. (AACSB: Communication; Use of IT; Reflective Thinking)

Marketing Ethics **Your Insurance Renewal Notice Could Be a Trap**

Consumers in the UK seem to be at the mercy of their own insurers. Hidden within the fine print of the renewal notices is the true cost of renewing the insurance, often as much as a 100 percent increase. This is despite the fact that there have been no claims on the insurance and perhaps the value of the insured asset has fallen since last year. Unwittingly, consumers have signed up for continuous payment to authorities. In effect, this means that consumers have agreed to continue to buy the insurance year over year, regardless of an increase in price, unless they contact the insurer and cancel it. If only cancelling insurance was that simple. If consumers fail to read the small print in their contracts carefully, they are hit by a cancellation fee. With higher percentages of consumers checking insurance quotes on price comparison websites, insurers still take the chance of inertia when the consumers receive their renewal notices. Insurers seem to rely on the fact that a certain percentage of consumers do not bother to read the documents, and if they do, they do not readily notice that the price is far higher than the previous year. The Financial Conduct Authority, which has responsibility for dealing with disputes arising out of financial services, receives around 500 complaints a year regarding insurance renewal. However, this is just the tip of the iceberg. In response to the bad publicity the practice has received in the media, the Association of British Insurers has proposed that renewal letters should state the amount that the consumer paid last year alongside the renewal price for the coming year. The suggestion is yet to be adopted.

3-11 Discuss what aspects of the competitive environment of the insurance industry might encourage this type of practice. (AACSB: Communication; Use of IT; Reflective Thinking)

3-12 Debate whether or not technology and access to price comparison websites can banish this type of fraudulent practice in the insurance industry. (AACSB: Communication; Use of IT; Reflective Thinking)

Marketing by the Numbers Tiny Markets

Many marketing decisions boil down to numbers. An important question is this: What is the sales potential in a given market? If the sales potential in a market is not large enough to warrant pursuing that market, then companies will not offer products and services to that market, even though a need may exist. Consider the market segment of infants and children. You've probably heard of heart procedures such as angioplasty and stents that are routinely performed on adults. But such heart procedures, devices, and related medications are not available for infants and children, despite the fact that almost 40,000 children a year are born in the United States with heart defects that oftentimes require repair. This is a life or death situation for many young patients, yet doctors must improvise by using devices designed and tested on adults. For instance, doctors use an adult kidney balloon on an infant's heart because it is the appropriate size for a newborn's aortic valve. However, this device is not approved for the procedure. Why are specific devices and medicines developed for the multibillion-dollar cardiovascular market not also designed for kids? It's a matter of economics—this segment of young consumers is just too small. One leading cardiologist attributed the discrepancy to a "profitability gap" between the children's market and the much more profitable adult market for treating heart disease. While this might make good economic sense for companies, it is little comfort to the parents of these small patients. Certainly there is a need for medical products to save children's lives. Still, companies are not pursuing this market.

3-13 Using the chain ratio method described in Appendix 2: Marketing by the Numbers, estimate the market sales potential for heart catheterization products to meet the needs of the infant and child segment. Assume that of the 40,000 children with heart defects each year, 60 percent will benefit from these types of products and that only 50 percent of their families have the financial resources to obtain such treatment. Also assume the average price for a device is $1,000. (AACSB: Communication; Analytical Reasoning)

3-14 Research the medical devices market and compare the market potential you estimated to the sales of various devices. Are companies justified in not pursuing the infant and child segment? (AACSB: Communication; Reflective Thinking)

Video Case Ecoist

At least one company has taken the old phrase "One man's trash is another man's treasure" and turned it into a business model. Ecoist is a company that uses discarded packaging materials from multinational brands like Coca-Cola, Frito-Lay, Disney, and Mars to craft high-end handbags that would thrill even the most discriminating fashionistas.

When the company first started in 2004, consumer perceptions of goods made from recycled materials weren't very positive. This video describes how Ecoist found opportunity in a growing wave of environmentalism. Not only does Ecoist capitalize on low-cost materials and the brand images of some of the world's major brands, it comes out smelling like a rose as it saves tons of trash from landfills.

After viewing the video featuring Ecoist, answer the following questions:

3-15 How engaged was Ecoist in analyzing the marketing environment before it launched its first company?

3-16 What trends in the marketing environment have contributed to the success of Ecoist?

3-17 Is Ecoist's strategy more about recycling or about creating value for customers? Explain.

Company Case Sony: Battling the Marketing Environment's "Perfect Storm"

With all the hype these days about companies like Apple, Google, Amazon, and Samsung, it's hard to remember that companies like Sony once ruled. In fact, not all that long ago, Sony was a high-tech rock star, a veritable merchant of cool. Not only was it the world's largest consumer electronics company, its history of innovative products—such as Trinitron TVs, Walkman portable music players, Handycam video recorders, and PlayStation video game consoles—had revolutionized entire industries. Sony's innovations drove pop culture, earned the adoration of the masses, and made money for the company. The Sony brand was revered as a symbol of innovation, style, and high quality.

Today, however, Sony is more a relic than a rock star, lost in the shadows of today's high-fliers. While Sony is still an enormous company with extensive global reach, Samsung overtook the former market leader as the world's largest consumer electronics company a decade ago and has been pulling away ever since. Likewise, Apple has pounded Sony with one new product after another. "When I was young, I had to have a Sony product," summarizes one analyst, "but for the younger generation today it's Apple." All of this has turned Sony's current "Make. Believe." brand promise into one that is more "make-believe."

Sony's declining popularity among consumers is reflected in its financial situation. For the most recent year, Samsung and Apple each tallied revenues exceeding $170 billion—more than double Sony's top line. Samsung's profits have surged in recent years while Sony's losses reached catastrophic levels. And whereas stock prices and brand values have skyrocketed for competitors, Sony's have reached new lows. Adding insult to injury, Moody's Investors Service recently cut Sony's credit rating to "junk" status.

How did Sony fall so hard so fast? The answer is a complex one. Sony never lost the capabilities that made it great. In fact, throughout the past decade, Sony was poised to sweep the markets for MP3 players, smartphones, online digital stores, and many other hit products that other companies have marketed successfully. But Sony was caught in the middle of a perfect storm of environmental forces that inhibited its growth and success. Some factors were beyond Sony's control. However, at the core of it all, Sony took its eye off the market, losing sight of the future by failing to adapt to important changes occurring all around it.

Hit on all Sides

For starters, Sony fell behind in technology. Sony built its once-mighty empire based on the innovative engineering and design of standalone electronics—TVs, CD players, and video game consoles. However, as Internet and digital technologies surged, creating a more connected and mobile world, standalone hardware was rapidly replaced by new connecting technologies, media, and content. As the world of consumer entertainment gave way to digital downloads and shared content accessed through PCs, iPods, smartphones, tablets, and Internet-ready TVs, Sony was late to adapt.

Behaving as though its market leadership could never be challenged, an arrogant Sony clung to successful old technologies rather than embracing new ones. For example, prior to the launch of Apple's first iPod in 2001, Sony had for three years been selling devices that would download and play digital music files. Sony had everything it needed to create an iPod/iTunes-type world, including its own recording company. But it passed up that idea in favor of continued emphasis on its then-highly successful CD business. "[Apple's] Steve Jobs figured it out, we figured it out, we didn't execute," said Sir Howard Stringer, former Sony CEO. "The music guys didn't want to see the CD go away."

Similarly, as the world's largest TV producer, Sony clung to its cherished Trinitron cathode-ray-tube technology. Meanwhile, Samsung, LG, and other competitors were moving rapidly ahead with flat screens. Sony eventually responded. But today, both Samsung and LG sell more TVs than Sony. Sony's TV business, once its main profit center, has lost nearly $8 billion over the last 10 years. Recently, in an effort to get back on its feet, Sony spun off its TV division into a standalone unit. But it faces a daunting uphill battle in a competitive landscape that is far different from the one in Sony's heyday. Not only does Sony continue to lose market share to Samsung and LG, but Chinese TV makers such as Haier, Hisense, and TCL are producing cutting edge flat panel offerings with a cost advantage that significantly undercuts Sony.

It was a similar story for Sony's PlayStation consoles, once the undisputed market leader and accounting for one-third of Sony's profits. Sony yawned when Nintendo introduced its innovative motion-sensing Nintendo Wii, dismissing it as a "niche game device." Instead, Sony engineers loaded up the PS3 with pricey technology that produced a loss of $300 per unit sold. Wii became a smash hit and the best-selling game console; the PS3 lost billions for Sony, dropping it from first place to third.

Even as a money loser, the PlayStation system, with its elegant blending of hardware and software, had all the right ingredients to make Sony a leader in the new world of digital entertainment distribution and social networking. Executives inside Sony even recognized the PlayStation platform as the "epitome of convergence," with the potential to create "a fusion of computers and entertainment." In other words, Sony could have had a strong competitive response to Apple's iTunes. But that vision never materialized, and Sony has lagged in the burgeoning business of connecting people to digital entertainment.

There are plenty of other examples of Sony's failure to capitalize on market trends despite the fact that it had the products to do so. Consider the Sony MYLO (or MY Life Online), a clever device released a year before the first iPhone that had the essence of everything that would eventually define the smartphone—a touch screen, Skype, a built-in camera, even apps. Or how about the long line of Sony Reader devices, the first of which was released a year before Amazon took the world by storm with its first Kindle.

The Turnaround

As Sony awoke to the reality of flattening revenues and plummeting profits, efforts were made to turn things around. In 2005, then-CEO Stringer moved in to put Sony back on track. To his credit, Stringer made a credible effort to reignite the company, developing a turnaround plan aimed at changing the Sony mind-set and moving the company into the new connected and mobile digital age. Stringer's efforts were slow to take root, meeting resistance by Sony's hardware-worshipping culture. "Whenever I mentioned content," he says, "people would roll their eyes because, 'This is an electronics company, and content is secondary.'" But even with its rigid structure and inflexible culture working against it, Sony's strengths kept it in the game. In fact, just a few years into Stringer's tenure, the once great consumer electronics giant began to show signs of life, as Sony's profits jumped 200 percent to $3.3 billion on rising revenue.

But if Sony didn't have enough challenges, this uptick occurred just as the Great Recession hit. A year later, Sony was right back where it started with a billion dollar loss. Stringer was quick to point out that if not for the global financial collapse and the yen trading near a post-war high, it would have been comfortably profitable.

After a few more years of negative profits, 2011 was to be Sony's comeback year. Its best batch of new products in over a decade was heading for store shelves, including a portable PlayStation player, a compact 24-megapixel camera, one of the most advanced smartphones on the market, a personal three-dimensional video viewer, and the company's first tablets. Perhaps more important, the company was ready to launch the Sony Entertainment Network—an iTunes-like global network that would finally combine Sony's strengths in movies, music, and video games to all its televisions, PCs, phones, and tablets. Analysts forecasted a profit of $2 billion.

But on March 11, 2011, Stringer received a text message at 4:30 a.m., after having just arrived in New York City. Eastern Japan had been devastated by an earthquake and tsunami. Nobody at Sony was hurt. In fact, Sony's employees dove into rescue efforts, fashioning rescue boats from foam shipping containers to assist in saving victims and ferrying supplies. But in the aftermath of the destruction, Sony shuttered 10 plants, disrupting the flow of Blu-ray discs, batteries, and many other Sony items.

In the wake of the extreme natural disasters, Sony's miseries had only just begun. A month later, a hacking attack invaded the company's Internet entertainment services. In what was determined to be the second-largest online data breach in U.S. history, Sony was forced to shut down the PlayStation Network. A short four months later, fires set by rioters in London destroyed a Sony warehouse and an estimated 25 million CDs and DVDs, gutting the inventory of 150 independent labels. And to round out the year, floods in Thailand shut down component plants, disrupting production and distribution of Sony cameras.

Sony's 2011 comeback year turned out to be big all right, but for all the wrong reasons. The projected $2 billion profit ended up as a $3.1 billion loss, marking a three-year losing streak. As Stringer prepared to fade away into retirement, Kazuo Hirai, Sony's emerging CEO, began speaking publicly of Sony's "sense of crisis." Indeed, Sony entered the record books the following year with a net loss in excess of $6 billion—its biggest ever.

Assessing the Damage

So in the end, just what is it that has caused Sony's fall from grace? Was it an addiction to hardware, an uncompetitive cost structure, the global financial crisis, natural disasters, computer hacking, or riots? In retrospect, all these elements of the marketing environment combined to deliver blow after blow. Sony's encounter with a perfect storm of environmental forces illustrates the havoc such forces can wreak—whether unforeseeable natural and economic events or more predictable turns in technology.

Throughout Sony's turbulent existence over the past decade, a few things remain clear. Sony is a company with a long history and strong legacy that refuses to give up. Even now, Hirai and others at Sony are firmly resolved to save the company. And with engineering and design at the core, they still have all the ingredients needed to become a total entertainment provider in today's market. Sony is a gaming console maker, a TV producer, a mobile company, a home device company, a movie studio, and a major recorded-music label. With renewed efforts toward cost-cutting and breaking down divisional walls, Sony's portfolio of new state-of-the-art products and the unifying umbrella of the Sony Entertainment Network show promise. Now, if Sony can just get the economy and Mother Nature to cooperate. . . .

Questions for Discussion

3-18 What microenvironmental factors have affected Sony's performance since 2000?

3-19 What macroenvironmental factors have affected Sony's performance during that period?

3-20 What stands in the way of Sony's success today?

3-21 Given Sony's current situation, what recommendations would you make to Hirai for the future of the company?

Sources: James McQuivey, "Sony Should Have Been a Digital Contender," *Forbes*, February 6, 2014, www.forbes.com/sites/forrester/2014/02/06/sony-should-have-been-a-digital-contender/; Kana Inagaki, "Sony Slashes Forecast to $1.1 Billion Annual Loss," *Wall Street Journal*, February 6, 2014, www.online.wsj.com/news/articles/SB10001424052702303496804579365813295595026; Daisuke Wakabayashi, "Sony Posts Loss, Curbing Stock's Rally," February 7, 2013, http://online.wsj.com/news/articles/SB10001424127887324590904578289103990967408; Cliff Edwards and Mariko Yasu, "Sony's Search for Cool. The Old-Fashioned Way," *Bloomberg Businessweek*, February 24, 2013, pp. 20–21; Kana Inagaki, "Moody's Cuts Sony Bond Rating to 'Junk'," *Wall Street Journal*, January 27, 2014, www.online.wsj.com/news/articles/SB10001424052702304007504579346001281768972; Al Lewis, "It's a Sony!' So What?" *Wall Street Journal*, February 9, 2014, www.online.wsj.com/news/articles/SB10001424052702304680904579367212204873836; and information from www.sony.net/SonyInfo/IR/, accessed June 2014.

MyMarketingLab

Go to **mymktlab.com** for the following Assisted-graded writing questions:

3-22 Discuss the impact of current trends in the economic environment on consumer spending and buying behavior. (AACSB: Communication; Reflective Thinking)

3-23 Discuss trends in the natural environment of which marketers must be aware and provide examples of companies' responses to them. (AACSB: Communication)

References

1. Based on information from Ashley Vance, "Microsoft Sees a New Image of Itself in Windows 8," *Business Week*, October 29, 2012, pp. 41–42; Spencer Jakab, "Microsoft Holds More Than Meets the Eye," *Wall Street Journal*, January 23, 2013, p. C1; Ashlee Vance and Dina Bass, "Microsoft's Office 2013 Is Software for the Cloud," *Bloomberg Businessweek,* January 29, 2013, www.businessweek.com/articles/2013-01-29/microsofts-old-software-comes-with-a-new-image; Ritsuko Ando and Bill Rigby, "Microsoft Swallows Nokia's Phone Business for $7.2 Billion," September 3, 2013, www.reuters.com/article/2013/09/03/us-microsoft-nokia-idUSBRE98202V20130903; "Microsoft Board Names Satya Nadella as CEO," *Microsoft News Center,* February 4, 2014, www.microsoft.com/en-us/news/press/2014/feb14/02-04newspr.aspx; and annual reports and other information from www.microsoft.com/investor/default.aspx, accessed September 2014.
2. See Rebecca Ellinor, "Crowd Pleaser," *Supply Management*, December 13, 2007, pp. 26–29; and information from www.loreal.co.in/_hi/_in/HTML/suppliers/values-partnership/values-mutual-benefits.aspx and www.lorealusa.com/profiles/suppliers.aspx, accessed September 2014.
3. Information from Robert J. Benes, Abbie Jarman, and Ashley Williams, "2007 NRA Sets Records," www.chefmagazine.com, accessed September 2007; and www.cokesolutions.com, accessed September 2014.
4. See www.community.officedepot.com/local.asp, www.community.officedepot.com/backpack.asp, http://officedepotfoundation.org/?page_id=164, and http://officedepotfoundation.org/?page_id=196, accessed September 2014. Listen Learn Care® is a registered trademark of Office Depot, Inc.

5. World POPClock, U.S. Census Bureau, at www.census.gov/popclock/, accessed September 2014. This Web site provides continuously updated projections of the U.S. and world populations.

6. U.S. Census Bureau projections and POPClock Projection, at www.census.gov/main/www/popclock.html, accessed September 2014.

7. Charles Kenny, "The Reproductive Recession," *Bloomberg Businessweek,* February 11, 2014, pp. 4–5.

8. Laura Rowley, "Baby Boomers Will Transform Aging in America, Panel Says," *Huffington Post*, April 2, 2012, www.huffingtonpost.com/2012/04/02/aging-in-america-baby-boomers-arianna-huffington_n_1397686.html.

9. See "Preparing for the Mature Consumer Boom," *Bloomberg,* September 17, 2013, www.bloomberg.com/infographics/2013-09-17/preparing-for-the-mature-consumer-boom.html; "What Is the Richest Target Audience of All," *Response: Multichannel Direct Marketing,* October 2013, p. 50; and Tracy Sestili, "5 Reasons Why You Should Market to Baby Boomers," *Social Media Today*, January 27, 2014, http://socialmediatoday.com/tracy-sestili/2115511/5-reasons-why-you-should-market-baby-boomers-45-65-year-olds.

10. See Matthew Boyle, "Aging Boomers Befuddle Marketers Aching for $15 Billion Prize," *Bloomberg,* September 17, 2013, www.bloomberg.com/news/2013-09-17/aging-boomers-befuddle-marketers-eying-15-trillion-prize.html; "50+ Active & Healthy Living," www.amazon.com/gp/browse.html/?node=5856180011, accessed September 2014; and www.boomnc.com/wp-content/uploads/Boom!_2014_Media_Kit_LR.pdf, accessed September 2014.

11. For more discussion, see Bernadette Turner, "Generation X. . . . Let's GO!" *New Pittsburgh Courier,* March 2–March 8, 2011, p. A11; Leonard Klie, "Gen X: Stuck in the Middle," *Customer Relationship Management,* February 2012, pp. 24–29; and Gavin O'Malley, "Gen X Proves Boon to Marketers," *Online Media Daily,* April 25, 2013, www.mediapost.com/publications/article/198964/gen-x-proves-boon-to-marketers.html.

12. See Joe Ruiz, "How Lowe's Is Sustaining Customer Relationships," *Maximize Social Business*, January 27, 2014, http://maximizesocialbusiness.com/lowes-sustaining-customer-relationships-12506/; and www.lowes.com/mobile, www.lowes.com, www.youtube.com/watch?v=zbFX7p6ZGTk, and www.pinterest.com/lowes/, accessed September 2014.

13. See Greg Petro, "Millennial Engagement and Loyalty—Make Them Part of the Process," *Forbes,* March 21, 2013, www.forbes.com/sites/gregpetro/2013/03/21/millennial-engagement-and-loyalty-make-them-part-of-the-process/.

14. Ellen Byron, "Marketing Decoder: Kitchen Appliances for 20-somethings," *Wall Street Journal*, June 25, 2013; Alan Wolf, "GE Develops Kitchen Line for Millennials," *Twice*, July 8, 2013, p. 44; and www.geappliances.com/products/artistry/, accessed September 2014.

15. See "Moxy Milan Malpensa Set to Open in September Followed by a Further Five Hotels in Europe by End of 2015," *Marriott New Center,* March 3, 2014, http://news.marriott.com/moxy-hotels/; and www.moxyhotels.com, accessed September 2014.

16. See Greg Smith, "Tweens 'R Shoppers: A Look at the Tween Market & Shopping Behavior," *POPAI,* March 2013, www.popai.com/store/downloads/POPAIWhitePaper-Tweens-R-Shoppers-2013.pdf; and Rory Kaluza, "A Few Tips on Targeting Generation Z," *Branding Magazine*, August 29, 2013, www.brandingmagazine.com/2013/08/29/tips-on-targeting-generation-z/.

17. See "GenZ: Digital in Their DNA"; and Shannon Bryant, "'Generation Z' Children More Tech-Savvy; Prefer Gadgets, Not Toys," *Marketing Forecast,* April 3, 2013, www.ad-ology.com/tag/tech-savvy-children/#.U5d9avldV8E.

18. Robert Klara, "It's Not Easy Being Tween," *Adweek,* June 27, 2012, www.adweek.com/print/141378; and www.shopjustice.com, accessed September 2014.

19. Heather Chaet, "The Tween Machine," *Adweek,* June 25, 2012, www.adweek.com/print/141357; and Greg Smith, "Tweens 'R Shoppers: A Look at the Tween Market & Shopping Behavior," *POPAI,* March 2013, accessed from www.popai.com/store/downloads/POPAIWhitePaper-Tweens-R-Shoppers-2013.pdf.

20. For statistics on family composition, see U.S. Census Bureau, "About Three in Four Parents Living with Children Are Married, Census Bureau Reports," November 25, 2013, www.census.gov/newsroom/releases/archives/families_households/cb13-199.html; and U.S. Census Bureau, "Households by Type, Age of Members, Region of Residence, and Age of Householder: 2013," Table H2, www.census.gov/hhes/families/data/cps2013H.html, accessed June 2014.

21. See U.S. Census Bureau, "Facts for Features," March 2013, www.census.gov/newsroom/releases/archives/facts_for_features_special_editions/cb13-ff04.html; U.S. Census Bureau, "America's Families and Living Arrangements: 2013," Table FG1, www.census.gov/hhes/families/data/cps2013F.html, accessed February 2014; and Bruce Horovitz, "Diversity Reaches New Levels in Honey Maid Ads," *USA Today,* March 10, 2014, www.usatoday.com/story/money/business/2014/03/10/honey-maid-mondelez-coca-cola-cheerios-diversity-commercials/6131151/.

22. Based on information from Bruce Horovitz, "Diversity Reaches New Levels in Honey Maid Ads," *USA Today,* March 10, 2014, www.usatoday.com/story/money/business/2014/03/10/honey-maid-mondelez-coca-cola-cheerios-diversity-commercials/6131151/; and www.youtube.com/watch?v=2xeanX6xnRU, accessed September 2014.

23. U.S. Census Bureau, "Geographical Mobility/Migration," www.census.gov/population/www/socdemo/migrate.html, accessed June 2014.

24. See U.S. Census Bureau, "Metropolitan and Micropolitan Statistical Areas," www.census.gov/population/metro/, accessed September 2014; U.S. Census Bureau, "Census Estimates Show New Patterns of Growth Nationwide," April 5, 2012, www.census.gov/newsroom/releases/archives/population/cb12-55.html; and "The 536 Micropolitan Statistical Areas of the United States of America," *Wikipedia,* http://en.wikipedia.org/wiki/List_of_Micropolitan_Statistical_Areas, accessed September 2014.

25. Mary C. Noonan and Jennifer L. Glass, "The Hard Truth about Telecommuting," *Monthly Labor Review*, June 2012, www.bls.gov/opub/mlr/2012/06/art3full.pdf; and "It's Unclearly Defined, but Telecommuting Is Fast on the Rise," *New York Times,* March 8, 2014, p. B5.

26. See "About WebEx," www.webex.com/why-webex/overview.html, accessed September 2014; www.gotomeeting.com, accessed September 2014; "What Is Cloud Computing?" www.salesforce.com/cloudcomputing, accessed September 2014; and http://nextspace.us/ and http://grindspaces.com, accessed September 2014.

27. U.S. Census Bureau, "Educational Attainment," www.census.gov/hhes/socdemo/education/, accessed June 2014.

28. See U.S. Census Bureau, "The 2012 Statistical Abstract: Education," Tables 229 and 276, www.census.gov/compendia/statab/cats/education.html; and U.S. Department of Labor, "Employment Projections: 2010–2020 Summary," February 1, 2012, www.bls.gov/ooh/.

29. See U.S. Census Bureau, "U.S. Population Projections," www.census.gov/population/projections/, accessed June 2013; U.S. Census Bureau, "America's Foreign Born in the Last 50 Years," www.census.gov/how/infographics/foreign_born.html, accessed June 2013; and U.S. Census Bureau, "2012 National Population Projections," www.census.gov/population/projections/data/national/2012.html, accessed June 2013.

30. See "Chinese American Investors Comfortable with Current Financial Situation, Confident about Financial Future," *Daily Finance,* June 4, 2013, www.dailyfinance.com/2013/06/04/chinese-american-investors-comfortable-with-curren/; "Multicultural Marketing Case Study: Wells Fargo's Asian Outreach," *DiversityInc,* www.diversityinc.com/diversity-management/multicultural-marketing-case-study-wells-fargos-asian-outreach/, accessed March 2014; and www.dae.com/, accessed March 2014.

31. Witeck Communications, "America's LGBT 2013 Buying Power Estimated at $830 Billion," November 18, 2013, www.witeck.com/pressreleases/lgbt-2013-buying-power.

32. For more discussion, see Leanne Italie, "Gay-Themed Ads Are Becoming More Mainstream," *Huffington Post,* March 6, 2013, www

.huffingtonpost.com/2013/03/06/gay-themed-ads-mainstream-_n_2821745.html; Stuart Elliott, "Commercials with a Gay Emphasis Are Moving to Mainstream Media," *New York Times,* June 26, 2013, p. B3; "Ad Campaigns Are Finally Reflecting Diversity of U.S.," *Advertising Age,* March 10, 2014, http://adage.com/print/292023; and www.aa.com/rainbow and www.facebook.com/AARainbowTeam, accessed September 2014.

33. Witeck-Combs Communications, "America's Disability Market at a Glance," http://www.witeck.com/wp/files/Americas-Disability-Market-at-a-Glance-FINAL-5-25-2006.pdf; U.S. Census Bureau, "Nearly 1 in 5 People Have a Disability in the U.S., Census Bureau Reports," press release, July 25, 2012, www.census.gov/newsroom/releases/archives/miscellaneous/cb12-134.html; and Christina Ng, "Huge Demographic Virtually Invisible in Media Wants to Be Seen," *ABC News*, May 29, 2013, http://abcnews.go.com/Business/disabled-community-media-marketing/story?id=19143489.

34. Based on information from "50 Most Innovative Companies: Azul—For Converting Bus Riders into Frequent Fliers," www.fastcompany.com/most-innovative-companies/2011/profile/azul.php; "Azul CEO Neeleman on Brazil, U.S. Airline Industry," *Bloomberg Businessweek,* December 14, 2012, accessed on www.businessweek.com/videos/2012-12-14/azul-ceo-neeleman-on-brazil-u-dot-s-dot-airline-industry; "Brazilian Airlines Face Challenges Ahead of 2014," *The Rio Times,* December 24, 2013, http://riotimesonline.com/brazil-news/rio-business/national-business/brazilian-airlines-face-challenges-ahead-of-2014/#; and www.voeazul.com.br/, accessed September 2014.

35. See U.S. Census Bureau, "Income, Poverty, and Health Insurance Coverage in the United States: 2012," Table 2, September 2013, www.census.gov/hhes/www/hlthins/data/incpovhlth.

36. See Dan Burrows, "Polar Vortex: 3 Winners, 3 Losers," *InvestorPlace*, January 9, 2014, http://investorplace.com/2014/01/polar-vortex-winners-losers-stocks/view-all/#.Uv5zE_ZuqcB; "Fed Confirms Bad Weather Hit to U.S. Economy in Early 2014," *Reuters,* March 6, 2014, http://in.reuters.com/article/2014/03/05/usa-economy-fed-idINDEEA240G220140305.

37. The 2030 Water Resources Group, www.2030wrg.org, accessed September 2014; and "The World's Water," *Pacific Institute,* www.worldwater.org/data.html, accessed September 2014.

38. Information from www.timberland.com and http://responsibility.timberland.com/, accessed September 2014.

39. See Maid Napolitano, "RFID Surges Ahead," *Materials Handling,* April 2012, pp. S48–S50; "Burberry Introduces Smart Personalization for Shoppers," *Integer,* March 25, 2013, http://shopperculture.integer.com/2013/03/burberry-introduces-smart-personalization-for-shoppers.html; and Bob Trebilcock, "RFID: Macy's Way," *Modern Materials Handling,* June 1, 2013, www.mmh.com/view/rfid_the_macys_way/inventory.

40. See "A $1 Billion Project to Remake the Disney World Experience, Using RFID," www.fastcodesign.com/1671616/a-1-billion-project-to-remake-the-disney-world-experience-using-rfid#1; and Brooks Barnes, "At Disney Parks, a Bracelet Meant to Build Loyalty (and Sales), *New York Times,* January 7, 2013, p. B1.

41. For this and other examples, see David Hessekiel, "A Good Thing: Cause Marketers Came Together in 2013," *Forbes,* December 31, 2013, www.forbes.com/sites/davidessekiel/2013/12/31/how-cause-marketing-evolved-in-2013/; www.itcanwait.com, accessed September 2014.

42. See "Warby Parker—Stylish Buy One Give One Eyewear Helps Restore Vision and Hope," *Shop with Meaning,* http://shopwithmeaning.org/warby-parker-glasses-stylish-buy-one-give-one-eyewear/, accessed June 2013; and "Warby Parker: Do Good," www.warbyparker.com/do-good/#home, accessed September 2014.

43. John Biggs, "Three Things Warby Parker Did to Launch a Successful Lifestyle Brand," *TechCrunch,* May 7, 2013, http://techcrunch.com/2013/05/07/the-three-things-warby-parker-did-to-launch-a-successful-lifestyle-brand/.

44. See "Statistics Every Cause Marketer Should Know," www.causemarketingforum.com/site/c.bkLUKcOTLkK4E/b.6448131/k.262B/Statistics_Every_Cause_Marketer_Should_Know.htm, accessed September 2014.

45. See www.yogiproducts.com/ and www.yogiproducts.com/our-story/our-story/, accessed September 2014.

46. Sherry Turkle, "The Flight from Conversation," *New York Times,* April 22, 2012, p. SR1.

47. See Stuart Elliott, "This Column Was 100% Made in America," *New York Times,* February 15, 2012; Brent Snavely, "Chrysler Keeps 'Imported from Detroit' Tagline," *USA Today,* April 24, 2013; and "Apple Kicks Off 'Made in USA' Marketing Push with High-End Mac Pro," *Advertising Age*, December 19, 2013, http://adage.com/print/245765/.

48. www.lohas.com, accessed September 2014.

49. See www.tomsofmaine.com/home, accessed September 2014.

50. See Stephen Daniells, "US Organic Food Market to Grow 14% from 2013-18," *Food Navigator,* January 3, 2014, www.foodnavigator-usa.com/Markets/US-organic-food-market-to-grow-14-from-2013-18; and Jill Ettinger, "U.S. Organic Food Sales to Continue to Skyrocket in 2014 and Beyond," *Organic Authority,* January 8, 2014, www.organicauthority.com/u-s-organic-food-sales-continue-to-skyrocket-in-2014-and-beyond/.

51. The Pew Forum on Religion & Public Life, "Nones on the Rise," www.pewforum.org/Unaffiliated/nones-on-the-rise.aspx, accessed October 9, 2012; and http://religions.pewforum.org/, accessed September 2014.

52. For more discussion, see Diana Butler Bass, "The End of Church," *Huffington Post*, February 18, 2012, www.huffingtonpost.com/diana-butler-bass/the-end-of-church_b_1284954.html.

53. See Brad Tuttle, "McDonald's Made the Right Move in Response to Gross 'Pink Slime,'" *Time,* February 5, 2014, http://time.com/4680/mcdonalds-made-the-right-move-in-response-to-gross-pink-slime/; and www.youtube.com/watch?v=Ua5PaSqKD6k, accessed September 2014.

4 Managing Marketing Information to Gain Customer Insights

Chapter Preview

In this chapter, we continue our exploration of how marketers gain insights into consumers and the marketplace. We look at how companies develop and manage information about important marketplace elements: customers, competitors, products, and marketing programs. To succeed in today's marketplace, companies must know how to turn mountains of marketing information into fresh customer insights that will help them deliver greater value to customers.

Let's start with a good story about marketing research and customer insights in action. When Pepsi's market share and sales recently took an embarrassing dip, putting the iconic brand in third place behind archrival Coca-Cola's Coke and Diet Coke brands, Pepsi turned to consumer research for answers. It launched an exhaustive nine-month global search for fresh consumer insights about just what it is that makes Pepsi different from Coke. The answer: Whereas Coke is *timeless*, Pepsi is *timely*. This simple but powerful consumer insight resulted in Pepsi's global "Live for Now" marketing campaign.

PEPSI'S MARKETING INSIGHT: Pepsi Drinkers "Live for Now"

Pepsi has long pitched itself to a now-generation of youthful cola drinkers, those young in mind and spirit. Almost 50 years ago, the brand invited consumers to "Come Alive! You're the Pepsi Generation!" Pepsi was different from Coca-Cola. "You've got a lot to live," went the jingle, "and Pepsi's got a lot to give."

But recently, PepsiCo's flagship cola brand began losing some of its youthful fizz. Partly to blame: U.S. soft drink consumption has been declining for the past eight years. But harder for PepsiCo to swallow, the Pepsi brand was losing ground in its century-long battle with archrival Coca-Cola, dropping from its perennial number-two position to number three, behind both Coca-Cola and Diet Coke. The embarrassing market-share slip sent a strong signal: The brand's positioning needed a pick-me-up.

To diagnose the issues behind the slide and find answers, PepsiCo launched an intense global consumer research effort. It set out to rediscover just what it is that makes Pepsi different from Coke. The company created a secretive, high-level research task force, located in an unmarked building in upstate New York. Charged with charting a new course for the Pepsi brand, the group embarked on an exhaustive nine-month worldwide search for new consumer insights.

The Pepsi task force left no stone unturned. It poured through reels of past Pepsi advertising. It fielded traditional focus groups, in-depth personal interviews, and lengthy quantitative surveys. Researchers and top executives participated in ethnographic studies, "moving in" with customers, observing them as they went about their daily lives, and immersing themselves in cultures throughout North and South America, Asia, Europe, Africa, and Australia.

The Pepsi research team discovered that the longtime iconic brand had lost sight of what it stands for and the role it plays in customers' lives. Top brands such as Nike, Disney, Starbucks, and Coca-Cola have a clear sense of their meaning. But Pepsi no longer had clear positioning that defined the essence of the brand, drove marketing and innovation, and fueled consumer engagement. In only the past few years, for example, Pepsi's positioning had jumped around from "Every Pepsi Refreshes the World" to "Summer Time Is Pepsi Time" to "Where There's Pepsi, There's Music."

So what does Pepsi mean to consumers? How does it differ from rival Coca-Cola in terms of consumer perceptions and feelings? The research task force boiled its extensive findings down to two simple but powerful customer insights. Whereas Coke is *timeless*, Pepsi is *timely*. Whereas Coca-Cola drinkers

Based on simple but powerful consumer insights gleaned from months of intensive consumer research, Pepsi's "Live for Now" marketing campaign has reenergized the Pepsi brand. "Live for Now" is "bringing back the roots of what Pepsi is all about."

seek *happiness*, Pepsi drinkers seek *excitement*. According to Brad Jakeman, Pepsi's president of global enjoyment and chief creative officer, Coca-Cola stands for moments of joy and happiness, and for protecting the culture and status quo. In contrast, Pepsi stands for creating culture rather than preserving it, and Pepsi customers would rather lead an exciting life than a happy one. Whereas Coca-Cola means belonging, Pepsi embraces individuality. "Brands that are timeless want to have museums," says Jakeman. "Pepsi is not a brand that belongs in a museum."

After scouring the planet for fresh consumer insights, Pepsi launched its "Live for Now" campaign, which urges consumers to capture the excitement of now.

Pepsi-Cola North America

Interestingly, such insights harken back to the old, youthful "choice of a new generation" positioning that built the Pepsi brand so powerfully decades ago. And despite its recent slide, Pepsi remains a formidable brand. Although it has never been the leading cola, Pepsi has always acted as if it were. According to Jakeman, Pepsi has done best when projecting the confidence and swagger of a leader, and Pepsi drinkers have always identified with that boldness. Looking forward, the key will be to regain that boldness and swagger. "This brand does not need to be reinvented," he asserts. "It needs to be reignited."

The "timely" versus "timeless" research insights—the idea of "capturing the excitement of now"—opened new creative doors for Pepsi. The result is a sweeping global marketing campaign—launched in mid-2012—called "Live for Now." Giving a kind of modern twist to the brand's classic "Pepsi Generation" positioning, the campaign provides a new rallying cry for the next generation of Pepsi drinkers. "Live for Now" is designed to shape culture, capture the excitement of the moment, and reestablish Pepsi's connection with entertainment and pop culture. To back the new campaign, PepsiCo increased its marketing budget by 50 percent, putting Pepsi's promotional spending at levels close to those of Coca-Cola.

"Live for Now" burst onto the scene with an abundance of traditional and digital media. The campaign has partnered with a full roster of music and sports stars, linking the brand with some of today's most exciting celebrities. For example, the first ads featured singer/rapper Nicki Minaj, whose hit "Moment 4 Life" contained lyrics made in heaven for Pepsi "Live for Now" commercials and videos ("I wish that I could have this moment for life. 'Cuz in this moment I just feel so alive"). Next, Pepsi inked a deal with Beyoncé that has had her pitching Pepsi's new message on everything from commercials and social media videos to Pepsi cans and a Super Bowl halftime extravaganza.

At the heart of the campaign, the interactive "Pepsi Pulse" Web site—what one analyst calls "a company-curated dashboard of pop culture"—serves as a portal to Pepsi's world of entertainment, featuring pop-culture information, entertainment news, and original content. Pepsi has also forged a music-related partnership with Twitter, and its Mi Pepsi Web site and Facebook page cater to Latino lifestyles and culture, urging customers to "Vive Hoy." Every aspect of the "Live for Now" campaign puts customers in the middle of the action. For example, during Super Bowl XLVII, Pepsi commercials and the Pepsi-sponsored halftime show featured youthful consumers as participants. "It really begins with the insight that Pepsi consumers want to be active participants, not observers of life," says a Pepsi marketer.

Pepsi's extensive research also showed that Pepsi drinkers around the globe are remarkably similar, giving the "Live for Now" positioning worldwide appeal. For example, in India, Pepsi's consumer research revealed that the country's young people are among the most optimistic in the world but are impatient for the future to happen sooner. So Pepsi TV ads in India feature brand endorsers such as cricket captain MS Dhoni, actress-turned-pop-singer Priyanka Chopra, and Bollywood star Ranbir Kapoor overcoming moments of impatience, interspersed with images of young people doing exciting spur-of-the-moment things. The "Live for Now" campaign tells young consumers that "there's nothing wrong with wanting something now," says a senior PepsiCo India marketer.

It's still too soon to tell how much "Live for Now" will reverse Pepsi's long-run fortunes, but initial sales and share results are encouraging. According to brand consultancy Interbrand—which last year included Pepsi as one of its top brands in terms of improved brand value—"Pepsi is making a comeback." It's clear that the folks at Pepsi have done their research homework. Based on what Pepsi's Jakeman describes as the "most-exhaustive and consumer-insights-led process" he's ever witnessed, the swagger is back at Pepsi. Backed by months and months of intensive consumer research, "Live for Now" is reenergizing the Pepsi brand, those who work on it, and those who drink it. According to one Pepsi bottler who cut his teeth in the industry back when the original "Pepsi Generation" campaign was in full stride, "Live for Now" is "bringing back the roots of what Pepsi is all about."[1]

Objective Outline

As the Pepsi Story highlights, good products and marketing programs begin with good customer information. Companies also need an abundance of information on competitors, resellers, and other actors and marketplace forces. But more than just gathering information, marketers must *use* the information to gain powerful *customer and market insights*.

Author Comment | Marketing information by itself has little value. The value is in the *customer insights* gained from the information and how marketers use these insights to make better decisions.

Marketing Information and Customer Insights

To create value for customers and build meaningful relationships with them, marketers must first gain fresh, deep insights into what customers need and want. Such customer insights come from good marketing information. Companies use these customer insights to develop a competitive advantage.

For example, when it began three years ago, social media site Pinterest needed to differentiate itself from the dozens, even hundreds, of existing social networking options.[2]

> Pinterest's research uncovered a key customer insight: Many people want more than just Twitter- or Facebook-like places to swap messages and pictures. They want a way to collect, organize, and share things on the Internet related to their interests and passions. So Pinterest created a social scrapbooking site, where people can create and share digital pinboards—theme-based image collections on things that inspire them. "Pinterest is your own little Internet of only the things you love," says the company. Pinterest's mission is to provide a platform of "inspiration and idea sharing" that connects people around the world through the "things they find interesting."

Pinterest users can upload their own images grouped by topics, pin existing online images, and discover and repin images from others' pinboards.

Thanks to this unique customer insight, Pinterest has been wildly popular. Today, more than 70 million Pinterest users, including some 20 percent of all Internet-using women, collectively pin more than 5 million articles a day and view more than 2.5 billion Pinterest pages a month. In turn, more than one-half million businesses use Pinterest to engage and inspire their customer communities. Sephora, for example, has found that its nearly 226,000 Pinterest followers spend fifteen times more than its Facebook fans.

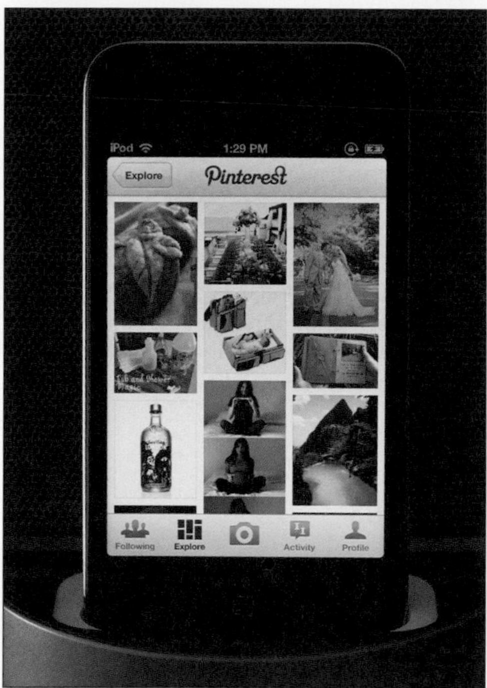

Key customer insights have helped make social scrapbooking site Pinterest wildly successful with its 70 million users. In turn, more than one-half million brands use Pinterest to engage and inspire their customer communities.

© Blaize Pascall/Alamy

Although customer and market insights are important for building customer value and engagement, these insights can be very difficult to obtain. Customer needs and buying motives are often anything but obvious—consumers themselves usually can't tell you exactly what they need and why they buy. To gain good customer insights, marketers must effectively manage marketing information from a wide range of sources.

Marketing Information and Today's "Big Data"

With the recent explosion of information technologies, companies can now generate and find marketing information in great quantities. The marketing world is filled to the brim with information from innumerable sources. Consumers themselves are now generating tons of marketing information. Through e-mail, text messaging, blogging, and social media, consumers now volunteer a tidal wave of bottom-up information to companies and to each other.

Far from lacking information, most marketing managers are overloaded with data and often overwhelmed by it. This problem is summed up in the concept of **big data**. The term *big data* refers to the huge and complex data sets generated by today's sophisticated information generation, collection, storage, and analysis technologies. Every day, the people and systems of the world generate an amazing 2.5 quintillion bytes of new data—about a trillion gigabytes of information each year. Put in perspective, that's enough data to fill 2.47 trillion good old CD-ROMs, a stack tall enough to go to the moon and back four times. If every word uttered by every human being who ever lived were written down and digitized, it would equal only two days' worth of the data being generated at today's rate.[3]

Big data
The huge and complex data sets generated by today's sophisticated information generation, collection, storage, and analysis technologies.

Big data presents marketers with both big opportunities and challenges. Companies that effectively tap this glut of big data can gain rich, timely customer insights. However, accessing and sifting through so much data is a daunting task. For example, when a company such as Pepsi monitors online discussions about its brands by searching key words in tweets, blogs, posts, and other sources, its servers take in a stunning 6 million public conversations a day, more than 2 billion a year. That's far more information than any manager can digest.[4] Thus, marketers don't need *more* information; they need *better* information. And they need to make better *use* of the information they already have.

Managing Marketing Information

Customer insights
Fresh marketing information-based understandings of customers and the marketplace that become the basis for creating customer value, engagement, and relationships.

The real value of marketing information lies in how it is used—in the **customer insights** that it provides. Based on such thinking, companies ranging from Coca-Cola to Google and GEICO are restructuring their marketing information and research functions. They are creating *customer insights teams,* headed by a senior marketing executive with representatives from all of the firm's functional areas. For example, Coca-Cola's vice president of marketing strategy and insights heads up a team of 25 strategists who develop strategy based on marketing research insights. Similarly, GEICO's Customer Insights team analyzes data from dozens of sources to gain insights into the GEICO customer experience, and then works with functional leaders across the organization to find ways to improve that experience.[5]

Customer insights groups collect customer and market information from a wide variety of sources, ranging from traditional marketing research studies to mingling with and observing consumers to monitoring social media conversations about the company and its products. They mine big data from sources far and wide. Then they *use* this information to develop important customer insights from which the company can create more value for its customers.

Thus, companies must design effective marketing information systems that give managers the right information, in the right form, at the right time and help them to use this information to create customer value and stronger customer relationships. A **marketing information system (MIS)** consists of people and procedures dedicated to assessing information needs, developing the needed information, and helping decision makers use the information to generate and validate actionable customer and market insights.

Marketing information system (MIS)
People and procedures dedicated to assessing information needs, developing the needed information, and helping decision makers to use the information to generate and validate actionable customer and market insights.

Figure 4.1 shows that the MIS begins and ends with information users—marketing managers, internal and external partners, and others who need marketing information. First, it interacts with these information users to assess information needs. Next, it interacts with the marketing environment to develop needed information through internal company databases, marketing intelligence activities, and marketing research. Finally, the MIS helps users to analyze and use the information to develop customer insights, make marketing decisions, and manage customer relationships.

Author Comment | The marketing information system begins and ends with users—assessing their information needs and then delivering information and insights that meet those needs.

Assessing Marketing Information Needs

The marketing information system primarily serves the company's marketing and other managers. However, it may also provide information to external partners, such as suppliers, resellers, or marketing services agencies. For example, Walmart's Retail Link system gives key suppliers access to information on everything from customers' buying patterns and store inventory levels to how many items they've sold in which stores in the past 24 hours.[6]

A good MIS balances the information users would *like* to have against what they really *need* and what is *feasible* to offer. Some managers will ask for whatever information they can get without thinking carefully about what they really need. Too much information can be as harmful as too little. Other managers may omit things they ought to know, or they may not know to ask for some types of information they should have. For example, managers might need to know about surges in favorable or unfavorable consumer discussions about their brands on blogs or social media. Because they do not know about these discussions, they do not think to ask about them. The MIS must monitor the marketing environment to provide decision makers with information they should have to make key marketing decisions.

Finally, the costs of obtaining, analyzing, storing, and delivering information can mount quickly. The company must decide whether the value of insights gained from additional information is worth the costs of providing it, and both value and cost are often hard to assess.

FIGURE | 4.1
The Marketing Information System

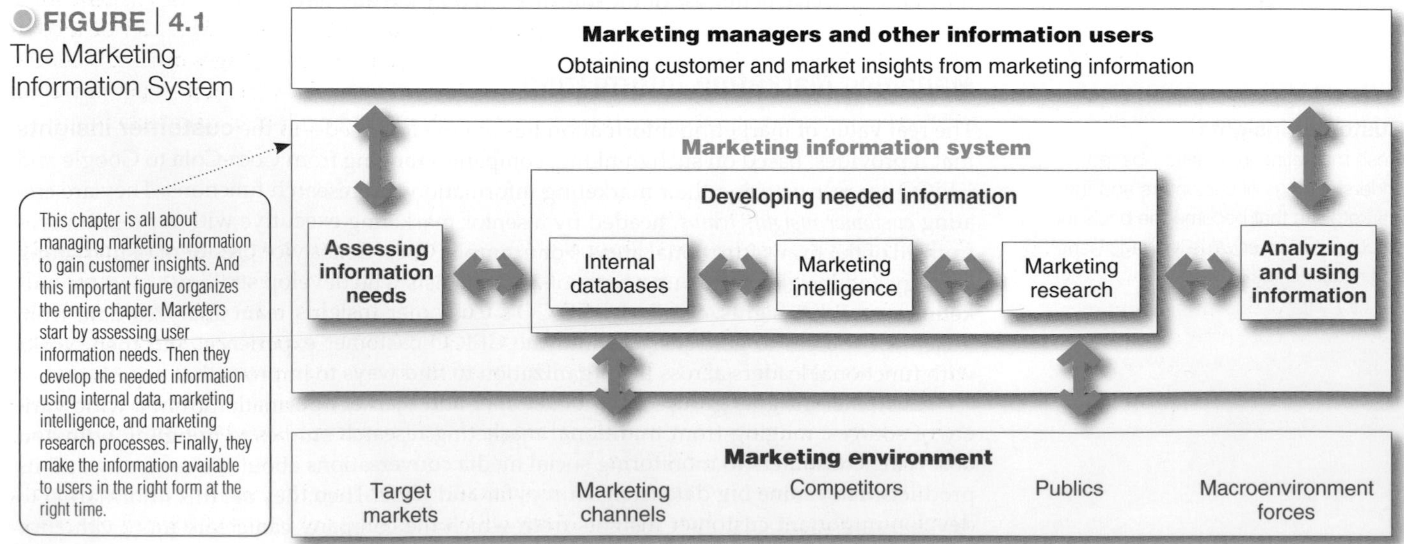

Marketing managers and other information users
Obtaining customer and market insights from marketing information
Marketing information system
Developing needed information
Assessing information needs
Internal databases
Marketing intelligence
Marketing research
Analyzing and using information
Marketing environment
Target markets
Marketing channels
Competitors
Publics
Macroenvironment forces
This chapter is all about managing marketing information to gain customer insights. And this important figure organizes the entire chapter. Marketers start by assessing user information needs. Then they develop the needed information using internal data, marketing intelligence, and marketing research processes. Finally, they make the information available to users in the right form at the right time.

Author Comment | The problem isn't *finding* information; the world is bursting with information from a glut of sources. The real challenge is to find the *right* information—from inside and outside sources—and turn it into customer insights.

Developing Marketing Information

Marketers can obtain the needed information from *internal data, marketing intelligence,* and *marketing research.*

Internal Data

Internal databases
Collections of consumer and market information obtained from data sources within the company network.

Many companies build extensive **internal databases**, collections of consumer and market information obtained from data sources within the company's network. Information in an internal database can come from many sources. The marketing department furnishes information on customer characteristics, in-store and online sales transactions, and Web and social media site visits. The customer service department keeps records of customer satisfaction or service problems. The accounting department provides detailed records of sales, costs, and cash flows. Operations reports on production, shipments, and inventories. The sales force reports on reseller reactions and competitor activities, and marketing channel partners provide data on sales transactions. Harnessing such information can provide powerful customer insights and competitive advantage.

For example, as part of its MyMacy's customer-centricity program, Macy's uses its huge internal database to glean customer insights and personalize customer engagements:[7]

● **Through its MyMacy's program, Macy's digs deeply into its huge customer database and uses the resulting insights to hyper-personalize its customers' shopping experiences. "Happy Birthday, Keri!"**

Courtesy of Gary Armstrong

> Macy's has assembled a vast shopper database containing reams of information on 33 million customer households and 500 million shopper transactions a year. Individual customer data include demographics, in-store and online purchases, style preferences and personal motivations, and even browsing patterns at Macy's Web and social media sites. ● Macy's then analyzes the data intensely and uses the resulting insights to coordinate and hyper-personalize each customer's shopping experiences. "The data they have on their customers is mind-boggling," says an analyst. "They're [the ultimate in] one-to-one marketing."
>
> For example, Macy's now sends out up to 500,000 unique versions of a single direct mail catalogue. "My book might look very different from [someone else's]," says the Macy's CMO. "I'm not such a great homemaker, but I am a cosmetic, shoe, and jewelry person, so what you might see in my book would be all of those categories." Similarly, under its "Intelligent Display" initiative, Macy's can track what customers browse on the company Web site, then have relevant display ads appear as they are browsing on other sites. Future MyMacy's actions will include data-informed e-mail, mobile, and Web and social media site customizations. The ultimate goal of the massive internal database effort, says the CMO, is to "put the customer at the center of all decisions."

Internal databases usually can be accessed more quickly and cheaply than other information sources, but they also present some problems. Because internal information is often collected for other purposes, it may be incomplete or in the wrong form for making marketing decisions. Data also ages quickly; keeping the database current requires a major effort. Finally, managing the mountains of information that a large company produces requires highly sophisticated equipment and techniques.

Competitive Marketing Intelligence

Competitive marketing intelligence
The systematic monitoring, collection, and analysis of publicly available information about consumers, competitors, and developments in the marketing environment.

Competitive marketing intelligence is the systematic monitoring, collection, and analysis of publicly available information about consumers, competitors, and developments in the marketplace. The goal of competitive marketing intelligence is to improve strategic decision making by understanding the consumer environment, assessing and tracking competitors' actions, and providing early warnings of opportunities and threats. Marketing intelligence techniques range from observing consumers firsthand to quizzing the company's own employees, benchmarking competitors' products, researching on the Internet, and monitoring social media buzz.

Good marketing intelligence can help marketers gain insights into how consumers talk about and engage with their brands. Many companies send out teams of trained observers to mix and mingle personally with customers as they use and talk about the company's products. Other companies—such as Dell, Cisco, PepsiCo, and MasterCard—have set up sophisticated digital command centers that routinely monitor brand-related online consumer and marketplace activity.

For example, MasterCard's digital intelligence command center—called the Conversation Suite—monitors, analyzes, and responds in real time to millions of online conversations around the world:[8]

MasterCard's Conversation Suite monitors online brand-related conversations across 43 markets and 26 languages. It tracks social networks, blogs, online and mobile video, and traditional media—any and every digital place that might contain relevant content or commentary on MasterCard. At MasterCard's Purchase, New York, headquarters, Conversation Suite staff huddle with managers from various MasterCard departments and business units in front of a giant 40-foot LED screen that displays summaries of ongoing global brand conversations, refreshed every four minutes. A rotating group of marketing and customer service people spends two or three hours a day in the command center. "It's a real-time focus group," says a MasterCard marketing executive. "We track all mentions of MasterCard and any of our products, plus the competition."

MasterCard uses what it sees, hears, and learns in the Conversation Suite to improve its products and marketing, track brand performance, and spark meaningful customer conversations and engagement. MasterCard is even training "social ambassadors" and "social concierges," who can join online conversations and engage customers and brand influencers directly. "Today, almost everything we do [across the company] is rooted in insights we're gathering from the Conversation Suite," says another manager. "[It's] transforming the way we do business."

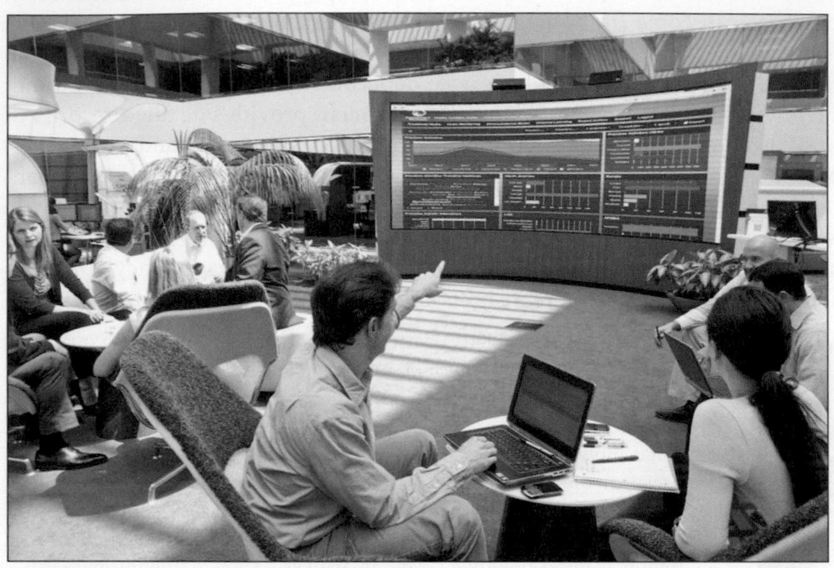

Competitive marketing intelligence: MasterCard's digital intelligence command center—called the Conversation Suite—monitors, analyzes, and responds in real time to millions of brand-related conversations across 43 markets and 26 languages around the world.

MasterCard

Companies also need to actively monitor competitors' activities. They can monitor competitors' Web and social media sites. For example, Amazon.com's Competitive Intelligence arm routinely purchases merchandise from competing sites to analyze and compare their assortment, speed, and service quality. Companies can use the Internet to search specific competitor names, events, or trends and see what turns up. And tracking consumer conversations about competing brands is often as revealing as tracking conversations about the company's own brands.

Firms use competitive marketing intelligence to gain early insights into competitor moves and strategies and to prepare quick competitive responses. For example, Samsung used intelligence gained from real-time monitoring of the social media activity surrounding the introduction of competitor Apple's new iPhone 5 line to capture record-breaking sales of its own signature Galaxy S smartphones.[9]

At the same time that Apple CEO Tim Cook was on stage in San Francisco unveiling the much-anticipated new iPhone 5, Samsung marketing and ad agency executives were huddled around their computers and TV screens in a Los Angeles war room hundreds of miles away watching events unfold. The Samsung strategists carefully monitored not only each new iPhone 5 feature as it was presented, but also the gush of online consumer commentary flooding blogs and social media channels. Even as the real-time consumer and competitive data surged in, the Samsung team began shaping a marketing response. By the time Cook had finished his iPhone 5 presentation two hours later, the Samsung team was already drafting a series on TV, print, and social media ads. The following week, just as the iPhone 5 was hitting store shelves, Samsung aired a 90-second "Fanboys" TV commercial. The ad mocked iPhone fans lined up outside Apple stores buzzing about the features of the new iPhone, only to be upstaged by passersby and their Samsung Galaxy smartphones ("The next big thing is already here!"). Lines in the ad were based on thousands upon thousands of actual Tweets and other social media interactions poking fun at or complaining about specific iPhone 5 features. The real-time-insights-based ad became the tech-ad sensation of the year (grabbing more than 70 million online views), allowing Samsung to rechannel excitement surrounding the iPhone 5 debut to sell a record number of its own Galaxy S phones.

Much competitor intelligence can be collected from people inside the company—executives, engineers and scientists, purchasing agents, and the sales force. The company can also obtain important intelligence information from suppliers, resellers, and key customers. Intelligence seekers can also pour through any of thousands of online databases. Some are free. For example, the U.S. Security and Exchange Commission's database provides a huge stockpile of financial information on public competitors, and the U.S. Patent Office and Trademark database reveals patents that competitors have filed. For a fee, companies can also subscribe to any of the more than 3,000 online databases and information search services, such as Hoover's, LexisNexis, and Dun & Bradstreet. Today's marketers have an almost overwhelming amount of competitor information only a few keystrokes away.

The intelligence game goes both ways. Facing determined competitive marketing intelligence efforts by competitors, most companies take steps to protect their own information. For example, Apple is obsessed with secrecy, and it passes that obsession along to its employees. "At Apple everything is a secret," says an insider. "Apple wants new products to remain in stealth mode until their release dates." Information leaks about new products before they are introduced gives the competition time to respond, raises customer expectations, and can steal thunder and sales from current products. So Apple employees are taught a "loose-lips-sink-ships" mentality: A T-shirt for sale in the company store reads, "I visited the Apple campus, but that's all I'm allowed to say."[10]

One self-admitted corporate spy advises that companies should try conducting marketing intelligence investigations of themselves, looking for potentially damaging information leaks. They should start by "vacuuming up" everything they can find in the public record, including job postings, court records, company advertisements and blogs, Web pages, press releases, online business reports, social media postings by customers and employees, and other information available to inquisitive competitors.[11]

The growing use of marketing intelligence also raises ethical issues. Some intelligence-gathering techniques may involve questionable ethics. Clearly, companies should take advantage of publicly available information. However, they should not stoop to snoop. With all the legitimate intelligence sources now available, a company does not need to break the law or accepted codes of ethics to get good intelligence.

Author Comment | Whereas marketing intelligence involves actively scanning the general marketing environment, marketing research involves more focused studies to gain customer insights relating to specific marketing decisions.

Marketing Research

In addition to marketing intelligence information about general consumer, competitor, and marketplace happenings, marketers often need formal studies that provide customer and market insights for specific marketing situations and decisions. For example, Budweiser wants to know what appeals will be most effective in its Super Bowl advertising. Yahoo! wants to know how Web searchers will react to a proposed redesign of its site. Or Samsung wants to know how many and what kinds of people will buy its next-generation, ultrathin televisions. In such situations, managers will need marketing research.

Marketing research
The systematic design, collection, analysis, and reporting of data relevant to a specific marketing situation facing an organization.

Marketing research is the systematic design, collection, analysis, and reporting of data relevant to a specific marketing situation facing an organization. Companies use marketing research in a wide variety of situations. For example, marketing research gives marketers insights into customer motivations, purchase behavior, and satisfaction. It can help them to assess market potential and market share or measure the effectiveness of pricing, product, distribution, and promotion activities.

Some large companies have their own research departments that work with marketing managers on marketing research projects. In addition, these companies—like their smaller counterparts—frequently hire outside research specialists to consult with management on specific marketing problems and to conduct marketing research studies. Sometimes firms simply purchase data collected by outside firms to aid in their decision making.

The marketing research process has four steps (see **Figure 4.2**): defining the problem and research objectives, developing the research plan, implementing the research plan, and interpreting and reporting the findings.

This first step is probably the most difficult but also the most important one. It guides the entire research process. It's frustrating to reach the end of an expensive research project only to learn that you've addressed the wrong problem!

FIGURE | 4.2
The Marketing Research Process

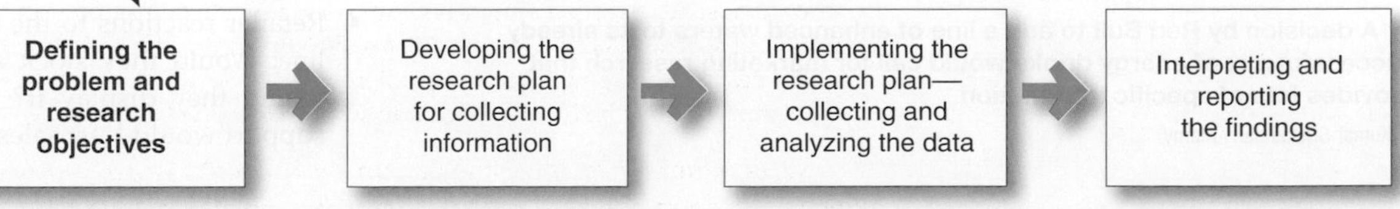

Defining the Problem and Research Objectives

Marketing managers and researchers must work together closely to define the problem and agree on research objectives. The manager best understands the decision for which information is needed, whereas the researcher best understands marketing research and how to obtain the information. Defining the problem and research objectives is often the hardest step in the research process. The manager may know that something is wrong, without knowing the specific causes.

Exploratory research
Marketing research to gather preliminary information that will help define problems and suggest hypotheses.

Descriptive research
Marketing research to better describe marketing problems, situations, or markets, such as the market potential for a product or the demographics and attitudes of consumers.

Causal research
Marketing research to test hypotheses about cause-and-effect relationships.

After the problem has been defined carefully, the manager and the researcher must set the research objectives. A marketing research project might have one of three types of objectives. The objective of **exploratory research** is to gather preliminary information that will help define the problem and suggest hypotheses. The objective of **descriptive research** is to describe things, such as the market potential for a product or the demographics and attitudes of consumers who buy the product. The objective of **causal research** is to test hypotheses about cause-and-effect relationships. For example, would a 10 percent decrease in tuition at a private college result in an enrollment increase sufficient to offset the reduced tuition? Managers often start with exploratory research and later follow with descriptive or causal research.

The statement of the problem and research objectives guides the entire research process. The manager and the researcher should put the statement in writing to be certain that they agree on the purpose and expected results of the research.

Developing the Research Plan

Once researchers have defined the research problem and objectives, they must determine the exact information needed, develop a plan for gathering it efficiently, and present the plan to management. The research plan outlines sources of existing data and spells out the specific research approaches, contact methods, sampling plans, and instruments that researchers will use to gather new data.

Research objectives must be translated into specific information needs. For example, suppose that Red Bull wants to know how consumers would react to a proposed new vitamin-enhanced water drink that would be available in several flavors and sold under the Red Bull name. Red Bull currently dominates the worldwide energy drink market with more than 43 percent of the market share worldwide—it sold more than $3.4 billion worth of energy drinks last year. And the brand recently introduced Red Bull Editions flavored energy drinks and Red Bull Total Zero, an energy drink for calorie-averse consumers.[12] A new line of enhanced, fizzless waters—akin to Glacéau's vitaminwater—might help Red Bull leverage its strong brand position even further. The proposed research might call for the following specific information:

A decision by Red Bull to add a line of enhanced waters to its already successful mix of energy drinks would call for marketing research that provides lots of specific information.

© Kumar Sriskandan / Alamy

- The demographic, economic, and lifestyle characteristics of current Red Bull customers. (Do current customers also consume enhanced-water products? Are such products consistent with their lifestyles? Or would Red Bull need to target a new segment of consumers?)
- The characteristics and usage patterns of the broader population of enhanced-water users: What do they need and expect from such products, where do they buy them, when and how do they use them, and what existing brands and price points are most popular? (The new Red Bull product would need strong, relevant positioning in the crowded enhanced-water market.)
- Retailer reactions to the proposed new product line: Would they stock and support it? Where would they display it? (Failure to get retailer support would hurt sales of the new drink.)

- Forecasts of sales and profits of both the new and current Red Bull products. (Will the new enhanced waters create new sales or simply take sales away from current Red Bull products? Will the new product increase Red Bull's overall profits?)

Red Bull's marketers will need these and many other types of information to decide whether or not to introduce the new product and, if so, the best way to do it.

The research plan should be presented in a *written proposal*. A written proposal is especially important when the research project is large and complex or when an outside firm carries it out. The proposal should cover the management problems addressed, the research objectives, the information to be obtained, and how the results will help management's decision making. The proposal also should include estimated research costs.

Secondary data
Information that already exists somewhere, having been collected for another purpose.

Primary data
Information collected for the specific purpose at hand.

To meet the manager's information needs, the research plan can call for gathering secondary data, primary data, or both. **Secondary data** consist of information that already exists somewhere, having been collected for another purpose. **Primary data** consist of information collected for the specific purpose at hand.

Gathering Secondary Data

Researchers usually start by gathering secondary data. The company's internal database provides a good starting point. However, the company can also tap into a wide assortment of external information sources.

Companies can buy secondary data from outside suppliers. For example, Nielsen sells shopper insight data from a consumer panel of more than 250,000 households in 25 countries worldwide, with measures of trial and repeat purchasing, brand loyalty, and buyer demographics. Experian Simmons carries out a full spectrum of consumer studies that provide a comprehensive view of the American consumer. The U.S. Yankelovich MONITOR service by The Futures Company sells information on important social and lifestyle trends. These and other firms supply high-quality data to suit a wide variety of marketing information needs.[13]

Using *commercial online databases*, marketing researchers can conduct their own searches of secondary data sources. ● General database services such as Dialog, ProQuest, and LexisNexis put an incredible wealth of information at the fingertips of marketing decision makers. Beyond commercial Web sites offering information for a fee, almost every industry association, government agency, business publication, and news medium offers free information to those tenacious enough to find their Web sites or apps.

Internet search engines can also be a big help in locating relevant secondary information sources. However, they can also be very frustrating and inefficient. For example, a Red Bull marketer Googling "enhanced-water products" would come up with more than 50,000 hits. Still, well-structured, well-designed online searches can be a good starting point to any marketing research project.

Secondary data can usually be obtained more quickly and at a lower cost than primary data. Also, secondary sources can sometimes provide data an individual company cannot collect on its own—information that either is not directly available or would be too expensive to collect. For example, it would be too expensive for Red Bull's marketers to conduct a continuing retail store audit to find out about the market shares, prices, and displays of competitors' brands. But those marketers can buy the

● **General database services such as Dialog, ProQuest, and LexisNexis put an incredible wealth of information at the fingertips of marketing decision makers.**

InfoScan service from SymphonyIRI Group, which provides this information based on scanner and other data from 34,000 retail stores in markets around the nation.[14]

Secondary data can also present problems. Researchers can rarely obtain all the data they need from secondary sources. For example, Red Bull will not find existing information regarding consumer reactions about a new enhanced-water line that it has not yet placed on the market. Even when data can be found, the information might not be very usable. The researcher must evaluate secondary information carefully to make certain it is *relevant* (fits the research project's needs), *accurate* (reliably collected and reported), *current* (up-to-date enough for current decisions), and *impartial* (objectively collected and reported).

Primary Data Collection

Secondary data provide a good starting point for research and often help to define research problems and objectives. In most cases, however, the company must also collect primary data. **Table 4.1** shows that designing a plan for primary data collection calls for a number of decisions on *research approaches*, *contact methods*, the *sampling plan*, and *research instruments*.

Research Approaches

Research approaches for gathering primary data include observation, surveys, and experiments. We discuss each one in turn.

Observational research
Gathering primary data by observing relevant people, actions, and situations.

Observational Research. **Observational research** involves gathering primary data by observing relevant people, actions, and situations. For example, food retailer Trader Joe's might evaluate possible new store locations by checking traffic patterns, neighborhood conditions, and the locations of competing Whole Foods, Fresh Market, and other retail chains.

Researchers often observe consumer behavior to glean customer insights they can't obtain by simply asking customers questions. For instance, Fisher-Price has established an observation lab in which it can observe the reactions little tots have to new toys. The Fisher-Price Play Lab is a sunny, toy-strewn space where lucky kids get to test Fisher-Price prototypes, under the watchful eyes of designers who hope to learn what will get them worked up into a new-toy frenzy.

Marketers not only observe what consumers do but also observe what consumers are saying. As discussed earlier, marketers now routinely listen in on consumer conversations on blogs, social networks, and Web sites. Observing such naturally occurring feedback can provide inputs that simply can't be gained through more structured and formal research approaches.

Ethnographic research
A form of observational research that involves sending trained observers to watch and interact with consumers in their "natural environments."

A wide range of companies now use **ethnographic research**. Ethnographic research involves sending observers to watch and interact with consumers in their "natural environments." The observers might be trained anthropologists and psychologists or company researchers and managers. For example, Coors insights teams frequent bars and other locations in a top-secret small-town location—they call it the "Outpost"—within a day's drive of Chicago. The researchers use the town as a real-life lab, hob-knobbing anonymously with bar patrons, supermarket shoppers, restaurant diners, convenience store clerks, and other

Table 4.1 | Planning Primary Data Collection

Research Approaches	Contact Methods	Sampling Plan	Research Instruments
Observation	Mail	Sampling unit	Questionnaire
Survey	Telephone	Sample size	Mechanical instruments
Experiment	Personal	Sampling procedure	
	Online		

townspeople to gain authentic insights how middle American consumers buy, drink, dine, and socialize around Coors and competing brands.[15]

P&G uses extensive ethnographic research to gain insights into serving the world's poor. Three years ago, P&G launched the "$2-a-Day Project," named for the average income of the people it targets worldwide. The project sends ethnographic researchers trekking through the jungles of Brazil, the slums of India, and farming villages in rural China seeking insights into the needs of very-low-income consumers. As an example, P&G researchers recently spent time with poor Chinese potato farmer Wei Xiao Yan, observing in detail as she washed her long black hair using only three cups of water. Her family's water supply is a precious commodity—it comes from storing rainwater. P&G must find affordable and practical solutions that both work in Wei's harsh environment while also supporting her needs to feel attractive.[16]

Ethnographic research: To better understand the needs of the world's poor, P&G sends researchers trekking through the jungles of Brazil, the slums of India, and farming villages in rural China to observe consumers in their "natural environments." Here, they watch Chinese potato farmer Wei Xiao Yan wash her long black hair with great care using only three cups of water.

Benjamin Lowy/Getty Images

Insights from P&G's $2-a-Day Project have already produced some successful new products for emerging markets—such as a skin-sensitive detergent for women who wash clothing by hand. In the works is a body cleanser formulated to clean without much water—it generates foam, which can be easily wiped away, instead of lather. Another product is a leave-in hair conditioner that requires no water at all. For underserved customers like Wei Xiao Yan, P&G has learned, it must develop products that are not just effective and affordable but are also aspirational.

Beyond conducting ethnographic research in physical consumer environments, many companies now routinely conduct *Netnography* research—observing consumers in a natural context on the Internet and mobile space. Observing people as they interact and move about in the online world can provide useful insights into both online and offline buying motives and behavior. And observing people's shopping patterns by tracking their mobile movement, both within and between stores, can provide retailers with valuable marketing information.[17]

Observational and ethnographic research often yield the kinds of details that just don't emerge from traditional research questionnaires or focus groups. Whereas traditional quantitative research approaches seek to test known hypotheses and obtain answers to well-defined product or strategy questions, observational research can generate fresh customer and market insights that people are unwilling or unable to provide. It provides a window into customers' unconscious actions and unexpressed needs and feelings.

In contrast, however, some things simply cannot be observed, such as attitudes, motives, or private behavior. Long-term or infrequent behavior is also difficult to observe. Finally, observations can be very difficult to interpret. Because of these limitations, researchers often use observation along with other data collection methods.

Survey research
Gathering primary data by asking people questions about their knowledge, attitudes, preferences, and buying behavior.

Survey Research. **Survey research**, the most widely used method for primary data collection, is the approach best suited for gathering descriptive information. A company that wants to know about people's knowledge, attitudes, preferences, or buying behavior can often find out by asking them directly.

The major advantage of survey research is its flexibility; it can be used to obtain many different kinds of information in many different situations. Surveys addressing almost any marketing question or decision can be conducted by phone or mail, in person, or online.

However, survey research also presents some problems. Sometimes people are unable to answer survey questions because they cannot remember or have never thought about what they do and why they do it. People may be unwilling to respond to unknown interviewers or about things they consider private. Respondents may answer survey questions even when they do not know the answer just to appear smarter or more informed. Or they may try to help the interviewer by giving pleasing answers. Finally, busy people may not take the time, or they might resent the intrusion into their privacy.

Experimental research
Gathering primary data by selecting matched groups of subjects, giving them different treatments, controlling related factors, and checking for differences in group responses.

Experimental Research. Whereas observation is best suited for exploratory research and surveys for descriptive research, **experimental research** is best suited for gathering causal information. Experiments involve selecting matched groups of subjects, giving them different treatments, controlling unrelated factors, and checking for differences in group responses. Thus, experimental research tries to explain cause-and-effect relationships.

For example, before adding a new sandwich to its menu, McDonald's might use experiments to test the effects on sales of two different prices it might charge. It could introduce the new sandwich at one price in one city and at another price in another city. If the cities are similar, and if all other marketing efforts for the sandwich are the same, then differences in sales in the two cities could be related to the price charged.

Contact Methods

Information can be collected by mail, telephone, personal interview, or online. **Table 4.2** shows the strengths and weaknesses of each contact method.

Mail, Telephone, and Personal Interviewing. *Mail questionnaires* can be used to collect large amounts of information at a low cost per respondent. Respondents may give more honest answers to more personal questions on a mail questionnaire than to an unknown interviewer in person or over the phone. Also, no interviewer is involved to bias respondents' answers.

However, mail questionnaires are not very flexible; all respondents answer the same questions in a fixed order. Mail surveys usually take longer to complete, and the response rate—the number of people returning completed questionnaires—is often very low. Finally, the researcher often has little control over the mail questionnaire sample. Even with a good mailing list, it is hard to control *who* at a particular address fills out the questionnaire. As a result of the shortcomings, more and more marketers are now shifting to faster, more flexible, and lower-cost e-mail, online, and mobile phone surveys.

Telephone interviewing is one of the best methods for gathering information quickly, and it provides greater flexibility than mail questionnaires. Interviewers can explain difficult

Table 4.2 | Strengths and Weaknesses of Contact Methods

	Mail	Telephone	Personal	Online
Flexibility	Poor	Good	Excellent	Good
Quantity of data that can be collected	Good	Fair	Excellent	Good
Control of interviewer effects	Excellent	Fair	Poor	Fair
Control of sample	Fair	Excellent	Good	Excellent
Speed of data collection	Poor	Excellent	Good	Excellent
Response rate	Poor	Poor	Good	Good
Cost	Good	Fair	Poor	Excellent

Source: Based on Donald S. Tull and Del I. Hawkins, *Marketing Research: Measurement and Method,* 7th ed. (New York: Macmillan Publishing Company, 1993). Adapted with permission of the authors.

questions and, depending on the answers they receive, skip some questions or probe on others. Response rates tend to be higher than with mail questionnaires, and interviewers can ask to speak to respondents with the desired characteristics or even by name.

However, with telephone interviewing, the cost per respondent is higher than with mail, online, or mobile questionnaires. Also, people may not want to discuss personal questions with an interviewer. The method introduces interviewer bias—the way interviewers talk, how they ask questions, and other differences that may affect respondents' answers. Finally, in this age of do-not-call lists and promotion-harassed consumers, potential survey respondents are increasingly hanging up on telephone interviewers rather than talking with them.

Personal interviewing takes two forms: individual interviewing and group interviewing. *Individual interviewing* involves talking with people in their homes or offices, on the street, or in shopping malls. Such interviewing is flexible. Trained interviewers can guide interviews, explain difficult questions, and explore issues as the situation requires. They can show subjects actual products, packages, advertisements, or videos and observe reactions and behavior. However, individual personal interviews may cost three to four times as much as telephone interviews.

Group interviewing consists of inviting 6 to 10 people to meet with a trained moderator to talk about a product, service, or organization. Participants normally are paid a small sum for attending. A moderator encourages free and easy discussion, hoping that group interactions will bring out actual feelings and thoughts. At the same time, the moderator "focuses" the discussion—hence the name **focus group interviewing**.

Focus group interviewing
Personal interviewing that involves inviting 6 to 10 people to gather for a few hours with a trained interviewer to talk about a product, service, or organization. The interviewer "focuses" the group discussion on important issues.

In traditional focus groups, researchers and marketers watch the focus group discussions from behind a one-way mirror and record comments in writing or on video for later study. Focus group researchers often use videoconferencing and Internet technology to connect marketers in distant locations with live focus group action. Using cameras and two-way sound systems, marketing executives in a far-off boardroom can look in and listen, using remote controls to zoom in on faces and pan the focus group at will.

Along with observational research, focus group interviewing has become one of the major qualitative marketing research tools for gaining fresh insights into consumer thoughts and feelings. In focus group settings, researchers not only hear consumer ideas and opinions, they can also observe facial expressions, body movements, group interplay, and conversational flows. However, focus group studies present some challenges. They usually employ small samples to keep time and costs down, and it may be hard to generalize from the results. Moreover, consumers in focus groups are not always open and honest about their real feelings, behavior, and intentions in front of other people.

To overcome these problems, many researchers are tinkering with the focus group design. Some companies use *immersion groups*—small groups of consumers who interact directly and informally with product designers without a focus group moderator present. Other researchers are changing the environments in which they conduct focus groups to help consumers relax and elicit more authentic responses. ● For example, Lexus hosted a series of "An Evening with Lexus" dinners with groups of customers in customers' homes:[18]

> According to Lexus group vice president and general manager Mark Templin, the best way to find out why luxury car buyers did or didn't become Lexus owners is to dine with them—up close and personal in their homes. At the first dinner, 16 owners of Lexus, Mercedes, BMW, Audi, Land Rover, and other high-end cars traded their perceptions of the Lexus brand over a sumptuous meal prepared by a famous chef at a home in Beverly Hills. Templin gained many actionable insights. For example, some owners viewed Lexus vehicles as unexciting. "Everyone had driven a Lexus at some point and had a great experience," he says. "But the Lexus they [had] wasn't as fun to drive as the car they have now. It's our challenge to show that Lexus is more fun

● **New focus group environments: Lexus USA general manager Mark Templin hosts "An Evening with Lexus" dinners with luxury car buyers to figure out why they did or didn't become Lexus owners.**

Courtesy of Lexus

to drive today than it was 15 years ago." Templin was also surprised to learn the extent to which the grown children of luxury car buyers influence what car they purchase. Now, Templin says, future Lexus marketing will also target young adults who may not buy luxury cars but who influence their parents' decisions.

Individual and focus group interviews can add a personal touch as opposed to more numbers-oriented research. "We get lots of research, and it tells us what we need to run our business, but I get more out of talking one-on-one," confirms Lexus's Templin. "It really comes to life when I hear people say it."

Online Marketing Research. The growth of the Internet has had a dramatic impact on how marketing research is conducted. Increasingly, researchers are collecting primary data through **online marketing research**: Internet and mobile surveys, online panels, experiments, and online focus groups and brand communities.

Online marketing research
Collecting primary data online through Internet surveys, online focus groups, Web-based experiments, or tracking of consumers' online behavior.

Online research can take many forms. A company can use the Internet or mobile technology as a survey medium: It can include a questionnaire on its Web or social media sites or use e-mail or mobile devices to invite people to answer questions. It can create online panels that provide regular feedback or conduct live discussions or online focus groups. Researchers can also conduct online experiments. They can experiment with different prices, headlines, or product features on different Web or mobile sites or at different times to learn the relative effectiveness of their offers. They can set up virtual shopping environments and use them to test new products and marketing programs. Or a company can learn about the behavior of online customers by following their click streams as they visit the online site and move to other sites.

The Internet is especially well suited to *quantitative* research—for example, conducting marketing surveys and collecting data. More than 80 percent of all Americans now use the Internet, making it a fertile channel for reaching a broad cross-section of consumers.[19] As response rates for traditional survey approaches decline and costs increase, the Internet is quickly replacing mail and the telephone as the dominant data collection methodology.

Internet-based survey research offers many advantages over traditional phone, mail, and personal interviewing approaches. The most obvious advantages are speed and low costs. By going online, researchers can quickly and easily distribute surveys to thousands of respondents simultaneously via e-mail or by posting them on selected online and mobile sites. Responses can be almost instantaneous, and because respondents themselves enter the information, researchers can tabulate, review, and share research data as the information arrives.

Online research also usually costs much less than research conducted through mail, phone, or personal interviews. Using the Internet eliminates most of the postage, phone, interviewer, and data-handling costs associated with the other approaches. Moreover, sample size has little impact on costs. Once the questionnaire is set up, there's little difference in cost between 10 respondents and 10,000 respondents on the Internet.

Its low cost puts online research well within the reach of almost any business, large or small. In fact, with the Internet, what was once the domain of research experts is now available to almost any would-be researcher. ● Even smaller, less sophisticated researchers can use online survey services such as Snap Surveys (www.snapsurveys.com) and SurveyMonkey (www.surveymonkey.com) to create, publish, and distribute their own custom online or mobile surveys in minutes.

Internet-based surveys also tend to be more interactive and engaging, easier to complete, and less intrusive than traditional phone or mail surveys. As a result, they usually garner higher response rates. The Internet is an excellent medium for reaching the hard-to-reach consumer—for example, the often-elusive teen, single, affluent, and well-educated audiences. It's also good

● **Online research: Thanks to survey services such as Snap Surveys, almost any business, large or small, can create, publish, and distribute its own custom online or mobile surveys in minutes.**

Snap Surveys

for reaching people who lead busy lives, from working mothers to on-the-go executives. Such people are well represented online, and they can respond in their own space and at their own convenience.

Just as marketing researchers have rushed to use the Internet for quantitative surveys and data collection, they are now also adopting *qualitative* Internet-based research approaches, such as online focus groups, blogs, and social networks. The Internet can provide a fast, low-cost way to gain qualitative customer insights.

Online focus groups
Gathering a small group of people online with a trained moderator to chat about a product, service, or organization and gain qualitative insights about consumer attitudes and behavior.

A primary qualitative Internet-based research approach is **online focus groups**. For example, online research firm FocusVision offers its InterVu service, which harnesses the power of Web conferencing to conduct focus groups with participants at remote locations, anywhere in the world, at any time. Using their own Webcams, InterVu participants can log on to focus sessions from their homes or offices and see, hear, and react to each other in real-time, face-to-face discussions.[20] Such focus groups can be conducted in any language and viewed with simultaneous translation. They work well for bringing together people from different parts of the country or world at low cost. Researchers can view the sessions in real time from just about anywhere, eliminating travel, lodging, and facility costs. Finally, although online focus groups require some advance scheduling, results are almost immediate.

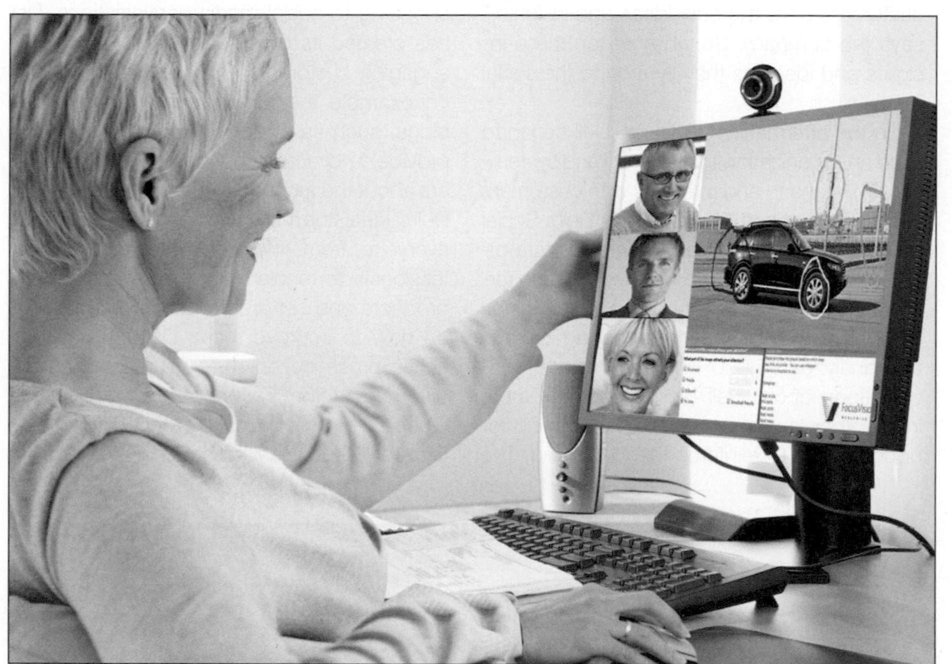

Online focus groups: FocusVision's InterVu service lets focus group participants at remote locations see, hear, and react to each other in real-time, face-to-face discussions.
FocusVision Worldwide, Inc.

Although growing rapidly, both quantitative and qualitative Internet-based research have some drawbacks. One major problem is controlling who's in the online sample. Without seeing respondents, it's difficult to know who they really are. To overcome such sample and context problems, many online research firms use opt-in communities and respondent panels. Alternatively, many companies are now developing their own custom social networks and using them to gain customer inputs and insights. For example, in addition to picking customers' brains in face-to-face events such as "An Evening with Lexus" dinners in customers' homes, Lexus has built an extensive online research community called the Lexus Advisory Board, which consists of 20,000 invitation-only Lexus owners representing a wide range of demographics, psychographics, and model ownership. Lexus regularly surveys the group to obtain input on everything from perceptions of the brand to customer relationships with dealers.[21]

Online Behavioral and Social Tracking and Targeting. Thus, in recent years, the Internet has become an important tool for conducting research and developing customer insights. But today's marketing researchers are going even further—well beyond online surveys, focus groups, and Internet communities. Increasingly, they are listening to and watching consumers by actively mining the rich veins of unsolicited, unstructured, "bottom-up" customer information already coursing around the Internet. Whereas traditional marketing research provides more logical consumer responses to structured and intrusive research questions, online listening provides the passion and spontaneity of unsolicited consumer opinions.

Tracking consumers online might be as simple as scanning customer reviews and comments on the company's brand site or on shopping sites such as Amazon.com or BestBuy.com. Or it might mean using sophisticated online-analysis tools to deeply analyze the mountains of consumer brand-related comments and messages found in blogs or on social media sites, such as Facebook, Yelp, YouTube, or Twitter. Listening to and engaging customers online can provide valuable insights into what consumers are saying or feeling about a brand. It can also provide opportunities for building positive brand experiences and relationships. Companies like Dell excel at listening online and responding quickly and appropriately. (See Real Marketing 4.1.)

Real Marketing 4.1 Dell Goes Social: Listening to and Engaging Customers Online

When it comes to listening, engaging, and responding to customers through online social media, Dell really gets it. The company has learned that good listening is an important part of building customer relationships. Similarly, not being a part of the social conversation can lead to serious missteps. It's not about controlling the online conversation; it's about making certain that the company knows what's being said about the brand and participates in the dialog. Today, Dell has become a poster child for using social media to listen to and connect with customers.

But Dell learned its social media lessons through hard experience. It all started a few years ago with a painful online incident—dubbed "Dell Hell"—that dramatically demonstrated the power of the social media in giving voice to consumer opinions and concerns, often to a company's detriment. It began with a brief but scathing blog entry by well-known tech blogger Jeff Jarvis of BuzzMachine about the many failings of his Dell computer and his struggles with Dell's customer support. "I just got a new Dell laptop and paid a fortune for the four-year, in-home service," raged Jarvis. "The machine is a lemon and the service is a lie." After detailing his problems with the laptop and the shortcomings of Dell's support, Jarvis signed off "DELL SUCKS. DELL LIES. Put that in your Google and smoke it, Dell."

In the old days, Jarvis's complaint, perhaps in the form of a letter to the editor in a local newspaper or a short commentary in an obscure technical journal, probably wouldn't have attracted much of an audience. But in today's superheated social media environment, Jarvis's blog post immediately went viral, becoming the third-most-linked-to post in the blogosphere the day it appeared. The ensuing online dialog unleashed a firestorm of complaints from customers who shared Jarvis's displeasure with Dell. Jarvis's headline—Dell Hell—became shorthand for the ability of a lone consumer using digital and social media to deliver a body blow to an unsuspecting business.

The Dell Hell incident opened Dell's eyes to the importance of social media in shaping brand conversations and opinions. If consumers are talking about your brand online, you need to be there too. Beyond monitoring the social media to catch and deal with the rants of disgruntled consumers, Dell also saw opportunities to use social media to proactively engage consumers, learn from them, and build positive brand experiences. Even before "Dell Hell," Michael Dell had seen social media as a perfect fit for a company with a deep heritage of working directly with customers. "Our customers have the best ideas and insights," says the company. So why not tap these insights and ideas as they fly around the social media?

In the aftermath of Dell Hell, Dell began to build an organization that actively and systematically listens to and interacts with customers online. At the heart of the effort is Dell's Social Media Listening Command Center, a state-of-the-art social media hub focused on monitoring, engaging, and responding to all things Dell online. The command center aggregates and analyzes 25,000 English-language conversations about Dell (and thousands more in 10 other languages) every day, looking for opportunities to reinforce the Dell brand. The Command Center isn't interested only in customer service or marketing matters. It sorts through oceans of online interactions that are important to all areas of Dell's business—from customer complaints, compliments, and support requests to product feedback and intelligence on an array of technology topics.

But beyond just listening in on and responding to social media conversations, Dell has created its own social media empire for engaging customers and other stakeholders. For example, the company now sponsors nine blogs, such as *Direct2Dell.com*, designed to provide "a direct exchange with Dell customers about the technology that connects us all." Dell's IdeaStorm site provides a forum where everyone from information technology professionals to regular folks can evaluate Dell's products and services and offer suggestions on how to improve them. Dell maintains an active presence on major public social media, ranging from Facebook, Twitter, LinkedIn, Google+, YouTube, Flickr, and Pinterest, to Brazil's Orkut, Germany's Xing, and China's

Listening and responding online: Dell's Social Media Listening Command Center aggregates and analyzes more than 6 million online conversations about Dell every year.

Geoff Livingston

Renren and YouKu social communities. Dell's participation in such social media goes well beyond the typical brand pages. All of Dell's social media efforts are designed to create and monitor consumer exchanges, gather feedback, provide customer service and support, and build customer relationships. Dell urges consumers to "get connected to Dell and let your voice be heard."

Dell's online listening and response culture pervades every aspect of its operations. At the top, Dell created the position of Listening Czar, an executive charged with making certain that social media are woven into the very fabric of the organization. It established a Social Outreach Services group, comprised of scores of dedicated social media support people who form a frontline response team that is ready to pounce on any hot topic or customer need, turning online rants into raves. Dell even has a social media governance team that helps promote a company-wide social media mindset. And in an effort to turn every employee into an online brand advocate, Dell set up a social media certification program that trains employees on how to get social in their jobs, technical support, and customer care. More than 7,500 Dell employees worldwide have become Dell Certified Social Media and Community Professionals.

Finally, to engage online influencers in an offline, in-person way, Dell now holds annual Consumer Advisory Panel (CAP) Days. During the two-day events, Dell invites 30 people active in social media to its headquarters to interact with Dell executives and discuss firsthand their thoughts about Dell's brand, products, Web and social media sites, and customer service. Dell teams take the feedback seriously—they know that the success of CAP Days depends on what happens *after* the customer advisors leave.

Thus, Dell has come a long way since its Dell Hell days. It now uses the social media skillfully to listen to, learn from, and engage its customers. Dell has become so good at social listening that it has formed a Social Media Services group that helps clients such as Caterpillar, Aetna, Kraft Foods, the American Red Cross, and others to develop their own social media strategies. Dell understands that conversations in the social media can shape customer attitudes and experiences as powerfully as a big-budget advertising campaign or a high-powered customer service or sales force. "Social media is far more than a tool," agrees Karen Quintos, Dell's chief marketing officer. "It's an extension of our brand. If your [customers] are in the social space, they are talking about your brand—so either engage and be part of the conversation or be left behind."

Sources: Based on information from Jennifer Rooney, "In Dell Social-Media Journey, Lessons for Marketers about the Power of Listening," *Forbes*, September 25, 2012, www.forbes.com/sites/jenniferrooney/2012/09/25/in-dell-social-media-journey-lessons-for-marketers-about-the-power-of-listening/2/; Jeff Jarvis, "Dell Lies. Dell Sucks." *BuzzMachine*, June 21, 2005, http://buzzmachine.com/2005/06/21/dell-lies-dell-sucks/; Liz Bullock, "How Dell Is Using Social Media to Deepen Customer Relationships and Build Trust," April 16, 2013, www.slideshare.net/LizBullock1/how-dell-is-using-social-media-to-deepen-customer-relationships-and-build-trust; "Dell Social Media," www.slideshare.net/dellsocialmedia, accessed July 2014; http://en.community.dell.com/dell-blogs/direct2dell/b/direct2dell/default.aspx, accessed September 2014; and "Dell Social Media Services: Experience to Transform and Lead," www.dell.com/learn/us/en/555/services/bpo-social-media-services, accessed September 2014.

Behavioral targeting
Using online consumer tracking data to target advertisements and marketing offers to specific consumers.

Information about what consumers do while trolling the vast expanse of the Internet—what searches they make, the sites they visit, how they shop, and what they buy—is pure gold to marketers. And today's marketers are busy mining that gold. Then, in a practice called **behavioral targeting**, marketers use the online data to target ads and offers to specific consumers. For example, if you place a mobile phone in your Amazon.com shopping cart but don't buy it, you might expect to see some ads for that very type of phone the next time you visit your favorite ESPN site to catch up on the latest sports scores.

The newest wave of Web analytics and targeting takes online eavesdropping even further—from *behavioral* targeting to *social* targeting. Whereas behavioral targeting tracks consumer movements across online sites, social targeting also mines individual online social connections and conversations from social networking sites. Research shows that consumers shop a lot like their friends and are much more likely to respond to ads from brands friends use. So, instead of just having a Zappos.com ad for running shoes pop up because you've recently searched online for running shoes (behavioral targeting), an ad for a specific pair of running shoes pops up because a friend that you're connected to via Twitter just bought those shoes from Zappos.com last week (social targeting).

Marketers watch what consumers say and do online, then use the resulting insights to personalize online shopping experiences. Is it sophisticated online research or "just a little creepy"?
©Andresr/Shutterstock.com

Online listening, behavioral targeting, and social targeting can help marketers to harness the massive amounts of consumer information swirling around the Internet. However, as marketers get more adept at trolling blogs, social networks, and other Internet domains, many critics worry about consumer privacy. At what point does sophisticated online research cross the line into consumer stalking? Proponents claim that behavioral and social targeting benefit more than abuse consumers by feeding back ads and products that are more relevant to their interests. But to many consumers and public advocates, following consumers online and stalking them with ads feels more than just a little creepy.

Regulators and others are stepping in. The Federal Trade Commission (FTC) has recommended the creation of a "Do Not Track" system (the Internet equivalent to the "Do Not Call" registry)—which would let people opt out of having their actions monitored online. Meanwhile, many major Internet browsers and social media have heeded the concerns by adding "Do Not Track" features to their services.[22]

Sampling Plan

Sample
A segment of the population selected for marketing research to represent the population as a whole.

Marketing researchers usually draw conclusions about large groups of consumers by studying a small sample of the total consumer population. A **sample** is a segment of the population selected for marketing research to represent the population as a whole. Ideally, the sample should be representative so that the researcher can make accurate estimates of the thoughts and behaviors of the larger population.

Designing the sample requires three decisions. First, *who* is to be studied (what *sampling unit*)? The answer to this question is not always obvious. For example, to learn about the decision-making process for a family automobile purchase, should the subject be the husband, the wife, other family members, dealership salespeople, or all of these? Second, *how many* people should be included (what *sample size*)? Large samples give more reliable results than small samples. However, larger samples usually cost more, and it is not necessary to sample the entire target market or even a large portion to get reliable results.

Finally, *how* should the people in the sample be *chosen* (what *sampling procedure*)? **Table 4.3** describes different kinds of samples. Using *probability samples*, each population member has a known chance of being included in the sample, and researchers can calculate confidence limits for sampling error. But when probability sampling costs too much or takes too much time, marketing researchers often take *nonprobability samples*, even though their sampling error cannot be measured. These varied ways of drawing samples have different costs and time limitations as well as different accuracy and statistical properties. Which method is best depends on the needs of the research project.

Research Instruments

In collecting primary data, marketing researchers have a choice of two main research instruments: *questionnaires* and *mechanical devices*.

Questionnaires. The questionnaire is by far the most common instrument, whether administered in person, by phone, by e-mail, or online. Questionnaires are very flexible—there are many ways to ask questions. Closed-ended questions include all the possible answers, and subjects make choices among them. Examples include multiple-choice questions and scale questions. Open-ended questions allow respondents to answer in their own words. In a survey of airline users, Southwest Airlines might simply ask, "What is your opinion of Southwest Airlines?" Or it might ask people to complete a sentence: "When I choose an airline, the

Table 4.3 | Types of Samples

Probability Sample	
Simple random sample	Every member of the population has a known and equal chance of selection.
Stratified random sample	The population is divided into mutually exclusive groups (such as age groups), and random samples are drawn from each group.
Cluster (area) sample	The population is divided into mutually exclusive groups (such as blocks), and the researcher draws a sample of the groups to interview.
Nonprobability Sample	
Convenience sample	The researcher selects the easiest population members from which to obtain information.
Judgment sample	The researcher uses his or her judgment to select population members who are good prospects for accurate information.
Quota sample	The researcher finds and interviews a prescribed number of people in each of several categories.

most important consideration is. . . ." These and other kinds of open-ended questions often reveal more than closed-ended questions because they do not limit respondents' answers.

Open-ended questions are especially useful in exploratory research, when the researcher is trying to find out *what* people think but is not measuring *how many* people think in a certain way. Closed-ended questions, on the other hand, provide answers that are easier to interpret and tabulate.

Researchers should also use care in the *wording* and *ordering* of questions. They should use simple, direct, and unbiased wording. Questions should be arranged in a logical order. The first question should create interest if possible, and difficult or personal questions should be asked last so that respondents do not become defensive.

● **Using mechanical instruments to monitor consumers: Some marketers are building supermarket "smart shelves" that track shopper demographics and purchases, supplying a wealth of insights into consumer shopping behavior.**

© Simon Belcher/Alamy

Mechanical Instruments. Although questionnaires are the most common research instrument, researchers also use mechanical instruments to monitor consumer behavior. Nielsen Media Research attaches people meters to television sets, cable boxes, and satellite systems in selected homes to record who watches which programs. Retailers use checkout scanners to record shoppers' purchases. Mondelez International—maker of Chips Ahoy!, Ritz crackers, Oreos, and other goodies—is even building supermarket "smart shelves." ● The shelves use sensors to analyze facial structures and other characteristics that identify a shopper's age and sex and determine if and when the shopper selects a product off the shelf. Along with supplying a wealth of insights into consumer shopping behavior, based on who's buying what, the smart shelves allow marketers to deliver real-time, personalized promotions via video screens on the shelves.[23]

Other mechanical devices measure subjects' physical responses to marketing offerings. Consider this example:[24]

> Time Warner's new MediaLab at its New York headquarters looks more like a chic consumer electronics store than a research lab. But the lab employs a nifty collection of high-tech observation techniques to capture the changing ways that today's viewers are using and reacting to television and Web content. The MediaLab uses biometric measures to analyze every show subjects watch, every site they visit, and every commercial they skip. Meanwhile, mechanical devices assess viewer engagement via physiological measures of skin temperature, heart rate, sweat level, leaning in, and facial and eye movements. Observers behind two-way mirrors or using cameras that peer over each subject's shoulder make real-time assessments of Web browsing behavior. In all, the deep consumer insights gained from MediaLab observations are helping Time Warner prepare for marketing in today's rapidly changing digital media landscape.

Still other researchers are applying *neuromarketing*, measuring brain activity to learn how consumers feel and respond. Marketing scientists using MRI scans and EEG devices have learned that tracking brain electrical activity and blood flow can provide companies with insights into what turns consumers on and off regarding their brands and marketing.

Companies ranging from PepsiCo and Disney to Google and Microsoft now hire neuromarketing research companies such as Sands Research, NeuroFocus, and EmSense to help figure out what people are really thinking. For example, PepsiCo's Frito-Lay worked with Nielsen's NeuroFocus to assess consumer motivations underlying the success of its Cheetos snack brand. After scanning the brains of carefully chosen consumers, NeuroFocus learned that part of what makes Cheetos a junk-food staple is the messy orange cheese dust—that's right, the neon stuff that gloms onto your fingers and then smears on your shirt or the couch cushions. As it turns out, the icky coating triggers a powerful brain response: a sense of "giddy subversion" that makes the messiness more than worth the trouble it causes. Using this finding, Frito-Lay successfully framed an entire advertising campaign around the mess Cheetos make. For its part, NeuroFocus won an award for outstanding advertising research.[25]

Although neuromarketing techniques can measure consumer involvement and emotional responses second by second, such brain responses can be difficult to interpret. Thus, neuromarketing is usually used in combination with other research approaches to gain a more complete picture of what goes on inside consumers' heads.

Implementing the Research Plan

The researcher next puts the marketing research plan into action. This involves collecting, processing, and analyzing the information. Data collection can be carried out by the company's marketing research staff or outside firms. Researchers should watch closely to make sure that the plan is implemented correctly. They must guard against problems with data collection techniques and technologies, data quality, and timeliness.

Researchers must also process and analyze the collected data to isolate important information and insight. They need to check data for accuracy and completeness and code it for analysis. The researchers then tabulate the results and compute statistical measures.

Interpreting and Reporting the Findings

The market researcher must now interpret the findings, draw conclusions, and report them to management. The researcher should not try to overwhelm managers with numbers and fancy statistical techniques. Rather, the researcher should present important findings and insights that are useful in the major decisions faced by management.

However, interpretation should not be left only to researchers. Although they are often experts in research design and statistics, the marketing manager knows more about the problem and the decisions that must be made. The best research means little if the manager blindly accepts faulty interpretations from the researcher. Similarly, managers may be biased. They might tend to accept research results that show what they expected and reject those that they did not expect or hope for. In many cases, findings can be interpreted in different ways, and discussions between researchers and managers will help point to the best interpretations. Thus, managers and researchers must work together closely when interpreting research results, and both must share responsibility for the research process and resulting decisions.

Author Comment | We've talked generally about managing customer relationships throughout the book. But here, "customer relationship management" (CRM) has a much narrower data-management meaning. It refers to capturing and using customer data from all sources to manage customer interactions, engage customers, and build customer relationships.

Analyzing and Using Marketing Information

Information gathered in internal databases and through competitive marketing intelligence and marketing research usually requires additional analysis. Managers may need help applying the information to gain customer and market insights that will improve their marketing decisions. This help may include advanced statistical analysis to learn more about the relationships within a set of data. Information analysis might also involve the application of analytical models that will help marketers make better decisions.

Once the information has been processed and analyzed, it must be made available to the right decision makers at the right time. In the following sections, we look deeper into analyzing and using marketing information.

Customer Relationship Management and Mining Big Data

The question of how best to analyze and use individual customer data presents special problems. In the current *big data* era, most companies are awash in information about their customers and the marketplace. Still, smart companies capture information at every possible customer *touch point*. These touch points include customer purchases, sales force contacts, service and support calls, Web and social media site visits, satisfaction surveys, credit and payment interactions, market research studies—every contact between a customer and a company.

Unfortunately, this information is usually scattered widely across the organization or buried deep in big data databases. To overcome such problems, many companies are now turning to **customer relationship management (CRM)** to manage detailed information about individual customers and carefully manage customer touch points to maximize customer loyalty.

Customer relationship management (CRM)
Managing detailed information about individual customers and carefully managing customer touch points to maximize customer loyalty.

CRM consists of sophisticated software and analytical tools from companies such as Salesforce.com, Oracle, Microsoft, and SAS that integrate customer and marketplace information from all sources, analyze it in depth, and apply the results to build stronger customer relationships. CRM integrates everything that a company's sales, service, and marketing teams know about individual customers, providing a 360-degree view of the customer relationship.

CRM analysts develop *big data warehouses* and use sophisticated *data mining* techniques to unearth the riches hidden in customer and marketplace data. A data warehouse is a company-wide database of finely detailed customer and market information that needs to be sifted through for gems. The purpose of a data warehouse is not only to gather information but also to pull it together into a central, accessible location. Then, once the data warehouse brings the data together, the company uses high-powered data mining and analytic techniques to sift through the mounds of big data and dig out interesting findings relevant to creating customer value.

Effective use of big data can lead to marketing opportunities. For example, The Weather Company (TWC), formerly The Weather Channel, has turned big data into a completely new business:[26]

> TWC has found big business in big data. It collects terabytes of data every day and uses it not only to predict the weather in millions of locations, but also to predict what consumers in those locations will buy. TWC has married more than 75 years' worth of weather data with aggregated consumer purchasing data. For example, air-conditioner sales increase during hot weather, but folks in Atlanta suffer three days longer than people in Chicago before running out to buy one. Such analysis has created a whole new business for TWC—selling ads based on big data analytics, which now generates half of the company's ad revenues.
>
> For example, P&G's Pantene and Puffs brands buy ads based on TWC's weather and consumption analytics. A woman checking The Weather Channel app in a humid locale receives an ad for Pantene Pro-V Smooth, a product formulated to tame frizzy hair. Checking the app again on a low humidity day or drier area results in seeing an ad for a volumizing product instead. Similarly, a consumer looking at a high pollen forecast receives an ad for Puffs facial tissues, with the message, "A face in need deserves Puffs indeed." According to TWC, weather has a significant influence on almost one-third of the world's buying every day. "The old paradigm of business and weather was cope and avoid," says TWC's vice president for weather analytics. "With [big data] technology, the paradigm is now anticipate and exploit." Thanks to TWC, companies can do just that in targeting where and when they run ads and promotions.

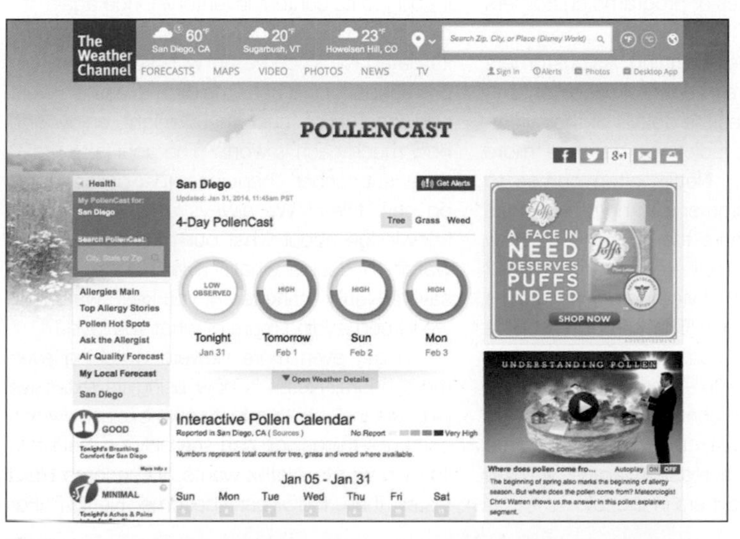

Big data: Based on The Weather Company's big data analytics, this Puff's ad ran in an area where TWC forecast heavy pollen. "A face in need deserves Puffs indeed!"

Courtesy The Weather Channel and The Procter & Gamble Company

By using CRM to understand customers better, companies can provide higher levels of customer service and develop deeper customer relationships. They can use big data and CRM to pinpoint high-value customers, target them more effectively, cross-sell the company's products, and create offers tailored to specific customer requirements. For example, Netflix maintains a bulging customer database, which it uses to fuel recommendations to subscribers, decide what programming to offer, and even develop its own exclusive content in the quest to serve its customers better (see Real Marketing 4.2).

CRM and big data benefits don't come without costs or risk, either in collecting the original data or in maintaining and mining it. The most common CRM mistake is to view CRM as a technology and software process only. Yet technology alone cannot build profitable customer relationships. Companies can't improve customer relationships by simply installing some new software. Instead, marketers should start with the fundamentals of managing customer relationships and *then* employ high-tech data solutions. They should focus first on the R—it's the *relationship* that CRM is all about.

Distributing and Using Marketing Information

Marketing information has no value until it is used to gain customer insights and make better marketing decisions. Thus, the marketing information system must make the information readily available to managers and others who need it, when they need it. In some cases, this means providing managers with regular performance reports, intelligence updates, and reports on the results of research studies.

But marketing managers may also need access to nonroutine information for special situations and on-the-spot decisions. For example, a sales manager having trouble with a large customer may want a summary of the account's sales and profitability over the past year. Or a brand manager may want to get a sense of the amount of the social media buzz surrounding the recent launch of a new product. These days, therefore, information distribution involves making information available in a timely, user-friendly way.

Real Marketing 4.2

Netflix Streams Success with Big Data and CRM

Americans now watch more movies and TV programs streamed via the Internet than they watch on DVDs and Blu-ray discs. And with its library of more than 60,000 titles, Netflix streams more movie and program content by far than any other video service. Netflix's 48 million paid subscribers watch more than 1.4 billion hours of movies and TV programs every month. During peak hours on any given day, a remarkable one-third of all downloads on the Internet are devoted to streamed programming from Netflix.

All of this comes as little surprise to avid Netflixers. But members might be startled to learn that while they are busy watching Netflix videos, Netflix is busy watching *them*—watching them very, very closely. Netflix tracks and analyzes heaps of customer data in excruciating detail. Then, it uses the big data insights to give customers exactly what they want. Netflix knows in depth what its audience wants to watch, and it uses this knowledge to fuel recommendations to subscribers, decide what programming to offer, and even develop its own exclusive content.

No company knows its customers better than Netflix. The company has mind-boggling access to real-time data on member viewing behavior and sentiments. Every day, Netflix tracks and parses member data on 3 million searches, 4 million ratings, and 30 million "plays." Netflix's bulging database contains every viewing detail for each and every individual subscriber—what shows they watch, time of day, on what devices, at what locations, even when they hit the pause, rewind, or fast-forward buttons during programs.

Netflix supplements this already-massive database with consumer information purchased from Nielsen, Facebook, Twitter, and other sources. Finally, the company employs experts to classify each video on hundreds of characteristics, such as talent, action, tone, genre, color, volume, scenery, and many, many others. Using this rich database, Netflix builds detailed subscriber profiles based on individual viewing habits and preferences. It then uses these profiles to personalize each customer's viewing experience. According to Netflix, there are 40 million different versions of Netflix, one for each individual subscriber worldwide.

For example, Netflix uses data on viewing history to make personalized recommendations. Wading through 60,000 titles to decide what to watch can be overwhelming. So when new customers sign up, Netflix asks them to rate their interest in movie and TV genres and to rate specific titles they have already seen. It then cross-references what people like with other similar titles to predict additional movies or programs customers will enjoy.

But that's just the beginning. As customers watch and rate more and more video content, and as Netflix studies the details of their viewing behavior, the predictions become more and more accurate. Netflix often comes to know individual customer viewing preferences better than customers themselves do. How accurate are Netflix's recommendations? Seventy-five percent of viewing activity results from these suggestions. That's important. The more subscribers watch, the more likely they are to stay with Netflix—viewers who watch at least 15 hours of content each month are 75 percent less likely to cancel. Accurate recommendations increase average viewing time, keeping subscribers in the fold.

Increased viewing also depends on offering the right content in the first place. But adding new programming is expensive—content licensing fees constitute the lion's share of Netflix's cost of goods sold. With so many new and existing movies and TV programs on the market, Netflix must be very selective in what it adds to its content inventory. Once again, it's big data to the rescue. Just as Netflix analyzes its database to come up with subscriber recommendations, it uses the data to assess what additional titles customers might enjoy and how much each is worth. The goal is to maximize subscriber "happiness-per-dollar-spent" on new titles. "We always use our in-depth knowledge about what our members love to watch to decide what's available on Netflix," says a Netflix marketer. "If you keep watching, we'll keep adding more of what you love."

To get even more viewers watching even more hours, Netflix is now using its extensive big data insights to add its own exclusive video content—things you can see only on Netflix. In its own words, Netflix wants "to become HBO faster than HBO can become Netflix." For

Netflix, big data, and CRM: While members are busy watching Netflix videos, Netflix is busy watching *them*—watching them very, very closely. Then, it uses the big data insights to give customers exactly what they want.

© OJO Images Ltd / Alamy (photo); © PSL Images / Alamy (logo)

example, Netflix stunned the media industry when it outbid both HBO and AMC by paying a stunning $100 million for exclusive rights to air the first two seasons of *House of Cards*, a U.S. version of a hit British political drama produced by Hollywood bigwigs David Fincher and Kevin Spacey.

To outsiders, the huge investment in *House of Cards* seemed highly risky. However, using its powerful database, Netflix was able to predict accurately which and how many existing members would watch the new *House of Cards* regularly, and how many new members would sign up because of the show. Netflix also used its viewer knowledge to pinpoint and personalize promotion of the exclusive new series. Rather than spending millions of dollars to promote the show broadly, Netflix tailored pitches to just the right members using viewer profiles and the recommendation feature. Before *House of Cards* premiered, based on their profiles, selected subscribers saw 1 of 10 different trailers of the show aimed at their specific likes and interests.

Thanks to Netflix's big data and CRM prowess, *House of Cards* was a smash hit. It brought in 3 million new subscribers in only the first three months. These new subscribers alone covered almost all of the $100 million investment. More important, a Netflix survey revealed that for the average *House of Cards* viewer, 86 percent were less likely to cancel because of the new program. Such success came as no surprise to Netflix. Its data had predicted that the program would be a hit before the director ever shouted "action."

Based on its success with *House of Cards*, Netflix developed a number of other original series, including *Hemlock Grove*, *Arrested Development*, and *Orange Is the New Black*, its most successful release to date. For traditional broadcast networks, the average success rate for new television shows is 35 percent. In contrast, Netflix is batting almost 70 percent. To continue the momentum, Netflix has committed $300 million a year to developing new original content. It plans to add at least five original titles annually, including drama series, comedy specials, movies, and documentaries.

As more and more high-quality video streams out of Netflix, more success streams in. Netflix's sales have spurted 60 percent during the past two years. Last year alone, membership grew by 25 percent, and Netflix's stock price quadrupled. Netflix thrives on using big data and CRM to know and serve its customers. The company excels at helping customers figure out just what they want to watch and to offer just the right content profitably. Says Netflix's chief communications officer, "Because we have a direct relationship with consumers, we *know* what people like to watch, and that helps us [immeasurably]."

Sources: David Carr, "Giving Viewers What They Want," *New York Times*, February 25, 2013, p. B1; Zach Bulygo, "How Netflix Uses Analytics to Select Movies, Create Content, and Make Multimillion Dollar Decisions," *Kissmetrics*, September 6, 2013, blog.kissmetrics.com/how-netflix-uses-analytics/; Rip Empson, "Netflix Tops HBO in Paid U.S. Subscribers as Members Stream 5 Billion Hours of Content in Q3," *Tech Crunch*, October 21, 2013, http://techcrunch.com/2013/10/21/netflix-tops-hbo-in-paid-u-s-subscribers-as-members-stream-5-billion-hours-of-content-in-q3/; Mark Rogowsky, "Hulu's Billion-Dollar Milestone: A Sign of Just How Far Behind Netflix It Has Fallen," *Forbes*, December 19, 2013, www.forbes.com/sites/markrogowsky/2013/12/19/hulus-billion-dollar-milestone-a-sign-of-just-how-far-behind-netflix-it-has-fallen/; Mike Snider, "Netflix, Adding Customers and Profits, Will Raise Prices," *USA Today*, April 22, 2014, www.usatoday.com/story/tech/2014/04/21/netflix-results/7965613/; and www.netflix.com, accessed July 2014.

Many firms use company *intranet* and internal CRM systems to facilitate this process. These systems provide ready access to research and intelligence information, customer contact information, reports, shared work documents, and more. For example, the CRM system at phone and online gift retailer 1-800-Flowers.com gives customer-facing employees real-time access to customer information. When a repeat customer calls, the system immediately pulls up data on previous transactions and other contacts, helping reps make the customer's experience easier and more relevant. For instance, if a customer usually buys tulips for his wife, the rep can talk about the best tulip selections and related gifts. Such connections result in greater customer satisfaction and loyalty and greater sales for the company. "We can do it in real time," says a 1-800-Flowers.com executive, "and it enhances the customer experience."[27]

In addition, companies are increasingly allowing key customers and value-network members to access account, product, and other data on demand through *extranets*. Suppliers, customers, resellers, and select other network members may access a company's extranet to update their accounts, arrange purchases, and check orders against inventories to improve customer service. For example, home improvement retailer Lowe's shares relevant sales, inventory, product development, and marketing information with suppliers via its LowesLink extranet. ● And Penske Truck Leasing's extranet site, MyFleetAtPenske.com, lets Penske business customers access all the data about their fleets in one spot and provides an array of tools and applications designed to help fleet managers manage their Penske accounts and maximize efficiency.[28]

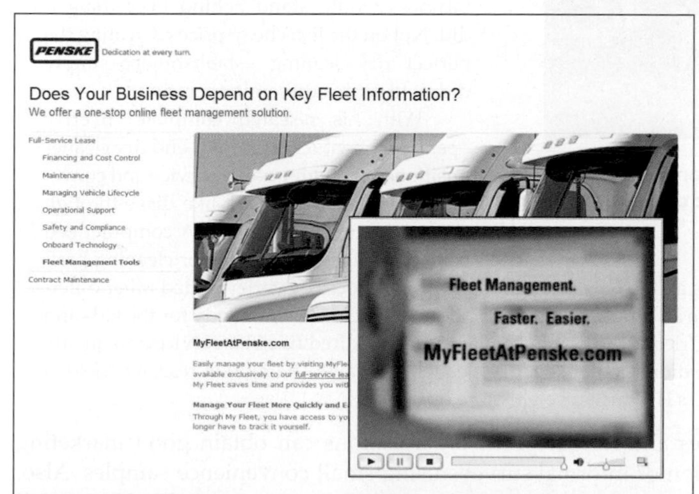

● **Extranets: Penske Truck Leasing's extranet site, *MyFleetAtPenske.com*, lets Penske customers access all of the data about their fleets in one spot and provides tools to help fleet managers manage their Penske accounts and maximize efficiency.**

Penske Truck Leasing

Thanks to modern technology, today's marketing managers can gain direct access to a company's information system at any time and from virtually anywhere. They can tap into the system from a home office, customer location, airport, or the local Starbucks—anyplace they can connect on a laptop, tablet, or smartphone. Such systems allow managers to get the information they need directly and quickly and tailor it to their own needs.

Author Comment | We finish this chapter by examining three special marketing information topics.

Other Marketing Information Considerations

This section discusses marketing information in two special contexts: marketing research in small businesses and nonprofit organizations and international marketing research. Then, we look at public policy and ethics issues in marketing research.

Marketing Research in Small Businesses and Nonprofit Organizations

Just like larger firms, small organizations need market information and the customer insights that it can provide. Managers of small businesses and not-for-profit organizations often think that marketing research can be done only by experts in large companies with big research budgets. True, large-scale research studies are beyond the budgets of most small organizations. However, many of the marketing research techniques discussed in this chapter also can be used by smaller organizations in a less formal manner and at little or no expense. ● Consider how one small-business owner conducted market research on a shoestring before even opening his doors:[29]

● **Before opening Bibbentuckers dry cleaner, owner Robert Byerley conducted research to gain insights into what customers wanted. First on the list: quality.**

Bibbentuckers

After a string of bad experiences with his local dry cleaner, Robert Byerley decided to open his own dry-cleaning business. But before jumping in, he conducted plenty of market research. He needed a key customer insight: How would he make his business stand out from the others? To start, Byerley spent an entire week online, researching the dry-cleaning industry. To get input from potential customers, using a marketing firm, Byerley held focus groups on the store's name, look, and brochure. He also took clothes to the 15 best competing cleaners in town and had focus group members critique their work. Based on his research, he made a list of features for his new business. First on his list: quality. His business would stand behind everything it did. Not on the list: cheap prices. Creating the perfect dry-cleaning establishment simply didn't fit with a discount operation.

With his research complete, Byerley opened Bibbentuckers, a high-end dry cleaner positioned on high-quality service and convenience. It featured a bank-like drive-through area with curbside delivery. A computerized barcode system read customer cleaning preferences and tracked clothes all the way through the cleaning process. Byerley added other differentiators, such as decorative awnings, TV screens, and refreshments (even "candy for the kids and a doggy treat for your best friend"). "I wanted a place . . . that paired five-star service and quality with an establishment that didn't look like a dry cleaner," he says. The market research yielded results. Today, Bibbentuckers is a thriving eight-store operation.

Thus, small businesses and not-for-profit organizations can obtain good marketing insights through observation or informal surveys using small convenience samples. Also, many associations, local media, and government agencies provide special help to small organizations. For example, the U.S. Small Business Administration offers dozens of free publications and a Web site (www.sba.gov) that give advice on topics ranging from starting, financing, and expanding a small business to ordering business cards. Other excellent resources for small businesses include the U.S. Census Bureau (www.census.gov) and the Bureau of Economic Analysis (www.bea.gov). Finally, small businesses can collect a considerable amount of information at very little cost online. They can scour competitor and customer Web and social media sites and use Internet search engines to research specific companies and issues.

In summary, secondary data collection, observation, surveys, and experiments can all be used effectively by small organizations with small budgets. However, although these informal research methods are less complex and less costly, they still must be conducted with care. Managers must think carefully about the objectives of the research, formulate questions in advance, recognize the biases introduced by smaller samples and less skilled researchers, and conduct the research systematically.[30]

International Marketing Research

International marketing research has grown tremendously over the past decade. International researchers follow the same steps as domestic researchers, from defining the research problem and developing a research plan to interpreting and reporting the results. However, these researchers often face more and different problems. Whereas domestic researchers deal with fairly homogeneous markets within a single country, international researchers deal with diverse markets in many different countries. These markets often vary greatly in their levels of economic development, cultures and customs, and buying patterns.

In many foreign markets, the international researcher may have a difficult time finding good secondary data. Whereas U.S. marketing researchers can obtain reliable secondary data from dozens of domestic research services, many countries have almost no research services at all. Some of the largest international research services operate in many countries. ● For example, The Nielsen Company (the world's largest marketing research company) has offices in more than 100 countries, from Schaumburg, Illinois, to Hong Kong to Nicosia, Cyprus. However, most research firms operate in only a relative handful of countries.[31] Thus, even when secondary information is available, it usually must be obtained from many different sources on a country-by-country basis, making the information difficult to combine or compare.

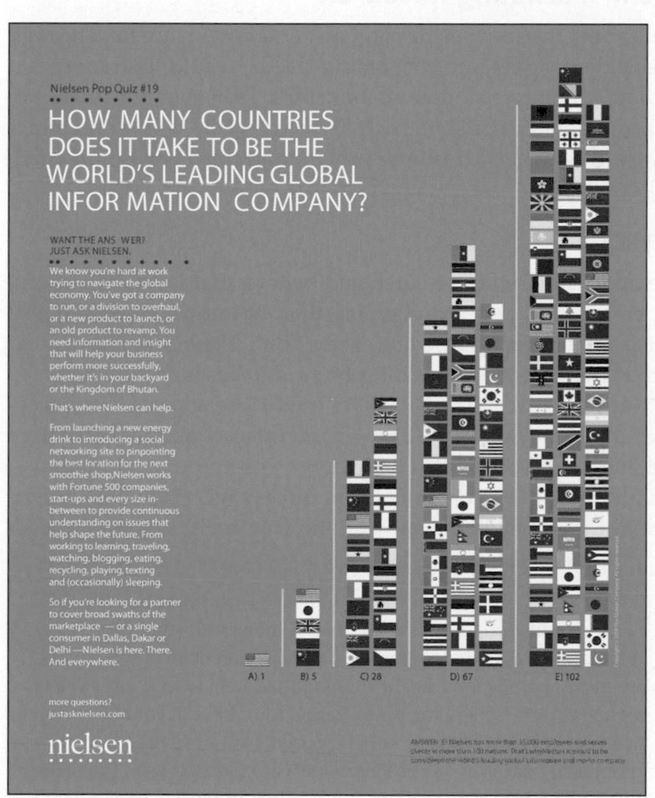

● **Some of the largest research services firms have large international organizations. Nielsen has offices in more than 100 countries.**

Because of the scarcity of good secondary data, international researchers often must collect their own primary data. However, obtaining primary data may be no easy task. For example, it can be difficult simply to develop good samples. U.S. researchers can use current telephone directories, e-mail lists, census tract data, and any of several sources of socioeconomic data to construct samples. However, such information is largely lacking in many countries.

Once the sample is drawn, the U.S. researcher usually can reach most respondents easily by telephone, by mail, online, or in person. However, reaching respondents is often not so easy in other parts of the world. Researchers in Mexico cannot rely on telephone, Internet, and mail data collection—most data collection is conducted door to door and concentrated in three or four of the largest cities. In some countries, few people have computers, let alone Internet access. For example, whereas there are 81 Internet users per 100 people in the United States, there are only 38 Internet users per 100 people in Mexico. In Madagascar, the number drops to 2 Internet users per 100 people. In some countries, the postal system is notoriously unreliable. In Brazil, for instance, an estimated 30 percent of the mail is never delivered; in Russia, mail delivery can take several weeks. In many developing countries, poor roads and transportation systems make certain areas hard to reach, making personal interviews difficult and expensive.[32]

Cultural differences from country to country cause additional problems for international researchers. Language is the most obvious obstacle. For example, questionnaires must be prepared in one language and then translated into the languages of each country researched. Responses then must be translated back into the original language for analysis and interpretation. This adds to research costs and increases the risks of error. Even within a given country, language can be a problem. For example, in India, English is the language of business, but consumers may use any of 14 "first languages," with many additional dialects.

Translating a questionnaire from one language to another is anything but easy. Many idioms, phrases, and statements mean different things in different cultures. For example, a Danish executive noted, "Check this out by having a different translator put back into English what you've translated from English. You'll get the shock of your life. I remember [an example in which] 'out of sight, out of mind' had become 'invisible things are insane.'"[33]

Consumers in different countries also vary in their attitudes toward marketing research. People in one country may be very willing to respond; in other countries, nonresponse can be a major problem. Customs in some countries may prohibit people from talking with strangers. In certain cultures, research questions often are considered too personal. For example, in many Muslim countries, mixed-gender focus groups are taboo, as is videotaping female-only focus groups. Even when respondents are *willing* to respond, they may not be *able* to because of high functional illiteracy rates.

Despite these problems, as global marketing grows, global companies have little choice but to conduct these types of international marketing research. Although the costs and problems associated with international research may be high, the costs of not doing it—in terms of missed opportunities and mistakes—might be even higher. Once recognized, many of the problems associated with international marketing research can be overcome or avoided.

Public Policy and Ethics in Marketing Research

Most marketing research benefits both the sponsoring company and its consumers. Through marketing research, companies gain insights into consumers' needs, resulting in more satisfying products and services and stronger customer relationships. However, the misuse of marketing research can also harm or annoy consumers. Two major public policy and ethics issues in marketing research are intrusions on consumer privacy and the misuse of research findings.

Intrusions on Consumer Privacy

Many consumers feel positive about marketing research and believe that it serves a useful purpose. Some actually enjoy being interviewed and giving their opinions. However, others strongly resent or even mistrust marketing research. They don't like being interrupted by researchers. They worry that marketers are building huge databases full of personal information about customers. Or they fear that researchers might use sophisticated techniques to probe our deepest feelings, track us as we browse and interact on the Internet, or peek over our shoulders as we shop and then use this knowledge to manipulate our buying.

For example, Target made some of its customers very uneasy recently when it used their buying histories to figure out that they had a baby on the way, including eerily accurate estimates of child gender and due date.[34]

Consumer privacy: Target made some customers uneasy when it used their buying histories to figure out things about them that even their family and friends didn't know. The chain's bulls-eye logo may now "send a shiver . . . down the closely-watched spines of some [Target shoppers]."

© Jonathan Larsen/Diadem Images / Alamy

Target gives every customer a Guest ID number, tied to their name, credit card, or e-mail address. It then tracks their purchases in detail, along with demographic information from other sources. By studying the buying histories of women who'd previously signed up for its baby registries, Target found that it could develop a "pregnancy prediction" score for each customer, based on their purchasing patterns across 25 product categories. It used this score to start sending personalized books of coupons for baby-related items to expectant parents, keyed to their pregnancy stages.

The strategy seemed to make good marketing sense—by hooking parents-to-be, Target could turn them into loyal buyers as their families developed. However, the strategy hit a snag when an angry man showed up at his local Target store, complaining that his high school-aged daughter was receiving Target coupons for cribs, strollers, and maternity clothes. "Are you trying to encourage her to get pregnant?" he demanded. The Target store manager apologized. But when he called to apologize again a few days later, he learned that Target's marketers had, in fact, known about the young woman's pregnancy before her father did. It turns out that many other customers were creeped out that Target knew about their pregnancies before they'd told even family and close friends. And they wondered what else Target might be tracking and profiling. As one reporter concluded: "The store's bulls-eye logo may now send a shiver . . . down the closely-watched spines of some [Target shoppers]."

When mining customer information, marketers must be careful not to cross over the privacy line. But there are no easy answers when it comes to marketing research and privacy. For example, is it a good or bad thing that marketers track and analyze consumers' online browsing or buying patterns to send them personalized promotions? Should we worry when marketers track consumer locations via their mobile phones to issue location-based ads and offers? Should we care that some retailers use mannequins with cameras hidden in one eye to record customer demographics and shopping behavior? Similarly, should we applaud or resent companies that monitor consumer discussions on Facebook, Twitter, YouTube, or other social media in an effort to be more responsive?[35]

Increasing consumer privacy concerns have become a major problem for the marketing research industry. Companies face the challenge of unearthing valuable but potentially sensitive consumer data while also maintaining consumer trust. At the same time, consumers wrestle with the trade-offs between personalization and privacy. They want to receive relevant, personalized offers that meet their needs but they worry or resent that companies may track them too closely. The key question: When does a company cross the line in gathering and using customer data? One recent study shows that nearly half of U.S. adults worry that they have little or no control over the personal information that companies gather about them online. Another survey found that 86 percent of Internet users have taken steps to remove or mask their digital footprints, such as removing cookies or encrypting e-mail.[36]

Failure to address privacy issues could result in angry, less cooperative consumers and increased government intervention. As a result, the marketing research industry is considering several options for responding to intrusion and privacy issues. One example is the Marketing Research Association's "Your Opinion Counts" and "Respondent Bill of Rights" initiatives to educate consumers about the benefits of marketing research and distinguish it from telephone selling and database building. The industry also has considered adopting broad standards, perhaps based on the International Chamber of Commerce's International Code of Marketing and Social Research Practice. This code outlines researchers' responsibilities to respondents and the general public. For example, it urges that researchers make their names and addresses available to participants and be open about the data they are collecting.[37]

Most major companies—including Facebook, Microsoft, IBM, Citigroup, American Express, and even the U.S. government—have now appointed a chief privacy officer (CPO), whose job is to safeguard the privacy of consumers who do business with the company. In the end, however, if researchers provide value in exchange for information, customers will gladly provide it. For example, Amazon.com's customers don't mind if the firm builds a database of products they buy as a way to provide future product recommendations. This saves time and provides value. The best approach is for researchers to ask only for the information they need, use it responsibly to provide customer value, and avoid sharing information without the customer's permission.

Use of research findings: The FTC recently ruled against POM Wonderful's research-based advertising claims that the brand could improve a user's health. POM is appealing the ruling.

Christopher Schall/Impact Photo

Misuse of Research Findings

Research studies can be powerful persuasion tools; companies often use study results as claims in their advertising and promotion. Today, however, many research studies appear to be little more than vehicles for pitching the sponsor's products. In fact, in some cases, research surveys appear to have been designed just to produce the intended effect. For example, a Black Flag survey once asked: "A roach disk . . . poisons a roach slowly. The dying roach returns to the nest and after it dies is eaten by other roaches. In turn these roaches become poisoned and die. How effective do you think this type of product would be in killing roaches?" Not surprisingly, 79 percent said effective.

However, few advertisers openly rig their research designs or blatantly misrepresent the findings—most abuses tend to be more subtle "stretches." Or disputes arise over the validity and use of research findings. Consider this example:

The FTC recently charged POM Wonderful—the pomegranate juice sold in the distinctive curvy bottle—and its parent company with making false and unsubstantiated health claims in its advertising. The disputed ads suggest that POM Wonderful Pomegranate Juice can prevent or treat heart disease, prostate cancer, and even erectile dysfunction. For instance, one ad boasted that

POM has "Super Health Powers!" while another proclaimed "I'm off to save prostates!" POM has stood behind its ad claims, asserting that they are backed by $35 million worth of company research showing that antioxidant-rich pomegranate products are good for you. The brand even retaliated during two years of legal wrangling with ads disputing the FTC and its allegations. But the FTC isn't buying the research behind POM's claims—it recently issued a final ruling ordering the brand to refrain from making claims that its products could improve a user's health unless backed by more stringent research. "When a company touts scientific research in its advertising, the research must squarely support the claims made," says the agency. "Contrary to POM Wonderful's advertising, the available scientific information does not prove that POM Juice . . . effectively treats or prevents these illnesses." POM Wonderful is currently appealing the FTC ruling.[38]

Recognizing that surveys can be abused, several associations—including the American Marketing Association, the Marketing Research Association, and the Council of American Survey Research Organizations (CASRO)—have developed codes of research ethics and standards of conduct. For example, the CASRO Code of Standards and Ethics for Survey Research outlines researcher responsibilities to respondents, including confidentiality, privacy, and avoidance of harassment. It also outlines major responsibilities in reporting results to clients and the public.[39]

In the end, however, unethical or inappropriate actions cannot simply be regulated away. Each company must accept responsibility for policing the conduct and reporting of its own marketing research to protect consumers' best interests and its own.

4 Reviewing the Concepts

OBJECTIVES REVIEW AND KEY TERMS

Objectives Review

To create value for customers and build meaningful relationships with them, marketers must first gain fresh, deep insights into what customers need and want. Such insights come from good marketing information. As a result of the recent explosion of "big data" and marketing technology, companies can now obtain great quantities of information, sometimes even too much. The challenge is to transform today's vast volume of consumer information into actionable customer and market insights.

Explain the importance of information in gaining insights about the marketplace and customers. *(pp 130–132)*

The marketing process starts with a complete understanding of the marketplace and consumer needs and wants. Thus, the company needs to turn sound consumer information into meaningful *customer insights* by which it can produce superior value for its customers. The company also requires information on competitors, resellers, and other actors and forces in the marketplace. Increasingly, marketers are viewing information not only as an input for making better decisions but also as an important strategic asset and marketing tool.

OBJECTIVE 2 **Define the marketing information system and discuss its parts.** *(pp 132–135)*

The *marketing information system* (*MIS*) consists of people and procedures for assessing information needs, developing the needed information, and helping decision makers use the information to generate and validate actionable customer and market insights. A well-designed information system begins and ends with users.

The MIS first *assesses information needs.* The MIS primarily serves the company's marketing and other managers, but it may also provide information to external partners. Then the MIS *develops information* from internal databases, marketing intelligence activities, and marketing research. *Internal databases* provide information on the company's own operations and departments. Such data can be obtained quickly and cheaply but often need to be adapted for marketing decisions. *Marketing intelligence* activities supply everyday information about developments in the external marketing environment, including listening and responding to the vast and complex digital environment. *Market research* consists of collecting information relevant to a specific marketing problem faced by the company. Last, the MIS helps users analyze and use the information to develop customer insights, make marketing decisions, and manage customer relationships.

OBJECTIVE 3 **Outline the steps in the marketing research process.** *(pp 135–148)*

The first step in the marketing research process involves *defining the problem and setting the research objectives*, which may be exploratory, descriptive, or causal research. The second step consists of *developing a research plan* for collecting data from primary and secondary sources. The third step calls for *implementing the marketing research plan* by gathering, processing, and analyzing the information. The fourth step consists of *interpreting and reporting the findings.* Additional information analysis helps marketing managers apply the information and provides them with sophisticated statistical procedures and models from which to develop more rigorous findings.

Both *internal* and *external* secondary data sources often provide information more quickly and at a lower cost than primary data sources, and they can sometimes yield information that a company cannot collect by itself. However, needed information might not exist in secondary sources. Researchers must also evaluate secondary information to ensure that it is *relevant*, *accurate*, *current*, and *impartial*.

Primary research must also be evaluated for these features. Each primary data collection method—*observational*, *survey*, and *experimental*—has its own advantages and disadvantages. Similarly, each of the various research contact methods—mail, telephone, personal interview, and online—has its own advantages and drawbacks.

OBJECTIVE 4 Explain how companies analyze and use marketing information. *(pp 148–152)*

Information gathered in internal databases and through marketing intelligence and marketing research usually requires more analysis. To analyze individual customer data, many companies have now acquired or developed special software and analysis techniques—called *customer relationship management* (*CRM*)—that integrate, analyze, and apply the mountains of individual customer and marketplace data contained in their databases.

Marketing information has no value until it is used to make better marketing decisions. Thus, the MIS must make the information available to managers and others who make marketing decisions or deal with customers. In some cases, this means providing regular reports and updates; in other cases, it means making nonroutine information available for special situations and on-the-spot decisions. Many firms use company intranets and extranets to facilitate this process. Thanks to modern technology, today's marketing managers can gain direct access to marketing information at any time and from virtually any location.

OBJECTIVE 5 Discuss the special issues some marketing researchers face, including public policy and ethics issues. *(pp 152–156)*

Some marketers face special marketing research situations, such as those conducting research in small business, not-for-profit, or international situations. Marketing research can be conducted effectively by small businesses and nonprofit organizations with limited budgets. International marketing researchers follow the same steps as domestic researchers but often face more and different problems. All organizations need to act responsibly concerning major public policy and ethical issues surrounding marketing research, including issues of intrusions on consumer privacy and misuse of research findings.

MyMarketingLab

Go to **mymktlab.com** to complete the problems marked with this icon .

Key Terms

OBJECTIVE 1

Big data (p 131)
Customer insights (p 131)
Marketing information system (MIS) (p 132)

OBJECTIVE 2

Internal databases (p 133)
Competitive marketing intelligence (p 133)

OBJECTIVE 3

Marketing research (p 135)
Exploratory research (p 136)
Descriptive research (p 136)
Causal research (p 136)
Secondary data (p 137)
Primary data (p 137)
Observational research (p 138)
Ethnographic research (p 138)
Survey research (p 139)
Experimental research (p 140)
Focus group interviewing (p 141)
Online marketing research (p 142)
Online focus groups (p 143)
Behavioral targeting (p 145)
Sample (p 146)

OBJECTIVE 4

Customer relationship management (CRM) (p 148)

DISCUSSION AND CRITICAL THINKING

Discussion Questions

4-1 What is *big data* and what opportunities and challenges does it provide for marketers? (AACSB: Communication; Reflective Thinking)

4-2 Explain how marketing intelligence differs from marketing research. (AACSB: Communication)

4-3 Are ethnographic studies carried out in your country or region? If so, find and discuss an example of this type of research. (AACSB: Communication)

4-4 How should marketing information be made available to managers to ensure that it encourages better marketing decisions? (AACSB: Communication)

4-5 Where does secondary data come from, and what checks are necessary before acting on such data? (AACSB: Communication)

Critical Thinking Exercises

4-6 In a small group, identify the steps a business organization might need to take to carry out market research in an overseas market. Suggest how the marketing research process needs to be framed. Discuss whether the business would be best advised to have someone do the research for it, or do it itself. (AACSB: Communication; Reflective Thinking)

4-7 Go to www.bized.co.uk/learn/business/marketing/research/index.htm and review the various resources available. Select one activity and present what you learned from that activity. (AACSB: Communication; Use of IT; Reflective Thinking)

4-8 Research the marketing research industry and develop a presentation describing various types of marketing research jobs and compensation for those jobs. Create a graphical representation to communicate your findings. (AACSB: Communication; Use of IT; Reflective Thinking)

MINICASES AND APPLICATIONS

Online, Mobile, and Social Media Marketing Online Snooping

Every second of every day, personal information is being indexed and processed. Every device we use has a unique address that is being broadcast if wireless networking is switched on. Many of us do not even realize that programs exist to find every picture you have ever posted online. Such programs can also pinpoint exactly where you were when you uploaded them. If you haven't set the right privacy settings, it is fairly easy to find out exactly where you live, your habits, and when you are at home and when you are out. Some services are specifically designed to scare people about the information they are unintentionally leaking to the world, such as pleaserobme.com. This shows you whether you are sharing your location and prompts you to change your privacy settings.

4-9 Make a detailed list of all the websites, online forums, social networks, and other web pages you have visited this week. What data have you left that could be of value to marketers? (AACSB: Communication; Use of IT)

4-10 Monetizing relevant data is the key to revealing its true value. Should marketers have access to the personal information of billions of people who use the Internet? Discuss how you would use data trails left by individuals on the Internet if you ran a business. (AACSB: Communication; Ethical Reasoning)

Marketing Ethics Research Ethics

As the Pepsi, P&G, and Lexus examples in the chapter illustrate, companies are increasingly using qualitative research methods such as observation, ethnography, and in-depth interviews to gain customer insights. However, qualitative research brings up ethical issues. Unlike quantitative data collection methods that use surveys or mechanical means, qualitative research puts researchers in close physical proximity to consumers—even in their homes—where the researchers may see or hear private and confidential things. Most research extends confidentiality to research subjects so they will be open in responding to questions, but what if a researcher learns something troublesome? For example, marketing research is advancing into more sensitive consumer behaviors related to product abuse and deviant behaviors, and consumers may reveal harmful or illegal behavior to the researcher. Alternatively, like all experiments, marketing research experiments, such as a researcher pretending to shoplift in a store to observe other customers' reactions, necessarily involve some type of deception. Such experiments can be conducted without customer knowledge, or customers may even be induced to participate in the deception. They may be told later and feel uncomfortable with their actions. These are just a few of the ethical issues related to qualitative marketing research.

4-11 What should marketing researchers do in situations such as those described? Visit www.iccindiaonline.org/policy_state/esomar.pdf and discuss whether the International Code of Marketing and Social Research Practice provides guidance in dealing with such issues. (AACSB: Communication; Ethical Reasoning)

4-12 Describe an example in which marketing research could cause harm to participants. Many companies have a review process similar to that required for government-funded research to ensure research participant safety, with most following the government's "Common Rule." Write a brief report explaining this rule and how you would apply it to your example. (AACSB: Communication; Reflective Thinking)

Marketing by the Numbers What's Your Sample?

Decisions are often made by businesses on the basis of fairly small samples in relation to the actual size of the population or number of customers. Thus, the future of products and services is often determined by relatively small numbers of people. But just how reliable are small-scale samples? Larger samples cost more money, take more time, and ultimately may not be any more accurate than a smaller sample. Are businesses and organizations right to rely so heavily on these small samples? Statistically speaking, a small sample is probably just as accurate.

4-13 Go to www.surveysystem.com/sscalc.htm to determine the appropriate sample size for a population in your country. Briefly explain what is meant by confidence interval and confidence level. Assuming a confidence interval of 5, how large should the sample of households be when desiring a 95 percent confidence level? How large for a 99 percent confidence level? (AACSB: Communication; Use of IT; Analytical Reasoning)

4-14 What sample sizes are necessary to cover the population of the whole region in which you live with a confidence interval of 5 and a 95 percent confidence level? Explain the effect population size has on a required sample size. (AACSB: Communication; Use of IT; Analytical Reasoning)

Video Case Domino's

As a delivery company, no one delivers better than Domino's. Its reputation for hot pizza in 30 minutes or less is ingrained in customers' minds. But not long ago, Domino's began hearing its customers talking about how its pizza was horrible. As a company that has long focused on solid marketing intelligence to make decisions, Domino's went to work on how it could change consumer perceptions about its pizza.

Through marketing research techniques, Domino's soon realized that it had to take a very risky step and completely recreate the pizza that it had been selling for over 40 years. This video illustrates how research not only enabled Domino's to come up with a winning recipe, but led to a successful promotional campaign that has made fans of Domino's pizza in addition to its delivery service.

After viewing the video featuring Domino's, answer the following questions:

4-15 Explain the role that marketing research played in the creation and launch of Domino's new pizza.

4-16 Are there more effective ways that Domino's could have gone about its research process?

4-17 Why did it take so long for Domino's to realize that customers didn't like its pizza? Was it an accident that it made this realization?

Company Case Oracle: Getting a Grip on Big Data

You may have heard the term *big data* and wondered just what it means. Consider this: Every day, the people and systems of the world generate 11 quintillion bytes of new data (that's 11 billion gigabytes). Last year, that added up to about four zettabytes of information. A zettabyte is a trillion gigabytes. Let's put that amount of data in perspective. If you were to put all that data on good old CD-ROMs, every person in the world would have been holding 773 of them at the end of the year. If you stacked all 5.4 trillion CDs on top of one another, it would create a column tall enough to go to the moon and back more than eight times. And you thought you had storage problems. This is big data.

The amount of data that we humans and our beloved machines generate has been growing exponentially. Consider that if every word uttered by every human being who ever lived were written down and digitized, it would only equal about one-half day's worth of the data that is being generated at today's rate. Of all the information that is stored today, more than 90 percent of it was created in the last two years alone. And of course, the data explosion isn't slowing down.

Just where does all that data come from? Every Google search, Facebook status update, YouTube video, text message, and purchase transaction generates data. There are now roughly 15 billion devices connected to the Internet; by the end of the decade, there will be 75 billion. It isn't just laptops and smartphones anymore. Fueling this explosion of connectivity is "The Internet of Things"—the development of smart machines that are talking to other smart machines. Utility meters, vending machines, appliances, automobiles, surgical devices, heavy industrial equipment, and even pets and shoes are now stuffed with technology that allows them to automatically collect consumption data and relay that information to the manufacturers, companies that own the systems that connect the machines, or any company that is willing to pay for such data.

Big Data: A Blessing and a Curse

This tsunami of data surging over corporations of all shapes and sizes is widely considered to be the most important issue in corporate strategy today. Ginni Rometty, CEO of IBM, recently predicted that big data will be the primary basis of competitive advantage in the future, calling it "the next natural resource." She thinks it will change how decisions are made, how value is created, and how value is delivered. Angela Ahrendts, CEO of Burberry, agrees. "Consumer data will be the biggest differentiator in the next two to three years. Whoever unlocks the reams of data and uses it strategically will win."

But harnessing and making sense of all this data is easier said than done. For decades, companies have made decisions based on data they've gathered from their own transactions and stored in relational databases. When a company designs its own databases, the information is organized and structured. However, the flood of data from new sources, most of which are external, is much less structured and often incompatible with a given company's own data systems. For example, how do you store a photo, a sound bite, a video clip, or a Facebook status update in a way that it can be combined with other data and mined for useful insights?

Most companies are simply overwhelmed by big data. In fact, only a small fraction of today's data is analyzed. It's challenging enough to get up to speed with data as it exists today, much less prepare for the increases in tomorrow's data flows. Companies need guidance from experts who can do most of the heavy lifting in gathering and making sense of all that information. They desperately need help in gleaning big data insights that will put them ahead of the competition in making decisions that will win with consumers, vendors, and partners.

Oracle to the Rescue

That's where Oracle comes in. Oracle has specialized in computer hardware and software products since 1977. Now the third-largest software maker (behind Microsoft and IBM), Oracle builds database management, resource planning, customer relationship management, and supply chain management systems. All this expertise, plus the visionary leadership of founder and CEO Larry Ellison, has moved Oracle to the forefront of gathering, organizing, and analyzing big data. Oracle claims that it "offers the broadest and most integrated portfolio of products to help you acquire and organize these diverse data sources and analyze them alongside your existing data to find new insights and capitalize on hidden relationships."

Oracle's portfolio includes software, platform (the architecture that connects software to hardware), and hardware products. According to Bob Evans, Oracle's Chief Communications Officer, "Oracle is the only tech company on Earth that has a full line at [each of these] levels." Oracle's portfolio of products is immense and includes database products that allow databases to collect, connect, integrate, and analyze. Its hardware systems include server products as well as big data appliances that are engineered to optimize all of Oracle's software products, as well as products from external sources.

With its completely integrated systems, Oracle can provide unique benefits to companies that other big data companies simply can't match. In the oil, gas, and mining industries, new machine-to-machine devices are being used to track exactly what's going into and coming out of each mine, reducing losses and maximizing profits. In the transportation industry, devices in shipping containers can monitor a shipment throughout its journey, keeping track of things like temperature, humidity, and even whether or not the container has been opened. And in the mobile services industry, virtual wallet services that let people pay for transactions with their phones are expanding rapidly and putting the capability in smartphones as well as traditional-feature phones. Oracle is at work in each of these situations, with expertise that lets clients gather and transmit data from enabled devices to systems that analyze the data in ways that provide better customer outcomes and maximize profits.

As an indication of Oracle's big data leadership and innovation, many of the products the company is now introducing to handle big data were designed well before terms such as *cloud computing* or even *big data* were being used. For example, the design of Oracle's Fusion applications—software suites designed to handle data management across corporate areas ranging from supply chain to human resources to customer relationship management—began in 2004. And Oracle began developing its most recent database product in 2007. Yet both of these product lines are optimized for the cloud, and both can be used on-site or over the Internet.

As another example of visionary development, Oracle's software-based enterprise applications have built-in social media capabilities. According to Abhay Parasnis, senior vice-president of Oracle Public Cloud, "Oracle's social relationship management capabilities bring social into everything and can light up our core large object applications with social capabilities." No other company has even attempted to do this, and it puts Oracle on the leading edge of pushing the industry to deliver the customer value benefits of social media.

Fighting for a Piece of the Pie

The recent developments in big data have sparked a frenzy of competitive activity. Large competitors such as Microsoft, IBM, and Dell are all grabbing for a piece of the big data pie, and a deluge of start-ups such as Hadapt, Precog, and Platfora are joining the fray. Oracle threw fuel on the fire with the recent release of its Sparc T5 server series. Oracle CEO Larry Ellison framed the advantages of the Sparc line this way: "You can go faster, but only if you're willing to pay 80 percent less than what IBM charges."

Facing Oracle's new line of faster and cheaper products, Colin Parris, general manager for IBM's Power systems, quickly downplayed the advantages of faster machines. He suggested that the race for faster processors is a thing of the past. Instead, today's companies are much more concerned about reliability, security, and cost effectiveness. But considering how fast the big data world is moving, the speed advantage has real world applications for executives who want to accelerate internal operations, make better decisions, and engage customers more intimately. When processes that formerly took weeks can be accomplished in just days, it provides a competitive advantage in numerous ways.

Despite Oracle's apparent sizable lead in the race to dominate big data, the data giant faces challenges. For starters, many companies large and small are finding that they can fulfill their big data needs more efficiently by using cheap hardware and open-source software. For example, years ago when Google faced the problem of indexing the Internet for its search engine, it built a huge database system comprised of cheap hardware and internally developed software that got the job done. And Google isn't alone.

Additionally, in the past eight quarters, Oracle has missed its financial goals three times. That's hard for Wall Street to swallow. Although big data represents only a portion of Oracle's overall business, many analysts observe that many of the big innovations are happening at smaller, more nimble companies. Thus, many talented employees are jumping ship from the big developers, leaving the likes of Oracle with high turnover and less innovative minds.

So although Oracle has the expertise and products to tackle today's big data needs, it also has its work cut out for it. However, even as the young and nimble start-ups nip at Oracle's heels and the other big dogs fight for positions on the big data porch, there is little question that no other single company is better poised to help companies use big data to optimize marketing opportunities.

Questions for Discussion

4-18 Discuss ways that Oracle could provide client customers with the ability to form better relationships with customers.

4-19 Discuss the similarities and differences between big data and the more traditional marketing research concepts found in Chapter 4.

4-20 Does competition from small start-ups really pose a big competitive threat to Oracle? Explain why or why not.

4-21 From a consumer point of view, what are some of the downsides to the developments in big data?

4-22 In the future, will consumers be more concerned about these downsides or less?

Sources: Steve Banker, "President of Oracle Speaks on Big Data at Oracle Supply Chain Conference," *Forbes*, February 10, 2014, www.forbes.com/sites/stevebanker/2014/02/10/president-of-oracle-speaks-on-big-data-at-oracle-supply-chain-conference/; Jessica Twentyman, "Data Can Be Source of Power," *Financial Times*, January 28, 2014, www.ft.com/intl/cms/s/0/89bad71c-81c5-11e3-87d5-00144feab7de.html#axzz2ttwQLNJr; Bob Evans, "Larry Ellison Doesn't Get the Cloud," *Forbes*, October 9, 2012, www.forbes.com/sites/oracle/2013/04/02/big-data-performance-speed-cost/; Bob Evans, "You Can Get a Chip Slower than the New Sparc T5, You Just Have to Pay More," *Forbes*, April 2, 2013, www.forbes.com/sites/oracle/2013/04/02/big-data-performance-speed-cost/; Tiernan Ray, "Internet of Things: Mammoth Morgan Stanley Note Tries To Explain It," *Barron's*, September 26, 2013, http://blogs.barrons.com/techtraderdaily/2013/09/26/internet-of-things-mammoth-morgan-stanley-note-tries-to-explain-it/; and www.oracle.com/us/technologies/big-data/index.html, accessed September 2014.

MyMarketingLab

Go to **mymktlab.com** for the following Assisted-graded writing questions:

4-23 What is neuromarketing and how is it useful in marketing research? Why is this research approach usually used with other approaches? (AACSB: Communication)

4-24 What are the similarities and differences when conducting research in another country versus the domestic market? (AACSB: Communication)

References

1. Based on information found in Karen Robinson-Jacobs, "Soda Sales Fall for Eight Straight Years, Posting Biggest Drop Since 2009," *Biz Beat Blog,* March 25, 2013, http://bizbeatblog.dallasnews.com/2013/03/soda-sales-fall-for-eighth-straight-year-see-biggest-drop-since-2009.html/; Natalie Zmuda, "Pepsi Tackles Identity Crisis after Fielding Biggest Consumer-Research Push in Decades," *Advertising Age*, May 7, 2012, pp. 1, 14; Natalie Zmuda, "Pepsi Debuts First Global Campaign," *Advertising Age*, April 30, 2012, http://adage.com/article/print/234379; Ravi Balakrishnan, "Is the 'Right Here Right Now' Campaign a Game Changer for Pepsi?" *The Economic Times (Online),* February 6, 2012, http://articles.economictimes.indiatimes.com/2013-02-06/news/36949962_1_homi-battiwalla-pepsico-india-surjo-dutt; Natalie Zmuda, "Pepsi Puts the Public in Super Bowl Spot," *Advertising Age,* January 7, 2013, p. 10; and "Best Global Brands 2013," *Interbrand,* www.interbrand.com/best-global-brands/2013/Pepsi, accessed February 2014.
2. See Craig Smith, "By the Numbers: 31 Amazing Pinterest Stats," *Digital Marketing Ramblings,* October 20, 2013, http://expandedramblings.com/index.php/pinterest-stats/; "Pinterest: What, Why, How, and Who?," *Just Creative,* April 24, 2012, http://justcreative.com/2012/04/24/pinterest-guide/; and Kevin Roose, "It's Time to Start Taking Pinterest Seriously," *New York Magazine,* October 24, 2013, http://nymag.com/daily/intelligencer/2013/10/time-to-start-taking-pinterest-seriously.html.
3. See "Big Data," *Wikipedia,* http://en.wikipedia.org/wiki/Big_data, accessed February 2014; and Yuyu Chen, "Marketers Still Struggle to Harness Power of Big Data," *ClickZ,* November 12, 2013, www.clickz.com/clickz/news/2303229/marketers-still-struggle-to-harness-power-of-big-data-study.
4. See Helen Leggatt, "IBM: Marketers Suffering from Data Overload," *BizReport,* October 12, 2011, www.bizreport.com/2011/10/ibm-marketers-suffering-data-overload.html#; Carey Toane, "Listening: The New Metric," *Strategy*, September 2009, p. 45; and Margarita Tartakovsky, "Overcoming Information Overload," *PsychCentral,* January 21, 2013, http://psychcentral.com/blog/archives/2013/01/21/overcoming-information-overload/.
5. See Piet Levy, "A Day with Stan Sthanunathan," *Marketing News,* February 28, 2011, pp. 11+; and "Customer Insights Analyst," http://jobs.geico.com/geico/customer-insights-analyst; accessed July 2014.
6. See www.walmartstores.com/Suppliers/248.aspx, accessed November 2014.
7. Based on information from "Macy's: 150+ Years of Customer Centricity," *Slideshare,* February 22, 2013, www.slideshare.net/imediaconnection/2013-2brandmacys; Allison Schiff, "Macy's CMO Shares Loyalty Insights at NRF Big Show," *Direct Marketing News*, January 16, 2012, www.dmnews.com/macys-cmo-shares-loyalty-insights-at-nrf-big-show/article/223344/; Emily Heitkamp, "Macy's Strategic Customer Focus: Love Your Loyals," *loyalty360,* September 19, 2013, http://loyalty360.org/resources/article/macys-strategic-customer-focus-love-your-loyals; and "Macy's Focuses on the Customer; Builds Comprehensive View Across Touch Points," Acxiom Case Study, www.acxiom.com/resources/macys-focuses-customer-builds-comprehensive-view-across-touch-points/, accessed September 2014.
8. Sheila Shayon, "MasterCard Harnesses the Power of Social with Innovative Conversation Suite," *brandchannel,* May 7, 2013, www.brandchannel.com/home/post/2013/05/07/MasterCard-Conversation-Suite-050713.aspx; Giselle Abramovich, "Inside Mastercard's Social Command Center," *Digiday,* May 9, 2013, http://digiday.com/brands/inside-mastercards-social-command-center/; and "MasterCard Conversation Suite Video," http://newsroom.mastercard.com/videos/mastercard-conversation-suite-video/, accessed September 2014.
9. Example based on information from Michal Lev-Ram, "Samsung's Road to Mobile Domination," *Fortune,* February 4, 2013, pp. 99–101; Jason Gilbert, "Samsung Mocks iPhone 5, Apple Fanboys

Again in New Galaxy S3 Commercial," *Huffington Post,* September 1, 2012, www.huffingtonpost.com/2012/09/20/samsung-mocks-iphone-5-commercial_n_1898443.html; Suzanne Vranica, "Tweets Spawn Ad Campaigns," *Wall Street Journal,* October 22, 2012, p. B5; and Shara Tibken, "Samsung Sends Spies to Uncover Apple's iPhone Line Phenom," *CNET News,* September 20, 2013, http://news.cnet.com/8301-1035_3-57603876-94.

10. See Adam Lashinsky, "The Secrets Apple Keeps," *Fortune,* February 6, 2012, pp. 85–94; and Megan Rose Dickey, "The Most Extreme Examples of Secrecy at Apple," *Business Insider,* July 22, 2013, www.businessinsider.com/the-most-extreme-examples-of-secrecy-at-apple-2013-7.

11. George Chidi, "Confessions of a Corporate Spy," *Inc.,* February 2013, pp. 72–77.

12. See http://biz.yahoo.com/ic/101/101316.html, accessed July 2014; "The Top 15 Energy Drink Brands," *Energy Fiend,* www.energyfiend.com/the-15-top-energy-drink-brands, accessed February 2014; and http://energydrink-us.redbull.com/red-bull-energy-drink, accessed September 2014.

13. For more on research firms that supply marketing information, see Jack Honomichl, "2013 Honomichl Top 50," special section, *Marketing News*, June 2013. Other information from www.nielsen.com/us/en/measurement/retail-measurement.html and http://thefuturescompany.com/what-we-do/us-yankelovich-monitor, accessed September 2014.

14. See www.iriworldwide.com/SolutionsandServices/Detail.aspx?ProductID=181, accessed September 2014.

15. E. J. Schultz, "Tapping into the Secret Town," *Advertising Age,* June 17, 2013, pp. 12–13.

16. See Jennifer Reingold, "Can P&G Make Money in Places Where People Earn $2 a Day?" *Fortune*, January 17, 2011, pp. 86–91; C. K. Prahalad, "Bottom of the Pyramid as a Source of Breakthrough Innovations," *Journal of Product Innovation Management*, January 2012, pp. 6–12; Jim Riley, "How Did P&G Reach the Top in China?" *tutor2u,* September 22, 2013, www.tutor2u.net/blog/index.php/business-studies/comments/how-did-pg-reach-the-top-in-china; and "P&G's Push into Rural China," www.youtube.com/watch?v=WvKmgP9A_5Y#t=47, accessed September 2013.

17. For more discussion of online ethnography and mobile phone tracking, see Robert V. Kozinets, "Netnography: The Marketer's Secret Weapon," March 2010, http://info.netbase.com/rs/netbase/images/Netnography_WP; http://en.wikipedia.org/wiki/Online_ethnography, accessed July 2014; and Sam Grobart, "Apple's Secret Retail Weapon Is Already in Your Pocket," *Bloomberg Businessweek,* October 16, 2013, www.businessweek.com/articles/2013-10-16/apples-secret-retail-weapon-is-already-in-your-pocket.

18. Example based on information found in "My Dinner with Lexus," *Automotive News,* November 29, 2010, http://www.autonews.com/article/20101129/RETAIL03/311299949/my-dinner-with-lexus; and "An Evening with Lexus," YouTube video, www.youtube.com/watch?v=LweS8EScADY, accessed December 2013.

19. See "Pew Internet: Health," *Pew Internet,* July 1, 2013, http://pewinternet.org/Commentary/2011/November/Pew-Internet-Health.aspx; and "Internet World Stats," www.internetworldstats.com/stats.htm, accessed November 2013.

20. For more information, see www.focusvision.com and www.youtube.com/watch?v=PG8RZl2dvNY, accessed February 2014.

21. Derek Kreindler, "Lexus Soliciting Customer Feedback with Lexus Advisory Board," August 24, 2010, *Automotive News*, www.autoguide.com/auto-news/2010/08/lexus-soliciting-customer-feedback-with-lexus-advisory-board.html; and www.lexusadvisoryboard.com, accessed February 2014.

22. For more discussion of online behavioral and social tracking and targeting, see Amit Avner, "How Social Targeting Can Lead to Discovery," *Adotas*, February 7, 2012, www.adotas.com/2012/02/how-social-targeting-can-lead-to-discovery/; Thomas Claburn, "Microsoft Finds People Want More Privacy Control," *Informationweek–Online,* January 24, 2013, www.informationweek.com/windows/security/microsoft-finds-people-want-more-privacy/240146932; Lisa M. Thomas, "We Know Where You've Been: Emerging Rules in Online Behavioral Advertising," *Computer and Internet Lawyer*, February 2013, pp. 16–19; and Somini Sengupta, "When Privacy Becomes a Business Imperative," *International New York Times,* March 3, 2013, www.nytimes.com/2013/03/04/technology/amid-do-not-track-effort-web-companies-race-to-look-privacy-friendly.html?_r=0.

23. See Clint Boulton, "Snack Maker Modernizes the Impulse Buy," *Wall Street Journal*, October 17, 2013, p. B4; Aaron Taube, "The Maker of Oreos Has Invented a Store Shelf that Spies on You While You're Shopping," *Business Insider*, October 18, 2013, www.businessinsider.com/mondelez-smart-shelf-technology-2013-10.

24. Based on information from "Time Warner Opens NYC Neuromarketing Lab," *Neuromarketing,* January 26, 2012, www.neurosciencemarketing.com/blog/articles/new-labs.htm; Amy Chozick, "These Lab Specimens Watch 3-D Television," *New York Times,* January 25, 2012, p. B3; and Sam Thielman, "Time Warner's Media Lab Knows What You Like to Watch," *Adweek,* February 4, 2013, www.adweek.com/news/technology/time-warner-s-media-lab-knows-what-you-watch-147045. Also see www.timewarnermedialab.com.

25. See Adam L. Penenberg, "NeuroFocus Uses Neuromarketing to Hack Your Brain," *Fast Company*, August 8, 2011, www.fastcompany.com/magazine/158/neuromarketing-intel-paypal; and Carmen Nobel, "Neuromarketing: Tapping into the 'Pleasure Center' of Consumers," *Forbes,* February 2, 2013, www.forbes.com/sites/hbsworkingknowledge/2013/02/01/neuromarketing-tapping-into-the-pleasure-center-of-consumers/. For other examples, see Roger Dooley, "Is Starbucks Coffee Too Cheap?" *Forbes,* October 14, 2013, www.forbes.com/sites/rogerdooley/2013/10/14/is-starbucks-coffee-too-cheap/; and "Microsoft Partners with Nielsen's NeuroFocus to Pin-Point Consumer Behavior," *Marketing,* June 2013, www.marketingmag.com.au/news/microsoft-partners-with-someone-to-do-something-with-the-brain-41575/#.UoOnSvmsh8G.

26. See "Up Next: The Weather Channel Forecasts the Business Value of Big Data," March 27, 2013, Microsoft News Center, www.microsoft.com/enterprise/en-ie/it-trends/big-data/articles/Up-Next-The-Weather-Channel-Forecasts-the-Business-Value-of-Big-Data.aspx#fbid=cx_oBHDwPyv; and Katherine Rosman, "Weather Channel Now Also Forecasts What You'll Buy," *Wall Street Journal,* August 14, 2013, http://online.wsj.com/news/articles/SB10001424127887323639704579012674092402660.

27. "1-800-Flowers.com Customer Connection Blooms with SAS Business Analytics," www.sas.com/success/1800flowers.html, accessed September 2014.

28. See www.loweslink.com and www.pensketruckleasing.com/leasing/precision/precision_features.html, accessed September 2014.

29. Based on information in Ann Zimmerman, "Small Business; Do the Research," *Wall Street Journal*, May 9, 2005, p. R3; with additional information and insights from John Tozzi, "Market Research on the Cheap," *BusinessWeek*, January 9, 2008, www.businessweek.com/smallbiz/content/jan2008/sb2008019_352779.htm; "Understanding the Basics of Small Business Market Research," *All Business,* www.allbusiness.com/marketing/market-research/2587-1.html#axzz2K8T92eOR, accessed February 2014; and www.bibbentuckers.com, accessed September 2014.

30. For some good advice on conducting market research in a small business, search "conducting market research," at www.sba.gov or see "Researching Your Market," *Entrepreneur*, www.entrepreneur.com/article/43024-1, accessed September 2014.

31. See "Top 25 Global Market Research Organizations," *Marketing News*, August 2013, p. 24; and www.nielsen.com/us/en/about-us.html and www.nielsen.com/us/en.html?worldWideSelected=true, accessed September 2014.

32. For these and other examples, see "From Tactical to Personal: Synovate's Tips for Conducting Marketing Research in Emerging Markets," *Marketing News*, April 30, 2011, pp. 20–22. Internet stats are from http://data.worldbank.org/indicator/IT.NET.USER.P2, accessed February 2014.

33. Subhash C. Jain, *International Marketing Management*, 3rd ed. (Boston: PWS-Kent, 1990), p. 338. For more discussion on international marketing research issues and solutions, see Warren J. Keegan and Mark C. Green, *Global Marketing*, 7th ed. (Upper Saddle River, NJ: Prentice Hall, 2013), pp. 170–201.

34. Based on information from Charles Duhigg, "Psst, You in Aisle 5," *New York Times,* February 19, 2012, p. MM30; and Kashmir Hill, "How Target Figured Out a Teen Girl Was Pregnant before Her Father Did," *Forbes,* February 16, 2012, www.forbes.com/sites/kashmirhill/2012/02/16/how-target-figured-out-a-teen-girl-was-pregnant-before-her-father-did/.

35. See Andrew Roberts, "In Some Stores, All Eyes Are on You," *Bloomberg Businessweek*, December 10, 2012, pp. 32–33; and "EyeSee Mannequin," www.almax-italy.com/en-US/ProgettiSpeciali/EyeSeeMannequin.aspx, accessed February 2014.

36. See Thomas Clayburn, "Microsoft Finds People Want More Privacy Control," *Informationweek–Online,* January 24, 2013, www.informationweek.com/windows/security/microsoft-finds-people-want-more-privacy/240146932; and Lee Rainie, Sara Kiesler, and Rougu Kang, "Anonymity, Privacy, and Security Online," *Pew Internet,* September 5, 2013, http://pewinternet.org/Reports/2013/Anonymity-online.aspx.

37. "ICC/ESOMAR International Code of Marketing and Social Research Practice," www.esomar.org/index.php/codes-guidelines.html, accessed September 2014. Also see "Respondent Bill of Rights," www.mra-net.org/ga/billofrights.cfm, accessed September 2014.

38. "FTC Complaint Charges Deceptive Advertising by POM Wonderful," September 27, 2010, www.ftc.gov/opa/2010/09/pom.shtm; Chris MacDonald, "Fruit Juice Ads and Sour Grapes," *Canadian Business*, July 16, 2012, p. 17; and Ashley Post, "FTC Issues Final Ruling against POM Wonderful," *Inside Counsel. Break News*, January 17, 2013; and Amanda Bronsted," POM Wonderful Fighting with Rival and FTC on Two Fronts, September 5, 2013, www.law.com/jsp/nlj/PubArticleNLJ.jsp?id=1202618143004.

39. Information at www.casro.org/?page=TheCASROCode&hhSearchTerms=%22code+and+standards%22, accessed September 2014.

5 Consumer Markets and Buyer Behavior

Chapter Preview

You've studied how marketers obtain, analyze, and use information to develop customer insights and assess marketing programs. In this chapter, we take a closer look at the most important element of the marketplace—customers. The aim of marketing is to engage consumers and affect how they think and act. To affect the *whats*, *whens*, and *hows* of buyer behavior, marketers must first understand the *whys*. In this chapter, we look at *final consumer* buying influences and processes. In the next chapter, we'll study the buyer behavior of *business customers*. You'll see that understanding buyer behavior is an essential but very difficult task.

To get a better sense of the importance of understanding consumer behavior, we begin by looking at GoPro. You may never have heard of GoPro, the small but fast-growing company that makes tiny, wearable HD video cameras. Yet few brands can match the avid enthusiasm and intense loyalty that GoPro has created in the hearts and minds of its customers. GoPro knows that, deep down, it offers much more than just durable little video cameras. More than that, it gives customers a way to share action-charged moments and emotions with friends.

GoPro: Be a HERO!

A growing army of GoPro customers—many of them extreme sports enthusiasts—are now strapping amazing little GoPro cameras to their bodies, or mounting them on anything from the front bumpers of race cars to the heels of skydiving boots, in order to capture the extreme moments of their lives and lifestyles. Then, they can't wait to share those emotion-packed GoPro moments with friends. In fact, the chances are good that you've seen many GoPro-created videos on YouTube or Facebook, or even on TV.

Maybe it's the one shot by the skier who sets off an avalanche in the Swiss Alps and escapes by parachuting off a cliff—that amateur video received 2.6 million YouTube views in nine months. Or maybe you saw the one where a seagull picks up a tourist's camera and takes off with it, capturing a bird's-eye view of a castle in Cannes, France (3 million views in seven months). Or what about the video of the mountain biker in Africa who is ambushed by a full-grown gazelle (more than 13 million views in four months)? A recent promotional video featuring five minutes of video clips captured by fans with the latest GoPro model snared more than 16 million YouTube views in only three months.

GoPro's avid customers have become evangelists for the brand. On average, they upload three new videos to YouTube every minute. In turn, the videos inspire new GoPro customers and even more video sharing. As a result, GoPro has become the world's hottest camera company. Last year, the young company sold a cool 3.8 million cameras, generating revenues of $986 million—nearly double the previous year's sales. GoPro already holds a 21.5 percent share of the digital camcorder market and an estimated 90 percent share of the wearable-camera market, and its sales are expected to double again this year.

What makes GoPro so successful? Part of the formula is the cameras themselves: GoPro cameras are marvels of modern technology, especially given their affordable starting price of only $200 to $400. At only about two inches wide and 2.21 ounces, a GoPro HD video camera looks like little more than a small gray box. But the lightweight, wearable or mountable GoPro is extremely versatile, and it packs amazing power for capturing stunning HD-quality video. A removable housing makes GoPro cameras waterproof to depths of 180 feet. And GoPro cameras are drop-proof from 3,000 feet (so claims one skydiver).

But GoPro knows that consumer behavior is driven by much more than just high-quality products with innovative features.

GoPro's runaway success comes from a deep-down understanding of what makes its customers tick. More than just selling tiny, wearable HD video cameras, GoPro helps people capture, share, and celebrate with others the most meaningful experiences in their lives.

GoPro's amazing little cameras let even the rankest video amateurs take stunning videos, giving them a way to celebrate the action-charged moments and emotions of their lives with others.
GoPro

The brand is all about what its cameras let customers *do*. GoPro users don't just want to take videos. More than that, they want to tell the stories and share the adrenaline-pumped emotions of the extreme moments in their lifestyles. "Enabling you to share your life through incredible photos and video is what we do," says GoPro. We "help people capture and share their lives' most meaningful experiences with others—to celebrate them together."

When people view a stunning GoPro video clip—like the one of New Zealand's Jed Mildon landing the first-ever BMX triple backflip captured by his helmet camera—to some degree, they experience what the subject experiences. They feel the passion and adrenaline. And when that happens, GoPro creates an emotional connection between the GoPro storyteller and the audience.

Thus, making good cameras is only the start of GoPro's success. GoPro founder Nick Woodman, himself an extreme sports junkie, talks about helping customers through four essential steps in their storytelling and emotion-sharing journeys: capture, creation, broadcast, and recognition. *Capture* is what the cameras do—shooting pictures and videos. *Creation* is the editing and production process that turns raw footage into compelling videos. *Broadcast* involves distributing the video content to an audience. *Recognition* is the payoff for the content creator. Recognition might come in the form of YouTube views or "Likes" and Shares" on Facebook. More probably, it's the enthusiastic oohs and ahs that their videos evoke from friends and family. The company's slogan sums up pretty well the consumer's deeper motivations: GoPro—Be a HERO.

So far, GoPro has focused primarily on the capture step of the overall customer storytelling experience. GoPro bills itself as the "World's Most Versatile Camera. Wear It. Mount It. Love It." It offers a seemingly endless supply of rigs, mounts, harnesses, straps, and other accessories that make GoPro cameras wearable or mountable just about anywhere. Users can strap the little cameras to their wrists or mount them on helmets. They can attach them to the tip of a snow ski, the bottom of a skateboard, or the underside of an RC helicopter. The handy little GoPro lets even the rankest video amateur capture some pretty incredible footage.

But Woodman knows that to keep growing, GoPro must broaden its offer to address the full range of customer needs and motivations—not just capture, but also creation, broadcast, and recognition. For example, on the creation side, GoPro offers free GoPro Studio software that makes it easier for users to create professional-quality videos from their GoPro content. On the broadcast side, with the GoPro app, users can view and play back photos and videos, then share their favorites with friends via e-mail, text, Instagram, Facebook, and other social media. GoPro has also partnered with YouTube to create a GoPro YouTube network offering a Wi-Fi plug-in that lets GoPro customers upload video directly from their cameras or using the mobile app. GoPro's YouTube channel long ago passed 200 million video views. As for recognition, GoPro now airs TV commercials created from the best videos submitted by customers at its Web site. GoPro's future lies in enabling and integrating the full user experience, from capturing video to sharing stories and life's emotions with others.

GoPro's rich understanding of what makes its customers tick is serving the young company well. Its enthusiastic customers are among the most loyal and engaged of any brand. For example, GoPro's Facebook fan base is more than 6.6 million and growing fast. To put that in perspective, much larger Canon USA has only 1.2 million Facebook followers; Panasonic has 253,000. Beyond uploading nearly half a million videos a year, GoPro fans interact heavily across a broad range of social media. "I think we have the most socially engaged online audience of any consumer brand in the world," claims Woodman.

All that customer engagement and enthusiasm has made GoPro the world's fastest-growing camera company. Today GoPro cameras are available in more than 35,000 stores in more than 100 countries, from small sports-enthusiast shops to REI, Best Buy, and Amazon.com. GoPro's remarkable little cameras have also spread beyond amateurs. They have become standard equipment for many professional filmmakers—whether it's the Discovery Channel or a news show team filming rescues, wildlife, and storms or the production crew of hit reality-TV shows such as *Deadliest Catch* taking pictures of underwater crab pots or the sides of ships in heavy seas. When stuntman Felix Baumgartner made his breathtaking 128,000-foot jump from the edge of space, he was wearing five GoPros. The use of GoPro equipment by professionals lends credibility that fuels even greater consumer demand.

Objective Outline

The moral of this story: Success begins with understanding customer needs and motivations. GoPro knows that it doesn't just make cameras. More than that, it enables customers to share important moments and emotions. Says Woodman: "We spent a lot of time recently thinking about, what are we really doing here? We know that our cameras are arguably the most socially networked consumer devices of our time, so it's clear we're not just building hardware." The company sums it up this way: "Dream it. Do it. Capture it with your GoPro. Capture and share your world."[1]

The GoPro story shows that factors at many levels affect consumer buying behavior. Buying behavior is never simple, yet understanding it is an essential task of marketing management. **Consumer buyer behavior** refers to the buying behavior of final consumers—individuals and households that buy goods and services for personal consumption. All of these final consumers combine to make up the **consumer market**. The American consumer market consists of more than 318 million people who consume more than $16 trillion worth of goods and services each year, making it one of the most attractive consumer markets in the world.[2]

Consumer buyer behavior
The buying behavior of final consumers—individuals and households that buy goods and services for personal consumption.

Consumer market
All the individuals and households that buy or acquire goods and services for personal consumption.

Consumers around the world vary tremendously in age, income, education level, and tastes. They also buy an incredible variety of goods and services. How these diverse consumers relate with each other and with other elements of the world around them impacts their choices among various products, services, and companies. Here we examine the fascinating array of factors that affect consumer behavior.

Author Comment | Despite the simple-looking model in Figure 5.1, understanding the *whys* of buying behavior is very difficult. Says one expert, "the mind is a whirling, swirling, jumbled mass of neurons bouncing around. . ."

Model of Consumer Behavior

Consumers make many buying decisions every day, and the buying decision is the focal point of the marketer's effort. Most large companies research consumer buying decisions in great detail to answer questions about what consumers buy, where they buy, how and how much they buy, when they buy, and why they buy. Marketers can study actual consumer purchases

FIGURE | 5.1
The Model of Buyer Behavior

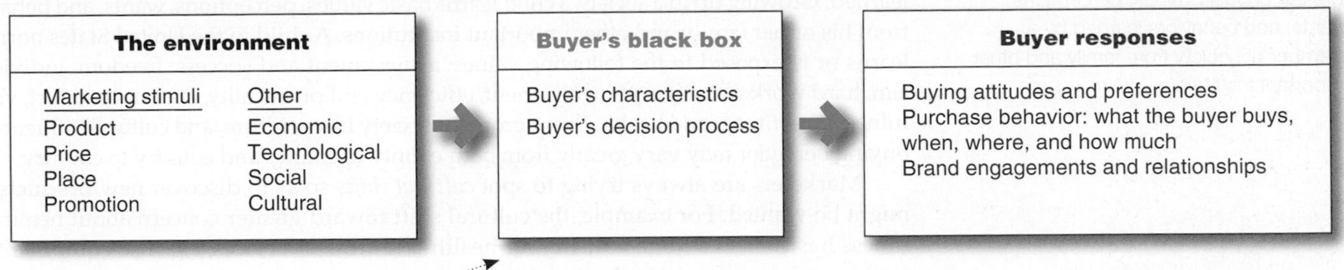

We can measure the whats, wheres, and whens of consumer buying behavior. But it's very diffcult to "see" inside the consumer's head and figure out the whys of buying behavior (that's why it's called the black box). Marketers spend a lot of time and dollars trying to figure out what makes customers tick.

to find out what they buy, where, and how much. But learning about the *whys* behind consumer buying behavior is not so easy—the answers are often locked deep within the consumer's mind. Often, consumers themselves don't know exactly what influences their purchases.

The central question for marketers is this: How do consumers respond to various marketing efforts the company might use? The starting point is the stimulus-response model of buyer behavior shown in **Figure 5.1**. This figure shows that marketing and other stimuli enter the consumer's "black box" and produce certain responses. Marketers must figure out what is in the buyer's black box.

Marketing stimuli consist of the four Ps: product, price, place, and promotion. Other stimuli include major forces and events in the buyer's environment: economic, technological, social, and cultural. All these inputs enter the buyer's black box, where they are turned into a set of buyer responses—the buyer's attitudes and preferences, brand engagements and relationships, and what he or she buys, when, where, and how much.

Marketers want to understand how the stimuli are changed into responses inside the consumer's black box, which has two parts. First, the buyer's characteristics influence how he or she perceives and reacts to the stimuli. Second, the buyer's decision process itself affects his or her behavior. We look first at buyer characteristics as they affect buyer behavior and then discuss the buyer decision process.

Author Comment | Many levels of factors affect our buying behavior—from broad cultural and social influences to motivations, beliefs, and attitudes lying deep within us. For example, why *did* you buy *that* specific phone you're carrying?

Characteristics Affecting Consumer Behavior

Consumer purchases are influenced strongly by cultural, social, personal, and psychological characteristics, as shown in **Figure 5.2**. For the most part, marketers cannot control such factors, but they must take them into account.

Cultural Factors

Cultural factors exert a broad and deep influence on consumer behavior. Marketers need to understand the role played by the buyer's *culture*, *subculture*, and *social class*.

FIGURE | 5.2
Factors Influencing Consumer Behavior

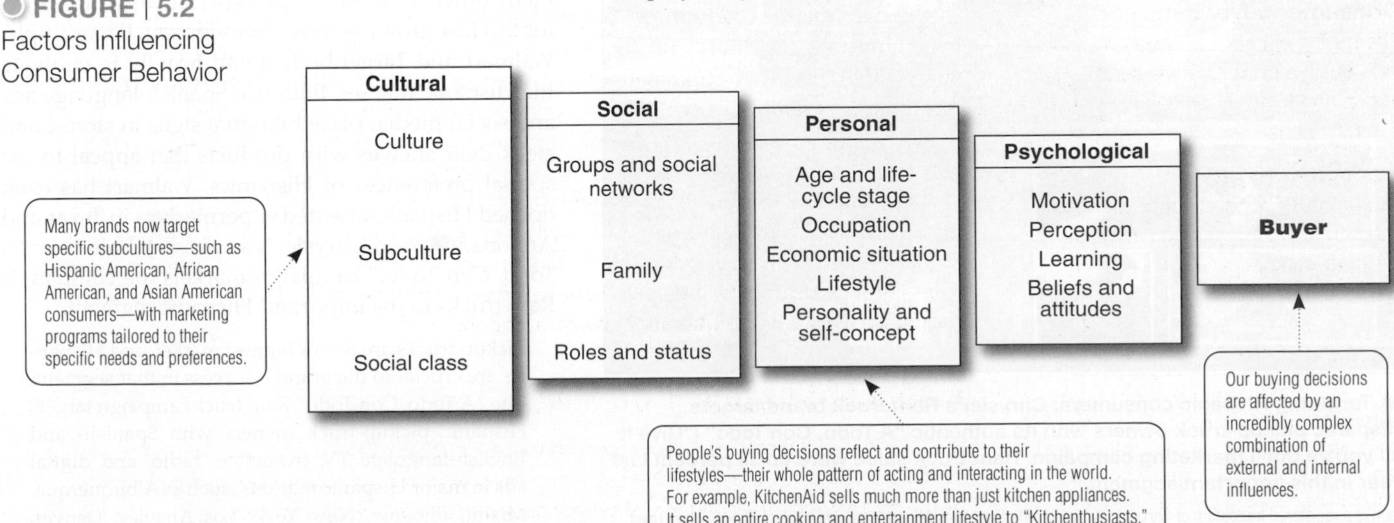

Culture

Culture
The set of basic values, perceptions, wants, and behaviors learned by a member of society from family and other important institutions.

Culture is the most basic cause of a person's wants and behavior. Human behavior is largely learned. Growing up in a society, a child learns basic values, perceptions, wants, and behaviors from his or her family and other important institutions. A child in the United States normally learns or is exposed to the following values: achievement and success, freedom, individualism, hard work, activity and involvement, efficiency and practicality, material comfort, youthfulness, and fitness and health. Every group or society has a culture, and cultural influences on buying behavior may vary greatly from both county to county and country to country.

Marketers are always trying to spot *cultural shifts* so as to discover new products that might be wanted. For example, the cultural shift toward greater concern about health and fitness has created a huge industry for health-and-fitness services, exercise equipment and clothing, organic foods, and a variety of diets.

Subculture

Subculture
A group of people with shared value systems based on common life experiences and situations.

Each culture contains smaller **subcultures**, or groups of people with shared value systems based on common life experiences and situations. Subcultures include nationalities, religions, racial groups, and geographic regions. Many subcultures make up important market segments, and marketers often design products and marketing programs tailored to their needs. Examples of three such important subculture groups are Hispanic American, African American, and Asian American consumers.

Hispanic American Consumers. Hispanics represent a large, fast-growing market. The nation's more than 55 million Hispanic consumers will have total annual buying power of $1.5 trillion by 2015, accounting for 11 percent of the nation's total buying power. The U.S. Hispanic population will surge to more than 128 million by 2060, close to one-third of the total U.S. population.[3]

Although Hispanic consumers share many characteristics and behaviors with the mainstream buying public, there are also distinct differences. They tend to be deeply family oriented and make shopping a family affair—children have a big say in what brands they buy. Older, first-generation Hispanic consumers tend to be very brand loyal and to favor brands and sellers who show special interest in them. Younger Hispanics, however, have shown increasing price sensitivity in recent years and a willingness to switch to store brands. Hispanics are more active on mobile and social networks than other segments, making digital medium ideal for reaching this segment.[4]

Within the Hispanic market, there exist many distinct subsegments based on nationality, age, income, and other factors. A company's product or message may be more relevant to one nationality over another, such as Mexicans, Costa Ricans, Argentineans, or Cubans. Companies must also vary their pitches across different Hispanic economic segments.

● Targeting Hispanic consumers: Chrysler's Ram truck brand targets Hispanic pickup-truck owners with its authentic "A Todo, Con Todo" ("Give it all you've got") marketing campaign. Ram truck sales were up 33 percent last year in this important segment.

Companies such as McDonald's, Walmart, Nestlé, State Farm, Chrysler, Verizon, Google, and many others have developed special targeting efforts for this fast-growing consumer segment. For example, Walmart and Target both spend heavily to cultivate the Hispanic market. Both use Spanish-language ads and social media, place bilingual signs in stores, and stock their shelves with products that appeal to the special preferences of Hispanics. Walmart has even opened Hispanic-oriented supermarkets in Texas and Arizona.[5] ● And Chrysler's successful three-year "A Todo, Con Todo," campaign markets the company's Ram trucks to the important Hispanic segment:[6]

> Pickup trucks are Ram's biggest market, and Hispanics are crucial to the brand's success in that segment. The "A Todo, Con Todo" Ram truck campaign targets Hispanic pickup-truck owners with Spanish- and English-language TV, magazine, radio, and digital ads in major Hispanic markets, such as Albuquerque, Miami, Phoenix, New York, Los Angeles, Denver, and numerous Texas communities. "A Todo, Con

Todo"—which translates as "To everything, with everything" (or "Give it all you've got")—appeals to authentic Hispanic values. The first ads in the series featured two Hispanic truck owners—Ascension Banuelos and Arturo Barcelo—who use their Ram trucks day in and day out for work and recreation. Banuelos manages a horse training ranch in Jacksboro, Texas, and owns a Ram 3500; Barcelo drives a Ram 1500 and owns a home-improvement construction company in Dallas. In the ads, these truck owners give unscripted, real-life testimonials about values that are important to them and how their Ram trucks fit serve values. An announcer concludes: "Finding a way to rise above, to push our limits further. The Ram 1500. Because success is not a destination, it's our journey. Ram. A Todo, Con Todo." Thanks largely to this campaign, Ram pickup truck sales to the important Hispanics segment were up 33 percent last year.

African American Consumers. The U.S. African American population is growing in affluence and sophistication. The nation's more than 42 million black consumers have more than $1 trillion of buying power. Although more price conscious than other segments, blacks are also strongly motivated by quality and selection. Brands are important.[7]

Many companies develop special products, appeals, and marketing programs for African American consumers. For example, last year Ford spent more than $15 million in African American–targeted advertising media. As just one example, it recently launched a multicultural campaign—called "Brand New"—to introduce its redesigned Ford Escape to the African American small SUV market:[8]

The campaign centers on the phrase "brand new," often used in the African American community to describe people who have tried something new or who have bettered themselves. "Brand New" also serves as an extension to the African American segment of Ford's brand-wide "Go Further" slogan. The humorous, documentary-style "Brand New" campaign creates a series of characters whose family lives are radically changed once they own an Escape. For instance, in the first commercial—aired during the finale of "The Game" on BET—the Brown family "gets all brand new" as their new Escape opens their eyes to new and exciting experiences such as kayaking, surfing, hiking, and even spelunking. Other ads introduce additional characters affected by the Brown's Ford Escape purchase, such as Stanley the gas station attendant who gets less business from the family thanks to the Escape's stingy EcoBoost feature, or Vince the Valet who loses out because the family uses the vehicle's Park Assist feature instead. The "Brand New" campaign—created by UniWorld, Ford's African American advertising agency—employs a full slate of black-oriented broadcast and print media, a campaign microsite (www.ford.com/benew), plus the Ford Escape YouTube channel and Facebook page and other social media. Ford has also created special African American campaigns for its Fusion and Focus models.

Asian American Consumers. Asian Americans are the most affluent U.S. demographic segment. A relatively well-educated and affluent segment, they now number more than 18 million, with annual buying power expected to approach $1 billion by 2017. Asian Americans are the second-fastest-growing subsegment after Hispanic Americans. And like Hispanic Americans, they are a diverse group. Chinese Americans constitute the largest group, followed by Filipinos, Asian Indians, Vietnamese, Korean Americans, and Japanese Americans. Yet, unlike Hispanics who all speak various dialects of Spanish, Asians speak many different languages. For example, ads for the 2010 U.S. Census ran in languages ranging from Japanese, Cantonese, Khmer, Korean, and Vietnamese to Thai, Cambodian, Hmong, Hinglish, and Taglish.[9]

As a group, Asian American consumers shop frequently and are the most brand conscious of all the ethnic groups. They can be fiercely brand loyal. As a result, many firms now target the Asian American market. ● AT&T learned that young Asian Americans are more than just a lucrative technology market in themselves—they also influence other consumers. So it created an innovative marketing campaign aimed at improving perceptions in this influential young segment:[10]

To raise perceptions of AT&T as an innovative and preferred brand among Asian-American youth, key influencers in its tech markets, AT&T created an engaging crowd-sourced, boy-meets-girl Web series called "Away We Happened." The low-cost series featured popular Asian youth celebrities Victor Kim and Jen Fromheadtotoe. AT&T partnered with Asian YouTube producer Wong Fu Productions to create the first episode. It then encouraged viewers to visit a Facebook app to submit their ideas for what happened next and vote on the best ideas for future episodes. The Effie-winning, six-episode series went viral, grabbing more than 13 million views over its six-week run and raising AT&T brand perceptions 50 percent among young Asian-American consumers.

● Targeting Asian American consumers: To improve perceptions among young Asian Americans, key influencers in its tech markets, AT&T created an engaging crowd-sourced, boy-meets-girl Web series called "Away We Happened."

Courtesy of AT&T Intellectual Property. Used with permission.

Cross-cultural marketing
Including ethnic themes and cross-cultural perspectives within a brand's mainstream marketing, appealing to consumer similarities across subcultural segments rather than differences.

Beyond targeting segments such as Hispanics, African Americans, and Asian Americans with specially tailored efforts, many marketers now embrace **cross-cultural marketing**—the practice of including ethnic themes and cross-cultural perspectives within their mainstream marketing. An example is a general-market commercial for Cheerios that featured an interracial family.[11] Cross-cultural marketing appeals to consumer similarities across subcultural segments rather than differences.

Many marketers are finding that insights gleaned from ethnic consumers can influence their broader markets. For example, today's youth-oriented lifestyle is influenced heavily by Hispanic and African American entertainers. So it follows that consumers expect to see many different cultures and ethnicities represented in the advertising and products they consume. For instance, McDonald's takes cues from African Americans, Hispanics, and Asians to develop menus and advertising in hopes of encouraging mainstream consumers to buy smoothies, mocha drinks, and snack wraps as avidly as they consume hip-hop and rock 'n' roll. "The ethnic consumer tends to set trends," says McDonald's chief marketing officer. "So they help set the tone for how we enter the marketplace." Thus, McDonald's might take an ad primarily geared toward African Americans and run it in general-market media. "The reality is that the new mainstream is multicultural," concludes one cross-cultural marketing expert.[12]

Social Class

Social class
Relatively permanent and ordered divisions in a society whose members share similar values, interests, and behaviors.

Almost every society has some form of social class structure. **Social classes** are society's relatively permanent and ordered divisions whose members share similar values, interests, and behaviors. Social scientists have identified the seven American social classes shown in **Figure 5.3**.

Social class is not determined by a single factor, such as income, but is measured as a combination of occupation, income, education, wealth, and other variables. In some social systems, members of different classes are reared for certain roles and cannot change their social positions. In the United States, however, the lines between social classes are not fixed and rigid; people can move to a higher social class or drop into a lower one.

Marketers are interested in social class because people within a given social class tend to exhibit similar buying behavior. Social classes show distinct product and brand

FIGURE | 5.3
The Major American Social Classes

Income Occupation Education Wealth

America's social classes show distinct brand preferences. Social class is not determined by a single factor but by a combination of all of these factors.

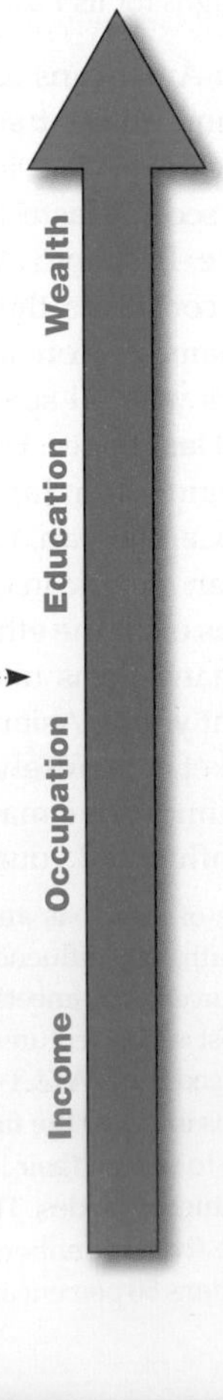

Upper Class
Upper Uppers (1 percent): The social elite who live on inherited wealth. They give large sums to charity, own more than one home, and send their children to the finest schools.

Lower Uppers (2 percent): Americans who have earned high income or wealth through exceptional ability. They are active in social and civic affairs and buy expensive homes, educations, and cars.

Middle Class
Upper Middles (12 percent): Professionals, independent businesspersons, and corporate managers who possess neither family status nor unusual wealth. They believe in education, are joiners and highly civic minded, and want the "better things in life."

Middle Class (32 percent): Average-pay white- and blue-collar workers who live on "the better side of town." They buy popular products to keep up with trends. Better living means owning a nice home in a nice neighborhood with good schools.

Working Class
Working Class (38 percent): Those who lead a "working-class lifestyle," whatever their income, school background, or job. They depend heavily on relatives for economic and emotional support, advice on purchases, and assistance in times of trouble.

Lower Class
Upper Lowers (9 percent): The working poor. Although their living standard is just above poverty, they strive toward a higher class. However, they often lack education and are poorly paid for unskilled work.

Lower Lowers (7 percent): Visibly poor, often poorly educated unskilled laborers. They are often out of work, and some depend on public assistance. They tend to live a day-to-day existence.

preferences in areas such as clothing, home furnishings, travel and leisure activity, financial services, and automobiles.

Social Factors

A consumer's behavior also is influenced by social factors, such as the consumer's *small groups*, *social networks*, *family*, and *social roles and status*.

Groups and Social Networks

Group
Two or more people who interact to accomplish individual or mutual goals.

Many small **groups** influence a person's behavior. Groups that have a direct influence and to which a person belongs are called *membership groups*. In contrast, *reference groups* serve as direct (face-to-face interactions) or indirect points of comparison or reference in forming a person's attitudes or behavior. People often are influenced by reference groups to which they do not belong. For example, an *aspirational group* is one to which the individual wishes to belong, as when a young basketball player hopes to someday emulate basketball star LeBron James and play in the NBA.

Marketers try to identify the reference groups of their target markets. Reference groups expose a person to new behaviors and lifestyles, influence the person's attitudes and self-concept, and create pressures to conform that may affect the person's product and brand choices. The importance of group influence varies across products and brands. It tends to be strongest when the product is visible to others whom the buyer respects.

Word-of-mouth influence
The impact of the personal words and recommendations of trusted friends, family, associates, and other consumers on buying behavior.

Word-of-Mouth Influence and Buzz Marketing. **Word-of-mouth influence** can have a powerful impact on consumer buying behavior. The personal words and recommendations of trusted friends, family, associates, and other consumers tend to be more credible than those coming from commercial sources, such as advertisements or salespeople. One recent study showed that 92 percent of consumers trust recommendations from friends and family above any form of advertising.[13] Most word-of-mouth influence happens naturally: Consumers start chatting about a brand they use or feel strongly about one way or the other. Often, however, rather than leaving it to chance, marketers can help to create positive conversations about their brands.

Opinion leader
A person within a reference group who, because of special skills, knowledge, personality, or other characteristics, exerts social influence on others.

Marketers of brands subjected to strong group influence must figure out how to reach **opinion leaders**—people within a reference group who, because of special skills, knowledge, personality, or other characteristics, exert social influence on others. Some experts call this group the *influentials* or *leading adopters*. When these influentials talk, consumers listen. Marketers try to identify opinion leaders for their products and direct marketing efforts toward them.

Buzz marketing involves enlisting or even creating opinion leaders to serve as "brand ambassadors" who spread the word about a company's products. For example, Nike created a ton of buzz worldwide during the 2012 London Olympics when it shod 400 of its Nike-sponsored athletes in can't-miss incandescent green/yellow Volt Flyknit shoes. The shoes became the talk of the Olympics. And pop star Lady Gaga routinely enlists her most passionate fans—she calls them the Little Monsters—to spread the word about her new music. Gaga frequently leaks snippets of unreleased songs exclusively through Little Monster networks to create advance buzz. With more than 40 million fans on Twitter and 60 million fans on Facebook, engaging these diehard fans creates a big marketplace wallop.[14]

Many companies turn everyday customers into brand evangelists. ● For instance, Philips turned users into brand ambassadors for its novel Wake-up Light lighting system:[15]

> A few years ago, Philips launched the first Wake-up Light—a bedside lighting system that simulated a natural sunrise, helping people to wake up more naturally and happily. At first, however, Philips had difficulty explaining the complex benefits of the wake-up concept to skeptical consumers. The solution: Create knowledgeable consumers advocates who could explain the product to others. Philips did this through an award-winning integrated media campaign called "Wake up the Town,"

● **Creating word of mouth: Philips' award-winning "Wake up the Town" word-of-mouth campaign created knowledgeable consumers who helped explain the benefits of its complex Wake-up Light bedside lighting system to others.**
Philips Consumer Lifestyle

in which it supplied the Wake-up Light to 200 residents in Longyearbyen, Norway—the northernmost town in the Arctic Circle. The town's 2,000 residents experience complete darkness 24 hours a day for 11 straight weeks each year. As you might imagine, waking up and starting the day in total darkness can be physically and mentally challenging. As the social experiment progressed, Philips asked consumers who used the Wake-up Light to honestly share their experiences on an interactive Web site, in blog posts, and on Facebook. Philips also arranged media interviews and posted video mini-documentaries on the site. The three-month word-of-mouth campaign paid off handsomely as potential buyers followed the stories of those using the light. Of the 200 participants in "Wake up the Town," 87 percent reported they were waking up feeling more refreshed, alert, and ready for the day; 98 percent reported that they would continue to use the Wake-up Light. During the campaign, purchase consideration in target markets in Sweden and the Netherlands grew by 17 percent and 45 percent, respectively. Unit demand grew by 29 percent.

Online social networks
Online social communities—blogs, social networking Web sites, and other online communities—where people socialize or exchange information and opinions.

Online Social Networks. Over the past several years, a new type of social interaction has exploded onto the scene—online social networking. **Online social networks** are online communities where people socialize or exchange information and opinions. Social networking communities range from blogs (Consumerist, Gizmodo, Zenhabits) and message boards (Craigslist) to social media sites (Facebook, Twitter, YouTube, Pinterest, and Foursquare) and virtual worlds (Second Life and Everquest). The new online forms of consumer-to-consumer and business-to-consumer dialog have big implications for marketers.

Marketers are working to harness the power of these new social networks and other "word-of-Web" opportunities to promote their products and build closer customer relationships. Instead of throwing more one-way commercial messages at consumers, they hope to use the Internet and mobile social networks to *interact* with consumers and become a part of their conversations and lives.

For example, Red Bull has an astounding 41 million friends on Facebook; Twitter and Facebook are the primary ways it communicates with college students. JetBlue listens in on customers on Twitter and often responds; one consumer recently tweeted "I'm getting on a JetBlue flight" and JetBlue tweeted back "You should try the smoked almonds [on board]." Dell sponsors nine blogs designed to provide "a direct exchange with Dell customers about the technology that connects us all." Even the Mayo Clinic uses social media extensively. It maintains Facebook, Flickr, and Twitter pages; a YouTube channel; smartphone patient apps that "put Mayo in your pocket wherever you are"; and a Sharing Mayo Clinic blog on which patients share their Mayo Clinic experiences and employees offer a behind-the-scenes view.

Most brands have built a comprehensive social media presence. Eco-conscious outdoor shoe and gear maker Timberland, for instance, has created an online community (http://community.timberland.com) that connects like-minded "Earthkeepers" with each other and the brand through a network that includes several Web sites, a Facebook page, a YouTube channel, Pinterest pinboards, a Bootmakers Blog, an e-mail newsletter, and several Twitter feeds. We will dig deeper into online social networks as a marketing tool in Chapter 17.

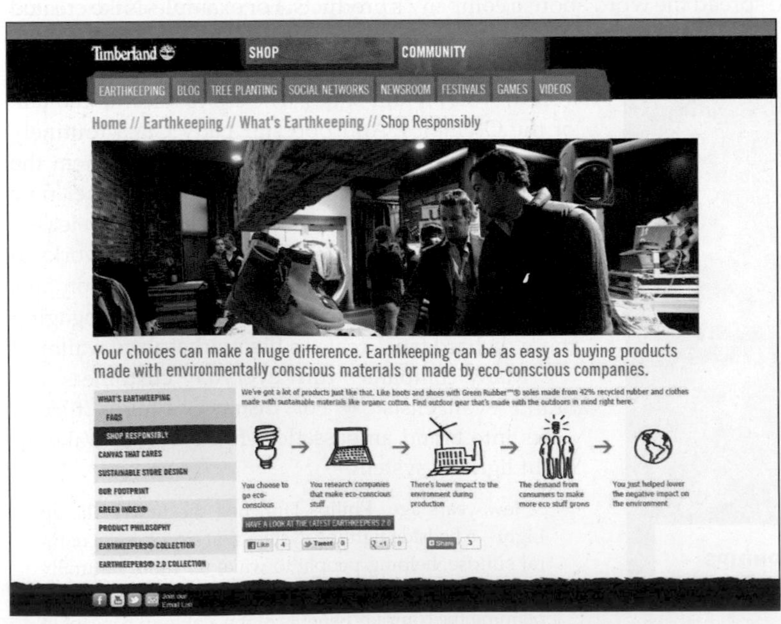
Timberland
SHOP
COMMUNITY
EARTHKEEPING BLOG TREE PLANTING SOCIAL NETWORKS NEWSROOM FESTIVALS GAMES VIDEOS
Home // Earthkeeping // What's Earthkeeping // Shop Responsibly
Your choices can make a huge difference. Earthkeeping can be as easy as buying products made with environmentally conscious materials or made by eco-conscious companies.

Using social networks: Timberland has created an extensive online community that connects like-minded "Earthkeepers" with each other and the brand through several Web sites, a Facebook page, a YouTube channel, a Bootmakers Blog, an e-mail newsletter, and several Twitter feeds.

Courtesy of Timberland

However, although much of the current talk about tapping social influence focuses on the Internet and social media, some 90 percent of brand conversations still take place the old-fashioned way—face to face.[16] So most effective word-of-mouth marketing programs begin with generating person-to-person brand conversations and integrating both offline and online social influence strategies. The goal is to create opportunities for customers to get involved with brands and then help them share their brand passions and experiences with others in both their real world and virtual social networks (see Real Marketing 5.1).

Family

Family members can strongly influence buyer behavior. The family is the most important consumer buying organization in society, and it has been researched extensively. Marketers are interested in the roles and influence of the husband, wife, and children on the purchase of different products and services.

Real Marketing 5.1

Word-of-Mouth Marketing: Sparking Brand Conversations and Helping Them Catch Fire

People love talking with others about things that make them happy—including their favorite products and brands. Say you really like JetBlue Airways—it flies with flair and gets you there at an affordable price. Or you just plain love your new little GoPro HERO3+ Black Edition video camera—it's too cool to keep to yourself. So you spread the good word about your favorite brands to anyone who will listen. In the old days, you'd have chatted up these brands with a few friends and family members. But these days, thanks to the Internet, social media, and mobile technology, anyone can share brand experiences with thousands, even millions, of other consumers digitally.

In response, marketers are now feverishly working to harness today's newfound technologies and get people interacting with each other about their brands, both online and offline. The aim is to inspire, nurture, and amplify brand conversations. Whether it entails seeding a product among high-potential consumers to get them talking, creating brand ambassadors, tapping into existing influentials and the social media, or developing conversation-provoking events and videos, the idea is to get people involved with and talking about the brand.

Generating successful word of mouth might be as simple as prompting Facebook Likes and Shares, Twitter streams, online reviews, blog commentaries, or YouTube videos. Even companies with small budgets can earn global exposure in the social media. For example, little-known start-up DollarShaveClub.com—which ships quality razors directly to customers for as little as one dollar a month—became an overnight sensation thanks largely to a single YouTube video. Founder Michael Dubin scraped together $4,500 to produce a clever video featuring himself, some corny props, a guy in a bear suit, and very salty language to pitch the new service. "Are the blades any good?" Dubin asks in the video. "No. Our blades are f***ing great," he answers. "So stop forgetting where you're going to buy your blades every month and start deciding where you're going to stack all those dollar bills I'm saving you." The edgy video went viral, and the word-of-mouth firestorm quickly earned DollarShaveClub.com more than 12 million YouTube views, 60,000 Twitter followers, 197,000 Likes on Facebook, dozens of response videos, and $10 million in venture capital funding.

But most successful social influence campaigns go well beyond a YouTube video or Facebook Likes. For example, many companies start by creating their own brand evangelists. That's what Ford did to introduce its Fiesta subcompact model in the United States. Under its now classic Fiesta Movement campaign, it handed out Fiestas to 100 young Millennial drivers—the target audience for the car—selected from 4,000 applicants. These "Fiesta Agents" lived with their cars for six months, all the while sharing their experiences via blogs, tweets, Facebook updates, and YouTube and Flickr posts. The highly successful Fiesta Movement campaign generated 58 percent pre-launch brand awareness among Fiesta's under-30 target consumers. The Fiesta ambassadors posted 50,000 items, generating 28 million social media views, 52,000 test drives, and 10,000 online vehicle reservations.

Five years later, the Fiesta Movement is still rolling. Most recently, Ford recruited 100 new Fiesta agents to create a year's worth of advertising for the 2014 Fiesta, including video clips to be used as commercials, digital ads, ads for social media such as Facebook and YouTube, and even magazine and newspaper ads. The Fiesta Movement has been so successful that Ford created similar social media evangelist campaigns for the Ford Escape ("Escape Routes") and its latest generation Ford Fusion ("Random Acts of Fusion").

Beyond creating their own ambassadors, companies looking to harness influence can work with the army of self-made influencers already plying the Internet—independent bloggers. Believe it or not, there are now almost as many people making a living as bloggers as there are lawyers. No matter what the interest area, there are probably hundreds of bloggers covering it. Moreover, research shows that 90 percent of bloggers post about their favorite and least favorite brands.

As a result, most companies try to form relationships with influential bloggers and online personalities. The key is to find bloggers who have strong networks of relevant readers, a credible voice, and a good fit with the brand. For example, companies ranging from P&G and McDonald's to Walmart work closely with influential "mommy bloggers." And you'll no doubt cross paths with the likes of climbers

Sparking word-of-mouth: Chubbies spreads its "shorts revolution" manifesto through both a booming social media presence and an army of brand face-to-face ambassadors on college campuses.

Chubbies Shorts

and skiers blogging for Patagonia, bikers blogging for Harley-Davidson, and foodies blogging for Whole Foods Market or Trader Joe's. Sometimes, bloggers and other social media mavens focus exclusively on a given brand. For example, StarbucksMelody.com is "an unofficial fan site for any and all Starbucks enthusiasts everywhere." TUAW is "The Unofficial Apple Weblog—a resource for all things Apple and beyond." Thanks to their independence, such blogs often generate more trustworthy buzz than a company's own blogs or online sites can.

Much of the word-of-mouth marketing frenzy today seems to center on creating online buzz. However, the majority of brand conversations still take place offline. According to one expert, some 90 percent of brand conversations still happen in the real world rather than the virtual one. So many marketers look beyond the digital world to create good old face-to-face brand conversations.

For example, Chubbies is a small but trendy and fast-growing start-up that targets young men with a line of "anti-cargo short shorts" (and a retro 5½-inch inseam). So far, the brand has marketed itself only through its social media presence. Avid Chubsters actively swap influence via pictures, videos, and stories on YouTube, Facebook, Twitter, Instagram, Pinterest, and the Chubbies Website and ChubsterNation blog. But now, Chubbies is building an army of face-to-face influencers, in the form of 140 student ambassadors at college campuses across the country. The ambassadors—what it calls its "thigh-liberating patriots"—spread the Chubster manifesto that "We don't do pants. We don't do cargos. We don't do capris. We do shorts and only shorts." "Pants are for work," they preach. Chubbies "are for having fun, or jumping off rocks, or playing beer pong, or climbing Everest." The ambassadors personally rally the faithful at tailgate parties and other campus events, expanding the ChubsterNation and sparking even more word-of-mouth for the irreverent brand.

Whether offline, online, or both, effective word-of-mouth marketing isn't something that just happens. And it's more than just building a following on Facebook. Marketers must build comprehensive programs that spark person-to-person brand conversations and then help them catch fire. The goal of word-of-mouth marketing is to "find and nurture true brand advocates [and to] encourage and amplify the narrative that naturally occurs," says one expert. It's about finding the company's best customers, giving them opportunities to become more involved, and helping them spread their brand passion and enthusiasm within their in-person and online social networks. "That's good advice to share with all your marketing friends and associates," advises another marketer.

Sources: Jack Neff, "Dollar Shave Club's Dubin Offers Tips for a Truly Viral Video," *Advertising Age*, July 18, 2012, http://adage.com/print/236099/; Stuart Feil, "Gift for Gab: What Marketers Are Doing to Encourage and Amplify Word-of-Mouth," *Adweek*, December 10, 2012, pp. W1–W2; Giselle Abramovich, "Why Ford Credits Social Media in Turnaround," *Digiday*, October 10, 2012, www.digiday.com/brands/why-ford-credits-social-media-in-turnaround/; Dale Buss, "Ford Restarts Fiesta Movement on Social Media with More Focus on Sales," *brandchannel*, February 19, 2013, www.brandchannel.com/home/post/2013/02/19/Ford-Fiesta-Movement-Remix-021913.aspx; Iris Mansour, "The New Face of Word-of-Mouth," *CNNMoney*, August 2013, http://management.fortune.cnn.com/2013/08/28/word-of-mouth-marketing/; Nellie Bowles, "Chubbies Shorts Popular with Troops," June 28, 2013, http://www.sfgate.com/style/article/Chubbies-shorts-popular-with-troops-4634821.php; www.chubbiesshorts.com/pages/manifesto, accessed March 2014; and www.escaperoutes.com, www.randomactsoffusion.com and www.fiestamovement.com, accessed September 2014.

Husband–wife involvement varies widely by product category and by stage in the buying process. Buying roles change with evolving consumer lifestyles. For example, in the United States, the wife traditionally has been considered the main purchasing agent for the family in the areas of food, household products, and clothing. But with more women working outside the home and the willingness of husbands to do more of the family's purchasing, all this is changing. A recent survey of men ages 18 to 64 found that 52 percent identify themselves as primary grocery shoppers in their households, and 39 percent handle most of their household's laundry. At the same time, today women outspend men three to two on new technology purchases and influence two-thirds of all new car purchases.[17]

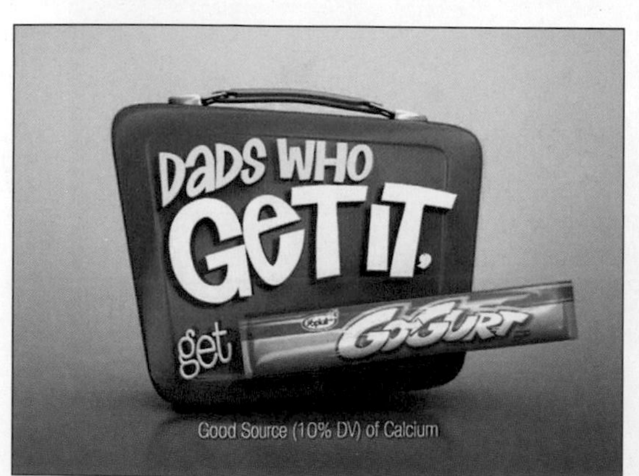

Changing family buying influences: One Go-Gurt ad shows a father packing Go-Gurt yogurt in his son's lunch as the child heads off to school. "Dads who get it, get Go-Gurt."

Used with permission of General Mills Marketing, Inc.

Such shifting roles signal a new marketing reality. Marketers in industries that have traditionally sold their products to only women or only men—from groceries and personal care products to cars and consumer electronics—are now carefully targeting the opposite sex. Other companies are showing their products in "modern family" contexts. For example, P&G's "My Tide" campaign has a commercial featuring a stay-at-home dad who does the household laundry using Tide Boost. A General Mills ad shows a father packing Go-Gurt yogurt in his son's lunch as the child heads off to school in the morning, with the slogan "Dads who get it, get Go-Gurt."

A recent ad for Samsung's Galaxy smartphone features a new dad at home swaddling a baby while mom is out running errands—with the help of his Samsung phone, of course. While holding the baby with one hand, the dad uses the Air Gesture feature to activate the phone, then requests "Hey Galaxy, search YouTube for swaddling tips." As he follows the resulting video, Smart Pause pauses the video automatically as he works through the steps. Crisis averted. When mom calls to see if there are any problems, the relieved dad reports, "No, we're having a dudes' day home. We're fiiiine."[18]

Children may also have a strong influence on family buying decisions. The nation's 36 million children ages 9 to 13 wield an estimated $43 billion in disposable income. They also influence an additional $200 billion that their families spend on them in areas such as food, clothing, entertainment, and personal care items. One study found that kids significantly influence family decisions about everything from what cars they buy to where they eat out and take vacations.[19]

Roles and Status

A person belongs to many groups—family, clubs, organizations, online communities. The person's position in each group can be defined in terms of both role and status. A role consists of the activities people are expected to perform according to the people around them. Each role carries a status reflecting the general esteem given to it by society.

People usually choose products appropriate to their roles and status. Consider the various roles a working mother plays. In her company, she may play the role of a brand manager; in her family, she plays the role of wife and mother; at her favorite sporting events, she plays the role of avid fan. As a brand manager, she will buy the kind of clothing that reflects her role and status in her company. At the game, she may wear clothing supporting her favorite team.

Personal Factors

A buyer's decisions also are influenced by personal characteristics such as the buyer's *age and life-cycle stage, occupation, economic situation, lifestyle,* and *personality and self-concept.*

Age and Life-Cycle Stage

People change the goods and services they buy over their lifetimes. Tastes in food, clothes, furniture, and recreation are often age related. Buying is also shaped by the stage of the family life cycle—the stages through which families might pass as they mature over time. Lifestage changes usually result from demographics and life-changing events—marriage, having children, purchasing a home, divorce, children going to college, changes in personal income, moving out of the house, and retirement. Marketers often define their target markets in terms of life-cycle stage and develop appropriate products and marketing plans for each stage.

One of the leading life-stage segmentation systems is the Nielsen PRIZM Lifestage Groups system. PRIZM classifies every American household into one of 66 distinct life-stage segments, which are organized into 11 major life-stage groups, based on affluence, age, and family characteristics. The classifications consider a host of demographic factors such as age, education, income, occupation, family composition, ethnicity, and housing; and behavioral and lifestyle factors, such as purchases, free-time activities, and media preferences.

The major PRIZM lifestage groups carry names such as "Striving Singles," "Midlife Success," "Young Achievers," "Sustaining Families," "Affluent Empty Nests," and "Conservative Classics," which in turn contain subgroups such as "Brite Lites, Li'l City," "Kids & Cul-de-Sacs," "Gray Power," and "Big City Blues." The "Young Achievers" group includes seven subsegments, with names like "Young Digerati," "Bohemian Mix," and "Young Influentials." The "Young Achievers" group consists of hip, single twenty-somethings who rent apartments in or close to metropolitan neighborhoods. Their incomes range from working class to well-to-do, but the entire group tends to be politically liberal, listen to alternative music, and enjoy lively nightlife.[20]

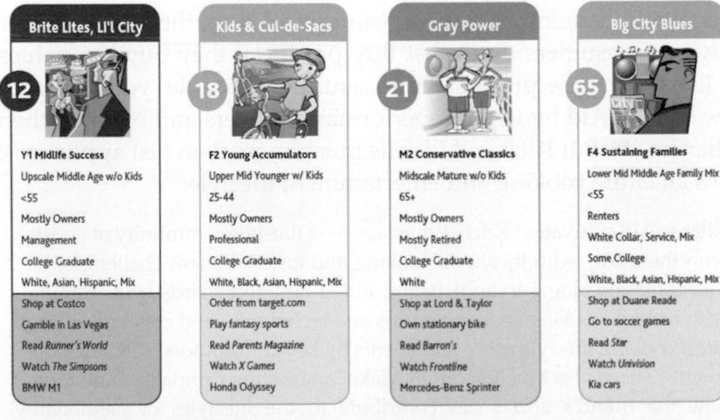

Life-stage segmentation: Nielsen's PRIZM organizes households into 66 distinct life-stage segments, with names such as "Brite Lites, Li'l City," "Kids & Cul-de-Sacs," "Gray Power," and "Big City Blues." Different life-stage segments exhibit different buying behaviors.

Different life-stage groups exhibit different buying behaviors. Life-stage segmentation provides a powerful marketing tool for marketers in all industries to better find, understand, and engage consumers. Armed with data about the makeup of consumer life stages, marketers can create actionable, personalized campaigns based on how people consume and interact with brands and the world around them.

Occupation

A person's occupation affects the goods and services bought. Blue-collar workers tend to buy more rugged work clothes, whereas executives buy more business suits. Marketers try to identify the occupational groups that have an above-average interest in their products and services. A company can even specialize in making products needed by a given occupational group.

For example, Carhartt makes rugged, durable, no-nonsense work clothes—what it calls "original equipment for the American worker. From coats to jackets, bibs to overalls . . . if the apparel carries the name Carhartt, the performance will be legendary." Its Web site has carried real-life testimonials of hard-working Carhartt customers. One electrician, battling the cold in Canada's arctic region, reported wearing Carhartt's lined Arctic bib overalls, Arctic jacket, and other clothing for more than two years without a single "popped button, ripped pocket seam, or stuck zipper." And a railroadman in northern New York, who's spent years walking rough railroad beds, climbing around trains, and switching cars in conditions ranging from extreme heat to frigid cold, called his trusty brown Carhartt jacket part of his "survival gear—like a bulletproof vest is to a policeman."[21]

Economic Situation

A person's economic situation will affect his or her store and product choices. Marketers watch trends in spending, personal income, savings, and interest rates. In today's more frugal times, most companies have taken steps to create more customer value by redesigning, repositioning, and repricing their products and services. For example, in recent years, upscale discounter Target has put more emphasis on the "Pay Less" side of its "Expect More. Pay Less." positioning promise.

Lifestyle
A person's pattern of living as expressed in his or her activities, interests, and opinions.

Similarly, in line with worldwide economic trends, smartphone makers who once offered only premium-priced phones are now offering lower-priced models for consumers both at home and in the world's emerging economies. Google's Motorola division recently unveiled an ultra-cheap Moto G phone, with most of the features offered on more expensive phones. And Apple introduced a lower-end, lower-priced version of its iPhone, the iPhone 5C. As their more affluent Western markets have become saturated and more competitive, the phone makers hope that their lower-priced phones will help them to compete effectively and grow in less-affluent emerging Eastern markets such as China and Southeast Asia.[22]

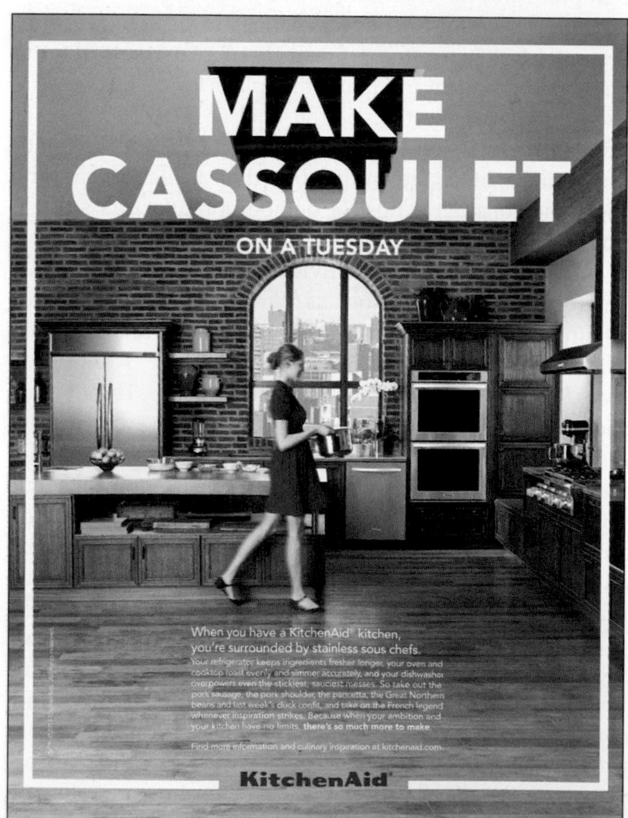

● **Lifestyles: KitchenAid sells much more than just high-performance kitchen appliances. It sells an entire cooking and entertainment lifestyle to "Kitchenthusiasts."**

Courtesy of Whirlpool Corporation. Photo © Melanie Acevedo/Stockland Martel.

Lifestyle

People coming from the same subculture, social class, and occupation may have quite different lifestyles. **Lifestyle** is a person's pattern of living as expressed in his or her psychographics. It involves measuring consumers' major AIO dimensions—activities (work, hobbies, shopping, sports, social events), interests (food, fashion, family, recreation), and opinions (about themselves, social issues, business, products). Lifestyle captures something more than the person's social class or personality. It profiles a person's whole pattern of acting and interacting in the world.

When used carefully, the lifestyle concept can help marketers understand changing consumer values and how they affect buyer behavior. Consumers don't just buy products; they buy the values and lifestyles those products represent. For example, you probably know KitchenAid by its high-performance mixers and other kitchen appliances. ● But KitchenAid sells much more than just appliances. It sells an entire cooking and entertainment lifestyle:[23]

> KitchenAid cultivates "Kitchenthusiasts"—a lifestyle community of "hosts with the most" who thrive on cooking and entertainment challenges. Its *Kitchenthusiast* blog, Facebook pages, and 11 Pinterest boards are brimming with recipes, cooking challenges, tips and techniques, and coverage of the latest cooking lifestyle news and events by key contributors. KitchenAid's recent "There's So Much More to Make" marketing campaign highlights how the brand's appliances contribute to the lifestyles of passionate Kitchenthusiasts. Says one ad: "When entertaining elates you, when every machine does incredible things, there's so much more to make."

Marketers look for lifestyle segments with needs that can be served through special products or marketing approaches. Such segments might be defined by anything from family characteristics or outdoor interests to the foods people eat. For example, fast-food chain Taco Bell recently repositioned itself as an experience brand, consistent with the lifestyles of its primary target customers, Millennials (see Real Marketing 5.2).

Personality and Self-Concept

Personality
The unique psychological characteristics that distinguish a person or group.

Each person's distinct personality influences his or her buying behavior. **Personality** refers to the unique psychological characteristics that distinguish a person or group. Personality is usually described in terms of traits such as self-confidence, dominance, sociability, autonomy, defensiveness, adaptability, and aggressiveness. Personality can be useful in analyzing consumer behavior for certain product or brand choices.

The idea is that brands also have personalities, and consumers are likely to choose brands with personalities that match their own. A *brand personality* is the specific mix of human traits that may be attributed to a particular brand. One researcher identified five brand personality traits: *sincerity* (down-to-earth, honest, wholesome, and cheerful), *excitement* (daring, spirited, imaginative, and up-to-date), *competence* (reliable, intelligent, and successful), *sophistication* (glamorous, upper class, charming), and *ruggedness* (outdoorsy and tough). "Your personality determines what you consume, what TV shows you watch, what products you buy, and [most] other decisions you make," says one consumer behavior expert.[24]

Most well-known brands are strongly associated with one particular trait: the Ford F150 with "ruggedness," Apple with "excitement," the *Washington Post* with "competence," Method with "sincerity," and Gucci with "class" and "sophistication." Hence, these brands will attract persons who are high on the same personality traits. JetBlue projects a "human" personality. Its recent "Air on the Side of Humanity" marketing campaign affirms that the airline cares about people. It's committed to award-winning customer service "for everyone, at every stage of the flying experience." The airline has been "Inspiring Humanity since 2000."[25]

Brand personality: Customers are likely to choose brands with personalities that match their own. JetBlue projects a "human" personality. It's been "inspiring humanity since 2000."
JetBlue

Many marketers use a concept related to personality—a person's *self-concept* (also called *self-image*). The idea is that people's possessions contribute to and reflect their identities—that is, "we are what we consume." Thus, to understand consumer behavior, marketers must first understand the relationship between consumer self-concept and possessions.

Psychological Factors

A person's buying choices are further influenced by four major psychological factors: *motivation, perception, learning,* and *beliefs and attitudes.*

Motivation

Motive (drive)
A need that is sufficiently pressing to direct the person to seek satisfaction of the need.

A person has many needs at any given time. Some are biological, arising from states of tension such as hunger, thirst, or discomfort. Others are psychological, arising from the need for recognition, esteem, or belonging. A need becomes a motive when it is aroused to a sufficient level of intensity. A **motive** (or **drive**) is a need that is sufficiently pressing to direct the person to seek satisfaction. Psychologists have developed theories of human motivation. Two of the most popular—the theories of Sigmund Freud and Abraham Maslow—carry quite different meanings for consumer analysis and marketing.

Sigmund Freud assumed that people are largely unconscious about the real psychological forces shaping their behavior. His theory suggests that a person's buying decisions are affected by subconscious motives that even the buyer may not fully understand. Thus, an aging baby boomer who buys a sporty BMW convertible might explain that he simply likes the feel of the wind in his thinning hair. At a deeper level, he may be trying to impress others with his success. At a still deeper level, he may be buying the car to feel young and independent again.

Real Marketing 5.2

Taco Bell: More Than Just Tacos, a "Live Más" Lifestyle

Years ago, Taco Bell practically invented the fast-food "value menu," with its "59¢–79¢–99¢" pricing structure. With slogans such as "The Cure for the Common Meal," "Make a Run for the Border," and "Think Outside the Bun," Taco Bell firmly established its affordable Mexican-inspired fare as a unique, "more-for-your-money" alternative to the mostly burgers and fries offered by dominant McDonald's and other fast-food competitors. Taco Bell grew rapidly into a $6-billion-a-year international brand.

In the early 2000s, however, consumer tastes began to change. Americans were looking for fresher, better-tasting, healthier eating options and more contemporary fast-casual atmospheres. Taco Bell's "food-as-fuel" marketing philosophy—its "fill them up, move them out" thinking—made the chain seem out of step with the times. After three straight years of flat sales, Taco Bell ended 2011 with a 1.4-percent decline in system-wide revenues. These dire results called for a shift in Taco Bell's strategy.

The shift began with the realization that customers want more from a fast-food restaurant than just lots of food on the cheap. More than "calories per dollar," they are seeking a food-eating experience, one that fits with and enhances their lifestyles. So in early 2012, Taco Bell shifted its positioning from "food as fuel" to "food as experience and lifestyle." It launched a new, innovative lifestyle marketing campaign—called "Live Más" ("más" is Spanish for "more"). Backed by a $280 million annual budget, the "Live Más" slogan is designed as a lifestyle rallying cry for Taco Bell's target customers, Millennials—young adults who consume a disproportionate share of fast and fast-casual food.

Taco Bell's aspirational "Live Más" message is crafted to inspire Millennials to try new things and to live life to the fullest. The first "Live Más" ad, called "Pockets," showed a hip, twenty-something man coming into a dim apartment as dawn breaks. He empties his pockets onto a table as he thinks back over the night he's had. Along with the standard wallet, keys, and smartphone, he tosses out a concert ticket stub, a matchbook from a 24-hour psychic, a pair of Kanji dice, and a strip of photo-booth images of himself with a young woman. The last item he pulls out is a blister pack of Taco Bell Fire Sauce, adorned with the new "Live Más" logo and the message, "You have chosen wisely." It's this last item that brings a smile to his face.

The "Live Más" lifestyle marketing campaign goes well beyond just advertising. For example, it includes new menu items aimed to please Millennial lifestyles. For example, in early 2012, Taco Bell unveiled cobranded Doritos Locos Tacos, like a standard Taco Bell taco or Taco Supreme, but wrapped in a tasty shell made from Nacho Cheese Doritos. Hungry Millennials gobbled up 100 million Doritos Locos Tacos in just the first 10 weeks, making it the most successful new-product launch in the company's 50-year history. The brand quickly added Cool Ranch and Fiery versions.

Recognizing that customers who want to "Live Más" might be looking to eat at just about any time of the day, Taco Bell is focusing on more day parts. For example, after a long absence from morning hours, Taco Bell is now rolling out a 7 A.M. to 11 A.M. breakfast menu. Options include breakfast burritos, the A.M. Cruchwrap, waffle tacos, and bite-size Cinnabon Delights. Similarly, Taco Bell's "Happier Hour" initiative targets between-meal-snack appetites from 2 P.M. to 5 P.M. daily, featuring new Mountain Dew frozen beverages and $1 Loaded Grillers. And for the late-night "Live Más" crowd, there's Fourthmeal, as in "You're out. You're hungry. You're doing Fourthmeal." In one ad—titled "After-Wedding Party"—a newlywed couple feasts on Taco Bell fare in the back of a limo, along with their groomsmen and maids-of-honor. The announcer concludes, "Fourthmeal—sometimes the best dinner is after the dinner."

To better engage targeted Millennials, Taco Bell now reaches them where they hang out—online, digital, and mobile. Befitting the Millennial lifestyle, a significant portion of the "Live Más" promotion budget goes to social media, digital tools, and other non-traditional channels. Beyond the usual Facebook, Twitter, and Pinterest, Taco Bell uses social media such as Vine, Pheed, and Snapchat for buzz-building announcements, limited-time promotions, and sneak peeks at new products. The revitalized chain watches and participates in online brand conversations with its "Fishbowl"—Taco Bell's own command center for monitoring social media and generating digital dialogue. For example, the brand achieved more 2 billion social media impressions for Cool Ranch Doritos Locos Tacos alone, before the product even launched.

Some analysts suggest that with "Live Más," Taco Bell is stretching too far beyond its core affordable fast-food positioning. "They're trying to suggest a lifestyle aspiration, but this seems an overreach for Taco Bell," says one restaurant-marketing consultant. "A tagline should embrace the DNA of the brand, which for Taco Bell is extraordinary value." Not so, says Taco Bell. Rather than abandoning the brand's "value" roots, says the company, the new tagline and other elements of the "Live Más" campaign underscore brand values dating back to its founding—"value, quality, relevance, and an exceptional experience." The "value" message still resonates in the

Taco Bell's innovative "Live más" marketing campaign targets the lifestyles of the brand's key target customers, Millennials.

Taco Bell Corp

campaign, but "Live más" also energizes the "relevance" and "experience" aspects of Taco Bell's long-standing value proposition.

The early results suggest that Taco Bell is right on track with "Live Más" and the new lifestyle positioning. The year following the introduction of the campaign, sales soared 8 percent, more than twice the gain of industry leader McDonald's. And last year, ad industry magazine *Advertising Age* named Taco Bell its Marketer of the Year, for going "into innovation overdrive, churning out a string of hot new products, game-changing menus, and an aggressive mix of traditional, social, and digital media that's hitting the mark with Millennials."

But for Taco Bell, becoming an experience and lifestyle brand isn't just about reversing sales declines and reaping marketing honors. It's about building for the future. Taco Bell recently announced plans to double its business to $14 billion by 2021, through a 40 percent increase in both number of stores and sales per store. Accomplishing that lofty objective will have both Taco Bell's customers *and* Taco Bell marketers shouting "Live Más!"

Sources: Maureen Morrison, "Sales Are Going Loco at Taco Bell, Ad Age's Marketer of the Year," *Advertising Age*, September 2, 2013, p. 2; Shirley Brady, "Taco Bell Promotes New 'Live Más' Tagline in New Campaign," *Brand Channel*, February 24, 2012, www.brandchannel.com/home/post/2012/02/24/Taco-Bell-Live-Mas-Doritos-Locos-Tacos-Spots-022412.aspx; Maureen Morrison, "Taco Bell to Exchange 'Think Outside the Bun' for 'Live Más,'" *Advertising Age*, February 21, 2012, adage.com/print/232849/; Mark Brandau, "Yum Plans to Double U.S. Taco Bell Sales," *Restaurant News*, May 22, 2013, nrn.com/quick-service/analysts-yum-plans-double-us-taco-bell-sales; Mark Brandau, "Taco Bell NBA Sponsorship to Emphasize Digital, Social Media," *Restaurant News*, October 18, 2013, nrn.com/social-media/taco-bell-nba-sponsorship-emphasize-digital-social-media; and various pages at www.tacobell.com, accessed September 2014.

The term *motivation research* refers to qualitative research designed to probe consumers' hidden, subconscious motivations. Consumers often don't know or can't describe why they act as they do. Thus, motivation researchers use a variety of probing techniques to uncover underlying emotions and attitudes toward brands and buying situations.

Many companies employ teams of psychologists, anthropologists, and other social scientists to carry out motivation research. One ad agency routinely conducts one-on-one, therapy-like interviews to delve into the inner workings of consumers. Another company asks consumers to describe their favorite brands as animals or cars (say, a Mercedes versus a Chevy) to assess the prestige associated with various brands. Still others rely on hypnosis, dream therapy, or soft lights and mood music to plumb the murky depths of consumer psyches.

Such projective techniques seem pretty goofy, and some marketers dismiss such motivation research as mumbo jumbo. But many marketers use such touchy-feely approaches, now sometimes called *interpretive consumer research,* to dig deeper into consumer psyches and develop better marketing strategies.

Abraham Maslow sought to explain why people are driven by particular needs at particular times. Why does one person spend a lot of time and energy on personal safety and another on gaining the esteem of others? Maslow's answer is that human needs are arranged in a hierarchy, as shown in **Figure 5.4**, from the most pressing at the bottom to

FIGURE | 5.4
Maslow's Hierarchy of Needs

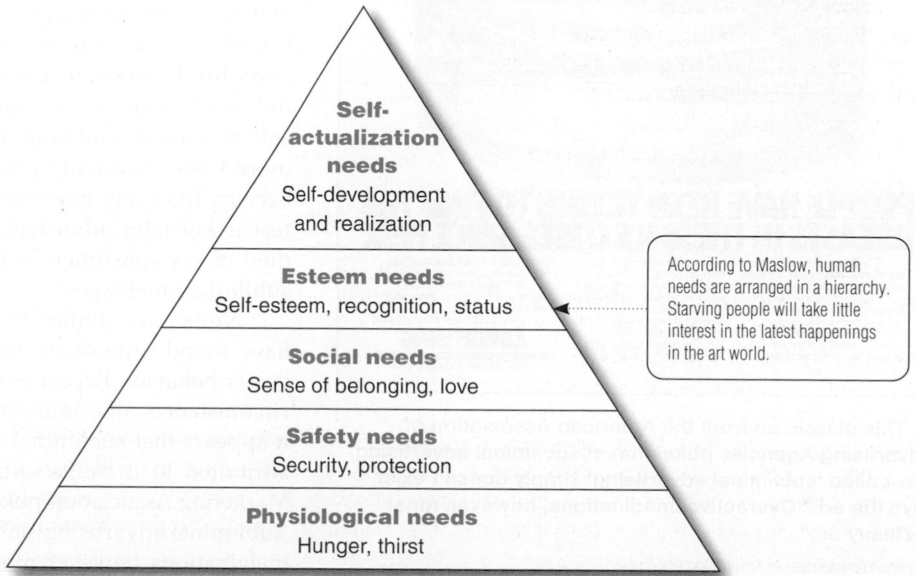

the least pressing at the top.[26] They include *physiological* needs, *safety* needs, *social* needs, *esteem* needs, and *self-actualization* needs.

A person tries to satisfy the most important need first. When that need is satisfied, it will stop being a motivator, and the person will then try to satisfy the next most important need. For example, starving people (physiological need) will not take an interest in the latest happenings in the art world (self-actualization needs) nor in how they are seen or esteemed by others (social or esteem needs) nor even in whether they are breathing clean air (safety needs). But as each important need is satisfied, the next most important need will come into play.

Perception

Perception
The process by which people select, organize, and interpret information to form a meaningful picture of the world.

A motivated person is ready to act. How the person acts is influenced by his or her own perception of the situation. All of us learn by the flow of information through our five senses: sight, hearing, smell, touch, and taste. However, each of us receives, organizes, and interprets this sensory information in an individual way. **Perception** is the process by which people select, organize, and interpret information to form a meaningful picture of the world.

People can form different perceptions of the same stimulus because of three perceptual processes: selective attention, selective distortion, and selective retention. People are exposed to a great amount of stimuli every day. For example, individuals are exposed to an estimated 3,000 to 5,000 ad messages every day. The cluttered digital environment adds 5.3 trillion online display ads shown each year, 400 million Tweets sent daily, 144,000 hours of video uploaded daily, and 4.75 billion pieces of content shared on Facebook every day.[27] It is impossible for people to pay attention to all the competing stimuli surrounding them. *Selective attention*—the tendency for people to screen out most of the information to which they are exposed—means that marketers must work especially hard to attract the consumer's attention.

Even noticed stimuli do not always come across in the intended way. Each person fits incoming information into an existing mind-set. *Selective distortion* describes the tendency of people to interpret information in a way that will support what they already believe. People also will forget much of what they learn. They tend to retain information that supports their attitudes and beliefs. *Selective retention* means that consumers are likely to remember good points made about a brand they favor and forget good points made about competing brands. Because of selective attention, distortion, and retention, marketers must work hard to get their messages through.

Interestingly, although most marketers worry about whether their offers will be perceived at all, some consumers worry that they will be affected by marketing messages without even knowing it—through *subliminal advertising*. More than 50 years ago, a researcher announced that he had flashed the phrases "Eat popcorn" and "Drink Coca-Cola" on a screen in a New Jersey movie theater every five seconds for 1/300th of a second. He reported that although viewers did not consciously recognize these messages, they absorbed them subconsciously and bought 58 percent more popcorn and 18 percent more Coke. Suddenly advertisers and consumer-protection groups became intensely interested in subliminal perception. Although the researcher later admitted to making up the data, the issue has not died. Some consumers still fear that they are being manipulated by subliminal messages.

This classic ad from the American Association of Advertising Agencies pokes fun at subliminal advertising. "So-called 'subliminal advertising' simply doesn't exist," says the ad. "Overactive imaginations, however, most certainly do."

American Association of Advertising Agencies

Numerous studies by psychologists and consumer researchers have found little or no link between subliminal messages and consumer behavior. Recent brain-wave studies have found that in certain circumstances, our brains may register subliminal messages. However, it appears that subliminal advertising simply doesn't have the power attributed to it by its critics. One classic ad from the American Marketing Association pokes fun at subliminal advertising. "So-called 'subliminal advertising' simply doesn't exist," says the ad. "Overactive imaginations, however, most certainly do."[28]

Learning
Changes in an individual's behavior arising from experience.

Learning

When people act, they learn. **Learning** describes changes in an individual's behavior arising from experience. Learning theorists say that most human behavior is learned. Learning occurs through the interplay of drives, stimuli, cues, responses, and reinforcement.

A *drive* is a strong internal stimulus that calls for action. A drive becomes a motive when it is directed toward a particular *stimulus object*. For example, a person's drive for self-actualization might motivate him or her to look into buying a camera. The consumer's response to the idea of buying a camera is conditioned by the surrounding cues. *Cues* are minor stimuli that determine when, where, and how the person responds. For example, the person might spot several camera brands in a shop window, hear of a special sale price, or discuss cameras with a friend. These are all cues that might influence a consumer's *response* to his or her interest in buying the product.

Suppose the consumer buys a Nikon camera. If the experience is rewarding, the consumer will probably use the camera more and more, and his or her response will be *reinforced*. Then the next time he or she shops for a camera, or for binoculars or some similar product, the probability is greater that he or she will buy a Nikon product. The practical significance of learning theory for marketers is that they can build up demand for a product by associating it with strong drives, using motivating cues, and providing positive reinforcement.

Belief
A descriptive thought that a person holds about something.

Attitude
A person's consistently favorable or unfavorable evaluations, feelings, and tendencies toward an object or idea.

Beliefs and Attitudes

Through doing and learning, people acquire beliefs and attitudes. These, in turn, influence their buying behavior. A **belief** is a descriptive thought that a person holds about something. Beliefs may be based on real knowledge, opinion, or faith and may or may not carry an emotional charge. Marketers are interested in the beliefs that people formulate about specific products and services because these beliefs make up product and brand images that affect buying behavior. If some of the beliefs are wrong and prevent purchase, the marketer will want to launch a campaign to correct them.

People have attitudes regarding religion, politics, clothes, music, food, and almost everything else. **Attitude** describes a person's relatively consistent evaluations, feelings, and tendencies toward an object or idea. Attitudes put people into a frame of mind of liking or disliking things, of moving toward or away from them. Our camera buyer may hold attitudes such as "Buy the best," "The Japanese make the best camera products in the world," and "Creativity and self-expression are among the most important things in life." If so, the Nikon camera would fit well into the consumer's existing attitudes.

● **Attitudes and beliefs are difficult to change; however, the Vidalia Onion Committee's award-winning Ogres and Onions campaign made believers of children and their delighted parents. Sales of bagged Vidalia onions shot up 30 percent.**

Vidalia® is a registered certification mark of Georgia Department of Agriculture

Attitudes are difficult to change. A person's attitudes fit into a pattern; changing one attitude may require difficult adjustments in many others. Thus, a company should usually try to fit its products into existing attitude patterns rather than attempt to change attitudes. Of course, there are exceptions. For example, trying to convince parents that their children would actually like onions—that's right, onions—seems like an uphill battle against prevailing attitudes. Convincing the children themselves seems like an even bigger challenge. However, the Vidalia Onion Committee (VOC), formed to promote one of Georgia's most important agricultural products, managed to do just that:[29]

> It can be hard selling children on the idea of eating onions. Onions have a strong smell, they can make you cry, and many kids simply refuse to eat them. So to help change these attitudes, the VOC developed a unique plan. ● It employed Shrek, the famous ogre from the hugely popular animated films. The inspiration came from a scene in the first Shrek film, in which Shrek explains ogres to his friend, Donkey. "Onions have layers, ogres have layers," says Shrek. "Ogres are like onions. End of story."
>
> The result was a national now-classic "Ogres and Onions" marketing campaign, launched to coincide with both the onion harvest and the premier of the latest Shrek film. The campaign featured giant Shrek placards in grocery store aisles alongside bags of Vidalia onions on which Shrek asked, "What do ogres and onions have in common?" At the Vidalia Onion Web site, Shrek offered kid-friendly Vidalia onion recipes. The award-winning campaign soon had kids clamoring for onions, and surprised and delighted parents responded. Sales of bagged Vidalia onions increased almost 30 percent for the season.

We can now appreciate the many forces acting on consumer behavior. The consumer's choice results from the complex interplay of cultural, social, personal, and psychological factors.

Author Comment | Some purchases are simple and routine, even habitual. Others are far more complex—involving extensive information gathering and evaluation—and are subject to sometimes subtle influences. For example, think of all that goes into a new car buying decision.

Types of Buying Decision Behavior

Buying behavior differs greatly for a tube of toothpaste, a smartphone, financial services, and a new car. More complex decisions usually involve more buying participants and more buyer deliberation. **Figure 5.5** shows the types of consumer buying behavior based on the degree of buyer involvement and the degree of differences among brands.

Complex Buying Behavior

Complex buying behavior
Consumer buying behavior in situations characterized by high consumer involvement in a purchase and significant perceived differences among brands.

Consumers undertake **complex buying behavior** when they are highly involved in a purchase and perceive significant differences among brands. Consumers may be highly involved when the product is expensive, risky, purchased infrequently, and highly self-expressive. Typically, the consumer has much to learn about the product category. For example, someone buying a new car might know what models, attributes, and accessories to consider or what prices to expect.

This buyer will pass through a learning process, first developing beliefs about the product, then attitudes, and then make a thoughtful purchase choice. Marketers of high-involvement products must understand the information-gathering and evaluation behavior of high-involvement consumers. They need to help buyers learn about product-class attributes and their relative importance. They need to differentiate their brand's features, perhaps by describing and illustrating the brand's benefits through printed promotional materials or in-depth online information and videos. They must motivate store salespeople and the buyer's acquaintances to influence the final brand choice.

Dissonance-Reducing Buying Behavior

Dissonance-reducing buying behavior
Consumer buying behavior in situations characterized by high involvement but few perceived differences among brands.

Dissonance-reducing buying behavior occurs when consumers are highly involved with an expensive, infrequent, or risky purchase but see little difference among brands. For example, consumers buying carpeting may face a high-involvement decision because carpeting is expensive and self-expressive. Yet buyers may consider most carpet brands in a given price range to be the same. In this case, because perceived brand differences are not large, buyers may shop around to learn what is available but buy relatively quickly. They may respond primarily to a good price or purchase convenience.

After the purchase, consumers might experience *postpurchase dissonance* (after-sale discomfort) when they notice certain disadvantages of the purchased carpet brand or hear favorable things about brands not purchased. To counter such dissonance, the marketer's after-sale communications should provide evidence and support to help consumers feel good about their brand choices.

Habitual Buying Behavior

Habitual buying behavior
Consumer buying behavior in situations characterized by low consumer involvement and few significant perceived brand differences.

Habitual buying behavior occurs under conditions of low-consumer involvement and little significant brand difference. For example, take table salt. Consumers have little involvement in this product category—they simply go to the store and reach for a brand. If they keep reaching for the same brand, it is out of habit rather than strong brand loyalty. Consumers appear to have low involvement with most low-cost, frequently purchased products.

In such cases, consumer behavior does not pass through the usual belief-attitude-behavior sequence. Consumers do not search extensively for information about the brands, evaluate brand characteristics, and make weighty decisions about which brands to buy. Because they are not highly involved with the product, consumers may not evaluate the

FIGURE | 5.5
Four Types of Buying Behavior
Source: Adapted from Henry Assael, *Consumer Behavior and Marketing Action* (Boston: Kent Publishing Company, 1987), p. 87. Used with permission of the author.

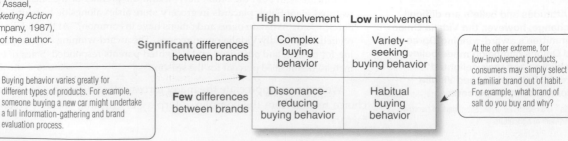

High involvement
Low involvement
Significant differences between brands
Few differences between brands
Complex buying behavior
Variety-seeking buying behavior
Dissonance-reducing buying behavior
Habitual buying behavior
Buying behavior varies greatly for different types of products. For example, someone buying a new car might undertake a full information-gathering and brand evaluation process.
At the other extreme, for low-involvement products, consumers may simply select a familiar brand out of habit. For example, what brand of salt do you buy and why?

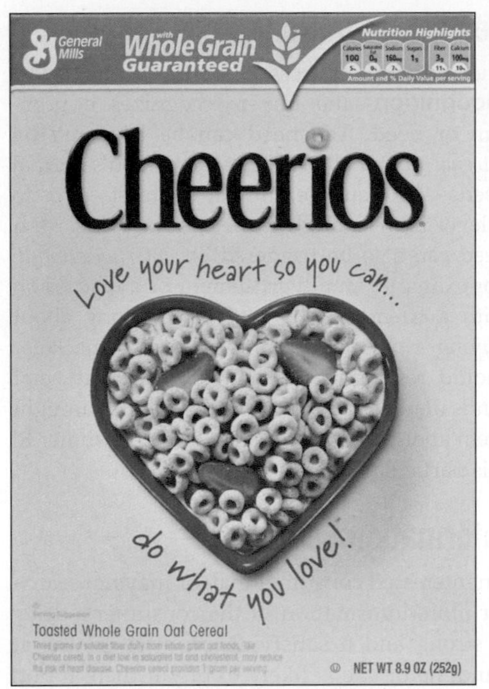
General Mills
Whole Grain Guaranteed
Nutrition Highlights
Cheerios
Love your heart so you can...
do what you love!
Toasted Whole Grain Oat Cereal
NET WT 8.9 OZ (252g)

To raise involvement, General Mills links its Cheerios brand to heart-healthy benefits. Cheerios tells consumers, "Love your heart so you can do what you love."

© Michael Neelon/Alamy

choice, even after purchase. Thus, the buying process involves brand beliefs formed by passive learning, followed by purchase behavior, which may or may not be followed by evaluation.

Because buyers are not highly committed to any brands, marketers of low-involvement products with few brand differences often use price and sales promotions to promote buying. Alternatively, they can add product features or enhancements to differentiate their brands from the rest of the pack and raise involvement. For example, take something as seemingly uncomplicated as breakfast cereal. To set its Cheerios brand apart, General Mills offers 16 different versions of the popular cereal, from regular, Multi Grain, and Honey Nut Cheerios to Apple Cinnamon, Fruity, and even Chocolate Cheerios. It also links Cheerios—originally called "Cheerioats"—to heart-healthy benefits, claiming that the brand is the only ready-to-eat cereal clinically proven to help lower "bad" cholesterol levels when eaten as part of a diet low in saturated fat and cholesterol. Cheerios tells consumers to "Love your heart so you can do what you love."

Variety-Seeking Buying Behavior

Consumers undertake **variety-seeking buying behavior** in situations characterized by low consumer involvement but significant perceived brand differences. In such cases, consumers often do a lot of brand switching. For example, when buying cookies, a consumer may hold some beliefs, choose a cookie brand without much evaluation, and then evaluate that brand during consumption. But the next time, the consumer might pick another brand out of boredom or simply to try something different. Brand switching occurs for the sake of variety rather than because of dissatisfaction.

Variety-seeking buying behavior
Consumer buying behavior in situations characterized by low consumer involvement but significant perceived brand differences.

In such product categories, the marketing strategy may differ for the market leader and minor brands. The market leader will try to encourage habitual buying behavior by dominating shelf space, keeping shelves fully stocked, and running frequent reminder advertising. Challenger firms will encourage variety seeking by offering lower prices, special deals, coupons, free samples, and advertising that presents reasons for trying something new.

Author Comment The actual purchase decision is part of a much larger buying process—starting with recognizing a need through how you feel after making the purchase. Marketers want to be involved throughout the entire buyer decision process.

The Buyer Decision Process

Now that we have looked at the influences that affect buyers, we are ready to look at how consumers make buying decisions. **Figure 5.6** shows that the buyer decision process consists of five stages: *need recognition, information search, evaluation of alternatives*, the *purchase decision*, and *postpurchase behavior*. Clearly, the buying process starts long before the actual purchase and continues long after. Marketers need to focus on the entire buying process rather than on the purchase decision only.

Figure 5.6 suggests that consumers pass through all five stages with every purchase in a considered way. But buyers may pass quickly or slowly through the buying decision process. And in more routine purchases, consumers often skip or reverse some of the stages. Much depends on the nature of the buyer, the product, and the buying situation. A woman buying her regular brand of toothpaste would recognize the need and go right to the purchase decision, skipping information search and evaluation. However, we use the model in Figure 5.6 because it shows all the considerations that arise when a consumer faces a new and complex purchase situation.

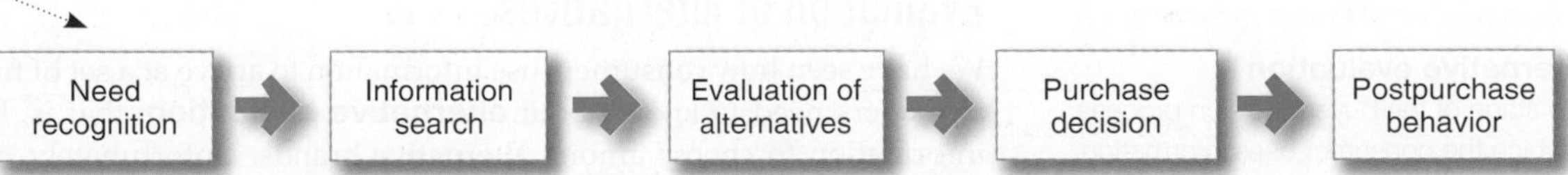
The buying process starts long before the actual purchase and continues long after. In fact, it might result in a decision not to buy. Therefore, marketers must focus on the entire buying process, not just the purchase decision.
Need recognition
Information search
Evaluation of alternatives
Purchase decision
Postpurchase behavior

FIGURE | 5.6
Buyer Decision Process

Need Recognition

The buying process starts with **need recognition**—the buyer recognizes a problem or need. The need can be triggered by *internal stimuli* when one of the person's normal needs—for example, hunger or thirst—rises to a level high enough to become a drive. A need can also be triggered by *external stimuli*. For example, an advertisement or a discussion with a friend might get you thinking about buying a new car. At this stage, the marketer should research consumers to find out what kinds of needs or problems arise, what brought them about, and how they led the consumer to this particular product.

Need recognition: This ad for National Geographic Kids reminds parents that, in these days of game consoles and social networking sites, they need to be certain that their children "make room for nature."

Courtesy National Geographic Society, Fox P2 Advertising, and Lung Animation.

Need recognition
The first stage of the buyer decision process, in which the consumer recognizes a problem or need.

Information search
The stage of the buyer decision process in which the consumer is motivated to search for more information.

Information Search

An interested consumer may or may not search for more information. If the consumer's drive is strong and a satisfying product is near at hand, he or she is likely to buy it then. If not, the consumer may store the need in memory or undertake an **information search** related to the need. For example, once you've decided you need a new car, at the least, you will probably pay more attention to car ads, cars owned by friends, and car conversations. Or you may actively search online, talk with friends, and gather information in other ways.

Consumers can obtain information from any of several sources. These include *personal sources* (family, friends, neighbors, acquaintances), *commercial sources* (advertising, salespeople, dealer and manufacturer Web and mobile sites, packaging, displays), *public sources* (mass media, consumer rating organizations, social media, online searches and peer reviews), and *experiential sources* (examining and using the product). The relative influence of these information sources varies with the product and the buyer.

Traditionally, consumers have received the most information about a product from commercial sources—those controlled by the marketer. The most effective sources, however, tend to be personal. Commercial sources normally *inform* the buyer, but personal sources *legitimize* or *evaluate* products for the buyer. Few advertising campaigns can be as effective as a next-door neighbor leaning over the fence and raving about a wonderful experience with a product you are considering.

Increasingly, that "neighbor's fence" is a digital one. Today, consumers share product opinions, images, and experiences freely across social media. And buyers can find an abundance of user-generated reviews alongside the products they are considering at sites ranging from Amazon.com or BestBuy.com to Yelp, TripAdvisor, Epinions, and Epicurious. Although individual user reviews vary widely in quality, an entire body of reviews often provides a reliable product assessment—straight from the fingertips of people like you who've actually purchased and experienced the product.

As more information is obtained, the consumer's awareness and knowledge of the available brands and features increase. In your car information search, you may learn about several brands that are available. The information might also help you to drop certain brands from consideration. A company must design its marketing mix to make prospects aware of and knowledgeable about its brand. It should carefully identify consumers' sources of information and the importance of each source.

Evaluation of Alternatives

Alternative evaluation
The stage of the buyer decision process in which the consumer uses information to evaluate alternative brands in the choice set.

We have seen how consumers use information to arrive at a set of final brand choices. Next, marketers need to know about **alternative evaluation**, that is, how consumers process information to choose among alternative brands. Unfortunately, consumers do not use a simple and single evaluation process in all buying situations. Instead, several evaluation processes are at work.

How consumers go about evaluating purchase alternatives depends on the individual consumer and the specific buying situation. In some cases, consumers use careful calculations and logical thinking. At other times, the same consumers do little or no evaluating. Instead, they buy on impulse and rely on intuition. Sometimes consumers make buying decisions on their own; sometimes they turn to friends, online reviews, or salespeople for buying advice.

Suppose you've narrowed your car choices to three brands. And suppose that you are primarily interested in four attributes—price, style, operating economy, and performance. By this time, you've probably formed beliefs about how each brand rates on each attribute. Clearly, if one car rated best on all the attributes, the marketer could predict that you would choose it. However, the brands will no doubt vary in appeal. You might base your buying decision mostly on one attribute, and your choice would be easy to predict. If you wanted style above everything else, you would buy the car that you think has the most style. But most buyers consider several attributes, each with different importance. By knowing the importance that you assigned to each attribute, the marketer could predict and affect your car choice more reliably.

Marketers should study buyers to find out how they actually evaluate brand alternatives. If marketers know what evaluative processes go on, they can take steps to influence the buyer's decision.

Purchase Decision

Purchase decision
The buyer's decision about which brand to purchase.

In the evaluation stage, the consumer ranks brands and forms purchase intentions. Generally, the consumer's **purchase decision** will be to buy the most preferred brand, but two factors can come between the purchase *intention* and the purchase *decision*. The first factor is the *attitudes of others*. If someone important to you thinks that you should buy the lowest-priced car, then the chances of you buying a more expensive car are reduced.

The second factor is *unexpected situational factors*. The consumer may form a purchase intention based on factors such as expected income, expected price, and expected product benefits. However, unexpected events may change the purchase intention. For example, the economy might take a turn for the worse, a close competitor might drop its price, or a friend might report being disappointed in your preferred car. Thus, preferences and even purchase intentions do not always result in an actual purchase choice.

Postpurchase behavior
The stage of the buyer decision process in which consumers take further action after purchase, based on their satisfaction or dissatisfaction.

Cognitive dissonance
Buyer discomfort caused by postpurchase conflict.

Postpurchase Behavior

The marketer's job does not end when the product is bought. After purchasing the product, the consumer will either be satisfied or dissatisfied and will engage in **postpurchase behavior** of interest to the marketer. What determines whether the buyer is satisfied or dissatisfied with a purchase? The answer lies in the relationship between the *consumer's expectations* and the product's *perceived performance*. If the product falls short of expectations, the consumer is disappointed; if it meets expectations, the consumer is satisfied; if it exceeds expectations, the consumer is delighted. The larger the gap between expectations and performance, the greater the consumer's dissatisfaction. This suggests that sellers should promise only what their brands can deliver so that buyers are satisfied.

● **Postpurchase cognitive dissonance: No matter what choice they make, consumers feel at least some postpurchase dissonance for every decision.**

Stephane Bidouze/Shutterstock.com

Almost all major purchases, however, result in **cognitive dissonance**, or discomfort caused by postpurchase conflict. After the purchase, consumers are satisfied with the benefits of the chosen brand and are glad to avoid the drawbacks of the brands not bought. However, every purchase involves compromise. So consumers feel uneasy about acquiring the drawbacks of the chosen brand and about losing the benefits of the brands not purchased. ● Thus, consumers feel at least some postpurchase dissonance for every purchase.[30]

Why is it so important to satisfy the customer? Customer satisfaction is a key to building profitable relationships with consumers—to keeping and growing consumers and reaping their customer lifetime value. Satisfied customers buy a product again, talk favorably to others about the product, pay less attention to competing brands and advertising, and buy other products from the company. Many marketers go beyond merely *meeting* the expectations of customers—they aim to *delight* customers.

A dissatisfied consumer responds differently. Bad word of mouth often travels farther and faster than good word of mouth. It can quickly damage consumer attitudes about a company and its products. But companies cannot simply wait for dissatisfied customers to volunteer their complaints. Most unhappy customers never tell the company about their problems. Therefore, a company should measure customer satisfaction regularly. It should set up systems that *encourage* customers to complain. In this way, the company can learn how well it is doing and how it can improve.

New product
A good, service, or idea that is perceived by some potential customers as new.

Adoption process
The mental process through which an individual passes from first hearing about an innovation to final adoption.

By studying the overall buyer decision process, marketers may be able to find ways to help consumers move through it. For example, if consumers are not buying a new product because they do not perceive a need for it, marketing might launch advertising messages that trigger the need and show how the product solves customers' problems. If customers know about the product but are not buying because they hold unfavorable attitudes toward it, marketers must find ways to change either the product or consumer perceptions.

Author Comment | Here we look at some special considerations in *new product* buying decisions.

The Buyer Decision Process for New Products

We now look at how buyers approach the purchase of new products. A **new product** is a good, service, or idea that is perceived by some potential customers as new. It may have been around for a while, but our interest is in how consumers learn about products for the first time and make decisions on whether to adopt them. We define the **adoption process** as the mental process through which an individual passes from first learning about an innovation to final adoption. *Adoption* is the decision by an individual to become a regular user of the product.[31]

The adoption process: To help get tentative consumers over the buying decision hump, SodaStream offers sales at retail, rebates, and other buying incentives—here a $20 cash-back rebate offer.

SodaStream

Stages in the Adoption Process

Consumers go through five stages in the process of adopting a new product:

Awareness. The consumer becomes aware of the new product but lacks information about it.

Interest. The consumer seeks information about the new product.

Evaluation. The consumer considers whether trying the new product makes sense.

Trial. The consumer tries the new product on a small scale to improve his or her estimate of its value.

Adoption. The consumer decides to make full and regular use of the new product.

This model suggests that marketers should think about how to help consumers move through these stages. For example, if SodaStream finds that many consumers are evaluating its home soda makers favorably but are still tentative about buying one, it might offer sales at retail, rebates, or other price incentives that help get consumers over the decision hump.

To help car buyers past purchase-decision hurdles following the economic meltdown in 2008, Hyundai offered a unique Hyundai Assurance Plan. It promised buyers who financed or leased new Hyundais that they could return them at no cost and with no harm to their credit rating if they lost their jobs or incomes within a year. Sales of the Hyundai Sonata surged 85 percent in the month following the start of the campaign. Chevrolet offered a similar "Love It or Return It" guarantee last year to help offset the still-tight economy. The guarantee gave uncertain buyers up to 60 days to return cars that had been driven fewer than 4,000 miles and had no damage.

Individual Differences in Innovativeness

People differ greatly in their readiness to try new products. In each product area, there are "consumption pioneers" and early adopters. Other individuals adopt new products much later. People can be classified into the adopter categories shown in **Figure 5.7**.[32] As shown by the curve, after a slow start, an increasing number of people adopt the new product. As successive groups of consumers adopt the innovation, it eventually reaches its cumulative saturation level. Innovators are defined as the first 2.5 percent of buyers to adopt a new idea (those beyond two standard deviations from mean adoption time); the early adopters are the next 13.5 percent (between one and two standard deviations); and then come early mainstream, late mainstream, and lagging adopters.

The five adopter groups have differing values. *Innovators* are venturesome—they try new ideas at some risk. *Early adopters* are guided by respect—they are opinion leaders in their communities and adopt new ideas early but carefully. *Early mainstream* adopters are deliberate—although they rarely are leaders, they adopt new ideas before the average person. *Late mainstream* adopters are skeptical—they adopt an innovation only after a majority of people have tried it. Finally, *lagging adopters* are tradition bound—they are suspicious of changes and adopt the innovation only when it has become something of a tradition itself.

This adopter classification suggests that an innovating firm should research the characteristics of innovators and early adopters in their product categories and direct initial marketing efforts toward them.

Influence of Product Characteristics on Rate of Adoption

The characteristics of the new product affect its rate of adoption. Some products catch on almost overnight. For example, Apple's iPod, iPhone, and iPad flew off retailers' shelves at an astounding rate from the day they were first introduced. Others take a longer time to gain acceptance. For example, the first HDTVs were introduced in the United States in the 1990s, but the percentage of U.S. households owning a high-definition set stood at only 12 percent by 2007. By the end of 2013, HDTV penetration was more than 85 percent.[33]

Five characteristics are especially important in influencing an innovation's rate of adoption. For example, consider the characteristics of HDTV in relation to the rate of adoption:

Relative advantage. The degree to which the innovation appears superior to existing products. HDTV offers substantially improved picture quality. This accelerated its rate of adoption.

Compatibility. The degree to which the innovation fits the values and experiences of potential consumers. HDTV, for example, is highly compatible with the lifestyles of the TV-watching public. However, in the early years, HDTV was not yet compatible with programming and broadcasting systems, which slowed adoption. As high-definition programs and channels became the norm, the rate of HDTV adoption increased rapidly.

FIGURE | 5.7
Adopter Categories Based on Relative Time of Adoption of Innovations

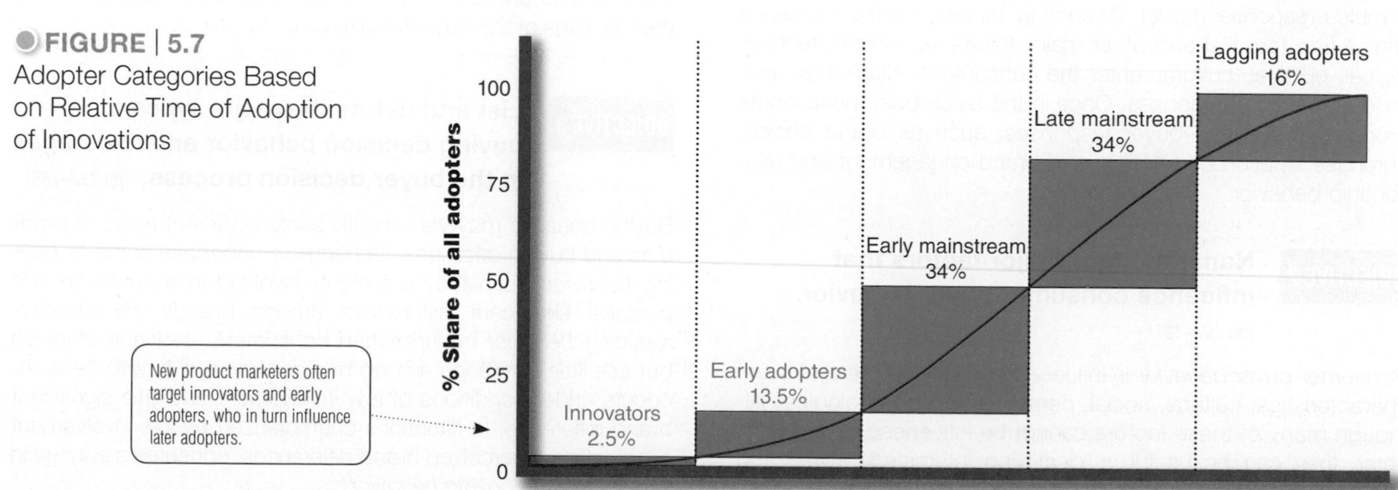

Complexity. The degree to which the innovation is difficult to understand or use. HDTVs are not very complex. Therefore, as more programming became available and prices fell, the rate of HDTV adoption increased faster than that of more complex innovations.

Divisibility. The degree to which the innovation may be tried on a limited basis. Early HDTVs and HD cable and satellite systems were very expensive, which slowed the rate of adoption. As prices fell, adoption rates increased.

Communicability. The degree to which the results of using the innovation can be observed or described to others. Because HDTV lends itself to demonstration and description, its use spread faster among consumers.

Other characteristics influence the rate of adoption, such as initial and ongoing costs, risk and uncertainty, and social approval. The new product marketer must research all these factors when developing the new product and its marketing program.

5 Reviewing the Concepts

OBJECTIVES REVIEW AND KEY TERMS

Objectives Review

The American consumer market consists of more than 317 million people who consume over $15 trillion worth of goods and services each year, making it one of the most attractive consumer markets in the world. Consumers vary greatly in terms of cultural, social, personal, and psychological makeup. Understanding how these differences affect *consumer buying behavior* is one of the biggest challenges marketers face.

Define the consumer market and construct a simple model of consumer buyer behavior. *(pp 166–167)*

The *consumer market* consists of all the individuals and households that buy or acquire goods and services for personal consumption. The simplest model of consumer buyer behavior is the stimulus-response model. According to this model, marketing stimuli (the four Ps) and other major forces (economic, technological, political, cultural) enter the consumer's "black box" and produce certain responses. Once in the black box, these inputs produce observable buyer responses, such as brand choice, purchase location and timing, and brand engagement and relationship behavior.

Name the four major factors that influence consumer buyer behavior. *(pp 167–181)*

Consumer buyer behavior is influenced by four key sets of buyer characteristics: cultural, social, personal, and psychological. Although many of these factors cannot be influenced by the marketer, they can be useful in identifying interested buyers and shaping products and appeals to serve consumer needs better. *Culture* is the most basic determinant of a person's wants and behavior. *Subcultures* are "cultures within cultures" that have distinct values and lifestyles and can be based on anything from age to ethnicity. Many companies focus their marketing programs on the special needs of certain cultural and subcultural segments, such as Hispanic American, African American, and Asian American consumers.

Social factors also influence a buyer's behavior. A person's *reference groups*—family, friends, social networks, professional associations—strongly affect product and brand choices. The buyer's age, life-cycle stage, occupation, economic circumstances, personality, and other *personal characteristics* influence his or her buying decisions. Consumer *lifestyles*—the whole pattern of acting and interacting in the world—are also an important influence on purchase decisions. Finally, consumer buying behavior is influenced by four major *psychological factors*: motivation, perception, learning, and beliefs and attitudes. Each of these factors provides a different perspective for understanding the workings of the buyer's black box.

List and define the major types of buying decision behavior and the stages in the buyer decision process. *(pp 182–186)*

Buying behavior may vary greatly across different types of products and buying decisions. Consumers undertake *complex buying behavior* when they are highly involved in a purchase and perceive significant differences among brands. *Dissonance-reducing behavior* occurs when consumers are highly involved but see little difference among brands. *Habitual buying behavior* occurs under conditions of low involvement and little significant brand difference. In situations characterized by low involvement but significant perceived brand differences, consumers engage in *variety-seeking buying behavior*.

When making a purchase, the buyer goes through a decision process consisting of *need recognition*, *information search*, *evaluation of alternatives*, *purchase decision*, and *postpurchase behavior*. The marketer's job is to understand the buyer's behavior at each stage and the influences that are operating. During *need recognition*, the consumer recognizes a problem or need that could be satisfied by a product or service in the market. Once the need is recognized, the consumer is aroused to seek more information and moves into the *information search* stage. With information in hand, the consumer proceeds to *alternative evaluation*, during which the information is used to evaluate brands in the choice set. From there, the consumer makes a *purchase decision* and actually buys the product. In the final stage of the buyer decision process, *postpurchase behavior*, the consumer takes action based on satisfaction or dissatisfaction.

OBJECTIVE 4 **Describe the adoption and diffusion process for new products.** *(pp 186–188)*

The product *adoption process* is made up of five stages: awareness, interest, evaluation, trial, and adoption. New-product marketers must think about how to help consumers move through these stages. With regard to the *diffusion process* for new products, consumers respond at different rates, depending on consumer and product characteristics. Consumers may be innovators, early adopters, early mainstream, late mainstream, or lagging adopters. Each group may require different marketing approaches. Marketers often try to bring their new products to the attention of potential early adopters, especially those who are opinion leaders. Finally, several characteristics influence the rate of adoption: relative advantage, compatibility, complexity, divisibility, and communicability.

MyMarketingLab

Go to **mymktlab.com** to complete the problems marked with this icon .

Key Terms

OBJECTIVE 1

Consumer buyer behavior (p 166)
Consumer market (p 166)

OBJECTIVE 2

Culture (p 168)
Subculture (p 168)
Cross-cultural marketing (p 170)
Social class (p 170)
Group (p 171)
Word-of-mouth influence (p 171)
Opinion leader (p 171)
Online social networks (p 172)
Lifestyle (p 176)
Personality (p 177)
Motive (drive) (p 177)
Perception (p 180)
Learning (p 181)
Belief (p 181)
Attitude (p 181)

OBJECTIVE 3

Complex buying behavior (p 182)
Dissonance-reducing buying behavior (p 182)
Habitual buying behavior (p 182)
Variety-seeking buying behavior (p 183)
Need recognition (p 184)
Information search (p 184)
Alternative evaluation (p 184)
Purchase decision (p 185)
Postpurchase behavior (p 185)
Cognitive dissonance (p 185)

OBJECTIVE 4

New product (p 186)
Adoption process (p 186)

DISCUSSION AND CRITICAL THINKING

Discussion Questions

5-1 What is subculture? Describe at least two subcultures to which you belong and identify any reference groups that might influence your consumption behavior. (AACSB: Communication; Diversity; Reflective Thinking)

5-2 Why are marketers interested in social factors such as the consumer's social roles and status, and what dimensions do they use to measure them? Describe your social factors along those dimensions and identify consumption-related activities based on your social factors. (AACSB: Communication; Reflective Thinking)

5-3 Describe the diffusion process for new products. How are consumers categorized in relation to this measure? (AACSB: Communication)

5-4 What characteristics of a new product affect its rate of adoption? How will each factor influence the rate of adoption of electric automobiles? (AACSB: Communication; Reflective Thinking)

Critical Thinking Exercises

5-5 Researchers study the role of personality on consumer purchase behavior. One research project—Beyond the Purchase—offers a range of surveys consumers can take to learn more about their own personality, in general, and their consumer personality, in particular. Register at www.beyondthepurchase.org/ and take the "Spending Habits" surveys, along with any of the other surveys that interest you. What do these surveys tell you about your general and consumer personality? Do you agree with the findings? Why or why not? (AACSB: Communication; Use of IT; Diversity; Reflective Thinking)

5-6 Malcolm Gladwell published a book entitled *The Tipping Point*. He describes the Law of the Few, Stickiness, and the Law of Context. Research these concepts and describe how understanding them helps marketers better understand and target consumers. (AACSB: Communication; Reflective Thinking)

5-7 In a small group, imagine that you are about to carry out a market research project using cameras in a general store. You will have posters stating that shoppers enter the store on the understanding that they are being observed. You are interested in how people move around the store and whether individuals from different cultures browse through products and shop in the same way. Create the poster that explains what you intend to do. You should state that for two hours per day the cameras will be switched off. (AACSB: Communication; Use of IT; Diversity; Reflective Thinking)

MINICASES AND APPLICATIONS

Online, Mobile, and Social Media Marketing **Blogvertorial**

Bloggers can be highly influential. On the one hand, we read their pieces because we value their opinions and ideas, but on the other, do we really know their motivations? In the UK, like many countries, there are strict rules about what you can and cannot claim in a conventional advertisement. However, there is a growing trend of social media and public relations agencies approaching bloggers to get them to "blogvertize" on their behalf. The agencies also insist that such bloggers make no mention of the fact that they are being paid to make positive statements about certain products and services. In the UK, under the Advertising Code, if such an arrangement came to the attention of the Advertising Standards Authority (ASA), the blogger could be subjected to investigation for having composed misleading advertising, but the blame would ultimately rest on the advertiser. The ASA clearly states that if money has changed hands, it is an advertisement and should be identified as such.

5-8 Have you encountered this type of blog posting before? Was it clear that the post was an advertisement? How might the fact that the blogger is being paid for an opinion change your view? Write a brief report of your observations. (AACSB: Use of IT; Communication; Reflective Thinking)

5-9 Are there clear rules in your country concerning blogvertorials, such as the U.S. Federal Trade Commission's disclosure rules on using social media for the promotion of products and services? If yes, can the rules help in controlling blogvertorials written in other countries? What sanctions should be imposed on those who promote blogvertorials without calling them so? (AACSB: Communication; Reflective Thinking)

Marketing Ethics **Liquid Gold**

Water is water, right? Not so! The maker of Beverly Hills 90H20 bills its "champagne of waters" as "The World's First Sommelier-Crafted Water." Champagne producers in France (the only region that can legally use the "champagne" label) were not pleased, especially since the water is sourced in California's Sierra Nevada Mountains. At $14 a bottle, this is not your everyday drinking water. The 7.5 alkalinity "silky" water is ideal for pairing with food and wine and comes in a hand-finished, triple-sealed, diamond-like bottle. It is only available in fine restaurants, gourmet markets, and luxury hotels. The 10,000 limited-edition bottles are individually numbered and decorated with custom art, making the bottle a collector's item. This isn't the first for luxury water, though, and is actually somewhat of a bargain. Fillico Beverly Hills (from Japan) costs $100 per bottle. That's without the gold or silver crown cap—you can double the price if you want that. Acqua di Cristallo Tributo a Modigliani gold-bottled water tops them all at $60,000 per bottle!

5-10 What buying factors are most likely affecting consumers who purchase luxury bottled water? (AACSB: Communication; Reflective Thinking)

5-11 Is it ethical to sell water, which is basically all the same, in a way that commands such high prices? Explain why or why not. (AACSB: Communication; Ethical Reasoning)

Marketing by the Numbers Evaluating Alternatives

One way consumers can evaluate alternatives is to identify important attributes and assess how purchase alternatives perform on those attributes. Consider the purchase of a tablet. Each attribute, such as screen size, is given a weight to reflect its level of importance to that consumer. Then the consumer evaluates each alternative on each attribute. For example, in the following table, price (weighted at 0.5) is the most important attribute for this consumer. The consumer believes that Brand C performs best on price, rating it 7 (higher ratings indicate higher performance). Brand B is perceived as performing the worst on this attribute (rating of 3). Screen size and available apps are the consumer's next most important attributes. Operating system is least important.

Attributes	Importance Weight (e)	Alternative Brands A	B	C
Screen size	0.2	4	6	2
Price	0.5	6	3	7
Operating system	0.1	5	5	4
Apps available	0.2	4	6	7

A score can be calculated for each brand by multiplying the importance weight for each attribute by the brand's score on that attribute. These weighted scores are then summed to determine the score for that brand. For example, $\text{Score}_{\text{Brand A}} = (0.2 \times 4) + (0.5 \times 6) + (0.1 \times 5) + (0.2 \times 4) = 0.8 + 3.0 + 0.5 + 0.8 = 5.1$. This consumer will select the brand with the highest score.

5-12 Calculate the scores for brands B and C. Which brand would this consumer likely choose? (AACSB: Communication; Analytic Reasoning)

5-13 Which brand is this consumer least likely to purchase? Discuss two ways the marketer of this brand can enhance consumer attitudes toward purchasing its brand. (AACSB: Communication; Reflective Thinking; Analytic Reasoning)

Video Case Goodwill Industries

Since 1902, Goodwill Industries has funded job training and placement programs through its chain of thrift stores. Although selling used clothing, furniture, and other items may not seem like big business, for Goodwill it amounts to more than $3 billion in annual sales. You might think of thrift stores as musty, low-class operations. But Goodwill is putting an end to such perceptions by focusing on consumer behavior concepts.

Like any good marketing company, Goodwill recognizes that not all customers are the same. This video demonstrates how Goodwill caters to different types of customers by recognizing the cultural, social, personal, and psychological factors that affect how customers make buying decisions. In this way, Goodwill maximizes customer value by offering the right mix of goods at unbeatable bargains.

After viewing the video featuring Goodwill, answer the following questions:

5-14 Describe different types of Goodwill customers.

5-15 Which of the four sets of factors affecting consumer behavior most strongly affects consumers' purchase decisions when shopping at Goodwill?

5-16 How does Goodwill's recognition of consumer behavior principles affect its marketing mix?

Company Case Veterinary Pet Insurance: Health Insurance for Our Furry—or Feathery—Friends

Health insurance for pets? Until recently, MetLife, Prudential, Northwestern Mutual, and most other large insurance companies haven't paid much attention to it. Instead, they've left that small piece of the insurance industry pie to more-focused niche companies. The largest of these peddlers of pet insurance (there are now 12 of them) is Veterinary Pet Insurance (VPI). And the business has become so lucrative that VPI was recently acquired by Nationwide, marking the first effort by large insurance companies to get into the business. VPI's mission is to "make the miracles of veterinary medicine affordable to all pet owners."

VPI was founded in 1980 by veterinarian Jack Stephens. He never intended to leave his practice, but his life took a dramatic turn when he visited a local grocery store and was identified by a client's daughter as "the man who killed Buffy." Stephens had euthanized the family dog two weeks earlier. He immediately began researching the possibility of creating medical pet insurance. "There is nothing more frustrating for a veterinarian than knowing that you can heal a sick patient, but the owner lacks the financial resources and instructs you to put the pet down," says Stephens. "I wanted to change that."

Pet insurance is a still-small but fast-growing segment of the insurance business. Insiders think the industry offers huge potential. Currently, 63 percent of all U.S. households own at least one pet. Collectively, Americans own some 83.3 million dogs, 95.6 million cats, and 8.3 million birds. And that doesn't include the hundreds of millions of pet fish, small animals, and reptiles. More than two-thirds have included their pets in holiday celebrations and one-third characterize their pet as a child. Some 42 percent of dogs now sleep in the same bed as their owners. Americans spend a whopping $55 billion a year on their pets, more than the gross domestic product of 121 countries in the world. They spend $14 billion of that on pet health care.

Unlike in Great Britain and Sweden, where almost half of all pet owners carry pet health insurance, relatively few pet owners in the United States now carry such coverage. However, according to recent studies, 41 percent of pet owners are at least somewhat worried they could not afford the medical bills for a sick cat or dog, and nearly 75 percent are willing to go into debt to pay for veterinary care for their furry—or feathery—companions. And for many pet medical procedures, they'd have to! If not diagnosed quickly, even a mundane ear infection in a dog can result in $1,000 worth of medical treatment. Ten days of dialysis treatment can reach $12,000 and cancer treatment as much as $40,000.

That's why Stephens started VPI. For a monthly fee ranging from $10 a month to $35 a month, VPI touts "plans for every pet and every budget." At the low end, plans cover accidents like broken bones and poisoning and carry a high deductible. The more expensive plans have a lower deductible and cover all types of diseases and conditions, even genetic issues. VPI plans help pay for office calls, prescriptions, treatments, lab fees, x-rays, surgery, and hospitalization.

Like its handful of competitors, VPI issues health insurance policies for dogs and cats. Unlike its competitors, VPI covers a menagerie of exotic pets as well. Among other critters, the Avian and Exotic Pet Plan covers birds, rabbits, ferrets, rats, guinea pigs, snakes, iguanas, chameleons, turtles, hedgehogs, and pot-bellied pigs. "There's such a vast array of pets," says a VPI executive, "and people love them. We have to respect that."

Unless you're a pet owner, you may not realize the kind of mischief pets can get into. A few years back, a VPI-insured dog got stuck in a refrigerator. While the dog chilled and waited for someone to rescue him, he took advantage of the opportunity and polished off an entire Thanksgiving ham. His owner eventually found him, complete with a licked-clean ham bone and a mild case of hypothermia that needed to be treated. In honor of this pooch, VPI began giving an award each year—appropriately called the VPI Hambone Award—to the most unusual pet insurance claim.

The first recipient of the VPI Hambone Award was an English bulldog named Lulu, who swallowed 15 baby pacifiers, a bottle cap, and a piece of a basketball. Others include Harley the pug who ate more than 100 rocks, Jojo the boxer who lost a tooth when he bit the tire of a moving delivery truck, and Peanut the dachshund-terrier mix who somehow buried himself after losing a fight with a skunk.

But perhaps Natasha, the Siberian Forest cat, presents the most harrowing survival story. Daryl Humdy of Oakland, California, arrived home just as his roommate was pulling his clothing out of the washing machine. Amongst the clothes was Natasha, shivering and crying. Apparently, while loading his laundry, the roommate went into the next room to grab more clothes, leaving the washing machine lid open. He returned, tossed in the clothes, shut the lid, and started the 35-minute cycle, detergent and all. How Natasha survived the entire wash-spin-rinse-spin process is anyone's guess. But after being treated for hypothermia and shock, Natasha was as good as new.

With stories like these happening every day, VPI is growing like a newborn puppy. VPI is by far the largest provider of pet insurance in the United States. Since its inception, VPI has issued more than one million policies, and it now serves more than 500,000 policyholders. Sales have grown rapidly, approaching $300 million in policy premiums in the coming year. That might not amount to much for the likes of MetLife, Prudential, or Northwestern Mutual, which rack up tens of billions of dollars in yearly revenues. But it's profitable business for small companies like VPI.

And there's room to grow. The cost of veterinary care has increased by an average of 6.8 percent over the past five years and will continue to increase in the future. More (and more expensive) procedures are being performed in specialties like cardiology, oncology, and ophthalmology. Even acupuncture, hospice, and writing prescriptions for medications like Prozac are part of a veterinarian's regular services. That helps explain why total pet insurance premiums in North America grew last year by 15 percent to $618 million. Yet with only about 3 percent of U.S. pet owners currently holding pet insurance policies, the potential for growth is very high. In fact, experts estimate that the North American market for pet insurance will swell to over a billion dollars.

As VPI pioneered the category of pet insurance in the United States, competitors took notice. Today, there are no less than 12 companies providing pet insurance to pet parents who want to protect the health and well-being of those they love. At one time, VPI held 95 percent of the pet insurance market. Its current share is down to just 53 percent. But with the industry experiencing double-digit growth each year, all that means is that VPI holds a smaller piece of a much larger pie. As a result, VPI's revenue growth won't be slowing down any time soon.

But VPI continues to pioneer new ways to provide for the well-being of beloved pets. For example, VPI has worked with major employers to have pet insurance added to the list of benefits from which employees can choose. Today, one out of three *Fortune* 500 companies offers VPI as a voluntary employment benefit, making VPI policies available to an astounding 67 million people. Companies like Chipotle Mexican Grill, Deloitte LLP, T-Mobile, and Wells Fargo have found this to be a fantastic incentive to pet-loving employees when it comes to recruitment and retention. Some companies cover the entire premium. All of them provide at least a discount on the cost of VPI's premiums.

Buyers who go in with their eyes only partially open may be in for some surprises when it comes to getting their claims paid. Like its competitors, VPI's policies carry limitations and exclusions, especially on the less expensive plans. Thus, there are plenty of cases where pet owners take their pets in for treatment of a disease or an accident, get sizable bills, and then find that their policies cover less than they expected. In some cases, they may find a policy doesn't cover their case at all. For example, some policies don't cover genetic illnesses. Others may cover a lifelong illness only during the year it is diagnosed. And then there are maximum benefit limitations that, at times, don't come close to covering the bills.

In such situations, customers may come away disgruntled, having paid insurance premiums for months or even years, only to find that they still have to pay a hefty vet bill. But online forums are also replete with stories like those of Lulu, JoJo, Peanut, and Natasha and from customers who feel that the insurance definitely paid off. Consider this glowing recommendation:

> I am so impressed with VPI insurance. My labrador, Jackson, has been dealing with severe allergies for years now and VPI insurance has taken care of all his needs. As he is only 4 yrs. old, when he recently herniated a disc in his back I really had no choice but to allow him to have surgery to correct the problem. If I didn't have VPI insurance it would have been an incredible financial burden. Not having to worry about the finances allowed me to concentrate on Jacksons' recovery. I am even more impressed that when renewal time came around, he was allowed to renew! I love VPI!

VPI can be a real comfort for policyholders. "I feel a lot better knowing that I have this coverage for my four-legged babies," says Carrie, another happy customer. VPI claims it will always "strive to make the miracles of modern medicine affordable." As more people become knowledgeable of VPI and share Carrie's point of view toward their pets, it's hard to think the pet insurance industry isn't just beginning to stretch its paws.

Questions for Discussion

5-17 Analyze the buyer decision process for a pet insurance customer.

5-18 Is the decision to buy pet insurance strictly an economic decision? Explain.

5-19 Explain how both positive and negative attitudes develop toward a brand like VPI. How might VPI change consumer attitudes toward the brand?

5-20 What explains the difference between pet insurance usage in the United States versus Great Britain or Sweden?

5-21 Will VPI continue to grow as it has in the past? Why or why not?

Sources: "Pets by the Numbers," January 30, 2014, www.humanesociety.org/issues/pet_overpopulation/facts/pet_ownership_statistics.html; "North American Pet Insurance Revenue Up 15%," *Packaged Facts*, November 15, 2013, www.packagedfacts.com/about/release.asp?id=3389; "Pets Are Serious Business for Marketers," *Forbes*, April 15, 2013, www.forbes.com/sites/onmarketing/2013/04/15/pets-are-serious-business-for-marketers/; "Facebook Saves Canine's Life," March 1, 2013, www.vpihamboneaward.com/nomination_year/2013/; "Lab Breaks Leg but Bounces Back from Bicycle Attack," January 1, 2013, www.vpihamboneaward.com/nomination_year/2013/; "Kitten Gets Stuck in Washing Machine, Creating Near 'Cat'astrophe," December 1, 2012, www.vpihamboneaward.com/nomination_year/2013/; "Customer Reviews," www.petinsurance.com/pet-insurance-reviews.aspx, accessed March 2014; and www.petinsurance.com, accessed March 2014.

MyMarketingLab

Go to **mymktlab.com** for the following Assisted-graded writing questions:

5-22 Define the consumer market and describe the four major set of factors that influence consumer buyer behavior. Which characteristics influenced you would attend? Are those the same characteristics that would influence you when deciding what to do on Saturday night? Explain. (AACSB: Communication; Reflective Thinking)

5-23 Explain the stages of the consumer buyer decision process and describe how you or your family went through this process to make a recent purchase. (AACSB: Communication; Reflective Thinking)

References

1. Based on information found in Tom Foster, "The GoPro Army," *Inc.*, January 26, 2012, www.inc.com/magazine/201202/the-gopro-army.html; Ryan Mac, "The Mad Billionaire behind GoPro: The World's Hottest Camera Company," *Forbes*, March 3, 2013, www.forbes.com/sites/ryanmac/2013/03/04/the-mad-billionaire-behind-gopro-the-worlds-hottest-camera-company/; Lauren Hockenson, "How GoPro Created a Billion Dollar Empire, Mashable, March 5, 2013, http://mashable.com/2013/03/05/gopro-camera/; Therese Poletti, "GoPro's Financials: A Profitable Surprise," *Marketing Watch*, May 19, 2014, www.marketwatch.com/story/gopros-financials-a-profitable-surprise-2014-05-19; and www.GoPro.com and http://gopro.com/about-us/, accessed September 2014.
2. Consumer expenditure figures from https://www.cia.gov/library/publications/the-world-factbook/geos/us.html. Population figures from the World POPClock, U.S. Census Bureau, www.census.gov/main/www/popclock.html, accessed September 2014. This Web site provides continuously updated projections of U.S. and world populations.
3. For these and other statistics, see Michael D. Hernandez, "Big Brands Target Hispanic Consumers, *USA Today*, September 23, 2013, www.usatoday.com/story/money/business/2013/09/22/big-brands-target-hispanic-consumers/2845009/; Advertising Age Hispanic Fact Pack, July 23, 2012, pp. 38–39; Lucia Moses, "Marketing to Hispanics," *Adweek*, May 13, 2013, pp. 18–19; "Population Projections," www.census.gov/population/projections/, accessed July 2014; and U.S. Census Bureau, "U.S. Census Bureau Projections Show a Slower Growing, Older, More Diverse Nation a Half Century from Now," www.census.gov/newsroom/releases/archives/population/cb12-243.html, accessed July 2014.
4. "Hispanics Lead as Web Users Who Are Truly Mobile-First," *eMarketer*, October 8, 2013, www.emarketer.com/Article/Hispanics-Lead-Web-Users-Who-Truly-Mobile-First/1010280.
5. Samantha Schmidt, "Target Steps Up Marketing to Hispanics," *Business Journal*, May 29, 2013, www.bizjournals.com/twincities/news/2013/05/29/targeting-the-hispanic-market.html.
6. Based on information from Dale Buss, "Ram Redoubles Reach-Out to Hispanic Pickup-Truck Buyers," *Forbes*, October 23, 2012, accessed from www.forbes.com/sites/dalebuss/2012/10/23/ram-redoubles-reach-out-to-hispanic-pickup-truck-buyers/; Tanya Irwin, "Ram Truck Hispanic Effort 'Most Comprehensive,'" *Marketing Daily*, September 28, 2011, www.mediapost.com/publications/article/159482/?print; Michael D. Hernandez, "Big Brands Target Hispanic Consumers," *USA Today*, September 23, 2013, www.usatoday.com/story/money/business/2013/09/22/big-brands-target-hispanic-consumers/2845009/; and www.ramtrucks-la.com/ accessed July 2014.
7. See Matthew Wallace Weeks, "Minority Buying Power Grows in 2013, According to Selig Center Repost," September 4, 2013, www.terry.uga.edu/news/releases/minority-buying-power-grows-in-2013-according-to-selig-center-report#.UozB_sSsh8E; U.S. Census Bureau, "U.S. Population Projections," https://www.census.gov/

population/projections, accessed November 2013; and information from "Reaching Black Consumers," www.reachingblackconsumers.com, accessed September 2014.

8. "Ford Debuts African-American Campaign for 2013 Escape with Humorous Creative," *Target Market News*, June 6, 2012, http://targetmarketnews.com/storyid06071201.htm; "UniWorld Group: Multi-Cultural Marketing: The Work," www.ford.com/benew/, accessed February 2014.

9. See U.S. Census Bureau, "Facts for Features: Asian/Pacific American Heritage Month: May 2013," www.census.gov/newsroom/releases/archives/facts_for_features_special_editions/cb13-ff09.html; Christine Birkner, "Asian-Americans in Focus," *Marketing News,* March 2013, p. 14; Gracie Zheng, "Nielsen Highlights the Buying Power of Asian Americans," May 5, 2013, http://v3con.com/2013/05/20/nielsen-highlights-the-buying-power-of-asian-americans/; and U.S. Census Bureau, "U.S. Population Projections," https://www.census.gov/population/projections, accessed March 2014.

10. See Liang Guo, "Crowdsourcing—AT&T and Wong Fu Productions 'Away We Happened,'" *Voices,* November 4, 2013, http://liyangnewmedia.wordpress.com/2013/11/04/crowdsourcing-att-and-wong-fu-productions-away-we-happened/; "Multicultural Media: Rezonate Media, AT&T, Away We Happened," December 28, 2012, www.mediapost.com/publications/article/190095/multicultural-media-rezonate-media-att-away-we.html; and AT&T "Away We Happened," www.effie.org/case_studies/case/2237, accessed September 2014.

11. See Stuart Elliott, "New Ad Organization to Promote Cross-Cultural Marketing," *New York Times,* August 30, 2013, http://www.nytimes.com/2013/08/31/business/media/new-ad-organization-to-promote-cross-cultural-marketing.html?_r=2&; and "Just Checking," www.youtube.com/watch?v=kYofm5d5Xdw&feature=youtu.be, accessed September 2014.

12. See Eleftheria Parpis, "Goodbye Color Codes," *Adweek,* September 27, 2010, pp. 24–25; "Ethnic Marketing: McDonald's Is Lovin' It," *Bloomberg BusinessWeek,* July 18, 2010, pp. 22–23; Alex Frias, "5 Tips to Refresh Your Multicultural Marketing Strategy in 2013," *Forbes,* February 8, 2013, www.forbes.com/sites/theyec/2013/02/08/5-tips-to-refresh-your-multicultural-marketing-strategy-in-2013/; Stuart Elliott, "New Ad Organization to Promote Cross-Cultural Marketing," *New York Times,* August 30, 2013, http://www.nytimes.com/2013/08/31/business/media/new-ad-organization-to-promote-cross-cultural-marketing.html?_r=2&; and The Cross-Cultural Marketing & Communications Association, "Total Market," www.theccmca.org/?page_id=3631; accessed September 2014.

13. Adam Bluestein, "Make Money in 2013 (and Beyond)," *Inc.,* December 2012/January 2013, pp. 58–65, here p. 64.

14. See "How Lady Gaga Co-Marketed New Album *ARTPOP* with Diehard Fans," *Forbes,* November 10, 2013, www.forbes.com/sites/jackiehuba/2013/11/10/how-lady-gaga-co-markets-new-album-artpop-with-diehard-fans/.

15. Based on information from Julie Liesse, "The Big Idea," *Advertising Age,* November 28, 2011, pp. C4–C6; and "Philips's 'Wake up the Town,'" www.ketchum.com/de/philips's-"wake-town", accessed September 2014.

16. Digital Strategy Consulting, "Word of Mouth Trends: How Advertising Influences Real-World Conversations," November 2, 2013, www.digitalstrategyconsulting.com/intelligence/2013/02/word_of_mouth_trends_how_advertising_influences_realworld_conversations_infographic.php.

17. Eve Tahmincioglu, "Majority of Dads Say They Do the Grocery Shopping," *Life Inc.,* June 15, 2012, http://lifeinc.today.com/_news/2012/06/15/12238737-majority-of-dads-say-they-do-the-grocery-shopping?lite; Samantha Murphy, "Stereotype Debunked: Women Buy More Technology Than Men," http://mashable.com/2012/01/09/women-and-technology/, accessed January 9, 2012; Chris Slocumb, "Women Outspend Men 3 to 2 on Technology Purchases," *ClarityQuest*, January 3, 2013, www.clarityqst.com/women-outspend-men-3-to-2-on-technology-purchases/; and David Koeppel, "Bromance at the Supermarket as More Men Shop," *Fiscal Times*, October 8, 2013, www.thefiscaltimes.com/Articles/2013/10/08/Bromance-Supermarket-More-Men-Shop.

18. See Melissa Hoffman, "Ad of the Day: Samsung Dad May Be the Swaddle Master but Kid Has Him Beat in This Galaxy S4 Spot," *Adweek,* June 5, 2013, www.adweek.com/news/advertising-branding/ad-day-samsung-150028; and www.youtube.com/watch?v=NApR0dDSuPM[, accessed July 2014.

19. See "Tweens 'R Shoppers: A Look at the Tween Market & Shopping Behavior," POPAI, March 7, 2013, www.popai.com/store/downloads/POPAIWhitePaper-Tweens-R-Shoppers-2013.pdf; and Michael R. Solomon, *Consumer Behavior,* 10th ed. (Upper Saddle River, NJ: Pearson Publishing, 2013), Chapter 10.

20. For more on the PRIZM lifestage segmentation, see "MyBestSegments: Nielsen PRIZM Lifestage Groups," www.claritas.com/MyBestSegments/Default.jsp?ID=7010&menuOption=learnmore&pageName=PRIZM%2BLifestage%2BGroups&segSystem=PRIZM, accessed September 2014.

21. See www.carhartt.com, accessed September 2014.

22. See "Apple Expected to Increase Marketing Presence Abroad with Low-Cost iPhone," *Advertising Age,* September 10, 2013, www.adage.com/print/244072; and Alistair Barr and Edward C. Baig, "Google Targets Low-End Smartphone Market with Moto G," *USA Today*, November 13, 2013, www.usatoday.com/story/tech/2013/11/13/google-motorola-moto-g/3516039/.

23. See Christopher Heine, "Appliance Brands Are Diving into Digital This Summer," *Adweek,* July 12, 2013, www.adweek.com/news/technology/appliance-brands-are-diving-digital-summer-150989; "KitchenAid 'So Much More' TV Commercial," www.youtube.com/watch?v=tr9KQQL5lgQ, accessed March 2014; and http://blog.kitchenaid.com/, www.pinterest.com/kitchenaidusa/, and www.kitchenaid.com/about-kitchenaid/, accessed September 2014.

24. See Jennifer Aaker, "Dimensions of Measuring Brand Personality," *Journal of Marketing Research*, August 1997, pp. 347–356; and Kevin Lane Keller, *Strategic Brand Management*, 4th ed. (Upper Saddle River, New Jersey: Pearson Publishing, 2012), Chapter 2.

25. See "Air on the Side of Humanity," September 17, 2013, www.mullen.com/air-on-the-side-of-humanity/; "The Newest Marketing Buzzword? Human." *Advertising Age,* September 20, 2013, www.adage.com/print/244261; and www.jetblue.com/corporate-social-responsibility/, accessed September 2014.

26. See Abraham H. Maslow, "A Theory of Human Motivation," *Psychological Review*, *50* (1943), pp. 370–396. Also see Maslow, *Motivation and Personality*, 3rd ed. (New York: HarperCollins Publishers, 1987); and Michael R. Solomon, *Consumer Behavior,* 11th ed. (Upper Saddle River, NJ: Prentice Hall, 2014), pp. 132–134.

27. See Ellen Moore, "Letter to My Colleague: We Can Do Better," *Adweek,* December 22, 2010, www.adweek.com/news/advertising-branding/letter-my-colleagues-we-can-do-better-104084; and Kelsey Libert and Kristin Tynski, "Research: The Emotions that Make Marketing Campaigns Go Viral," *Harvard Business Review,* October 24, 2013, http://blogs.hbr.org/2013/10/research-the-emotions-that-make-marketing-campaigns-go-viral/.

28. For more reading, see Lawrence R. Samuel, *Freud on Madison Avenue: Motivation Research and Subliminal Advertising in America* (Philadelphia: University of Pennsylvania Press, 2010); Charles R. Acland, *Swift Viewing: The Popular Life of Subliminal Influence* (Duke University Press, 2011); Christopher Shea, "The History of Subliminal Ads," *Wall Street Journal*, February 15, 2012, http://blogs.wsj.com/ideas-market/2012/02/15/the-history-of-subliminal-ads/;

and Dominic Green, "15 Corporate Logos that Contain Subliminal Messaging," *Business Insider,* May 11, 2013, www.businessinsider.com/subliminal-messages-in-12-popular-logos-2013-5#.

29. Example based on information found in John Berman, "Shrek Boosts Vidalia Onion Sales," June 29, 2010, http://abcnews.go.com/WN/shrek-boosts-vidalia-onion-sales/story?id=11047273; and "Vidalia Onion Committee Cinches Triple Crown of National Marketing Awards," October 20, 2011, www.vidaliaonion.org/news/vidalia_onion_committee_cinches_triple_crown_of_national_-marketing_awards. Vidalia® is a registered certification mark of Georgia Department of Agriculture.

30. See Leon Festinger, *A Theory of Cognitive Dissonance* (Stanford, CA: Stanford University Press, 1957); Cynthia Crossen, "'Cognitive Dissonance' Became a Milestone in the 1950s Psychology," *Wall Street Journal*, December 12, 2006, p. B1; and Anupam Bawa and Purva Kansal, "Cognitive Dissonance and the Marketing of Services: Some Issues," *Journal of Services Research*, October 2008–March 2009, p. 31.

31. The following discussion draws from the work of Everett M. Rogers. See his *Diffusion of Innovations*, 5th ed. (New York: Free Press, 2003).

32. Based on Rogers, *Diffusion of Innovation*, p. 281. For more discussion, see http://en.wikipedia.org/wiki/Everett_Rogers, accessed September 2014.

33. Ken Werner, "HDTV Expert—UHD-TV, Small OLEDs, and Market Forecasting," *HDTV Magazine*, October 31, 2013, www.hdtvmagazine.com/columns/2013/10/hdtv-expert-uhdtv-small-oleds-and-market-forecasting.php.

6 Business Markets and Business Buyer Behavior

Chapter Preview

In the previous chapter, you studied *final consumer* buying behavior and factors that influence it. In this chapter, we'll do the same for *business customers*—those that buy goods and services for use in producing their own products and services or for resale to others. As when selling to final buyers, firms marketing to businesses must engage business customers and build profitable relationships with them by creating superior customer value.

To start, let's look at a startup company from Egypt. KarmSolar provides custom solar energy applications to the agricultural and industrial markets, and also provides help with financial analysis and other challenges that its clients face when switching to solar power. To succeed in these business-to-business markets, KarmSolar must do more than just design and distribute good products. It must work closely and deeply with its business customers to become a strategic, problem-solving partner.

KARMSOLAR: Building Partnerships and Providing Cheap Sustainable Solutions

KarmSolar Inc. is an Egyptian company founded in October 2011 with the sole purpose of providing cost-competitive renewable energy solutions to the Egyptian market and the MENA region. But to be able to do that, KarmSolar needed an edge, a niche, a selling point that would set it apart from the competition. Solar energy has been used for years, but it was always disregarded as a practical alternative when designing a commercial or agricultural project. This fact can be attributed to many social and economical factors; however, the main reason is the lack of awareness and understanding of the technology. It has been regarded as a space-age technology that is too expensive to be applied in industrial solutions, but this is far from the truth.

The real challenge for KarmSolar was to convince customers and consumers that solar energy is cheaper than conventional fuels. And to add to the challenges KarmSolar faced, the Egyptian government subsidizes all conventional energy sources, including natural gas, diesel, and electricity, provided by the government, making KarmSolar's investment in solar energy appear to be an enormous undertaking at first glance. KarmSolar executives knew they could compete in the consumer products segment as a startup and could not sell universal, ready-made products that can operate under any conditions, and for these two reasons another business strategy had to be adopted.

KarmSolar's business-to-business model is based on the provision of custom-designed commercial solar energy applications and solutions to clients in the off-grid agricultural and industrial market. The solutions are custom designed to meet the unique needs of each client, with the end goal of providing the client with a commercially viable energy solution. With a very high potential for growth and expansion, KarmSolar started creating long-lasting partnerships with its clients by providing comprehensive solutions with innovative solar energy solutions. "The key to winning clients in our field is in understanding their challenges, and in providing them with innovative and sustainable energy solutions to help them reduce their operating costs and consequently achieve their breakthrough results," says Ahmed Zahran, KarmSolar CEO.

At this point, research had been under way for several years, and the market demand for high-capacity energy solutions was high, but solar energy could only offer small-scale capacities, and with a very high markup. Naturally, the gap was filled by diesel and natural gas generators. KarmSolar had to be innovative: "We had to customize, and come up with a turnkey innovative technology that would change people's perception of solar energy, and we did," says Xavier Auclair, Chief of Innovation and technology. KarmSolar's solution utilizes the

"Our relationship with our customers is based on trust. We offer them the means to grow and increase their profitability." For KarmSolar, it's not a one-off sale; it's a partnership that results in mutual benefits and business growth.

varying intensity of solar radiation to provide the highest throughput and maximize the utilization of client assets.

For KarmSolar's clients, the decision to invest in a solar power generation plant is anything but easy. It is a very tiring process that involves calculating and forecasting the economics and financials of such an investment. This makes it extremely important for KarmSolar when providing the comprehensive solution to help with all financial and economical studies required for the sale. KarmSolar acts as a problem-solving partner; it has to get involved in the client's problems to understand that client's challenges. And this strategy has been very successful for both parties, providing mutual growth potential.

KarmSolar works closely with its customers, offering training, support, and education, and developing a mutually beneficial partnership in the process.

"Like any other business segment in Egypt, off-grid agriculture is highly wasteful; we do not provide solar energy as a cheaper alternative for fossil fuels only, we also help the farms understand how they are wasting their resources, like water, fertilizers, and energy, and how they can increase their efficiency and minimize their costs," says Mohamed Fadly, KarmSolar's Innovation Officer. KarmSolar now operates with a partnership mentality in all relationships with business clients, which in turn sell their products to the market.

Every sale for KarmSolar counts, and thus is handled with great care and attention; every project has different characteristics and conditions, which results in the complex and comprehensive nature of the solutions. For KarmSolar, it is not a sale—it is a partnership. "Our relationship with our customers is based on trust. We offer them the means to grow and increase their profitability; we engage them in the design and make sure they get what they need," says Yumna Madi, KarmSolar's Chief Business Development Officer. The business strategy KarmSolar uses is simple, and it is based on the mutual benefit and growth of both businesses.

KarmSolar's competitive edge comes from its ability to stay one step ahead of the competition. Notes Madi, "We continuously invest in research and development to make sure we are always ahead of our competition. Our price is the first thing customers ask about. And we have to stay appealing." The only way for KarmSolar, which is a top-level solar technology integrator, to keep prices down and stay competitive in the market is by innovating and driving out all losses in its solutions. "We provide trainings to the clients; we provide after sale support. And we teach them how to use our solutions effectively," notes Madi. This wasn't easy at the beginning, and this is why KarmSolar created a web-based software program called Solar Management Interface, or SMI. This is how KarmSolar simplifies its services and makes it easier for business clients to understand and interact with the solar power solution.

Driven by a passion to make a difference and a dream to make solar energy viable for all business sectors, KarmSolar acts as the engine for off-grid urbanization. Its products are not in your kitchen or living room, but some of your food might have been watered with solar-powered pumps as it was grown, or refrigerated by a solar-powered compressor before being shipped.[1]

Objective Outline

In One way or another, most large companies sell to other organizations. Companies such as Boeing, DuPont, IBM, Caterpillar, and countless other firms sell *most* of their products to other businesses. Even large consumer-products companies, which make products used by final consumers, must first sell their products to other businesses. For example, General Mills makes many familiar consumer brands—Big G cereals (Cheerios, Wheaties, Trix, Chex, Total, Fiber One), baking products (Pillsbury, Betty Crocker, Bisquick, Gold Medal flour), snacks (Nature Valley, Bugles, Chex Mix), Yoplait yogurt, Häagen-Dazs ice cream, and many others. But to sell these products to consumers, General Mills must first sell them to its wholesaler and retailer customers, who in turn serve the consumer market.

Business buyer behavior
The buying behavior of organizations that buy goods and services for use in the production of other products and services that are sold, rented, or supplied to others.

Business buying process
The decision process by which business buyers determine which products and services their organizations need to purchase and then find, evaluate, and choose among alternative suppliers and brands.

Business buyer behavior refers to the buying behavior of organizations that buy goods and services for use in the production of other products and services that are sold, rented, or supplied to others. It also includes the behavior of retailing and wholesaling firms that acquire goods to resell or rent to others at a profit. In the **business buying process**, business buyers determine which products and services their organizations need to purchase and then find, evaluate, and choose among alternative suppliers and brands. *Business-to-business (B-to-B) marketers* must do their best to understand business markets and business buyer behavior. Then, like businesses that sell to final buyers, they must engage business customers and build profitable relationships with them by creating superior customer value.

Author Comment | Business markets operate "behind the scenes" to most consumers. Most of the things you buy involve many sets of business purchases before you ever see them.

Business Markets

The business market is *huge*. In fact, business markets involve far more dollars and items than do consumer markets. For example, think about the large number of business transactions involved in the production and sale of a single set of Goodyear tires. Various suppliers sell Goodyear the rubber, steel, equipment, and other goods that it needs to produce tires.

Goodyear then sells the finished tires to retailers, which in turn sell them to consumers. Thus, many sets of *business* purchases were made for only one set of *consumer* purchases. In addition, Goodyear sells tires as original equipment to manufacturers that install them on new vehicles and as replacement tires to companies that maintain their own fleets of company cars, trucks, or other vehicles.

In some ways, business markets are similar to consumer markets. Both involve people who assume buying roles and make purchase decisions to satisfy needs. However, business markets differ in many ways from consumer markets. The main differences are in *market structure and demand*, the *nature of the buying unit*, and the *types of decisions and the decision process* involved.

Market Structure and Demand

The business marketer normally deals with *far fewer but far larger buyers* than the consumer marketer does. Even in large business markets, a few buyers often account for most of the purchasing. For example, when Goodyear sells replacement tires to final consumers, its potential market includes millions of car owners around the world. But its fate in business markets depends on getting orders from only a handful of large automakers.

Further, many business markets have *inelastic and more fluctuating demand*. The total demand for many business products is not much affected by price changes, especially in the short run. A drop in the price of leather will not cause shoe manufacturers to buy much more leather unless it results in lower shoe prices that, in turn, increase consumer demand for shoes. And the demand for many business goods and services tends to change more—and more quickly—than does the demand for consumer goods and services. A small percentage increase in consumer demand can cause large increases in business demand.

Derived demand
Business demand that ultimately comes from (derives from) the demand for consumer goods.

Finally, business demand is **derived demand**—it ultimately derives from the demand for consumer goods. Consumers buy Intel processors only when they buy PCs, tablets, smartphones, and other devices with Intel processors inside them from producers such as HP, Dell, Lenovo, Samsung, Sony, and Toshiba. And demand for Gore-Tex fabrics derives from consumer purchases of outdoor apparel brands made from Gore-Tex. If consumer demand for these products increases, so does the demand for the Intel processors or Gore-Tex fabrics they contain. Therefore, B-to-B marketers sometimes promote their products directly to final consumers to increase business demand. For example, Intel's long-running Intel Inside consumer marketing campaign consists of ads and promotions extoling the virtues of both Intel processors and the brands that contain them:[2]

> During the recent holiday season, Intel opened pop-up retail stores in major cities—called Intel Experience Stores—featuring the latest products from Dell, Asus, Lenovo, Acer, Sony, HP, Samsung, Toshiba, and other Intel-based brands. Intel also partnered with retailers such as Best Buy to set up online sites featuring Intel-based products (*BestBuy.com/IntelExperience*). And it posted an online holiday buying guide promoting Intel Atom-powered laptop and tablet brands. Intel even collaborated recently with Toshiba to produce several award-winning social media film series, called "Inside," "The Beauty Inside," and "The Power Inside." ● For example, the 63-episode "The Beauty Inside" series followed the story of Alex, a man who wakes up every day as the same person but in a different body, forcing him to explore his inner self. Each episode featured actual brand fans who gave Alex hundreds of different faces. The film engaged consumers deeply and got even strangers discussing their own central identities, all celebrating the essential fact that "it's what's inside that counts" (which just happens to be Intel's core marketing message). The award-winning film captured 70 million views and 26 million interactions. It even won an Emmy for Outstanding New Approach to Daytime Programing at the 40th Annual Daytime Emmy Awards. Based on its success, Intel and Toshiba followed with "The Power Inside," a comedy/Sci-Fi adventure in which the hero calls on the power inside his Toshiba laptop and the power inside himself to defend earth from a race of extraterrestrial moustaches and unibrows which take over people's faces.

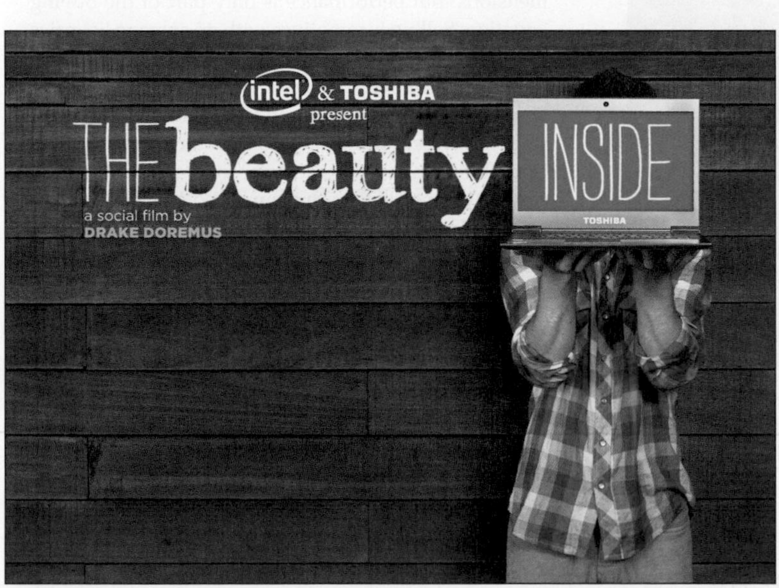

● **Derived demand: As part of its long-running Intel Inside campaign, Intel partnered with Toshiba to produce the award-winning social media film series, "The Beauty Inside," which engaged consumers with the message "it's what's inside that counts." Both Intel and Toshiba benefited.**

Courtesy Intel and Toshiba American Information Systems, Inc.

In all, the series garnered over 200 million views and the Intel Inside campaign has boosted demand for both Intel processors and the products containing them, benefiting both Intel and its business partners.

Nature of the Buying Unit

Compared with consumer purchases, a business purchase usually involves *more decision participants* and a *more professional purchasing effort*. Often, business buying is done by trained purchasing agents who spend their working lives learning how to buy better. The more complex the purchase, the more likely it is that several people will participate in the decision-making process. Buying committees composed of technical experts and top management are common in the buying of major goods. Beyond this, B-to-B marketers now face a new breed of higher-level, better-trained supply managers. Therefore, companies must have well-trained marketers and salespeople to deal with these well-trained buyers.

Types of Decisions and the Decision Process

Business buyers usually face *more complex* buying decisions than do consumer buyers. Business purchases often involve large sums of money, complex technical and economic considerations, and interactions among people at many levels of the buyer's organization. The business buying process also tends to be *longer* and *more formalized*. Large business purchases usually call for detailed product specifications, written purchase orders, careful supplier searches, and formal approval.

Supplier development
Systematic development of networks of supplier-partners to ensure an appropriate and dependable supply of products and materials for use in making products or reselling them to others.

Finally, in the business buying process, the buyer and seller are often much *more dependent* on each other. B-to-B marketers may roll up their sleeves and work closely with their customers during all stages of the buying process—from helping customers define problems, to finding solutions, to supporting after-sale operation. They often customize their offerings to individual customer needs. In the short run, sales go to suppliers who meet buyers' immediate product and service needs. In the long run, however, business-to-business marketers keep customers by meeting current needs *and* by partnering with them to help solve their problems. ● For example, consider the buying process for GE's diesel locomotives:[3]

● **Business buyer decision process: In selling locomotives with an average list price of $2.2 million, GE's real challenge is to win buyers' business by building day-in, day-out, year-in, year-out partnerships with them based on close collaboration.**

GE Transportation

> GE locomotives might not seem glamorous to you, but they are beautiful brutes to those who buy and use them. Performance plays an important role in the locomotive buyer's decision, and GE locomotives outperform competing engines on most important dimensions. But performance is only part of the buying equation. Selling locomotives with an average list price of $2.2 million involves a tortuously long buying process, dozens or even hundreds of decision makers, and layer upon layer of subtle and not-so-subtle buying influences. GE's real challenge is to win buyers' business by building day-in, day-out, year-in, year-out, problem-solving partnerships with them based on close collaboration. More than just "selling locomotives," GE wins contracts by partnering strategically with customers to help them translate performance into moving passengers and freight more efficiently and reliably. For example, CSX Transportation (CSXT), one of GE's largest customers, has purchased hundreds of GE locomotives in recent years. According to a CSXT purchasing executive, the company "evaluates many cost factors before awarding . . . a locomotive contract. Environmental impact, fuel consumption, reliability, serviceability [are] all key elements in this decision." But as important is "the value of our ongoing partnership with GE."

As in GE's case, in recent years, relationships between most customers and suppliers have been changing from downright adversarial to close and chummy. In fact, many customer companies are now practicing **supplier development**, systematically developing networks of supplier-partners to ensure a dependable supply of the products and materials that they use in making their own products or reselling to others. For example,

Walmart doesn't have a "Purchasing Department"; it has a "Supplier Development Department." The giant retailer knows that it can't just rely on spot suppliers who might be available when needed. Instead, Walmart manages a huge network of supplier-partners that help provide the hundreds of billions of dollars of goods that it sells to its customers each year.

Author Comment | Business buying decisions can range from routine to incredibly complex, involving only a few or very many decision makers and buying influences.

Business Buyer Behavior

At the most basic level, marketers want to know how business buyers will respond to various marketing stimuli. **Figure 6.1** shows a model of business buyer behavior. In this model, marketing and other stimuli affect the buying organization and produce certain buyer responses. To design good marketing strategies, marketers must understand what happens within the organization to turn stimuli into purchase responses.

Within the organization, buying activity consists of two major parts: the *buying center*, composed of all the people involved in the buying decision, and the *buying decision process*. The model shows that the buying center and the buying decision process are influenced by internal organizational, interpersonal, and individual factors as well as external environmental factors.

The model in Figure 6.1 suggests four questions about business buyer behavior: What buying decisions do business buyers make? Who participates in the business buying process? What are the major influences on buyers? How do business buyers make their buying decisions?

Major Types of Buying Situations

Straight rebuy
A business buying situation in which the buyer routinely reorders something without any modifications.

Modified rebuy
A business buying situation in which the buyer wants to modify product specifications, prices, terms, or suppliers.

New task
A business buying situation in which the buyer purchases a product or service for the first time.

There are three major types of buying situations.[4] In a **straight rebuy**, the buyer reorders something without any modifications. It is usually handled on a routine basis by the purchasing department. To keep the business, "in" suppliers try to maintain product and service quality. "Out" suppliers try to find new ways to add value or exploit dissatisfaction so that the buyer will consider them.

In a **modified rebuy**, the buyer wants to modify product specifications, prices, terms, or suppliers. The "in" suppliers may become nervous and feel pressured to put their best foot forward to protect an account. "Out" suppliers may see the modified rebuy situation as an opportunity to make a better offer and gain new business.

A company buying a product or service for the first time faces a **new task** situation. In such cases, the greater the cost or risk, the larger the number of decision participants and the greater the company's efforts to collect information. The new task situation is the marketer's greatest opportunity and challenge. The marketer not only tries to reach as many key buying influences as possible, but also provides help and information. The buyer makes the fewest decisions in the straight rebuy and the most in the new task decision.

Many business buyers prefer to buy a complete solution to a problem from a single seller rather than buying separate products and services from several suppliers and putting them together. The sale often goes to the firm that provides the most complete *system* for

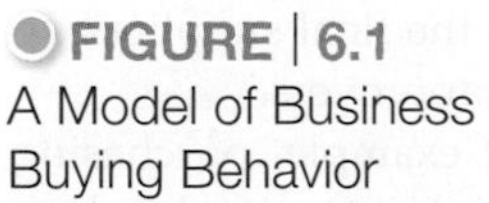
FIGURE | 6.1
A Model of Business Buying Behavior

In some ways, business markets are similar to consumer markets—this model looks a lot like the model of consumer buyer behavior presented in Figure 5.1. But there are some major differences, especially in the nature of the buying unit, the types of decisions made, and the decision process.

The environment
Marketing stimuli
Other stimuli
Product
Price
Place
Promotion
Economic
Technological
Political
Cultural
Competitive

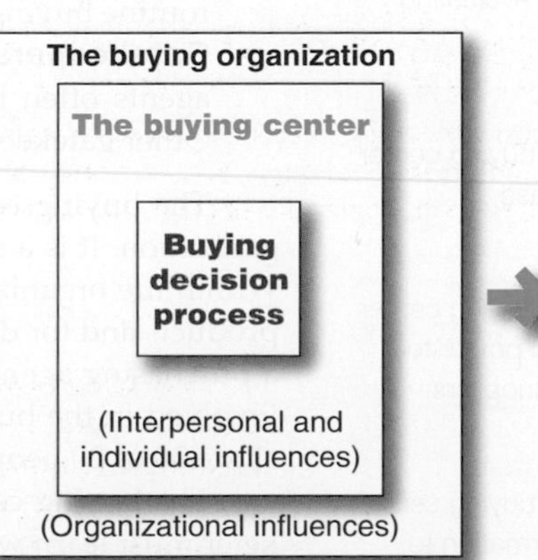

Solutions selling: Delivering a fun and safe experience for Six Flags guests requires careful and effective management of thousands of park assets across its 19 regional theme parks. IBM works hand-in-hand with Six Flags to provide not just software, but a complete solution.

Wirelmage

meeting the customer's needs and solving its problems. Such **systems selling** (or **solutions selling**) is often a key business marketing strategy for winning and holding accounts. Consider IBM and its customer Six Flags Entertainment Corporation:[5]

> Six Flags operates 19 regional theme parks across the United States, Mexico, and Canada, featuring exciting rides and water attractions, world-class roller coasters, and special shows and concerts. To deliver a fun and safe experience for guests, Six Flags must carefully and effectively manage thousands of park assets—from rides and equipment to buildings and other facilities. Six Flags needed a tool for managing all those assets efficiently and effectively across its far-flung collection of parks. So it turned to IBM, which has software—called Maximo Asset Management software—that handles that very problem well.
>
> But IBM didn't just hand the software over to Six Flags with best wishes for happy implementation. Instead, IBM's Maximo Professional Services group combined the software with an entire set of services designed to get and keep the software up and running. IBM is working hand-in-hand with Six Flags to customize the application and strategically implement it across Six Flags's far-flung facilities, along with on-site immersion training and planning workshops. "We've implemented the solution at five parks to date, and as the implementation team completes each deployment, they move to the next property," says Six Flags's director of corporate project management. "We have one implementation team to make sure that all the deployments across our parks are consistent." IBM will work with Six Flags throughout the process. Thus, IBM isn't just selling the software, it's selling a complete solution to Six Flags's complex asset management problem.

Systems selling (or **solutions selling**)
Buying a packaged solution to a problem from a single seller, thus avoiding all the separate decisions involved in a complex buying situation.

Buying center
All the individuals and units that play a role in the purchase decision-making process.

Users
Members of the buying organization who will actually use the purchased product or service.

Influencers
People in an organization's buying center who affect the buying decision; they often help define specifications and also provide information for evaluating alternatives.

Buyers
People in an organization's buying center who make an actual purchase.

Deciders
People in an organization's buying center who have formal or informal power to select or approve the final suppliers.

Gatekeepers
People in an organization's buying center who control the flow of information to others.

Participants in the Business Buying Process

Who does the buying of the trillions of dollars' worth of goods and services needed by business organizations? The decision-making unit of a buying organization is called its **buying center**. It consists of all the individuals and units that play a role in the business purchase decision-making process. This group includes the actual users of the product or service, those who make the buying decision, those who influence the buying decision, those who do the actual buying, and those who control buying information.

The buying center includes all members of the organization who play any of five roles in the purchase decision process.[6]

- **Users** are members of the organization who will use the product or service. In many cases, users initiate the buying proposal and help define product specifications.
- **Influencers** often help define specifications and also provide information for evaluating alternatives. Technical personnel are particularly important influencers.
- **Buyers** have formal authority to select the supplier and arrange terms of purchase. Buyers may help shape product specifications, but their major role is in selecting vendors and negotiating. In more complex purchases, buyers might include high-level officers participating in the negotiations.
- **Deciders** have formal or informal power to select or approve the final suppliers. In routine buying, the buyers are often the deciders, or at least the approvers.
- **Gatekeepers** control the flow of information to others. For example, purchasing agents often have authority to prevent salespersons from seeing users or deciders. Other gatekeepers include technical personnel and even personal secretaries.

The buying center is not a fixed and formally identified unit within the buying organization. It is a set of buying roles assumed by different people for different purchases. Within the organization, the size and makeup of the buying center will vary for different products and for different buying situations. For some routine purchases, one person—say, a purchasing agent—may assume all the buying center roles and serve as the only person involved in the buying decision. For more complex purchases, the buying center may include 20 or 30 people from different levels and departments in the organization.

The buying center concept presents a major marketing challenge. The business marketer must learn who participates in the decision, each participant's relative influence, and what evaluation criteria each decision participant uses. This can be difficult.

The buying center usually includes some obvious participants who are involved formally in the buying decision. For example, the decision to buy a corporate jet will probably involve the company's CEO, the chief pilot, a purchasing agent, some legal staff, a member of top management, and others formally charged with the buying decision. It may also involve less obvious, informal participants, some of whom may actually make or strongly affect the buying decision. Sometimes, even the people in the buying center are not aware of all the buying participants. For example, the decision about which corporate jet to buy may actually be made by a corporate board member who has an interest in flying and who knows a lot about airplanes. This board member may work behind the scenes to sway the decision. Many business buying decisions result from the complex interactions of ever-changing buying center participants.

Major Influences on Business Buyers

Business buyers are subject to many influences when they make their buying decisions. Some marketers assume that the major influences are economic. They think buyers will favor the supplier who offers the lowest price or the best product or the most service. They concentrate on offering strong economic benefits to buyers. Such economic factors are very important to most buyers, especially in a tough economy. However, business buyers actually respond to both economic and personal factors. Far from being cold, calculating, and impersonal, business buyers are human and social as well. They react to both reason and emotion.

Today, most B-to-B marketers recognize that emotion plays an important role in business buying decisions. Consider this example:[7]

IF YOU'RE NOT LIFTING SHEETROCK® ULTRALIGHT PANELS, WHAT ARE YOU LIFTING?

Emotions play a role in business buying. The emotion-charged images in this B-to-B ad convey the message that USG's Ultralight wallboard panels remove some of the weight from the backs and shoulders of its customers.

USG Corporation

USG Corporation is a leading manufacturer of gypsum wallboard and other building materials for the construction and remodeling industries. Given its construction contractor, dealer, and builder audience, you might expect USG's B-to-B ads to focus heavily on the performance features and benefits, such as strength, impact resistance, ease of installation, and costs. USG does promote these benefits. However, a recent marketing campaign for USG's Sheetrock Ultralight wallboard panels also packed a decidedly more emotional wallop. Ultralight panels offer performance equal to or better than standard gypsum wallboard but are 30 percent lighter. That makes them easier to lift, carry, and install, reducing worker fatigue. Instead of just stating that Ultralight is lighter, USG's award-winning advertising campaign—called the "Weight Has Been Lifted"—visualized this benefit using dramatic, emotion-charged imagery showing that it's literally removing some weight from the backs and shoulders of its customers. Ads show contractors struggling to carry enormous objects such as a car, a giant anchor, a grand piano, or an elephant or dinosaur. The tagline: "If you're not lifting Ultralight Panels, what are you lifting?"

Figure 6.2 lists various groups of influences on business buyers—environmental, organizational, interpersonal, and individual. Business buyers are heavily influenced by

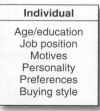

FIGURE | 6.2
Major Influences on Business Buying Behavior

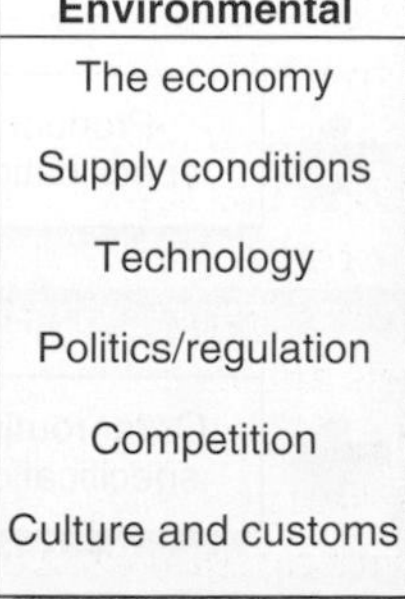
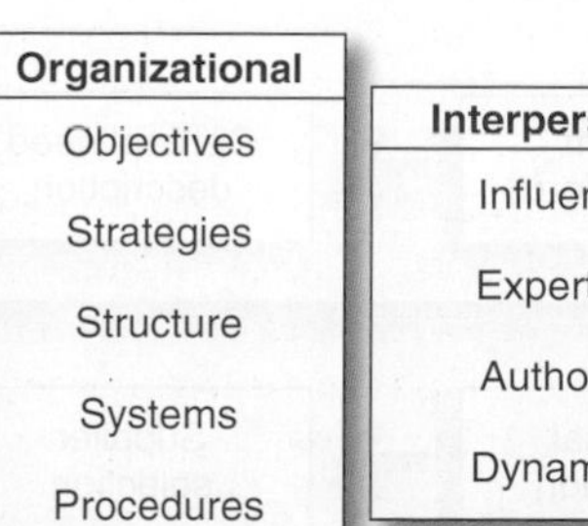
Like consumer buying decisions in Figure 5.2, business buying decisions are affected by an incredibly complex combination of environmental, interpersonal, and individual influences, but with an extra layer of organizational factors thrown into the mix.
Environmental
The economy
Supply conditions
Technology
Politics/regulation
Competition
Culture and customs
Organizational
Objectives
Strategies
Structure
Systems
Procedures
Interpersonal
Influence
Expertise
Authority
Dynamics
Individual
Age/education
Job position
Motives
Personality
Preferences
Buying style
Buyers

factors in the current and expected *economic environment*, such as the level of primary demand, the economic outlook, and the cost of money. Another environmental factor is the *supply* of key materials. Many companies now are more willing to buy and hold larger inventories of scarce materials to ensure adequate supply. Business buyers also are affected by *technological*, *political*, and *competitive* developments in the environment. Finally, *culture and customs* can strongly influence business buyer reactions to the marketer's behavior and strategies, especially in the international marketing environment (see Real Marketing 6.1). The business buyer must watch these factors, determine how they will affect the buyer, and try to turn these challenges into opportunities.

Organizational factors are also important. Each buying organization has its own objectives, strategies, structure, systems, and procedures, and the business marketer must understand these factors well. Questions such as these arise: How many people are involved in the buying decision? Who are they? What are their evaluative criteria? What are the company's policies and limits on its buyers?

The buying center usually includes many participants who influence each other, so *interpersonal factors* also influence the business buying process. However, it is often difficult to assess such interpersonal factors and group dynamics. Buying center participants do not wear tags that label them as "key decision maker" or "not influential." Nor do buying center participants with the highest rank always have the most influence. Participants may influence the buying decision because they control rewards and punishments, are well liked, have special expertise, or have a special relationship with other important participants. Interpersonal factors are often very subtle. Whenever possible, business marketers must try to understand these factors and design strategies that take them into account.

Each participant in the business buying decision process brings in personal motives, perceptions, and preferences. These *individual factors* are affected by personal characteristics such as age, income, education, professional identification, personality, and attitudes toward risk. Also, buyers have different buying styles. Some may be technical types who make in-depth analyses of competitive proposals before choosing a supplier. Other buyers may be intuitive negotiators who are adept at pitting the sellers against one another for the best deal.

The Business Buying Process

Figure 6.3 lists the eight stages of the business buying process.[8] Buyers who face a new task buying situation usually go through all stages of the buying process. Buyers making modified or straight rebuys, in contrast, may skip some of the stages. We will examine these steps for the typical new task buying situation.

Problem Recognition

Problem recognition
The first stage of the business buying process in which someone in the company recognizes a problem or need that can be met by acquiring a good or a service.

The buying process begins when someone in the company recognizes a problem or need that can be met by acquiring a specific product or service. **Problem recognition** can result from internal or external stimuli. Internally, the company may decide to launch a new product that requires new production equipment and materials. Or a machine may break down and need new parts. Perhaps a purchasing manager is unhappy with a current supplier's product quality, service, or prices. Externally, the buyer may get some new ideas at a trade show, see an ad, or receive a call from a salesperson who offers a better product or a lower price.

In fact, in their advertising, business marketers often alert customers to potential problems and then show how their products and services provide solutions. For example, consulting firm Accenture's award-winning "High Performance. Delivered." B-to-B ads do this. One Accenture ad points to the urgent need for a business to get up to speed with digital technology. "Accenture Digital can help you attract more customers." the ad states, showing moths drawn to

FIGURE | 6.3
Stages of Business Buying Behavior

Buyers facing new, complex buying decisions usually go through all of these stages. Those making rebuys often skip some of the stages. Either way, the business buying process is usually much more complicated than this simple flow diagram suggests.

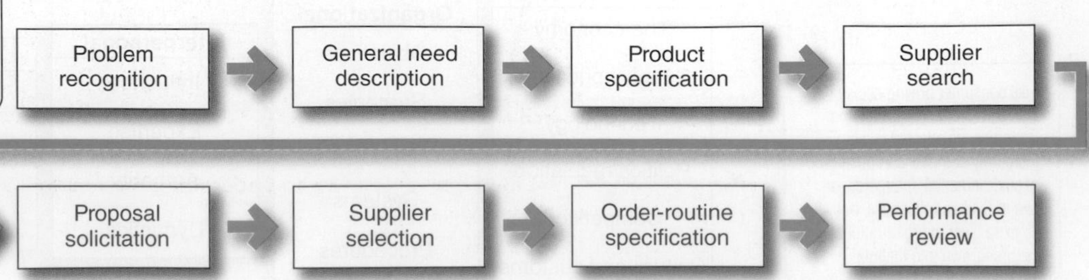

Real Marketing 6.1

International Marketing Manners

Picture this: Consolidated Amalgamation, Inc., thinks it's time that the rest of the world enjoyed the same fine products it has offered American consumers for two generations. It dispatches Vice President Harry E. Slicksmile to Europe, Asia, and Africa to explore the territory. Mr. Slicksmile stops first in London, where he makes short work of some bankers—he rings them up on the phone. He handles Parisians with similar ease: After securing a table at La Tour d'Argent, he greets his luncheon guest, the director of an industrial engineering firm, with the words, "Just call me Harry, Jacques." In Germany, Mr. Slicksmile is a powerhouse. Whisking through a flashy multimedia presentation with an ultra-compact projector, he shows 'em that this Georgia boy knows how to make a buck.

Mr. Slicksmile next swings through Saudi Arabia, where he coolly presents a potential client with a multimillion-dollar proposal in a classy pigskin binder. Heading on to Moscow, Harry strikes up a conversation with the Japanese businessman sitting next to him on the plane. Harry complements the man's cufflinks several times, recognizing him as a man of importance. As the two say good-bye, the man gifts his cufflinks to Harry, presents his business card with both hands, and bows at the waist. Harry places his hand firmly on the man's back to express sincere thanks, then slips his own business card into the man's shirt pocket.

Harry takes Russia by storm as he meets with the CEO of a start-up tech firm. Feeling very at ease with the Russia executive, Harry sheds his suit coat, leans back, crosses one foot over the other knee, and slips his hands into his pockets. At his next stop in Beijing, China, Harry talks business over lunch with a group of Chinese executives. After completing the meal, he drops his chopsticks into his bowl of rice and presents each guest with a gift as a gesture of his desire to do business with them—an elegant Tiffany clock.

A great tour, sure to generate a pile of orders, right? Wrong. Six months later, Consolidated Amalgamation has nothing to show for the extended trip but a stack of bills. Abroad, they weren't wild about Harry.

This hypothetical case has been exaggerated for emphasis. Americans are seldom such dolts. But experts say success in international business has a lot to do with knowing the territory and its people. By learning English and extending themselves in other ways, the world's business leaders have met Americans more than halfway. In contrast, Americans too often do little except assume that others will march to their music. "We want things to be 'American' when we travel. Fast. Convenient. Easy. So we become 'ugly Americans' by demanding that others change," says one American world trade expert. "I think more business would be done if we tried harder."

Poor Harry tried, all right, but in all the wrong ways. The British do not, as a rule, make deals over the phone as much as Americans do. It's not so much a "cultural" difference as a difference in approach. A proper Frenchman neither likes instant familiarity nor refers to strangers by their first names. "That poor fellow, Jacques, probably wouldn't show anything, but he'd not be pleased," explains an expert on French business practices.

Harry's flashy presentation would likely have been a flop with the Germans, who dislike overstatement and showiness. And to the Saudi Arabians, the pigskin binder would have been considered vile. An American salesperson who actually presented such a binder was unceremoniously tossed out of the country, and his company was blacklisted from working with Saudi businesses.

Harry also committed numerous faux pas with his new Japanese acquaintance. Because the Japanese strive to please others, especially when someone admires their possessions, the executive likely felt obligated rather than pleased to give up his cuff-links. Harry's "hand on the back" probably labeled him as disrespectful and presumptuous. Japan, like many Asian countries, is a "no-contact culture" in which even shaking hands is a strange experience. Harry made matters worse with his casual treatment of the business cards. Japanese people revere the business card as an extension of self and as an indicator of rank. They do not hand it to people; they present it—with both hands.

Things didn't go well in Russia, either. Russian business people maintain a conservative, professional appearance, with dark suits and dress shoes. Taking one's coat off during negotiations of any kind is taken as a sign of

International marketing manners: To compete successfully in global markets, companies must help their managers to understand the needs, customs, and cultures of international business buyers.

©David Crockett/Shutterstock

weakness. Placing hands in one's pockets is considered rude, and showing the bottoms of one's shoes is a disgusting gesture. Similarly, in China, Harry casually dropping his chopsticks could have been misinterpreted as an act of aggression. Stabbing chopsticks into a bowl of rice and leaving them signifies death to the Chinese. The clocks Harry offered as gifts might have confirmed such dark intentions. To "give a clock" in Chinese sounds the same as "seeing someone off to his end."

Thus, to compete successfully in global markets, or even to deal effectively with international firms in their home markets, companies must help their managers to understand the needs, customs, and cultures of international business buyers. Several companies now offer smartphone apps that provide tips to international travelers and help prevent them from making embarrassing mistakes while abroad. Cultures around the world differ greatly, and marketers must dig deeply to make certain they adapt to these differences. "When doing business in a foreign country and a foreign culture . . . take nothing for granted," advises an international business specialist. "Turn every stone. Ask every question. Dig into every detail."

Sources: Portions adapted from Susan Harte, "When in Rome, You Should Learn to Do What the Romans Do," *The Atlanta Journal-Constitution,* January 22, 1990, pp. D1, D6. Additional information and examples can be found in Susan Adams, "Business Etiquette Tips for International Travel," *Forbes,* June 6, 2012, www.forbes.com/sites/susanadams/2012/06/15/business-etiquette-tips-for-international-travel/; Janette S. Martin and Lillian H. Cheney, *Global Business Etiquette* (Santa Barbara, CA: Praeger Publishers, 2013); "Learn Tips to Do Business in China," *The News-Sentinel*, February 9, 2012, www.news-sentinel.com; and www.cyborlink.com, accessed September 2014.

General need description
The stage in the business buying process in which a buyer describes the general characteristics and quantity of a needed item.

a brightly lit smartphone screen. Accenture's solution: "We're helping clients leverage mobility not only to connect with customers—but also employees, businesses, and machines on Web-enabled devices of every kind. That's high performance, delivered."[9] Other ads in the series tell success stories of how Accenture has helped client companies recognize and solve a variety of other problems.

Our approach to mobility can help you attract more customers.
Are your customers drawn to you? We're helping clients leverage mobility not only to connect with customers – but also employees, businesses and machines on web-enabled devices of every kind. With critical experience in mobile solutions in industry after industry, we can help create opportunities that increase productivity, enhance collaboration and drive more transactions. That's high performance, delivered.
High performance. Delivered.
accenture
consulting | technology | outsourcing

Problem recognition: This Accenture ad alerts customers to the problem of getting up to speed on mobile technology, then suggests a solution. It promises "High Performance. Delivered."
©Accenture TBWA\Chiat\Day Worldwide

General Need Description

Having recognized a need, the buyer next prepares a **general need description** that describes the characteristics and quantity of the needed item. For standard items, this process presents few problems. For complex items, however, the buyer may need to work with others—engineers, users, consultants—to define the item. The team may want to rank the importance of reliability, durability, price, and other attributes desired in the item. In this phase, the alert business marketer can help the buyers define their needs and provide information about the value of different product characteristics.

Product Specification

The buying organization next develops the item's technical **product specifications**, often with the help of a value analysis engineering team. *Product value analysis* is an approach to cost reduction in which components are studied carefully to determine if they can be redesigned, standardized, or made by less costly methods of production. The team decides on the best product characteristics and specifies them accordingly. Sellers, too, can use value analysis as a tool to help secure a new account. By showing buyers a better way to make an object, outside sellers can turn straight rebuy situations into new task situations that give them a chance to obtain new business.

Supplier Search

The buyer now conducts a **supplier search** to find the best vendors. The buyer can compile a small list of qualified suppliers by reviewing trade directories, doing online searches, or phoning other companies for recommendations. Today, more and more companies are turning to the Internet to find suppliers. For marketers, this has leveled the playing field—the Internet gives smaller suppliers many of the same advantages as larger competitors.

The newer the buying task, and the more complex and costly the item, the greater the amount of time the buyer will spend searching for suppliers. The supplier's task is to get listed in major directories and build a good reputation in the marketplace. Salespeople should watch for companies in the process of searching for suppliers and make certain that their firm is considered.

Product specification
The stage of the business buying process in which the buying organization decides on and specifies the best technical product characteristics for a needed item.

Supplier search
The stage of the business buying process in which the buyer tries to find the best vendors.

Proposal Solicitation

In the **proposal solicitation** stage of the business buying process, the buyer invites qualified suppliers to submit proposals. In response, some suppliers will refer the buyer to its Web site or promotional materials or send a salesperson to call on the prospect. However, when the item is complex or expensive, the buyer will usually require detailed written proposals or formal presentations from each potential supplier.

Proposal solicitation
The stage of the business buying process in which the buyer invites qualified suppliers to submit proposals.

Business marketers must be skilled in researching, writing, and presenting proposals in response to buyer proposal solicitations. Proposals should be marketing documents, not just technical documents. Presentations should inspire confidence and should make the marketer's company stand out from the competition.

Supplier Selection

The members of the buying center now review the proposals and select a supplier or suppliers. During **supplier selection**, the buying center often will draw up a list of the desired supplier attributes and their relative importance. Such attributes include product and service quality, reputation, on-time delivery, ethical corporate behavior, honest communication, and competitive prices. The members of the buying center will rate suppliers against these attributes and identify the best suppliers.

Supplier selection
The stage of the business buying process in which the buyer reviews proposals and selects a supplier or suppliers.

Buyers may attempt to negotiate with preferred suppliers for better prices and terms before making the final selections. In the end, they may select a single supplier or a few suppliers. Many buyers prefer multiple sources of supplies to avoid being totally dependent on one supplier and to allow comparisons of prices and performance of several suppliers over time. Today's supplier development managers want to develop a full network of supplier-partners that can help the company bring more value to its customers.

Order-Routine Specification

The buyer now prepares an **order-routine specification**. It includes the final order with the chosen supplier or suppliers and lists items such as technical specifications, quantity needed, expected delivery time, return policies, and warranties. In the case of maintenance, repair, and operating items, buyers may use blanket contracts rather than periodic purchase orders. A blanket contract creates a long-term relationship in which the supplier promises to resupply the buyer as needed at agreed prices for a set time period.

Order-routine specification
The stage of the business buying process in which the buyer writes the final order with the chosen supplier(s), listing the technical specifications, quantity needed, expected time of delivery, return policies, and warranties.

Many large buyers now practice *vendor-managed inventory*, in which they turn over ordering and inventory responsibilities to their suppliers. Under such systems, buyers share sales and inventory information directly with key suppliers. The suppliers then monitor inventories and replenish stock automatically as needed. For example, most major suppliers to large retailers such as Walmart, Target, The Home Depot, and Lowe's assume vendor-managed inventory responsibilities.

Performance Review

In this stage, the buyer reviews supplier performance. The buyer may contact users and ask them to rate their satisfaction. The **performance review** may lead the buyer to continue, modify, or drop the arrangement. The seller's job is to monitor the same factors used by the buyer to make sure that the seller is giving the expected satisfaction.

Performance review
The stage of the business buying process in which the buyer assesses the performance of the supplier and decides to continue, modify, or drop the arrangement.

In all, the eight-stage buying-process model shown in Figure 6.3 provides a simple view of the business buying as it might occur in a new task buying situation. However, the actual process is usually much more complex. In the modified rebuy or straight rebuy situation, some of these stages would be compressed or bypassed. Each organization buys in its own way, and each buying situation has unique requirements.

Different buying center participants may be involved at different stages of the process. Although certain buying-process steps usually do occur, buyers do not always follow them in the same order, and they may add other steps. Often, buyers will repeat certain stages of the process. Finally, a customer relationship might involve many different types of purchases ongoing at a given time, all in different stages of the buying process. The seller must manage the total *customer relationship*, not just individual purchases.

E-Procurement and Online Purchasing

E-procurement
Purchasing through electronic connections between buyers and sellers—usually online.

Advances in information technology have changed the face of the B-to-B marketing process. Online purchasing, often called **e-procurement**, has grown rapidly in recent years. Virtually unknown a decade and a half ago, online purchasing is standard procedure for most companies today. E-procurement gives buyers access to new suppliers, lowers purchasing costs, and hastens order processing and delivery. In turn, business marketers can connect with customers online to share marketing information, sell products and services, provide customer support services, and maintain ongoing customer relationships.

Companies can do e-procurement in any of several ways. They can conduct *reverse auctions*, in which they put their purchasing requests online and invite suppliers to bid for the business. Or they can engage in online *trading exchanges*, through which companies work collectively to facilitate the trading process. Companies also can conduct e-procurement by setting up their own *company buying sites*. For example, GE operates a company trading site on which it posts its buying needs and invites bids, negotiates terms, and places orders. Or companies can create *extranet links* with key suppliers. For instance, they can create direct procurement accounts with suppliers such as Dell or Staples, through which company buyers can purchase equipment, materials, and supplies directly. ● Staples operates a business-to-business procurement division called Staples Advantage, which serves the office supplies and services buying needs of businesses of any size, from 20 employees to the *Fortune* 1000.

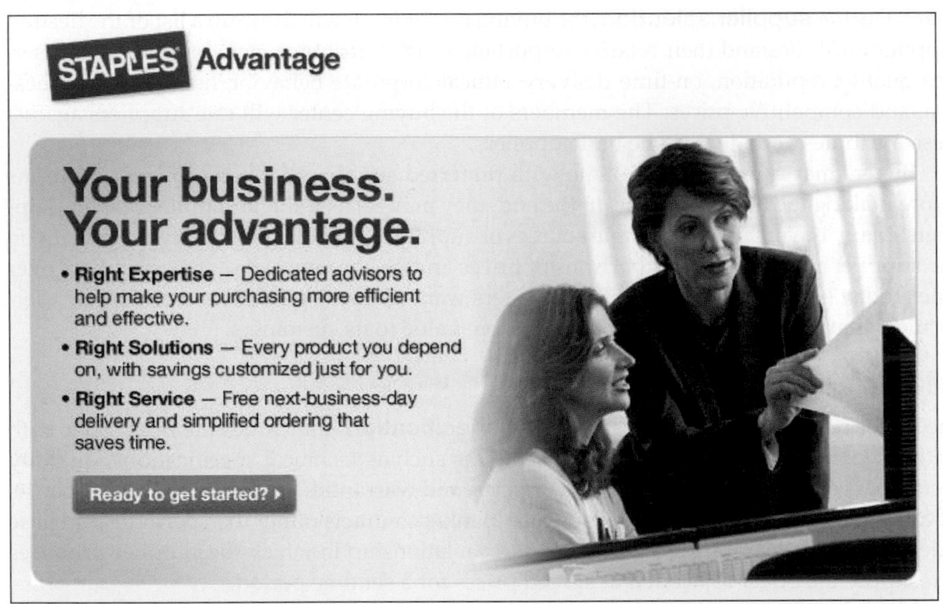

● **Online buying: Staples operates a business-to-business procurement division called Staples Advantage, which serves the office supplies and services buying needs of business customers of any size.**
Staples

B-to-B marketers can help customers online and build stronger customer relationships by creating well-designed, easy-to-use Web sites. For example, *BtoB* magazine rated the site of Shaw Floors—a market leader in flooring products—as one of its "10 great B-to-B Web sites." The site helps Shaw build strong links with its business and trade customers:[10]

> At one time, flooring manufacturer Shaw Floors' Web site was nothing more than "brochureware." Today, however, the site is a true interactive experience. At the site, design and construction professionals as well as customers can "see"—virtually—the company's many product lines. At the popular "Try on a Floor" area, designers or retailers can even work with final buyers to upload digital images of an actual floor and put any of the company's many carpets on it to see how they look. They can select various lines and colors immediately without digging through samples. And the extremely detailed images can be rotated and manipulated so a designer, for example, can show a client what the pile of the carpet looks like and how deep it is.
>
> The Shaw Floors site also provides a rich set of easy-to-navigate resources for Shaw retailers. The "For Retailers" area lets retail-partners search the company's products, make inventory checks, track order status, or order brochures for their stores. At the Shaw AdSource area, retailers can find resources to create their own ads. The Shaw Web Studio lets retailers—many of which are mom-and-pop stores—download the photography, catalog engines, and other tools they need to build their own Web sites. "So many retailers don't have the time or money to build their own online presence," says Shaw's interactive marketing manager, "so this really helps them."

More generally, today's business-to-business marketers are using a wide range of digital and social marketing approaches—from Web sites, blogs, and smartphone apps to mainstream social media such as Facebook, LinkedIn, YouTube, and Twitter to reach business customers and manage customer relationships anywhere, at any time. Digital and social media marketing has rapidly become *the* new space for engaging business customers (see Real Marketing 6.2).

Real Marketing 6.2

B-to-B Social Marketing: *The* Space to Engage Business Customers

There's a hot new video on YouTube these days, featured at the Makino Machine Tools YouTube channel. It shows Makino's D500 five-axis vertical machining center in action, with metal chips flying as the machinery mills a new industrial part. Sound exciting? Probably not to you. But to the right industrial customer, the video is downright spellbinding. "Wow," says one viewer, "that's a new concept to have the saddle ride in Y rather than X. Is that a rigidity enhancement?" In all, the video has been viewed more than 33,000 times, mostly by current or prospective Makino customers. For B-to-B marketer Makino, that's great exposure.

When you think of digital marketing and social media, you most likely think of marketing to final consumers. But today, most business-to-business marketers, like Makino, have also upped their use of these new approaches to reach and engage business customers. The use of digital and social media channels in business marketing isn't just growing, it's exploding. Even as most major B-to-B marketers are cutting back on traditional media and event marketing, they are ramping up their use of everything from Web sites, blogs, mobile apps, e-newsletters, and proprietary online networks to mainstream social media such as Facebook, LinkedIn, Google+, YouTube, SlideShare, and Twitter.

Digital and social media have become *the* space in which to engage B-to-B customers and strengthen customer relationships. Again, consider Makino, a leading manufacturer of metal cutting and machining technology:

> Makino employs a wide variety of social media initiatives that inform customers and enhance customer relationships. For example, it hosts an ongoing series of industry-specific Webinars that position the company as an industry thought leader. Makino produces about three Webinars each month and offers a library of more than 100 on topics ranging from optimizing machine tool performance to discovering new metal-cutting processes. Webinar content is tailored to specific industries, such as aerospace or medical, and is promoted through carefully targeted banner ads and e-mails. The Webinars help to build Makino's customer database, generate leads, build customer relationships, and prepare the way for salespeople by providing relevant information and educating customers online.
>
> Makino even uses Twitter, Facebook, and YouTube to inform customers and prospects about the latest Makino innovations and events and to vividly demonstrate the company's machines in action. The results have been gratifying. "We've shifted dramatically into the [digital] marketing area," says Makino's marketing manager. "It speeds up the sales cycle and makes it more efficient—for both the company and the customer. The results have been outstanding."

Compared with traditional media and sales approaches, digital and social media can create greater customer engagement and interaction. B-to-B marketers know that they aren't really targeting *businesses,* they are targeting *individuals* in those businesses who affect buying decisions. "We are selling business-to-people," notes one B-to-B marketer. And today's business buyers are always connected. They have their digital devices—whether PCs, tablets, or smartphones—hardwired to their brains. As one B-to-B marketer puts it, "Being at work is no longer a place; it is a state of mind."

Digital and social media can play an important role in engaging today's always-connected business buyers in a way that personal selling alone cannot. Instead of the old model of sales reps calling on business customers at work or maybe meeting up with them at trade shows, the new digital approaches facilitate anytime, anywhere connections between a wide range of people in the selling and customer organizations. It gives both sellers and buyers more control of and access to important information. B-to-B marketing has always been social network marketing, but today's digital environment offers an exciting array of new networking tools and applications.

No company seems to grasp the new digital and social media opportunities more fully than one of the oldest companies around—IBM. At over 100 years old and with more than 434,000 employees in 170 countries, Big Blue is as fresh and relevant as ever when it comes to social media. It uses a decentralized approach to social media. "We represent our brand online the way it always has been," says an IBM social media executive. "Our brand is largely shaped by the interactions that [IBMers] have with customers."

B-to-B social media: Machining tool manufacturer Makino engages its business customers through extensive digital and social marketing—everything from proprietary online communities and Webinars to Facebook, YouTube, and Twitter.

Courtesy of Makino, Inc. Facebook is a trademark of Facebook, Inc.

From that perspective, IBM encourages employees to talk publicly in the social media—to each other and to customers—and lets them go about it with no intervention or oversight. And go about it they do. Thousands of IBMers are the voice of the company. There are 100,000 IBMers using 17,000 internal blogs and 53,000 members plying IBM's own internal Facebook-like network. "Run an online search for 'IBM blog' and you'll find countless IBMers posting publically on everything from service-oriented architecture to sales to parenthood," says one analyst. "If you want to blog at IBM, you simply start." IBM employees by the tens of thousands or even hundreds of thousands are also actively involved on Twitter, LinkedIn, Facebook, YouTube, and many other public social media.

All this IBMer-led social networking drives an incredible amount of interaction among IBM employees, customers, and suppliers. For example, an IBM "innovation jam" can include a diverse group of as many as 500,000 people inside and outside the company. Such online interactions helped spawn what is now a major IBM movement, Smarter Planet—an initiative that puts the collective minds and tools at IBM and outside the company toward solving issues ranging from rush-hour traffic to natural disaster response.

Whether it's IBM's decentralized approach to digital and social media or Makino's more focused and deliberate one, B-to-B marketers are discovering just how effective these new networking channels can be for engaging and interacting with business customers. Digital and social marketing aren't passing B-to-B fads; they signal a new way of doing business. Gone are the days when B-to-B marketers can just push out information about their products and services in a sales call or at a marketing event. Instead, marketers need to engage customers in meaningful and relevant ways, whenever and wherever customers demand it, 24 hours a day, 7 days a week. As one B-to-B social media director states, "Customer expectations have changed. Customers want, on demand, to have a say in how they interact with you as a company." Says another social media expert, "Social media is how the current and next generation of B-to-B customers is choosing to learn about new solutions and stay current on brands."

Sources: Sara Roncero-Menedez, "Marketers Are Putting Their Money and Confidence in Social Media," *Mashable,* November 1, 2013, http://mashable.com/2013/11/01/b2b-marketing-infographic/; Elizabeth Sullivan, "One to One," *Marketing News*, May 15, 2009, pp. 10–13; Sean Callahan, "Is B2B Marketing Really Obsolete?" *btobonline.com*, January 17, 2011; Casey Hibbard, "How IBM Uses Social Media to Spur Employee Innovation," *Socialmediaexaminer.com*, February 2, 2010; "Analytics, Content, and Apps Are Hot Topics at 'BtoB's SF NetMarketing Breakfast," *BtoB,* February 17, 2012, www.btobonline.com/article/20120217/EVENT02/302179995/; David Kiron, "How IBM Builds Vibrant Social Communities," *MIT Sloan Management Review,* June 2012; Louis Columbus, "B2B Marketers Need to Get Real about Social Media and Customer Engagement," *Forbes,* January 17, 2013, www.forbes.com/sites/louiscolumbus/2013/01/17/b2b-marketers-need-to-get-real-about-social-media-and-customer-engagement/print/; and www.collaborationjam.com and www.youtube.com/user/MakinoMachineTools, accessed September 2014.

Business-to-business e-procurement yields many benefits. First, it shaves transaction costs and results in more efficient purchasing for both buyers and suppliers. E-procurement reduces the time between order and delivery. And an online-powered purchasing program eliminates the paperwork associated with traditional requisition and ordering procedures and helps an organization keep better track of all purchases. Finally, beyond the cost and time savings, e-procurement frees purchasing people from a lot of drudgery and paperwork. In turn, it frees them to focus on more-strategic issues, such as finding better supply sources and working with suppliers to reduce costs and develop new products.

The rapidly expanding use of e-procurement, however, also presents some problems. For example, at the same time that the Internet makes it possible for suppliers and customers to share business data and even collaborate on product design, it can also erode decades-old customer–supplier relationships. Many buyers now use the power of the Internet to pit suppliers against one another and search out better deals, products, and turnaround times on a purchase-by-purchase basis.

Author Comment | These two nonbusiness organizational markets provide attractive opportunities for many companies. Because of their unique nature, we give them special attention here.

Institutional and Government Markets

So far, our discussion of organizational buying has focused largely on the buying behavior of business buyers. Much of this discussion also applies to the buying practices of institutional and government organizations. However, these two nonbusiness markets have additional characteristics and needs. In this final section, we address the special features of institutional and government markets.

Institutional Markets

The **institutional market** consists of schools, hospitals, nursing homes, prisons, and other institutions that provide goods and services to people in their care. Institutions differ from

Institutional market
Schools, hospitals, nursing homes, prisons, and other institutions that provide goods and services to people in their care.

one another in their sponsors and their objectives. For example, Tenet Healthcare runs 80 for-profit hospitals in 14 states, generating $9.2 billion in annual revenues. By contrast, the Shriners Hospitals for Children is a nonprofit organization with 23 facilities that provide free specialized health care for children, whereas the government-run Veterans Affairs Medical Centers located across the country provide special services to veterans.[11] Each institution has different buying needs and resources.

Institutional markets can be huge. Consider the massive and expanding U.S. prisons economy:

> Some 7.4 million Americans, more than the individual populations of 38 of the 50 states, are in prison, on parole, or on probation. Criminal correction spending is outpacing budget growth in education, transportation, and public assistance. For instance, during the last two decades, state and federal spending on prisons grew by 127 percent, six times the growth rate of spending on higher education. U.S. prisons, which hold 2.2 million adults, spend about $80 billion annually to keep those facilities running—on average almost $35,000 per year per prisoner. "One year in prison [in New Jersey] costs more than one year at Princeton," remarks one analyst. The ultimate captive market, it translates into plenty of work for companies looking to break into the prison market. "Our core business touches so many things—security, medicine, education, food service, maintenance, technology—that it presents a unique opportunity for any number of vendors to do business with us," says an executive at Corrections Corporation of America, the largest private prison operator in the country.[12]

Many institutional markets are characterized by low budgets and captive patrons. For example, hospital patients have little choice but to eat whatever food the hospital supplies. A hospital purchasing agent has to decide on the quality of food to buy for patients. Because the food is provided as a part of a total service package, the buying objective is not profit. Nor is strict cost minimization the goal—patients receiving poor-quality food will complain to others and damage the hospital's reputation. Thus, the hospital purchasing agent must search for institutional food vendors whose quality meets or exceeds a certain minimum standard and whose prices are low.

Many marketers set up separate divisions to meet the special characteristics and needs of institutional buyers. For example, Nestlé Professional helps institutional foodservice customers find creative meal solutions using Nestlé's broad assortment of food and beverage brands. Similarly, P&G's Procter & Gamble Professional Division markets professional cleaning and laundry formulations and systems to educational, healthcare, and other institutional and commercial customers.[13]

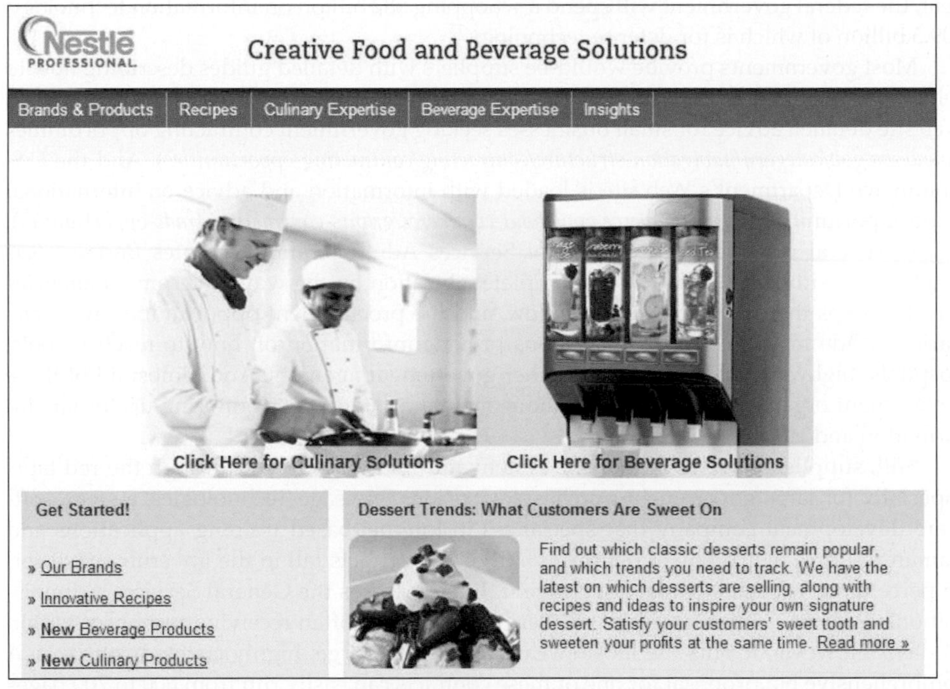

Institutional markets: Nestlé Professional helps institutional foodservice customers find creative meal solutions using Nestlé's broad assortment of food and beverage brands.

Government Markets

Government market
Governmental units—federal, state, and local—that purchase or rent goods and services for carrying out the main functions of government.

The **government market** offers large opportunities for many companies, both big and small. In most countries, government organizations are major buyers of goods and services. In the United States alone, federal, state, and local governments contain more than 89,000 buying units that purchase more than $1 trillion in goods and services each year.[14] Government buying and business buying are similar in many ways. But there are also differences that must be understood by companies that wish to sell products and services to governments. To succeed in the government market, sellers must locate key decision makers, identify the factors that affect buyer behavior, and understand the buying decision process.

Government organizations typically require suppliers to submit bids, and normally they award the contract to the lowest bidder. In some cases, a governmental unit will make allowances for the supplier's superior quality or reputation for completing contracts on time. Governments will also buy on a negotiated contract basis, primarily in the case of complex projects involving major R&D costs and risks, and in cases where there is little competition.

Government organizations tend to favor domestic suppliers over foreign suppliers. A major complaint of multinationals operating in Europe is that each country shows favoritism toward its nationals in spite of superior offers that are made by foreign firms. The European Economic Commission is gradually removing this bias.

Like consumer and business buyers, government buyers are affected by environmental, organizational, interpersonal, and individual factors. One unique thing about government buying is that it is carefully watched by outside publics, ranging from Congress to a variety of private groups interested in how the government spends taxpayers' money. Because their spending decisions are subject to public review, government organizations require considerable documentation from suppliers, who often complain about excessive paperwork, bureaucracy, regulations, decision-making delays, and frequent shifts in procurement personnel.

Given all the red tape, why would any firm want to do business with the U.S. government? The reasons are quite simple: The U.S. government is the world's largest buyer of products and services—more than $500 billion worth each year—and its checks don't bounce. The government buys everything from socks to stealth bombers. For example, this year, the federal government will spend a whopping $82 billion on information technology, $39.5 billion of which is for defense technology.[15]

Most governments provide would-be suppliers with detailed guides describing how to sell to the government. For example, the U.S. Small Business Administration provides on its Web site detailed advice for small businesses seeking government contracting opportunities (*www.sba.gov/category/navigation-structure/contracting/contracting-opportunities*). And the U.S. Commerce Department's Web site is loaded with information and advice on international trade opportunities (*www.commerce.gov/about-commerce/grants-contracting-trade-opportunities*).

In several major cities, the General Services Administration operates *Business Service Centers* with staffs to provide a complete education on the way government agencies buy, the steps that suppliers should follow, and the procurement opportunities available. Various trade magazines and associations provide information on how to reach schools, hospitals, highway departments, and other government agencies. And almost all of these government organizations and associations maintain Internet sites offering up-to-date information and advice.

Still, suppliers have to master the system and find ways to cut through the red tape, especially for large government purchases. Consider Envisage Technologies, a small software development company that specializes in Internet-based training applications and human resource management platforms. All of its contracts fall in the government sector; 65 percent are with the federal government. Envisage uses the General Services Administration's Web site to gain access to smaller procurements, often receiving responses within 14 days. However, it puts the most sweat into seeking large, highly coveted contracts. A comprehensive bid proposal for one of these contracts can easily run from 600 to 700 pages because of federal paperwork requirements. And the company's president estimates that to prepare a single bid proposal, the firm has spent as many as 5,000 man-hours over the course of a few years.[16]

Noneconomic criteria also play a growing role in government buying. Government buyers are asked to favor depressed business firms and areas; small business firms; minority-owned firms; and business firms that avoid race, gender, or age discrimination. Sellers need to keep these factors in mind when seeking government business.

Many companies that sell to the government have not been very marketing oriented for a number of reasons. Total government spending is determined by elected officials rather than by any marketing effort to develop this market. Government buying has emphasized price, making suppliers invest their effort in technology to bring costs down. When the product's characteristics are specified carefully, product differentiation is not a marketing factor. Nor do advertising or personal selling matter much in winning bids on an open-bid basis.

Several companies, however, have established separate government marketing departments, including GE, Boeing, and Goodyear. Other companies sell primarily to government buyers, such as Lockheed Martin, which makes 82 percent of its sales from the U.S. government, either as a prime contractor or a subcontractor. These companies anticipate government needs and projects, participate in the product specification phase, gather competitive intelligence, prepare bids carefully, and produce stronger communications to describe and enhance their companies' reputations.

Other companies have established customized marketing programs for government buyers. For example, Dell has specific business units tailored to meet the needs of federal as well as state and local government buyers. Dell offers its customers tailor-made Premier Web pages that include special pricing, online purchasing, and service and support for each city, state, and federal government entity.

During the past decade, a great deal of the government's buying has gone online. The Federal Business Opportunities Web site (*www.fbo.gov*) provides a single point of entry through which commercial vendors and government buyers can post, search, monitor, and retrieve opportunities solicited by the entire federal contracting community. The three federal agencies that act as purchasing agents for the rest of government have also launched Web sites supporting online government purchasing activity. The General Services Administration, which influences more than one-quarter of the federal government's total procurement dollars, has set up a GSA Advantage! Web site (*www.gsaadvantage.gov*). The Defense Logistics Agency offers an Internet Bid Board System (*www.dibbs.bsm.dla.mil*) for purchases by America's military services. And the Department of Veterans Affairs facilitates e-procurement through its VA Advantage! Web site (*https://VAadvantage.gsa.gov*).

Such sites allow authorized defense and civilian agencies to buy everything from office supplies, food, and information technology equipment to construction services through online purchasing. The General Services Administration, the Defense Logistics Agency, and the Department of Veterans Affairs not only sell stocked merchandise through their Web sites but also create direct links between government buyers and contract suppliers. For example, the branch of the Defense Logistics Agency that sells 160,000 types of medical supplies to military forces transmits orders directly to vendors such as Bristol-Myers Squibb. Such online systems promise to eliminate much of the hassle sometimes found in dealing with government purchasing.[17]

6 Reviewing the Concepts

OBJECTIVES REVIEW AND KEY TERMS

Objectives Review

Business markets and consumer markets are alike in some key ways. For example, both include people in buying roles who make purchase decisions to satisfy needs. But business markets also differ in many ways from consumer markets. For one thing, the business market is *huge*, far larger than the consumer market. Within the United States alone, the business market includes organizations that annually purchase trillions of dollars' worth of goods and services.

OBJECTIVE 1 Define the business market and explain how business markets differ from consumer markets. *(pp 198–201)*

The *business market* comprises all organizations that buy goods and services for use in the production of other products and services or for the purpose of reselling or renting them to others at a profit. As compared to consumer markets, business markets usually have fewer but larger buyers. Business demand is derived demand, which tends to be more inelastic and fluctuating than consumer demand. The business buying decision usually involves more, and more professional, buyers. Business buyers usually face more complex buying decisions, and the buying process tends to be more formalized. Finally, business buyers and sellers are often more dependent on each other.

OBJECTIVE 2 Identify the major factors that influence business buyer behavior. *(pp 201–204)*

Business buyers make decisions that vary with the three types of *buying situations*: straight rebuys, modified rebuys, and new tasks. The decision-making unit of a buying organization—the *buying center*—can consist of many different persons playing many different roles. The business marketer needs to know the following: Who are the major buying center participants? In what decisions do they exercise influence and to what degree? What evaluation criteria does each decision participant use? The business marketer also needs to understand the major environmental, organizational, interpersonal, and individual influences on the buying process.

OBJECTIVE 3 List and define the steps in the business buying decision process. *(pp 204–210)*

The *business buying decision process* itself can be quite involved, with eight basic stages: problem recognition, general need description, product specification, supplier search, proposal solicitation, supplier selection, order-routine specification, and performance review. Buyers who face a new task buying situation usually go through all stages of the buying process. Buyers making modified or straight rebuys may skip some of the stages. Companies must manage the overall customer relationship, which often includes many different buying decisions in various stages of the buying decision process.

Advances in information technology have given birth to "e-procurement," by which business buyers are purchasing all kinds of products and services online. The Internet gives business buyers access to new suppliers, lowers purchasing costs, and hastens order processing and delivery. However, e-procurement can also erode customer-supplier relationships. Still, business marketers are increasingly connecting with customers online to share marketing information, sell products and services, provide customer support services, and maintain ongoing customer relationships.

OBJECTIVE 4 Compare the institutional and government markets and explain how institutional and government buyers make their buying decisions. *(pp 210–213)*

The *institutional market* consists of schools, hospitals, prisons, and other institutions that provide goods and services to people in their care. These markets are characterized by low budgets and captive patrons. The *government market*, which is vast, consists of government units—federal, state, and local—that purchase or rent goods and services for carrying out the main functions of government.

Government buyers purchase products and services for defense, education, public welfare, and other public needs. Government buying practices are highly specialized and specified, with open bidding or negotiated contracts characterizing most of the buying. Government buyers operate under the watchful eye of the U.S. Congress and many private watchdog groups. Hence, they tend to require more forms and signatures and respond more slowly and deliberately when placing orders.

MyMarketingLab

Go to **mymktlab.com** to complete the problems marked with this icon .

Key Terms

OBJECTIVE 1

Business buyer behavior (p 198)
Business buying process (p 198)
Derived demand (p 199)
Supplier development (p 200)

OBJECTIVE 2

Straight rebuy (p 201)
Modified rebuy (p 201)
New task (p 201)
Systems selling (solutions selling) (p 202)
Buying center (p 202)
Users (p 202)
Influencers (p 202)
Buyers (p 202)
Deciders (p 202)
Gatekeepers (p 202)

OBJECTIVE 3

Problem recognition (p 204)
General need description (p 206)
Product specification (p 206)
Supplier search (p 206)
Proposal solicitation (p 207)
Supplier selection (p 207)
Order-routine specification (p 207)
Performance review (p 207)
E-procurement (p 208)

OBJECTIVE 4

Institutional market (p 211)
Government market (p 211)

DISCUSSION AND CRITICAL THINKING

Discussion Questions

6-1 Explain how the market structure and demand differ for business markets compared to consumer markets. (AACSB: Communication; Reflective Thinking)

6-2 Explain what a business marketer needs to know and what he or she needs to understand about the customer. (AACSB: Communication; Reflective Thinking)

6-3 Discuss the three main buying situations. (AACSB: Communication)

6-4 Assess how advances in information technology have had an impact on B-to-B buying process and identify what aspects have remained the same. (AACSB: Communication; Reflective Thinking)

6-5 Compare the institutional and government markets and explain how institutional and government buyers make their buying decisions. (AACSB: Communication)

Critical Thinking Exercises

6-6 *Kaizen. Seiri. Seiton. Seiso. Seiketsu. Shitsako. Jishuken.* These Japanese words are related to continuous quality improvement and are applied in supplier development programs, particularly Toyota's. Research Toyota's Production System (TPS) and describe how these concepts are applied in supplier development. (AACSB: Communication; Multicultural and Diversity)

6-7 Interview a business person to learn how purchases are made in his or her organization. Ask this person to describe a straight rebuy, a modified rebuy, and a new-task buying situation that took place recently or of which he or she is aware (define them if necessary). Did the buying process differ based on the type of product or purchase situation? Ask the business person to explain the role he or she played in a recent purchase and to discuss the factors that influenced the decision. Write a brief report of your interview by applying the concepts you learned in this chapter regarding business buyer behavior. (AACSB: Communication; Reflective Thinking)

6-8 The United States government is the world's largest purchaser of goods and services, spending more than $460 billion per year. By law, 23 percent of all government buying must be targeted to small firms. In a small group, visit the Small Business Administration's Government Contracting Classroom at www.sba.gov/content/government-contracting-classroom to learn how small businesses can take advantage of government contracting opportunities. Complete one of the self-paced online courses and develop a brochure explaining the process to small business owners. (AACSB: Communication; Reflective Thinking; Use of IT)

MINICASES AND APPLICATIONS

Online, Mobile, and Social Media Marketing E-Procurement and Mobile Procurement

Many businesses outsource certain functions to save costs. For example, your university may contract with Barnes & Noble to run its bookstore or Aramark for its foodservice. One teaching hospital in New York outsourced its coding and billing service for just one department and saved $1.35 million on billing services. The hospital might not have saved that much if it hadn't used MedPricer's e-sourcing platform to find the right supplier at the right cost for the job. E-sourcing, or e-procurement, is changing the way buyers and sellers do business. However, e-sourcing and reverse e-auctions are old news. The new kid on the block is mobile procurement, which offers a cloud-based platform that reduces the search, order, and approval cycle and offers analytics-on-the go. Most large companies have adopted some form of e-sourcing, and a recent study found that 30 percent plan to adopt mobile procurement and supply chain function mobile applications within the next year.

6-9 Discuss the advantages of e-procurement to both buyers and sellers. What are the disadvantages? (AACSB: Communication; Reflective Thinking)

6-10 Research mobile procurement and discuss the roles in the buying center that are impacted most by this technology. (AACSB: Communication; Reflective Thinking)

Marketing Ethics Pay to Stay

UK-based Premier, Foods with a net income of $1.34 billion, found itself at the center of a controversy in December 2014. It emerged that the business was charging suppliers for the right to sell them goods and services. The business was approaching the end of a process to cut down the number of suppliers from 2,800 to 1,230. The controversial scheme asked suppliers to make investment payments in return for contracts from Premier. Gavin Darby, the CEO of Premier, quickly responded to the criticism and claimed that the whole scheme had been misunderstood. The investment payment, which the media had dubbed "pay to stay," was, Darby claimed, simply an alternative to discount negotiations. Within 48 hours after the UK Business Secretary referred the matter to the Competition and Markets Authority (CMA) to investigate, the scheme was under review by Premier. Premier's share price was hit very badly and consumers started responding negatively to the news, seemingly boycotting many of the company's household brands.

6-11 Research your own country's rules about this kind of relationship and type of deal between suppliers and major companies. Explain how this might work to the mutual benefit of both parties. Do you think that it is beneficial to consumers? (AACSB: Communication; Reflective Thinking)

6-12 If there were illegal payments or deals being made between suppliers and major companies, what sanctions should be taken against them? Explain your point of view. (AACSB: Communication; Ethical Reasoning)

Marketing by the Numbers NAICS

The North American Industry Classification System (NAICS) code is very useful for marketers. It replaces the old product-based Standard Industrial Classification (SIC) system introduced in the 1930s. The NAICS system classifies businesses by production processes, better reflecting changes in the global economy, especially in the service and technology industries. It was developed jointly by the United States, Canada, and Mexico in 1997 in concert with the North American Free Trade Agreement (NAFTA), providing a common classification system for the three countries and better compatibility with the International Standard Industrial Classification (ISIC) system. This six-digit number (in some cases, 7 or 10 digits) is very useful for understanding business markets.

6-13 What do the six digits of the NAICS code represent? What industry is represented by the NAICS code 721110? How many businesses comprise this code? (AACSB: Communication)

6-14 How can marketers use NAICS codes to better deliver customer satisfaction and value? (AACSB: Communication; Reflective Thinking)

Video Case Eaton

With approximately 70,000 employees in more than 150 countries and annual revenues of nearly $12 billion, Eaton is one of the world's largest suppliers of diversified industrial goods. Eaton has been known for products that make cars peppier and 18-wheelers safer to drive. But a recent restructuring has made Eaton a powerhouse in the growing field of power management. In short, Eaton is making electrical, hydraulic, and mechanical power systems more accessible to and more efficient for its global customers. But Eaton isn't successful only because of the products and services that it sells. It is successful because it works closely with its business customers to help them solve their problems and create better products and services of their own. Eaton is known for high-quality, dependable customer service and product support. In this manner, Eaton builds strong relationships with its clients.

After viewing the video featuring Eaton, answer the following questions:

6-15 What is Eaton's value proposition?

6-16 Who are Eaton's customers? Describe Eaton's customer relationships.

6-17 Discuss the different ways that Eaton provides value beyond that which customers can provide for themselves.

Company Case Cisco Systems: Solving Business Problems through Collaboration

You've heard of Cisco. It's the company known for those catchy "Tomorrow starts here" ads. But while you may have seen its ads and other promotions, Cisco Systems is not for regular consumers like you. In fact, after ten years of trying to establish a presence in the world of consumer products, the company recently sold Linksys and its home networking business, shut down its Flip video business, and otherwise dissolved various other product lines marketed to folks like you and me. In doing so, Cisco has clearly defined itself as what it has always been since it started selling network products commercially in the 1980s—a tried and true business-to-business company. In fact, it earned honors as *Advertising Age*'s 2013 "BtoB Best Marketer." Cisco's core business is comprised of routers, switches, and advanced network technologies—the things that keep the data moving around cyberspace 24/7. But ever since the dot-com bust, Cisco has been pioneering the next generation of networking tools, from cybersecurity to videoconferencing to cloud systems.

This story is about much more than just a tech giant that makes the equipment companies need to run their Internet and intranet activities. It's about a forward-thinking firm that has transitioned from a hardware company to a leadership consultancy. In the process, there is one concept that seems to be the main driver of Cisco's business with other organizations: customer collaboration. Cisco is all about collaborating with its business customers to help vem better collaborate internally with employees as well as externally with suppliers, partners, and their customers.

Collaboration Within and Without

John Chambers became the CEO of Cisco way back in 1995, when annual revenues were a mere $1.2 billion. He successfully directed the growth of Cisco as a hardware provider. But following the dot-com bust in the early 2000s, he knew the world had become a different place. In response, he engineered a massive, radical, and often bumpy reorganization of the company. Chambers turned Cisco inside out and created a culture of 75,000 employees that truly thrives on collaboration. As such, Cisco is the perfect laboratory where new products are developed, used, and then sold to external clients. Cisco doesn't just manufacture hardware and software that makes all the sharing activity possible—it's the expert on how to use it. All this collaboration has helped Cisco's business explode, hitting $48 billion last year.

Perhaps Cisco's advertising campaign, "Tomorrow starts here," best illustrates the company's philosophy. The campaign highlights the Internet of Everything (IoE)—Cisco's term for bringing people, processes, data, and equipment together through networked connections—and the benefits that come to an organization when it utilizes its network of people more effectively. As the campaign points out, the next big thing is "lots of things—all waking up. . . . Trees will talk to networks will talk to scientists about climate change. Cars will talk to road sensors will talk to stoplights about traffic efficiency. The ambulance will talk to patient records will talk to doctors about saving lives."

According to Cisco, the pragmatic approach of the campaign helps customers understand how Cisco's IoE technologies can increase profits, speed up the development and execution of strategic insights, sustain a competitive advantage, and be more secure throughout all of it. This campaign has helped Cisco become the 13th most valuable brand in the world at the same time it has communicated why companies need Cisco's products and services.

Chambers tells the story of how Cisco began its transition from hardware into services. "Our customers literally pulled us kicking and screaming into providing consultancy," says Chambers. Some years ago, the CEO of financial services company USAA asked Chambers to help the company figure out what to do with the Internet. Chambers replied that Cisco wasn't in the Internet consulting business. But when USAA committed to giving all its networking business to Cisco if it would take the job, Chambers proclaimed "We are in that business!" Now, Cisco has both the products and the knowledge to help other companies succeed on the Internet.

A turning point for Chambers in further understanding the impact that Cisco can have on clients was the Great Sichuan Earthquake near Chengdu, China.

> Tae Yoo, a 19-year Cisco veteran, supervises the company's social responsibility efforts and sits on the China strategy board and the emerging-countries council. "I had always been a believer in collaboration," she says, but after the earthquake, "I saw it really happen. Our local team immediately mobilized, checking in with employees, customers, NGO partners. The council got people on the phone, on [video conference], to give us a complete assessment of what was happening locally. We connected West China Hospital to a specialized trauma center in Maryland via the network." High-level medical centers from the other side of the world were able to weigh in on diagnostics remotely. Cisco employees were on the ground helping rural areas recover and rebuild homes and schools. Within 14 days, Yoo continues, "I walked over to the China board with a complete plan and $45 million to fund it." That number ultimately grew to more than $100 million. "Our business is growing 30 percent year over year there," Chambers says, adding that Cisco has committed to investing $16 billion in public–private partnerships in China. "No one has the reach and trust that we do. No one could offer the help that we could."

Collaboration Benefits

Cisco management knows that number one on most CEOs' lists is to break down the communication barriers between a company and its customers, suppliers, and partners. According to Jim Grubb, Chambers' longtime product-demo sidekick, "If we can accelerate the productivity of scientists who are working on the next solar technology because we're hooking them together, we're doing a great thing for the world." Doing a great thing for the world, while selling a ton of routers and switches.

But while routers and switches still account for most of Cisco's business, the really interesting developments are far more cutting edge. Consider Cisco's involvement in what it calls the Smart+Connected Communities initiative. Perhaps the best example of a smart and connected community is New Songdo City in South Korea, a soon-to-be-completed city the size of downtown Boston being built from scratch on a man-made island in the Yellow Sea. Cisco was hired as the technology partner for this venture and is teaming up with the construction company, architects, 3M, and United Technologies as partners in the instant-city business.

Cisco's involvement goes way beyond installing routers, switches, and citywide Wi Fi. The networking giant is wiring every square inch of the city with electronic synapses. Through trunk lines under the streets, filaments will branch out through every wall and fixture like a nervous system. Cisco is intent on having this city run on information, with its control room playing the part of New Songdo's brain stem.

Not content to simply sell the plumbing, Cisco will operate services layered on top of its hardware. Imagine a city where every home and office is wired to Cisco videoconferencing screens. Engineers will listen, learn, and release new Cisco-branded services for modest monthly fees. Cisco intends to bundle urban necessities—water, power, traffic, communications, and entertainment—into a single, Internet-enabled utility. This isn't just big brother stuff. This Cisco system will allow New Songdo to reach new heights in environmental sustainability and efficiency. Because of these efficiencies, the cost for such services to residents will be cheaper as well.

Smart cities make one of Cisco's other businesses all the more relevant. Studies show that telecommuting produces enormous benefits for companies, communities, and employees. For example, telecommuters have higher job satisfaction. For that reason, they are more productive, giving back as much as 60 percent of their commuting time to the company. There is even evidence that people like working from home so much that they would be willing to work for less pay. An overwhelming majority of telecommuters produce work in a more timely manner with better quality. Their ability to communicate with co-workers is at least as good and in many cases better than when they work in the office. With products like Cisco Virtual Office and the expertise that Cisco offers to go with it, Sun Microsystems saved $68 million. It also reduced carbon emissions by 29,000 metric tons.

Cisco has also recently unveiled a set of Internet-based communication products to enhance organizations' collaborative activities. Cisco says this is all about making business more people-centric than document-centric. Its cloud-based WebEx suite promises to empower customers to "connect with anyone, anywhere, any time." In addition to WebEx Mail, WebEx Meetings provides "better meetings from beginning to end" with high-definition video conferencing that incorporates presentations, file sharing, and simultaneous use of applications, all from a computer or mobile device. WebEx Social—a sort of Facebook for corporations—allows the free flow of information to increase exponentially over existing products because they exist behind an organization's firewall with no filters, lawyers, or security issues to get in the way. And other WebEx products provide for training, customer service and IT support, and large scale online events and Webinars.

A Bright Future

"Tomorrow starts here" isn't just a tagline—it's a call to action. And as Cisco's campaign points out, the next big thing is "not that far away." Cisco has weathered tough economic times in recent years, emerging stronger, more flexible, and better poised for growth in new markets. During the decade of the 2000s, Cisco acquired 48 venture-backed companies. In the last four years, the company acquired 32 more, giving it ownership of dozens of new collaboration technologies. With these resources—and $50 billion in cash that it has stowed away—Cisco is now expanding into 30 different markets, each with the potential to produce $1 billion a year in revenue. Moving forward, the company has committed to adding 20 percent more new-market businesses annually. And because Cisco enters a new market only when it's confident that it can gain a 40 percent share, the chance of failure is far below normal.

The collaboration market has been estimated at $35 billion, a figure that will grow substantially in years to come. Because Cisco is the leader in this emerging industry, analysts have no problem accepting John Chambers' long-term goal of 12 to 17 percent revenue growth per year. Cisco has demonstrated that it has the product portfolio and the leadership structure necessary to pull it off. One thing is for sure. Cisco is no longer just a plumber, providing the gizmos and gadgets necessary to make the Internet go around. It is a networking leader, a core competency that will certainly make it a force to be reckoned with for years to come.

Questions for Discussion

6-18 Discuss the nature of the market structure and demand for Cisco's products.

6-19 Given the industries in which Cisco competes, what are the implications for the major types of buying situations?

6-20 What specific customer benefits likely result from the Cisco products mentioned in the case?

6-21 Discuss the customer buying process for one of Cisco's products. Discuss the selling process. In what ways do these processes differ from those found in buying and selling a broadband router for home use?

6-22 Is the relationship between Cisco's own collaborative culture and the products and services it sells something that could work for all companies? Consider this issue for a consumer products company like P&G.

Sources: Christine Crandell, "Cisco's User Is the Most Disruptive Force at Work," *Forbes*, March 12, 2014, www.forbes.com/sites/christinecrandell/2014/03/12/ciscos-user-is-the-most-disruptive-force-at-work/; Ellen McGirt, "How Cisco's CEO John Chambers Is Turning the Tech Giant Socialist," *Fast Company*, November 25, 2008, www.fastcompany.com/1093654/how-ciscos-ceo-john-chambers-turning-tech-giant-socialist; Greg Lindsay, "Cisco's Big Bet on New Songdo," *Fast Company*, February 1, 2010, www.fastcompany.com/1514547/ciscos-big-bet-new-songdo-creating-cities-scratch; "BtoB's Best Marketers: Blair Christie, Cisco Systems," *Advertising Age*, October 15, 2013, http://adage.com/article/btob/btob-s-marketers-blair-christie-cisco-systems/290420/; and information from www.cisco.com/web/about/ac79/innov/IoE.html and www.webex.com/products/web-conferencing/features.html, accessed July 2014.

MyMarketingLab

Go to **mymktlab.com** for the following Assisted-graded writing questions:

6-23 What is supplier development and why are companies practicing it? (AACSB: Communication; Reflective Thinking)

6-24 Describe how online purchasing has changed the business-to-business marketing process and discuss the advantages and disadvantages of electronic purchasing.

References

1. Information from www.karmsolar.com/, as well as an interview with Ahmed Zahraan, KarmSolar's CEO; Yumna Madi, KarmSolar's Chief Business Development Officer; Xavier Auclair, KarmSolar's Chief of Innovation and Technology; and Mohamed Fadly, KarmSolar's Technology Innovation Officer, interviews conducted November 18, 2012.
2. Based on information from Jessica Hansen, "Intel Opens Pop-up Retail Stores Featuring the Latest Intel-Based Devices for the Holidays," November 22, 2013, http://newsroom.intel.com/community/intel_newsroom/blog/2013/11/22/intel-opens-pop-up-retail-stores-featuring-the-latest-intel-based-devices-for-the-holidays; Beth Snyder Bulik, "What's Inside Intel/Toshiba's 'Beauty Inside,'" *Advertising Age,* November 12, 2013, http://adage.com/print/245136/; and www.youtube.com/watch?v=RMrcAQeDHbI, accessed September 2013.
3. See "CSX Transportation Takes Delivery of 300th Evolution Series Locomotive from GE," *Bloomberg*, July 19, 2007, www.bloomberg.com/apps/news?pid=newsarchive&sid=a79WICjr0_RI; and www.getransportation.com/locomotives, accessed September 2014.
4. This classic categorization was first introduced in Patrick J. Robinson, Charles W. Faris, and Yoram Wind, *Industrial Buying Behavior and Creative Marketing* (Boston: Allyn & Bacon, 1967). Also see Philip Kotler and Kevin Lane Keller, *Marketing Management*, 14th ed. (Upper Saddle River, NJ: Prentice Hall, 2012), Chapter 7.
5. Based on information from "Six Flags Entertainment Corporation: Improving Business Efficiency with Enterprise Asset Management," July 12, 2012, www-01.ibm.com/software/success/cssdb.nsf/CS/LWIS-8W5Q84?OpenDocument&Site=default&cty=en_us; and www-01.ibm.com/software/tivoli/products/maximo-asset-mgmt/, accessed September 2014.
6. See Frederick E. Webster Jr. and Yoram Wind, *Organizational Buying Behavior* (Upper Saddle River, NJ: Prentice Hall, 1972), pp. 78–80. Also see Jorg Brinkman and Markus Voeth, "An Analysis of Buying Center Decisions Through the Sales Force," *Industrial Marketing Management*, October 2007, p. 998; and Philip Kotler and Kevin Lane Keller, *Marketing Management*, 14th ed. (Upper Saddle River, NJ: Prentice Hall, 2012), pp. 188–191.
7. Based on information from "USG Print Campaign," *Communications Arts,* June 6, 2012, www.commarts.com/exhibit/usg-corporation-print.html; "BtoB's Best—Integrated Campaign: USG Corp.," October 8, 2012, www.btobonline.com/article/20121008/ADVERTISING02/310089984/btobs-best-integrated-campaign-less-than-200-000-usg-corp; Kate Maddox, "BtoB's Best Marketers," *BtoB,* October 15, 2013, www.btobonline.com/article/20131015/PEOPLE0303/310149942/btobs-best-marketers-linda-mcgovern-usg-corp; and www.usg.com/company/about-usg.html and www.theweighthasbeenlifted.com, accessed September 2014.
8. Robinson, Faris, and Wind, *Industrial Buying Behavior*, p. 14. Also see Philip Kotler and Kevin Lane Keller, *Marketing Management*, pp. 197–203.

9. For more ads in this series, see www.accenture.com/us-en/company/overview/advertising/Pages/brand-print-advertising.aspx, accessed March 2015.

10. For this and other examples, see "10 Great Web Sites," *BtoB Online*, September 13, 2010; and Karen J. Bannon, "10 Great BtoB Web Sites: Overview," *BtoB Online*, September 19, 2011. Other information from www.shawfloors.com/About-Shaw/Retailer-Support, accessed September 2014.

11. Information from www.shrinershospitalsforchildren.org/Hospitals.aspx; and www.tenethealth.com/about/pages/default.aspx, accessed September 2014.

12. Brian Resnick, "Chart: One Year of Prison Costs More Than One Year at Princeton," *The Atlantic*, November 1, 2011, www.theatlantic.com/national/archive/2011/11/chart-one-year-of-prison-costs-more-than-one-year-at-princeton/247629/; and Alan Bluestein, "Marketing: Prison Bound," *Inc.*, February 2012, pp. 96–97; "One Nation Behind Bars," *Economist*, August 17, 2013, www.economist.com/news/leaders/21583680-eric-holders-ideas-locking-up-fewer-americans-are-welcome-do-not-go-far-enough-one.

13. See www.nestleprofessional.com/united-states/en/Pages/home.aspx and www.pgpro.com, accessed September 2014.

14. Henry Canaday, "Government Contracts," *Selling Power*, June 2008, pp. 59–62; Niraj Chokshi, "There's about One 'Government Unit' for Every 3,566 People in the U.S.," *Washington Post*, September 4, 2013, www.washingtonpost.com/blogs/govbeat/wp/2013/09/04/theres-about-one-governmental-unit-for-every-3566-people-in-the-u-s/; "2012 Census of Governments," www.census.gov/govs/cog2012/, accessed March 2014; and "State & Local Government Finances & Employment: Government Units," www.census.gov/compendia/statab/cats/state_local_govt_finances_employment/governmental_units.html, accessed March 2014.

15. Chris Isidore, "Uncle Sam's Outsourcing Tab: $517 Billion," *CNNMoney*, June 10, 2013, http://money.cnn.com/2013/06/10/news/economy/outsourced-federal-government/; and Adam Mazmanian, "IT Spending up 2 Percent in President's Budget," *FCW*, April 10, 2013, http://fcw.com/articles/2013/04/10/obama-budget-it-breakdowns.aspx.

16. Based on communications with Ari Vidali, CEO of Envisage Technologies, January 2012.

17. See "GSA Organization Overview," www.gsa.gov/portal/content/104438, accessed September 2014; "Defense Logistics Agency: Medical Supply Chain," www.dscp.dla.mil/sbo/medical.asp, accessed September 2014; and Department of Veterans Affairs Office of Acquisition & Material Management, www.va.gov/oal/business/dbwva.asp, accessed September 2014.

7 Customer-Driven Marketing Strategy
Creating Value for Target Customers

Chapter Preview

So far, you've learned what marketing is and about the importance of understanding consumers and the marketplace environment. With that as a background, you're now ready to delve deeper into marketing strategy and tactics. This chapter looks further into key customer-driven marketing strategy decisions—dividing up markets into meaningful customer groups (*segmentation*), choosing which customer groups to serve (*targeting*), creating market offerings that best serve targeted customers (*differentiation*), and positioning the offerings in the minds of consumers (*positioning*). The chapters that follow explore the tactical marketing tools—the four Ps—by which marketers bring these strategies to life.

To open our discussion of segmentation, targeting, differentiation, and positioning, let's look at AirAsia. Despite fierce competition in the airline industry, AirAsia is thriving due to careful customer segmentation and targeting strategy. Combined with strong marketing efforts and booming demand, AirAsia is looking to the future with expansion in mind.

AIRASIA: Success in Targeting the Right Markets

AirAsia started its operations in 2001 as the first Asian budget airline, founded by Tony Fernandes. He started the company by buying out a failing airline company in Malaysia. The airline was originally owned by the Malaysian government, which eventually sold it to Fernandes for a small price of 25 pence. Although AirAsia had generated a lot of money, Fernandes decided to turn the company around by developing a different marketing direction through the segmentation, targeting, and positioning process. An opportunity to target a market looking for short-haul and inexpensive flights presented itself, and Fernandes transformed the company into a low-cost carrier with flights to destinations across Asia. The company began with 2 planes in 2002, and it is now up to 170 planes with over 121 routes. About 42.6 million people fly with AirAsia around the world. The airline offers over 400 flights daily from Malaysia, Thailand, Indonesia, and Singapore, among other cities. AirAsia combined a strong marketing plan with technological advancement in developing its strategy for success.

A major part of its strategy was identifying the right target market to focus on and developing the right marketing mix and operations to engage the market competitively. The main vision of AirAsia is to become the largest airline in Asia and to better connect millions of people at low cost. AirAsia also aims for high aircraft utilization, which it has achieved with the fastest plane turnaround time—only 25 minutes—thus ensuring high productivity while keeping costs low. Another aspect of AirAsia's strategy is being known as the low-fare, no-frills airline, a key part of its competitive advantage. Basically, AirAsia provides passengers with customized services and doesn't compromise on quality concerning the basic services of an airline. Finally, the airline's lean distribution system offers a variety of channels through which customers can reserve bookings and buy their tickets. AirAsia also continues to invest in and enhance its brand image, and advertising dollars go toward generating publicity and creating promotional campaigns that raise awareness of the brand.

AirAsia has a very clear vision of just which markets it wants to serve and how. It targets the price-conscious passenger with no-frills service and low fares.

AirAsia also continues to focus on friendly and personal service care for its customers. Employees are encouraged to provide high-quality service to passengers, and are often hired for their customer service skills. Such employees provide a strong foundation for the value AirAsia's customers get for their money. Customer reviews on Skytrack show that the airline has a three-star ranking, with customers noting that the employees are pleasant, efficient, and helpful. As is to be expected, some customers complain of problems when there are flight delays, especially when there are no explanations or apologies for the situation. Most are happy with the low-cost fares and are aware of the additional charges for in-flight food and beverages and are not really concerned about the added costs. Thus, the majority of the target market seems to be attracted to AirAsia's pricing strategy.

During the initial startup stages, AirAsia began to focus on price-conscious consumers, targeting leisure and business travelers who were concerned about high costs. AirAsia's main strategy is to target markets within a 3 ½-hour flight time from its hubs, which gives the company access to about 500 million people living in Southeast Asia. The growing populations of Malaysia, Thailand, and Indonesia are a big market for AirAsia. The targets within these markets include individuals who may not have been able to afford air travel or who didn't previously have access to airlines, as many airlines do not service such price-conscious markets.

AirAsia has developed a competitive advantage by targeting price-conscious, short-haul travelers who don't mind no-frills service if it means lower fares.

© farang / 123RF

At first, AirAsia started with a simple product developed for this market: a short-haul flight with no frills for the price-conscious customer. To cut costs, AirAsia provided narrow seats so that planes could accommodate more passengers, offered only one class of seating, and did not offer a frequent-flyer program allowing for discounts. In addition, many of the airline's hubs were located in secondary airports to reduce associated airport fees, and the short ground waits for flights mean AirAsia skips many of the processes of higher-cost airlines. In sum, AirAsia's strategy is to lower internal operating costs.

To provide customers with the best possible service, Air Asia relies on Internet technology. For example, online booking services are key channels for distributing its services. AirAsia's strong yield management system makes seats available at different price ranges at different points in time—reservations made earlier are cheaper than those booked later, and routes in higher demand also have higher ticket prices.

Combined, these strategies have helped to increase AirAsia's revenue by nearly 4 percent. The company's net income increased by 3.36 percent to about $1.49 billion in 2013 from 2012. AirAsia has the world's lowest unit cost of $0.023 per available seat kilometer (ASK). It has a breakeven load factor of 52%. It has also decided to hedge a huge amount of its fuel requirement until 2017. Moreover, AirAsia's aircraft turnaround time is just 25 minutes and its airplanes are utilized 13 hours per day. The CEO of AirAsia, Aireen Omar, noted that the cash position of the airline is strong and greater profits are expected in the year to come due to the high demand for its services. To meet the demand, AirAsia has set up subsidiaries in other countries, including the Philippines, Thailand, and Japan.

However, AirAsia must face a number of key challenges, including rising fuel prices and higher labor costs, as well as the need to upgrade its infrastructure, which is currently inadequate to handle the company's growth. Air Asia also finds itself having to compete with newcomers to the market, the latest being Lion Air from Indonesia and VietJetAir from Vietnam. Both airlines are entering the market by working with local partners to create Thai Lion Air and Thai VietJetAir. AirAsia must deal with these changes to continue to target its budget-conscious market, or risk becoming another Oasis Airline, which failed in its ability to keep costs low. AirAsia's current strategies for facing these challenges include hedging fuel prices and plans to buy 475 more planes by 2026. According to forecasts, Asia's annual growth in air travel will be about 6.6 percent through 2031 as the economy continues to grow, and AirAsia expects to launch more routes in order to take advantage of the higher demand.[1]

Objective Outline

OBJECTIVE 1 Define the major steps in designing a customer-driven marketing strategy: market segmentation, targeting, differentiation, and positioning.
Customer-Driven Marketing Strategy (pp 222–223)

OBJECTIVE 2 List and discuss the major bases for segmenting consumer and business markets.
Market Segmentation (pp 223–232)

OBJECTIVE 3 Explain how companies identify attractive market segments and choose a market-targeting strategy.
Market Targeting (pp 232–238)

OBJECTIVE 4 Discuss how companies differentiate and position their products for maximum competitive advantage.
Differentiation and Positioning (pp 238–247)

Companies today recognize that they cannot appeal to all buyers in the marketplace—or at least not to all buyers in the same way. Buyers are too numerous, widely scattered, and varied in their needs and buying practices. Moreover, companies themselves vary widely in their abilities to serve different market segments. Instead, like P&G, companies must identify the parts of the market they can serve best and most profitably. They must design customer-driven marketing strategies that build the right relationships with the right customers.

Thus, most companies have moved away from mass marketing and toward *target marketing:* identifying market segments, selecting one or more of them, and developing products and marketing programs tailored to each. Instead of scattering their marketing efforts (the "shotgun" approach), firms are focusing on the buyers who have greater interest in the values they create best (the "rifle" approach).

Figure 7.1 shows the four major steps in designing a customer-driven marketing strategy. In the first two steps, the company selects the customers that it will serve. **Market segmentation** involves dividing a market into smaller segments of buyers with distinct needs, characteristics, or behaviors that might require separate marketing strategies or mixes. The company identifies different ways to segment the market and develops profiles of the resulting market segments. **Market targeting** (or **targeting**) consists of evaluating each market segment's attractiveness and selecting one or more market segments to enter.

In the final two steps, the company decides on a value proposition—how it will create value for target customers. **Differentiation** involves actually differentiating the firm's

Market segmentation
Dividing a market into smaller segments of buyers with distinct needs, characteristics, or behaviors that might require separate marketing strategies or mixes.

Market targeting (targeting)
Evaluating each market segment's attractiveness and selecting one or more segments to enter.

Differentiation
Differentiating the market offering to create superior customer value.

FIGURE | 7.1
Designing a Customer-Driven Market Strategy

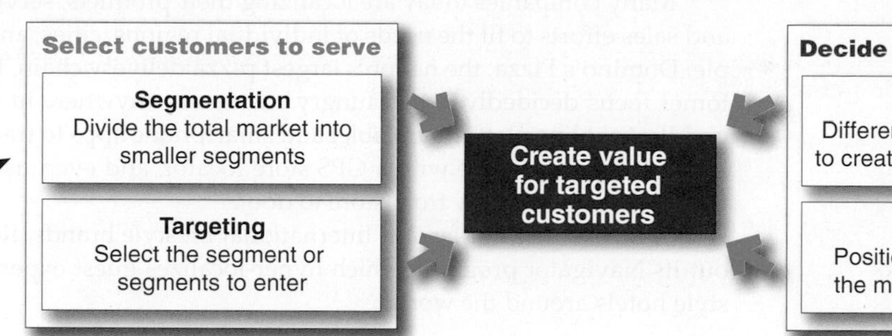
In concept, marketing boils down to two questions: (1) Which customers will we serve? and (2) How will we serve them? Of course, the tough part is coming up with good answers to these simple sounding yet difficult questions. The goal is to create more value for the customers we serve than competitors do.
Select customers to serve
Segmentation
Divide the total market into smaller segments
Targeting
Select the segment or segments to enter
Create value for targeted customers
Decide on a value proposition
Differentiation
Differentiate the market offering to create superior customer value
Positioning
Position the market offering in the minds of target customers

Positioning
Arranging for a market offering to occupy a clear, distinctive, and desirable place relative to competing products in the minds of target consumers.

market offering to create superior customer value. **Positioning** consists of arranging for a market offering to occupy a clear, distinctive, and desirable place relative to competing products in the minds of target consumers. We discuss each of these steps in turn.

Author Comment | Market segmentation addresses the first simple-sounding marketing question: What customers will we serve?

Market Segmentation

Buyers in any market differ in their wants, resources, locations, buying attitudes, and buying practices. Through market segmentation, companies divide large, heterogeneous markets into smaller segments that can be reached more efficiently and effectively with products and services that match their unique needs. In this section, we discuss four important segmentation topics: segmenting consumer markets, segmenting business markets, segmenting international markets, and the requirements for effective segmentation.

Segmenting Consumer Markets

There is no single way to segment a market. A marketer has to try different segmentation variables, alone and in combination, to find the best way to view market structure. **Table 7.1** outlines variables that might be used in segmenting consumer markets. Here we look at the major *geographic, demographic, psychographic,* and *behavioral* variables.

Geographic segmentation
Dividing a market into different geographical units, such as nations, states, regions, counties, cities, or even neighborhoods.

Geographic Segmentation

Geographic segmentation calls for dividing the market into different geographical units, such as nations, regions, states, counties, cities, or even neighborhoods. A company

Table 7.1 | Major Segmentation Variables for Consumer Markets

Segmentation Variable	Examples
Geographic	Nations, regions, states, counties, cities, neighborhoods, population density (urban, suburban, rural), climate
Demographic	Age, life-cycle stage, gender, income, occupation, education, religion, ethnicity, generation
Psychographic	Social class, lifestyle, personality
Behavioral	Occasions, benefits, user status, usage rate, loyalty status

may decide to operate in one or a few geographical areas or operate in all areas but pay attention to geographical differences in needs and wants.

Many companies today are localizing their products, services, advertising, promotion, and sales efforts to fit the needs of individual regions, cities, and neighborhoods. For example, Domino's Pizza, the nation's largest pizza delivery chain, keeps its marketing and customer focus decidedly local. Hungry customers anywhere in the nation can use the pizza peddler's online platform or tablet and smartphone apps to track down local coupon offers, locate the nearest store with a GPS store locator, and even use Domino's Pizza Tracker to follow their pies locally from store to door.[2]

Similarly, one of Marriott International lifestyle brands, Renaissance Hotels has rolled out its Navigator program, which hyper-localizes guest experiences at each of its 155 lifestyle hotels around the world:[3]

> Renaissance Hotels' Navigator program puts a personal and local face on each location by "micro-localizing" recommendations for guests' food, shopping, entertainment, and cultural experiences at each destination. The program is anchored by on-site Renaissance Hotels "Navigators" at each location. Whether it's Omar Bennett, a restaurant-loving Brooklynite at the Renaissance New York Times Square Hotel, or James Elliott at the St. Pancras Renaissance London Hotel, a history buff and local pub expert, Navigators are extensively trained locals who are deeply passionate about the destination and often have a personal connection to the locale. Based on their own personal experiences and ongoing research, they work with guests personally to help them experience "the hidden gems throughout the neighborhood of each hotel through the eyes of those who know it best."
>
> In addition, Renaissance Hotels engages locals in each city to participate by inviting them to follow their local Navigator via social media, as well as adding their own favorites to the system, creating each hotel's own version of Yelp. Navigators then cull through submitted tips and feature the best recommendations alongside their own, for sharing within the hotel lobby or on its Web site and social media channels. Since introducing the hyper-localized Navigator program as part of Renaissance Hotels' "Live Life to Discover" campaign two years ago, the hotel's Web site traffic has grown more than 80 percent, Facebook likes have exploded from 40,000 to more than 915,000, and Twitter followers have surged from 5,000 to 61,000.

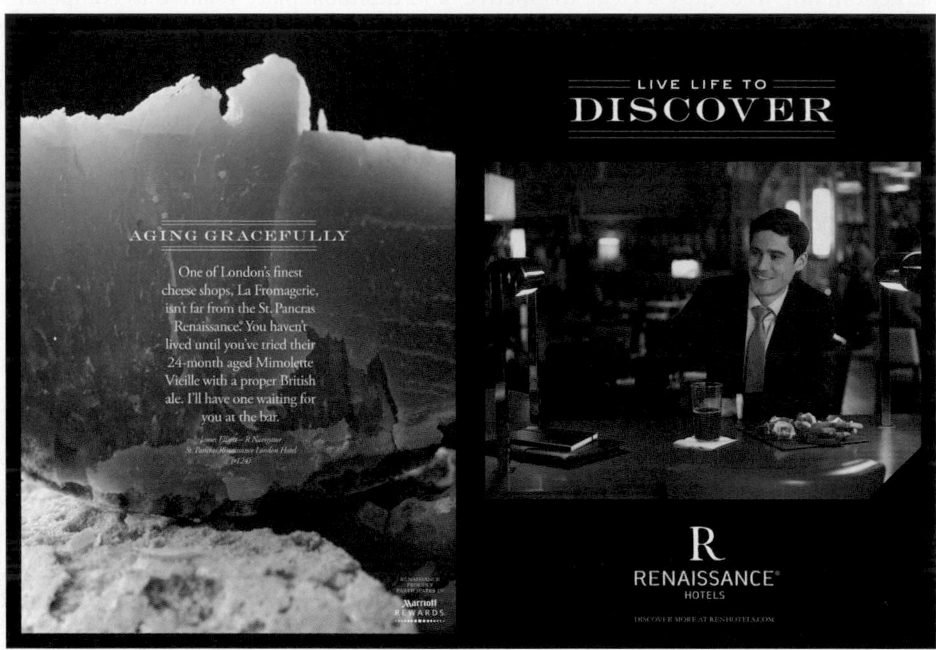

Geographic segmentation: Renaissance Hotels' Navigators and "Live Life to Discover" program help guests to experience "the hidden gems within the neighborhood of each hotel through the eyes of those who know it best."

Renaissance Hotels, Marriott International, Marriott Rewards

Demographic Segmentation

Demographic segmentation
Dividing the market into segments based on variables such as age, life-cycle stage, gender, income, occupation, education, religion, ethnicity, and generation.

Demographic segmentation divides the market into segments based on variables such as age, life-cycle stage, gender, income, occupation, education, religion, ethnicity, and generation. Demographic factors are the most popular bases for segmenting customer groups. One reason is that consumer needs, wants, and usage rates often vary closely with demographic variables. Another is that demographic variables are easier to measure than most other types of variables. Even when marketers first define segments using other bases, such as benefits sought or behavior, they must know a segment's demographic characteristics to assess the size of the target market and reach it efficiently.

Age and life-cycle segmentation
Dividing a market into different age and life-cycle groups.

Age and Life-Cycle Stage. Consumer needs and wants change with age. Some companies use **age and life-cycle segmentation**, offering different products or using different marketing approaches for different age and life-cycle groups. For example, Kraft promotes JELL-O to children as a fun snack, one that "taught the world to wiggle." For adults, it's a tasty, guilt-free indulgence—"the most sweet-tooth satisfaction 10 calories can hold." Similarly, although LEGO has typically targeted youthful users, it also markets kits that appeal more to adults. Its Mindstorms series, for instance, includes a $350, 601-piece R3PTAR robot snake kit that includes sensors, software, and motors to control the creature's movement and speech.[4]

Other companies offer brands that target specific age or life-stage groups. For example, whereas most tablet makers have been busy marketing their devices to grown-ups, Amazon has spotted a tinier tablet market. Feedback from parents suggested that they were handing their entertainment-packed Kindle Fire tablet over to their young children for entertainment, education, and babysitting purposes. To tap this young-family market, Amazon introduced FreeTime Unlimited, a multimedia subscription service targeted toward 3- to 8-year-olds. Complete with parental controls, the service provides access to a treasure trove of G-rated movies, games, and books, including premium content from Nickelodeon, Disney, Sesame Street, and DC Comics. Not only does FreeTime Unlimited generate revenues for Amazon, it helps sell more Kindle Fire tablets to young families.[5]

Marketers must be careful to guard against stereotypes when using age and life-cycle segmentation. For example, although some 80-year-olds fit the stereotypes of doddering shut-ins with fixed incomes, others ski and play tennis. Similarly, whereas some 40-year-old couples are sending their children off to college, others are just beginning new families. Thus, age is often a poor predictor of a person's life cycle, health, work or family status, needs, and buying power.

Gender segmentation
Dividing a market into different segments based on gender.

Gender. **Gender segmentation** has long been used in marketing clothing, cosmetics, toiletries, toys, and magazines. For example, P&G was among the first to use gender segmentation with Secret, a brand specially formulated for a woman's chemistry, packaged and advertised to reinforce the female image.

More recently, the men's personal care industry has exploded, and many cosmetics brands that previously catered mostly to women—from L'Oréal, Nivea, and Sephora to Unilever's Dove brand—now successfully market men's lines. For example, L'Oréal's Men Expert line includes a host of products with decidedly unmanly names such as Men's Expert Vita Lift SPF 15 Anti-Wrinkle & Firming Moisturizer and Men's Expert Hydra-Energetic Ice Cold Eye Roller (for diminishing under-eye dark circles). Dove's Men+Care line crafts a more masculine position by offering practical solutions to men's personal care problems. Calling itself "The authority on man maintenance," Dove's Men+Care provides a full line of body washes ("skin care built in"), body bars ("fight skin dryness"), antiperspirants ("tough on sweat, not on skin"), face care ("take better care of your face"), and hair care ("3X stronger hair").[6]

Gender segmentation: GoldieBlox markets engineering toys for girls. "Move over Barbie, there's a new girl in town. And she's wearing overalls and construction boots."
GoldieBlox, Inc.

Going in the other direction, GoldieBlox markets a collection of engineering toys for girls. Designed by a female engineer from Stanford University, the brand's goal is "to get girls building" and to inspire a future generation of female engineers. Aimed at girls 5 to 9 years old, GoldieBlox consists of story books and construction sets that require young girls to solve a series of construction challenges. Initially funded by more than a quarter of a million dollars raised via crowdfunding platform Kickstarter, the innovative product has recently won two Toy Industry Foundation Toy of the Year awards—Educational and People's Choice. As one writer notes, "Move over Barbie, there's a new girl in town. And she's wearing overalls and construction boots."[7]

Income segmentation
Dividing a market into different income segments.

Income. The marketers of products and services such as automobiles, clothing, cosmetics, financial services, and travel have long used **income segmentation**. Many companies target affluent consumers with luxury goods and convenience services. Other marketers use high-touch marketing programs to court the well-to-do. In the extreme, for example, one Chinese entrepreneur plans to build a luxurious gambling casino in Macau, a Chinese territory that has become the world epicenter for gaming (it generates six times the gambling revenues of Las Vegas). The casino resort, named "Louis XIII," will cater to the world's ultra-wealthy, with 200 luxury rooms, including a 20,000-square-foot abode that will rent out for $130,000 per night. Minimum bets will be $650, invitation-only artisan boutiques will sell jewelry items priced at $1 million to $100 million, and guests will be chauffeured around in red Rolls-Royce Phantoms.[8]

However, not all companies that use income segmentation target the affluent. For example, many retailers—such as the Dollar General, Family Dollar, and Dollar Tree store chains—successfully target low- and middle-income groups. The core market for such stores is represented by families with incomes under $30,000. When Family Dollar real estate experts scout locations for new stores, they look for lower-middle-class neighborhoods where people wear less-expensive shoes and drive old cars that drip a lot of oil. With their low-income strategies, dollar stores are now the fastest-growing retailers in the nation.

Psychographic Segmentation

Psychographic segmentation
Dividing a market into different segments based on social class, lifestyle, or personality characteristics.

Psychographic segmentation divides buyers into different segments based on social class, lifestyle, or personality characteristics. People in the same demographic group can have very different psychographic characteristics.

In Chapters 5, we discussed how the products people buy reflect their *lifestyles*. As a result, marketers often segment their markets by consumer lifestyles and base their marketing strategies on lifestyle appeals. For example, retailer Anthropologie, with its whimsical, "French flea market" store atmosphere, sells a Bohemian-chic lifestyle to which its young women customers aspire. And VF Corporation offers a closet full of more than 30 premium lifestyle brands that "fit the lives of consumers the world over, from commuters to cowboys, surfers to soccer moms, sports fans to rock bands."[9]

VF is the nation's number-one jeans maker, with brands such as Lee, Riders, Rustler, and Wrangler. But jeans are not the only focus for VF. The company's brands are carefully separated into five major lifestyle segments—Jeanswear, Imagewear (workwear), Outdoor and Action Sports, Sportswear, and Contemporary. The North Face and Timberland brands, both part of the Outdoor unit, offer top-of-the-line gear and apparel for outdoor enthusiasts. From the Sportswear unit, Nautica focuses on people who enjoy high-end casual apparel inspired by sailing and the sea. Vans began as a skate shoemaker, and Reef features surf-inspired footwear and apparel. In the Contemporary unit, Lucy features upscale active-wear, whereas 7 for All Mankind supplies premium denim and accessories sold in boutiques and high-end department stores such as Saks and Nordstrom. At the other end of the spectrum, Horace Small, part of the Imagewear unit, markets uniforms for police and fire departments and other first responders. No matter who you are, says the company, "We fit your life."

Differentiated marketing: VF Corporation offers a closet full of over 30 premium lifestyle brands, each of which "taps into consumer aspirations to fashion, status, and well-being" in a well-defined segment.
VF Corporation

Marketers also use *personality* variables to segment markets. For example, different soft drinks target different personalities. On the one hand, Mountain Dew projects a youthful, rebellious, adventurous, go-your-own-way personality. Its ads remind customers that "It's different on the Mountain." By contrast, Coca-Cola Zero appears to target more mature, practical, and cerebral but good-humored personality types. Its subtly humorous ads promise "Real Coca-Cola taste and zero calories."

Marketers sometimes refer to brand-focused psychographic segments as *brand "tribes"*—communities of core customers with shared characteristics, brand experiences, and strong affinities for a particular brand.[10] For example, outfitter REI's core customers are passionate about the great outdoors and share this belief as members of the REI tribe. The Apple tribe consists of stylish, tech-savvy nonconformists. Home Depot targets a core psychographic segment of dedicated do-it-yourself enthusiasts; the Nike tribe consists of high-performance athletes. Often, brands in the same product category target very different tribes. For example, although both Dunkin' Donuts and Starbucks are snack and coffee shops, their brand tribes are as different as day and night (see Real Marketing 7.1).

Real Marketing 7.1

Dunkin' Donuts: Targeting the Average Joe

A few years back, Dunkin' Donuts paid dozens of faithful customers in Phoenix, Chicago, and Charlotte, North Carolina, $100 a week to buy coffee at Starbucks instead. At the same time, the no-frills coffee chain paid Starbucks customers to make the opposite switch. When it later debriefed the two groups, Dunkin' says it found them so polarized that company researchers dubbed them "tribes," each of whom loathed the very things that made the other tribe loyal to their coffee shop. Dunkin' fans viewed Starbucks as pretentious and trendy, whereas Starbucks loyalists saw Dunkin' as plain and unoriginal. "I don't get it," one Dunkin' regular told researchers after visiting Starbucks. "If I want to sit on a couch, I stay at home."

Dunkin' Donuts is rapidly expanding into a national coffee powerhouse, on par with Starbucks, the nation's largest coffee chain. But the research confirmed a simple fact: Dunkin' is not Starbucks. In fact, it doesn't want to be. To succeed, Dunkin' must have its own clear vision of just which customers it wants to serve and how. Dunkin' and Starbucks target very different customers, who want very different things from their favorite coffee shops. Starbucks is strongly positioned as a sort of high-brow "third place"—outside the home and office—featuring couches, eclectic music, and art-splashed walls. Dunkin' has a decidedly more low-brow, "everyman" kind of appeal.

Dunkin' Donuts built itself on serving simple fare at a reasonable price to working-class customers. It gained a reputation as a morning pit stop where everyday folks could get their daily donut and caffeine fix. But recently, to broaden its appeal and fuel expansion, the chain has been moving upscale—a bit, but not too far. It has spiffed up its stores and added new menu items, such as lattes and non-breakfast items such as breaded chicken sandwiches with barbeque sauce. Dunkin' has also made dozens of store and atmosphere redesign changes, big and small, ranging from adding free Wi-Fi, digital menu boards, and more electrical outlets for laptops and smartphones to playing relaxing background music. Dunkin' franchisees can now redecorate in any of four Starbucks-esque color schemes, including "Dark Roast," "Cappuccino Blend," and "Jazz Brew," which features "dark orange and brown cozy booth seating, as well as hanging light fixtures that lend a soft glow to wall murals printed with words such as 'break,' 'fresh' and 'quality'."

However, as it inches upscale, Dunkin' Donuts is being careful not to alienate its traditional customer base. There are no couches in the remodeled stores. Dunkin' even renamed a new hot sandwich a "stuffed melt" after customers complained that calling it a "panini" was too fancy; it then dropped it altogether when faithful customers thought it was too messy. "We're walking [a fine] line," says the chain's vice president of consumer insights. "The thing about the Dunkin' tribe is, they see through the hype."

Dunkin' Donuts' research showed that, although loyal customers want nicer stores, they were bewildered and turned off by the atmosphere at Starbucks. They groused that crowds of laptop users made it difficult to find a seat. They didn't like Starbucks' "tall," "grande," and "venti" lingo for small, medium, and large coffees. And they couldn't understand why anyone would pay so much for a cup of coffee. "It was almost as though they were a group of Martians talking about a group of Earthlings," says an executive from Dunkin's advertising agency. The Starbucks customers that Dunkin' paid to switch were equally uneasy in Dunkin' shops. "The Starbucks people couldn't bear that they weren't special anymore," says the ad executive.

Such opposing opinions aren't surprising, given the differences in the two stores' customers. Dunkin's customers include more middle-income blue- and white-collar workers across all age, race, and income demographics. By contrast, Starbucks targets a higher income, more professional group. But Dunkin' researchers concluded that it was more the ideal, rather than income, that set the two tribes apart: Dunkin's tribe members want to be part of a crowd, whereas members of the Starbucks tribe want to stand out as individuals. "You could open a Dunkin' Donuts right next to Starbucks and get two completely different types of consumers," says one retailing expert.

Over the past several years, both Dunkin' Donuts and Starbucks have grown rapidly, each targeting its own tribe of customers and riding the wave of America's growing thirst for coffee. Now, both are looking for more growth by convincing "grab-and-go" morning customers to visit later in the day and stick around longer. Although still smaller than Starbucks—which captures a 33 percent U.S. market share versus Dunkin's

Psychographic segmentation: Dunkin' Donuts successfully targets the "Dunkin' tribe"—not the Starbucks coffee snob but the average Joe. Dunkin' Donuts isn't like Starbucks—it doesn't want to be."

Getty Images News

16 percent share—Dunkin' is currently the nation's fastest-growing snack and coffee chain. It hopes that the recent repositioning and upgrades will help keep that momentum going. Dunkin' plans to double its number of U.S. stores by 2020.

However, in refreshing its stores and positioning, Dunkin' Donuts has stayed true to the needs and preferences of the Dunkin' tribe. Dunkin' is "not going after the Starbucks coffee snob," says one analyst, it's "going after the average Joe." So far so good. For seven years running, Dunkin' Donuts has ranked number one in the coffee category in a leading customer loyalty and engagement survey, ahead of number-two Starbucks. According to the survey, Dunkin' Donuts was the top brand for consistently meeting or exceeding customer expectations with respect to taste, quality, and customer service.

Dunkin' Donuts' targeting and positioning are pretty well summed up in its popular ad slogan "America Runs on Dunkin'." No longer just a morning pit stop, Dunkin now bills itself as America's favorite all-day, everyday stop for coffee and baked goods. "We remain committed to keeping America running with our great coffee, baked goods, and snacks served in a friendly environment at a great value," says Dunkin's chief global marketing officer. Nothing too fancy—just meeting the everyday, all-day needs of the Dunkin' tribe.

Sources: Quotes and other information from Leslie Patton, "Dunkin' Donuts Adds Jazz to Get Less Pit and More Stop," *Bloomberg Businessweek,* June 7, 2013, www.bloomberg.com/news/2013-06-07/dunkin-donuts-adds-jazz-to-get-less-pit-and-more-stop.html; Leslie Patton, "Starbucks Turns to Happy Hour to Bring in More Traffic," *Bloomberg Businessweek,* February 1, 2012, www.businessweek.com/news/2012-02-01/starbucks-turns-to-happy-hour-to-bring-in-more-traffic-retail.html; Janet Adamy, "Battle Brewing: Dunkin' Donuts Tries to Go Upscale, But Not Too Far," *Wall Street Journal*, April 8, 2006, p. A1; "Brand Keys Ranks Dunkin' Donuts Number One in Coffee Customer Loyalty and Packaged Coffee Customer Loyalty," February 19, 2013, http://news.dunkindonuts.com; and www.dunkindonuts.com, and www.dunkinbrands.com, accessed September 2014.

Behavioral Segmentation

Behavioral segmentation
Dividing a market into segments based on consumer knowledge, attitudes, uses of a product, or responses to a product.

Occasion segmentation
Dividing the market into segments according to occasions when buyers get the idea to buy, actually make their purchase, or use the purchased item.

Benefit segmentation
Dividing the market into segments according to the different benefits that consumers seek from the product.

Behavioral segmentation divides buyers into segments based on their knowledge, attitudes, uses, or responses concerning a product. Many marketers believe that behavior variables are the best starting point for building market segments.

Occasions. Buyers can be grouped according to occasions when they get the idea to buy, actually make their purchases, or use the purchased items. **Occasion segmentation** can help firms build up product usage. Campbell's advertises its soups more heavily in the cold winter months, and Home Depot runs special springtime promotions for lawn and garden products. For more than a decade, Starbucks has welcomed the autumn season with its Pumpkin Spice Latte (PSL). Sold only in the fall, to date, the coffee chain has sold more than 200 million cups of the eagerly anticipated concoction. "I've never been happier about burning my tongue with a hot beverage," tweeted a Starbucks customer recently.[11]

Still other companies try to boost consumption by promoting usage during nontraditional occasions. For example, most consumers drink orange juice in the morning, but orange growers have promoted drinking orange juice as a cool, healthful refresher at other times of the day. Similarly, whereas consumers tend to drink soft drinks later in the day, Mountain Dew introduced Mtn Dew A.M. (a mixture of Mountain Dew and orange juice) to increase morning consumption. And Taco Bell's First Meal campaign attempts to build business by promoting Mtn Dew A.M. along with the chain's A.M. Crunchwrap and other breakfast items as a great way to start the day.

Benefit segmentation: Schwinn makes bikes for every benefit segment. For example, Schwinn's urban bikes are "for riders who want a functional, durable, and stylish bike to commute or ride casually in urban areas."

Schwinn Bicycles

Benefits Sought. A powerful form of segmentation is grouping buyers according to the different *benefits* that they seek from a product. **Benefit segmentation** requires finding the major benefits people look for in a product class, the kinds of people who look for each benefit, and the major brands that deliver each benefit.

For example, people buying bicycles are looking for any number of benefits, from competitive racing and sports performance to recreation, fitness, touring, transportation, and just plain fun. To meet varying benefit preferences, Schwinn makes affordable, quality bikes in seven major benefit groups: cruisers, hybrid, bike path, mountain, road, urban, and kids. *Bike path* bikes are "Perfect for riders who want a comfortable and easy-riding bike with convenient features for casual riding over all surfaces." Schwinn's *urban* bikes are "for riders who want a functional, durable, and stylish bike to commute or ride casually in urban areas."

In all, Schwinn makes more than 50 different lines of bikes, each designed for a specific benefit segment or subsegment. For example, Schwinn's Lakeshore bike (priced at an affordable $170 to $220) is a steel frame classic cruiser bike with coaster brakes that sells at mass retailers. It allows for "relaxing exercise" and comes with a rack on the back, handy for running errands. In contrast, the high-tech Vestige bike (priced at $1,470) is a sustainably designed urban bike, with a frame made of natural, biodegradable flax fibers and coated in water-soluble paint. The Vestige's fenders and grips are made of bamboo, and the bike can be purchased only through select dealers. The Schwinn Vestige combines style with function and has a low carbon footprint.

User Status. Markets can be segmented into nonusers, ex-users, potential users, first-time users, and regular users of a product. Marketers want to reinforce and retain regular users, attract targeted nonusers, and reinvigorate relationships with ex-users. Included in the potential users group are consumers facing life-stage changes—such as new parents and newlyweds—who can be turned into heavy users. For example, to get new parents off to the right start, P&G makes certain that its Pampers Swaddlers are the diaper most U.S. hospitals provide for newborns. And to capture newly engaged couples who will soon be equipping their new kitchens, upscale kitchen and cookware retailer Williams-Sonoma takes the usual bridal registry a step further. Through a program called "The Store Is Yours," it opens its stores after hours, by appointment, exclusively for individual couples to visit and make their wish lists. About half the people who register are new to the Williams-Sonoma brand.

Usage Rate. Markets can also be segmented into light, medium, and heavy product users. Heavy users are often a small percentage of the market but account for a high percentage of total consumption. For instance, Carl's Jr. and Hardee's restaurants, both owned by parent company CKE Restaurants, focus on a target of "young, hungry men." These young male customers, ages 18 to 34, fully embrace the chain's "If you're gonna eat, eat like you mean it" positioning. That means they wolf down a lot more Thickburgers and other indulgent items featured on the chains' menus. ● To attract this audience, the company is known for its steamy hot-models-in-bikinis commercials, featuring models such as Kate Upton, Padma Lakshmi, and Nina Agdal to heat up the brands' images. Such ads clearly show "what our target audience of young, hungry guys like," says CKE's chief executive.[12]

● **Targeting heavy users: Sister chains Hardee's and Carl's Jr. use steamy hot-models-in-bikinis commercials to attract an audience of "young, hungry men," who wolf down a lot more of the chains' featured Thickburgers and other indulgent items than consumers in other segments.**

CKE Restaurants/Splash News/Newscom

Loyalty Status. A market can also be segmented by consumer loyalty. Consumers can be loyal to brands (Tide), stores (Target), and companies (Apple). Buyers can be divided into groups according to their degree of loyalty. Some consumers are completely loyal—they buy one brand all the time and can't wait to tell others about it. For example, whether they own a MacBook computer, an iPhone, or an iPad, Apple devotees are granite-like in their devotion to the brand. At one end are the quietly satisfied Apple users, folks who own one or several Apple devices and use them for browsing, texting, e-mail, and social networking. At the other extreme, however, are the Apple zealots—the so-called MacHeads or Macolytes—who can't wait to tell anyone within earshot of their latest Apple gadget. Such loyal Apple devotees helped keep Apple afloat during the lean years a decade ago, and they are now at the forefront of Apple's huge iPod, iTunes, and iPad empire.

Other consumers are somewhat loyal—they are loyal to two or three brands of a given product or favor one brand while sometimes buying others. Still other buyers show no loyalty to any brand—they either want something different each time they buy, or they buy whatever's on sale.

A company can learn a lot by analyzing loyalty patterns in its market. It should start by studying its own loyal customers. Highly loyal customers can be a real asset. They often promote the brand through personal word of mouth and social media. Some companies actually put loyalists to work for the brand. For example, Patagonia relies on its most tried-and-true customers—what it calls Patagonia ambassadors—to field test products in harsh environments, provide input for "ambassador-driven" lines of apparel and gear, and share their product experiences with others.[13] In contrast, by studying its less-loyal buyers, a company can detect which brands are most competitive with its own. By looking at customers who are shifting away from its brand, the company can learn about its marketing weaknesses and take actions to correct them.

Using Multiple Segmentation Bases

Marketers rarely limit their segmentation analysis to only one or a few variables. Rather, they often use multiple segmentation bases in an effort to identify smaller, better-defined target groups. Several business information services—such as Nielsen, Acxiom, and Experian—provide multivariable segmentation systems that merge geographic, demographic, lifestyle, and behavioral data to help companies segment their markets down to zip codes, neighborhoods, and even households.

Using Experian's mosaic USA segmentation system, marketers can paint a surprisingly precise picture of who you are and what you might buy. Mosaic USA segments carry colorful names such as Colleges and Cafes, Birkenstocks and Beemers, Bohemian Groove, Hispanic Harmony, Rolling the Dice, Small Town Shallow Pockets, and True Grit Americans that help bring the segments to life.

©StockLite/Shutterstock

One of the leading consumer segmentation systems is Experian's Mosaic USA system. It classifies U.S. households into one of 71 lifestyle segments and 19 levels of affluence, based on specific consumer demographics, interests, behaviors, and passions. Mosaic USA segments carry exotic names such as *Birkenstocks and Beemers, Bohemian Groove, Sports Utility Families, Colleges and Cafes, Hispanic Harmony, Rolling the Dice, Small Town Shallow Pockets*, and *True Grit Americans*.[14] Such colorful names help bring the segments to life.

For example, the *Birkenstocks and Beemers* group is located in the Middle Class Melting Pot level of affluence and consists of 40- to 65-year-olds who have achieved financial security and left the urban rat race for rustic and artsy communities located near small cities. They find spirituality more important than religion. *Colleges and Cafes* consumers are part of the Singles and Starters affluence level and are mainly white, under-35 college graduates who are still finding themselves. They are often employed as support or service staff related to a university. They don't make much money and tend to not have any savings.

Mosaic USA and other such systems can help marketers to segment people and locations into marketable groups of like-minded consumers. Each segment has its own pattern of likes, dislikes, lifestyles, and purchase behaviors. For example, *Bohemian Groove* consumers, part of the Significant Singles group, are urban singles aged 45 to 65 living in apartments in smaller cities such as Sacramento, CA, and Harrisburg, PA. They tend to be laid back, maintain a large circle of friends, and stay active in community groups. They enjoy music, hobbies, and the creative arts. When they go out to eat, they choose places such as the Macaroni Grill or Red Robin. Their favorite TV channels are Bravo, Lifetime, Oxygen, and TNT, and they watch two times more *CSI* than the average American. Using the Mosaic system, marketers can paint a surprisingly precise picture of who you are and what you might buy.

Such rich segmentation provides a powerful tool for marketers of all kinds. It can help companies identify and better understand key customer segments, reach them more efficiently, and tailor market offerings and messages to their specific needs.

Segmenting Business Markets

Consumer and business marketers use many of the same variables to segment their markets. Business buyers can be segmented geographically, demographically (industry, company size), or by benefits sought, user status, usage rate, and loyalty status. Yet, business marketers also use some additional variables, such as customer *operating characteristics, purchasing approaches, situational factors*, and *personal characteristics*.

Almost every company serves at least some business markets. For example, Starbucks has developed distinct marketing programs for each of its two business segments: the office coffee segment and the food service segment. In the office coffee and vending segment, Starbucks Office Coffee Solutions markets a variety of workplace coffee services to businesses of any size, helping them to make Starbucks coffee and related products available to their employees in their workplaces. Starbucks helps these business customers design the best office solutions involving its coffees (the Starbucks or Seattle's Best brands), teas

(Tazo), syrups, and branded paper products and methods of serving them—portion packs, single cups, or vending. The Starbucks Foodservice division teams up with businesses and other organizations—ranging from airlines, restaurants, colleges, and hospitals to baseball stadiums—to help them serve the well-known Starbucks brand to their own customers. Starbucks provides not only the coffee, tea, and paper products to its food service partners, but also equipment, training, and marketing and merchandising support.[15]

Many companies establish separate systems for dealing with larger or multiple-location customers. For example, Steelcase, a major producer of office furniture, first divides customers into seven segments: biosciences, higher education, U.S. and Canadian governments, state and local governments, health care, professional services, and retail banking. Next, company salespeople work with independent Steelcase dealers to handle smaller, local, or regional Steelcase customers in each segment. But many national, multiple-location customers, such as ExxonMobil or IBM, have special needs that may reach beyond the scope of individual dealers. Therefore, Steelcase uses national account managers to help its dealer networks handle national accounts.

Segmenting International Markets

Few companies have either the resources or the will to operate in all, or even most, of the countries that dot the globe. Although some large companies, such as Coca-Cola or Sony, sell products in more than 200 countries, most international firms focus on a smaller set. Operating in many countries presents new challenges. Different countries, even those that are close together, can vary greatly in their economic, cultural, and political makeup. Thus, just as they do within their domestic markets, international firms need to group their world markets into segments with distinct buying needs and behaviors.

Companies can segment international markets using one or a combination of several variables. They can segment by *geographic location*, grouping countries by regions such as Western Europe, the Pacific Rim, South Asia, or Africa. Geographic segmentation assumes that nations close to one another will have many common traits and behaviors. Although this is often the case, there are many exceptions. For example, some U.S. marketers lump all Central and South American countries together. However, the Dominican Republic is no more like Brazil than Italy is like Sweden. Many Central and South Americans don't even speak Spanish, including more than 200 million Portuguese-speaking Brazilians and the millions in other countries who speak a variety of Indian dialects.

Intermarket (cross-market) segmentation
Forming segments of consumers who have similar needs and buying behaviors even though they are located in different countries.

World markets can also be segmented based on *economic factors*. Countries might be grouped by population income levels or by their overall level of economic development. A country's economic structure shapes its population's product and service needs, and therefore the marketing opportunities it offers. For example, many companies are now targeting the BRIC countries—Brazil, Russia, India, and China—which are fast-growing developing economies with rapidly increasing buying power.

Countries can also be segmented by *political and legal factors* such as the type and stability of government, receptivity to foreign firms, monetary regulations, and amount of bureaucracy. *Cultural factors* can also be used, grouping markets according to common languages, religions, values and attitudes, customs, and behavioral patterns.

Segmenting international markets based on geographic, economic, political, cultural, and other factors presumes that segments should consist of clusters of countries. However, as new communications technologies, such as satellite TV and the Internet, connect consumers around the world, marketers can define and reach segments of like-minded consumers no matter where in the world they are. Using **intermarket segmentation** (also called **cross-market segmentation**), they form segments of consumers who have similar needs and buying behaviors even though they are located in different countries.

Intermarket segmentation: Coca-Cola targets teens the world over through universal teen themes, such as music.
Getty Images for Coca-Cola

For example, Lexus targets the world's well-to-do—the "global elite" segment—regardless of their country. Retailer H&M targets fashion-conscious but frugal shoppers in 43 countries with its low-priced, trendy apparel and accessories. And Coca-Cola creates special programs to target teens, core consumers of its soft drinks the world over. By 2020, one-third of the world's population—some 2.5 billion people—will be under 18 years of age. Coca-Cola reaches this important market through the universal teen themes, such as music. For example, it recently joined forces with Spotify to provide a global music network that helps teens discover new music, connect with other music-loving teens, and share their experiences with friends worldwide both online and offline.[16]

Requirements for Effective Segmentation

Clearly, there are many ways to segment a market, but not all segmentations are effective. For example, buyers of table salt could be divided into blonde and brunette customers. But hair color obviously does not affect the purchase of salt. Furthermore, if all salt buyers bought the same amount of salt each month, believed that all salt is the same, and wanted to pay the same price, the company would not benefit from segmenting this market.

To be useful, market segments must be

- *Measurable.* The size, purchasing power, and profiles of the segments can be measured.
- *Accessible.* The market segments can be effectively reached and served.
- *Substantial.* The market segments are large or profitable enough to serve. A segment should be the largest possible homogeneous group worth pursuing with a tailored marketing program. It would not pay, for example, for an automobile manufacturer to develop cars especially for people whose height is greater than seven feet.
- *Differentiable.* The segments are conceptually distinguishable and respond differently to different marketing mix elements and programs. If men and women respond similarly to marketing efforts for soft drinks, they do not constitute separate segments.
- *Actionable.* Effective programs can be designed for attracting and serving the segments. For example, although one small airline identified seven market segments, its staff was too small to develop separate marketing programs for each segment.

Author Comment | After dividing the market into segments, it's time to answer that first seemingly simple marketing strategy question we raised in Figure 7.1: Which customers will the company serve?

Market Targeting

Market segmentation reveals the firm's market segment opportunities. The firm now has to evaluate the various segments and decide how many and which segments it can serve best. We now look at how companies evaluate and select target segments.

Evaluating Market Segments

In evaluating different market segments, a firm must look at three factors: segment size and growth, segment structural attractiveness, and company objectives and resources. First, a company wants to select segments that have the right size and growth characteristics. But "right size and growth" is a relative matter. The largest, fastest-growing segments are not always the most attractive ones for every company. Smaller companies may lack the skills and resources needed to serve larger segments. Or they may find these segments too competitive. Such companies may target segments that are smaller and less attractive, in an absolute sense, but that are potentially more profitable for them.

The company also needs to examine major structural factors that affect long-run segment attractiveness.[17] For example, a segment is less attractive if it already contains many strong and aggressive *competitors* or if it is easy for *new entrants* to come into the segment. The existence of many actual or potential *substitute products* may limit prices and the profits that can be earned in a segment. The relative *power of buyers* also affects segment attractiveness. Buyers with strong bargaining power relative to sellers will try to force prices down, demand more services, and set competitors against one another—all at the expense of seller profitability. Finally, a segment may be less attractive if it contains *powerful suppliers* that can control prices or reduce the quality or quantity of ordered goods and services.

Even if a segment has the right size and growth and is structurally attractive, the company must consider its own objectives and resources. Some attractive segments can be dismissed quickly because they do not mesh with the company's long-run objectives. Or the company may lack the skills and resources needed to succeed in an attractive segment. For example, the economy segment of the automobile market is large and growing. But given its objectives and resources, it would make little sense for luxury-performance carmaker

FIGURE | 7.2
Market-Targeting Strategies

This figure covers a broad range of targeting strategies, from mass marketing (virtually no targeting) to individual marketing (customizing products and programs to individual customers). An example of individual marketing: At mymms.com you can order a batch of M&M's with your face and personal message printed on each little candy.

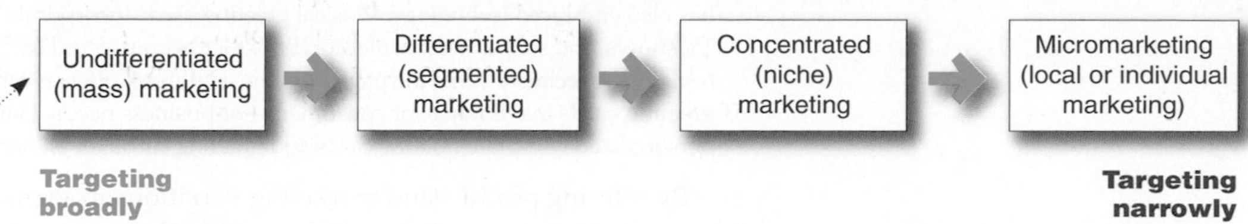

BMW to enter this segment. A company should only enter segments in which it can create superior customer value and gain advantages over its competitors.

Selecting Target Market Segments

Target market
A set of buyers sharing common needs or characteristics that the company decides to serve.

After evaluating different segments, the company must decide which and how many segments it will target. A **target market** consists of a set of buyers who share common needs or characteristics that the company decides to serve. Market targeting can be carried out at several different levels. **Figure 7.2** shows that companies can target very broadly (*undifferentiated marketing*), very narrowly (*micromarketing*), or somewhere in between (*differentiated or concentrated marketing*).

Undifferentiated Marketing

Undifferentiated (mass) marketing
A market-coverage strategy in which a firm decides to ignore market segment differences and go after the whole market with one offer.

Using an **undifferentiated marketing** (or **mass marketing**) strategy, a firm might decide to ignore market segment differences and target the whole market with one offer. Such a strategy focuses on what is *common* in the needs of consumers rather than on what is *different*. The company designs a product and a marketing program that will appeal to the largest number of buyers.

As noted earlier in the chapter, most modern marketers have strong doubts about this strategy. Difficulties arise in developing a product or brand that will satisfy all consumers. Moreover, mass marketers often have trouble competing with more-focused firms that do a better job of satisfying the needs of specific segments and niches.

Differentiated Marketing

Differentiated (segmented) marketing
A market-coverage strategy in which a firm decides to target several market segments and designs separate offers for each.

Using a **differentiated marketing** (or **segmented marketing**) strategy, a firm decides to target several market segments and designs separate offers for each. As we saw in the chapter-opening story, P&G markets at least six different laundry detergent brands in the United States (Tide, Gain, Cheer, Era, Dreft, and Bold), which compete with each other on supermarket shelves. Then, P&G further segments each detergent brand to serve even narrower niches. For example, you can buy any of the dozens of versions of Tide—from original Tide, Tide Coldwater, or Tide Pods to Tide Free & Gentle, Tide plus Febreze, or Tide with a Touch of Downy.

Perhaps no brand practices differentiated marketing like Hallmark Cards.[18]

Hallmark vigorously segments the greeting card market. In addition to its broad Hallmark card line and popular sub-branded lines such as the humorous Shoebox Greetings, Hallmark has introduced lines targeting a dozen or more specific segments. Fresh Ink targets 18- to 39-year-old women. Hallmark Warm Wishes offers hundreds of affordable 99-cent cards. Hallmark's three ethnic lines—Mahogany, Sinceramente Hallmark, and Tree of Life—target African-American, Hispanic, and Jewish

Differentiated marketing: In addition to its broad Hallmark card line, Hallmark vigorously segments the greeting card market, with shelves full of popular sub-branded lines.

© Kristoffer Tripplaar/Alamy

consumers, respectively. Hallmark's newer Journeys line of encouragement cards focuses on such challenges as fighting cancer, coming out, and battling depression. Specific greeting cards benefit charities such as (PRODUCT) RED, UNICEF, and the Susan G. Komen Race for the Cure. Hallmark has also embraced technology. Musical greeting cards incorporate sound clips from popular movies, TV shows, and songs. Recordable storybooks let people record each page of a book and have it played back as the recipient turns the pages. Online, Hallmark offers e-cards as well as personalized printed greeting cards that it mails for consumers. For business needs, Hallmark Business Expressions offers personalized corporate holiday cards and greeting cards for all occasions and events.

By offering product and marketing variations to segments, companies hope for higher sales and a stronger position within each market segment. Developing a stronger position within several segments creates more total sales than undifferentiated marketing across all segments. Thanks to its differentiated approach, Hallmark's brands account for more than 44 percent of the greeting cards purchased in the United States. Similarly, P&G's multiple detergent brands capture four times the market share of its nearest rival.[19]

But differentiated marketing also increases the costs of doing business. A firm usually finds it more expensive to develop and produce, say, 10 units of 10 different products than 100 units of a single product. Developing separate marketing plans for separate segments requires extra marketing research, forecasting, sales analysis, promotion planning, and channel management. And trying to reach different market segments with different advertising campaigns increases promotion costs. Thus, the company must weigh increased sales against increased costs when deciding on a differentiated marketing strategy.

Concentrated Marketing

Concentrated (niche) marketing
A market-coverage strategy in which a firm goes after a large share of one or a few segments or niches.

When using a **concentrated marketing** (or **niche marketing**) strategy, instead of going after a small share of a large market, a firm goes after a large share of one or a few smaller segments or niches. For example, Whole Foods Market has more than 360 stores and over $13 billion in sales, compared with goliaths such as Kroger (more than 3,600 stores and sales of $96 billion) and Walmart (close to 10,000 stores and sales of $469 billion).[20] Yet, over the past five years, the smaller, more upscale retailer has grown faster and more profitably than either of its giant rivals. Whole Foods thrives by catering to affluent customers who the Walmarts of the world can't serve well, offering them "organic, natural, and gourmet foods, all swaddled in Earth Day politics." In fact, a typical Whole Foods customer is more likely to boycott the local Walmart than to shop at it.

Through concentrated marketing, the firm achieves a strong market position because of its greater knowledge of consumer needs in the niches it serves and the special reputation it acquires. It can market more *effectively* by fine-tuning its products, prices, and programs to the needs of carefully defined segments. It can also market more *efficiently*, targeting its products or services, channels, and communications programs toward only consumers that it can serve best and most profitably.

Niching lets smaller companies focus their limited resources on serving niches that may be unimportant to or overlooked by larger competitors. Many companies start as nichers to get a foothold against larger, more resourceful competitors and then grow into broader competitors. For example, Southwest Airlines began by serving intrastate, no-frills commuters in Texas but is now one of the nation's largest airlines. And Enterprise Rent-A-Car began by building a network of neighborhood offices rather than competing with Hertz and Avis in airport locations. Enterprise is now the nation's largest car rental company.

Today, the low cost of setting up shop on the Internet makes it even more profitable to serve seemingly miniscule niches. Small businesses, in particular, are realizing riches from serving small niches on the Web. Consider online women's clothing nicher Modcloth.com:[21]

Concentrated marketing: Thanks to the reach and power of online marketing, online women's clothing nicher ModCloth.com has attracted a devoted following.

Modcloth Inc.

While her high-school classmates were out partying with friends or shopping at the mall, Susan Gregg Koger was squirreled away in her bedroom, sorting through vintage clothing she'd found at local thrift shops and dreaming up her own online business. At the tender age of 17, she and her boyfriend, now husband, Eric Koger, launched ModCloth.com out of their Carnegie Mellon dorm rooms. Despite these modest beginnings, thanks to the power of the Internet, the fledgling company soared. Today, only a decade later, ModCloth.com boasts more than 450 employees, 700 independent designers, and a closet full of one-of-a-kind finds. ModCloth.com's unique selection of indie clothing, engaging promotions on The ModCloth blog and various social media, and Web interactivity—such as letting customers play a big role in selecting featured apparel and even its design direction—have attracted a devoted following. The site draws more than 2 million visitors per month. ModCloth's revenues exceeded $100 million last year and the company is growing at 40 percent annually.

Concentrated marketing can be highly profitable. At the same time, it involves higher-than-normal risks. Companies that rely on one or a few segments for all of their business will suffer greatly if the segment turns sour. Or larger competitors may decide to enter the same segment with greater resources. In fact, many large companies develop or acquire niche brands of their own. For example, Coca-Cola's Venturing and Emerging Brands unit markets a cooler full of niche beverages. Its brands include Honest Tea (the nation's number one organic bottled tea brand), NOS (an energy drink popular among auto enthusiasts), FUZE (a fusion of tea, fruit, and other flavors), Zico (pure premium coconut water), Odwalla (natural beverage and bars that "bring goodness to your life"), and many others. Such brands let Coca-Cola compete effectively in smaller, specialized markets, and some will grow into future powerhouse brands.[22]

Micromarketing

Micromarketing
Tailoring products and marketing programs to the needs and wants of specific individuals and local customer segments; it includes *local marketing* and *individual marketing*.

Local marketing
Tailoring brands and marketing to the needs and wants of local customer segments—cities, neighborhoods, and even specific stores.

Differentiated and concentrated marketers tailor their offers and marketing programs to meet the needs of various market segments and niches. At the same time, however, they do not customize their offers to each individual customer. **Micromarketing** is the practice of tailoring products and marketing programs to suit the tastes of specific individuals and locations. Rather than seeing a customer in every individual, micromarketers see the individual in every customer. Micromarketing includes *local marketing* and *individual marketing*.

Local Marketing. **Local marketing** involves tailoring brands and promotions to the needs and wants of local customer groups—cities, neighborhoods, and even specific stores. For example, department store chain Macy's has rolled out a localization program called My Macy's in which merchandise is customized under 69 different geographical districts. At stores around the country, Macy's sales clerks record local shopper requests and pass them along to district managers. In turn, blending the customer requests with store transaction data, the district managers customize the mix of merchandise in their stores. So, for instance, Macy's stores in Michigan stock more locally made Sanders chocolate candies. In Orlando, Macy's carries more swimsuits in stores near waterparks and more twin bedding in stores near condominium rentals. The chain stocks extra coffee percolators in its Long Island stores, where it sells more of the 1960s must-haves than anywhere else in the country. In all, the "My Macy's" strategy is to meet the needs of local markets, making the giant retailer seem smaller and more in touch.[23]

Advances in communications technology have given rise to new high-tech versions of location-based marketing. Thanks to the explosion in net-connected smartphones with GPS capabilities and location-based social networks, companies can now track consumers' whereabouts closely and gear their offers accordingly. Using location-based social media check-in services such as Foursquare or Shopkick and local-marketing deal-of-the-day services such as Groupon or LivingSocial, retailers can engage consumers with local deals and information.

Increasingly, location-based marketing is going mobile, reaching on-the-go consumers as they come and go in key local market areas. It's called *SoLoMo (social+local+mobile)* marketing:[24]

With the rise of smartphones and tablets that integrate geo-location technology such as GPS, marketers are now tapping into what experts call the Social Local Mobile (SoLoMo) revolution. SoLoMo refers to the ability of companies to give on-the-go consumers local information and deals fast, wherever they may be. Services such as Foursquare and Groupon, and retailers ranging from REI and Starbucks to Walgreens, have jumped onto the SoLoMo bandwagon, primarily in the form of smartphone and tablet apps.

Mobile app Shopkick excels at SoLoMo. It sends special offers and rewards to shoppers simply for checking into client stores such as Target, American Eagle, Best Buy, or Crate&Barrel. When shoppers are near a participating store, the Shopkick app on their phone picks up a signal from the store and spits out store coupons, deal alerts, and product information. When Shopkickers

Increasingly, local marketing is going mobile. Mobile app Shopkick excels at SoLoMo (Social Local Mobile) by sending rewards and special offers to shoppers for simply walking into client stores such as Target, American Eagle, Best Buy, or Crate&Barrel.

Shopkick

walk into their favorite retail stores, the app automatically checks them in and they rack up rewards points or "kicks." If they buy something, they get even more kicks. Users can use their kicks for discounted or free merchandise of their own choosing. Shopkick helps users get the most out of their efforts by mapping out potential kicks in a given geographic area. Shopkick has grown quickly to become one of the nation's top five shopping apps, with more than 6 million users.

Local marketing has some drawbacks, however. It can drive up manufacturing and marketing costs by reducing the economies of scale. It can also create logistics problems as companies try to meet the varied requirements of different local markets. Still, as companies face increasingly fragmented markets, and as new supporting technologies develop, the advantages of local marketing often outweigh the drawbacks.

Individual Marketing. In the extreme, micromarketing becomes **individual marketing**—tailoring products and marketing programs to the needs and preferences of individual customers. Individual marketing has also been labeled one-to-one marketing, mass customization, and markets-of-one marketing.

Individual marketing
Tailoring products and marketing programs to the needs and preferences of individual customers.

The widespread use of mass marketing has obscured the fact that for centuries consumers were served as individuals: The tailor custom-made a suit, the cobbler designed shoes for an individual, and the cabinetmaker made furniture to order. Today, new technologies are permitting many companies to return to customized marketing. Detailed databases, robotic production and flexible manufacturing, and interactive media such as smartphones and the Internet have combined to foster mass customization. *Mass customization* is the process by which firms interact one to one with masses of customers to design products and services tailor-made to individual needs.

Individual marketing has made relationships with customers more important than ever. Just as mass production was the marketing principle of the twentieth century, interactive marketing is becoming a marketing principle for the twenty-first century. The world appears to be coming full circle—from the good old days when customers were treated as individuals to mass marketing when nobody knew your name, and then back again.

Companies these days are hyper-customizing everything from food to artwork, earphones, sneakers, and motorcycles.[25]

At mymms.com, candy lovers can buy M&M's embossed with images of their kids or pets; at mixmyown.com, nutrition-minded folks can create their own healthy cereal mix. JH Audio in Orlando makes music earphones based on molds of customers' ears to provide optimized fit and better and safer sound. The company even laser prints designs on the tiny ear buds—some people request a kid for each ear; others prefer a dog. The PUMA Factory sneaker customization Web site lets customers pick their own fabrics and tailor their PUMA shoes to taste. "It's a place for you to match your shoes to your favorite team or oldest t-shirt, paint by numbers, and innovate outside the lines," says PUMA. On a much larger scale, Harley-Davidson's H-D1 factory customization program lets customers go online, design their own Harley, and get it in as little as four weeks. It invites customers to explore some 8,000 ways to create their own masterpiece. "You dream it. We build it," says the company.

Individual marketing: The PUMA Factory sneaker customization Web site lets customers tailor their PUMA shoes to taste. "You know what works—what styles, what textures, what colors. Customize your sneakers whatever way you want."

PUMA SE

Business-to-business marketers are also finding new ways to customize their offerings. For example, John Deere manufactures seeding equipment that can be configured in more than 2 million versions to individual customer specifications. The seeders are produced one at a time, in any sequence, on a single production line. Mass customization provides a way to stand out against competitors.

Choosing a Targeting Strategy

Companies need to consider many factors when choosing a market-targeting strategy. Which strategy is best depends on the company's resources. When the firm's resources are limited, concentrated marketing makes the most sense. The best strategy also depends on the degree of product variability. Undifferentiated marketing is more suited for uniform products, such as grapefruit or steel. Products that can vary in design, such as cameras and cars, are more suited to differentiation or concentration. The product's life-cycle stage also must be considered. When a firm introduces a new product, it may be practical to launch one version only, as undifferentiated marketing or concentrated marketing may make the most sense. In the mature stage of the product life cycle, however, differentiated marketing often makes more sense.

Another factor is *market variability*. If most buyers have the same tastes, buy the same amounts, and react the same way to marketing efforts, undifferentiated marketing is appropriate. Finally, *competitors' marketing strategies* should be considered. When competitors use differentiated or concentrated marketing, undifferentiated marketing can be suicidal. Conversely, when competitors use undifferentiated marketing, a firm can gain an advantage by using differentiated or concentrated marketing, focusing on the needs of buyers in specific segments.

Socially Responsible Target Marketing

Smart targeting helps companies become more efficient and effective by focusing on the segments that they can satisfy best and most profitably. Targeting also benefits consumers—companies serve specific groups of consumers with offers carefully tailored to their needs. However, target marketing sometimes generates controversy and concern. The biggest issues usually involve the targeting of vulnerable or disadvantaged consumers with controversial or potentially harmful products.

Socially responsible targeting: Critics worry that children may be especially vulnerable to targeted marketing messages subtly embedded within digital content and viewed on personal, small-screen devices that are beyond even the most watchful parent's eye.

For example, fast-food chains have generated controversy over the years by their attempts to target inner-city minority consumers. They've been accused of pitching their high-fat, salt-laden fare to low-income, urban residents who are much more likely than suburbanites to be heavy consumers. Similarly, big banks and mortgage lenders have been criticized for targeting consumers in poor urban areas with attractive adjustable-rate home mortgages that they can't really afford.

Children are seen as an especially vulnerable audience. Marketers in a wide range of industries—from cereal, soft drinks, and fast food to toys and fashion—have been criticized for their marketing efforts directed toward children. Critics worry that enticing premium offers and high-powered advertising appeals will overwhelm children's defenses. In recent years, for instance, McDonald's has been criticized by various health advocates and parent groups concerned that its popular Happy Meals offers—featuring trinkets and other items tied in with children's movies such as *The LEGO Movie*—create a too-powerful connection between children and the often fat- and calorie-laden meals. Some critics have even asked McDonald's to retire its iconic Ronald McDonald character. McDonald's has responded by putting the Happy Meal on a diet, cutting the overall calorie count by 20 percent, adding fruit to every meal, and promoting Happy Meals only with milk, water, and juice. For two weeks during one month last year, McDonald's replaced the toys in its Happy Meals with specially developed children's books containing nutritional messages.[26]

The digital era may make children even more vulnerable to targeted marketing messages. Traditional child-directed TV and print ads usually contain obvious pitches that are easily detected and controlled by parents. However, marketing in digital media may be subtly embedded within the content and viewed by children on personal, small-screen devices that are beyond even the most watchful parent's eye. Such marketing might take the form of immersive "advergames"—video games specifically designed to engage children with products. Or they might consist of embedded ads, quizzes, or product placements that let marketers cross-promote branded products, TV shows, popular characters, or other marketable entities.

For example, free video games offered at Barbie.com let children help Barbie "build 'n style" her "perf mansion" or play "princess charm school games" with her. At Nickelodeon's The Club—an "online virtual world for kids"—young children can create an avatar and immerse themselves in "Super Spongy Square Games" with SpongeBob SquarePants or browse the Power Rangers Samurai store. Kraft's free "Jiggle-It" app engages kids by letting them watch a JELL-O cube dance to their favorite songs; the brand's "Dinner, Not Art" app lets them create digital macaroni art, helping to promote the company's Kraft Macaroni and Cheese. Some watchers see such marketing as adding value for both the children and the marketers—promoting child creativity and entertainment while engaging the child in brand-related experiences. Others, however, worry that it constitutes "stealth marketing" that takes advantage of children who can't yet tell the difference between commercial and entertainment or educational content. "Kids are not as savvy to the methods and motives of advertisers," concludes one analyst. "Young kids are more gullible."[27]

To encourage responsible children's advertising, the Children's Advertising Review Unit, the advertising industry's self-regulatory agency, has published extensive children's advertising guidelines that recognize the special needs of child audiences. Still, critics feel that more should have been done, especially concerning online and digital marketing. Some have even called for a complete ban on advertising to children.

Not all attempts to target children, minorities, or other special segments draw such criticism. In fact, most provide benefits to targeted consumers. For example, Pantene markets Relaxed and Natural hair products to women of color. Samsung markets the Jitterbug, an easy-to-use phone, directly to seniors who need a simpler mobile phone with bigger buttons, large screen text, and a louder speaker. And Colgate makes a large selection of toothbrush shapes and toothpaste flavors for children—from Colgate SpongeBob SquarePants Mild Bubble Fruit toothpaste to Colgate Dora the Explorer character toothbrushes. Such products help make tooth brushing more fun and get children to brush longer and more often.

More broadly, the growth of the Internet, smartphones, and other carefully targeted direct media has raised fresh concerns about potential targeting abuses. The Internet and mobile marketing allow more precise targeting, letting the makers of questionable products or deceptive advertisers zero in on the most vulnerable audiences. Unscrupulous marketers can now send tailor-made, deceptive messages by e-mail directly to millions of unsuspecting consumers. For example, the Federal Bureau of Investigation's Internet Crime Complaint Center Web site alone received more than 289,000 complaints last year.[28]

Today's marketers are also using sophisticated analytical techniques to track consumers' digital movements and to build detailed customer profiles containing highly personal information. Such profiles can then be used to hypertarget individual consumers with personalized brand messages and offers. Hypertargeting can benefit both marketers and consumers, getting the right brand information into the hands of the right customers. However, taken too far or used wrongly, hypertargeting can harm consumers more than benefit them. Marketers must use these new targeting tools responsibly (see Real Marketing 7.2).

Thus, in target marketing, the issue is not really *who* is targeted but rather *how* and for *what*. Controversies arise when marketers attempt to profit at the expense of targeted segments—when they unfairly target vulnerable segments or target them with questionable products or tactics. Socially responsible marketing calls for segmentation and targeting that serve not just the interests of the company but also the interests of those targeted.

Author Comment | At the same time that the company is answering the first simple-sounding question (Which customers will we serve?), it must be asking the second question (How will we serve them?). For example, Ritz-Carlton hotels serve the top 5 percent of corporate and leisure travelers. Its parallel value proposition is "The Ritz-Carlton Experience"—one that "enlivens the senses, instills a sense of well-being, and fulfills even the unexpressed wishes and needs of our guests."

Differentiation and Positioning

Beyond deciding which segments of the market it will target, the company must decide on a *value proposition*—how it will create differentiated value for targeted segments and what positions it wants to occupy in those segments. A **product position** is the way a product is *defined by consumers* on important attributes—the place the product occupies in consumers' minds relative to competing products. Products are made in factories, but brands happen in the minds of consumers.

Real Marketing 7.2

Hypertargeting: Walking a Fine Line between Serving Customers and Stalking Them

How well does your smartphone know you? What stories could your laptop tell? In truth, your digital devices probably know more about you than you know about yourself. Smartphones and other digital equipment have become fundamental extensions of our lives. Whatever you do—at work, at play, socializing, shopping—your phone, tablet, laptop, or desktop is almost always a part of the action. These devices go where you go, entertain you, connect you with friends, take you browsing and shopping, feed you news and information, and listen in on even your most intimate voice, text, and e-mail conversations. They know where you live, with whom you interact, what you search for, what you buy, and what you do for fun. And more and more, these devices are sharing all that personal information with marketers, who in turn use it to create hypertargeted brand messages and promotions crafted just for you.

In the old days (really only a year or two ago) marketers gathered information about consumers' digital doings using cookies—those small bits of data sent from Web sites or third parties and stored in user's Web browsers. But cookies don't work with mobile devices and apps. So as mobile and app usage has soared, and as cookie-blocking technologies have improved, marketers have sought new ways to track consumers as they move about digitally.

As a result, companies have now developed sophisticated new ways to extract intimate insights about consumers that border on wizardry. For example, a string of high-tech mobile advertising service start-ups—with intriguing names such as Drawbridge, Flurry, Velti, and SessionM—are developing technologies that can put together amazingly detailed profiles of smartphone users—who they are, where they go, what they do, who they know, and what they like and don't like. For brands and marketers, such information is pure gold.

The mobile advertising companies use different methods to track consumers. Drawbridge creates partnerships with online publishers and advertising exchanges to track online activity—every time a user visits a Web site or uses a mobile app, the partners send a notification to Drawbridge. In contrast, Flurry works with publishers to embed its software directly into their apps—so far, its software can be found in 350,000 apps on more than 1.2 billion devices. The companies then apply statistical modeling to analyze the mountain of data they collect, assign identifiers to individual users, and ferret out user characteristics and behavior patterns.

And here's the real wizardry: By tracking individual digital activity, the services can link several different devices—a smartphone, home computer, work computer, and tablet—to the same person, even if the devices themselves aren't connected. Every person's data profile is unique—kind of like a fingerprint. So Drawbridge, Flurry, and the other services can use the profiles to identify individuals no matter what device they are using.

For example, suppose that you regularly check your Snapchat Snaps in bed every morning from your smartphone. Then, while eating breakfast at the kitchen table, you use your laptop to browse the latest entertainment news on TMZ and to check a few social media sites. Between your morning classes, you use your phone to text friends and your tablet to do a little online browsing. In the afternoon, during breaks at your job, you use a company desktop to monitor your favorite sites and make a purchase at Amazon.com. At home that evening, you catch up on your favorite TV shows, exchange messages with friends, and do some online research for a class project, jumping back and forth between your phone, tablet, and laptop.

The entire time, chances are good that the information brokers are peering over your shoulder. Based on your unique pattern of browsing and carousing, one of the data services may well have identified your unique digital fingerprint. Not surprisingly, when you're signed into Google, Facebook, or Amazon .com, those companies can track your activities on their sites across devices. But companies like Drawbridge, once they've figured you out, can follow you across all activities and devices even if you aren't logged in.

This uncanny ability to follow unique users across devices lets mobile advertising services like Drawbridge and Flurry help marketers craft mobile ads and promotions that reach carefully targeted users with exactly the right message at just the right moment. So if you use your work computer to check on airline tickets to travel home for the holidays, that night you might see an Expedia ad on your phone offering a low price on a ticket for that same route and date. Drawbridge can define user profiles so precisely that it can often distinguish between different family members using the

Socially responsible targeting: Marketers have developed sophisticated new ways to extract intimate insights about consumers that border on wizardry. But hypertargeting walks a fine line between "serving" consumers and "stalking" them.

Andrew Bret Wallis/Getty Images

same devices and then target ads accordingly. Such targeting accuracy has attracted a host of blue chip brands to Drawbridge and similar services, from Expedia, Ford, and Fidelity Investments to Quiznos and Groupon.

Marketers argue that all of this up-close-and-personal information and hypertargeting better serves both customers and a company. Customers receive tailored, relevant information and offers from brands that really interest them. However, many consumer privacy advocates are concerned that such intimate information in the hands of unscrupulous marketers or other parties could result in more harm or concern than benefit to consumers. Even responsible marketers worry that customers will be put off by what they view less as "getting to know me better to serve me better" and more as "stalking" and "profiling." Companies like Drawbridge are careful in how they position their services. They don't call it tracking. "Tracking is a dirty word," says a Drawbridge executive. Instead, Drawbridge is "observing your behaviors and connecting your profile to mobile devices," he says elliptically.

Some information seems far too sensitive for use in hypertargeting. For example, targeting based on health, financial, or personal activity profiles could cause consumers embarrassment, discomfort, or damage. Consider revelations about certain prescription drug medications, financial planning or debt counseling, or private leisure activities. For instance, imagine having a taboo ad pop up on your work computer while your boss is looking over your shoulder, or while you are making a presentation to colleagues. Or consider that someone targeting customized ads based on your travel plans also knows when your home will likely be unattended. And who's to protect the privacy of children and other vulnerable groups and shield them from the advances of overzealous marketers? Although most consumers are willing to share some personal information if it means getting better service or deals, many consumers worry that marketers might go too far.

Thus, with today's super-sophisticated behavioral targeting tools, marketers walk a fine line between serving consumers and stalking them. Most marketers want to do the right thing with hypertargeting—focusing on the right customers with personalized offers that meet their exacting needs. They want to build trusted relationships with customers by serving them, not harming them. But responsible hypertargeting calls for proactively guarding the rights and sensitivities of those being targeted. Marketers who cross the line risk the wrath of advocates, legislators, and consumers themselves.

Sources: Kate Kay, "Three Big Privacy Changes to Plan for in 2014," *Advertising Age*, January 3, 2014, http://adage.com/print/290885/; Claire Cain Miller and Somini Sengupta, "Selling Secrets of Phone Users to Advertisers," *New York Times*, October 6, 2013, p. A1; George Fox, "When Online Marketers Target Mobile Device Users, Nothing's Out of Bounds," *ECN Magazine*, October 28, 2013, www.ecnmag.com/blogs/2013/10/when-online-marketers-target-mobile-device-users-nothing's-out-bounds; and Katy Bachman, "FTC's Ad Regulator Plans to Focus Heavily on Native and Mobile," *Adweek*, January 5, 2014, www.adweek.com/print/154693.

Product position
The way a product is defined by consumers on important attributes—the place the product occupies in consumers' minds relative to competing products.

Method laundry detergent is positioned as a smarter, easier, and greener detergent; Dreft is positioned as the gentle detergent for baby clothes. At IHOP, you "Come hungry. Leave happy." At Olive Garden, "When You're Here, You're Family." In the automobile market, the Nissan Versa and Honda Fit are positioned on economy, Mercedes and Cadillac on luxury, and Porsche and BMW on performance. Folger's Coffee is "The best part of wakin' up"; Honest Tea is "Refreshingly Honest," with "Brewed organic tea leaves. Real ingredients." Home improvement store Lowe's helps you "Never stop improving." And IKEA does more than just sell affordable home furnishings; it's the "Life improvement store."

Consumers are overloaded with information about products and services. They cannot reevaluate products every time they make a buying decision. To simplify the buying process, consumers organize products, services, and companies into categories and "position" them in their minds. A product's position is the complex set of perceptions, impressions, and feelings that consumers have for the product compared with competing products.

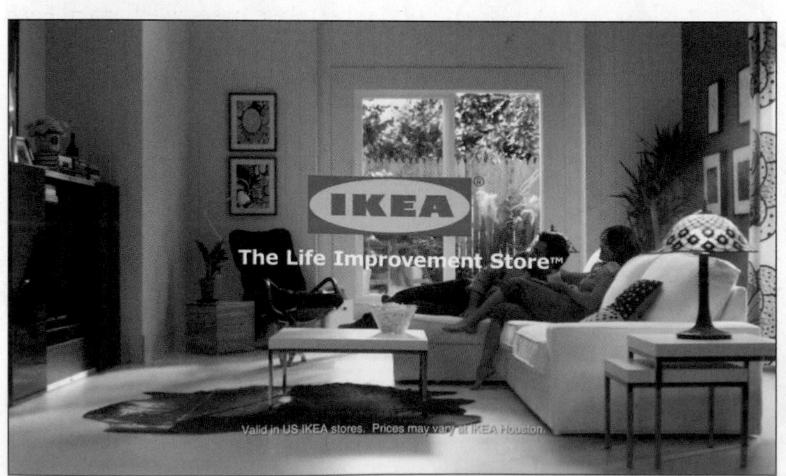

Positioning: IKEA does more than just sell affordable home furnishings; it's the "Life improvement store."

Used with the permission of Inter IKEA Systems B.V.

Consumers position products with or without the help of marketers. But marketers do not want to leave their products' positions to chance. They must *plan* positions that will give their products the greatest advantage in selected target markets, and they must design marketing mixes to create these planned positions.

Positioning Maps

In planning their differentiation and positioning strategies, marketers often prepare *perceptual positioning maps* that show consumer perceptions of their brands versus those of competing products on important buying dimensions. **Figure 7.3** shows a positioning

FIGURE | 7.3
Positioning Map: Large Luxury SUVs
Source: Based on data provided by WardsAuto.com and Edmunds.com, 2014.

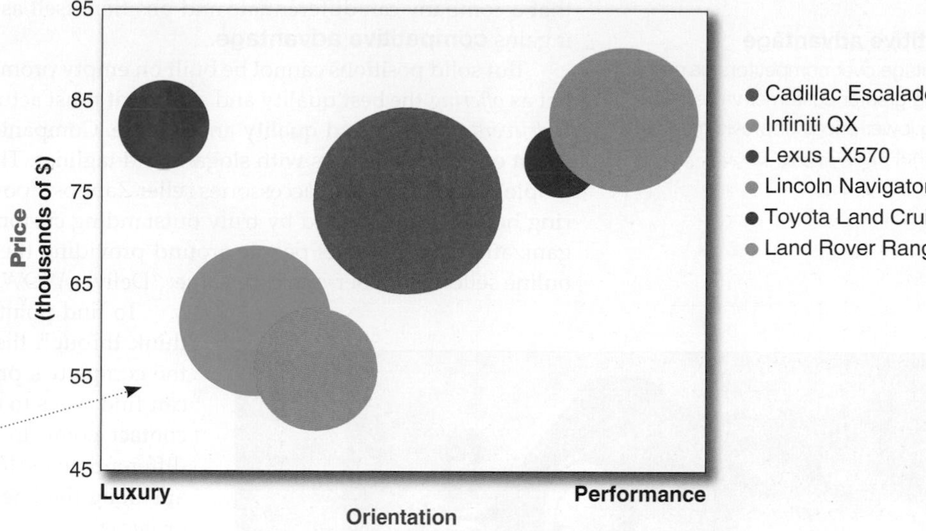

The location of each circle shows where consumers position a brand on two dimensions: price and luxury-performance orientation. The size of each circle indicates the brand's relative market share in the segment. Thus, Toyota's Land Cruiser is a niche brand that is perceived to be relatively expensive and more performance oriented.

map for the U.S. large luxury SUV market.[29] The position of each circle on the map indicates the brand's perceived positioning on two dimensions: price and orientation (luxury versus performance). The size of each circle indicates the brand's relative market share.

Thus, customers view the market-leading Cadillac Escalade as a moderately priced, large, luxury SUV with a balance of luxury and performance. The Escalade is positioned on urban luxury, and, in its case, "performance" probably means power and safety performance. You'll find no mention of off-road adventuring in an Escalade ad.

By contrast, the Range Rover and the Land Cruiser are positioned on luxury with nuances of off-road performance. For example, the Toyota Land Cruiser began in 1951 as a four-wheel-drive, Jeep-like vehicle designed to conquer the world's most grueling terrains and climates. In recent years, the Land Cruiser has retained this adventure and performance positioning but with luxury added. Its Web site brags of "legendary off-road capability," with off-road technologies such as an Acoustic Control Induction System to get the most out of the RPMs, "so you can make molehills out of mountains." Despite its ruggedness, however, the company notes that "its available Bluetooth hands-free technology, DVD entertainment, and a sumptuous interior have softened its edges."

Choosing a Differentiation and Positioning Strategy

Some firms find it easy to choose a differentiation and positioning strategy. For example, a firm well known for quality in certain segments will go after this position in a new segment if there are enough buyers seeking quality. But in many cases, two or more firms will go after the same position. Then each will have to find other ways to set itself apart. Each firm must differentiate its offer by building a unique bundle of benefits that appeals to a substantial group within the segment.

Above all else, a brand's positioning must serve the needs and preferences of well-defined target markets. For example, as discussed previously, although both Dunkin' Donuts and Starbucks are coffee and snack shops, they target very different customers, who want very different things from their favorite coffee seller. Starbucks targets more upscale professionals with more high-brow positioning. In contrast, Dunkin' Donuts targets the "average Joe" with a decidedly more low-brow, "everyman" kind of positioning. Yet each brand succeeds because it creates just the right value proposition for its unique mix of customers.

The differentiation and positioning task consists of three steps: identifying a set of differentiating competitive advantages on which to build a position, choosing the right competitive advantages, and selecting an overall positioning strategy. The company must then effectively communicate and deliver the chosen position to the market.

Identifying Possible Value Differences and Competitive Advantages

To build profitable relationships with target customers, marketers must understand customer needs and deliver more customer value better than competitors do. To the extent that a company can differentiate and position itself as providing superior customer value, it gains **competitive advantage**.

Competitive advantage
An advantage over competitors gained by offering greater customer value, either by having lower prices or providing more benefits that justify higher prices.

But solid positions cannot be built on empty promises. If a company positions its product as *offering* the best quality and service, it must actually differentiate the product so that it *delivers* the promised quality and service. Companies must do much more than simply shout out their positions with slogans and taglines. They must first *live* the slogan. For example, online shoes and accessories seller Zappos' "powered by service" positioning would ring hollow if not backed by truly outstanding customer care. Zappos aligns its entire organization and all of its people around providing the best possible customer service. The online seller's number-one core value: "Deliver WOW through service."[30]

To find points of differentiation, marketers must think through the customer's entire experience with the company's product or service. An alert company can find ways to differentiate itself at every customer contact point. In what specific ways can a company differentiate itself or its market offer? It can differentiate along the lines of *product, services, channels, people,* or *image*.

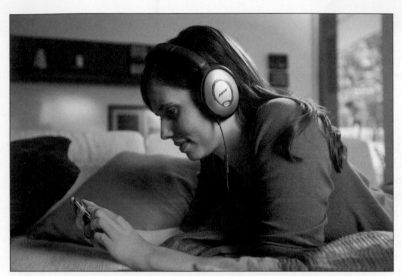

● **Product differentiation: Premium audio brand Bose promises "better sound through research—an innovative, high-quality listening experience."**
Image of Bose Headphones used with permission of Bose Corporation.

Through *product differentiation*, brands can be differentiated on features, performance, or style and design. ● Thus, premium audio brand Bose positions its audio products on the innovative, high-quality listening experiences it gives users. Bose promises "better sound through research." By gaining the approval of the American Heart Association as an approach to a healthy lifestyle, Subway differentiates itself as the healthy fast-food choice. And SodaStream positions itself as an alternative to bottled carbonated waters and soft drinks. It promises a simple, convenient, ecofriendly process for turning home tap water into fresh, homemade soda with no heavy bottles to carry, store, and recycle. SodaStream gives you "smart. simple. soda."

Beyond differentiating its physical product, a firm can also differentiate the services that accompany the product. Some companies gain *services differentiation* through speedy, convenient, or careful delivery. For example, First Convenience Bank of Texas offers "Real Hours for Real People"; it is open seven days a week, including evenings. Others differentiate their service based on high-quality customer care. In an age where customer satisfaction with airline service is in constant decline, Singapore Airlines sets itself apart through extraordinary customer care and the grace of its flight attendants. "Everyone expects excellence from us," says the international airline. "[So even] in the smallest details of flight, we rise to each occasion and deliver the Singapore Airlines experience."[31]

Firms that practice *channel differentiation* gain competitive advantage through the way they design their channel's coverage, expertise, and performance. Amazon.com and GEICO, for example, set themselves apart with their smooth-functioning direct channels. Companies can also gain a strong competitive advantage through *people differentiation*—hiring and training better people than their competitors do. People differentiation requires that a company select its customer-contact people carefully and train them well. For example, Disney World trains its theme park people thoroughly to ensure that they are competent, courteous, friendly, and upbeat—from the hotel check-in agents, to the monorail drivers, to the ride attendants, to the people who sweep Main Street USA. Each employee is carefully trained to understand customers and to "make people happy."

Even when competing offers look the same, buyers may perceive a difference based on company or brand *image differentiation*. A company or brand image should convey a product's distinctive benefits and positioning. Developing a strong and distinctive image calls for creativity and hard work. A company cannot develop an image in the public's mind overnight by using only a few ads. If Ritz-Carlton means quality, this image must be supported by everything the company says and does.

Symbols, such as the McDonald's golden arches, the colorful Google logo, the Twitter bird, the Nike swoosh, or Apple's "bite mark" logo, can provide strong company or brand recognition and image differentiation. The company might build a brand around a famous person, as Nike did with its Michael Jordan, Kobe Bryant, and LeBron James basketball shoe and apparel collections. Some companies even become associated with colors, such as Coca-Cola (red), IBM (blue), or UPS (brown). The chosen symbols, characters, and other image elements must be communicated through advertising that conveys the company's or brand's personality.

Choosing the Right Competitive Advantages

Suppose a company is fortunate enough to discover several potential differentiations that provide competitive advantages. It now must choose the ones on which it will build its positioning strategy. It must decide how many differences to promote and which ones.

How Many Differences to Promote. Many marketers think that companies should aggressively promote only one benefit to the target market. Former advertising executive Rosser Reeves, for example, said a company should develop a *unique selling proposition (USP)* for each brand and stick to it. Each brand should pick an attribute and tout itself as "number one" on that attribute. Buyers tend to remember number one better, especially in this overcommunicated society. Thus, Walmart promotes its unbeatable low prices and Burger King promotes personal choice—"have it your way."

Other marketers think that companies should position themselves on more than one differentiator. This may be necessary if two or more firms are claiming to be best on the same attribute. For example, with its "Expect More. Pay Less." positioning, Targets sets itself apart from Walmart by adding a touch of class to its low prices.

Today, in a time when the mass market is fragmenting into many small segments, companies and brands are trying to broaden their positioning strategies to appeal to more segments. ● For example, whereas Gatorade originally offered a sports drink positioned only on performance hydration, the brand now offers an entire G Series of sports drinks that provide at least three primary benefits. G Series "fuels your body before, during, and after practice, training, or competition." Gatorade Prime 01 is positioned as "pre-game fuel" that provides energy *before* exercise. Gatorade G2 Thirst Quencher is for use "in the moment of activity" *during* exercise. Finally, Gatorade Recover 03 is positioned as a post-game recovering beverage that provides protein for recovery *after* exercise. Clearly, many buyers want these multiple benefits. The challenge is to convince them that one brand can do it all.

● Positioning on multiple competitive advantages: The Gatorade G Series "fuels your body before, during, and after" exercise.

Pepsi-Cola North America, Inc.

Which Differences to Promote. Not all brand differences are meaningful or worthwhile, and each difference has the potential to create company costs as well as customer benefits. A difference is worth establishing to the extent that it satisfies the following criteria:

- *Important.* The difference delivers a highly valued benefit to target buyers.
- *Distinctive.* Competitors do not offer the difference, or the company can offer it in a more distinctive way.
- *Superior.* The difference is superior to other ways that customers might obtain the same benefit.
- *Communicable.* The difference is communicable and visible to buyers.
- *Preemptive.* Competitors cannot easily copy the difference.
- *Affordable.* Buyers can afford to pay for the difference.
- *Profitable.* The company can introduce the difference profitably.

Many companies have introduced differentiations that failed one or more of these tests. When the Westin Stamford Hotel in Singapore once advertised itself as the world's tallest hotel, it was a distinction that was not important to most tourists; in fact, it turned many off. Similarly, Coca-Cola's now classic product failure—New Coke—failed the superiority and importance tests among core Coca-Cola drinkers. Extensive blind taste tests showed that 60 percent of all soft drink consumers chose a new, sweeter Coca-Cola formulation over the original Coke, and 52 percent chose it over Pepsi. So the brand dropped its original-formula Coke and, with much fanfare, replaced it with New Coke, a sweeter, smoother version. However, in its research, Coca-Cola overlooked the many intangibles that have made Coca-Cola so popular for 125 years. To loyal Coke drinkers, the original beverage stands alongside baseball, apple pie, and the Statue of Liberty as an American institution. As it turns out, Coca-Cola differentiates its brand not just by taste, but by tradition. By dropping the original formula, Coca-Cola trampled on the sensitivities of the huge core of loyal Coke drinkers who loved Coke just the way it was. After only three months, the company brought the classic Coke back.

Thus, choosing competitive advantages on which to position a product or service can be difficult, yet such choices may be crucial to success. Choosing the right differentiators can help a brand stand out from the pack of competitors. For example, when Nokia introduced its Lumia 1020 smartphone, it didn't position the phone only on attributes shared with competing models, such as user interface and speed. It positioned it as a smartphone with a 41 megapixel camera with a "reinvented zoom" and "full HD video" that fits today's digital lifestyles.

Selecting an Overall Positioning Strategy

Value proposition
The full positioning of a brand—the full mix of benefits on which it is positioned.

The full positioning of a brand is called the brand's **value proposition**—the full mix of benefits on which a brand is differentiated and positioned. It is the answer to the customer's question "Why should I buy your brand?" BMW's "ultimate driving machine" value proposition hinges on performance but also includes luxury and styling, all for a price that is higher than average but seems fair for this mix of benefits.

Figure 7.4 shows possible value propositions on which a company might position its products. In the figure, the five green cells on the top and right represent winning value propositions—differentiation and positioning that give the company a competitive advantage. The pink cells at the lower left, however, represent losing value propositions. The center orange cell represents at best a marginal proposition. In the following sections, we discuss the five winning value propositions: more for more, more for the same, the same for less, less for much less, and more for less.

More for More. *More-for-more* positioning involves providing the most upscale product or service and charging a higher price to cover the higher costs. A more-for-more market offering not only offers higher quality, it also gives prestige to the buyer. It symbolizes status and a loftier lifestyle. Four Seasons hotels, Rolex watches, Starbucks coffee, Mercedes automobiles, SubZero appliances—each claims superior quality, craftsmanship, durability, performance, or style, and therefore charges a higher price. When Apple premiered its iPhone, it offered higher-quality features than a traditional mobile phone, with a hefty price tag to match.

FIGURE | 7.4
Possible Value Propositions

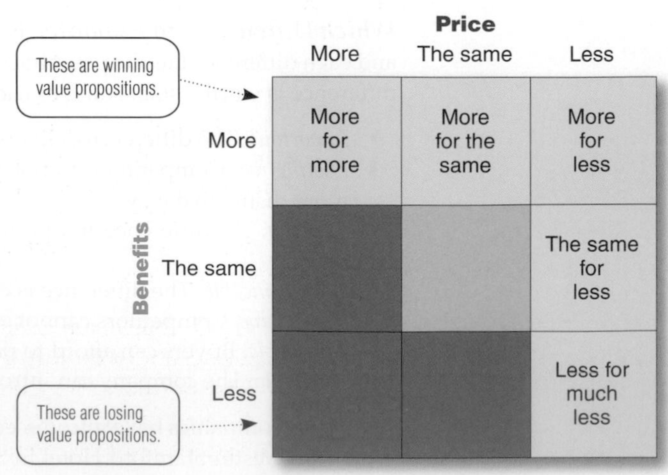

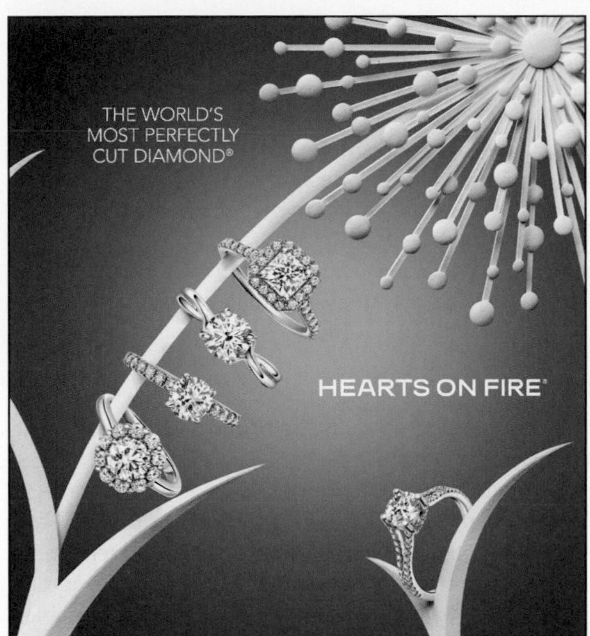

More-for-more positioning: Hearts On Fire diamonds have created a more-for-more niche as "The World's Most Perfectly Cut Diamond—for those who expect more and give more in return."

Used with permission of Hearts On Fire Company, LLC

Similarly, the marketers of Hearts On Fire diamonds have created a more-for-more niche as "The World's Most Perfectly Cut Diamond." Hearts On Fire diamonds have a unique "hearts and arrow" design. When viewed under magnification from the bottom, a perfect ring of eight hearts appears; from the top comes a perfectly formed Fireburst of light. Hearts On Fire diamonds aren't for everyone, says the company. "Hearts On Fire is for those who expect more and give more in return." The brand commands a 15 to 20 percent price premium over comparable competing diamonds.[32]

Although more-for-more can be profitable, this strategy can also be vulnerable. It often invites imitators who claim the same quality but at a lower price. For example, more-for-more brand Starbucks now faces "gourmet" coffee competitors ranging from Dunkin' Donuts to McDonald's. Also, luxury goods that sell well during good times may be at risk during economic downturns when buyers become more cautious in their spending. The recent gloomy economy hit premium brands, such as Starbucks, the hardest.

More for the Same. A company can attack a competitor's value proposition by positioning its brand as offering more for the same price. For example, Target positions itself as the "upscale discounter." It claims to offer more in terms of store atmosphere, service, stylish merchandise, and classy brand image but at prices comparable to those of Walmart and other discounters. Toyota introduced its Lexus line with a *more-for-the-same* (or even more-for-less) value proposition versus Mercedes and BMW. Its first headline read: "Perhaps the first time in history that trading a $72,000 car for a $36,000 car could be considered trading up." It communicated the higher quality of its new Lexus through rave reviews in car magazines and a widely distributed video showing side-by-side comparisons of Lexus and Mercedes automobiles. It published surveys showing that Lexus dealers were providing customers with better sales and service experiences. Many Mercedes owners switched to Lexus, and the Lexus repurchase rate grew to 60 percent, twice the industry average.

The Same for Less. Offering *the same for less* can be a powerful value proposition—everyone likes a good deal. Discount stores such as Walmart and "category killers" such as Best Buy, PetSmart, David's Bridal, and DSW Shoes use this positioning. They don't claim to offer different or better products. Instead, they offer many of the same brands as department stores and specialty stores but at deep discounts based on superior purchasing power and lower-cost operations. Other companies develop imitative but lower-priced brands in an effort to lure customers away from the market leader. For example, Amazon.com offers the Kindle Fire tablet, which sells for less than 40 percent of the price of the Apple iPad or Samsung Galaxy tablet.

Less for Much Less. A market almost always exists for products that offer less and therefore cost less. Few people need, want, or can afford "the very best" in everything they buy. In many cases, consumers will gladly settle for less-than-optimal performance or give up some of the bells and whistles in exchange for a lower price. For example, many travelers seeking lodgings prefer not to pay for what they consider unnecessary extras, such as a pool, an attached restaurant, or mints on the pillow. Hotel chains such as Ramada Limited, Holiday Inn Express, and Motel 6 suspend some of these amenities and charge less accordingly.

Less-for-much-less positioning involves meeting consumers' lower performance or quality requirements at a much lower price. For example, Family Dollar and Dollar General stores offer more affordable goods at very low prices. Costco warehouse stores offer less merchandise selection and consistency and much lower levels of service; as a result, they charge rock-bottom prices.

More for Less. Of course, the winning value proposition would be to offer *more for less.* Many companies claim to do this. And, in the short run, some companies can actually achieve such lofty positions. For example, when it first opened for business, Home Depot had arguably the best product selection, the best service, *and* the lowest prices compared to local hardware stores and other home improvement chains.

Yet in the long run, companies will find it very difficult to sustain such best-of-both positioning. Offering more usually costs more, making it difficult to deliver on the "for-less" promise. Companies that try to deliver both may lose out to more focused competitors. For example, facing determined competition from Lowe's stores, Home Depot must now decide whether it wants to compete primarily on superior service or on lower prices.

All said, each brand must adopt a positioning strategy designed to serve the needs and wants of its target markets. *More for more* will draw one target market, *less for much less* will draw another, and so on. Thus, in any market, there is usually room for many different companies, each successfully occupying different positions. The important thing is that each company must develop its own winning positioning strategy, one that makes the company special to its target consumers.

Developing a Positioning Statement

Positioning statement
A statement that summarizes company or brand positioning using this form: To (target segment and need) our (brand) is (concept) that (point of difference).

Company and brand positioning should be summed up in a **positioning statement**. The statement should follow the form: To (target segment and need) our (brand) is (concept) that (point of difference).[33] ● Here is an example using the popular digital information management application Evernote: "To busy multitaskers who need help remembering things, Evernote is a digital content management application that makes it easy to capture and remember moments and ideas from your everyday life using your computer, phone, tablet, and the Web."

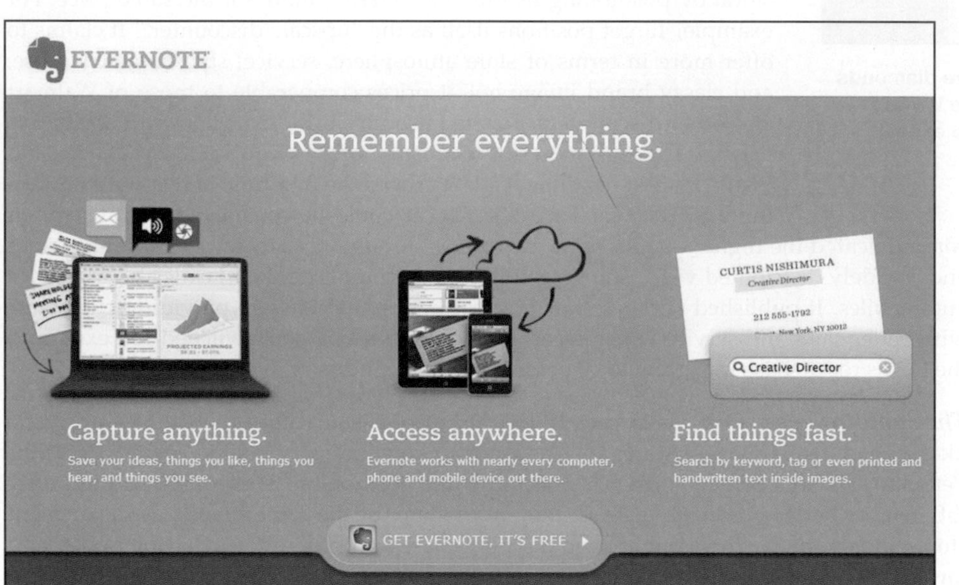

● **Positioning statement: Evernote is positioned as a digital content management application that helps busy people to capture and remember moments and ideas and find them fast later.**

Evernote Corporation

Note that the positioning statement first states the product's membership in a category (digital content management application) and then shows its point of difference from other members of the category (easily capture moments and ideas and remember them later). Evernote helps you "remember everything" by letting you take notes, capture photos, create to-do lists, and record voice reminders, and then makes them easy to find and access using just about any device, anywhere—at home, at work, or on the go.

Placing a brand in a specific category suggests similarities that it might share with other products in the category. But the case for the brand's superiority is made on its points of difference. For example, the U.S. Postal Service ships packages just like UPS and FedEx, but it differentiates its Priority Mail from competitors with convenient, low-price, flat-rate shipping boxes and envelopes. "If it fits, it ships," promises the Post Office.

Communicating and Delivering the Chosen Position

Once it has chosen a position, the company must take strong steps to deliver and communicate the desired position to its target consumers. All the company's marketing mix efforts must support the positioning strategy.

Positioning the company calls for concrete action, not just talk. If the company decides to build a position on better quality and service, it must first *deliver* that position. Designing the marketing mix—product, price, place, and promotion—involves working out the tactical details of the positioning strategy. Thus, a firm that seizes on a more-for-more position knows that it must produce high-quality products, charge a high price, distribute through high-quality dealers, and advertise in high-quality media. It must hire and train more service people, find retailers that have a good reputation for service, and develop sales and advertising messages that broadcast its superior service. This is the only way to build a consistent and believable more-for-more position.

Companies often find it easier to come up with a good positioning strategy than to implement it. Establishing a position or changing one usually takes a long time. In contrast, positions that have taken years to build can quickly be lost. Once a company has built the desired position, it must take care to maintain the position through consistent performance and communication. It must closely monitor and adapt the position over time to match changes in consumer needs and competitors' strategies. However, the company should avoid abrupt changes that might confuse consumers. Instead, a product's position should evolve gradually as it adapts to the ever-changing marketing environment.

7 Reviewing the Concepts

OBJECTIVES REVIEW AND KEY TERMS

Objectives Review

In this chapter, you learned about the major elements of a customer-driven marketing strategy: segmentation, targeting, differentiation, and positioning. Marketers know that they cannot appeal to all buyers in their markets, or at least not to all buyers in the same way. Therefore, most companies today practice *target marketing*—identifying market segments, selecting one or more of them, and developing products and marketing mixes tailored to each.

OBJECTIVE 1 Define the major steps in designing a customer-driven marketing strategy: market segmentation, targeting, differentiation, and positioning. *(pp 222–223)*

A customer-driven marketing strategy begins with selecting which customers to serve and determining a value proposition that best serves the targeted customers. It consists of four steps. *Market segmentation* is the act of dividing a market into distinct segments of buyers with different needs, characteristics, or behaviors who might require separate products or marketing mixes. Once the groups have been identified, *market targeting* evaluates each market segment's attractiveness and selects one or more segments to serve. *Differentiation* involves actually differentiating the market offering to create superior customer value. *Positioning* consists of positioning the market offering in the minds of target customers. A customer-driven marketing strategy seeks to build the *right relationships* with the *right customers*.

OBJECTIVE 2 List and discuss the major bases for segmenting consumer and business markets. *(pp 223–232)*

There is no single way to segment a market. Therefore, the marketer tries different variables to see which give the best segmentation opportunities. For consumer marketing, the major segmentation variables are geographic, demographic, psychographic, and behavioral. In *geographic segmentation*, the market is divided into different geographical units, such as nations, regions, states, counties, cities, or even neighborhoods. In *demographic segmentation*, the market is divided into groups based on demographic variables, including age, life-cycle stage, gender, income, occupation, education, religion, ethnicity, and generation. In *psychographic segmentation*, the market is divided into different groups based on social class, lifestyle, or personality characteristics. In *behavioral segmentation*, the market is divided into groups based on consumers' knowledge, attitudes, uses, or responses concerning a product.

Business marketers use many of the same variables to segment their markets. But business markets also can be segmented by business *demographics* (industry, company size), *operating characteristics*, *purchasing approaches*, *situational factors*, and *personal characteristics*. The effectiveness of the segmentation analysis depends on finding segments that are *measurable*, *accessible*, *substantial*, *differentiable*, and *actionable*.

OBJECTIVE 3 Explain how companies identify attractive market segments and choose a market-targeting strategy. *(pp 232–238)*

To target the best market segments, the company first evaluates each segment's size and growth characteristics, structural attractiveness, and compatibility with company objectives and resources. It then chooses one of four market-targeting strategies—ranging from very broad to very narrow targeting. The seller can ignore segment differences and target broadly using *undifferentiated* (or *mass*) *marketing*. This involves mass producing, mass distributing, and mass promoting the same product in about the same way to all consumers. Or the seller can adopt *differentiated marketing*—developing different market offers for several segments. *Concentrated marketing* (or *niche marketing*) involves focusing on one or a few market segments only. Finally, *micromarketing* is the practice of tailoring products and marketing programs to suit the tastes of specific individuals and locations. Micromarketing includes *local marketing* and *individual marketing*. Which targeting strategy is best depends on company resources, product variability, product life-cycle stage, market variability, and competitive marketing strategies.

Discuss how companies differentiate and position their products for maximum competitive advantage. *(pp 238–247)*

Once a company has decided which segments to enter, it must decide on its *differentiation and positioning strategy*. The differentiation and positioning task consists of three steps: identifying a set of possible differentiations that create competitive advantage, choosing advantages on which to build a position, and selecting an overall positioning strategy.

The brand's full positioning is called its *value proposition*—the full mix of benefits on which the brand is positioned. In general, companies can choose from one of five winning value propositions on which to position their products: more for more, more for the same, the same for less, less for much less, or more for less. Company and brand positioning are summarized in positioning statements that state the target segment and need, the positioning concept, and specific points of difference. The company must then effectively communicate and deliver the chosen position to the market.

MyMarketingLab

Go to **mymktlab.com** to complete the problems marked with this icon .

Key Terms

OBJECTIVE 1

Market segmentation (p 222)
Market targeting (targeting) (p 223)
Differentiation (p 223)
Positioning (p 223)

OBJECTIVE 2

Geographic segmentation (p 223)
Demographic segmentation (p 224)
Age and life-cycle segmentation (p 224)
Gender segmentation (p 225)
Income segmentation (p 225)
Psychographic segmentation (p 226)
Behavioral segmentation (p 228)
Occasion segmentation (p 228)
Benefit segmentation (p 228)
Intermarket (cross-market) segmentation (p 231)

OBJECTIVE 3

Target market (p 233)
Undifferentiated (mass) marketing (p 233)
Differentiated (segmented) marketing (p 233)
Concentrated (niche) marketing (p 234)
Micromarketing (p 235)
Local marketing (p 235)
Individual marketing (p 236)

OBJECTIVE 4

Product position (p 238)
Competitive advantage (p 242)
Value proposition (p 244)
Positioning statement (p 246)

DISCUSSION AND CRITICAL THINKING

Discussion Questions

7-1 Name and describe the four major steps in designing a customer-driven marketing strategy. (AACSB: Communication)

7-2 Compare and contrast consumer and business market segmentation. (AACSB: Communication)

7-3 Explain how the effectiveness of market segments is tested. (AACSB: Communication)

7-4 Explain value proposition and identify the five winning propositions. (AACSB: Communication

7-5 Discuss the nature and the value of a company or brand positioning statement. What is its purpose? (AACSB: Communication)

Critical Thinking Exercises

7-6 Marketing segmentation is widely used by advertisers in promoting products to potential consumers. Find examples of local print ads that match each of the major consumer segmentation variables. What is the target market for each ad? Why has the advertiser chosen a particular segmentation variable for each ad? (AACSB: Communication; Reflective Thinking)

7-7 In a small group, develop a customer-driven marketing strategy that would work for a new business or product in your country or region. Follow the steps described in this chapter to provide a framework for your proposal. (AACSB: Communication; Reflective Thinking)

7-8 Form a small group and create an idea for a new reality television show. Using the form provided in the chapter, develop a positioning statement for this television show. What competitive advantage does the show have over existing shows? How many and which differences would you promote? (AACSB: Communication; Reflective Thinking)

MINICASES AND APPLICATIONS

Online, Mobile, and Social Media Marketing SoLoMo (Social + Local + Mobile)

Imagine walking into a retail store that has very little merchandise on display. Technology company Hointer is allowing retailers to do just that. For example, the company's store in Seattle only has one of every style of clothing hanging on display, seemingly floating in the air. With the store app, customers simply scan the tag to get information about each product, read reviews by others, access media clips, and request that the product be added to their fitting room. Once in the fitting room, customers can request other sizes or styling advice via a tablet on the wall or through the mobile app on their phones. Customers return products they don't want through one chute and another size is delivered through another chute in about 30 seconds. With one click, customers can check out on a mobile device or at the sales counter, and they can share their purchases with others on Instagram, Facebook, or Twitter. Sales associates still exist, but they are likely using the associate's tools to monitor customers' choices and suggest matching items of clothing and accessories. All this is possible with Hointer's suite of SoLoMo tools for retailers—eTag, Digital Connections, Omnicart, Associate Tools, and Whoosh Fitting Room.

7-9 Search the Internet to find other examples of retailers using SoLoMo to target and engage potential customers, or describe how you have used a retailer's app in this manner. (AACSB: Communication; Use of IT; Reflective Thinking)

7-10 Do manufacturers use SoLoMo? Find examples of or make suggestions as to how manufacturers can use this type of targeting. (AACSB: Communication; Reflective Thinking)

Marketing Ethics Unrealistic Bodies

With more than a third of American children and adolescents overweight, you would think that Mattel's slender Barbie doll would be a good role model for little girls. Not so, according to some critics. If Barbie was a real woman, she would have less than 17 percent body fat, a neck too thin to hold her head up, a waist too small to house a full liver and intestines, and ankles and feet too tiny to walk. One group of researchers estimated the likelihood of a woman having Barbie's body at one in 100,000. Yet some women strive for impossible bodies, with more than 20 million suffering from eating disorders such as anorexia and bulimia. Other research has shown that 40 to 60 percent of preadolescent girls are concerned about their weight, and almost 70 percent of elementary-aged girls who read magazines say the pictures of thin models influence their perceptions of an ideal weight. Statistics like these cause consumer advocacy groups such as the Campaign for a Commercial-Free Childhood (CCFC) to call for action, especially when targeting young girls. For example, the CCFC is concerned about Mattel's Barbie Be Anything, Do Everything partnership with the Girl Scouts, in which Daisy and Brownie scouts (that is, kindergarten through third graders) can play an interactive game on the Girl Scouts' Web site and earn Barbie participation badges to wear on their uniforms.

7-11 Do you think it is wrong for Mattel and other doll manufacturers to market dolls with unrealistic body proportions to young girls? Explain why you think that way. Discuss other examples of marketers targeting females with unrealistic body concepts. (AACSB: Communication; Ethical Reasoning)

7-12 Give an example of a company that is countering this trend by offering more realistic dolls for young girls. (AACSB: Communication; Reflective Thinking)

Marketing by the Numbers USAA

USAA is a financial services company formed in 1922 by 25 Army officers who came together to insure each other's automobiles because they were deemed too high-risk to insure. USAA now has almost 25,000 employees and more than 9 million member customers. It consistently ranks in the top 10 automobile insurance companies and offers other types of insurance as well as banking, investment, retirement, and financial planning services. USAA practices a niche marketing strategy—it targets only active and former military personnel and their immediate families. Members earn the right to be customers by serving in the military and can pass that on to their spouses and children. The company was originally even more restrictive, targeting only military officers. However, in 1996, eligibility was extended to enlisted personnel and is now extended to people who served and were honorably discharged from the military and their immediate family members.

7-13 Discuss the factors used to evaluate the usefulness of the military segment. (AACSB: Communication; Reflective Thinking)

7-14 Using the chain ratio method described in Appendix 2: Marketing by the Numbers, estimate the market potential in the military (active duty and veterans) market. Be sure to state any assumptions you make. (AACSB: Communication; Use of IT; Analytical Reasoning)

Video Case Boston Harbor Cruises

Since 1926, Boston Harbor Cruises has been providing customers with memorable experiences on ocean-going vessels in and around the Boston area. But these days, the term *cruise* has different meanings for the four-generation family business. To thrive in good economic times and in bad, Boston Harbor Cruises has progressively targeted various types of customers with its different boats and different services. Sight-seeing trips around Boston Harbor, whale-watching tours, fast ferry service to Cape Cod, dinner and wedding cruises, and a high-speed thrill ride are among Boston Harbor Cruises' offerings. It even offers commuter services and off-shore construction support. Targeting this diverse customer base has become even more challenging as Boston Harbor Cruises has further differentiated the market into local customers, domestic vacationers, and international travelers.

After viewing the video featuring Boston Harbor Cruises, answer the following questions:

7-15 On what main variables has Boston Harbor Cruises focused in segmenting its markets?

7-16 Which target marketing strategy best describes the efforts of Boston Harbor Cruises? Support your choice.

7-17 How does Boston Harbor Cruises use the concepts of differentiation and positioning to build relationships with the right customers?

Company Case Bentley Motors: Differentiation and Positioning in International Markets

The mission of Bentley Motors, the definitive British luxury car company, to produce best cars in their class, has remained unchanged since it was expressed eloquently by its founder Walter Owen Bentley in London in 1919. Located in Crewe, England, since 1946 and owned since 1998 by Volkswagen AG, Bentley Motors is an international company developing and crafting one of the world's most desirable luxury cars.

There are many unmistakable characteristics that define a Bentley—distinctive design, handcrafted luxury, supreme comfort, ultimate performance, and a refined and exhilarating driving experience. Yet it is the company's brand imaging through differentiation and positioning that makes the quintessentially British brand unique today. To many, owning a Bentley is not about getting from A to B but more about cruising with flair infused with advanced technology and breathtaking power as well as time-hallowed tradition and classic hand craftsmanship at the pinnacle of British luxury motoring. Based largely on the concept of "Britishness" in image and design, Bentley has succeeded in differentiating its position in the global luxury car market through a market-driven strategy based on responsive cross-market segmentation.

Cross-Market Segmentation

The traditional markets of Bentley Motors are the United States, the United Kingdom, and Europe, which were identified by the company using two of the traditional international market segmentation variables: the level of a nation's economic development and per capita gross domestic product (GDP). Bentley had enjoyed high sales in these economically developed markets, especially in the boom of the 1980s. In the 1990s, it struggled to reach a similar level of sales, which led to a major investment in the facility, new-product development, and brand repositioning in 1999. The brand reached the height of its heyday in the 1920s and 1930s, and the Bentley Boys winning the 24-hour race in LeMans in 2003 seemed to emulate victories of the past. Its new Arnage T luxury sports sedan won critical acclaim from the motoring press worldwide soon after, and the Continental GT, launched in 2004, was seen as one of the most successful launches of any car in Bentley's history.

However, sales in its traditional markets slumped in 2008 due to the global financial crisis triggered by the collapse of Lehman Brothers in September 2008. Some orders for its cars were cancelled immediately, and sales dropped by 24 percent that year compared to 2007. When the company was forced to stage a seven-week production shutdown in the spring of 2009 due to the slump, it started to search for new markets to increase sales. It realized that the use of the more traditional market segmentation variables such as age, gender, education, and level of economic development does not seem to reflect the real aspects of market behavior, especially the burgeoning purchasing power of the well-to-do in the big emerging markets such as Brazil, Russia, India, and China. The result of the search was the identification of a thriving consumer segment that transcends the national boundaries of these nations. Despite being located in nations featuring low per capita income, this segment of consumers has the greatest global consumption growth and represents rapidly growing buying power for luxury goods ranging from ultra-luxury cars to designer handbags.

Targeting

Operating in markets of both developed and emerging economies presents challenges for Bentley. It was clear from day one that it targeted members of high-income groups who want to buy into the symbolism and history of the Bentley brand, even though the prospect customers would inherently know that they could purchase a vehicle with similar performance and specifications for less than half the price. Bentley is aware that the needs and preferences of its target groups in the emerging economies may differ from those of its prospects in developed economies, who are typically older or retired males, highly educated, and high earners. In comparison, Bentley's target consumers in emerging markets are often the young, less educated entrepreneurs who share a number of important commonalties. They have a strong appetite for Western-branded luxury goods, from which they expect superior quality as a fundamental attribute associated with these goods—quality may mean design, materials used, technology, performance, and craftsmanship, but also attributes such as the tradition and the heritage of the country of origin, unique traits, and perceived superiority and exclusivity. Recognizing the differences and the opportunity to be had from differentiating its targeting efforts, Bentley launched its value proposition based on "Britishness" in its newly found markets while refreshing its original value proposition of luxury, performance, and exclusivity in its traditional markets.

Differentiation and Positioning

The Bentley brand concept is based on the premise that a consumer who regards luxury car brand characteristics as important or desirable, and is in the market for such a luxury product, should be attracted to the brand. Bentley is aware that for its brand to be unique, it must have imagery and symbolic meaning to a consumer. In other words, it must stand for a lifestyle or an attitude and communicate this to its cross-market consumer bases.

Although owned by the German Volkswagen AG group, which enjoys a perception of creditability and originality, Bentley brands itself as a quintessentially distinctive luxury brand originating in Crewe, England, with a fusion of heritage and cutting-edge technology. It defines its cars by the important attributes of tradition and hand craftsmanship, relative to those of speed and performance used by its competitors. It focuses on the emotional benefits of its cars and has stayed true to this proposition through an integrated, high-touch differentiation and positioning program tailored to the carefully defined well-to-do groups in each of its markets.

Bentley offers an exclusive collection of limited non-motoring products produced under license from its equally exclusive partners. Ettinger for Bentley offers luxury leather travel products in vibrant colors from the Bentley color palette, hand-stitched in England from Bentley's own hides. Through Estede, Bentley offers a limited edition, high-end range of sunglasses and ophthalmic frames featuring the famous winged B emblem and presented in a Bentley leather presentation box. Through Zai, a Swiss maker of luxury ski equipment known for its craft and exclusivity, Bentley offers innovative ski products handmade in Switzerland with support from the Bentley Styling Studio in England.

Bentley has also teamed up with luxury hospitality brands to reinforce its value proposition through Bentley Places that embody the values and the spirit of Bentley around the world. The Bentley Room at London's Mosimann's is an inimitably British blend of style and tradition with a dash of Bentley décor and detailing. The dining room was designed by Caulder Moore, who also designed the Bentley Living Room at the company's headquarters in Crewe. The Bentley Suite at the exclusive St. Regis Hotel in New York—built by John Jacob Astor IV in 1904—provides guests with the luxury, craftsmanship, and style associated with the Bentley brand.

In its traditional markets of the United States, the United Kingdom, and Europe, Bentley, through its dealerships, regularly invites customers to take part in national golf tournaments that culminate in a cross-national event held in differing worldwide locations; the winner is crowned with the Bentley "Continental Cup." These events bring together golfers from different continents with a common interest in golf and Bentley and help to refresh and reinforce its image of luxury and exclusivity.

In its newly found markets in the emerging economies, Bentley increases publicity to raise awareness of its brand through motor shows, exhibitions, openings of grand showrooms, and signing of exclusive dealerships to highlight the craftsmanship, quality, and luxury of a Bentley car and the authenticity of the Bentley name. All these events take place in the most economically developed and fashionable metropolitan areas, such as Sao Paulo in Brazil; Shanghai, Shenzhen, and Beijing in China; and Mumbai in India.

Bentley stays true to its English heritage and makes sure that its targeted marketing programs are steeped in its "Britishness." In the biggest Bentley brand exhibition ever held outside Crewe, the World of Bentley exhibition held in Shanghai in 2009 featured a myriad of exhibits devoted to telling the Bentley story of craftsmanship, style, luxury, and heritage originated in England. Bentley has long stood alone as the world's premier maker of handcrafted cars, and it did not disappoint in Shanghai.

The Bentley Design Studio gave the crowds a rare chance to glance into its celebrated tradition of designing the "grand tour" automobile: a Bentley stylist at work, sketching its future, inspired by its past. Bentley woodwork and trim experts demonstrated Bentley's unrivalled craftsmanship in an interactive and fun-filled display of how the company brought the English way of life into dynamic designs of luxurious motor cars. In the words of Geoff Dowding, Bentley's Regional Manager for East Asia, "The Chinese just love the Britishness."

Bentley's high-touch positioning through tailored marketing programs in its new markets played a key role in the company's recovery since the sales slumps in 2008. China is now second to the United States as Bentley's largest market. In 2014, the company delivered 2,191 cars to Chinese customers in the first three quarters of the year. The prominent presence of its dealerships, 38 by December 2014, is set to further expand in the next 12 months as the latest high-performance coupe and convertible Continental models are introduced to Chinese customers. In 2013, Bentley exceeded the 10,000 sales figure with 10,120. By 2018, it hopes to reach 15,000 sales per year.

The Road Ahead

In summary, Bentley targets high-income segments, and builds its brand by serving a luxury segment of the car market. It produces superior-quality products distributed through exclusive dealerships and is never shy about charging a typically high price. It is strongly positioned as a quintessentially British brand steeped with tradition and heritage, and it communicates this proposition through consistent and believable associations with high-end brands in the luxury consumer goods and hospitality sectors. In doing so, it draws its existing and prospective customers to style, luxury, prestige, heritage, and exclusivity.

Through these well-tuned competitive advantages, it had sold well in its traditional markets until the economic downturn in 2008, when buyers became more cautious in their spending. It has since recovered following expansion into high-consumption growth segments in the emerging economies by carrying out effective cross-market segmentation, targeting, and positioning.

The pent-up demand for luxury cars in the emerging economies remains strong, with Bentley and other European sports car brands all reporting strong sales and orders. However, there are already signs of a slowdown in some of Bentley's new markets, such as China, which reported the slowest economic growth in the past decade. Furthermore, increasing sales aggressively in these new markets may imply less distinctiveness and exclusivity for the Bentley brand.

However, as long as Bentley remains true to its pinnacle positioning of building the best car in its class with heritage, tradition, and cutting-edge technology, it can look forward to ample opportunities in the years to come, especially in the existing emerging economies as well as those in the making, such as Vietnam, Cambodia, Kazakhstan, and the Philippines, where the nouveau rich have just started to appreciate the quintessentially British tradition and heritage that is embodied in Bentley.

Questions for Discussion

7-18 What is international market segmentation? What challenges does it pose to Bentley?

7-19 Using the full spectrum of segmentation variables, describe how Bentley segments and targets the international luxury car market.

7-20 Has Bentley differentiated and positioned its brand effectively? Explain.

7-21 Given the economic downturn in developed economies and the slowdown in emerging economies such as China, will Bentley continue to grow? Why or why not?

Sources: Based on information from Andrew Hopps, "A Study into Aspiration and Brand Preference in the Luxury Car Market," MSc in Business Management thesis, 2003; Manchester Metropolitan University and Louise Lucas, "Slowdown Reduces Thirst for Scotch," *Financial Times*, October 2, 2012, http://www.ft.com/cms/s/0/0266cbb4-0cae-11e2-a73c-144feabdc0.html#axzz2HJDcgl89 and www.bentleymotors.com, accessed November 2014.

MyMarketingLab

Go to **mymktlab.com** for the following Assisted-graded writing questions:

7-22 How can marketers use behavioral segmentation in consumer markets? Give an example for each method of behavioral segmentation. (AACSB: Communication; Reflective Thinking)

7-23 Is it appropriate that marketers focus on such a young market with high-priced clothing? (AACSB: Communication; Reflective Thinking; Ethical Reasoning)

References

1. "How Air Asia Founder Tony Fernandes' Dream Came True," BBC News, November 1, 2010, www.bbc.co.uk/news/business-11647205; "AirAsia Posts Third Straight Profit Gain on Budget Travel Demand," Bloomberg.com, November 21, 2012, www.bloomberg.com/news/2012-11-21/airasia-posts-third-straight-profit-gain-on-budgettravel-demand.html; and Dimitrious Buhalis, "eAirlines: Strategic and Tactical Use of ICTs in the Airline Industry," Airlinequality.com, http://www.airlinequality.com/Forum/air_asia.html, accessed November 2014.

2. See https://order.dominos.com/en/pages/content/content.jsp?page=apps&so=hpnf&panelnumber=3&panelname=apps, accessed September 2014.

3. See Joan Voight, "Marriott Chain Adds Some Local Flavor," *Adweek,* January 7, 2013, p. 9; "Renaissance Hotels Launches New Navigator Program to Help Guests Discover 'Hidden Gems' of Various Cities around the World," January 8, 2013, www.adweek.com/print/146321; and http://renaissance-hotels.marriott.com/r-navigator, accessed September 2014.

4. See Katarina Gustafsson, "Rebuilding Lego for Today's Kids," *Bloomberg Businessweek,* November 7, 2013, www.businessweek.com/articles/2013-11-07/lego-launches-toys-more-complex-than-blocks-fit-for-digital-age; and www.lego.com/en-us/mindstorms/products/starter-robots/r3ptar/, accessed September 2014.

5. Sarah Perez, "Amazon's Kindle FreeTime Becomes an Even Better Babysitter, with New Educational Feature that Tells Kids to 'Learn First,' Play Later," *Tech Crunch,* December 9, 2013, http://techcrunch.com/2013/12/09/amazons-kindle-freetime-becomes-an-even-better-babysitter-with-new-educational-feature-that-tells-kids-to-learn-first-play-later/; Keenan Mayo, "Amazon Eyes the Kids' Tablet Market," *Bloomberg Businessweek*, December 12, 2012, p. 34; and www.amazon.com/gp/feature.html?ie=UTF8&docId=1000863021, accessed September 2014.

6. See Matthew Boyle, "Yes, Real Men Drink Beer and Use Skin Moisturizer," *Bloomberg Businessweek,* October 3, 2013, www.businessweek.com/articles/2013-10-03/men-now-spend-more-on-toiletries-than-on-shaving-products; and www.dovemencare.com/, accessed September 2014.

7. See Oliver Wainwright, "Meet GoldieBlox: The Toy Designed to Get Girls Interested in Engineering," *The Guardian,* October 16, 2012, www.theguardian.com/artanddesign/architecture-design-blog/2012/oct/16/goldieblox-toy-girls-engineering-gender; Sarah Barness, "GoldieBlox, World's Coolest Toys for Girls, Could Win a Super Bowl TV Spot," *Huffington Post,* November 15, 2013, www.huffingtonpost.com/2013/11/14/goldieblox-superbowl_n_4269101.html; and www.goldieblox.com/, accessed September 2014.

8. Kate O'Keeffe, "The Wizard of Macau," *Wall Street Journal,* December 13, 2013, http://online.wsj.com/news/articles/SB10001424052702303997604579238361987195446.

9. See www.vfc.com/brands, accessed September 2014.

10. For more on brand tribes, see Tina Sharkey, "What's Your Tribe?" *Forbes,* January 25, 2012, www.forbes.com/sites/tinasharkey/2012/01/25/whats-your-tribe-tap-into-your-core-consumers-aspirations-like-nike-gatorade-babycenter-and-rei-do/; Seth Godin, *Tribes: We Need You to Lead Us* (Portfolio, 2008); "Brand Trialism," *Wikipedia,* http://en.wikipedia.org/wiki/Brand_tribalism, accessed September 2014.

11. Lisa Fleisher, "Pumpkin Spice Latte, the Drink That Almost Wasn't," *Wall Street Journal,* August 30, 2013, http://blogs.wsj.com/corporate-intelligence/2013/08/30/pumpkin-spice-latte-the-drink-that-almost-wasnt/; and www.starbucks.com/menu/drinks/espresso/pumpkin-spice-latte, accessed September 2014.

12. See Lisa Jennings, "CKE: Advertising, Turkey Burgers Drive Sales," *Restaurant News,* April 12, 2013, http://nrn.com/latest-headlines/cke-advertising-turkey-burgers-drive-sales; and Meaghan Murphy, "Nina Agdal Follows Kate Upton as Carl's Jr. Spokesmodel, Lands Super Bowl Commercial," *Fox News,* February 1, 2013, www.foxnews.com/entertainment/2013/02/01/nina-agdal-follows-kate-upton-as-carl-jr-spokesmodel-lands-super-bowl/.

13. See www.patagonia.com/us/ambassadors, accessed September 2014.

14. For this and other information on Experian's Mosaic USA system, see www.experian.com/marketing-services/consumer-segmentation.html and http://classic.demographicsnow.com/Templates/static/mosaicPDF/K40%20Bohemian%20Groove.PDF, accessed September 2014.

15. See www.starbucksfs.com and http://starbucksocs.com/, accessed September 2014.

16. See Jay Moy, "Every Song Has a Place: Coca-Cola, Spotify Launch Groundbreaking Social Music App," June 11, 2013, www.coca-colacompany.com/coca-cola-music/every-song-has-a-place-coca-cola-spotify-launch-groundbreaking-social-music-app; and www.coca-cola.com/music, accessed September 2014.

17. See Michael Porter, *Competitive Advantage* (New York: Free Press, 1985), pp. 4–8, 234–236. For a more recent discussion, see Philip Kotler and Kevin Lane Keller, *Marketing Management*, 14th ed. (Upper Saddle River, NJ: Prentice Hall, 2012), p. 232.

18. Example adapted from Kotler and Keller, *Marketing Management*, p. 233. Also see Brad van Auken, "Leveraging the Brand: Hallmark Case Study," January 11, 2008, www.brandstrategyinsider.com; "Hallmark Breaks Out of Special-Occasion Mold," *Advertising Age,* July 6, 2011, www.adage.com/print/228558; and www.hallmark.com, accessed September 2014.

19. Carl Franzen, "Sorry for Your Loss: Hallmark Struggles to Update Its Card Empire," *The Verge,* September 4, 2013, www.theverge.com/2013/9/4/4579832/sorry-for-your-loss-hallmark-struggles-to-update-its-card-empire.

20. Store information found at www.walmartstores.com, www.wholefoodsmarket.com, and www.kroger.com, accessed September 2014.

21. Based on information from "America's Fastest-Growing Retailer," *Inc.*, September 1, 2010; David Moin, "Modcloth's M.O.," *Women's Wear Daily*, June 15, 2011; Jordan Speer, "Get Feedback. It Closes the Loop," *Apparel,* November 2011, p. 2; Lauren Indvik, "How ModCloth Went from a College Dorm to $100 Million a Year," *Mashable,* August 13, 2013, http://mashable.com/2013/08/13/modcloth-scaling/; and www.modcloth.com, accessed September 2014.

22. See Jack Neff, "Making the Case for the Titans," *Advertising Age,* October 7, 2013, p. 14.

23. See Cotton Timberlake, "With Stores Nationwide, Macy's Goes Local," *Bloomberg BusinessWeek,* October 4–10, 2010, pp. 21–22; Robert Klara, "For the New Macy's, All Marketing Is Local," *Adweek,* June 7, 2010, pp. 25–26; "Macy's Launches Millennial Strategy," *MRketplace,* March 22, 2012, www.mrketplace.com/30516/macys-launches-millennial-strategy/#; and Jim Tierney, "Macy's Confident in My Macy's, Magic Selling Customer Engagemnt Strategies," *Loyalty 360,* August 15, 2013, http://loyalty360.org/resources/article/macys-confident-in-my-macys-magic-selling-customer-engagement-strategies.

24. Based on information found in Samantha Murphy, "SoLoMo Revolution Picks Up Where Hyperlocal Search Left Off," *Mashable*, January 12, 2012, http://mashable.com/2012/01/12/solomo-hyperlocal-search/; "Localeze/15miles Fifth Annual comScore Local Search Usage Study Reveals SoLoMo Revolution Has Taken Over," *Business Wire,* February 29, 2012; Joe Ruiz, "What Is SoMoLo and Why Is It Important to Marketers?" *Business2Community,* February 1, 2013, www.business2community.com/marketing/what-is-somolo-and-why-is-it-important-to-marketers-0395281; and www.shopkick.com, accessed April 2014. For examples of successful retailer and brand SoLoMo efforts, see Jennifer Lingerfelt, "What Airlines and Hotels Can Learn from Starbucks, Coca-Cola and Sephora's Approach to SoLoMo," *loyalty360,* May 18, 2013, http://loyalty360.org/loyalty-today/article/what-airlines-and-hotels-can-learn-from-starbucks-coca-cola-and-sephoras-ap; and "Walgreens SoLoMo Case Study," Strategic Marketing Solutions, www.strategicdriven.com/offers/Strategic-Marketing-Solutions-SoLoMo-Walgreens-Case-Study.pdf, accessed September 2014.

25. Based on information found in Arlene Weintraub, "Is Mass Customization the Future of Retailing?" *Entrepreneur,* November 14, 2013, www.entrepreneur.com/article/229869; Gwendolyn Bounds, "The Rise of Holiday Me-tailers," *Wall Street Journal,* December 8, 2010, p. D1; Abbey Klaassen, "Harley-Davidson Breaks Consumer-Created Work from Victors & Spoils," *Advertising Age,* February 14, 2012, http://adage.com/print/148873; and http://factory.puma.com/en/about and www.harley-davidson.com/en_US/Content/Pages/H-D1_Customization/h-d1_customization.html, accessed September 2014.

26. See "McDonald's Introduces New Automatic Offerings of Fruit in Every Happy Meal," *PRNewswire,* January 20, 2012; "Judge Dismisses Happy Meal Lawsuit," *Advertising Age,* April 4, 2012, http://adage.com/print/233946; Allison Aubrey, "McDonald's Says Bye-Bye to Sugary Sodas in Happy Meals," *NPR,* September 26, 2013, www.npr.org/blogs/thesalt/2013/09/26/226564560/mcdonalds-says-bye-bye-to-sugary-sodas-in-happy-meals; and Maria Godoy, "Catcher in the Fry? McDonald's Happy Meals with a Side of Books," *NPR,* October 10, 2013, www.npr.org/blogs/thesalt/2013/10/10/231531070/catcher-in-the-fry-mcdonalds-happy-meals-with-a-side-of-books.

27. "Marketing to Kids: Toy Sellers' Bonanza or Parental Danger Zone?" Knowledge@Wharton, December 5, 2012, http://knowledge.wharton.upenn.edu/article.cfm?articleid=3127. Examples based on information from www.barbie.com/activities/fun_games/#whats-hot and www.nick.com/club/, accessed September 2014.

28. See "IC3 2012 Internet Crime Report Released," May 14, 2013, www.ic3.gov/media/2013/130514.aspx.

29. SUV sales data furnished by www.WardsAuto.com, accessed March 2013. Price data from www.edmunds.com, accessed March 2013.

30. See "Zappos Family Core Values," http://about.zappos.com/our-unique-culture/zappos-core-values; and http://about.zappos.com/, accessed September 2014.

31. Quote from "Singapore Airlines: Company Information," www.singaporeair.com, accessed September 2014.

32. See www.heartsonfire.com/Learn-About-Our-Diamonds.aspx, accessed September 2014.

33. See Bobby J. Calder and Steven J. Reagan, "Brand Design," in Dawn Iacobucci, ed., *Kellogg on Marketing* (New York: John Wiley & Sons, 2001), p. 61. For more discussion, see Kotler and Keller, *Marketing Management*, 14th ed., Chapter 10.

8 Products, Services, and Brands
Building Customer Value

Chapter Preview After examining customer-driven marketing strategy, we now take a deeper look at the marketing mix: the tactical tools that marketers use to implement their strategies, engage customers, and deliver superior customer value. In this and the next chapter, we will study how companies develop and manage products and brands. Then, in the chapters that follow, we look at pricing, distribution, and marketing communication tools. The product and brand are usually the first and most basic marketing consideration. We start with a seemingly simple question: What *is* a product? As it turns out, the answer is not so simple.

Before starting into the chapter, let's look at an interesting brand story. Marketing is all about building brands that connect deeply with customers. So, when you think about top brands, which ones pop up first? Maybe it's traditional megabrands such as Coca-Cola, Nike, or McDonald's. Or maybe a trendy tech brand such as Google, Facebook, or Amazon. But if we asked you to focus on sports entertainment, you'd probably name ESPN. When it comes to your life and sports, ESPN probably has it covered.

THE ESPN BRAND: Every Sport Possible—Now

When you think about ESPN, you probably don't think of it as a "brand." You think of it as a cable TV network, a Web site or mobile app, or perhaps a magazine. ESPN is all of those things. But more than that, ESPN is a brand experience—a meaningful part of customers' lives that goes well beyond the cable networks, publications, and other media entities it comprises. To consumers, ESPN is synonymous with sports entertainment, and is inexorably linked with their sports memories, realities, and anticipations.

In 1979, entrepreneur Bill Rasmussen took a daring leap and founded the round-the-clock sports network ESPN (Entertainment and Sports Programming Network). Despite many early skeptics—a 24-hour sports network?—ESPN is now a multibillion-dollar sports empire and a "can't-live-without-it" part of the daily routine for hundreds of millions of people worldwide. Today, ESPN is recognized and revered as much as iconic megabrands such as Coca-Cola, Nike, Apple, and Google. No matter who you are, chances are good that ESPN has touched you in some meaningful way. And no matter what the sport or where, ESPN seems to be everywhere at once.

Here's a brief summary of the incredible variety of entities tied together under the ESPN brand:

Television: From its original groundbreaking cable network, the ESPN brand has sprouted seven additional networks—ESPN3D, ESPN2, ESPN Classic, ESPNEWS, ESPNU, ESPN Deportes (Spanish language), and the Longhorn Network. With its signal now flowing into almost 100 million U.S. households at an industry-topping cost of $5 per household per month—TNT is a distant second at $1.16—ESPN is by far the most-sought cable network. Additionally, ESPN International serves fans through 24 international networks in 58 countries and territories across all seven continents. ESPN is the home of the NBA Finals, WNBA, *Monday Night Football*, NASCAR, IndyCar, the NHRA, college football, college basketball, tennis's Grand Slam events, golf's Masters, the U.S. Open and British Open, World Cup Soccer, the Little League World Series, and more. This list grows every year as ESPN continues to outbid the major broadcast networks to capture the rights to many major sports events. ESPN has certainly answered the question of whether cable TV has the mass appeal needed to support major sports events. For 14 straight years, American men have named ESPN their favorite channel.

Radio: Sports radio is thriving, and ESPN operates the largest sports radio network, broadcasting more than 9,000 hours of content annually to 24 million listeners through 450 U.S.

The ever-expanding ESPN brand is recognized and revered as much as iconic megabrands such as Coca-Cola, Nike, or Google. When it comes to your life and sports, chances are good that ESPN plays a meaningful role.

affiliates plus 45 Spanish-language ESPN Deportes stations in major markets. Overseas, ESPN has radio and syndicated radio programs in 11 countries.

Online: ESPN.com is the leading sports Web site, with an average audience of 77,000 per minute, 52 percent more than its closest rival. ESPNRadio.com is the most-listened-to online sports destination, with one million unique visitors per month. ESPN's Podcasts are downloaded more than 358 million times per year. With literally dozens of global and market-specific sites, ESPN more than dominates.

With access to content from television, radio, and print, ESPN has a plentiful supply of material to feed its digital efforts. But ESPN is also leading the game in the exploding mobile arena. It employs a "mobile first" strategy, in which it orients all of its Web sites around mobile, thus optimizing performance. Now, ESPN delivers mobile sports content via all major U.S. wireless providers—including real-time scores, stats, late-breaking news, and video-on-demand. Its mobile sites and apps lead the sports category in unique visitors and average audience per minute. The digital strategy has led to ESPN3, a multi-screen live 24/7 sports network available at no cost to 85 million homes that receive their high-speed Internet connection from an affiliated service provider. ESPN3 viewers can stream ESPN coverage on their computers, tablets, or smartphones.

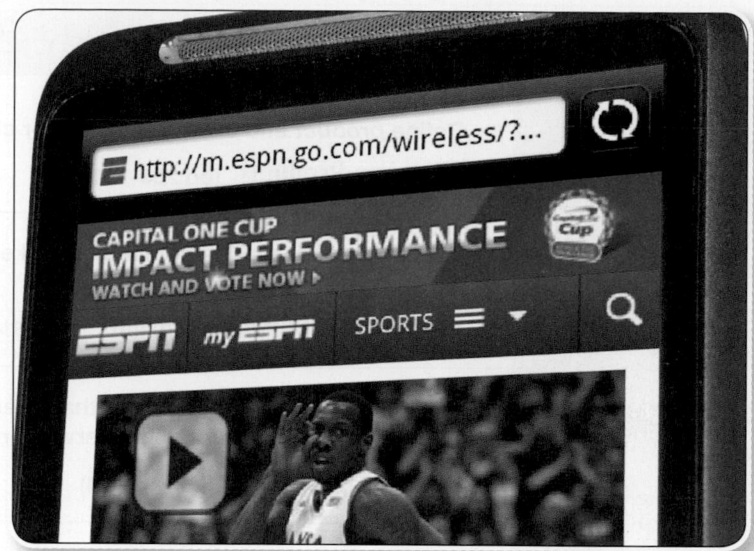

ESPN is more than just a collection of cable networks, online and mobile sites, and publications. The ESPN brand is synonymous with sports entertainment, inexorably linked with consumers' sports memories, realities, and anticipations.

© M40S Photos/Alamy

Publishing: When ESPN first published *ESPN The Magazine* in 1998, critics gave it little chance against mighty *Sports Illustrated*. Yet, with its bold look, bright colors, and unconventional format, the ESPN publication now serves more than 14 million readers each month and continues to grow. Last year, digital-only consumption of the magazine jumped 50 percent to nearly 1 million readers per issue. By comparison, a relatively stagnant *Sports Illustrated* is struggling to make the shift to a digital world.

As if all this weren't enough, ESPN also manages events, including the X Games, Winter X Games, ESPN Outdoors (featuring the Bassmaster Classic), the Skins Games, the Jimmy V Classic, and several football bowl games. It also develops ESPN-branded consumer products and services, including CDs, DVDs, video games, apparel, and even golf schools. If reading all this makes you hungry, you may be near an ESPN Zone, which includes a sports-themed restaurant, interactive games, and sports-related merchandise sales. You'll now find ESPN content in airports and on planes, in health clubs, and even on gas station video panels. All this translates into annual revenues of $8.5 billion, making ESPN more important to the parent Walt Disney Company than the Disneyland and Disney World theme parks combined.

What ties it all together? The ESPN brand's customer-focused mission: It wants to serve sports enthusiasts "wherever sports are watched, listened to, discussed, debated, read about, or played." ESPN has a philosophy known as "best available screen." It knows that when fans are at home, they'll watch the big 50-inch flat screen. But during the morning hours, smartphones light up more. During the day, desktops dominate, and in the evening, tablet activity increases. ESPN is on a crusade to know when, where, and under what conditions fans will reach for which device, and to provide the most seamless, high-quality experience for them.

It's no surprise, then, that sports fans around the world love their ESPN. To consumers everywhere, ESPN means sports. Tech savvy, creative, and often irreverent, the well-managed, ever-extending brand continues to build meaningful customer experiences and relationships. If it has to do with your life and sports—large or small—ESPN covers it for you, anywhere you are, 24/7. Perhaps the company should rename ESPN to stand for Every Sport Possible—Now.[1]

Objective Outline

OBJECTIVE 1	**Define *product* and describe the major classifications of products and services.** What Is a Product? (pp 256–261)
OBJECTIVE 2	**Describe the decisions companies make regarding their individual products and services, product lines, and product mixes.** Product and Service Decisions (pp 261–268)
OBJECTIVE 3	**Identify the four characteristics that affect the marketing of services and the additional marketing considerations that services require.** Services Marketing (pp 268–274)
OBJECTIVE 4	**Discuss branding strategy—the decisions companies make in building and managing their brands.** Branding Strategy: Building Strong Brands (pp 274–284)

As the ESPN story shows, in their quest to create customer relationships, marketers must build and manage products and brands that connect with customers. This chapter begins with a deceptively simple question: *What is a product?* After addressing this question, we look at ways to classify products in consumer and business markets. Then we discuss the important decisions that marketers make regarding individual products, product lines, and product mixes. Next, we examine the characteristics and marketing requirements of a special form of product—services. Finally, we look into the critically important issue of how marketers build and manage product and service brands.

Author Comment | As you'll see, this is a deceptively simple question with a very complex answer. For example, think back to the opening ESPN story. What is the ESPN "product"?

What Is a Product?

We define a **product** as anything that can be offered to a market for attention, acquisition, use, or consumption that might satisfy a want or need. Products include more than just tangible objects, such as cars, computers, or mobile phones. Broadly defined, *products* also include services, events, persons, places, organizations, and ideas, or a mixture of these. Throughout this text, we use the term *product* broadly to include any or all of these entities. Thus, an Apple iPhone, a Toyota Camry, and a Caffé Mocha at Starbucks are products. But so are a trip to Las Vegas, Schwab online investment services, your Facebook page, and advice from your family doctor.

Product
Anything that can be offered to a market for attention, acquisition, use, or consumption that might satisfy a want or need.

Because of their importance in the world economy, we give special attention to services. **Services** are a form of product that consists of activities, benefits, or satisfactions offered for sale that are essentially intangible and do not result in the ownership of anything. Examples include banking, hotel, airline travel, retail, wireless communication, and home-repair services. We will look at services more closely later in this chapter.

Service
An activity, benefit, or satisfaction offered for sale that is essentially intangible and does not result in the ownership of anything.

Products, Services, and Experiences

Products are a key element in the overall *market offering*. Marketing mix planning begins with building an offering that brings value to target customers. This offering becomes the basis on which the company builds profitable customer relationships.

A company's market offering often includes both tangible goods and services. At one extreme, the market offer may consist of a *pure tangible good*, such as soap, toothpaste, or salt; no services accompany the product. At the other extreme are *pure services*, for which the market offer consists primarily of a service. Examples include a doctor's exam and financial services. Between these two extremes, however, many goods-and-services combinations are possible.

Today, as products and services become more commoditized, many companies are moving to a new level in creating value for their customers. To differentiate their offers, beyond simply making products and delivering services, they are creating and managing customer *experiences* with their brands or companies.

Experiences have always been an important part of marketing for some companies. Disney has long manufactured dreams and memories through its movies and theme parks—it wants theme park cast members to deliver a thousand "small wows" to every customer. And Nike has long declared, "It's not so much the shoes but where they take you." Today, however, all kinds of firms are recasting their traditional goods and services to create experiences. For example, Verizon's newly redesigned Smart Stores don't just sell phones. They create lifestyle experiences that encourage customers to visit more often, hang around, and experience the wonders of mobile technology:[2]

You probably don't much look forward to visiting your wireless carrier's retail store—you maybe stop by every few years to upgrade your phone in exchange for extending your contract. But Verizon is trying to change all that. It's remodeling some 1,700 retail stores nationwide, turning them into "Smart Stores"—what one observer calls "rec rooms for geeks." The aim is to create a new retail experience, one that helps customers to discover how Verizon technology can enhance their mobile lifestyles. Verizon has already opened a prototype store at the Mall of America in Minneapolis. The store is organized into interactive mobile lifestyle zones, where customers can try out gadgets, apps, and gear relevant to their lifestyle needs running on the Verizon network. For example, a "Get Fit" zone caters to active sports and fitness buffs; a "Have Fun" zone focuses on gamers; a "Home and On the Go" zone is for folks interested in home monitoring and energy management. In the Workshop area, Verizon specialists hold classes in front of a large digital display screen and share tips about getting the most out of mobile devices and Verizon's services. With the new stores, Verizon hopes to build deeper brand engagement and customer relationships by serving as a guide for its wireless customers. "We want to talk with them about all the ways they can use their devices," says a Verizon executive.

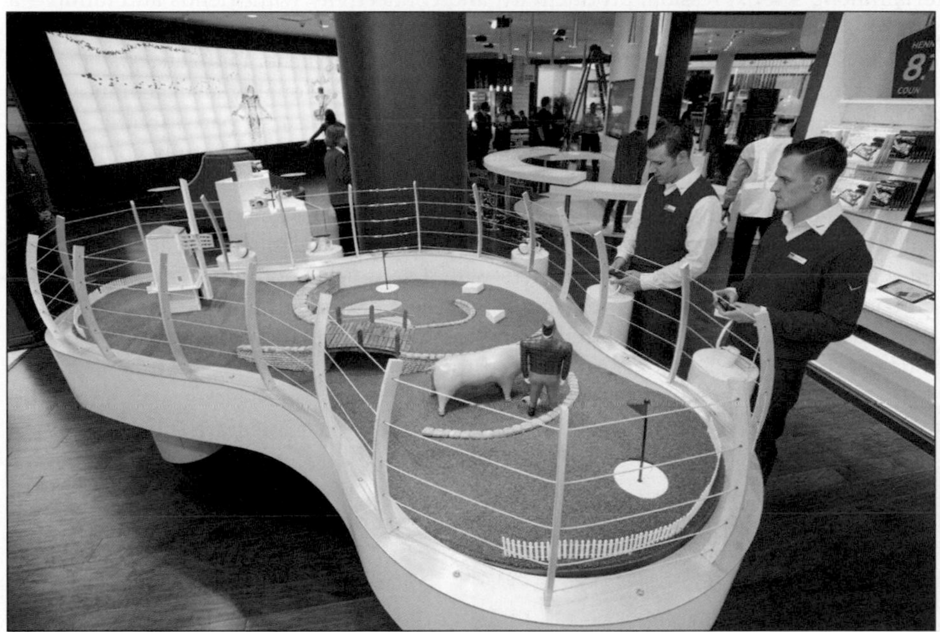

Creating customer experiences: Verizon's redesigned Smart Stores don't just sell phones. They create lifestyle experiences—a kind of "rec room for geeks," in which customers can hang around and experience the wonders of mobile technology.
AP Images for Verizon Wireless

Levels of Product and Services

Product planners need to think about products and services on three levels (see **Figure 8.1**). Each level adds more customer value. The most basic level is the *core customer value*, which addresses the question: *What is the buyer really buying?* When designing products, marketers must first define the core, problem-solving benefits or services that consumers seek.

FIGURE | 8.1
Three Levels of Product

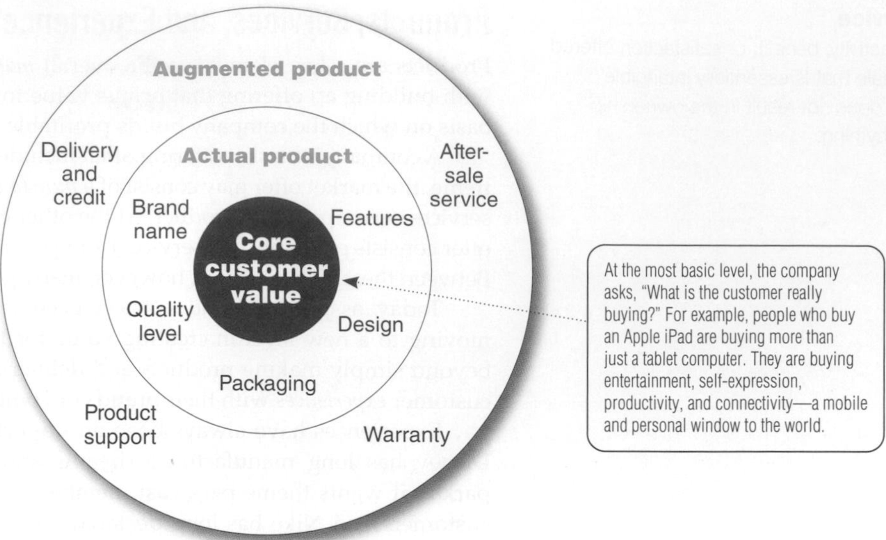
Augmented product
Actual product
Core customer value
Delivery and credit
After-sale service
Brand name
Features
Quality level
Design
Packaging
Product support
Warranty
At the most basic level, the company asks, "What is the customer really buying?" For example, people who buy an Apple iPad are buying more than just a tablet computer. They are buying entertainment, self-expression, productivity, and connectivity—a mobile and personal window to the world.

A woman buying lipstick buys more than lip color. Charles Revson of Revlon saw this early: "In the factory, we make cosmetics; in the store, we sell hope." And people who buy an Apple iPad are buying much more than just a tablet computer. They are buying entertainment, self-expression, productivity, and connectivity with friends and family—a mobile and personal window to the world.

At the second level, product planners must turn the core benefit into an *actual product*. They need to develop product and service features, a design, a quality level, a brand name, and packaging. For example, the iPad is an actual product. Its name, parts, styling, operating system, features, packaging, and other attributes have all been carefully combined to deliver the core customer value of staying connected.

Finally, product planners must build an *augmented product* around the core benefit and actual product by offering additional consumer services and benefits. The iPad is more than just a digital device. It provides consumers with a complete connectivity solution. Thus, when consumers buy an iPad, Apple and its resellers also might give buyers a warranty on parts and workmanship, quick repair services when needed, and a Web site to use if they have problems or questions. Apple also provides access to a huge assortment of apps and accessories, along with an iCloud service that integrates buyers' photos, music, documents, apps, calendars, contacts, and other content across all of their devices from any location.

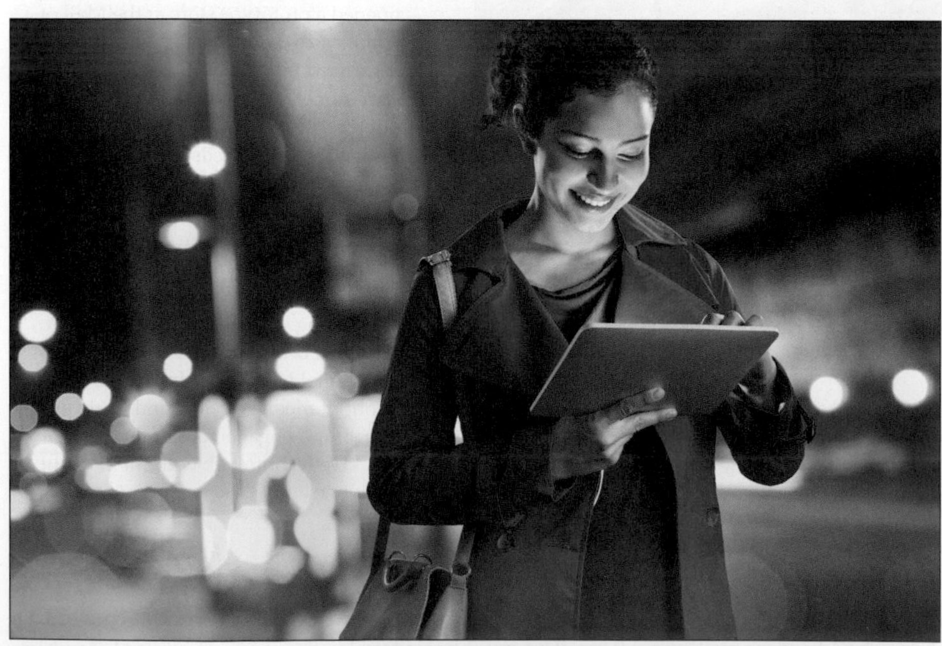

Core, actual, and augmented product: People who buy an iPad are buying much more than a tablet computer. They are buying entertainment, self-expression, productivity, and connectivity—a mobile and personal window to the world.

Betsie Van der Meer/Getty Images

Consumers see products as complex bundles of benefits that satisfy their needs. When developing products, marketers first must identify the *core customer value* that consumers seek from the product. They must then design the *actual* product and find ways to *augment* it to create customer value and a full and satisfying brand experience.

Product and Service Classifications

Products and services fall into two broad classes based on the types of consumers who use them: *consumer products* and *industrial products*. Broadly defined, products also include other marketable entities such as experiences, organizations, persons, places, and ideas.

Consumer Products

Consumer product
A product bought by final consumers for personal consumption.

Convenience product
A consumer product that customers usually buy frequently, immediately, and with minimal comparison and buying effort.

Shopping product
A consumer product that the customer, in the process of selecting and purchasing, usually compares on such attributes as suitability, quality, price, and style.

Specialty product
A consumer product with unique characteristics or brand identification for which a significant group of buyers is willing to make a special purchase effort.

Unsought product
A consumer product that the consumer either does not know about or knows about but does not normally consider buying.

Consumer products are products and services bought by final consumers for personal consumption. Marketers usually classify these products and services further based on how consumers go about buying them. Consumer products include *convenience products, shopping products, specialty products,* and *unsought products*. These products differ in the ways consumers buy them and, therefore, in how they are marketed (see **Table 8.1**).

Convenience products are consumer products and services that customers usually buy frequently, immediately, and with minimal comparison and buying effort. Examples include laundry detergent, candy, magazines, and fast food. Convenience products are usually low priced, and marketers place them in many locations to make them readily available when customers need or want them.

Shopping products are less frequently purchased consumer products and services that customers compare carefully on suitability, quality, price, and style. When buying shopping products and services, consumers spend much time and effort in gathering information and making comparisons. Examples include furniture, clothing, major appliances, and hotel services. Shopping product marketers usually distribute their products through fewer outlets but provide deeper sales support to help customers in their comparison efforts.

Specialty products are consumer products and services with unique characteristics or brand identifications for which a significant group of buyers is willing to make a special purchase effort. Examples include specific brands of cars, high-priced photography equipment, designer clothes, gourmet foods, and the services of medical or legal specialists. A Lamborghini automobile, for example, is a specialty product because buyers are usually willing to travel great distances to buy one. Buyers normally do not compare specialty products. They invest only the time needed to reach dealers carrying the wanted products.

Unsought products are consumer products that the consumer either does not know about or knows about but does not normally consider buying. Most major new innovations are unsought until the consumer becomes aware of them through advertising. Classic examples of known but unsought products and services are life insurance, preplanned funeral services, and blood donations to the Red Cross. By their very nature, unsought products require a lot of advertising, personal selling, and other marketing efforts.

Table 8.1 | Marketing Considerations for Consumer Products

	Type of Consumer Product			
Marketing Considerations	**Convenience**	**Shopping**	**Specialty**	**Unsought**
Customer buying behavior	Frequent purchase; little planning, little comparison or shopping effort; low customer involvement	Less frequent purchase; much planning and shopping effort; comparison of brands on price, quality, and style	Strong brand preference and loyalty; special purchase effort; little comparison of brands; low price sensitivity	Little product awareness or knowledge (or, if aware, little or even negative interest)
Price	Low price	Higher price	High price	Varies
Distribution	Widespread distribution; convenient locations	Selective distribution in fewer outlets	Exclusive distribution in only one or a few outlets per market area	Varies
Promotion	Mass promotion by the producer	Advertising and personal selling by both the producer and resellers	More carefully targeted promotion by both the producer and resellers	Aggressive advertising and personal selling by the producer and resellers
Examples	Toothpaste, magazines, and laundry detergent	Major appliances, televisions, furniture, and clothing	Luxury goods, such as Rolex watches or fine crystal	Life insurance and Red Cross blood donations

Industrial Products

Industrial product
A product bought by individuals and organizations for further processing or for use in conducting a business.

Industrial products are those products purchased for further processing or for use in conducting a business. Thus, the distinction between a consumer product and an industrial product is based on the *purpose* for which the product is purchased. If a consumer buys a lawn mower for use around home, the lawn mower is a consumer product. If the same consumer buys the same lawn mower for use in a landscaping business, the lawn mower is an industrial product.

The three groups of industrial products and services are materials and parts, capital items, and supplies and services. *Materials and parts* include raw materials as well as manufactured materials and parts. Raw materials consist of farm products (wheat, cotton, livestock, fruits, vegetables) and natural products (fish, lumber, crude petroleum, iron ore). Manufactured materials and parts consist of component materials (iron, yarn, cement, wires) and component parts (small motors, tires, castings). Most manufactured materials and parts are sold directly to industrial users. Price and service are the major marketing factors; branding and advertising tend to be less important.

Capital items are industrial products that aid in the buyer's production or operations, including installations and accessory equipment. Installations consist of major purchases such as buildings (factories, offices) and fixed equipment (generators, drill presses, large computer systems, elevators). Accessory equipment includes portable factory equipment and tools (hand tools, lift trucks) and office equipment (computers, fax machines, desks). These types of equipment have shorter lives than do installations and simply aid in the production process.

The final group of industrial products is *supplies and services*. Supplies include operating supplies (lubricants, coal, paper, pencils) and repair and maintenance items (paint, nails, brooms). Supplies are the convenience products of the industrial field because they are usually purchased with a minimum of effort or comparison. Business services include maintenance and repair services (window cleaning, computer repair) and business advisory services (legal, management consulting, advertising). Such services are usually supplied under contract.

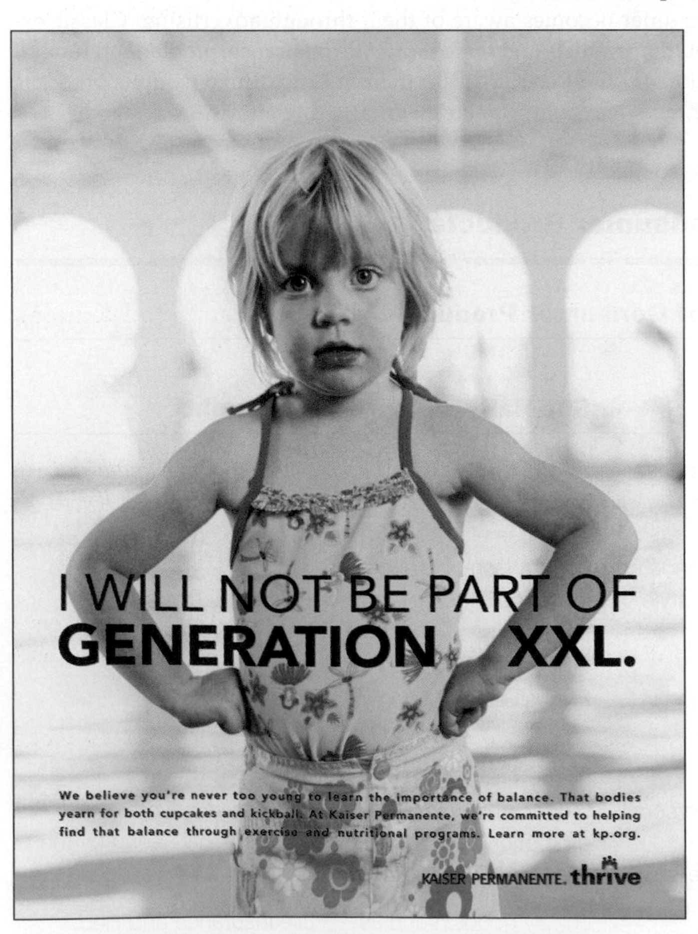

● **Organization marketing: Kaiser Permanente's "Thrive" campaign markets the organization as a total health advocate that helps its members get healthy, stay healthy, and thrive.**

Organizations, Persons, Places, and Ideas

In addition to tangible products and services, marketers have broadened the concept of a product to include other market offerings: organizations, persons, places, and ideas.

Organizations often carry out activities to "sell" the organization itself. *Organization marketing* consists of activities undertaken to create, maintain, or change the attitudes and behavior of target consumers toward an organization. Both profit and not-for-profit organizations practice organization marketing. Business firms sponsor public relations or *corporate image marketing* campaigns to market themselves and polish their images.

For example, Kaiser Permanente's long-running "Thrive" campaign markets the health maintenance organization (HMO) not just as a health-care company, but as a total health advocate. Whereas "competitors [stand] for health care," says the company, "Kaiser Permanente [stands] for health." The award-winning "Thrive" campaign promotes prevention and wellness through healthy lifestyles that will help Kaiser Permanente members and their families get healthy, stay healthy, and thrive. Some ads show people exercising or focus on healthy eating choices ("I scream, You scream. We all scream for green beans."). ● Another ad shows a determined, trim, and fit young girl who declares, "I will not be part of Generation XXL." Still other ads show how Kaiser Permanente accomplishes major health-care breakthroughs behind the scenes so that its members can thrive and enjoy the everyday moments of their lives to the fullest.[3]

People can also be thought of as products. *Person marketing* consists of activities undertaken to create, maintain, or change attitudes or behavior toward particular people. People ranging from presidents, entertainers, and sports figures to professionals such as doctors, lawyers, and architects use person marketing to build their reputations. And businesses, charities, and other organizations use well-known personalities to help sell their products or causes. For example, P&G's Cover Girl brand is represented by well-known celebrities such as Ellen DeGeneres, P!nk, and Sofia Vergara. The skillful use of marketing can turn a person's name into a powerhouse brand. For example, The Food Network's celebrity chef Rachael Ray is a one-woman marketing phenomenon, with her own daytime talk show, cookware and cutlery brands, dog food brand (Nutrish), and even her own brand of EVOO (extra virgin olive oil, for those not familiar with Rayisms).

Place marketing involves activities undertaken to create, maintain, or change attitudes or behavior toward particular places. Cities, states, regions, and even entire nations compete to attract tourists, new residents, conventions, and company offices and factories. The New Orleans city Web site shouts "Go NOLA" and markets annual events such as Mardi Gras festivities and the New Orleans Jazz and Heritage Festival. Michigan invites visitors to experience Pure Michigan: unspoiled nature, lakes that feel like oceans, miles of cherry orchards, glorious sunsets, and nighttime skies scattered with stars. And Brand USA, a public–private marketing partnership created by a recent act of Congress, promotes the United States as a tourist destination to international travelers. Its mission is to "represent the true greatness of America—from sea to shining sea" through country-by-country ads and promotions and a DiscoverAmerica.com Web site that features destinations, U.S. travel information and tips, and travel planning tools.[4]

Ideas can also be marketed. In one sense, all marketing is the marketing of an idea, whether it is the general idea of brushing your teeth or the specific idea that Crest toothpastes create "healthy, beautiful smiles for life." Here, however, we narrow our focus to the marketing of *social ideas*. This area has been called **social marketing** and consists of using traditional business marketing concepts and tools to create behaviors that will create individual and societal well-being.

Social marketing
The use of commercial marketing concepts and tools in programs designed to influence individuals' behavior to improve their well-being and that of society.

Social marketing programs cover a wide range of issues. The Ad Council of America (www.adcouncil.org), for example, has developed dozens of social advertising campaigns involving issues ranging from health care, education, and environmental sustainability to human rights and personal safety. But social marketing involves much more than just advertising. It involves a broad range of marketing strategies and marketing mix tools designed to bring about beneficial social change.[5]

Author Comment Now that we've answered the "What is a product?" question, we dig into the specific decisions that companies must make when designing and marketing products and services.

Product and Service Decisions

Marketers make product and service decisions at three levels: individual product decisions, product line decisions, and product mix decisions. We discuss each in turn.

Individual Product and Service Decisions

Figure 8.2 shows the important decisions in the development and marketing of individual products and services. We will focus on decisions about *product attributes*, *branding*, *packaging*, *labeling*, and *product support services*.

Product and Service Attributes

Developing a product or service involves defining the benefits that it will offer. These benefits are communicated and delivered by product attributes such as *quality*, *features*, and *style and design*.

Product quality
The characteristics of a product or service that bear on its ability to satisfy stated or implied customer needs.

Product Quality. **Product quality** is one of the marketer's major positioning tools. Quality affects product or service performance; thus, it is closely linked to customer value and satisfaction. In the narrowest sense, quality can be defined as "no defects." But most

FIGURE | 8.2
Individual Product Decisions

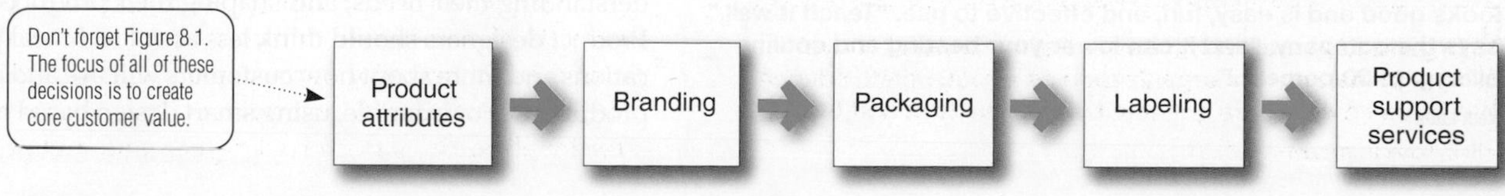
Don't forget Figure 8.1. The focus of all of these decisions is to create core customer value.
Product attributes
Branding
Packaging
Labeling
Product support services

marketers go beyond this narrow definition. Instead, they define quality in terms of creating customer value and satisfaction. The American Society for Quality defines quality as the characteristics of a product or service that bear on its ability to satisfy stated or implied customer needs. Similarly, Siemens defines quality this way: "Quality is when our customers come back and our products don't."[6]

Total quality management (*TQM*) is an approach in which all of the company's people are involved in constantly improving the quality of products, services, and business processes. For most top companies, customer-driven quality has become a way of doing business. Today, companies are taking a *return-on-quality* approach, viewing quality as an investment and holding quality efforts accountable for bottom-line results.

Product quality has two dimensions: level and consistency. In developing a product, the marketer must first choose a *quality level* that will support the product's positioning. Here, product quality means *performance quality*—the product's ability to perform its functions. For example, a Rolls-Royce provides higher performance quality than a Chevrolet: It has a smoother ride, lasts longer, and provides more hand craftsmanship, luxury, and "creature comforts." Companies rarely try to offer the highest possible performance quality level; few customers want or can afford the high levels of quality offered in products such as a Rolls-Royce automobile, a Viking range, or a Rolex watch. Instead, companies choose a quality level that matches target market needs and the quality levels of competing products.

Beyond quality level, high quality also can mean high levels of quality consistency. Here, product quality means *conformance quality*—freedom from defects and consistency in delivering a targeted level of performance. All companies should strive for high levels of conformance quality. In this sense, a Chevrolet can have just as much quality as a Rolls-Royce. Although a Chevy doesn't perform at the same level as a Rolls-Royce, it can just as consistently deliver the quality that customers pay for and expect.

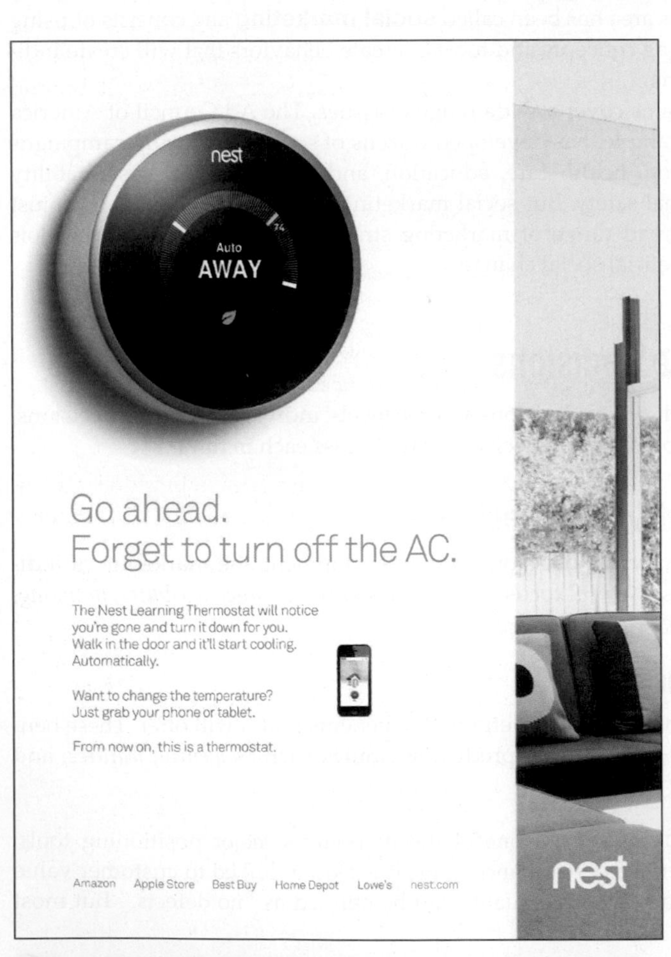

nest
Auto
AWAY
Go ahead.
Forget to turn off the AC.
The Nest Learning Thermostat will notice you're gone and turn it down for you. Walk in the door and it'll start cooling. Automatically.
Want to change the temperature? Just grab your phone or tablet.
From now on, this is a thermostat.
Amazon Apple Store Best Buy Home Depot Lowe's nest.com
nest

Through award-winning, consumer-driven design, Nest Labs created the Nest Learning Thermostat, a sleek device that both looks good and is easy, fun, and effective to use. "Teach it well," says the company, "and it can lower your heating and cooling bills up to 20 percent."

Nest Labs

Product Features. A product can be offered with varying features. A stripped-down model, one without any extras, is the starting point. The company can then create higher-level models by adding more features. Features are a competitive tool for differentiating the company's product from competitors' products. Being the first producer to introduce a valued new feature is one of the most effective ways to compete.

How can a company identify new features and decide which ones to add to its product? It should periodically survey buyers who have used the product and ask these questions: How do you like the product? Which specific features of the product do you like most? Which features could we add to improve the product? The answers to these questions provide the company with a rich list of feature ideas. The company can then assess each feature's *value* to customers versus its *cost* to the company. Features that customers value highly in relation to costs should be added.

Product Style and Design. Another way to add customer value is through distinctive *product style and design*. Design is a larger concept than style. *Style* simply describes the appearance of a product. Styles can be eye catching or yawn producing. A sensational style may grab attention and produce pleasing aesthetics, but it does not necessarily make the product *perform* better. Unlike style, *design* is more than skin deep—it goes to the very heart of a product. Good design contributes to a product's usefulness as well as to its looks.

Good design doesn't start with brainstorming new ideas and making prototypes. Design begins with observing customers, understanding their needs, and shaping their product-use experience. Product designers should think less about technical product specifications and more about how customers will use and benefit from the product. For example, using smart design based on deep insights into consumer needs, Nest Labs created a home heating and cooling thermostat that's not just pretty to look at but also packed with easy-to-access customer benefits:[7]

> The Nest Learning Thermostat looks great—its sleek, clean, curved design and neutral brushed-silver finish create a chameleon effect that grounds the device within its environment. But the Nest Learning Thermostat's beauty is more than just skin deep. Earlier programmable thermostats were too complicated to use, and the units looked clunky and antiquated. So Nest Labs assembled a corps of Silicon Valley designers who reinvented the thermostat to fit the needs of today's smartphone generation. The result is the Nest Learning Themostat, which—all by itself—learns from your preferences, behaviors, and surroundings and then optimizes your heating and cooling schedule to keep you comfortable while you're at home and saving energy while you're away. Users can also control the device simply via WIFI, at home or away, using a laptop, tablet, or smartphone app.
>
> Thus, Nest Labs has transformed the lowly home thermostat into a device that you're not only proud to hang on your wall but also a cool, connected device that's easy, fun, and effective to use. Thanks to good design, the nifty little Nest Learning Thermostat sold out for months shortly after launch. Based on the thermostat's huge success, Nest Labs applied the same design magic to create an equally smart smoke detector, which alerts homeowners by alarm, voice, or phone messages if it senses smoke. The detector also interacts with Nest thermostats to shut off the furnace if it detects carbon monoxide. Good design pays in more ways than one. Founded in 2010, the incredibly successful company was acquired in 2014 by Google for $3.2 billion.

Branding

Brand
A name, term, sign, symbol, or design, or a combination of these, that identifies the products or services of one seller or group of sellers and differentiates them from those of competitors.

Perhaps the most distinctive skill of professional marketers is their ability to build and manage brands. A **brand** is a name, term, sign, symbol, or design, or a combination of these, that identifies the maker or seller of a product or service. Consumers view a brand as an important part of a product, and branding can add value to a consumer's purchase. Customers attach meanings to brands and develop brand relationships. As a result, brands have meaning well beyond a product's physical attributes. ● Consider this story:[8]

> One Tuesday evening in January, Joshua Bell, one of the world's finest violinists, played at Boston's stately Symphony Hall before a packed audience who'd paid an average of $100 a seat. Based on the well-earned strength of the "Joshua Bell brand," the talented musician routinely drew standing-room-only audiences at all of his performances around the world. Three days later, however, as part of a *Washington Post* social experiment, Bell found himself standing in a Washington, D.C., metro station, dressed in jeans, a T-shirt, and a Washington Nationals baseball cap. As morning commuters streamed by, Bell pulled out his $4 million Stradivarius violin, set the open case at his feet, and began playing the same revered classics he'd played in Boston. During the next 45 minutes, some 1,100 people passed by but few stopped to listen. Bell earned a total of $32. No one recognized the "unbranded" Bell, so few appreciated his artistry. What does that tell you about the meaning of a strong brand?

Branding has become so strong that today hardly anything goes unbranded. Salt is packaged in branded containers, common nuts and bolts are packaged with a distributor's

● **The meaning of a strong brand: The "branded" and "unbranded" Joshua Bell—The premier musician packs concert halls at an average of $100 or more a seat but made only $32 as a street musician at a Washington, D.C., metro station.**
NBC via Getty Images (left); The Washington Post/Getty Images (right)

label, and automobile parts—spark plugs, tires, filters—bear brand names that differ from those of the automakers. Even fruits, vegetables, dairy products, and poultry are branded—Cuties mandarin oranges, Dole Classic iceberg salads, Horizon Organic milk, Perdue chickens, and Eggland's Best eggs.

Branding helps buyers in many ways. Brand names help consumers identify products that might benefit them. Brands also say something about product quality and consistency—buyers who always buy the same brand know that they will get the same features, benefits, and quality each time they buy. Branding also gives the seller several advantages. The seller's brand name and trademark provide legal protection for unique product features that otherwise might be copied by competitors. Branding helps the seller to segment markets. For example, rather than offering just one general product to all consumers, Toyota can offer the different Lexus, Toyota, and Scion brands, each with numerous sub-brands—such as Camry, Corolla, Prius, Matrix, Yaris, Tundra, and Land Cruiser.

Finally, a brand name becomes the basis on which a whole story can be built about a product's special qualities. For example, the Cuties brand of pint-sized mandarins sets itself apart from ordinary oranges by promising "Kids love Cuties because Cuties are made for kids." They are a healthy snack that's "perfect for little hands": sweet, seedless, kid-sized, and easy to peel.[9] Building and managing brands are perhaps the marketer's most important tasks. We will discuss branding strategy in more detail later in the chapter.

Packaging

Packaging
The activities of designing and producing the container or wrapper for a product.

Packaging involves designing and producing the container or wrapper for a product. Traditionally, the primary function of the package was to hold and protect the product. In recent times, however, packaging has become an important marketing tool as well. Increased competition and clutter on retail store shelves means that packages must now perform many sales tasks—from attracting buyers, to communicating brand positioning, to closing the sale. Not every customer will see a brand's advertising, social media pages, or other promotions. However, all consumers who buy and use a product will interact regularly with its packaging. Thus, the humble package represents prime marketing space.

Companies are realizing the power of good packaging to create immediate consumer recognition of a brand. For example, an average supermarket stocks about 43,000 items; the average Walmart supercenter carries 142,000 items. The typical shopper makes three out of four purchase decisions in stores and passes by some 300 items per minute. In this highly competitive environment, the package may be the seller's best and last chance to influence buyers. So the package itself has become an important promotional medium.[10]

Poorly designed packages can cause headaches for consumers and lost sales for the company. Think about all those hard-to-open packages, such as DVD cases sealed with impossibly sticky labels, packaging with finger-splitting wire twist-ties, or sealed plastic clamshell containers that cause "wrap rage" and send thousands of people to the hospital each year with lacerations and puncture wounds. Another packaging issue is overpackaging—as when a tiny USB flash drive in an oversized cardboard and plastic display package is delivered in a giant corrugated shipping carton. Overpackaging creates an incredible amount of waste, frustrating those who care about the environment.

Amazon recently launched a multiyear Frustration-Free Packaging initiative to alleviate both wrap rage and overpackaging. The online retailer now works with more than 2,000 companies, such as Fisher-Price, Mattel, Unilever, Microsoft, and others, to create smaller, easy-to-open, recyclable packages that use less packaging material and no frustrating plastic clamshells or wire ties. It currently offers more than 200,000 such items and to date has shipped over 75 million of them to 175 countries. In the process, the initiative has eliminated nearly 60 million square feet of cardboard and 25 million pounds of packaging waste.[11]

Innovative packaging can give a company an advantage over competitors and boost sales. ● For example, PUMA recently replaced the traditional shoebox with an attractive and functional yet environmentally friendly alternative—the Clever Little Bag:[12]

> In their search for the next generation of shoe packaging, PUMA's designers spent 21 months road testing 40 shoebox prototypes, checking on their potential environmental impact from production and transport through use and future re-use. They came up with what PUMA calls the Clever Little Bag with a big impact. The new container—which consists of a light cardboard insert that slides seamlessly into a colorful, reusable red bag—uses 65 percent less paper to make and reduces water, energy, and fuel consumption during manufacturing by more than 60 percent a year. Because it takes up less space and weight, the new container also reduces

Innovative packaging: PUMA's next-generation shoe packaging—The Clever Little Bag—is more than just friendly to the environment, it's also very friendly to consumers' sensibilities and the company's bottom line. Pretty clever, huh?

PUMA SE

carbon emissions during shipping by 10,000 tons a year. What's more, everything is 100 percent recyclable. In all, PUMA's Clever Little Bag is more than just friendly to the environment, it's also very friendly to consumers' likes and the company's bottom line. Pretty clever, huh?

In recent years, product safety has also become a major packaging concern. We have all learned to deal with hard-to-open "childproof" packaging. Due to the rash of product tampering scares in the 1980s, most drug producers and food makers now put their products in tamper-resistant packages. In making packaging decisions, the company also must heed growing environmental concerns. Fortunately, like Puma, many companies have gone "green" by reducing their packaging and using environmentally responsible packaging materials.

Labeling

Labels range from simple tags attached to products to complex graphics that are part of the packaging. They perform several functions. At the very least, the label *identifies* the product or brand, such as the name Sunkist stamped on oranges. The label might also *describe* several things about the product—who made it, where it was made, when it was made, its contents, how it is to be used, and how to use it safely. Finally, the label might help to *promote* the brand, support its positioning, and connect with customers. For many companies, labels have become an important element in broader marketing campaigns.

Labels and brand logos can support the brand's positioning and add personality to the brand. In fact, brand labels and logos can become a crucial element in the brand–customer connection. Customers often become strongly attached to logos as symbols of the brands they represent. Consider the feelings evoked by the logos of companies such as Coca-Cola, Google, Twitter, Apple, and Nike. Logos must be redesigned from time to time. For example, brands ranging from Yahoo! and eBay to Wendy's have successfully adapted their logos to keep them contemporary and to meet the needs of new interactive media such as the Web and mobile apps and browsers. However, companies must take care when changing such important brand symbols.

For example, when Gap introduced a more contemporary redesign of its familiar old logo—the well-known white text on a blue square—customers went ballistic and imposed intense online pressure. Gap reinstated the old logo after only one week. Similarly, when American Airlines replaced its familiar 45-year-old "AA eagle" logo with a more modern version, the new logo became a flashpoint for both brand fans and detractors. Although the brand redesign was probably overdue, fans lamented the loss of the classic design, whereas detractors claimed that the millions spent on repainting all of American's planes should have been invested in improving the airline's customer service. Such examples "highlight a powerful connection people have to the visual representations of their . . . brands," says an analyst.[13]

Brand labels and logos: When American Airlines modernized its familiar old "AA eagle" logo, the new logo became a flashpoint for both brand fans and detractors.

Associated Press (new); Mark Fairhurst/ZUMA Press/Newscom (old)

Along with the positives, there has been a long history of legal concerns about packaging and labels. The Federal Trade Commission Act of 1914 held that false, misleading, or deceptive labels or packages constitute unfair competition. Labels can mislead customers, fail to describe important ingredients, or fail to include needed safety warnings. As a result, several federal and state laws regulate labeling. The most prominent is the Fair Packaging and Labeling Act of 1966, which set mandatory labeling requirements, encouraged voluntary industry packaging standards, and allowed federal agencies to set packaging regulations in specific industries.

Labeling has been affected in recent times by *unit pricing* (stating the price per unit of a standard measure), *open dating* (stating the expected shelf life of the product), and *nutritional labeling* (stating the nutritional values in the product). The Nutritional Labeling and Educational Act of 1990 requires sellers to provide detailed nutritional information on food products, and recent sweeping actions by the Food and Drug Administration (FDA) regulate the use of health-related terms such as *low fat*, *light*, and *high fiber*. Sellers must ensure that their labels contain all the required information.

Product Support Services

Customer service is another element of product strategy. A company's offer usually includes some support services, which can be a minor part or a major part of the total offering. Later in this chapter, we will discuss services as products in themselves. Here, we discuss services that augment actual products.

Support services are an important part of the customer's overall brand experience. For example, L.L.Bean—the iconic American outdoor apparel and equipment retailer—knows good marketing doesn't stop with making the sale. Keeping customers happy *after* the sale is the key to building lasting relationships.[14]

NOTICE

I do not consider a sale complete until goods are worn out and customer still satisfied.

We will thank anyone to return goods that are not perfectly satisfactory.

Should the person reading this notice know of anyone who is not satisfied with our goods, I will consider it a favor to be notified.

Above all things we wish to avoid having a dissatisfied customer.

L.L.Bean

Customer service: For more than 100 years, L.L.Bean has been going the extra mile for customers. As founder Leon Leonwood Bean put it: "I do not consider a sale complete until [the] goods are worn out and the customer [is] still satisfied."

L.L.Bean Inc.

Year after year, L.L.Bean lands in the top ten of virtually every list of top service companies, including J.D. Power's most recent list of "customer service champions." The customer-service culture runs deep at L.L. Bean. More than 100 years ago, Leon Leonwood Bean founded the company on a philosophy of complete customer satisfaction, expressed in the following guarantee: "I do not consider a sale complete until [the] goods are worn out and the customer [is] still satisfied." To this day, customers can return any item, no questions asked, even decades after purchase.

The company's customer-service philosophy is perhaps best summed up in founder L.L.'s answer to the question, What is a customer? His answer still forms the backbone of the company's values: "A customer is the most important person ever in this company—in person or by mail. A customer is not dependent on us, we are dependent on him. A customer is not an interruption of our work, he is the purpose of it. We are not doing a favor by serving him, he is doing us a favor by giving us the opportunity to do so. A customer is not someone to argue or match wits with. Nobody ever won an argument with a customer. A customer is a person who brings us his wants. It is our job to handle them profitably to him and to ourselves." Adds former L.L.Bean CEO Leon Gorman: "A lot of people have fancy things to say about customer service, but it's just a day-in, day-out, ongoing, never-ending, persevering, compassionate kind of activity."

The first step in designing support services is to survey customers periodically to assess the value of current services and obtain ideas for new ones. Once the company has assessed the quality of various support services to customers, it can take steps to fix problems and add new services that will both delight customers and yield profits to the company.

Many companies now use a sophisticated mix of phone, e-mail, online, social media, mobile, and interactive voice and data technologies to provide support services that were not possible before. For example, home improvement store Lowe's offers a vigorous dose of customer service at both its store and online locations that makes shopping easier, answers customer questions, and handles problems. Customers can access Lowe's extensive support by phone, e-mail (CareTW@lowes.com), Web site, mobile app, and Twitter via @LowesCares. The Lowe's Web site and mobile app link to a buying guide and how-to library. In its stores, Lowe's has equipped employees with 42,000 iPhones filled with custom apps and add-on hardware, letting them perform service tasks such as checking inventory at nearby stores, looking up specific customer purchase histories, sharing how-to videos, and checking competitor prices—all without leaving the customer's side.[15]

Product Line Decisions

Product line
A group of products that are closely related because they function in a similar manner, are sold to the same customer groups, are marketed through the same types of outlets, or fall within given price ranges.

Beyond decisions about individual products and services, product strategy also calls for building a product line. A **product line** is a group of products that are closely related because they function in a similar manner, are sold to the same customer groups, are marketed through the same types of outlets, or fall within given price ranges. For example, Nike produces several lines of athletic shoes and apparel, and Marriott offers several lines of hotels.

The major product line decision involves *product line length*—the number of items in the product line. The line is too short if the manager can increase profits by adding items; the line is too long if the manager can increase profits by dropping items. Managers need to analyze their product lines periodically to assess each item's sales and profits and understand how each item contributes to the line's overall performance.

A company can expand its product line in two ways: by *line filling* or *line stretching*. *Product line filling* involves adding more items within the present range of the line. There are several reasons for product line filling: reaching for extra profits, satisfying dealers, using excess capacity, being the leading full-line company, and plugging holes to keep out competitors. However, line filling is overdone if it results in cannibalization and customer confusion. The company should ensure that new items are noticeably different from existing ones.

Product mix (or product portfolio)
The set of all product lines and items that a particular seller offers for sale.

Product line stretching occurs when a company lengthens its product line beyond its current range. The company can stretch its line downward, upward, or both ways. Companies located at the upper end of the market can stretch their lines *downward*. A company may stretch downward to plug a market hole that otherwise would attract a new competitor or to respond to a competitor's attack on the upper end. Or it may add low-end products because it finds faster growth taking place in the low-end segments. Companies can also stretch their product lines *upward*. Sometimes, companies stretch upward to add prestige to their current products. Or they may be attracted by a faster growth rate or higher margins at the higher end.

● **Product line stretching and filling: Samsung's bulging Galaxy mobile devices line now offers a size for any need or preference, including smartphones, "phablets," tablets, and even a wristwatch-like wearable smartphone, the Galaxy Gear.**

© Oleksiy Maksymenko Photography/Alamy

● Over the past few years Samsung has both stretched and filled its Galaxy line of premium smartphone and tablet mobile devices. Samsung started the Galaxy line with a 4″ smartphone, then quickly added a 10.1″ tablet. It now offers a bulging Galaxy line that includes a size for any need or preference. The basic Galaxy smartphones come with 5″ screens. The popular Galaxy Note "phablet" comes with a 5.7″ screen in what Samsung calls "the best of both" between a phone and tablet. Galaxy Tab buyers can now choose among any of three sizes—7″, 8″, and 10.1″. To top things off, Samsung offers the Galaxy Gear, a wristwatch-like wearable Galaxy smartphone. The Galaxy line still caters heavily to the top end of its markets. But to address the fastest-growing smartphone segment—phones that sell for less than $300 contract-free—Samsung is rumored to have lower-priced Galaxy models in the works. As a result, through artful stretching and filling, Samsung's successful Galaxy line has broadened its appeal, improved its competitive position, and boosted growth.

Product Mix Decisions

An organization with several product lines has a product mix. A **product mix** (or **product portfolio**) consists of all the product lines and items that a particular seller offers for sale. For example, The Clorox Company is best known for its CLOROX bleach. But, in fact, Clorox is a $5.6 billion firm that makes and markets a full product mix consisting of dozens of familiar lines and brands. Clorox divides its overall product mix into five major lines: Cleaning, Household, Lifestyle, Professional, and International.[16] Each product line consists of many brands and items.

A company's product mix has four important dimensions: width, length, depth, and consistency. Product mix *width* refers to the number of different product lines the company carries. For example, Clorox has a fairly contained product mix that fits its mission to "make everyday life better, every day." By contrast, GE manufactures as many as 250,000 items across a broad range of categories, from light bulbs to medical equipment, jet engines, and diesel locomotives.

Product mix *length* refers to the total number of items a company carries within its product lines. Clorox carries several brands within each line. For example, its cleaning line includes CLOROX, FORMULA 409, LIQUID PLUMBER, SOS, PINE-SOL, TILEX, HANDI-WIPES, and others. The lifestyle line contains the KC MASTERPIECE, BRITA, HIDDEN VALLEY, and BURT'S BEES brands, among others.

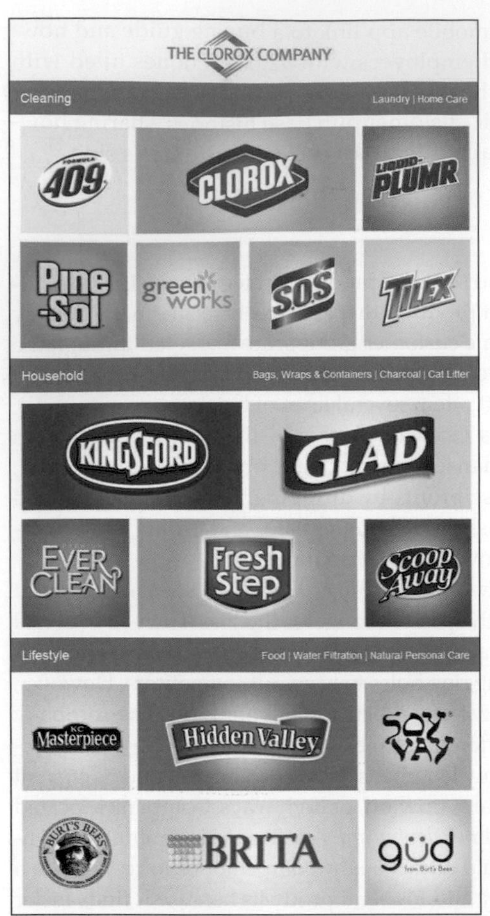

The product mix: The Clorox Company has a nicely contained product mix consistent with its mission to "make everyday life better every day."

Product mix *depth* refers to the number of versions offered for each product in the line. The Clorox brand contains a deep assortment of items and varieties, including disinfecting wipes, floor cleaners, stain removers, and bleach products. Each variety comes in a number of product forms, formulations, scents, and sizes. For example, you can buy CLOROX Regular Bleach, CLOROX Scented Bleach, CLOROX Bleach Foamer, CLOROX High Efficiency Bleach, CLOROX UltimateCare Bleach (gentle for delicate fabrics), or any of a dozen other varieties.

Finally, the *consistency* of the product mix refers to how closely related the various product lines are in end use, production requirements, distribution channels, or some other aspect. The Clorox Company's product lines are consistent insofar as they are primarily consumer products and go through the same distribution channels. The lines are less consistent insofar as they perform different functions for buyers.

These product mix dimensions provide the handles for defining the company's product strategy. A company can increase its business in four ways. It can add new product lines, widening its product mix. In this way, its new lines build on the company's reputation in its other lines. A company can lengthen its existing product lines to become a more full-line company. It can add more versions of each product and thus deepen its product mix. Finally, a company can pursue more product line consistency—or less—depending on whether it wants to have a strong reputation in a single field or in several fields.

From time to time, a company may also have to streamline its product mix to pare out marginally performing lines and to regain its focus. For example, as discussed in the previous chapter, P&G pursues a megabrand strategy built around 25 billion-dollar brands in the household care and beauty and grooming categories. During the past decade, the consumer products giant has sold off dozens of major brands that no longer fit either its evolving focus or the billion-dollar threshold, ranging from Jif peanut butter, Crisco shortening, Folgers coffee, Pringles snack chips, and Sunny Delight drinks to Noxema skin care products, Right Guard deodorant, and Aleve pain reliever. Such pruning is essential for maintaining a focused, healthy product mix.

Author Comment | As noted at the start of this chapter, services are "products," too—intangible ones. So all the product topics we've discussed so far apply to services as well as to physical products. However, in this section, we focus on the special characteristics and marketing needs that set services apart.

Services Marketing

Services have grown dramatically in recent years. Services now account for 80 percent of the U.S. gross domestic product (GDP). Services are growing even faster in the world economy, making up almost 64 percent of the gross world product.[17]

Service industries vary greatly. *Governments* offer services through courts, employment services, hospitals, military services, police and fire departments, the postal service, and schools. *Private not-for-profit organizations* offer services through museums, charities, churches, colleges, foundations, and hospitals. In addition, a large number of *business organizations* offer services—airlines, banks, hotels, insurance companies, consulting firms, medical and legal practices, entertainment and telecommunications companies, real estate firms, retailers, and others.

The Nature and Characteristics of a Service

A company must consider four special service characteristics when designing marketing programs: intangibility, inseparability, variability, and perishability (see **Figure 8.3**).

FIGURE | 8.3
Four Service Characteristics

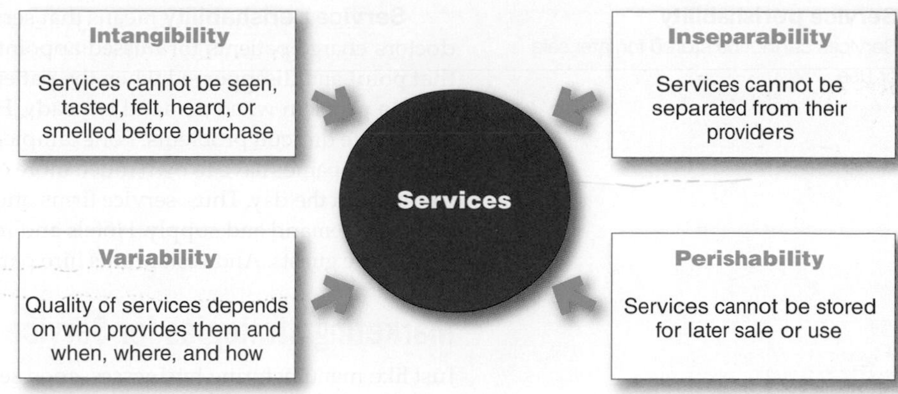

Although services are "products" in a general sense, they have special characteristics and marketing needs. The biggest differences come from the fact that services are essentially intangible and that they are created through direct interactions with customers. Think about your experiences with an airline or Google versus Nike or Apple.

Service intangibility
Services cannot be seen, tasted, felt, heard, or smelled before they are bought.

Service intangibility means that services cannot be seen, tasted, felt, heard, or smelled before they are bought. For example, people undergoing cosmetic surgery cannot see the result before the purchase. Airline passengers have nothing but a ticket and a promise that they and their luggage will arrive safely at the intended destination, hopefully at the same time. To reduce uncertainty, buyers look for *signals* of service quality. They draw conclusions about quality from the place, people, price, equipment, and communications that they can see.

Therefore, the service provider's task is to make the service tangible in one or more ways and send the right signals about quality. The Mayo Clinic does this well:[18]

Service inseparability
Services are produced and consumed at the same time and cannot be separated from their providers.

Service variability
The quality of services may vary greatly depending on who provides them and when, where, and how they are provided.

When it comes to hospitals, most patients can't really judge "product quality." It's a very complex product that's hard to understand, and you can't try it out before buying it. So when considering a hospital, most people unconsciously search for evidence that the facility is caring, competent, and trustworthy. The Mayo Clinic doesn't leave these things to chance. Rather, it offers patients organized and honest evidence of its dedication to "providing the best care to every patient every day."

Inside, staff is trained to act in a way that clearly signals Mayo Clinic's concern for patient wellbeing. For example, doctors regularly follow up with patients at home to see how they are doing, and they work with patients to smooth out scheduling problems. The clinic's physical facilities also send the right signals. They've been carefully designed to offer a place of refuge, show caring and respect, and signal competence. Looking for external confirmation? Go online and hear directly from those who've been to the clinic or work there. The Mayo Clinic now uses social networking—everything from blogs to Facebook and YouTube—to enhance the patient experience. For example, on the Sharing Mayo Clinic blog (http://sharing.mayoclinic.org), patients and their families retell their Mayo experiences, and Mayo employees offer behind-the-scenes views. The result? Highly loyal customers who willingly spread the good word to others, building one of the most powerful brands in health care.

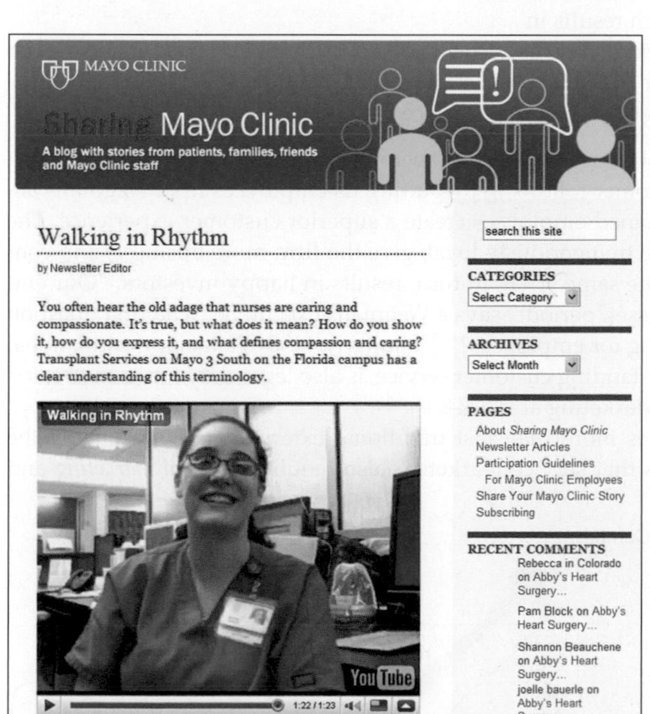

By providing customers with organized, honest evidence of its capabilities, the Mayo Clinic has built one of the most powerful brands in health care. Its Sharing Mayo Clinic blog lets you hear directly from those who have been to the clinic or who work there.

Mayo Clinic

Physical goods are produced, then stored, then later sold, and then still later consumed. In contrast, services are first sold and then produced and consumed at the same time. **Service inseparability** means that services cannot be separated from their providers, whether the providers are people or machines. If a service employee provides the service, then the employee becomes a part of the service. And customers don't just buy and use a service, they play an active role in its delivery. Customer coproduction makes *provider–customer interaction* a special feature of services marketing. Both the provider and the customer affect the service outcome.

Service variability means that the quality of services depends on who provides them as well as when, where, and how they are provided. For example, some hotels—say, Marriott—have reputations for providing better service than others. Still, within a given Marriott hotel, one registration-counter employee may be cheerful and efficient, whereas another standing just a few feet away may be grumpy and slow. Even the quality of a single Marriott employee's service varies according to his or her energy and frame of mind at the time of each customer encounter.

Service perishability
Services cannot be stored for later sale or use.

Service perishability means that services cannot be stored for later sale or use. Some doctors charge patients for missed appointments because the service value existed only at that point and disappeared when the patient did not show up. The perishability of services is not a problem when demand is steady. However, when demand fluctuates, service firms often have difficult problems. For example, because of rush-hour demand, public transportation companies have to own much more equipment than they would if demand were even throughout the day. Thus, service firms often design strategies for producing a better match between demand and supply. Hotels and resorts charge lower prices in the off-season to attract more guests. And restaurants hire part-time employees to serve during peak periods.

Marketing Strategies for Service Firms

Just like manufacturing businesses, good service firms use marketing to position themselves strongly in chosen target markets. FedEx promises to take your packages "faster, farther"; Angie's List offers "Reviews you can trust." At Hampton, "We love having you here." And St. Jude Children's Hospital is "Finding cures. Saving children." These and other service firms establish their positions through traditional marketing mix activities. However, because services differ from tangible products, they often require additional marketing approaches.

The Service Profit Chain

Service profit chain
The chain that links service firm profits with employee and customer satisfaction.

In a service business, the customer and the front-line service employee *interact* to co-create the service. Effective interaction, in turn, depends on the skills of front-line service employees and on the support processes backing these employees. Thus, successful service companies focus their attention on both their customers and their employees. They understand the **service profit chain**, which links service firm profits with employee and customer satisfaction. This chain consists of five links:[19]

- *Internal service quality.* Superior employee selection and training, a quality work environment, and strong support for those dealing with customers, which results in . . .
- *Satisfied and productive service employees.* More satisfied, loyal, and hardworking employees, which results in . . .
- *Greater service value.* More effective and efficient customer value creation, engagement, and service delivery, which results in . . .
- *Satisfied and loyal customers.* Satisfied customers who remain loyal, make repeat purchases, and refer other customers, which results in . . .
- *Healthy service profits and growth.* Superior service firm performance.

For example, supermarket chain Wegmans—a perennial customer service champion—has developed a cult-like customer following by putting its employees first. Wegmans believes that happy, superbly trained employees create a superior customer experience. The resulting happy customers are tremendously loyal, give the firm more business, and convince other customers to do the same. That, in turn, results in happy investors. "Our employees are our number one asset, period," says a Wegmans executive. "The first question [we] ask is 'Is this the best thing for employees?'"[20] Similarly, HSBC, a major multinational bank with a reputation for outstanding customer service, is also legendary for its motivated and satisfied employees (see Marketing at Work 8.1).

Service marketing requires more than just traditional external marketing using the four Ps. **Figure 8.4** shows that service marketing also requires *internal marketing* and

FIGURE | 8.4
Three Types of Service Marketing

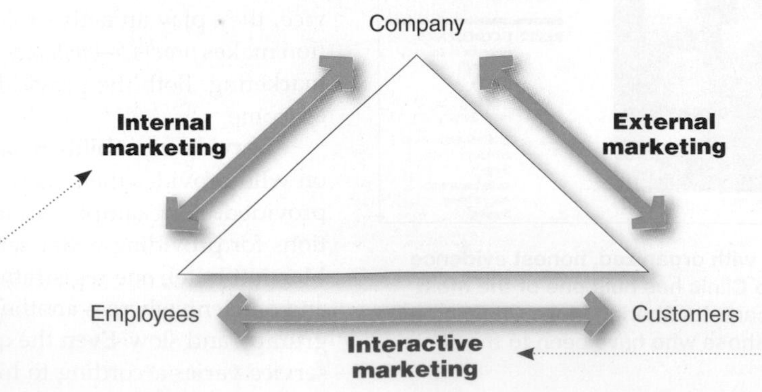
Company
Internal marketing
External marketing
Employees
Customers
Interactive marketing
Service firms must sell customer-contact employees on the importance of delighting customers. At Four Seasons Hotels, the most important guideline is the golden rule: "Do unto others. . . ."
Then service firms must help employees master the art of interacting with customers. At Four Seasons Hotels, employees quickly learn that guests paying $1,000 a night "expect to have their minds read."

Real Marketing 8.1 HSBC: Internal Marketing Drives Overall Excellence

Due to their intangible nature, providing services as a form of business is a great challenge, but doing so in a volatile economic climate is even more challenging. Whether regarding loans, mortgages, current accounts, insurance products, or other services, most bank customers are now better informed and more demanding. So, succeeding in the business of providing financial services requires more than the basic efforts; a significant level of customer orientation is in order, especially as competition becomes stiffer. This is one of the key areas where HSBC, one of the world's leading banks, scores very high in the perception of financial services customers. The bank operates across 80 countries and territories and serves over 60 million customers with various needs, and evidence suggests that the organization is growing by the day. It is noteworthy that as big as it is in structure, from the top to the bottom of the organization, the focus of the entire workforce is predominantly and clearly centered on customer satisfaction. However, the bank acknowledges an important factor that is very significant to its success—its employees.

The belief of the bank is that for the customer to be satisfied, it is very important to take care of the employees, as they are the ones who meet and interact with customers regularly and work toward delighting and giving them the utmost satisfaction desired in their various transactions. The logic is that sound external marketing that is focused on customer satisfaction should be preceded by an excellent practice of internal marketing. This is evident in the bank's three core group values, which can be simply summarized in this expression: HSBC people are open, connected, and dependable. To actualize this philosophy and maintain success in the marketplace, HSBC is strongly committed to its internal marketing, which is simply about identifying the needs of the employees and meeting them effectively to create satisfied employees who have the desired sense of life and professional fulfillment. The opportunities and motivation for employees are wide-ranging and attractive. As a large financial organization, the bank is in a position to offer its employees thousands of different job opportunities and positions, ranging from customer service and corporate and commercial banking to IT and human resource management. Accordingly, the bank matches these with several benefits and rewards, such as competitive salary, a contributory pension scheme, employee assistance programs, and flexible working policies. And for some roles, it also incentivizes staff members with performance-related bonus schemes, private health care, and life assurance and insurance. Closely related to this are the bank's programs for training and development, which enrich the staff's work experience. The approach adopted for training and development of staff at HSBC is special because it gives the employee control over his or her training programs through a portal it calls "My Learning." Using this link, the employee can access all the learning opportunities available to him or her. The bank also has an efficient learning and development team composed of seasoned training professionals who work closely with various units in the organization for the training and development programs of their staff members. The flexibility associated with these programs makes them very popular among the staff. In this existing arrangement, a staff member can access paper-based training programs, online training opportunities, and video-based programs. The ultimate aim of the bank is to ensure enduring job satisfaction among the staff, as the management sees this as a worthwhile investment. It is not surprising that the bank was named one of the top employers in the UK for women in The Times Top 50 Employers for Women in 2013. Antonio Simoes, who heads HSBC UK, emphasizes the bank's values when he expresses pride in offering equal employment opportunities to different kinds of men and women, reflective of the company's own diverse customer base and commitment to gender balance.

Another key feature of the bank's internal marketing program is its flexible benefits packages for employees. Besides the

HSBC bank operates in around 80 countries and territories and serves over 60 million customers worldwide, leveraging its employees' happiness to send out positive brand messages in the external marketplace.

competitive regular payments it offers its staff, HSBC's overtime payment is excellent. In response to the views of employees, the bank tailors its benefits packages to the specific needs of the staff. For example, benefits can be tailored to employees' interests in providing for the future, breakdown coverage, and child care, among other options. The bank simply calls this "My Choice."

So, to those who wonder why HSBC's staff members are so customer-focused—always welcoming customers with smiles and courtesy, and strongly committed to the business of delighting customers—the key answers lie in the employees' motivation levels, morale, and career development paths in the organization. HSBC has proven that winning in the tough post-recession marketplace is not only about formulating a sound marketing strategy, but also about taking care of those who take care of its customers.

Sources: Based on information from "HSBC: About Us," www.hsbc.co.uk/1/2//about-us;"HSBC: For a Great Career, Start Here," www.jobs.hsbc.co.uk/14-en/HSBC.aspx; "HSBC and You," www.jobs.hsbc.co.uk/108-en/YouAndHSBC.aspx; "Managing the Most of the Recruitment Process," www.jobs.hsbc.co.uk/111-en/FeaturesAndPromotions.aspx; "HSBC: Diversity," www.jobs.hsbc.co.uk/113-en/Diversity.aspx; and "HSBC: Employee Handbook," www.jobs.hsbc.co.uk/SIP_STORAGE/files/5/235.pdf; www.hsbc.com/about-hsbc; https://hsbc.tbs.aon.com, accessed November 2014.

Internal marketing
Orienting and motivating customer-contact employees and supporting service employees to work as a team to provide customer satisfaction.

interactive marketing. **Internal marketing** means that the service firm must orient and motivate its customer-contact employees and supporting service people to work as a team to provide customer satisfaction. Marketers must get everyone in the organization to be customer centered. In fact, internal marketing must *precede* external marketing. For example, Four Seasons Hotels and Resorts starts by hiring the right people and carefully orienting and inspiring them to give unparalleled customer service. The idea is to make certain that employees themselves believe in the brand so that they can authentically deliver the brand's promise to customers.

Interactive marketing
Training service employees in the fine art of interacting with customers to satisfy their needs.

Interactive marketing means that service quality depends heavily on the quality of the buyer–seller interaction during the service encounter. In product marketing, product quality often depends little on how the product is obtained. But in services marketing, service quality depends on both the service deliverer and the quality of delivery. Service marketers, therefore, have to master interactive marketing skills. Thus, Four Seasons selects only people with an innate "passion to serve" and instructs them carefully in the fine art of interacting with customers to satisfy their every need. All new hires complete three months of training to help them improve their customer-interaction skills.

Today, as competition and costs increase, and as productivity and quality decrease, more service marketing sophistication is needed. Service companies face three major marketing tasks: They want to increase their *service differentiation*, *service quality*, and *service productivity*.

Managing Service Differentiation

In these days of intense price competition, service marketers often complain about the difficulty of differentiating their services from those of competitors. To the extent that customers view the services of different providers as similar, they care less about the provider than the price. The solution to price competition is to develop a differentiated offer, delivery, and image.

The *offer* can include innovative features that set one company's offer apart from competitors' offers. For example, some retailers differentiate themselves by offerings that take you well beyond the products they stock. ● Dick's Sporting Goods has grown from a single bait-and-tackle store in Binghamton, New York, into a 588-store, $5.8 billion sporting goods megaretailer in 46 states by offering interactive services that set it apart from ordinary sporting goods stores. Customers can sample shoes on Dick's indoor footwear track, test golf clubs with an on-site golf swing analyzer and putting green, shoot bows in its archery range, and receive personalized fitness product guidance from an in-store team of fitness trainers. Such differentiated services help make Dick's "the ultimate sporting goods destination store for core athletes and outdoor enthusiasts."[21]

Service companies can differentiate their service *delivery* by having more able and reliable customer-contact people, developing a superior physical environment in which the service product is delivered, or designing a superior delivery process. For example, many

Service differentiation: Dick's Sporting Goods differentiates itself by offering services that go well beyond the products it stocks.

© Ian Dagnall/Alamy

grocery chains now offer online shopping and home delivery as a better way to shop than having to drive, park, wait in line, and tote groceries home. And most banks offer mobile phone apps that allow you to more easily transfer money and check account balances. Many even allow mobile check deposits. "Sign, snap a photo, and submit a check from anywhere," says one Citibank ad. "It's easier than running to the bank."

Finally, service companies also can work on differentiating their *images* through symbols and branding. Aflac adopted the duck as its advertising symbol. Today, the duck is immortalized through stuffed animals, golf club covers, and free ringtones and screensavers. The well-known Aflac duck helped make the big but previously unknown insurance company memorable and approachable. Other well-known service characters and symbols include the GEICO gecko, Progressive Insurance's Flo, McDonald's golden arches, Allstate's "good hands," the Twitter bird, and Wendy's freckled, red-haired, pigtailed spokesperson.

Managing Service Quality

A service firm can differentiate itself by delivering consistently higher quality than its competitors provide. Like manufacturers before them, most service industries have now joined the customer-driven quality movement. And like product marketers, service providers need to identify what target customers expect in regard to service quality.

Unfortunately, service quality is harder to define and judge than product quality. For instance, it is harder to agree on the quality of a haircut than on the quality of a hair dryer. Customer retention is perhaps the best measure of quality; a service firm's ability to hang onto its customers depends on how consistently it delivers value to them.

Top service companies set high service-quality standards. They watch service performance closely, both their own and that of competitors. They do not settle for merely good service—they strive for 100 percent defect-free service. A 98 percent performance standard may sound good, but using this standard, the U.S. Postal Service would lose or misdirect 440,000 pieces of mail each hour, and U.S. pharmacies would misfill more than 75.3 million prescriptions each week.[22]

Unlike product manufacturers who can adjust their machinery and inputs until everything is perfect, service quality will always vary, depending on the interactions between employees and customers. As hard as they may try, even the best companies will have an occasional late delivery, burned steak, or grumpy employee. However, good *service recovery* can turn angry customers into loyal ones. In fact, good recovery can win more customer purchasing and loyalty than if things had gone well in the first place.

For example, Southwest Airlines has a proactive customer communications team whose job is to find the situations in which something went wrong—a mechanical delay, bad weather, a medical emergency, or a berserk passenger—then remedy the bad experience quickly, within 24 hours, if possible.[23] The team's communications to passengers, usually e-mails these days, have three basic components: a sincere apology, a brief explanation of what happened, and a gift to make it up, usually a voucher in dollars that can be used on their next Southwest flight. Surveys show that when Southwest handles a delay situation well, customers score it 14 to 16 points higher than on regular on-time flights.

These days, social media such as Facebook and Twitter can help companies root out and remedy customer dissatisfaction with service. Consider Marriott International:[24]

> John Wolf, Marriott Hotel's director of public relations, heads a team of Marriott people who work full-time monitoring the company's Twitter feed and other social media. The team seeks

out people who are complaining about problems they've had at Marriott. "We'd rather know that there's an issue than not know it, and we'd rather be given the opportunity to solve the problem," Wolf says. This strategy helps Marriott to solve customer problems as they arise and to recover previously dissatisfied customers. For example, when the team discovered an unhappy Marriott regular tweeting and blogging about an experience at a Marriott hotel that resulted in a ruined pair of shoes and big dry cleaning bill, they contacted him directly via Twitter, asking for his contact information. The next day, the disgruntled customer received a personal call from Marriott offering an explanation, a sincere apology, and a generous amount of reward points added to his account to be applied to future stays at Marriott. The result: a once-again happy and loyal customer who now blogged and tweeted to others about his positive experience.

Managing Service Productivity

With their costs rising rapidly, service firms are under great pressure to increase service productivity. They can do so in several ways. They can train current employees better or hire new ones who will work harder or more skillfully. Or they can increase the quantity of their service by giving up some quality. Finally, a service provider can harness the power of technology. Although we often think of technology's power to save time and costs in manufacturing companies, it also has great—and often untapped—potential to make service workers more productive.

However, companies must avoid pushing productivity so hard that doing so reduces quality. Attempts to streamline a service or cut costs can make a service company more efficient in the short run. But that can also reduce its longer-run ability to innovate, maintain service quality, or respond to consumer needs and desires. For example, some airlines have learned this lesson the hard way as they attempt to economize in the face of rising costs. Passengers on most airlines now encounter "time-saving" check-in kiosks rather than personal counter service. And most airlines have stopped offering even the little things for free—such as in-flight snacks—and now charge extra for everything from checked luggage to aisle seats. The result is a plane full of disgruntled customers. In their attempts to improve productivity, many airlines have mangled customer service.

Managing service productivity: Companies should be careful not to take things too far. For example, in their attempts to improve productivity, some airlines have mangled customer service.

AP Photo/Rick Bowmer

Thus, in attempting to improve service productivity, companies must be mindful of how they create and deliver customer value. They should be careful not to take *service* out of the service. In fact, a company may purposely lower service productivity in order to improve service quality, in turn allowing it to maintain higher prices and profit margins.[25]

Author Comment | A brand represents everything that a product or service *means* to consumers. As such, brands are valuable assets to a company. For example, when you hear someone say "Coca-Cola," what do you think, feel, or remember? What about "Target"? Or "Google"?

Branding Strategy: Building Strong Brands

Some analysts see brands as *the* major enduring asset of a company, outlasting the company's specific products and facilities. John Stewart, former CEO of Quaker Oats, once said, "If this business were split up, I would give you the land and bricks and mortar, and I would keep the brands and trademarks, and I would fare better than you." A former CEO of McDonald's declared, "If every asset we own, every building, and every piece of equipment were destroyed in a terrible natural disaster, we would be able to borrow all the money to replace it very quickly because of the value of our brand. . . . The brand is more valuable than the totality of all these assets."[26]

Thus, brands are powerful assets that must be carefully developed and managed. In this section, we examine the key strategies for building and managing product and service brands.

Brand Equity and Brand Value

Brands are more than just names and symbols. They are a key element in the company's relationships with consumers. Brands represent consumers' perceptions and feelings about a product and its performance—everything that the product or the service *means* to consumers. In the final analysis, brands exist in the heads of consumers. As one well-respected marketer once said, "Products are created in the factory, but brands are created in the mind." Adds Jason Kilar, former CEO of the online video service Hulu, "A brand is what people say about you when you're not in the room."[27]

Brand equity
The differential effect that knowing the brand name has on customer response to the product or its marketing.

A powerful brand has high *brand equity*. **Brand equity** is the differential effect that knowing the brand name has on customer response to the product and its marketing. It's a measure of the brand's ability to capture consumer preference and loyalty. A brand has positive brand equity when consumers react more favorably to it than to a generic or unbranded version of the same product. It has negative brand equity if consumers react less favorably than to an unbranded version.

Brands vary in the amount of power and value they hold in the marketplace. Some brands—such as Coca-Cola, Nike, Disney, GE, McDonald's, Harley-Davidson, and others—become larger-than-life icons that maintain their power in the market for years, even generations. Other brands—such as Google, Facebook, Apple, ESPN, and Wikipedia—create fresh consumer excitement and loyalty. These brands win in the marketplace not simply because they deliver unique benefits or reliable service. Rather, they succeed because they forge deep connections with customers. People really do have relationships with brands. ● For example, to devoted Vespa fans around the world, the brand stands for much more than just a scooter. It stands for "La Vespa Vida," a carefree, stylish lifestyle. Colorful, cute, sleek, nimble, efficient—the Vespa brand represents the freedom to roam wherever you wish and "live life with passion."[28]

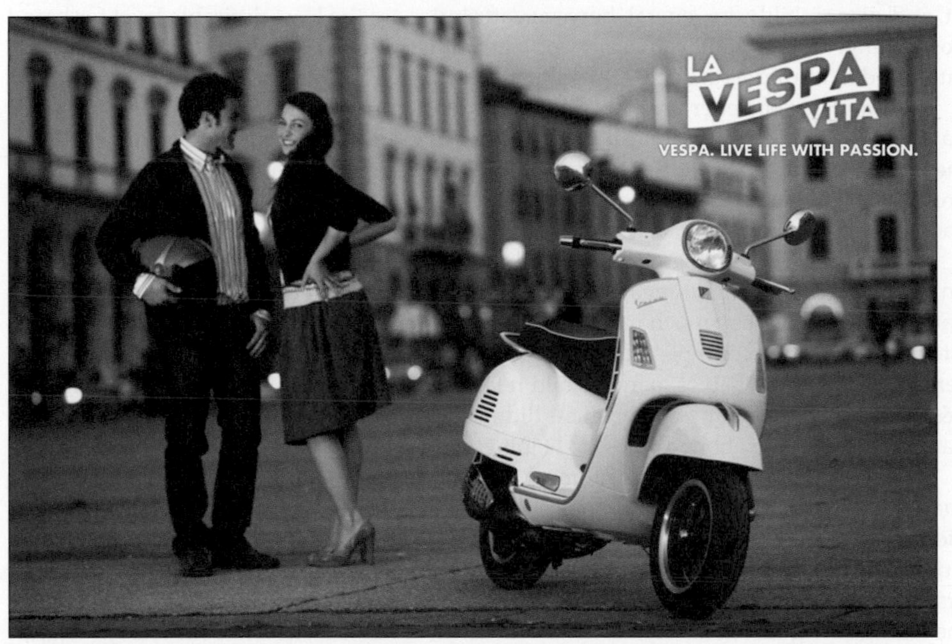

● Consumers' relationship with brands: To devoted Vespa fans around the world, the brand stands for much more than just a scooter. It stands for "La Vespa Vita"—living life with passion.

Courtesy of Piaggio Group

Ad agency Young & Rubicam's BrandAsset Valuator measures brand strength along four consumer perception dimensions: *differentiation* (what makes the brand stand out), *relevance* (how consumers feel it meets their needs), *knowledge* (how much consumers know about the brand), and *esteem* (how highly consumers regard and respect the brand). Brands with strong brand equity rate high on all four dimensions. The brand must be distinct, or consumers will have no reason to choose it over other brands. However, the fact that a brand is highly differentiated doesn't necessarily mean that consumers will buy it. The brand must stand out in ways that are relevant to consumers' needs. Even a differentiated, relevant brand is far from a shoe-in. Before consumers will respond to the brand, they must first know about and understand it. And that familiarity must lead to a strong, positive consumer–brand connection.[29]

Thus, positive brand equity derives from consumer feelings about and connections with a brand. Consumers sometimes bond *very* closely with specific brands. As perhaps the ultimate expression of brand devotion, a surprising number of people—and not just Harley-Davidson fans—have their favorite brand tattooed on their bodies. Whether it's contemporary new brands such as Facebook or Amazon or old classics like Harley or Converse, strong brands are built around an ideal of engaging consumers in some relevant way.

Brand value
The total financial value of a brand.

A brand with high brand equity is a very valuable asset. **Brand value** is the total financial value of a brand. Measuring such value is difficult. However, according to one estimate, the brand value of Apple is a whopping $185 billion, with Google at $113.6 billion, IBM at $112.5 billion, McDonald's at $90 billion, Coca-Cola at $78.4 billion, and Microsoft at

$70 billion. Other brands rating among the world's most valuable include AT&T, China Mobile, GE, Walmart, and Amazon.com.[30]

High brand equity provides a company with many competitive advantages. A powerful brand enjoys a high level of consumer brand awareness and loyalty. Because consumers expect stores to carry the particular brand, the company has more leverage in bargaining with resellers. Because a brand name carries high credibility, the company can more easily launch line and brand extensions. A powerful brand also offers the company some defense against fierce price competition.

Above all, however, a powerful brand forms the basis for building strong and profitable customer relationships. The fundamental asset underlying brand equity is *customer equity*—the value of customer relationships that the brand creates. A powerful brand is important, but what it really represents is a profitable set of loyal customers. The proper focus of marketing is building customer equity, with brand management serving as a major marketing tool. Companies need to think of themselves not as portfolios of brands but as portfolios of customers.

Building Strong Brands

Branding poses challenging decisions to the marketer. **Figure 8.5** shows that the major brand strategy decisions involve *brand positioning*, *brand name selection*, *brand sponsorship*, and *brand development*.

Brand Positioning

Marketers need to position their brands clearly in target customers' minds. They can position brands at any of three levels.[31] At the lowest level, they can position the brand on *product attributes*. For example, P&G invented the disposable diaper category with its Pampers brand. Early Pampers marketing focused on attributes such as fluid absorption, fit, and disposability. In general, however, attributes are the least desirable level for brand positioning. Competitors can easily copy attributes. More important, customers are not interested in attributes as such—they are interested in what the attributes will do for them.

A brand can be better positioned by associating its name with a desirable *benefit*. Thus, Pampers can go beyond technical product attributes and talk about the resulting containment and skin-health benefits from dryness. Some successful brands positioned on benefits are FedEx (guaranteed on-time delivery), Nike (performance), Walmart (save money), and Facebook (connections and sharing).

The strongest brands go beyond attribute or benefit positioning. They are positioned on strong *beliefs and values*, engaging customers on a deep, emotional level. For example, to parents, Pampers mean much more than just containment and dryness. The Pampers Web site (www.pampers.com) positions Pampers as a "love, sleep, and play" brand that's concerned about happy babies, parent–child relationships, and total baby care. Says a former P&G executive, "Our baby care business didn't start growing aggressively until we changed Pampers from being about dryness to helping mom with her baby's development."[32]

Successful brands engage customers on a deep, emotional level. Advertising agency Saatchi & Saatchi suggests that brands should strive to become *lovemarks*, products or services that "inspire loyalty beyond reason." Brands ranging from Apple, Disney, Nike, and Coca-Cola to Google and Pinterest have achieved this status with many of their customers. Lovemark brands pack an emotional wallop. Customers don't just like these brands, they have strong emotional connections with them and love them unconditionally.[33] Brands don't have to be big or legendary to be classified as lovemarks. Consider Shake Shack, which began 10 years ago as a lowly hot dog cart in Manhattan and grew into a small burger chain with a big, almost cult-like following. The occasionally epic lines at local Shake Shacks testify to its status as a lovemark brand.

When positioning a brand, the marketer should establish a mission for the brand and a vision of what the brand must be and do. A brand is the company's promise to deliver a specific

Brands are powerful assets that must be carefully developed and managed. As this figure suggests, building strong brands involves many challenging decisions.

Brand positioning	Brand name selection	Brand sponsorship	Brand development
Attributes Benefits Beliefs and values	Selection Protection	Manufacturer's brand Private brand Licensing Co-branding	Line extensions Brand extensions Multibrands New brands

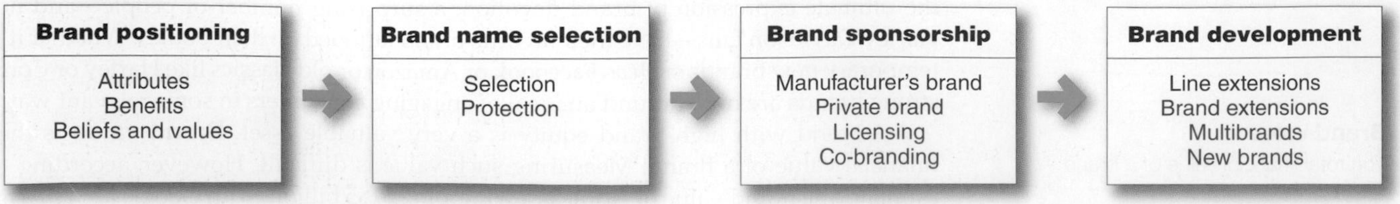

FIGURE | **8.5** Major Brand Strategy Decisions

Brands don't have to be big or legendary to be classified as lovemarks. The occasionally epic lines at local Shake Shacks testify to its lovemark status.

Sports Illustrated/Getty Images

set of features, benefits, services, and experiences consistently to buyers. The brand promise must be clear, simple, and honest. Motel 6, for example, offers clean rooms, low prices, and good service but does not promise expensive furnishings or large bathrooms. In contrast, The Ritz-Carlton offers luxurious rooms and a truly memorable experience but does not promise low prices.

Brand Name Selection

A good name can add greatly to a product's success. However, finding the best brand name is a difficult task. It begins with a careful review of the product and its benefits, the target market, and proposed marketing strategies. After that, naming a brand becomes part science, part art, and a measure of instinct.

Desirable qualities for a brand name include the following: (1) It should suggest something about the product's benefits and qualities: Beautyrest, Lean Cuisine, Snapchat, Pinterest. (2) It should be easy to pronounce, recognize, and remember: iPad, Tide, Jelly Belly, Twitter, JetBlue. (3) The brand name should be distinctive: Panera, Swiffer, Zappos, Nest. (4) It should be extendable—Amazon.com began as an online bookseller but chose a name that would allow expansion into other categories. (5) The name should translate easily into foreign languages. Before changing its name to Exxon, Standard Oil of New Jersey rejected the name Enco, which it learned meant a stalled engine when pronounced in Japanese. (6) It should be capable of registration and legal protection. A brand name cannot be registered if it infringes on existing brand names.

Choosing a new brand name is hard work. After a decade of choosing quirky names (Yahoo!, Google) or trademark-proof made-up names (Novartis, Aventis, Accenture), today's style is to build brands around names that have real meaning. For example, names like Silk (soy milk), Method (home products), Smartwater (beverages), and Blackboard (school software) are simple and make intuitive sense. But with trademark applications soaring, *available* new names can be hard to find. Try it yourself. Pick a product and see if you can come up with a better name for it. How about Moonshot? Tickle? Vanilla? Treehugger? Simplicity? Google them and you'll find that they are already taken.

Once chosen, the brand name must be protected. Many firms try to build a brand name that will eventually become identified with the product category. Brand names such as Kleenex, JELL-O, BAND-AID, Scotch Tape, Velcro, Formica, Magic Marker, Post-it notes, and Ziploc have succeeded in this way. However, their very success may threaten the company's rights to the name. Many originally protected brand names—such as cellophane, aspirin, nylon, kerosene, linoleum, yo-yo, trampoline, escalator, thermos, and shredded wheat—are now generic names that any seller can use.

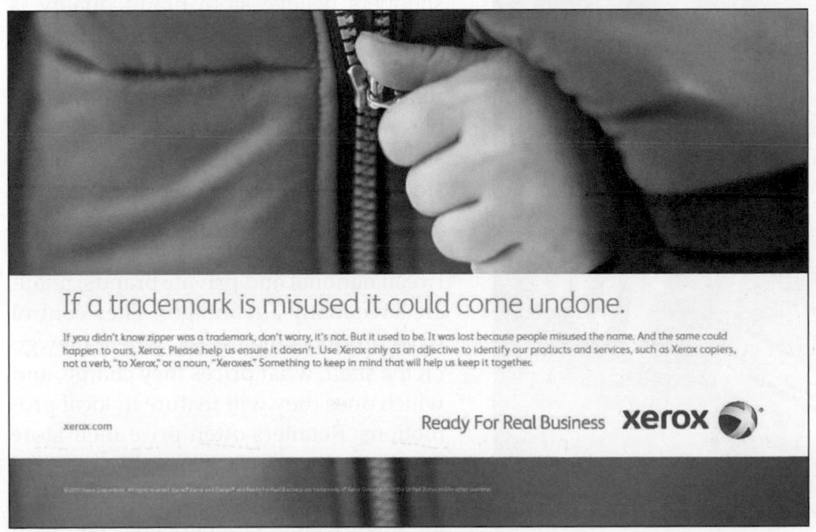

If a trademark is misused it could come undone.
If you didn't know zipper was a trademark, don't worry, it's not. But it used to be. It was lost because people misused the name. And the same could happen to ours, Xerox. Please help us ensure it doesn't. Use Xerox only as an adjective to identify our products and services, such as Xerox copiers, not a verb, "to Xerox," or a noun, "Xeroxes." Something to keep in mind that will help us keep it together.
xerox.com
Ready For Real Business
xerox

Protecting a brand name: This ad asks people to use the Xerox name only as an adjective to identify its products and services (such as "Xerox copiers"), not as a verb ("to Xerox" something) or a noun ("I'll make a Xerox").

Associated Press

To protect their brands, marketers present them carefully using the word *brand* and the registered trademark symbol, as in "BAND-AID® Brand Adhesive Bandages." Even the long-standing "I am stuck on BAND-AID 'cause BAND-AID's stuck on me" jingle has now become "I am stuck on BAND-AID brand 'cause BAND-AID's stuck on me." Similarly, a recent Xerox advertisement notes that a brand name can be lost if people misuse it. The ad asks people to use the Xerox name only as an adjective to identify its products and services (such as "Xerox copiers"), not as a verb ("to Xerox" something) or a noun ("I'll make a Xerox").

Brand Sponsorship

A manufacturer has four sponsorship options. The product may be launched as a *national brand* (or *manufacturer's brand*), as when Samsung and Kellogg sell their output under their own brand names (the Samsung Galaxy tablet or Kellogg's Frosted Flakes). Or the manufacturer may sell to resellers who give the product a *private brand* (also called a *store brand* or *distributor brand*). Although most manufacturers create their own brand names, others market *licensed brands*. Finally, two companies can join forces and *co-brand* a product. We discuss each of these options in turn.

Store brand (or **private brand**)
A brand created and owned by a reseller of a product or service.

National Brands versus Store Brands. National brands (or manufacturers' brands) have long dominated the retail scene. In recent times, however, increasing numbers of retailers and wholesalers have created their own **store brands** (or **private brands**). Store brands have been gaining strength for more than two decades, but recent tighter economic times have created a store-brand boom. Studies show that consumers are now buying even more private brands, which on average yield a 30 percent savings.[34] More frugal times give store brands a boost as consumers become more price-conscious and less brand-conscious.

In fact, store brands have grown much faster than national brands in recent years. Over the past three years, annual sales of private-brand grocery goods have grown at twice the rate of national brands. Private labels now account for more than 18 percent of supermarket dollar sales and almost 17 percent of drugstore dollar sales. Similarly, for apparel sales, private-label brands—such as Hollister, The Limited, Arizona Jean Company (JCPenney), and Xhilaration (Target)—now capture a 50 percent share of all U.S. apparel sales, up from 25 percent a decade ago.[35]

Many large retailers skillfully market a deep assortment of store-brand merchandise. ● For example, Walmart's private brands—Great Value food products; Sam's Choice beverages; Equate pharmacy, health, and beauty products; White Cloud brand toilet tissue and diapers; Simple Elegance laundry products; and Canopy outdoor home products—account for a whopping 20 percent of its sales. Its private-label brands alone generate more sales than all P&G brands combined, and Walmart's Great Value is the nation's largest single food brand. At the other end of the grocery spectrum, upscale Whole Foods Market offers an array of store-brand products under its 365 Everyday Value brand, from organic Canadian maple syrup and frozen chicken Caesar pizza to chewy children's multivitamins and organic whole-wheat pasta.[36]

Once known as "generic" or "no-name" brands, today's store brands are shedding their image as cheap knockoffs of national brands. Store brands now offer much greater selection, and they are rapidly achieving name-brand quality. In fact, retailers such as Target and Trader Joe's are out-innovating many of their national-brand competitors. As a result, consumers are becoming loyal to store brands for reasons besides price. Recent research showed that 80 percent of all shoppers believe store brand quality is equal to or better than that of national brands. "Sometimes I think they don't actually know what is a store brand," says one retail analyst.[37] In some cases, consumers are even willing to pay more for store brands that have been positioned as gourmet or premium items.

● **The popularity of store brands has soared recently. Walmart's store brands account for a whopping 25 percent of its sales, and its Great Value brand is the nation's largest single food brand.**
SIPA USA-KT/SIPA/Newscom

In the so-called *battle of the brands* between national and private brands, retailers have many advantages. They control what products they stock, where they go on the shelf, what prices they charge, and which ones they will feature in local promotions. Retailers often price their store brands lower than comparable national brands and feature the price differences in side-by-side comparisons on store shelves. Although store brands can be hard to establish and costly to stock and promote, they also yield higher profit margins for the reseller. And they give resellers exclusive products that cannot be bought from competitors, resulting in greater store traffic and loyalty. Fast-growing retailer Trader Joe's, which carries 85 percent store brands, largely controls its own brand destiny, rather than relying on producers to make and manage the brands it needs to serve its customers best.[38]

To compete with store brands, national brands must sharpen their value propositions, especially when appealing to today's more frugal consumers. Many national brands are fighting back by rolling out more discounts and coupons to defend their market share. In the long run, however, leading brand marketers must compete by investing in new brands, new features, and quality improvements that set them apart. They must design strong advertising programs to maintain high awareness and preference. And they must find ways to partner with major distributors to find distribution economies and improve joint performance.

For example, in response to the recent surge in private-label sales, consumer product giant Procter & Gamble has redoubled its efforts to develop and promote new and better products, particularly at lower price points. "We invest $2 billion a year in research and development, $400 million on consumer knowledge, and about 10 percent of sales on advertising," says P&G's CEO. "Store brands don't have that capacity." As a result, P&G brands still dominate in their categories. For example, its Tide, Gain, Cheer, and other premium laundry detergent brands capture a combined 50-percent share of the $8.6 billion North American detergent market.[39]

Licensing. Most manufacturers take years and spend millions to create their own brand names. However, some companies license names or symbols previously created by other manufacturers, names of well-known celebrities, or characters from popular movies and books. For a fee, any of these can provide an instant and proven brand name.

Apparel and accessories sellers pay large royalties to adorn their products—from blouses to ties and linens to luggage—with the names or initials of well-known fashion innovators such as Calvin Klein, Tommy Hilfiger, Gucci, or Armani. Sellers of children's products attach an almost endless list of character names to clothing, toys, school supplies, linens, dolls, lunch boxes, cereals, and other items. Licensed character names range from classics such as Sesame Street, Disney, Barbie, Star Wars, Scooby Doo, Hello Kitty, and Dr. Seuss characters to the more recent Doc McStuffins, Monster High, Angry Birds, and Ben 10. And currently, numerous top-selling retail toys are products based on television shows and movies.

Name and character licensing has grown rapidly in recent years. Annual retail sales of licensed products worldwide have grown from only $4 billion in 1977 to $55 billion in 1987 and more than $230 billion today. Licensing can be a highly profitable business for many companies. For example, Disney is the world's biggest licensor with a studio full of hugely popular characters, from the Disney Princesses and Disney Fairies to heroes from *Toy Story* and *Cars*, to classic characters such as Mickey and Minnie Mouse. Disney characters reaped a reported $39.3 billion in worldwide merchandise sales last year. By themselves, the Disney Princesses made $1.5 billion in North American retail sales.[40]

Co-branding
The practice of using the established brand names of two different companies on the same product.

Co-branding: KitKat and Google teamed up to name the latest version of Google's Android operating system—Android KitKat. Co-branding added a touch of fun, familiarity, and exposure to both brands.
ASSOCIATED PRESS

Co-branding. **Co-branding** occurs when two established brand names of different companies are used on the same product. Co-branding offers many advantages. Because each brand operates in a different category, the combined brands create broader consumer appeal and greater brand equity. For example, Benjamin Moore and Pottery Barn joined forces to create a special collection of Benjamin Moore paint colors designed to perfectly coordinate with Pottery Barn's unique furnishings and accents. Taco Bell and Doritos teamed up to create the Doritos Locos Taco. Taco Bell sold more than 100 million of the tacos in just the first 10 weeks and quickly added Cool Ranch and Fiery versions.[41]

Seemingly unlikely partners KitKat and Google co-branded the latest Android KitKat operating system. Google has traditionally named versions of its Android operating system after sweet treats (because Android devices "make our lives so sweet"), with names such as Cupcake, Honeycomb, and Jelly Bean. This time, it named the new version "after one of our favorite chocolate treats, KitKat." In turn, KitKat launched specially branded KitKat candy bars featuring the Android robot. The co-branding effort added a touch or fun, familiarity, and exposure to both brands.

Co-branding can take advantage of the complementary strengths of two brands. It also allows a company to expand its existing brand into a category it might otherwise have difficulty entering alone. For example, Nike and Apple co-branded the Nike+iPod Sport Kit, which lets runners link their Nike shoes with their iPods to track and enhance running performance in real time. "Your iPod Nano [or iPod Touch] becomes your coach. Your personal trainer. Your favorite workout companion." The Nike+iPod arrangement gives Apple a presence in the sports and fitness market. At the same time, it helps Nike bring new value to its customers.[42]

Co-branding can also have limitations. Such relationships usually involve complex legal contracts and licenses. Co-branding partners must carefully coordinate their advertising, sales promotion, and other marketing efforts. Finally, when co-branding, each partner must trust that the other will take good care of its brand. If something damages the reputation of one brand, it can tarnish the co-brand as well.

Brand Development

A company has four choices when it comes to developing brands (see **Figure 8.6**). It can introduce *line extensions, brand extensions, multibrands,* or *new brands.*

Line extension
Extending an existing brand name to new forms, colors, sizes, ingredients, or flavors of an existing product category.

Line Extensions. **Line extensions** occur when a company extends existing brand names to new forms, colors, sizes, ingredients, or flavors of an existing product category. For example, over the years, KFC has extended its "finger lickin' good" chicken lineup well beyond original recipe, bone-in Kentucky fried chicken. It now offers grilled chicken, boneless fried chicken, chicken tenders, hot wings, chicken bites, and, most recently, KFC Go Cups—chicken and potato wedges in a handy car-cup holder that lets customers snack on the go.

A company might introduce line extensions as a low-cost, low-risk way to introduce new products. Or it might want to meet consumer desires for variety, use excess capacity, or simply command more shelf space from resellers. However, line extensions involve some risks. An overextended brand name might cause consumer confusion or lose some of its specific meaning.

For example, in its efforts to offer something for everyone—from basic burger buffs to practical parents to health-minded fast-food seekers—McDonald's has created a menu bulging with options. Some customers find the crowded menu a bit overwhelming, and offering so many choices has complicated the chain's food assembly process and slowed service at counters and drive-throughs. The extended menu may also be confusing the chain's positioning. According to one analyst, McDonald's "doesn't have a clear marketing message right now."[43]

At some point, additional extensions might add little value to a line. For instance, the original Doritos Tortilla Chips have morphed into a U.S. roster of more than 20 different types of chips and flavors, plus dozens more in foreign markets. Flavors include everything from Nacho Cheese and Pizza Supreme to Blazin' Buffalo & Ranch, Fiery Fusion, and Salsa Verde. Or how about duck-flavored Gold Peking Duck Chips or wasabi-flavored Mr. Dragon's Fire Chips (Japan)? Although the line seems to be doing well with global sales of nearly $5 billion, the original Doritos chips seem like just another flavor.[44] And

FIGURE | 8.6
Brand Development Strategies

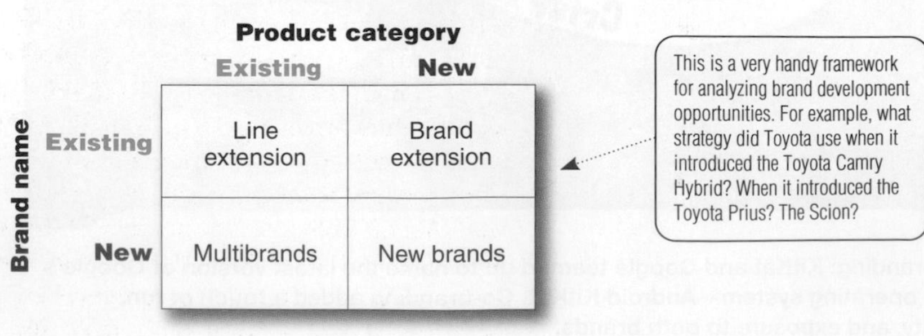

Brand extensions: P&G has leveraged the strength of its Mr. Clean brand to launch new lines, including Mr. Clean-branded car washes.

The Procter & Gamble Company

how much would adding yet another flavor steal from Doritos' own sales versus those of competitors? A line extension works best when it takes sales away from competing brands, not when it "cannibalizes" the company's other items.

Brand Extensions. A **brand extension** extends a current brand name to new or modified products in a new category. For example, Starbucks has extended its retail coffee shops by adding packaged supermarket coffees, a chain of teahouses (Teavana Fine Teas + Tea Bar), and even a single-serve home coffee, espresso, and latte machine—the Verismo. And P&G has leveraged the strength of its Mr. Clean household cleaner brand to launch several new lines: cleaning pads (Magic Eraser), bathroom cleaning tools (Magic Reach), and home auto cleaning kits (Mr. Clean AutoDry). It even launched Mr. Clean-branded car washes.

Brand extension
Extending an existing brand name to new product categories.

A brand extension gives a new product instant recognition and faster acceptance. It also saves the high advertising costs usually required to build a new brand name. At the same time, a brand extension strategy involves some risk. The extension may confuse the image of the main brand—for example, how about Zippo perfume or Dr. Pepper marinades? Brand extensions such as Cheetos lip balm, Heinz pet food, and Life Savers gum met early deaths.[45] And if a brand extension fails, it may harm consumer attitudes toward other products carrying the same brand name. Furthermore, a brand name may not be appropriate to a particular new product, even if it is well made and satisfying—would you consider flying on Hooters Air or wearing an Evian water-filled padded bra (both failed)? Thus, before transferring a brand name to a new product, marketers must research how well the extension fits the parent brand's associations, as well as how much the parent brand will boost the extension's market success (see Real Marketing 8.2).

Multibrands. Companies often market many different brands in a given product category. For example, in the United States, PepsiCo markets at least eight brands of soft drinks (Pepsi, Sierra Mist, Mountain Dew, Manzanita Sol, Mirinda, IZZE, Tropicana Twister, and Mug root beer), three brands of sports and energy drinks (Gatorade, AMP Energy, Starbucks Refreshers), four brands of bottled teas and coffees (Lipton, SoBe, Starbucks, and Tazo), three brands of bottled waters (Aquafina, H2OH!, and SoBe), and nine brands of fruit drinks (Tropicana, Dole, IZZE, Lipton, Looza, Ocean Spray, and others). Each brand includes a long list of sub-brands. For instance, SoBe consists of SoBe Teas & Elixers, SoBe Lifewater, SoBe Lean, and SoBe Lifewater with Coconut Water. Aquafina includes regular Aquafina, Aquafina Flavorsplash, and Aquafina Sparkling.

Multibranding offers a way to establish different features that appeal to different customer segments, lock up more reseller shelf space, and capture a larger market share. For example, although PepsiCo's many brands of beverages compete with one another on supermarket shelves, the combined brands reap a much greater overall market share than any single brand ever could. Similarly, by positioning multiple brands in multiple segments, Pepsi's eight soft drink brands combine to capture much more market share than any single brand could capture by itself.

A major drawback of multibranding is that each brand might obtain only a small market share, and none may be very profitable. The company may end up spreading its resources over many brands instead of building a few brands to a highly profitable level. These companies should reduce the number of brands they sell in a given category and set up tighter screening procedures for new brands. This happened to GM, which in recent years has cut numerous brands from its portfolio, including Saturn, Oldsmobile, Pontiac, Hummer, and Saab. Similarly, as part of its recent turnaround, Ford dropped its Mercury line, sold off Volvo, and pruned the number of Ford nameplates from 97 to fewer than 20. Says Ford CEO Alan Mulally, "I mean, we had 97 [models, for goodness] sake! How you gonna make 'em all cool? You gonna come in at 8 a.m. and say 'from 8 until noon I'm gonna make No. 64 cool? And then I'll make No. 17 cool after lunch?' It was ridiculous."[46]

Real Marketing 8.2

Brand Extensions: Consumers Say "Yeah!" or "Huh?"

These days, a large majority of new products—tens of thousands of them every year—are extensions of already-successful brands. Compared with building new brands, extensions can create immediate new-product familiarity and acceptance. For example, it's not just any new wireless charging mat for your mobile devices, it's a Duracell Powermat. And it's not just a new, no-name over-the-counter sleep-aid, it's Vicks ZzzQuil. Extensions such as the Duracell Powermat and Vicks ZzzQuil make good sense—they connect well with the core brand's values and build on its strengths.

But for every sensible and successful brand extension, there are puzzlers that leave you scratching your head and asking, "Huh? What were they thinking?" For example, how about Gerber food for adults (including a lip-smacking pureed sweet-and-sour pork and chicken Madeira)? Or how would you feel about quaffing a can of Exxon fruit punch or Kodak quencher? Other misbegotten attempts to stretch a good name include Cracker Jack cereal, Smucker's premium ketchup, Carnation pet food, and Fruit of the Loom laundry detergent. Not only were these extensions epic flops themselves, they threatened to sully the reputations of the base brands they extended. Huh? Really. What *were* they thinking?

What separates brand extension hits from misses? According to brand extension consultancy Parham | Santana, the success of a brand extension rests on three pillars: the extension should have a logical fit with the parent brand; the parent brand should give the extension a competitive advantage in a new category; and the extension should offer significant sales and profit potential.

It's the "fit factor" that seems to drive the other two pillars. The value of any brand is its good name, which it earns over time. People become loyal to it; they trust it to deliver a consistent set of attributes. You can't just take a familiar brand name and slap it on a product in another category. Instead, a good extension should fit logically with its parent brand. But brands are complex perceptual and emotional entities, so fit can be hard to define. One way to assure fit is to focus on the brand's core product portfolio.

Consider the recent introduction of Planters Peanut Butter. For more than 100 years, the Planters brand has focused on one type of product—nuts. Cashews, almonds, pistachios, walnuts, sunflower seeds, and, of course, peanuts. No brand is more strongly associated with America's favorite nut. The company's mascot—the 100-year-old, monocled Mr. Peanut—is one of the best-known icons in advertising history. Given Planters' focus on nuts in general, and on peanuts in particular, extending the brand to include peanut butter seems obvious. Consumers appear to agree. Only nine months after its introduction, Planters Peanut Butter had achieved a profitable, mid-single-digit share in a mature and highly competitive market.

Other well-known brands, however, have squandered consumer trust by attaching their good names to something totally out of character. For example, Louis Sherry No Sugar Added Gorgonzola Cheese Dressing was everything that the Louis Sherry brand—known for its rich chocolate candies and ice cream—shouldn't be: sugarless, cheese, and salad dressing. Similarly, Zippo, the company that's been making quality refillable lighters for more than 80 years, recently extended its brand with a perfume, named Zippo The Woman. The perfume has an attractive fruity and floral fragrance, and it comes in a frosted pink container that looks like a lighter, complete with the classic Zippo flip top. Unfortunately, however, no matter how good it smells, perfume has little to do with the Zippo brand's core competency of "all things flame." As a result, in a recent Parham | Santana survey, consumers voted Zippo The Woman as the worst brand extension of the past year. Zippo, what were you thinking?

Even when a new product seems to associate well with a brand's core values, consumers may not make the connection. For example, back in the early 1990s, Clorox investigated several cleaning-related extensions, from laundry detergents to carpet cleaners. That seemed to make sense, given Clorox's association with cleaning. But consumers rejected these new-product concepts, worried that cleaning products from a bleach company might damage the colors in their clothes or carpets. More than just "cleaning," consumers associated the Clorox brand with "cleaning, disinfecting, and stain fighting." So rather than trying to change those brand perceptions, Clorox leveraged them with products such as Clorox Toilet Bowl Cleaner, now the bestselling brand in its category with a 35 percent market share. Other successful brand extensions include Clorox Disinfecting Wipes, Clorox Clean-Up (designed to clean and disinfect stains on a variety of surfaces), and Clorox OxiMagic (a multi-purpose stain remover spray that works on both laundry and household stains).

Good fit goes both ways. Just as an extension should fit the parent brand, the parent brand should give the extension competitive advantage in its new category. The result is sales and profit success. For example, consumers

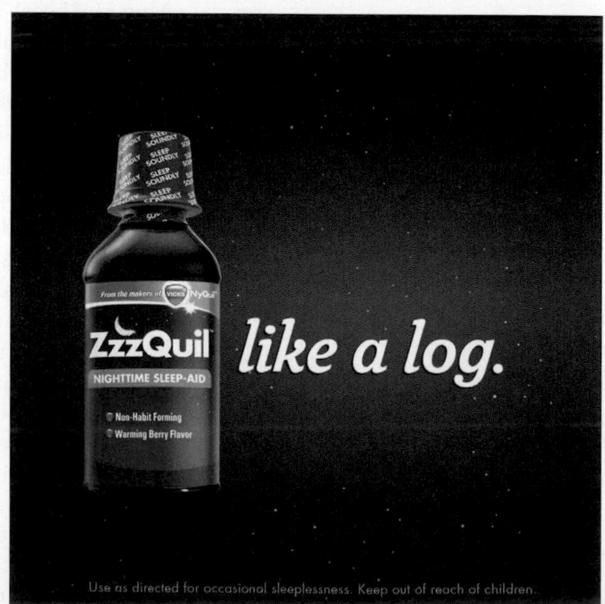

Brand extensions: A good brand extension should fit the parent brand; the parent brand should give the extension competitive advantage in its new category. Above, it's not just a new, no-name over-the-counter sleep-aid, it's Vicks ZzzQuil.

The Procter & Gamble Company

have long associated the Vicks NyQuil brand with relieving cold symptoms so that they could get a better night's sleep. So the Vicks ZzzQuil name gave the extension a substantial boost in the sleep-aids segment. Similarly, when FedEx created FedEx TechConnect, a service that handles technology configuring, repairing, and refurbishing for businesses, the FedEx brand's established reputation for speed, reliability, and accessibility gave the new service immediate credibility over competitors.

Of course, when it comes to brand extensions, most consumers don't stop to think about the "three pillars" or other factors of success. Instead, the simply react. And according to Parham | Santana's president, consumers usually have instantaneous, almost visceral responses to brand extensions. An extension either makes sense or it doesn't. In his words, "Some folks say 'Yeah!' and some just say 'Huh?'" What were they thinking?

Sources: Based on information from Robert Klara, "The Best (and Worst) Brand Extensions," *Adweek*, February 4, 2013, pp. 26–27; Brad Tuttle, "Why Some Brand Extensions Are Brilliant and Others Are Just Awkward," *Time*, February 7, 2013, http://business.time.com/2013/02/07/why-some-brand-extensions-are-brilliant-and-others-are-just-awkward/; Gary Belsky, "These Companies Stretched Their Brands to Make Even Bigger Bucks," *Time*, March 13, 2012, business .time.com/2012/03/14/the-10-best-brand-extensions-ever-according-to-me/; Denise Lee Yohn, "Great Brands Aim for Customers' Hearts, Not Their Wallets," *Forbes*, January 2014, www.forbes.com/sites/onmarketing/2014/01/08/ great-brands-aim-for-customers-hearts-not-their-wallets/; www.clorox.com/products, www.duracellpowermat.com, and www.zzzquil.com, accessed September 2014.

New Brands. A company might believe that the power of its existing brand name is waning, so a new brand name is needed. Or it may create a new brand name when it enters a new product category for which none of its current brand names are appropriate. For example, Toyota created the separate Lexus brand aimed at luxury car consumers and the Scion brand, targeted toward Millennial consumers.

As with multibranding, offering too many new brands can result in a company spreading its resources too thin. And in some industries, such as consumer packaged goods, consumers and retailers have become concerned that there are already too many brands, with too few differences between them. Thus, P&G, PepsiCo, Kraft, and other large marketers of consumer products are now pursuing megabrand strategies—weeding out weaker or slower-growing brands and focusing their marketing dollars on brands that can achieve the number-one or number-two market share positions with good growth prospects in their categories.

Managing Brands

Companies must manage their brands carefully. First, the brand's positioning must be continuously communicated to consumers. Major brand marketers often spend huge amounts on advertising to create brand awareness and build preference and loyalty. For example, worldwide, Coca-Cola spends almost $3 billion annually to advertise its many brands, GM spends $3.2 billion, Unilever spends $7.4 billion, and P&G spends an astounding $10.6 billion.[47]

Such advertising campaigns can help create name recognition, brand knowledge, and perhaps even some brand preference. However, the fact is that brands are not maintained by advertising but by customers' *engagement* with brands and customers' *brand experiences*. Today, customers come to know a brand through a wide range of contacts and touch points. These include advertising but also personal experience with the brand, word of mouth and social media, company Web pages and mobile apps, and many others. The company must put as much care into managing these touch points as it does

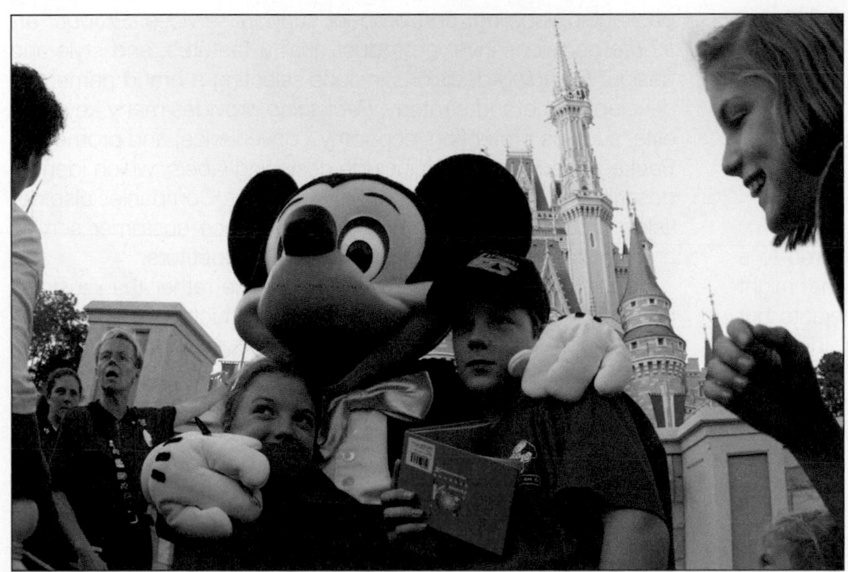

Managing brands requires managing "touch points." Says a former Disney executive: "A brand is a living entity, and it is enriched or undermined cumulatively over time, the product of a thousand small gestures."

Joe Raedle/Getty Images

into producing its ads. ● As one former Disney top executive put it: "A brand is a living entity, and it is enriched or undermined cumulatively over time, the product of a thousand small gestures."[48]

The brand's positioning will not take hold fully unless everyone in the company lives the brand. Therefore, the company needs to train its people to be customer centered. Even better, the company should carry on internal brand building to help employees understand and be enthusiastic about the brand promise. Many companies go even further by training and encouraging their distributors and dealers to serve their customers well.

Finally, companies need to periodically audit their brands' strengths and weaknesses. They should ask: Does our brand excel at delivering benefits that consumers truly value? Is the brand properly positioned? Do all of our consumer touch points support the brand's positioning? Do the brand's managers understand what the brand means to consumers? Does the brand receive proper, sustained support? The brand audit may turn up brands that need more support, brands that need to be dropped, or brands that must be rebranded or repositioned because of changing customer preferences or new competitors.

8 Reviewing the Concepts

OBJECTIVES REVIEW AND KEY TERMS

Objectives Review

A product is more than a simple set of tangible features. Each product or service offered to customers can be viewed on three levels. The *core customer value* consists of the core problem-solving benefits that consumers seek when they buy a product. The *actual product* exists around the core and includes the quality level, features, design, brand name, and packaging. The *augmented product* is the actual product plus the various services and benefits offered with it, such as a warranty, free delivery, installation, and maintenance.

Define *product* and describe the major classifications of products and services. *(pp 256–261)*

Broadly defined, a *product* is anything that can be offered to a market for attention, acquisition, use, or consumption that might satisfy a want or need. Products include physical objects but also services, events, persons, places, organizations, ideas, or mixtures of these entities. *Services* are products that consist of activities, benefits, or satisfactions offered for sale that are essentially intangible, such as banking, hotel, tax preparation, and home-repair services.

Products and services fall into two broad classes based on the types of consumers who use them. *Consumer products*—those bought by final consumers—are usually classified according to consumer shopping habits (convenience products, shopping products, specialty products, and unsought products). *Industrial products*—those purchased for further processing or for use in conducting a business—include materials and parts, capital items, and supplies and services. Other marketable entities—such as organizations, persons, places, and ideas—can also be thought of as products.

OBJECTIVE 2

Describe the decisions companies make regarding their individual products and services, product lines, and product mixes. *(pp 261–268)*

Individual product decisions involve product attributes, branding, packaging, labeling, and product support services. *Product attribute* decisions involve product quality, features, and style and design. *Branding* decisions include selecting a brand name and developing a brand strategy. *Packaging* provides many key benefits, such as protection, economy, convenience, and promotion. Package decisions often include designing *labels*, which identify, describe, and possibly promote the product. Companies also develop *product support services* that enhance customer service and satisfaction and safeguard against competitors.

Most companies produce a product line rather than a single product. A *product line* is a group of products that are related in function, customer-purchase needs, or distribution channels. All product lines and items offered to customers by a particular seller make up the *product mix*. The mix can be described by four dimensions: width, length, depth, and consistency. These dimensions are the tools for developing the company's product strategy.

OBJECTIVE 3

Identify the four characteristics that affect the marketing of services and the additional marketing considerations that services require. *(pp 268–274)*

Services are characterized by four key aspects: they are *intangible*, *inseparable*, *variable*, and *perishable*. Each characteristic poses problems and marketing requirements. Marketers work to find ways to make the service more tangible, increase the productivity of providers who are inseparable from their products, standardize quality in the face of variability, and improve demand movements and supply capacities in the face of service perishability.

Good service companies focus attention on *both* customers and employees. They understand the *service profit chain*, which links service firm profits with employee and customer satisfaction. Services marketing strategy calls not only for external marketing but also for *internal marketing* to motivate employees and *interactive marketing* to create service delivery skills among service providers. To succeed, service marketers must create *competitive differentiation*, offer high *service quality*, and find ways to increase *service productivity*.

OBJECTIVE 4 **Discuss branding strategy—the decisions companies make in building and managing their brands.** *(pp 274–284)*

Some analysts see brands as *the* major enduring asset of a company. Brands are more than just names and symbols; they embody everything that the product or the service *means* to consumers. *Brand equity* is the positive differential effect that knowing the brand name has on customer response to the product or the service. A brand with strong brand equity is a very valuable asset.

In building brands, companies need to make decisions about brand positioning, brand name selection, brand sponsorship, and brand development. The most powerful *brand positioning* builds around strong consumer beliefs and values. *Brand name selection* involves finding the best brand name based on a careful review of product benefits, the target market, and proposed marketing strategies. A manufacturer has four *brand sponsorship* options: it can launch a *national brand* (or manufacturer's brand), sell to resellers that use a *private brand*, market *licensed brands*, or join forces with another company to *co-brand* a product. A company also has four choices when it comes to developing brands. It can introduce *line extensions*, *brand extensions*, *multibrands*, or *new brands*.

Companies must build and manage their brands carefully. The brand's positioning must be continuously communicated to consumers. Advertising can help. However, brands are not maintained by advertising but by customers' *brand experiences*. Customers come to know a brand through a wide range of contacts and interactions. The company must put as much care into managing these touch points as it does into producing its ads. Companies must periodically audit their brands' strengths and weaknesses.

MyMarketingLab

Go to **mymktlab.com** to complete the problems marked with this icon .

Key Terms

OBJECTIVE 1

Product (p 256)
Service (p 256)
Consumer product (p 259)
Convenience product (p 259)
Shopping product (p 259)
Specialty product (p 259)
Unsought product (p 259)
Industrial product (p 260)
Social marketing (p 261)

OBJECTIVE 2

Product quality (p 261)
Brand (p 263)
Packaging (p 264)
Product line (p 267)
Product mix (product portfolio) (p 267)

OBJECTIVE 3

Service intangibility (p 269)
Service inseparability (p 269)
Service variability (p 269)
Service perishability (p 270)
Service profit chain (p 270)
Internal marketing (p 272)
Interactive marketing (p 272)

OBJECTIVE 4

Brand equity (p 275)
Brand value (p 275)
Store brand (private brand) (p 278)
Co-branding (p 279)
Line extension (p 280)
Brand extension (p 281)

DISCUSSION AND CRITICAL THINKING

Discussion Questions

8-1 What is a service? Can services be differentiated as consumer services and industrial services? (AACSB: Communication; Reflective Thinking)

8-2 Most companies produce a product line rather than a single product. Why is this? (AACSB: Communication)

8-3 Explain why a services marketing strategy needs a mix of external, internal, and interactive marketing in order to succeed.

8-4 What is a brand? Describe the brand sponsorship options available to marketers and provide an example of each. (AACSB: Communication)

8-5 Discuss how service providers differentiate their services from those of competitors and provide examples. (AACSB: Communication)

Critical Thinking Exercises

8-6 The Food and Drug Administration recently announced a proposal to change the standard nutrition label on food items. In a small group, research the proposed changes and create a report explaining them. Include history on nutrition labels in your presentation. (AACSB: Communication; Use of IT; Reflective Thinking)

8-7 A product's package must satisfy many criteria, such as sustainability, convenience, safety, efficiency, functionality, and marketing. Research "packaging awards" and develop a presentation analyzing an award-winning product packaging effort. Describe the organization hosting the award competition, the criteria for selecting winners, and one of the award winning packages. (AACSB: Communication; Use of IT)

8-8 Find five examples of service-provider attempts to reduce service intangibility. (AACSB: Communication; Reflective Thinking)

MINICASES AND APPLICATIONS

Online, Mobile, and Social Media Marketing **Funeral Plans**

According to the UK price comparison site Compare the Market, the cost of funerals is rising on average at a rate of 7 percent per year. The Funeral Planning Authority (FPA) estimates that the average cost of a UK funeral is over $5,000. With costs rising, the market for funeral plans has increased, with over 1,20,000 packages sold on a yearly basis. This is a considerable rise compared to 10 years ago when less than 40,000 were sold each year. The FPA states that there are 909,091 active plans (worth an estimated $5 billion) in the UK and that this total will break the 1 million mark in 2015. It has been estimated that pre-paid funeral plans cover 1 in 10 funerals in the UK. In 2014, Golden Charter, one of the biggest providers of funeral plans, had a 21 percent growth in sales and its market share increased from 36.9 percent to 41.7 percent. The other two dominant market leaders are the Co-operative Group and Dignity. The three companies control the bulk of the market. The funeral business as a whole is estimated to be worth around $3 billion per year in funeral costs, despite falling death rates. Pre-paid funeral plans used to be an unsought product or service, but they are certainly becoming more and more popular.

8-9 Describe the nature of unsought products and why they might be so notoriously difficult for a company to sell to consumers. (AACSB: Communication; Reflective Thinking)

8-10 Discuss other examples of unsought products and services and how consumers can be convinced to buy them. (AACSB: Communication; Reflective Thinking)

Marketing Ethics **$450 Starbucks Gift Card**

For the second year right around the holidays, Starbucks offered the Limited Edition Medal Starbucks Card for $450, entitling the holder to $400 of Starbucks drinks, goodies, and gold-level Starbucks membership status. The other $50 was to cover the cost to make the handcrafted, rose-colored, laser-etched steel card. Sounds crazy, doesn't it? Well, 1,000 of the super-premium cards, which could only be purchased at the luxury goods Web site Gilt.com, sold out within minutes. Then they popped up on eBay selling at $500 to $1,000! The premium cards are refillable, allowing owners elite exclusivity. Some criticized Starbucks, claiming it is a card "for the 1%" and saying it is "all about status" and that holders of the premium card have something others don't. Starbucks also rolled out a pricey brew for the other 99 percent, charging $7 a cup.

8-11 What is it about Starbucks that allows the company to sell a gift card for $50 more than the $400 in merchandise the card can purchase? Should a brand be allowed to do that? (AACSB: Communication; Reflective Thinking; Ethical Reasoning)

8-12 How has Starbucks positioned its brand? Could this premium gift card offer or $7 cup of coffee harm Starbucks' brand image? (AACSB: Communication; Reflective Thinking)

Marketing by the Numbers **Pop-Tarts Gone Nutty!**

Kellogg's, maker of Pop-Tarts, recently introduced Pop-Tarts Gone Nutty! The new product includes flavors such as peanut butter and chocolate peanut butter. Although the new Gone Nutty! product will reap a higher wholesale price for the company ($1.20 per 8-count package of the new product versus $1.00 per package for the original product), it also comes with higher variable costs ($0.55 per 8-count package for the new product versus $0.30 per 8-count package for the original product).

8-13 What brand development strategy is Kellogg's undertaking? (AACSB: Communication; Reflective Thinking)

8-14 Assume the company expects to sell 5 million packages of Pop-Tarts Gone Nutty! in the first year after introduction but expects that 80 percent of those sales will come from buyers who would normally purchase existing Pop-Tart flavors (that is, cannibalized sales). Assuming the sales of regular Pop-Tarts are normally 300 million packages per year and that the company will incur an increase in fixed costs of $500,000 during the first year to launch Gone Nutty!, will the new product be profitable for the company? Refer to the discussion of cannibalization in Appendix 2: Marketing by the Numbers for an explanation regarding how to conduct this analysis. (AACSB: Communication; Analytical Reasoning)

Video Case Life is good

You're probably familiar with Life Is good. The company's cheerful logo is prominently featured on everything from T-shirts to dog collars and seems to exude a positive vibe. Although this company has found considerable success in selling its wares based on a happy brand image, consumers aren't getting the complete image that Life Is good founders intended. This video illustrates the challenges a company faces in balancing the role of the customer and the role of the company in determining the meaning of a brand.

After viewing the video featuring Life Is good, answer the following questions:

8-15 What are people buying when they purchase a Life Is good product?

8-16 What factors have contributed to the Life Is good brand image?

8-17 What recommendations would you make to Life Is good regarding brand development strategies?

Company Case Mavi Jeans: Jeans That Fit

Founded in 1991 by Sait Akarlılar, Mavi Jeans designs and sells a collection of denim and other apparel. Mavi apparel is sold in specialty stores, department stores, and chains in 50 countries, including the United States, Germany, Australia, and Russia. The company was founded in 1991 by Sait Akarlılar and operates more than 280 retail stores in many major cities; of these, six are flagship stores, including those in New York, Vancouver, and Berlin. Mavi apparel is available at more than 4,000 points of sale worldwide. Global sales reached $300 million in 2012, and the company has been growing about 30 percent annually in recent years.

Mavi had been manufacturing private-label jeans since 1984 for brands such as Lee, Calvin Klein, Armani, and Tommy Hilfiger. Building on this experience, Mavi, which means "blue" in Turkish, quickly became a success in Turkey due to the high-quality denim used and the fashionable designs. In 1994 the brand was introduced in Europe, and 1996 was an important year for the company, as a customs union agreement between Turkey and the European Union (EU) opened up a new era of increasing opportunities in EU countries. Although the customs agreement heated up the competition in Turkey, Mavi became the number one brand in Turkey, replacing Levi's. That same year, the company built the largest jeans production facility in Europe in Istanbul.

In 1996, Mavi entered the North American market, and not in a way one would expect from an apparel manufacturer from a developing country. Mavi was sold in high-end retailers such as Bloomingdales and Nordstrom, targeting fashion-conscious buyers. It was a challenging move; after all, jeans are as much a part of American life as Coca Cola. Sait Akarlılar, being a young Turk, knew that if Mavi succeeded in the United States, success in other markets would be easier. Although Mavi apparel carried a higher price than mainstream brands, quality and price attracted teenagers and college students. The brand gained huge visibility as the choice of Chelsea Clinton, Cher, and some MTV hosts.

The company opened its flagship store in New York City in Union Square, near New York University. In 2001, Mavi took on a move that was a first in the industry: it transferred the menu concept to fashion. Customers could order outfit combinations from menus hanging behind the checkout counters. Customers could purchase already-paired jeans, shirt, and shoes, for instance, and salespeople actually dressed similar to service providers in a fast-food restaurant. The company has not disclosed what percentage of sales comes from menu-item sales, but the practice is still used in Turkey.

Mavi Jeans has become one of the most well-known jeans brands globally, as foretold by its 1999 campaign motto "we've gone too far." The first Mavi store opened at Sharjah Mega Mall in the UAE in June 2013, with plans under way to open Mavi stores in the Dubai Mall and Abu Dhabi Mall. Celebrities known to like Mavi include Avril Lavigne, Kate Winslet, Hillary Duff, Jason Biggs, Annie Lenox, Billy Zane, Lady Gaga, Fergie, Hayden Panetterie, Zac Efron, and Carly Rae Jepsen, among others.

Keeping Up the Brand Image

From the beginning, Mavi Jeans heavily emphasized the "fit," as in the slogan "Mavi fits." Its jeans were designed to be comfortable, and size availability for different styles was important. The state-of-the-art plant in Istanbul was designed to have flexibility in production, as flexibility helps to cater to the different tastes and physical characteristics of customers dispersed in many countries.

Mavi jeans are not just comfortable, but also fashionable; Mavi is a brand for fashion-conscious young people. In addition to styling and denim quality, many designer labels can be identified by a worn-in appearance. This special style requires additional processing and handling, which can actually cost more than the fabric itself. Mavi has been successful in keeping its prices on the lower side of the designer jean price continuum, so that the price–quality combination is attractive for target buyers. For example, Mavi's Molly, a popular design for women, is priced at about twice the cost of a pair of Levi's 501 jeans.

The brand is built around the jeans culture and young customers, and it emphasizes a Mediterranean feeling in fashion. The company considers the brand as exotic and inspirational, contemporary and accessible. Building on the Mediterranean feel, in 2005 Mavi started to feature evil eye beads on its products. These are eye-shaped amulets of dark blue with a blue eye at the center, which are believed to protect against "evil eye"; such charms are a popular souvenir in Greece and Turkey. In

2007, the Anatolian yemeni (a headscarf of loose cotton) was featured in the collection globally. The Mediterranean feel is also reflected in the design of some stores, such as the flagship store in New York.

"Mavi fits" is understood not just as fitting the bodies of customers, but their lifestyles as well. This necessitates following the ever-changing youth culture. It is a constant challenge to remain fresh in the eyes of the target market. The company employs a very young, multicultural design team. This helps the company to not age with its customers, and keep up with the global pop culture. In addition to the in-house design teams in Turkey, the United States, Canada, Australia, and Italy, the company collaborates with designers and consultants from different parts of the world. To name a few, Adriano Goldshmied (considered the world's best jeans designer by many experts), Venucia de Russi, and Rıfat Ozbek were among those who worked with Mavi Jeans. Preparing a collection for a jeans brand was a first for Rıfat Ozbek, whose clientele list includes Madonna, Diana Ross, and the late Princess Diana.

Mavi tries a similar approach in its advertising campaigns. Olivero Toscani and Emir Kusturica took part in a recent ad campaign; Toscani is an Italian photographer known for the Benetton campaigns of the 1980s and 1990s, and Kusturica is Serbian filmmaker, a two-time winner of the Palme D'Or award of the Cannes film festival. Mavi also features celebrities carefully chosen for different markets. For instance, Kıvanc Tatlıtug˘, a Turkish model-actor, is featured in Middle East, where Turkish soap operas are extremely popular. Other faces of Mavi include Francisco Lachowski and Adriana Lima; Lima was featured on a global scale for the fall/winter campaign of 2012.

Top management considers travel as very important for identifying new trends worldwide. Ersin Akarlılar, son of the founder and a manager in the company, once said he spent about two-thirds of his time on the road, chasing new ideas across the globe. A visit to Rio by Ersin's sister Elif led to the introduction of a Latin line to the brand's collection.

Mavi Jeans is an active company in public relations and contributions to the society. For example, some stores are developed into more than a shopping place. The NYC flagship store has a gallery for up-and-coming artists, and exhibits short films by filmmakers twice a month. The company issues the *Maviology* magazine, and sponsors the Mavi Cup collegiate basketball championship in Turkey. When the company introduced its organic cotton jeans line in 2006, only a few companies had gone before it.

What Is Ahead

Having established operations in many major markets, Mavi is trying to keep a balance between strengthening its position in certain markets and further expansion. The company expects a 30 percent annual increase in upcoming years, and hopes to hit the $500 million mark by 2016. The priority in terms of the collection is to further expand the women's line, which is becoming more colorful.

Questions for Discussion

8-18 What factors contributed to the success of Mavi Jeans?

8-19 How would you define the company's target market? What is the current positioning strategy? Briefly explain Mavi's four Ps.

8-20 What are customers of Mavi actually buying? How do you evaluate the "menu" approach?

8-21 What recommendations would you make to help Mavi keep up the brand image and enhance the connection to the target market?

Sources: Based on information from Pelin Turget, "Making the Perfect Fit", *Time*, February 23, 2003, www.time.com/time/magazine/article/0,9171,425833,00.html, and Ceyhan Konu, "Mavi, 2012'nin ilk ceyreg˘ indeyuzde 50 buyudu", *Turkishtime*, May 9, 2012, www.turkishtimedergi.com/perakende/mavi-2012nin-ilk-ceyreginde-yuzde-50-buyudu/ and http://tr.mavi.com/corporate and www.mavi-store.com, http://www.turkofamerica.com/index.php?option=comcontent&task=view&id=506&Itemid=161, accessed November, 2014.

MyMarketingLab

Go to **mymktlab.com** for the following Assisted-graded writing questions:

8-22 Describe the four characteristics of services that marketers must consider when designing marketing programs. How do the services offered by a doctor's office differ from those offered by a bank? (AACSB: Communication; Reflective Thinking)

8-23 List the names of the store brands found in the following stores: Walmart, Best Buy, and Whole Foods. Identify the private label brands of another retailer of your choice and compare the price and quality of one of the products to a comparable national brand. (AACSB: Communication; Reflective Thinking)

References

1. See Anthony Kosner, "Mobile First: How ESPN Delivers to the Best Available Screen," *Forbes*, January 30, 2012, www.forbes.com/sites/anthonykosner/2012/01/30/mobile-first-how-espn-delivers-to-the-best-available-screen/2/; Nick Summers, "Big, Bigger, Biggest," *Newsweek*, January 23, 2012, p. 4; Kenneth R. Gosselin, "ESPN in the Zone," *McClatchy-Tribune Business News,* January 20, 2013; Derek Thompson, "The Global Dominance of ESPN," *The Atlantic,* August 14, 2013, www.theatlantic.com/magazine/archive/2013/09/the-most-valuable-network/309433/; and information from http://espnmediazone.com/us/about-espn/ and www.espn.com, accessed September 2014.
2. Based on information from Joshua Brustein, "Verizon Has a Class for You," *Bloomberg Businessweek,* November 20, 2013, www.businessweek.com/articles/2013-11-20/verizon-has-a-class-for-you; and Robin Nicole, "Verizon Destination Store Opens at Mall of America," November 19, 2013, www.verizonwireless.com/news/article/2013/11/verizon-destination-store-unveiling.html.
3. See "Kaiser Permanente: Health Isn't an Industry. It's a Cause," www.c-e.com/work/clients/Kaiser-Permanente.html, accessed September 2014.
4. See www.neworleansonline.com, www.michigan.org, and www.thebrandusa.com, accessed September 2014.
5. For more on social marketing, see Alan R. Andreasen, *Social Marketing in the 21st Century* (Thousand Oaks, CA: Sage Publications, 2006); Philip Kotler and Nancy Lee, *Social Marketing: Influencing Behaviors for Good*, 4th ed. (Thousand Oaks, CA: Sage Publications, 2011); and www.adcouncil.org and www.i-socialmarketing.org, accessed September 2014.
6. Quotes and definitions from Philip Kotler, *Marketing Insights from A to Z* (Hoboken, NJ: Wiley, 2003), p. 148; and www.asq.org/glossary/q.html, accessed September 2014.
7. Based on information from "Nest Labs Introduces the World's First Learning Thermostat," October 25, 2011, www.nest.com/press/nest-labs-introduces-worlds-first-learning-thermostat/; Katie Fehrenbacher, "'Hundreds of Thousands' of Nest Learning Thermostats Sold," *GigaOM,* September 4, 2012, http://gigaom.com/2012/09/04/hundreds-of-thousands-of-nest-learning-thermostats-sold/; Claire Cane Miller, "Is 2014 the Year of the Connected Home?" *New York Times,* January 3, 2014, http://bits.blogs.nytimes.com/2014/01/03/is-2014-the-year-of-the-connected-home/?_r=0; Alexei Oreskovic, "Google to Acquire Nest for $3.2 billion in Cash," *Reuters,* January 13, 2014, http://finance.yahoo.com/news/google-acquire-nest-3-2-212257046.html; and www.nest.com/living-with-nest/, accessed September 2014.
8. Based on information from Gene Weingarten, "Pearls before Breakfast," *Washington Post,* April 8, 2007, www.washingtonpost.com/wp-dyn/content/article/2007/04/04/AR2007040401721.html; and "Stop and Hear the Music," www.youtube.com/watch?v=hnOPu0_YWhw, accessed September 2014.
9. See http://cutieskids.com/what-is-a-cutie/, accessed September 2014.
10. See "3 in 4 Grocery Purchase Decisions Being Made In-Store," *MarketingCharts*, May 15, 2012, www.marketingcharts.com/direct/3-in-4-grocery-purchase-decisions-being-made-in-store-22094; "FMI—Supermarket Facts," www.fmi.org/research-resources/supermarket-facts, accessed April 2014; and "Our Retail Divisions," http://news.walmart.com/news-archive/2005/01/07/our-retail-divisions, accessed April 2014.
11. See Mary Mazzoni, "Amazon Continues Its Battle against 'Wrap Rage,'" *Triple Pundit,* December 9, 2013, www.triplepundit.com/2013/12/amazon-continues-battle-against-wrap-rage/; "The Gallery of Wrap Rage," www.amazon.com/Packaging-Videos-Green/b?ie=UTF8&node=1234279011, accessed September 2014.
12. Based on information from "PUMA Clever Little Bag," www.idsa.org/puma-clever-little-bag, accessed March 2012; and http://brand.puma.com/cleverworld/cleverlittlepackaging, accessed September 2014.
13. See "Leggo Your Logo," *Adweek,* December 6, 2010, p. 12; "New Gap Logo a Neural Failure," October 10, 2010, www.newscientist.com/blogs/shortsharpscience/2010/10/-normal-0-false-false-2.html; "Marketer in the News," *Marketing,* February 9, 2011, p. 8; Robert Klara, "New American Airlines Logo Triggers Ire and a Sense of Déjà vu," *Adweek,* January 18, 2013, www.adweek.com/print/146659; Emile Futterman, "9 Major Logo Redesigns: Yahoo and Beyond," *The Next Web,* September 13, 2013, http://thenextweb.com/dd/2013/09/05/9-major-logo-redesigns/#!saOXg; and www.designboom.com/design/futurebrand-american-airlines-rebrand/, accessed September 2014.
14. Based on information from "Company Values," www.llbean.com/customerService/aboutLLBean/company_values.html; www.llbean.com/customerService/aboutLLBean/company_history.html?nav=s1-ln; and other pages at www.llbean.com, accessed September 2014.
15. See Anna Rose Welch, "Lowe's Leverages Mobile Initiatives to Improve Customer Experience," *Integrated Solutions for Retailers,* November 21, 2013, www.retailsolutionsonline.com/doc/lowe-s-leverages-mobile-initiatives-to-improve-customer-experience-0001; and www.lowes.com/cd_Contact+Us_347544179_, www.lowes.com/how-to-library; www.lowes.com/webapp/wcs/stores/servlet/ContactUsLandingPageView, and https://twitter.com/LowesCares, accessed September 2014.
16. Information on The Clorox Company's product mix from www.thecloroxcompany.com/products/our-brands/, accessed September 2014.

17. See "Table 1.2.5 Gross Domestic Product by Major Type of Product," U.S. Bureau of Economic Analysis, January 27, 2012, www.bea.gov/national/nipaweb/TableView.asp?SelectedTable=19&Freq=Qtr&FirstYear=2009&LastYear=2011; and "List of Countries by GDP Sector Composition," http://en.wikipedia.org/wiki/List_of_countries_by_GDP_sector_composition, accessed April 2014.

18. Based on information from Leonard Berry and Neeli-Bendapudi, "Clueing in Customers," *Harvard Business Review*, February 2003, pp. 100–106; Jeff Hansel, "Mayo Hits the Blogosphere," *McClatchy-Tribune Business News*, January 22, 2009; "Mayo Clinic Model of Care," www.mayo.edu/pmts/mc4200-mc4299/mc4270.pdf, accessed September 2014; and www.mayoclinic.org, accessed September 2014.

19. See James L. Heskett, W. Earl Sasser, Jr., and Leonard A. Schlesinger, *The Service Profit Chain: How Leading Companies Link Profit and Growth to Loyalty, Satisfaction, and Value* (New York: Free Press, 1997); and Heskett, Sasser, and Schlesinger, *The Value Profit Chain: Treat Employees Like Customers and Customers Like Employees* (New York: Free Press, 2003). Also see John Marshall and Dave Mayer, "Activate a Brand Internally," *Marketing Management,* Winter 2012, pp. 37–44.

20. David Rohde, "The Anti-Walmart: The Secret Sauce of Wegmans Is People," *The Atlantic,* March 23, 2012, www.theatlantic.com/business/archive/2012/03/the-anti-walmart-the-secret-sauce-of-wegmans-is-people/254994/. Also see Carmine Gallo, "How Wegmans, Apple Store, and Ritz-Carlton Win Loyal Customers," *Forbes,* December 11, 2012, www.forbes.com/sites/carminegallo/2012/12/11/how-wegmans-apple-store-and-the-ritz-carlton-wins-loyal-customers/.

21. See annual reports and information at http://phx.corporate-ir.net/phoenix.zhtml?c=132215&p=irol-irhome, accessed July 2014.

22. See "United States: Prescription Drugs," www.statehealthfacts.org/profileind.jsp?sub=66&rgn=1&cat=5, accessed April 2014; and "Postal Facts," http://about.usps.com/who-we-are/postal-facts/welcome.htm, accessed July 2014.

23. See Terry Maxon, "Horrible Flight? Airlines' Apology Experts Will Make It Up to You," *McClatchy-Tribune News Service*, August 24, 2010; Katie Morell, "Lessons from Southwest Airlines' Stellar Customer Service," *ehotelier.com,* August 29, 2012, http://ehotelier.com/hospitality-news/item.php?id=23931_0_11_0M_C; and Micah Solomon, "Customer Service: What Southwest Knows and You Don't (Hint: Being Nice Isn't Enough)," *Forbes,* September 22, 2013, www.forbes.com/sites/micahsolomon/2013/09/22/not-hiring-jerks-isnt-enough-your-systems-have-to-love-your-customers-too/.

24. Based on information from Sarah Kessler, "The Future of the Hotel Industry and Social Media," *Mashable!*, October 19, 2010, http://mashable.com/2010/10/18/hotel-industry-social-media/; and Jeff Williams, "Marriott's SM Team Gets It," *HD Leader,* September 14, 2010, http://hdleader.com/2010/09/14/marriotts-sm-team-gets-it/. Also see https://twitter.com/MarriottIntl, accessed September 2014.

25. For more discussion on the trade-offs between service productivity and service quality, see Roland T. Rust and Ming-Hui Huang, "Optimizing Service Productivity," *Journal of Marketing,* March 2012, pp. 47–66.

26. See "McAtlas Shrugged," *Foreign Policy*, May–June 2001, pp. 26–37; and Philip Kotler and Kevin Lane Keller, *Marketing Management*, 14th ed. (Upper Saddle River: Pearson Publishing, 2012), p. 256.

27. Quotes from Jack Trout, "'Branding' Simplified," *Forbes*, April 19, 2007, www.forbes.com; and a presentation by Jason Kilar at the Kenan-Flagler Business School, University of North Carolina at Chapel Hill, Fall 2009.

28. Pete Pachal, "Love Your Vespa? Now You Can Do It Officially on Social Media," *Mashable*, August 21, 2012, http://mashable.com/2012/08/21/la-vespa-vita/; and www.lavespavita.com/, accessed September 2014.

29. For more on Young & Rubicam's BrandAsset Valuator, see W. Ronald Lane, Karen Whitehill King, and Tom Reichert, *Kleppner's Advertising Procedure*, 18th ed. (Upper Saddle River, NJ: Pearson Prentice Hall, 2011), pp. 83–84; "Brand Asset Valuator," *Value-BasedManagement.net*, www.valuebasedmanagement.net/methods_brand_asset_valuator.html, accessed June 2014; and http://bavconsulting.com, accessed June 2014.

30. See Millward Brown Optimor, "BrandZ Top 100 Most Valuable Global Brands," www.millwardbrown.com/brandz/2013/Top100/Docs/2013_BrandZ_Top100_Chart.pdf. Also see "Best Global Brands," www.interbrand.com/en/best-global-brands/2013/top-100-list-view.aspx.

31. See Scott Davis, *Brand Asset Management*, 2nd ed. (San Francisco: Jossey-Bass, 2002). For more on brand positioning, see Kotler and Keller, *Marketing Management*, 14th ed., Chapter 10.

32. See "For P&G, Success Lies in More Than Merely a Dryer Diaper," *Advertising Age*, October 15, 2007, p. 20; Jack Neff, "Just How Well-Defined Is Your Brand's Ideal?" *Advertising Age,* January 16, 2012, p. 4; and www.pampers.com, accessed September 2014.

33. See Aaron Ahuvia Rajeev and Richard P. Bagozzi, "Brand Love," *Journal of Marketing,* March 2012, pp. 1–16; and www.saatchi.com/the_lovemarks_company and www.lovemarks.com, accessed September 2014.

34. "Store Brands Prices Stay Hot During the Coldest Months, Saving Shoppers 30% on Average," *PRNewswire*, February 12, 2013, www.prnewswire.com/news-releases/store-brands-prices-stay-hot-during-the-coldest-months-saving-shoppers-30-on-average-190846991.html.

35. See "Store Brands Growing across All Channels," http://plma.com/storeBrands/sbt13.html, accessed January 2014; Stephanie Strom, "Groceries Are Cleaning Up in Store-Brand Aisles," *New York Times,* October 2, 2013, p. B1; and "IRI: Private and National Brands Should Combine Strengths for Growth," *Store Brands Decisions,* January 7, 2014, www.storebrandsdecisions.com/news/2014/01/07/iri-private-and-national-brands-should-combine-strengths-for-growth-.

36. See "Top 35 Private Label Retailers," *Private Label Buyer*, October 2, 2013, www.privatelabelbuyer.com/articles/87669-top-35-private-label-retailers; and www.wholefoodsmarket.com/about-our-products/product-lines/365-everyday-value, accessed September 2014.

37. Scott Davis, "How Target, Walgreens, and Home Depot Have Forever Changed the Private Label Game," *Forbes,* www.forbes.com/sites/scottdavis/2013/05/23/how-target-walgreens-and-home-depot-have-forever-changed-the-private-label-game/; and Stephanie Strom, "Groceries Are Cleaning Up in Store-Brand Aisles," *New York Times,* October 2, 2013, p. B1.

38. See "Top 35 Private Label Retailers," *Private Label Buyer*, October 2, 2013, www.privatelabelbuyer.com/articles/87669-top-35-private-label-retailers.

39. "P&G Targets Thrifty Customers with Cheaper Tide," *Trefis*, September 11, 2013, www.trefis.com/stock/pg/articles/205189/pg-targets-thrifty-customers-with-cheaper-tide-detergent/2013-09-11.

40. "Top 150 Global Licensors Account for More Than $230 Billion in Retail Sales," *PRNewswire*, May 16, 2013, www.prnewswire.com/news-releases/top-150-global-licensors-account-for-more-than-230-billion-in-retail-sales-207686201.html; "Disney Princess, Star Wars, Hello Kitty Topped $1B Each in Licensed Merchandise Sales in 2012," *PRNewswire,* October 21, 2013, www.prnewswire.com/news-releases/disney-princess-star-wars-hello-kitty-topped-1b-each-in-licensed-merchandise-sales-in-2012-228647991.html.

41. See Austin Carr, "The Hard Sell at Taco Bell," Fast Company, July/August 2013, pp. 36–38; www.tacobell.com/food/menuitem/Doritos-Locos-Tacos-Supreme, accessed September 2014.

42. Quote from www.apple.com/ipod/nike/, accessed April 2014.

43. Julie Jargon, "At McDonald's, Salads Don't Sell," *Wall Street Journal,* October 13, 2013, http://online.wsj.com/news/articles/SB10001424052702304384104579139871559464960.

44. See "The Brand That Launched 1000 Ships," *Bloomberg Businessweek,* October 3–October 9, 2011, p. 30; and www.fritolay.com/our-snacks/doritos.html, accessed September 2014.

45. For interesting lists of good and bad brand extension candidates, see Christina Austin, "See the 10 Worst Brand Extensions Currently on the Market," *Business Insider,* February 9, 2013, www.businessinsider.com/the-10-worst-brand-extensions-2013-2?op=1; and Brad Tuttle, "Why Some Brand Extensions Are Brilliant and Others Are Just Awkward," *Time,* February 7, 2013, http://business.time.com/2013/02/07/why-some-brand-extensions-are-brilliant-and-others-are-just-awkward/.

46. Paul Hochman, "Ford's Big Reveal," *Fast Company*, April 2010, pp. 90–95.

47. "Global Marketers 2013," *Advertising Age*, December 9, 2013, p. 17.

48. Stephen Cole, "Value of the Brand," *CA Magazine*, May 2005, pp. 39–40. Also see "The Power of Customer Service," *Fortune,* December 3, 2012, www.timeincnewsgroupcustompub.com/sections/121203_Disney.pdf; and "Customer Engagement," http://thewaltdisneycompany.com/citizenship/community/consumer-engagement, accessed September 2014.

9 New Product Development and Product Life-Cycle Strategies

Chapter Preview

In previous chapters, you've learned how marketers manage and develop products and brands. In this chapter, we examine two additional product topics: developing new products and managing products through their life cycles. New products are the lifeblood of an organization. However, new product development is risky, and many new products fail. So, the first part of this chapter lays out a process for finding and growing successful new products. Once introduced, marketers then want their products to enjoy long and happy lives. In the second part of this chapter, you'll see that every product passes through several life-cycle stages, and each stage poses new challenges requiring different marketing strategies and tactics. Finally, we wrap up our product discussion by looking at two additional considerations: social responsibility in product decisions and international product and services marketing.

For openers, consider Google, one of the world's most innovative companies. Google seems to come up with an almost unending flow of knock-your-eye-out new technologies and services. If it has to do with finding, refining, or using information, there's probably an innovative Google solution for it. At Google, innovation isn't just a process, it's in the very spirit of the place.

GOOGLE: The New Product Moonshot Factory

Google is wildly innovative. Over the past decade, it has become a top-five fixture in every list of most-innovative companies. Google simply refuses to get comfortable with the way things are. Instead, it innovates constantly, plunging into new markets and taking on new competitors.

As a result, Google is also spectacularly successful. Despite formidable competition from giants such as Microsoft and Yahoo!, Google's share in its core business—online search—stands at a decisive 86 percent globally, more than five times the market shares of all other competitors combined. The company also dominates in paid online and mobile search-advertising revenue. Searches accounted for a majority of Google's $60 billion in revenues last year, 20 percent of which filtered down into profits. And Google is growing at a blistering rate—its revenues have more than doubled in just the past three years.

But Google is rapidly becoming much more than just an online search and advertising company. Google's mission is "to organize the world's information and make it universally accessible and useful." In Google's view, information is a kind of natural resource—one to be mined, refined, and universally distributed. That idea unifies what would otherwise appear to be a widely diverse set of Google projects, such as mapping the world, creating wearable computer technology, amassing the world's largest video library, or even providing for the early detection of flu epidemics. If it has to do with harnessing and using information, Google's got it covered in some innovative way.

Google knows how to innovate. At many companies, new product development is a cautious, step-by-step affair that might take years to unfold. In contrast, Google's freewheeling new product development process moves at the speed of light. The nimble innovator implements major new products and services in less time than it takes competitors to refine and approve an initial idea. As one Google executive explains, "The hardest part about indoctrinating people into our culture is when engineers show me a prototype and I'm like, 'Great, let's go!' They'll say, 'Oh, no, it's not ready.' I tell them, 'The Googly thing is to launch it early [as a beta product] and then to iterate, learning what the market wants—and making it great.'"

When it comes to new product development at Google, there are no two-year plans. The company's new product planning looks ahead only four to five months. Google would rather

Google's famously chaotic innovation process has unleashed a seemingly unending flurry of diverse new products. But at Google, innovation is more than a process. It's part of the company's DNA. "Where does innovation happen at Google? It happens everywhere."

see projects fail quickly than see a carefully planned, drawn-out project fail. Whereas even highly innovative companies such as Apple prefer the safety of a "perfect-it-before-you-sell-it" approach, at Google, it's all about "launching and iterating." When Google developers face two paths and aren't sure which one to take, they invariably take the quickest one.

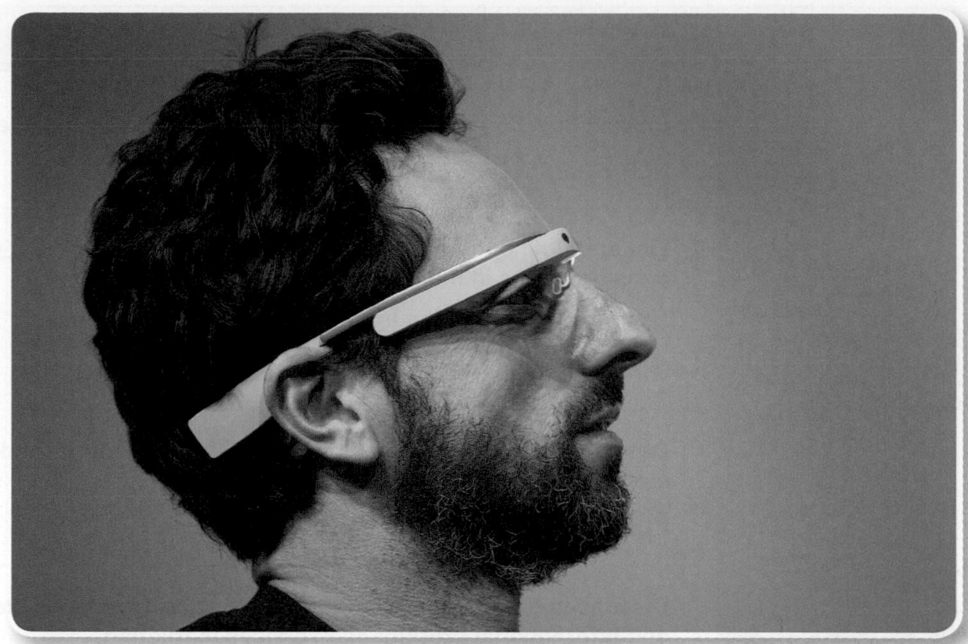

Google's innovation machine is renowned for producing new product "moonshots," such as Google Glass, the wearable smart-devices that have everyone buzzing.

Bloomberg via Getty Images

Google's famously chaotic innovation process has unleashed a seemingly unending flurry of diverse products, most of which are market leaders in their categories. These include an e-mail service (Gmail), a digital media store (Google Play), an online payment service (Google Wallet), a photo sharing service (Google Picasa), a mobile operating system (Google Android), an ultrahigh-speed residential broadband network (Google Fiber), a cloud-friendly Internet browser (Chrome), projects for mapping and exploring the world (Google Maps and Google Earth), and even an early warning system for flu outbreaks in your area (Google Flu Trends).

Google's most recent innovations are taking it well beyond simply organizing and searching for information. The company is now leading the way in harnessing the potential of the Internet to connect virtually everything in people's lives. For example, Google recently paid an eyeball-bending $3.2 billion—twice what it paid for YouTube—to acquire Nest Labs, a maker of smart thermostats and smoke alarms. Nest has reimagined these lowly home appliances into connected, digital devices worthy of the smartphone age, making them fun, easy, and efficient to use. Although it may seem like Google paid a lot for a little with Nest, with Google's substantial resources and innovation prowess, Nest may soon be helping you run your entire home, a huge potential market. As one analyst explains, "This is about whose service—Google, Amazon, Apple, Microsoft, and others—is going to coordinate your smart home for you."

If the concept of Internet-connected smart homes seems a bit far-fetched for Google, that's pretty tame next to some of the company's other grand ideas. Google's innovation machine is renowned for "moonshots"—futuristic longshots that, if successful, will profoundly change how people live. According to one Google engineer, Google co-founders Larry Page and Sergey Brin "have this idea that incremental improvements are not good enough. The standard for success is whether we can get these [moonshots] into the world and do audacious things."

To foster moonshots, Google created Google X—a secretive research lab and kind of nerd heaven charged with developing things that seem audacious even for Google. "Anything which is a huge problem for society we'll sign up for," says the innovation unit's director. Google X's most notable innovation so far is Google Glass—the wearable smart-devices that have everyone buzzing. But behind the secret curtain are numerous other futuristic projects, such as Google's driverless car—a project once thought to be pure science fiction but now surprisingly close to reality. Imagine buying something online, then having an automated Google Car pull up to your home and a Google Humanoid jump out to deliver the package to your door. Seem farfetched? Maybe not. Google is now a leading robotics developer.

Google is open to new product ideas from just about any source. But the company also places responsibility for innovation on every employee. Google is famous for its Innovation Time-Off program, which encourages engineers and developers to spend 20 percent of their time—one day a week—developing their own "cool and wacky" new product ideas. In the end, at Google, innovation is more than a process—it's part of the company's DNA. "Where does innovation happen at Google? It happens everywhere," says a Google research scientist.

Talk to Googlers at various levels and departments, one powerful theme emerges: These people feel that their work can change the world. The marvel of Google is its ability to continue to instill a sense of creative fearlessness and ambition in its employees. Prospective hires are often asked, "If you could change the world using Google's resources, what would you build?" But here, this isn't a goofy or even theoretical question: Google wants to know because thinking—and building—on that scale is what Google does. When it comes to innovation, Google is different. But the difference isn't tangible. It's in the air—in the spirit of the place.[1]

Objective Outline

As the Google story suggests, companies that excel at developing and managing new products reap big rewards. Every product seems to go through a life cycle: It is born, goes through several phases, and eventually dies as newer products come along that create new or greater value for customers.

This product life cycle presents two major challenges: First, because all products eventually decline, a firm must be good at developing new products to replace aging ones (the challenge of *new product development*). Second, a firm must be good at adapting its marketing strategies in the face of changing tastes, technologies, and competition as products pass through stages (the challenge of *product life-cycle strategies*). We first look at the problem of finding and developing new products and then at the problem of managing them successfully over their life cycles.

New product development
The development of original products, product improvements, product modifications, and new brands through the firm's own product development efforts.

Author Comment | New products are the lifeblood of a company. As old products mature and fade away, companies must develop new ones to take their place. For example, the iPhone and iPad have been around for less than eight years but are now Apple's two top-selling products.

New Product Development Strategy

A firm can obtain new products in two ways. One is through *acquisition*—by buying a whole company, a patent, or a license to produce someone else's product. The other is through the firm's own **new product development** efforts. By *new products* we mean original products, product improvements, product modifications, and new brands that the firm develops through its own research and development (R&D) efforts. In this chapter, we concentrate on new product development.

New products are important to both customers and the marketers who serve them: They bring new solutions and variety to customers' lives, and they are a key source of growth for companies. In today's fast-changing environment, many companies rely on new products for the majority of their growth. For example, new products have almost completely transformed Apple in recent years. The iPhone and iPad—neither of which was available just eight years ago—are now the company's two biggest-selling products, with the iPhone bringing in more than half of Apple's total revenues.[2]

Yet innovation can be very expensive and very risky. New products face tough odds. By one estimate, 66 percent of all new products introduced by established companies fail within two years. By another, 96 percent of all innovations fail to return their development costs.[3] Why do so many new products fail? There are several reasons. Although an idea may be good, the company may overestimate market size. The actual product may be poorly designed. Or it might be incorrectly positioned, launched at the wrong time, priced too high, or poorly advertised. A high-level executive might push a favorite idea despite poor marketing research findings. Sometimes the costs of product development are higher than expected, and sometimes competitors fight back harder than expected.

So, companies face a problem: They must develop new products, but the odds weigh heavily against success. To create successful new products, a company must understand its consumers, markets, and competitors and develop products that deliver superior value to customers.

Author Comment | Companies can't just hope that they'll stumble across good new products. Instead, they must develop a systematic new product development process.

The New Product Development Process

Rather than leaving new products to chance, a company must carry out strong new product planning and set up a systematic, customer-driven *new product development process* for finding and growing new products. **Figure 9.1** shows the eight major steps in this process.

Idea Generation

Idea generation
The systematic search for new product ideas.

New product development starts with **idea generation**—the systematic search for new product ideas. A company typically generates hundreds—even thousands—of ideas to find a few good ones. Major sources of new product ideas include internal sources and external sources such as customers, competitors, distributors and suppliers, and others.

Internal Idea Sources

Using *internal sources*, the company can find new ideas through formal R&D. However, according to one study, only 33 percent of companies surveyed rated traditional R&D as a leading source of innovation ideas. In contrast, 41 percent of companies identified customers as a key source, followed by heads of company business units (35 percent), employees (33 percent), and the sales force (17 percent).[4]

Thus, beyond its internal R&D process, a company can pick the brains of its own people—from executives to salespeople to scientists, engineers, and manufacturing staff. Many companies have developed successful internal social networks and *intrapreneurial* programs that encourage employees to develop new product ideas. For example, Google's Innovation Time-Off program has resulted in blockbuster product ideas ranging from Gmail and Ad Sense to Google News. A similar program at 3M, called Dream Days, has long encouraged employees to spend 15 percent of their working time on their own projects, resulting in Post-it Notes and many other successful products.[5]

Tech companies such as Facebook and Twitter sponsor periodic "hackathons," in which employees take a day or a week away from their day-to-day work to develop new ideas. LinkedIn, the 250-million-member professional social media network, holds "hackdays," a Friday each month when it encourages employees to work on whatever they want that will

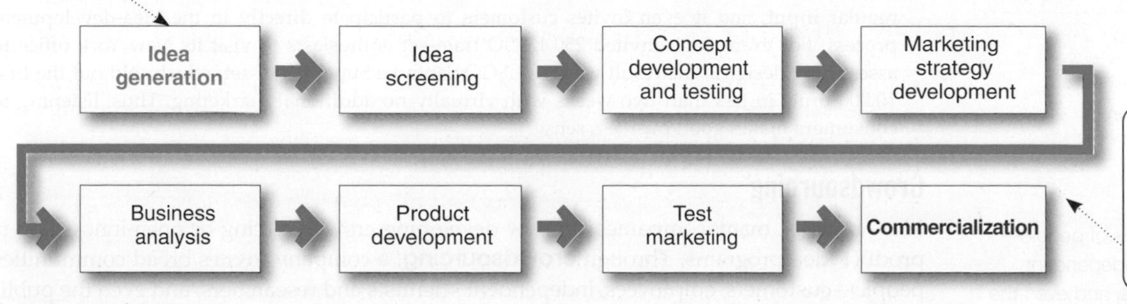
New product development starts with good new product ideas—lots of them. For example, Cisco's I-Prize crowdsourcing challenge attracted 824 ideas from 2,900 innovators representing more than 156 countries.
Idea generation
Idea screening
Concept development and testing
Marketing strategy development
Business analysis
Product development
Test marketing
Commercialization
The remaining steps reduce the number of ideas and develop only the best ones into profitable products. Of the 824 ideas from Cisco's I-Prize challenge, only a handful are being developed.

FIGURE | 9.1
Major Stages in New Product Development

benefit the company. LinkedIn takes the process a step further with its InCubator program, under which employees can form teams each quarter that pitch innovative new ideas to LinkedIn executives. If approved, the team gets up to 90 days away from its regular work to develop the idea into reality. So far, the program has produced proposals for new products and business lines, internal tools, and human resources programs developed by employees from all over the company.[6]

External Idea Sources

Companies can also obtain good new product ideas from any of a number of external sources. For example, *distributors and suppliers* can contribute ideas. Distributors are close to the market and can pass along information about consumer problems and new product possibilities. Suppliers can tell the company about new concepts, techniques, and materials that can be used to develop new products. Walmart invites its thousands of would-be suppliers to submit product ideas and supporting videos through its "Get on the Shelf" program. The retailer then invites its millions of customers nationwide to vote online for the products they'd most like to see on its shelves. Recent winners include an Elvis Pressley Home Bedding Collection and SKRIBS Customizable Wristbands.[7]

Competitors are another important source. Companies watch competitors' ads to get clues about their new products. They buy competing new products, take them apart to see how they work, analyze their sales, and decide whether they should bring out a new product of their own. Other idea sources include trade magazines, shows, Web sites, and seminars; government agencies; advertising agencies; marketing research firms; university and commercial laboratories; and inventors.

New product ideas from customers: The LEGO CUUSOO Web site invites users to submit and vote on product ideas. LEGO Minecraft Micro World racked up the required 10,000 votes in less than 48 hours.

Perhaps the most important sources of new product ideas are *customers* themselves. The company can analyze customer questions and complaints to find new products that better solve consumer problems. Or it can invite customers to share suggestions and ideas. For example, the Danish-based LEGO Group, maker of the classic LEGO plastic bricks that have been fixtures in homes around the world for more than 60 years, systematically taps users for new product ideas and input:[8]

> In 2008, LEGO teamed with Japanese design co-creation platform firm CUUSOO SYSTEM to launch the LEGO CUUSOO Web site. At the site, LEGO invites users to submit ideas for "the LEGO set of their dreams" and to vote for other users' ideas. Ideas supported by 10,000 votes are reviewed internally with a chance of being put into production. Consumers who have their ideas chosen earn 1 percent of the total net sales of the product. So far, the efforts of LEGO CUUSOO fans have resulted in dozens of major product ideas and six new products. One recent release is the LEGO Back to the Future DeLorean Time Machine, which lets users build the classic time-traveling car in LEGO bricks. The idea pulled in the required 10,000 votes in nine months. During that time, the idea was viewed more than 400,000 times and attracted over 2,000 comments. A previous LEGO CUUSOO idea, the highly successful LEGO Minecraft Micro World, racked up its 10,000 votes in less that 48 hours.
>
> On a broader level, in developing new product ideas, LEGO actively taps into the AFOL (adult fans of LEGO) community. It has created a roster of customer ambassadors who provide regular input, and it even invites customers to participate directly in the idea-development process. For example, it invited 250 LEGO train-set enthusiasts to visit its New York office to assess new designs. The result was the LEGO Santa Fe Super Chief set, which sold out the first 10,000 units in less than two weeks with virtually no additional marketing. Thus, listening to consumers makes good business sense.

Crowdsourcing

Crowdsourcing
Inviting broad communities of people—customers, employees, independent scientists and researchers, and even the public at large—into the new product innovation process.

More broadly, many companies are now developing crowdsourcing or open-innovation new product idea programs. Through **crowdsourcing**, a company invites broad communities of people—customers, employees, independent scientists and researchers, and even the public at large—into the innovation process. Tapping into a breadth of sources—both inside and outside the company—can produce unexpected and powerful new ideas (see Real Marketing 9.1).

Real Marketing 9.1

Crowdsourcing: Throwing the Innovation Doors Wide Open

Today, crowdsourcing is big business. You're probably most familiar with consumer-generated marketing efforts in which companies invite customers to help them create new advertising or product ideas. PepsiCo's Frito-Lay division is well known for doing this. For example, its annual Doritos Crash the Super Bowl ad competition generates award-winning, consumer-produced Super Bowl ads every year. And its Frito-Lay "Do Us a Flavor" competition invites consumers to submit and vote on new flavors for Lays potato chips. These highly successful crowdsourcing campaigns generate heaps of customer involvement and buzz. Last year's "Do Us a Flavor" contest alone produced more than 4 million new flavor ideas.

But today's crowdsourcing is about much more than just clever consumer contests that build buzz. Companies ranging from giants like P&G, Under Armor, and Samsung to manufacturing start-ups like Quirky are throwing the innovation doors wide open, inviting broad communities of people—customers, employees, independent scientists and researchers, and even the public at large—into the new product innovation process. Consider the following examples.

Procter & Gamble

P&G has long set the gold standard for breakthrough innovation and new product development in its industry. P&G's Tide detergent was the first synthetic laundry detergent for automatic washing machines, its Pampers brand was the first successful disposable diaper, and P&G's Febreze was the first air freshener that eliminated odors rather than just covering them up. Such breakthrough innovations have been pivotal in P&G's incredible growth and success.

Until recently, most of P&G's innovations came from within its own R&D labs. P&G employs more than 8,000 R&D researchers in 26 facilities around the globe, some of the best research talent in the world. But P&G's research labs alone simply can't provide the quantity of innovation required to meet the growth needs of the $84 billion company.

So about 12 years ago, P&G began inviting outside partners to help develop new products and technologies. It launched P&G Connect + Develop, a major crowdsourcing program that invites entrepreneurs, scientists, engineers, and other researchers—even consumers themselves—to submit ideas for new technologies, product designs, packaging, marketing models, research methods, engineering, or promotion—anything that has the potential to create better products that will help P&G meet its goal of "improving more consumers' lives."

P&G isn't looking to replace its 8,000 researchers; it wants to leverage them better. Through careful crowdsourcing, it could extend its inside people with millions of brilliant minds outside. Through Connect + Develop, says the company, "Together, we can do more than either of us could do alone."

Today, thanks to Connect + Develop, P&G has a truly global open-innovation network. More than 50 percent of its innovations involve some kind of external partner. So far, the program has resulted in more than 2,000 successful agreements. The long list of successful Connect + Develop products includes, among others, Tide Pods, Tide Total Care, Olay Regenerist, Swiffer Dusters, Glad ForceFlex Bags, CoverGirl Eyewear, the Oral B Pulsonic toothbrush, and Mr. Clean Magic Eraser. P&G Connect + Develop is "at the heart of how P&G innovates."

Under Armour

Sports apparel maker Under Armour knows that no matter how many top-notch developers it has inside, sometimes the only way to produce good outside-the-box ideas is by going outside the company. So Under Armour sponsors a semi-annual Future Show Innovation Challenge, a competition that is part crowdsourcing and part new product *American Idol* but all business in its quest to find The Next Big Thing. The Future Show invites inventors from around the nation to submit new product ideas. From thousands of entries, an Under Armour team culls 12 finalists, who go before a panel of seven judges to pitch their products in a splashy, *Shark Tank*-like reality TV setting. The winner earns $25,000 and a contract to work with Under Armour to help develop the winning product.

Under Armour founder and CEO Kevin Plank started the company with his innovative idea for a shirt that pulled moisture away from the body to keep athletes dry. Since then, the now-$2-billion-a-year company has built its reputation on innovative but pricy sports gear. The Future Show is one more way to keep Under Armour on the cutting edge of innovation. "We don't have all the good ideas," says Plank. The goal of the Future Show Challenge is to "cajole top innovators to come to Under Armour first with gee-whizzers."

The first winner, and Plank's favorite so far, is a made-for-athletes zipper—the UA MagZip—that can be zipped easily with only one hand. Under Armour's internal R&D team had been trying to develop a better zipper for two years but "we couldn't get it to work," says the company's innovation chief. The crowdsourced zipper will soon show up in stores on 400,000 Under Armour jackets and could eventually be used in all Under Armour outerwear. That simple zipper is just one of dozens of creative new product ideas from Future Show. But by itself, it makes the entire crowdsourcing effort worthwhile.

Quirky

It's not just big companies such as P&G and Under Armour that use crowdsourcing. Quirky is a promising $50-million company built solely around crowdsourcing. Based on the notion that ordinary people have extraordinary ideas, Quirky manufactures products from everyday inventors. It taps into an online community of 500,000 members who submit inventive new product ideas, in the form of "a napkin sketch, a sentence, or a fully baked product." The company receives more than 2,000 ideas a week. The community then votes for its favorites, and each week, in a live Webcast from Quirky's New York headquarters, company executives, industry experts, and community members debate the merits of submitted ideas and select three or four for development.

Quirky then handles all of the difficult design, production, legal, and marketing details in turning chosen ideas into marketable products. Crowdsourcing plays a role throughout, as the Quirky community provides input on everything from design to the product's name, packaging, tagline, and price. Products that make it through development are shipped off to one of five global distribution centers, then to any of more than 35,000 retail locations, including Target, Bed Bath & Beyond, Best Buy, Amazon.com, and even QVC.

Inventors whose ideas become products and people who contribute to improving those products share in royalties based on product sales. Of the more than 100 products that Quirky has put on store shelves in its brief history, not one has lost money. The company's top seller to date is a clever pivoting power strip called Pivot Power. Sales of the Pivot Power are approaching a million units, and the product promises to make its 24-year-old amateur inventor more than $2 million by the end of the year.

The P&Gs, PepsiCos, and Under Armours of the world operate on a scale that dwarfs the Quirky. Yet, small Quirky perhaps best illustrates the raw power of crowdsourcing, the democratization of product development in its purest form. As one Target representative concludes, "Nobody is innovating at the pace that Quirky is."

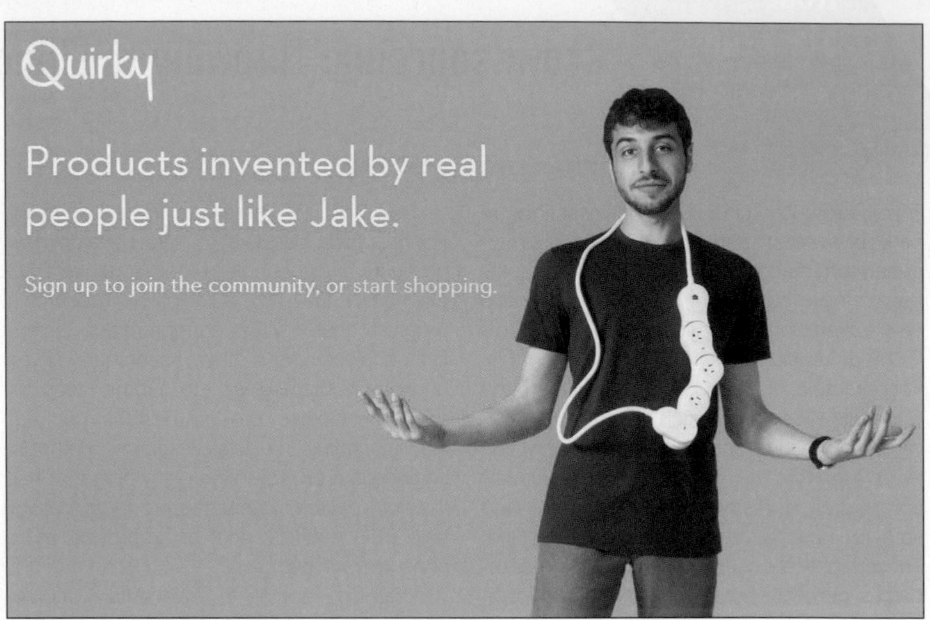

Crowdsourcing: New product start-up Quirky best illustrates the raw power of crowdsourcing in its purest form. "Nobody is innovating at the pace that Quirky is."
Quirky

Sources: Based on information from Kurt Wagner, "Five Brands That Got Fans to Lend a Hand," *Fortune*, June 24, 2013, www.money.cnn.com/gallery/leadership/2013/06/24/crowdsourcing-brands.fortune/; Dale Buss, "P&G Enhances Connect + Develop Innovation Pipeline," *BrandChannel*, February 13, 2013, www.brandchannel.com/home/post/2013/02/13/PG-Connect-Develop-Website-021313.aspx; Larry Huston and Nabil Sakkab, "Connect and Develop: Inside Procter & Gamble's New Model for Innovation," *Harvard Business Review*, March 2006, pp. 2–9; Bruce Horovitz, "Under Armour Seeks Ideas for Its Next Big Thing," *USA Today*, October 20, 2013; Josh Dean, "Is This the World's Most Creative Manufacturer?" *Inc.*, October 2013, pp. 95–114; and www.pgconnectdevelop.com and www.quirky.com, accessed September 2014.

Companies large and small, across all industries, are using crowdsourcing rather than relying only on their own R&D labs to produce all of the needed new product innovations. For example, Samsung recently launched an Open Innovation Program, by which it connects broadly with outside collaborators and entrepreneurs to develop new products and technologies. The program's mission is to break down the walls surrounding its own innovation process and open the doors to fresh new ideas from outside the company. Through the program, Samsung creates alliances with top industry and university researchers around the world, participates actively in industrywide forums, works with suppliers on innovation, and seeks out and invests in promising start-up companies. "In the 21st century, no company can do all the research alone," says a Samsung executive, "and we see it as critically important to partner with [others] across the world to build and strengthen a vibrant research community."[9]

Rather than creating and managing their own crowdsourcing platforms, companies can use third-party crowdsourcing networks, such as InnoCentive, TopCoder, CloudSpokes, and jovoto. For example, organizations ranging from Audi, Microsoft, and Nestlé to Swiss Army Knife maker Victorinox have tapped into jovoto's network of 50,000 creative professionals for ideas and solutions, offering prizes of $100 to $100,000. ● For the past three years, Victorinox has used jovoto to capture new designs for a limited fashion edition of its Swiss Army Knife. The aim of fashion designs is to attract younger buyers to the venerable

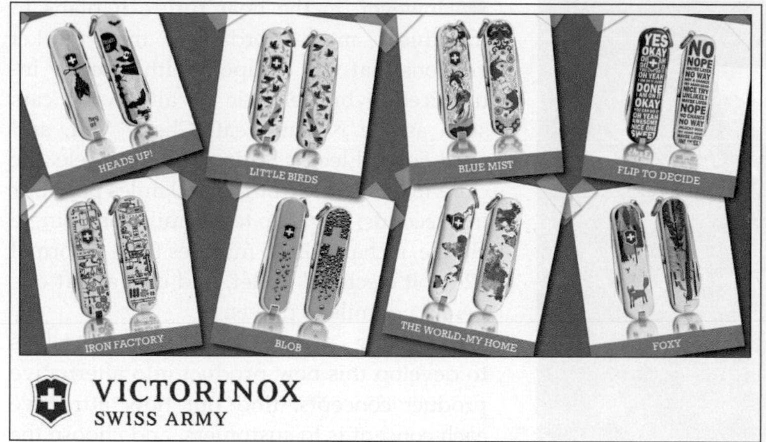

Victorinox used third-party crowdsourcing network jovoto to capture creative designs for limited fashion editions of its venerable Swiss Army Knife. The crowdsourced designed models had 20 percent better sales success than any previous internally created limited editions.
Victorinox AG

old product. The first year, more than 1,000 artists submitted designs via jovoto. The limited edition, consisting of 10 designs selected after review by jovoto community members and voting on Facebook by Victorinox brand fans, had 20 percent better sales success than any previous internally created limited edition models.[10]

Crowdsourcing can produce a flood of innovative ideas. In fact, opening the floodgates to anyone and everyone can overwhelm the company with ideas—some good and some bad. For example, when Cisco Systems sponsored an open-innovation effort called I-Prize, soliciting ideas from external sources, it received more than 820 distinct ideas from more than 2,900 innovators from 156 countries. "The evaluation process was far more labor-intensive than we'd anticipated," says Cisco's chief technology officer. It required "significant investments of time, energy, patience, and imagination . . . to discern the gems hidden within rough stones." In the end, a team of six Cisco people worked full-time for three months to carve out 32 semifinalist ideas, as well as nine teams representing 14 countries in six continents for the final phase of the competition.[11]

Truly innovative companies don't rely only on one source or another for new product ideas. Instead, they develop extensive innovation networks that capture ideas and inspiration from every possible source, from employees and customers to outside innovators and multiple points beyond.

Idea Screening

Idea screening
Screening new product ideas to spot good ones and drop poor ones as soon as possible.

The purpose of idea generation is to create a large number of ideas. The purpose of the succeeding stages is to *reduce* that number. The first idea-reducing stage is **idea screening**, which helps spot good ideas and drop poor ones as soon as possible. Product development costs rise greatly in later stages, so the company wants to go ahead only with those product ideas that will turn into profitable products.

Many companies require their executives to write up new product ideas in a standard format that can be reviewed by a new product committee. The write-up describes the product or the service, the proposed customer value proposition, the target market, and the competition. It makes some rough estimates of market size, product price, development time and costs, manufacturing costs, and rate of return. The committee then evaluates the idea against a set of general criteria.

One marketing expert describes an R-W-W ("real, win, worth doing") new product screening framework that asks three questions. First, *Is it real?* Is there a real need and desire for the product and will customers buy it? Is there a clear product concept and will such a product satisfy the market? Second, *Can we win?* Does the product offer a sustainable competitive advantage? Does the company have the resources to make such a product a success? Finally, *Is it worth doing?* Does the product fit the company's overall growth strategy? Does it offer sufficient profit potential? The company should be able to answer yes to all three R-W-W questions before developing the new product idea further.[12]

Concept Development and Testing

Product concept
A detailed version of the new product idea stated in meaningful consumer terms.

An attractive idea must then be developed into a **product concept**. It is important to distinguish between a product idea, a product concept, and a product image. A *product idea* is an idea for a possible product that the company can see itself offering to the market. A *product concept* is a detailed version of the idea stated in meaningful consumer terms. A *product image* is the way consumers perceive an actual or potential product.

Concept Development

Suppose a car manufacturer has developed a practical battery-powered, all-electric car. Its initial prototype is a sleek, sporty roadster convertible that sells for more than $100,000.[13]

Tesla is introducing more-affordable mass-market models will travel more than 300 miles on a single charge, recharge in 45 minutes from a normal 120-volt electrical outlet, and cost about one penny per mile to power.
AFP/Getty Images

However, in the near future it plans to introduce more-affordable, mass-market versions that will compete with recently introduced hybrid-electric or all-electric cars such as the Nissan Leaf, Chevy Volt, and Ford Focus Electric. This 100 percent electric car will accelerate from 0 to 60 miles per hour in 4 seconds, travel up to 300 miles on a single charge, recharge in 45 minutes from a normal 120-volt electrical outlet, and cost about one penny per mile to power.

Looking ahead, the marketer's task is to develop this new product into alternative product concepts, find out how attractive each concept is to customers, and choose the best one. It might create the following product concepts for this electric car:

- *Concept 1.* An affordably priced midsize car designed as a second family car to be used around town for running errands and visiting friends.
- *Concept 2.* A mid-priced sporty compact appealing to young singles and couples.
- *Concept 3.* A "green" car appealing to environmentally conscious people who want practical, no-polluting transportation.
- *Concept 4.* A high-end midsize utility vehicle appealing to those who love the space SUVs provide but lament the poor gas mileage.

Concept Testing

Concept testing
Testing new product concepts with a group of target consumers to find out if the concepts have strong consumer appeal.

Concept testing calls for testing new product concepts with groups of target consumers. The concepts may be presented to consumers symbolically or physically. Here, in more detail, is concept 3:

> An efficient, fun-to-drive, battery-powered compact car that seats four. This 100 percent electric wonder provides practical and reliable transportation with no pollution. It goes 300 miles on a single charge and costs pennies per mile to operate. It's a sensible, responsible alternative to today's pollution-producing gas-guzzlers. Its fully equipped base price is $28,800.

Many firms routinely test new product concepts with consumers before attempting to turn them into actual new products. For some concept tests, a word or picture description might be sufficient. However, a more concrete and physical presentation of the concept will increase the reliability of the concept test. After being exposed to the concept, consumers then may be asked to react to it by answering questions similar to those in **Table 9.1**.

The answers to such questions will help the company decide which concept has the strongest appeal. For example, the last question asks about the consumer's intention to buy. Suppose 2 percent of consumers say they "definitely" would buy, and another 5 percent say "probably." The company could project these figures to the full population in this target group to estimate sales volume. Even then, however, the estimate is uncertain because people do not always carry out their stated intentions.

Marketing Strategy Development

Marketing strategy development
Designing an initial marketing strategy for a new product based on the product concept.

Suppose the carmaker finds that concept 3 for the electric car tests best. The next step is **marketing strategy development**, designing an initial marketing strategy for introducing this car to the market.

The *marketing strategy statement* consists of three parts. The first part describes the target market; the planned value proposition; and the sales, market-share, and profit goals for the first few years. Thus:

> The target market is younger, well-educated, moderate- to high-income individuals, couples, or small families seeking practical, environmentally responsible transportation. The car will be

Table 9.1 | Questions for the All-Electric Car Concept Test

1. Do you understand the concept of a battery-powered electric car?
2. Do you believe the claims about the car's performance?
3. What are the major benefits of an all-electric car compared with a conventional car?
4. What are its advantages compared with a gas-electric hybrid car?
5. What improvements in the car's features would you suggest?
6. For what uses would you prefer an all-electric car to a conventional car?
7. What would be a reasonable price to charge for the car?
8. Who would be involved in your decision to buy such a car? Who would drive it?
9. Would you buy such a car (definitely, probably, probably not, definitely not)?

positioned as more fun to drive and less polluting than today's internal combustion engine or hybrid cars. The company will aim to sell 50,000 cars in the first year, at a loss of not more than $15 million. In the second year, the company will aim for sales of 90,000 cars and a profit of $25 million.

The second part of the marketing strategy statement outlines the product's planned price, distribution, and marketing budget for the first year:

> The battery-powered all-electric car will be offered in three colors—red, white, and blue—and will have a full set of accessories as standard features. It will sell at a base retail price of $28,800, with 15 percent off the list price to dealers. Dealers who sell more than 10 cars per month will get an additional discount of 5 percent on each car sold that month. A marketing budget of $50 million will be split 40-30-30 among a national media campaign, online and social media marketing, and local event marketing. Advertising, the Web and mobile sites, and various social media content will emphasize the car's fun spirit and low emissions. During the first year, $100,000 will be spent on marketing research to find out who is buying the car and what their satisfaction levels are.

The third part of the marketing strategy statement describes the planned long-run sales, profit goals, and marketing mix strategy:

> We intend to capture a 3 percent long-run share of the total auto market and realize an after-tax return on investment of 15 percent. To achieve this, product quality will start high and be improved over time. Price will be raised in the second and third years if competition and the economy permit. The total marketing budget will be raised each year by about 10 percent. Marketing research will be reduced to $60,000 per year after the first year.

Business Analysis

Business analysis
A review of the sales, costs, and profit projections for a new product to find out whether these factors satisfy the company's objectives.

Once management has decided on its product concept and marketing strategy, it can evaluate the business attractiveness of the proposal. **Business analysis** involves a review of the sales, costs, and profit projections for a new product to find out whether they satisfy the company's objectives. If they do, the product can move to the product development stage.

To estimate sales, the company might look at the sales history of similar products and conduct market surveys. It can then estimate minimum and maximum sales to assess the range of risk. After preparing the sales forecast, management can estimate the expected costs and profits for the product, including marketing, R&D, operations, accounting, and finance costs. The company then uses the sales and costs figures to analyze the new product's financial attractiveness.

Product Development

Product development
Developing the product concept into a physical product to ensure that the product idea can be turned into a workable market offering.

For many new product concepts, a product may exist only as a word description, a drawing, or perhaps a crude mock-up. If the product concept passes the business test, it moves into **product development**. Here, R&D or engineering develops the product concept into

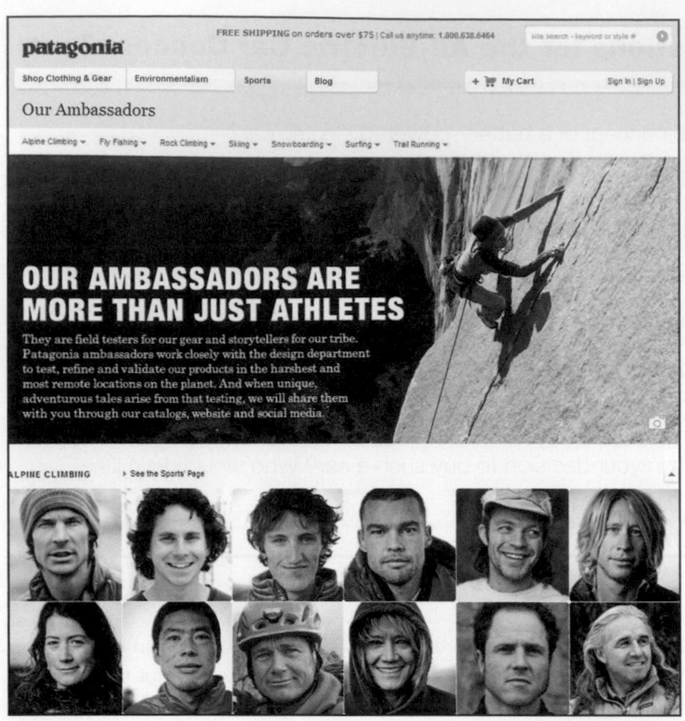

Product testing: Patagonia uses tried-and-true customers—its Patagonia Ambassadors—to help field test its products under harsh conditions and help designers refine them.

Patagonia, Inc.

a physical product. The product development step, however, now calls for a huge jump in investment. It will show whether the product idea can be turned into a workable product.

The R&D department will develop and test one or more physical versions of the product concept. R&D hopes to design a prototype that will satisfy and excite consumers and that can be produced quickly and at budgeted costs. Developing a successful prototype can take days, weeks, months, or even years depending on the product and prototype methods.

Often, products undergo rigorous tests to make sure that they perform safely and effectively, or that consumers will find value in them. Companies can do their own product testing or outsource testing to other firms that specialize in testing.

Marketers often involve actual customers in product development and testing. For example, Patagonia selects tried-and-true customers—called Patagonia Ambassadors—to work closely with its design department to field test and refine its products under harsh conditions. Similarly, Carhartt, maker of durable workwear and outerwear, has enlisted an army of Groundbreakers, "hard working men and women to help us create our next generation of products." These volunteers take part in live chats with Carhartt designers, review new product concepts, and field test products that they helped to create.[14]

A new product must have the required functional features and also convey the intended psychological characteristics. The all-electric car, for example, should strike consumers as being well built, comfortable, and safe. Management must learn what makes consumers decide that a car is well built. To some consumers, this means that the car has "solid-sounding" doors. To others, it means that the car is able to withstand a heavy impact in crash tests. Consumer tests are conducted in which consumers test-drive the car and rate its attributes.

Test Marketing

Test marketing
The stage of new product development in which the product and its proposed marketing program are tested in realistic market settings.

If the product passes both the concept test and the product test, the next step is **test marketing**, the stage at which the product and its proposed marketing program are introduced into realistic market settings. Test marketing gives the marketer experience with marketing a product before going to the great expense of full introduction. It lets the company test the product and its entire marketing program—targeting and positioning strategy, advertising, distribution, pricing, branding and packaging, and budget levels.

The amount of test marketing needed varies with each new product. When introducing a new product requires a big investment, when the risks are high, or when management is not sure of the product or its marketing program, a company may do a lot of test marketing. For instance, Taco Bell took three years and 45 prototypes before introducing Doritos Locos Tacos, now the most successful product launch in the company's history. And Starbucks spent 20 years developing Starbucks VIA instant coffee—one of its most risky product rollouts ever—and several months testing the product in Starbucks shops in Chicago and Seattle before releasing it nationally. The testing paid off. The Starbucks VIA line now accounts for more than $300 million in sales annually.[15]

However, test marketing costs can be high, and testing takes time that may allow market opportunities to slip by or competitors to gain advantages. A company may do little or no test marketing when the costs of developing and introducing a new product are low, or when management is already confident about the new product. For example, companies often do not test market simple line extensions or copies of competitors' successful products. Companies may also shorten or skip testing to take advantage of fast-changing market developments. That's what Post Foods did when it launched Honey Bunches of Oats Greek Honey Crunch cereal:[16]

When a Post Foods cereal executive informally mentioned to buyers from Walmart and Target that Post was considering a new cereal concept—mixing trendy Greek yogurt with breakfast

Companies sometimes shorten or skip test marketing to take advantage of fast-changing market developments, as Post did in launching Post Honey Bunches of Oats Greek Honey Crunch cereal in record time.

©2013 Post Foods, LLC

cereal—the buyers loved the idea. In fact, they loved it so much that they wanted the product on their shelves within six months to take advantage of the Greek yogurt trend. The problem: Post still hadn't invented or market tested the cereal, a process that usually takes a year or more. "We had the nation's biggest retailer and No. 2 retailer give us a slot to deliver this," says a Post product-development executive. And deliver it they did. Post undertook a crash program to overcome technical development challenges while at the same time developing packaging and marketing programs for the new cereal. The result: Post Honey Bunches of Oats Greek Honey Crunch cereal went from concept to store shelf in less than six months, the fastest rollout in Post history. That left almost no time for market testing before launch. However, given the market opportunity, the risks of launching the new product without testing were well worth taking. "Luckily, the product [ended up testing] very well," says the Post executive.

As an alternative to extensive and costly standard test markets, companies can use controlled test markets or simulated test markets. In *controlled test markets*, such as SymphonyIRI's BehaviorScan, new products and tactics are tested among controlled panels of shoppers and stores.[17] By combining information on each test consumer's purchases with consumer demographic and TV viewing information, BehaviorScan can provide store-by-store, week-by-week reports on the sales of tested products and the impact of in-store and in-home marketing efforts. Using *simulated test markets*, researchers measure consumer responses to new products and marketing tactics in laboratory stores or simulated online shopping environments. Both controlled test markets and simulated test markets reduce the costs of test marketing and speed up the process.

Commercialization

Commercialization
Introducing a new product into the market.

Test marketing gives management the information needed to make a final decision about whether to launch the new product. If the company goes ahead with **commercialization**—introducing the new product into the market—it will face high costs. For example, the company may need to build or rent a manufacturing facility. And, in the case of a major new consumer product, it may spend hundreds of millions of dollars for advertising, sales promotion, and other marketing efforts in the first year. For instance, to introduce the Surface tablet, Microsoft spent close to $400 million on an advertising blitz that spanned TV, print, radio, outdoor, the Internet, events, public relations, and sampling. Similarly, Tide spent $150 million on a campaign to launch Tide Pods in the highly competitive U.S. laundry detergent market.[18]

A company launching a new product must first decide on introduction *timing*. If the new product will eat into the sales of other company products, the introduction may be delayed. If the product can be improved further, or if the economy is down, the company may wait until the following year to launch it. However, if competitors are ready to introduce their own competing products, the company may push to introduce its new product sooner.

Next, the company must decide *where* to launch the new product—in a single location, a region, the national market, or the international market. Some companies may quickly introduce new models into the full national market. Companies with international distribution systems may introduce new products through swift global rollouts. For example, Microsoft launched its Windows 8 operating system with a massive $1 billion global marketing campaign spanning 42 countries. The initial launch featured a series of events that began with preview parties in Shanghai and New York City and the opening of 31 pop-up stores worldwide.[19]

Author Comment | Above all else, new product development must focus on creating customer value. Says a senior Samsung executive, "We get our ideas from the market. The market is the driver."

Managing New Product Development

The new product development process shown in Figure 9.1 highlights the important activities needed to find, develop, and introduce new products. However, new product development involves more than just going through a set of steps. Companies must take a holistic approach to managing this process. Successful new product development requires a customer-centered, team-based, and systematic effort.

Customer-Centered New Product Development

Above all else, new product development must be customer centered. When looking for and developing new products, companies often rely too heavily on technical research in their R&D laboratories. But like everything else in marketing, successful new product development begins with a thorough understanding of what consumers need and value. **Customer-centered new product development** focuses on finding new ways to solve customer problems and create more customer-satisfying experiences.

Customer-centered new product development
New product development that focuses on finding new ways to solve customer problems and create more customer-satisfying experiences.

One study found that the most successful new products are ones that are differentiated, solve major customer problems, and offer a compelling customer value proposition. Another study showed that companies that directly engage their customers in the new product innovation process had twice the return on assets and triple the growth in operating income of firms that did not. Thus, customer involvement has a positive effect on the new product development process and product success.[20]

Intuit—maker of financial software such as TurboTax, QuickBooks, and Quicken—is a strong proponent of customer-driven new product development:[21]

> Intuit follows a "Design for Delight (D4D)" development philosophy that products should delight customers by providing experiences that go beyond their expectations. Design for Delight starts with customer empathy—knowing customers better than they know themselves. To that end, each year, Intuit conducts 10,000 hours of what it calls "follow-me-homes," in which design employees observe firsthand how customers use its products at home and at work. They look to understand problems and needs that even customers themselves might not recognize. Based on customer observations, the next D4D step is to "go broad, go narrow"—developing many customer-driven product ideas, then narrowing them down to one or a few great ideas for products that will solve customer problems. The final D4D step involves turning the great ideas into actual products and services that create customer delight, collecting customer feedback steadily throughout the development process.
>
> Intuit works relentlessly to embed Design for Delight concepts deeply into its culture. "You've got feel it," says the company's vice president of design innovation. "It can't be in your head. It's got to be in your heart. It's got to be in your gut. And we want to put it in our products." Thanks to customer-centered new product development, Intuit's revenues have grown to $4.2 billion annually, a 40 percent increase in just the past four years.

HOW WE INNOVATE

DEEP CUSTOMER EMPATHY

GO BROAD TO GO NARROW

DELIGHT

RAPID EXPERIMENTS WITH CUSTOMERS

intuit. simplify the business of life

TurboTax QuickBooks Quicken Mint

Customer-centered new product development: Financial software maker Intuit follows a "Design for Delight" philosophy that products should delight customers by providing experiences that go beyond their expectations.

Thus, today's innovative companies get out of the research lab and connect with customers in search of fresh ways to meet customer needs. Customer-centered new product development begins and ends with understanding customers and involving them in the process.

Team-Based New Product Development

Good new product development also requires a total-company, cross-functional effort. Some companies organize their new product development process into the orderly sequence of steps shown in Figure 9.1, starting with idea generation and ending with commercialization. Under this *sequential product development* approach, one company department works individually to complete its stage of the process before passing the new product along to the next department and stage. This orderly, step-by-step process can help bring control to complex and risky projects. But it can also be dangerously slow. In fast-changing, highly competitive markets, such slow-but-sure product development can result in product failures, lost sales and profits, and crumbling market positions.

Team-based new product development
New product development in which various company departments work closely together, overlapping the steps in the product development process to save time and increase effectiveness.

To get their new products to market more quickly, many companies use a **team-based new product development** approach. Under this approach, company departments work closely together in cross-functional teams, overlapping the steps in the product development process to save time and increase effectiveness. Instead of passing the new product from department to department, the company assembles a team of people from various departments that stays with the new product from start to finish. Such teams usually include people from the marketing, finance, design, manufacturing, and legal departments and even supplier and customer companies. In the sequential process, a bottleneck at one phase can seriously slow an entire project. In the team-based approach, however, if one area hits snags, it works to resolve them while the team moves on.

The team-based approach does have some limitations, however. For example, it sometimes creates more organizational tension and confusion than the more orderly sequential approach. However, in rapidly changing industries facing increasingly shorter product life cycles, the rewards of fast and flexible product development far exceed the risks. Companies that combine a customer-centered approach with team-based new product development gain a big competitive edge by getting the right new products to market faster.

Systematic New Product Development

Finally, the new product development process should be holistic and systematic rather than compartmentalized and haphazard. Otherwise, few new ideas will surface, and many good ideas will sputter and die. To avoid these problems, a company can install an *innovation management system* to collect, review, evaluate, and manage new product ideas.

The company can appoint a respected senior person to be its innovation manager. It can set up Web-based idea management software and encourage all company stakeholders—employees, suppliers, distributors, dealers—to become involved in finding and developing new products. It can assign a cross-functional innovation management committee to evaluate proposed new product ideas and help bring good ideas to market. It can also create recognition programs to reward those who contribute the best ideas.

The innovation management system approach yields two favorable outcomes. First, it helps create an innovation-oriented company culture. It shows that top management supports, encourages, and rewards innovation. Second, it will yield a larger number of new product ideas, among which will be found some especially good ones. The good new ideas will be more systematically developed, producing more new product successes. No longer will good ideas wither for the lack of a sounding board or a senior product advocate.

Thus, new product success requires more than simply thinking up a few good ideas, turning them into products, and finding customers for them. It requires a holistic approach for finding new ways to create valued customer experiences, from generating and screening new product ideas to creating and rolling out want-satisfying products to customers.

More than this, successful new product development requires a whole-company commitment. At companies known for their new product prowess, such as Google, Samsung, Apple, 3M, P&G, and GE, the entire culture encourages, supports, and rewards innovation. ● Again, consider Samsung:[22]

● **Samsung's entire culture encourages and supports innovation. Every product has to pass the customer "Wow!" test or it goes straight back to development.**
ASSOCIATED PRESS

> Not many years ago, Samsung was a copycat consumer electronics brand you bought if you couldn't afford Sony, then the world's most coveted consumer electronics brand. In the mid-1990s, however, Samsung made an inspired decision. It turned its back on cheap knock-offs and set out to overtake rival Sony. To dethrone the consumer electronics giant, however, Samsung first had to change its entire culture, from copycat to leading-edge. To out-*sell* Sony, Samsung first had to out-*innovate* Sony.
>
> To make that happen, Samsung hired a crop of fresh, young designers and managers who unleashed a torrent of new products—not humdrum, me-too products, but sleek, bold, and beautiful products targeted to high-end users. Samsung called them "lifestyle works of art." Every new product had to pass the "Wow!" test: If it didn't get a "Wow!" reaction during market testing, it went straight back to development. Beyond innovative technology and stylish designs, Samsung put the customer at the core of its innovation movement.

Its primary goal was to improve the customer experience and bring genuine change to people's lives in everything it did.

Today, thanks to its whole-company culture of innovation, the Samsung brand holds a high-end, cutting-edge aura that rivals or even exceeds that of Apple, long considered to be the keeper of all things cool. Samsung is now by far the world's largest consumer electronics company, with sales two and one-half times those of Sony and 25 percent greater than Apple's.

New Product Development in Turbulent Times

When tough economic times hit, or when a company faces financial difficulties, management may be tempted to reduce spending on new product development. However, such thinking is usually shortsighted. By cutting back on new products, the company may make itself less competitive during or after the downturn. In fact, tough times might call for even greater new product development, as the company struggles to better align its market offerings with changing consumer needs and tastes. In difficult times, innovation more often helps than hurts in making the company more competitive and positioning it better for the future.

Companies such as Apple, Google, Samsung, and Amazon keep the innovations flowing during down economic times. For example, Apple created its blockbuster iPod, iPhone, and iTunes innovations in the midst of some very difficult times it faced more than a decade ago. Those innovations not only saved the company, they propelled it into the innovative powerhouse it is today. Thus, rain or shine, good times or bad, a company must continue to innovate and develop new products if it wants to grow and prosper.

Author Comment | A company's products are born, grow, mature, and then decline, just as living things do. To remain vital, the firm must continually develop new products and manage them effectively throughout their life cycles.

Product Life-Cycle Strategies

After launching the new product, management wants that product to enjoy a long and happy life. Although it does not expect the product to sell forever, the company wants to earn a decent profit to cover all the effort and risk that went into launching it. Management is aware that each product will have a life cycle, although its exact shape and length is not known in advance.

Product life cycle (PLC)
The course of a product's sales and profits over its lifetime.

Figure 9.2 shows a typical **product life cycle (PLC)**, the course that a product's sales and profits take over its lifetime. The PLC has five distinct stages:

1. *Product development* begins when the company finds and develops a new product idea. During product development, sales are zero, and the company's investment costs mount.
2. *Introduction* is a period of slow sales growth as the product is introduced in the market. Profits are nonexistent in this stage because of the heavy expenses of product introduction.
3. *Growth* is a period of rapid market acceptance and increasing profits.
4. *Maturity* is a period of slowdown in sales growth because the product has achieved acceptance by most potential buyers. Profits level off or decline because of increased marketing outlays to defend the product against competition.
5. *Decline* is the period when sales fall off and profits drop.

FIGURE | 9.2
Sales and Profits over the Product's Life from Inception to Decline

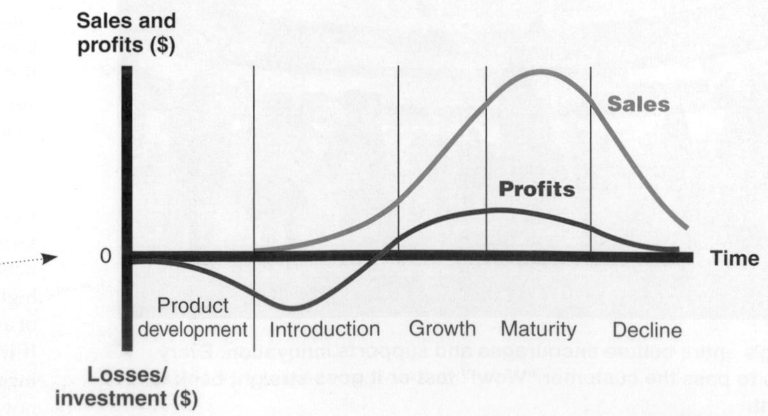

Some products die quickly; others stay in the mature stage for a long, long time. For example, TABASCO sauce has been around for more than 140 years. Even then, to keep the product young, the company has added a full line of flavors (such as Sweet & Spicy and Chipotle) and a kitchen cabinet full of new TABASCO products (such as spicy beans, a chili mix, and jalapeno nacho slices).

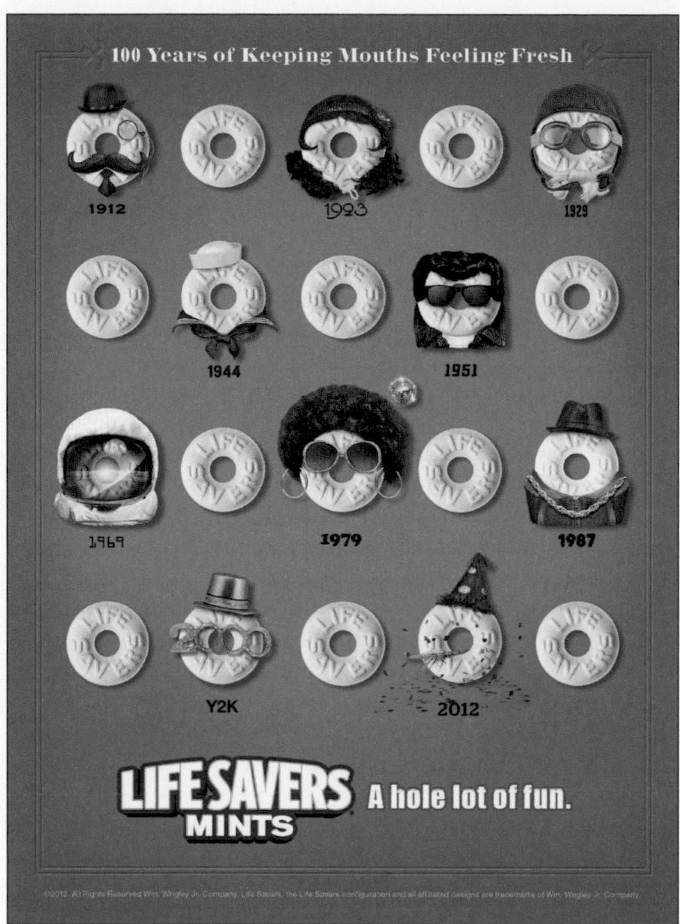

100 Years of Keeping Mouths Feeling Fresh
1912
1923
1929
1944
1951
1969
1979
1987
Y2K
2012
LIFE SAVERS MINTS
A hole lot of fun.

● Product life cycle: Some products die quickly; others stay in the mature stage for a long, long time. Life Savers Mints recently celebrated "100 years of keeping mouths feeling fresh."

The Wrigley Company

Not all products follow all five stages of the PLC. Some products are introduced and die quickly; others stay in the mature stage for a long, long time. Some enter the decline stage and are then cycled back into the growth stage through strong promotion or repositioning. It seems that a well-managed brand could live forever. Venerable brands like Coca-Cola, Gillette, Budweiser, Guinness, American Express, Wells Fargo, Kikkoman, and TABASCO sauce, for instance, are still going strong after more than 100 years. Guinness beer has been around for more than 250 years, ● Life Savers Mints recently celebrated "100 years of keeping mouths feeling fresh," and TABASCO sauce brags that it's "over 140 years old and still able to totally whup your butt!"

The PLC concept can describe a *product class* (gasoline-powered automobiles), a *product form* (SUVs), or a *brand* (the Ford Escape). The PLC concept applies differently in each case. Product classes have the longest life cycles; the sales of many product classes stay in the mature stage for a long time. Product forms, in contrast, tend to have the standard PLC shape. Product forms such as "dial telephones," "VHS tapes," and "film cameras" passed through a regular history of introduction, rapid growth, maturity, and decline.

A specific brand's life cycle can change quickly because of changing competitive attacks and responses. For example, although laundry soaps (product class) and powdered detergents (product form) have enjoyed fairly long life cycles, the life cycles of specific brands have tended to be much shorter. Today's leading U.S. brands of powdered laundry soap are Tide and Gain; the leading brands 100 years ago were Fels-Naptha, Octagon, and Kirkman.

The PLC concept also can be applied to what are known as styles, fashions, and fads. Their special life cycles are shown in ● **Figure 9.3**. A **style** is a basic and distinctive mode of expression. For example, styles appear in homes (colonial, ranch, transitional), clothing (formal, casual), and art (realist, surrealist, abstract). Once a style is invented, it may last for generations, passing in and out of vogue. A style has a cycle showing several periods of renewed interest.

Style
A basic and distinctive mode of expression.

Fashion
A currently accepted or popular style in a given field.

Fad
A temporary period of unusually high sales driven by consumer enthusiasm and immediate product or brand popularity.

A **fashion** is a currently accepted or popular style in a given field. For example, the more formal "business attire" look of corporate dress of the 1980s and 1990s gave way to the "business casual" look of the 2000s and 2010s. Fashions tend to grow slowly, remain popular for a while, and then decline slowly.

Fads are temporary periods of unusually high sales driven by consumer enthusiasm and immediate product or brand popularity.[23] A fad may be part of an otherwise normal life cycle, as in the case of recent surges in the sales of poker chips and accessories. Or the fad may comprise a brand's or product's entire life cycle. Pet Rocks are a classic example. Upon hearing his friends complain about how expensive it was to care for their dogs, advertising copywriter Gary Dahl joked about his pet rock. He soon wrote a spoof of a dog-training manual for it, titled *The Care and Training of Your Pet Rock*. Soon Dahl was selling some 1.5 million ordinary beach pebbles at $4 a pop. Yet the fad, which broke one October, had

● **FIGURE | 9.3**
Styles, Fashions, and Fads

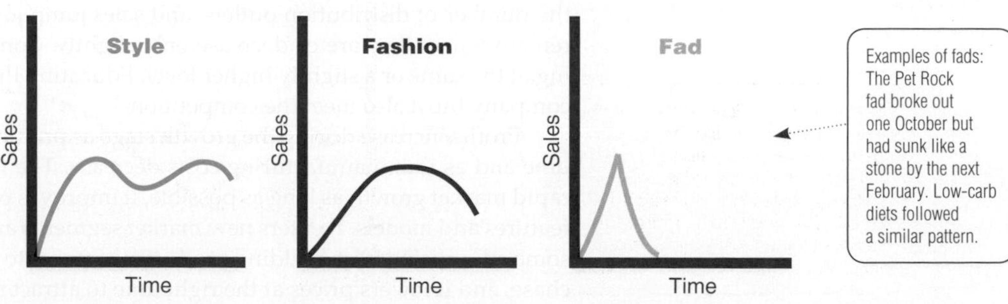

sunk like a stone by the next February. Dahl's advice to those who want to succeed with a fad: "Enjoy it while it lasts." Other examples of fads include Silly Bandz, Furbies, Crocs, and Pogs.[24]

Marketers can apply the product life-cycle concept as a useful framework for describing how products and markets work. And when used carefully, the PLC concept can help in developing good marketing strategies for the different life-cycle stages. However, using the PLC concept for forecasting product performance or developing marketing strategies presents some practical problems. For example, in practice, it is difficult to forecast the sales level at each PLC stage, the length of each stage, and the shape of the PLC curve. Using the PLC concept to develop marketing strategy also can be difficult because strategy is both a cause and a result of the PLC. The product's current PLC position suggests the best marketing strategies, and the resulting marketing strategies affect product performance in later stages.

Moreover, marketers should not blindly push products through the traditional product life-cycle stages. Instead, marketers often defy the "rules" of the life cycle and position or reposition their products in unexpected ways. By doing this, they can rescue mature or declining products and return them to the growth phase of the life cycle. Or they can leapfrog obstacles that slow consumer acceptance and propel new products forward into the growth phase.

The moral of the product life cycle is that companies must continually innovate; otherwise, they risk extinction. No matter how successful its current product lineup, a company must skillfully manage the life cycles of existing products for future success. And to grow, the company must develop a steady stream of new products that bring new value to customers.

We looked at the product development stage of the PLC in the first part of this chapter. We now look at strategies for each of the other life-cycle stages.

Introduction Stage

Introduction stage
The PLC stage in which a new product is first distributed and made available for purchase.

The **introduction stage** starts when a new product is first launched. Introduction takes time, and sales growth is apt to be slow. Well-known products such as frozen foods and HDTVs lingered for many years before they entered a stage of more rapid growth.

In this stage, as compared to other stages, profits are negative or low because of the low sales and high distribution and promotion expenses. Much money is needed to attract distributors and build their inventories. Promotion spending is relatively high to inform consumers of the new product and get them to try it. Because the market is not generally ready for product refinements at this stage, the company and its few competitors produce basic versions of the product. These firms focus their selling on those buyers who are the most ready to buy.

A company, especially the *market pioneer*, must choose a launch strategy that is consistent with the intended product positioning. It should realize that the initial strategy is just the first step in a grander marketing plan for the product's entire life cycle. If the pioneer chooses its launch strategy to make a "killing," it may be sacrificing long-run revenue for the sake of short-run gain. The pioneer has the best chance of building and retaining market leadership if it plays its cards correctly from the start.

Growth Stage

Growth stage
The PLC stage in which a product's sales start climbing quickly.

If the new product satisfies the market, it will enter a **growth stage**, in which sales will start climbing quickly. The early adopters will continue to buy, and later buyers will start following their lead, especially if they hear favorable word of mouth. Attracted by the opportunities for profit, new competitors will enter the market. They will introduce new product features, and the market will expand. The increase in competitors leads to an increase in the number of distribution outlets, and sales jump just to build reseller inventories. Prices remain where they are or decrease only slightly. Companies keep their promotion spending at the same or a slightly higher level. Educating the market remains a goal, but now the company must also meet the competition.

Profits increase during the growth stage as promotion costs are spread over a large volume and as unit manufacturing costs decrease. The firm uses several strategies to sustain rapid market growth as long as possible. It improves product quality and adds new product features and models. It enters new market segments and new distribution channels. It shifts some advertising from building product awareness to building product conviction and purchase, and it lowers prices at the right time to attract more buyers.

In the growth stage, the firm faces a trade-off between high market share and high current profit. By spending a lot of money on product improvement, promotion, and distribution, the company can capture a dominant position. In doing so, however, it gives up maximum current profit, which it hopes to make up in the next stage.

Maturity Stage

Maturity stage
The PLC stage in which a product's sales growth slows or levels off.

At some point, a product's sales growth will slow down, and it will enter the **maturity stage**. This maturity stage normally lasts longer than the previous stages, and it poses strong challenges to marketing management. Most products are in the maturity stage of the life cycle, and therefore most of marketing management deals with the mature product.

The slowdown in sales growth results in many producers with many products to sell. In turn, this overcapacity leads to greater competition. Competitors begin marking down prices, increasing their advertising and sales promotions, and upping their product development budgets to find better versions of the product. These steps lead to a drop in profit. Some of the weaker competitors start dropping out, and the industry eventually contains only well-established competitors.

Although many products in the mature stage appear to remain unchanged for long periods, most successful ones are actually evolving to meet changing consumer needs. Product managers should do more than simply ride along with or defend their mature products—a good offense is the best defense. They should consider modifying the market, product offering, and marketing mix.

In *modifying the market*, the company tries to increase consumption by finding new users and new market segments for its brands. For example, brands such as Harley-Davidson and Axe fragrances, which have typically targeted male buyers, are introducing products and marketing programs aimed at women. Conversely, Weight Watchers and Bath & Body Works, which have typically targeted women, have created products and programs aimed at men.

The company may also look for ways to increase usage among present customers. For example, 3M recently ran a marketing campaign to inspire more usage of its Post-it products:[25]

> The Post-It Brand's "Go Ahead" campaign hopes to convince customers that the sticky pieces of paper are good for much more than just scribbling temporary notes and reminders. Instead, it positions Post-it Notes as a means of self-expression by showing creative, nontraditional ways that consumers around the world use them. In the past, 3M promoted mostly functional uses of Post-it products, but research showed that consumers have a surprisingly strong emotional relationship with the brand. "They're using it to communicate, using it to collaborate, using it to organize themselves," says a 3M marketing executive. The "Go ahead" campaign was motivated by customers' "quirky and inspired uses of our product."
>
> An initial ad shows people on a college campus blanketing a wall outside a building with Post-it Notes answering the question, "What inspires you?" "Share on a real wall," the announcer explains. Other scenes show a young man filling a wall with mosaic artwork created from multiple colors of Post-it notes, teachers using Post-it Notes to enliven their classrooms, and a man posting a "Morning, beautiful" note on the bathroom mirror as his wife is brushing her teeth. "Go ahead," says the announcer, "keep the honeymoon going." The ad ends with a hand peeling Post-it Notes off a pad one by one to reveal new, unexpected uses: "Go ahead, Connect," "Go ahead, Inspire," and "Go ahead, Explore."

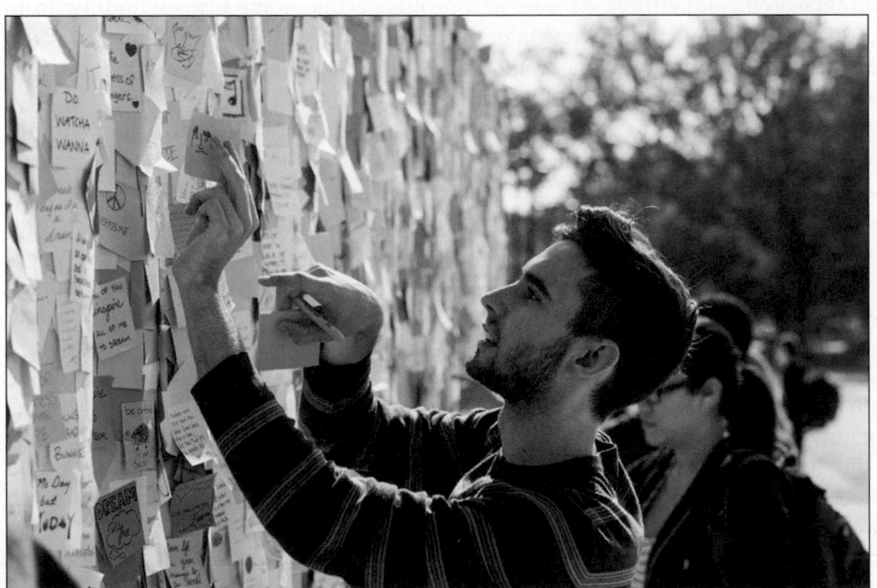

Inspiring more usage: The Post-it Brand from 3M's "Go ahead" campaign portrays Post-it Notes as good for much more than just scribbling temporary notes and reminders. Instead, they are a means of self-expression.

The company might also try *modifying the product*—changing characteristics such as quality, features, style, packaging, or technology platforms to retain current users or attract new ones. Thus, to freshen up their products for today's technology-obsessed children, many classic toy and game makers are creating new digital versions or add-ons for old favorites. More than 75 percent of children 8 years old and younger now use mobile devices such as tablets and smartphones. So toy makers are souping up their products to meet the tastes of the new generation. For example, the electronic banking edition of Monopoly uses bank cards instead of paper money, Hot Wheels cars can zoom across an iPad using the Hot Wheels Apptivity app, and the Barbie Photo Fashion doll has a digital camera built in.[26]

Finally, the company can try *modifying the marketing mix*—improving sales by changing one or more marketing mix elements. The company can offer new or improved services to buyers. It can cut prices to attract new users and competitors' customers. It can launch a better advertising campaign or use aggressive sales promotions—trade deals, cents-off, premiums, and contests. In addition to pricing and promotion, the company can also move into new marketing channels to help serve new users.

Kellogg used all of these market, product, and marketing mix modification approaches to keep its 50+-year-old Special K brand from sinking into decline. Introduced in 1957 as a healthful, high-protein cereal, Special K had matured by the 1990s—sales were flat and the brand had lost its luster. To reinvigorate the brand, Kellogg first extended the cereal line to include a variety of cereal flavors, such as Red Berries, Vanilla Almond, and Chocolatey Delight. Then, it stretched Special K beyond cereals, turning it into a healthful, slimming lifestyle brand. The expanded line now includes meal and snack bars, protein waters and shakes, crackers and chips, and fruit crisps. To attract new users and more usage, Kellogg promotes My Special K weight-management plans online and via a mobile app, which are built around Special K products. "Whether your goal is to finally slip into those skinny jeans or you're just looking to become a little more fit and fabulous, the Special K Challenge is a great way to kick-start a better you!" The Special K brand-rejuvenation efforts paid off. The Special K line has grown steadily over the past 15 years and now accounts for more than $2 billion in annual sales.[27]

Decline Stage

The sales of most product forms and brands eventually dip. The decline may be slow, as in the cases of stamps and oatmeal cereal, or rapid, as in the cases of VHS tapes. Sales may plunge to zero, or they may drop to a low level where they continue for many years. This is the **decline stage**.

Decline stage
The PLC stage in which a product's sales fade away.

Sales decline for many reasons, including technological advances, shifts in consumer tastes, and increased competition. As sales and profits decline, some firms withdraw from the market. Those remaining may prune their product offerings. In addition, they may drop smaller market segments and marginal trade channels, or they may cut the promotion budget and reduce their prices further.

Carrying a weak product can be very costly to a firm, and not just in profit terms. There are many hidden costs. A weak product may take up too much of management's time. It often requires frequent price and inventory adjustments. It requires advertising and sales-force attention that might be better used to make "healthy" products more profitable. A product's failing reputation can cause customer concerns about the company and its other products. The biggest cost may well lie in the future. Keeping weak products delays the search for replacements, creates a lopsided product mix, hurts current profits, and weakens the company's foothold on the future.

For these reasons, companies must identify products in the decline stage and decide whether to maintain, harvest, or drop them. Management may decide to *maintain* its brand, repositioning or reinvigorating it in hopes of moving it back into the growth stage of the product life cycle. P&G has done this with several brands, including Mr. Clean and Old Spice. And LEGO found a way to reinvigorate its brand by returning to its core and making its well-known system the anchor of all new products (see Real Marketing 9.2).

Management may decide to *harvest* the product, which means reducing various costs (plant and equipment, maintenance, R&D, advertising, sales force), hoping that sales hold up. If successful, harvesting will increase the company's profits in the short run. Finally, management may decide to *drop* the product from its line. The company can sell the product to another firm or simply liquidate it at salvage value. In recent years, P&G has sold off several lesser or declining brands, such as Folgers coffee, Crisco oil, Comet cleanser, Sure

Real Marketing 9.2

LEGO: An Old Brand Story with a New Beginning

The LEGO brand has had a long and eventful product life cycle. Founded by joiner and carpenter Ole Kirk Kristiansen, who started making wooden toys in 1932, LEGO has since been owned by the same family for three generations. The LEGO brick was invented in 1958, and it has been the mortar of many childhood memories. The name LEGO comes from the Danish words for "play well," and this has been the core thought behind the brand's entire lifetime. Every life has a beginning and an end, and every life is a cycle of different stages; this also holds true for many brands. The product life cycle is normally described as consisting of a product development phase, an introduction phase, a growth phase, a maturity phase, and a decline phase, but this simple picture does not always hold for the stories of real brands. As for LEGO, the brick itself has not changed much, but the brand has evolved over the years. In the beginning, the LEGO bricks were just small plastic bricks for building. In 1974, LEGO developed small human figures to go with the bricks, adding a touch of personality to the LEGO universe. In 1980, teaching material became part of the concept and the focus on learning became more explicit. In 1997, LEGO entered the digital age, adding computer games and other items to its product line. The company seemed to be doing well in the 1990s and was one of the most recognized global brands and the second largest toymaker in the world. The toy industry may seem like a cozy industry, but it is a highly competitive environment. In the 2000s, LEGO experienced some hard times. LEGO made some poor decisions in the late 1990s and the beginning of the 2000s, and suffered its first financial loss in 1998. Sales still looked good, but costs had escalated on all fronts. Different explanations have been cited as the reason for its problems—for example, an overdiversified product line, more innovative products absorbing the attention of children, demographic changes, cheaper products from low-cost producers, an out-of-control creativity culture in the company's innovation department, and an outdated supply chain. LEGO hit rock bottom in 2003, where it looked like the end for the old family business. This would seem like a standard product life cycle, where the old brand entered its decline phase, but had time really run out for the old LEGO brick? LEGO's mission is to inspire and develop the builders of tomorrow. LEGO aims to support children in learning systematically and creative problem solving. These are skills needed in the twenty-first century.

The LEGO story could have ended here, but the company managed to turn things around. The first turnaround attempt failed. The growing complexity of the company was making a textbook turnaround impossible. The second attempt was a slow-it-down approach launched by its present CEO. This meant that LEGO returned to the core of its business—the little plastic brick. It also meant careful cash management, reducing product complexity, and reconnecting with customers. The turnaround succeeded, with 2006 being the turning point. In 2013, results showed nine years of consecutive growth, a 9.9 percent increase in revenue to kr 25,382 million (about $4,265 million), a profit before tax of kr 6,119 million (about $1,028 million), and a global market share of 8.6 percent. LEGO's focus is not on being the biggest but on being the best. The strategy of LEGO at this stage is niche differentiation and excellence. Its focus is on sustainable growth in line with the core values. The innovation focus has been adjusted so that it is more customer oriented. There are two focus areas: (1) developing the next generation of existing products and existing play themes, and (2) developing fundamentally new products and playing experiences (always anchored in the well-known LEGO system). An example of such a new product is LEGO Speed Champions—a new partnership with three major automobile manufacturers, Ferrari, MacLaren, and Porsche beginning in spring 2015. The result is a new line of LEGO bricks designed to be able to make some of the most iconic high-speed cars in the world. Among the new products available are a large red Ferrari truck, the Ferrari F14 T racing car, and a McLaren Mercedes pit stop set featuring the McLaren Mercedes MP4-29.

LEGO resurrects itself with a new story, building on its old foundations of delivering high-quality bricks, despite a tumultuous history, as it sets new benchmarks in manufacturing and quality control with dynamic, consumer-sustaining business plans.

The Internet plays an important role in keeping in touch with users. LEGO is also putting a lot more weight on marketing research and including users in product development. An example of this is the LEGO Friends concept. A challenge for LEGO has always been to reach out to girls above the age of five years—an important segment considering the situation in the toy market. This is where LEGO can find new growth potential. In order to reach this audience, LEGO had to gather more knowledge and insight into the preferences and playing patterns of girls above the age of five. This was done through observations in private homes, questionnaires, focus groups, interviews with girls, and systematic feedback from parents of girls. This resulted in the new product line LEGO Friends, specifically designed to appeal to girls, within the LEGO system.

Many companies have made a successful return to their roots, but not after leaving their core in order to keep up with technological developments. This is what makes LEGO special. LEGO is proof that even though technological and demographic developments pose huge threats to many companies, it is important to not immediately assume that this is the case for all companies. LEGO represents one of those few companies that experienced high growth and decline, but still managed to find a new source of growth—only, in LEGO's case, the source is not entirely new.

It has capitalized on its key strength, the LEGO brick. Balancing the old and the new is not an easy task for LEGO. The classic brick has to be constantly renewed so that consumers do not lose interest in buying new bricks even though they already have piles of old ones; at the same time, the old values and system have to persist so that they are recognizable, and even 30-year-old bricks fit with new products. The LEGO saga is the story of an old brand that seemed outdated, but has managed to prolong its life cycle and resurrect a brand new story.

Sources: Based on information from the LEGO Group, "Progress Report 2012," http://aboutus.lego.com/en-us/progress-report, accessed October 2013; Keith Oliver, Edouard Samakh, and Peter Heckmann, "Rebuilding Lego, Brick by Brick," http://toostep.com/insight/rebuilding-lego-brickby-brick, accessed October 2013; BBC News, "LEGO Becomes World's Second-Biggest Toymaker," September 5, 2013, http://www.bbc.co.uk/news/business-23968860; Maggie Starvish, "HBS Cases: LEGO," *HBS Working Knowledge*, March18, 2013, http://hbswk.hbs.edu/item/7170.html; www.b.dk/sites/default/files.../2920515-lego.docx; David Robertson and Per Hjuler, "Innovating a Turnaround at Lego," *Harvard Business Review*, September 2009; and A. O'Connell, "LEGO CEO Jørgen Vig Knudstorp on Leading Through Survival and Growth," *Harvard Business Review*, January 2009; http://www.lego.com/en-us/aboutus/news-room/2014/november/lego-speed-champions, accessed November, 2014.

deodorant, Duncan Hines cake mixes, and Jif peanut butter. If the company plans to find a buyer, it will not want to run down the product through harvesting.

Table 9.2 summarizes the key characteristics of each stage of the PLC. The table also lists the marketing objectives and strategies for each stage.[28]

Author Comment | Let's look at just a few more product topics, including regulatory and social responsibility issues and the special challenges of marketing products internationally.

Additional Product and Service Considerations

We wrap up our discussion of products and services with two additional considerations: social responsibility in product decisions and issues of international product and services marketing.

Product Decisions and Social Responsibility

Marketers should carefully consider public policy issues and regulations regarding acquiring or dropping products, patent protection, product quality and safety, and product warranties.

Regarding new products, the government may prevent companies from adding products through acquisitions if the effect threatens to lessen competition. Companies dropping products must be aware that they have legal obligations, written or implied, to their suppliers, dealers, and customers who have a stake in the dropped product. Companies must also obey U.S. patent laws when developing new products. A company cannot make its product illegally similar to another company's established product.

Manufacturers must comply with specific laws regarding product quality and safety. The Federal Food, Drug, and Cosmetic Act protects consumers from unsafe and adulterated food, drugs, and cosmetics. Various acts provide for the inspection of sanitary conditions

Table 9.2 | Summary of Product Life-Cycle Characteristics, Objectives, and Strategies

	Introduction	Growth	Maturity	Decline
Characteristics				
Sales	Low sales	Rapidly rising sales	Peak sales	Declining sales
Costs	High cost per customer	Average cost per customer	Low cost per customer	Low cost per customer
Profits	Negative	Rising profits	High profits	Declining profits
Customers	Innovators	Early adopters	Mainstream adopters	Lagging adopters
Competitors	Few	Growing number	Stable number beginning to decline	Declining number
Marketing objectives	Create product engagement and trial	Maximize market share	Maximize profit while defending market share	Reduce expenditure and milk the brand
Strategies				
Product	Offer a basic product	Offer product extensions, service, and warranty	Diversify brand and models	Phase out weak items
Price	Use cost-plus	Price to penetrate market	Price to match or beat competitors	Cut price
Distribution	Build selective distribution	Build intensive distribution	Build more intensive distribution	Go selective: phase out unprofitable outlets
Advertising	Build product awareness among early adopters and dealers	Build engagement and interest in the mass market	Stress brand differences and benefits	Reduce to level needed to retain hard-core loyals
Sales Promotion	Use heavy sales promotion to entice trial	Reduce to take advantage of heavy consumer demand	Increase to encourage brand switching	Reduce to minimal level

Source: Based on Philip Kotler and Kevin Lane Keller, *Marketing Management,* 14th ed. (Upper Saddle River, NJ: Prentice Hall, 2012), p. 317. © 2012. Printed and Electronically reproduced by permission of Pearson Education, Inc., Upper Saddle River, New Jersey.

in the meat- and poultry-processing industries. Safety legislation has been passed to regulate fabrics, chemical substances, automobiles, toys, and drugs and poisons. The Consumer Product Safety Act of 1972 established the Consumer Product Safety Commission, which has the authority to ban or seize potentially harmful products and set severe penalties for violation of the law.

If consumers have been injured by a product with a defective design, they can sue manufacturers or dealers. A recent survey of manufacturing companies found that product liability was the second-largest litigation concern, behind only labor and employment matters. Tens of thousands of product liability suits are now tried in U.S. district courts each year. Although manufacturers are found to be at fault in only a small percentage of all product liability cases, when they are found guilty, awards can run into the tens or even hundreds of millions of dollars. Class-action suits can run into the billions. For example, after it recalled 11 million vehicles for acceleration-pedal-related issues, Toyota faced more than 100 class-action and individual lawsuits and ended up paying a $1.6 billion settlement to compensate owners for financial losses associated with the defect.[29]

This litigation phenomenon has resulted in huge increases in product liability insurance premiums, causing big problems in some industries. Some companies pass these higher rates along to consumers by raising prices. Others are forced to discontinue high-risk product lines. Some companies are now appointing *product stewards*, whose job is to protect consumers from harm and the company from liability by proactively ferreting out potential product problems.

International Product and Services Marketing

International product and services marketers face special challenges. First, they must figure out what products and services to introduce and in which countries. Then they must decide how much to standardize or adapt their products and services for world markets.

On the one hand, companies would like to standardize their offerings. Standardization helps a company develop a consistent worldwide image. It also lowers the product design, manufacturing, and marketing costs of offering a large variety of products. On the other hand, markets and consumers around the world differ widely. Companies must usually respond to these differences by adapting their product offerings. For example, by carefully tailoring its products to local tastes in China, PepsiCo has become the largest snack-and-beverage company in the world's second-biggest economy:[30]

Global product adaptation: Lay's famously funky Chinese chip flavors include cucumber (a best-seller), iced lemon tea, "Numb & Spicy Hot Pot," and "Sha La Cui," a concoction that tastes like a baked salad.

Frito-Lay

PepsiCo has found that success in China's huge beverage and snack markets depends on carefully adapting its many brands—such as Pepsi, Lay's, Gatorade, and Quaker—to the tastes of Chinese consumers. Its large food and beverage innovation center in Shanghai employs consumer and food researchers, product developers, experimental kitchens, and even a pilot manufacturing plant, all devoted to pinpointing and pinging the unique palates of Chinese consumers. And before new product concepts ever hit the market, they are sampled extensively by local taste testers—often local homemakers.

While not likely to be favorites in Western markets, PepsiCo's Chinese lineup includes lip-smackers such as hot and sour fish soup potato chips, white fungus oatmeal, and blueberry Gatorade. Lay's famously funky Chinese chip flavors include cucumber (a best-seller), iced lemon tea, "Numb & Spicy Hot Pot," and "Sha La Cui," a concoction designed to taste like a baked salad. The Chinese market holds huge potential for PepsiCo. For example, China's 1.35 billion people now consume an average of only about one small bag of potato chips every two to four weeks, compared with 15 bags in that period in the United States. Skillful product adaptation has helped PepsiCo achieve double-digit growth in this important market.

Service marketers also face special challenges when going global. Some service industries have a long history of international operations. For example, the commercial banking industry was one of the first to grow internationally. Banks had to provide global services to meet the foreign exchange and credit needs of their home-country clients who wanted to sell overseas. In recent years, many banks have become truly global. Germany's Deutsche Bank, for example, serves more than 19 million customers through 2,984 branches in more than 70 countries. For its clients around the world who wish to grow globally, Deutsche Bank can raise money not only in Frankfurt but also in Zurich, London, Paris, Tokyo, and Moscow.[31]

Professional and business services industries, such as accounting, management consulting, and advertising, have also globalized. The international growth of these firms followed the globalization of the client companies they serve. For example, as more clients employ worldwide marketing and advertising strategies, advertising agencies have responded by globalizing their own operations. McCann Worldgroup, a large U.S.-based advertising and marketing services agency, operates in more than 110 countries. It serves international clients such as Coca-Cola, GM, ExxonMobil, Microsoft, MasterCard, Johnson & Johnson, and Unilever in markets ranging from the United States and Canada to Korea and Kazakhstan. Moreover, McCann Worldgroup is one company in the Interpublic Group of Companies, an immense, worldwide network of advertising and marketing services companies.[32]

Retailers are among the latest service businesses to go global. As their home markets become saturated, American retailers such as Walmart, Office Depot, and Saks Fifth Avenue are expanding into faster-growing markets abroad. For example, since 1991, Walmart has entered 27 countries outside the United States; its international division's sales account for 29 percent of total sales. Foreign retailers are making similar moves. Asian shoppers can now buy American products in French-owned Carrefour stores. Carrefour—the world's fourth-largest retailer behind Walmart, Costco, and the U.K.'s Tesco—now operates almost 10,000 stores in 33 countries. It is the leading retailer in Europe, Brazil, and Argentina and the largest foreign retailer in China.[33]

The trend toward growth of global service companies will continue, especially in banking, airlines, telecommunications, and professional services. Today, service firms are no longer simply following their manufacturing customers. Instead, they are taking the lead in international expansion.

9 Reviewing the Concepts

OBJECTIVES REVIEW AND KEY TERMS

Objectives Review

A company's current products face limited life spans and must be replaced by newer products. But new products can fail—the risks of innovation are as great as the rewards. The key to successful innovation lies in a customer-focused, holistic, total-company effort; strong planning; and a systematic new product development process.

OBJECTIVE 1 Explain how companies find and develop new product ideas. *(pp 294–295)*

Companies find and develop new product ideas from a variety of sources. Many new product ideas stem from *internal sources*. Companies conduct formal R&D, or they pick the brains of their employees, urging them to think up and develop new product ideas. Other ideas come from *external sources*. Companies track *competitors'* offerings and obtain ideas from *distributors and suppliers* who are close to the market and can pass along information about consumer problems and new product possibilities.

Perhaps the most important sources of new product ideas are customers themselves. Companies observe customers, invite them to submit their ideas and suggestions, or even involve customers in the new product development process. Many companies are now developing *crowdsourcing* or *open-innovation* new product idea programs, which invite broad communities of people—customers, employees, independent scientists and researchers, and even the general public—into the new product innovation process. Truly innovative companies do not rely only on one source or another for new product ideas.

OBJECTIVE 2 List and define the steps in the new product development process and the major considerations in managing this process. *(pp 295–306)*

The new product development process consists of eight sequential stages. The process starts with *idea generation*. Next comes *idea screening,* which reduces the number of ideas based on the company's own criteria. Ideas that pass the screening stage continue through *product concept development,* in which a detailed version of the new product idea is stated in meaningful consumer terms. This stage includes *concept testing,* in which new product concepts are tested with a group of target consumers to determine whether the concepts have strong consumer appeal. Strong concepts proceed to *marketing strategy development,* in which an initial marketing strategy for the new product is developed from the product concept. In the *business-analysis* stage, a review of the sales, costs, and profit projections for a new product is conducted to determine whether the new product is likely to satisfy the company's objectives. With positive results here, the ideas become more concrete through *product development* and *test marketing* and finally are launched during *commercialization*.

New product development involves more than just going through a set of steps. Companies must take a systematic, holistic approach to managing this process. Successful new product development requires a customer-centered, team-based, systematic effort.

OBJECTIVE 3 Describe the stages of the product life cycle and how marketing strategies change during a product's life cycle. *(pp 306–312)*

Each product has a *life cycle* marked by a changing set of problems and opportunities. The sales of the typical product follow an S-shaped curve made up of five stages. The cycle begins with the *product development* stage in which the company finds and develops a new product idea. *The introduction stage* is marked by slow growth and low profits as the product is distributed to the market. If successful, the product enters a *growth stage,* which offers rapid sales growth and increasing profits. Next comes a *maturity stage* in which the product's sales growth slows down and profits stabilize. Finally, the product enters a *decline stage* in which sales and profits dwindle. The company's task during this stage is to recognize the decline and decide whether it should maintain, harvest, or drop the product. The different stages of the PLC require different marketing strategies and tactics.

OBJECTIVE 4 Discuss two additional product issues: socially responsible product decisions and international product and services marketing. *(pp 312–315)*

Marketers must consider two additional product issues. The first is *social responsibility*. This includes public policy issues and regulations involving acquiring or dropping products, patent protection, product quality and safety, and product warranties. The second involves the special challenges facing international product and services marketers. International marketers must decide how much to standardize or adapt their offerings for world markets.

MyMarketingLab

Go to **mymktlab.com** to complete the problems marked with this icon ✪.

Key Terms

OBJECTIVE 1

New product development (p 294)

OBJECTIVE 2

Idea generation (p 295)
Crowdsourcing (p 296)
Idea screening (p 299)
Product concept (p 299)
Concept testing (p 300)
Marketing strategy development (p 300)
Business analysis (p 301)
Product development (p 301)
Test marketing (p 302)
Commercialization (p 303)
Customer-centered new product development (p 304)
Team-based new product development (p 305)

OBJECTIVE 3

Product life cycle (PLC) (p 306)
Style (p 307)
Fashion (p 307)
Fad (p 307)
Introduction stage (p 308)
Growth stage (p 308)
Maturity stage (p 309)
Decline stage (p 310)

DISCUSSION AND CRITICAL THINKING

Discussion Questions

9-1 Why is it increasingly the case that customers are vital in the creation of innovative new products and services? How has this come about? (AACSB: Communication; Reflective Thinking)

✪ **9-2** What decisions must be made once a company decides to go ahead with commercialization for a new product? (AACSB: Communication)

✪ **9-3** What is the purpose and the importance of the business-analysis stage in the process of developing a new product? What happens after this vital stage? (AACSB: Communication)

9-4 What options are open to a business when their product or service reaches the decline stage? Explain. (AACSB: Communication; Reflective Thinking)

Critical Thinking Exercises

9-5 It appears that the sky is the limit regarding ideas for smartphone/tablet apps. In a small group, create an idea for a new app related to (1) business, (2) health, (3) education, (4) sports, and (5) shopping. (AACSB: Communication; Use of IT; Reflective Thinking)

9-6 Develop a presentation illustrating the launch and progress of a new consumer product in your own country or region in the past five years. Focus on how the business has used the four Ps. Identify any specifics that have determined how the four Ps have been balanced and whether this strategy has worked. (AACSB: Communication; Reflective Thinking)

✪ **9-7** The "Internet of Things"—a term that refers to everyday objects being connected to the Internet—is growing. Thermostats, ovens, cars, toothbrushes, and even baby clothes are connecting to the Internet. Research this phenomenon and suggest five innovative product ideas connected to the "Internet of Things." (AACSB: Communication; Use of IT; Reflective Thinking)

MINICASES AND APPLICATIONS

Online, Mobile, and Social Media Marketing Reading Rainbow App

You may have grown up watching LeVar Burton on PBS's *Reading Rainbow* show. He hosted the children's educational show for 26 years and now has taken it mobile. Burton purchased the rights to the show and launched a *Reading Rainbow* mobile app, making it the App Store's top-grossing app in less than a year. The app is free to try, but a $9.99 per month or $29.99 per six-month subscription allows kids unlimited access to the library and adventures on themed islands such as the Animal Kingdom and others from the iconic television show, as well as new adventure field trips. Kids have gobbled up more than 10 million books. Audio and video storytelling brings books to life for children, and interactive elements encourage curiosity and learning. Adventures incorporate segments from the TV show and brand new video. Up to five children in a household can customize their own reading adventures, and reading lists are suggested based on their abilities and interests. The parent dashboard lets parents monitor their child's reading progress. LeVar Burton personally starts each day with a "Good morning, y'all" tweet followed by 15 to 20 more tweets each day to his followers. The service is always expanding, offering new adventures that are often based on user feedback through social media.

9-8 In what stage of the product life cycle is the *Reading Rainbow* television program? Has the mobile app changed that? Explain. (AACSB: Communication; Reflective Thinking)

9-9 Discuss other existing products that have created new life for the product by embracing Internet, mobile, or social media platforms. Suggest an app for another tangible product or service that does not currently use online, mobile, or social media, along with ways to encourage customer engagement and social sharing for the brand. (AACSB: Communication; Use of IT; Reflective Thinking)

Marketing Ethics There Is No Such Thing as a Miracle

Miracle Mineral Solution (MMS) can cure AIDS, Ebola, cancer, and malaria. Or at least that is what the website tells potential customers. The inventor and chief advocate of the product is Jim Humble. There is little evidence to support the fact that MMS does anything to patients aside from making them feel worse than they did before they tried it. The U.S. Food and Drug Administration (FDA) is typical in its conclusions about the so-called miracle drug. The FDA identifies it as 28 percent sodium chlorite, which, when mixed with an acid (as recommended), produces a potent form of bleach. The product's label suggests high oral doses for the maximum effect. The FDA states the oral doses will produce nothing but nausea, vomiting, dehydration, and diarrhea. Humble claims to have "treated" 100,000 patients in Africa alone with MMS, and he has used it to treat cancer patients in Mexico and other parts of the world. It is also clear that MMS has been used on pancreatic and lung cancer patients in developing countries. In the UK, for example, a support group reports those selling MMS to relevant authorities. Meanwhile, Humble and those who believe in MMS dispense it to patients around the world. In New Zealand around 2,000 patients have been sold the product, and the Australian Medical Association reports that 10 people have been poisoned by MMS over the past five years. They want it banned.

9-10 Discuss the ethical issues surrounding unproven products such as MMS. Do you think that these products should be banned before independent assessment? (AACSB: Communication; Ethical Reasoning)

9-11 Discuss the impact of unethical and unfounded product claims such as these on those in the developing world desperate to be cured of fatal diseases. (AACSB: Communication; Reflective Thinking)

Marketing by the Numbers Dental House Calls

With the population aging and patients who dread sitting in a sterile dental office, dentists are finding an opportunity in dental house calls. The Blende Dental Group has taken its service on the road in San Francisco and New York City, performing everything from routine exams and cleanings to root canals. Some patients are wealthy and prefer the personal service, whereas others are elderly homebounds who cannot get out to the dentist's office. Recreating a dental office in a home requires additional equipment, such as a portable X-ray machine that looks like a ray gun, sterile water tanks, a dental drill, lights, and a laptop. A portable X-ray machine alone costs $8,000. Refer to Appendix 2: Marketing by the Numbers to answer the following questions.

9-12 What types of fixed costs are associated with this service? Estimate the total fixed costs for this additional service, and, assuming a contribution margin of 40 percent, determine the amount of sales necessary to break even on this increase in fixed costs to offer this additional service. (AACSB: Communication; Analytical Thinking)

9-13 What other factors must a dentist consider before offering this service in addition to his or her in-office service? (AACSB: Communication; Reflective Thinking)

Video Case Subaru

When a company has a winning product, it has it made. Or does it? Subaru is a winning company (one of the few automotive companies to sustain growth and profits in hard economic times) with various winning products, including the Impreza, Legacy, Forester, and Outback. But what happens when any one product starts to decline in popularity? This video demonstrates how Subaru constantly engages in new product development as part of its efforts to manage the product life cycle for each of its models. Subaru is focused on both developing the next version of each existing model and developing possible new models to boost its product portfolio.

After viewing the video featuring Subaru, answer the following questions:

9-14 Discuss the product life cycle in relation to one Subaru product.

9-15 How do shifting consumer trends affect Subaru's products?

9-16 Has Subaru remained customer oriented in its new product efforts? Explain.

Company Case 3M: Where Innovation Is a Way of Life

In recent years, companies topping the world's "most innovative" lists typically have been high-tech leaders such as Google, Apple, Samsung, and Amazon. When thinking of companies that set the world on fire with one revolutionary product after another, the image of a stodgy company that originated in the mining industry more than 100 years ago is hardly the icon. But although 3M may not be as flashy as today's high-tech headliners, it's anything but stodgy.

3M—the Minnesota Mining and Manufacturing Company—is a multinational powerhouse with more than $30 billion in annual sales. Year-after-year, with machine-like precision, 20 percent of 3M's sales filter down as operating profits, allowing the company to increase its dividend to shareholders—something it has done every year for the past 56 years.

3M sells more than 50,000 products in nearly 200 countries across dozens of industries, including office products, construction, telecommunications, electronics, health care, aerospace, and automotive. Among its products are some of the world's most recognizable consumer brands, such as Scotch tape, Nexcare first aid products, Filtrete home filtration products, and Post-it Notes. But 3M's portfolio is also packed with hundreds of brands that most people have never heard of—such as Pruven waste bags for picking up dog poop.

The unusual breadth of 3M's product portfolio is both a blessing and a curse for the company. Having a hand in so many industries shields the company from overreliance on any given market. Even when multiple industries are down, many more are doing just fine. That explains 3M's financial strength. But it also explains why 3M has a hard time thrilling Wall Street. Even a hit new product doesn't make much of a difference in 3M's steady but unspectacular growth rate—one that is consistently in the low single digits.

Like 3M, the company's current CEO, Inge Thulin, is methodical and understated. He keeps a long-term focus and places strong emphasis on maintaining 3M's reliable profitability. But Thulin is also interested in stoking the fire just a bit, to put a little more heat under sales growth. One of the first things Thulin did as CEO was to trim 3M's annual sales growth goal from 7 or 8 percent—a goal the company consistently missed—to between 4 and 6 percent. Then, as the world watched, 3M's organic sales growth grew to 5.8 percent. And under Thulin's leadership, 3M is now on track to maintain that stronger growth rate.

How did Thulin do it? The same way 3M has been doing it for decades. At the core of 3M's success is its business model—organic growth comes from innovation and the creation of market-changing products. Such market-changing products have at times created entirely new industries. 3M has sustained this type of innovation decade after decade by fostering a deep culture of innovation, encouraging collaboration, and maintaining a dedication to research and development.

Culture of Innovation

From its earliest days, 3M created a culture of innovation by allowing team members to take risks in a protected environment. 3M knows that it must try thousands of product ideas to hit the new product jackpot. One well-worn slogan at 3M is, "You have to kiss a lot of frogs to find a prince." "Kissing frogs" often means making mistakes, but 3M accepts blunders and dead ends as a normal part of creativity and innovation. In fact, its philosophy seems to be "If you aren't making mistakes, you probably aren't doing anything."

As it turns out, "blunders" have turned into some of 3M's most successful products. Old-timers at 3M love to tell the story about the chemist who accidentally spilled a new chemical on her sneakers. Some days later, she noticed that the spots hit by the chemical had not gotten dirty—an attractive benefit. It was that discovery that eventually led to the creation of Scotchgard fabric protector. They tell about the early 3M scientist who had a deathly fear of shaving with a straight razor. So he invented a very fine, waterproof sandpaper, which he used to sand the stubble from his face each morning. Although this invention never caught on as a shaving solution, it became one of 3M's best-selling products—wet-dry sandpaper, now used for a wide variety of commercial and industrial applications.

And then there's the one about 3M scientist Spencer Silver. Silver started out to develop a superstrong adhesive; instead, he came up with one that didn't stick very well at all. He sent the apparently useless substance on to other 3M researchers to see whether they could find something to do with it. Nothing happened for several years. Then 3M scientist Arthur Fry had an idea. As a choir member in a local church, Mr. Fry was having trouble marking places in his hymnal—the little scraps of paper he used kept falling out. He tried dabbing some of Mr. Silver's weak glue on one of the scraps. It stuck nicely and later peeled off without damaging the book. Thus were born 3M's Post-it Notes, a product that is now one of the top selling office supply products in the world.

One of the ways 3M fosters a culture of innovation is by encouraging everyone to look for new products. The company's renowned "15 percent rule" allows all employees to spend up to 15 percent of their time "bootlegging"—working on projects of personal interest whether those projects directly benefit the company or not. And yet, there is a vibe throughout the company regarding these precious six hours a week. Who knows where the next Post-it Note will come from? "It's one of the things that sets 3M apart as an innovative company . . . giving every one of our employees the ability to follow their instincts to take advantage of opportunities for the company," says Kurt Beinlich, a technical director who oversees a 70-person lab team. "It's really shaped what and who 3M is."

Encouraging Collaboration

While 3M's 15 percent program has inspired other companies to follow suit (both Google and HP apply their own versions), it's a rare perk in the corporate world. Not only is it an expense, but to be successful it takes a lot more than simply giving employees the time. Experts suggest that this kind of program works best at companies where there is a high level of collaboration across employees and departments.

3M has that collaboration in spades. One example is an annual event that is simple but has a huge impact. The event resembles a middle school science fair, as employees from dozens of 3M divisions make cardboard posters describing their 15-percent-time project. Employees hang out next to their posters, await feedback, and look for potential collaborators. Wayne Maurer, an R&D manager in 3M's abrasives division, refers to it as a chance for people to unhinge their "inner geek." "For technical people, it's the most passionate and engaged event we have at 3M."

The event isn't just an opportunity to show off; it has actually moved projects through the development phase to commercialization. Past projects that have made it to market include clear bandages, optical films that reflect light, and painter's tape that prevents bleeding. The event has even put new life in projects that have sat on a back burner for years.

One employee had an idea for creating a sandpaper with reshaped grit particles that wouldn't dull so quickly. But after playing around with the idea for a while, he shelved it and moved on to other things. Fifteen years later, the employee resurrected the project during his 15 percent time and made a poster in hopes of getting some ideas that would move the project along. With the help of new employees and new technology, 3M discovered that a particle's sharp, pyramid-like shape became more durable with a change in the mixing order of the ingredients. That discovery led to the launch of Cubitron II, sandpaper that acts more like a cutting tool. On the market since 2009, it still stumps other companies trying to create copycat products.

Emphasis on R&D

There are few companies that provide more support for research and development than 3M. For years, 3M invested 6 percent of sales every year in R&D. But in recent years, that spending had been cut to just 5.5 percent—a small difference on paper, but one that Thulin believes is significant. "Those long-term investments are needed to get the growth engine up and going." If such investments are reduced, Thulin believes, "you will kill the business." That's why 3M's R&D expenditures are once again up to 6 percent. Thulin believes R&D "is the heartbeat of this company and it's a competitive advantage for us." By comparison, the average of R&D expenses across corporations is about 3 percent. For the most recent year, Apple spent 4.5 billion on R&D, a company record that still amounted to only 2.6 percent of sales.

But it isn't just the amount of money that is important for a successful R&D program. It's how the money is used. In addition to increasing the R&D allotment, Thulin is putting more priority on the 3M technologies that have the most potential for growth. Among these technologies are films designed to protect everything from smartphones to kitchen appliances, and a construction wrap that will outperform DuPont's Tyvek as a weather-resistant barrier for homes and buildings.

But Thulin's plan for allocating R&D funds also includes eliminating 3M units with poor financial performance, or those that aren't a good fit with the company's core strengths. For Thulin, it's nothing personal; it's strictly business. Last year, 3M sold Scientific Anglers, which makes fishing line and other related products. Thulin believed there was little symbiosis between developments in that product line and other 3M technologies.

And although Thulin's plan also focuses on high-tech areas, it also recognizes the importance of a broad portfolio that includes low-tech items—such as doggie doo bags. In fact, 3M is committed to a broad range of pet-care supplies. "You cannot have only high-tech in every category because then you will not get space in the shops," says Thulin, recognizing that mass retailers want to purchase full lines of products within and across categories from manufacturers.

3M will likely never have growth rates matching Apple, Facebook, or even Microsoft in its heyday. But it will also likely never experience the potential downturns that even the biggest companies eventually face. 3M's long-term dedication to innovative new products and technologies has sustained the company for decades, and there's no reason to expect that this will change. And who knows—the next "big thing" may just have "3M" stamped on it instead of "Apple."

Questions for Discussion

9-17 Based on concepts discussed in this chapter, describe the factors that have contributed to 3M's new product success.

9-18 Is 3M's product development process customer centered? Why or why not?

9-19 Considering the product life cycle, what challenges does 3M face in managing its product portfolio?

9-20 Are there limits to how broad 3M's product portfolio can grow? Explain.

9-21 Is it possible for 3M to maintain steady growth and profitability *and* raise that growth to much higher levels?

Sources: Kevin Mahoney, "2 MN Cos. Make Fortune's List of 'World's Most Admired'", *Twin Cities Mag*, February 27, 2014, http://tcbmag.com/News/Recent-News/2014/February/2-MN-Cos-Make-Fortunes-List-Of-Worlds-Most-Admir; "Here Is Why We Think 3M Is Worth $140," *Forbes*, March 6, 2014, www.forbes.com/sites/greatspeculations/2014/03/06/here-is-why-we-think-3m-is-worth-140/; James R. Hagerty, "50,000 Products but 3M Still Searching for Growth," *Wall Street Journal*, November 18, 2013, p. B1; Kaomi Goetz, "How 3M Gave Everyone Days Off and Created an Innovation Dynamo," *Fast Company*, February 1, 2011, www.fastcodesign.com/1663137/how-3m-gave-everyone-days-off-and-created-an-innovation-dynamo.

MyMarketingLab

Go to **mymktlab.com** for the following Assisted-graded writing questions:

9-22 Define crowdsourcing and explain why companies use it in new product development. Describe an example of a company using crowdsourcing this way. (AACSB: Communication; Reflective Thinking)

9-23 Discuss the special challenges facing international product and service marketers. (AACSB: Communication)

References

1. Based on information found in Brad Stone, "Inside the Moonshot Factory," *Bloomberg Businessweek*, May 22, 2013, pp. 56–61; Chuck Salter, "Google: The Faces and Voices of the World's Most Innovative Company," *Fast Company,* March 2008, pp. 74–88; John Markoff, "Google Puts Money on Robots, Using the Man Behind Android," *New York Times*, December 4, 2013, p. 1; Larry Popelka, "Google Is Winning the Innovation War Against Apple," *Bloomberg Businessweek*, May 20, 2013, www.businessweek.com/articles/2013-05-20/google-is-winning-the-innovation-war-against-apple; Ben Paynter, "Google: For Adding Fiber to Our Internet Diet," *Fast Company*, February 11, 2013, www.fastcompany.com/most-innovative-companies/2013/google; Rolfe Winkler and Daisuke Wakabayashi, "Google to Buy Nest Labs for $3.2 Billion," *Wall Street Journal*, January 13, 2014; and www.google.com and http://investor.google.com/financial/tables.html, accessed September 2014.
2. Austino Fontevecchia, "Apple's Strong iPhone Sales Mask Falling Revenue per Unit as Gross Margins Contract," *Forbes,* July 22, 2013, www.forbes.com/sites/afontevecchia/2013/07/23/apples-strong-iphone-sales-mask-falling-revenue-per-unit-as-gross-margins-contract/.
3. Marsha Lindsey, "8 Ways to Ensure Your New-Product Launch Succeeds," *Fast Company,* April 3, 2012, www.fastcompany.com/1829483/8-ways-ensure-your-new-product-launch-succeeds; and Vijaya Kumar, "Improving the Success Rate of New Product Introduction through Digital Social Media," *PDMA,* August 27, 2013, www.pdma.org/p/bl/et/blogid=2&blogaid=115.
4. See Paul Sloane, "Source of Innovative Ideas," *Yahoo! Voices*, June 16, 2010, http://voices.yahoo.com/sources-innovative-ideas-6185898.html; and "R&D Spending Returns to Pre-Recession Levels, Finds Booz & Company Global Innovation 1000 Study," October 10, 2012, www.booz.com/global/home/press/display/51296501.
5. For these and other examples, see Dan Schawbel, "Why Companies Want You to Become an Intrapreneur," *Forbes,* September 9, 2013, www.forbes.com/sites/danschawbel/2013/09/09/why-companies-want-you-to-become-an-intrapreneur/; and "Time to Think," http://solutions.3m.com/innovation/en_US/stories/time-to-think, accessed September 2014.
6. Kevin Scott, "The LinkedIn [in]cubator," December 7, 2012, http://blog.linkedin.com/2012/12/07/linkedin-incubator/; and www.linkedin.com/static?key=what_is_linkedin, accessed September 2014.
7. "Walmart Crowdsources New Product Ideas," *Brand Channel,* January 23, 2012, www.brandchannel.com/home/post/2012/01/23/walmart-get-on-the-shelf-012312.aspx; "Walmart's Get on the Shelf Winners," *YouTube,* January 3, 2014, www.youtube.com/watch?v=-6y-f37rm74.
8. Based on information from Matthew Kronsberg, "How Lego's Great Adventure in Geek-Sourcing Snapped into Place and Boosted the Brand," *Fast Company,* February 2, 2012, www.fastcompany.com/1812959/lego-cuusoo-minecraft-lord-of-rings-hayabusa; Yun Mi Antorini and Albert M. Muniz, Jr., "The Benefits and Challenges of Collaborating with User Communities," *Research Technology Management*, May/June 2013, pp. 21–28; Kurt Wagner, "5 Brands That Got Fans to Lend a Hand," *Fortune,* June 24, 2013, http://money.cnn.com/gallery/leadership/2013/06/24/crowdsourcing-brands.fortune/; and http://lego.cuusoo.com/, accessed September 2014.
9. "Samsung Is Fueling Its Future with Open Innovation," *InnoCentive*, October 23, 2103, www.innocentive.com/blog/2013/10/23/samsung-is-fueling-its-future-with-open-innovation/.
10. See "Victorinox Success!" September 2012, www.jovoto.com/blog/2012/09/success-story-victorinox/; Bastian Unterberg et al., *Crowdstorm: The Future of Ideas, Innovation, and Problem Solving Is Collaboration* (Somerset, NJ: Wiley, 2013), pp. 175–177; and http://victorinox.jovoto.com and www.jovoto.com/clients, accessed September 2014.
11. Guido Jouret, "Inside Cisco's Search for the Next Big Idea," *Harvard Business Review*, September 2009, pp. 43–45; Geoff Livingston, "Real Challenges to Crowdsourcing for Social Good," *Mashable*, October 12, 2010, http://mashable.com/2010/10/12/social-good-crowdsourcing; and www.cisco.com/web/solutions/iprize/index.html, accessed June 2014.
12. See George S. Day, "Is It Real? Can We Win? Is It Worth Doing?" *Harvard Business Review*, December 2007, pp. 110–120.
13. This example is based on Tesla Motors and information obtained from www.teslamotors.com, accessed April 2014. Also see Ryan Bradley, "Full Charge Ahead," *Fortune,* February 4, 2013, pp. 10–13; Leah Hunter, "How Tesla Protects the Romance of Driving while Disrupting the Industry," *Co.Design,* November 7, 2013, www.fastcodesign.com/3021312; and "Electric Car," *Wikipedia,* http://en.wikipedia.org/wiki/Electric_car, accessed September 2014.
14. Information from www.patagonia.com/us/ambassadors and www.carhartt.com/webapp/wcs/stores/servlet/FieldTestingView?langId=-1&storeId=10051&catalogId=10101, accessed September 2014.
15. See Maureen Morrison, "Marketer of the Year: Taco Bell," *Advertising Age,* September 2, 2013, pp. 15–16; Susan Berfield, "Baristas, Patrons Steaming over Starbucks VIA," *Bloomberg BusinessWeek*, November 13, 2009; and Tamara Walsh, "Starbucks Makes a Big Bet on New Product Mix in 2014," *The Motley Fool,* January 8, 2014, www.fool.com/investing/general/2014/01/08/starbucks-makes-a-big-bet-on-new-product-mix-in-20.aspx.
16. Based on information from "How Post Pulled off a Six-Month Cereal Launch," *Advertising Age,* February 10, 2013, p. 12.
17. For information on BehaviorScan Rx, see www.symphonyiri.com/?TabId=159&productid=75, accessed June 2014.
18. See Jack Neff, "P&G Reinvents Laundry with $150 Million Tide Pods Launch," *Advertising Age*, April 26, 2011, www.adage.com/print/227208/; and Sheila Shayon, "Microsoft Unleashes Global Marketing Blitz for Windows 8, New Devices," *BrandChannel*, October 25, 2012, www.brandchannel.com/home/post/2012/10/25/Microsoft-Global-Windows-8-Launch-102512.aspx.
19. Beth Snyder Bulik, "Microsoft Spends $1B on Operating System Launch, But Are Ads Windows-Washing?" *Advertising Age*, October 29, 2012, p. 10; and Mary Jo Foley, "Microsoft to Open Its

Holiday Pop-Up Retail Stores on October 26," *ZDNet*, October 2, 2012, www.zdnet.com/microsoft-to-open-its-holiday-pop-up-retail-stores-on-october-26-7000005113/.

20. See Robert G. Cooper, "Formula for Success," *Marketing Management*, March–April 2006, pp. 19–23; Christoph Fuchs and Martin Schreier, "Customer Empowerment in New Product Development," *Product Innovation Management*, January 2011, pp. 17–32; and Robert Safien, "The Lessons of Innovation," *Fast Company,* March 2012, p. 18.

21. See Chris O'Brien, "How Intuit became a Pioneer of 'Delight,'" *Los Angeles Times,* May 10, 2013; Bob Thompson, "Delight, by Design. Innovation Sets Intuit Apart as a Customer-Centric Leader," *Customer Think,* June 6, 2013, http://customerthink.com/delight_by_design_innovation_sets_intuit_apart_as_customer_centric_leader/; Intuit: Immersive Customer Experience, Michele Marut and Duncan Wannamaker," *Design for Experience Awards,* http://awards.designforexperience.com/gallery/2013/promoting-empathy-for-users/intuit, accessed June 2014; and http://investors.intuit.com/financial-information/annual-reports/default.aspx and intuitlabs.com/innovation.html, accessed September 2014.

22. Based in part on information from Min-Jeong Lee, "Samsung Chases 'Wow' Moment," *Wall Street Journal,* March 12, 2013, http://online.wsj.com/news/articles/SB10001424127887324096404578355781939805000; Max Chafkin, "Samsung: For Elevating Imitation to an Art Form," *Fast Company,* March 2013, p. 108; and information from www.sony.com, www.Apple.com, and www.samsung.com, accessed September 2014.

23. This definition is based on one found in Bryan Lilly and Tammy R. Nelson, "Fads: Segmenting the Fad-Buyer Market," *Journal of Consumer Marketing*, Vol. 20, No. 3, 2003, pp. 252–265.

24. See Katya Kazakina and Robert Johnson, "A Fad's Father Seeks a Sequel," *New York Times*, May 30, 2004, www.nytimes.com; John Schwartz, "The Joy of Silly," *New York Times*, January 20, 2008, p. 5; "Drew Guarini, "11 Surprising Product Fads," *Huffington Post,* August 8, 2012, www.huffingtonpost.com/2012/08/22/product-fads_n_1819710.html#slide=1410262; and www.crazyfads.com, accessed September 2014.

25. Based on information from Stuart Elliott, "3M Says, 'Go Ahead, Make Something of It,'" *New York Times,* January 28, 2013, www.nytimes.com/2013/01/28/business/mutfund/3m-says-go-ahead-make-something-of-it.html?pagewanted=2&tntemail0=y&_r=3&emc=tnt; and "Post-it Brand. Go Ahead," www.youtube.com/watch?v=F1zOJTonK5s, accessed September 2014.

26. Stephanie Clifford, "Go Digitally, Directly to Jail? Classic Toys Learn New Clicks," *New York Times,* February 25, 2012; Anya Kamenetz, "Study: 75% of Kids Under Age 8 Use Mobile Devices," *Fast Company*, October 28, 2013, www.fastcompany.com/3020755/fast-feed/study-75-of-kids-under-age-8-use-mobile-devices; and http://mattelapptivity.com/app-toys-games/hot-wheels/, accessed September 2014.

27. Elaine Wong, "Kellogg Makes Special K a Way of Life," *Adweek*, June 7, 2010, p. 18; and www.kelloggs.com, www.specialk.com, and www.specialk.com/en_us/plans.html, accessed September 2014.

28. For a more comprehensive discussion of marketing strategies over the course of the PLC, see Philip Kotler and Kevin Lane Keller, *Marketing Management*, 14th ed. (Upper Saddle River, NJ: Prentice Hall, 2012), pp. 310–317.

29. Jaclyn Trop, "Toyota Will Pay $1.6 Billion Over Faulty Accelerator Suit," *New York Times*, July 20, 2013, p. 3B.

30. Based on information from "How PepsiCo Dreams Up New Products in China," *Advertising Age,* December 9, 2013, http://adage.com/print/245558; Louise Ho, "PepsiCo's Strategy Wins Market Share," *Global Times,* December 4, 2013, www.globaltimes.cn/content/829870.shtml#.Uu_5Q_ldV8F; Laurie Burkett, "PepsiCo Chips Away at China," *Wall Street Journal*, July 11, 2012, p. B3; and "PepsiCo's Greater China Region: Driving Growth and Innovation," PepsiCo, October 24, 2013, www.pepsico.com/Story/PepsiCos-Greater-China-Region--Driving-Growth-and-Innovation102420131193.html.

31. Information from www.db.com, accessed September 2014.

32. Information from www.interpublic.com and www.mccann.com, accessed September 2014.

33. See "Global Powers of Retailing 2014," http://www2.deloitte.com/content/dam/Deloitte/global/Documents/Consumer-Business/dttl_CB_Global-Powers-of-Retailing-2014.pdf; "Walmart Corporate International," http://corporate.walmart.com/our-story/locations, accessed September 2014; and information from www.carrefour.com, accessed September 2014.

10 Pricing
Understanding and Capturing Customer Value

Chapter Preview

In this chapter, we look at the second major marketing mix tool—pricing. If effective product development, promotion, and distribution sow the seeds of business success, effective pricing is the harvest. Firms successful at creating customer value with the other marketing mix activities must still capture some of this value in the prices they earn. In this chapter, we discuss the importance of pricing, dig into three major pricing strategies, and look at internal and external considerations that affect pricing decisions. In the next chapter, we examine some additional pricing considerations and approaches.

For openers, let's examine pricing at JCPenney. Over the past two decades, Penney's has steadily lost ground to discount and department store rivals and specialty retail chains. To turn things around, the venerable old chain set out to radically reinvent itself. At the core of the risky transformation was a sweeping new pricing strategy—called Fair and Square pricing—that aimed to put "value" back into Penney's price-value equation. The results were disastrous, leaving JCPenney in a desperate struggle to find the right pricing formula. This dramatic story illustrates the challenges of finding a successful pricing strategy.

JCPENNEY: Struggling to Find a Successful Pricing Strategy

In early 2012, JCPenney ran ads showing shoppers screaming in frustration after missing out on limited-time sales events, arduously clipping coupons, or standing in long lines at night to get "blowout" prices. "Enough. Is. Enough." concluded each ad in stark red letters. At JCPenney's Facebook page, consumers were greeted with more messages spoofing promotion-crazy retailers with pitches to "enjoy our biggest and best-ever crazy and exhausting and totally confusing sale."

The "Enough. Is. Enough." ad campaign announced that things would now be different at JCPenney. With what it called "Fair and Square" pricing, Penney's halted coupons, doorbuster deals, and nonstop markdowns on artificially inflated prices. In their place, the chain launched a simplified everyday low pricing scheme with only occasional special promotions. Not only would the new pricing make life easier for promotion-weary customers, JCPenney's promised, but it would also put much-needed money into the company's till.

Over the previous decade, JCPenney had been steadily losing ground to discounters and department store rivals such as Walmart, Target, Kohl's, and Macy's on the one hand, and to nimbler specialty store retailers such as Bed, Bath & Beyond on the other. By 2011, JCPenney's annual sales had bottomed out at $17 billion, half of what they had been only a decade earlier.

Desperate for a turnaround, the 110-year-old retailer hired a new CEO, Ron Johnson, who first cut his retailing teeth at Target and then worked wonders for a decade as head of retail operations at Apple. Johnson announced that JCPenney would undergo a radical $1 billion, four-year transformation, one of the most sweeping retail makeovers in history, designed to radically reinvent the JCPenney customer experience. Penney's began making seismic changes across almost every aspect of its operations and marketing.

For starters, Johnson began putting the "department" back in department stores. By 2015, he announced, each JCPenney store would be reorganized into a collection of 80 to 100 brand stores-within-a-store—a kind of "Main Street" of in-store brand shops spread along wider, less-cluttered aisles and featuring higher quality merchandise. Such operational changes were revolutionary for JCPenney.

But the lynchpin of JCPenney's revitalization was a new "Fair and Square" pricing strategy. As Penney's had fallen

Desperate for a turnaround, JCPenney set out to radically reinvent itself. But its risky new "Fair and Square" pricing strategy failed dismally, leaving the retailer in a desperate struggle to find the right pricing formula. JCPenney's very survival hangs in the balance.

behind rivals in recent years, it had come to rely on deep and frequent discounts to drive sales. When Johnson arrived at JCPenney, the retailer was holding some 590 separate sales each year. Such sales were crushing margins and profits. Almost 75 percent of JCPenney's merchandise was being sold at discounts of 50 percent or more, and less than 1 percent was sold at full price.

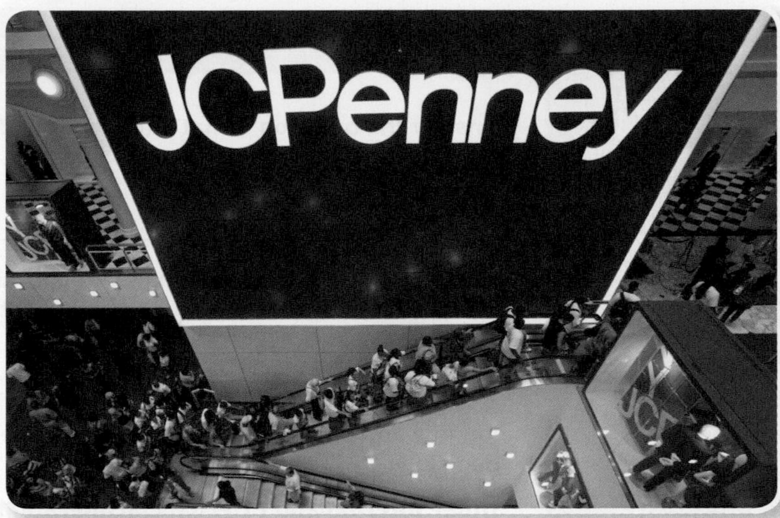

JCPenney faces a serious pricing challenge, one that's all too familiar to many retailers today: It can't live with sale prices, but it can't live without them either.

ASSOCIATED PRESS

JCPenney's new pricing ditched deep discounts and endless rounds of sales and coupons in favor of lower everyday prices. For starters, Penney's cut its regular retail prices by about 40 percent across the board. It then installed a simpler, steadier three-tiered pricing scheme: "Everyday" prices (red sales tags) featured regular lower prices on most merchandise throughout the store. "Month-long value" prices (white tags) applied to limited monthly themed sales events, such as "back-to-school" pricing in August. "Best prices" (blue tags) offered clearance prices on the first and third Fridays of every month.

All three sets of prices employed simplified tags and signage, with prices ending in "0," rather than ".99" or ".50," to suggest good value. And tags listed only one price, rather than making "previously priced at" comparisons. The Fair and Square pricing goal was to offer fair, predictable prices for the value received. JCPenney wanted to convey this message to consumers: Why play the "wait for the rock-bottom price" game when you can get good low prices every day on what you want, when you want it?

"Fair and square" pricing seemed to make sense, and the retail industry waited with anxious anticipation to see how JCPenney's promising transformation strategy would work out. The answer: It was an absolute disaster. In the year following implementation of the new strategy, deal-prone JCPenney regulars, still looking for deep discounts, reacted badly. JCPenney's sales plunged to the lowest levels in 25 years.

The critics piled on, asserting that Johnson should have changed pricing more gradually, allowing more time to implement the stores-within-a-store concept and to reorient core customers. Johnson himself admitted that he'd underestimated how much JCPenney customers valued coupons and sales. As a result, by year's end, Penney's had reversed some of its pricing changes, once again offering regular sales. It even added back "suggested retail price" comparisons to some price tags. And everyday ads were urging customers to check out PCPenney's "unbelievably low prices every day" and to "Compare. Save. Smile."

Despite these reversals, however, the chain remained committed to the new everyday value pricing. Sales focused on only selected items important to driving sales during key events and holidays. JCPenney still relied on many fewer sales than in the old days, and it retained the new, cleaner pricing look. But the moderated pricing strategy failed to mollify Penney's old core customers or to bring in new customers. Sales and profits continued to plunge. By the end of 2012, annual sales had dropped 25 percent to just $13 billion—down a stomach-churning $4 billion in only one year—and losses mounted to a cool $1 billion. JCPenney's stock price fell to $17 a share, less than half its pre-Johnson levels.

Under pressure from shareholders and the JCPenney board of directors, Ron Johnson stepped down as CEO after only a brief two years. Ironically, Penney's reappointed former CEO Mike Ullman, whose policies and performance had led to Johnson replacing him in the first place. Within weeks, JCPenney was running ads apologizing to loyal customers for going astray and asking them to "Come Back to JCPenney." Although it retained some elements of the new strategy, Penney's once again began to feature regular sale prices, discounts, coupons, and many other pre-Fair and Square pricing tactics. By the end of 2013, the return toward business as usual seemed to have stabilized sales. But JCPenney faced a projected loss of $1.5 billion, its biggest ever, and the retailer begun closing underperforming stores and cutting jobs to help stem the losses. The company's stock price slid to a dismal $6 a share.

Moving forward, JCPenney now faces a serious pricing conundrum, one that's all too familiar to many retailers today: It can't live with sale prices, but it can't live without them either. The chain's previous diet of constant deals and deep discounts produced growing losses. However, its attempts to wean customers off endless deals and move to everyday fair pricing produced even more dire results. Its current pricing approach appears to straddle the most recent Fair and Square pricing approach and the old deals-and-discounts strategy. That leaves the vexing question: Can JCPenney succeed—or even survive—using a combination of two failed pricing strategies? As one JCPenney executive stated bluntly: "I think that the consumer is ultimately going to decide that for us."[1]

Objective Outline

Pricing: No matter what the state of the economy, companies should sell value, not price.
magicoven/Shutterstock.com

Companies today face a fierce and fast-changing pricing environment. Value-seeking customers have put increased pricing pressure on many companies. Thanks to tight economic times in recent years, the pricing power of the Internet, and value-driven retailers such as Walmart, today's more frugal consumers are pursuing spend-less strategies. In response, it seems that almost every company has been looking for ways to cut prices.

Yet, cutting prices is often not the best answer. Reducing prices unnecessarily can lead to lost profits and damaging price wars. It can cheapen a brand by signaling to customers that price is more important than the customer value a brand delivers. Instead, in both good economic times and bad, companies should sell value, not price. In some cases, that means selling lesser products at rock-bottom prices. But in most cases, it means persuading customers that paying a higher price for the company's brand is justified by the greater value they gain.

What Is a Price?

In the narrowest sense, **price** is the amount of money charged for a product or a service. More broadly, price is the sum of all the values that customers give up to gain the benefits of having or using a product or service. Historically, price has been the major factor affecting buyer choice. In recent decades, however, nonprice factors have gained increasing importance. Even so, price remains one of the most important elements that determine a firm's market share and profitability.

Price
The amount of money charged for a product or service, or the sum of the values that customers exchange for the benefits of having or using the product or service.

Price is the only element in the marketing mix that produces revenue; all other elements represent costs. Price is also one of the most flexible marketing mix elements. Unlike product features and channel commitments, prices can be changed quickly. At the same time, pricing is the number-one problem facing many marketing executives, and many companies do not handle pricing well. Some managers view pricing as a big headache, preferring instead to focus on other marketing mix elements.

However, smart managers treat pricing as a key strategic tool for creating and capturing customer value. Prices have a direct impact on a firm's bottom line. A small percentage improvement in price can generate a large percentage increase in profitability. More important, as part of a company's overall value proposition, price plays a key role in creating customer value and building customer relationships. So, instead of shying away from pricing, smart marketers are embracing it as an important competitive asset.[2]

Author Comment | Setting the right price is one of the marketer's most difficult tasks. A host of factors come into play. But as the opening story about JCPenney illustrates, finding and implementing the right pricing strategy is critical to success.

Major Pricing Strategies

The price the company charges will fall somewhere between one that is too low to produce a profit and one that is too high to produce any demand. **Figure 10.1** summarizes the major considerations in setting prices. Customer perceptions of the product's value set the ceiling for its price. If customers perceive that the product's price is greater than its value, they will not buy the product. Likewise, product costs set the floor for a product's price. If the company prices the product below its costs, the company's profits will suffer. In setting its price between these two extremes, the company must consider several external and internal factors, including competitors' strategies and prices, the overall marketing strategy and mix, and the nature of the market and demand.

Figure 10.1 suggests three major pricing strategies: customer value-based pricing, cost-based pricing, and competition-based pricing.

Author Comment | Like everything else in marketing, good pricing starts with *customers* and their perceptions of value.

Customer Value-Based Pricing

In the end, the customer will decide whether a product's price is right. Pricing decisions, like other marketing mix decisions, must start with customer value. When customers buy a product, they exchange something of value (the price) to get something of value (the benefits of having or using the product). Effective customer-oriented pricing involves understanding how much value consumers place on the benefits they receive from the product and setting a price that captures that value.

Customer value-based pricing
Setting price based on buyers' perceptions of value rather than on the seller's cost.

Customer value-based pricing uses buyers' perceptions of value as the key to pricing. Value-based pricing means that the marketer cannot design a product and marketing program and then set the price. Price is considered along with all other marketing mix variables *before* the marketing program is set.

Figure 10.2 compares value-based pricing with cost-based pricing. Although costs are an important consideration in setting prices, cost-based pricing is often product driven. The company designs what it considers to be a good product, adds up the costs of making the product, and sets a price that covers costs plus a target profit. Marketing must then convince buyers that the product's value at that price justifies its purchase. If the price turns out to be too high, the company must settle for lower markups or lower sales, both resulting in disappointing profits.

Value-based pricing reverses this process. The company first assesses customer needs and value perceptions. It then sets its target price based on customer perceptions of value. The targeted value and price drive decisions about what costs can be incurred and the resulting product design. As a result, pricing begins with analyzing consumer needs and value perceptions, and the price is set to match perceived value.

FIGURE | 10.1
Considerations in Setting Price

If customers perceive that a product's price is greater than its value, they won't buy it. If the company prices the product below its costs, profits will suffer. Between the two extremes, the "right" pricing strategy is one that delivers both value to the customer and profits to the company.

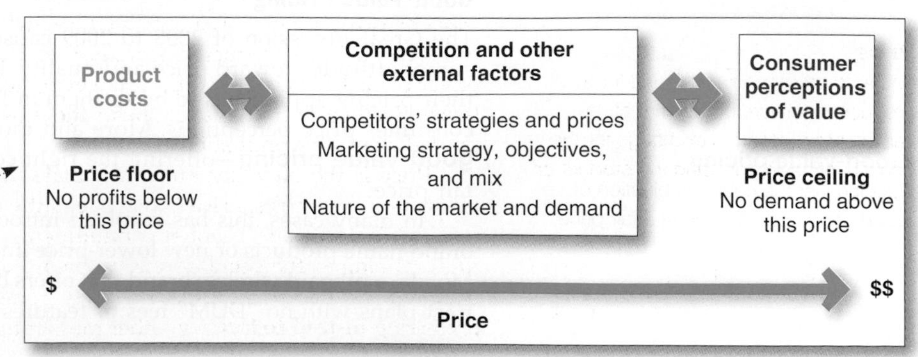

FIGURE | 10.2 Value-Based Pricing versus Cost-Based Pricing

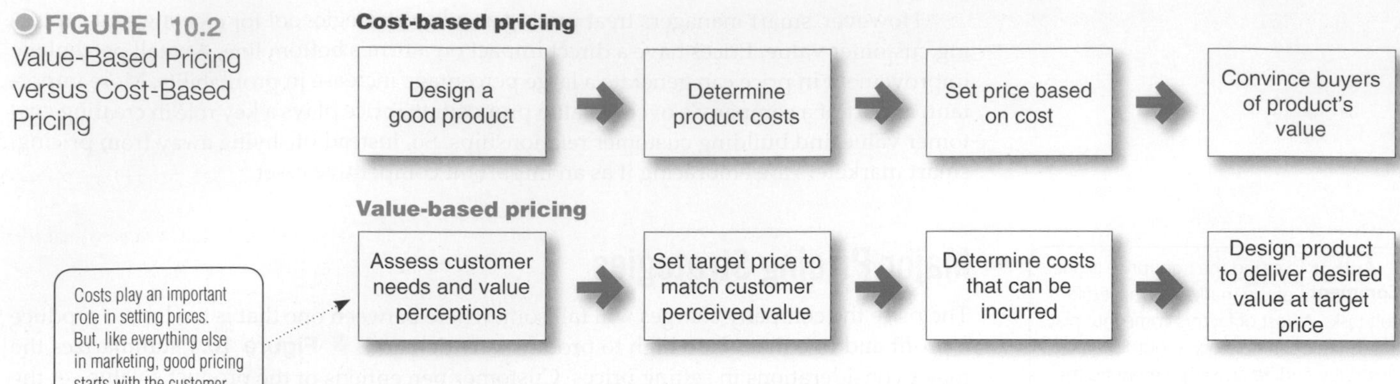

It's important to remember that "good value" is not the same as "low price." For example, some owners consider a luxurious Patek Philippe watch a real bargain, even at eye-popping prices ranging from $20,000 to $500,000:[3]

> Listen up here, because I'm about to tell you why a certain watch costing $20,000, or even $500,000, isn't actually expensive, but is in fact a tremendous value. Every Patek Philippe watch is handmade by Swiss watchmakers from the finest materials and can take more than a year to make. Still not convinced? Beyond keeping precise time, Patek Philippe watches are also good investments. They carry high prices but retain or even increase their value over time. Many models achieve a kind of cult status that makes them the most coveted timepieces on the planet. But more important than just a means of telling time or a good investment is the sentimental and emotional value of possessing a Patek Philippe. These watches are unique possessions steeped in precious memories, making them treasured family assets. According to the company, "The purchase of a Patek Philippe is often related to a personal event—a professional success, a marriage, or the birth of a child—and offering it as a gift is the most eloquent expression of love or affection." A Patek Philippe watch is made not to last just one lifetime, but many. Says one ad: "You never actually own a Patek Philippe, you merely look after it for the next generation." That makes it a real bargain, even at twice the price.

A company will often find it hard to measure the value customers attach to its product. For example, calculating the cost of ingredients in a meal at a fancy restaurant is relatively easy. But assigning value to other measures of satisfaction such as taste, environment, relaxation, conversation, and status is very hard. Such value is subjective; it varies both for different consumers and different situations.

Still, consumers will use these perceived values to evaluate a product's price, so the company must work to measure them. Sometimes, companies ask consumers how much they would pay for a basic product and for each benefit added to the offer. Or a company might conduct experiments to test the perceived value of different product offers. According to an old Russian proverb, there are two fools in every market—one who asks too much and one who asks too little. If the seller charges more than the buyers' perceived value, the company's sales will suffer. If the seller charges less, its products sell very well, but they produce less revenue than they would if they were priced at the level of perceived value.

We now examine two types of value-based pricing: *good-value pricing* and *value-added pricing*.

Good-Value Pricing

The Great Recession of 2008 to 2009 caused a fundamental and lasting shift in consumer attitudes toward price and quality. In response, many companies have changed their pricing approaches to bring them in line with changing economic conditions and consumer price perceptions. More and more, marketers have adopted the strategy of **good-value pricing**—offering the right combination of quality and good service at a fair price.

Good-value pricing
Offering just the right combination of quality and good service at a fair price.

In many cases, this has involved introducing less-expensive versions of established brand name products or new lower-price lines. For example, T-Mobile added GoSmart Mobile, a prepaid wireless brand that offers budget-conscious consumers low-cost, no contract plans with no "DUM" fees or features—as in you get "FreeDUM in wireless" with

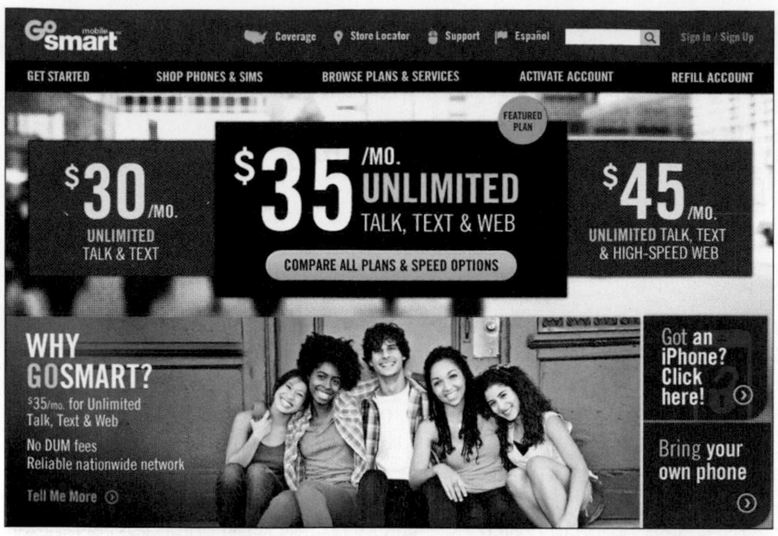

Good-value pricing: In line with thriftier times, T-Mobile added GoSmart mobile, a prepaid wireless brand that offers budget-conscious consumers low-cost, no contract plans that give them "FreeDUM in wireless."

©T-Mobile USA, Inc. Used with permission. (image of people) © Peathegee Inc/Blend Images/Corbis

no DUM contracts, no DUM caps, and no DUM hidden fees. And Walmart is test-marketing an extreme-value store brand called Price First. Priced even lower than the retailer's already-low-priced Great Value brand, Price First invites thrift-conscious customer s to "Choose our lowest-priced brand for all your grocery staples."[4]

In other cases, good-value pricing has involved redesigning existing brands to offer more quality for a given price or the same quality for less. Some companies even succeed by offering less value but at very low prices. For example, the ALDI supermarket chain has established an impressive good-value pricing position by which it gives customers "more 'mmm' for the dollar" (see Real Marketing 10.1).

ALDI practices an important type of good-value pricing at the retail level called *everyday low pricing* (*EDLP*). EDLP involves charging a constant, everyday low price with few or no temporary price discounts. Other retailers such as Costco and Lumber Liquidators practice EDLP. However, the king of EDLP is Walmart, which practically defined the concept. Except for a few sale items every month, Walmart promises everyday low prices on everything it sells. In contrast, *high-low pricing* involves charging higher prices on an everyday basis but running frequent promotions to lower prices temporarily on selected items. Department stores such as Sears and Macy's practice high-low pricing by having frequent sale days, early-bird savings, and bonus earnings for store credit-card holders.

Value-Added Pricing

Value-added pricing
Attaching value-added features and services to differentiate a company's offers and charging higher prices.

Value-based pricing doesn't mean simply charging what customers want to pay or setting low prices to meet competition. Instead, many companies adopt **value-added pricing** strategies. Rather than cutting prices to match competitors, they attach value-added features and services to differentiate their offers and thus support their higher prices. For example, even as frugal consumer spending habits linger, some movie theater chains are *adding* amenities and charging *more* rather than cutting services to maintain lower admission prices:[5]

Some theater chains are turning their multiplexes into smaller, roomier luxury outposts. The new premium theaters offer value-added features such as online reserved seating, high-backed leather executive or rocking chairs with armrests and footrests, the latest in digital sound and super-wide screens, dine-in restaurants serving fine food and drinks, and even valet parking. For example, AMC Theatres (the second-largest American theater chain) operates more than 50 theaters with some kind of enhanced food and beverage amenities, including Fork & Screen (upgraded leather seating, seat-side service, extensive menu including dinner offerings, beer, wine, and cocktails) and Cinema Suites (additional upscale food offerings in addition to premium cocktails and an extensive wine list, seat-side service, red leather reclining chairs, and eight to nine feet of spacing between rows).

So at the Cinema Suites at the AMC Easton 30 with IMAX in Columbus, Ohio, bring on the mango margaritas! For $9 to $15 a ticket (depending on the time and day), moviegoers are treated to reserved seating, a strict 21-and-over-only policy, reclining leather seats, and the opportunity to pay even more to have dinner and drinks brought to their seats. Such theaters are so successful that AMC plans to add more. "Once people experience it," says a company spokesperson, "more often than not they don't want to go anywhere else."

Value-added pricing: Rather than cutting services to maintain lower admission prices, premium theaters such as AMC's Cinema Suites are adding amenities and charging more. "Once people experience it, . . . they don't want to go anywhere else."

Courtesy of AMC Theaters

Real Marketing 10.1

ALDI: Impressively High Quality at Impossibly Low Prices, Every Day

When asked to name the world's largest grocery chains, you'd probably come up with Walmart, the world's largest retailer; and maybe Kroger, the largest U.S. grocery-only merchant. One name that probably wouldn't come to mind is Germany-based discount grocer ALDI. Yet, surprisingly, with more than $73 billion in annual revenues and over 10,000 stores in 17 countries, ALDI is the world's ninth-largest retailer overall and the second-largest grocery-only retailer behind Kroger. What's more, ALDI is taking the United States and other country markets by storm, growing faster than any of its larger rivals.

How does ALDI do it? Its simple formula for success is no secret. In fact, it's almost a cliché: Give customers a basic assortment of good-quality everyday items at everyday-extra low prices. These days, many grocers brag about low prices. But at ALDI, they are an absolute fact. The rapidly expanding chain promises customers "Simply Smarter Shopping," driven by a long list of "ALDI Truths" by which it delivers "impressively high quality at impossibly low prices." (ALDI Truth #1: When deciding between eating well and saving money, always choose both.)

ALDI has redesigned the food shopping experience to reduce costs and give customers prices that it claims are up to 50 percent lower than those of rival supermarkets. To keep costs and prices down, ALDI operates smaller, energy-saving stores (about one-third the size of traditional supermarkets), and each store carries only about 1,400 of the fastest-moving grocery items (the typical supermarket carries about 40,000 items). Almost 95 percent of its items are ALDI store brands. So, ALDI claims, customers are paying for the product itself, not national brand advertising and marketing. Also, ALDI does no promotional pricing or price matching—it just sticks with its efficient everyday very low prices (ALDI Truth #12: We don't match other stores' prices because that would mean raising ours).

In trimming costs and passing savings along to customers, ALDI leaves no stone unturned. Even customers themselves help to keep costs low: They bring their own bags (or purchase them from ALDI for a small charge), bag their own groceries (ALDI provides no baggers), return shopping carts on their own (to get back a 25-cent deposit), and pay with cash or a debit card (no credit cards accepted). But to ALDI fans, the savings make it all worthwhile (ALDI Truth #14: You can't eat frills, so why pay for them?).

Whereas ALDI cuts operating costs to the bone, it doesn't scrimp on quality. With its preponderance of store brands, ALDI exercises complete control over the quality of the products on its shelves, and the chain promises that everything it sells is certifiably fresh and tasty. ALDI Truth #60—We make delicious cost a lot less—makes it clear that the chain promises more than just low prices. ALDI backs this promise with a Double Guarantee on all items: "If for any reason you are not 100-percent satisfied with any product, we will gladly replace the product AND refund your money."

To improve the quality of its assortment, ALDI has progressively added items that aren't usually associated with "discounted" groceries. Beyond the typical canned, boxed, and frozen food basics, ALDI carries fresh meat, baked goods, and fresh produce. It also carries an assortment of regular and periodic specialty goods, such as Mama Cozzi's Pizza Kitchen Meat Trio Focaccia, Appetitos Spinach Artichoke Dip, and All Natural Mango Salsa. ALDI even offers a selection of organic foods. With such items, and with its clean, bright stores, ADLI targets not just low-income customers, but frugal middle-class and upper-middle-class customers as well.

None of this is news to German shoppers, who have loved ALDI for decades. In Germany, the chain operates more than 4,200 stores, accounting for over 28 percent of the market. That might explain why Walmart gave up in Germany just nine years after entering the market. Against competitors like ALDI, Walmart's normally low prices were just too expensive for frugal German consumers.

ALDI's no-frills basic approach isn't for everyone. Whereas some shoppers love the low prices, basic assortments, and simple store atmosphere, others can't imagine life without at least some of the luxuries and amenities offered by rivals. But most people who shop at ALDI quickly become true believers. Testimonials from converts litter the Internet. "I just recently switched to ALDI from a 'premium' grocery store . . . and the savings blow me away!" proclaims one customer. "Shoot, I wish

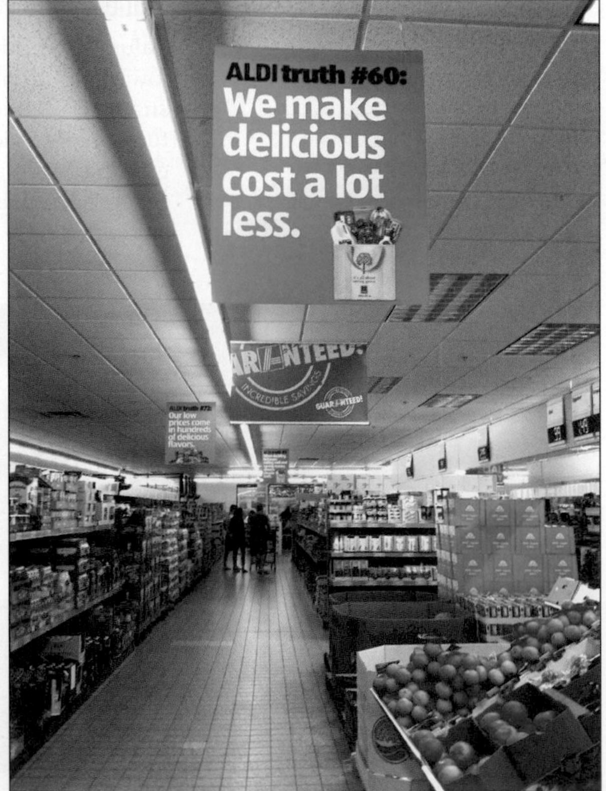

Good-value pricing: ALDI keeps costs low so that it can offer customers "impressively high quality at impossibly low prices" every day.

Keri Miksza

I had some pom-poms, because I am so totally team ALDI!" Says another fervent fan:

> I will probably never grocery shop anywhere else! As a family of three on a very strict budget, I usually scour the sale papers and coupons looking to save. I usually make two or three different stops on my grocery trips and do my shopping every two weeks. We budget $200 a month for groceries and I usually come in right under that amount. Today at ALDI I got everything on my list, plus about 20 extra items not on the list, and my total was only $86! I cannot believe how much I saved! ALDI is now my immediate go-to grocery store!

Many customers also wax enthusiastic about their favorite ALDI products, items they can't live without and can't get anywhere else.

With tradition behind it and its can't-lose operating and marketing model, ALDI plans for rapid U.S. expansion. The company has quickly grown to more than 1,300 stores in 32 states. That's a huge accomplishment compared with, say, British discount chain Tesco, the world's second largest retailer, which exited the U.S. market with heavy losses after only seven years. ALDI still has plenty of room for more growth. It has a $3 billion plan to open 130 U.S. stores a year, expanding by 50 percent to 1,950 stores by 2018. With its proven everyday-extra low-pricing strategy, ALDI will likely accomplish or even exceed that goal. That's good news for the company but also for customers. When ALDI comes to your neighborhood, "Your wallet and taste buds are in for a treat" (ALDI Truth #34).

Sources: Walter Loeb, "Why Aldi and Lidl Have What It Takes to Beat the Best and the Biggest," *Forbes*, October 30, 2013, www.forbes.com/sites/walterloeb/2013/10/30/why-aldi-and-lidl-have-what-it-takes-to-beat-the-best-and-the-biggest/; Leslie Patton, "Aldi Plans to Expand U.S. Store Count by 50% in Next Five Years," *Businessweek*, December 20, 2013, www.businessweek.com/news/2013-12-20/aldi-plans-to-expand-u-dot-s-dot-store-count-by-50-percent-in-next-five-years; "Top 250 Global Powers of Retailing 2014," Deloitte, p. G12, www2.deloitte.com/global/en/pages/consumer-business/articles/global-powers-of-retailing-2014.html; and www.aldi.us, www.aldi.us/en/new-to-aldi/aldi-truths/, and www.aldi.us/en/new-to-aldi/switch-save/, accessed September 2014.

Author Comment | Costs set the floor for price, but the goal isn't always to *minimize* costs. In fact, many firms invest in higher costs so that they can claim higher prices and margins (think back about Patek Philippe watches). The key is to manage the *spread* between costs and prices—how much the company makes for the customer value it delivers.

Cost-Based Pricing

Whereas customer value perceptions set the price ceiling, costs set the floor for the price that the company can charge. **Cost-based pricing** involves setting prices based on the costs of producing, distributing, and selling the product plus a fair rate of return for the company's effort and risk. A company's costs may be an important element in its pricing strategy.

Cost-based pricing
Setting prices based on the costs of producing, distributing, and selling the product plus a fair rate of return for effort and risk.

Some companies, such as Walmart or Southwest Airlines, work to become the *low-cost producers* in their industries. Companies with lower costs can set lower prices that result in smaller margins but greater sales and profits. However, other companies—such as Apple, BMW, and Steinway—intentionally pay higher costs so that they can add value and claim higher prices and margins. For example, it costs more to make a "handcrafted" Steinway piano than a Yamaha production model. But the higher costs result in higher quality, justifying an average $87,000 price. The key is to manage the spread between costs and prices—how much the company makes for the customer value it delivers.

Types of Costs

Fixed costs (overhead)
Costs that do not vary with production or sales level.

Variable costs
Costs that vary directly with the level of production.

Total costs
The sum of the fixed and variable costs for any given level of production.

A company's costs take two forms: fixed and variable. **Fixed costs** (also known as **overhead**) are costs that do not vary with production or sales level. For example, a company must pay each month's bills for rent, heat, interest, and executive salaries regardless of the company's level of output. **Variable costs** vary directly with the level of production. Each PC produced by HP involves a cost of computer chips, wires, plastic, packaging, and other inputs. Although these costs tend to be the same for each unit produced, they are called variable costs because the total varies with the number of units produced. **Total costs** are the sum of the fixed and variable costs for any given level of production. Management wants to charge a price that will at least cover the total production costs at a given level of production.

The company must watch its costs carefully. If it costs the company more than its competitors to produce and sell a similar product, the company will need to charge a higher price or make less profit, putting it at a competitive disadvantage.

Costs at Different Levels of Production

To price wisely, management needs to know how its costs vary with different levels of production. For example, suppose Texas Instruments (TI) built a plant to produce 1,000 calculators per day. **Figure 10.3A** shows the typical short-run average cost curve (SRAC).

FIGURE | 10.3
Cost per Unit at Different Levels of Production per Period

What's the point of all the cost curves in this and the next few figures? Costs are an important factor in setting price, and companies must understand them well!

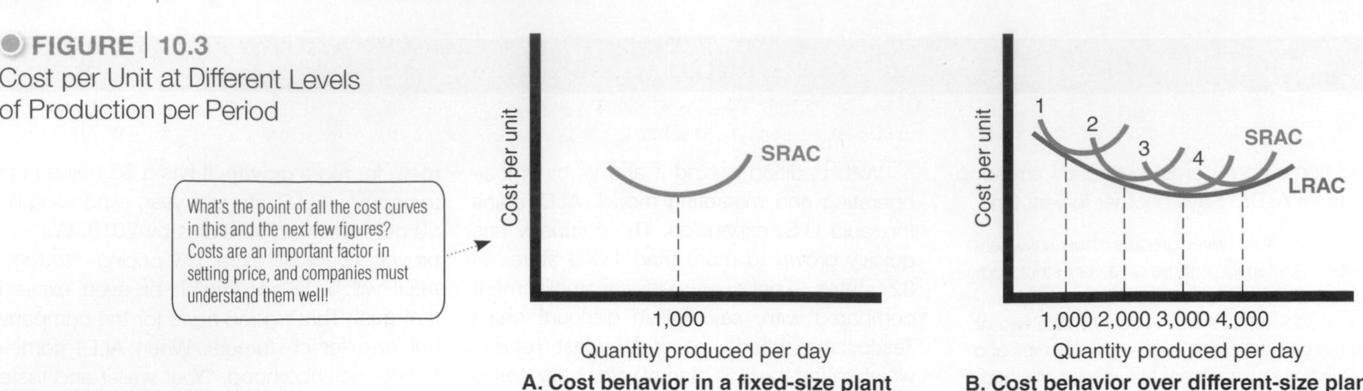

It shows that the cost per calculator is high if TI's factory produces only a few per day. But as production moves up to 1,000 calculators per day, the average cost per unit decreases. This is because fixed costs are spread over more units, with each one bearing a smaller share of the fixed cost. TI can try to produce more than 1,000 calculators per day, but average costs will increase because the plant becomes inefficient. Workers have to wait for machines, the machines break down more often, and workers get in each other's way.

If TI believed it could sell 2,000 calculators a day, it should consider building a larger plant. The plant would use more efficient machinery and work arrangements. Also, the unit cost of producing 2,000 calculators per day would be lower than the unit cost of producing 1,000 units per day, as shown in the long-run average cost (LRAC) curve (**Figure 10.3B**). In fact, a 3,000-capacity plant would be even more efficient, according to Figure 10.3B. But a 4,000-daily production plant would be less efficient because of increasing diseconomies of scale—too many workers to manage, paperwork slowing things down, and so on. Figure 10.3B shows that a 3,000-daily production plant is the best size to build if demand is strong enough to support this level of production.

Costs as a Function of Production Experience

Suppose TI runs a plant that produces 3,000 calculators per day. As TI gains experience in producing calculators, it learns how to do it better. Workers learn shortcuts and become more familiar with their equipment. With practice, the work becomes better organized, and TI finds better equipment and production processes. With higher volume, TI becomes more efficient and gains economies of scale. As a result, the average cost tends to decrease with accumulated production experience. This is shown in **Figure 10.4**.[6] Thus, the average cost of producing the first 100,000 calculators is $10 per calculator. When the company has produced the first 200,000 calculators, the average cost has fallen to $8.50. After its accumulated production experience doubles again to 400,000, the average cost is $7. This drop in the average cost with accumulated production experience is called the **experience curve** (or the **learning curve**).

FIGURE | 10.4
Cost per Unit as a Function of Accumulated Production: The Experience Curve

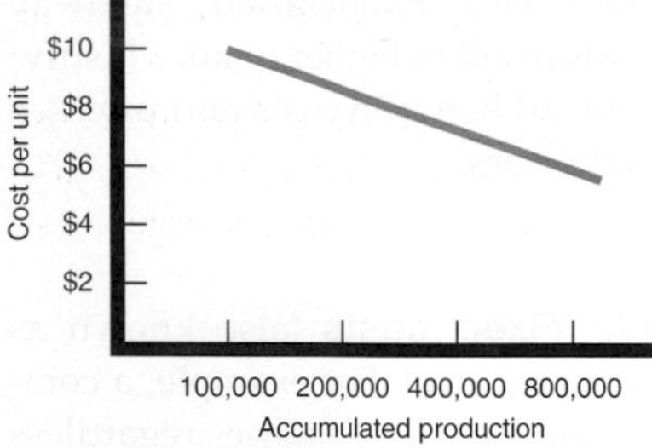

If a downward-sloping experience curve exists, this is highly significant for the company. Not only will the company's unit production cost fall, but it will fall faster if the company makes and sells more during a given time period. But the market has to stand ready to buy the higher output. And to take advantage of the experience curve, TI must get a large market share early in the product's life cycle. This suggests the following pricing strategy: TI should price its calculators low; its sales will then increase, and its costs will decrease through gaining more experience, and then it can lower its prices further.

Some companies have built successful strategies around the experience curve. However, a single-minded focus on reducing costs and exploiting the experience curve will not always work. Experience-curve pricing carries some major risks. The aggressive pricing might give the product a cheap image. The strategy also assumes that competitors are weak and not willing to fight it out by meeting the company's price cuts. Finally, while the company is building volume under one technology, a competitor may find a lower-cost technology that lets it start at prices lower than those of the market leader, which still operates on the old experience curve.

Experience curve (learning curve)
The drop in the average per-unit production cost that comes with accumulated production experience.

Cost-Plus Pricing

The simplest pricing method is **cost-plus pricing** (or **markup pricing**)—adding a standard markup to the cost of the product. Construction companies, for example, submit job bids by estimating the total project cost and adding a standard markup for profit. Lawyers,

Cost-plus pricing (markup pricing)
Adding a standard markup to the cost of the product.

accountants, and other professionals typically price by adding a standard markup to their costs. Some sellers tell their customers they will charge cost plus a specified markup; for example, aerospace companies often price this way to the government.

To illustrate markup pricing, suppose a toaster manufacturer had the following costs and expected sales:

Variable cost	$10
Fixed costs	$300,000
Expected unit sales	50,000

Then the manufacturer's cost per toaster is given by the following:

$$\text{unit cost} = \text{variable cost} + \frac{\text{fixed costs}}{\text{unit sales}} = \$10 + \frac{\$300{,}000}{50{,}000} = \$16$$

Now suppose the manufacturer wants to earn a 20 percent markup on sales. The manufacturer's markup price is given by the following:[7]

$$\text{markup price} = \frac{\text{unit cost}}{(1 - \text{desired return on sales})} = \frac{\$16}{1 - .2} = \$20$$

The manufacturer would charge dealers $20 per toaster and make a profit of $4 per unit. The dealers, in turn, will mark up the toaster. If dealers want to earn 50 percent on the sales price, they will mark up the toaster to $40 ($20 + 50% of $40). This number is equivalent to a *markup on cost* of 100 percent ($20/$20).

Does using standard markups to set prices make sense? Generally, no. Any pricing method that ignores demand and competitor prices is not likely to lead to the best price. Still, markup pricing remains popular for many reasons. First, sellers are more certain about costs than about demand. By tying the price to cost, sellers simplify pricing; they do not need to make frequent adjustments as demand changes. Second, when all firms in the industry use this pricing method, prices tend to be similar, so price competition is minimized. Third, many people feel that cost-plus pricing is fairer to both buyers and sellers. Sellers earn a fair return on their investment but do not take advantage of buyers when buyers' demand becomes great.

Break-Even Analysis and Target Profit Pricing

Break-even pricing (target return pricing)
Setting price to break even on the costs of making and marketing a product, or setting price to make a target return.

Another cost-oriented pricing approach is **break-even pricing** (or a variation called **target return pricing**). The firm tries to determine the price at which it will break even or make the target return it is seeking.

Target return pricing uses the concept of a *break-even chart*, which shows the total cost and total revenue expected at different sales volume levels. **Figure 10.5** shows a break-even chart for the toaster manufacturer discussed here. Fixed costs are $300,000 regardless

FIGURE | 10.5
Break-Even Chart for Determining Target Return Price and Break-Even Volume

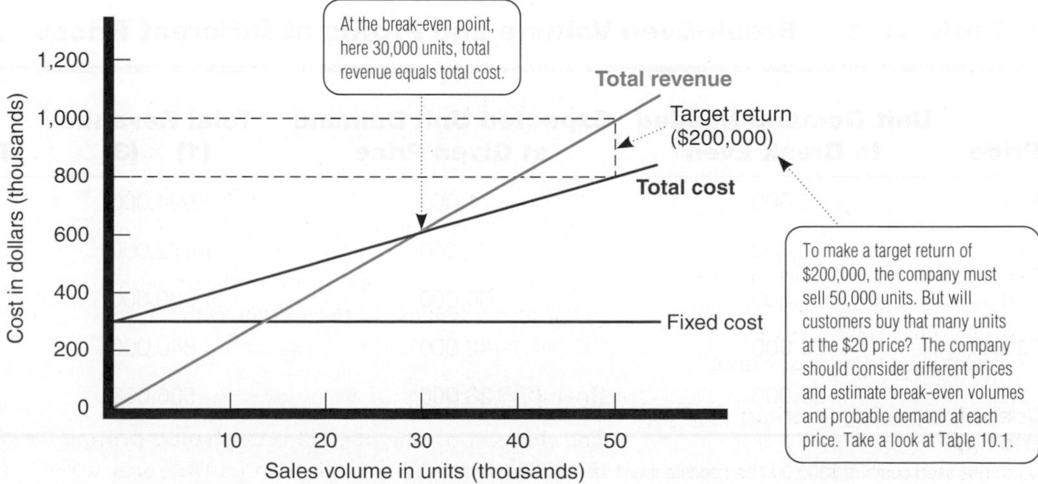
At the break-even point, here 30,000 units, total revenue equals total cost.
Total revenue
Target return ($200,000)
Total cost
Fixed cost
To make a target return of $200,000, the company must sell 50,000 units. But will customers buy that many units at the $20 price? The company should consider different prices and estimate break-even volumes and probable demand at each price. Take a look at Table 10.1.
Cost in dollars (thousands)
1,200
1,000
800
600
400
200
0
10
20
30
40
50
Sales volume in units (thousands)

of sales volume. Variable costs are added to fixed costs to form total costs, which rise with volume. The total revenue curve starts at zero and rises with each unit sold. The slope of the total revenue curve reflects the price of $20 per unit.

The total revenue and total cost curves cross at 30,000 units. This is the *break-even volume*. At $20, the company must sell at least 30,000 units to break even, that is, for total revenue to cover total cost. Break-even volume can be calculated using the following formula:

$$\text{break-even volume} = \frac{\text{fixed cost}}{\text{price} - \text{variable cost}} = \frac{\$300{,}000}{\$20 - \$10} = 30{,}000$$

If the company wants to make a profit, it must sell more than 30,000 units at $20 each. Suppose the toaster manufacturer has invested $1,000,000 in the business and wants to set a price to earn a 20 percent return, or $200,000. In that case, it must sell at least 50,000 units at $20 each. If the company charges a higher price, it will not need to sell as many toasters to achieve its target return. But the market may not buy even this lower volume at the higher price. Much depends on price elasticity and competitors' prices.

The manufacturer should consider different prices and estimate break-even volumes, probable demand, and profits for each. This is done in **Table 10.1**. The table shows that as price increases, the break-even volume drops (column 2). But as price increases, the demand for toasters also decreases (column 3). At the $14 price, because the manufacturer clears only $4 per toaster ($14 less $10 in variable costs), it must sell a very high volume to break even. Even though the low price attracts many buyers, demand still falls below the high break-even point, and the manufacturer loses money. At the other extreme, with a $22 price, the manufacturer clears $12 per toaster and must sell only 25,000 units to break even. But at this high price, consumers buy too few toasters, and profits are negative. The table shows that a price of $18 yields the highest profits. Note that none of the prices produce the manufacturer's target return of $200,000. To achieve this return, the manufacturer will have to search for ways to lower the fixed or variable costs, thus lowering the break-even volume.

Author Comment | In setting prices, the company must also consider competitors' prices. No matter what price it charges—high, low, or in between—the company must be certain to give customers superior value for that price.

Competition-Based Pricing

Competition-based pricing involves setting prices based on competitors' strategies, costs, prices, and market offerings. Consumers will base their judgments of a product's value on the prices that competitors charge for similar products.

Competition-based pricing
Setting prices based on competitors' strategies, prices, costs, and market offerings.

In assessing competitors' pricing strategies, the company should ask several questions. First, how does the company's market offering compare with competitors' offerings in terms of customer value? If consumers perceive that the company's product or service provides greater value, the company can charge a higher price. If consumers perceive less value relative to competing products, the company must either charge a lower price or change customer perceptions to justify a higher price.

Next, how strong are current competitors and what are their current pricing strategies? If the company faces a host of smaller competitors charging high prices relative to the value

Table 10.1 | Break-Even Volume and Profits at Different Prices

Price	Unit Demand Needed to Break Even	Expected Unit Demand at Given Price	Total Revenue (1) × (3)	Total Costs*	Profit (4) – (5)
$14	75,000	71,000	$994,000	$1,010,000	–$16,000
16	50,000	67,000	1,072,000	970,000	102,000
18	37,500	60,000	1,080,000	900,000	180,000
20	30,000	42,000	840,000	720,000	120,000
22	25,000	23,000	506,000	530,000	–$24,000

*Assumes fixed costs of $300,000 and constant unit variable costs of $10.

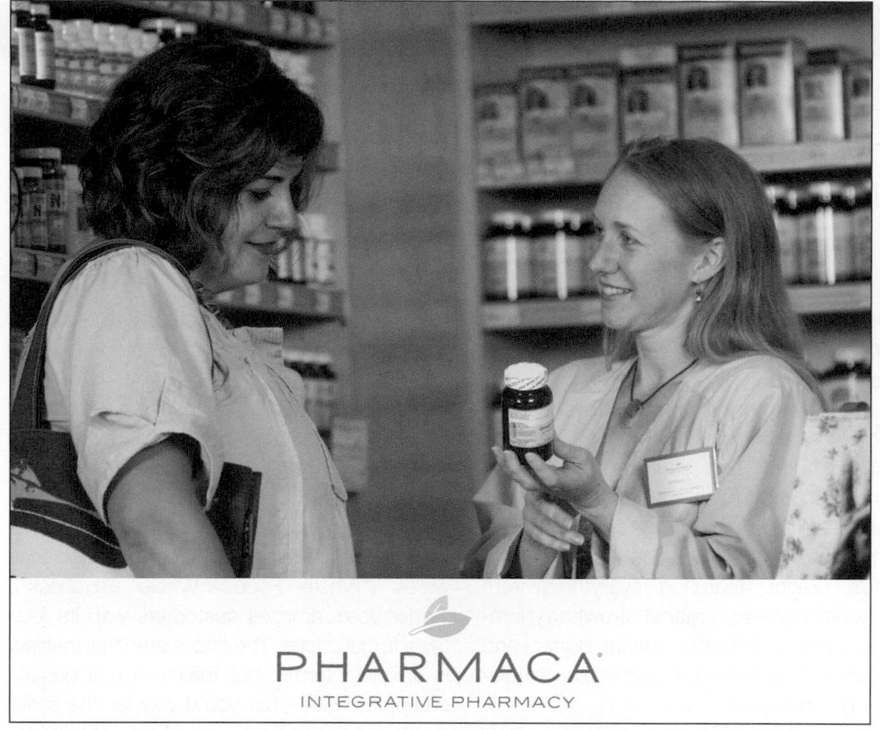

Pricing against larger, lower-price competitors: Pharmaca targets small niches with value-added services at higher prices. It's the relationships with Pharmaca's highly qualified professional staff, not low prices, that bring customers back.

Photo courtesy Pharmaca Integrative Pharmacy

they deliver, it might charge lower prices to drive weaker competitors from the market. If the market is dominated by larger, lower-price competitors, the company may decide to target unserved market niches with value-added products and services at higher prices. For example, consider Pharmaca Integrative Pharmacy:[8]

> In a market saturated with CVSs, Rite-Aids, and Walgreens, pharmacy nicher Pharmaca wants to be much more than a traditional drugstore. Instead, at its two dozen and growing brick-and-mortar stores and its robust online site, Pharmaca positions itself as an upscale total wellness resource center. Sometimes dubbed "the Whole Foods of pharmacies," Pharmaca carries only a limited sprinkling of mainstream consumer brands amidst a much broader assortment of high-end natural, organic, and alternative products, everything from organic chocolates to spa skin care brands to mineral makeup lines.
>
> Like a typical drugstore, Pharmaca fills prescriptions for traditional medicines. But what sets it apart from a Walgreens or CVS is its highly-skilled staff of integrative healthcare professionals—nutritionists, herbalists, aestheticians, homeopaths, and naturopathic doctors—all dressed in lab coats, milling the aisles, and ready to assist customers. Their goal is to get to know customers and help them take charge of their own wellness by treating the whole person—from the skin to the bones to the mind. Pharmaca's high-end products and professional staff mean higher prices; a typical customer receipt is three times greater than in a traditional drugstore. But Pharmaca customers aren't looking for low prices. "When customers develop faith in a practitioner, they become much more loyal to the store," says CEO Mark Panzer. It's those relationships, not low prices, that keep customers coming back.

What principle should guide decisions about what price to charge relative to those of competitors? The answer is simple in concept but often difficult in practice: No matter what price you charge—high, low, or in between—be certain to give customers superior value for that price.

Author Comment | Now that we've looked at the three general pricing strategies—value-, cost-, and competitor-based pricing—let's dig into some of the many other factors that affect pricing decisions.

Other Internal and External Considerations Affecting Price Decisions

Beyond customer value perceptions, costs, and competitor strategies, the company must consider several additional internal and external factors. Internal factors affecting pricing include the company's overall marketing strategy, objectives, and marketing mix, as well as other organizational considerations. External factors include the nature of the market and demand and other environmental factors.

Overall Marketing Strategy, Objectives, and Mix

Price is only one element of the company's broader marketing strategy. So, before setting price, the company must decide on its overall marketing strategy for the product or service. Sometimes, a company's overall strategy is built around its price and value story. For example, grocery retailer Trader Joe's unique price-value positioning has made it one of the nation's fastest-growing, most popular food stores. Trader Joe's understands that success comes not just from what products you offer customers or from the prices you charge. It comes from offering the combination of products, prices, and store operations that produces the greatest customer *value*—what customers get for the prices they pay (see Real Marketing 10.2).

Real Marketing 10.2

Trader Joe's Unique Price-Value Positioning: "Cheap Gourmet"

On an early July morning in Manhattan's Chelsea neighborhood, a large and enthusiastic crowd has already gathered. The occasion: Trader Joe's is opening a new store, and waiting shoppers are sharing their joy over the arrival of the trendy retailer in their neighborhood. Trader Joe's is more than a grocery store, it's a cultural experience. Its shelves are packed with goods that are at the same time both exotic luxuries and affordable. Whether it's organic creamy Valencia peanut butter or cage-free eggs, Thai lime-and-chili cashews, or Belgian butter waffle cookies, you'll find them only at Trader Joe's. Within moments of the new store's opening, the deluge of customers makes it almost impossible to navigate the aisles. They line up 10 deep at checkouts with carts full of Trader Joe's exclusive $2.99 Charles Shaw wine—aka "Two-Buck Chuck"—and an assortment of other exclusive gourmet products at impossibly low prices. All of this has made Trader Joe's one of the nation's hottest retailers.

Trader Joe's isn't really a gourmet food store. Then again, it's not a discount food store either. It's actually a bit of both. Trader Joe's has put its own special twist on the food price-value equation—call it "cheap gourmet." It offers gourmet-caliber, one-of-a-kind products at bargain prices, all served up in a festive, vacation-like atmosphere that makes shopping fun. However you define it, Trader Joe's inventive price-value positioning has earned it an almost cult-like following of devoted customers who love what they get from Trader Joe's for the prices they pay.

Trader Joe's describes itself as an "island paradise" where "value, adventure, and tasty treasures are discovered, every day." Shoppers bustle and buzz amid cedar-plank-lined walls and fake palm trees as a ship's bell rings out occasionally at checkout, alerting them to special announcements. Unfailingly helpful and cheery associates in aloha shirts chat with customers about everything from the weather to menu suggestions for dinner parties. At the Chelsea store opening, workers greeted customers with high-fives and free cookies. Customers don't just shop at Trader Joe's; they experience it.

Shelves bristle with an eclectic assortment of gourmet-quality grocery items. Trader Joe's stocks only a limited assortment of about 4,000 products (compared with the 50,000 items found in a typical grocery store). However, the assortment is uniquely Trader Joe's, including special concoctions of gourmet packaged foods and sauces, ready-to-eat soups, fresh and frozen entrees, snacks, and desserts—all free of artificial colors, flavors, and preservatives. Trader Joe's is a gourmet foodie's delight, featuring everything from kettle corn cookies, organic strawberry lemonade, creamy Valencia peanut butter, and fair trade coffees to kimchi fried rice and triple-ginger ginger snaps.

Another thing that makes Trader Joe's products so special is that you just can't get most of them elsewhere. For example, try finding Ginger Cats cookies or quinoa and black bean tortilla chips at some other store. More than 85 percent of the store's brands are private label goods, sold exclusively by Trader Joe's. If asked, almost any customer can tick off a ready list of Trader Joe's favorites that they just can't live without—a list that quickly grows. People come in intending to buy a few favorites and quickly fill a cart. "They just seem to turn their customers on," says one food industry analyst.

A special store atmosphere, exclusive gourmet products, helpful and attentive associates—this all sounds like a recipe for high prices. Not so at Trader Joe's. Whereas upscale competitors such as Whole Foods Market charge upscale prices to match their wares ("Whole Foods, Whole Paycheck"), Trader Joe's amazes customers with its relatively frugal prices. The prices aren't all that low in absolute terms, but they're a real bargain compared with what you'd pay for the same quality and coolness elsewhere. "At Trader Joe's, we're as much about value as we are about great food," says the company. "So you can afford to be adventurous without breaking the bank."

How does Trader Joe's keep its gourmet prices so low? It carefully shapes nonprice elements to support its overall price-value strategy. For starters, Trader Joe's has lean operations and a near-fanatical focus on saving money. To keep costs down, Trader Joe's typically locates

Trader Joe's unique price-value strategy has earned it an almost cult-like following of devoted customers who love what they get for the prices they pay.

its stores in low-rent, out-of-the-way locations, such as suburban strip malls. Its small store size with small back rooms and limited product assortment result in reduced facilities and inventory costs. Trader Joe's stores save money by eliminating large produce sections and expensive on-site bakery, butcher, deli, and seafood shops. And for its private label brands, Trader Joe's buys directly from suppliers and negotiates hard on price.

Finally, the frugal retailer saves money by spending almost nothing on advertising, and it offers no coupons, discount cards, or special promotions of any kind. Trader Joe's unique combination of quirky products and low prices produces so much word-of-mouth promotion and buying urgency that the company doesn't really need to advertise or price promote. The closest thing to an official promotion is the company's Web site, mobile app, or *The Fearless Flyer* monthly e-newsletter. Trader Joe's most potent promotional weapon is its army of faithful followers. Trader Joe's customers have even started their own fan Web sites, such as www.traderjoesfan.com, where they discuss new products and stores, trade recipes, and swap their favorite Trader Joe's stories.

Thus, building the right price-value formula has made Trader Joe's one of the nation's fastest-growing and most popular food stores. Its more than 415 stores in 32 states now reap annual sales of an estimated $11.4 billion, more than double its sales five years ago. Trader Joe's stores pull in an amazing $1,750 per square foot, more than twice the supermarket industry average. *Consumer Reports* recently ranked Trader Joe's, along with Wegmans, as the best supermarket chain in the nation.

It's all about value and price—what you get for what you pay. Just ask Trader Joe's regular Chrissi Wright, found early one morning browsing her local Trader Joe's in Bend, Oregon.

> Chrissi expects she'll leave Trader Joe's with eight bottles of the popular Charles Shaw wine priced at $2.99 each tucked under her arms. "I love Trader Joe's because they let me eat like a yuppie without taking all my money," says Wright. "Their products are gourmet, often environmentally conscientious and beautiful . . . and, of course, there's Two-Buck Chuck—possibly the greatest innovation of our time."

Sources: Based on information from Emma Sapong, "Trader Joe's Has Them Wowed," *McClatchy-Tribune Business News,* February 17, 2013; "Top 35 Private Label Retailers," *Private Label Buyer*, October 2, 2013, www.privatelabelbuyer.com/articles/87669-top-35-private-label-retailers; Anna Sowa, "Trader Joe's: Why the Hype?" *McClatchy-Tribune Business News,* March 27, 2008; Beth Kowitt, "Inside the Secret World of Trader Joe's," *Fortune*, August 23, 2010, pp. 86–96; Laura Huchzermeyer, "What's So Great About Trader Joe's? Cookie Butter and 3,000 Other Products," *Bizmology,* September 23, 2013, http://bizmology.hoovers.com/2013/09/23/whats-so-great-about-trader-joes-cookie-butter-and-3000-other-private-label-products/; "SN's Top 75 Retailers & Wholesalers 2014," *Supermarket News,* http://supermarketnews.com/trader-joe-s-co-2014; and www.traderjoes.com, accessed September 2014.

If a company has selected its target market and positioning carefully, then its marketing mix strategy, including price, will be fairly straightforward. For example, Amazon positions its Kindle Fire tablet as offering the same (or even more) for less, and prices it at 40 percent less than Apple's iPad and Samsung's Galaxy tablets. It recently began targeting families with young children, positioning the Kindle Fire as the "perfect family tablet," with models priced as low as $159, bundled with Kindle FreeTime, an all-in-one subscription service starting at $2.99 per month that brings together books, games, educational apps, movies, and TV shows for kids ages 3 through 8. Thus, the Kindle pricing strategy is largely determined by decisions on market positioning.

Pricing may play an important role in helping to accomplish company objectives at many levels. A firm can set prices to attract new customers or profitably retain existing ones. It can set prices low to prevent competition from entering the market or set prices at competitors' levels to stabilize the market. It can price to keep the loyalty and support of resellers or avoid government intervention. Prices can be reduced temporarily to create excitement for a brand. Or one product may be priced to help the sales of other products in the company's line.

Price decisions must be coordinated with product design, distribution, and promotion decisions to form a consistent and effective integrated marketing mix program. Decisions made for other marketing mix variables may affect pricing decisions. For example, a decision to position the product on high-performance quality will mean that the seller must charge a higher price to cover higher costs. And producers whose resellers are expected to support and promote their products may have to build larger reseller margins into their prices.

Target costing
Pricing that starts with an ideal selling price, then targets costs that will ensure that the price is met.

Companies often position their products on price and then tailor other marketing mix decisions to the prices they want to charge. Here, price is a crucial product-positioning factor that defines the product's market, competition, and design. Many firms support such price-positioning strategies with a technique called **target costing**. Target costing reverses the usual process of first designing a new product, determining its cost, and then asking, "Can we sell it for that?" Instead, it starts with an ideal selling price based on customer

Nonprice positioning: Luxury smartphone maker Vertu puts very high value into its products and charges sky-high prices to match that value. Average price: nearly $6,000.

Vertu

value considerations and then targets costs that will ensure that the price is met. For example, when Honda initially designed the Honda Fit, it began with a $13,950 starting price point and highway mileage of 33 miles per gallon firmly in mind. It then designed a stylish, peppy little car with costs that allowed it to give target customers those values.

Other companies deemphasize price and use other marketing mix tools to create *nonprice* positions. Often, the best strategy is not to charge the lowest price but rather to differentiate the marketing offer to make it worth a higher price. For example, luxury smartphone maker Vertu puts very high value into its products and charges premium prices to match that value. Vertu phones are made from high-end materials such as titanium and sapphire crystal, and each phone is hand-assembled by a single craftsman in England. Phones come with additional services such as Vertu Concierge, which helps create personal, curated user experiences and recommendations. Vertu phones sell for an average price of $6,000, with top models going for more than $10,000. But target customers recognize Vertu's very high quality and are willing to pay more to get it.[9]

Some marketers even position their products on *high* prices, featuring high prices as part of their product's allure. For example, Grand Marnier offers a $225 bottle of Cuvée du Cent Cinquantenaire cognac that's marketed with the tagline "Hard to find, impossible to pronounce, and prohibitively expensive." And Titus Cycles, a premium bicycle manufacturer, features its high prices in its advertising. One ad humorously shows a man giving his girlfriend a "cubic zirconia" engagement ring so that he can purchase a Titus Vuelo for himself. Suggested retail price: $7,750.00.

Thus, marketers must consider the total marketing strategy and mix when setting prices. But again, even when featuring price, marketers need to remember that customers rarely buy on price alone. Instead, they seek products that give them the best value in terms of benefits received for the prices paid.

Organizational Considerations

Management must decide who within the organization should set prices. Companies handle pricing in a variety of ways. In small companies, prices are often set by top management rather than by the marketing or sales departments. In large companies, pricing is typically handled by divisional or product managers. In industrial markets, salespeople may be allowed to negotiate with customers within certain price ranges. Even so, top management sets the pricing objectives and policies, and it often approves the prices proposed by lower-level management or salespeople.

In industries in which pricing is a key factor (airlines, aerospace, steel, railroads, oil companies), companies often have pricing departments to set the best prices or help others set them. These departments report to the marketing department or top management. Others who have an influence on pricing include sales managers, production managers, finance managers, and accountants.

The Market and Demand

As noted earlier, good pricing starts with an understanding of how customers' perceptions of value affect the prices they are willing to pay. Both consumer and industrial buyers balance the price of a product or service against the benefits of owning it. Thus, before setting prices, the marketer must understand the relationship between price and demand for the company's product. In this section, we take a deeper look at the price–demand relationship and how it varies for different types of markets. We then discuss methods for analyzing the price–demand relationship.

Pricing in Different Types of Markets

The seller's pricing freedom varies with different types of markets. Economists recognize four types of markets, each presenting a different pricing challenge.

Under *pure competition*, the market consists of many buyers and sellers trading in a uniform commodity, such as wheat, copper, or financial securities. No single buyer or seller has much effect on the going market price. In a purely competitive market, marketing research, product development, pricing, advertising, and sales promotion play little or no role. Thus, sellers in these markets do not spend much time on marketing strategy.

Under *monopolistic competition*, the market consists of many buyers and sellers trading over a range of prices rather than a single market price. A range of prices occurs because sellers can differentiate their offers to buyers. Because there are many competitors, each firm is less affected by competitors' pricing strategies than in oligopolistic markets. Sellers try to develop differentiated offers for different customer segments and, in addition to price, freely use branding, advertising, and personal selling to set their offers apart. ● Thus, Honda sets its Odyssey minivan apart through strong branding and advertising, reducing the impact of price. Its tongue-in-cheek "Van of Your Dreams" advertisements tell parents "the new Odyssey has everything one would dream about in a van, if one had dreams about vans." Beyond the standard utility features you'd expect in a van, Honda tells them, you'll also find yourself surrounded by a dazzling array of technology, a marvel of ingenuity, even a built-in vacuum.

● **Pricing in monopolistic competition: Honda sets its Odyssey minivan apart through strong branding and advertising, reducing the impact of price. Its tongue-in-cheek "Van of Your Dreams" ads tell parents "the new Odyssey has everything one would dream about in a van, if one had dreams about vans."**

Print advertisement provided courtesy of American Honda Motor Co., Inc.

Under *oligopolistic competition*, the market consists of only a few large sellers. For example, only four companies—Verizon, AT&T, Sprint, and T-Mobile—control more than 90 percent of the U.S. wireless service provider market. Because there are few sellers, each seller is alert and responsive to competitors' pricing strategies and marketing moves. In a *pure monopoly*, the market is dominated by one seller. The seller may be a government monopoly (the U.S. Postal Service), a private regulated monopoly (a power company), or a private unregulated monopoly (De Beers and diamonds). Pricing is handled differently in each case.

Analyzing the Price–Demand Relationship

Demand curve
A curve that shows the number of units the market will buy in a given time period, at different prices that might be charged.

Each price the company might charge will lead to a different level of demand. The relationship between the price charged and the resulting demand level is shown in the **demand curve** in ● **Figure 10.6**. The demand curve shows the number of units the market will buy in a given time period at different prices that might be charged. In the normal case, demand and price are inversely related—that is, the higher the price, the lower the demand. Thus, the company would sell less if it raised its price from P_1 to P_2. In short, consumers with limited budgets probably will buy less of something if its price is too high.

Understanding a brand's price–demand curve is crucial to good pricing decisions. ConAgra Foods learned this lesson when pricing its Banquet frozen dinners:[10]

> When ConAgra tried to cover higher commodity costs by raising the list price of Banquet dinners from $1 to $1.25, consumers turned up their noses to the higher price. Sales dropped, forcing ConAgra to sell off excess dinners at discount prices. It turns out that "the key component

FIGURE | 10.6
Demand Curves

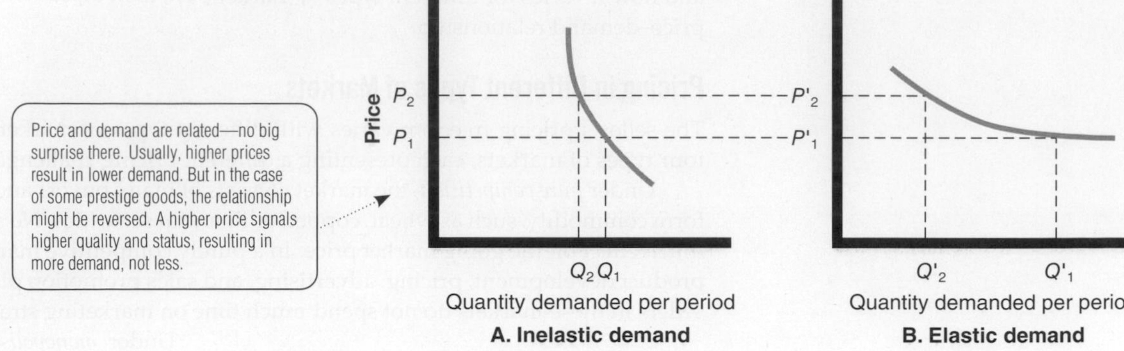
Price and demand are related—no big surprise there. Usually, higher prices result in lower demand. But in the case of some prestige goods, the relationship might be reversed. A higher price signals higher quality and status, resulting in more demand, not less.
Price
P_2
P_1
P'_2
P'_1
Q_2 Q_1
Quantity demanded per period
A. Inelastic demand
Q'_2
Q'_1
Quantity demanded per period
B. Elastic demand

for Banquet dinners—the key attribute—is you've got to be at $1," says ConAgra's CEO Gary Rodkin. "Everything else pales in comparison to that." Banquet dinner prices are now back to a buck a dinner. To make money at that price, ConAgra has done a better job of managing costs by shrinking portions and substituting less expensive ingredients for costlier ones. More than just Banquet dinners, ConAgra prices all of its frozen and canned products at under $1 per serving. Consumers are responding well to the brand's efforts to keep prices down. After all, where else can you find dinner for $1?

Most companies try to measure their demand curves by estimating demand at different prices. The type of market makes a difference. In a monopoly, the demand curve shows the total market demand resulting from different prices. If the company faces competition, its demand at different prices will depend on whether competitors' prices stay constant or change with the company's own prices.

Price Elasticity of Demand

Price elasticity
A measure of the sensitivity of demand to changes in price.

Marketers also need to know **price elasticity**—how responsive demand will be to a change in price. If demand hardly changes with a small change in price, we say demand is *inelastic*. If demand changes greatly, we say the demand is *elastic*.

If demand is elastic rather than inelastic, sellers will consider lowering their prices. A lower price will produce more total revenue. This practice makes sense as long as the extra costs of producing and selling more do not exceed the extra revenue. At the same time, most firms want to avoid pricing that turns their products into commodities. In recent years, forces such as deregulation and the instant price comparisons afforded by the Internet and other technologies have increased consumer price sensitivity, turning products ranging from telephones and computers to new automobiles into commodities in some consumers' eyes.

The Economy

Economic conditions can have a strong impact on the firm's pricing strategies. Economic factors such as a boom or recession, inflation, and interest rates affect pricing decisions because they affect consumer spending, consumer perceptions of the product's price and value, and the company's costs of producing and selling a product.

In the aftermath of the Great Recession of 2008 to 2009, many consumers rethought the price–value equation. They tightened their belts and become more value conscious. Consumers have continued their thriftier ways well beyond the economic recovery. As a result, many marketers have increased their emphasis on value-for-the-money pricing strategies.

The most obvious response to the new economic realities is to cut prices and offer discounts. Thousands of companies have done just that. Lower prices make products more affordable and help spur short-term sales. However, such price cuts can have undesirable long-term consequences. Lower prices mean lower margins. Deep discounts may cheapen a brand in consumers' eyes. And once a company cuts prices, it's difficult to raise them again when the economy recovers.

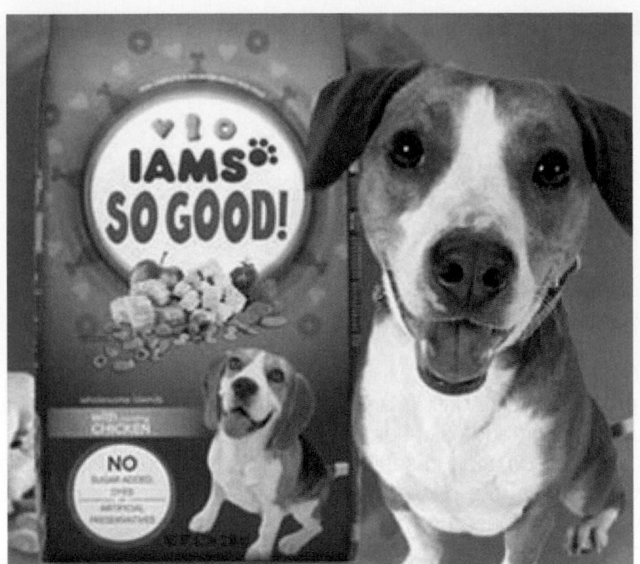

● **Pricing and the economy: In line with tighter consumer budgets and thriftier spending habits, P&G launched Iams So Good dog food, a line designed as a "more accessible" addition to its premium Iams brand.**

The Procter & Gamble Company

Rather than cutting prices, many companies have instead shifted their marketing focus or added more affordable lines to their product mixes. For example, in line with tighter consumer budgets and thriftier spending habits, P&G has added lower-price versions of its premium brands to make them more affordable. It has introduced "Basic" versions of its Bounty and Charmin brands that sell for less. It brought back its Vidal Sassoon Pro Series hair products line as an affordable alternative to the company's higher-priced Pantene brand. ● And P&G recently launched Iams So Good dog food, a line designed as a "more accessible" addition to its premium Iams brand. Making Iams "more accessible" is "a big move for us," says a P&G marketing executive. In these thriftier times, "we realize a lot of our brands need to 'tier down' to appeal to more consumers." Iams So Good is positioned as a "100 percent wholesome" product without added sugar, dyes, and artificial ingredients. The brand's lower prices are conveyed mostly through store displays and packaging.[11]

Other companies are holding their price positions but redefining the "value" in their value propositions. Consider upscale grocery retailer Whole Foods Market:[12]

> Whole Foods Market, the upscale grocer known for its pricy organic products, now finds itself fending off swarms of new organic rivals—from natural foods stores to traditional supermarkets—all competing for today's more thrift-minded customers. In response, Whole Foods has subtly increased its emphasis on affordable options and adopted some of the selling tactics used by lower-price competitors. For example, in many stores, Whole Foods has added more conventional fruits and vegetables at lower prices than organic offerings. And alongside grass-fed beef in some markets, customers might find items such as frozen meatballs and vacuum-packed fish fillets. The retailer's *The Whole Deal* in-store and online value guide gives customers coupons and deals, budget-friendly recipes, and money-saving tips. Other tactics include one-day sales on selected items, and even "flash" sales promoted on Facebook and [T]witter that last only a few hours.
>
> At the same time, however, Whole Foods Market is reinforcing its core up-market positioning by convincing shoppers that, for what you get, Whole Foods's regular products and prices offer good value as well. When it comes to quality food, price isn't everything. The upscale retailer has even assigned workers to serve as "value tour guides" to escort shoppers around stores and point out the value in both sale and regular items. As one tour guide notes, "Value means getting a good exchange for your money." As a result of subtle shifts in its value strategy, Whole Foods Market is meeting the challenges of thriftier times in a way that preserves all the things that have made it special to customers through the years.

Remember, even in tough economic times, consumers do not buy based on prices alone. They balance the price they pay against the value they receive. For example, despite selling its shoes for as much as $150 a pair, Nike commands the highest consumer loyalty of any brand in the footwear segment. Customers perceive the value of Nike's products and the Nike ownership experience to be well worth the price. Thus, no matter what price they charge—low or high—companies need to offer great *value for the money*.

Other External Factors

Beyond the market and the economy, the company must consider several other factors in its external environment when setting prices. It must know what impact its prices will have on other parties in its environment. How will *resellers* react to various prices? The company should set prices that give resellers a fair profit, encourage their support, and help them to sell the product effectively. The *government* is another important external influence on pricing decisions. Finally, *social concerns* may need to be taken into account. In setting prices, a company's short-term sales, market share, and profit goals may need to be tempered by broader societal considerations. We will examine public policy issues in pricing in Chapter 11.

10 Reviewing the Concepts

OBJECTIVES REVIEW AND KEY TERMS

Objectives Review

Companies today face a fierce and fast-changing pricing environment. Firms successful at creating customer value with the other marketing mix activities must still capture some of this value in the prices they earn. This chapter examines the importance of pricing, general pricing strategies, and the internal and external considerations that affect pricing decisions.

OBJECTIVE 1 **Answer the question "What is a price?" and discuss the importance of pricing in today's fast-changing environment.** *(pp 324–325)*

Price can be defined narrowly as the amount of money charged for a product or service. Or it can be defined more broadly as the sum of the values that consumers exchange for the benefits of having and using the product or service. The pricing challenge is to find the price that will let the company make a fair profit by getting paid for the customer value it creates.

Despite the increased role of nonprice factors in the modern marketing process, price remains an important element in the marketing mix. It is the only marketing mix element that produces revenue; all other elements represent costs. More important, as a part of a company's overall value proposition, price plays a key role in creating customer value and building customer relationships. Smart managers treat pricing as a key strategic tool for creating and capturing customer value.

OBJECTIVE 2 **Identify the three major pricing strategies and discuss the importance of understanding customer value perceptions, company costs, and competitor strategies when setting prices.** *(pp 325–333)*

Companies can choose from three major pricing strategies: customer value-based pricing, cost-based pricing, and competition-based pricing. *Customer value-based pricing* uses buyers' perceptions of value as the basis for setting price. Good pricing begins with a complete understanding of the value that a product or service creates for customers and setting a price that captures that value. Customer perceptions of the product's value set the ceiling for prices. If customers perceive that a product's price is greater than its value, they will not buy the product.

Companies can pursue either of two types of value-based pricing. *Good-value pricing* involves offering just the right combination of quality and good service at a fair price. EDLP is an example of this strategy. *Value-added pricing* involves attaching value-added features and services to differentiate the company's offers and support charging higher prices.

Cost-based pricing involves setting prices based on the costs for producing, distributing, and selling products plus a fair rate of return for effort and risk. Company and product costs are an important consideration in setting prices. Whereas customer value perceptions set the price ceiling, costs set the floor for pricing. However, cost-based pricing is product driven rather than customer driven. The company designs what it considers to be a good product and sets a price that covers costs plus a target profit. If the price turns out to be too high, the company must settle for lower markups or lower sales, both resulting in disappointing profits. If the company prices the product below its costs, its profits will also suffer. Cost-based pricing approaches include *cost-plus pricing* and *break-even pricing* (or target profit pricing).

Competition-based pricing involves setting prices based on competitors' strategies, costs, prices, and market offerings. Consumers base their judgments of a product's value on the prices that competitors charge for similar products. If consumers perceive that the company's product or service provides greater value, the company can charge a higher price. If consumers perceive less value relative to competing products, the company must either charge a lower price or change customer perceptions to justify a higher price.

OBJECTIVE 3 **Identify and define the other important external and internal factors affecting a firm's pricing decisions.** *(pp 333–339)*

Other *internal* factors that influence pricing decisions include the company's overall marketing strategy, objectives, and marketing mix, as well as organizational considerations. Price is only one element of the company's broader marketing strategy. If the company has selected its target market and positioning carefully, then its marketing mix strategy, including price, will be fairly straightforward. Common pricing objectives might include customer retention and building profitable customer relationships, preventing competition, supporting resellers and gaining their support, or avoiding government intervention. Price decisions must be coordinated with product design, distribution, and promotion decisions to form a consistent and effective marketing program. Finally, in order to coordinate pricing goals and decisions, management must decide who within the organization is responsible for setting price.

Other *external* pricing considerations include the nature of the market and demand and environmental factors such as the economy, reseller needs, and government actions. Ultimately, the customer decides whether the company has set the right price. The customer weighs the price against the perceived values of using the product—if the price exceeds the sum of the values, consumers will not buy. So the company must understand such concepts as demand curves (the price–demand relationship) and price elasticity (consumer sensitivity to prices).

Economic conditions can have a major impact on pricing decisions. The Great Recession caused consumers to rethink the price–value equation, and consumers have continued their thriftier ways well beyond the economic recovery. Marketers have responded by increasing their emphasis on value-for-the-money pricing strategies. No matter what the economic times, however, consumers do not buy based on prices alone. Thus, no matter what price they charge—low or high—companies need to offer superior value for the money.

MyMarketingLab

Go to **mymktlab.com** to complete the problems marked with this icon ✪.

Key Terms

OBJECTIVE 1

Price (p 324)

OBJECTIVE 2

Customer value-based pricing (p 325)
Good-value pricing (p 326)
Value-added pricing (p 327)
Cost-based pricing (p 329)
Fixed costs (overhead) (p 329)
Variable costs (p 329)
Total costs (p 329)
Experience curve (learning curve) (p 330)
Cost-plus pricing (markup pricing) (p 330)
Break-even pricing (target return pricing) (p 331)
Competition-based pricing (p 332)

OBJECTIVE 3

Target costing (p 335)
Demand curve (p 337)
Price elasticity (p 338)

DISCUSSION AND CRITICAL THINKING

Discussion Questions

10-1 How would you explain the term *pricing challenge?* (AACSB: Communication)

✪ **10-2** Name and describe the types of costs marketers must consider when setting prices. Describe the types of cost-based pricing and the methods of implementing each. (AACSB: Communication)

10-3 List common pricing objectives. Also, identify the various factors that price decisions must be coordinated with. (AACSB: Communication)

✪ **10-4** Name and describe the four types of markets recognized by economists and discuss the pricing challenges posed by each. (AACSB: Communication)

✪ **10-5** What other issues beyond the market and the economy must marketers consider when setting prices? (AACSB: Communication)

Critical Thinking Exercises

✪ **10-6** If you've ever traveled to another country, such as Germany, you may have noticed that the price on a product is the total amount you actually pay when you checkout. That is, no sales tax is added to the purchase price at the checkout as it is in the United States. That is because many countries impose a value added tax (VAT). In a small group, research value added taxes and debate whether or not such taxes benefit consumers. Do marketers support or dislike these types of taxes? (AACSB: Communication; Reflective Thinking)

10-7 In a small group, discuss your perceptions of value and how much you are willing to pay for the following products: automobiles, frozen dinners, jeans, and athletic shoes. Are there differences among members of your group? Explain why those differences exist. Discuss some examples of brands of these products that are positioned to deliver different value to consumers. (AACSB: Communication; Reflective Thinking)

10-8 What is the Consumer Price Index (CPI)? Select one of the reports available at www.bls.gov/cpi/home.htm and create a presentation on price changes over the past two years. Discuss reasons for that change. (AACSB: Communication; Use of IT; Reflective Thinking)

MINICASES AND APPLICATIONS

Online, Mobile, and Social Media Marketing Sold Out

Even before tickets went on general sale for the Rugby World Cup 2015, tickets were being offered on the secondary market for up to $14,000 for a $200 ticket. This equates to around 44 times the face value of the ticket. The 1 million general sale tickets were later offered for sale by ballot. The overpriced tickets were thought to have been legitimately secured hospitality packages bought by an individual or company in the hope that a big profit could be made them. At the same time, tickets for the final match of the sports competition were being offered at around $7,000 each. Although there is no suggestion that StubHub or Viagogo, the two resale sites in this case, had done anything illegal in hosting a third-party sale, it does illustrate the fact that within minutes of an event's tickets being available online, they might be sold out. In many cases, tickets are being offered even before the tickets are officially on sale, and at inflated prices. The ticket resellers need to be fairly confident that they can secure the tickets. This is usually done with the help of specially programmed software that they use to ensure their ticket orders get to the front of the queue, making a huge profit for them.

10-9 Is there a ticket resale market active in your own country? How does ticketing work? Are tickets bought directly or via agents and brokers? Write a report on the ticketing industry in your country. (AACSB: Communication; Use of IT)

10-10 Inflated ticket prices can reflect very badly on the sport, event, or celebrity, even though the activities of resellers have nothing to do with them. Discuss how resellers could be cut out of the market. (AACSB: Communication; Use of IT)

Marketing Ethics Psychology of Mobile Payments

Consumers love to play games on their mobile devices, and Japanese consumers seem to be the most passionate. Mobile game publishers in Japan have mastered the art of getting as much revenue as possible from players—some earning more than $4 million per day. The makers of *Puzzle & Dragons* have seemingly cracked the revenue code by using the psychology of mobile payments to squeeze more revenue from players by encouraging them to play longer. One *Puzzle & Dragons* secret was to issue its own virtual currency, called magic stones, so consumers don't feel like they are spending real money for chances to enhance play. Then, the game offers a little reward at the end with a reminder of what is lost if the player doesn't take the offer. Limited-time sales offer monsters to use in battle for just a few magic stones, and if players run out of space, the game reminds them that they will lose their monsters if they don't purchase more space. All the while, mathematicians and statisticians work behind the scenes to track game play and make it easier or more challenging to keep players engaged and spending. One expert called *Puzzle & Dragons* "truly diabolical" in convincing players to pay and play more. These and other game producers' tactics have propelled Japan's game revenue alone to exceed revenue from all apps in the United States.

10-11 Is it ethical for game producers to use game playing data to encourage consumers to spend more? Explain why or why not. (AACSB: Communication; Ethical Reasoning)

10-12 Is this similar to the "freemium" model used by many U.S. game producers? Explain this model and discuss examples of games that use this model. (AACSB: Communication; Reflective Thinking; Ethical Reasoning)

Marketing by the Numbers Pricey Sheets

Many luxury sheets cost less than $200 to make but sell for more than $500 in retail stores. Some cost even more—consumers pay almost $3,000 for Frett'e "Tangeri Pizzo" king-size luxury linens. The creators of a new brand of luxury linens, called Boll & Branch, have entered this market and are determining the price at which to sell their sheets directly to consumers online. They want to price their sheets lower than most brands but still want to earn an adequate margin on sales. The sheets come in a luxurious box that can be reused to store lingerie, jewelry, or other keepsakes. The Boll & Branch brand touts fair trade practices when sourcing its high-grade long-staple organic cotton from India. Given the cost information below, refer to Appendix 2: Marketing by the Numbers to answer the following questions.

	Cost/King-size Set
Raw Cotton	$28.00
Spinning/Weaving/Dyeing	$12.00
Cut/Sew/Finishing	$10.00
Material Transportation	$ 3.00
Factory Fee	$16.00
Inspection and Import Fees	$14.00
Ocean Freight/Insurance	$ 5.00
Warehousing	$ 8.00
Packaging	$15.00
Promotion	$30.00
Customer Shipping	$15.00

10-13 Given the cost per king-size sheet set above, and assuming the manufacturer has total fixed costs of $500,000 and estimates first year sales will be 50,000 sets, determine the price to consumers if the company desires a 40 percent margin on sales. (AACSB: Communication; Analytical Reasoning)

10-14 If the company decides to sell through retailers instead of directly to consumers online, to maintain the consumer price you calculated in the previous question, at what price must it sell the product to a wholesaler who then sells it to retailers? Assume wholesalers desire a 10 percent margin and retailers get a 20 percent margin, both based on their respective selling prices. (AACSB: Communication; Analytical Reasoning)

Video Case Smashburger

Hamburgers are America's favorite food. Consumers spend more than $100 billion on the beef sandwiches every year. But despite America's infatuation with burgers, there is often considerable dissatisfaction among consumers based on hamburger quality and value. Many customers just aren't happy with what is served up at market-leading fast-food outlets. They want a better burger, and they won't hesitate to pay a higher price to get one. Enter Smashburger. Started just a few years ago in Denver, Colorado, Smashburger is now a rapidly expanding nationwide chain. And all this growth started during a severe economic downturn despite Smashburger's average lunch check of $8. Many customers pay as much as $10 or $12 for a burger, fries, and shake. The Smashburger video shows how this small start-up employed pricing strategy to pull off a seemingly impossible challenge. After viewing the video featuring Smashburger, answer the following questions:

10-15 Discuss the three major pricing strategies in relation to Smashburger. Which of these three do you think is the company's core strategic strategy?

10-16 What effect does Smashburger's premium price have on consumer perceptions? How did a restaurant with a premium-priced product and little track record take off during a recession?

10-17 Is Smashburger's success based on novelty alone or will it continue to succeed?

Company Case Cath Kidston: Nostalgic Fantasy That Creates Value for Consumers

This case study examines the pricing strategy of Cath Kidston, a UK-based company that sells furnishings, home and personal accessories, and clothes, operating mainly in the UK, Europe, and Asia regions.

How much are you willing to pay for a key ring? The market price charges just a bit more than $1. But would you pay $2 for a comparable product? How about $7? A low-price strategy is often used by companies if their products are not well differentiated. Although a low-price strategy might seem attractive, especially in an economic downturn, some companies are focusing on creating value for customers and adopting customer-value-added pricing strategy. Cath Kidston Ltd is one UK-based company which understands that sometimes it pays to charge more.

Cath Kidston's key rings sell for roughly $7 to $10, whereas the market price charges less than a third of that. To understand how Cath Kidston has succeeded with this pricing strategy, let's look at what makes the brand so special. The cheery colors and fun patterns Cath Kidston created allows it not to focus on price-sensitive market segments but instead lure customers with a value-added pricing strategy. It is important for a brand to create something that people respond to with their hearts, which is a sure-fire way to breed success for a brand. Cath Kidston is a brand that is confident in its design style and fun in its character.

From Humble Beginnings

Cath Kidston Ltd was founded in 1993 when designer Cath Kidston opened a tiny shop in London's Holland Park with a $23,800 investment in her business, selling towels, vintage fabrics and wallpaper, and brightly painted "junk" furniture she remembered fondly from her childhood. Cath Kidston's clever reworking of traditional English country style made her tiny shop soon become a cult success. Today, the brand carries a wide product range, everything from furnishings, crockery, cutlery, cloths, toys, china, bed linen, and bags, to women's and children's wear and accessories, charging price premiums that fans are gladly paying.

In 2012, Cath Kidston had 57 shops and concessions in the UK, 2 in Ireland, 27 in Japan, 7 in South Korea, 3 in Thailand, and 1 in Taiwan. The business is also driven by successful web, mail-order, and wholesale divisions, with UK, Euro, and U.S. transactional Web sites. Cath Kidston has become a powerhouse of British design and retail, up there with the likes of Burberry and Pringle.

Design is core part of Cath Kidston's brand. However, it is more than the vintage-inspired patterns and the stunning shop interiors. Walk into any Cath Kidston shop and you are able to "experience" the brand that other retail shops do not offer. And this "experience" permeates Cath Kidston's Web sites and all of its printed communications. If you are a fan, you can feel the essence of the brand in every aspect. In color psychology terms, Cath Kidston is pure spring—fun, creative, warm, inspiring, and young, adding a splash of color and vintage charm to a routine day.

Cath Kidston not only offers a wide product range but is actually a lifestyle store. You can buy almost everything for your home, children, or yourself. The broad product range maximizes the brand's appeal and means that it works for both gift and personal purchases. Cath Kidston allows its brand personality (fun and brightness) to shine through its brand identity (colors and typography), hence becoming a brand consumers can fall in love with.

Value Versus Price

In certain respects, cross-comparing personal products such as key rings can be problematic, because there is so much variation in both features and price. But consider some popular Cath Kidston products. Its scarves sell for roughly $77, whereas comparable products from apparel retailers such as Marks & Spencer or Monsoon range from roughly $20 to $55. Cath Kidston's plastic-coated fabric bags sell from roughly $56 to $104, whereas other apparel retailers only charge similar prices for their leather bags. The fantasy of the English country childhood that Cath Kidston creates for customers enables the brand to charge price premiums as compared to competitors, such as John Lewis, Marks & Spencer, and Monsoon. For the fans of Cath Kidston, her products excite them in a way that IKEA and other competitors cannot hope to grasp.

In terms of competition, in the product category of home accessories, Cath Kidston competes directly with UK retailers like John Lewis and Marks & Spencer. In the clothing category, apparel retailers such as Monsoon and Marks & Spencer are the key competitors of Cath Kidston, while it competes with retailers like IKEA in the furniture category. Compared to its main competitors, the weakness of Cath Kidston is that its product offerings are still relatively limited and narrow. However, Cath Kidston's unique strength is its product design offers its customers a strong personal statement and identity that other competitors find hard to achieve. The biggest challenge for the Cath Kidston brand is to continue its success with the traditional English country style and fun brand character, while satisfying its loyal customers with innovative product design and product line extension.

Retro Brands in Hard Times

Given the harsh economic climate, you might expect to see the cheerful floral prints that made Cath Kidston a household name withering a little. However, Cath Kidston has survived the recession very well, selling the retro styling and a rose-tinted antidote to an uncertain world in the uncertain economic climate. The brand is now a seemingly recession-proof "global lifestyle brand." In 2009, while other brands were chalking up serious losses due to the economic downturn, Cath Kidston saw profits leap by 60 percent, and sales rose from roughly $30 to $49 million. The reason for this phenomenon is that in these uncertain times, consumers, although cash-conscious, have an appetite for nostalgia. The products of Cath Kidston fulfil consumer needs for value and meaning, because they are inspired by a comforting and familiar 1950s aesthetic.

For Cath Kidston, its premium pricing strategy coincided with a trend of consumer preference toward nostalgia, which seemed to provide comfort in the time of recession. Thus, the value derived from Cath Kidston products was enough to justify the high prices for many of its products. In an economic downturn, consumers want a bit of security and comfort, and this trend shows in the recession of the 1990s and today. UK retailers such as Asda reported a surge in sales of nostalgic brands, as people seem to look back to their childhood in an attempt to cheer themselves up. Consumers want the comfort and security that retro brands can give them, reminding them of their childhoods and even their parents' childhoods.

In times of economic downturn, people are worried about the credit crunch and losing jobs, and thus brands that act as an antidote to anxiety will do well. A lot of people didn't see the most recent economic crisis coming, and that makes them nervous about looking forward. The reflex is to seek comfort in things that refer to the past. Also, as people stay at home more in a recession time to reduce consumption, stylish home comforts become more important, which also helps explain why Cath Kidston has done well in hard times.

Cath Kidston is conquering the world with her floral and polka dot designs, and it is not surprising to see how such a powerful brand can divide people. Consumers either love it or hate it. For those who hate it, the products of Cath Kidston look like the junk from a late granny's attic. However, as the key target audiences of Cath Kidston are 30- to 40-year-old middle-class working women, their strong purchasing power sustains the growth of the brand.

Spotting the brand's potential to expand in all directions, Cath Kidston embarked on a series of collaborations, including a range of mobile phones for Nokia, eco-bags for the UK supermarket chain Tesco, a flower-covered Sky TV box, tents for Millets, and radios for the retro-styled Roberts range. To the fans of Cath Kidston, the brand offers them a dream of a simpler and nicer world that make them think of happy childhoods, homemade cakes, picnics, and the seaside.

In 2010, Cath Kidston became the subject of a high-profile buyout, when a $159 million deal saw the sale of Cath Kidston Ltd to a newly incorporated company owned by the U.S. private equity firm TA Associates. Cath Kidston Ltd had an equality sale valuing it at $119 million, while the funder and designer Cath Kidston retained her remaining 30 percent share, valued at $39.75 million, and continued her design role for the brand.

Pressing on with Price Premiums

The core idea of the Cath Kidston brand is a product-centric strategy. The control and expansion of the brand to a wider product range is still the focus after the shifting of company ownership. The product-centric concept of a brand is a business model that embodies perhaps the most essential brand ingredient for business success: simplicity. By 2014, there were 59 shops in the UK and Ireland, with a further 54 in Spain and the Far East, including Japan, South Korea, and China. The brand is pressing on with its nostalgic designs that create value for its customers, justifying the premium price of its products.

Questions for Discussion

10-18 Does Cath Kidston's pricing strategy truly differentiate it from the competition?

10-19 Has Cath Kidston executed value-based pricing, cost-based pricing, or competition-based pricing? Explain.

10-20 Could Cath Kidston have been successful as a design-focused product marketer had it employed a low-price strategy? Explain.

10-21 Is Cath Kidston's pricing strategy sustainable? Explain.

Sources: Beth Hale, "Cath Kidston to Pocket £50m from Sale of Brand 20 Years After Shop Assistant Created Famous Nostalgic Designs," *DailyMail*, February 23, 2010, www.dailymail.co.uk/femail/article-1252954/Cath-Kidston-pocket-30m-sale-brand-20-years-shop-assistantcreated-famous-nostalgic-designs.html; Kathryn Hopkins, "Designer Cath Kidston in Deal to Sell off Her Retail Empire," *Guardian*, March 7,2010, www.guardian.co.uk/business/2010/mar/07/cath-kidston-privateequity-buyout; Rachel Porter, "The REAL Domestic Goddess: How CathKidston Is Conquering the World with Her Floral and Polka Dot Designs,"*Daily Mail*, August 11, 2009, www.dailymail.co.uk/femail/article-1205665/The-REAL-domestic-goddess-How-Cath-Kidston-conquering-worldfloral-polka-dot-designs.html; and other information from www.cathkidston.co.uk/, accessed November, 2014.

MyMarketingLab

Go to **mymktlab.com** for the following Assisted-graded writing questions:

10-23 Define price elasticity and discuss why it is important for marketers to understand this concept. (AACSB: Communication; Reflective Thinking)

10-24 Why are consumers so concerned about the price of gas and why are they willing to search out stations with lower prices? (AACSB: Communication; Reflective Thinking)

References

1. Based on information from John Kell, "JCPenney to Close 33 Stores, Cut 2,000 Jobs," *Wall Street Journal*, January 14, 2014, p. B2; Kyle Stock, "Is JC Penney Giving Away the Store?", *Bloomberg Businessweek,* December 4, 2013, www.businessweek.com/articles/2013-12-04/is-jc-penney-giving-away-the-store; Brad Tuttle, "JCPenney Reintroduces Fake Prices," *Time*, May 2, 2013, http://business.time.com/2013/05/02/jc-penney-reintroduces-fake-prices-and-lots-of-coupons-too-of-course/; Natalie Zmuda, "JC Penney Reinvention Is Bold Bet, but Hardly Fail-Safe," *Advertising Age*, January 30, 2012, pp. 1, 22; Steve Denning, "JCPenney: Was Ron Johnson's Strategy Wrong?" *Forbes,* April 9, 2013, www.forbes.com/sites/stevedenning/2013/04/09/j-c-penney-was-ron-johnsons-strategy-wrong/; and http://ir.jcpenney.com/phoenix.zhtml?c=70528&p=irol-irHome, accessed July 2014.
2. For more on the importance of sound pricing strategy, see Thomas T. Nagle, John Hogan, and Joseph Zale, *The Strategy and Tactics of Pricing: A Guide to Growing More Profitably*, 5th ed. (Upper Saddle River, NJ: Prentice Hall, 2011), Chapter 1.
3. See Megan Willett, "How Swiss Watchmaker Patek Philippe Handcrafts Its Famous $500,000 Watches," *Business Insider,* July 12, 2013, www.businessinsider.com/how-a-patek-philippe-watch-is-made-2013-7; and www.patek.com/contents/default/en/values.html, accessed September 2014.
4. See "Walmart Puts Price First with Extreme Value Store Brand. *Store Brand Decisions,* November 5, 2013, www.storebrandsdecisions.com/news/2013/11/05/walmart-puts-price-first-with-extreme-value-store-brand-; "GoSmart Mobile Launches Nationwide No-Contract Wireless Service for Budget-Conscious Consumers," *PRNewswire,* February 19, 2013; Jacob Kastrenakes, "T-Mobile Giving Free Facebook Access to GoSmart Prepaid Users without a Data Plan," *The Verge,* December 23, 2013, www.theverge.com/2013/12/23/5238540/gosmart-free-facebook-data-t-mobile; and www.gosmartmobile.com/, accessed September 2014.
5. See Maria Puente, "Theaters Turn Up the Luxury," *USA Today*, March 12, 2010, p. 1A; "iPic Entertainment and Alberta Development Partners Announce Visionary Luxury Movie Theater Escape Planned for Dallas," *PR Newswire,* January 23, 2013; and information from http://dinein.amctheatres.com, accessed June 2014.
6. Accumulated production is drawn on a semilog scale so that equal distances represent the same percentage increase in output.
7. The arithmetic of markups and margins is discussed in Appendix 2, Marketing by the Numbers available online.
8. Based on information from "Pharmaca Integrative Pharmacy," *Retail Merchandiser*, May/June 2010, p. 30; Rachel Brown, "Pharmaca Marries Mainstream," *WWD,* May 11, 2007, p. 10; Amanda Gaines and Lisa Marshall, "Transform Your Store," *Natural Foods Merchandiser*, January 2012, pp. 23+; Michael Johnsen, "Personalizing High-Touch Retailing," *Drug Store News*, April 22, 2013, p. 112; and www.pharmaca.com, accessed September 2014.
9. See Stan Schroeder, "Vertu's Luxury Android Smartphone Costs $10,000, *Mashable,* February 12, 2013, http://mashable.com/2013/02/12/vertu-ti/; Matt Vella, "The Ulter-Luxe Phone," *Fortune,* April 29, 2013, pp. 10–12; Lara O'Reilly, "Vertu Seeks to Broaden Appeal with Marketing," *Marketing Week,* October 13, 2013, www.marketingweek.co.uk/news/vertu-seeks-to-broaden-appeal-with-marketing/4008105.article; and www.vertu.com, accessed September 2014.
10. Based on information found in Joseph Weber, "Over a Buck for Dinner? Outrageous," *BusinessWeek*, March 9, 2009, p. 57; and Tom Mulier and Matthew Boyle, "Dollar Dinners from ConAgra's Threatened by Costs," *Bloomberg Businessweek,* August 19, 2010, www.businessweek.com.
11. See Stuart Elliott, "Courting Thrifty Shoppers with Quality and Value," *New York Times,* June 3, 2013, p. B4; and http://www.iams.com/dog-food/about-so-good-dog-food, accessed September 2014.
12. For more information, see Annie Gasparro, "Whole Foods Aims to Alter 'Price Perception' as It Expands," *Wall Street Journal,* February 15, 2012; Julie Jargon, "Whole Foods' Battle for the Organic Shopper," *Wall Street Journal,* August 13, 2013, B1; http://online.wsj.com/news/articles/SB1000142412788732345510457901516213 5676136; and www.wholefoodsmarket.com/about-our-products/whole-deal, accessed September 2014.

11 Pricing Strategies
Additional Considerations

Chapter Preview In the previous chapter, you learned that price is an important marketing mix tool for both creating and capturing customer value. You explored the three main pricing strategies—customer value-based, cost-based, and competition-based pricing—and the many internal and external factors that affect a firm's pricing decisions. In this chapter, we'll look at some additional pricing considerations: new product pricing, product mix pricing, price adjustments, and initiating and reacting to price changes. We close the chapter with a discussion of public policy and pricing.

For openers, let's examine the importance of pricing in online retailing. In case you haven't noticed, there's a war going on—between Walmart, by far the world's largest retailer, and Amazon, the planet's largest online merchant. Each combatant brings an arsenal of potent weapons to the battle. For now, the focus is on price. But in the long run, it'll take much more than low prices to win this war. The spoils will go to the company that delivers the best overall online customer experience and value for the price.

AMAZON VS. WALMART: A Price War for Online Supremacy

"Walmart to Amazon: Let's Rumble" read the headline. Ali had Frazier. Coke has Pepsi. The Yankees have the White Sox. And now, the two retail heavyweights are waging a war all their own. The objective? Online supremacy. The weapon of choice? Prices, at least for now—not surprising, given the two combatants' long-held low-cost positions.

Each side is formidable in its own right. Walmart dominates offline retailing. It's price-driven "Save money. Live Better." positioning has made it far and away the world's biggest retailer, and the world's largest company to boot. In turn, Amazon is the "Walmart of the Web"—our online general store. Although Walmart's yearly sales total an incredible $469 billion, more than 6.3 times Amazon's $75 billion annually, Amazon's online sales are 7.5 times greater than Walmart's online sales. By one estimate, Amazon captures a full one-third of all online buying worldwide.

Why does Walmart worry about Amazon? After all, online sales currently account for only about 5 percent of total U.S. retail sales. Walmart captures most of its business through its more than 11,000 brick-and-mortar stores—online buying accounts for only a trifling 2 percent of its total sales. But this battle isn't about now, it's about the future. Although still a small market by Walmart's standards, online sales are growing at three times the rate of physical-world sales. Within the next decade, online and mobile buying will capture as much as a third of all retail sales. Because Amazon owns online, its revenues have soared an average of almost 30 percent annually over the past three years. Meanwhile, Walmart's earthbound sales have grown at less than 5 percent a year during that period. At that rate, Amazon's revenues will reach $100 billion within the next year, reaching that mark faster than any other company in history.

Amazon has shown a relentless ambition to offer more of almost everything online. It started by selling only books, but now sells everything from books, movies, and music to consumer electronics, home and garden products, clothing, jewelry, toys, tools, and even groceries. Thus, Amazon's online prowess now looms as a significant threat to Walmart. If Amazon's expansion continues and online sales spurt as predicted, the digital merchant will eat further and further into Walmart's bread-and-butter store sales.

Walmart, the world's largest retailer, and Amazon, the world's largest online merchant, are fighting a war for online supremacy. The weapon of choice? Prices, at least for now. But in the long run, winning the war will take much more than just low prices.

But Walmart isn't about to let that happen without a fight. Instead, it's taking the battle to Amazon's home territory—the Internet and mobile buying. It started with the tactics it knows best—low costs and prices. Through aggressive pricing, Walmart is now fighting for every dollar consumers spend online. If you compare prices at Walmart.com and Amazon.com, you'll find a price war raging across a broad range of products.

In a price war, Walmart would seem to have the edge. Low costs and prices are in the company's DNA. Through the years, Walmart has used its efficient operations and immense buying power to slash prices and thrash one competitor after another. But Amazon is not like most other competitors. Its network is optimized for online shopping, and the Internet seller isn't saddled with the costs of running physical stores. As a result, Amazon has been able to match or even beat Walmart at its own pricing game online. The two giants now seem pretty much stalemated on low prices, giving neither much of an advantage there. In fact, in the long run, reckless price cutting will likely do more damage than good to both Walmart and Amazon. So, although low prices will be crucial, they won't be enough to win over online buyers. Today's online shoppers want it all, low prices *and* selection, speed, convenience, and a satisfying overall shopping experience.

Walmart versus Amazon online: Achieving online supremacy will take more than just waging and winning an online price war. The spoils will go to the company that delivers the best overall online customer experience and value for the price.

(top) Bloomberg via Getty Images; (bottom) © digitallife / Alamy

For now, Amazon seems to have the upper hand on most of the important nonprice buying factors. Its made-for-online distribution network speeds orders to buyers' homes quickly and efficiently—including same-day delivery in some markets. Amazon's online assortment outstrips even Walmart's, and the Web wizard is now moving into groceries, an area that currently accounts for 55 percent of Walmart's sales. As for Amazon's lack of physical stores—no problem. Amazon's heavily used mobile app lets customers shop Amazon.com even as they are browsing Walmart's stores. Finally, Amazon's unmatched, big data-driven customer interface creates personalized, highly satisfying online buying experiences. Amazon regularly rates among the leaders in customer satisfaction across all industries.

By contrast, Walmart came late to online selling. It's still trying to figure out how to efficiently deliver goods into the hands of online shoppers. As its online sales have grown, the store-based giant has patched together a makeshift online distribution network out of unused corners of its store distribution centers. And the still-mostly-store retailer has yet to come close to matching Amazon's online customer buying experience. So even with its impressive low-price legacy, Walmart finds itself playing catch-up online. "We're starting to gain traction," says Walmart's CEO, but "we still have a long ways to go."

To catch up, Walmart is investing heavily to create a next-generation fulfillment network. Importantly, it's taking advantage of a major asset that Amazon can't match—an opportunity to integrate online buying with its massive network of brick-and-mortar stores. For example, Walmart is experimenting with fulfilling online orders more quickly and cheaply by having workers in stores pluck and pack items and mail or deliver them to customers' homes. Two-thirds of the U.S. population lives within five miles of a Walmart store, offering the potential for 30-minute delivery.

And by combining its online and offline operations, Walmart can provide some unique services, such as free and convenient pickup and returns of online orders in stores (Walmart's site gives you three buying options: "online," "in-store," and "site-to-store"). Using Walmart's Web site and mobile app can also smooth in-store shopping. They let customers prepare shopping lists in advance, locate products by aisle to reduce wasted shopping time, and use their smartphones at checkout with preloaded

Objective Outline

OBJECTIVE 1	**Describe the major strategies for pricing new products.** New Product Pricing Strategies (pp 349–350)
OBJECTIVE 2	**Explain how companies find a set of prices that maximizes the profits from the total product mix.** Product Mix Pricing Strategies (pp 350–352)
OBJECTIVE 3	**Discuss how companies adjust their prices to take into account different types of customers and situations.** Price Adjustment Strategies (pp 352–360)
OBJECTIVE 4	**Discuss the key issues related to initiating and responding to price changes.** Price Changes (pp 360–365)
OBJECTIVE 5	**Overview the social and legal issues that affect pricing decisions.** Public Policy and Pricing (pp 365–367)

digital coupons applied automatically. Customers who pick up online orders in the store can pay with cash, opening up online shopping to the 20 percent of Walmart customers who don't have bank accounts or credit cards. For customers who do pay online, Walmart is testing in-store lockers where customers can simply go to an assigned locker for pickup.

Who will win the battle for the hearts and dollars of online buyers? Certainly, low prices will continue to be important. But achieving online supremacy will involve much more than just waging and winning an online price war. It will require delivering low prices *plus* selection, convenience, and a world-class online buying experience—something that Amazon perfected long ago. For Walmart, catching and conquering Amazon online will require time, resources, and skills far beyond its trademark everyday low prices. As Walmart's president of global e-commerce puts it, the important task of winning online "will take the rest of our careers and as much as we've got [to invest]. This isn't a project. It's about the future of the company."[1]

As the Walmart–Amazon story suggests, and as we learned in the previous chapter, pricing decisions are subject to a complex array of company, environmental, and competitive forces. To make things even more complex, a company does not set a single price but rather a *pricing structure* that covers different items in its line. This pricing structure changes over time as products move through their life cycles. The company adjusts its prices to reflect changes in costs and demand and to account for variations in buyers and situations. As the competitive environment changes, the company considers when to initiate price changes and when to respond to them.

This chapter examines additional pricing approaches used in special pricing situations or to adjust prices to meet changing situations. We look in turn at *new product pricing* for products in the introductory stage of the product life cycle, *product mix pricing* for related products in the product mix, *price adjustment tactics* that account for customer differences and changing situations, and strategies for initiating and responding to *price changes*.

Author Comment | Pricing new products can be especially challenging. Just think about all the things you'd need to consider in pricing a new smartphone, say the first Apple iPhone. Even more, you need to start thinking about the price—along with many other marketing considerations—at the very beginning of the design process.

New Product Pricing Strategies

Pricing strategies usually change as the product passes through its life cycle. The introductory stage is especially challenging. Companies bringing out a new product face the challenge of setting prices for the first time. They can choose between two broad strategies: *market-skimming pricing* and *market-penetration pricing*.

Market-Skimming Pricing

Market-skimming pricing (price skimming)
Setting a high price for a new product to skim maximum revenues layer by layer from the segments willing to pay the high price; the company makes fewer but more profitable sales.

Many companies that invent new products set high initial prices to *skim* revenues layer by layer from the market. Apple frequently uses this strategy, called **market-skimming pricing** (or **price skimming**). When Apple first introduced the iPhone, its initial price was as high as $599 per phone. The phones were purchased only by customers who really wanted the sleek new gadget and could afford to pay a high price for it. Six months later, Apple dropped the price to $399 for an 8-GB model and $499 for the 16-GB model to attract new buyers. Within a year, it dropped prices again to $199 and $299, respectively, and you can now get a basic 8-GB model for free with a wireless phone contract. In this way, Apple has skimmed the maximum amount of revenue from the various segments of the market.

Market skimming makes sense only under certain conditions. First, the product's quality and image must support its higher price, and enough buyers must want the product at that price. Second, the costs of producing a smaller volume cannot be so high that they cancel the advantage of charging more. Finally, competitors should not be able to enter the market easily and undercut the high price.

Market-Penetration Pricing

Market-penetration pricing
Setting a low price for a new product in order to attract a large number of buyers and a large market share.

Rather than setting a high initial price to skim off small but profitable market segments, some companies use **market-penetration pricing**. Companies set a low initial price to *penetrate* the market quickly and deeply—to attract a large number of buyers quickly and win a large market share. The high sales volume results in falling costs, allowing companies to cut their prices even further. For example, Samsung has used penetration pricing to quickly build demand for its mobile devices in fast-growing emerging markets.[2]

In Kenya, Nigeria, and other Africa countries, Samsung recently unveiled an affordable yet full-function Samsung Galaxy Pocket model that sells for only about $120 with no contract. ● The Samsung Pocket is designed and priced to encourage millions of first-time African buyers to trade up to smartphones from their more basic handsets. Samsung also offers a line of Pocket models in India, selling for as little as $77. Through penetration pricing, the world's largest smartphone maker hopes to make quick and deep inroads into India's exploding mobile device market, which consists of mostly first-time users and accounts for nearly one-quarter of all smartphones sold globally each year. Samsung's penetration pricing has set off a price war in India with Apple, which has responded in emerging markets with heavy discounts and more affordable models of its own. Apple iPhones have typically sold for more than $300 in India, limiting Apple's market share to only about 2 percent there.

● **Penetration pricing: Samsung has used low initial prices to make quick and deep inroads into emerging mobile device markets such as Africa and India.**

Bloomberg via Getty Images

Several conditions must be met for this low-price strategy to work. First, the market must be highly price sensitive so that a low price produces more market

Table 11.1 | Product Mix Pricing

Pricing Situation	Description
Product line pricing	Setting prices across an entire product line
Optional-product pricing	Pricing optional or accessory products sold with the main product
Captive-product pricing	Pricing products that must be used with the main product
By-product pricing	Pricing low-value by-products to get rid of or make money on them
Product bundle pricing	Pricing bundles of products sold together

growth. Second, production and distribution costs must decrease as sales volume increases. Finally, the low price must help keep out the competition, and the penetration pricer must maintain its low-price position. Otherwise, the price advantage may be only temporary.

Author Comment | Most individual products are part of a broader product mix and must be priced accordingly. For example, Gillette prices its Fusion razors low. But once you buy the razor, you're a captive customer for its higher-margin replacement cartridges.

Product Mix Pricing Strategies

The strategy for setting a product's price often has to be changed when the product is part of a product mix. In this case, the firm looks for a set of prices that maximizes its profits on the total product mix. Pricing is difficult because the various products have related demand and costs and face different degrees of competition. We now take a closer look at the five product mix pricing situations summarized in **Table 11.1**: *product line pricing*, *optional-product pricing*, *captive-product pricing*, *by-product pricing*, and *product bundle pricing*.

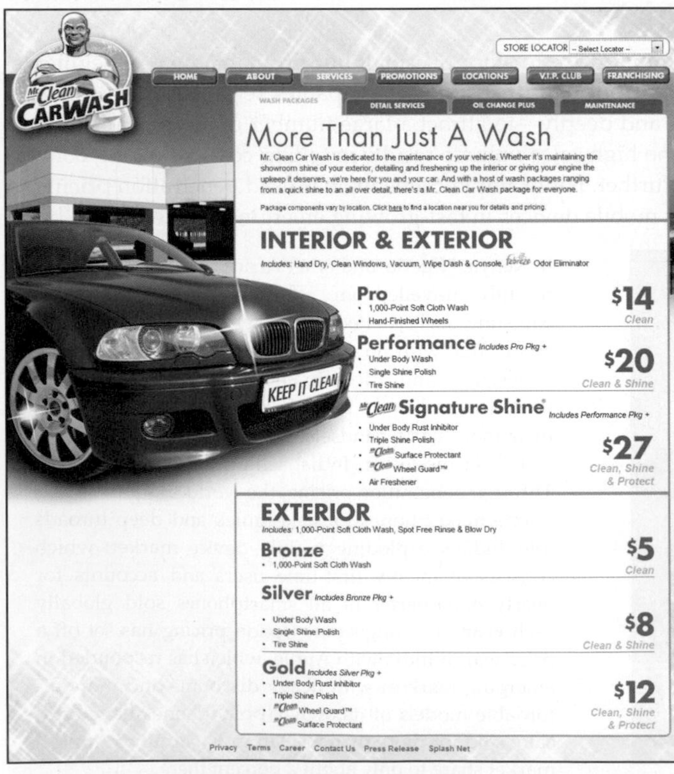

Product line pricing: Mr. Clean car washes offer a complete line of wash packages priced from $5 for the basic Bronze wash to $27 for the feature-loaded Mr. Clean Signature Shine package.

The Procter & Gamble Company

Product Line Pricing

Companies usually develop product lines rather than single products. For example, Rossignol offers seven different collections of alpine skis of all designs and sizes, at prices that range from $150 for its junior skis, such as Fun Girl, to more than $1,100 for a pair from its Radical racing collection. It also offers lines of Nordic and backcountry skis, snowboards, and ski-related apparel. In **product line pricing**, management must determine the price steps to set between the various products in a line.

The price steps should take into account cost differences between products in the line. More important, they should account for differences in customer perceptions of the value of different features. For example, at a Mr. Clean car wash, you can choose from any of six wash packages, ranging from a basic exterior-clean-only "Bronze" wash for $5; to an exterior clean, shine, and protect "Gold" package for $12; to an interior-exterior "Signature Shine" package for $27 that includes the works, from a thorough cleaning inside and out to a tire shine, underbody rust inhibitor, surface protectant, and even air freshener. The car wash's task is to establish perceived value differences that support the price differences.

Optional-Product Pricing

Many companies use **optional-product pricing**—offering to sell optional or accessory products along with the main product. For example, a car buyer may choose to order a navigation system and premium entertainment system. Refrigerators come with optional ice makers. And when you order a new computer,

Product line pricing
Setting the price steps between various products in a product line based on cost differences between the products, customer evaluations of different features, and competitors' prices.

Optional-product pricing
The pricing of optional or accessory products along with a main product.

Captive-product pricing
Setting a price for products that must be used along with a main product, such as blades for a razor and games for a video-game console.

you can select from a bewildering array of processors, hard drives, docking systems, software options, and service plans. Pricing these options is a sticky problem. Companies must decide which items to include in the base price and which to offer as options.

Captive-Product Pricing

Companies that make products that must be used along with a main product are using **captive-product pricing**. Examples of captive products are razor blade cartridges, video games, printer cartridges, single-serve coffee pods, and e-books. Producers of the main products (razors, video-game consoles, printers, single-cup coffee brewing systems, and tablet computers) often price them low and set high markups on the supplies. For example, Amazon makes little or no profit on its Kindle readers and tablets. It hopes to more than make up for thin margins through sales of digital books, music, movies, subscription services, and other content for the devices. "We want to make money when people use our devices, not when they buy our devices," declares Amazon CEO Jeff Bezos.[3]

Captive products can account for a substantial portion of a brand's sales and profits. ● For example, only about 27 percent of Keurig's revenues come from the sale of its single-cup brewing systems. The bulk of the brand's revenues—nearly 73 percent—comes from captive sales of its K-Cup portion packs.[4] However, companies that use captive-product pricing must be careful. Finding the right balance between the main-product and captive-product prices can be tricky. Even more, consumers trapped into buying expensive captive products may come to resent the brand that ensnared them.

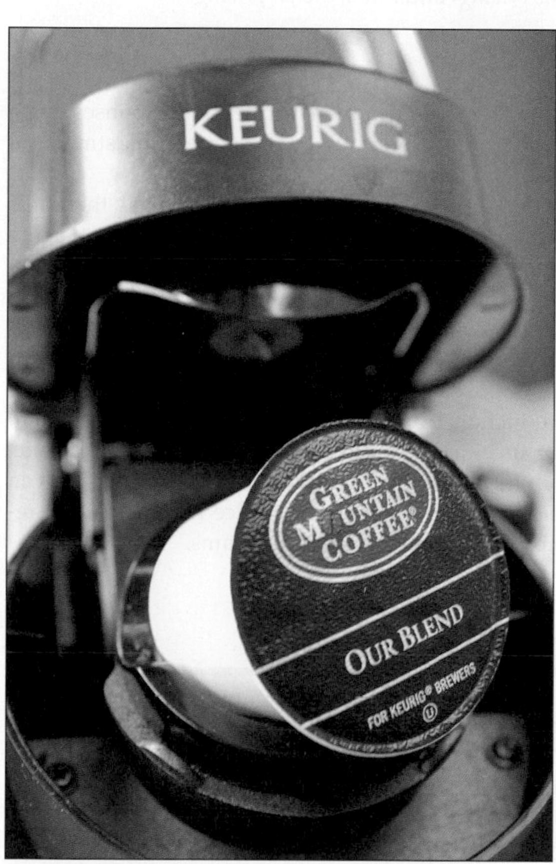

● **Captive product pricing: Nearly 73 percent of Keurig's sales come from its K-Cup portion packs. The brand must find the right balance between main-product and captive-product prices.**
ASSOCIATED PRESS

For example, customers of single-cup coffee brewing systems may cringe at what they must pay for those handy little coffee portion packs. Although they might seem like a bargain when compared on a cost-per-cup basis versus Starbucks, the pods' prices can seem like highway robbery when broken down by the pound. One investigator calculated the cost of pod coffee at a shocking $51 per pound.[5] At those prices, you'd be better off cost-wise brewing a big pot of premium coffee and pouring out the unused portion. For many buyers, the convenience and selection offered by single-cup brewing systems outweigh the extra costs. However, such captive product costs might make others avoid buying the device in the first place or cause discomfort during use after purchase.

In the case of services, captive-product pricing is called *two-part pricing*. The price of the service is broken into a *fixed fee* plus a *variable usage rate*. Thus, at Six Flags and other amusement parks, you pay a daily ticket or season pass charge plus additional fees for food and other in-park features.

By-Product Pricing

Producing products and services often generates by-products. If the by-products have no value and if getting rid of them is costly, this will affect the pricing of the main product. Using **by-product pricing**, the company seeks a market for these by-products to help offset the costs of disposing of them and help make the price of the main product more competitive.

The by-products themselves can even turn out to be profitable—turning trash into cash. For example, Coca-Cola converts waste from its beverage-making operations into profitable by-products. Nothing goes to waste, not even orange peels:[6]

By-product pricing
Setting a price for by-products in order to make the main product's price more competitive.

> To make its Simply Orange, Minute Maid, and other orange juice brands, Coca-Cola and its fruit-procuring partner, Cutrale, squeeze a lot of oranges. Together each year, the two companies buy and process some 50 million boxes of oranges from Florida growers alone. That's a lot of orange juice, but it also leaves behind a lot of orange peels. Rather than paying to have the peels hauled way, however, Coca-Cola and Cutrale turn them into valuable by-products. Every part of the orange is put to good use. Essential oils are extracted, bottled, and sold for everything from food flavorings to household cleaners. What's left is pressed into pellets sold for livestock feed. Even the Simply Orange bottles you buy at your supermarket might soon be made in part from left-over orange peels. Coca-Cola's newly developed bio-PET Plant Bottles contain orange peels and other agricultural by-products from the company's food processing operations.

Product Bundle Pricing

Product bundle pricing
Combining several products and offering the bundle at a reduced price.

Using **product bundle pricing**, sellers often combine several products and offer the bundle at a reduced price. For example, fast-food restaurants bundle a burger, fries, and a soft drink at a "combo" price. Bath & Body Works offers "three-fer" deals on its soaps and lotions (such as three antibacterial soaps for $10). And Comcast, Time Warner, Verizon, and other telecommunications companies bundle TV service, phone service, and high-speed Internet connections at a low combined price. Price bundling can promote the sales of products consumers might not otherwise buy, but the combined price must be low enough to get them to buy the bundle.

Author Comment | Setting the base price for a product is only the start. The company must then adjust the price to account for customer and situational differences. When was the last time you paid the full suggested retail price for something?

Price Adjustment Strategies

Companies usually adjust their basic prices to account for various customer differences and changing situations. Here we examine the seven price adjustment strategies summarized in **Table 11.2**: *discount and allowance pricing, segmented pricing, psychological pricing, promotional pricing, geographical pricing, dynamic pricing*, and *international pricing*.

Discount and Allowance Pricing

Most companies adjust their basic price to reward customers for certain responses, such as paying bills early, volume purchases, and off-season buying. These price adjustments—called *discounts* and *allowances*—can take many forms.

Discount
A straight reduction in price on purchases during a stated period of time or of larger quantities.

One form of **discount** is a *cash discount*, a price reduction to buyers who pay their bills promptly. A typical example is "2/10, net 30," which means that although payment is due within 30 days, the buyer can deduct 2 percent if the bill is paid within 10 days. A *quantity discount* is a price reduction to buyers who buy large volumes. A seller offers a *functional discount* (also called a *trade discount*) to trade-channel members who perform certain functions, such as selling, storing, and record keeping. A *seasonal discount* is a price reduction to buyers who buy merchandise or services out of season.

Allowance
Promotional money paid by manufacturers to retailers in return for an agreement to feature the manufacturer's products in some way.

Allowances are another type of reduction from the list price. For example, *trade-in allowances* are price reductions given for turning in an old item when buying a new one. Trade-in allowances are most common in the automobile industry, but they are also given for other durable goods. *Promotional allowances* are payments or price reductions that reward dealers for participating in advertising and sales-support programs.

Table 11.2 | Price Adjustments

Strategy	Description
Discount and allowance pricing	Reducing prices to reward customer responses such as volume purchases, paying early, or promoting the product
Segmented pricing	Adjusting prices to allow for differences in customers, products, or locations
Psychological pricing	Adjusting prices for psychological effect
Promotional pricing	Temporarily reducing prices to spur short-run sales
Geographical pricing	Adjusting prices to account for the geographic location of customers
Dynamic pricing	Adjusting prices continually to meet the characteristics and needs of individual customers and situations
International pricing	Adjusting prices for international markets

Segmented Pricing

Segmented pricing
Selling a product or service at two or more prices, where the difference in prices is not based on differences in costs.

Companies will often adjust their basic prices to allow for differences in customers, products, and locations. In **segmented pricing**, the company sells a product or service at two or more prices, even though the difference in prices is not based on differences in costs.

Segmented pricing takes several forms. Under *customer-segment pricing*, different customers pay different prices for the same product or service. Museums and movie theaters, for example, may charge a lower admission for students and senior citizens. Under *product form pricing*, different versions of the product are priced differently but not according to differences in their costs. For instance, a round-trip economy seat on a flight from New York to London might cost $1,000, whereas a business-class seat on the same flight might cost $4,700 or more. Although business-class customers receive roomier, more comfortable seats and higher-quality food and service, the differences in costs to the airlines are much less than the additional prices to passengers. However, to passengers who can afford it, the additional comfort and services are worth the extra charge.

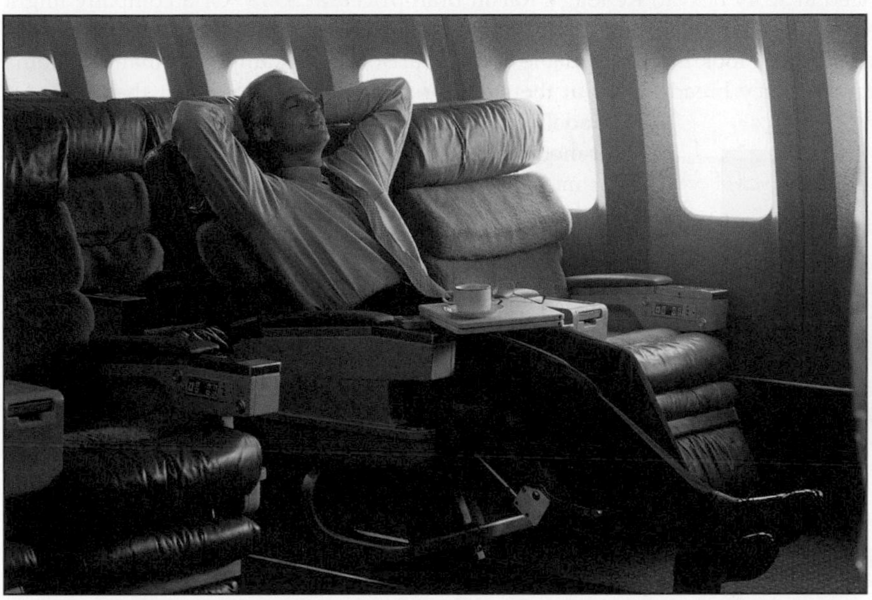

Product-form pricing: A roomier business class seat on a flight from New York to London is many times the price of an economy seat on the same flight. To customers who can afford it, the extra comfort and service are worth the extra charge.

Using *location-based pricing*, a company charges different prices for different locations, even though the cost of offering each location is the same. For instance, state universities charge higher tuition for out-of-state students, and theaters vary their seat prices because of audience preferences for certain locations. Finally, using *time-based pricing*, a firm varies its price by the season, the month, the day, and even the hour. For example, movie theaters charge matinee pricing during the daytime, and resorts give weekend and seasonal discounts.

For segmented pricing to be an effective strategy, certain conditions must exist. The market must be segmentable, and segments must show different degrees of demand. The costs of segmenting and reaching the market cannot exceed the extra revenue obtained from the price difference. Of course, the segmented pricing must also be legal.

Most important, segmented prices should reflect real differences in customers' perceived value. Consumers in higher price tiers must feel that they're getting their extra money's worth for the higher prices paid. By the same token, companies must be careful not to treat customers in lower price tiers as second-class citizens. Otherwise, in the long run, the practice will lead to customer resentment and ill will. For example, in recent years, the airlines have incurred the wrath of frustrated customers at both ends of the airplane. Passengers paying full fare for business- or first-class seats often feel that they are being gouged. At the same time, passengers in lower-priced coach seats feel that they're being ignored or treated poorly.

Psychological Pricing

Price says something about the product. For example, many consumers use price to judge quality. A $100 bottle of perfume may contain only $3 worth of scent, but some people are willing to pay the $100 because this price indicates something special.

Psychological pricing
Pricing that considers the psychology of prices and not simply the economics; the price is used to say something about the product.

In using **psychological pricing**, sellers consider the psychology of prices, not simply the economics. For example, consumers usually perceive higher-priced products as having higher quality. When they can judge the quality of a product by examining it or by calling on past experience with it, they use price less to judge quality. But when they cannot judge quality because they lack the information or skill, price becomes an important quality signal. For instance, who's the better lawyer, one who charges $50 per hour or one who charges $500 per hour? You'd have to do a lot of digging into the respective lawyers' credentials to answer this question objectively; even then, you might not be able to judge accurately. Most of us would simply assume that the higher-priced lawyer is better.

Reference prices
Prices that buyers carry in their minds and refer to when they look at a given product.

Another aspect of psychological pricing is **reference prices**—prices that buyers carry in their minds and refer to when looking at a given product. The reference price might be formed by noting current prices, remembering past prices, or assessing the buying situation. Sellers can influence or use these consumers' reference prices when setting price. For example, a grocery retailer might place its store brand of bran flakes and raisins cereal priced at $2.49 next to Kellogg's Raisin Bran priced at $3.79. Or a company might offer more expensive models that don't sell very well to make its less expensive but still-high-priced models look more affordable by comparison. For example, Williams-Sonoma once offered a fancy bread maker at the steep price of $279. However, it then added a $429 model. The expensive model flopped but sales of the cheaper model doubled.[7]

For most purchases, consumers don't have all the skill or information they need to figure out whether they are paying a good price. They don't have the time, ability, or inclination to research different brands or stores, compare prices, and get the best deals. ● Instead, they may rely on certain cues that signal whether a price is high or low. Interestingly, such pricing cues are often provided by sellers, in the form of sales signs, price-matching guarantees, loss-leader pricing, and other helpful hints.

Even small differences in price can signal product differences. A 9 or 0.99 at the end of a price often signals a bargain. You see such prices everywhere. For example, browse the online sites of top discounters such as Target, Best Buy, or Overstock.com, where almost every price ends in 9. In contrast, high-end retailers might favor prices ending in a whole number (for example, $6, $25, or $200). Others use 00-cent endings on regularly priced items and 99-cent endings on discount merchandise.

Although actual price differences might be small, the impact of such psychological tactics can be big. For example, in one study, people were asked how likely they were to choose among LASIK eye surgery providers based only on the prices they charged: $299 or $300. The actual price difference was only $1, but the study found that the psychological difference was much greater. Preference ratings for the providers charging $300 were much higher. Subjects perceived the $299 price as significantly less, but the lower price also raised stronger concerns about quality and risk. Some psychologists even argue that each digit has symbolic and visual qualities that should be considered in pricing. Thus, eight (8) is round and even and creates a soothing effect, whereas seven (7) is angular and creates a jarring effect.[8]

● **Psychological pricing: What do the prices marked on this tag suggest about the product and buying situation?**

© Tetra Images/Alamy

Promotional Pricing

Promotional pricing
Temporarily pricing products below the list price, and sometimes even below cost, to increase short-run sales.

With **promotional pricing**, companies will temporarily price their products below list price—and sometimes even below cost—to create buying excitement and urgency. Promotional pricing takes several forms. ● A seller may simply offer *discounts* from normal prices to increase sales and reduce inventories. Sellers also use *special-event pricing* in certain seasons to draw more customers. Thus, TVs and other consumer electronics are promotionally priced in November and December to attract holiday shoppers into the stores. *Limited-time offers*, such as online *flash sales*, can create buying urgency and make buyers feel lucky to have gotten in on the deal.

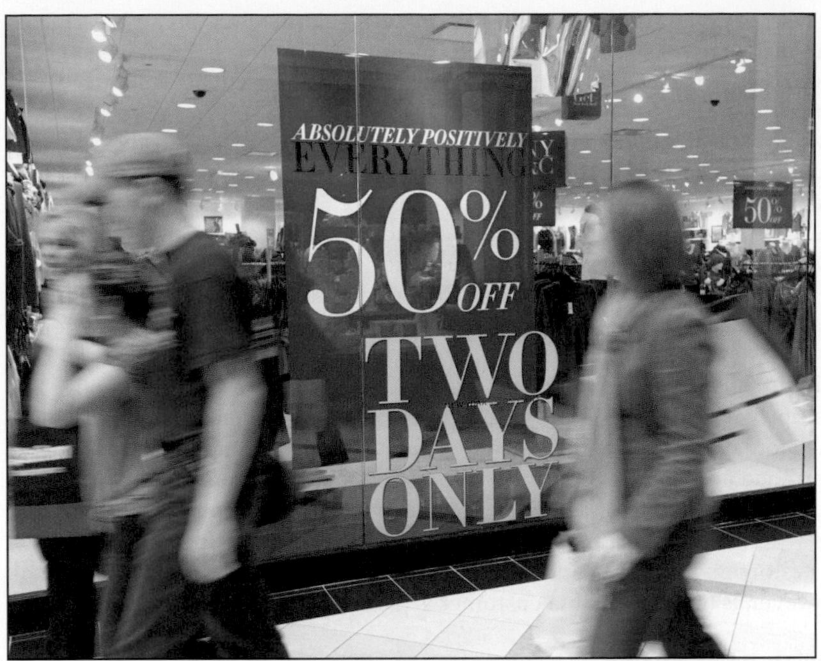

Promotional pricing: Companies offer promotional prices to create buying excitement and urgency.

Bloomberg via Getty Images

Manufacturers sometimes offer *cash rebates* to consumers who buy the product from dealers within a specified time; the manufacturer sends the rebate directly to the customer. Rebates have been popular with automakers and producers of mobile phones and small appliances, but they are also used with consumer packaged goods. Some manufacturers offer *low-interest financing, longer warranties*, or *free maintenance* to reduce the consumer's "price." This practice has become another favorite of the auto industry.

Promotional pricing can help move customers over humps in the buying decision process. For example, to encourage its voice-plan customers to "break free" from WiFi-only tablets and add its 4G LTE mobile Internet services, T-Mobile recently offered discounts of up to $100 on T-Mobile 4G tablets, plus 1GB of free 4G LTE data monthly for up to eight months (and 200MB of free data monthly for as long as they own the tablet). Such aggressive price promotions can provide powerful buying and switching incentives.[9]

Promotional pricing, however, can have adverse effects. During most holiday seasons, for example, it's an all-out bargain war. Marketers carpet-bomb consumers with deals, causing buyer wear-out and pricing confusion. Used too frequently, price promotions can create "deal-prone" customers who wait until brands go on sale before buying them. In addition, constantly reduced prices can erode a brand's value in the eyes of customers.

Marketers sometimes become addicted to promotional pricing, especially in tight economic times. They use price promotions as a quick fix instead of sweating through the difficult process of developing effective longer-term strategies for building their brands. For example, as recounted in the Chapter 10 opening story, JCPenney has long relied on a steady diet of coupons, markdowns, and nonstop sales to pull customers through the doors. Although these promotional practices have been destructive to JCPenney's image and profitability, they've become so ingrained that the retailer is finding it difficult to stop offering them. To avoid such problems, companies must be careful to balance short-term sales incentives against long-term brand building.

Geographical Pricing

A company also must decide how to price its products for customers located in different parts of the United States or the world. Should the company risk losing the business of more-distant customers by charging them higher prices to cover the higher shipping costs? Or should the company charge all customers the same prices regardless of location? We will look at five **geographical pricing** strategies for the following hypothetical situation:

Geographical pricing
Setting prices for customers located in different parts of the country or world.

> The Peerless Paper Company is located in Atlanta, Georgia, and sells paper products to customers all over the United States. The cost of freight is high and affects the companies from which customers buy their paper. Peerless wants to establish a geographical pricing policy. It is trying to determine how to price a $10,000 order to three specific customers: Customer A (Atlanta), Customer B (Bloomington, Indiana), and Customer C (Compton, California).

FOB-origin pricing
A geographical pricing strategy in which goods are placed free on board a carrier; the customer pays the freight from the factory to the destination.

One option is for Peerless to ask each customer to pay the shipping cost from the Atlanta factory to the customer's location. All three customers would pay the same factory price of $10,000, with Customer A paying, say, $100 for shipping; Customer B, $150; and Customer C, $250. Called **FOB-origin pricing**, this practice means that the goods are placed *free on board* (hence, *FOB*) a carrier. At that point, the title and responsibility pass to the customer, who pays the freight from the factory to the destination. Because each customer picks up its own cost, supporters of FOB pricing feel that this is the fairest way to assess freight charges. The disadvantage, however, is that Peerless will be a high-cost firm to distant customers.

Uniform-delivered pricing
A geographical pricing strategy in which the company charges the same price plus freight to all customers, regardless of their location.

Uniform-delivered pricing is the opposite of FOB pricing. Here, the company charges the same price plus freight to all customers, regardless of their location. The freight charge is set at the average freight cost. Suppose this is $150. Uniform-delivered pricing therefore results in a higher charge to the Atlanta customer (who pays $150 freight instead of $100) and a lower charge to the Compton customer (who pays $150 instead of $250). Although the Atlanta customer would prefer to buy paper from another local paper company that uses FOB-origin pricing, Peerless has a better chance of capturing the California customer.

Zone pricing
A geographical pricing strategy in which the company sets up two or more zones. All customers within a zone pay the same total price; the more distant the zone, the higher the price.

Zone pricing falls between FOB-origin pricing and uniform-delivered pricing. The company sets up two or more zones. All customers within a given zone pay a single total price; the more distant the zone, the higher the price. For example, Peerless might set up an East Zone and charge $100 freight to all customers in this zone, a Midwest Zone in which it charges $150, and a West Zone in which it charges $250. In this way, the customers within a given price zone receive no price advantage from the company. For example, customers in Atlanta and Boston pay the same total price to Peerless. The complaint, however, is that the Atlanta customer is paying part of the Boston customer's freight cost.

Basing-point pricing
A geographical pricing strategy in which the seller designates some city as a basing point and charges all customers the freight cost from that city to the customer.

Using **basing-point pricing**, the seller selects a given city as a "basing point" and charges all customers the freight cost from that city to the customer location, regardless of the city from which the goods are actually shipped. For example, Peerless might set Chicago as the basing point and charge all customers $10,000 plus the freight from Chicago to their locations. This means that an Atlanta customer pays the freight cost from Chicago to Atlanta, even though the goods may be shipped from Atlanta. If all sellers used the same basing-point city, delivered prices would be the same for all customers, and price competition would be eliminated.

Freight-absorption pricing
A geographical pricing strategy in which the seller absorbs all or part of the freight charges in order to get the desired business.

Finally, the seller who is anxious to do business with a certain customer or geographical area might use **freight-absorption pricing**. Using this strategy, the seller absorbs all or part of the actual freight charges to get the desired business. The seller might reason that if it can get more business, its average costs will decrease and more than compensate for its extra freight cost. Freight-absorption pricing is used for market penetration and to hold on to increasingly competitive markets.

Dynamic and Internet Pricing

Dynamic pricing
Adjusting prices continually to meet the characteristics and needs of individual customers and situations.

Throughout most of history, prices were set by negotiation between buyers and sellers. *Fixed-price* policies—setting one price for all buyers—is a relatively modern idea that arose with the development of large-scale retailing at the end of the nineteenth century. Today, most prices are set this way. However, some companies are now reversing the fixed-pricing trend. They are using **dynamic pricing**—adjusting prices continually to meet the characteristics and needs of individual customers and situations.

Dynamic pricing is especially prevalent online, where the Internet seems to be taking us back to a new age of fluid pricing. Such pricing offers many advantages for marketers. For example, Internet sellers such as L.L.Bean, Amazon.com, or Dell can mine their databases to gauge a specific shopper's desires, measure his or her means, instantaneously tailor offers to fit that shopper's behavior, and price products accordingly.

Services ranging from retailers, airlines, and hotels to sports teams change prices on the fly according to changes in demand, costs, or competitor pricing, adjusting what they charge for specific items on a daily, hourly, or even continuous basis. Done well, dynamic pricing can help sellers to optimize sales and serve customers better. However, done poorly, it can trigger margin-eroding price wars and damage customer relationships and trust. Companies must be careful not to cross the fine line between smart dynamic pricing strategies and damaging ones (see Real Marketing 11.1).

In the extreme, some companies customize their offers and prices based on the specific characteristics and behaviors of individual customers, mined from online browsing and purchasing histories. These days, online offers and prices might well be based on what

Real Marketing 11.1

Dynamic Pricing: The Wonders and Woes of Real-Time Price Adjustments

These days, it seems every seller knows what prices competitors are charging—for anything and everything it sells, minute by minute, and down to the penny. What's more, today's technologies give sellers the flexibility to adjust their own prices on the fly. This often results in some pretty zany pricing dynamics.

For example, during a recent Black Friday weekend, the prices charged for the latest version of an Xbox game, Dance Central, experienced some head-spinning dips and dives. The day before Thanksgiving, Amazon marked the game down to $49.96, matching Walmart's price and beating Target's price by three cents. On Thanksgiving Day, Amazon slashed that price in half to just $24.99, matching Best Buy's Thanksgiving Day special. Walmart responded quickly with a rock-bottom price of $15, which Amazon matched immediately. "What kind of pricing lunacy is this?" you ask. Welcome to the wonders and woes of dynamic pricing.

On the plus side, dynamic pricing can help sellers optimize sales and serve customers better by aligning prices with competitor offers and market conditions. For example, airlines routinely use dynamic pricing to constantly adjust fares for specific flights, depending on competitor pricing and anticipated seat availability. As any frequent flyer knows, if you call now to book a seat on a flight to sunny Florida next week, you'll get one price. Try again an hour later and you'll get a different price—maybe higher, maybe lower. Book the same seat a month in advance and you'll probably pay a lot less.

Dynamic pricing isn't just about sellers optimizing their returns. It also puts pricing power into the hands of consumers, as alert shoppers take advantage of the constant price skirmishes among sellers. By using online price checkers and shopping apps to monitor prices, consumers can snap up good deals or leverage retailer price-matching policies. In fact, today's fluid pricing sometimes gives buyers too much of an upper hand. With price-checking and online-ordering now at the shopper's fingertips, even giant retailers such as Target, Walmart, and Best Buy have fallen victim to "showrooming"—whereby shoppers check merchandise and prices in store-retailer showrooms, then buy the goods online.

Stores like Best Buy are in turn using dynamic pricing to combat showrooming, or even turn it into an advantage. For example, Best Buy Canada now provides its sales associates with mobile price checkers of their own that they can use with every transaction to check the competing prices in real time. Associates can often show customers that Best Buy actually has the best prices on most items. When Best Buy's price isn't lowest, associates are instructed to beat the lower-priced competitor—online or offline—by 10 percent. Once it has neutralized price as a buying factor, Best Buy reasons, it can convert showroomers into in-store buyers with its nonprice advantages of service, immediacy, convenient locations, and easy returns.

As the Best Buy example illustrates, dynamic pricing doesn't just happen in the fast-shifting online environment. For example, discount department store Kohl's has replaced static price tags with digital ones. These digital tags can be centrally controlled to change prices dynamically on individual items within a given store or across the entire chain. The technology lets Kohl's apply Internet-style dynamic pricing, changing prices as conditions dictate without the time and costs of changing physical tags.

Beyond using dynamic pricing to match competitors, many sellers use it to adjust prices based on customer characteristics or buying situations. Some sellers vary prices they charge different customers based on customer purchase histories or personal data. Some companies offer special discounts to customers with more items in their shopping carts. Online travel agent Orbitz has even been known to charge higher prices to Mac and iPad users because Apple fans have higher average household incomes.

Most consumers are surprised to learn that it's perfectly legal under most circumstances to charge different prices to different customers based on their buying behaviors. In fact, one survey found that two-thirds of online shoppers thought the practice was illegal. When they learned that it was not illegal, nearly nine out of ten thought it should be.

Legal or not, dynamic pricing doesn't always sit well with customers. Done poorly, it can cause customer confusion, frustration, or even resentment, damaging hard-won customer relationships. Consider this Amazon shopper's experience:

> Nancy Plumlee had just taken up mahjong, a Chinese game of tiles similar to rummy. She browsed Amazon.com and, after sifting through several pages of options, settled on a set for $54.99. She placed it in her [shopping cart] and continued shopping for some scorecards and game accessories. A few minutes later, she scanned the cart and noticed the $54.99 had jumped to $70.99. Plumlee thought she was going crazy. She checked her computer's viewing history and, indeed, the game's original price was listed at $54.99. Determined, she cleared out the cart and tried again. [This time,] the game's price jumped from $54.99 to $59.99. "That just doesn't feel like straight-up business honesty. Shame on Amazon," said Plumlee, who called [Amazon] and persuaded the online retailer to refund her $5.

Uber's "surge pricing": App-based car service Uber uses dynamic pricing to adjust its rates to meet market conditions. Some customers are shocked, but Uber alerts customers in advance about its pricing.

Associated Press

It is sometimes difficult to locate the fine line between a smart dynamic pricing strategy and one that crosses the line, doing more damage to customer relationships than good to the company's bottom line. Consider Uber, an app-based car dispatch service serving many major U.S. cities that lets customers summon taxis, cars, or other transportation using texts or the company's phone app:

Uber uses a form of dynamic pricing called "surge pricing." Under normal circumstances, Uber customers pay reasonable fares. However, using Uber in periods of surging demand can result in shocking price escalations. For example, on one recent stormy, holiday-Saturday night in Manhattan, Uber charged—and got—fares that were more than eight times the usual. Although Uber's app warned customers of heightened fares before processing their requests, many customers were outraged. They commented, e-mailed, and tweeted their displeasure with messages charging the company with price gouging. One customer shared an Instagram photo of a taxi receipt for $415. "That is robbery!" tweeted another. However, despite the protests, Uber experienced no subsequent drop in demand in the New York City area. It seems that, to most people who can afford Uber, convenience and prestige are the deciding factors, not price. "No one is forcing you to use the service," adds one commenter. "Don't like it? Take [your own] cab. Or public transportation. Or walk."

Thus, used well, dynamic pricing can help sellers to optimize sales and profits by keeping track of competitor pricing and quickly adjusting to marketplace changes. Used poorly, however, it can trigger margin-eroding price wars and damage customer relationships and trust. Too often, dynamic pricing takes the form of a pricing "arms race" among sellers, putting too much emphasis on prices at the expense of other important customer value-building elements. Companies must be careful to keep pricing in balance. As one Best Buy marketer states, pricing—dynamic or otherwise—remains "just one part of the equation. There's the right assortment, convenience, expedited delivery, customer service, warranty. All of these things matter to the customer."

Sources: Andrew Nusca, "The Future of Retail Is Dynamic Pricing. So Why Can't We Get It Right?", *ZDNet,* October 2, 2013, www.zdnet.com/the-future-of-retail-is-dynamic-pricing-so-why-cant-we-get-it-right-7000021444/; Randall Stross, "Digital Tags Help Ensure the Price Is Right," *New York Times,* February 9, 2013, www.nytimes.com/2013/02/10/technology/digital-tags-help-ensure-that-the-price-is-right.html?_r=0; Laura Gunderson, "Amazon's 'Dynamic' Prices Get Some Static," *The Oregonian,* May 5, 2012, http://blog.oregonlive.com/complaintdesk/2012/05/amazons_dynamic_prices_get_som.html; Thorin Klosowski, "How Web Sites Vary Prices Based on Your Information," *Lifehacker,* January 7, 2013, http://lifehacker.com/5973689; David P; Schulz, "Changing Direction," *Stores,* March 2013, www.stores.org/STORES%20Magazine%20March%202013/changing-direction; Jessi Hempel, "Why Surge-Pricing Fiasco Is Great for Uber," *CNNMoney,* December 30, 2013, http://tech.fortune.cnn.com/2013/12/30/why-the-surge-pricing-fiasco-is-great-for-uber/; Victor Fiorillo, "Will Everyone Please Shut Up about Under Surge Pricing?" *Philadelphia Magazine,* December 18, 2013, www.phillymag.com/news/2013/12/18/uber-surge-pricing/; and Alison Griswold, "Everybody Hates Surge Pricing," *Slate,* April 24, 2014, www.slate.com/articles/business/moneybox/2014/04/uber_style_surge_pricing_does_the_system_make_sense_for_d_c_cabs.html.

specific customers search for and buy, how much they pay for other purchases, and whether they might be willing and able to spend more. For example, a consumer who recently went online to purchase a first-class ticket to London or customize a new Mercedes coupe might later get a higher quote on a new Bose Wave Radio. By comparison, a friend with a more modest online search and purchase history might receive an offer of 5 percent off and free shipping on the same radio.[10]

Although such dynamic pricing practices seem legally questionable, they're not. Dynamic pricing is legal as long as companies do not discriminate based on age, gender, location, or other similar characteristics. Dynamic pricing makes sense in many contexts—it adjusts prices according to market forces and consumer preferences. But marketers need to be careful not to use dynamic pricing to take advantage of certain customer groups, thereby damaging important customer relationships.

The practice of online pricing, however, goes both ways, and consumers often benefit from online and dynamic pricing. Thanks to the Internet, the centuries-old art of haggling is suddenly back in vogue. For example, consumers can negotiate prices at online auction sites and exchanges. Want to sell that antique pickle jar that's been collecting dust for generations? Post it on eBay or Craigslist. Want to name your own price for a hotel room or rental car? Visit Priceline.com or another reverse auction site. Want to bid on a ticket to a hot show or sporting event? Check out Ticketmaster.com, which offers an online auction service for event tickets.

● Also thanks to the Internet, consumers can get instant product and price comparisons from thousands of vendors at price comparison sites such as Yahoo! Shopping, Epinions.com, and PriceGrabber.com, or using mobile apps such as TheFind, eBay's RedLaser, Google Shopper, or Amazon's Price Check. For example, the RedLaser mobile app lets customers scan barcodes or QR codes (or search by voice or image) while shopping in stores. It then searches online and at nearby stores to provide thousands of reviews and

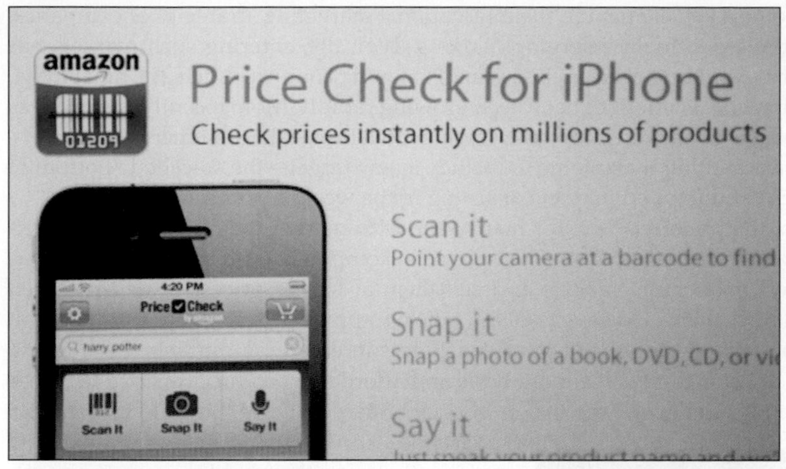

Dynamic and Internet pricing: Using mobile apps such as Amazon's Price Check, consumers can get instant price comparisons on millions of products.

Bloomberg via Getty Images

comparison prices, and even offers buying links for immediate online purchasing. Armed with this information, consumers can often negotiate better in-store prices.

In fact, many retailers are finding that ready online access to comparison prices is giving consumers *too* much of an edge. Store retailers ranging from Target and Best Buy to Brookstone and GNC are now devising strategies to combat the consumer practice of *showrooming*. Consumers armed with smartphones now routinely come to stores to see an item, compare prices online while in the store, and then buy the item online at a lower price. Such behavior is called showrooming because consumers use retailers' stores as de facto "showrooms" for online resellers such as Amazon.com.

This past holiday season, Best Buy launched an advertising campaign—called "Your Ultimate Holiday Showroom"—designed to directly combat showrooming:[11]

> In the campaign, a host of popular celebrities pitched Best Buy as a better shopping experience than buying from online-only retailers like Amazon.com. They touted Best Buy advantages, such as assistance by well-trained associates, the ability to order online and pick up in store, and Best Buy's low-price guarantee. "Showrooming . . . is not the ideal experience," says a Best Buy marketer, ". . . to do research at home, go to the store, do more research, then hit pause, go home and order and hope it arrives on time. There's a better way." That better way would be shopping and buying at Best Buy, the ultimate holiday showroom. Most consumers reacted positively to the light-hearted campaign, which helped lift holiday store traffic. However, the real challenge for Best Buy is to convert shoppers to buyers. Some customers remained skeptics. As one consumer tweeted regarding the "Ultimate Showroom" ads: "Dear Best Buy, I'm glad you know your place as a showroom. Love, everyone who shops at Amazon."

International Pricing

Companies that market their products internationally must decide what prices to charge in different countries. In some cases, a company can set a uniform worldwide price. For example, Boeing sells its jetliners at about the same price everywhere, whether the buyer is in the United States, Europe, or a third-world country. However, most companies adjust their prices to reflect local market conditions and cost considerations.

The price that a company should charge in a specific country depends on many factors, including economic conditions, competitive situations, laws and regulations, and the nature of the wholesaling and retailing system. Consumer perceptions and preferences also may vary from country to country, calling for different prices. Or the company may have different marketing objectives in various world markets, which require changes in pricing strategy. For example, Apple introduces sophisticated, feature-rich, premium smartphones in carefully segmented mature markets in highly developed countries using a market-skimming pricing strategy. By contrast, it's now under pressure to discount older models and develop a more basic phone for sizable but less affluent markets in developing countries, supported by penetration pricing.

Costs play an important role in setting international prices. Travelers abroad are often surprised to find that goods that are relatively inexpensive at home may carry outrageously higher price tags in other countries. A pair of Levi's selling for $30 in the United States might go for $63 in Tokyo and $88 in Paris. A McDonald's Big Mac selling for a modest $4.20 in the United States might cost $7.85 in Norway or $5.65 in Brazil, and an Oral-B toothbrush selling for $2.49 at home may cost $10 in China. Conversely, a Gucci handbag going for only $140 in Milan, Italy, might fetch $240 in the United States. In some cases, such *price escalation* may result from differences in selling strategies or market conditions. In most instances, however, it is simply a result of the higher costs of selling in another country—the additional costs of operations, product modifications, shipping and insurance, import tariffs and taxes, exchange-rate fluctuations, and physical distribution.

Price has become a key element in the international marketing strategies of companies attempting to enter less affluent emerging markets. Typically, entering such markets has meant targeting the exploding middle classes in developing countries such as China, India, Russia, and Brazil, whose economies have been growing rapidly. More recently, however, as the weakened global economy has slowed growth in both domestic and emerging markets, many companies are shifting their sights to include a new target—the so-called "bottom of the pyramid," the vast untapped market consisting of the world's poorest consumers.

Not long ago, the preferred way for many brands to market their products in developing markets—whether consumer products or cars, computers, and smartphones—was to paste new labels on existing models and sell them at higher prices to the privileged few who could afford them. However, such a pricing approach put many products out of the reach of the tens of millions of poor consumers in emerging markets. As a result, many companies developed smaller, more basic and affordable product versions for these markets. For example, Unilever—the maker of such brands as Dove, Sunsilk, Lipton, and Vaseline—shrunk its packaging and set low prices that even the world's poorest consumers could afford. It developed single-use packages of its shampoo, laundry detergent, face cream, and other products that it could sell profitably for just pennies a pack. As a result, today, more than half of Unilever's revenues come from emerging economies.[12]

International pricing: To lower prices in emerging markets, such as Indonesia shown here, Unilever developed smaller, single-use packets of its Sunsilk, Ponds, Dove, and other brands that sell at prices even the world's poorest consumers can afford.

Bloomberg via Getty Images

Although this strategy has been successful for Unilever, most companies are learning that selling profitably to the bottom of the pyramid requires more than just repackaging or stripping down existing products and selling them at low prices. Just like more well-to-do consumers, low-income buyers want products that are both functional *and* aspirational. Thus, companies today are innovating to create products that not only sell at very low prices but also give bottom-of-the-pyramid consumers more for their money, not less (see Real Marketing 11.2).

International pricing presents many special problems and complexities. We discuss international pricing issues in more detail in Chapter 19.

Author Comment | When and how should a company change its price? What if costs rise, putting the squeeze on profits? What if the economy sags and customers become more price sensitive? Or what if a major competitor raises or drops its prices? As Figure 11.1 suggests, companies face many price-changing options.

Price Changes

After developing their pricing structures and strategies, companies often face situations in which they must initiate price changes or respond to price changes by competitors.

Initiating Price Changes

In some cases, the company may find it desirable to initiate either a price cut or a price increase. In both cases, it must anticipate possible buyer and competitor reactions.

Initiating Price Cuts

Several situations may lead a firm to consider cutting its price. One such circumstance is excess capacity. Another is falling demand in the face of strong price competition or a weakened economy. In such cases, the firm may aggressively cut prices to boost sales and market share. But as the airline, fast-food, automobile, retailing, and other industries have learned in recent years, cutting prices in an industry loaded with excess capacity may lead to price wars as competitors try to hold on to market share.

A company may also cut prices in a drive to dominate the market through lower costs. Either the company starts with lower costs than its competitors, or it cuts prices in the hope

Real Marketing 11.2

International Pricing: Targeting the Bottom of the Pyramid

Many companies are now waking up to a shocking statistic. Of the roughly 7 billion people on this planet, 4 billion of them (that's 57 percent) live in poverty. Known as the "bottom of the pyramid," the world's poor might not seem like a promising market. However, despite their paltry incomes, as a group, these consumers represent an eye-popping $5 trillion in annual purchasing power. Moreover, this vast segment is largely untapped. The world's poor often have little or no access to even the most basic products and services taken for granted by more affluent consumers. As the weakened global economy has flattened domestic markets and slowed the growth of emerging middle-class markets, companies are increasingly looking to the bottom of the pyramid for fresh growth opportunities.

But how can a company sell profitably to consumers with incomes below the poverty level? For starters, the *price* has got to be right. And in this case, says one analyst, "right" means "lower than you can imagine." With this in mind, many companies have made their products more affordable simply by offering smaller package sizes or lower-tech versions of current products. For example, in Nigeria, P&G sells a Gillette razor for 23 cents, a 1-ounce package of Ariel detergent for about 10 cents, and a 10-count pack of one-diaper-a-night Pampers for $2.30. Although there isn't much margin on products selling for pennies apiece, P&G is succeeding through massive volume.

Consider Pampers: Nigeria alone produces some 6 million newborns each year, almost 50 percent more than the United States, a country with twice the population. Nigeria's astounding birthrate creates a huge, untapped market for Pampers diapers, P&G's top-selling brand. However, the typical Nigerian mother spends only about 5,000 naira a month, about $30, on household purchases. P&G's task is to make Pampers affordable to this mother and to convince her that Pampers are worth some of her scarce spending. To keep costs and prices low in markets like Nigeria, P&G invented an absorbent diaper with fewer features. Although much less expensive, the diaper still functions at a high level. When creating such affordable new products, says an R&D manager at P&G, "Delight, don't dilute." That is, the diaper needs to be priced low, but it also has to do what other cheap diapers don't—keep a baby comfortable and dry for 12 hours.

Even with the right diaper at the right price, selling Pampers in Nigeria presents a challenge. In the West, babies typically go through numerous disposable diapers a day. In Nigeria, however, most babies are in cloth diapers. To make Pampers more acceptable and even more affordable for Nigerians, P&G markets the diapers as a one-a-day item. According to company ads, "One Pampers equals one dry night." The campaign tells mothers that keeping babies dry at night helps them to get a good night's sleep, which in turn helps them to grow and achieve. The message taps into a deep sentiment among Nigerians, unearthed by P&G researchers, that their children will have a better life than they do. Thus, thanks to affordable pricing, a product that meets customers' needs, and relevant positioning, Pampers sales are booming. In Nigeria, the name Pampers is now synonymous with diapers.

As P&G has learned, in most cases, selling profitably to the bottom of the pyramid takes much more than just developing single-use packets and pennies-apiece pricing. It requires broad-based innovation that produces not just lower prices but also new products that give people in poverty more for their money, not less. As another example, consider how Indian appliance company Godrej & Boyce used customer-driven innovation to successfully tap the market for low-priced refrigerators in India:

> Because of their high cost to both buy and operate, traditional compressor-driven refrigerators had penetrated only 18 percent of the Indian market. But rather than just produce a cheaper, stripped-down version of its higher-end refrigerators, Godrej assigned a team to study the needs of Indian consumers with poor or no refrigeration. The semi-urban and rural people the team observed typically earned 5,000 to 8,000 rupees (about $125 to $200) a month, lived in single-room dwellings with four or five family members, and changed residences frequently. Unable to afford conventional refrigerators, these consumers were making do with communal,

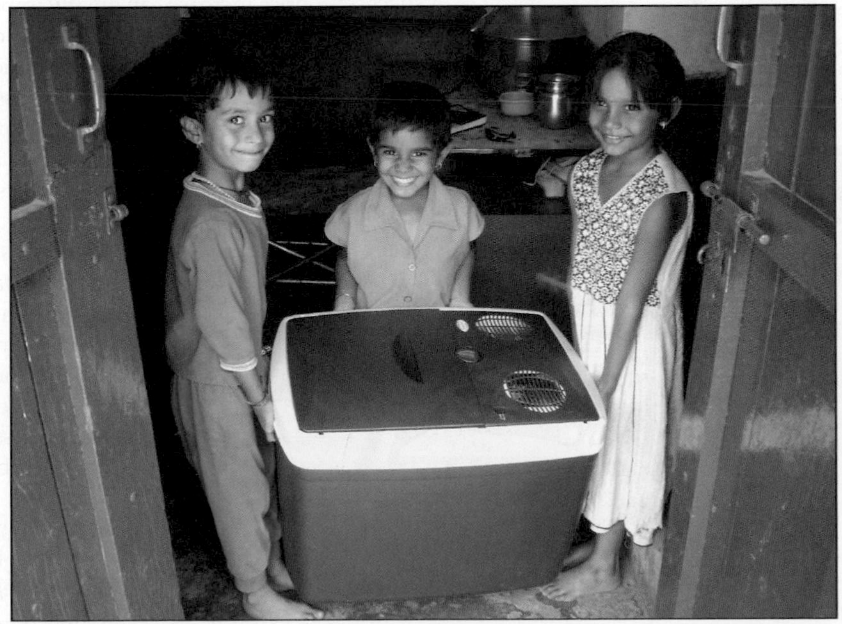

Selling to the world's poor: At only $69, Godrej's ChotuKool ("little cool") does a better job of meeting the needs of low-end Indian consumers at half the price of even the most basic conventional refrigerator.

Courtesy Godrej & Boyce Mfg. Co. Ltd.

usually second-hand ones. But even the shared fridges usually contained only a few items. Their users tended to shop daily and buy only small quantities of vegetables and milk. Moreover, electricity was unreliable, putting even the little food they wanted to keep cool at risk.

Godrej concluded that the low-end segment had little need for a conventional high-end refrigerator; it needed a fundamentally new product. So Godrej invented the ChotuKool ("little cool"), a candy red, top-opening, highly-portable, dorm-size unit that has room for the few items users want to keep fresh for a day or two. Rather than a compressor and refrigerant, the miserly little unit uses a chip that cools when current is applied, and its top-opening design keeps cold air inside when the lid is opened. In all, the ChotuKool uses less than half the energy of a conventional refrigerator and can run on a battery during the power outages common in rural villages. The best part: At only $69, "little cool" does a better job of meeting the needs of low-end consumers at half the price of even the most basic traditional refrigerator.

Thus, the bottom of the pyramid offers huge untapped opportunities to companies that can develop the right products at the right prices. And companies such as P&G are moving aggressively to capture these opportunities. P&G has set lofty goals for acquiring new customers, moving the company's emphasis from the developed West, where it currently gets most of its revenue, to the developing economies of Asia and Africa.

But successfully tapping these new developing markets will require more than just shipping out cheaper versions of existing products. "Our innovation strategy is not just diluting the top-tier product for the lower-end consumer," says P&G's CEO. "You have to discretely innovate for every one of those consumers on that economic curve, and if you don't do that, you'll fail."

Sources: Based on information from David Holthaus, "Pampers: P&G's No. 1 Growth Brand," *Cincinnati.com*, April 17, 2011, http://news.cincinnati.com/article/20110417/BIZ01/104170337/; Mya Frazier, "How P&G Brought the Diaper Revolution to China," *CBS News*, January 7, 2010, www.cbsnews.com/8301-505125_162-51379838/; David Holthaus, "Health Talk First, Then a Sales Pitch," April 17, 2011, *Cincinnati.com*, http://news.cincinnati.com/article/20110417/BIZ01/104170344/; Matthew J. Eyring, Mark W. Johnson, and Hari Nair, "New Business Models in Emerging Markets," *Harvard Business Review*, January–February 2011, pp. 89–95; C. K. Prahalad, "Bottom of the Pyramid as a Source of Breakthrough Innovations," *Journal of Product Innovation Management*, January 2012, pp. 6–12; Erik Simanis, "Reality Check at the Bottom of the Pyramid," *Harvard Business Review*, June 2012, pp. 120–125; "Marketing Innovative Devices for the Base of the Pyramid," Hystra Consulting, March 2013, http://hystra.com/marketing-devices; and "The State of Consumption Today," *Worldwatch Institute*, www.worldwatch.org/node/810, accessed September 2014.

of gaining market share that will further cut costs through larger volume. For example, computer and electronics maker Lenovo uses an aggressive low-cost, low-price strategy to increase its share of the PC market in developing countries.

Initiating Price Increases

A successful price increase can greatly improve profits. For example, if the company's profit margin is 3 percent of sales, a 1 percent price increase will boost profits by 33 percent if sales volume is unaffected. A major factor in price increases is cost inflation. Rising costs squeeze profit margins and lead companies to pass cost increases along to customers. Another factor leading to price increases is over-demand: When a company cannot supply all that its customers need, it may raise its prices, ration products to customers, or both—consider today's worldwide oil and gas industry.

When raising prices, the company must avoid being perceived as a *price gouger*. For example, when gasoline prices rise rapidly, angry customers often accuse the major oil companies of enriching themselves at the expense of consumers. Customers have long memories, and they will eventually turn away from companies or even whole industries that they perceive as charging excessive prices. In the extreme, claims of price gouging may even bring about increased government regulation.

There are some techniques for avoiding these problems. One is to maintain a sense of fairness surrounding any price increase. Price increases should be supported by company communications telling customers why prices are being raised.

Wherever possible, the company should consider ways to meet higher costs or demand without raising prices. For example, it might consider more cost-effective ways to produce or distribute its products. It can "unbundle" its market offering, removing features, packaging, or services and separately

Initiating price increases: When gasoline prices rise rapidly, angry consumers often accuse the major oil companies of enriching themselves by gouging customers.

Louis DeLuca/Dallas Morning News/Corbis

pricing elements that were formerly part of the offer. Or it can shrink the product or substitute less-expensive ingredients instead of raising the price. P&G recently did this with Tide by holding price while shrinking 100-ounce containers to 92 ounces and 50-ounce containers to 46 ounces, creating a more than 8 percent price increase per ounce without changing package prices. Similarly, Kimberly-Clark raised Kleenex prices by "desheeting"—reducing the number of sheets of toilet paper or facial tissues in each package. And a regular Snickers bar now weighs 1.86 ounces, down from 2.07 ounces in the past, effectively increasing prices by 11 percent.[13]

Buyer Reactions to Price Changes

Customers do not always interpret price changes in a straightforward way. A price *increase*, which would normally lower sales, may have some positive meanings for buyers. For example, what would you think if Rolex *raised* the price of its latest watch model? On the one hand, you might think that the watch is even more exclusive or better made. On the other hand, you might think that Rolex is simply being greedy by charging what the traffic will bear.

Similarly, consumers may view a price *cut* in several ways. For example, what would you think if Rolex were to suddenly cut its prices? You might think that you are getting a better deal on an exclusive product. More likely, however, you'd think that quality had been reduced, and the brand's luxury image might be tarnished. A brand's price and image are often closely linked. A price change, especially a drop in price, can adversely affect how consumers view the brand.

Competitor Reactions to Price Changes

A firm considering a price change must worry about the reactions of its competitors as well as those of its customers. Competitors are most likely to react when the number of firms involved is small, when the product is uniform, and when the buyers are well informed about products and prices.

How can the firm anticipate the likely reactions of its competitors? The problem is complex because, like the customer, the competitor can interpret a company price cut in many ways. It might think the company is trying to grab a larger market share or that it's doing poorly and trying to boost its sales. Or it might think that the company wants the whole industry to cut prices to increase total demand.

The company must guess each competitor's likely reaction. If all competitors behave alike, this amounts to analyzing only a typical competitor. In contrast, if the competitors do not behave alike—perhaps because of differences in size, market shares, or policies—then separate analyses are necessary. However, if some competitors will match the price change, there is good reason to expect that the rest will also match it.

Responding to Price Changes

Here we reverse the question and ask how a firm should respond to a price change by a competitor. The firm needs to consider several issues: Why did the competitor change the price? Is the price change temporary or permanent? What will happen to the company's market share and profits if it does not respond? Are other competitors going to respond? Besides these issues, the company must also consider its own situation and strategy and possible customer reactions to price changes.

Figure 11.1 shows the ways a company might assess and respond to a competitor's price cut. Suppose the company learns that a competitor has cut its price and decides that this price cut is likely to harm its sales and profits. It might simply decide to hold its current price and profit margin. The company might believe that it will not lose too much market share, or that it would lose too much profit if it reduced its own price. Or it might decide that it should wait and respond when it has more information on the effects of the competitor's price change. However, waiting too long to act might let the competitor get stronger and more confident as its sales increase.

If the company decides that effective action can and should be taken, it might make any of four responses. First, it could *reduce its price* to match the competitor's price. It may decide that the market is price sensitive and that it would lose too much market share to the lower-priced competitor. However, cutting the price will reduce the company's profits in the short run. Some companies might also reduce their product quality, services, and

FIGURE | 11.1
Responding to Competitor Price Changes

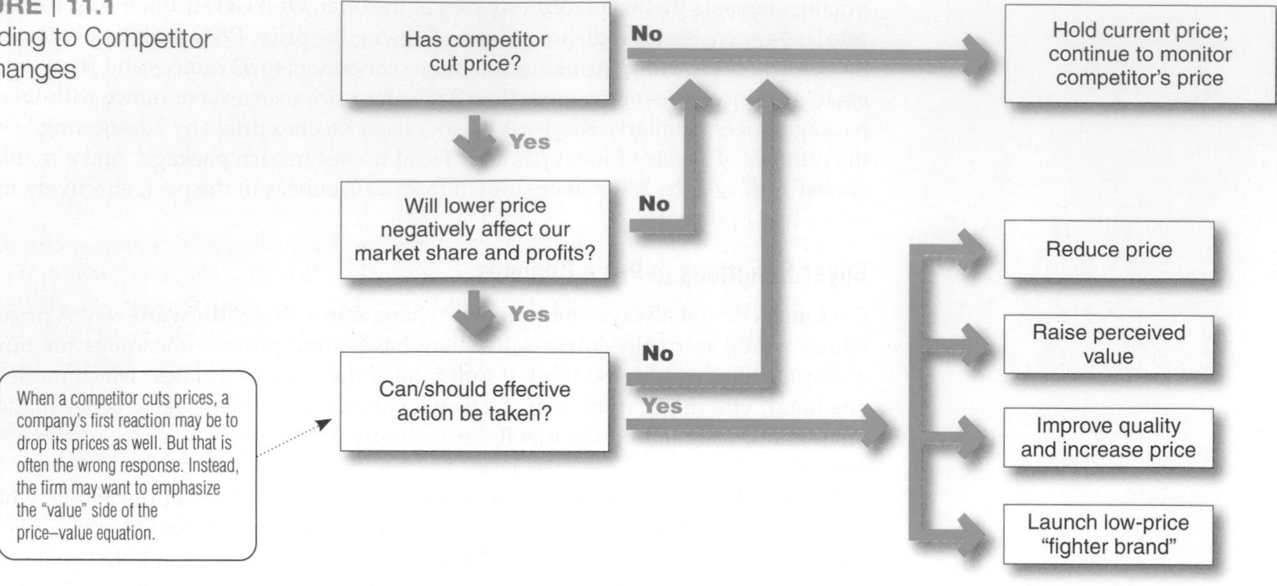

marketing communications to retain profit margins, but this will ultimately hurt long-run market share. The company should try to maintain its quality as it cuts prices.

Alternatively, the company might maintain its price but *raise the perceived value* of its offer. It could improve its communications, stressing the relative value of its product over that of the lower-price competitor. The firm may find it cheaper to maintain price and spend money to improve its perceived value than to cut price and operate at a lower margin. Or, the company might *improve quality* and *increase price*, moving its brand into a higher price–value position. The higher quality creates greater customer value, which justifies the higher price. In turn, the higher price preserves the company's higher margins.

Finally, the company might launch a *low-price "fighter brand"*—adding a lower-price item to the line or creating a separate lower-price brand. This is necessary if the particular market segment being lost is price sensitive and will not respond to arguments of higher quality. Starbucks did this when it acquired Seattle's Best Coffee, a brand positioned with working-class, "approachable-premium" appeal compared to the more professional, full-premium appeal of the main Starbucks brand. Seattle's Best coffee is generally cheaper than the parent Starbucks brand. As such, at retail, it competes more directly with Dunkin' Donuts, McDonald's, and other mass-premium brands through its franchise outlets and through partnerships with Subway, Burger King, Delta, AMC theaters, Royal Caribbean cruise lines, and others. On supermarket shelves, it competes with store brands and other mass-premium coffees such as Folgers Gourmet Selections and Millstone.[14]

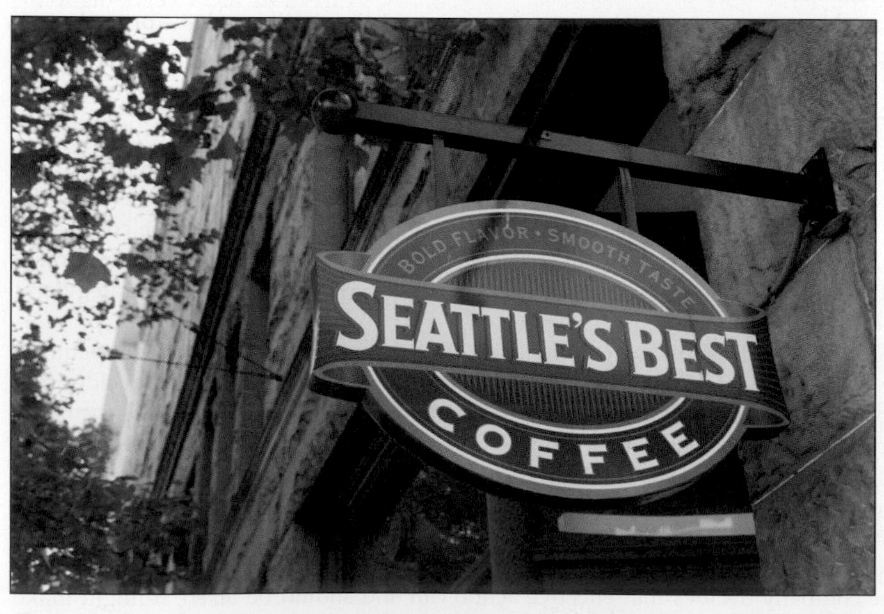

Fighter brands: Starbucks has positioned its Seattle's Best Coffee unit to compete more directly with the "mass-premium" brands sold by Dunkin' Donuts, McDonald's, and other lower-priced competitors.

To counter store brands and other low-price entrants in a tighter economy, P&G turned a number of its brands into fighter brands. Luvs disposable diapers give parents "premium leakage protection for less than pricier brands." And P&G offers popular budget-priced basic versions of several of its major brands. For example, Charmin Basic "holds up at a great everyday price," and Puffs Basic gives you "Everyday softness. Everyday value." And Tide Simply Clean & Fresh is about 35 percent cheaper than regular

Tide detergent. However, companies must use caution when introducing fighter brands, as such brands can tarnish the image of the main brand. In addition, although they may attract budget buyers away from lower-priced rivals, they can also take business away from the firm's higher-margin brands.

Author Comment | Pricing decisions are often constrained by social and legal issues. For example, think about the pharmaceuticals industry. Are rapidly rising prescription drug prices justified? Or are the drug companies unfairly lining their pockets by gouging consumers who have few alternatives? Should the government step in?

Public Policy and Pricing

Price competition is a core element of our free-market economy. In setting prices, companies usually are not free to charge whatever prices they wish. Many federal, state, and even local laws govern the rules of fair play in pricing. In addition, companies must consider broader societal pricing concerns. In setting their prices, for example, pharmaceutical firms must balance their development costs and profit objectives against the sometimes life-and-death needs of drug consumers.

The most important pieces of legislation affecting pricing are the Sherman Act, the Clayton Act, and the Robinson-Patman Act, initially adopted to curb the formation of monopolies and regulate business practices that might unfairly restrain trade. Because these federal statutes can be applied only to interstate commerce, some states have adopted similar provisions for companies that operate locally.

Figure 11.2 shows the major public policy issues in pricing. These include potentially damaging pricing practices within a given level of the channel (price-fixing and predatory pricing) and across levels of the channel (retail price maintenance, discriminatory pricing, and deceptive pricing).[15]

Pricing within Channel Levels

Federal legislation on *price-fixing* states that sellers must set prices without talking to competitors. Otherwise, price collusion is suspected. Price-fixing is illegal per se—that is, the government does not accept any excuses for price-fixing. As such, companies found guilty of these practices can receive heavy fines. Recently, governments at the state and national levels have been aggressively enforcing price-fixing regulations in industries ranging from gasoline, insurance, and concrete to credit cards, CDs, and computer chips. Price-fixing is also prohibited in many international markets. For example, Apple was recently fined $670,000 on price-fixing charges for its iPhones in Taiwan.[16]

Sellers are also prohibited from using *predatory pricing*—selling below cost with the intention of punishing a competitor or gaining higher long-run profits by putting competitors out of business. This protects small sellers from larger ones that might sell items below cost temporarily or in a specific locale to drive them out of business. The biggest problem is determining just what constitutes predatory pricing behavior. Selling below cost to unload excess inventory is not considered predatory; selling below cost to drive out competitors is. Thus, a given action may or may not be predatory depending on intent, and intent can be very difficult to determine or prove.

In recent years, several large and powerful companies have been accused of predatory pricing. However, turning an accusation into a lawsuit can be difficult. For example,

FIGURE | 11.2
Public Policy Issues in Pricing

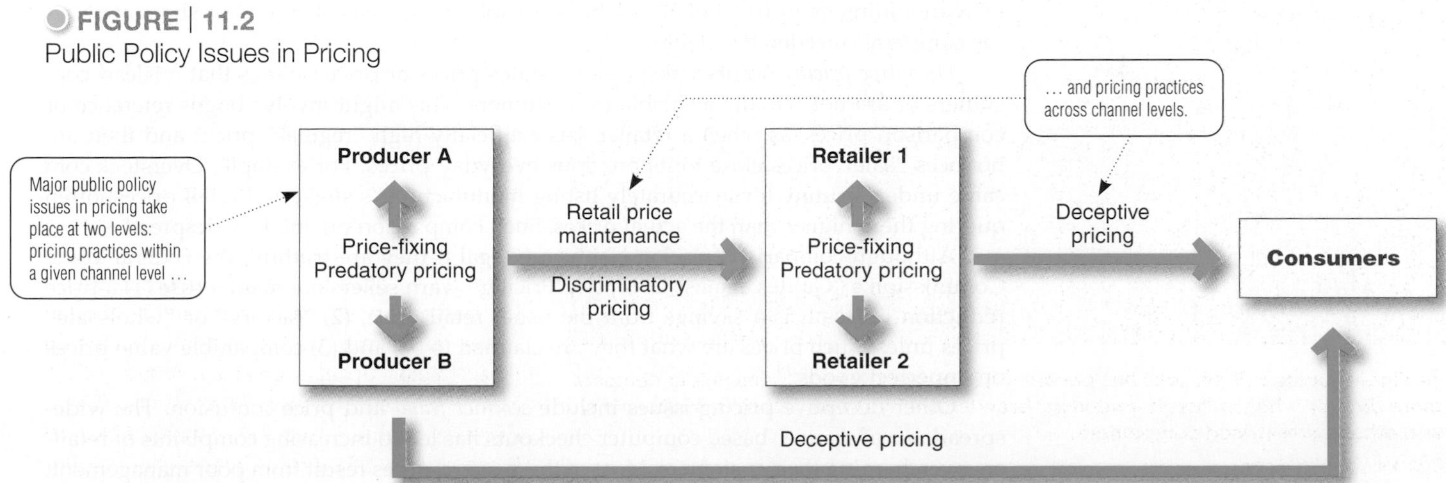

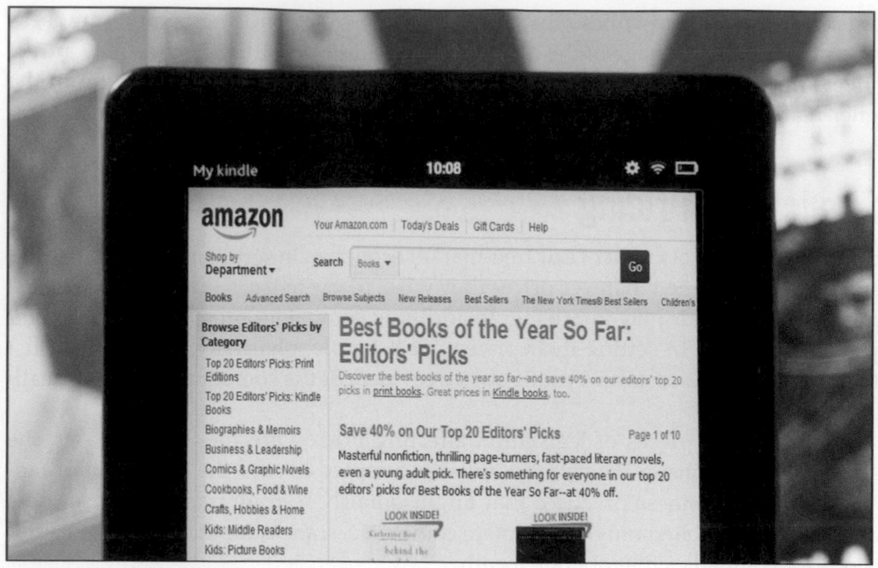

Predatory pricing: Some industry critics have accused Amazon.com of pricing books at fire-sale prices that harm competing booksellers. But is it predatory pricing or just plain good competitive marketing?

Christopher Schall | Impact Photo

many publishers and booksellers have expressed concerns about Amazon.com's predatory practices, especially its book pricing:[17]

> Many booksellers and publishers complain that Amazon.com's book pricing policies are destroying their industry. During past holiday seasons, Amazon has sold top-10 bestselling hardback books as loss leaders at cut-rate prices of less than $10 each. And Amazon now sells e-books at fire-sale prices in order to win customers for its Kindle e-reader. Such very low book prices have caused considerable damage to competing booksellers, many of whom view Amazon's pricing actions as predatory. Says one observer, "The word 'predator' is pretty strong, and I don't use it loosely, but . . . I could have sworn we had laws against predatory pricing. I just don't understand why [Amazon's pricing] is not an issue." Still, no predatory pricing charges have ever been filed against Amazon. It would be extremely difficult to prove that such loss-leader pricing is purposefully predatory as opposed to just plain good competitive marketing.

Pricing across Channel Levels

The Robinson-Patman Act seeks to prevent unfair *price discrimination* by ensuring that sellers offer the same price terms to customers at a given level of trade. For example, every retailer is entitled to the same price terms from a given manufacturer, whether the retailer is REI or a local bicycle shop. However, price discrimination is allowed if the seller can prove that its costs are different when selling to different retailers—for example, that it costs less per unit to sell a large volume of bicycles to REI than to sell a few bicycles to the local dealer.

The seller can also discriminate in its pricing if the seller manufactures different qualities of the same product for different retailers. The seller has to prove that these differences are proportional. Price differentials may also be used to "match competition" in "good faith," provided the price discrimination is temporary, localized, and defensive rather than offensive.

Laws also prohibit *retail (or resale) price maintenance*—a manufacturer cannot require dealers to charge a specified retail price for its product. Although the seller can propose a manufacturer's *suggested* retail price to dealers, it cannot refuse to sell to a dealer that takes independent pricing action, nor can it punish the dealer by shipping late or denying advertising allowances. For example, the Florida attorney general's office investigated Nike for allegedly fixing the retail price of its shoes and clothing. It was concerned that Nike might be withholding items from retailers who were not selling its most expensive shoes at prices the company considered suitable.

Deceptive pricing occurs when a seller states prices or price savings that mislead consumers or are not actually available to consumers. This might involve bogus reference or comparison prices, as when a retailer sets artificially high "regular" prices and then announces "sale" prices close to its previous everyday prices. For example, Overstock.com came under scrutiny for inaccurately listing manufacturer's suggested retail prices, often quoting them higher than the actual prices. Such comparison pricing is widespread.

Although comparison pricing claims are legal if they are truthful, the Federal Trade Commission's "Guides against Deceptive Pricing" warn sellers not to advertise (1) a price reduction unless it is a savings from the usual retail price, (2) "factory" or "wholesale" prices unless such prices are what they are claimed to be, and (3) comparable value prices on imperfect goods.[18]

Other deceptive pricing issues include *scanner fraud* and price confusion. The widespread use of scanner-based computer checkouts has led to increasing complaints of retailers overcharging their customers. Most of these overcharges result from poor management, such as a failure to enter current or sale prices into the system. Other cases, however, involve intentional overcharges.

Many federal and state statutes regulate against deceptive pricing practices. For example, the Automobile Information Disclosure Act requires automakers to attach a statement on new vehicle windows stating the manufacturer's suggested retail price, the prices of optional equipment, and the dealer's transportation charges. However, reputable sellers go beyond what is required by law. Treating customers fairly and making certain that they fully understand prices and pricing terms is an important part of building strong and lasting customer relationships.

11 Reviewing the Concepts

OBJECTIVES REVIEW AND KEY TERMS

Objectives Review

In this chapter, we examined some additional pricing considerations—new product pricing, product mix pricing, price adjustments, initiating and reacting to prices changes, and pricing and public policy. A company sets not a single price but rather a *pricing structure* that covers its entire mix of products. This pricing structure changes over time as products move through their life cycles. The company adjusts product prices to reflect changes in costs and demand and account for variations in buyers and situations. As the competitive environment changes, the company considers when to initiate price changes and when to respond to them.

OBJECTIVE 1 Describe the major strategies for pricing new products. (pp 349–350)

Pricing is a dynamic process, and pricing strategies usually change as the product passes through its life cycle. The introductory stage—setting prices for the first time—is especially challenging. The company can decide on one of several strategies for pricing innovative new products: It can use *market-skimming pricing* by initially setting high prices to "skim" the maximum amount of revenue from various segments of the market. Or it can use *market-penetrating pricing* by setting a low initial price to penetrate the market deeply and win a large market share. Several conditions must be set for either new product pricing strategy to work.

OBJECTIVE 2 Explain how companies find a set of prices that maximizes the profits from the total product mix. (pp 350–352)

When the product is part of a product mix, the firm searches for a set of prices that will maximize the profits from the total mix. In *product line pricing*, the company determines the price steps for the entire product line it offers. In addition, the company must set prices for *optional products* (optional or accessory products included with the main product), *captive products* (products that are required for using the main product), *by-products* (waste or residual products produced when making the main product), and *product bundles* (combinations of products at a reduced price).

OBJECTIVE 3 Discuss how companies adjust their prices to take into account different types of customers and situations. (pp 352–360)

Companies apply a variety of *price adjustment strategies* to account for differences in consumer segments and situations. One is *discount and allowance pricing*, whereby the company establishes cash, quantity, functional, or seasonal discounts, or varying types of allowances. A second strategy is *segmented pricing*, where the company sells a product at two or more prices to accommodate different customers, product forms, locations, or times. Sometimes companies consider more than economics in their pricing decisions, using *psychological pricing* to better communicate a product's intended position. In *promotional pricing*, a company offers discounts or temporarily sells a product below list price as a special event, sometimes even selling below cost as a loss leader. Another approach is *geographical pricing*, whereby the company decides how to price to distant customers, choosing from such alternatives as FOB-origin pricing, uniform-delivered pricing, zone pricing, basing-point pricing, and freight-absorption pricing. Using *dynamic pricing*, a company can adjust prices continually to meet the characteristics and needs of individual customers and situations. Finally, *international pricing* means that the company adjusts its price to meet different conditions and expectations in different world markets.

OBJECTIVE 4 Discuss the key issues related to initiating and responding to price changes. (pp 360–365)

When a firm considers initiating a *price change*, it must consider customers' and competitors' reactions. There are different implications to *initiating price cuts* and *initiating price increases*. Buyer reactions to price changes are influenced by the meaning customers see in the price change. Competitors' reactions flow from a set reaction policy or a fresh analysis of each situation.

There are also many factors to consider in responding to a competitor's price changes. The company that faces a price change initiated by a competitor must try to understand the competitor's intent as well as the likely duration and impact of the change. If a swift reaction is desirable, the firm should preplan its reactions to different possible price actions by competitors. When facing a competitor's price change, the company might sit tight, reduce its own price, raise perceived quality, improve quality and raise price, or launch a fighter brand.

OBJECTIVE 5 **Overview the social and legal issues that affect pricing decisions.** *(pp 365–367)*

Many federal, state, and even local laws govern the rules of fair pricing. Also, companies must consider broader societal pricing concerns. The major public policy issues in pricing include potentially damaging pricing practices *within* a given level of the channel, such as price-fixing and predatory pricing. They also include pricing practices *across* channel levels, such as retail price maintenance, discriminatory pricing, and deceptive pricing. Although many federal and state statutes regulate pricing practices, reputable sellers go beyond what is required by law. Treating customers fairly is an important part of building strong and lasting customer relationships.

MyMarketingLab

Go to **mymktlab.com** to complete the problems marked with this icon .

Key Terms

OBJECTIVE 1

Market-skimming pricing (price skimming) (p 349)
Market-penetration pricing (p 349)

OBJECTIVE 2

Product line pricing (p 350)
Optional-product pricing (p 350)
Captive-product pricing (p 351)
By-product pricing (p 351)
Product bundle pricing (p 352)

OBJECTIVE 3

Discount (p 352)
Allowance (p 352)
Segmented pricing (p 353)
Psychological pricing (p 353)
Reference prices (p 354)
Promotional pricing (p 354)
Geographical pricing (p 355)
FOB-origin pricing (p 355)
Uniform-delivered pricing (p 356)
Zone pricing (p 356)
Basing-point pricing (p 356)
Freight-absorption pricing (p 356)
Dynamic pricing (p 356)

DISCUSSION AND CRITICAL THINKING

Discussion Questions

11-1 Explain the essential nature of pricing and why it is necessary to switch strategies over the course of a product or service life cycle. What is particularly important about setting prices for the first time? (AACSB: Communication; Reflective Thinking)

11-2 Define captive-product pricing and give examples. What must marketers be concerned about when implementing this type of pricing? (AACSB: Communication)

11-3 What is geographical pricing? What kinds of options are available to a company using this type of pricing? (AACSB: Communication)

11-4 What factors does a company need to consider when responding to a competitor's price change? What is the process and why are these steps important? (AACSB: Communication)

11-5 Briefly discuss the major policy issues across levels of the channel of distribution. (AACSB: Communication)

Critical Thinking Exercises

11-6 You are an owner of a small independent chain of coffee houses competing head-to-head with Starbucks. The retail price your customers pay for coffee is exactly the same as at Starbucks. The wholesale price you pay for roasted coffee beans has increased by 25 percent. You know that you cannot absorb this increase and that you must pass it on to your customers. However, you are concerned about the consequences of an open price increase. Discuss three alternative price-increase strategies that address these concerns. (AACSB: Communication; Reflective Thinking)

11-7 Identify three online price-comparison shopping sites or apps and shop for a product you are interested in purchasing. Compare the price ranges given at the three sites. Based on your search, determine a "fair" price for the product. (AACSB: Communication; Use of IT; Reflective Thinking)

11-8 One psychological pricing tactic is "just-below" pricing. It is also called "9-ending" pricing because prices usually end in the number 9 (or 99). In a small group, have each member select five different products and visit a store to learn the price of those items. Is there a variation among the items and stores with regard to 9-ending pricing? Why do marketers use this pricing tactic? (AACSB: Communication; Reflective Thinking)

MINICASES AND APPLICATIONS

Online, Mobile, and Social Media Marketing **Online Price Glitches**

Walmart's recent online price glitches—erroneous prices accidentally posted on the Web—is just one in a string of Web price glitches haunting sellers. The error led to very low prices for regularly higher-priced items such as treadmills, televisions, and computer monitors, with some priced under $10. Word spread quickly through social media and consumers rushed to place orders before Walmart wised up. No one was interested in purchasing the incorrectly priced Lysol for $100 or the Kool-Aid packets for $70, but they sure wanted to take advantage of the steals. Social media made matters worse as lucky customers tweeted about the deals. Web sites such as FatWallet and SlickDeals also sent e-mail alerts for "possible PMs"—price mistakes—discussed in forums. Walmart was not alone, however. Amazon incorrectly priced DVDs at more than 75 percent off the actual price, Dell priced a $1,000 computer at $25, Sears offered an iPad2 for $69, Best Buy priced a 52-inch HDTV for just $10, Zappos site 6pm.com capped all prices at $49.99, Delta airlines had flights priced as low as $12, and a glitch on the American Airlines Web site gave away flights for free! Walmart reacted by cancelling the orders and offering buyers a $10 e-gift card, but American Airlines and Zappos honored the mistakenly priced orders at a cost in the millions. Most online price glitches, if caught before the item is shipped, are not honored by the seller.

11-9 Research the legal requirements regarding orders resulting from a pricing mistake. Must sellers honor such orders? Write a report of what you learn. (AACSB: Communication; Reflective Thinking)

11-10 Research these and other online pricing glitches and summarize what marketers did that was well and/or not well received by consumers. What suggestions would you make to marketers for handling such problems? (AACSB: Communication; Reflective Thinking)

Marketing Ethics **Breaking the Law or Cultural Norm?**

Tokyo-headquartered Bridgestone Corporation, the world's largest tire and rubber producer, recently agreed to plead guilty to price-fixing along with 25 other Japanese automotive suppliers. Twenty-eight executives were involved and pled guilty to the charges; some face prison sentences. Bridgestone and other suppliers were charged with conspiring to fix prices, rig bids, and allocate sales of parts sold to Japanese automakers Toyota, Isuzu, Nissan, Suzuki, and Fuji Heavy Industries in the United States during most of the 2000s. The company was slapped with a whopping $425 million criminal fine, more than double any of the other offenders' fines. In 2011, Bridgestone paid a $28 million fine for conspiring to fix prices with competitors in the marine hose industry but did not disclose that it was conducting the same activity in the automotive industry. The U.S. Justice Department didn't take kindly to that—hence the much larger fine this time. Collaboration among competitors is not unusual and is accepted in many Eastern cultures, such as Japan. Perhaps that is why the conspiracy continued for so many years. It involved Japanese suppliers selling to Japanese manufacturers, albeit in the United States.

11-11 No U.S.-based automotive manufacturers were victimized by this price-fixing scheme by Japan-based suppliers selling to Japan-based buyers in the United States. Should companies from different cultures that seem to accept such practices be punished so severely? (AACSB: Communication; Ethical Reasoning; Reflective Thinking)

11-12 Discuss other recent examples of price fixing. (AACSB: Communication; Reflective Thinking)

Marketing by the Numbers **Louis Vuitton Price Increase**

One way to maintain exclusivity for a brand is to raise its price. That's what luxury fashion and leather goods maker Louis Vuitton did. The company did not want the brand to become overexposed and too common, so it raised prices 10 percent and is slowing its expansion in China. The Louis Vuitton brand is the largest contributor to the company's $13.3 billion revenue from its fashion and leather division, accounting for $8 billion of those sales. It might seem counterintuitive to want to encourage fewer customers to purchase a company's products, but when price increases, so does the product's contribution margin, making each sale more profitable. Thus, sales can drop and the company can still maintain the same profitability as before the price hike.

11-13 If the company's original contribution margin was 40 percent, calculate the new contribution margin if price is increased 10 percent. Refer to Appendix 2, Marketing by the Numbers, paying attention to endnote 6 on the price change explanation in which the analysis is done by setting price equal to $1.00. (AACSB: Communications; Analytic Reasoning)

11-14 Determine by how much sales can drop and let the company still maintain the total contribution it had when the contribution margin was 40 percent. (AACSB: Communication; Analytic Reasoning)

Video Case Hammerpress

Printing paper goods may not sound like the best business to get into these days. But Hammerpress is a company that is carving out a niche in this old industry. And Hammerpress is doing it by returning to old technology. Today's printing firms use computer-driven graphic design techniques and printing processes. But Hammerpress creates greeting cards, calendars, and business cards that are hand-crafted by professional artists and printed using traditional letterpress technology.

When it comes to competing, this presents both opportunities and challenges. While Hammerpress's products certainly stand out as works of art, the cost for producing such goods is considerably higher than the industry average. This video illustrates how Hammerpress employs dynamic pricing techniques in order to meet the needs of various customer segments and thrive in a competitive environment.

After viewing the video featuring Hammerpress, answer the following questions:

11-15 How does Hammerpress employ the concept of dynamic pricing?

11-16 Discuss the three major pricing strategies in relation to Hammerpress. Which of these three do you think is the company's core strategic strategy?

11-17 Does it make sense for Hammerpress to compete in product categories where the market dictates a price that is not profitable for the company? Explain.

Company Case Coach: Riding the Wave of Premium Pricing

Victor Luis stood looking out the window of his office on 34th Street in Manhattan's Hell's Kitchen neighborhood. It had been just over a year since he had taken over as CEO of Coach, Inc., a position that had previously been held by Lewis Frankfort for 28 years. Under Frankfort's leadership, it seemed Coach could do no wrong. Indeed, over the previous decade, the 73-year-old company had seen its revenues skyrocket from about $1 billion to over $5 billion as its handbags became one of the most coveted luxury items for women in the United States and beyond. On top of that, the company's $1 billion bottom line—a 20 percent net margin—was typical. Coach's revenues made it the leading handbags seller in the nation. The brand's premium price and profit margins made the company a Wall Street darling.

Right around the time Luis took over, however, Coach's fortunes began to shift. Although the company had experienced promising results with expansion into men's lines and international markets, it had just recorded the fourth straight quarter of declining revenues in the United States, a market that accounted for 70 percent of its business. North American comparable sales were down by a whopping 21 percent over the previous year. Once the trendsetter, for two years in a row Coach lost market share to younger and more nimble competitors. Investors were jittery, causing Coach's stock price to drop by nearly 50 percent in just two years. After years of success, it now seemed that Coach could do little right.

Artisanal Origins

In a Manhattan loft in 1941, six artisans formed a partnership called Gail Leather Products and ran it as a family-owned business. Employing skills handed down from generation to generation, the group handcrafted a collection of leather goods, primarily wallets and billfolds. Five years later, the company hired Miles and Lillian Cahn—owners of a leather handbag manufacturing firm—and by 1950, Miles was running things.

As the business grew, Cahn took particular interest in the distinctive properties of the leather in baseball gloves. The gloves were stiff and tough when new, but with use they became soft and supple. Cahn developed a method that mimicked the wear-and-tear process, making a leather that was stronger, softer, and more flexible. As an added benefit, the worn leather also absorbed dye to a greater degree, producing deep, rich tones. When Lillian Cahn suggested adding women's handbags to the company's low-margin line of wallets, the Coach brand was born.

Over the next 20 years, Coach's uniquely soft and feminine cowhide bags developed a reputation for their durability. Coach bags also became known for innovative features and bright colors, rather than the usual browns and tans. As the Coach brand expanded into shoes and accessories, it also became known for attractive integrated hardware pieces—particularly the silver toggle that remains an identifying feature of the Coach brand today. In 1985, the Cahns sold Coach to the Sara Lee Corporation, which housed the brand within its Hanes Group. Lewis Frankfort became Coach's director and took the brand into a new era of growth and development.

Under Frankfort's leadership, Coach grew from a relatively small company to a widely recognized global brand. This growth not only included new designs for handbags and new product lines, but a major expansion of outlets as well. When Frankfort assumed the top position, Coach had only six boutiques located within department stores and a flagship Coach store on Madison

Avenue. By the time Frankfort stepped down, there were more than 900 Coach stores in North America, Asia, and Europe, with hundreds of Coach boutiques in department stores throughout those same markets as well as in Latin America, the Middle East, and Australia. In addition to the brick-and-mortar outlets, Coach had developed a healthy stream of online sales through its Web sites.

High Price Equals High Sales

With the expansion in Coach's product lines and distribution outlets, women everywhere were drawn to the brand's quality and style. But perhaps more than anything, they were attracted to the brand as a symbol of luxury, taste, and success. Over the years, Coach had taken great care to find an optimal price point, well above that of ordinary department store brands. Whereas stores that carried Coach products also sold mid-tier handbag brands for moderate prices, Coach bags were priced as much as five times higher.

It might seem that such a high price would scare buyers off. To the contrary. As Coach's reputation grew, women aspired to own its products. And although the price of a Coach bag is an extravagance for most buyers, it is still within reach for even middle-class women who want to splurge once in a while. And with comparable bags from Gucci, Fendi, or Prada priced five to ten times higher, a Coach bag is a relative bargain.

With its image as an accessible status symbol, Coach was one of the few luxury brands that maintained steady growth and profits throughout the Great Recession. And it did so without discounting its prices. Fearing that price cuts would damage the brand's image, Coach instead introduced its "Poppy" line at prices about 30 percent lower than regular Coach bags. Coach concentrated on its factory stores in outlet malls. And it maintained an emphasis on quality to drive perceptions of value. As a result, Coach's devoted customer base remained loyal throughout the tough times.

At about the same time, Coach also invested in new customers. It opened its first men's-only store, stocked with small leather goods, travel accessories, footwear, jewelry, and swimsuits. Coach also expanded men's collections in other stores. As a result, its revenue from men's products doubled in one year. The company saw similar success with international customers, pressing hard into Europe, China, and other Asian markets.

But just as it seemed that Coach was untouchable, the brand showed signs of frailty. Coach's U.S. handbag business started slowing down. During Luis's first year on the job, Coach's share of the U.S. handbag market fell from 19 percent to 17.5 percent—the second straight year for such a loss. During that same period, Michael Kors, Coach's biggest competitive threat, saw its market share increase from 4.5 percent to 7 percent. Up-and-comers Kate Spade and Tory Burch also saw increases. Because the U.S. market accounted for such a large portion of the company's business, overall revenue took a dip despite the brand's growth in new markets.

What's the Problem?

Many factors could be blamed. During the most recent holiday season, Coach had to contend with the same problem many other retailers faced—less traffic in shopping malls. But Kate Spade and Michael Kors, which operate their own stores and sell through department stores in malls just as Coach does, experienced double-digit gains during the same period. Coach's performance also ran counter to the dynamics of the handbag and accessory market as a whole, which grew by nearly 10 percent over the previous year.

The difference in sales trends between Coach and its competitors have led some analysts to speculate that the long-time leader has lost its eye for fashion. "These guys are definitely losing share," said analyst Brian Yarbrough. "Fashionwise, they're missing the beat." Yarbrough isn't alone. Many others assert that, under the same creative direction for 17 years, Coach's designs have grown stale.

Then there is the issue of Coach's price structure—in short, Coach may have taken the premium price point too far. "Coach tried to eliminate coupon promotions tied directly to its discount outlets, which are the company's biggest source of revenue, and which attract customers looking to stretch their dollars," said one luxury retail expert. "The number of people willing and able to pay a premium for luxury brands, like Coach, is getting small as this weak economy continues." However, price alone would not explain why Coach's business slid at the same time that sales by comparably priced competitors rose. Additionally, while Coach's North American revenues were down last year, sales of its high-end handbags (priced above $400) actually increased.

Some analysts have also questioned the effect of Coach's popularity on its image of exclusivity. A luxury brand's image and customer aspirations often rest on the fact that not everyone can afford it. But Coach has become so accessible, anyone that wants a Coach product can usually find a way to buy one. This availability has been fostered by Coach's outlet stores—company-owned stores that carry prior season merchandise, seconds, and lower-quality lines at much lower prices. With the number of customers drawn in by low prices, Coach's outlet stores now account for a sizable 60 percent of revenues and an even higher percentage of unit sales. Combine that with a healthy secondary market through eBay and other Web sites, and Coach products are no longer as exclusive as they once were.

Although new as CEO, Luis has been with Coach for the past eight years and oversaw Coach's international expansion. And although Frankfort has stepped down, he is still involved as chairman of the board. Led by these seasoned fashion executives, Coach has a turnaround plan. For starters, the company has hired a new creative director who, according to Luis, is "providing a fashion relevance for the brand like we have never had." Both the fashion and investment worlds anxiously await the first designs from the new regime.

In addition to the creative and design changes, Coach is rebalancing its product portfolio. To win back shoppers, Coach will be positioned as a lifestyle brand with greater expansion into footwear, clothing, and accessories. Additionally, the company will increase the number of handbag offerings priced at $400 or more, a move that could raise the average price point of Coach's handbags. With all that the brand has at stake, those in charge will not give up easily. The question is, will the new strategy restore Coach to its former glory days?

Questions for Discussion

11-18 What challenges does Coach face relative to pricing its vast product line?

11-19 Based on principles from the chapter, explain how price affects customer perceptions of the Coach brand.

11-20 How has increased competition at Coach's price points affected the brand's performance?

11-21 Will the plan proposed by current Coach leadership be successful in reversing the brand's slide in market share? Why or why not?

11-22 What recommendations would you make to Coach?

Sources: Andrew Marder, "Coach, Inc. Can't Get It Together," *Motley Fool*, April 30, 2014, www.fool.com/investing/general/2014/04/30/coach-inc-cant-get-it-together.aspx; Phil Wahba, "Coach Sales in North America Plummet as Market Share Erodes," *Reuters*, January 22, 2014, http://in.reuters.com/article/2014/01/22/coach-results-idINL3N0KW3V920140122; Ashley Lutz, "Coach Is Slipping Fast, and It Can All Be Traced to One Major Mistake," *Business Insider*, October 22, 2012, www.businessinsider.com/coach-is-losing-its-value-2012-10; and additional information taken from www.coach.com/online/handbags/genWCM-10551-10051-en-/Coach_US/CompanyInformation/InvestorRelations/CompanyProfile, accessed May 2014.

MyMarketingLab

Go to **mymktlab.com** for the following Assisted-graded writing questions:

11-23 Explain how businesses implement segmented pricing and discuss conditions necessary for success. (AACSB: Communication; Reflective Thinking)

11-24 Any charge that is not airfare is referred to as ancillary revenue for airlines—and they are cleaning up on it to the tune of $20 billion a year. While consumers can avoid some fees, such as those for food, preferred seating, and wi-fi, the majority can't avoid baggage fees. What type of pricing strategies are airlines using? Is it ethical for airlines to charge baggage fees? (AACSB: Communication; Ethical Reasoning)

References

1. Based on information from Tom Gara, "When Elephants Fight: The Great Wal-Mart-Amazon War of 2013," *Wall Street Journal*, March 28, 2013, http://blogs.wsj.com/corporate-intelligence/2013/03/28/when-elephants-fight-the-great-wal-mart-amazon-war-of-2013; Farhad Manjoo, "Walmart's Evolution from Big Box Giant to E-Commerce Innovator," *Fast Company*, November 26, 2012, www.fastcompany.com/3002948/walmarts-evolution-big-box-giant-e-commerce-innovator; Shelly Banjo, "Walmart's E-Stumble with Amazon," *Wall Street Journal,* June 19, 2013, http://online.wsj.com/news/articles/SB10001424127887323566804578553301017702818; and www.walmart.com and www.amazon.com, accessed September 2014.
2. "Lower Cost Samsung GALAXY Unveiled in Kenya," *BiztechAfrica,* May 23, 2014, www.biztechafrica.com/article/lower-cost-samsung-samsung-galaxy-unveiled-kenya/2967/#.Uvo4bfldV8F; Ed Sutherland, "Apple vs Samsung Price War in India," *iDownloadBlog,* April 17, 2013, www.idownloadblog.com/2013/04/17/apple-samsung-india-price-war/; Panjaj Mishra, "Apple Turns to Old iPhone Models, and Lower Prices, to Woo Users In India," *TechCrunch,* January 17, 2014, http://techcrunch.com/2014/01/17/apple-turns-to-old-iphone-models-and-lower-prices-to-woo-users-in-india/; and "Samsung Galaxy Pocket Neo," www.mysmartprice.com/mobile/samsung-galaxy-pocket-neo-msp2810, accessed March 2014.
3. Karis Hustad, "Kindle Fire HDX Keeps Amazon's Low Price, Adds Extra Features," *Christian Science Monitor,* September 26, 2013, www.csmonitor.com/Innovation/2013/0926/Kindle-Fire-HDX-keeps-Amazon-s-low-price-adds-extra-features.
4. See information found at http://investor.keuriggreenmountain.com/annuals-proxies.cfm, accessed September 2014.
5. See Oliver Strand, "With Coffee, the Price of Individualism Can Be High," *New York Times,* February 8, 2012, p. D6; and "$51 per Pound: The Deceptive Cost of Single-Serve Coffee," *New York Times,* www.thekitchn.com/51-per-pound-the-deceptive-cost-of-single-serve-coffee-the-new-york-times-165712, accessed February 2014.
6. Example based on information from Duane Stanford, "Coke Engineers Its Orange Juice—With an Algorithm," *Bloomberg Businessweek,* January 31, 2013, www.businessweek.com/articles/2013-01-31/coke-engineers-its-orange-juice-with-an-algorithm#p2.
7. For this and other examples, see Peter Coy, "Why the Price Is Rarely Right," *Bloomberg Businessweek*, February 1 & 8, 2010, pp. 77–78.
8. See Anthony Allred, E. K. Valentin, and Goutam Chakraborty, "Pricing Risky Services: Preference and Quality Considerations," *Journal of Product and Brand Management*, Vol. 19, No. 1, 2010, p. 54; Kenneth C. Manning and David E. Sprott, "Price Endings, Left-Digit Effects, and Choice," *Journal of Consumer Research*, August 2009, pp. 328–336; Martin Lindstrom, "The Psychology behind the Sweet Spots of Pricing," *Fast Company,* March 27, 2012, www.fastcompany.com/1826172/psychology-behind-sweet-spots-pricing; and Travis Nichols, "A Penny Saved: Psychological Pricing," *Gumroad,* October 18, 2013, http://blog.gumroad.com/post/64417917582/a-penny-saved-psychological-pricing.
9. See "Get Up To $100 Off Our Most Popular Tablets!" www.t-mobile.com/landing/free-mobile-internet-data.html?cmpid=WTR_PB_vVDAYcs2&002=2201628&004=7544714199&005=39867426325&006=30844130079&007=Search&008=&025=c&026=&gclid=CKy8ppGbmr8CFdBi7AodKXMAxA, accessed July 2014.
10. See Justin D. Martin, "Dynamic Pricing: Internet Retailers Are Treating Us Like Foreign Tourists in Egypt," *Christian Science Monitor*, January 7, 2011; Patrick Rishe, "Dynamic Pricing: The Future of Ticket Pricing in Sports," *Forbes,* January 6, 2012, www.forbes.com/sites/prishe/2012/01/06/dynamic-pricing-the-future-of-ticket-pricing-in-sports/; and Mike Southon, "Time to Ensure the Price Is Right," *Financial Times,* January 21, 2012, p. 30.
11. See Natalie Zmuda, "Best Buy Tries to Co-Opt 'Showrooming' This Holiday Season," *Advertising Age,* October 29, 2013, http://adage.com/print/244993/; and Meredith Derby Berg, "Is Best Buy's 'Showrooming' Campaign Working?" *Advertising Age,* December 26, 2013, http://adage.com/print/245831/.

12. Matthew Boyle, "Unilever: Taking on the World, One Stall at a Time," *Bloomberg Businessweek,* January 7, 2013, pp. 18–20; and Martinne Geller, "Unilever Sticks with Emerging Markets as Sales Rebound," *Reuters,* January 21, 2014, http://uk.reuters.com/article/2014/01/21/uk-unilever-results-idUKBREA0K09A20140121.

13. See Serena Ng, "Toilet-Tissue 'Desheeting' Shrinks Rolls, Plumps Margins," *Wall Street Journal,* July 24, 2013, http://online.wsj.com/news/articles/SB10001424127887323971204578626223494483866; and Serena Ng, "At P&G, New Tide Comes In, Old Price Goes Up," *Wall Street Journal,* February 10, 2014, http://online.wsj.com/news/articles/SB10001424052702304450904579368852980301572.

14. Information from "Starbuck's Kid Brother Grows Up Fast," *Bloomberg Businessweek,* April 25–May 1, 2011, pp. 26–27; "Seattle's Best Coffee: Forget the Flowers, Poems, and Chocolate," *Marketing Weekly News,* February 25, 2012, p. 585; and www.seattlesbest.com and www.starbucks.com, accessed September 2014.

15. For discussions of these issues, see Dhruv Grewel and Larry D. Compeau, "Pricing and Public Policy: A Research Agenda and Overview of the Special Issue," *Journal of Public Policy and Marketing*, Spring 1999, pp. 3–10; Walter L. Baker, Michael V. Marn, and Craig C. Zawada, *The Price Advantage* (Hoboken, New Jersey: John Wiley & Sons, 2010), Appendix 2; and Thomas T. Nagle, John E. Hogan, and Joseph Zale, *The Strategy and Tactics of Pricing*, 5th ed. (Upper Saddle River, NJ: Prentice Hall, 2011).

16. See Tim Worstall, "Apple Fined $670,000 in Taiwan for Price Fixing," *Forbes,* December 25, 2013, www.forbes.com/sites/timworstall/2013/12/25/apple-fined-670000-in-taiwan-for-price-fixing.

17. Based on information found in Lynn Leary, "Publishers and Booksellers See a 'Predatory' Amazon," *NPR Books,* January 23, 2012, www.npr.org/2012/01/23/145468105; and Allison Frankel, "Bookstores Accuse Amazon (not Apple!)," and Andrew Albanese, "Court Denies Bid to Examine Amazon's E-book Pricing," *Publishers Weekly,* November 14, 2013, http://www.publishersweekly.com/pw/by-topic/digital/content-and-e-books/article/60002-court-denies-bid-to-examine-amazon-s-e-book-pricing.html.

18. "FTC Guides against Deceptive Pricing," www.ecfr.gov/cgi-bin/text-idx?c=ecfr&sid=dfafb89837c306cf5b010b5bde15f041&rgn=div5&view=text&node=16:1.0.1.2.16&idno=16, accessed September 2014.

12 Marketing Channels

Delivering Customer Value

Chapter Preview We now look at the third marketing mix tool—distribution. Companies rarely work alone in creating value for customers and building profitable customer relationships. Instead, most are only a single link in a larger supply chain and marketing channel. As such, a firm's success depends not only on how well *it* performs but also on how well its *entire marketing channel* competes with competitors' channels. The first part of this chapter explores the nature of marketing channels and the marketer's channel design and management decisions. We then examine physical distribution—or logistics—an area that has grown dramatically in importance and sophistication. In the next chapter, we'll look more closely at two major channel intermediaries: retailers and wholesalers.

We start by looking at Netflix. Through innovative distribution, Netflix has become the world's largest video subscription service. But as baseball great Yogi Berra, known more for his mangled phrasing than for his baseball prowess, once said, "The future ain't what it used to be." To stay atop the churning video distribution industry, Netflix must continue to innovate at a break-neck pace or risk being pushed aside.

NETFLIX'S CHANNEL INNOVATION: Finding the Future by Abandoning the Past

Time and again, Netflix has innovated its way to the top in the distribution of video entertainment. In the early 2000s, Netflix's revolutionary DVD-by-mail service put all but the most powerful movie-rental stores out of business. In 2007, Netflix's then groundbreaking move into digital streaming once again revolutionized how people accessed movies and other video content. Now, with Netflix leading the pack, video distribution has become a boiling, roiling pot of emerging technologies and high-tech competitors, one that offers both stomach-churning risks and mind-bending opportunities.

Just ask Blockbuster. Only a few years ago, the giant brick-and-mortar movie-rental chain flat-out owned the industry. Then along came Netflix, the fledgling DVD-by-mail service. First thousands, then millions, of subscribers were drawn to Netflix's innovative distribution model—no more trips to the video store, no more late fees, and a selection of more than 100,000 titles that dwarfed anything Blockbuster could offer. Even better, Netflix's $5-a-month subscription rate cost little more than renting a single video from Blockbuster. In 2010, as Netflix surged, once-mighty Blockbuster fell into bankruptcy.

The Blockbuster riches-to-rags story underscores the turmoil that typifies today's video distribution business. In only the past few years, a glut of video access options has materialized. At the same time that Netflix ascended and Blockbuster plunged, Coinstar's Redbox came out of nowhere to build a novel national network of $1-a-day DVD-rental kiosks. Then high-tech start-ups such as Hulu—with its high-quality, ad-supported free access to movies and current TV shows—began pushing digital streaming via the Internet.

All along the way, Netflix has acted boldly to stay ahead of the competition. For example, in 2007, rather than sitting on the success of its still-hot DVD-by-mail business, Netflix and its CEO, Reed Hastings, set their sights on a then-revolutionary new video distribution model: Deliver the Netflix service to every Internet-connected screen, from laptops to Internet-ready TVs to mobile phones and other Wi-Fi-enabled devices. Netflix began by launching its Watch Instantly service, which let Netflix members stream movies instantly to their computers as part of their monthly membership fee, even if it came at the expense of Netflix's still-booming DVD business.

Although Netflix didn't pioneer digital streaming, it poured resources into improving the technology and building the largest streaming library. It built a huge subscriber base and sales

Time and again, Netflix has innovated its way to the top in the distribution of video entertainment. But to stay atop its boiling, roiling industry, Netflix must keep the distribution innovation pedal to the metal.

and profits soared. With its massive physical DVD library and a streaming library of more than 20,000 high-definition movies accessible via 200 different Internet-ready devices, it seemed that nothing could stop Netflix.

But Netflix's stunning success drew a slew of resourceful competitors. In 2010, video giants such as Google's YouTube and Apple's iTunes began renting movie downloads, and Hulu introduced subscription-based Hulu Plus. To stay ahead, even to survive, Netflix needed to keep the innovation pedal to the metal. So in the summer of 2011, in an ambitious but risky move, CEO Hastings made an all-in bet on digital streaming. He split off Netflix's still-thriving DVD-by-mail service into a separate business named Qwikster and required separate subscriptions for DVD rentals and streaming (at a startling 60 percent price increase for customers using both). The Netflix name would now stand for nothing but digital streaming, which would be the primary focus of the company's future growth.

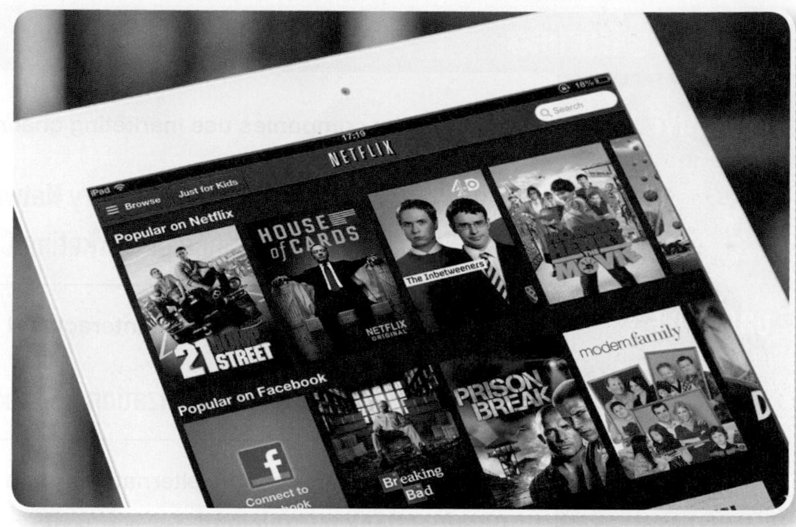

Netflix's innovative distribution strategy: From DVDs by mail, to Watch Instantly, to video streaming on almost any device, Netflix has stayed ahead of the howling pack by doing what it does best—revolutionize distribution. What's next?

© M40S Photos/Alamy

Although perhaps visionary, Netflix's abrupt changes didn't sit well with customers. Some 800,000 subscribers dropped the service, and Netflix's stock price plummeted by almost two-thirds. To repair the damage, within only weeks, Netflix admitted its blunder and reversed its decision to set up a separate Qwikster operation. However, despite the setback, Netflix retained its separate, higher pricing for DVDs by mail. Netflix rebounded quickly, replacing all of its lost subscribers and then some. What's more, with a 60 percent higher price, revenues and profits rose as well. Netflix's stock price was once again skyrocketing.

Now more than ever, Hastings seems bent on speeding up the company's leap from success in DVDs to success in streaming. Although customers can still access Netflix's world's-biggest DVD library, the company's promotions and online site barely mention that option. The focus is now squarely on streaming video. Netflix's current 48 million paid subscribers watch an astounding 1.4 billion hours of movies and TV programs every month.

Despite its continuing success, Netflix knows that it can't rest its innovation machine. Competition continues to move at a blurring rate. For example, Amazon's Prime Instant Video offers instant streaming of thousands of movies and TV shows to Amazon Prime members at no extra cost. Google has moved beyond its YouTube rental service with Google Play, an all-media entertainment portal for movies, music, e-books, and apps. Comcast offers Xfinity Streampix, which lets subscribers stream older movies and television programs via their TVs, laptops, tablets, or smartphones. Coinstar and Verizon have now joined forces to form Redbox Instant by Verizon, which offers subscription-based streaming of older movies and newer pay-per-view content. And Apple and Samsung are creating smoother integration with streaming content via smart TVs.

Moving ahead, as the industry settles into streaming as the main delivery model, content—not just delivery—will be a key to distancing Netflix from the rest of the pack. Given its head start, Netflix remains well ahead in the content race. However, Amazon, Hulu Plus, and other competitors are working feverishly to sign contracts with big movie and TV content providers. But so is Netflix. It recently scored a big win with a Disney exclusive—soon, Netflix will be the only place viewers can stream Disney's deep catalog and new releases from Walt Disney Animation, Marvel, Pixar, and Lucasfilm.

But as content-licensing deals with movie and television studios become harder to get, in yet another innovative video distribution twist, Netflix and its competitors are now developing their own original content at a feverish pace. Once again, Netflix appears to have the upper hand. For example, it led the way with the smash hit *House of Cards,* a U.S. version of a hit British political drama series produced by Hollywood bigwigs David Fincher and Kevin Spacey. Based on its huge success with *House of Cards,* Netflix developed a number of other original series, including *Hemlock Grove, Lillyhammer,* and *Orange Is the New Black*, its most successful release to date. Such efforts have left the rest of the video industry scrambling to keep up. And Netflix is just getting started. It plans to invest $300 million a year in developing new original content, adding at least five original titles annually.

Thus, from DVDs by mail, to Watch Instantly, to video streaming on almost any device, to developing original content, Netflix has stayed ahead of the howling pack by doing what it does best—innovate and revolutionize distribution. What's next? No one really knows. But one thing seems certain: Whatever's coming, if Netflix doesn't lead the change, it risks being left behind—and quickly. In this fast-changing business, new tricks grow old in a hurry. To stay ahead, as one headline suggests, Netflix must "find its future by abandoning its past."[1]

Objective Outline

As the Netflix story shows, good distribution strategies can contribute strongly to customer value and create competitive advantage for a firm. But firms cannot bring value to customers by themselves. Instead, they must work closely with other firms in a larger value delivery network.

Author Comment These are pretty hefty terms for a really simple concept: A company can't go it alone in creating customer value. It must work within a broader network of partners to accomplish this task. Individual companies and brands don't compete; their entire value delivery networks do.

Supply Chains and the Value Delivery Network

Producing a product or service and making it available to buyers requires building relationships not only with customers but also with key suppliers and resellers in the company's *supply chain*. This supply chain consists of upstream and downstream partners. Upstream from the company is the set of firms that supply the raw materials, components, parts, information, finances, and expertise needed to create a product or service. Marketers, however, have traditionally focused on the downstream side of the supply chain—the *marketing channels* (or *distribution channels*) that look toward the customer. Downstream marketing channel partners, such as wholesalers and retailers, form a vital link between the firm and its customers.

The term *supply chain* may be too limited, as it takes a *make-and-sell* view of the business. It suggests that raw materials, productive inputs, and factory capacity should serve as the starting point for market planning. A better term would be *demand chain* because it suggests a *sense-and-respond* view of the market. Under this view, planning starts by identifying the needs of target customers, to which the company responds by organizing a chain of resources and activities with the goal of creating customer value.

Value delivery network
A network composed of the company, suppliers, distributors, and, ultimately, customers who partner with each other to improve the performance of the entire system in delivering customer value.

Yet, even a demand chain view of a business may be too limited because it takes a step-by-step, linear view of purchase-production-consumption activities. Instead, most large companies today are engaged in building and managing a complex, continuously evolving value delivery network. As defined in Chapter 2, a **value delivery network** is made up of the company, suppliers, distributors, and, ultimately, customers who "partner" with each other to improve the performance of the entire system. ● For example, adidas makes great sports shoes and apparel. But to make and market just one of its many lines—say, its new adidas originals line of retro shoes and vintage street wear—adidas manages a huge network of people within the company. It also coordinates the efforts of thousands of suppliers, retailers ranging from Foot Locker to online seller Zappos, and advertising agencies and other marketing service firms that must work together to create customer value and establish the line's "unite all originals" positioning.

● **Value delivery network: In making and marketing even just its adidas originals line, adidas manages a huge network of people within the company plus thousands of outside suppliers, resellers, and marketing firms that must work together to create customer value and establish the line's "unite all originals" positioning.**
adidas

This chapter focuses on marketing channels—on the downstream side of the value delivery network. We examine four major questions concerning marketing channels: What is the nature of marketing channels and why are they important? How do channel firms interact and organize to do the work of the channel? What problems do companies face in designing and managing their channels? What role do physical distribution and supply chain management play in attracting and satisfying customers? In the next chapter, we will look at marketing channel issues from the viewpoints of retailers and wholesalers.

Author Comment In this section, we look at the downstream side of the value delivery network—the marketing channel organizations that connect the company and its customers. To understand their value, imagine life without retailers—say, without grocery stores or department stores.

The Nature and Importance of Marketing Channels

Few producers sell their goods directly to final users. Instead, most use intermediaries to bring their products to market. They try to forge a **marketing channel** (or **distribution channel**)—a set of interdependent organizations that help make a product or service available for use or consumption by the consumer or business user.

A company's channel decisions directly affect every other marketing decision. Pricing depends on whether the company works with national discount chains, uses high-quality specialty stores, or sells directly to consumers online. The firm's sales force and communications decisions depend on how much persuasion, training, motivation, and support its channel partners need. Whether a company develops or acquires certain new products may depend on how well those products fit the capabilities of its channel members.

Marketing channel (distribution channel)
A set of interdependent organizations that help make a product or service available for use or consumption by the consumer or business user.

Companies often pay too little attention to their distribution channels—sometimes with damaging results. In contrast, many companies have used imaginative distribution systems to gain a competitive advantage. Enterprise Rent-A-Car revolutionized the car-rental business by setting up off-airport rental offices. Apple turned the retail music business on its head by selling music for the iPod via the Internet on iTunes. FedEx's creative and imposing distribution system made it a leader in express package delivery. And Amazon.com forever changed the face of retailing and became the Walmart of the Internet by selling anything and everything without using physical stores.

Distribution channel decisions often involve long-term commitments to other firms. For example, companies such as Ford, McDonald's, or Nike can easily change their advertising, pricing, or promotion programs. They can scrap old products and introduce new ones as market tastes demand. But when they set up distribution channels through contracts with franchisees, independent dealers, or large retailers, they cannot readily replace these channels with company-owned stores or Internet sites if the conditions change. Therefore, management must design its channels carefully, with an eye on both today's likely selling environment and tomorrow's as well.

How Channel Members Add Value

Why do producers give some of the selling job to channel partners? After all, doing so means giving up some control over how and to whom they sell their products. Producers use intermediaries because they create greater efficiency in making goods available to target markets. Through their contacts, experience, specialization, and scale of operation, intermediaries usually offer the firm more than it can achieve on its own.

Figure 12.1 shows how using intermediaries can provide economies. Figure 12.1A shows three manufacturers, each using direct marketing to reach three customers. This system requires nine different contacts. Figure 12.1B shows the three manufacturers working through one distributor, which contacts the three customers. This system requires only six contacts. In this way, intermediaries reduce the amount of work that must be done by both producers and consumers.

From the economic system's point of view, the role of marketing intermediaries is to transform the assortments of products made by producers into the assortments wanted by consumers. Producers make narrow assortments of products in large quantities, but consumers want broad assortments of products in small quantities. Marketing channel members buy large quantities from many producers and break them down into the smaller quantities and broader assortments desired by consumers.

For example, Unilever makes millions of bars of Lever 2000 hand soap each week. However, you most likely only want to buy a few bars at a time. Therefore, big food, drug, and discount retailers, such as Safeway, Walgreens, and Target, buy Lever 2000 by the truckload and stock it on their stores' shelves. In turn, you can buy a single bar of Lever 2000, along with a shopping cart full of small quantities of toothpaste, shampoo, and other related products, as you need them. Thus, intermediaries play an important role in matching supply and demand.

In making products and services available to consumers, channel members add value by bridging the major time, place, and possession gaps that separate goods and services from those who use them. Members of the marketing channel perform many key functions. Some help to complete transactions:

- *Information.* Gathering and distributing information about consumers, producers, and other actors and forces in the marketing environment needed for planning and aiding exchange.
- *Promotion.* Developing and spreading persuasive communications about an offer.
- *Contact.* Finding and engaging prospective buyers.

FIGURE | 12.1
How a Distributor Reduces the Number of Channel Transactions

Marketing channel intermediaries make buying a lot easier for consumers. Again, think about life without grocery retailers. How would you go about buying that 12-pack of Coke or any of the hundreds of other items that you now routinely drop into your shopping cart?

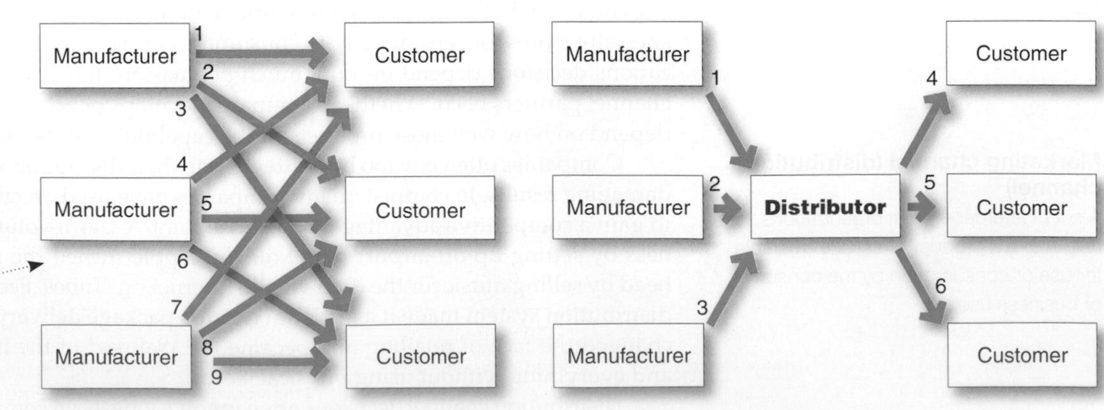

A. Number of contacts without a distributor **B. Number of contacts with a distributor**

- *Matching.* Shaping offers to meet the buyer's needs, including activities such as manufacturing, grading, assembling, and packaging.
- *Negotiation.* Reaching an agreement on price and other terms so that ownership or possession can be transferred.

Others help to fulfill the completed transactions:

- *Physical distribution.* Transporting and storing goods.
- *Financing.* Acquiring and using funds to cover the costs of the channel work.
- *Risk taking.* Assuming the risks of carrying out the channel work.

The question is not *whether* these functions need to be performed—they must be—but rather *who* will perform them. To the extent that the manufacturer performs these functions, its costs go up; therefore, its prices must be higher. When some of these functions are shifted to intermediaries, the producer's costs and prices may be lower, but the intermediaries must charge more to cover the costs of their work. In dividing the work of the channel, the various functions should be assigned to the channel members that can add the most value for the cost.

Number of Channel Levels

Companies can design their distribution channels to make products and services available to customers in different ways. Each layer of marketing intermediaries that performs some work in bringing the product and its ownership closer to the final buyer is a **channel level**. Because both the producer and the final consumer perform some work, they are part of every channel.

Channel level
A layer of intermediaries that performs some work in bringing the product and its ownership closer to the final buyer.

Direct marketing channel
A marketing channel that has no intermediary levels.

Indirect marketing channel
A marketing channel containing one or more intermediary levels.

The *number of intermediary levels* indicates the *length* of a channel. **Figure 12.2** shows both consumer and business channels of different lengths. Figure 12.2A shows several common consumer distribution channels. Channel 1, called a **direct marketing channel**, has no intermediary levels—the company sells directly to consumers. For example, Mary Kay Cosmetics and Amway sell their products through home and office sales parties and online Web sites and social networks; companies ranging from GEICO insurance to Omaha Steaks sell directly to customers via the Internet, mobile, and telephone. The remaining channels in Figure 12.2A are **indirect marketing channels**, containing one or more intermediaries.

FIGURE | 12.2
Consumer and Business Marketing Channels

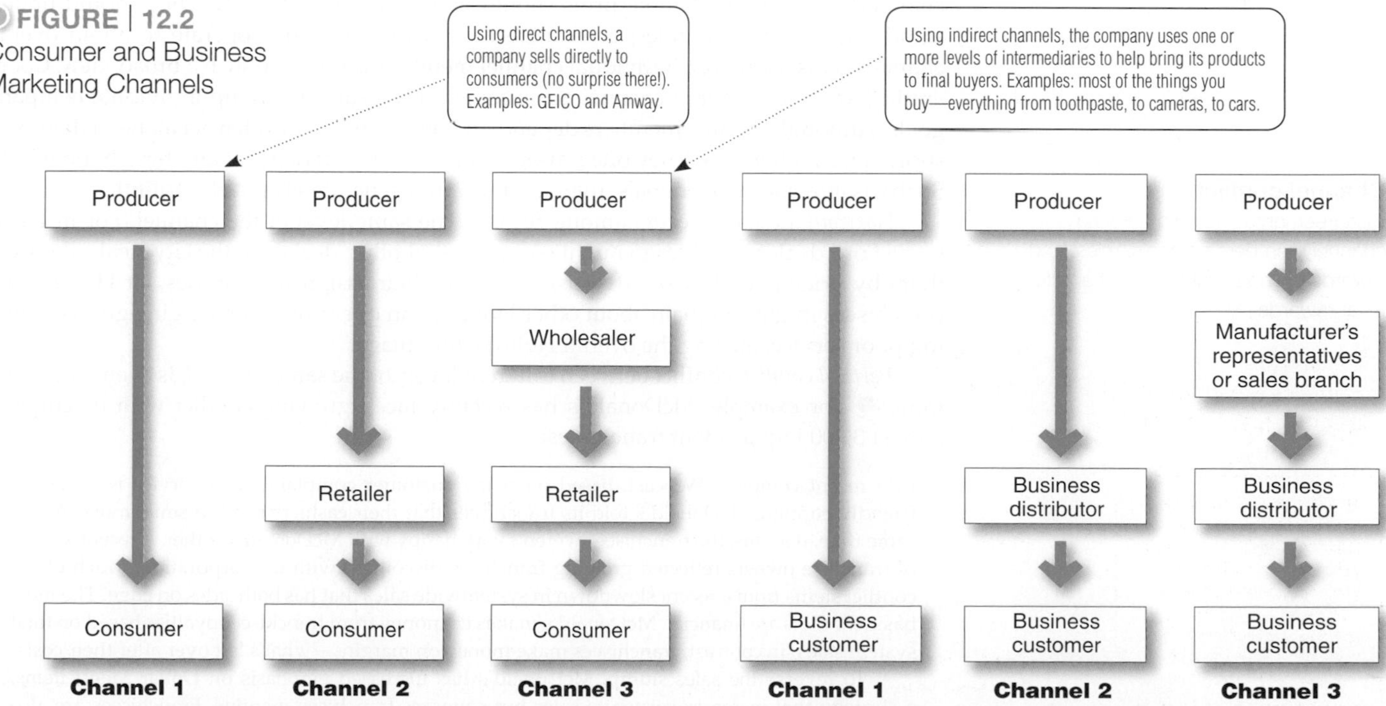

Figure 12.2B shows some common business distribution channels. The business marketer can use its own sales force to sell directly to business customers. Or it can sell to various types of intermediaries, which in turn sell to these customers. Although consumer and business marketing channels with even more levels can sometimes be found, these are less common. From the producer's point of view, a greater number of levels means less control and greater channel complexity. Moreover, all the institutions in the channel are connected by several types of *flows*. These include the *physical flow* of products, the *flow of ownership*, the *payment flow*, the *information flow*, and the *promotion flow*. These flows can make even channels with only one or a few levels very complex.

Author Comment | Channels are made up of more than just boxes and arrows on paper. They are behavioral systems consisting of real companies and people who interact to accomplish their individual and collective goals. Like groups of people, sometimes they work well together and sometimes they don't.

Channel Behavior and Organization

Distribution channels are more than simple collections of firms tied together by various flows. They are complex behavioral systems in which people and companies interact to accomplish individual, company, and channel goals. Some channel systems consist of only informal interactions among loosely organized firms. Others consist of formal interactions guided by strong organizational structures. Moreover, channel systems do not stand still—new types of intermediaries emerge and whole new channel systems evolve. Here we look at channel behavior and how members organize to do the work of the channel.

Channel Behavior

A marketing channel consists of firms that have partnered for their common good. Each channel member depends on the others. For example, a Ford dealer depends on Ford to design cars that meet customer needs. In turn, Ford depends on the dealer to attract customers, persuade them to buy Ford cars, and service the cars after the sale. Each Ford dealer also depends on other dealers to provide good sales and service that will uphold the brand's reputation. In fact, the success of individual Ford dealers depends on how well the entire Ford marketing channel competes with the channels of other auto manufacturers.

Each channel member plays a specialized role in the channel. For example, Samsung's role is to produce electronics products that consumers will like and create demand through national advertising. Best Buy's role is to display these Samsung products in convenient locations, answer buyers' questions, and complete sales. The channel will be most effective when each member assumes the tasks it can do best.

Ideally, because the success of individual channel members depends on the overall channel's success, all channel firms should work together smoothly. They should understand and accept their roles, coordinate their activities, and cooperate to attain overall channel goals. However, individual channel members rarely take such a broad view. Cooperating to achieve overall channel goals sometimes means giving up individual company goals. Although channel members depend on one another, they often act alone in their own short-run best interests. They often disagree on who should do what and for what rewards. Such disagreements over goals, roles, and rewards generate **channel conflict**.

Channel conflict
Disagreements among marketing channel members on goals, roles, and rewards—who should do what and for what rewards.

Horizontal conflict occurs among firms at the same level of the channel. For instance, some Ford dealers in Chicago might complain that other dealers in the city steal sales from them by pricing too low or advertising outside their assigned territories. Or Holiday Inn franchisees might complain about other Holiday Inn operators overcharging guests or giving poor service, hurting the overall Holiday Inn image.

Vertical conflict, conflict between different levels of the same channel, is even more common. ● For example, McDonald's has recently faced growing conflict with its corps of almost 3,000 independent franchisees:

> In a recent company Webcast, based on rising customer complaints that service isn't fast or friendly enough, McDonald's told its franchisees that their cashiers need to smile more. At the same time, it seems, the franchisees weren't very happy with McDonald's, either. A recent survey of franchise owners reflected growing franchisee discontent with the corporation. Much of the conflict stems from a recent slowdown in systemwide sales that has both sides on edge. The most basic conflicts are financial. McDonald's makes its money from franchisee royalties based on total system sales. In contrast, franchisees make money on margins—what's left over after their costs.
>
> To reverse the sales slump, McDonald's has increased emphasis on Dollar Menu items, a strategy that increases corporate sales but squeezes franchisee margins. Franchisees are also grumbling about adding popular but more complex menu items, such as Snack Wraps, that

THIRST
BEGONE!

Channel conflict: Growing McDonald's franchisee discontent may explain the increasing lack of smiles on the faces of both McDonald's cashiers and customers. "There's a huge connection" between franchisee satisfaction and customer service.

ASSOCIATED PRESS

increase the top line for McDonald's but add preparation and staffing costs for franchisees while slowing down service. McDonald's is also asking franchisees to make costly restaurant upgrades and overhauls. As one survey respondent summarized, there's "too much reliance on price-pointing and discounting to drive top-line sales, which is where the corporate cow feeds." In all, the survey rates McDonald's current franchisee relations at a decade-low 1.93 out of a possible 5, in the "fair" to "poor" range. That fact might explain both the lack of smiles and the increasing customer complaints. According to one restaurant consultant, "there's a huge connection" between franchisee satisfaction and customer service.[2]

Some conflict in the channel takes the form of healthy competition. Such competition can be good for the channel; without it, the channel could become passive and noninnovative. For example, the McDonald's conflict with its franchisees might represent normal give-and-take over the respective rights of the channel partners. However, severe or prolonged conflict can disrupt channel effectiveness and cause lasting harm to channel relationships. McDonald's should manage the channel conflict carefully to keep it from getting out of hand.

Vertical Marketing Systems

For the channel as a whole to perform well, each channel member's role must be specified, and channel conflict must be managed. The channel will perform better if it includes a firm, agency, or mechanism that provides leadership and has the power to assign roles and manage conflict.

Conventional distribution channel
A channel consisting of one or more independent producers, wholesalers, and retailers, each a separate business seeking to maximize its own profits, perhaps even at the expense of profits for the system as a whole.

Historically, *conventional distribution channels* have lacked such leadership and power, often resulting in damaging conflict and poor performance. One of the biggest channel developments over the years has been the emergence of *vertical marketing systems* that provide channel leadership. **Figure 12.3** contrasts the two types of channel arrangements.

A **conventional distribution channel** consists of one or more independent producers, wholesalers, and retailers. Each is a separate business seeking to maximize its own profits, perhaps even at the expense of the system as a whole. No channel member has much control over the other members, and no formal means exists for assigning roles and resolving channel conflict.

FIGURE | 12.3
Comparison of Conventional Distribution Channel with Vertical Marketing System

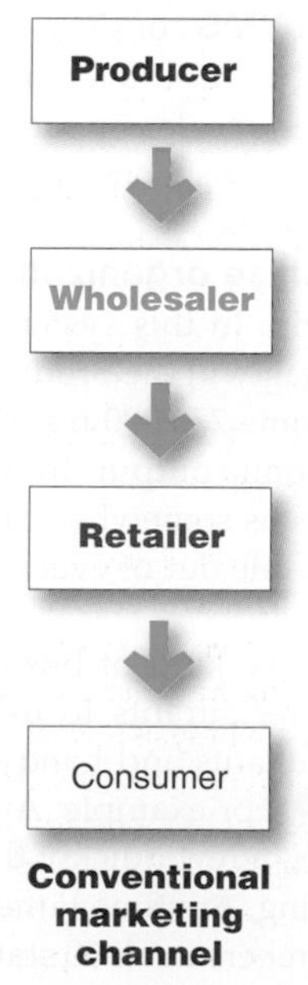
Producer
Wholesaler
Retailer
Consumer
Conventional marketing channel

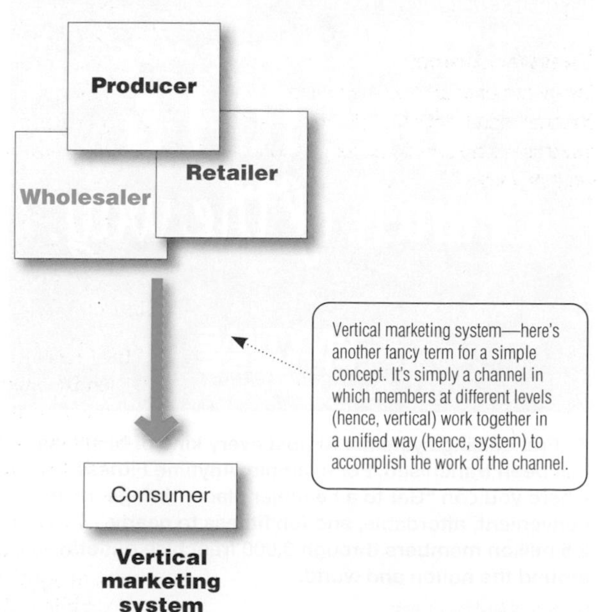
Producer
Retailer
Wholesaler
Consumer
Vertical marketing system
Vertical marketing system—here's another fancy term for a simple concept. It's simply a channel in which members at different levels (hence, vertical) work together in a unified way (hence, system) to accomplish the work of the channel.

Vertical marketing system (VMS) A channel structure in which producers, wholesalers, and retailers act as a unified system. One channel member owns the others, has contracts with them, or has so much power that they all cooperate.

In contrast, a **vertical marketing system (VMS)** consists of producers, wholesalers, and retailers acting as a unified system. One channel member owns the others, has contracts with them, or wields so much power that they must all cooperate. The VMS can be dominated by the producer, the wholesaler, or the retailer.

We look now at three major types of VMSs: *corporate*, *contractual*, and *administered*. Each uses a different means for setting up leadership and power in the channel.

Corporate VMS

Corporate VMS A vertical marketing system that combines successive stages of production and distribution under single ownership—channel leadership is established through common ownership.

A **corporate VMS** integrates successive stages of production and distribution under single ownership. Coordination and conflict management are attained through regular organizational channels. For example, Sherwin-Williams, the largest U.S. coatings manufacturer, sells its Sherwin-Williams-branded products exclusively through more than 4,000 company-owned retail paint stores. And grocery giant Kroger owns and operates 37 manufacturing plants—17 dairies, 9 deli or bakery plants, 5 grocery plants, 2 beverage plants, 2 cheese plants, and 2 meat plants—that give it factory-to-store channel control over 40 percent of the more than 11,000 private-label items found on its shelves.[3]

Contractual VMS A vertical marketing system in which independent firms at different levels of production and distribution join together through contracts.

Integrating the entire distribution chain—from its own design and manufacturing operations to distribution through its own managed stores—has turned Spanish clothing chain Zara into the world's fastest-growing fast-fashion retailer:[4]

In recent years, fashion retailer Zara has attracted a near cultlike clientele of shoppers swarming to buy its "cheap chic"—stylish designs that resemble those of big-name fashion houses but at moderate prices. However, Zara's amazing success comes not just from *what* it sells, but from *how fast* its cutting-edge distribution system *delivers* what it sells. Zara delivers fast fashion—*really* fast fashion. Thanks to vertical integration, Zara can take a new fashion concept through design, manufacturing, and store-shelf placement in as little as three weeks, whereas competitors such as Gap, Benetton, or H&M often take six months or more. And the resulting low costs let Zara offer the very latest midmarket chic at downmarket prices.

Speedy design and distribution allows Zara to introduce a copious supply of new fashions—at three times the rate of competitor introductions. Then, Zara's distribution system supplies its stores with small shipments of new merchandise twice a week, compared with competing chains' outlets, which get large shipments seasonally, usually just four to six times per year. The combination of a large number of timely new fashions delivered in frequent small batches gives Zara stores a continually updated merchandise mix that brings customers back more often. Fast turnover also results in less outdated and discounted merchandise. "Instead of betting on tomorrow's hot look," says one analyst, "Zara can wait to see what customers are actually buying—and make that."

Franchising systems: Almost every kind of business has been franchised. For example, Anytime Fitness, where you can "Get to a healthier place," brings convenient, affordable, and fun fitness to nearly 2.5 million members through 3,000 franchise outlets around the nation and world.

Courtesy of Anytime Fitness

Contractual VMS

A **contractual VMS** consists of independent firms at different levels of production and distribution that join together through contracts to obtain more economies or sales impact than each could achieve alone. Channel members coordinate their activities and manage conflict through contractual agreements.

The **franchise organization** is the most common type of contractual relationship. In this system, a channel member called a *franchisor* links several stages in the production-distribution process. In the United States alone, some 770,000 franchise outlets account for more than $830 billion of economic output. Industry analysts estimate that a new franchise outlet opens somewhere in the United States every eight minutes and that about one out of every 12 retail business outlets is a franchised business.[5]

Almost every kind of business has been franchised—from motels and fast-food restaurants to dental centers and dating services, from wedding consultants and handyman services to funeral homes and fitness centers. For example, Anytime Fitness, where you can "Get to a healthier place," grew quickly through franchising. Only a decade or so after its founding, Anytime Fitness now operates nearly 3,000 clubs with 2.5 million members in all 50 states and 23 countries.[6]

Franchise organization
A contractual vertical marketing system in which a channel member, called a franchisor, links several stages in the production-distribution process.

There are three types of franchises. The first type is the *manufacturer-sponsored retailer franchise system*—for example, Ford and its network of independent franchised dealers. The second type is the *manufacturer-sponsored wholesaler franchise system*—Coca-Cola licenses bottlers (wholesalers) in various world markets that buy Coca-Cola syrup concentrate and then bottle and sell the finished product to retailers locally. The third type is the *service-firm-sponsored retailer franchise system*—for example, Burger King and its nearly 12,100 franchisee-operated restaurants around the world. Other examples can be found in everything from auto rentals (Hertz, Avis), apparel retailers (The Athlete's Foot, Plato's Closet), and motels (Holiday Inn, Hampton Inn) to supplemental education (Huntington Learning Center, Kumon) and personal services (Great Clips, Mr. Handyman, Anytime Fitness).

The fact that most consumers cannot tell the difference between contractual and corporate VMSs shows how successfully the contractual organizations compete with corporate chains. The next chapter presents a fuller discussion of the various contractual VMSs.

Administered VMS

Administered VMS
A vertical marketing system that coordinates successive stages of production and distribution through the size and power of one of the parties.

In an **administered VMS**, leadership is assumed not through common ownership or contractual ties but through the size and power of one or a few dominant channel members. Manufacturers of a top brand can obtain strong trade cooperation and support from resellers. For example, GE, P&G, and Apple can command unusual cooperation from many resellers regarding displays, shelf space, promotions, and price policies. In turn, large retailers such as Walmart, Home Depot, Kroger, and Walgreen can exert strong influence on the many manufacturers that supply the products they sell.

Horizontal marketing system
A channel arrangement in which two or more companies at one level join together to follow a new marketing opportunity.

For example, in the normal push and pull between Walmart and its consumer goods supplier, giant Walmart—the biggest grocer in the United States with a 25 percent share of all U.S. grocery sales—usually gets its way. Take Clorox Company, for instance. Although the company's strong consumer brand preference gives it significant negotiating power, Walmart simply holds more cards. Sales to Walmart make up 26 percent of Clorox's sales, whereas Clorox products account for only one-third of 1 percent of Walmart's purchases, making Walmart by far the dominant partner. Things get even worse for Cal-Maine Foods and its Eggland's Best brand, which relies on Walmart for nearly one-third of its sales but tallies only about one-tenth of 1 percent of Walmart's volume. For such brands, maintaining a strong relationship with the giant retailer is crucial.[7]

Horizontal Marketing Systems

Another channel development is the **horizontal marketing system**, in which two or more companies at one level join together to follow a new marketing opportunity. By working together, companies can combine their financial, production, or marketing resources to accomplish more than any one company could alone.

Companies might join forces with competitors or noncompetitors. They might work with each other on a temporary or permanent basis, or they may create a separate company. For example, competing big media companies Fox Broadcasting, Disney-ABC, and NBCUniversal (Comcast) jointly own and market Hulu, the successful online subscription service that provides on-demand streaming of TV shows, movies, and other video content. Together, they compete more effectively against digital streaming competitors such as Netflix. Walmart partners with noncompetitor McDonald's to place "express" versions of McDonald's restaurants in Walmart stores. McDonald's benefits from Walmart's heavy store traffic, and Walmart keeps hungry shoppers from needing to go elsewhere to eat.

Horizontal marketing systems: General Mills and Nestlé operate a joint venture—Cereal Partners Worldwide—that markets General Mills Big G cereal brands outside North America.

Such channel arrangements also work well globally. For example, competitors General Mills and Nestlé operate a joint venture—Cereal Partners Worldwide—to market General Mills BigG cereal brands in 130 countries outside North America. General Mills supplies a kitchen cabinet full of quality cereal brands, whereas Nestlé contributes its extensive international distribution channels and local market knowledge. The 30-year-old alliance produces $1.1 billion in revenues for General Mills.[8]

Multichannel Distribution Systems

Multichannel distribution system
A distribution system in which a single firm sets up two or more marketing channels to reach one or more customer segments.

In the past, many companies used a single channel to sell to a single market or market segment. Today, with the proliferation of customer segments and channel possibilities, more and more companies have adopted **multichannel distribution systems**. Such multichannel marketing occurs when a single firm sets up two or more marketing channels to reach one or more customer segments.

Figure 12.4 shows a multichannel marketing system. In the figure, the producer sells directly to consumer segment 1 using catalogs, telemarketing, online, and mobile channels and reaches consumer segment 2 through retailers. It sells indirectly to business segment 1 through distributors and dealers and to business segment 2 through its own sales force.

These days, almost every large company and many small ones distribute through multiple channels. For example, John Deere sells its familiar green-and-yellow lawn and garden tractors, mowers, and outdoor power products to consumers and commercial users through several channels, including John Deere retailers, Lowe's home improvement stores, and online. It sells and services its tractors, combines, planters, and other agricultural equipment through its premium John Deere dealer network. And it sells large construction and forestry equipment through selected large, full-service John Deere dealers and their sales forces.

Multichannel distribution systems offer many advantages to companies facing large and complex markets. With each new channel, the company expands its sales and market coverage and gains opportunities to tailor its products and services to the specific needs of diverse customer segments. But such multichannel systems are harder to control, and they can generate conflict as more channels compete for customers and sales. For example, when John Deere first began selling selected consumer products through Lowe's home improvement stores, many of its independent dealers complained loudly. To avoid such conflicts in its Internet marketing channels, the company routes all of its online sales to John Deere dealers.

Changing Channel Organization

Disintermediation
The cutting out of marketing channel intermediaries by product or service producers or the displacement of traditional resellers by radical new types of intermediaries.

Changes in technology and the explosive growth of direct and online marketing are having a profound impact on the nature and design of marketing channels. One major trend is toward **disintermediation**—a big term with a clear message and important consequences. Disintermediation occurs when product or service producers cut out intermediaries and go directly to final buyers or when radically new types of channel intermediaries displace traditional ones.

FIGURE | 12.4
Multichannel Distribution System

Most large companies distribute through multiple channels. For example, you could buy a familiar green-and-yellow John Deere lawn tractor from a neighborhood John Deere dealer or from Lowe's. A large farm or forestry business would buy larger John Deere equipment from a premium full-service John Deere dealer and its sales force.

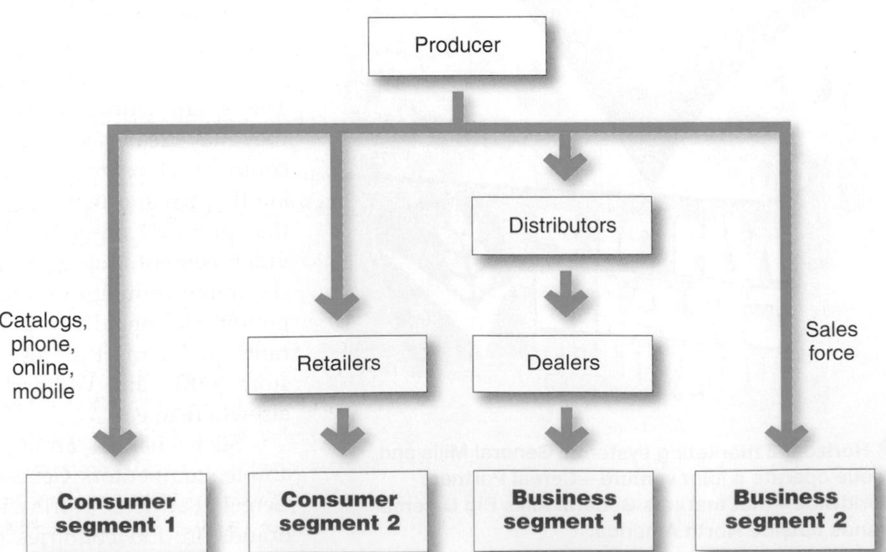

Thus, in many industries, traditional intermediaries are dropping by the wayside, as is the case with online marketers taking business from traditional brick-and-mortar retailers. For example, online music download services such as iTunes and Amazon MP3 have pretty much put traditional music-store retailers out of business. In turn, streaming music services such as Spotify and Vevo are now disintermediating digital download services—digital downloads peaked last year while music streaming increased 32 percent. Similarly, Amazon.com almost single-handedly bankrupted the nation's number-two bookseller, Borders, in less than 10 years. And the burgeoning online-only merchant has recently forced highly successful store retailers such as Best Buy to dramatically rethink their entire operating models. In fact, many retailing experts question whether stores like Best Buy can compete in the long run against online rivals.[9]

Disintermediation presents both opportunities and problems for producers and resellers. Channel innovators who find new ways to add value in the channel can displace traditional resellers and reap the rewards. In turn, traditional intermediaries must continue to innovate to avoid being swept aside. For example, superstore booksellers Borders and Barnes & Noble pioneered huge book selections and low prices, sending most small independent bookstores into ruin. Then, along came Amazon.com, which threatened even the largest brick-and-mortar bookstores. Now, both offline and online sellers of physical books are being threatened by digital book downloads and e-readers. Rather than yielding to digital developments, however, Amazon.com is leading them with its highly successful Kindle e-readers and tablets. By contrast, Barnes & Noble—the giant that put so many independent bookstores out of business—was a latecomer with its struggling Nook e-reader and now finds itself locked in a battle for survival.[10]

Disintermediation: Barnes & Noble—the giant that helped put so many independent bookstores out of business—is now locked in a battle for survival against online booksellers and digital e-book downloads.

Bloomberg via Getty Images

Like resellers, to remain competitive, product and service producers must develop new channel opportunities, such as the Internet and other direct channels. However, developing these new channels often brings them into direct competition with their established channels, resulting in conflict. To ease this problem, companies often look for ways to make going direct a plus for the entire channel. For example, Stanley Black & Decker knows that many customers would prefer to buy its power tools and outdoor power equipment directly from the company online. But selling directly through its Web and mobile sites would create conflicts with important and powerful retail partners, such as Home Depot, Walmart, Sears, and Amazon.com. So, although Stanley Black & Decker's online sites provide detailed information about the company's products, you can't buy a Black & Decker cordless drill, laser level, leaf blower, power garden shears, or anything else there. Instead, the Black & Decker site refers you to resellers' sites and stores. Thus, Black & Decker's direct marketing helps both the company and its channel partners.

Author Comment | Like everything else in marketing, good channel design begins with analyzing customer needs. Remember, marketing channels are really *customer value delivery networks.*

Channel Design Decisions

We now look at several channel design decisions manufacturers face. In designing marketing channels, manufacturers struggle between what is ideal and what is practical. A new firm with limited capital usually starts by selling in a limited market area. In this case, deciding on the best channels might not be a problem: The problem might simply be how to convince one or a few good intermediaries to handle the line.

If successful, the new firm can branch out to new markets through existing intermediaries. In smaller markets, the firm might sell directly to retailers; in larger markets, it might sell through distributors. In one part of the country, it might grant exclusive franchises; in another, it might sell through all available outlets. Then it might add an Internet store that sells directly to hard-to-reach customers. In this way, channel systems often evolve to meet market opportunities and conditions.

Marketing channel design
Designing effective marketing channels by analyzing customer needs, setting channel objectives, identifying major channel alternatives, and evaluating those alternatives.

For maximum effectiveness, however, channel analysis and decision making should be more purposeful. **Marketing channel design** calls for analyzing consumer needs, setting channel objectives, identifying major channel alternatives, and evaluating those alternatives.

Analyzing Consumer Needs

As noted previously, marketing channels are part of the overall *customer value delivery network*. Each channel member and level adds value for the customer. Thus, designing the marketing channel starts with finding out what target consumers want from the channel. Do consumers want to buy from nearby locations or are they willing to travel to more distant and centralized locations? Would customers rather buy in person, by phone, or online? Do they value breadth of assortment or do they prefer specialization? Do consumers want many add-on services (delivery, installation, repairs), or will they obtain these services elsewhere? The faster the delivery, the greater the assortment provided, and the more add-on services supplied, the greater the channel's service level.

Providing the fastest delivery, the greatest assortment, and the most services, however, may not be possible, practical, or desired. The company and its channel members may not have the resources or skills needed to provide all the desired services. Also, providing higher levels of service results in higher costs for the channel and higher prices for consumers. The success of modern discount retailing shows that consumers will often accept lower service levels in exchange for lower prices.

Meeting customers' channel service needs: Ace Hardware positions itself as "The helpful place." To loyal Ace customers, the convenience of smaller stores and the personal service they receive are well worth Ace's somewhat higher prices.

© ZUMA Press, Inc./Alamy

Many companies, however, position themselves on higher service levels, and customers willingly pay the higher prices. For example, your local independently owned Ace Hardware store probably provides more personalized service, a more convenient location, and less shopping hassle than the nearest huge Home Depot or Lowe's store. As a result, it also charges somewhat higher prices. To loyal Ace customers, the convenience and higher service levels are well worth the price. Ace positions itself as "The helpful place." Says the company: "While others have become large and impersonal, at Ace, we've remained small and very personal. That's why we say a visit to Ace is like a visit to your neighbor." In his review on Yelp, one loyal Ace customer agrees:[11]

> I have become a convert from Lowe's/Home Depot to Ace for two reasons. For one, it's much easier to get in and out of and it's closer to my house. Second, and most importantly, upon entering the store a knowledgeable employee will greet me and ask how they may help. Then they will lead me to where I need to go and boom, I'm done. At Lowe's I end up wandering around the caverns of that building—back and forth, is it here? down there? did I pass it?—until I'm exhausted. At Ace, the time and energy saved more than makes up for an increase in cost. Plus, they're very friendly.

Thus, companies must balance consumer needs not only against the feasibility and costs of meeting these needs but also against customer price preferences.

Setting Channel Objectives

Companies should state their marketing channel objectives in terms of targeted levels of customer service. Usually, a company can identify several segments wanting different levels of service. The company should decide which segments to serve and the best channels to use in each case. In each segment, the company wants to minimize the total channel cost of meeting customer service requirements.

The company's channel objectives are also influenced by the nature of the company, its products, its marketing intermediaries, its competitors, and the environment. For example, the company's size and financial situation determine which marketing functions it can handle itself and which it must give to intermediaries. Companies selling perishable products, for example, may require more direct marketing to avoid delays and too much handling.

In some cases, a company may want to compete in or near the same outlets that carry competitors' products. For example, Maytag and other appliance makers want their products displayed alongside competing brands to facilitate comparison shopping. In other cases, companies may avoid the channels used by competitors. The Pampered Chef, for instance, sells directly to consumers through its corps of more than 60,000 consultants worldwide rather than going head-to-head with other kitchen tool makers for scarce positions in retail stores. And Stella & Dot sells its quality jewelry through more than 30,000 independent reps—called stylists—who hold Tupperware-like in-home "trunk shows."[12] GEICO and USAA primarily market insurance and banking products to consumers via phone and Internet channels rather than through agents.

Finally, environmental factors such as economic conditions and legal constraints may affect channel objectives and design. For example, in a depressed economy, producers will want to distribute their goods in the most economical way, using shorter channels and dropping unneeded services that add to the final price of the goods.

Identifying Major Alternatives

When the company has defined its channel objectives, it should next identify its major channel alternatives in terms of the *types* of intermediaries, the *number* of intermediaries, and the *responsibilities* of each channel member.

Types of Intermediaries

A firm should identify the types of channel members available to carry out its channel work. Most companies face many channel member choices. For example, until recently, Dell sold directly to final consumers and business buyers only through its sophisticated phone and Internet marketing channel. It also sold directly to large corporate, institutional, and government buyers using its direct sales force. However, to reach more consumers and match competitors such as Samsung and Apple, Dell now sells indirectly through retailers such as Best Buy, Staples, and Walmart. It also sells indirectly through value-added resellers, independent distributors and dealers that develop computer systems and applications tailored to the special needs of small- and medium-sized business customers.

Using many types of resellers in a channel provides both benefits and drawbacks. For example, by selling through retailers and value-added resellers in addition to its own direct channels, Dell can reach more and different kinds of buyers. However, the new channels will be more difficult to manage and control. In addition, the direct and indirect channels will compete with each other for many of the same customers, causing potential conflict. In fact, Dell often finds itself "stuck in the middle," with its direct sales reps complaining about competition from retail stores, whereas its value-added resellers complain that the direct sales reps are undercutting their business.

Intensive distribution
Stocking the product in as many outlets as possible.

Exclusive distribution
Giving a limited number of dealers the exclusive right to distribute the company's products in their territories.

Number of Marketing Intermediaries

Companies must also determine the number of channel members to use at each level. Three strategies are available: intensive distribution, exclusive distribution, and selective distribution. Producers of convenience products and common raw materials typically seek **intensive distribution**—a strategy in which they stock their products in as many outlets as possible. These products must be available where and when consumers want them. For example, toothpaste, candy, and other similar items are sold in millions of outlets to provide maximum brand exposure and consumer convenience. Kraft, Coca-Cola, Kimberly-Clark, and other consumer goods companies distribute their products in this way.

● **Exclusive distribution: Breitling watches—positioned as "Instruments for Professionals" and with prices to match—are sold by only a few authorized dealers in any given market area.**

Associated Press

By contrast, some producers purposely limit the number of intermediaries handling their products. The extreme form of this practice is **exclusive distribution**, in which the producer gives only a limited number of dealers the exclusive right to distribute its products in their territories. Exclusive distribution is often found in the distribution of luxury brands. ● For example, Breitling watches—positioned as "Instruments for Professionals" and selling at prices from $5,000 to more than $100,000—are sold by only a few authorized dealers in any given market area. Exclusive distribution enhances Breitling's distinctive positioning and earns greater dealer support and customer service.

Selective distribution
The use of more than one but fewer than all of the intermediaries that are willing to carry the company's products.

Between intensive and exclusive distribution lies **selective distribution**—the use of more than one but fewer than all of the intermediaries who are willing to carry a company's products. Most consumer electronics, furniture, and home appliance brands are distributed in this manner. For example, Whirlpool and GE sell their major appliances through dealer networks and selected large retailers. By using selective distribution, they can develop good working relationships with selected channel members and expect a better-than-average selling effort. Selective distribution gives producers good market coverage with more control and less cost than does intensive distribution.

Responsibilities of Channel Members

The producer and the intermediaries need to agree on the terms and responsibilities of each channel member. They should agree on price policies, conditions of sale, territory rights, and the specific services to be performed by each party. The producer should establish a list price and a fair set of discounts for the intermediaries. It must define each channel member's territory, and it should be careful about where it places new resellers.

Mutual services and duties need to be spelled out carefully, especially in franchise and exclusive distribution channels. For example, McDonald's provides franchisees with promotional support, a record-keeping system, training at Hamburger University, and general management assistance. In turn, franchisees must meet company standards for physical facilities and food quality, cooperate with new promotion programs, provide requested information, and buy specified food products.

Evaluating the Major Alternatives

Suppose a company has identified several channel alternatives and wants to select the one that will best satisfy its long-run objectives. Each alternative should be evaluated against economic, control, and adaptability criteria.

Using *economic criteria*, a company compares the likely sales, costs, and profitability of different channel alternatives. What will be the investment required by each channel alternative, and what returns will result? The company must also consider *control issues*. Using intermediaries usually means giving them some control over the marketing of the product, and some intermediaries take more control than others. Other things being equal, the company prefers to keep as much control as possible. Finally, the company must apply *adaptability criteria*. Channels often involve long-term commitments, yet the company wants to keep the channel flexible so that it can adapt to environmental changes. Thus, to be considered, a channel involving long-term commitments should be greatly superior on economic and control grounds.

Designing International Distribution Channels

International marketers face many additional complexities in designing their channels. Each country has its own unique distribution system that has evolved over time and changes very slowly. These channel systems can vary widely from country to country. Thus, global marketers must usually adapt their channel strategies to the existing structures within each country.

In some markets, the distribution system is complex and hard to penetrate, consisting of many layers and large numbers of intermediaries. For example, many Western companies find Japan's distribution system difficult to navigate. It's steeped in tradition and very complex, with many distributors touching the product before it arrives on the store shelf.

At the other extreme, distribution systems in developing countries may be scattered, inefficient, or altogether lacking. For example, China and India are huge markets—each with a population well over 1 billion people. However, because of inadequate distribution systems, most companies can profitably access only a small portion of the population located in each country's most affluent cities. Rural markets in both countries are highly decentralized, made of many distinct submarkets, each with its own subculture. China's distribution system is so fragmented that logistics costs to wrap, bundle, load, unload, sort, reload, and transport goods amount to 18 percent of the nation's GDP, far higher than in most other countries. (In comparison, U.S. logistics costs account for about 8.5 percent of the nation's GDP.) After years of effort, even Walmart executives admit that they have been unable to assemble an efficient supply chain in China.[13]

Sometimes local conditions can greatly influence how a company distributes products in global markets. For example, in low-income neighborhoods in Brazil where consumers have limited access to supermarkets, Nestlé supplements its distribution with thousands of self-employed salespeople who sell Nestlé products from refrigerated carts door to door. And in crowded cities in Asia and Africa, fast-food restaurants such as McDonald's and KFC offer delivery:[14]

> Whereas Americans who want a quick meal delivered to their homes are likely to order in Chinese, people in China and elsewhere around the world are now ordering in from McDonald's or KFC. In big cities such as Beijing, Cairo, and Tokyo, where crowded streets and high real estate costs make drive-thrus impractical, delivery is becoming an important part of fast-food strategy. ● In these markets, McDonald's and KFC now dispatch legions of motorbike delivery drivers in colorful uniforms to dispense Big Macs and buckets of chicken to customers who call in. In McDonald's Asia/Pacific, Middle East, and Africa division, more than 1,500 of its 8,800 restaurants now offer "McDelivery." "We've used the slogan, 'If you can't come to us, we'll come to you,'" says the division's president. More than 30 percent of McDonald's total sales in Egypt and 12 percent of its Singapore sales come from delivery. Similarly, for KFC, delivery accounts for nearly half of all sales in Kuwait and a third of sales in Egypt.

● **The McDonald's delivery guy: In cities like Beijing, Seoul, and Cairo, armies of motorbike delivery drivers outfitted in colorful uniforms and bearing food in specially designed boxes strapped to their backs make their way through bustling traffic to deliver Big Macs.**

Li shengli Imaginechina

Thus, international marketers face a wide range of channel alternatives. Designing efficient and effective channel systems between and within various country markets poses a difficult challenge. We discuss international distribution decisions further in Chapter 19.

Author Comment | Now it's time to implement the chosen channel design and work with selected channel members to manage and motivate them.

Channel Management Decisions

Once the company has reviewed its channel alternatives and determined the best channel design, it must implement and manage the chosen channel. **Marketing channel management** calls for selecting, managing, and motivating individual channel members and evaluating their performance over time.

Marketing channel management
Selecting, managing, and motivating individual channel members and evaluating their performance over time.

Selecting Channel Members

Producers vary in their ability to attract qualified marketing intermediaries. Some producers have no trouble signing up channel members. For example, when Toyota first introduced its Lexus line in the United States, it had no trouble attracting new dealers. In fact, it had to turn down many would-be resellers.

At the other extreme are producers that have to work hard to line up enough qualified intermediaries. For example, Swedish firm NEVS, which purchased the venerable old Saab automobile brand out of bankruptcy in 2011, is now attempting to sell its cars via the Internet because the Saab dealer network no longer exists. As another example, when Timex first tried to sell its inexpensive watches through regular jewelry stores, most jewelry stores refused to carry them. The company then managed to get its watches into mass-merchandise outlets. This turned out to be a wise decision because of the rapid growth of mass merchandising.

Even established brands may have difficulty gaining and keeping their desired distribution, especially when dealing with powerful resellers. For example, you won't find

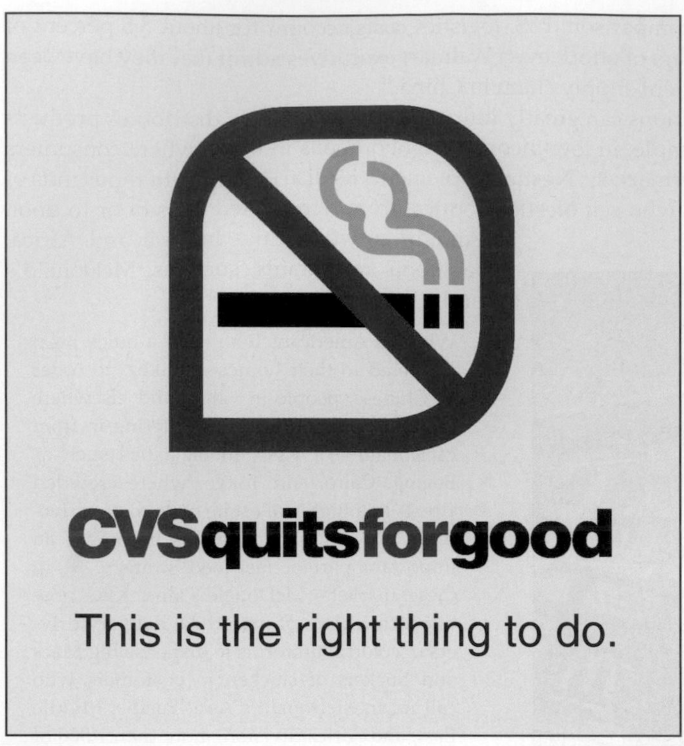

CVSquitsforgood
This is the right thing to do.

Selecting channels: Even established brands may have difficulty keeping desired channels. CVS Caremark's decision to stop selling cigarettes left tobacco companies seeking new sales channels.

CVS Caremark Corporation

Marlboro, Winston, Camel, or any other cigarette brand at your local CVS pharmacy store. CVS Caremark recently announced that it will no longer sell cigarettes in its stores, despite the resulting loss of more than $2 billion in annual sales. "This is the right thing to do," says the company. "We came to the decision that cigarettes and providing healthcare just don't go together in the same setting." Target dropped cigarettes nearly 20 years ago, and public advocates are pressuring Walmart to do the same. If the major discount stores and other drugstore chains such as Walgreens and Rite Aid follow suit, Philip Morris, R.J. Reynolds, and other tobacco companies will have to seek new channels for selling their brands.[15]

When selecting intermediaries, the company should determine what characteristics distinguish the better ones. It will want to evaluate each channel member's years in business, other lines carried, location, growth and profit record, cooperativeness, and reputation.

Managing and Motivating Channel Members

Once selected, channel members must be continuously managed and motivated to do their best. The company must sell not only *through* the intermediaries but also *to* and *with* them. Most companies see their intermediaries as first-line customers and partners. They practice strong *partner relationship management* to forge long-term partnerships with channel members. This creates a value delivery system that meets the needs of both the company *and* its marketing partners.

In managing its channels, a company must convince suppliers and distributors that they can succeed better by working together as a part of a cohesive value delivery system. Companies must work in close harmony with others in the channel to find better ways to bring value to customers. Thus, Amazon and P&G work closely to accomplish their joint goal of selling consumer package goods profitably online. Through its Vendor Flex program, Amazon operates within P&G warehouses to reduce distribution costs and speed up delivery, benefiting both the partnering companies and the customers they jointly serve (see Real Marketing 12.1).

Similarly, heavy-equipment manufacturer Caterpillar works hand-in-hand with its superb dealer network—together they dominate the world's construction, mining, and logging equipment business:

> Heavy-equipment manufacturer Caterpillar produces innovative, high-quality industrial equipment products. But ask anyone at Caterpillar and they'll tell you that the most important reason for Caterpillar's dominance is its outstanding distribution network of 189 independent dealers in more than 180 countries. Dealers are the ones on the front line. Once the product leaves the factory, the dealers take over. They're the ones that customers see. So rather than selling to or through its dealers, Caterpillar treats dealers as inside partners. When a big piece of Caterpillar equipment breaks down, customers know that they can count on both Caterpillar and its dealer network for support. A strong dealer network makes for a strong Caterpillar, and the other way around. On a deeper level, dealers play a vital role in almost every aspect of Caterpillar's operations, from product design and delivery to service and support. As a result of its close partnership with dealers, the big Cat is purring. Caterpillar dominates the world's markets for heavy construction, mining, and logging equipment. Its familiar yellow tractors, crawlers, loaders, bulldozers, and trucks capture well over a third of the worldwide heavy-equipment business, more than twice that of number two Komatsu.

Many companies are now installing integrated high-tech partnership relationship management (PRM) systems to coordinate their whole-channel marketing efforts. Just as they use customer relationship management (CRM) software systems to help manage relationships with important customers, companies can now use PRM and supply chain management (SCM) software to help recruit, train, organize, manage, motivate, and evaluate relationships with channel partners.

Real Marketing 12.1

Amazon and P&G: Taking Channel Partnering to a New Level

Until recently, if you ordered Bounty paper towels, Pampers diapers, Charmin toilet paper, or any of the dozens of other P&G consumer products from Amazon.com, they probably came to your doorstep by a circuitous distribution route. The paper towels, for example, might well have been produced in P&G's large northeastern Pennsylvania factory and shipped by the trailer-truck load to its nearby Tunkhannock warehouse, where they were unloaded and repacked with other P&G goods and shipped to Amazon's Dinwiddie, Virginia, fulfillment center. At the fulfillment center, they were unloaded and shelved, and then finally picked and packed by Amazon employees for shipment to you via UPS, FedEx, or the USPS.

But today, in a move that could turn consumer package goods distribution upside down, Amazon and P&G are quietly blazing a new, simpler, lower-cost distribution trail for such goods. Now, for example, at the Pennsylvania warehouse, rather than reloading truckloads of P&G products and shipping them to Amazon fulfillment centers, P&G employees simply cart the goods to a fenced-off area inside their own warehouse. The fenced-in area is run by Amazon. From there, Amazon employees pack, label, and ship items directly to customers who've ordered them online. Amazon calls this venture Vendor Flex—and it's revolutionizing how people buy low-priced, low-margin everyday household products.

Amazon's Vendor Flex program offers big potential for both Amazon and supplier-partners like P&G. Americans currently buy only about 2 percent of their nonfood consumer package goods online. Boosting online sales of these staples to 6 percent—the percentage that the Internet now captures of overall retail sales—would give Amazon an additional $10 billion a year in revenues, up from the current $2 billion.

But there's a reason why household staples have lagged behind other kinds of products in online sales. Such goods have long been deemed too bulky or too cheap to justify the high shipping costs involved with Internet selling. To sell household staples profitably online, companies like Amazon and P&G must work together to streamline the distribution process and reduce costs. That's where Vendor Flex comes in.

Vendor Flex takes channel partnering to an entirely new level. Co-locating "in the same tent" creates advantages for both partners. For Amazon, Vendor Flex reduces the costs of storing bulky items, such as diapers and toilet paper, in its own distribution centers, and it frees up space in Amazon's centers for more higher-margin goods. The sharing arrangement lets Amazon extend its consumer package goods selection without building more distribution center space. For example, the P&G warehouse also stocks other popular P&G household brands, from Gillette razors to Pantene shampoo to Iams pet food. Finally, locating at the source guarantees Amazon immediate availability and facilitates quick delivery of P&G products to customers.

P&G also benefits from the Vendor Flex partnership. It saves money by cutting out the costs of transporting goods to Amazon's fulfillment centers, which in turn lets it charge more competitive prices to the e-commerce giant. And although P&G is a superb in-store brand marketer, it is still a relative newcomer to online selling, one of the company's top priorities. By partnering more closely with Amazon, P&G gets Amazon's expert help in moving its brands online.

Amazon considers household staples to be one of its next big frontiers for Internet sales. Its presence inside the P&G Pennsylvania warehouse is just the tip of the iceberg for Vendor Flex. Amazon and P&G quietly began sharing warehouse space three years ago, and the online merchant has set up shop inside at least seven other P&G distribution centers worldwide, including facilities in Japan and Germany. Amazon is also inside or talking with other major consumer goods suppliers—from Kimberly Clark to Georgia Pacific to Seventh Generation—about co-locating distribution facilities. Moreover, Amazon has invested heavily to build an infrastructure for profitably selling all kinds of everyday household items to consumers online. For example, in late 2010, Amazon acquired Quidsi, the owner of Diapers.com and Soap.com, online retailers of baby products and household essentials. Since the Amazon acquisition, Quidsi has added a half-dozen new sites selling, among other things, toys (YoYo.com), pet supplies (Wag.com), premium beauty products (BeautyBar.com), and home products (Casa.com).

Vendor Flex looks like a win-win for everyone involved—Amazon, P&G, and final consumers. However, the close Amazon–P&G partnership has caused some grumbling among other important channel participants. For example, what about Walmart, P&G's largest customer by far? The giant store retailer is locked in a fierce online battle with Amazon, yet one of its largest suppliers appears to be giving Amazon preferential treatment. At the same time, Amazon's courtship of P&G may upset other important suppliers that compete

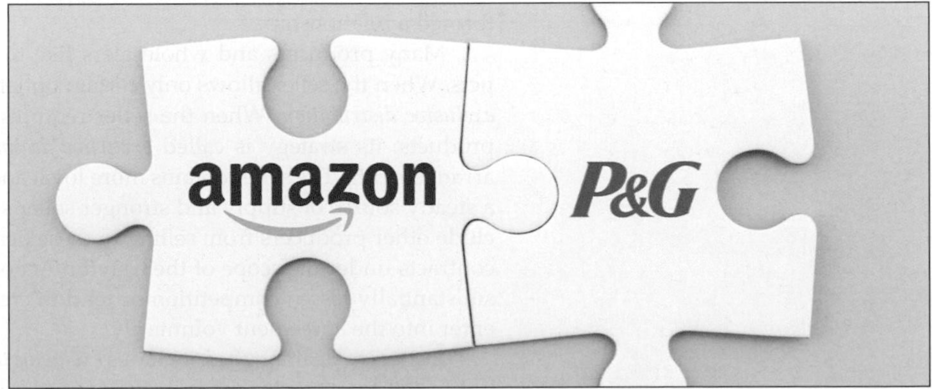

Partnering in the distribution channel: Under Amazon's Vendor Flex program, P&G and Amazon share warehouse facilities, creating distribution cost and delivery advantages for both partners.

© raywoo/Fotolia; © grzegorz knec/Alamy

with P&G on Amazon's site. Both P&G and Amazon must be careful that their close Vendor Flex relationship doesn't damage other important channel partnerships.

More broadly, some analysts assert that even with Vendor Flex, Amazon won't be able to sell products such as paper towels, detergent, or shaving cream profitably online. They reason that the margins on such items are simply too low to cover shipping costs. Amazon is already losing an estimated $1 billion to $2 billion annually on its Amazon Prime shipping program. And, they suggest, if there is money to be made by shipping a heavy jug of Tide or a bulky 3-pack of Bounty paper towels from P&G's warehouse to your front door, P&G would have been doing that long ago.

However, such doom-and-gloom predictions seem to overlook recent rapid changes in the distribution landscape, especially in online retailing. Mega-shippers like UPS and FedEx are continuing to drive down small-package delivery times and costs. And Amazon is moving aggressively toward same-day delivery in major market areas, including grocery and related items. The Vendor Flex program seems to align well with such distribution trends.

As for the Amazon–P&G Vendor Flex partnership, it looks like an ideal match for both companies. If P&G wants to be more effective in selling its brands online, what better partner could it have than Amazon, the undisputed master of online retailing? If Amazon wants to be more effective in selling household staples, what better partner could it have than P&G, the acknowledged master of consumer package goods marketing? Together, under Amazon's Vendor Flex, these respective industry leaders can flex their distribution muscles to their own benefit, and to the benefit of the consumers they jointly serve.

Sources: Serena Ng, "Soap Opera: Amazon Moves In with P&G," *Wall Street Journal*, October 15, 2013, p. A1; Andre Mouton, "Amazon Considers 'Co-Creation' with Procter & Gamble," *USA Today*, October 21, 2013, www.usatoday.com/story/tech/2013/10/21/amazon-proctor-gamble-products/3143773/; and David Streitfeld, "Amazon to Raise Fees as Revenue Disappoints," *New York Times*, January 31, 2014, p. B1.

Evaluating Channel Members

The company must regularly check channel member performance against standards such as sales quotas, average inventory levels, customer delivery time, treatment of damaged and lost goods, cooperation in company promotion and training programs, and services to the customer. The company should recognize and reward intermediaries that are performing well and adding good value for consumers. Those that are performing poorly should be assisted or, as a last resort, replaced.

Finally, companies need to be sensitive to the needs of their channel partners. Those that treat their partners poorly risk not only losing their support but also causing some legal problems. The next section describes various rights and duties pertaining to companies and other channel members.

Public Policy and Distribution Decisions

For the most part, companies are legally free to develop whatever channel arrangements suit them. In fact, the laws affecting channels seek to prevent the exclusionary tactics of some companies that might keep another company from using a desired channel. Most channel law deals with the mutual rights and duties of channel members once they have formed a relationship.

Many producers and wholesalers like to develop exclusive channels for their products. When the seller allows only certain outlets to carry its products, this strategy is called *exclusive distribution*. When the seller requires that these dealers not handle competitors' products, its strategy is called *exclusive dealing*. Both parties can benefit from exclusive arrangements: The seller obtains more loyal and dependable outlets, and the dealers obtain a steady source of supply and stronger seller support. But exclusive arrangements also exclude other producers from selling to these dealers. This situation brings exclusive dealing contracts under the scope of the Clayton Act of 1914. They are legal as long as they do not substantially lessen competition or tend to create a monopoly and as long as both parties enter into the agreement voluntarily.

Exclusive dealing often includes *exclusive territorial agreements*. The producer may agree not to sell to other dealers in a given area, or the buyer may agree to sell only in its own territory. The first practice is normal under franchise systems as a way to increase dealer enthusiasm and commitment. It is also perfectly legal—a seller has no legal obligation to sell through more outlets than it wishes. The second practice, whereby the producer tries to keep a dealer from selling outside its territory, has become a major legal issue.

Producers of a strong brand sometimes sell it to dealers only if the dealers will take some or all of the rest of its line. This is called *full-line forcing*. Such *tying agreements* are not necessarily illegal, but they violate the Clayton Act if they tend to lessen competition substantially. The practice may prevent consumers from freely choosing among competing suppliers of these other brands.

Finally, producers are free to select their dealers, but their right to terminate dealers is somewhat restricted. In general, sellers can drop dealers "for cause." However, they cannot drop dealers if, for example, the dealers refuse to cooperate in a doubtful legal arrangement, such as exclusive dealing or tying agreements.

Author Comment Marketers used to call this plain-old "physical distribution." But as these titles suggest, the topic has grown in importance, complexity, and sophistication.

Marketing Logistics and Supply Chain Management

In today's global marketplace, selling a product is sometimes easier than getting it to customers. Companies must decide on the best way to store, handle, and move their products and services so that they are available to customers in the right assortments, at the right time, and in the right place. Logistics effectiveness has a major impact on both customer satisfaction and company costs. Here we consider the nature and importance of logistics management in the supply chain, the goals of the logistics system, major logistics functions, and the need for integrated supply chain management.

Marketing logistics (physical distribution)
Planning, implementing, and controlling the physical flow of materials, final goods, and related information from points of origin to points of consumption to meet customer requirements at a profit.

Supply chain management
Managing upstream and downstream value-added flows of materials, final goods, and related information among suppliers, the company, resellers, and final consumers.

Nature and Importance of Marketing Logistics

To some managers, marketing logistics means only trucks and warehouses. But modern logistics is much more than this. **Marketing logistics**—also called **physical distribution**—involves planning, implementing, and controlling the physical flow of goods, services, and related information from points of origin to points of consumption to meet customer requirements at a profit. In short, it involves getting the right product to the right customer in the right place at the right time.

In the past, physical distribution planners typically started with products at the plant and then tried to find low-cost solutions to get them to customers. However, today's *customer-centered* logistics starts with the marketplace and works backward to the factory or even to sources of supply. Marketing logistics involves not only *outbound logistics* (moving products from the factory to resellers and ultimately to customers) but also *inbound logistics* (moving products and materials from suppliers to the factory) and *reverse logistics* (reusing, recycling, refurbishing, or disposing of broken, unwanted, or excess products returned by consumers or resellers). That is, it involves the entirety of **supply chain management**—managing upstream and downstream value-added flows of materials, final goods, and related information among suppliers, the company, resellers, and final consumers, as shown in **Figure 12.5**.

The logistics manager's task is to coordinate the activities of suppliers, purchasing agents, marketers, channel members, and customers. These activities include forecasting, information systems, purchasing, production planning, order processing, inventory, warehousing, and transportation planning.

Companies today are placing greater emphasis on logistics for several reasons. First, companies can gain a powerful competitive advantage by using improved logistics to give customers better service or lower prices. Second, improved logistics can yield tremendous cost savings to both a company and its customers. As much as 20 percent of an average product's price is accounted for by shipping and transport alone. This far exceeds the cost of advertising and many other marketing costs. American companies spend $1.33 trillion each year—about 8.5 percent of GDP—to wrap, bundle, load, unload, sort, reload, and transport goods. That's more than the total national GDPs of all but 13 countries worldwide.[16]

Logistics: As this huge stockpile of shipping containers suggests, American companies spend about $1.33 trillion each year—8.5 percent of U.S. GDP—to wrap, bundle, load, unload, sort, reload, and transport goods.

E.G. Pors/Shutterstock.com

FIGURE | 12.5
Supply Chain Management

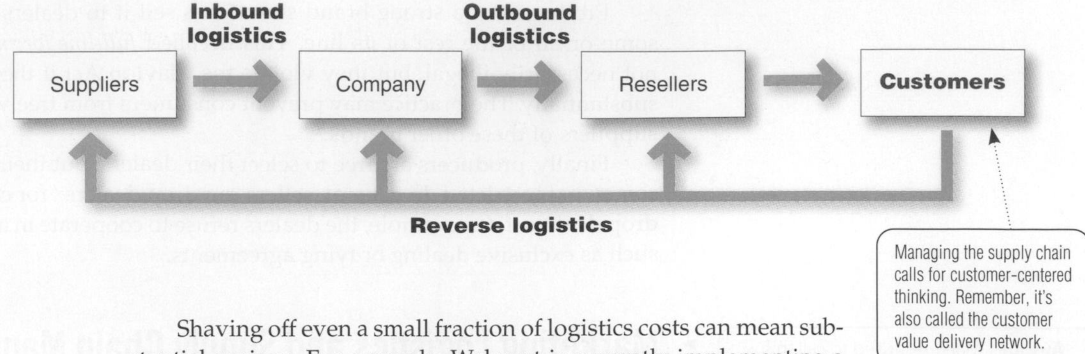

Managing the supply chain calls for customer-centered thinking. Remember, it's also called the customer value delivery network.

Shaving off even a small fraction of logistics costs can mean substantial savings. For example, Walmart is currently implementing a program of logistics improvements through more efficient sourcing, better inventory management, and greater supply chain productivity that will reduce supply chain costs by 5 to 15 percent over five years—that's a whopping $4 billion to $12 billion.[17]

Third, the explosion in product variety has created a need for improved logistics management. For example, in 1916 the typical Piggly Wiggly grocery store carried only 605 items. Today, a Piggly Wiggly carries a bewildering stock of between 20,000 and 35,000 items, depending on store size. A Walmart Supercenter store carries more than 140,000 products, 30,000 of which are grocery products.[18] Ordering, shipping, stocking, and controlling such a variety of products presents a sizable logistics challenge.

Improvements in information technology have also created opportunities for major gains in distribution efficiency. Today's companies are using sophisticated supply chain management software, Internet-based logistics systems, point-of-sale scanners, RFID tags, satellite tracking, and electronic transfer of order and payment data. Such technology lets them quickly and efficiently manage the flow of goods, information, and finances through the supply chain.

Finally, more than almost any other marketing function, logistics affects the environment and a firm's environmental sustainability efforts. Transportation, warehousing, packaging, and other logistics functions are typically the biggest supply chain contributors to the company's environmental footprint. At the same time, they also provide one of the most fertile areas for cost savings. In other words, developing a *green supply chain* is not only environmentally responsible but can also be profitable (see Real Marketing 12.2). Here's a simple example:[19]

> Consumer package goods maker SC Johnson made a seemingly simple but smart—and profitable—change in the way it packs its trucks. Under the old system, a load of its Ziploc products filled a truck trailer before reaching the maximum weight limit. In contrast, a load of Windex glass cleaner hit the maximum weight before the trailer was full. By strategically mixing the two products, SC Johnson found it could send the same amount of products with 2,098 fewer shipments, while burning 168,000 fewer gallons of diesel fuel and eliminating 1,882 tons of greenhouse gasses. Thus, smart supply chain thinking not only helped the environment, it also saved the company money. Says the company's director of environmental issues, "Loading a truck may seem simple, but making sure that a truck is truly full is a science. Consistently hitting a trailer's maximum weight provided a huge opportunity to reduce our energy consumption, cut our greenhouse gas emissions, and save money [in the bargain.]" Thus, green supply chains aren't just something companies have to do, they make good business sense.

Goals of the Logistics System

Some companies state their logistics objective as providing maximum customer service at the least cost. Unfortunately, as nice as this sounds, no logistics system can *both* maximize customer service *and* minimize distribution costs. Maximum customer service implies rapid delivery, large inventories, flexible assortments, liberal returns policies, and other services—all of which raise distribution costs. In contrast, minimum distribution costs imply slower delivery, smaller inventories, and larger shipping lots—which represent a lower level of overall customer service.

The goal of marketing logistics should be to provide a *targeted* level of customer service at the least cost. A company must first research the importance of various distribution services to customers and then set desired service levels for each segment. The objective is to maximize *profits*, not sales. Therefore, the company must weigh the benefits of providing higher levels of service against the costs. Some companies offer less service than their competitors and charge a lower price. Other companies offer more service and charge higher prices to cover higher costs.

Real Marketing 12.2

Greening the Supply Chain: It's the Right Thing to Do—and It's Profitable, Too

You may remember the old song in which Kermit the Frog laments, "It's not easy bein' green." That's often as true for a company's supply chains as it is for the Muppet. Greening up a company's channels often takes substantial commitment, ingenuity, and investment. Although challenging, however, today's supply channels are getting ever greener.

Companies have many reasons for reducing the environmental impact of their supply chains. For one thing, in the not-too-distant future, if companies don't green up voluntarily, a host of "green laws" and sustainability regulations enacted around the world will require them to do so. For another, many large customers—from Nike to Walmart to the federal government—are demanding it. Environmental sustainability has become an important factor in supplier selection and performance evaluation, so suppliers need to think green or put their relationships with prime customers at risk. Perhaps even more important than *having* to do it, designing more environmentally responsible supply chains is simply the *right* thing to do. It's one more way that companies can contribute to saving our world for future generations.

But that's all pretty heady stuff. As it turns out, companies have a more immediate and practical reason for turning their supply chains green. Not only are green channels good for the world, they're also good for a company's bottom line. Companies green their supply chains through greater efficiency, and greater efficiency means lower costs and higher profits. This cost-savings side of environmental responsibility makes good sense. The very logistics activities that create the biggest environmental footprint—such as transportation, warehousing, and packaging—are also the ones that account for a lion's share of logistics costs, especially in an age of scarce resources and soaring energy prices. Although it may require an up-front investment, in the long run, greening up channels usually costs less.

Here are just a few examples of how creating greener supply chains can benefit both the environment and a company's bottom line:

- *Stonyfield Farm.* As the world's largest yogurt maker grew over the years, inefficiencies crept into its distribution system. So Stonyfield worked with Ryder Systems, the large transportation and logistics services firm, to design a new logistics system that cut distribution costs at the same time that it improved customer service levels and dramatically reduced the company's carbon footprint. After evaluating the Stonyfield network, Ryder helped Stonyfield set up a small, dedicated truck fleet, including fuel-efficient hybrid vehicles, to make regional deliveries in New England. It then replaced Stonyfield's national less-than-truckload distribution network with a regional multistop truckload system. As a result, Stonyfield now moves more product in fewer but fuller trucks, cutting in half the number of miles traveled. In all, the changes produced a 40 percent reduction in transportation-related carbon dioxide emissions while knocking an eye-popping 14 percent off Stonyfield's transportation costs. Says Stonyfield's director of logistics, "We're surprised. We understand that environmental responsibility can be profitable. We expected some savings, but not really in this range."
- *Nike.* The iconic sports shoe and apparel company has developed a sweeping strategy for greening every phase of its supply chain. For example, Nike recently teamed with Levi's, REI, Target, and other members of the Sustainable Apparel Coalition to develop the Higg Index—a tool that measures how a single apparel product impacts the environment across the entire supply chain. Based in part on Nike's years-old Materials Sustainability Index, the Higg Index lets Nike work with suppliers and distributors to reduce the supply chain's environmental footprint. For instance, during just the past three years, the more than 900 contract factories that make Nike footwear worldwide have reduced their carbon emissions by 6 percent, despite production increases of 20 percent. That's equivalent to an emissions savings equal to more than 1 billion car-miles.

  Nike has found that even seemingly simple supply chain adjustments can produce big benefits. For example, Nike sources its

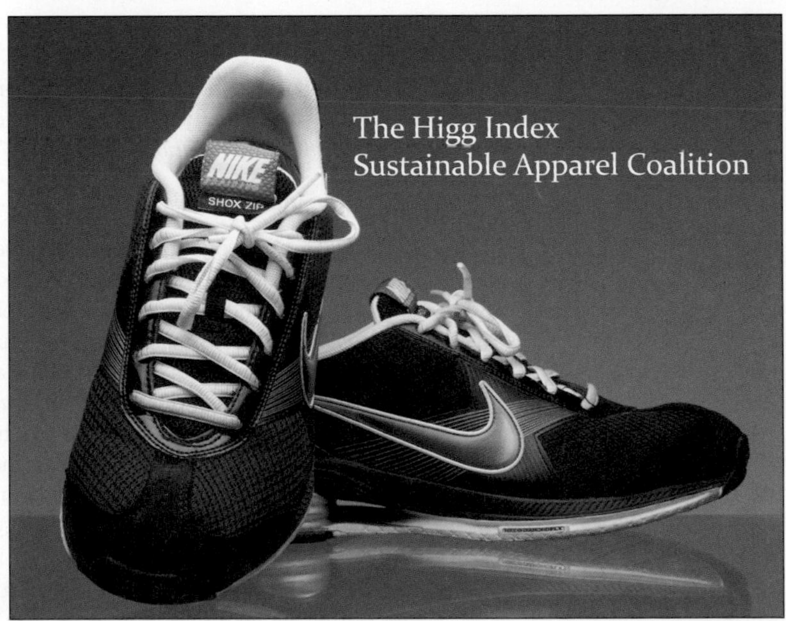

Green supply chains: Nike has developed a sweeping strategy for greening its supply chain. The Higg Index lets Nike work with suppliers and distributors to reduce the supply chain's environmental footprint.

shoes in Asia, but most are sold in North America. Until about a decade ago, the shoes were shipped from factory to store by air freight. After analyzing distribution costs more carefully, Nike shifted a sizable portion of its cargo to ocean freight. That simple shoes-to-ships shift reduced emissions per product by 4 percent, making environmentalists smile. But it also put a smile on the faces of Nike's accountants by saving the company some $8 million a year in shipping costs.

- *Walmart.* The world's largest retailer is often criticized for its huge carbon footprint. But it turns out that Walmart may be the world's biggest green-channels champion. Among dozens of other major greening initiatives, the giant retailer has worked diligently to reduce the environmental impact of its huge fleet of more than 7,000 trucks. "Within the transportation function," says the head of Walmart's sustainability efforts, "we want to accomplish three goals: fill every trailer to capacity; drive those trailers the fewest miles possible; and use the most efficient equipment. All these efforts drive sustainability, as well as operational efficiency."

    To accomplish those objectives, Walmart has installed hybrid engines and more efficient tires, adopted alternative fuels, and developed more effective load-management and routing systems. As a result, during the past five years, Walmart's fleet has delivered 361 million more cases of product in 287 million fewer miles, reducing carbon emissions by 25 percent and cutting a big chunk out of distribution costs.

    Walmart also works with its throng of more than 100,000 global suppliers to help them clean up their environmental acts. For example, it recently set a goal to reduce overall supplier packaging by 5 percent. Given Walmart's size, even small changes make a substantial impact. For instance, a slight change in the design of one supplier's shoeboxes resulted in a 43 percent reduction in the amount of paper required to make them. In only 10 months, that Walmart-led design improvement cut out 692 tons of paper from shoeboxes crossing Walmart's check-out scanners. That equates to saving 2,500 trees, 400,000 pounds of solid waste, 2.4 million gallons of water, and 14.5 billion BTUs. The change also resulted in an eye-opening 28 percent reduction in supply chain costs.

So when it comes to supply chains, Kermit might be right—it's not easy bein' green. But it's now more necessary than ever, and it can pay big returns. It's a challenging area, says one supply chain expert, "but if you look at it from a pure profit-and-loss perspective, it's also a rich one." Another expert concludes, "It's now easier than ever to build a green supply chain without going into the red, while actually saving cash along the way."

Sources: Based on information from Ryan Boccelli and Mark Swenson, "Improving Transportation and Supply Chain Efficiency while Reducing Your Carbon Footprint," http://investors.ryder.com/files/doc_downloads/stonyfield_ryder_carbon.pdf, accessed June 2014; Jessica Stillman, "Green Cred: Sustainability a Cost-Cutting Move for Suppliers," *Forbes*, December 11, 2012, www.forbes.com/sites/ups/2012/12/11/green-cred-sustainability-a-cost-cutting-move-for-suppliers/; William Hoffman, "Supplying Sustainability," *Traffic World*, April 7, 2008; "Supply Chain Standard: Going Green without Going into the Red," *Logistics Manager*, March 2009, p. 22; Amy Westervelt, "Target, Nike, Levi's Join Forces on Sustainable Clothing," *Forbes*, July 26, 2012, www.forbes.com/sites/amywestervelt/2012/07/26/target-nike-levis-join-forces-on-sustainable-clothing/; Joseph O'Reilly, "Green Logistics the Walmart Way," *Inbound Logistics*, June 2013, www.inboundlogistics.com/cms/article/green-logistics-the-walmart-way/; and www.nikeresponsibility.com/, www.nikeresponsibility.com/report/content/chapter/manufacturing, and http://corporate.walmart.com/global-responsibility/environment-sustainability, accessed September 2014.

Major Logistics Functions

Given a set of logistics objectives, the company designs a logistics system that will minimize the cost of attaining these objectives. The major logistics functions are *warehousing*, *inventory management*, *transportation*, and *logistics information management*.

Warehousing

Production and consumption cycles rarely match, so most companies must store their goods while they wait to be sold. For example, Snapper, Toro, and other lawn mower manufacturers run their factories all year long and store up products for the heavy spring and summer buying seasons. The storage function overcomes differences in needed quantities and timing, ensuring that products are available when customers are ready to buy them.

A company must decide on *how many* and *what types* of warehouses it needs and *where* they will be located. The company might use either *storage warehouses* or *distribution centers*. Storage warehouses store goods for moderate to long periods. In contrast, **distribution centers** are designed to move goods rather than just store them. They are large and highly automated warehouses designed to receive goods from various plants and suppliers, take orders, fill them efficiently, and deliver goods to customers as quickly as possible.

Distribution center
A large, highly automated warehouse designed to receive goods from various plants and suppliers, take orders, fill them efficiently, and deliver goods to customers as quickly as possible.

For example, Home Depot operates 18 giant Rapid Deployment Centers (RDCs)—huge, highly mechanized distribution centers that supply almost all of the daily needs of Home Depot's more than 2,200 stores around the country. The RDC in Westfield, Massachusetts, covers 657,000 square feet under a single roof (13 football fields) and serves some 115 Home Depot stores throughout New England. Nothing is stored at the RDCs. Instead, they are "pass-through" centers at which product shipments are received from suppliers, processed, and efficiently redistributed to individual Home Depot stores. The RDCs provide a maximum

72-hour turnaround from the time products reach the center until their delivery to stores, where 80 percent go directly to the sales floor. With such rapid and accurate delivery, individual Home Depot stores can improve merchandise availability to customers while at the same time carrying less in-store stock and reducing inventory costs.[20]

Like almost everything else these days, warehousing has seen dramatic changes in technology in recent years. Outdated materials-handling methods are steadily being replaced by newer, computer-controlled systems requiring fewer employees. Computers and scanners read orders and direct lift trucks, electric hoists, or robots to gather goods, move them to loading docks, and issue invoices. For example, to improve efficiency in its massive distribution centers, Amazon recently purchased robot maker Kiva Systems:[21]

> When you buy from Amazon, the chances are still good that your order will be plucked from warehouse shelves by human hands. However, the humans in Amazon's distribution centers are increasingly being assisted by an army of squat, ottoman-size, day-glo orange robots. The robots bring racks of merchandise to workers, who in turn fill boxes. Dubbed the "magic shelf," racks of items simply materialize in front of workers, with red lasers pointing to items to be picked. The robots then drive off and new shelves appear. The super-efficient robots work tirelessly 16 hours a day, seven days a week. They never complain about the workload or ask for pay raises, and they are pretty much maintenance free. "When they run low on power, they head to battery-charging terminals," notes one observer, "or, as warehouse personnel say, 'They get themselves a drink of water.'"

High-tech distribution centers: Amazon employs a team of super-retrievers—in day-glo orange—to keep its warehouse humming.

Brent Humphreys/Redux Pictures

Inventory Management

Inventory management also affects customer satisfaction. Here, managers must maintain the delicate balance between carrying too little inventory and carrying too much. With too little stock, the firm risks not having products when customers want to buy. To remedy this, the firm may need costly emergency shipments or production. Carrying too much inventory results in higher-than-necessary inventory-carrying costs and stock obsolescence. Thus, in managing inventory, firms must balance the costs of carrying larger inventories against resulting sales and profits.

Many companies have greatly reduced their inventories and related costs through *just-in-time* logistics systems. With such systems, producers and retailers carry only small inventories of parts or merchandise, often enough for only a few days of operations. New stock arrives exactly when needed, rather than being stored in inventory until being used. Just-in-time systems require accurate forecasting along with fast, frequent, and flexible delivery so that new supplies will be available when needed. However, these systems result in substantial savings in inventory-carrying and inventory-handling costs.

Marketers are always looking for new ways to make inventory management more efficient. In the not-too-distant future, handling inventory might even become fully automated. For example, in Chapter 3 we discussed RFID or "smart tag" technology, by which small transmitter chips are embedded in or placed on products and packaging for everything from flowers and razors to tires. "Smart" products could make the entire supply chain—which accounts for nearly 75 percent of a product's cost—intelligent and automated.

Companies using RFID know, at any time, exactly where a product is located physically within the supply chain. "Smart shelves" would not only tell them when it's time to reorder but also place the order automatically with their suppliers. Such exciting new information technology is revolutionizing distribution as we know it. Many large and resourceful marketing companies, such as Walmart, Macy's, P&G, Kraft, and IBM, are investing heavily to make the full use of RFID technology a reality.[22]

Transportation

The choice of transportation carriers affects the pricing of products, delivery performance, and the condition of goods when they arrive—all of which will affect customer satisfaction.

Transportation: In shipping goods to their warehouses, dealers, and customers, companies can choose among many transportation modes, including truck, rail, water, pipeline, and air. Much of today's shipping requires multiple modes.
Thanapun/Shutterstock

In shipping goods to its warehouses, dealers, and customers, the company can choose among five main transportation modes: truck, rail, water, pipeline, and air, along with an alternative mode for digital products—the Internet.

Trucks have increased their share of transportation steadily and now account for 40 percent of total cargo ton-miles moved in the United States. U.S. trucks travel more than 397 billion miles a year—more than double the distance traveled 25 years ago—carrying 9.2 billion tons of freight. According to the American Trucking Association, 80 percent of U.S. communities depend solely on trucks for their goods and commodities. Trucks are highly flexible in their routing and time schedules, and they can usually offer faster service than railroads. They are efficient for short hauls of high-value merchandise. Trucking firms have evolved in recent years to become full-service providers of global transportation services. For example, large trucking firms now offer everything from satellite tracking, Internet-based shipment management, and logistics planning software to cross-border shipping operations.[23]

Railroads account for 26 percent of the total cargo ton-miles moved. They are one of the most cost-effective modes for shipping large amounts of bulk products—coal, sand, minerals, and farm and forest products—over long distances. In recent years, railroads have increased their customer services by designing new equipment to handle special categories of goods, providing flatcars for carrying truck trailers by rail (piggyback), and providing in-transit services such as the diversion of shipped goods to other destinations en route and the processing of goods en route.

Water carriers, which account for 7 percent of the cargo ton-miles, transport large amounts of goods by ships and barges on U.S. coastal and inland waterways. Although the cost of water transportation is very low for shipping bulky, low-value, nonperishable products such as sand, coal, grain, oil, and metallic ores, water transportation is the slowest mode and may be affected by the weather. *Pipelines*, which account for 17 percent of the cargo ton-miles, are a specialized means of shipping petroleum, natural gas, and chemicals from sources to markets. Most pipelines are used by their owners to ship their own products.

Although *air* carriers transport less than 1 percent of the cargo ton-miles of the nation's goods, they are an important transportation mode. Airfreight rates are much higher than rail or truck rates, but airfreight is ideal when speed is needed or distant markets have to be reached. Among the most frequently airfreighted products are perishables (such as fresh fish, cut flowers) and high-value, low-bulk items (technical instruments, jewelry). Companies find that airfreight also reduces inventory levels, packaging costs, and the number of warehouses needed.

The *Internet* carries digital products from producer to customer via satellite, cable, phone wire, or wireless signal. Software firms, the media, music and video companies, and education all make use of the Internet to transport digital products. The Internet holds the potential for lower product distribution costs. Whereas planes, trucks, and trains move freight and packages, digital technology moves information bits.

Multimodal transportation
Combining two or more modes of transportation.

Shippers also use **multimodal transportation**—combining two or more modes of transportation. Eight percent of the total cargo ton-miles are moved via multiple modes. *Piggyback* describes the use of rail and trucks; *fishyback*, water and trucks; *trainship*, water and rail; and *airtruck*, air and trucks. Combining modes provides advantages that no single mode can deliver. Each combination offers advantages to the shipper. For example, not only is piggyback cheaper than trucking alone, but it also provides flexibility and convenience.

Most logistics carriers now recognize the importance of multimodal transportation, regardless of their main line of activity. For example, Union Pacific, primarily a rail carrier, offers "door-to-door shipping" coordination for its business customers. According to one Union Pacific ad: "The end of the tracks is just the beginning of our capabilities. Every day, we coordinate rail, trucks, and ocean carriers for thousands of companies—many without tracks to their doors. That would be a challenge if we were just a railroad, but we're not. We're logistics experts."

Logistics Information Management

Companies manage their supply chains through information. Channel partners often link up to share information and make better joint logistics decisions. From a logistics perspective, flows of information, such as customer transactions, billing, shipment and inventory levels, and even customer data, are closely linked to channel performance. Companies need simple, accessible, fast, and accurate processes for capturing, processing, and sharing channel information.

Information can be shared and managed in many ways, but most sharing takes place through *electronic data interchange* (*EDI*), the digital exchange of data between organizations, which primarily is transmitted via the Internet. Walmart, for example, requires EDI links with its more than 100,000 suppliers through its Retail Link sales data system. If new suppliers don't have the required EDI capability, Walmart will work with them to find and implement the needed tools.[24]

In some cases, suppliers might actually be asked to generate orders and arrange deliveries for their customers. Many large retailers—such as Walmart and Home Depot—work closely with major suppliers such as P&G or Moen to set up *vendor-managed inventory (VMI)* systems or *continuous inventory replenishment* systems. Using VMI, the customer shares real-time data on sales and current inventory levels with the supplier. The supplier then takes full responsibility for managing inventories and deliveries. Some retailers even go so far as to shift inventory and delivery costs to the supplier. Such systems require close cooperation between the buyer and seller.

Integrated Logistics Management

Integrated logistics management
The logistics concept that emphasizes teamwork—both inside the company and among all the marketing channel organizations—to maximize the performance of the entire distribution system.

Today, more and more companies are adopting the concept of **integrated logistics management**. This concept recognizes that providing better customer service and trimming distribution costs require *teamwork*, both inside the company and among all the marketing channel organizations. Inside, the company's various departments must work closely together to maximize its own logistics performance. Outside, the company must integrate its logistics system with those of its suppliers and customers to maximize the performance of the entire distribution network.

Cross-Functional Teamwork inside the Company

Most companies assign responsibility for various logistics activities to many different departments—marketing, sales, finance, operations, and purchasing. Too often, each function tries to optimize its own logistics performance without regard for the activities of the other functions. However, transportation, inventory, warehousing, and information management activities interact, often in an inverse way. Lower inventory levels reduce inventory-carrying costs. But they may also reduce customer service and increase costs from stockouts, backorders, special production runs, and costly fast-freight shipments. Because distribution activities involve strong trade-offs, decisions by different functions must be coordinated to achieve better overall logistics performance.

The goal of integrated supply chain management is to harmonize all of the company's logistics decisions. Close working relationships among departments can be achieved in several ways. Some companies have created permanent logistics committees composed of managers responsible for different physical distribution activities. Companies can also create supply chain manager positions that link the logistics activities of functional areas. For example, P&G has created product supply managers who manage all the supply chain activities for each product category. Many companies have a vice president of logistics or a supply chain VP with cross-functional authority.

Finally, companies can employ sophisticated, system-wide supply chain management software, now available from a wide range of software enterprises large and small, from SAP and Oracle to Infor and Logility. For example, Logility offers Logility Voyager Solutions, a suite of software tools for managing

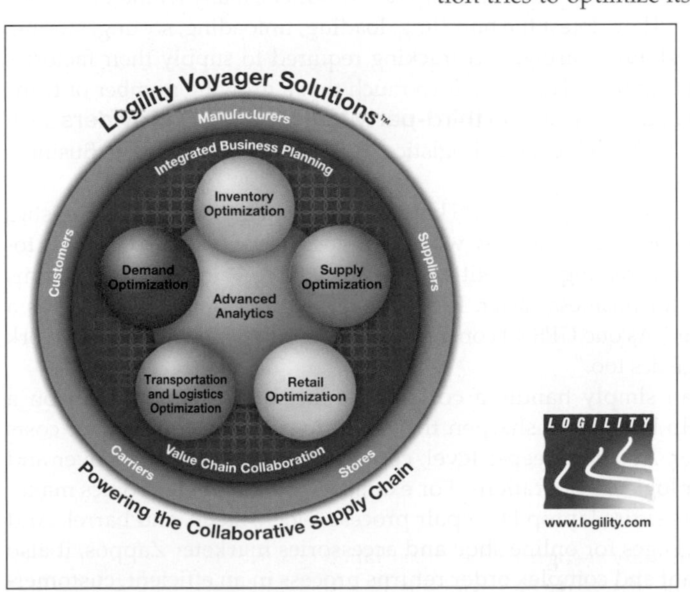

Integrated logistics management: Logility's Voyager Solutions software offers tools for managing every aspect of the supply chain, from value chain collaboration to inventory optimization to transportation and logistics management.
Logility, Inc.

every aspect of the supply chain, from value chain collaboration to inventory optimization to transportation and logistics management. The important thing is that the company must coordinate its logistics, inventory investments, demand forecasting, and marketing activities to create high market satisfaction at a reasonable cost.

Building Logistics Partnerships

Companies must do more than improve their own logistics. They must also work with other channel partners to improve whole-channel distribution. The members of a marketing channel are linked closely in creating customer value and building customer relationships. One company's distribution system is another company's supply system. The success of each channel member depends on the performance of the entire supply chain. For example, IKEA can create its stylish but affordable furniture and deliver the "IKEA lifestyle" only if its entire supply chain—consisting of thousands of merchandise designers and suppliers, transport companies, warehouses, and service providers—operates at maximum efficiency and with customer-focused effectiveness.

Smart companies coordinate their logistics strategies and forge strong partnerships with suppliers and customers to improve customer service and reduce channel costs. Many companies have created *cross-functional, cross-company teams*. For example, Nestlé's Purina pet food unit has a team of dozens of people working in Bentonville, Arkansas, the home base of Walmart. The Purina Walmart team members work jointly with their counterparts at Walmart to find ways to squeeze costs out of their distribution system. Working together benefits not only Purina and Walmart but also their shared, final consumers.

Other companies partner through *shared projects*. For example, many large retailers conduct joint in-store programs with suppliers. Home Depot allows key suppliers to use its stores as a testing ground for new merchandising programs. The suppliers spend time at Home Depot stores watching how their product sells and how customers relate to it. They then create programs specially tailored to Home Depot and its customers. Clearly, both the supplier and the customer benefit from such partnerships. The point is that all supply chain members must work together in the cause of bringing value to final consumers.

Third-Party Logistics

Although most big companies love to make and sell their products, many loathe the associated logistics "grunt work." They detest the bundling, loading, unloading, sorting, storing, reloading, transporting, customs clearing, and tracking required to supply their factories and get products to their customers. They hate it so much that a growing number of firms now outsource some or all of their logistics to **third-party logistics (3PL) providers** such as Ryder, Penske Logistics, BAX Global, DHL Logistics, FedEx Logistics, and UPS Business Solutions.

Third-party logistics (3PL) provider
An independent logistics provider that performs any or all of the functions required to get a client's product to market.

For example, as discussed in Chapter 6, UPS knows that, for many companies, logistics can be a real nightmare. But logistics is exactly what UPS does best. To UPS, logistics is today's most powerful force for creating competitive advantage. "We ❤ logistics," proclaims UPS. "It makes running your business easier. It can make your customers happier. It's a whole new way of thinking." As one UPS ad concludes: "We love logistics. Put UPS to work for you and you'll love logistics too."

At one level, UPS can simply handle a company's package shipments. But on a deeper level, UPS can help businesses sharpen their own logistics systems to cut costs and serve customers better. At a still deeper level, companies can let UPS take over and manage part or all of their logistics operations. For example, consumer electronics maker Toshiba lets UPS handle its entire laptop PC repair process—lock, stock, and barrel. And UPS not only delivers packages for online shoe and accessories marketer Zappos, it also manages Zappos' important and complex order returns process in an efficient, customer-pleasing way.[25]

3PL providers like UPS can help clients tighten up sluggish, overstuffed supply chains; slash inventories; and get products to customers more quickly and reliably. According to one report, 86 percent of *Fortune* 500 companies use 3PL (also called *outsourced logistics* or *contract logistics*) services. General Motors, P&G, and Walmart each use 50 or more 3PLs.[26]

Companies use third-party logistics providers for several reasons. First, because getting the product to market is their main focus, using these providers makes the most sense, as they can often do it more efficiently and at lower cost. Outsourcing typically results in a 15 to 30 percent cost savings. Second, outsourcing logistics frees a company to focus more intensely on its core business. Finally, integrated logistics companies understand increasingly complex logistics environments.

12 Reviewing the Concepts

OBJECTIVES REVIEW AND KEY TERMS

Objectives Review

Some companies pay too little attention to their distribution channels; others, however, have used imaginative distribution systems to gain a competitive advantage. A company's channel decisions directly affect every other marketing decision. Management must make channel decisions carefully, incorporating today's needs with tomorrow's likely selling environment.

OBJECTIVE 1 Explain why companies use marketing channels and discuss the functions these channels perform. *(pp 376–380)*

In creating customer value, a company can't go it alone. It must work within an entire network of partners—a value delivery network—to accomplish this task. Individual companies and brands don't compete, their entire value delivery networks do.

Most producers use intermediaries to bring their products to market. They forge a *marketing channel* (or *distribution channel*)—a set of interdependent organizations involved in the process of making a product or service available for use or consumption by the consumer or business user. Through their contacts, experience, specialization, and scale of operation, intermediaries usually offer the firm more than it can achieve on its own.

Marketing channels perform many key functions. Some help *complete transactions* by gathering and distributing *information* needed for planning and aiding exchange, developing and spreading persuasive *communications* about an offer, performing *contact* work (finding and communicating with prospective buyers), *matching* (shaping and fitting the offer to the buyer's needs), and entering into *negotiation* to reach an agreement on price and other terms of the offer so that ownership can be transferred. Other functions help to *fulfill* the completed transactions by offering *physical distribution* (transporting and storing goods), *financing* (acquiring and using funds to cover the costs of the channel work), and *risk taking* (assuming the risks of carrying out the channel work.

OBJECTIVE 2 Discuss how channel members interact and how they organize to perform the work of the channel. *(pp 380–385)*

The channel will be most effective when each member assumes the tasks it can do best. Ideally, because the success of individual channel members depends on overall channel success, all channel firms should work together smoothly. They should understand and accept their roles, coordinate their goals and activities, and cooperate to attain overall channel goals. By cooperating, they can more effectively sense, serve, and satisfy the target market.

In a large company, the formal organization structure assigns roles and provides needed leadership. But in a distribution channel composed of independent firms, leadership and power are not formally set. Traditionally, distribution channels have lacked the leadership needed to assign roles and manage conflict. In recent years, however, new types of channel organizations have appeared that provide stronger leadership and improved performance.

OBJECTIVE 3 Identify the major channel alternatives open to a company. *(pp 385–389)*

Channel alternatives vary from direct selling to using one, two, three, or more intermediary *channel levels*. Marketing channels face continuous and sometimes dramatic change. Three of the most important trends are the growth of *vertical*, *horizontal*, and *multichannel marketing systems*. These trends affect channel cooperation, conflict, and competition.

Channel design begins with assessing customer channel service needs and company channel objectives and constraints. The company then identifies the major channel alternatives in terms of the *types* of intermediaries, the *number* of intermediaries, and the *channel responsibilities* of each. Each channel alternative must be evaluated according to economic, control, and adaptive criteria. *Channel management* calls for selecting qualified intermediaries and motivating them. Individual channel members must be evaluated regularly.

OBJECTIVE 4 Explain how companies select, motivate, and evaluate channel members. *(pp 389–393)*

Producers vary in their ability to attract qualified marketing intermediaries. Some producers have no trouble signing up channel members, whereas others have to work hard to line up enough qualified intermediaries. When selecting intermediaries, the company should evaluate each channel member's qualifications and select those that best fit its channel objectives.

Once selected, channel members must be continuously motivated to do their best. The company must sell not only *through* the intermediaries but also *with* them. It should forge strong partnerships with channel members to create a marketing system that meets the needs of both the manufacturer *and* the partners.

OBJECTIVE 5 Discuss the nature and importance of marketing logistics and integrated supply chain management. *(pp 393–401)*

Marketing logistics (or *physical distribution*) is an area of potentially high cost savings and improved customer satisfaction. Marketing logistics addresses not only *outbound logistics* but also *inbound logistics* and *reverse logistics*. That is, it involves the entire *supply chain management*—managing value-added flows between suppliers, the company, resellers, and final users. No logistics system can both maximize customer service and minimize distribution costs. Instead, the goal of logistics management is to provide a *targeted* level of service at the least cost. The major logistics functions are *warehousing*, *inventory management*, *transportation*, and *logistics information management*.

The *integrated supply chain management concept* recognizes that improved logistics requires teamwork in the form of close working relationships across functional areas inside the company and across various organizations in the supply chain. Companies can achieve logistics harmony among functions by creating cross-functional logistics teams, integrative supply manager positions, and senior-level logistics executive positions with cross-functional authority. Channel partnerships can take the form of cross-company teams, shared projects, and information-sharing systems. Today, some companies are outsourcing their logistics functions to third-party logistics (3PL) providers to save costs, increase efficiency, and gain faster and more effective access to global markets.

MyMarketingLab

Go to **mymktlab.com** to complete the problems marked with this icon .

Key Terms

OBJECTIVE 1

Value delivery network (p 377)
Marketing channel (distribution channel) (p 377)
Channel level (p 379)
Direct marketing channel (p 379)
Indirect marketing channel (p 379)

OBJECTIVE 2

Channel conflict (p 380)
Conventional distribution channel (p 381)
Vertical marketing system (VMS) (p 382)
Corporate VMS (p 382)
Contractual VMS (p 382)
Franchise organization (p 382)
Administered VMS (p 383)
Horizontal marketing system (p 383)
Multichannel distribution system (p 384)
Disintermediation (p 384)

OBJECTIVE 3

Marketing channel design (p 386)
Intensive distribution (p 387)
Exclusive distribution (p 387)
Selective distribution (p 388)

OBJECTIVE 4

Marketing channel management (p 389)

OBJECTIVE 5

Marketing logistics (physical distribution) (p 393)
Supply chain management (p 393)
Distribution center (p 396)
Multimodal transportation (p 398)
Integrated logistics management (p 399)
Third-party logistics (3PL) provider (p 400)

DISCUSSION AND CRITICAL THINKING

Discussion Questions

12-1 Describe the key functions of marketing channel members. How do they assist the overall process of distribution between manufacturers and consumers?

✪ **12-2** Explain where power and leadership lie in a distribution channel with independent members. (AACSB: Communication)

✪ **12-3** Is it common for manufacturers to develop exclusive arrangements with resellers in your country? Are there problems with such arrangements, and are they legal?

12-4 Describe intermodal transportation and list the different combinations used to distribute products and the benefits of using this mode of transportation. (AACSB: Communication)

✪ **12-5** Are third-party logistics providers used in your country or region? Explain why they are or are not used. (AACSB: Communication)

Critical Thinking Exercises

12-6 Pharmaceutical counterfeiting is a worldwide problem. It is as far from being a victimless crime as possible. Research whether this is a major issue in your country or region. What steps are being taken by the government and manufacturers to combat this type of crime? Write a report on the situation and the initiatives to fight counterfeit drugs. Suggest ways in which the problem can be tackled. (AACSB: Communication; Reflective Thinking)

12-7 The franchise organization is the most common type of vertical marketing system. It has become a global phenomenon. What type of franchise opportunities are there in your country or region? Visit www.franchisedirect.com/internationalfranchises/ to identify them. Write a report describing a chosen franchise. Identify what type of franchise it represents and research the local market opportunities for its products or services. (AACSB: Communication; Use of IT; Reflective Thinking)

12-8 Although most big companies love to create and sell, many loathe the associated logistics. They dislike the bundling, loading, unloading, sorting, storing, reloading, transporting, customs clearing, and tracking that go with selling products. For companies that do dislike taking care of logistics, what could be the advantages of using third-party logistics (3PL) providers? Investigate how the growth of third-party logistics has affected distribution in your own country. (AACSB: Communication; Reflective Thinking)

MINICASES AND APPLICATIONS

Online, Mobile, and Social Media Marketing **Self-Publishing**

Do you think that you have what it takes to write a bestselling novel? In the past, authors had to go through traditional publishing houses to print and distribute their work, but technology has turned the publishing industry on its head. Although aspiring authors could always self-publish a book, selling it through the traditional channels—book stores—was only a pipedream for most. But that has all changed thanks to the Internet and social media. Amazon's Kindle Direct Publishing is a popular platform for self-publishers, but others such as Smashwords, Author Solutions, and Fast-Pencil offer similar services with hundreds of thousands of authors and titles. For example, Amanda Hocking's self-published e-book sales caught the attention of a publisher, and now the former social worker is a millionaire. Self-published books have grown nearly 300 percent in less than 10 years, with the majority being e-books. Almost 40 percent of readers now own e-readers, such as Kindles and iPads. That creates opportunities for anyone wanting to distribute their works to these avid readers. For example, after being turned away by traditional publishers, author Christine Bronstein created her own online social network to promote her book, *Nothing But the Truth, So Help Me God: 51 Women Reveal the Power of Positive Female Connection*, which launched on Amazon and Barnes and Noble sites. She's even expanded access to her readers. For just $19.95 (no copy edit) or $94.95 (copy edited), you can publish your own *Nothing But the Truth, So Help Me God: My Story* at http://nothingbutthetruth.com/submit.

12-9 Visit a self-publishing site such as Amazon's Kindle Direct (https://kdp.amazon.com/) and create a presentation to give to aspiring authors about distributing their works this way. (AACSB: Communication; Use of IT; Reflective Thinking)

✪ **12-10** What other industries' channel of distribution has been impacted dramatically by online, mobile, and social media? (AACSB: Communication; Reflective Thinking)

Marketing Ethics **Ethical Sourcing**

Lush, an international retailer for fresh handmade cosmetics, was launched in 1995 by the same creative team that has designed many amazing products for The Body Shop. In the less than 20 years since its establishment, Lush has grown to a network of over 850 stores in more than 50 countries worldwide and over 6,000 employees. From the outset, the company has been keen on ensuring that it sourced its product ingredients ethically. This has become its key USP, and together with stance against animal testing and the ethos of making fresh cosmetics, the business stands apart from most of its competitors. It does mean that the prices of its products are marginally higher, but this is offset by the unique minimalist packaging and general vibe of the brand. When Lush looks for suppliers it considers the whole picture; it takes into account the conditions under which the workers may operate, and also considers how the production of the ingredients affects the environment. For Lush, it is important that the ingredients used for the cosmetics are vegetarian, are not tested on animals, and have minimal impact as far as transportation is concerned. Today, the company indirectly supports 400 women in Ghana who supply fair-trades shea butter and has stopped using palm oil from Indonesia in order to protect the natural habitat of the orangutan. It also buys directly from small farmers in Tunisia, Costa Rica, the Dominican Republic, and Laos.

12-11 Write a brief report on a business of your choice that supports ethical sourcing. What criteria are used to establish the ethical standards under which the company operates? (AACSB: Communication; Reflective Thinking)

12-12 Should ethical sourcing be the default standard for all businesses? (AACSB: Communication; Reflective Thinking; Ethical Reasoning)

Marketing by the Numbers Tyson Expanding Distribution

Tyson Foods is the largest U.S. beef and chicken supplier, processing more than 100,000 head of cattle and 40-plus million chickens weekly. Their primary distribution channels are supermarket meat departments. However, the company is now expanding distribution into convenience stores. There are almost 150,000 gas stations and convenience stores where the company would like to sell hot Buffalo chicken bites near the checkout. This is a promising channel, as sales are growing considerably at these retail outlets and profit margins on prepared foods are higher than selling raw meat to grocery stores. Tyson will have to hire 10 more sales representatives at a salary of $45,000 each to expand into this distribution channel because many of these types of stores are independently owned. Each convenience store is expected to generate an average of $50,000 in revenue for Tyson. Refer to Appendix 2: Marketing by the Numbers to answer the following questions.

12-13 If Tyson's contribution margin is 30 percent on this product, what increase in sales will it need to break even on the increase in fixed costs to hire the new sales reps? (AACSB: Communication; Analytical Reasoning)

12-14 How many new retail accounts must the company acquire to break even on this tactic? What average number of accounts must each new rep acquire? (AACSB: Communication; Analytical Reasoning)

Video Case Gaviña Gourmet Coffee

These days, there seems to be plenty of coffee to go around. So how does a small-time coffee roaster like Gaviña make it in an industry dominated by big players? By carefully crafting a distribution strategy that moves its products into the hands of consumers.

Without a big advertising budget, Gaviña has creatively pursued channel partners in the grocery, restaurant, and hospitality industries. Now, major chains like McDonald's and Publix make Gaviña's coffees available to the public. This video also illustrates the impact of distribution strategy on supply chain and product development issues.

After viewing the video featuring Gaviña, answer the following questions:

12-15 Apply the concept of the supply chain to Gaviña.

12-16 Sketch out as many consumer and business channels for Gaviña as you can. How does each of these channels meet distinct customer needs?

12-17 How has Gaviña's distribution strategy affected its product mix?

Company Case Corning: Feeding Innovation through the Supply Chain

Sometime around 1960, scientists at Corning made a significant advance while experimenting with ways to strengthen glass. Using a recently developed method that involved dipping glass in a hot potassium salt bath, they discovered that adding aluminum oxide to the glass before dipping produced a product with never-before-seen strength and durability. The scientists hurtled everything they could think of at this new super glass, including frozen chickens at high speeds, and even dropped it from the top of their nine-story building. They found that the new glass could withstand 100,000 pounds of pressure per square inch (normal glass can only handle about 7,000).

This super glass, Corning assumed, would surely be embraced by manufacturers of products ranging from eyeglasses to phone booths, prison windows, and automobile windshields. Corning named the glass Chemcor and put it on the market. But most potential customer companies did not deem the strength benefits of Chemcor worth the premium price mandated by its high cost of production. Making matters worse, when it did break, Chemcor had the potential to explode, leading the few companies that had placed orders to recall their products. When Corning realized that it had created an expensive upgrade nobody wanted, it shelved Chemcor in 1971.

Getting By with a Little Help from Suppliers . . .

When Amory Houghton, Sr., founded Corning in 1851, not even he could have foreseen the vast array of products his company would develop—products that would literally revolutionize the twenty-first century. Most people in the 1850s thought of glass as, well, just glass. But Corning thought differently. It went on to develop innovative products that would change the way people live, including light bulbs, television tubes, cookware, ceramic substrates, optical fiber, active-liquid crystal displays, and even missile nose cones. Corning achieved these feats because Houghton established research and development as the company's foundation.

From its origins, Corning has relied upon sound relationships with suppliers and customers to keep the innovation machine churning. On the supply side, producing the quantities of glass that pour off the Corning production lines requires massive amounts of sand (silicon dioxide). But because sand has such a high melting point, other chemicals—such as sodium oxide—are used to lower the melting point, making glass easier and cheaper to produce. Corning also relies on many elements and chemicals to give different types of glass their useful qualities. For example, Chemcor contains not only silicon dioxide, but also aluminum, magnesium, and sodium.

To keep the right kinds of chemicals and other raw materials flowing, price and quality are only baseline criteria at Corning. To maximize long-term success for itself and for its suppliers, Corning has also established a Supplier Code of Conduct. The Code ensures that all supplier operations are conducted within the laws, customs, and cultural norms of the regions where Corning does business. It also ensures that they comply with the company's own corporate values. Corning invests considerable energy in selecting suppliers. The Code of Conduct includes specific criteria regarding ethics, labor, health and safety, and environmental concerns. On the surface, such criteria seem to have little to do with making glass. But Corning knows that such factors can ultimately affect the quality, price, and availability of the raw materials the company needs for making its products.

. . . and from the Supplied

Some of Corning's products are consumer products. For example, take Corningware. Corning scientist Don Stookey found that product by accident when a faulty temperature controller allowed a sample of photosensitive glass to reach 1,600 degrees rather than the intended 1,100 degrees. He thought the result would be a blob of melted glass and a ruined furnace. On closer inspection, however, Stookey discovered that he had a milky white plate that was lighter than aluminum, harder than high-carbon steel, and far stronger than regular soda-lime glass. When he dropped it on the floor, instead of shattering, it bounced. When Corningware hit the market in 1959, it was a space-age wonder.

But most of Corning's products are supplied to manufacturers as components or raw materials in other products such as televisions and automobiles. That's where successful outcomes depend most on good supplier relationships. In this case, however, Corning is the supplier. Always on the lookout for ways to forge new relationships with manufacturing customers, Corning came up with an idea in 2005 when Motorola released the Razr V3, a mobile flip phone that featured a glass screen instead of the usual high-impact plastic. Maybe Chemcor—the super strong glass that Corning had shelved in 1971—would make a good glass for mobile phones. The company quickly formed a team to explore the possibilities and codenamed the project Gorilla Glass. Its team's main goal was to reduce the thickness of the glass from its current 4 millimeters to something that could be used in a phone.

As the team was making progress on the thickness issue, Corning CEO Wendell Weeks received a phone call that would give Gorilla Glass its big chance. The call came from late Apple founder Steve Jobs. Jobs and Weeks had collaborated previously. In fact, Weeks had pitched to Jobs the idea of using laser-based microprojection technologies—something Corning scientists were toying with—to provide larger screens for increasingly smaller phones. Jobs said the idea was dumb and that he was working on something better—a device whose entire surface was a display. The world would soon know that product as the iPhone.

Jobs was relentless in getting the iPhone's design just right. A plastic face just wasn't good enough, he insisted. The iPhone would need a "silky, tough, smooth piece of glass." The problem was that no such glass product was commercially available. However, Jobs had heard about Corning's Gorilla Glass and thought it had potential. So he put in the call to Wendell Weeks.

Jobs explained that he needed a piece of smooth, clear glass that would resist scratches and breaking and act as a conductor for touch-screen technology. It also needed to be 1.3 millimeters thick. Weeks explained that Gorilla Glass might meet Jobs' needs but was nowhere near that thin. Undaunted, Jobs gave Weeks a seemingly impossible mandate—make millions of square feet of Gorilla Glass, make it ultrathin, and have it ready in six months, because the iPhone would be on store shelves in seven months.

The mandate posed many unknowns for Gorilla Glass. The product had never been mass-produced, and it was unclear that a process could be developed to produce the quantity of glass that Apple needed. Weeks was also uncertain whether Gorilla Glass could be made so thin and still retain its strength. Even if these issues could be ironed out, how long would it take? So in responding to Jobs, Weeks did what any risk-taking CEO would do. He said, "Yes." Then he formed a team to make it happen.

With such a tight deadline, Corning had no time to develop a new manufacturing process. Instead, the team adapted a process the company was already using called fusion draw. This process could produce thinner glass while also speeding up the process. To maintain the desired toughness characteristics, the team tweaked the existing Gorilla Glass recipe. It changed the levels of several of the glass's seven individual components and added one new secret ingredient. But there was still one hitch. Corning only had one factory—in Harrodsburg, Kentucky—capable of producing glass by means of fusion draw. That plant's seven production lines were already going full blast to meet the demand for sold-out LCD glass for TV panels. However, the factory was somehow able to squeeze Apple's initial Gorilla Glass order into one of its production lines. Incredibly, and ahead of schedule, Corning produced enough 1.3 millimeter Gorilla Glass to cover seven football fields.

The rest, as they say, is history. Every iPhone and iPad that Apple has ever sold features Gorilla Glass. Beyond that, the state-of-the-art Corning material is featured on nearly 3 billion devices worldwide across 2,450 different product models, including smartphones, tablets, notebooks, and TVs. In all, Corning supplies the glass for devices to 33 different companies. If you regularly touch or swipe a gadget, you have likely touched Gorilla Glass. In 2007, Corning sold $20 million worth of Gorilla Glass. Today, it accounts for over $1 billion of the company's $8 billion total annual revenues. In fact, display technologies as a whole contribute 37 percent to Corning's total revenues and 78 percent to its bottom line.

But quantity doesn't begin to characterize the impact of Corning's relationships with manufacturers. In only a handful of years, a simple thing like a glass display has gone from a component to an aesthetic. When a user touches the outer layer of Gorilla Glass, the body closes the circuit between an electrode beneath the screen and the glass itself, transforming motion into data. It's a seamless partition that connects people's physical selves with the infinite digital world—so seamless, in fact, that most people have a hard time determining exactly where that partition exists.

The Ongoing Need for Good Supplier Relationships

The Corning Harrodsburg factory continues to churn out Gorilla Glass in five-square-foot panels. Robotic arms put the panels in wooden crates that are trucked to Louisville, Kentucky, and loaded onto a westbound train. When they reach the coast, they are loaded onto freighters and shipped off to a Corning facility in China, where they receive a finishing bath and are cut into gadget-sized rectangles.

But Corning's partnerships with customers like Apple are more important today than ever. For starters, Gorilla Glass isn't entirely unbreakable. Manufacturers round up broken devices that get returned and send them back to Corning where a team tries to replicate the activities that caused the breaks. The research provides vital information for developing new glass. If Corning learns how Gorilla Glass typically breaks, it can try to prevent those breaks in future products by altering the composition of the glass or tweaking the chemicals that strengthen it.

And Corning needs customer help in developing new versions of Gorilla Glass. New designs require ever-more-stringent specifications. A few years after the first iPhone hit the market, Corning released Gorilla Glass 2—20 percent thinner and stronger than the original—in response to the demands of Apple, Samsung, Google, and others who desired to make thinner devices. Just over a year later, Gorilla Glass 3 was introduced—40 percent more scratch resistant than Version 2. "Today, glass still breaks, and glass still scratches," says Dave Velasquez, director of marketing and commercial operations for Gorilla Glass. "Until those things go to zero, the customer is not going to be happy."

Future designs will call for even more radical glass. Corning now has an antimicrobial version of Gorilla Glass. And then there's Willow, a product born out of Gorilla Glass. Willow is durable and light—a 100-micron-thick sheet of glass that bends and flexes like transparent paper. This is glass, not plastic. Corning is working with manufacturers for possible product platforms such as flexible smartphones, roll-up OLED displays (organic LED displays), and even flexible solar cells. And for applications that require a three-dimensional shape, Corning now has the capability to form Gorilla Glass into any 3D shape. While this may sound like a gimmick, experts predict that the market for flexible and 3D displays will reach $41 billion by 2020. For Corning, that represents incremental revenues of $3 billion.

It's these customer partnerships that have kept Corning on the cutting edge of innovation. Corning has had a successful partnership with Samsung in the television display industry dating back to the early days of television itself. That partnership continues today in the form of Samsung Corning Precision Materials, a joint-venture that combines Samsung's display technology and Corning's glass expertise in the production of OLED displays—displays used by Samsung and sold to other companies. If partnerships like this are any indication, it doesn't take a looking glass to see that the future looks very bright for Corning.

Questions for Discussion

12-18 As completely as possible, sketch the value chain for Corning from raw materials to finished consumer goods.

12-19 Is Corning a producer, a consumer, or an intermediary? Explain.

12-20 Discuss Corning's channel management procedures. Do Apple and Samsung have similar procedures in place?

12-21 Identify all the reasons why Corning's partnerships are essential to its success.

12-22 With respect to marketing channels, what are some threats to Corning's future?

Sources: Alex Barinka, "Corning Aims to Improve Its Gorilla Glass Screens," *Businessweek*, January 16, 2014, www.businessweek.com/articles/2014-01-16/corning-aims-to-improve-its-gorilla-glass-screens; Stephanie Mlot, "Antimicrobial Gorilla Glass Kills Touch-Screen Germs," *PCMag,* January 3, 2014, www.pcmag.com/article2/0,2817,2429145,00.asp; "3D-Shaped Gorilla Glass May Boost Corning's Revenue," *Forbes*, January 13, 2014, www.forbes.com/sites/greatspeculations/2014/01/13/3d-shaped-gorilla-glass-may-boost-cornings-revenue/; Bryan Gardiner, "Glass Works: How Corning Created the Ultrathin, Ultrastrong Material of the Future," *Wired*, September 24, 2012, www.wired.com/wiredscience/2012/09/ff-corning-gorilla-glass/all/; and information from www.corning.com/about_us/index.aspx and www.corninggorillaglass.com, accessed July 2014.

MyMarketingLab

Go to **mymktlab.com** for the following Assisted-graded writing questions:

12-23 Describe multichannel distribution systems and the advantages and disadvantages of using them. (AACSB: Communication; Reflective Thinking)

12-24 Experts are predicting that cable and satellite television will become obsolete because of the Internet. With respect to the channel of distribution, what trend does this reflect? Is it right for Comcast to use data limits to lessen competition? (AACSB: Communication; Ethical Reasoning)

References

1. Based on information from Rip Empson, "Netflix Tops HBO in Paid U.S. Subscribers as Members Stream 5 Billion Hours of Content in Q3," *Tech Crunch,* October 21, 2013, http://techcrunch.com/2013/10/21/netflix-tops-hbo-in-paid-u-s-subscribers-as-members-stream-5-billion-hours-of-content-in-q3/; Ronald Grover and Cliff Edwards, "Can Netflix Find Its Future by Abandoning Its Past?" *Bloomberg Businessweek,* September 26–October 2, 2011, pp. 29–30; Stu Woo and Ian Sherr, "Netflix Recovers Subscribers," *Wall Street Journal,* January 26, 2012, p. B1; David Carr, "Giving Viewers What They Want," *New York Times*, February 25, 2013, p. B1; Brian Stelter, "Netflix Grabs a Slice of Star Wars," *CNNMoney,* February 13, 2014, http://money.cnn.com/2014/02/13/technology/netflix-star-wars/; Mike Snider, "Netflix, Adding Customers and Profits, Will Raise Prices," *USA Today,* April 22, 2014, www.usatoday.com/story/tech/2014/04/21/netflix-results/7965613/; and www.netflix.com, accessed September 2014.
2. Based on information from Joe Cahill, "Mind Your Franchisees, Mayor McCheese," *Crain's Chicago Business*, April 26, 2013, www.chicagobusiness.com/article/20130426/BLOGS10/130429841; and "McDonald's Customer Service Push Irritates Some Franchisees," *Chicago Business Journal*, April 17, 2014, www.bizjournals.com/chicago/news/2013/04/17/mcdonalds-riding-fine-line-franchisees.html.
3. See http://investors.sherwin-williams.com/; and "The Kroger Co. Fact Book," http://ir.kroger.com/phoenix.zhtml?c=106409&p=irol-reportsAnnual, accessed September 2014.
4. See "Fashion Forward; Inditex," *The Economist,* March 24, 2012, pp. 63–64; Susan Berfield, "Zara's Fast-Fashion Edge," *Bloomberg Businessweek,* November 14, 2013, www.businessweek.com/articles/2013-11-14/2014-outlook-zaras-fashion-supply-chain-edge; and information from the Inditex Press Dossier, www.inditex.com/en/press/information/press_kit, accessed September 2014.

5. Franchising facts from "The State of the Franchise Economy in 2013," http://franchiseeconomy.com/wp-content/uploads/2013/09/The-State-Of-The-Franchise-Economy-In-2013-9-17-13.pdf; www.azfranchises.com/franchisefacts.htm, accessed May 2013. Also see "Franchise Business Economic Outlook for 2014," January 13, 2014, http://franchiseeconomy.com/wp-content/uploads/2014/01/Franchise_Business_Outlook_January_2014-1-13-13.pdf.

6. See "Meet the Top Franchise of 2014," *Entrepreneur,* December 19, 2013, www.entrepreneur.com/article/230291#; and www.anytimefitness.com/, accessed September 2014.

7. See Eric Platt, "22 Companies That Are Addicted to Walmart," June 13, 2012, *Business Insider,* www.businessinsider.com/22-companies-who-are-completely-addicted-to-walmart-2012-6#; and Stacy Mitchell, "Will Walmart Replace the Supermarket?" *Salon,* March 28, 2013, www.salon.com/2013/03/28/will_walmart_replace_the_supermarket_partner/.

8. See "General Mills: Joint Ventures," www.generalmills.com/en/Company/Businesses/International/Joint_ventures.aspx, accessed September 2014.

9. For more discussion, see Eleazar David Melendez, "Best Buy Is Still Alive, but How?" *Huffington Post,* August 20, 2014, www.huffingtonpost.com/2013/08/20/best-buy-turnaround_n_3786695.html; Matthew Yglesias, "Best Buy 'Still Basically Sucks' Despite Successful Turnaround," *Huffington Post*, September 9, 2013, www.huffingtonpost.com/2013/09/20/best-buy-turnaround_n_3962408.html; and Steve Knopper, "Beats Enters Streaming Wars," *Rolling Stone,* February 13, 2014, p. 15.

10. Matt Townsend, "The End," *Bloomberg Businessweek,* July 25, 2013, pp. 52–55; and Julie Bosman, "Bookseller Cuts Jobs at Division for Nook," *New York Times,* February 11, 2014, p. B3.

11. See "Ace Town & Country Hardware: Recommended Reviews," *Yelp*, www.yelp.com/biz/ace-town-and-country-hardware-chapel-hill-2, accessed September 2014; and www.acehardware.com/corp/index.jsp?page=about, accessed September 2014.

12. See http://new.pamperedchef.com/company-facts and www.stelladot.com/trunkshow, accessed September 2014.

13. See "Ministry of Commerce Tackles China's High Logistics Costs," *WantChinaTimes.com*, November 30, 2013, www.wantchinatimes.com/news-subclass-cnt.aspx?id=20131130000004&cid=1102; and Benjamin Robertson, "Walmart Keeps on Expansion Path in China," *South China Morning Post,"* December 19, 2013, www.scmp.com/business/companies/article/1385419/walmart-keeps-expansion-path-china.

14. Based on information from Julie Jargon, "Asia Delivers for McDonald's," *Wall Street Journal*, December 13, 2011, http://online.wsj.com/article/SB10001424052970204397704577074982151549316.html; "Feel Like a Burger? Dial M for McDonald's Japan," *Asia Pulse*, January 23, 2012; and McDonald's annual reports, www.aboutmcdonalds.com/mcd/investors/annual_reports.html, accessed September 2014.

15. See Stephanie Strom, "CVS Vows to Quit Selling Tobacco Products," *New York Times,* February 5, 2014, p. B1; and http://info.cvscaremark.com/cvs-insights/cvs-quits, accessed September 2014.

16. See Rosalyn Wilson, "24th Annual State of Logistics Report: Is This the New Normal?," www.fmsib.wa.gov/reports/powerPoints/RosalynWilsonStateofLogisticsReport2013.pdf, August 21, 2013.

17. William B. Cassidy, "Walmart Squeezes Costs from Supply Chain," *Journal of Commerce,* January 5, 2010; and "Walmart to Save $150 Million Thanks to Sustainability Programs," *Triple Pundit,* October 16, 2012, www.triplepundit.com/2012/10/walmart-save-150-million-sustainability-programs/.

18. Andy Brack, "Piggly Wiggly Center Offers Info-Packed Field Trip," *Charleston Currents*, January 4, 2010, www.charlestoncurrents.com/issue/10_issues/10.0104.htm; and information from http://en.wikipedia.org/wiki/Piggly_wiggly and http://news.walmart.com/news-archive/2005/01/07/our-retail-divisions, accessed June 2014.

19. Bill Mongrelluzzo, "Supply Chain Expert Sees Profits in Sustainability," *Journal of Commerce*, March 11, 2010, www.joc.com/logistics-economy/sustainability-can-lead-profits-says-expert; SC Johnson example from "SC Johnson Reduces Greenhouse Gasses by the Truckload," CRS Press Release, www.csrwire.com/press_releases/22882-SC-Johnson-Reduces-Greenhouse-Gases-by-the-Truckload. Also see "SC Johnson Receives U.S. EPA 2013 SmartWay Excellence Award," October 13, 2013, www.scjohnson.com/en/press-room/press-releases/10-23-2013/SC-Johnson-Receives-2013-SmartWay-Excellence-Award.aspx.

20. See Ted LaBorde, "Home Depot Opens New Record Limited Distribution Center in Westfield," *masslive.com*, December 14, 2010, www.masslive.com/news/index.ssf/2010/12/home_depot_opens_new_rapid_dep.html; "Home Depot Distribution Efficiencies Improve In-Stock Positions," *Retailed Info Systems News*, November 21, 2011, http://risnews.edgl.com/retail-best-practices/Home-Depot-Distribution-Efficiencies-Improve-In-Stock-Positions76905; "Home Depot Bridges Gap Between Online and In-Store," *Retail Info Systems News,* December 17, 2013; and www.homedepot.com, accessed September 2014.

21. See Scott Kirsner, "Amazon Acquisition Puts Amazon Rivals in Awkward Spot," *Boston Globe,* December 1, 2013, www.bostonglobe.com/business/2013/12/01/will-amazon-owned-robot-maker-sell-tailer-rivals/FON7bVNKvfzS2sHnBHzfLM/story.html; and www.kivasystems.com, accessed September 2014.

22. See Maida Napolitano, "RFID Surges Ahead," *Logistics Management,* April 2012, pp. 47–49; "Research and Markets: Global RFID Market Forecast to 2014," *Business Wire*, April 2012; and Bob Trebilcock, "RFID: The Macy's Way," *Modern Materials Handling*, June 1, 2013, www.mmh.com/article/rfid_the_macys_way.

23. Bureau of Transportation Statistics, "Pocket Guide to Transportation 2014," January 2014, www.rita.dot.gov/bts/sites/rita.dot.gov.bts/files/publications/pocket_guide_to_transportation/2014/; and American Trucking Association, www.trucking.org/News_and_Information_Reports_Industry_Data.aspx, accessed February 2014.

24. See Walmart's supplier requirements at http://corporate.walmart.com/suppliers, accessed September 2014.

25. For this and other UPS examples and information, see "Toshiba Laptop Repair," accessed at http://pressroom.ups.com/Video/Toshiba+Laptop+Repair, May 2013; and www.thenewlogistics.com and www.ups.com/content/us/en/about/facts/worldwide.html, accessed June 2014.

26. "3PL Customers Report Identifies Service Trends, 3PL Market Segment Sizes and Growth Rates," Armstrong & Associates, Inc., July 11, 2013, www.3plogistics.com/PR_3PL_Customers-2013.htm.

13 Retailing and Wholesaling

Chapter Preview

We now look more deeply into the two major intermediary marketing channel functions: retailing and wholesaling. You already know something about retailing—retailers of all shapes and sizes serve you every day, both in stores and online. However, you probably know much less about the hoard of wholesalers working behind the scenes. In this chapter, we examine the characteristics of different kinds of retailers and wholesalers, the marketing decisions they make, and trends for the future.

When it comes to white goods wholesalers in Europe, you have to start with BEKO. This mega-supplier from Turkey has reshaped the meaning of modern domestic appliances. BEKO's focus on customer value through innovative design, strong supply chain management, and investment in a portfolio of recognized brands has helped the company become a global player in the home appliance and electronics market.

BEKO: The Leading Wholesaler from Turkey

Turkey is better known for the exotic bazaars and ancient monuments of old Istanbul than for its factories. Yet, over the last 20 years the reality has changed dramatically. Turkey now produces more than half of the televisions sold in Europe and has also become a significant production base for household appliances. Founded in 1955, Arçelik Group is the leader of the Turkish consumer durables sector and a key player in the international arena. Arçelik Group possesses 10 brands and generates more than 50 percent of its revenues from international operations. It belongs to the largest conglomerate in Turkey, Koç Group, which is active in four core industries internationally—energy, automotive, financial services, and durable goods—and was ranked as the world's 273rd largest company by *Fortune* magazine in 2009.

BEKO is the international brand of Arçelik Group and is one of the top 10 home appliance brands in the world. The BEKO brand continues its steady growth in global markets, especially in Western and Eastern Europe. It is the leading oven/cooker, cooling, and freezer brand in the UK and one of the fastest-growing washing machine and dishwasher brands.

BEKO's rich product range covers a wide variety of white goods, including refrigerators, freezers, washing machines, tumble dryers, dishwashers, cookers, vacuum cleaners, and air conditioning units, as well as consumer electronics, encompassing more than 3,500 active product models. BEKO is currently spread out over 100 countries and develops various smart solutions to cater to the needs of different people, different cultures, and different ways of life. To serve this wide market, eight production facilities are located in Turkey but factories can also be found in Russia, Romania, and China.

BEKO's ambition is to prove that Turkish engineering can provide quality as well as quantity. Innovation and development are important, too, as shown by the more than 850 employees in its research and development (R&D) center. BEKO adheres to the highest standards in the industry. This strategy is in line with BEKO's philosophy, which aims to make people's lives easier and to demonstrate the importance of the emotional value attached to the brand.

BEKO stands to be a consumer-focused brand delivering technology and efficient solutions with functional design. Supporting this approach, BEKO has received many international awards acknowledging both its flair for innovation and energy efficiency. Some of the awards include the Energy Saving Trust award, Plus X award, and iF and RedDot Design awards.

BEKO's continuous innovation and improvements, coupled with long-term relationships with suppliers, are laying the foundation for global success in the twenty-first century.

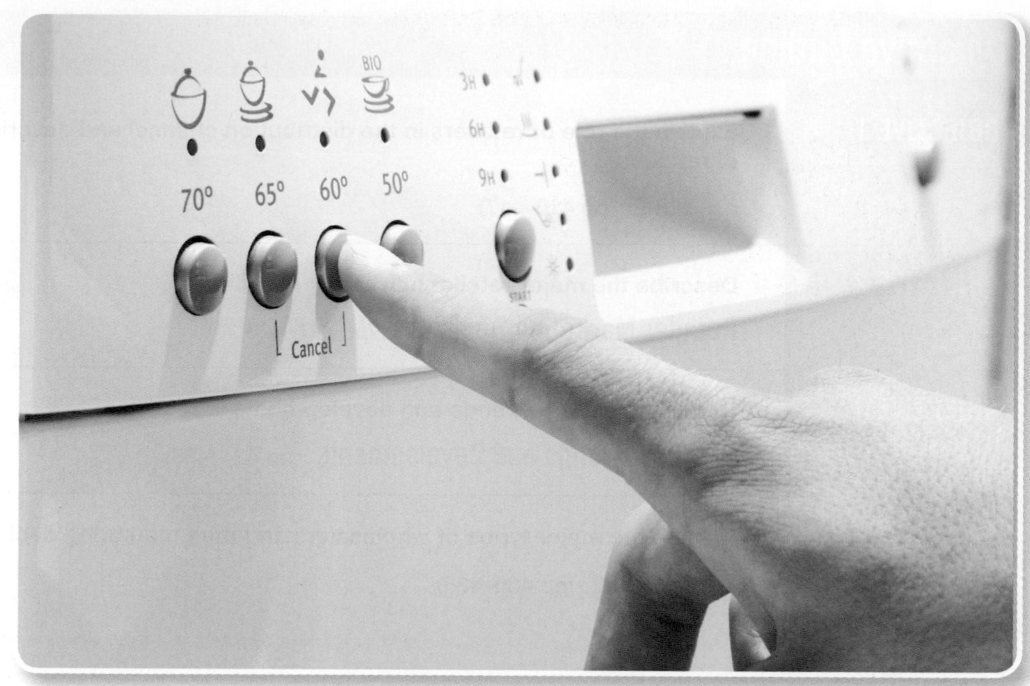

BEKO produces a wide range of electronic goods, from washing machines to plasma TVs, demonstrating that Turkish engineering can offer quantity and quality.

© fbhenrg/Fotolia.com

What is behind this spectacular success? First, unlike to many global firms, BEKO puts its human resources at the center of its strategy. To accomplish this, specific facilities and training opportunities are available to employees to make sure that they remain up to date on the latest developments. Trustworthiness, continuity, and responsibility for all its working partners and the work environment in general symbolize BEKO's commitment to sustainability. Health and retirement benefits, social and cultural activities, sports recreational facilities, and food and transport services are available to employees. Remuneration is based on performance and capability, and includes generous bonus schemes.

Second, BEKO is very respectful of its customers. This is developed in many areas, including BEKO's Web site, salesperson training, and product innovation. It is also evident in the company's sponsorship activities, which aim to give back to communities. The company regularly publishes a sustainability report to ensure that it aligns itself with the best socially responsible corporations in the world. To support the environment and future generations, BEKO has set a new vision: "Respect the Globe, Respected Globally."

In addition, the success of BEKO relies heavily on innovation and the possibilities for distinguishing BEKO from the competition. BEKO achieves this through its high-quality, long-lasting product range offers and its products' distinctive features, which rely on innovative technical aspects and an elegant look. Designers around the world compete for their product to be crowned the BEKO design. The strongest designs are then tested by a range of consumers. BEKO has become a leader, championing consumer participation and co-creation and utilizing consumer ideas in the design process.

So, how does BEKO make a profit with such an inclusive strategy that focuses heavily on social responsibility in such a competitive environment? As in many modern retail organizations, a low-cost structure has been put in place in BEKO's production and distribution facilities. Technology and innovation in both management and production are developed, and continuous improvement is built into all systems and processes. The approach is made possible through total quality management, total productive management, and Six Sigma methodologies for cost reduction, quality control, process improvement, and flexible structures. Purchasing has a great influence on the whole process.

Suppliers want to share BEKO's philosophy, business rules, and ethics (including a list of prohibited materials) to collectively and mutually benefit from the BEKO organization. Suppliers are also expected to comply with a code of conduct that complies with the European Committee of Domestic Equipment Manufacturers. BEKO and its suppliers mutually sign "purchasing contracts" to define working conditions.

Despite BEKO's incredible success over the past two decades, it faces some huge challenges ahead as many markets other than developed economies in the West are opening up rapidly. Arçelik's position in the global marketplace had been significantly strengthened through a wave of acquisitions. In 2002, the BEKO Group purchased the 127-year-old German brand Blomberg, the 117-year-old Austrian brand Elektra Bregenz, and cooker brands of the UK and Ireland— Leisure and Flavel—as well as Arctic, Romania's largest household appliances manufacturer. In 2007, the Group incorporated Grundig, the leading consumer electronics brand of Germany. BEKO also emphasizes its presence in promising areas such as Azerbaijan, Lebanon, Lithuania, Georgia, Poland, the Russian Federation, Romania, the Ukraine, Algeria, and Libya.

Turkey's unique geographical position between Asia and Europe and its long trading heritage are creating good conditions for growth in many areas where traditional brands lack cultural affinities.

Still, even as BEKO improves its image, the Turkish internal market is very much cared for. BEKO is a source of cultural pride in a rapidly growing population of over 70 million inhabitants, many under the age of 24. Contrary to its European competitors, BEKO can also rely on strong internal demand.[1]

Objective Outline

OBJECTIVE 1	**Explain the role of retailers in the distribution channel and describe the major types of retailers.** Retailing (pp 410–417)
OBJECTIVE 2	**Describe the major retailer marketing decisions.** Retailer Marketing Decisions (pp 417–423)
OBJECTIVE 3	**Discuss the major trends and developments in retailing.** Retailing Trends and Developments (pp 424–430)
OBJECTIVE 4	**Explain the major types of wholesalers and their marketing decisions.** Wholesaling (pp 430–435)

The BEKO story sets the stage for examining the fast-changing world of today's retailers. This chapter looks at *retailing* and *wholesaling*. In the first section, we look at the nature and importance of retailing, the major types of store and nonstore retailers, the decisions retailers make, and the future of retailing. In the second section, we discuss these same topics as they apply to wholesalers.

Author Comment | You already know a lot about retailers. You deal with them every day—store retailers, service retailers, online and mobile retailers, and others.

Retailing

What is retailing? We all know that Costco, Home Depot, Macy's, and Target are retailers, but so are Amazon.com, the local Hampton Inn, and a doctor seeing patients. **Retailing** includes all the activities involved in selling products or services directly to final consumers for their personal, nonbusiness use. Many institutions—manufacturers, wholesalers, and retailers—do retailing. But most retailing is done by **retailers**, businesses whose sales come *primarily* from retailing.

Retailing
All the activities involved in selling goods or services directly to final consumers for their personal, nonbusiness use.

Retailer
A business whose sales come *primarily* from retailing.

Shopper marketing
Focusing the entire marketing process on turning shoppers into buyers as they approach the point of sale, whether during in-store, online, or mobile shopping.

Retailing plays a very important role in most marketing channels. Last year, retailers accounted for more than $5 trillion of sales to final consumers.[2] Retailers play an important role in connecting brands with consumers in the final phases of the buying process and at the point of purchase. In fact, many marketers are now embracing the concept of **shopper marketing**, focusing the entire marketing process—from product and brand development to logistics, promotion, and merchandising—toward turning shoppers into buyers as they approach the point of sale.

Of course, every well-designed marketing effort focuses on customer buying behavior. What differentiates the concept of shopper marketing is the suggestion that these efforts should be coordinated around the shopping process itself. For example, P&G follows a "store back" concept, in which all marketing ideas need to be effective at the store-shelf level and work back from there. The strategy builds around what P&G calls

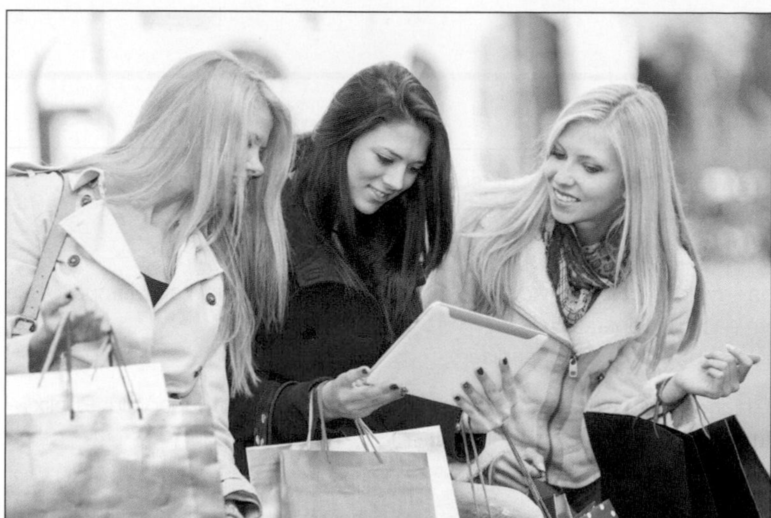

Shopper marketing: The dramatic growth in online and mobile shopping has added new dimensions to "point of purchase." Influencing consumers' buying decisions as they shop now involves efforts aimed at online search and in-store, online, and mobile shopping.

the "First Moment of Truth"—the critical three to seven seconds that a shopper considers a product on a store shelf.[3]

The dramatic growth of online and mobile shopping has added new dimensions to shopper marketing. The retailing "moment of truth" no longer takes place only in stores. Instead, Google defines a "zero moment of truth," when consumers begin the buying process by searching for and learning about products online. Today's consumers are increasingly *omnichannel buyers*, who make little distinction between in-store and online shopping, and for whom the path to a retail purchase runs across multiple channels. For these buyers, a particular purchase might consist of researching a product online and buying it from an online retailer, without ever setting foot into a retail store. Alternatively, they might use a smartphone to research a purchase on the fly, or even in retail store aisles. For example, it's common to see a consumer examining an item on a shelf at Target while at the same time using a mobile app to check product reviews and prices at Amazon.com. Thus, shopper marketing isn't just about in-store buying these days. Influencing consumers' buying decisions as they shop involves efforts aimed at online search and in-store, online, and mobile shopping.[4]

Although most retailing is still done in retail stores, in recent years direct and online retailing have been growing much faster than store retailing. We discuss direct and online retailing in detail later in this chapter and in Chapter 17. For now, we will focus on store retailing.

Types of Retailers

Retail stores come in all shapes and sizes—from your local hairstyling salon or family-owned restaurant to national specialty chain retailers such as REI or Williams-Sonoma to megadiscounters such as Costco or Walmart. The most important types of retail stores are described in Table 13.1 and discussed in the following sections. They can be classified in terms of several characteristics, including the *amount of service* they offer, the breadth and depth of their *product lines*, the *relative prices* they charge, and how they are *organized*.

Amount of Service

Different types of customers and products require different amounts of service. To meet these varying service needs, retailers may offer one of three service levels: self-service, limited service, and full service.

Self-service retailers serve customers who are willing to perform their own *locate-compare-select* process to save time or money. Self-service is the basis of all discount operations and is typically used by retailers selling convenience goods (such as supermarkets) and nationally branded, fast-moving shopping goods (such as Target or Kohl's). *Limited-service retailers*, such as Sears or JCPenney, provide more sales assistance because they carry more shopping goods about which customers need information. Their increased operating costs result in higher prices.

Full-service retailers, such as high-end specialty stores (for example, Tiffany or Williams-Sonoma) and first-class department stores (such as Nordstrom or Neiman Marcus) assist customers in every phase of the shopping process. Full-service stores usually carry more specialty goods for which customers need or want assistance or advice. They provide more services, which results in much higher operating costs. These higher costs are passed along to customers as higher prices.

Product Line

Specialty store
A retail store that carries a narrow product line with a deep assortment within that line.

Retailers can also be classified by the length and breadth of their product assortments. Some retailers, such as **specialty stores**, carry narrow product lines with deep assortments within those lines. Today, specialty stores are flourishing. The increasing use of market

Table 13.1 | Major Store Retailer Types

Type	Description	Examples
Specialty store	A store that carries a narrow product line with a deep assortment, such as apparel stores, sporting-goods stores, furniture stores, florists, and bookstores.	REI, Sunglass Hut, Sephora, Williams-Sonoma
Department store	A store that carries several product lines—typically clothing, home furnishings, and household goods—with each line operated as a separate department managed by specialist buyers or merchandisers.	Macy's, Sears, Neiman Marcus
Supermarket	A relatively large, low-cost, low-margin, high-volume, self-service operation designed to serve the consumer's total needs for grocery and household products.	Kroger, Safeway, SuperValu, Publix
Convenience store	A relatively small store located near residential areas, open long hours seven days a week, and carrying a limited line of high-turnover convenience products at slightly higher prices.	7-Eleven, Stop-N-Go, Circle K, Sheetz
Discount store	A store that carries standard merchandise sold at lower prices with lower margins and higher volumes.	Walmart, Target, Kohl's
Off-price retailer	A store that sells merchandise bought at less-than-regular wholesale prices and sold at less than retail. These include *factory outlets* owned and operated by manufacturers; *independent off-price retailers* owned and run by entrepreneurs or by divisions of larger retail corporations; and *warehouse* (*or wholesale*) *clubs* selling a limited selection of goods at deep discounts to consumers who pay membership fees.	Mikasa (factory outlet); TJ Maxx (independent off-price retailer); Costco, Sam's Club, BJ's (warehouse clubs)
Superstore	A very large store that meets consumers' total needs for routinely purchased food and nonfood items. This includes *supercenters*, combined supermarket and discount stores, and *category killers*, which carry a deep assortment in a particular category.	Walmart Supercenter, SuperTarget, Meijer (discount stores); Best Buy, PetSmart, Staples, Bed Bath & Beyond (category killers)

segmentation, market targeting, and product specialization has resulted in a greater need for stores that focus on specific products and segments.

Department store
A retail store that carries a wide variety of product lines, each operated as a separate department managed by specialist buyers or merchandisers.

By contrast, **department stores** carry a wide variety of product lines. In recent years, department stores have been squeezed between more focused and flexible specialty stores on the one hand and more efficient, lower-priced discounters on the other. In response, many have added promotional pricing to meet the discount threat. Others have stepped up the use of store brands and single-brand *designer shops* to compete with specialty stores. Still others are trying direct and online selling. Service remains the key differentiating factor. Retailers such as Nordstrom, Saks, Neiman Marcus, and other high-end department stores are doing well by emphasizing exclusive merchandise and high-quality service.

Supermarket
A large, low-cost, low-margin, high-volume, self-service store that carries a wide variety of grocery and household products.

Supermarkets are the most frequently visited type of retail store. Today, however, they are facing slow sales growth because of slower population growth and an increase in competition from discounters (Walmart, Costco, and Dollar General) on the one hand and specialty food stores (Whole Foods Market, Trader Joe's, ALDI, Sprouts) on the other. Supermarkets also have been hit hard by the rapid growth of out-of-home eating over the past two decades. In fact, supermarkets' share of the groceries and food market plunged from 66 percent in 2000 to 48 percent last year.[5]

In the battle for "share of stomachs," some supermarkets have moved upscale, providing improved store environments and higher-quality food offerings, such as from-scratch bakeries, gourmet deli counters, natural foods, and fresh seafood departments. Others, however, are attempting to compete head-on with large discounters such as Costco and

In the battle for "share of stomach," regional supermarket chain WinCo successfully competes head-on with large discounters such as Costco and Walmart. It's rapidly becoming "Walmart's worst nightmare."

WinCo Foods, Inc.

Walmart by cutting costs, establishing more-efficient operations, and lowering prices. WinCo, a fast-growing regional discount-grocery chain in the western United States, has done this successfully:[6]

> You probably haven't heard of WinCo yet. But you can bet that Walmart and Costco are keeping a close eye on the small discount-grocery chain. In fact, according to one supermarket-retailing expert, WinCo is fast becoming "Walmart's worst nightmare." In its markets, WinCo (short for "Winning Company") positions itself directly against mighty Walmart as "The Supermarket Low Price Leader." And that's more than just a slogan—WinCo doesn't just match Walmart's prices; it often undercuts them. WinCo keeps prices low through low-cost, efficient operations. The chain often cuts out distributors and buys goods at lower costs directly from farms and factories. Its large, efficient, no-frills stores carry a limited assortment of basic fast-moving merchandise. WinCo's customers help to keep costs down by bagging their own groceries and paying cash (no credit cards accepted). Finally, the employee-owned chain has a reputation for treating its employees right in terms of pay, benefits, and pensions. The result is a cheerful, highly-motivated, productive workforce that genuinely contributes to the company's low-cost success. Why should Walmart and Costco worry about WinCo? The rapidly-growing chain expects to double in size every five to seven years. According to the retailing expert, "WinCo is really unstoppable at this point."

Convenience stores are small stores that carry a limited line of high-turnover convenience goods. After several years of stagnant sales, these stores are now experiencing growth. Many convenience store chains have tried to expand beyond their primary market of young, blue-collar men by redesigning their stores to attract female shoppers. They are shedding the image of a "truck stop" where men go to buy gas, beer, cigarettes, or shriveled hotdogs on a roller grill and are instead offering freshly prepared foods and cleaner, safer, more-upscale environments.

Convenience store
A small store, located near a residential area, that is open long hours seven days a week and carries a limited line of high-turnover convenience goods.

For example, consider 7-Eleven, which is providing new reasons to say "Oh thank heaven—it's 7-Eleven":[7]

> Long known as a haven for Slurpees, Big Gulps, hot dogs spinning on a roller, self-serve nachos with cheese and chili, smokes, beer, and bags of chips, 7-Eleven is changing both its fare and its image. To meet evolving consumer tastes and stiffer competition from the likes of Dunkin' Donuts and Starbucks—which now offer fresh food to on-the-go customers—7-Eleven is stocking its shelves with healthier options, developed by a company team of culinary and food science experts. More health-conscious customers will now find an expanding menu of snack and meal items under 400 calories, such as yogurt parfaits, salads, bags of carrots and celery, fresh subs, Smart turkey sandwiches on whole wheat bread, and a Bistro Snack Protein Pack— carrots, hummus, pita rounds, cheddar cheese, and grapes in a meal-to-go box. The chain is also resizing and single-sizing existing products. Over the next three years, 7-Eleven plans to boost its sales of high-margin fresh foods to 20 percent, twice the current level. The goal is to offer "what the consumer now wants, which is tasty, healthy, fresh food choices," says 7-Eleven's CEO. The change means less reliance on decreasing cigarette sales and aligns the chain with the latest consumer buying trends.

Superstore
A store much larger than a regular supermarket that offers a large assortment of routinely purchased food products, nonfood items, and services.

Category killer
A giant specialty store that carries a very deep assortment of a particular line.

Service retailer
A retailer whose product line is actually a service; examples include hotels, airlines, banks, colleges, and many others.

Superstores are much larger than regular supermarkets and offer a large assortment of routinely purchased food products, nonfood items, and services. Walmart, Target, Meijer, and other discount retailers offer *supercenters*, very large combination food and discount stores. Whereas a traditional grocery store brings in about $320,000 a week in sales, a supercenter brings in about $1.4 million a week. Walmart, which opened its first supercenter in 1988, now has more than 3,200 supercenters in North America and is opening new ones at a rate of about 120 per year.[8]

Recent years have also seen the rapid growth of superstores that are actually giant specialty stores, the so-called **category killers** (for example, Best Buy, Home Depot, PetSmart, and Bed Bath & Beyond). They feature stores the size of airplane hangars that carry a very deep assortment of a particular line. Category killers are found in a wide range of categories, including electronics, home-improvement products, books, baby gear, toys, home goods, party goods, sporting goods, and even pet supplies.

Finally, for many retailers, the product line is actually a service. **Service retailers** include hotels and motels, banks, airlines, restaurants, colleges, hospitals, movie theaters, tennis clubs, bowling alleys, repair services, hair salons, and dry cleaners. Service retailers in the United States are growing faster than product retailers.

Relative Prices

Retailers can also be classified according to the prices they charge (see Table 13.1). Most retailers charge regular prices and offer normal-quality goods and customer service. Others offer higher-quality goods and service at higher prices. Retailers that feature low prices are discount stores and "off-price" retailers.

Discount store
A retail operation that sells standard merchandise at lower prices by accepting lower margins and selling at higher volume.

Discount Stores. A **discount store** (for example, Target, Kohl's, or Walmart) sells standard merchandise at lower prices by accepting lower margins and selling higher volume. The early discount stores cut expenses by offering few services and operating in warehouse-like facilities in low-rent, heavily traveled districts. Today's discounters have improved their store environments and increased their services, while at the same time keeping prices low through lean, efficient operations.

Leading "big-box" discounters, such as Walmart, Costco, and Target, now dominate the retail scene. However, even "small-box" discounters are thriving in the current economic environment. For example, dollar stores are now today's fastest-growing retail format. Back in the day, dollar stores sold mostly odd-lot assortments of novelties, factory overruns, close-outs, and outdated merchandise—most priced at $1. Not anymore. ● Dollar General, the nation's largest small-box discount retailer, makes a powerful value promise for the times: "Save time. Save money. Every day":[9]

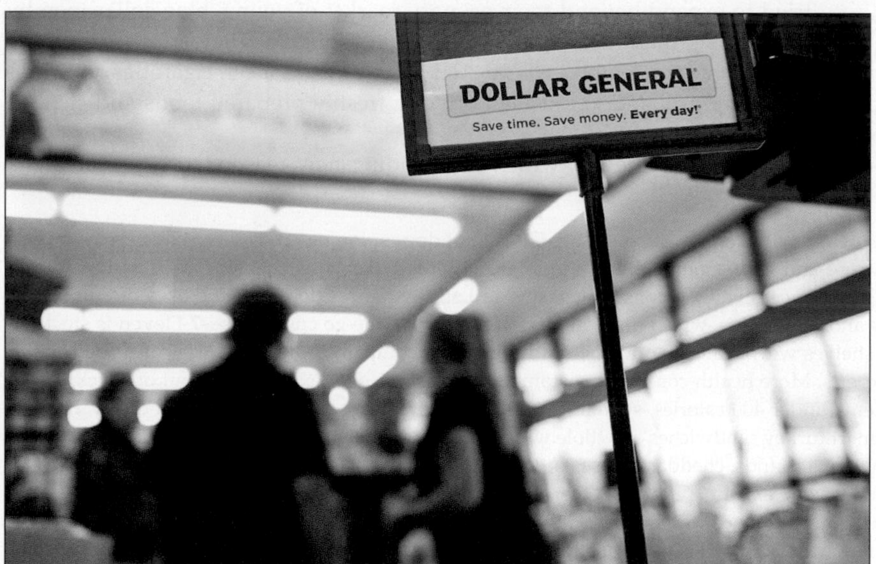

● **Discounter Dollar General, the nation's largest small-box discount retailer, makes a powerful value promise for the times: "Save time. Save money. Every day."**
Bloomberg via Getty Images

Dollar General's slogan isn't just for show. It's a careful statement of the store's value promise. The retailer's goal is to keep shopping simple by offering only a selected assortment of popular brands at everyday low prices in small and convenient locations. Dollar General's slimmed-down product line and smaller stores (you could fit more than 25 Dollar General stores inside the average Walmart supercenter) add up to a quick trip—the average customer is in and out of the store in less than 10 minutes. And its prices on the popular brand-name products it carries are an estimated 20 to 40 percent lower than grocery store prices. Put it all together, and things are sizzling right now at Dollar General. Moreover, the fast-growing retailer is well positioned for the future. We "see signs of a new consumerism," says Dollar General's CEO, "as people shift where they shop, switch to lower-cost brands, and stay generally more frugal." Convenience and low prices, it seems, never go out of style.

Off-price retailer
A retailer that buys at less-than-regular wholesale prices and sells at less than retail.

Independent off-price retailer
An off-price retailer that is independently owned and operated or a division of a larger retail corporation.

Off-Price Retailers. As the major discount stores traded up, a new wave of **off-price retailers** moved in to fill the ultralow-price, high-volume gap. Ordinary discounters buy at regular wholesale prices and accept lower margins to keep prices down. By contrast, off-price retailers buy at less-than-regular wholesale prices and charge consumers less than retail. Off-price retailers can be found in all areas, from food, clothing, and electronics to no-frills banking and discount brokerages.

The three main types of off-price retailers are *independents*, *factory outlets*, and *warehouse clubs*. **Independent off-price retailers** either are independently owned and run or are divisions of larger retail corporations. Although many off-price operations are run by smaller independents, most large off-price retailer operations are owned by bigger retail chains. Examples include store retailers such as TJ Maxx and Marshalls, which are owned by TJX Companies, and online sellers such as Overstock.com. TJ Maxx promises brand name and designer fashions for 20 to 60 percent off department store prices. How does it fulfill this promise? Its buyer are constantly on the lookout for deals. "So when a designer overproduces and department stores overbuy," says the company, "we swoop in, negotiate the lowest possible price, and pass the savings on."[10]

Factory outlet
An off-price retailing operation that is owned and operated by a manufacturer and normally carries the manufacturer's surplus, discontinued, or irregular goods.

Factory outlets—manufacturer-owned and operated stores by firms such as J. Crew, Gap, Levi Strauss, and others—sometimes group together in *factory outlet malls* and *value-retail centers*. At these centers, dozens of outlet stores offer prices as much as 50 percent below retail on a wide range of mostly surplus, discounted, or irregular goods. Whereas outlet malls consist primarily of manufacturers' outlets, value-retail centers combine manufacturers' outlets with off-price retail stores and department store clearance outlets.

These malls in general are now moving upscale—and even dropping *factory* from their descriptions. A growing number of outlet malls now feature luxury brands such as Coach, Polo Ralph Lauren, Dolce&Gabbana, Giorgio Armani, Burberry, and Versace. As consumers become more value-minded, even upper-end retailers are accelerating their factory outlet strategies, placing more emphasis on outlets such as Nordstrom Rack, Neiman Marcus Last Call, Bloomingdale's Outlets, and Saks Off 5th. Many companies now regard outlets not simply as a way of disposing of problem merchandise but as an additional way of gaining business for fresh merchandise. The combination of highbrow brands and lowbrow prices found at outlets provides powerful shopper appeal, especially in thriftier times.

Warehouse club
An off-price retailer that sells a limited selection of brand name grocery items, appliances, clothing, and other goods at deep discounts to members who pay annual membership fees.

Warehouse clubs (also known as *wholesale clubs* or *membership warehouses*), such as Costco, Sam's Club, and BJ's, operate in huge, drafty, warehouse-like facilities and offer few frills. However, they offer ultralow prices and surprise deals on selected branded merchandise. Warehouse clubs have grown rapidly in recent years. These retailers appeal not only to low-income consumers seeking bargains on bare-bones products but also to all kinds of customers shopping for a wide range of goods, from necessities to extravagances.

Consider Costco, now the nation's second-largest retailer, behind Walmart. Low price is an important part of Costco's equation, but what really sets Costco apart is the products it carries and the sense of urgency that it builds into the Costco shopper's store experience:[11]

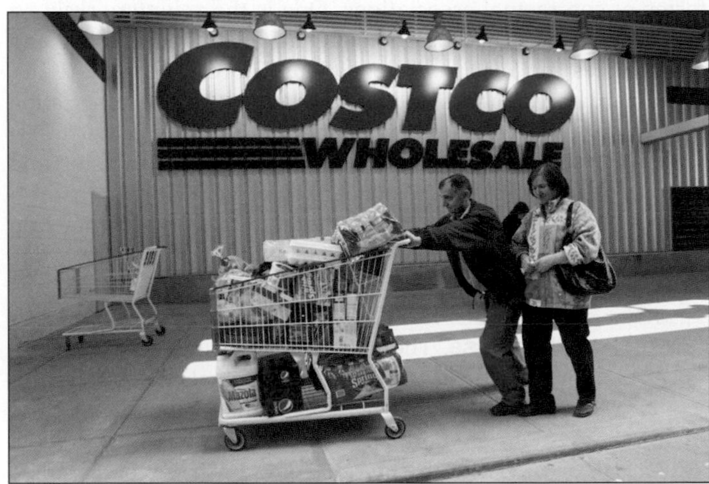

Warehouse clubs: Costco is a retail treasure hunt, where both low-end and high-end products meet deep-discount prices.
Suzanne Dechillo/The New York Times

Costco is a retail treasure hunt, where both low-end and high-end products meet deep-discount prices. Alongside the gallon jars of peanut butter and 2,250-count packs of Q-Tips, Costco offers an ever-changing assortment of high-quality products—even luxuries—all at tantalizingly low margins. Last year, Costco sold more than 109 million hot dog and soda combinations (still only $1.50 as they have been for more than 20 years). At the same time, it sold more than 100,000 carats of diamonds at up to $100,000 per item. It is the nation's biggest baster of poultry (more than 60 million rotisserie chickens a year at $4.99) but also the country's biggest seller of fine wines (including the likes of a Chateau Cheval Blanc Premier Grand Cru Classe at $1,750 a bottle).

Each Costco store is a theater of retail that creates buying urgency and excitement. Mixed in with its regular stock of staples, Costco features a glittering, constantly shifting array of one-time specials, such as discounted Prada bags, Calloway golf clubs, or Kenneth Cole bags—deals you just won't find anywhere else. In fact, of the 4,000 items that Costco carries, 1,000 are designated as "treasure items" (Costco's words). The changing assortment and great prices keep people of all kinds coming back, wallets in hand. There was a time when only the great, unwashed masses shopped at off-price retailers, but Costco has changed all that. Now, even people who don't have to pinch pennies shop there.

Organizational Approach

Although many retail stores are independently owned, others band together under some form of corporate or contractual organization. Table 13.2 describes four major types of retail organizations—*corporate chains*, *voluntary chains*, *retailer cooperatives*, and *franchise organizations*.

Corporate chains
Two or more outlets that are commonly owned and controlled.

Corporate chains are two or more outlets that are commonly owned and controlled. They have many advantages over independents. Their size allows them to buy in large quantities at lower prices and gain promotional economies. They can hire specialists to

Table 13.2 | Major Types of Retail Organizations

Type	Description	Examples
Corporate chain	Two or more outlets that are commonly owned and controlled. Corporate chains appear in all types of retailing but they are strongest in department stores, discount stores, food stores, drugstores, and restaurants.	Macy's (department stores), Target (discount stores), Kroger (grocery stores), CVS (drugstores)
Voluntary chain	Wholesaler-sponsored group of independent retailers engaged in group buying and merchandising.	Independent Grocers Alliance (IGA), Do-It Best (hardware), Western Auto (auto supply), True Value (hardware)
Retailer cooperative	Group of independent retailers who jointly establish a central buying organization and conduct joint promotion efforts.	Associated Grocers (groceries), Ace Hardware (hardware)
Franchise organization	Contractual association between a franchisor (a manufacturer, wholesaler, or service organization) and franchisees (independent businesspeople who buy the right to own and operate one or more units in the franchise system).	McDonald's, Subway, Pizza Hut, Jiffy Lube, Meineke Mufflers, 7-Eleven

Franchise
A contractual association between a manufacturer, wholesaler, or service organization (a franchisor) and independent businesspeople (franchisees) who buy the right to own and operate one or more units in the franchise system.

deal with areas such as pricing, promotion, merchandising, inventory control, and sales forecasting.

The great success of corporate chains caused many independents to band together in one of two forms of contractual associations. One is the *voluntary chain*—a wholesaler-sponsored group of independent retailers that engages in group buying and common merchandising. Examples include the Independent Grocers Alliance (IGA), Western Auto, and Do-It Best hardware stores. The other type of contractual association is the *retailer cooperative*—a group of independent retailers that bands together to set up a jointly owned, central wholesale operation and conduct joint merchandising and promotion efforts. Examples are Associated Grocers and Ace Hardware. These organizations give independents the buying and promotion economies they need to meet the prices of corporate chains.

Another form of contractual retail organization is a **franchise**. The main difference between franchise organizations and other contractual systems (voluntary chains and retail cooperatives) is that franchise systems are normally based on some unique product or service; a method of doing business; or the trade name, goodwill, or patent that the franchisor has developed. Franchising has been prominent in fast-food restaurants, motels, health and fitness centers, auto sales and service dealerships, and real estate agencies.

However, franchising covers a lot more than just burger joints and fitness centers. Franchises have sprung up to meet just about any need. For example, Mad Science Group franchisees put on science programs for schools, scout troops, and birthday parties. H&R Block provides tax-preparation services, and Supercuts offers affordable, anytime, walk-in haircuts. Mr. Handyman provides repair services for homeowners, while Merry Maids tidies up their houses. And Soccer Shots offers programs that give kids ages 2 to 8 an introduction to basic soccer skills at daycare centers, schools, and parks.

Franchising covers a lot more than just burger joints and fitness centers. For example, Soccer Shots franchisees offer programs that give kids ages 2 to 8 an introduction to basic soccer skills.

Soccer Shots Franchising

Franchises now command about 45 percent of all retail sales in the United States. These days, it's nearly impossible to stroll down a city block or drive on a city street without seeing a McDonald's, Subway, Jiffy Lube, or Holiday Inn. One of the best-known and most successful franchisers, McDonald's, now has more than 34,000 stores in 118 countries, including more than 14,000 in the United States. It serves 69 million customers a day and racks up more than $97 billion in annual system-wide sales. More than 80 percent of McDonald's restaurants worldwide are owned and operated by franchisees. Gaining fast is Subway, one of the fastest-growing franchise restaurants, with system-wide sales of $18.1 billion and more than 41,000 shops in 105 countries, including more than 25,500 in the United States.[12]

Retailer Marketing Decisions

Retailers are always searching for new marketing strategies to attract and hold customers. In the past, retailers attracted customers with unique product assortments and more or better services. Today, the assortments and services of various retailers are looking more and more alike. You can find most consumer brands not only in department stores but also in mass-merchandise discount stores, off-price discount stores, and all over the Internet. Thus, it's now more difficult for any one retailer to offer exclusive merchandise.

Service differentiation among retailers has also eroded. Many department stores have trimmed their services, whereas discounters have increased theirs. In addition, customers have become smarter and more price sensitive. They see no reason to pay more for identical brands, especially when service differences are shrinking. For all these reasons, many retailers today are rethinking their marketing strategies.

As shown in **Figure 13.1**, retailers face major marketing decisions about *segmentation and targeting*, *store differentiation and positioning*, and the *retail marketing mix*.

Segmentation, Targeting, Differentiation, and Positioning Decisions

Retailers must first segment and define their target markets and then decide how they will differentiate and position themselves in these markets. Should they focus on upscale, midscale, or downscale shoppers? Do target shoppers want variety, depth of assortment, convenience, or low prices? Until they define and profile their markets, retailers cannot make consistent decisions about product assortment, services, pricing, advertising, store décor, online and mobile site design, or any of the other decisions that must support their positions.

Too many retailers, even big ones, fail to clearly define their target markets and positions. For example, what market does Sears target? For what is the department store known? What is its value proposition versus, say, Walmart on one hand and Macy's or Nordstrom on the other? If you're having trouble answering those questions, you're not alone—so is Sears's management.

FIGURE | 13.1
Retailer Marketing Strategies

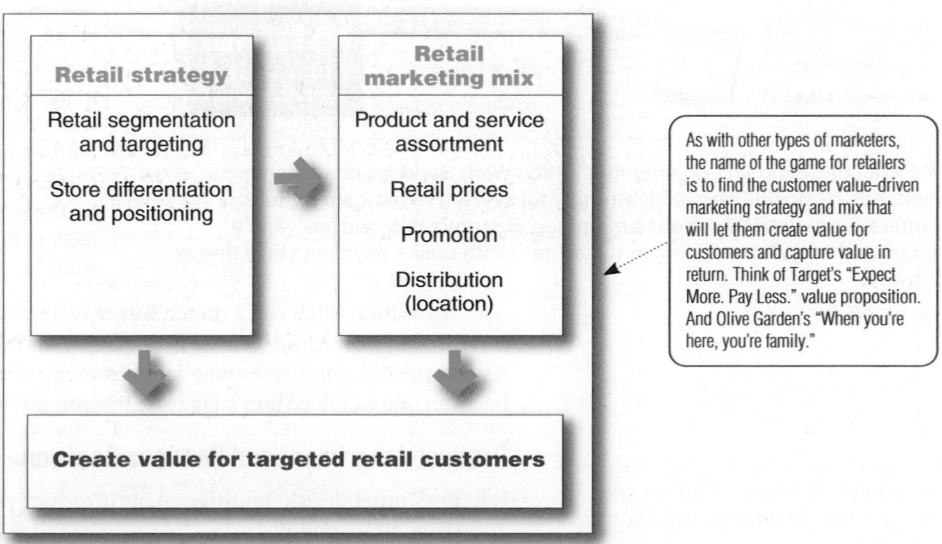

For well over a century, Sears was America's iconic retailer. Its well-known slogan, "Where America Shops," was more than just an advertising tagline—it was a meaningful positioning statement. Almost every American relied on Sears for everything from basic apparel and home goods to appliances and tools. But during the past two decades, once-mighty Sears has lost its way. Squeezed between lower-priced big-box discount stores on the one hand, and trendier, more targeted upscale department and specialty stores on the other, Sears has gotten lost in the murky middle. Its old "Where America Shops" positioning has little meaning these days for a store with little more than one-twentieth the sales of competitor Walmart. It seems that about the only thing Sears has going for it these days is that everything it sells is always on sale. However, price is not a convincing value proposition for Sears, which has trouble matching the low prices of competitors such as Walmart, Target, or Kohl's. Now in a financial tailspin, some analysts even predict that once-dominant Sears will soon disappear entirely. To once again position Sears as the place "Where America Shops," the retailer must first answer the question, "Why should people shop at Sears?"

By contrast, successful retailers define their target markets well and position themselves strongly. For example, Trader Joe's has established its "cheap gourmet" value proposition. Walmart is powerfully positioned on low prices and what those always-low prices mean to its customers. And highly successful outdoor products retailer Bass Pro Shops positions itself strongly as being "as close to the Great Outdoors as you can get indoors!"

With solid targeting and positioning, a retailer can compete effectively against even the largest and strongest competitors. For example, compare little Which Wich Superior Sandwiches to giant Subway. Which Wich has about 300 stores and $125 million in sales; Subway has more than 41,000 stores worldwide and system-wide sales of $18 billion. How does Which Wich compete with one of the world's largest franchise chains? It doesn't—at least not directly. ● Which Wich succeeds by carefully positioning itself *away* from Subway.[13]

● **Retail targeting and positioning: Which Wich Superior Sandwiches succeeds by positioning itself strongly away from larger competitors. It offers more than 50 varieties of unique customizable "wiches" and a "positive energy" from being in the store—both unlike anything you'll find at Subway.**

www.WhichWich.com

Sandwiches are where it's at these days. If you're craving something between two slices of bread, you have no end of choices, from a basic Subway sub to more exotic creations from Panera Bread, McAlister's Deli, Au Bon Pain, or Potbelly Sandwich Shop. But Which Wich Superior Sandwiches stands out from the pack as the ultimate "have it your way" sandwich place. It offers more than 50 varieties of customizable "wiches"—unlike anything you'll find at Subway—from the signature Wicked (loaded with five meats and three cheeses), to unique items such as the Thank You Turkey (with stuffing and cranberry sauce) and the Elvis Wich (peanut butter, bacon, sweet honey, and fresh banana). Customers use red Sharpies to mark up preprinted menus on sandwich bags, starting with one of the 50 sandwich bases and customizing it with their choices of everything from breads to mustards to veggies. The possibilities for personalization are endless. And instead of standing in a cafeteria-style line as you would at Subway, at Which Wich you hand your bag to the cashier, grab a drink and chips, have a seat, and wait to hear your name called. While you're eating, use the red Sharpie to draw on your bag, then hang your "artwork" on the community wall. It's not just the food that sets Which Wich apart, says the company, "it's a feeling, that positive energy, you get from being in our store."

So, Which Wich can't match Subway's massive economies of scale, incredible volume purchasing power, ultraefficient logistics, and low prices. But then again, it doesn't even try. By positioning itself away from Subway and other large competitors, Which Wich has become one of the nation's fastest-growing fast-casual restaurant chains.

Product Assortment and Services Decision

Retailers must decide on three major product variables: product assortment, services mix, and store atmosphere.

The retailer's *product assortment* should differentiate it while matching target shoppers' expectations. One strategy is to offer a highly targeted product assortment: Lane Bryant carries plus-size clothing, Brookstone offers an unusual assortment of gadgets and gifts, and BatteryDepot.com offers about every imaginable kind of replacement battery. Alternatively, a retailer can differentiate itself by offering merchandise that no other competitor carries, such as store brands or national brands on which it holds exclusive rights. For example, Kohl's gets exclusive rights to carry well-known labels such as Simply Vera by Vera Wang and a Food Network-branded line of kitchen tools, utensils, and appliances. Kohl's also offers its own private-label lines, such as Sonoma, Croft & Barrow, Candies, and Apt. 9.

The *services mix* can also help set one retailer apart from another. For example, some retailers invite customers to ask questions or consult service representatives in person or via phone or keyboard. Home Depot offers a diverse mix of services to do-it-yourselfers, from "how-to" classes and "do-it-herself" and kid workshops to a proprietary credit card. Nordstrom delivers top-notch service and promises to "take care of the customer, no matter what it takes."

The *store's atmosphere* is another important element in the reseller's product arsenal. Retailers want to create a unique store experience, one that suits the target market and moves customers to buy. Many retailers practice *experiential retailing*. For example, L.L. Bean has turned its flagship retail store in Freeport, Maine, into an adventure center, where customers can experience the store's goods before buying them:[14]

> Customers don't just shop at L.L.Bean's flagship store in Freeport, they *experience* it. Sure, the company's several stores on the Freeport campus offer a full assortment of outdoor apparel and gear. But more than that, they create outdoor experiences. For example, along with selling camping, fishing, hiking, boating, home furnishings, and other goods, L.L.Bean offers a slate of free in-store, hands-on clinics, in which knowledgeable experts share tips and techniques to help customers prepare for their own outdoor adventures. Clinics cover everything from tying knots and fishing flies to roadside bike repair to compass navigation and even stargazing. Customers seeking more depth can sign up for one of L.L.Bean's Outdoor Discovery Schools programs in snowshoeing, cross-country skiing, stand-up paddleboarding, fly fishing, biking, birdwatching, canoeing, hunting, or any of a dozen other outdoor activities.
>
> L.L.Bean plans to turn the Freeport campus into a full-fledged outdoor adventure center, where customers can hike, bike, golf, kayak, or even go seal watching or fishing at nearby Cisco Bay. The adventure center pulls in more customers, who in turn buy more goods. L.L.Bean's flagship store and Freeport campus attract more than 3 million visitors a year, making them Maine's second-most popular tourist destination behind Acadia National Park. The Freeport campus may soon become a model for additional L.L.Bean adventure centers in other states. The company plans to open 35 new stores in the next five years.

Experiential retailing: L.L.Bean has turned its flagship retail store in Freeport, Maine, into an adventure center, where customers can experience goods before buying them.

Photos courtesy of L.L.Bean

Today's digital technologies present many new challenges and opportunities for shaping retail experiences. The surge in online and mobile shopping has changed retail customer behaviors and expectations. As a result, a wide range of store retailers—from high-tech sellers such as AT&T to high-touch sellers like Audi and Build-A-Bear—are digitizing the in-store experience. They are merging the physical and digital worlds to create new-age experiential retailing environments (see Real Marketing 13.1).

Successful retailers carefully orchestrate virtually every aspect of the consumer store experience. The next time you step into a retail store—whether it sells consumer electronics, hardware, or high fashion—stop and carefully consider your surroundings. Think about the store's layout and displays. Listen to the background music. Check out the colors. Smell the smells. Chances are good that everything in the store, from the layout and lighting to the music and even the colors and smells, has been carefully orchestrated to help shape the customers' shopping experiences—and open their wallets.

Real Marketing 13.1

Digitizing the In-Store Retail Experience

There's a flashy new store on Michigan Avenue in downtown Chicago's high-end retail district known as the Magnificent Mile. The store is bright and inviting, with sights and sounds designed to pull people in and get them to linger longer. Customers sit at any of dozens of stations, sampling the latest phone apps and electronic gadgetry. Enthusiastic, iPad-wielding associates mingle with customers, talking tech and dispensing hands-on help and advice. With 130 digital screens and an 18-foot video wall, every aspect of the open space is designed to engage customers about future wireless technologies and services. It feels more like a techy neighborhood hangout than a place to buy products.

A gleaming new Apple store? Think again. This is AT&T's new flagship store. But the resemblance to Apple's groundbreaking retail concept is no mistake. Dozens of diverse retail chains—from high-tech sellers like AT&T to high-touch merchants such as Audi and Build-A-Bear—are remaking their stores in the image of Apple's open marketplace prototypes. But even more, with the surge in digital, online, and mobile technologies invading the retail space, these store chains are blazing new ground. They are digitizing in-store retail—transforming the traditional in-store experience by infusing digital and online technologies into their physical store environments. It's the future of store retailing, but it's already happening.

When they first walk into AT&T's new store, customers quickly realize that it's like nothing they've seen before. "One of my favorite comments from a recent patron . . . was that it was like walking into a Web site," says AT&T's president of retail. Organized into zones and stations, the store's technology immerses customers in multimedia and interpersonal experiences. In the Explorer Lounge, customers can play with and learn about the latest apps. At the App Bar, "apptenders" give one-on-one or group demos, which are displayed on the Apps Wall for others to follow along. The 18-foot-high Connect Wall features a giant interactive video screen that displays customer interactions with content and product information, visible to the entire store and to passers-by outside. Lifestyle Boutiques organize products, apps, and accessories by customer needs, such as Get Fit, Be Productive, and Share Your Life. At the Experience Platform, customers can interact with AT&T products for home security and automation, entertainment, music, and automobiles.

Although it might seem that the store is all about products and technologies, the real focus is on the customer experience. The store is designed to let customers interact with devices and services, understand how they work, and experience the impact the devices can have on their lives. In one store area, for example, customers can experience how Jawbone's Up Bracelet integrates with a smartphone app to monitor health and fitness by tracking sleep, eating, and movement patterns. In another, a Nissan Leaf is set up to interactively demonstrate various auto-based apps that help customers solve problems, such as monitoring how fast their teenagers are driving. The store is a physical manifestation of AT&T's "It's what you do with what we do" marketing campaign. "We used to sell phones," says the AT&T executive. "Now we've shifted to offering solutions."

Digitizing in-store retail is an obvious fit for a technology retailer like AT&T. But companies in a wide range of other industries are also pioneering the concept. Take German automaker Audi, for instance. In the lead-up to the XXX Summer Olympics in London, Audi threw open the doors to its first Audi City, a stunningly innovative digitized showroom in London's busy Piccadilly Circus area.

Rather than displaying a sea of shiny new vehicles, the Audi City showroom contains very few actual cars, and future Audi showrooms may have none at all. Instead, Audi City is all-digital. Prospective customers use touchscreens and Kinect-style cameras to design and manipulate virtual, life-size cars of their dreams displayed on massive screens surrounding the showroom space. When they've finished, a video shows the car they've designed in action, complete with the exact sound of the chosen engine in full stereo fidelity. The car is then loaded onto a memory stick that the customer can take for later remembering and sharing.

The idea of buying a car without actually seeing it flies in the face of auto retailing tradition. But these car-buying times are anything but traditional. Audi sees digitization as a way to fit showrooms into smaller urban settings and to overcome the limitations of physical dealerships. With 12 different models, each with up to six different trim levels, all with numerous options, no physical dealership can have every possible model on hand. Virtual showrooms, however, can present every model in Audi's extensive portfolio in every possible permutation.

Digitizing in-store retail: AT&T's flagship Chicago showroom infuses digital and online technologies into a physical store environment to let customers experience the impact of its devices and services on their lives. It's "like walking into a Web site."

Moreover, customers can call them up instantly and make changes on the fly.

So far, the Audi City virtual experience is producing very real-world results. Audi City showrooms in London, Beijing, and Dubai are outselling their traditional counterparts by 70 percent, with an average increase in margin per vehicle of 30 percent. And the digitized auto lounges are bringing more new customers through the doors. Ninety percent of Audi City visitors are new to the brand.

The digitized showroom is finding its way into every industry imaginable. Consider Build-A-Bear Workshop. No stranger to retail innovation, Build-A-Bear revolutionized the in-store experience when it burst into America's malls almost 20 years ago with unique stores that were part showroom, part factory, and part theme park. With the original Build-A-Bear format, children moved from station to station, constructing and customizing their stuffed bears and watching them come to life before their very eyes.

But as smartphones, tablets, and other digital devices changed the way children play, Build-A-Bear saw its sales decline and losses mount. Now, however, rather than fighting digital-age developments, Build-A-Bear is deploying them. Today's Build-A-Bear stores are designed to engage the new generation of digitally adept children. A large video screen at the front of the store uses movement technology to greet children, engage them with interactive games, and introduce store features. From there, each of the eight stations in the bear-building process is enhanced by touchscreens and digital features that give young bear-builders more hands-on involvement and more design options. Kids can even give their finished bear a virtual bath before fluffing it with real air.

For AT&T, Audi, and Build-A-Bear, retailing is nothing new. Each has been in brick-and-mortar retailing for years, with hundreds of showrooms worldwide. But these forward-looking retailers are now betting on a digitized in-store future. AT&T plans to roll out six or seven elements of its Michigan Avenue store to each of its 2,300 other stores. Audi plans to open 20 more Audi City showrooms by 2015. And Build-A-Bear has already updated each of its more than 400 stores with its new digital workstations. As AT&T's president of retail points out, digitization is more than just electronic whiz-bang. "It's all about creating [relevant customer experiences and] interactions rather than just transactions."

Sources: Christopher Heine, "The Store of the Future Has Arrived," *Adweek*, June 3, 2013, www.adweek.com/print/149900; Nicole Giannopoulos, "A 'Magnificent' In-Store Experience," *Retail Info Systems News*, June 10, 2013, http://risnews.edgl.com/magazine/June-2013/A--Magnificent--In-Store-Experience86772; Elizabeth Olson, "Build-A-Bear Goes High Tech," *New York Times*, September 27, 2012, p. B3; Rajesh Setty, "Re-Imagining the Retail Experience: The Audi City Store," *Huffington Post*, December 29, 2013, www.huffingtonpost.com/rajesh-setty/re-imagining-the-retail-e_b_4514046.html; and www.youtube.com/watch?v=GDdPN6mVLPM, accessed September 2014.

For example, retailers choose the colors in their logos and interiors carefully: Black suggests sophistication, orange is associated with fairness and affordability, white signifies simplicity and purity (think Apple stores), and blue connotes trust and dependability (financial institutions use it a lot). And most large retailers have developed signature scents that you smell only in their stores:[15]

> Bloomingdale's uses different essences in different departments: the soft scent of baby powder in the baby store, coconut in the swimsuit area, lilacs in intimate apparel, and sugar cookies and evergreen scent during the holiday season. Anytime Fitness pipes in "Inspire," a eucalyptus-mint fragrance to create a uniform scent from store to store and mask that "gym" smell. Sheraton Hotels employs Welcoming Warmth, a mix of fig, Jasmine, and freesia; whereas Westin Hotel & Resorts disperses White Tea, which attempts to provide the indefinable "Zen-retreat" experience. Scents can subtly reinforce a brand's imagery and positioning. For example, luxury men's fashion brand Hugo Boss chose a signature smooth, musky scent for all of its stores. "We wanted it to feel like coming home," says a Hugo Boss marketer. Similarly, the Hard Rock Café Hotel in Orlando added a scent of the ocean in its lobby to help guests imagine checking into a seaside resort (even though the hotel is located an hour from the coast). To draw customers into the hotel's often-overlooked downstairs ice cream shop, the hotel put a sugar cookie aroma at the top of the stairs and a whiff of waffle cone at the bottom. Ice cream sales jumped 45 percent in the following six months.

Such *experiential retailing* confirms that retail stores are much more than simply assortments of goods. They are environments to be experienced by the people who shop in them.

Price Decision

A retailer's price policy must fit its target market and positioning, product and service assortment, the competition, and economic factors. All retailers would like to charge high markups and achieve high volume, but the two seldom go together. Most retailers seek *either* high markups on lower volume (most specialty stores) *or* low markups on higher volume (mass merchandisers and discount stores).

Thus, 110-year-old Bergdorf Goodman caters to the upper crust by selling apparel, shoes, and jewelry created by designers such as Chanel, Prada, Hermes, and Jimmy Choo. The up-market retailer pampers its customers with services such as a personal shopper and in-store showings of the upcoming season's trends with cocktails and hors d'oeuvres. By contrast, TJ Maxx sells brand-name clothing at discount prices aimed at middle-class Americans. As it stocks new products each week, the discounter provides a treasure hunt for bargain shoppers. "No sales. No gimmicks." says the retailer. "Just brand name and designer fashions for you . . . for up to 60 percent off department store prices."

Retailers must also decide on the extent to which they will use sales and other price promotions. Some retailers use no price promotions at all, competing instead on product and service quality rather than on price. For example, it's difficult to imagine Bergdorf Goodman holding a two-for-the-price-of-one sale on Chanel handbags, even in a tight economy. Other retailers—such as Walmart, Costco, ALDI, and Family Dollar—practice *everyday low pricing (EDLP)*, charging constant, everyday low prices with few sales or discounts.

Still other retailers practice *high-low pricing*—charging higher prices on an everyday basis, coupled with frequent sales and other price promotions, to increase store traffic, create a low-price image, or attract customers who will buy other goods at full prices. Recent tighter economic times caused a rash of high-low pricing, as retailers poured on price cuts and promotions to coax bargain-hunting customers into their stores. Which pricing strategy is best depends on the retailer's overall marketing strategy, the pricing approaches of its competitors, and the economic environment.

Promotion Decision

Retailers use various combinations of the five promotion tools—advertising, personal selling, sales promotion, public relations (PR), and direct and social media marketing—to reach consumers. They advertise in newspapers and magazines and on radio and television. Advertising may be supported by newspaper inserts and catalogs. Store salespeople greet customers, meet their needs, and build relationships. Sales promotions may include in-store demonstrations, displays, sales, and loyalty programs. PR activities, such as new-store openings, special events, newsletters and blogs, store magazines, and public service activities, are also available to retailers.

Most retailers also interact digitally with customers using Web sites and digital catalogs, online ads and video, social media, mobile ads and apps, blogs, and e-mail. Almost every retailer, large or small, maintains a full social media presence. For example, giant Walmart leads the way with a whopping 34 million Facebook Likes, 37,000 Pinterest followers, 446,000 Twitter followers, and 15,000 YouTube subscribers. By contrast, Fairway Market, the small but fast-growing metropolitan New York grocery chain that carries a huge product assortment—from "sky-high piles" of produce to overflowing bins of fresh seafood to hand-roasted coffee—has only 86,000 Facebook Likes. But Fairway isn't complaining—that's nearly twice as many Facebook Likes per million dollars of sales as mighty Walmart.[16]

Digital promotions let retailers reach individual customers with carefully targeted messages. ● For example, to compete more effectively against online rivals, CVS distributes personalized versions of its weekly circulars to the chain's ExtraCare loyalty program members. Called myWeekly Ad, customers can view their circulars by logging into their personal accounts at CVS.com on computers, tablets, or smartphones. Based on ExtraCare members' characteristics and previous purchases, the personalized promotions highlight sales items and special offers of special interest to each specific customer. With the myWeekly Ad program, "We're trying to get people to change their behavior," says the CVS marketer heading up the effort, "going online for a much more personalized experience" rather than checking weekly circulars.[17]

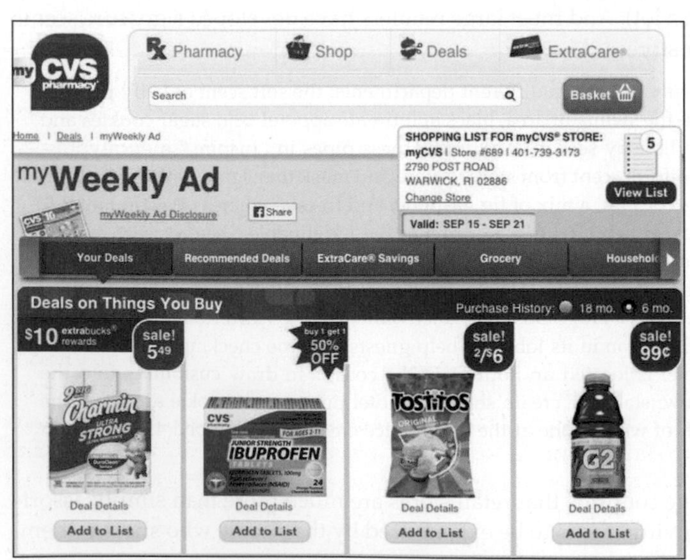

● **Retailer promotion: Most retailers interact digitally with customers using Web sites and digital catalogs, mobile and social media, and other digital platforms. CVS's myWeekly Ad program distributes personalized versions of its weekly circulars to the chain's ExtraCare loyalty program members.**

CVS Caremark Corporation

Place Decision

Retailers often point to three critical factors in retailing success: location, location, and location! It's very important that retailers select locations that are accessible to the target market in areas that are consistent with the retailer's positioning. For example, Apple locates its stores in high-end malls and trendy shopping districts—such as the "Magnificent Mile" on Chicago's Michigan Avenue or Fifth Avenue in Manhattan—not low-rent strip malls on the edge of town. By contrast, to keep costs down and support its "cheap gourmet" positioning, Trader Joe's places its stores in lower-rent, out-of-the-way locations. Small retailers may have to settle for whatever locations they can find or afford. Large retailers, however, usually employ specialists who use advanced methods to select store locations.

Most stores today cluster together to increase their customer pulling power and give consumers the convenience of one-stop shopping. Central business districts were the main form of retail cluster until the 1950s. Every large city and town had a central business district with department stores, specialty stores, banks, and movie theaters. When people began moving to the suburbs, however, many of these central business districts, with their traffic, parking, and crime problems, began to lose business. In recent years, many cities have joined with merchants to revive downtown shopping areas, generally with only mixed success.

Shopping center
A group of retail businesses built on a site that is planned, developed, owned, and managed as a unit.

A **shopping center** is a group of retail businesses built on a site that is planned, developed, owned, and managed as a unit. A *regional shopping center*, or *regional shopping mall*, the largest and most dramatic shopping center, has from 50 to more than 100 stores, including two or more full-line department stores. It is like a covered mini-downtown and attracts customers from a wide area. A *community shopping center* contains between 15 and 50 retail stores. It normally contains a branch of a department store or variety store, a supermarket, specialty stores, professional offices, and sometimes a bank. Most shopping centers are *neighborhood shopping centers* or *strip malls* that generally contain between 5 and 15 stores. These centers, which are close and convenient for consumers, usually contain a supermarket, perhaps a discount store, and several service stores—dry cleaner, drugstore, hardware store, local restaurant, or other stores.[18]

A newer form of shopping center is the so-called power center. *Power centers* are huge unenclosed shopping centers consisting of a long strip of retail stores, including large, free-standing anchors such as Walmart, Home Depot, Costco, Best Buy, Michaels, PetSmart, and OfficeMax. Each store has its own entrance with parking directly in front for shoppers who wish to visit only one store.

In contrast, *lifestyle centers* are smaller, open-air malls with upscale stores, convenient locations, and nonretail activities, such as a playground, skating rink, hotel, dining establishments, and a movie theater complex. In fact, the original power center and lifestyle center concepts are now morphing into hybrid lifestyle-power centers that combine the convenience and community feel of a neighborhood center with the brute force of a power center. Meanwhile, traditional regional shopping malls are adding lifestyle elements—such as fitness centers, common areas, and multiplex theaters—to make themselves more social and welcoming. In all, today's centers are more like places to hang out rather than just places to shop. "The line between shopping, entertainment, and community building has blurred," says one analyst. "Shopping centers aren't just places to buy things. They're social centers, places for entertainment, and employment hubs."[19]

The past few years have brought hard times for shopping centers. Many experts suggest that the country has long been "overmalled." Not surprisingly, the Great Recession hit shopping malls hard. Consumer spending cutbacks forced many retailers—small and large—out of business, increasing mall vacancy rates. Power centers were especially hard hit as their big-box retailer tenants such as Circuit City, Borders, Mervyns, and Linens N Things went out of business and others such as Best Buy, Barnes & Noble, and Office Depot reduced the number or size of their stores. Some of the pizzazz has also went out of lifestyle centers, whose upper-middle-class shoppers suffered most during the recession.

As the economy has improved, however, malls of all types have rebounded a bit. Many power centers, for example, are filling their empty space with a broader range of retailers, from the likes of Ross Dress for Less, Boot Barn, Nordstrom Rack, and other off-price retailers to dollar stores, warehouse grocers, and traditional discounters like Walmart and Target.[20]

Retailing Trends and Developments

Retailers operate in a harsh and fast-changing environment, which offers threats as well as opportunities. Consumer demographics, lifestyles, and spending patterns are changing rapidly, as are retailing technologies. To be successful, retailers need to choose target segments carefully and position themselves strongly. They need to take the following retailing developments into account as they plan and execute their competitive strategies.

Tighter Consumer Spending

Following many years of good economic times for retailers, the Great Recession turned many retailers' fortunes from boom to bust. Even as the economy has recovered, retailers will feel the effects of changed consumer spending patterns well into the future.

Some retailers actually benefit from a down economy. For example, as consumers cut back and looked for ways to spend less on what they bought, big discounters such as Costco scooped up new business from bargain-hungry shoppers. Similarly, lower-priced fast-food chains, such as McDonald's, took business from their pricier eat-out competitors.

For other retailers, however, tighter consumer spending meant tough times. During and following the recession, several large and familiar retailers declared bankruptcy or closed their doors completely—including household names such as Linens N Things, Circuit City, KB Toys, Borders Books, and Sharper Image, to name a few. Other retailers, from Macy's and Home Depot to Starbucks, laid off employees, cut their costs, and offered deep price discounts and promotions aimed at luring cash-strapped customers back into their stores.

Value positioning: Facing tighter consumer spending, Home Depot adopted a thriftier theme: "More saving. More doing."

(logo) The Home Depot,/(photo) iofoto/Shutterstock.com

As the economy has improved, and as consumers have retained their more frugal spending ways, many retailers have added new value pitches to their positioning. For example, Home Depot replaced its older "You can do it. We can help." theme with a thriftier one: "More saving. More doing." Retailers ranging from Walmart to Macy's and Whole Foods Market are boosting their emphasis on more economical private label brands. Publix, the nation's largest employee-owned supermarket chain, has outperformed rivals by helping customers get the most out of today's tighter food budgets:[21]

> Despite its own rising purchasing and transportation costs, Publix introduced Publix Essentials, a consumer program that reduced its prices for basics such as bread, milk, and laundry detergent by as much as 20 percent. In addition, Publix began a Savings Made Easy program that offers Meal Deal and Thrifty Tips advice to customers trying to stretch their shopping dollars. "In today's economy, Publix is working hard to help," says the chain. "In addition to lowering prices on groceries you need most, we're giving you simple strategies for saving." Says one retail consultant, "Publix is always at its best when the economy is at its worst." Customers seem to agree. According to the American Customer Satisfaction Index (ACSI), for the 20th consecutive year, Publix is the highest-ranking supermarket for customer satisfaction.

When reacting to economic difficulties, retailers must be careful that their short-run actions don't damage their long-run images and positions. For example, drastic price discounting can increase immediate sales but damage brand loyalty. Instead of relying on cost-cutting and price reductions, retailers should focus on building greater customer value within their long-term store positioning strategies.

New Retail Forms, Shortening Retail Life Cycles, and Retail Convergence

New retail forms continue to emerge to meet new situations and consumer needs, but the life cycle of new retail forms is getting shorter. Department stores took about 100 years to reach the mature stage of the life cycle; more recent forms, such as warehouse stores, reached maturity in about 10 years. In such an environment, seemingly solid retail positions can crumble quickly. Of the top 10 discount retailers in 1962 (the year that the first Walmart, Kmart, Target, and Kohl's stores first opened), not one still exists today. Even the most successful retailers can't sit back with a winning formula. To remain successful, they must keep adapting.

New retail forms are always emerging. The most recent blockbuster retailing trend is the advent of online retailing, by both online-only and brick-and-mortar retailers, via

Web sites, mobile apps, and social media. But lesser innovations occur regularly. For example, many retailers are now using limited-time *pop-up stores* that let them promote their brands to seasonal shoppers and create buzz in busy areas. During holiday seasons, for instance, Toys "R" Us sets up temporary pop-up toy boutiques, many located in vacant mall locations. Brazilian Sandal maker Havaianas is known for opening temporary seasonal pop-up shops at beaches, festivals, and other summer hot spots around the world. This past summer, it opened a 1,200 square foot pop-up space in New York City's busy meatpacking district, featuring the largest assortment of its sandals to be found in Manhattan. Even the Girl Scouts of Greater New York have gotten into the act, opening pop-up shops across New York City during a recent cookie-selling season. "Our birthday is right around the corner," said one ad celebrating 100 years of Girl Scouts, "and so are our cookies." The online and mobile equivalent is *flash sales* sites, such as Nordstrom's HauteLook and Amazon's MyHabit, which host time-limited sales events on top fashion and lifestyle brands. Similarly, Zulily flashes sales on products for moms, babies, and kids; and Groupon offers flash deals on travel through Groupon Getaways.[22]

New retail forms: Many retailers, such as Brazilian sandal maker Havaianas, use temporary pop-up shops to promote their brands to seasonal shoppers and create buzz in busy areas.

Alpargatas S.A.

Today's retail forms appear to be converging. Increasingly, different types of retailers now sell the same products at the same prices to the same consumers. For example, you can buy brand name home appliances at department stores, discount stores, home-improvement stores, off-price retailers, electronics superstores, and a slew of online sites that all compete for the same customers. If you can't find the microwave oven you want at Sears, you can step across the street and find one for a better price at Lowe's or Best Buy—or just order one online from Amazon.com or even RitzCamera.com. This merging of consumers, products, prices, and retailers is called *retail convergence*. Such convergence means greater competition for retailers and greater difficulty in differentiating the product assortments of different types of retailers.

The Rise of Megaretailers

The rise of huge mass merchandisers and specialty superstores, the formation of vertical marketing systems, and a rash of retail mergers and acquisitions have created a core of superpower megaretailers. With their size and buying power, these giant retailers can offer better merchandise selections, good service, and strong price savings to consumers. As a result, they grow even larger by squeezing out their smaller, weaker competitors.

The megaretailers have shifted the balance of power between retailers and producers. A small handful of retailers now controls access to enormous numbers of consumers, giving them the upper hand in their dealings with manufacturers. For example, you may never have heard of specialty coatings and sealants manufacturer RPM International, but you've probably used one or more of its many familiar do-it-yourself brands—such as Rust-Oleum paints, Plastic Wood and Dap fillers, Mohawk and Watco finishes, and Testors hobby cements and paints—all of which you can buy at your local Home Depot store. Home Depot is a very important customer to RPM, accounting for a significant share of its consumer sales. However, Home Depot's sales of $74 billion are almost 20 times RPM's sales of $4 billion. As a result, the giant retailer can, and often does, use this power to wring concessions from RPM and thousands of other smaller suppliers.[23]

Growth of Direct, Online, Mobile, and Social Media Retailing

Most consumers still make a majority of their purchases the old-fashioned way: They go to a store, find what they want, plunk down their cash or credit cards, and bring home the goods. However, consumers now have a broad array of nonstore alternatives, including direct and digital shopping via Web sites, mobiles apps, and social media. As we'll discuss in Chapter 17, direct and digital marketing are currently the fastest-growing forms of marketing.

Today, thanks to advanced technologies, easier-to-use and enticing online sites and mobile apps, improved online services, and the increasing sophistication of search technologies, online retailing is thriving. In fact, although it currently accounts for only about 5.8 percent of total U.S. retail sales, online buying is growing at a much brisker pace than retail buying as a whole. Last year's U.S. online retail sales reached an estimated $263 billion, up 16.9 percent over the previous year versus a 4.2 percent increase in overall retail sales. Online retail will reach an estimated $370 billion by 2017.[24]

Retailer online sites, mobile apps, and social media also influence a large amount of in-store buying. An estimated 46 percent of total U.S. retail sales were either transacted directly or influenced by online research. An estimated 15 percent of all online sales now take place on mobile devices, a number that will grow to 25 percent by 2017. And according to a recent survey, nearly 20 percent of online holiday shoppers made at least some purchases based on personal connections or promotions on Facebook. Retailers of all kinds rely on social media to engage their buyer communities. For example, whereas Walmart leads among retailers in Facebook Likes, Nordstrom is tops in Pinterest followers. iTunes leads in Twitter followers, but Whole Foods Market comes in a close second. Victoria's Secret is second only to iTunes among retailers in YouTube subscribers.[25]

The spurt in online, mobile, and social media retailing is both a blessing and a curse to store retailers. Although it gives them new channels for engaging and selling to customers, it also creates more competition from online-only retailers. To the dismay of some store retailers, many shoppers now check out merchandise at physical-store showrooms but then buy it online using a computer or mobile device, sometimes while in the store—a process called **showrooming**. These days, as many as half of all shoppers who buy products online first check them out at a traditional store. Many retailers have been hit hard by showrooming. Today, however, many store retailers are developing strategies to counter showrooming. Others are even embracing it as an opportunity to highlight the advantages of shopping in stores versus online-only retailers (see Real Marketing 13.2).[26]

Showrooming
The shopping practice of coming into retail store showrooms to check out merchandise and prices but instead buying from an online-only rival, sometimes while in the store.

Thus, it's no longer a matter of customers deciding whether to shop in a store *or* shop online. Increasingly, customers are merging store, Web sites, social media, and mobile outlets into a single shopping process. ● The Internet and digital devices have spawned a whole new breed of shopper and way of shopping. Whether shopping for electronics, consumer products, cars, homes, or medical care, many people just can't buy anything unless they first look it up online and get the lowdown. And they've gotten used to buying anywhere, anytime—whether it's in the store, online, on the go, or even online while in the store.

● **The digital age has spawned a whole new breed of shopper—people who just can't buy anything unless they first look it up online and get the lowdown.**

©Zurijeta/Shutterstock

All types of retailers now employ direct and online channels. The Web and mobile online sales of large brick-and-mortar retailers, such as Walmart, Target, Staples, and Best Buy, are increasing rapidly. Many large online-only retailers—Amazon.com, Zappos.com, Netflix, Overstock.com, online travel companies such as Travelocity.com and Expedia.com, and others—have made it big on the Internet. At the other extreme, hordes of niche marketers have used the Internet to reach new markets and expand their sales.

Still, much of the anticipated growth in online sales will go to multichannel retailers—the click-and-brick marketers who can successfully merge the virtual and physical worlds. In a recent ranking of the top 25 online retail sites, 15 were owned by store-based retail chains. Another study showed that, among the top 500 online retailers, online sales by store chains were growing 8 percent faster than those of online-only retailers and 40 percent faster than overall e-commerce.[27]

Real Marketing 13.2

Shopping 2.0: Shopping in Stores But Buying Online Versus Getting More in Store

The periodic emergence of low-margin merchants is not new to the retail scene. Not so long ago, catalogue showrooms were considered as key low-cost competitors to traditional city center shops. Nowadays, with advanced mobile technologies, consumers can—at the touch of an app—engage in price comparison while still in the shop, a practice referred to as *showrooming*. Smartphones have indeed revolutionized the shopping experience by giving consumers faster access to larger volumes of information than ever before. Shoppers who like to try before they buy can use physical storefronts to look at, touch, and try on products, before scanning the barcode to make sure they've gotten the best price. In a recent report from Forrester, 41 percent of U.S. consumers said they had showroomed and then later chose to buy online specifically because of better prices.

Furthermore, 50 percent of those engaging in this trend were 25 to 34 years old. In Turkey, another compounding effect involves the use of retail apps from the main retailers and malls to learn about new products during the week, then discussing this information via social networking sites such as Twitter with friends to form an opinion, and then, during the weekend while shopping at the mall, using price comparison apps such as barcode scanners and Amazon's price-checking features. For young Turkish consumers (70 percent of whom own a smartphone), the mobile is now their favorite shopping companion, and retailers need to respond. Showrooming is often regarded as taboo for traditional retailers, but recently some of them are for the first time turning showrooming into a positive and profitable experience.

The case of the Istanbul Cevahir Shopping and Entertainment Centre, one of the world's largest shopping malls, put showrooming 2.0 to the test. The center is home to 12 cinemas, including a cinema for children; a classical variety of mall food; and diverse entertainment, including Atlantis, a covered thematic play park; a private theater; a bowling hall; and even a small roller coaster, all under one roof, presenting a new way of shopping and living. The mix of store global and local brands is underlined as important and provides advantages over the online channel: shoppers shop in groups, and all tastes need to be available in one place. The mall has been designed to provide a high-tech experience. The facilities, among many, range from free Wi-Fi to the availability of location-aware offers, a Twitter and Facebook fan page, touchscreens for digital signage and directory (two-way digital communications between mobile devices and digital signage), ambient music zones, high-definition LED displays, high-tech shopping carts, and security cameras linked with the possibility of a photo souvenir. QR codes and RFID technologies have also been integrated in most displays, and intelligent shelves are available in most stores, allowing the emerging advantages of augmented reality to be leveraged.

Think of a bridal registry: you walk through your chosen store with a handheld scanner and scan the items you want to buy or hope to receive as gifts. Each of your friends can then place an order at the register or online, and then choose the pick-up date and location. The list is checked by the to-be-married couple, and if they decide they don't want something, they can change any product—free of charge. What's more, they know that the exact item in the exact shade of red, for example, is going to be exactly what they have asked for. The online catalogue can allow for a greater stock to be made available by varying sizes and colors for each item, even those unavailable in the smaller stores in rural areas where many friends might live. By repurposing basic models such as the bridal registry, retailers can now guarantee that they are not only drawing their customers back in the store, but that they're making sure they offer those customers a service that the online competitors can't.

For instance, through augmented reality, IBM Research launched in 2012 an application that allows in-store consumers to use their smartphones to scan a product or an aisle. The result is a digital overlay of products meeting the consumer's dietary needs, coupons on those specific products, and, in all, a rather fun experience. In Turkey, over half of smartphone users have used QR codes through ambient marketing offers, and about

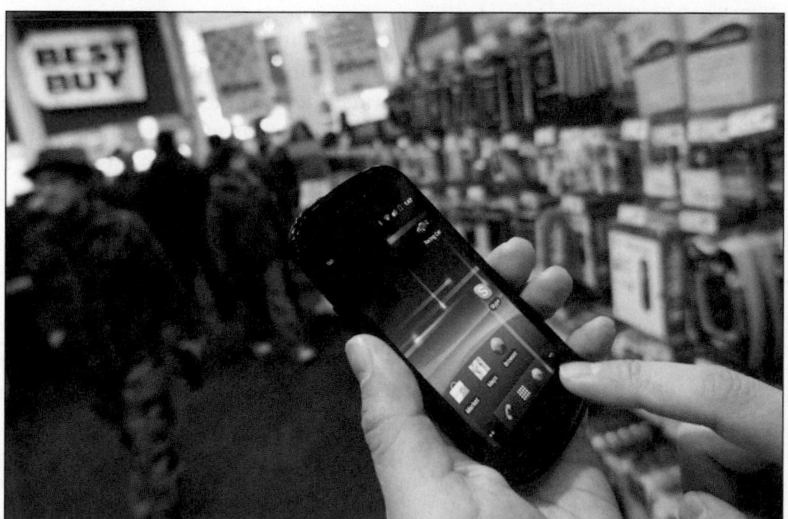

Showrooming: The now-common practice of viewing products in stores but buying them online presents serious challenges to store retailers. Rather than fighting showrooming, store retailers should embrace it as a way to showcase their strengths.

ZUMA Press/Newscom

half of that is in-store use. About 10 percent of users with mobile devices in the store view available coupons. Whether it's by using old technologies (bridal registries) or new technologies (augmented reality), retailers have the ability to make convenient services foster purchases, prevent overstocking, and secure customer loyalty. These efforts are also in line with day-to-day behavior of shoppers. Shoppers shop with a directional list, not detailed enough to do a lot of direct price comparison; each shopping trip often involves a "basket of goods" rather than a unique item, making it hard to compare prices on all.

As such, the most powerful way to use showrooming is not to try to stop it, but to embrace it, by allowing customers to order online and pick up items in the stores, and, while they are there, add to their purchases. Of the top 10 retailers, 70 percent provide in-store pick-up for e-commerce orders along with consistent, transparent pricing, as well as promotions. This effort is often supported via a wider range of the retailer's own brand products or more exclusive in-store-only lines that cannot be directly duplicated by online retailers. Moreover, if the customer is connected, he or she can be tracked; in addition, data such as the customer's location in the store can be used as an engagement tool linked to loyalty programs.

Near-field communication (NFC) technology also offers a plethora of opportunities. It allows browsing customers to tap products to get excerpts, reviews, or any other information the store wants to include. From there, customers are able to add the product to their lists or wish lists, or buy the product in any available format (tangible or digital), bringing the vast inventory of products available online into the physical store. On another side, a Wi-Fi network and overlay location information showing where the shopper is in the store can result in "heat maps" that can show which products are most vulnerable to being tried out in the store but ultimately bought for less online. The challenge for the modern shopping mall, hence, rests more in a managerial shift toward embracing mobile technologies and showrooming rather than resisting them. As in co-creation, co-production and service dominate the debate, as noted by Denegri-Knott, and following Kozinet et al., the desires of producers and consumers are more similar and interdependent than often thought, and overlap more commonly than would be expected.

Sources: Based on information from R. Kozinet, J. F. Sherry, D. Storm, A. Duhachek, K. Nuttavuthisit, and B. Deberry-Spence, "Ludic Agency and Retail Spectacle," *Journal of Consumer Research*, vol. 31, no. 3, 2004, pp. 658–672; J. Denegri-Knott, "Consumers Behaving Badly: Deviation or Innovation? Power Struggles on the Web," *Journal of Consumer Behaviour*, vol. 5, no.1, 2006, pp. 82–94; and www.digitalartsonline.co.uk/ news/interactive-design/ibm-developing-augmented-reality-app-that-identifies-products-without-qr-codes/, www.forrester.com/ Nine+Percent+Of+US+Customers +Showroom+Long+Live+Showrooming/-/E-PRE7384, accessed November, 2014.

For example, thanks largely to rapid growth in online sales, upscale home products retailer Williams-Sonoma now captures more than half of its total revenues from its direct-to-consumer channel. Like many retailers, Williams-Sonoma has discovered that many of its best customers visit and shop both online and offline. Beyond just offering online shopping, the retailer engages customers through online communities, social media, mobile apps, a blog, and special online programs. "The Internet has changed the way our customers shop," says Williams-Sonoma CEO Laura Alber, "and the online brand experience has to be inspiring and seamless."[28]

Growing Importance of Retail Technology

Retail technologies have become critically important as competitive tools. Progressive retailers are using advanced information technology (IT) and software systems to produce better forecasts, control inventory costs, interact electronically with suppliers, send information between stores, and even sell to customers within stores. They have adopted sophisticated systems for checkout scanning, RFID inventory tracking, merchandise handling, information sharing, and customer interactions.

Perhaps the most startling advances in retail technology concern the ways in which retailers are connecting with consumers. Today's customers have gotten used to the speed and convenience of buying online and to the control that the Internet gives them over the buying process. The Internet lets consumers shop when they like and where they like, with instant access to gobs of information about competing products and prices. At the same time, Web sites, blogs, social media, and mobile apps give retailers a whole new avenue for establishing brand connections and community with customers. No real-world store can do all that.

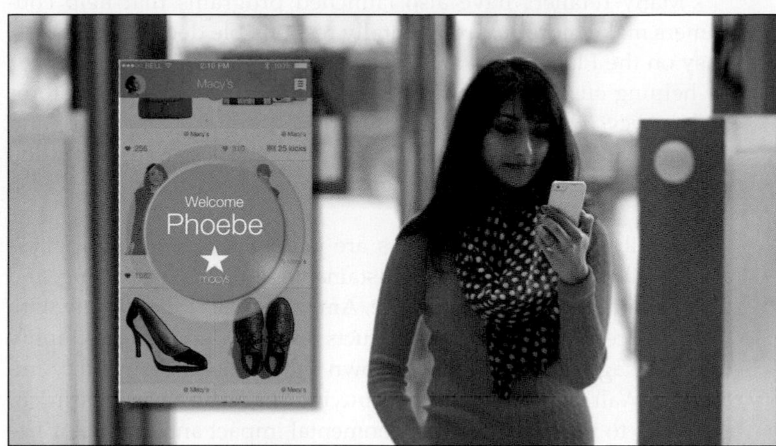

Retail technology: Macy's uses Shopkick's shopBeacon to engage consumers in the store and personalize their shopping experiences.

Shopkick, Inc.

Increasingly, retailers are bringing online and digital technologies into their physical stores. Many retailers now routinely use technologies ranging from touchscreen kiosks and handheld shopping assistants to interactive dressing-room mirrors and virtual sales associates. Macy's uses Shopkick's shopBeacon indoor positioning system to engage customers digitally as they shop around its stores. When opted-in customers enter a Macy's store, a Bluetooth signal wakes up the shopBeacon app on their smartphone or tablet, which welcomes them and alerts them to location-specific rewards, deals, discounts, and product recommendations within the store. The technology can also link in-store and at-home browsing; if the customer "likes" a specific product online, shopBeacon can remind them where to find it in the store and maybe pass along a for-you-only deal. The goal of shopBeacon is to engage Macy's tech-savvy and social customers as a trusted companion and to personalize their in-store shopping experience.[29]

But the future of technology in retailing lies in merging online and offline shopping into a seamless shopping experience. It's not a matter of online retailing growing while physical retailing declines. Instead, both will be important, and the two must be integrated. For example, Walmart's goal is to merge online, social media, and mobile innovations with physical stores to give customers an "anytime, anywhere" shopping experience.[30]

To augment in-store shopping, Walmart formed @WalmartLabs, which develops mobile and social media platforms that make shopping easier, more accessible, and more fun. For example, the retailer's Walmart Gifts gift-finder app applies data from users' Facebook Likes, comments, status updates, and other data to recommend the best products for customers and gifts for their friends. The retailer's feature-rich mobile apps let customers create smart shopping lists, scan barcodes and check prices, access product information, and scan coupons in real time—all from a smartphone or tablet, at home, at work, in the store, or anywhere in between. Customers will soon be able to use their smartphones in self-checkout lines. Walmart is even working on a voice-activated app that will summon an associate for assistance when the customer enters the store. The Walmart SocialStore team at @WalmartLabs is exploring other new in-store social media, mobile, and kiosk technologies that will both assist customers as they shop and help stores get to know and serve their customers better.[31]

Green Retailing

Today's retailers are increasingly adopting environmentally sustainable practices. They are greening up their stores and operations, promoting more environmentally responsible products, launching programs to help customers be more responsible, and working with channel partners to reduce their environmental impact.

At the most basic level, most large retailers are making their stores more environmentally friendly through sustainable building design, construction, and operations. For example, all new Kohl's stores are constructed with recycled and regionally sourced building materials, water-efficient landscaping and plumbing fixtures, and ENERGY STAR-rated roofs that reduce energy usage. Inside, new Kohl's stores use occupancy sensor lighting for stockrooms, dressing rooms, and offices; energy management systems to control heating and cooling; and a recycling program for cardboard boxes, packaging, and hangers. "Kohl's cares," says the store. "From large-scale initiatives like constructing environmentally friendly buildings to everyday practices like recycling hangers, we're taking big steps to ensure we leave a smaller footprint."[32]

Retailers are also greening up their product assortments. For example, the Safeway grocery chain offers its own Bright Green line of home care products, featuring cleaning and laundry soaps made with biodegradable and naturally derived ingredients, energy-efficient light bulbs, and paper products made from a minimum of 60 percent recycled content. And

Green retailing: Safeway offers its own Bright Green line of home care products, including cleaning and laundry products made from biodegradable and naturally derived ingredients.

Safeway Inc.

clothing retailer H&M has launched an eco-friendly "Conscious Collection," clothing made from materials such as organic cotton and recycled fibers. Such products can both boost sales and lift the retailer's image as a responsible company.

Many retailers have also launched programs that help consumers make more environmentally responsible decisions. Staples' Easy on the Planet program "makes it easier to make a difference" by helping customers to identify green products sold in its stores and to recycle printer cartridges, mobile phones, computers, and other office technology products. Staples recycles some 30 million printer cartridges and 10 million pounds of old technology each year.[33]

Finally, many large retailers are joining forces with suppliers and distributors to create more sustainable products, packaging, and distribution systems. For example, Amazon.com works closely with the producers of many of the products it sells to reduce and simplify their packaging. And beyond its own substantial sustainability initiatives, Walmart wields its huge buying power to urge its army of suppliers to improve their environmental impact and practices. The retailer has even developed a worldwide Sustainable Product Index, by which it rates suppliers. It plans to translate the index into a simple rating for consumers to help them make more sustainable buying choices.

Green retailing yields both top- and bottom-line benefits. Sustainable practices lift a retailer's top line by attracting consumers looking to support environmentally friendly sellers and products. They also help the bottom line by reducing costs. For example, Amazon.com's reduced-packaging efforts increase customer convenience and eliminate "wrap rage" while at the same time saving packaging costs. And Kohl's earth-friendly and environmentally friendly buildings not only appeal to customers and help save the planet but also cost less to operate.

Global Expansion of Major Retailers

Retailers with unique formats and strong brand positions are increasingly moving into other countries. Many are expanding internationally to escape saturated home markets. Over the years, some giant U.S. retailers, such as McDonald's, have become globally prominent as a result of their marketing prowess. Others, such as Walmart, are rapidly establishing a global presence. Walmart, which now operates more than 6,300 stores in 26 non-U.S. markets, sees exciting global potential. Its international division alone last year racked up sales of more than $135 billion, almost 88 percent more than rival Target's *total* sales of $72 billion.[34]

However, most U.S. retailers are still significantly behind Europe and Asia when it comes to global expansion. Although 8 of the world's top 20 retailers are U.S. companies, only 4 of these retailers have set up stores outside North America (Walmart, Home Depot, Costco, and Best Buy). Of the 12 non-U.S. retailers in the world's top 20, 8 have stores in at least 10 countries. Foreign retailers that have gone global include France's Carrefour, Groupe Casino, and Auchan chains; Germany's Metro, Lidl, and ALDI chains; Britain's Tesco; and Japan's Seven & I.[35]

International retailing presents challenges as well as opportunities. Retailers can face dramatically different retail environments when crossing countries, continents, and cultures. Simply adapting the operations that work well in the home country is usually not enough to create success abroad. Instead, when going global, retailers must understand and meet the needs of local markets.

Wholesaling
All the activities involved in selling goods and services to those buying for resale or business use.

Wholesaler
A firm engaged *primarily* in wholesaling activities.

Author Comment | Whereas retailers primarily sell goods and services directly to final consumers for personal use, wholesalers sell primarily to those buying for resale or business use. Because wholesalers operate behind the scenes, they are largely unknown to final consumers. But they are very important to their business customers.

Wholesaling

Wholesaling includes all the activities involved in selling goods and services to those buying them for resale or business use. Firms engaged *primarily* in wholesaling activities are called **wholesalers.**

Wholesalers buy mostly from producers and sell mostly to retailers, industrial consumers, and other wholesalers. As a result, many of the nation's largest and most important wholesalers are largely unknown to final consumers. For example, you may never have heard of Grainger, even though it's very well known and much valued by its more than 2 million business and institutional customers in more than 150 countries:[36]

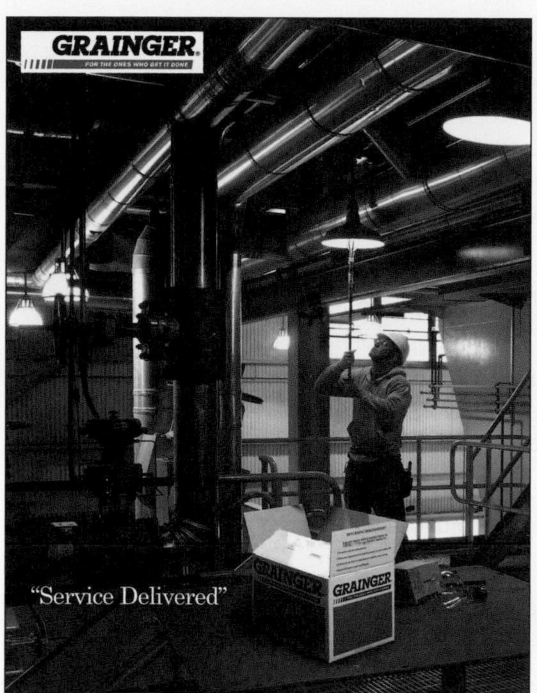

Wholesaling: Many of the nation's largest and most important wholesalers—like Grainger—are largely unknown to final consumers. But they are very well known and much valued by the business customers they serve.

W. W. Grainger, Inc.

> Grainger may be the biggest market leader you've never heard of. It's a $9 billion business that offers more than 1.2 million maintenance, repair, and operating (MRO) products from 4,800 manufacturers in 23 countries to over 2 million active customers. Through its branch network, service centers, sales reps, catalog, and online and social media sites, Grainger links customers with the supplies they need to keep their facilities running smoothly—everything from light bulbs, cleaners, and display cases to nuts and bolts, motors, valves, power tools, test equipment, and safety supplies. Grainger's 709 branches, 33 strategically located distribution centers, more than 23,500 employees, and innovative Web sites handle more than 115,000 transactions a day. Grainger's customers include organizations ranging from factories, garages, and grocers to schools and military bases.
>
> Grainger operates on a simple value proposition: to make it easier and less costly for customers to find and buy MRO supplies. It starts by acting as a one-stop shop for products needed to maintain facilities. On a broader level, it builds lasting relationships with customers by helping them find *solutions* to their overall MRO problems. Acting as consultants, Grainger sales reps help buyers with everything from improving their supply chain management to reducing inventories and streamlining warehousing operations.
>
> So, how come you've never heard of Grainger? Perhaps it's because the company operates in the not-so-glamorous world of MRO supplies, which are important to every business but not so important to consumers. More likely, it's because Grainger is a wholesaler. And like most wholesalers, it operates behind the scenes, selling mostly to other businesses.

Why are wholesalers important to sellers? For example, why would a producer use wholesalers rather than selling directly to retailers or consumers? Simply put, wholesalers add value by performing one or more of the following channel functions:

- *Selling and promoting.* Wholesalers' sales forces help manufacturers reach many small customers at a low cost. The wholesaler has more contacts and is often more trusted by the buyer than the distant manufacturer.
- *Buying and assortment building.* Wholesalers can select items and build assortments needed by their customers, thereby saving much work.
- *Bulk breaking.* Wholesalers save their customers money by buying in carload lots and breaking bulk (breaking large lots into small quantities).
- *Warehousing.* Wholesalers hold inventories, thereby reducing the inventory costs and risks of suppliers and customers.
- *Transportation.* Wholesalers can provide quicker delivery to buyers because they are closer to buyers than are producers.
- *Financing.* Wholesalers finance their customers by giving credit, and they finance their suppliers by ordering early and paying bills on time.
- *Risk bearing.* Wholesalers absorb risk by taking title and bearing the cost of theft, damage, spoilage, and obsolescence.
- *Market information.* Wholesalers give information to suppliers and customers about competitors, new products, and price developments.
- *Management services and advice.* Wholesalers often help retailers train their salesclerks, improve store layouts and displays, and set up accounting and inventory control systems.

Types of Wholesalers

Merchant wholesaler
An independently owned wholesale business that takes title to the merchandise it handles.

Wholesalers fall into three major groups (see Table 13.3): *merchant wholesalers, brokers and agents*, and *manufacturers' and retailers' branches and offices.* **Merchant wholesalers** are the largest single group of wholesalers, accounting for roughly 50 percent of all wholesaling. Merchant wholesalers include two broad types: full-service wholesalers and limited-service wholesalers. *Full-service wholesalers* provide a full set of services, whereas the various

Table 13.3 | Major Types of Wholesalers

Type	Description
Merchant wholesalers	Independently owned businesses that take title to all merchandise handled. There are full-service wholesalers and limited-service wholesalers.
Full-service wholesalers	Provide a full line of services: carrying stock, maintaining a sales force, offering credit, making deliveries, and providing management assistance. Full-service wholesalers include wholesale merchants and industrial distributors.
Wholesale merchants	Sell primarily to retailers and provide a full range of services. General merchandise wholesalers carry several merchandise lines, whereas general line wholesalers carry one or two lines in great depth. Specialty wholesalers specialize in carrying only part of a line.
Industrial distributors	Sell to manufacturers rather than to retailers. Provide several services, such as carrying stock, offering credit, and providing delivery. May carry a broad range of merchandise, a general line, or a specialty line.
Limited-service wholesalers	Offer fewer services than full-service wholesalers. Limited-service wholesalers are of several types:
Cash-and-carry wholesalers	Carry a limited line of fast-moving goods and sell to small retailers for cash. Normally do not deliver.
Truck wholesalers (or truck jobbers)	Perform primarily a selling and delivery function. Carry a limited line of semiperishable merchandise (such as milk, bread, snack foods), which is sold for cash as deliveries are made to supermarkets, small groceries, hospitals, restaurants, factory cafeterias, and hotels.
Drop shippers	Do not carry inventory or handle the product. On receiving an order, drop shippers select a manufacturer, who then ships the merchandise directly to the customer. Drop shippers operate in bulk industries, such as coal, lumber, and heavy equipment.
Rack jobbers	Serve grocery and drug retailers, mostly in nonfood items. Rack jobbers send delivery trucks to stores, where the delivery people set up toys, paperbacks, hardware items, health and beauty aids, or other items. Rack jobbers price the goods, keep them fresh, set up point-of-purchase displays, and keep inventory records.
Producers' cooperatives	Farmer-owned members that assemble farm produce for sale in local markets. Producers' cooperatives often attempt to improve product quality and promote a co-op brand name, such as Sun-Maid raisins, Sunkist oranges, or Diamond nuts.
Mail-order or Web wholesalers	Send catalogs to or maintain Web sites for retail, industrial, and institutional customers featuring jewelry, cosmetics, specialty foods, and other small items. Its primary customers are businesses in small outlying areas.
Brokers and agents	Do not take title to goods. The main function is to facilitate buying and selling, for which they earn a commission on the selling price. Generally specialize by product line or customer type.
Brokers	Bring buyers and sellers together and assist in negotiation. Brokers are paid by the party who hired the broker and do not carry inventory, get involved in financing, or assume risk. Examples include food brokers, real estate brokers, insurance brokers, and security brokers.
Agents	Represent either buyers or sellers on a more permanent basis than brokers do. There are four types:
Manufacturers' agents	Represent two or more manufacturers of complementary lines. Often used in such lines as apparel, furniture, and electrical goods. A manufacturer's agent is hired by small manufacturers who cannot afford their own field sales forces and by large manufacturers who use agents to open new territories or cover territories that cannot support full-time salespeople.

Type	Description
Selling agents	Have contractual authority to sell a manufacturer's entire output. The selling agent serves as a sales department and has significant influence over prices, terms, and conditions of sale. Found in product areas such as textiles, industrial machinery and equipment, coal and coke, chemicals, and metals.
Purchasing agents	Generally have a long-term relationship with buyers and make purchases for them, often receiving, inspecting, warehousing, and shipping the merchandise to buyers. Purchasing agents help clients obtain the best goods and prices available.
Commission merchants	Take physical possession of products and negotiate sales. Used most often in agricultural marketing by farmers who do not want to sell their own output. Take a truckload of commodities to a central market, sell it for the best price, deduct a commission and expenses, and remit the balance to the producers.
Manufacturers' and retailers' branches and offices	Wholesaling operations conducted by sellers or buyers themselves rather than operating through independent wholesalers. Separate branches and offices can be dedicated to either sales or purchasing.
Sales branches and offices	Set up by manufacturers to improve inventory control, selling, and promotion. Sales branches carry inventory and are found in industries such as lumber and automotive equipment and parts. Sales offices do not carry inventory and are most prominent in the dry goods and notions industries.
Purchasing offices	Perform a role similar to that of brokers or agents but are part of the buyer's organization. Many retailers set up purchasing offices in major market centers, such as New York and Chicago.

limited-service wholesalers offer fewer services to their suppliers and customers. The different types of limited-service wholesalers perform varied specialized functions in the distribution channel.

Brokers and *agents* differ from merchant wholesalers in two ways: They do not take title to goods, and they perform only a few functions. Like merchant wholesalers, they generally specialize by product line or customer type. A **broker** brings buyers and sellers together and assists in negotiation. **Agents** represent buyers or sellers on a more permanent basis. *Manufacturers' agents* (also called *manufacturers' representatives*) are the most common type of agent wholesaler. The third major type of wholesaling is that done in **manufacturers' and retailers' branches and offices** by sellers or buyers themselves rather than through independent wholesalers.

Broker
A wholesaler who does not take title to goods and whose function is to bring buyers and sellers together and assist in negotiation.

Agent
A wholesaler who represents buyers or sellers on a relatively permanent basis, performs only a few functions, and does not take title to goods.

Manufacturers' and retailers' branches and offices
Wholesaling by sellers or buyers themselves rather than through independent wholesalers.

Wholesaler Marketing Decisions

Wholesalers now face growing competitive pressures, more-demanding customers, new technologies, and more direct-buying programs on the part of large industrial, institutional, and retail buyers. As a result, they have taken a fresh look at their marketing strategies. As with retailers, their marketing decisions include choices of segmentation and targeting, differentiation and positioning, and the marketing mix—product and service assortments, price, promotion, and distribution (see **Figure 13.2**).

Segmentation, Targeting, Differentiation, and Positioning Decisions

Like retailers, wholesalers must segment and define their target markets and differentiate and position themselves effectively—they cannot serve everyone. They can choose a target group by size of customer (for example, large retailers only), type of customer (convenience stores only), the need for service (customers who need credit), or other factors. Within the target group, they can identify the more profitable customers, design stronger offers, and build better relationships with them. They can propose automatic reordering systems, establish management-training and advisory systems, or even sponsor a voluntary chain.

FIGURE | 13.2
Wholesaler Marketing Strategies

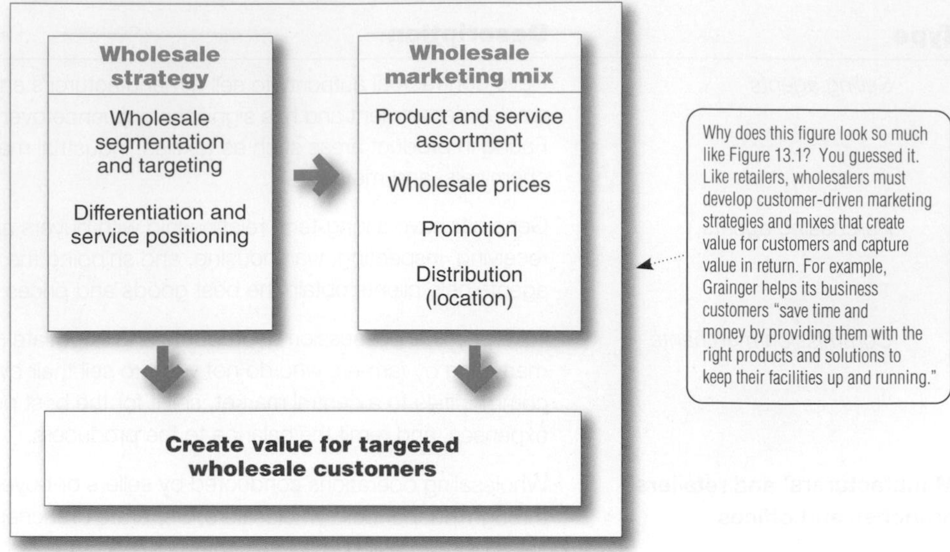
Wholesale strategy
Wholesale segmentation and targeting
Differentiation and service positioning
Wholesale marketing mix
Product and service assortment
Wholesale prices
Promotion
Distribution (location)
Create value for targeted wholesale customers
Why does this figure look so much like Figure 13.1? You guessed it. Like retailers, wholesalers must develop customer-driven marketing strategies and mixes that create value for customers and capture value in return. For example, Grainger helps its business customers "save time and money by providing them with the right products and solutions to keep their facilities up and running."

They can discourage less-profitable customers by requiring larger orders or adding service charges to smaller ones.

Marketing Mix Decisions

Like retailers, wholesalers must decide on product and service assortments, prices, promotion, and place. Wholesalers add customer value though the *products and services* they offer. They are often under great pressure to carry a full line and stock enough for immediate delivery. But this practice can damage profits. Wholesalers today are cutting down on the number of lines they carry, choosing to carry only the more profitable ones. They are also rethinking which services count most in building strong customer relationships and which should be dropped or paid for by the customer. The key for companies is to find the mix of services most valued by their target customers.

Price is also an important wholesaler decision. Wholesalers usually mark up the cost of goods by a standard percentage—say, 20 percent. Expenses may run 17 percent of the gross margin, leaving a profit margin of 3 percent. In grocery wholesaling, the average profit margin is often less than 2 percent. The recent recession put heavy pressure on wholesalers to cut their costs and prices. As their retail and industrial customers face sales and margin declines, these customers turn to wholesalers, looking for lower prices. Wholesalers may, in turn, cut their margins on some lines to keep important customers. They may also ask suppliers for special price breaks in cases when they can turn them into an increase in the supplier's sales.

Although *promotion* can be critical to wholesaler success, most wholesalers are not promotion minded. They use largely scattered and unplanned trade advertising, sales promotion, personal selling, and public relations. Many are behind the times in personal selling; they still see selling as a single salesperson talking to a single customer instead of as a team effort to sell, build, and service major accounts. Wholesalers also need to adopt some of the nonpersonal promotion techniques used by retailers. They need to develop an overall promotion strategy and make greater use of supplier promotion materials and programs. Digital and social media are playing an increasingly important role. For example, Grainger maintains an active presence on Facebook, YouTube, Twitter, LinkedIn, and Google+. It also provides a feature-rich mobile app. On its YouTube channel, Grainger lists more than 500 videos on topics ranging from the company and its products and services to keeping down inventory costs.

Finally, *distribution* (location) is important. Wholesalers must choose their locations, facilities, and Web locations carefully. There was a time when wholesalers could locate in low-rent, low-tax areas and invest little money in their buildings, equipment, and systems. Today, however, as technology zooms forward, such behavior results in outdated systems for material handling, order processing, and delivery.

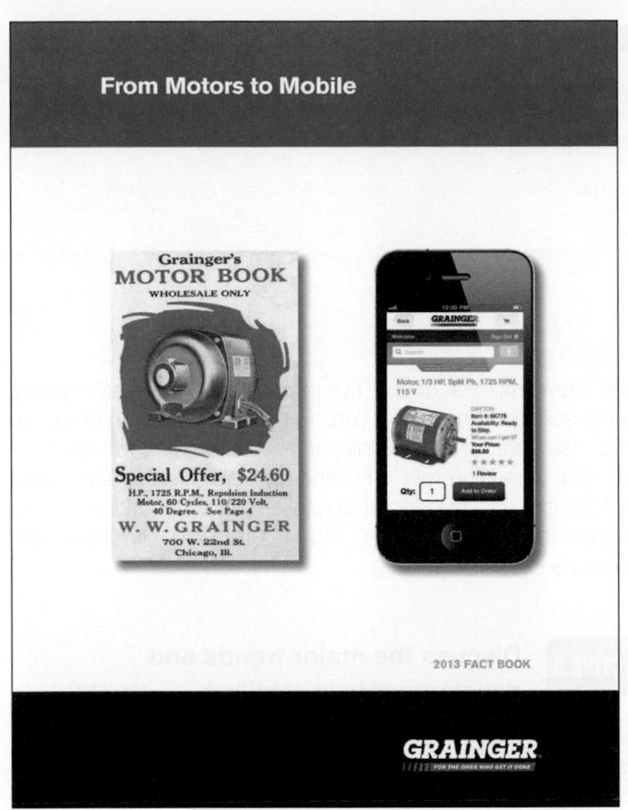

From Motors to Mobile
Grainger's
MOTOR BOOK
WHOLESALE ONLY
Special Offer, $24.60
W. W. GRAINGER
700 W. 22nd St.
Chicago, Ill.
2013 FACT BOOK
GRAINGER

Wholesaler marketing: Progressive wholesalers like Grainger maintain an active presence in online, mobile, and social media. For example, online and mobile purchasing now account for 80 percent of Grainger's total sales.

W. W. Grainger, Inc.

Instead, today's large and progressive wholesalers have reacted to rising costs by investing in automated warehouses and IT systems. Orders are fed from the retailer's information system directly into the wholesaler's, and the items are picked up by mechanical devices and automatically taken to a shipping platform where they are assembled. Most large wholesalers use technology to carry out accounting, billing, inventory control, and forecasting. Modern wholesalers are adapting their services to the needs of target customers and finding cost-reducing methods of doing business. They are also transacting more business online. For example, e-commerce is Grainger's fastest-growing sales channel, making Grainger the 13th largest e-tailer in the United States and Canada. Online and mobile purchasing now account for 36 percent of the wholesaler's total sales.[37]

Trends in Wholesaling

Today's wholesalers face considerable challenges. The industry remains vulnerable to one of its most enduring trends—the need for ever-greater efficiency. Recent tighter economic conditions have led to demands for even lower prices and the winnowing out of suppliers who are not adding value based on cost and quality. Progressive wholesalers constantly watch for better ways to meet the changing needs of their suppliers and target customers. They recognize that their only reason for existence comes from adding value, which occurs by increasing the efficiency and effectiveness of the entire marketing channel.

As with other types of marketers, the goal is to build value-adding customer relationships. McKesson provides an example of progressive, value-adding wholesaling. The company is a diversified health-care-services provider and the nation's leading wholesaler of pharmaceuticals, health and beauty care, home health care, and medical supply and equipment products. To survive, especially in a tight economic environment, McKesson has to be more cost effective than manufacturers' sales branches. Thus, the company has built efficient automated warehouses, established direct computer links with drug manufacturers, and created extensive online supply management and accounts receivable systems for customers. It offers retail pharmacists a wide range of online resources, including supply management assistance, catalog searches, real-time order tracking, and an account management system. It has also created solutions such as automated pharmaceutical-dispensing machines that assist pharmacists by reducing costs and improving accuracy. Retailers can even use the McKesson systems to maintain prescription histories and medical profiles on their customers.

McKesson's medical-surgical supply and equipment customers receive a rich assortment of online solutions and supply management tools, including an online order management system and real-time information on products and pricing, inventory availability, and order status. According to McKesson, it adds value in the channel by providing "supply, information, and health care management products and services designed to reduce costs and improve quality across healthcare."[38]

The distinction between large retailers and large wholesalers continues to blur. Many retailers now operate formats such as wholesale clubs and supercenters that perform many wholesale functions. In return, some large wholesalers are setting up their own retailing operations. For example, SuperValu is the nation's largest food wholesaler, and it's also one of the country's largest food retailers. About half of the company's sales come from its Cub Foods, Save-A-Lot, Farm Fresh, Hornbacher's, Shop 'n Save, and Shoppers stores. In fact, SuperValu now bills itself as "America's neighborhood grocer."[39]

Wholesalers will continue to increase the services they provide to retailers—retail pricing, cooperative advertising, marketing and management information services, accounting services, online transactions, and others. However, both the more value-focused environment and the demand for increased services have put the squeeze on wholesaler profits. Wholesalers that do not find efficient ways to deliver value to their customers will soon drop by the wayside. Fortunately, the increased use of computerized, automated, and Internet-based systems will help wholesalers contain the costs of ordering, shipping, and inventory holding, thus boosting their productivity.

13 Reviewing the Concepts

OBJECTIVES REVIEW AND KEY TERMS

Objectives Review

Retailing and wholesaling consist of many organizations bringing goods and services from the point of production to the point of use. In this chapter, we examined the nature and importance of retailing, the major types of retailers, the decisions retailers make, and the future of retailing. We then examined these same topics for wholesalers.

OBJECTIVE 1 Explain the role of retailers in the distribution channel and describe the major types of retailers. *(pp 410–417)*

Retailing includes all the activities involved in selling goods or services directly to final consumers for their personal, nonbusiness use. Retailers play an important role in connecting brands to consumers in the final phases of the buying process. *Shopper marketing* involves focusing the entire marketing process on turning shoppers into buyers as they approach the point of sale, whether during in-store, online, or mobile shopping.

Retail stores come in all shapes and sizes, and new retail types keep emerging. Store retailers can be classified by the *amount of service* they provide (self-service, limited service, or full service), *product line sold* (specialty stores, department stores, supermarkets, convenience stores, superstores, and service businesses), and *relative prices* (discount stores and off-price retailers). Today, many retailers are banding together in corporate and contractual *retail organizations* (corporate chains, voluntary chains, retailer cooperatives, and franchise organizations).

OBJECTIVE 2 Describe the major retailer marketing decisions. *(pp 417–423)*

Retailers are always searching for new marketing strategies to attract and hold customers. They face major marketing decisions about segmentation and targeting, store differentiation and positioning, and the retail marketing mix.

Retailers must first segment and define their target markets and then decide how they will differentiate and position themselves in these markets. Those that try to offer "something for everyone" end up satisfying no market well. By contrast, successful retailers define their target markets well and position themselves strongly.

Guided by strong targeting and positioning, retailers must decide on a retail marketing mix—product and services assortment, price, promotion, and place. Retail stores are much more than simply an assortment of goods. Beyond the products and services they offer, today's successful retailers carefully orchestrate virtually every aspect of the consumer store experience. A retailer's price policy must fit its target market and positioning, products and services assortment, and competition. Retailers use various combinations of the five promotion tools—advertising, personal selling, sales promotion, PR, and direct marketing—to reach consumers. Online, mobile, and social media tools are playing an ever-increasing role in helping retailers to engage customers. Finally, it's very important that retailers select locations that are accessible to the target market in areas that are consistent with the retailer's positioning.

OBJECTIVE 3 Discuss the major trends and developments in retailing. *(pp 424–430)*

Retailers operate in a harsh and fast-changing environment, which offers threats as well as opportunities. Following years of good economic times for retailers, retailers have now adjusted to the new economic realities and more thrift-minded consumers. New retail forms continue to emerge. At the same time, however, different types of retailers are increasingly serving similar customers with the same products and prices (retail convergence), making differentiation more difficult. Other trends in retailing include the rise of megaretailers; the rapid growth of direct, online, and social media retailing; the growing importance of retail technology; a surge in green retailing; and the global expansion of major retailers.

OBJECTIVE 4 Explain the major types of wholesalers and their marketing decisions. *(pp 430–435)*

Wholesaling includes all the activities involved in selling goods or services to those who are buying for the purpose of resale or business use. Wholesalers fall into three groups. First, *merchant wholesalers* take possession of the goods. They include *full-service wholesalers* (wholesale merchants and industrial distributors) and *limited-service wholesalers* (cash-and-carry wholesalers, truck wholesalers, drop shippers, rack jobbers, producers' cooperatives, and mail-order wholesalers). Second, *brokers* and *agents* do not take possession of the goods but are paid a commission for aiding companies in buying and selling. Finally, *manufacturers' and retailers' branches and offices* are wholesaling operations conducted by non-wholesalers to bypass the wholesalers.

Like retailers, wholesalers must target carefully and position themselves strongly. And, like retailers, wholesalers must decide on product and service assortments, prices, promotion, and place. Progressive wholesalers constantly watch for better ways to meet the changing needs of their suppliers and target customers. They recognize that, in the long run, their only reason for existence comes from adding value, which occurs by increasing the efficiency and effectiveness of the entire marketing channel. As with other types of marketers, the goal is to build value-adding customer relationships.

MyMarketingLab

Go to **mymktlab.com** to complete the problems marked with this icon .

Key Terms

OBJECTIVE 1

Retailing (p 410)
Retailer (p 410)
Shopper marketing (p 410)
Specialty store (p 411)
Department store (p 412)
Supermarket (p 412)
Convenience store (p 413)
Superstore (p 413)
Category killer (p 413)
Service retailer (p 413)
Discount store (p 414)
Off-price retailer (p 414)
Independent off-price retailer (p 414)
Factory outlet (p 415)
Warehouse club (p 415)
Corporate chains (p 415)
Franchise (p 416)

OBJECTIVE 2

Shopping center (p 423)

OBJECTIVE 3

Showrooming (p 426)

OBJECTIVE 4

Wholesaling (p 430)
Wholesaler (p 430)
Merchant wholesaler (p 431)
Broker (p 433)
Agent (p 433)
Manufacturers' and retailers' branches and offices (p 433)

DISCUSSION AND CRITICAL THINKING

Discussion Questions

13-1 Explain how the mix of different retailer types is changing and the current trends in this regard. (AACSB: Communication; Reflective Thinking)

13-2 Define the essential nature of retailing and describe its function and role. (AACSB: Communication)

13-3 What is meant by the term *retail marketing mix,* and what does it involve that is specific to retailing? (AACSB: Communication)

13-4 Are wholesalers common in your country or region? Do they add value to the channels of distribution? (AACSB: Communication)

13-5 Compare and contrast brokers and agents with merchant wholesalers. (AACSB: Communication; Reflective Thinking)

Critical Thinking Exercises

13-6 Visit a local mall and evaluate five stores. What type of retailer is each of these stores? What is the target market for each? How is each store positioned? Do the retail atmospherics of each store enhance this positioning effectively to attract and satisfy the target market? (AACSB: Communication; Reflective Thinking)

13-7 Deciding on a target market and positioning for a retail store are very important marketing decisions. In a small group, develop the concept for a new retail store. What is the target market for your store? How is your store positioned? What retail atmospherics will enhance this positioning effectively to attract and satisfy your target market? (AACSB: Communication; Reflective Thinking)

13-8 The majority of shoppers agree that online reviews can be very helpful. However, some online reviews are fake. Research this issue and write a report on how to spot fake online reviews and the steps online retailers take to minimize fake reviews. (AACSB: Communication; Use of IT; Reflective Thinking)

MINICASES AND APPLICATIONS

Online, Mobile, and Social Media Marketing Guilty as Charged

Small businesses often need to come up with a unique angle to attract media attention. Sizzle and Grill in Cardiff, South Wales, UK, is home to 40 different mega-meals. As a result, the online buzz about the food makes sure every night at the restaurant is a busy night. The owner, Paul Stevens, knew he would have to come up with something special when the challenge to eat his 69-oz mixed grill, in an hour, was completed by seven people. He introduced the 96-oz steak and a 61/2-pound burger. The restaurant had become the prime venue for raucous nights out, including hen and stag parties. It has also attracted the interest of the national media. The problem with excessive media publicity and nonstop attention on social media is that the next big story hits the headlines with an immediate and sometimes damaging effect. For example, in April 2014, no important newspaper, radio station, or TV channel could miss reporting on Stevens pleading guilty to 18 hygiene offenses and two counts of benefit fraud.

13-9 Find an example of a local retailer in your community that uses online, mobile, and social media marketing. Interview the owner of the store or restaurant and ask about the challenges and successes he or she has experienced when implementing this strategy. (AACSB: Communication; Use of IT; Reflective Thinking)

13-10 Create a presentation to give to local retailers explaining how they can effectively use online, mobile, and social media marketing to engage customers and enhance their business. (AACSB: Communication; Reflective Thinking)

Marketing Ethics Footloose and Tax Free

In the UK in the summer of 2013, there were mass protests and discourse regarding several global brands operating in the country. Starbucks, Google, Amazon, and Vodafone immediately came under fire. Shortly afterward, the Arcadia Group, Boots, and Fortnum & Mason were singled out for attention. The reason: they were all avoiding paying UK taxes on UK sales. Everything they were doing was legal. It was tax avoidance, not tax evasion. Starbucks, with sales of almost $500 million, had paid no corporation tax. It was paying royalties to a Dutch sister company, buying coffee beans in Switzerland, and paying extortionate interest on loans to other parts of the business. Meanwhile, Amazon, with sales of $5.5 billion, had somehow contrived to pay less than $3 million in tax. Similarly, Google, with a turnover of $640 million, had paid under $10 million in tax. How is this legally achieved? The first tried-and-tested method is to locate facilities in low-tax jurisdictions, as Starbucks located its coffee wholesaling business in Switzerland. Google's UK operation is actually based in the Republic of Ireland and Bermuda. The second method is known as transfer pricing. By locating factories, services, and distribution in low-tax countries, the business is able to bill the subsidiary in a high-tax country. In effect, the money is siphoned out of the high-tax country into a low-tax one.

13-11 Why do global businesses use such strategies? Are the financial benefits greater than the loss in customer confidence and trust? (AACSB: Communication; Reflective Thinking)

13-12 Consider the Marketplace Fairness Act of 2013 that would enable state governments in the United States to collect sales taxes from online retailers. Discuss the impact this act will have on small retailers. (AACSB: Communication; Ethical Reasoning; Reflective Thinking)

Marketing by the Numbers Inventory Management

Stock turnover is a way to measure stock performance. It is an indication of the number of times the stock has been "turned over" or replaced over a given period of time. This is a measurement of sales performance too, as the higher the rate, the better the stock, and the business, is performing. If the rate is low, then the stock is taking some time to sell, which means that the business has cash tied up in the stock, which affects its cash flow. In order to work out stock turnover, it is necessary to calculate the value of the opening stock and the value of the closing stock over a period of time.

13-13 Refer to Appendix 2, Marketing by the Numbers, and determine the average stock of a business with an opening stock of $24,000 and a closing stock of $36,000. (AACSB: Communication; Analytical Reasoning)

13-14 If a company has sold goods worth $210,000, what is the stock turnover ratio? Is this a good or bad ratio, in your opinion? (AACSB: Communication; Reflective Thinking)

Video Case Home Shopping Network

Shopping on television has been around almost as long as television itself. But the Home Shopping Network (HSN) made it a full-time endeavor in 1982, giving birth to a new retail outlet. Since then, HSN has been a pioneer in products, presentation, and order taking. The company has sold millions of products and has been known for giving an outlet to legitimate products that otherwise would not reach customers.

But what does a company do when the very retail channel that it depends upon starts to fizzle out? This video illustrates how HSN has met the challenges of a changing marketplace to continue its innovative methods for reaching its customer base.

After viewing the video featuring HSN, answer the following questions:

13-15 How has HSN differentiated itself from other retailers through each element of the retail marketing mix?

13-16 Discuss the concept of the retail life cycle as it relates to HSN.

13-17 Do you think HSN has a bright future? Why or why not?

Company Case Leader Price: Good Quality, Low Price

Leader Price has emerged as one of France's leading discount stores. It presents itself as "the smart choice for living well." In a society known for seeking value-oriented items and practicing responsible spending, Leader Price has reached a well-earned spot among the major players in the country. Leader Price Holding was founded in 1998 as a subsidiary of Groupe Casino, which ranks as the fifth biggest food retailer in France. It came in to complete the group's already existing brands, which are the Giant Casino hypermarkets; Casino supermarkets; Monoprix, which is targeted at an urban clientele and emphasizes high quality; Petit Casino markets, which are small convenience stores; and, finally, Naturalia, which carries only organic products and caters to the health conscious.

In food retailing in France, hypermarkets are dominating the sector. The turnover of Carrefour, the market leader, in 2013 was 76,127 million euros, whereas Groupe Casino's turnover amounted to 48,645 million euros, but it is worth noting that the number of stores owned by Carrefour is 10,102, whereas those owned by Groupe Casino total 12,000. Of course, as most of Carrefour's stores are of large square footage and are usually located on the outskirts of urban areas, even with fewer stores than its competitors it is able to exceed their numbers. In terms of discount stores, the German Lidl and Aldi have the largest market shares of hard discount stores in France. With the hype of discount retailing in France, even the largest chains have been trying to develop their versions of discount stores. French names such as Carrefour, Casino, and Leclerc have launched a new arm of discount stores.

Leader Price is unique in the way it portrays itself as committed to providing French families with their entire daily needs with simplicity. Its unique selling proposition is offering low prices while maintaining quality. The array of products is carefully selected so that the consumer doesn't need to look elsewhere for better value for the money. This also makes the shopping experience a simple and pleasant one, as the number of products is limited in each category. Besides regular fast-moving consumer goods, Leader Price sells a variety of seasonal fresh fruits, vegetables, and meats supplied every day to guarantee quality.

Most Leader Price stores are located in places where parking is easy; in urban areas, they are usually located right outside of an underground exit, making them difficult to miss. In 2010, after a drop in sales early in the year, the chain took two major steps to control the situation. A new design for the store's logo and interior was developed, and it started selling products of national brands from outside the Leader Price branded range. The new design was a successful attempt to make its stores more visually pleasing and to enhance the shopping experience. At the beginning, its stores looked somewhat dull, like many typical discount stores, but with the renewal, they were transformed: well organized, well lit, and inviting. The introduction of national brands also allowed Leader Price to compete not only with other discount stores but also with small convenience stores such as Carrefour City, a subsidiary of Carrefour aimed at urbanites. Currently, Leader Price has 600 stores in France and has also extended to other European countries, such as Belgium. Now, Groupe Casino intends to focus on international expansion, whichs include opening a significant number of stores across South America and Southeast Asia, both regions with major growth potential.

Range of Products

The way Leader Price works is by carrying a small number of products compared to other retail stores. It currently sells 4,000 products, 3,000 of which are branded Leader Price and produced by the chain itself. These range from toilet paper to chocolates to shampoo. They usually are similar to existing products in terms of packaging and with slight alterations in the names. The prices are cut compared to the original product. An example of this is Leader Price's Pralina, which competes with Nutella. Of the 4,000 products, 300 are from large brands such as Coca Cola, Lipton, Mars, and Evian, to name a few. These products are usually discounted and are cheaper than if purchased anywhere else. The reason Leader Price chose to sell products from various other brands was to attract customers who are loyal to certain brands; this way there would be no reason for them to choose another regular supermarket or convenience store over Leader Price, as they are now able to find the products for which they prefer a certain brand as well as discounted versions of the products for which they have no particular brand loyalty. The final 700 products come from several product lines also created by Leader Price. These 700 products are differentiated from the 3,000 products labeled Leader Price in order to render them more noticeable to customers who are likely to have the need or the desire to buy them. These lines include Leader Price Baby, Leader Price Kids, Leader Price Bio, Leader Price Fine Ligne, L'avenir En Vert, and Selection de nos Region.

This array of product lines gives Leader Price the ability to reach and cater to a very wide audience. For example, the babies and kids categories can attract families with babies and children, who in fact represent 22 percent of French households. They may have a tight budget and find it convenient to go to one store where they can fill their shopping carts with all their daily needs. The Bio selection offers packaged organic food, which is becoming more and more sought after. The market size of these products in France reached $6.6 billion in 2014 and is forecasted to exceed $8 billion in 2018; thus by including such products on its shelves, Leader Price is guaranteed a share of the booming market. The disadvantage of packaged organic foods is that they are generally more expensive than their nonorganic counterparts. A hard discount store overcomes the problem because the prices are cut, so customers can buy the products at a more reasonable price than at a regular supermarket. Leader Price also caters to the health conscious with the Fine Ligne selection, which provides low-fat and low-calorie versions of products such as yogurt and cereal.

Eco-Friendly and Fair Trade

Leader Price does not miss out on the chance to offer ecologically friendly products. For the French consumer market, it is important that shops show their engagement and responsibility toward the planet. The opportunity to make a positive contribution to the preservation of the environment is welcomed by most consumers, but unfortunately it comes at a high price. Again, Leader Price overcomes this problem. Finally, the French are known to have high esteem for their culture; accordingly, they take pride in their local produce and have a taste for fine cheese and wine. The idea of a discount store may give the impression that the products sold are of low quality, processed, and far from natural. Leader Price breaks this stereotype by making available a line of products that offers delicacies such as cheeses and nuts from different regions of France.

In 2009, Leader Price began to include fair-trade-certified products under its name. These appeared in categories such as tea, rice, chocolate, and fruit juice. The packages have the label of the Max Havelaar Foundation, a fair-trade movement present in France. In general, fair-trade products are found to be from 10 to 30 percent more expensive than their regular counterparts. The French National Commission of Fair Trade carried out research in 2010 aiming to find out the level of awareness and consumption of fair-trade products among the population; 62 percent of the people surveyed responded as having bought a fair-trade product at least once in the past year. Among the people surveyed, only 22 percent, however, said they bought these products at least once a month. What Leader Price does differently is that it gives those who wish to contribute to protecting local producers from exploitation the chance to do so at a more attainable price, usually 3 to 4 percent cheaper than other stores.

Leader Price's promotional strategy includes discount vouchers and catalogues with further price cuts on designated products as well as momentary offers. The strategy does not stop here. The chain has enlisted Jean Pierre Coffe, a TV and radio presenter as well as cook and food critic, to endorse its products and write recipes for its Web site. A regular supermarket would not have to do that, but a discount store in a country where food plays a lead role in the quotidian life has to prove that it is capable of offering people the exact same culinary experience at a lower price. The idea is to show that buying discounted products does not mean that one cannot prepare sophisticated meals.

At Leader Price there is something for everyone, including those looking for staples and those looking to consume responsibly. Despite the fact that the stores only carry 4,000 products, they manage to reach a large segment of the market and satisfy the various needs of their customers. This is the result of a careful choice of products, a clear brand identity, and agile responsiveness to the ever-changing trends of the French retail market.

Questions for Discussion

13-18 Describe Leader Price according to the different types of retailers discussed in the chapter.

13-19 As a retail brand, assess the Leader Price strategy with respect to segmentation, targeting, differentiation, and positioning.

13-20 List all the reasons why Leader Price has been able to compete with regular convenience stores.

13-21 Would the Leader Price model be successful in your country? What would have to be changed to adapt to your culture? Support your answer.

13-22 How can Leader Price expand its selection of products in a way that will cater to more customers?

Sources: Fiona Briggs, "Retail Chinn-wag: Leader Price Launches New Concept and Broadens Offer to Revitalise Flagging Sales," *Retail Times*, October 2010, http://retailtimes.co.uk/retail-chinn-wag-leader-pricelaunches-new-concept-and-broadens-offer-to-revitalise-flagging-sales;Agri-Food Trade Services, "France—How to Cope with a Traditional Marketplace," Agriculture and Agri-Food Canada, 2011, www.ats-sea.agr.gc.ca/eur/5722-eng.htm; Institut National de la Statistique desetudes economiques, "Tableaux de l'Économie Française," 2012, www.insee.fr/fr/themes/document.asp? ref_id=T12F034. www.gov.mb.ca/agriculture/statistics/agrifood/france_organic_packaged_food_en.pdf;"Leader Price devient equitable," *Lineaires*, August 2009, www.lineaires.com/LA-DISTRIBUTION/Les-actus/Leader-Price-devientequitable-23274; "Les Français et le commerce equitable," *Je ConsommeEquitable*, www.jeconsommeequitable.fr/je-pratique/enquetes/313-lesfrancais-et-le-commerce-equitable.html, accessed November 2012; "Rankings and Profiles of the Top Retailers in France," Retail Index, Veraart Research, n.d., www.retail-index.com/HomeSearch/Topr etailersinEuropebycountry/ToprankingretailersinFrance .asp&xgt, accessed November 2012; and information from www.groupe-casino.fr, www.leaderprice.fr, www.maxhavelaarfrance.org, and www.leaderprice.fr/ investisseurs, accessed November 2014.

MyMarketingLab

Go to **mymktlab.com** for the following Assisted-graded writing questions:

13-23 What is retail convergence? Has it helped or harmed small retailers? (AACSB: Communication; Reflective Thinking)

13-24 Explain how wholesalers add value in the channel of distribution. (AACSB: Communication)

References

1. M. Sevkli, S.C.L. Koh, S. Zaim, M. Demirbag, and E. Tatoglu, "An Application of Data Envelopment Analytic Hierarchy Process for Supplier Selection: A Case Study of BEKO in Turkey," *International Journal of Production Research,* Vol. 45 (9), pp. 1973–2003; Jim Boulden, "Turkey Switches on to TV Market," CNN International.com, January 17, 2005, http://edition.cnn.com/2005/ BUSINESS/01/17/turkey.beko/; "BEKO Elektronik A.S. to Show MHP Demonstration at IFA," August 29, 2005, www.thefreelibrary.com/Beko+Elektronik+A.S.+to+Show+MHP+Demonstration+at+IFA-a0135589881; "BEKO Technologies—Latest Company News," September 9, 2010, www.engineeringtalk.com/news/bek/bek198.html; Ozcivelek Rukiye, Zontul, Haluk, "Insights into the ICT Industry in Turkey," Institute for Prospective Technological Studies, 2004, http://fiste.jrc.ec.europa.eu/download/EUR21392%20FINAL%20Turkish%20report.pdf; and Arçelik Annual Report (2009), Arçelik A. S., available at www.arcelikas.com.tr.
2. See "Monthly and Annual Retail Trade," U.S. Census Bureau, www.census.gov/retail/, accessed March 2014.
3. Jack Neff, "P&G Pushes Design in Brand-Building Strategy," April 12, 2010, http://adage.com/print?article_id=143211; and Gil Press, "What Do CMOs Want? On Big Data, Better Focus, and Moments of Truth," *Forbes,* November 25, 2013, www.forbes.com/sites/gilpress/2013/11/25/what-do-cmos-want-on-big-data-better-focus-and-moments-of-truths/.
4. For more on digital aspects of shopper marketing, see Christopher Heine, ""Marketing to the Omnichannel Shopper," *Adweek,* June 3, 2013, pp. S1–S2; John Balla, "Customer Love—It's All about the Connection," *loyalty360,* February 14, 2014, http://loyalty360.org/loyalty-today/article/customer-love-its-all-about-the-connection; www.shoppermarketingmag.com/home/, accessed June 2014; and "ZMOT," *Google Digital Services*, www.zeromomentoftruth.com/, accessed September 2014.
5. See Annie Gasparro and Timothy W. Martin, "What's Wrong with America's Supermarkets?" *Wall Street Journal*, July 13, 2012, p. B1; Jennifer Haderspeck, "Competing for Consumer Share," *Beverage Industry*, January 2013, pp. 38, 40; and "U.S. Supermarkets Gain Share: Report," *Supermarket News,* May 30, 2013, http://supermarketnews.com/retail-amp-financial/us-supermarkets-gain-share-report.
6. Jon Springer, "Pricing: WinCo Keeps Costs Down and Velocity High," *Supermarket News,* April 29, 2013, http://supermarketnews.com/retail-amp-financial/pricing-winco-keeps-costs-down-and-velocity-high#ixzz2uLcJzlvN; Brad Tuttle, "Meet the Low-Key, Low-Cost Grocery Chain Being Called 'Walmart's Worst Nightmare,'" *Time,* August 7, 2013, http://business.time.com/2013/08/07/meet-the-low-key-low-cost-grocery-chain-being-called-wal-marts-worst-nightmare/; and www.wincofoods.com, accessed September 2014.
7. Based on information from Stephanie Strom, "7-Eleven Shifts Focus to Healthier Food Options," *New York Times*, December 24, 2012, www.nytimes.com/2012/12/25/business/7-eleven-stores-focus-on-healthier-food-options.html?partner=rss&emc=rss; Jonathon Berr, "7-Eleven Goes on a Healthy Kick," *MSN Money,* September 13, 2013, http://money.msn.com/now/post--7-eleven-goes-on-a-health-kick; and http://corp.7-eleven.com, accessed September 2014.
8. Karen Brune Mathis, "Wal-Mart Supercenters Top Count of Southeast Regional Retailers," *Jacksonville Daily Record,* October 19, 2012, www.jaxdailyrecord.com/showstory.php?Story_id=537805; http://corporate.walmart.com/, accessed June 2014; and "Supermarket Facts," www.fmi.org/research-resources/supermarket-facts, accessed September 2014.
9. See "Dollar General to Open 635 New Stores and Create More Than 6,000 New Jobs in 2013," January 23, 2013, http://newscenter.dollargeneral.com/article_display.cfm?article_id=1848; and Christopher Matthews, "Will Dollar Stores Rule the Retail World?" *Time,* April 1, 2013, http://business.time.com/2013/04/01/will-dollar-stores-rule-the-retail-world/.
10. "How We Do It," http://tjmaxx.tjx.com/store/jump/topic/how-we-do-it/2400087, accessed September 2014.
11. Based on information from "2013 Top 250 Global Retailers," *Stores,* January 2014; Matthew Boyle, "Why Costco Is So Addictive," *Fortune*, October 25, 2006, pp. 126–132; Rick Aristotle Munarriz, "For Costco, $1.50 Hot Dog Combos and $4.99 Chickens Aren't Enough," *Daily Finance*, October 10, 2013, www.dailyfinance.com/2013/10/10/costco-earnings-disappointment-analysis-hot-dogs-chicken/; and www.costco.com and http://www.costco.com/insider-guide-amazing-facts.html, accessed September 2014.
12. Company and franchising information from "2013 Franchise Times Top 200 Franchise Systems," *Franchise Times*, October 2013, www.franchisetimes.com/pdf/Top-200-2013.pdf, www.score.org/resources/should-i-buy-franchise; and www.aboutmcdonalds.com/mcd and www.subway.com/subwayroot/About_Us/default.aspx, accessed September 2014.

13. Numbers from "2013 Franchise Times Top 200 Franchise Systems," *Franchise Times*, October 2013, www.franchisetimes.com/pdf/Top-200-2013.pdf. See also www.whichwich.com and www.whichwich.com/about_us, accessed September 2014.

14. Based on information from "How Do You See This Experiential Retailing Trend Working Its Way across Retail?" *Integrated Retailing,* www.integratedretailing.com/?p=131, accessed September 2014; and www.llbean.com, www.llbean.com/llb/shop/1000001692?nav=ftlink, and www.llbean.com/llb/shop/1000001704?page=campus-lander#, accessed September 2014.

15. See Yelena Moroz Alpert, "How Color Affects Your Spending," *Real Simple,* March 2013, p. 148; James Archer, "Let Them Sniff, Customers Will Buy More," *Inc.*, January 23, 2013, www.inc.com/james-archer/let-them-sniff-customers-will-buy-more.html; Justine Sharrock, "How Manufactured Smells Are Making People Shop Longer and Kill Better," *BuzzFeed,* March 15, 2013, www.buzzfeed.com/justinesharrock/how-manufactured-smells-are-making-people-shop-longer-and-ki; Alexandra Sifferlin, "My Nose Made Me Buy It," *Time*, December 16, 2013, http://healthland.time.com/2013/12/16/my-nose-made-me-buy-it-how-retailers-use-smell-and-other-tricks-to-get-you-to-spend-spend-spend/; and www.scentair.com/why-scentair-scent-studies/, accessed September 2014.

16. See various social media sites for Walmart and Fairway, accessed June 2014.

17. "CVS/pharmacy Revolutionizes the Way Customers Experience the Sales Circular with Launch of myWeekly Ad," October 17, 2013, http://info.cvscaremark.com/newsroom/press-releases/cvspharmacy-revolutionizes-way-customers-experience-sales-circular-launch; Stuart Elliott, "For CVS Regulars, Ads Tailored Just to Them," *New York Times,* October 10, 2013, www.nytimes.com/2013/10/11/business/media/for-cvs-regulars-ads-tailored-just-to-them.html?_r=0; and www.cvs.com, accessed September 2014.

18. For definitions of these and other types of shopping centers, see "Dictionary," *American Marketing Association*, www.marketingpower.com/_layouts/Dictionary.aspx, accessed September 2014.

19. See "Brick by Brick: The State of the Shopping Center," Nielsen, May 17, 2013, http://nielsen.com/us/en/reports/2013/brick-by-brick-the-state-of-the-shopping-center.html; "It's the End of the Mall as We Know It," *Real Estate Weekly*, February 22, 2013, www.rew-online.com/2013/02/22/its-the-end-of-the-mall-as-we-know-it/; and Judy Keen, "As Enclosed Malls Decline, 'Lifestyle Centers' Proliferate," MINNPOST, August 30, 2013, www.minnpost.com/cityscape/2013/08/enclosed-malls-decline-lifestyle-centers-proliferate.

20. See Joe Gose, "How Shopping Power Centers Survived a Big Retail Route," *Investors.com,* December 12, 2013, http://news.investors.com/121213-682722-power-centers-adapt-as-discount-retailers-thrive.htm?ven=djcp&src=aurlabo; and Randyl Drummer, "New Wave of Retail Tenants Filling Power Centers," *CoStar,* November 12, 2013, www.costar.com/News/Article/New-Wave-of-Retail-Tenants-Filling-Power-Centers/154356.

21. Timothy W. Martin, "May I Help You?" *Wall Street Journal*, April 22, 2009, http://online.wsj.com/article/SB124025177889535871.html; "The Top 10 Companies by Revenue," *Inc.*, August 22, 2011, www.inc.com/ss/2011-inc-5000-top-10-companies-revenue; "The American Customer Satisfaction Index," www.theacsi.org/index.php?option=com_content&view=article&id=12&Itemid=110, accessed March 2013; and www.publix.com, accessed March 2013.

22. See "A Summer's Worth of Pop-Up Shops in NYC," *Guest of a Guest,* http://guestofaguest.com/new-york/nyc/a-summers-worth-of-pop-up-shops-in-nyc&slide=5, accessed March 2014; "Find Your Nearest Girl Scout Cookie Pop-Up Shop," www.girlscoutsnyc.org/media-center/video/8-girl-scouts-of-greater-ny-promotional-ads, accessed March 2014; Lauren Sherman, "Pop-Up Shops Prove to Be More than Just a Passing Trend, *Fashionista*, November 7, 2013, http://fashionista.com/2013/11/pop-up-shops-prove-to-be-more-than-just-a-passing-trend/; Selena Larson, "How Zulily Escaped the Flash-Sales Curse," *ReadWrite,* December 26, 2013, http://readwrite.com/2013/12/06/zulily-success-flash-sales-sites-ecommerce#awesm=~ox53XxjqgL06LX.

23. See www.rpminc.com/leading-brands/consumer-brands, accessed September 2014.

24. "60% of U.S. Retail Sales Will Involve the Web by 2017," *Internet Retailer*, October 30, 2013, www.internetretailer.com/2013/10/30/60-us-retail-sales-will-involve-web-2017; and U.S. Census Bureau News, "Quarterly Retail E-Commerce Sales, 4rd Quarter 2013," February 18, 2014, www.census.gov/retail/mrts/www/data/pdf/ec_current.pdf.

25. See Lucia Moses, "Data Points: Mobile Shopping," *Adweek,* May 20, 2013, pp. 20–21; and "Retail Social Media Top 10," *Retail Customer Experience.com,* January 10, 2013, www.retailcustomerexperience.com/blog/9655/Retail-Social-Media-Top-10-Infographic.

26. See Ann Zimmerman, "Can Retailers Halt 'Showrooming'?" *Wall Street Journal,* April 11, 2012, p. B1; "Data Points: Spending It," *Adweek,* April 16, 2012, pp. 24–25; and "Consumers Visit Retailers, Then Go Online for Cheaper Sources," *Adweek,* March 14, 2013, www.adweek.com/print/147777; and 60% of U.S. Retail Sales Will Involve the Web by 2017," *Internet Retailer*, October 30, 2013, www.internetretailer.com/2013/10/30/60-us-retail-sales-will-involve-web-2017.

27. "Top 500 Guide," *Internet Retailer*, www.top500guide.com/top-500/the-top-500-list/, accessed June 2014; and "Store-Based Retailers Take the Early Lead among Top 500 Retailers in Online Sales Growth," *Internet Retailer,* February 18, 2014, www.internetretailer.com/2014/02/18/store-based-retailers-take-early-lead-among-top-500.

28. J. A. Graham, "Williams-Sonoma—Well Done But Not Over-Cooked," *Foolish Blogging Network*, February 6, 2013, http://beta.fool.com/le-kitkat/2013/02/06/williams-sonoma-well-done-over-cooked/22873/; Adam Blair, "Williams-Sonoma Invests $75M in Fast-Growing, Profitable E-Commerce," *RIS,* March 22, 2011, http://risnews.edgl.com/retail-best-practices/Williams-Sonoma-Invests-$75M-in-Fast-Growing,-Profitable-E-Commerce71523; and Paul Demery, "E-Commerce Becomes More Dominant at Williams-Sonoma," *Internet Retailer*, August 20, 2013, www.internetretailer.com/2013/08/30/e-commerce-becomes-more-dominant-williams-sonoma.

29. For another example, see "American Eagle Outfitters and Shopkick Announce 100-Store Trial of New shopBeacon Technology," *PRNewswire*, January 16, 2014, www.prnewswire.com/news-releases/american-eagle-outfitters-and-shopkick-announce-100-store-trial-of-new-shopbeacon-technology-240487111.html; and Ingrid Lunden, "Shopkick Starts 100-Store iBeacon Trial for American Eagle, Biggest Apparel Rollout Yet," *TechCrunch*, January 16, 2014, http://techcrunch.com/2014/01/16/shopkick-starts-100-store-ibeacon-trial-for-american-eagle-outfitters-the-biggest-apparel-rollout-yet/.

30. See Mark J. Miller, "Walmart and Apple Test Mobile Self-Checkouts," *Brand Channel,* September 5, 2012, www.brandchannel.com/home/?tag=/%40WalmartLabs; and "Our Strategy: Winning in Global E-Commerce," *Walmart 2012 Annual Report*, www.walmartstores.com/sites/annual-report/2012/WalMart_AR.pdf, March 2013, pp. 12–13; and www.walmartlabs.com, accessed September 2014.

31. See "Walmart Labs: Social," www.walmartlabs.com/social/, accessed June 2014; Mark J. Miller, "Walmart and Apple Test Mobile Self-Checkouts," *Brand Channel,* September 5, 2012, www.brandchannel.com/home/?tag=/%40WalmartLabs; and "Our Strategy: Winning in Global E-Commerce," *Walmart 2012 Annual Report*, www.walmartstores.com/sites/annual-report/2012/WalMart_AR.pdf, March 2013, pp. 12–13.

32. "Kohl's Opens Eight New Stores Creating Approximately 1,000 Jobs," *Business Wire,* March 8, 2012; and www.kohlsgreenscene.com, accessed June 2014. See also US EPA, "Top 30 Retail," January 27, 2014, www.epa.gov/greenpower/toplists/top30retail.htm.

33. See www.staples.com/sbd/cre/marketing/easy-on-the-planet/recycling-and-eco-services.html, accessed September 2014.

34. See http://news.walmart.com/walmart-facts/corporate-financial-fact-sheet, accessed September 2014.

35. See "Global Powers of Retailing 2014," *Deloitte*, January 2014, accessed at http://www2.deloitte.com/content/dam/Deloitte/global/Documents/Consumer-Business/dttl_CB_Global-Powers-of-Retailing-2014.pdf.

36. Grainger facts and other information are from the "Grainger: Beyond the Box Fact Book," accessed at http://invest.grainger.com/phoenix.zhtml?c=76754&p=irol-irFactBook and www.grainger.com, accessed September 2014.

37. "Top 500 Guide," *Internet Retailer*, www.top500guide.com/top-500/the-top-500-list, accessed March 2014; and www.grainger.com, accessed June 2014.

38. Information from "About Us," www.mckesson.com; and "Supply Management Online," http://mckessonbop.com/solutions-services/mckesson-connect/, accessed September 2014.

39. Facts from Michael Garry, "2013 Power 50: Sam Duncan, No. 1 in Wholesalers," *Supermarket News,* July 15, 2013, http://supermarketnews.com/people/2013-power-50-sam-duncan-no1-wholesalers; and www.supervalu.com, accessed September 2014.

14 Engaging Customers and Communicating Customer Value

Integrated Marketing Communications Strategy

Chapter Preview

In this and the next three chapters, we'll examine the last of the marketing mix tools—promotion. Companies must do more than just create customer value. They must also clearly and persuasively communicate that value. Promotion is not a single tool but rather a mix of several tools. Ideally, under the concept of *integrated marketing communications*, a company will carefully coordinate these promotion elements to engage customers and build a clear, consistent, and compelling message about the organization and its brands.

We begin by introducing the various promotion mix tools. Next, we'll examine the rapidly changing communications environment—especially the addition of new digital and social media and the need for integrated marketing communications. Finally, we discuss the steps in developing marketing communications and the promotion budgeting process. In the next three chapters, we'll present the specific marketing communications tools: advertising and public relations (Chapter 15); personal selling and sales promotion (Chapter 16); and direct, online, mobile, and social media marketing (Chapter 17).

Let's start by looking at a good integrated marketing communications campaign. In an industry characterized by constantly shifting promotional themes, Chick-fil-A's remarkably enduring "Eat Mor Chikin" campaign—featuring an unlikely herd of quirky cows—has successfully engaged customers, communicated the brand's personality and positioning, and made Chick-fil-A one of America's most successful quick-service restaurant chains.

CHICK-FIL-A: A Remarkably Enduring Integrated Marketing Communications Campaign

Nearly two decades ago, regional fast-food chain Chick-fil-A set out in search of a promotion strategy that would set it apart from its big-three fast-food competitors—burger joints McDonald's, Burger King, and Wendy's. Chick-fil-A's strength had always been its signature fried chicken sandwich—you still won't find anything but chicken on the menu. But somehow, just saying "we make good chicken sandwiches" wasn't enough. Chick-fil-A needed a creative "big idea"—something memorable that would communicate the brand's unique value proposition.

What it came up with—of all things—was an improbable herd of renegade black-and-white cows that couldn't spell. Their message: "Eat Mor Chikin." Their goal: to convince consumers to switch from hamburgers to chicken. Acting in their own self-interest, the fearless cows realized that when people eat chicken, they don't eat beef. So in 1995, the first mischievous cow, paintbrush in mouth, painted "Eat Mor Chikin" on a billboard. From that first billboard, the effort has now grown to become one of the most consistent and enduring integrated marketing communications campaigns in history, a full multimedia campaign that has forever changed the burger-eating landscape.

The key to the "Eat Mor Chikin" campaign's success lies in its remarkable consistency. As industry publication *Advertising Age* pointed out when it recently crowned Chick-fil-A as its runner-up marketer of the year, "Often, the smartest marketing is the most patient marketing." And few promotion campaigns

Chick-fil-A's remarkably enduring "Eat Mor Chikin" integrated marketing communications campaign is more than just an advertising campaign. The renegade cows have "become part of our passion and our brand."

have been more persistently patient than this one. For nearly 20 years, Chick-fil-A has stuck steadfastly to its simple but potent "Eat Mor Chikin" message, and the brand's racscally cows have now become pop culture icons.

Building on the basic "Eat Mor Chikin" message, Chick-fil-A keeps the campaign fresh with an ever-changing mix of clever message executions and innovative media placements. Today, you find the cows just about anywhere and everywhere—from traditional television, print, and radio ads, to imaginative sales promotions and event sponsorships, to online social media and smartphone apps, with an occasional water tower still thrown in.

For example, in a TV ad promoting Chick-fil-A's growing breakfast menu, the pesky cows set off car alarm after car alarm, awakening an apartment building full of tenants to the message, "Wake up—itz chikin time." In print ads, the cows promote menu staples with taglines like "Milk shakes—the after chikin dinner drink." Billboards sport quotes such as "Lose that burger belly." During election years, the cows show their nonpartisanship with phrases like "Vote chikin. Itz not right wing or left." The ubiquitous cows even pull zany stunts, such as parachuting into football stadiums with signs reading "Du the wave. Eat the chikin."

Although the "Eat Mor Chikin" campaign has made plentiful use of the traditional media, it is perhaps the nontraditional promotional tactics that have won the cows a special place in the hearts of Chick-fil-A's fiercely loyal customers. Shortly after the start of the campaign, the company began its now-packed promotional merchandise catalogue with an annual cow-themed calendar. This year, it offered the first ever digital calendar, titled "Royal T-Bones," and paid tribute to some of the brand's more famous bovine royalty, such as Queen Elizabrisket—"though her appearance was soft, this skirt steak could be counted on to lead calfkind through tough times"—and Emperor Napoloin Bovinapart, the cow that "wasn't just a two-time emperor—he was also great commander of the militeryaki." Today, Chick-fil-A loyalists snap up large quantities of cow-themed mugs, T-shirts, stuffed animals, refrigerator magnets, laptop cases, and dozens of other items. These promotional items not only generate revenue, they also help to strengthen company-customer engagement while at the same time spreading the brand's "Eat Mor Chikin" message.

Chick-fil-A further engages customers through an assortment of in-store promotional events. Every July, for example, the company promotes "Cow Appreciation Day ("cow bells welcome")," on which customers who show up at any Chick-fil-A store dressed as a cow get a free meal. Last year, nearly 600,000 cow-clad customers cashed in on the event. And when a new Chick-fil-A restaurant opens, under the chain's "First 100" promotion, fans who camp out for 24 hours in advance of the opening get a chance to be one of the lucky 100 who win free Chick-fil-A meals for a year. While waiting, they'll likely meet Chick-fil-A CEO Dan Cathy—known for his customer-centered leadership style—who often camps out overnight with customers, signing T-shirts, posing for pictures, and ultimately handing out those vouchers for a free year's worth of Chick-fil-A.

For nearly two decades, Chick-fil-A has stuck steadfastly to its simple but potent "Eat Mor Chikin" message, and the brand's racscally cows have now become pop culture icons.
PR Newswire

Most recently, Chick-fil-A has taken its "Eat Mor Chikin" message to social media, including Facebook, YouTube, Pinterest, and Twitter. When the company first plotted its social media strategy a few years back, it discovered that it already had a robust Facebook fan page with some 25,000 fans. The page was created by customer Brandy Bitzer, a true Chick-fil-A brand evangelist. In a genuine gesture of customer appreciation, Chick-fil-A joined forces with Bitzer, who continues to administer the page while the company provides assets to fuel enthusiasm for the brand. The strategy is working. Today, the Chick-fil-A Facebook page boasts more than 7.4 million fans. It's packed with information, customer-engaging communications, and plenty of cow advice like "Eat chikin or I'll de-friend u."

These days, you never know where the quirky cows will show up next. But no matter where you see them—on TV, in a sports arena, on your smartphone, or in your local Chick-fil-A restaurant—the long-standing brand message remains consistent. Over the years, the "Eat Mor Chikin" campaign has racked up a who's who list of major advertising awards and honors. More important, the campaign has helped to engage customers and communicate Chick-fil-A's personality and positioning, making it one of the nation's most successful quick-service chains.

Chick-fil-A's more than 1,775 restaurants in 39 states rang up $5 billion in sales last year. Since the first Chick-fil-A store opened, the company has posted revenue increases for

Objective Outline

46 straight years. Since the "Eat Mor Chikin" campaign began, Chick-fil-A sales have increased more than 7.5-fold. The average Chick-fil-A restaurant now pulls in more sales per year—over $3.3 million—than the average McDonald's, despite being open only six days a week (all Chick-fil-A stores are famously closed on Sundays for both practical and spiritual reasons). Chick-fil-A is now America's number-one chicken chain, and its phenomenal growth has contributed greatly to number-two KFC's falling market share in the category.

In all, Chick-fil-A's now-classic but still-contemporary integrated marketing communications campaign "has been more successful than we ever imagined it could be," concludes the company's senior vice president of marketing. "The Cows started as part of our advertising campaign, and now they have become part of our passion and our brand." Who knows what the cows can accomplish in yet another 5 or 10 years. Whatever the future brings, the Chick-fil-A message will still be loud and clear: Eat Mor Chikin![1]

Building good customer relationships calls for more than just developing a good product, pricing it attractively, and making it available to target customers. Companies must also *communicate* their value propositions to customers, and what they communicate should not be left to chance. All communications must be planned and blended into carefully integrated programs. Just as good communication is important in building and maintaining any other kind of relationship, it is a crucial element in a company's efforts to engage customers and build profitable customer relationships.

Author Comment | The promotion mix is the marketer's bag of tools for engaging and communicating with customers and other stakeholders. To deliver a clear and compelling message, each tool must be carefully coordinated under the concept of *integrated marketing communications* (IMC).

The Promotion Mix

A company's total **promotion mix**—also called its **marketing communications mix**—consists of the specific blend of advertising, public relations, personal selling, sales promotion, and direct marketing tools that the company uses to engage consumers, persuasively communicate customer value, and build customer relationships. The five major promotion tools are defined as follows:[2]

- **Advertising**. Any paid form of nonpersonal presentation and promotion of ideas, goods, or services by an identified sponsor.
- **Sales promotion**. Short-term incentives to encourage the purchase or sale of a product or service.
- **Personal selling**. Personal customer interactions by the firm's sales force for the purpose of engaging customers, making sales, and building customer relationships.
- **Public relations**. Building good relations with the company's various publics by obtaining favorable publicity, building up a good corporate image, and handling or heading off unfavorable rumors, stories, and events.
- **Direct and digital marketing**. Engaging directly with carefully targeted individual consumers and customer communities to both obtain an immediate response and build lasting customer relationships.

Promotion mix (marketing communications mix)
The specific blend of promotion tools that the company uses to persuasively communicate customer value and build customer relationships.

Advertising
Any paid form of nonpersonal presentation and promotion of ideas, goods, or services by an identified sponsor.

Sales promotion
Short-term incentives to encourage the purchase or sale of a product or a service.

Personal selling
Personal presentation by the firm's sales force for the purpose of engaging customers, making sales, and building customer relationships.

Each category involves specific promotional tools that are used to communicate with customers. For example, *advertising* includes broadcast, print, online, mobile, outdoor, and other forms. *Sales promotion* includes discounts, coupons, displays, and demonstrations. *Personal selling* includes sales presentations, trade shows, and incentive programs. *Public relations (PR)* includes press releases, sponsorships, events, and Web pages. And *direct and digital marketing* includes direct mail, catalogs, online and social media, mobile marketing, and more.

At the same time, marketing communication goes beyond these specific promotion tools. The product's design, its price, the shape and color of its package, and the stores that sell it—*all* communicate something to buyers. Thus, although the promotion mix is the company's primary engagement and communications activity, the entire marketing mix—promotion, *as well as* product, price, and place—must be coordinated for greatest impact.

Author Comment | IMC is a *really* hot marketing topic these days. No other area of marketing is changing so quickly and profoundly. A big part of the reason is the huge surge in customer engagement through digital media—online, mobile, and social media marketing.

Integrated Marketing Communications

In past decades, marketers perfected the art of mass marketing: selling highly standardized products to masses of customers. In the process, they developed effective mass-media communication techniques to support these strategies. Large companies now routinely invest millions or even billions of dollars in television, magazine, or other mass-media advertising, reaching tens of millions of customers with a single ad. Today, however, marketing managers face some new marketing communications realities. Perhaps no other area of marketing is changing so profoundly as marketing communications, creating both exciting and challenging times for marketing communicators.

Public relations (PR)
Building good relations with the company's various publics by obtaining favorable publicity, building up a good corporate image, and handling or heading off unfavorable rumors, stories, and events.

Direct and digital marketing
Engaging directly with carefully targeted individual consumers and customer communities to both obtain an immediate response and build lasting customer relationships.

The New Marketing Communications Model

Several major factors are changing the face of today's marketing communications. First, *consumers* are changing. In this digital, wireless age, consumers are better informed and more communications empowered. Rather than relying on marketer-supplied information, they can use the Internet, social media, and other technologies to find information on their own. They can connect easily with other consumers to exchange brand-related information or even create their own brand messages and experiences.

Second, *marketing strategies* are changing. As mass markets have fragmented, marketers are shifting away from mass marketing. More and more, they are developing focused marketing programs designed to build closer relationships with customers in more narrowly defined micromarkets.

Finally, sweeping advances in *digital technology* are causing remarkable changes in the ways companies and customers communicate with each other. The digital age has spawned a host of new information and communication tools—from smartphones and tablets to satellite and cable television systems to the many faces of the Internet (brand Web sites, e-mail, blogs, social media and online communities, the mobile Web, and so much more). These explosive developments have had a dramatic impact on marketing communications. Just as mass marketing once gave rise to a new generation of mass-media communications, the new digital and social media have given birth to a more targeted, social, and engaging marketing communications model.

Although network television, magazines, newspapers, and other traditional mass media remain very important, their dominance is declining. In their place, advertisers are now adding a broad selection of more-specialized and highly targeted media to engage smaller customer segments with more personalized, interactive content. The new media range from specialty cable television channels and made-for-the-Web videos to online display ads, Internet catalogs, e-mail and texting, blogs, mobile coupons and other content, and social media such as Twitter, Facebook, Google+, and Pinterest. Such new media have taken marketing by storm.

Some advertising industry experts even predict that the old mass-media communications model will eventually become obsolete. Mass-media costs are rising, audiences are shrinking, ad clutter is increasing, and viewers are gaining control of message exposure through technologies such as video streaming or DVRs that let them skip disruptive television commercials. As a result, the skeptics suggest, marketers are shifting ever-larger portions of their marketing budgets away from old-media mainstays and moving them to online, social, mobile, and other new-age media.

In recent years, although TV still dominates as an advertising medium with a 38 percent share of U.S. ad spending, its growth has stagnated. Spending in magazines, newspapers, and radio has lost ground. Meanwhile, digital media have come from nowhere during the past few years to account for more than 27 percent of U.S. advertising spending, second only to TV. By far the fastest-growing ad-spending category, digital's share is expected to grow to 31 percent by 2017. P&G, the world's biggest advertiser, now spends a full third of its marketing budget on digital media.[3]

In some cases, marketers are skipping traditional media altogether. For example, when Rovio introduced the Angry Birds Space version of its popular game, it used only online video. It began by posting a 20-second video teaser containing only the game title and launch date—that video landed 2.2 million online views. Next, in an inspired move, Rovio teamed with NASA and astronaut Don Petit to do a video in outer space on the International Space Station, which demonstrated the actual physics of a stuffed Angry Bird in space—that video went viral. Six millions views and a few days later, Rovio released a video trailer briefly introducing the game's characters, which grabbed another cool 1 million views in only two days. Finally, at launch time, Rovio posted a two-minute video fully introducing the new game. In total, the award-winning online video campaign reaped an astonishing 134 million views and 168,570 social shares.[4]

The new marketing communications model: Rovio Entertainment introduced the Angry Birds Space version of its popular game using only an online video campaign. The campaign reaped an astonishing 134 million views and 168,570 social shares.

Similarly, eco-friendly household products maker Method recently employed a full but digital-only promotional campaign themed "Clean happy."[5] The campaign used zero ads in traditional media like TV or magazines. Instead, the centerpiece of the campaign was a two-minute brand video that could be watched only on YouTube and on Method's Facebook and Web pages. That video was followed at monthly intervals by four other clips that focused on individual Method products. The campaign also employed online media ads, as well as a major presence in social media and blogs. The "Clean happy" campaign fit both Method's grass-roots personality and its budget. The campaign ran a first-year budget of only about $3.5 million, compared with the whopping $150 million or so that rival P&G might spend to bring out a single new product, such as its Tide Pods detergent packets. Method ran the digital-only campaign for a full year before beginning to bring it to TV.

In the new marketing communications world, rather than using old approaches that interrupt customers and force-feed them mass messages, new media formats let marketers reach smaller communities of consumers in more interactive, engaging ways. For example, think about television viewing these days. Consumers can now watch their favorite programs on just about anything with a screen—on televisions but also laptops, mobile phones, or tablets. And they can choose to watch programs whenever and wherever they wish, often without commercials. Increasingly, some programs, ads, and videos are being produced only for Internet viewing.

Despite the shift toward new digital media, however, traditional mass media still capture a large share of the promotion budgets of most major marketing firms, a fact that probably won't change quickly. Thus, rather than the old-media model collapsing completely, most industry insiders foresee a shifting mix of both traditional mass media and a wide array of online, mobile, and social media that engage more-targeted consumer communities in a more-personalized, interactive way. Many advertisers and ad agencies are still grappling with this transition. In the end, however, regardless of the communications channel, the key is to integrate all of these media in a way that best engages customers, communicates the brand message, and enhances the customer's brand experiences.

As the marketing communications environment shifts, so will the role of marketing communicators. Rather than just creating and placing "TV ads" or "print ads" or "Facebook display ads," many marketers now view themselves more broadly as **content marketing** managers. As such, they create, inspire, and share brand messages and conversations with and among customers across a fluid mix of *paid, owned, earned,* and *shared* communication channels. These channels include media that are both traditional and new, and controlled and not controlled (see Real Marketing 14.1).

Content marketing
Creating, inspiring, and sharing brand messages and conversations with and among consumers across a fluid mix of paid, owned, earned, and shared channels.

The Need for *Integrated* Marketing Communications

The shift toward a richer mix of media and brand content approaches poses a problem for marketers. Consumers today are bombarded by brand content from a broad range of sources. But consumers don't distinguish between content sources the way marketers do. In the consumer's mind, brand content from different sources—whether it's a Super Bowl ad, in-store display, mobile app, or a friend's social media post—all become part of a single message about the brand or company. Conflicting content from these different sources can result in confused company images, brand positions, and customer relationships.

All too often, companies fail to integrate their various communication channels. The result is a hodgepodge of brand content to consumers. Mass-media ads say one thing, whereas an in-store promotion sends a different signal, and the company's Internet site, e-mails, social media pages, or videos posted on YouTube say something altogether different. The problem is that these communications often come from different parts of the company. Advertising messages are planned and implemented by the advertising department or an ad agency. Other company departments or agencies are responsible for public relations (PR), sales promotion events, and online or social media content. However, whereas companies may have separated their communications tools, customers don't. Mixed content from these sources results in blurred brand perceptions by consumers.

The new world of online, mobile, social media marketing presents tremendous opportunities but also big challenges. It can "give companies increased access to their customers, fresh insights into their preferences, and a broader creative palette to work with," says one marketing executive. But "the biggest issue is complexity and fragmentation . . . the amount of choice out there," says another. The challenge is to "make it come together in an organized way."[6]

To that end, more companies today are adopting the concept of **integrated marketing communications (IMC)**. Under this concept, as illustrated in **Figure 14.1**, the company carefully integrates its many communication channels to deliver a clear, consistent, and compelling message about the organization and its brands.

Integrated marketing communications (IMC)
Carefully integrating and coordinating the company's many communications channels to deliver a clear, consistent, and compelling message about the organization and its products.

Integrated marketing communications calls for recognizing all touch points where the customer may encounter content about the company and its brands. Each contact with the brand will deliver a message—whether good, bad, or indifferent. The company's goal should be to deliver a consistent and positive message at each contact. Integrated marketing

Real Marketing 14.1

Just Don't Call It Advertising: It's Content Marketing

In the good old days, life seemed so simple for advertisers. When a brand needed an advertising campaign, everybody knew what that meant. The brand team and ad agency came up with a creative strategy, developed a media plan, produced and placed a set of TV commercials and magazine or newspaper ads, and maybe issued a press release to stir up some news. But in these digital times, the old practice of placing "advertisements" in well-defined "media" within the tidy framework of a carefully managed "advertising campaign" just doesn't work anymore.

Instead, the lines are rapidly blurring between traditional advertising and new digital, social media, and mobile content. To be relevant, today's brand messages must be social, mobile, interactively engaging, and multi-platformed. Says one industry insider: "Today's media landscape keeps getting more diverse—it's broadcast, cable, and streaming; it's online, tablet, and smartphone; it's video, rich media, social media, branded content, banners, apps, in-app advertising, and interactive technology products."

The new digital landscape has called into question the very definition of advertising. "What Is Advertising Anyway?" asks one provocative headline. Call it whatever you want, admonishes another, but "Just *Don't* Call It Advertising." Instead, according to many marketers these days, it's "content marketing," creating and distributing a broad mix of compelling content that engages customers, builds relationships with and among them, and moves them to action. To feed today's digital and social media machinery, and to sustain "always-on" consumer conversations, brands need a constant supply of fresh content across a breadth of traditional and digital platforms.

Many advertisers and marketers now view themselves more broadly as *content marketing managers* who create, inspire, share, and curate marketing content—both their own content and that created by consumers and others. Rather than using traditional media breakdowns, they subscribe to a new framework that builds on how and by whom marketing content is created, controlled, and distributed. The new classification identifies four major types of media: paid, owned, earned, and shared (POES):

Paid media—promotional channels paid for by the marketer, including traditional media (such as TV, radio, print, or outdoor) and online and digital media (paid search ads, Web and social media display ads, mobile ads, or e-mail marketing).

Owned media—promotional channels owned and controlled by the company, including company Web sites, corporate blogs, owned social media pages, proprietary brand communities, sales forces, and events.

Earned media—PR media channels, such as television, newspapers, blogs, online video sites, and other media not directly paid for or controlled by the marketer but that include the content because of viewer, reader, or user interest.

Shared media—media shared by consumers with other consumers, such as social media, blogs, mobile media, and viral channels, as well as traditional word-of-mouth.

In the past, advertisers have focused on traditional paid (broadcast, print) or earned (public relations) media. Now, however, content marketers are rapidly adding the new digital generation of owned (Web sites, blogs, brand communities) and shared (online social, mobile, e-mail) media. Whereas a successful paid ad used to be an end in itself, marketers are now developing integrated marketing content that leverages the combined power of all the POES channels. Thus, many TV ads often aren't just TV ads any more. They're "video content" you might see anywhere—on a TV screen but also on a tablet or phone. Other video content looks a lot like TV advertising but was never intended for TV, such as made-for-online videos posted on Web sites or social media. Similarly, printed brand messages and pictures no longer appear only in carefully crafted magazine ads or catalogs. Instead, such content, created by a variety of sources, pops up in anything from formal ads and online brand pages to mobile and social media and independent blogs.

The new "content marketing" campaigns look a lot different from the old "advertising" campaigns. For example, to move beyond its long-running, traditional "Intel Inside" advertising, Intel recently teamed with computer maker Toshiba to produce an award-winning social media film series, called "Inside." Enlisting the talents of Hollywood directors and actors, the engaging series blurs the lines between advertising, social media, and entertainment. The most recent series, a comedy/Sci-Fi adventure called "The Power Inside," chronicles the efforts of a Scooby-Doo squad of twenty-somethings to foil the plans of aliens

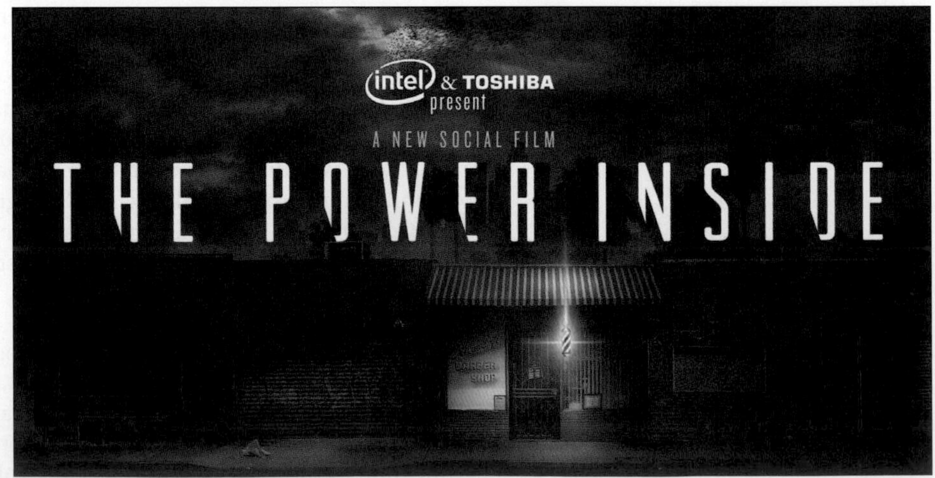

Content marketing: Intel's and Toshiba's award-winning "Inside" social media film series blurs the line between advertising, social media, and entertainment, creating high levels of customer–brand engagement for the two brands.

Courtesy Intel and Toshiba American Information Systems, Inc.

intent on taking over the world by disguising themselves as mustaches and unibrows. Intel-powered Toshiba Ultrabooks play a central role, but the subtle product placement doesn't come across as an ad.

"The Power Inside" was released in six episodes on YouTube, with traffic driven through Facebook and Twitter (shared media), a dedicated microsite (owned media), and ads placed on Skype and Spotify (paid media). Awareness and popularity of the series were driven higher by mentions and articles in independent blogs and the press (earned media). "The Power Inside" earned even more publicity when its launch coincided perfectly with the awarding of a Daytime Emmy and the coveted Cannes Grand Prix award to the previous Intel/Toshiba series, "The Beauty Inside." In all, the integrated, multi-platform content marketing campaign created high levels of customer-brand engagement for the two brands.

Careful integration across the POES channels can produce striking communications results. Consider Samsung's "Life's a Photo. Take It." campaign to launch its Web-connected Galaxy Camera in 18 regions worldwide. To show how easily images taken by the camera can be shared instantly anytime, anyplace, Samsung chose 32 prominent Instagramers ("the world's most social photographers") and challenged them to use the new camera to prove that their cities—from London, Amsterdam, Berlin, Madrid, and Milan to Paris, Sydney, and San Francisco—were the most photogenic in the world. Their photos were uploaded to Tumblr, and fans voted for their favorites via Tumblr, Facebook, Twitter, and Pinterest. The winning city—Berlin—hosted a massive final event, where influencers invited from across Europe took photos with the connected camera and saw them projected onto giant, inflatable, 3D projection cubes.

The "Life's a Photo. Take It." campaign, with its rich mix of marketing content, was an unqualified success. During its three-month run, the campaign reached more than 79 million people worldwide. Awareness of the Galaxy Camera rose 58 percent; purchase intent jumped 115 percent. The campaign won a 2013 Interactive Advertising Bureau MIXX award for content marketing, sparking a flurry of additional publicity. Finally, the social media campaign served as a foundation for a series of paid television ads. In the end, Samsung reignited a product category that many considered to be waning—dedicated digital cameras—and became the market leader in Web-connected digital imaging.

So, we can't just call it "advertising" anymore. Today's shifting and sometimes chaotic marketing communications environment calls for more than simply creating and placing ads in well-defined and controlled media spaces. Rather, today's marketing communicators must be marketing content strategists, creators, connectors, and catalysts who manage brand conversations with and among customers and help those conversations catch fire across a fluid mix of channels. That's a tall order, but with today's new thinking, anything is POES–ible!

Sources: Randall Rothenberg, "What Is Advertising Anyway?" *Ad Week*, September 16, 2013, p. 15; Joan Voight, "Intel and Toshiba Peddle Product Placement in Branded Film 'The Power Inside,'" *Ad Week*, July 29, 2013, www.adweek.com/print/151476; Peter Himler, "Paid, Earned & Owned: Revisited," *The Flack*, June 21, 2011, http://flatironcomm.com/2011/06/paid-earned-owned-revisited/; Paul Nolan, "The C Word: What Is Content Marketing," *Sales & Marketing Management*, January/February 2014; "Samsung's Galaxy Camera," 2013 AIB MIXX Awards Winners Gallery, www.iab.net/mixxawards/gallery2013/strategies-and-objectives/content-marketing.html; http://samsungcamera.tumblr.com/latest; "Life's a Photo, Take It," Jam, www.spreadingjam.com/our-work/samsung/life-s-a-photo-take-it, accessed September 2014; and "'Life's a Photo. Take It'—Campaign Overview," *Vice*, www.vice.com/sgc/lifes-a-photo-take-it-campaign-overview, accessed September 2014.

communications ties together all of the company's messages and images. Its television and print ads have the same brand message as its e-mail and personal selling communications. And its PR materials are consistent with Web site, online, social media, and mobile marketing content.

FIGURE | 14.1
Integrated Marketing Communications

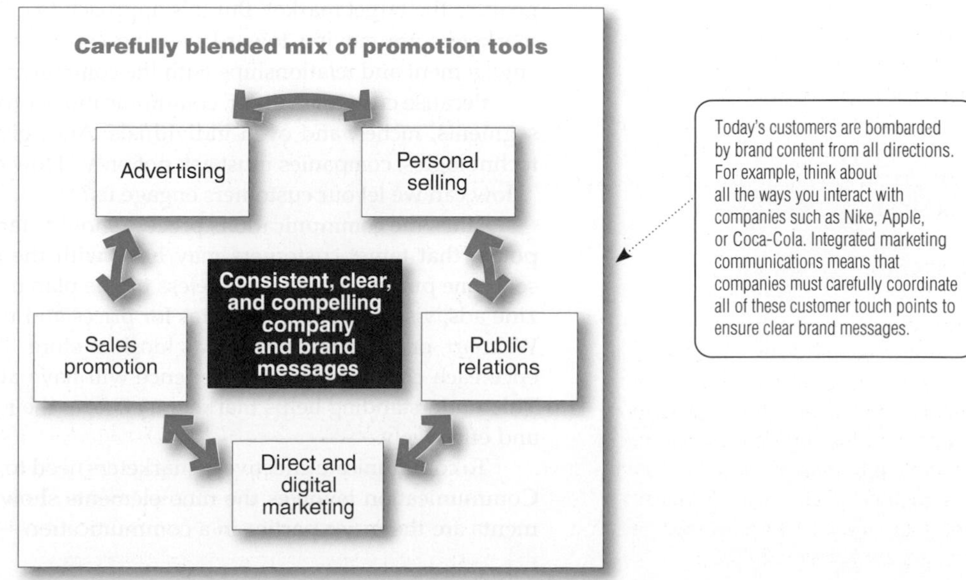
Carefully blended mix of promotion tools
Advertising
Personal selling
Consistent, clear, and compelling company and brand messages
Sales promotion
Public relations
Direct and digital marketing
Today's customers are bombarded by brand content from all directions. For example, think about all the ways you interact with companies such as Nike, Apple, or Coca-Cola. Integrated marketing communications means that companies must carefully coordinate all of these customer touch points to ensure clear brand messages.

Often, different media play unique roles in engaging, informing, and persuading consumers. For example, a recent study showed that more than two-thirds of advertisers and their agencies are planning video ad campaigns that stretch across multiple viewing platforms, such as traditional TV and digital, mobile, and social media. Such *digital video ad convergence*, as it's called, combines TV's core strength—vast reach—with digital's better targeting, interaction, and engagement.[7] These varied media and roles must be carefully coordinated under the overall marketing communications plan.

A great example of a well-integrated marketing communications effort is Coca-Cola's recent "Mirage" campaign. Built around two Super Bowl XLVII ads, the campaign integrated the clout of traditional big-budget TV advertising with the interactive power of social media to create real-time customer engagement with the Coke brand:[8]

> Coca-Cola's "Mirage" tells the story of three bands of desert vagabonds—Cowboys, Showgirls, and *Mad Max*-inspired "Badlanders"—as they trek through the blazing-hot desert pursuing the same elusive mirage—a frosty bottle of Coca-Cola. The Mirage campaign began two weeks before the Super Bowl with a 30-second teaser ad on *American Idol* and posted on YouTube and other online destinations inviting fans to visit CokeChase.com to get to know the story and teams. Then, during the big game, a 60-second Mirage ad set up the exciting chase, with a cliff-hanging close that urged viewers to visit CokeChase.com, where they could help decide the outcome by casting votes for their favorite team and throwing obstacles in front of rival teams. During the rest of the game, Coca-Cola listening teams monitored related activity on major social media, and put fans in the middle of the action by posting real-time chase updates on Facebook, YouTube, and Twitter and chase photos on Tumblr and Instagram. After the end of the game, a second Mirage ad announced the chase team with the most viewer votes—the Showgirls, in their glam pink and silver outfits, won the Coke. But the real winner was Coca-Cola. The Mirage campaign exceeded all expectations. In addition to the usual huge Super Bowl audience numbers, during the game, the campaign captured an eye-popping 8.2 million online and social-media interactions and 910,000 votes, far exceeding the brand's internal goals of 1.6 million interactions and 400,000 votes.

In the past, no one person or department was responsible for thinking through the communication roles of the various promotion tools and coordinating the promotion mix. To help implement integrated marketing communications, some companies have appointed a marketing communications director who has overall responsibility for the company's communications efforts. This helps to produce better communications consistency and greater sales impact. It places the responsibility in someone's hands—where none existed before—to unify the company's image as it is shaped by thousands of company activities.

Author Comment | To develop effective marketing communications, you must first understand the general communication process.

A View of the Communication Process

Integrated marketing communications involves identifying the target audience and shaping a well-coordinated promotional program to obtain the desired audience response. Too often, marketing communications focus on immediate awareness, image, or preference goals in the target market. But this approach to communication is too shortsighted. Today, marketers are moving toward viewing communications *as* managing ongoing customer engagement and relationships with the company and its brands.

Because customers differ, communications programs need to be developed for specific segments, niches, and even individuals. And, given today's interactive communications technologies, companies must ask not only "How can we engage our customers?" but also "How can we let our customers engage us?"

Thus, the communications process should start with an audit of all the potential touch points that target customers may have with the company and its brands. For example, someone purchasing a new wireless phone plan may talk to others, see television or magazine ads, visit various online sites for prices and reviews, and check out plans at Best Buy, Walmart, or a wireless provider's kiosk or store. The marketer needs to assess what influence each communication experience will have at different stages of the buying process. This understanding helps marketers allocate their communication dollars more efficiently and effectively.

To communicate effectively, marketers need to understand how communication works. Communication involves the nine elements shown in **Figure 14.2**. Two of these elements are the major parties in a communication—the *sender* and the *receiver*. Another two

FIGURE | 14.2
Elements in the Communication Process

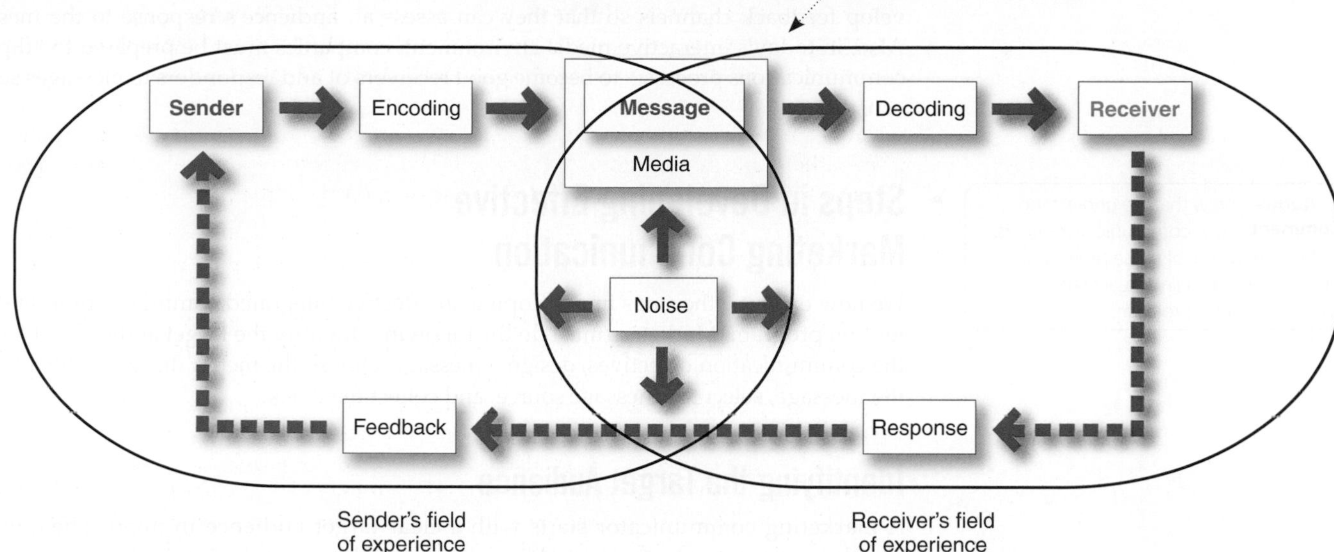
There is a lot going on in this figure! For example, apply this model to McDonald's. To create great advertising—such as its long-running "i'm lovin' it" campaign—McDonald's must thoroughly understand its customers and how communication works.
Sender
Encoding
Message
Media
Decoding
Receiver
Noise
Feedback
Response
Sender's field of experience
Receiver's field of experience

are the major communication tools—the *message* and the *media*. Four more are major communication functions—*encoding*, *decoding*, *response*, and *feedback*. The last element is *noise* in the system. Definitions of these elements follow and are applied to a McDonald's "i'm lovin' it" television commercial.

- *Sender.* The *party sending the message* to another party—here, McDonald's.
- *Encoding.* The process of *putting thought into symbolic form*—for example, McDonald's ad agency assembles words, sounds, and illustrations into a TV advertisement that will convey the intended message.
- *Message.* The *set of symbols* that the sender transmits—the actual McDonald's ad.
- *Media.* The *communication channels* through which the message moves from the sender to the receiver—in this case, television and the specific television programs that McDonald's selects.
- *Decoding.* The process by which the receiver *assigns meaning to the symbols* encoded by the sender—a consumer watches the McDonald's commercial and interprets the words and images it contains.
- *Receiver.* The *party receiving the message* sent by another party—the customer who watches the McDonald's ad.
- *Response.* The *reactions of the receiver* after being exposed to the message—any of hundreds of possible responses, such as the consumer likes McDonald's better, is more likely to eat at McDonald's next time, hums the "i'm lovin' it" jingle, or does nothing.
- *Feedback.* The part of the *receiver's response communicated back to the sender*—McDonald's research shows that consumers are either struck by and remember the ad or they write or call McDonald's, praising or criticizing the ad or its products.
- *Noise.* The *unplanned static or distortion* during the communication process, which results in the receiver getting a different message than the one the sender sent—the consumer is distracted while watching the commercial and misses its key points.

For a message to be effective, the sender's encoding process must mesh with the receiver's decoding process. The best messages consist of words and other symbols that are familiar to the receiver. The more the sender's field of experience overlaps with that of the receiver, the more effective the message is likely to be. Marketing communicators may not always *share* the customer's field of experience. For example, an advertising copywriter from one socioeconomic level might create ads for customers from another level—say, wealthy business owners. However, to communicate effectively, the marketing communicator must *understand* the customer's field of experience.

This model points out several key factors in good communication. Senders need to know what audiences they wish to reach and what responses they want. They must be good at encoding messages that take into account how the target audience decodes them. They must send messages through media that reach target audiences, and they must develop feedback channels so that they can assess an audience's response to the message. Also, in today's interactive media environment, companies must be prepared to "flip" the communications process—to become good receivers of and responders to messages sent by consumers.

Author Comment | Now that we understand how communication works, it's time to turn all of those promotion mix elements into an actual marketing communications program.

Steps in Developing Effective Marketing Communication

We now examine the steps in developing an effective integrated communications and promotion program. Marketers must do the following: Identify the target audience, determine the communication objectives, design a message, choose the media through which to send the message, select the message source, and collect feedback.

Identifying the Target Audience

A marketing communicator starts with a clear target audience in mind. The audience may be current users or potential buyers, those who make the buying decision or those who influence it. The audience may be individuals, groups, special publics, or the general public. The target audience will heavily affect the communicator's decisions on *what* will be said, *how* it will be said, *when* it will be said, *where* it will be said, and *who* will say it.

Determining the Communication Objectives

Buyer-readiness stages
The stages consumers normally pass through on their way to a purchase: awareness, knowledge, liking, preference, conviction, and, finally, the actual purchase.

Once the target audience has been defined, marketers must determine the desired response. Of course, in many cases, they will seek a *purchase* response. But purchase may result only after a lengthy consumer decision-making process. The marketing communicator needs to know where the target audience now stands and to what stage it needs to be moved. The target audience may be in any of six **buyer-readiness stages**, the stages consumers normally pass through on their way to making a purchase. These stages are *awareness*, *knowledge*, *liking*, *preference*, *conviction*, and *purchase* (see **Figure 14.3**).

The marketing communicator's target market may be totally unaware of the product, know only its name, or know only a few things about it. Thus, the marketer must first build *awareness* and *knowledge*. For example, to introduce consumers to its innovative new Microsoft Surface tablet, Microsoft spent an estimated $190 million on marketing in only the first 10 months. The current campaign introduces the Surface 2 tablet as the "One device for everything in your life"—it's lighter and thinner than a laptop but with a click-in keyboard and fuller features than competing tablets. The extensive introductory campaign used a broad range of traditional, digital, mobile, social, and in-store media to quickly create awareness and knowledge across the entire market.[9]

Assuming that target consumers *know* about a product, how do they *feel* about it? Once potential buyers know about Microsoft's Surface tablet, marketers want to move them through successively stronger stages of feelings toward the model. These stages include *liking* (feeling favorable about the Surface), *preference* (preferring the Surface to competing tablets), and *conviction* (believing that the Surface is the best tablet for them).

A goal of marketing in general, and of marketing communications in particular, is to move target customers through the buying process. Once again, it all starts with understanding customer needs and wants.

FIGURE | 14.3
Buyer-Readiness Stages

One device
for everything
in your life.
surface.com
The new Surface is lighter, thinner and much more than a tablet. With an available click-in keyboard and Microsoft Office, you can multi-task like a pro. It's all you need to get it all done.
Start
Surface
Microsoft

Moving customers through the buyer-readiness stages: Microsoft used an extensive $190 million marketing campaign to create awareness and knowledge for its innovative new Microsoft Surface tablet.

Microsoft

Microsoft Surface marketers use a combination of promotion mix tools to create positive feelings and conviction. Initial TV commercials help build anticipation and an emotional brand connection. Images and videos on the Microsoft Surface's YouTube, Facebook, and Pinterest pages engage potential buyers and demonstrate the product's use and features. Press releases and other PR activities help keep the buzz going about the product. A packed microsite (microsoft.com/surface) provides additional information and buying opportunities.

Finally, some members of the target market might be convinced about the product but not quite get around to making the *purchase*. The communicator must lead these consumers to take the final step. To help reluctant consumers over such hurdles, Microsoft might offer buyers special promotional prices and upgrades, and support the product with comments and reviews from customers at its Web and social media sites and elsewhere.

Of course, marketing communications alone cannot create positive feelings and purchases for the Surface. The product itself must provide superior value for the customer. In fact, outstanding marketing communications can actually speed the demise of a poor product. The more quickly potential buyers learn about a poor product, the more quickly they become aware of its faults. Thus, good marketing communications call for "good deeds followed by good words."

Designing a Message

Having defined the desired audience response, the communicator then turns to developing an effective message. Ideally, the message should get *attention*, hold *interest*, arouse *desire*, and obtain *action* (a framework known as the *AIDA model*). In practice, few messages take the consumer all the way from awareness to purchase, but the AIDA framework suggests the desirable qualities of a good message.

When putting a message together, the marketing communicator must decide what to say (*message content*) and how to say it (*message structure* and *format*).

Message Content

The marketer has to figure out an appeal or theme that will produce the desired response. There are three types of appeals: rational, emotional, and moral. *Rational appeals* relate to the audience's self-interest. They show that the product will produce the desired benefits. Examples are messages showing a product's quality, economy, value, or performance. Thus, an ad for Aleve makes this matter-of-fact claim: "More pills doesn't mean more pain relief. Aleve has the strength to keep back, body, and arthritis pain away all day with fewer pills than Tylenol." And a Weight Watchers' ad states this simple fact: "The diet secret to end all diet secrets is that there is no diet secret."

Emotional appeals attempt to stir up either negative or positive emotions that can motivate purchase. Communicators may use emotional appeals ranging from love, joy, and humor to fear and guilt. Advocates of emotional messages claim that they attract more attention and create more belief in the sponsor and the brand. The idea is that consumers often feel before they think, and persuasion is emotional in nature.

Good storytelling in a commercial often strikes an emotional chord. For example, Anheuser-Busch aired two emotional Budweiser commercials during Super Bowl XLVIII. The first ad, called "Puppy Love," portrayed the special, heart-warming relationship between a Budweiser Clydesdale and a puppy, who were separated and then reunited. The second commercial, another tears-of-joy affair called "A Hero's Welcome," recounted a Budweiser-arranged welcome home for a young American soldier, complete with a home-town parade and a ride on the famed Clydesdale-drawn Budweiser wagon. Neither commercial said anything at all about the qualities of Budweiser beer. But both ads made deep emotional connections between the Budweiser brand and viewers.

Emotional appeals: Budweiser's top-rated "Puppy Love" Super Bowl commercial said nothing at all about the qualities of Budweiser beer. But it made deep emotional connections between the Budweiser brand and viewers.

Associated Press

"Puppy Love" rated a clear number one in the *USA Today* Ad Meter Rankings and was shared online more than 1.3 million times by the morning following the Super Bowl. Within two months, it had chalked up nearly 50 million YouTube views. Similarly, "A Hero's Welcome" placed third in the Ad Metter rankings and grabbed another 9 million YouTube views. Moreover, both ads were rated by one source among the top-five Super Bowl XLVIII ads based on attributes such as persuasion, relevance, information, attention, change, desire, and watchability.[10]

Moral appeals are directed to an audience's sense of what is "right" and "proper." They are often used to urge people to support social causes, such as a cleaner environment or aid to the disadvantaged. For example, the United Way's Live United campaign urges people to give back to their communities—to "Live United. Make a difference. Help create opportunities for everyone in your community." An EarthShare ad urges environmental involvement by reminding people that "We live in the house we all build. Every decision we make has consequences. . . . We choose the world we live in, so make the right choices. . . ."

Message Structure

Marketers must also decide how to handle three message structure issues. The first is whether to draw a conclusion or leave it to the audience. Research suggests that, in many cases, rather than drawing a conclusion, the advertiser is better off asking questions and letting buyers come to their own conclusions.

The second message structure issue is whether to present the strongest arguments first or last. Presenting them first gets strong attention but may lead to an anticlimactic ending.

The third message structure issue is whether to present a one-sided argument (mentioning only the product's strengths) or a two-sided argument (touting the product's strengths while also admitting its shortcomings). Usually, a one-sided argument is more effective in sales presentations—except when audiences are highly educated or likely to hear opposing claims or when the communicator has a negative association to overcome. In this spirit, Heinz ran the message "Heinz Ketchup is slow good," and Listerine ran the message "Listerine tastes bad twice a day." In such cases, two-sided messages can enhance an advertiser's credibility and make buyers more resistant to competitor attacks.

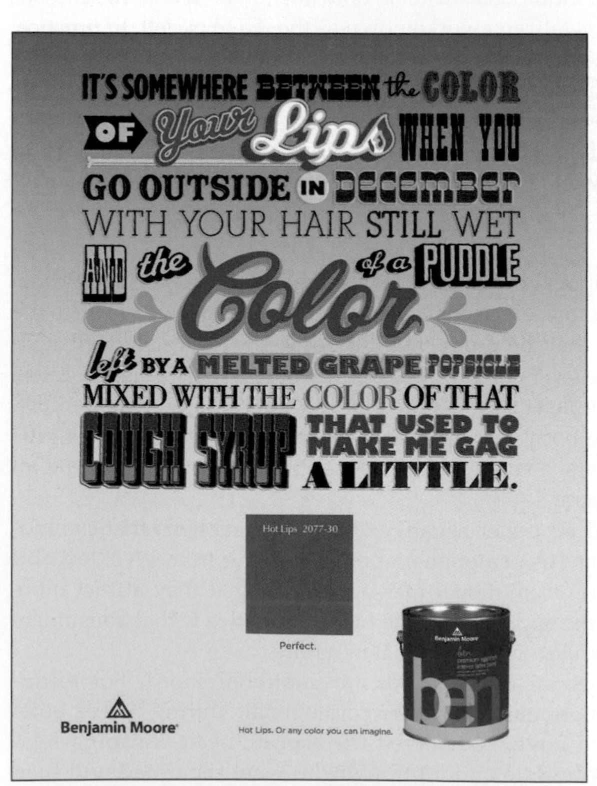

Message format: To attract attention and engage customers, marketers can use novelty and contrast, eye-catching headlines, and distinctive formats, as in this Benjamin Moore ad.

Courtesy of Benjamin Moore Paints

Message Format

The marketing communicator also needs a strong *format* for the message. In a print ad, the communicator has to decide on the headline, copy, illustration, and colors. To attract attention, advertisers can use novelty and contrast; eye-catching pictures and headlines; distinctive formats; message size and position; and color, shape, and movement. For example, striking Benjamin Moore paint ads consist mostly of a single long headline in mixed fonts balanced against a color swatch and background that illustrate the color discussed in the headline. One ad describes Benjamin Moore's Hot Lips paint color this way: "It's somewhere between the color of your lips when you go outside in December with your hair still wet and the color of a puddle left by a melted grape popsicle mixed with the color of that cough syrup that used to make me gag a little. Hot lips. Perfect."

Presenters plan every detail carefully, from start to finish. If the message is to be communicated by television or video, the communicator must incorporate motion, pace, and sound. If the message is carried on the product or its package, the communicator must watch texture, scent, color, size, and shape. For example, color alone can enhance message recognition for a brand. One study suggests that color increases brand recognition by up to 80 percent—think about Target (red), McDonald's (yellow and red), John Deere (green and yellow), Twitter (blue), or UPS (brown). Thus, in designing effective marketing communications, marketers must consider color and other seemingly unimportant details carefully.

Choosing Communication Channels and Media

The communicator must now select the *channels of communication*. There are two broad types of communication channels: *personal* and *nonpersonal*.

Personal Communication Channels

Personal communication channels
Channels through which two or more people communicate directly with each other, including face to face, on the phone, via mail or e-mail, or even through an Internet "chat."

In **personal communication channels**, two or more people communicate directly with each other. They might communicate face to face, on the phone, via mail or e-mail, or even through texting or an Internet chat. Personal communication channels are effective because they allow for personal addressing and feedback.

Some personal communication channels are controlled directly by the company. For example, company salespeople contact business buyers. But other personal communications about the product may reach buyers through channels not directly controlled by the company. These channels might include independent experts—consumer advocates, bloggers, and others—making statements to buyers. Or they might be neighbors, friends, family members, associates, or other consumers talking to target buyers, in person or via social media or other interactive media. This last channel, **word-of-mouth influence**, has considerable effect in many product areas.

Word-of-mouth influence
Personal communications about a product between target buyers and neighbors, friends, family members, and associates.

Personal influence carries great weight, especially for products that are expensive, risky, or highly visible. One survey found that recommendations from friends and family are far and away the most powerful influence on consumers worldwide: More than 50 percent of consumers said friends and family are the number one influence on their awareness and purchase. Another study found that 90 percent of customers trust recommendations from people they know and 70 percent trust consumer opinions posted online, whereas trust in ads runs from a high of about 62 percent to less than 24 percent, depending on the medium.[11] Is it any wonder, then, that few consumers buy a big-ticket item before checking out what existing users have to say about the product at a site such as Amazon.com? Who hasn't made an Amazon purchase based on another customer's review or the "Customers who bought this also bought . . ." section; or decided against purchase because of negative customer reviews?

Buzz marketing
Cultivating opinion leaders and getting them to spread information about a product or a service to others in their communities.

Companies can take steps to put personal communication channels to work for them. For example, as we discussed in Chapter 5, they can create *opinion leaders* for their brands—people whose opinions are sought by others—by supplying influencers with the product on attractive terms or by educating them so that they can inform others. **Buzz marketing** involves cultivating opinion leaders and getting them to spread information about a product or a service to others in their communities. For example, Ford's successful and long-running Fiesta Movement campaign hands out Fiestas to selected consumers, turning them into "Fiesta Agents." These brand ambassadors then create buzz by sharing their experiences via blogs, tweets, Facebook updates, YouTube videos, and other social media interactions.[12]

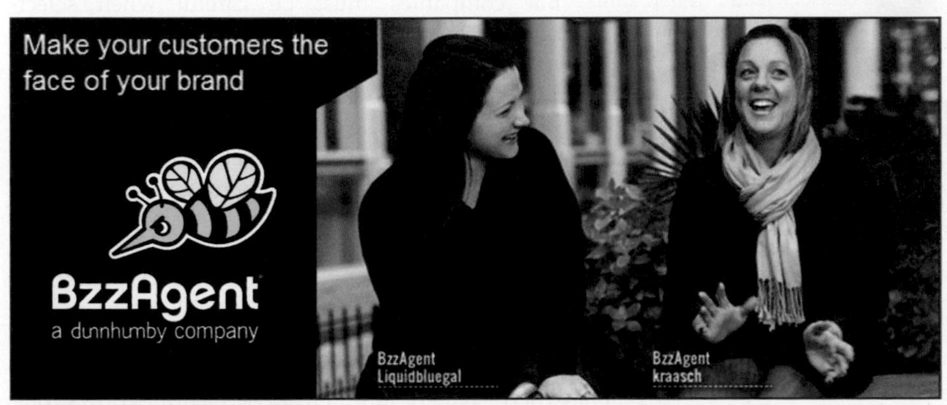

Buzz marketing: Social marketing firm BzzAgent turns a brand's actual users into influential brand advocates.
dunnhumby

Social marketing firm BzzAgent takes a different approach to creating buzz. It creates customers for a client brand, then turns them into influential brand advocates:[13]

> BzzAgent has assembled a volunteer army of natural-born buzzers, millions of actual shoppers around the world who are highly active in social media

and who love to talk about and recommend products. Once a client signs on, BzzAgent searches its database and selects "agents" that fit the profiles of the product's target customers. Selected volunteers receive product samples, creating a personal brand experience. BzzAgent then urges the agents to share their honest opinions of the product through face-to-face conversations and via tweets, Facebook posts, online photo and video sharing, blogs, and other social sharing venues. If the product is good, the positive word of mouth spreads quickly. If the product is iffy—well, that's worth learning quickly as well. BzzAgent advocates have successfully buzzed the brands of hundreds of top marketing companies, from P&G, Nestle, Coca-Cola, and Estee Lauder to Kroger, Disney, and Dunkin' Donuts. BzzAgent's appeal is its authenticity. The agents aren't scripted. Instead, the company tells its advocates, "Here's the product; if you believe in it, say whatever you think. Bzz is no place for excessive, repetitive, or unauthentic posts."

Nonpersonal Communication Channels

Nonpersonal communication channels
Media that carry messages without personal contact or feedback, including major media, atmospheres, and events.

Nonpersonal communication channels are media that carry messages without personal contact or feedback. They include major media, atmospheres, and events. Major *media* include print media (newspapers, magazines, direct mail), broadcast media (television, radio), display media (billboards, signs, posters), and online media (e-mail and company Web sites). *Atmospheres* are designed environments that create or reinforce the buyer's leanings toward buying a product. Thus, lawyers' offices and banks are designed to communicate confidence and other qualities that might be valued by clients. *Events* are staged occurrences that communicate messages to target audiences. For example, public relations departments arrange grand openings, shows and exhibits, public tours, and other events.

Nonpersonal communication affects buyers directly. In addition, using mass media often affects buyers indirectly by causing more personal communication. For example, communications might first flow from television, magazines, and other mass media to opinion leaders and then from these opinion leaders to others. Thus, opinion leaders step between the mass media and their audiences and carry messages to people who are less exposed to media. Interestingly, marketers often use nonpersonal communication channels to replace or stimulate personal communications by embedding consumer endorsements or word-of-mouth testimonials in their ads and other promotions.

Selecting the Message Source

In either personal or nonpersonal communication, the message's impact also depends on how the target audience views the communicator. Messages delivered by highly credible sources are more persuasive. Thus, many food companies promote to doctors, dentists, and other health-care providers to motivate these professionals to recommend specific food products to their patients. And marketers hire celebrity endorsers—well-known athletes, actors, musicians, and even cartoon characters—to deliver their messages. ● A host of NBA superstars lend their images to brands such as Nike, McDonald's, and Coca-Cola. Taylor Swift endorses Diet Coke, Keds, and CoverGirl, and Beyoncé endorses Pepsi and L'Oréal, among other brands.

● **Using celebrity endorsers to represent brands—Beyoncé speaks for Pepsi.**

Pepsi-Cola North America, Inc.

But companies must be careful when selecting celebrities to represent their brands. Picking the wrong spokesperson can result in embarrassment and a tarnished image. For example, a dozen or more big brands—including Nike, Anheuser-Busch, Radio Shack, Oakley, Trek bikes, and Giro helmets—faced embarrassment when pro cyclist Lance Armstrong was stripped of his Tour de France titles and banned for life from competitive cycling for illegal use of performance-enhancing drugs. Previously considered a model brand spokesman, Armstrong once earned nearly $20 million in endorsement income in a single year. "Arranged marriages between brands and celebrities are inherently risky," notes one expert. "Ninety-nine percent of celebrities do a strong job for their brand partners," says another, "and 1 percent goes off the rails."[14] More than ever, it's important to pick the right celebrity for the brand (see Real Marketing 14.2).

Real Marketing 14.2 Celebrity Endorsers: Finding the Right Celebrity for the Brand

Ever since Red Rock Cola hired baseball legend Babe Ruth to endorse its soft drink in the late 1930s, companies have been paying big bucks to have their products associated with big-name celebrities. Brands seek an endorser's "halo effect"—the positive association that surrounds a product after a popular celebrity has pitched it.

As evidence of the popularity of celebrities in today's marketing, check out recent Super Bowl advertising. Over the past few years, big-budget Super Bowl ads have showcased stars ranging from Jerry Seinfeld (Acura), Clint Eastwood (Chrysler), Kim Kardashian (Skechers), and Elton John (Pepsi) to Stephen Colbert (Wonderful Pistachios), John Stamos (Dannon), Ben Kingsley (Jaguar), Arnold Schwarzenegger (Anheuser-Busch), Scarlett Johansson (Soda Stream), and a host of others.

Celebrity endorsements are big business, for both the brands and the endorsers. For example, Nike spends an estimated half-billion dollars a year to pay celebrities to hawk its goods. But the payoff appears to be well worth the price. For example, Nike's Jordan Brand subsidiary (Air Jordan currently sponsors 19 active NBA players, including Chris Paul, Carmelo Anthony, and Ray Allen) enjoys annual revenues topping $1 billion and reaps a 58 percent share of the U.S. basketball shoe market, outselling even parent company Nike, a distant number two with 34 percent. In turn, even though he hasn't played professional basketball in over a decade, Michael Jordan earns $80 million annually from endorsement deals with Nike (worth $60 million by itself), Gatorade, Hanes, and other big brands.

However, although linking up with the right celebrity can add substantial appeal to a brand, using celebrities doesn't guarantee success. For example, according to one study, ads with celebrities are on average 3 percent less effective than ads without them. "During last year's Super Bowl," says an analyst, "ads without celebrities performed 9.2 percent better than those with celebrities." In fact, "ads with animals performed 21 percent better than ads with celebrities." Moreover, celebrity partnerships can create difficulties. When a major celebrity deal turns sour, or when a celebrity falls from grace, it can tarnish rather than enhance a brand's image.

Despite the potential pitfalls, however, celebrity endorsements are bigger today than ever. By one estimate, celebrities now appear in roughly one-fifth of all ads. In fact, the age-old technique is moving into dynamic new areas, in line with the social media revolution. Beyond simply employing celebs as brand icons or ad spokespeople, many marketers are putting them squarely in the middle of consumers' social dialogue. For example, Twitter is now at the center of a new celebrity endorsement revolution.

Nowhere was that more evident than at the 2014 Academy Awards. Host Ellen DeGeneres used a Samsung Galaxy Note 3 phone to tweet out selfies to her 25 million followers (Samsung was a major sponsor of the Oscars for the fifth year in a row). The most famous moment, called by some the "best selfie ever," featured DeGeneres, Kevin Spacey, Angelina Jolie, Brad Pitt, Julia Roberts, Meryl Streep, Bradley Cooper, Channing Tatum, and Jennifer Lawrence. The tweet shattered President Obama's election-night photo record with 2.7 million re-tweets, crashing the Twitter network. Samsung sponsored 10 tweets from DeGeneres that night as well as donating $1.5 million each to two of Ellen's charities of choice. And on Ellen DeGeneres's talk show the next day, everyone in the audience received a brand new Samsung Galaxy Note 3.

Such sponsored tweets have become the latest celebrity endorsement rage as top Twitter personalities post brand-related plugs to their followers. Less popular celebrities such as Lance Bass get paid as little as $650 per sponsored tweet. But top stars like Kim Kardashian routinely pull in as much as $20,000 for quips like, "Pregnancy lips . . . @ EOS to the rescue! LOL," accompanied by a photo of her using EOS lip balm. At the other extreme, P&G struck a deal with Kevin Jonas for rights to announce news of the birth of the pop singer's first daughter, as well as distributing the first baby picture via the Dreft detergent Twitter feed and Facebook page.

Having celebrities tweet about a brand can add instant interest to the message. But many marketers question the effectiveness of this latest celebrity endorsement trend. For starters, only about 9.5 percent of U.S. adults even use Twitter, and only a fraction of those follow a given celebrity. And by itself, the brief, "drive-by" nature of the typical Twitter campaign isn't likely to build a long-term celebrity–brand relationship or have much brand-building impact. Still, as with many other promotional efforts today, marketers are

Celebrity endorsers: Academy Awards host Ellen DeGeneres used a Samsung Galaxy Note 3 phone to tweet out epic selfies to her 25 million followers. One was retweeted a record 2.7 million times, crashing the Twitter network.

Associated Press

working feverishly to make more effective use of celebrities in social media.

The success of celebrity endorsements seems to come down to matching the right celebrity with the right brand. Too often, endorsement deals come off to consumers as offhand paid commercial pairings of the celebrity and the brand. For example, a recent music video ad for Hot Pockets microwavable sandwiches featuring Snoop Dogg rapping to Kate Upton and Larry King left audiences mystified. But a Kardashian sister tweeting about cosmetic products is a no-brainer. And there's perhaps no better endorsement fit than professional athletes and the shoes they wear. After Lebron James won his second NBA title with the Miami Heat, sales of his signature Nike shoes rose by 50 percent.

The best use of celebrities requires that kind of authenticity. Thanks to success stories like Nike's, although the whos and hows might change to fit the shifting marketing communications environment, celebrity power will likely remain an important element in the marketing of many brands. "We live in a celebrity-crazed culture," concludes one analyst. "Advertisers will never abandon them."

Sources: Kurt Badenhausen, "How Michael Jordan Still Earns $80 Million a Year," *Forbes*, February 14, 2013, www.forbes.com/sites/kurtbadenhausen/2013/02/14/how-michael-jordan-still-earns-80-million-a-year/; Liat Kornowski, "Celebrity Sponsored Tweets: What the Stars Get Paid for Advertising in 140 Characters," *Huffington Post*, May 30, 2013, www.huffingtonpost.com/2013/05/30/celebrity-sponsored-tweets_n_3360562.html; Abby Johnson, "Super Bowl Commercials: What Makes Them Effective?" *WebProNews,* January 31, 2012, http://www.webpronews.com/super-bowl-commercials-what-makes-them-effective-2012-01; Joyce Chen, "Snoop Dogg, Kate Upton Join Together for Trippy Hot Pockets Music Video Ad," *Us Weekly*, October 8, 2013, www.usmagazine.com/celebrity-news/news/snoop-dogg-kate-upton-join-together-for-trippy-hot-pockets-music-video-ad-2013810; Lucia Moses, "Why Celebrity Weeklies Should Worry about Dreft's Baby Notice,"*Adweek*, February 4, 2014, www.adweek.com/news/advertising-branding/why-celebrity-weekies-should-worry-about-drefts-baby-notice-155467; and James Nye, "Psst, Don't Tell Samsung: Ellen Uses Oscar Sponsor's Galaxy for Her Onstage Stunts," *Mail Online*, March 3, 2014, www.dailymail.co.uk/news/article-2572343/.

Collecting Feedback

After sending the message or other brand content, the communicator must research its effect on the target audience. This involves asking target audience members whether they remember the content, how many times they saw it, what points they recall, how they felt about the content, and their past and present attitudes toward the brand and company. The communicator would also like to measure behavior resulting from the content—how many people bought the product, talked to others about it, or visited the store.

Feedback on marketing communications may suggest changes in the promotion program or in the product offer itself. For example, Macy's uses television and newspaper advertising to inform area consumers about its stores, services, and merchandising events. Suppose feedback research shows that 80 percent of all shoppers in an area recall seeing the store's ads and are aware of its merchandise and sales. Sixty percent of these aware shoppers have visited a Macy's store in the past month, but only 20 percent of those who visited were satisfied with the shopping experience.

These results suggest that although promotion is creating *awareness*, Macy's stores aren't giving consumers the *satisfaction* they expect. Therefore, Macy's needs to improve the shopping experience while staying with the successful communications program. In contrast, suppose research shows that only 40 percent of area consumers are aware of the store's merchandise and events, only 30 percent of those aware have shopped recently, but 80 percent of those who have shopped return soon to shop again. In this case, Macy's needs to strengthen its promotion program to take advantage of its power to create customer satisfaction in the store.

Author Comment In this section, we'll look at the promotion budget-setting process and at how marketers blend the various marketing communication tools into a smooth-functioning integrated promotion mix.

Setting the Total Promotion Budget and Mix

We have looked at the steps in planning and sending communications to a target audience. But how does the company determine its total *promotion budget* and the division among the major promotional tools to create the *promotion mix*? By what process does it blend the tools to create integrated marketing communications? We now look at these questions.

Setting the Total Promotion Budget

One of the hardest marketing decisions facing a company is how much to spend on promotion. John Wanamaker, the department store magnate, once said, "I know that half

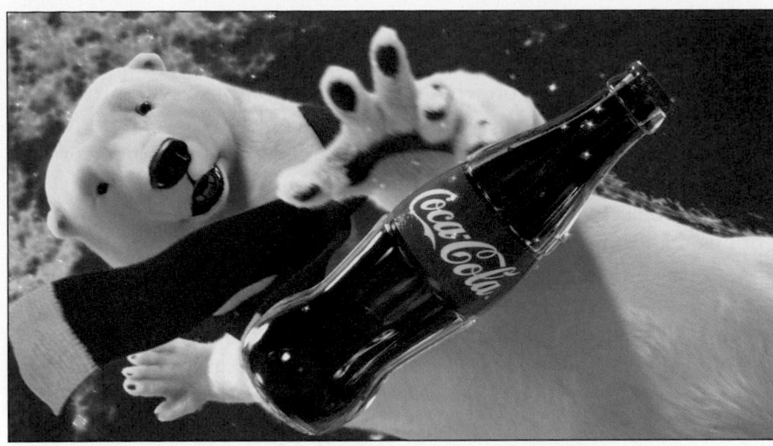

Setting the promotion budget is one of the hardest decisions facing a company. Coca-Cola spends hundreds of millions of dollars annually, but is that "half enough or twice too much"?
Associated Press

of my advertising is wasted, but I don't know which half. I spent $2 million for advertising, and I don't know if that is half enough or twice too much." Thus, it is not surprising that industries and companies vary widely in how much they spend on promotion. Promotion spending may be 10–12 percent of sales for consumer packaged goods, 20 percent for cosmetics, and only 1.9 percent for household appliances. Within a given industry, both low and high spenders can be found.[15]

How does a company determine its promotion budget? Here, we look at four common methods used to set the total budget for advertising: the *affordable method*, the *percentage-of-sales method*, the *competitive-parity method*, and the *objective-and-task method*.

Affordable Method

Affordable method
Setting the promotion budget at the level management thinks the company can afford.

Some companies use the **affordable method**: They set the promotion budget at the level they think the company can afford. Small businesses often use this method, reasoning that the company cannot spend more on advertising than it has. They start with total revenues, deduct operating expenses and capital outlays, and then devote some portion of the remaining funds to advertising.

Unfortunately, this method of setting budgets completely ignores the effects of promotion on sales. It tends to place promotion last among spending priorities, even in situations in which advertising is critical to the firm's success. It leads to an uncertain annual promotion budget, which makes long-range market planning difficult. Although the affordable method can result in overspending on advertising, it more often results in underspending.

Percentage-of-Sales Method

Percentage-of-sales method
Setting the promotion budget at a certain percentage of current or forecasted sales or as a percentage of the unit sales price.

Other companies use the **percentage-of-sales method**, setting their promotion budget at a certain percentage of current or forecasted sales. Or they budget a percentage of the unit sales price. The percentage-of-sales method is simple to use and helps management think about the relationships between promotion spending, selling price, and profit per unit.

Despite these claimed advantages, however, the percentage-of-sales method has little to justify it. It wrongly views sales as the *cause* of promotion rather than as the *result*. Although studies have found a positive correlation between promotional spending and brand strength, this relationship often turns out to be effect and cause, not cause and effect. Stronger brands with higher sales can afford the biggest ad budgets.

Thus, the percentage-of-sales budget is based on the availability of funds rather than on opportunities. It may prevent the increased spending sometimes needed to turn around falling sales. Because the budget varies with year-to-year sales, long-range planning is difficult. Finally, the method does not provide any basis for choosing a *specific* percentage, except what has been done in the past or what competitors are doing.

Competitive-Parity Method

Competitive-parity method
Setting the promotion budget to match competitors' outlays.

Still other companies use the **competitive-parity method**, setting their promotion budgets to match competitors' outlays. They monitor competitors' advertising or get industry promotion spending estimates from publications or trade associations and then set their budgets based on the industry average.

Two arguments support this method. First, competitors' budgets represent the collective wisdom of the industry. Second, spending what competitors spend helps prevent promotion wars. Unfortunately, neither argument is valid. There are no grounds for believing that the competition has a better idea of what a company should be spending on promotion than does the company itself. Companies differ greatly, and each has its own special promotion needs. Finally, there is no evidence that budgets based on competitive parity prevent promotion wars.

Objective-and-Task Method

Objective-and-task method
Developing the promotion budget by (1) defining specific promotion objectives, (2) determining the tasks needed to achieve these objectives, and (3) estimating the costs of performing these tasks. The sum of these costs is the proposed promotion budget.

The most logical budget-setting method is the **objective-and-task method**, whereby the company sets its promotion budget based on what it wants to accomplish with promotion. This budgeting method entails (1) defining specific promotion objectives, (2) determining the tasks needed to achieve these objectives, and (3) estimating the costs of performing these tasks. The sum of these costs is the proposed promotion budget.

The advantage of the objective-and-task method is that it forces management to spell out its assumptions about the relationship between dollars spent and promotion results. But it is also the most difficult method to use. Often, it is hard to figure out which specific tasks will achieve the stated objectives. For example, suppose Samsung wants a 95-percent-awareness level for its latest smartphone model during the six-month introductory period. What specific advertising messages, marketing content, and media schedules should Samsung use to attain this objective? How much would this content and media cost? Samsung management must consider such questions, even though they are hard to answer.

Author Comment | In this section, we'll look at how marketers blend the various marketing communication tools into a smooth-functioning, integrated, and engaging promotion mix.

Shaping the Overall Promotion Mix

The concept of integrated marketing communications suggests that the company must blend the promotion tools carefully into a coordinated *promotion mix*. But how does it determine what mix of promotion tools to use? Companies within the same industry differ greatly in the design of their promotion mixes. For example, cosmetics maker Mary Kay spends most of its promotion funds on personal selling and direct marketing, whereas competitor CoverGirl spends heavily on consumer advertising. We now look at factors that influence the marketer's choice of promotion tools.

The Nature of Each Promotion Tool

Each promotion tool has unique characteristics and costs. Marketers must understand these characteristics in shaping the promotion mix.

Advertising. Advertising can reach masses of geographically dispersed buyers at a low cost per exposure, and it enables the seller to repeat a message many times. For example, television advertising can reach huge audiences. Nearly 112 million Americans watched the most recent Super Bowl, more than 43 million people watched at least part of the last Academy Awards broadcast, and as many as 22 million avid fans tuned in each week for the latest season of *NCIS*. What's more, a popular TV ad's reach can be extended through online and social media. ● For example, in addition to the 100+ million TV viewers, Microsoft's inspiring and effective Super Bowl XLVIII ad "Empowering"—about how technology improves our lives and empowers us all to make the impossible possible—drew more than 3.7 YouTube views during the ensuing two months. For companies that want to reach a mass audience, TV is the place to be.[16]

● **TV advertising has vast reach. Microsoft's inspiring Super Bowl XLVIII ad, "Empowering"—about how technology improves our lives—drew 100+ million TV viewers and triggered millions of online views and shares.**
Microsoft

Beyond its reach, large-scale advertising says something positive about the seller's size, popularity, and success. Because of advertising's public nature, consumers tend to view advertised products as more legitimate. Advertising is also very expressive; it allows the company to dramatize its products through the artful use of visuals, print, sound, and color. On the one hand, advertising can be used to build up a long-term image for a product (such as Coca-Cola ads). On the other hand, advertising can trigger quick sales (as when Kohl's advertises weekend specials).

Advertising also has some shortcomings. Although it reaches many people quickly, advertising is impersonal and lacks the direct persuasiveness of company salespeople. For the most part, advertising can carry on only a one-way communication with an audience, and the audience does not feel that it has to pay attention or respond. In addition, advertising can be very costly. Although some advertising forms, such as newspaper and radio advertising, can be done on smaller budgets, other forms, such as network TV advertising, require very large budgets. For example, the one-minute Microsoft "Empowering" Super Bowl ad discussed above cost $8 million for media time alone, not counting the costs of producing the ad.

Personal Selling. Personal selling is the most effective tool at certain stages of the buying process, particularly in building up buyers' preferences, convictions, and actions. It involves personal interaction between two or more people, so each person can observe the other's needs and characteristics and make quick adjustments. Personal selling also allows all kinds of customer relationships to spring up, ranging from matter-of-fact selling relationships to personal friendships. An effective salesperson keeps the customer's interests at heart to build a long-term relationship by solving a customer's problems. Finally, with personal selling, the buyer usually feels a greater need to listen and respond, even if the response is a polite "No thank-you."

These unique qualities come at a cost, however. A sales force requires a longer-term commitment than does advertising—although advertising can be turned up or down, the size of a sales force is harder to change. Personal selling is also the company's most expensive promotion tool, costing companies on average $600 or more per sales call, depending on the industry.[17] U.S. firms spend up to three times as much on personal selling as they do on advertising.

Sales Promotion. Sales promotion includes a wide assortment of tools—coupons, contests, discounts, premiums, and others—all of which have many unique qualities. They attract consumer attention, engage consumers, offer strong incentives to purchase, and can be used to dramatize product offers and boost sagging sales. Sales promotions invite and reward quick response. Whereas advertising says, "Buy our product," sales promotion says, "Buy it now." Sales promotion effects can be short lived, however, and often are not as effective as advertising or personal selling in building long-run brand preference and customer relationships.

Public Relations. Public relations is very believable—news stories, features, sponsorships, and events seem more real and believable to readers than ads do. PR can also reach many prospects who avoid salespeople and advertisements—the message gets to buyers as "news and events" rather than as a sales-directed communication. And, as with advertising, public relations can dramatize a company or product. Marketers tend to underuse public relations or use it as an afterthought. Yet a well-thought-out public relations campaign used with other promotion mix elements can be very effective and economical.

Direct and Digital Marketing. The many forms of direct and digital marketing—from direct mail, catalogs, and telephone marketing to online, mobile, and social media—all share some distinctive characteristics. Direct marketing is more targeted: It's usually directed to a specific customer or customer community. Direct marketing is immediate and personalized: Messages can be prepared quickly—even in real time—and tailored to appeal to specific consumers or brand groups. Finally, direct marketing is interactive: It allows a dialogue between the marketing team and the consumer, and messages can be altered depending on the consumer's response. Thus, direct and digital marketing are well suited to highly targeted marketing efforts, creating customer engagement, and building one-to-one customer relationships.

Promotion Mix Strategies

Marketers can choose from two basic promotion mix strategies: *push* promotion or *pull* promotion. **Figure 14.4** contrasts the two strategies. The relative emphasis given to the specific promotion tools differs for push and pull strategies. A **push strategy** involves "pushing" the product through marketing channels to final consumers. The producer directs its marketing activities (primarily personal selling and trade promotion) toward channel members to induce them to carry the product and promote it to final consumers. For example, John Deere does very little promoting of its lawn mowers, garden tractors, and other residential consumer products to final consumers. Instead, John Deere's sales force works with Lowe's, Home Depot, independent dealers, and other channel members, who in turn push John Deere products to final consumers.

Push strategy
A promotion strategy that calls for using the sales force and trade promotion to push the product through channels. The producer promotes the product to channel members who in turn promote it to final consumers.

Using a **pull strategy**, the producer directs its marketing activities (primarily advertising, consumer promotion, and direct and digital media) toward final consumers to induce them to buy the product. For example, Unilever promotes its Axe grooming products directly to its young male target market using TV and print ads, its Web and social media brand sites, and other channels. If the pull strategy is effective, consumers will then demand the brand from retailers, such as CVS, Walgreens, or Walmart, which will in turn demand it from Unilever. Thus, under a pull strategy, consumer demand "pulls" the product through the channels.

Pull strategy
A promotion strategy that calls for spending a lot on consumer advertising and promotion to induce final consumers to buy the product, creating a demand vacuum that "pulls" the product through the channel.

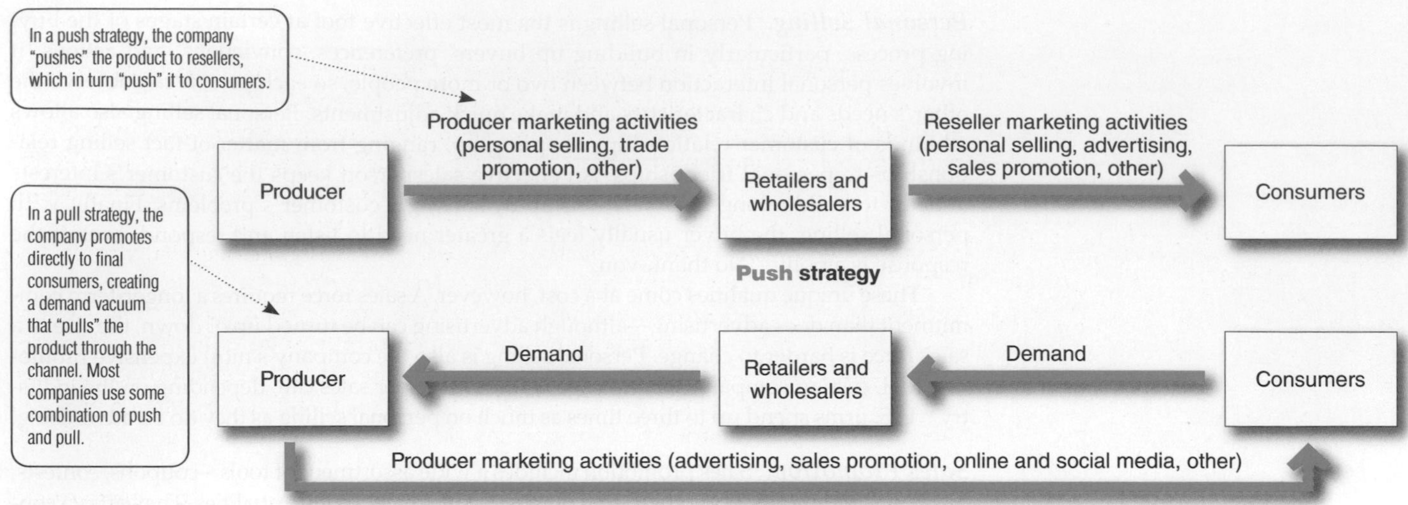

FIGURE | 14.4
Push versus Pull Promotion Strategy

Some industrial-goods companies use only push strategies; likewise, some direct marketing companies use only pull strategies. However, most large companies use some combination of both. For example, Unilever spends more than $9.1 billion worldwide each year on consumer marketing and sales promotions to create brand preference and pull customers into stores that carry its products.[18] At the same time, it uses its own and distributors' sales forces and trade promotions to push its brands through the channels, so that they will be available on store shelves when consumers come calling.

Companies consider many factors when designing their promotion mix strategies, including the type of product and market. For example, the importance of different promotion tools varies between consumer and business markets. Business-to-consumer companies usually pull more, putting more of their funds into advertising, followed by sales promotion, personal selling, and then public relations. In contrast, business-to-business marketers tend to push more, putting more of their funds into personal selling, followed by sales promotion, advertising, and public relations.

Integrating the Promotion Mix

Having set the promotion budget and mix, the company must now take steps to see that each promotion mix element is smoothly integrated. Guided by the company's overall communications strategy, the various promotion elements should work together to carry the firm's unique brand messages and selling points. Integrating the promotion mix starts with customers. Whether it's advertising, personal selling, sales promotion, public relations, or digital and direct marketing, communications at each customer touch point must deliver consistent marketing content and positioning. An integrated promotion mix ensures that communications efforts occur when, where, and how *customers* need them.

To achieve an integrated promotion mix, all of the firm's functions must cooperate to jointly plan communications efforts. Many companies even include customers, suppliers, and other stakeholders at various stages of communications planning. Scattered or disjointed promotional activities across the company can result in diluted marketing communications impact and confused positioning. By contrast, an integrated promotion mix maximizes the combined effects of all a firm's promotional efforts.

Socially Responsible Marketing Communication

In shaping its promotion mix, a company must be aware of the many legal and ethical issues surrounding marketing communications. Most marketers work hard to communicate openly and honestly with consumers and resellers. Still, abuses may occur, and public policy makers have developed a substantial body of laws and regulations to govern advertising, sales promotion, personal selling, and direct marketing. In this section, we discuss issues regarding advertising, sales promotion, and personal selling. We discuss digital and direct marketing issues in Chapter 17.

Advertising and Sales Promotion

By law, companies must avoid false or deceptive advertising. Advertisers must not make false claims, such as suggesting that a product cures something when it does not. They must avoid ads that have the capacity to deceive, even though no one actually may be deceived. An automobile cannot be advertised as getting 32 miles per gallon unless it does so under typical conditions, and diet bread cannot be advertised as having fewer calories simply because its slices are thinner.

Sellers must avoid bait-and-switch advertising that attracts buyers under false pretenses. For example, a large retailer advertised a sewing machine at $179. However, when consumers tried to buy the advertised machine, the seller downplayed its features, placed faulty machines on showroom floors, understated the machine's performance, and took other actions in an attempt to switch buyers to a more expensive machine. Such actions are both unethical and illegal.

A company's trade promotion activities also are closely regulated. For example, under the Robinson-Patman Act, sellers cannot favor certain customers through their use of trade promotions. They must make promotional allowances and services available to all resellers on proportionately equal terms.

Beyond simply avoiding legal pitfalls, such as deceptive or bait-and-switch advertising, companies can use advertising and other forms of promotion to encourage and promote socially responsible programs and actions. For example, General Mills's Nature Valley brand promotes a lot more than just Granola Bars, Greek Yogurt Protein Bars, Breakfast Biscuits, and other healthy snacks. It also promotes a strong commitment to preserving nature.[19] "We love nature and having fun in it," says the brand. The Nature Valley Web and social media brand sites devote almost as much attention to the topic of taking care of nature as to marketing specific products. The brand heavily promotes its Preserve the Parks initiative, which supports restoration projects in America's national parks through donations and volunteer hours. ● It also promotes the Nature Valley Trail View project, which uses street-view technology to provide glimpses online into America's national parks. "To pull it off," says the brand, "we hiked, climbed, and captured over 400 miles of 360° photo-views on trails across the country. We hope it inspires others to join us in enjoying and preserving one of the most amazing resources we have." By promoting its mission of taking care of the great outdoors, Nature Valley benefits both its "The Taste Nature Intended" positioning and the natural environment that its customers love.

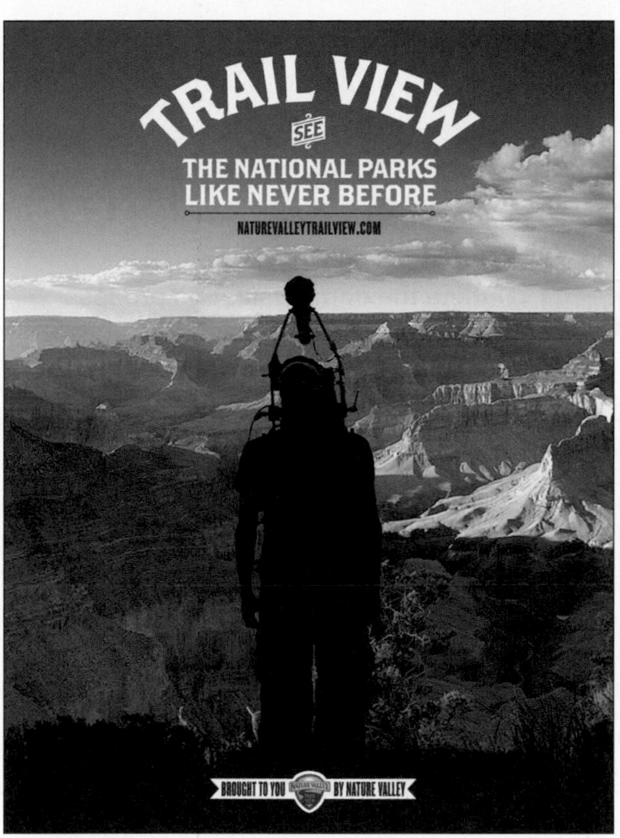

● Promoting socially responsible programs and actions: Nature Valley promotes a lot more than just Granola Bars and other healthy snacks. It also promotes a strong commitment to preserving nature. "We love nature and having fun in it," says the brand.

Used with permission of General Mills Marketing, Inc.

Personal Selling

A company's salespeople must follow the rules of "fair competition." Most states have enacted deceptive sales acts that spell out what is not allowed. For example, salespeople may not lie to consumers or mislead them about the advantages of buying a particular product. To avoid bait-and-switch practices, salespeople's statements must match advertising claims.

Different rules apply to consumers who are called on at home or who buy at a location that is not the seller's permanent place of business versus those who go to a store in search of a product. Because people who are called on may be taken by surprise and may be especially vulnerable to high-pressure selling techniques, the Federal Trade Commission (FTC) has adopted a *three-day cooling-off rule* to give special protection to customers who are not seeking products. Under this rule, customers who agree in their own homes, workplace, dormitory, or facilities rented by the seller on a temporary basis—such as hotel rooms, convention centers, and restaurants—to buy something costing more than $25 have 72 hours in which to cancel a contract or return merchandise and get their money back—no questions asked.

Much personal selling involves business-to-business trade. In selling to businesses, salespeople may not offer bribes to purchasing agents or others who can influence a sale. They may not obtain or use technical or trade secrets of competitors through bribery or industrial espionage. Finally, salespeople must not disparage competitors or competing products by suggesting things that are not true.

14 Reviewing the Concepts

OBJECTIVES REVIEW AND KEY TERMS

Objectives Review

In this chapter, you learned how companies use integrated marketing communications (IMC) to communicate customer value. Modern marketing calls for more than just creating customer value by developing a good product, pricing it attractively, and making it available to target customers. Companies also must clearly and persuasively engage current and prospective consumers and *communicate* that value to them. To do this, they must blend five promotion mix tools, guided by a well-designed and implemented IMC strategy.

OBJECTIVE 1 Define the five promotion mix tools for communicating customer value. (p 447)

A company's total *promotion mix*—also called its *marketing communications mix*—consists of the specific blend of *advertising, personal selling, sales promotion, public relations,* and *direct and digital marketing* tools that the company uses to engage consumers, persuasively communicate customer value, and build customer relationships. *Advertising* includes any paid form of nonpersonal presentation and promotion of ideas, goods, or services by an identified sponsor. In contrast, *public relations* focuses on building good relations with the company's various publics. *Personal selling* is personal presentation by the firm's sales force for the purpose of making sales and building customer relationships. Firms use *sales promotion* to provide short-term incentives to encourage the purchase or sale of a product or service. Finally, firms seeking immediate response from targeted individual customers use *direct and digital marketing* tools to engage directly with customers and cultivate relationships with them.

OBJECTIVE 2 Discuss the changing communications landscape and the need for integrated marketing communications. (pp 447–452)

The explosive developments in communications technology and changes in marketer and customer communication strategies have had a dramatic impact on marketing communications. Advertisers are now adding a broad selection of more-specialized and highly targeted media and content—including online, mobile, and social media—to reach smaller customer segments with more-personalized, interactive messages. As they adopt richer but more fragmented media and promotion mixes to reach their diverse markets, they risk creating a communications hodgepodge for consumers. To prevent this, companies are adopting the concept of *integrated marketing communications (IMC)*. Guided by an overall IMC strategy, the company works out the roles that the various promotional tools and marketing content will play and the extent to which each will be used. It carefully coordinates the promotional activities and the timing of when major campaigns take place.

OBJECTIVE 3 Outline the communication process and the steps in developing effective marketing communications. (pp 452–460)

The communication process involves nine elements: two major parties (sender, receiver), two communication tools (message, media), four communication functions (encoding, decoding, response, and feedback), and noise. To communicate effectively, marketers must understand how these elements combine to communicate value to target customers.

In preparing marketing communications, the communicator's first task is to *identify the target audience* and its characteristics. Next, the communicator has to determine the *communication objectives* and define the response sought, whether it be *awareness*, *knowledge*, *liking*, *preference*, *conviction*, or *purchase*. Then a *message* should be constructed with an effective content and structure. *Media* must be selected, both for personal and nonpersonal communication. The communicator must find highly credible sources to deliver messages. Finally, the communicator must collect *feedback* by watching how much of the market becomes aware, tries the product, and is satisfied in the process.

OBJECTIVE 4 Explain the methods for setting the promotion budget and factors that affect the design of the promotion mix. (pp 460–465)

The company must determine how much to spend for promotion. The most popular approaches are to spend what the company can afford, use a percentage of sales, base promotion on competitors' spending, or base it on an analysis and costing of the communication objectives and tasks. The company has to divide the *promotion budget* among the major tools to create the *promotion mix*. Companies can pursue a *push* or a *pull* promotional strategy—or a combination of the two. The best specific blend of promotion tools depends on the type of product/market, the buyer's readiness stage, and the PLC stage. People at all levels of the organization must be aware of the many legal and ethical issues surrounding marketing communications. Companies must work hard and proactively at communicating openly, honestly, and agreeably with their customers and resellers.

MyMarketingLab

Go to **mymktlab.com** to complete the problems marked with this icon .

Key Terms

OBJECTIVE 1

Promotion mix (or marketing communications mix) (p 447)
Advertising (p 447)
Sales promotion (p 447)
Personal selling (p 447)
Public relations (PR) (p 447)
Direct and digital marketing (p 447)

OBJECTIVE 2

Content marketing (p 449)
Integrated marketing communications (IMC) (p 449)

OBJECTIVE 3

Buyer-readiness stages (p 454)
Personal communication channels (p 457)
Word-of-mouth influence (p 457)
Buzz marketing (p 457)
Nonpersonal communication channels (p 458)

OBJECTIVE 4

Affordable method (p 461)
Percentage-of-sales method (p 461)
Competitive-parity method (p 461)
Objective-and-task method (p 462)
Push strategy (p 463)
Pull strategy (p 463)

DISCUSSION AND CRITICAL THINKING

Discussion Questions

14-1 Identify the promotion mix tools used for immediate response from customers. (AACSB: Communication)

14-2 Why is there a need for integrated marketing communications and how do marketers go about implementing it? (AACSB: Communication; Reflective Thinking)

14-3 How might a marketer or a marketing communicator determine the communication objectives and the response sought while developing an effective integrated communications and promotion program? (AACSB: Communication; Reflective Thinking)

14-4 Name and describe the two basic promotion mix strategies. In which strategy is advertising more important? (AACSB: Communication; Reflective Thinking)

14-5 What is the Federal Trade Commission's three-day cooling-off rule? Why was it put in place? (AACSB: Communication)

Critical Thinking Exercises

14-6 In a small group, select a company and research its marketing communications activities for the past several years. Has the company changed its advertising campaign in that time? Has the type of appeal remained the same or has it changed? Create a presentation of your findings. (AACSB: Communication; Use of IT; Reflective Thinking)

14-7 Marketers use Q Scores to determine a celebrity's appeal to his or her target audience. Research Q Scores and write a report of a celebrity's Q Score for the past several years. If the score changed considerably, what could be the reason? What other types of Q Scores are there besides scores for celebrities? (AACSB: Communication; Reflective Thinking)

14-8 Find three examples of advertisements that incorporate socially responsible marketing in the message. Some companies are criticized for exploiting social issues or organizations by promoting them for their own gain. Do the examples you found do that? Explain. (AACSB: Communication; Ethical Reasoning; Reflective Thinking)

MINICASES AND APPLICATIONS

Online, Mobile, and Social Media Marketing **Spot the Difference**

Online newspapers and magazines need most of the content they publish to be current, up to date, and in vogue. However, very few readers actually want to pay to access that content. The solution seems simple—use thinly disguised advertorial content instead. Interestingly, the more the content is read, the greater the advertising revenue. To many readers, it would appear that only a few online content sites are prepared to take the risk of paying a proper journalist or travel writer to create an article or a piece of high quality. Instead, content is either advertorial material or fairly dull practical advice. This also means that opportunities of making a living for journalists are dwindling. The subscription systems put people off, and it is impossible to subscribe to only a specific section of a newspaper or magazine to keep up with news and events from a specific perspective. A great deal of writing on news and media sites has become an integral part of public relations rather than conventional journalism. Some sites simply reprint press releases without comment or changes. Others will turn to business organizations that have customized-content providers to create a piece for them in different styles to match the look of different news Web sites. A major marketing trend has been to create content for brands. This has blurred the fine line between paid media coverage or advertisements and earned media coverage, which is more about convincing a journalist that a brand deserves to be written about. This has also created a conflict between different parts of the marketing industry. PR specialists would suggest that they are better placed to write the customized content and that they can find a newsworthy story for a brand. Advertising specialists claim they are the ones with the greatest affinity with advertorials, and they would know better how to make something stand out. As the distinctions between opinionated news content and customized content, also presented with a clear opinion and purpose, become ever more blurred, it is becoming increasingly difficult for the reader to tell the difference. As advertising revenue becomes more diluted with increased competition, should we blame the media for looking for a new income stream? Brands deserve their own story too, and it looks like the media is ready to write it for them.

14-9 Find examples of advertorials on various news Web sites. Create a presentation with screen shots showing the content and how it is identified. Has the content been shared with others via social media? (AACSB: Communication; Use of IT)

14-10 Should there be a clear warning on content that it has been sponsored or customized? Should there be legislation or guidelines to identify and control this activity? (AACSB: Communication; Reflective Thinking)

Marketing Ethics **Western Stereotypes**

In January 2014, the Japanese airline All Nippon Airways (ANA) was forced to pull a TV advertisement after being accused of racist stereotyping by viewers. The TV commercial featured two Japanese men in ANA uniforms. They were discussing, in English with Japanese subtitles, how they could boost the image of ANA as an international airline. The punch line of the commercial saw one of them suggesting that they change the image of Japanese people. The camera then cut back to the other man who was now wearing a blonde wig and a long rubber nose. These are stereotypical Japanese images of what Westerners look like. This is by no means the first, and probably not the last, time potentially racist stereotyping of Westerners has been employed in Japanese advertisements. In 2013, Toshiba featured a Japanese girl with a blonde wig and a fake nose in an advertisement for a bread maker. In 2010, Nagasaki Prefecture promoted its foreign-designed buildings with Japanese tourists wearing blonde wigs and big noses. At other times, Westerners have been portrayed as hapless visitors, a role that has not been met with viewers' approval.

14-11 Westerners are comparatively rare in countries such as Japan. Is it right to portray them in this way? Explain why or why not. (AACSB: Communication; Reflective Thinking; Ethical Reasoning)

14-12 Find other examples of marketing strategies that have employed racial stereotypes that could be considered inappropriate by viewers outside of a specific culture. (AACSB: Communication; Reflective Thinking)

Marketing by the Numbers **Advertising-to-Sales Ratios**

Using the percent-of-sales method, an advertiser sets its budget at a certain percentage of current or forecasted sales. However, determining what percentage to use is not always clear. Many marketers look at industry averages and competitor spending for comparisons. Web sites and trade publications publish data regarding industry averages to guide marketers in setting the percentage to use.

14-13 Find industry advertising-to-sales ratio data. Why do some industries have higher advertising-to-sales ratios than others? (AACSB: Communication; Use of IT; Reflective Thinking)

14-14 Determine the advertising-to-sales ratios for two competing companies and compare them to the industry advertising-to-sales ratio found above. Why do you think there is a difference between competitors and the industry average? (AACSB: Communication; Use of IT; Analytical Reasoning; Reflective Thinking)

Video Case **OXO**

For over 20 years, OXO has put its well-known kitchen gadgets into almost every home in the United States through word-of-mouth, product placement, and other forms of nontraditional promotional techniques. But OXO has decided to enter the world of broadcast advertising as it attempts to meet the challenges of a more competitive environment.

This video demonstrates how a successful company can remain on top through modifying its promotional mix. With its Good Grips, SteeL, Candela, Tot, and Staples/OXO brands, OXO has expanded its advertising efforts with a major new campaign and, in the process, is proving that good-old advertising is still a good bet.

After viewing the video featuring OXO, answer the following questions:

14-15 Why has OXO chosen to change its promotional strategy at this time?

14-16 Describe OXO's overall advertising strategy.

14-17 Is OXO abandoning its old promotional methods? How is OXO blending a new advertising strategy with the promotional techniques that have made it a success?

Company Case Snickers: Achieving Promotional Integration with a Universal Appeal—Hunger

Over the years, many Super Bowl ads have scored well with viewers and provided a big boost to their brands. Snickers aired one such ad during the 2010 Super Bowl. In the ad, during a neighborhood pickup football game, Golden Girl Betty White appeared as a player who was "playing like Betty White." After biting into a Snickers, however, the football player turned back into himself and the play ensued. The ad ended with the now famous slogan, "You're not you when you're hungry," followed by the tagline, "Snickers satisfies."

This ad proved to be a turning point for Snickers. It generated tremendous buzz for the brand. According to Nielsen, it was the "best-liked spot" of that year's Super Bowl. It had the highest score on *USA Today*'s Ad Meter and received top honors from many other sources. It went viral, racking up millions of views online. It sparked endless free media for the candy bar brand. It even marked a comeback for Betty White, who went on to host *Saturday Night Live* and score numerous roles on television shows, including that of octogenarian Elka Ostrovsky on the TV Land series *Hot in Cleveland*.

But this promotional event was far more than just a single hit ad. It became the cornerstone for a long-term integrated campaign that would eventually see Snickers become the best-selling confection on the planet.

Satisfying from the Start

Not only is Snickers now the biggest candy bar brand, it's one of the oldest. In the late 1920s, a young Mars Inc. started developing a candy bar to complement its own Milky Way. Combining common candy bar ingredients like chocolate, nougat, caramel, and whole peanuts, it came up with a winning formula. Heartier than most candy bars, Snickers acted more like a meal than a snack. The brand was an instant success, even selling initially at four times the price of the Milky Way bar. Within a decade, the company was mass-marketing the Snickers in global markets.

In 1979, Ted Bates Worldwide coined the tagline, "Snickers really satisfies," a direct reference to the bar's stomach filling properties. Often pitched as a meal alternative, Snickers targeted young athletic males. One classic print ad showed an approving mother sending her son off to football practice with a Snickers bar.

Snickers enjoyed years of growth before saturating that market and winding up in a rut characterized by flat sales growth and a loss of market share. Mars decided to take the brand in a new strategic direction. It set out to create an integrated marketing campaign that would retain the essence of the brand but achieve greater growth by appealing to new markets.

However, developing an effective integrated campaign is easier said than done. These days, companies everywhere are shooting for one and agencies claim to offer one. But in reality, true integration of marketing communications is rarely achieved. Integration requires more than merely using the same language or symbols in every element of the campaign. At a minimum, an integrated campaign must work equally well across TV, online, print, and outdoor media. Beyond that, the campaign's message must take a unique aspect of the brand and present it in a way that is both powerful and engaging, thus motivating consumers to act.

But Mars found a winning campaign created by agency BBDO. The agency started with the unique attribute that had been associated with Snickers for decades—"satisfying." Although the famous tagline "Snickers satisfies" had been used to primarily target young men, BBDO found that the line was far more robust. By appending "Snickers satisfies" with "You're not you when you're hungry," the brand tapped into a powerful and universal emotional appeal—hunger—relevant to a much broader audience. After all, who can't relate to hunger? "Now, Snickers is talking to the factory worker, the office worker, the college student," says one marketing expert. It's as powerful for women as it is for men. And it works across world cultures.

A Global Campaign

The Snickers "You're not you when you're hungry" campaign has spawned plenty of traditional mass-media ads—dozens of different television ads have run in more than 80 different countries. The campaign draws heavily on well-known local celebrities. One memorable ad features Robin Williams as a football coach instructing his team to "kill them—with kindness," by making balloon animals and tea cosies. In another, lumberjack Roseanne Barr complains "My back hurts!" just before she is flattened by an enormous log being moved by a crane. In a more recent ad introducing the new Snickers Bites, a poker-playing Kenny G is pronounced "a buzzkill when you're hungry" by one of his buddies at the table. The Snickers team lets local markets plug their own celebrities. In the UK, hunger turns footballers in a locker room into Joan Collins and Stephanie Beacham. In Latin America, its men on BMX bikes turning into Mexican singer Anahí.

But such traditional media advertising serves as only one pillar of this integrated campaign. The "You're not you when you're hungry" message has also rolled out across Facebook, Twitter, and other social networks. In the UK, celebrities tweeted things that were, for them, completely out of character. Supermodel Katie Price posted about quantitative easing, liquidity in the bond market, and the political economy. Footballer Rio Ferdinand posted about the joys of knitting. Cricketer Ian Botham waxed eloquent about learning to play the cello. And boxer Amir Khan tweeted about stamp collecting. These celebrity tweets were followed by an additional tweet showing them eating a Snickers accompanied by the "You're not you" tagline. The out-of-character tweets created lots of buzz, including a mention in Parliament. "It's come to something," exclaimed the UK's Chief Secretary to the Treasury, Danny Alexander, "When Katie Price's tweets make more sense on the economy than the Labour front bench."

Other elements illustrate the Snickers campaign's flexibility across media platforms, such as print and outdoor, with or without celebrities. One ad shows three sprinters in start position on a track, one of them facing the wrong direction. Another shows four soccer players in position to block a direct kick, all covering their crotches save one who is gazing off into the distance. One print ad gets the point across without using humans at all. In an extreme reversal of roles, it shows a zebra in hot pursuit of a lion. Each simple visual is accented by a cross section of the inside of a Snickers bar and the phrase, "You're not you when you're hungry. Snickers satisfies."

The campaign not only illustrates integration across different media types, it also accomplishes one of the most important feats of a modern promotional campaign—integration through content sharing. For example, ads like the Betty White Super Bowl spot themselves get things rolling. But other ads, tweets, and social media posts by the brand also spur sharing. For example, Snickers' 11 million Facebook fans receive frequent messages such as "Slow afternoon? Might be time for your secret SNICKERS stash," accompanied by a picture of a Snickers bar in an office desk drawer. On average, thousands of fans "like" each message and often place them in newsfeeds where they are seen by tens of thousands more.

A more complex example is a live stunt captured and edited into a short YouTube film for the Australian market. Actors posing as workers at a downtown Melbourne construction site shouted out to female passersby. But rather than sexist catcalls and suggestive comments, in line with the "You're not you" theme, the workers shouted out empowering statements. Women were clearly caught off guard by statements such as "I'd like to show *you* the respect you deserve!" and "A woman's place is where she chooses." One worker gets a woman's attention by shouting out, "You know what I'd like to see?" She is noticeably amused when he continues, "A society in which the objectification of women makes way for gender-neutral interaction free from assumptions and expectations." The clip ends with one of the workers leading the others in a rousing call. "What do we want? Equality! What don't we want? Misogony!" Within weeks, the clip had racked up more than 3 millions views on the Snickers Australia brand channel.

Year after Year, It Keeps on Satisfying

After more than four years, Mars Inc. continues to infuse the various elements of its global promotional campaigns with the "Snickers satisfies" and "You're not you when you're hungry" taglines. How has it kept this campaign going on such a broad and global scale? "You're not you" strikes at the core of a universal human emotion—that a person gets a bit cranky and out of sorts when he or she hasn't eaten for a while. "Peanut power was always at the heart of the brand," explains Debra Sandler, president of Mars Chocolate North America. By retaining the key word "satisfies," Mars retained all the brand familiarity it earned through years of promoting the old slogan. But by taking a storytelling approach and illustrating the effect that hunger has on people, Mars gave the brand a more emotional and powerful appeal. The message today is that Snickers is "the bar of substance that sorts you out," says Sandler.

It's sometimes difficult to measure the success of an integrated marketing campaign. The fact that Mars has kept this campaign running suggests that the effort is succeeding in spades. And in the case of "You're not you when you're hungry," the numbers seem to say it all. Prior to the start of the campaign in 2010, the iconic chocolate bar was losing share in a very competitive market. But not long after Betty White made her Super Bowl debut, Snickers surpassed both Trident gum and Mars's own M&M's to become the bestselling confection on Earth. With a portfolio that now includes Snickers Dark, Snickers Almond, Snickers Peanut Butter Squared, Snickers Bites, and Snickers Ice Cream bars, the Snickers franchise now contributes more than $3.5 billion to Mars Inc.'s $33 billion revenues. All this just goes to show that an integrated message combining a salient brand attribute with a compelling emotional appeal can live on indefinitely.

Questions for Discussion

14-18 Which promotional mix elements does Snickers use?

14-19 How does this Snickers campaign demonstrate the characteristics of integration?

14-20 What grade would you give Snickers on integration effectiveness?

14-21 What challenges does Mars Inc. face in maintaining the success it has achieved with the "You're not you" campaign?

14-22 What recommendations would you make to Mars Inc. for future Snickers promotional efforts?

Sources: David Gianatasio, "Construction Workers Yell Messages of Empowerment to Women in Snickers Stunt," *Ad Week*, March 26, 2014, www.adweek.com/print/156541; Robert Klara, "How Snickers Fired a Quarterback, Hired a Zebra, and Tweaked One of Advertising's Most Famous Tag Lines," *Ad Week*, February 27, 2014, www.adweek.com/print/155873; E. J. Schultz, "Behind the Snickers Campaign that Launched a Global Comeback," *Advertising Age*, October 4, 2013, http://adage.com/print/244593; David Benady, "Nike, Snickers and Fosters Have Created Powerful Integrated Campaigns—So What's Their Secret?" *The Guardian*, August 19, 2013, www.theguardian.com/best-awards/powerful-integrated-campaigns-secret; "Snickers UK Campaign: Clever Use of Twitter," *Bhatnaturally,* July 22, 2012, www.bhatnaturally.com/featured/snickers-uk-campaign-clever-use-of-twitter/.

MyMarketingLab

Go to **mymktlab.com** for the following Assisted-graded writing questions:

14-23 Name and describe the types of appeals marketers use when designing marketing communication messages. What message structure issues must be considered when creating messages? (AACSB: Communication)

14-24 Select an advertisement for a national brand. What type of appeal is the advertiser using? Describe the message structure used. Create an advertisement for the brand that communicates the same information but uses a different type of appeal and message structure. (AACSB: Communication; Reflective Thinking)

References

1. Based on information from "The Cow Campaign: A Brief History," www.chick-fil-a.com/Cows/Campaign-History, accessed June 2014; "Company Fact Sheet," www.chick-fil-a.com/Company/Highlights-Fact-Sheets, accessed June 2014; Thomas Pardee, "Armed with a Beloved Product and a Strong Commitment to Customer Service, Fast Feeder Continues to Grow," *Advertising Age,* October 18, 2010, http://adage.com/print/146491/; Brian Morrissey, "Chick-fil-A's Strategy: Give Your Fans Something to Do," *AdWeek*, October 3, 2009, www.adweek.com/print/106477; and information from various other pages and press releases at www.chick-fil-a.com and www.chick-fil-a.com/Pressroom/Press-Releases, accessed September 2014.

2. For other definitions, see www.marketingpower.com/_layouts/Dictionary.aspx, accessed September 2014.

3. "US Total Media Ad Spend Inches Up, Pushed by Digital," *eMarketer*, August 22, 2013, www.emarketer.com/Article/US-Total-Media-Ad-Spend-Inches-Up-Pushed-by-Digital/1010154; Serena Ng and Suzanne Vranica, "P&G Shifts Marketing Dollars to Online, Mobile," *Wall Street Journal,* August 1, 2013, http://online.wsj.com/news/articles/SB10001424127887323681904578641993173406444; "Total Media Ad Spend Continues Slow and Steady Trajectory," *eMarketer*, December 26, 2013, www.emarketer.com/Article/Total-Media-Ad-Spend-Continues-Slow-Steady-Trajectory/1010485; and Anthony Ha, "IAB Report: US Internet Ad Revenue Grew to $42.8 Billion in 2013, Overtaking Broadcast TV," *Tech Crunch,* April 10, 2014, http://techcrunch.com/2014/04/10/iab-2013-report/.

4. Chris Anderson, "The 'Angry Birds in Space' Video Marketing Campaign," *The Video Marketer,* March 22, 2012, http://blog.wooshii.com/the-angry-birds-in-space-video-marketing-campaign/; and "Samsung, Wieden & Kennedy Rule *Ad Age*'s 2013 Viral Video Awards," *Advertising Age,* April 16, 2013, http://adage.com/print/240900/.

5. See Stuart Elliott, "Ad for Method Celebrates the Madness," *New York Times,* March 12, 2012, p. B1; "Method Brings 'Clean Happy' Campaign to TV," *Business Wire,* March 4, 2013, www.businesswire.com/news/home/20130304005445/en/Method-Brings-%E2%80%9CClean-Happy%E2%80%9D-Campaign-TV; and http://methodhome.com/cleanhappy/, accessed September 2014.

6. See Jon Lafayette, "4A's Conference: Agencies Urged to Embrace New Technologies," *Broadcasting & Cable,* March 8, 2011, www.broadcastingcable.com/news/advertising-and-marketing/4as-conference-agencies-urged-embrace-new-technologies/52550; and David Gelles, "Advertisers Rush to Master Fresh Set of Skills," *Financial Times,* March 7, 2012, www.ft.com/intl/cms/s/0/8383bbae-5e20-11e1-b1e9-00144feabdc0.html#axzz1xUrmM3KK.

7. See "Advertisers Blend Digital and TV for Well-Rounded Campaigns," *eMarketer,* March 12, 2014, www.emarketer.com/Article/Advertisers-Blend-Digital-TV-Well-Rounded-Campaigns/1010670.

8. See "Thrill of the Chase: Coca-Cola Invites Fans to Shape Storyline of Big Game Ad," *Coca-Cola Journey,* January 25, 2013, www.coca-colacompany.com/stories/thrill-of-the-chase-coca-cola-invites-fans-to-shape-storyline-of-big-game-ad; Dale Buss, "Super Bowl Ad Watch: Crowdsourcing Peaks with Coke's 'Mirage' Campaign, *BrandChannel,* January 22, 2013, www.brandchannel.com/home/post/2013/01/22/SuperBowl-Coke-012213.aspx; and Natalie Zmuda, "Watching the Super Bowl from Coca-Cola's War Room(s)," *Advertising Age,* February 4, 2013, http://adage.com/print/239582/.

9. See John McDermott, "Microsoft Doubles Down on Surface Despite $900 Million Write-Down," September 23, 2013, http://adage.com/print/244326/; and Todd Wasserman, "Believe It: Microsoft Surface Is Turning Out to Be a Moneymaker," *Mashable,* January 23, 2014, http://mashable.com/2014/01/23/microsoft-surface-money-maker/.

10. See Steve Lepore, "The Complete 2014 Super Bowl Ad Meter Results," *USA Today,* February 4, 2014; p. B1+; "Super Bowl 2014 Ads: Facts and Figures," *MarketingCharts,* February 6, 2014, www.marketingcharts.com/wp/traditional/super-bowl-2014-ads-facts-and-figures-39421/; and www.youtube.com/watch?v=uQB7QRyF4p4; and www.youtube.com/watch?v=K7L5QByvXOQ, accessed September 2014.

11. Jonah Bloom, "The Truth Is: Consumers Trust Fellow Buyers Before Marketers," *Advertising Age,* February 13, 2006, p. 25; and "Jack Morton Publishes New Realities 2012 Research," press release, January 26, 2012, www.jackmorton.com/news/article.aspx?itemID=106.

12. See www.fiestamovement.com/, accessed September 2014.

13. www.bzzagent.com and http://about.bzzagent.com/, accessed September 2014.

14. T. L. Stanley, "Dancing with the Stars," *Brandweek,* March 8, 2010, pp. 10–12; and Chris Isidore, "Lance Armstrong: How He'll Make Money Now," *CNNMoney,* January 18, 2013, http://money.cnn.com/2013/01/16/news/companies/armstrong-endorsements/.

15. For more on advertising spending by company and industry, see "100 Leading National Advertisers: U.S. Ad Spending by Category," *Advertising Age,* June 24, 2013, pp. 14–22; and "2014 Marketing Fact Pack," *Advertising Age,* December 30, 2014, pp. 8–12.

16. See "Super Bowl 2014 Ratings Set New Record," *CBS News*, February 3, 2014, www.cbsnews.com/news/super-bowl-2014-ratings-set-new-record/; Ryan Faughnder, "Oscar 2014 Draws 43 Million Viewers, Biggest Audience in 10 Years," *Los Angeles Times*, March 3, 2014; "2013 TV Ratings Winners," *Malay Mail Online*, December 21, 2013, www.themalaymailonline.com/showbiz/article/2013-tv-ratings-winners-ncis-sunday-night-football-and-the-big-bang-theory; "Super Bowl 2014 Ads: Facts and Figures," *MarketingCharts*, February 6, 2014, www.marketingcharts.com/wp/traditional/super-bowl-2014-ads-facts-and-figures-39421/; and www.youtube.com/watch?v=qaOvHKG0Tio, accessed September 2014.

17. See discussions at Mike Ishmael, "The Cost of a Sales Call," October 22, 2012, http://4dsales.com/the-cost-of-a-sales-call/; Jeff Green, "The New Willy Loman Survives by Staying Home," *Bloomberg Businessweek,* January 14–January 20, 2013, pp. 16–17; and "What Is the Real Cost of a B2B Sales Call?" www.marketing-playbook.com/sales-marketing-strategy/what-is-the-real-cost-of-a-b2b-sales-call, accessed September 2014.

18. Jack Neff, "Unilever Plans to Cut 800 Marketers as It Slashes Agency Fees, Products," *Advertising Age*, December 5, 2013, http://adage.com/article/news/unilever-eliminate-800-marketers-globally-cut-launches/245542/.

19. See www.naturevalley.com; www.naturevalleytrailview.com; and www.naturevalley.com/preserve-the-parks, accessed September 2014.

15 Advertising and Public Relations

Chapter Preview

After an analysis of overall IMC planning, we dig more deeply into the specific marketing communication tools. In this chapter, we explore advertising and public relations (PR). Advertising involves communicating the company's or brand's value proposition by using paid media to inform, persuade, and remind consumers. PR involves building good relations with various company publics—from consumers and the general public to the media, investor, donor, and government publics. As with all the promotion mix tools, advertising and PR must be blended into the overall IMC program. In Chapters 16 and 17, we will discuss the remaining promotion mix tools: personal selling, sales promotion, and direct and digital marketing.

Let's start by looking at an outstanding advertising campaign. Two decades ago, GEICO was a little-known nicher in the U.S. auto-insurance industry. But now, thanks in large part to an industry-changing, big-budget advertising program, featuring an enduring tagline and a likeable but unlikely spokes-lizard, GEICO has muscled its way to the number-two position in its ultra-competitive industry. The message: Good advertising really does matter. Here's the story.

GEICO: From Bit Player to Behemoth through Good Advertising

Founded in 1936, GEICO initially targeted a select customer group of government employees and noncommissioned military officers with exceptional driving records. Unlike its competitors, GEICO had no agents. Instead, the auto insurer marketed directly to customers, keeping its costs low and passing on the savings in the form of lower premiums. For nearly 60 years, GEICO's marketing relied almost entirely on direct mail and telephone advertising.

In 1994, however, when GEICO decided to expand its customer base, it knew that it must also expand its marketing. So it entered the world of mass media, a shift that would dramatically change the face of insurance advertising. GEICO started slowly, spending a paltry $10 million to launch its first national TV, radio, and print ads. Then, in 1996, billionaire investor Warren Buffett bought the company and famously told the marketing group "money is no object" when it comes to growing the business, so "speed things up." Did it ever. Over the next 10 years, GEICO's ad spending jumped 50-fold, to more than $500 million a year.

By now, you know a lot about GEICO and its smooth-talking gecko. But at the start, the insurer faced a tough task—introducing a little-known brand with a funny name to a national audience. Like all good advertising, the GEICO campaign began with a simple but compelling theme, one that highlights the convenience and savings advantages of GEICO's direct-to-customers system. To this day, every single one of the hundreds of ads and other content pieces in the GEICO campaign has driven home the now-familiar pitch: "15 minutes could save you 15 percent or more on car insurance."

But what really set GEICO's advertising apart was the inspired way the company chose to bring its value proposition to life. At the time, competitors were using serious and sentimental pitches—"You're in good hands with Allstate" or "Like a good neighbor, State Farm is there." To make its advertising stand out, GEICO decided to deliver its punch line with humor. The creative approach worked and sales began to climb.

In trying to grow the brand, it become apparent that customers had difficulty pronouncing the GEICO name (which stands for Government Employees Insurance Company). Too often, GEICO became "gecko." Enter the charismatic green lizard. In

Thanks in large part to an industry-changing, big-budget advertising program, featuring an enduring tagline and a likeable but unlikely spokes-lizard, GEICO has muscled its way to the number-two position in its ultra-competitive industry.

1999, GEICO ran a 15-second spot in which the now-famous, British-accented gecko calls a press conference and pleads: "I am a gecko, not to be confused with GEICO, which could save you hundreds on car insurance. So stop calling me." The ad was supposed to be a one-time "throwaway," but consumers quickly flooded the company with calls and letters begging to see more of the gecko. The rest, as they say, is history.

Although the gecko remains GEICO's iconic spokesman, one lizard could take the company only so far. So over the years, to keep its pitch fresh and entertaining, GEICO has supplemented the gecko ads with a continuous flow of clever, buzzworthy new executions telling the brand's value story. Early on, when GEICO first went online, the campaign employed a clutch of cultured cavemen, insulted by the company's advertising slogan, "It's so easy to use GEICO.com, even a caveman could do it." Later, in response to the question, "Can switching to GEICO really save you 15 percent or more on car insurance?", the "Rhetorical Questions" campaign responded, "Is Ed 'Too Tall' Jones too tall?", "Was Abe Lincoln honest?", and "Did the little piggy cry 'wee wee wee' all the way home?" That last ad introduced the world to Maxwell, the talking pig who went on to star in his own GEICO campaign, emphasizing GEICO's growing digital, social, and mobile advances.

In a more recent installment of the campaign, bluegrass pickers Ronny and Jimmy drove home GEICO's money saving benefits in a dozen different "Happier than . . ." ads. Each ad began with a seemingly unrelated scenario. Then, on a small stage nearby, mandolin-playing Ronny and guitar-picking Jimmy struck up the music. "You know Jimmy," said Ronnie, "folks who save hundreds of dollars switching to GEICO sure are happy." "How happy, Ronny?" asked Jimmy. Depending on the ad, Ronny deadpanned "Happier than Paul Revere with a cell phone," or "Happier than Gallagher at a farmer's market," or "Happier than Dracula participating at a blood drive." One ad in the series promoted yet another GEICO character to pop culture icon status—the wildly popular Caleb the Camel who struts through the office every Wednesday rejoicing "It's hump day," suggesting that GEICO customers are "Happier than a camel on hump day." The swaggering Caleb would go on to star in other GEICO commercials and even appeared in the pregame show of Super Bowl XLVIII.

"No matter how many GEICO ads you've seen over the years—and it's a bunch—they never seem to grow stale," observes one expert. The company's chief marketing officer explains, "We're trying to stay ever-present in the consumer's mind but not bore them and have them just tune out yet another GEICO ad." However, no matter how varied, each minicampaign has a distinctly GEICO flavor, and every single ad closes strongly with the crucial "15 minutes could save you 15 percent" tagline.

The GEICO tagline is now so well-recognized that in the most recent minicampaign—"Did you know?"—the brand even pokes a little fun at itself. The commercials show one person reading a GEICO "15 percent" ad while a second person observes, "Everybody knows that." The first person then responds, "Well, did you know . . ." followed by a humorous (though fictional) fact. For instance, after revealing that "Old MacDonald was a really bad speller," one ad shows a farmer participant being eliminated from a spelling bee when he spells "cow" "C-O-W . . . E-I-E-I-O." Each ad concludes, "GEICO: 15 minutes could save you, well . . . you know."

For nearly 20 years, GEICO's advertising and charismatic gecko have creatively and relentlessly driven home the brand's value proposition: "15 minutes could save you 15 percent or more on car insurance."
GEICO

Along with fresh content, GEICO has also adapted its content delivery to the fast-changing digital times. The brand was one of the first in its industry to provide customers with mobile apps and options for obtaining quotes, buying policies, and managing their accounts. The company is also an acknowledged leader in the use of online and social media, ranking third in the insurance industry behind only full-line insurers Allstate and State Farm in social media performance and digital customer engagement.

GEICO continues to invest heavily in advertising and content marketing, outspending every other insurance company in measured media by a nearly two-to-one margin. Its annual advertising budget, now nearly $1 billion, makes GEICO the fifth-most-advertised U.S. megabrand. However, the brand's creative and relentless advertising messaging, plus its heavy investment, have paid big dividends. The once little-known GEICO brand now enjoys well over 90 percent awareness among insurance shoppers. And after years of double-digit market share gains, GEICO recently passed Allstate to move into second place in the ultra-competitive U.S. car-insurance market.

Moreover, beyond spurring GEICO's spectacular growth, the brand's advertising has changed the way the entire insurance industry markets its products. In what was once a yawn-provoking category, competitors ranging from Allstate (with "Mayhem") to Progressive (with "Flo") are now injecting humor and interest in their own advertising campaigns. "This strategy is absolutely working for GEICO," asserts one analyst. It's "a testament to how GEICO has used advertising to evolve from a bit player to a behemoth," says another.[1]

Objective Outline

As we discussed in the previous chapter, companies must do more than simply create customer value. They must also engage target customers and clearly and persuasively communicate that value to them. In this chapter, we take a closer look at two marketing communications tools: *advertising* and *public relations*.

Author Comment You already know a lot about advertising—you are exposed to it every day. But here we'll look behind the scenes at how companies make advertising decisions.

Advertising

Advertising can be traced back to the very beginnings of recorded history. Archaeologists working in countries around the Mediterranean Sea have dug up signs announcing various events and offers. The Romans painted walls to announce gladiator fights and the Phoenicians painted pictures on large rocks to promote their wares along parade routes. During the golden age in Greece, town criers announced the sale of cattle, crafted items, and even cosmetics. An early "singing commercial" went as follows: "For eyes that are shining, for cheeks like the dawn/For beauty that lasts after girlhood is gone/For prices in reason, the woman who knows/Will buy her cosmetics from Aesclyptos."

Advertising
Any paid form of nonpersonal presentation and promotion of ideas, goods, or services by an identified sponsor.

Modern advertising, however, is a far cry from these early efforts. U.S. advertisers now run up an estimated annual bill of more than $140 billion on measured advertising media; worldwide ad spending is an estimated $518 billion. P&G, the world's largest advertiser, last year spent almost $5 billion on U.S. advertising and $10.6 billion worldwide.[2]

Although advertising is used mostly by business firms, a wide range of not-for-profit organizations, professionals, and social agencies also use advertising to promote their causes to various target publics. In fact, the 49th largest advertising spender is a not-for-profit organization—the U.S. government, which advertises in many ways. For example,

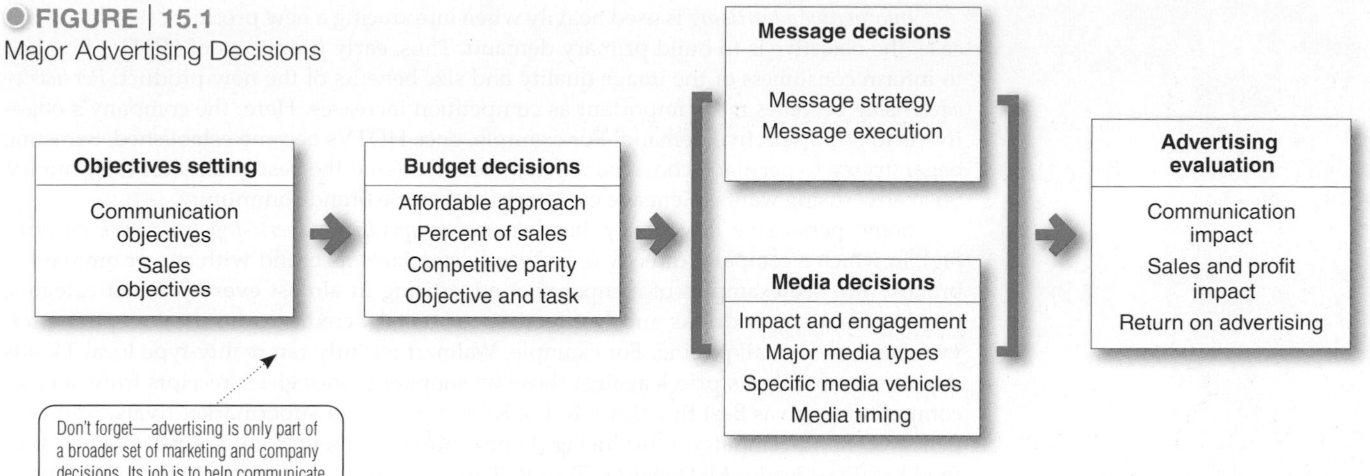

FIGURE | 15.1
Major Advertising Decisions

its Centers for Disease Control spent $48 million on the second year of an anti-smoking advertising campaign titled "Tips from a Former Smoker," showing people who have paid dearly due to smoking-related diseases.[3] Advertising is a good way to engage, inform, and persuade, whether the purpose is to sell Coca-Cola worldwide, help smokers kick the habit, or educate people in developing nations on how to lead healthier lives.

Marketing management must make four important decisions when developing an advertising program (see **Figure 15.1**): *setting advertising objectives, setting the advertising budget, developing advertising strategy (message decisions and media decisions),* and *evaluating advertising campaigns.*

Setting Advertising Objectives

The first step is to set *advertising objectives*. These objectives should be based on past decisions about the target market, positioning, and the marketing mix, which define the job that advertising must do in the total marketing program. The overall advertising objective is to help engage customers and build customer relationships by communicating customer value. Here, we discuss specific advertising objectives.

Advertising objective
A specific communication *task* to be accomplished with a specific *target* audience during a specific period of *time*.

An **advertising objective** is a specific communication *task* to be accomplished with a specific *target* audience during a specific period of *time*. Advertising objectives can be classified by their primary purpose—to *inform, persuade,* or *remind*. **Table 15.1** lists examples of each of these specific objectives.

Table 15.1 | Possible Advertising Objectives

Informative Advertising	
Communicating customer value	Suggesting new uses for a product
Building a brand and company image	Informing the market of a price change
Telling the market about a new product	Describing available services and support
Explaining how a product works	Correcting false impressions
Persuasive Advertising	
Building brand preference	Persuading customers to purchase now
Encouraging switching to a brand	Creating customer engagement
Changing customer perceptions of product value	Building brand community
Reminder Advertising	
Maintaining customer relationships	Reminding consumers where to buy the product
Reminding consumers that the product may be needed in the near future	Keeping the brand in a customer's mind during off-seasons

Informative advertising is used heavily when introducing a new product category. In this case, the objective is to build primary demand. Thus, early producers of HDTVs first had to inform consumers of the image quality and size benefits of the new product. *Persuasive advertising* becomes more important as competition increases. Here, the company's objective is to build selective demand. For example, once HDTVs became established, Samsung began trying to persuade consumers that *its* brand offered the best quality for their money. Such advertising wants to engage customers and create brand community.

Some persuasive advertising has become *comparative advertising* (or *attack advertising*), in which a company directly or indirectly compares its brand with one or more other brands. You see examples of comparative advertising in almost every product category, ranging from sports drinks and fast food to car rentals, credit cards, wireless phone services, and even retail pricing. For example, Walmart recently ran reality-type local TV ads directly comparing its prices against those on shopper cash-register receipts from specific competitors such as Best Buy, Toys 'R' Us, Kroger, and other supermarket rivals. And Taco Bell's recent ad campaign introducing its new breakfast menu took a direct poke at fast-food breakfast leader McDonald's. Taco Bell ads employed a slew of actual people named Ronald McDonald as Taco Bell spokespeople. "It's not surprising these guys are loving Taco Bell's new Waffle Taco," says one ad. "What's surprising is who they are." An online "behind-the-scenes" video drew millions of YouTube views.[4]

Microsoft has recently run an extensive campaign directly comparing its Bing search engine and Windows computers to Google's leading search engine and other products:

> It all began with Microsoft's "Bing It On" campaign, which directly challenged consumers to make side-by-side comparisons of its Bing search engine results to Google search results without knowing which results were from which search engine. According to Microsoft, to the surprise of many people, those making the comparison choose Bing over Google by a 2-to-1 margin. ● Microsoft next launched an aggressive "Scroogled" campaign, which attacked Google's search engine for "Scroogling" users by exploiting their personal data with everything from invasive ads in Gmail to sharing data with app developers to maximize advertising profits. "For an honest search engine," said the Scroogled ads, "try Bing." More recent Scroogled attack ads have disparaged Google Chromebook laptops—inexpensive stripped-down, Web-only machines that Google and partners like Acer, Samsung, and HP market as an alternative to full-fledged laptops. The hard-hitting Scroogled ads point out that Chromebooks won't run Microsoft Windows and other popular programs like Office, iTunes, and Photoshop and suggest that a Chromebook is "pretty much a brick" when not connected to the Internet. Although controversial, the Scroogled campaign has been effective in getting many consumers to look at Bing and other Microsoft products in a new light versus competitor Google.[5]

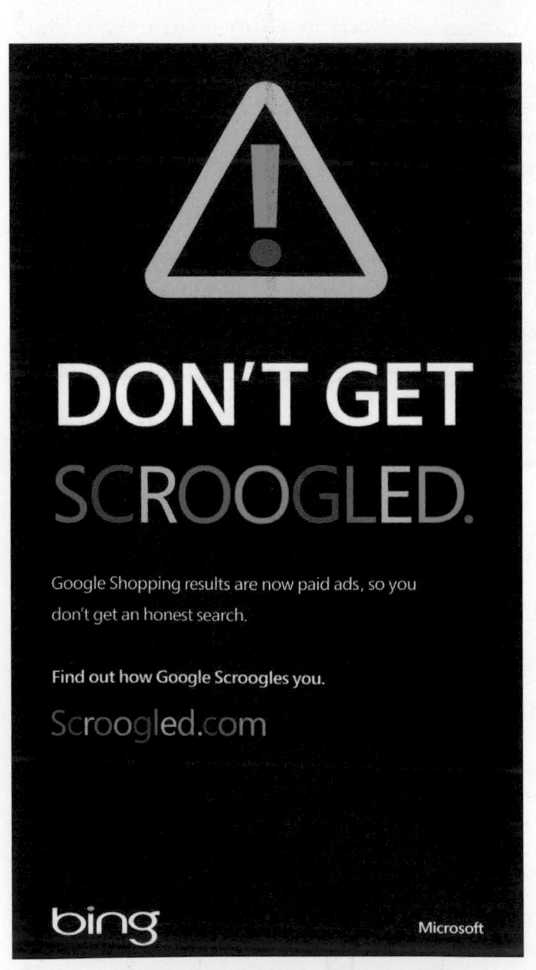

● Comparative advertising: Microsoft's hard-hitting "Scroogled" campaign directly challenges competitor Google. "For an honest search engine, try Bing."

Microsoft

Advertisers should use comparative advertising with caution. All too often, such ads invite competitor responses, resulting in an advertising war that neither competitor can win. Upset competitors might also take more drastic action, such as filing complaints with the self-regulatory National Advertising Division of the Council of Better Business Bureaus or even filing false-advertising lawsuits. For example, Walmart has responded to attorneys general in several states over complaints lodged by Toys "R" Us, Best Buy, and several regional supermarkets concerning its comparative pricing ads.[6]

Reminder advertising is important for mature products; it helps to maintain customer relationships and keep consumers thinking about the product. Expensive Coca-Cola television ads primarily build and maintain the Coca-Cola brand relationship rather than inform consumers or persuade them to buy it in the short run.

Advertising's goal is to help move consumers through the buying process. Some advertising is designed to move people to immediate action. For example, a direct-response television ad by Weight Watchers urges consumers to go online and sign up right away, and a Best Buy newspaper insert for a weekend sale encourages immediate store visits. However, many ads focus on building or strengthening long-term customer relationships. For example, a Nike television ad in which well-known athletes work through extreme challenges in their Nike gear never directly asks for a sale. Instead, the goal is to engage customers and somehow change the way they think or feel about the brand.

Setting the Advertising Budget

Advertising budget
The dollars and other resources allocated to a product or a company advertising program.

After determining its advertising objectives, the company next sets its **advertising budget** for each product. Four commonly used methods for setting promotion budgets are discussed in Chapter 14. Here we discuss some specific factors that should be considered when setting the advertising budget.

A brand's advertising budget often depends on its *stage in the product life cycle.* For example, new products typically need relatively large advertising budgets to build awareness and to gain consumer trial. In contrast, mature brands usually require lower budgets as a ratio to sales. *Market share* also impacts the amount of advertising needed: Because building the market or taking market share from competitors requires larger advertising spending than does simply maintaining current share, low-share brands usually need more advertising spending as a percentage of sales.

Also, brands in a market with many competitors and high advertising clutter must be advertised more heavily to be noticed above the noise in the marketplace. Undifferentiated brands—those that closely resemble other brands in their product class (soft drinks, laundry detergents)—may require heavy advertising to set them apart. When the product differs greatly from those of competitors, advertising can be used to point out the differences to consumers.

No matter what method is used, setting the advertising budget is no easy task. How does a company know if it is spending the right amount? Some critics charge that large consumer packaged-goods firms tend to spend too much on advertising and that business-to-business marketers generally underspend on advertising. They claim that, on the one hand, the large consumer companies use lots of image advertising without really knowing its effects. They overspend as a form of "insurance" against not spending enough. On the other hand, business advertisers tend to rely too heavily on their sales forces to bring in orders. They underestimate the power of company and product image in preselling industrial customers. Thus, they do not spend enough on advertising to build customer awareness and knowledge.

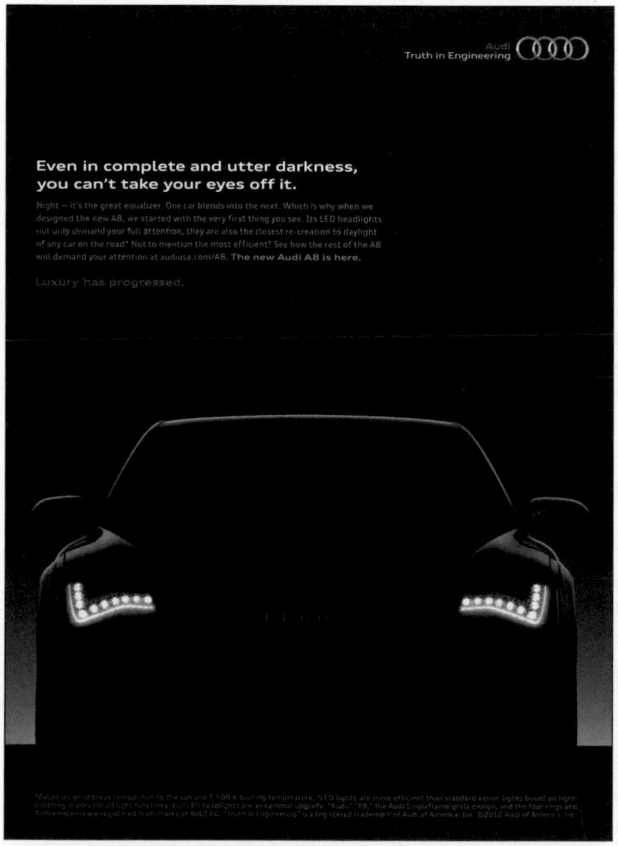

Companies such as Coca-Cola and Kraft have built sophisticated statistical models to determine the relationship between promotional spending and brand sales, and to help determine the "optimal investment" across various media. Still, because so many factors affect advertising effectiveness, some controllable and others not, measuring the results of advertising spending remains an inexact science. In most cases, managers must rely on large doses of judgment along with more quantitative analysis when setting advertising budgets.

As a result of such thinking, advertising is one of the easiest budget items to cut when economic times get tough. Cuts in brand-building advertising appear to do little short-term harm to sales. For example, in the wake of the recent recession, U.S. advertising expenditures plummeted 12 percent over the previous year. In the long run, however, slashing ad spending may cause long-term damage to a brand's image and market share. In fact, companies that can maintain or even increase their advertising spending while competitors are decreasing theirs can gain competitive advantage.

For example, during the recent Great Recession, while competitors were cutting back, car maker Audi actually increased its marketing and advertising spending. Audi "kept its foot on the pedal while everyone else [was] pulling back," said an Audi ad executive. "Why would we go backwards now when the industry is generally locking the brakes and cutting spending?" As a result, Audi's brand awareness and buyer consideration reached record levels during the recession, outstripping those of BMW, Mercedes, and Lexus, and positioning Audi strongly for the postrecession era. Audi is now one of the hottest auto brands on the market, neck and neck with BMW and Mercedes in global luxury car sales.[7]

Setting the promotion budget: Promotion spending is one of the easiest items to cut in tough economic times. But Audi gained competitive advantage by keeping its foot on the promotion pedal as competitors retrenched.

Used with permission of Audi of America.

Developing Advertising Strategy

Advertising strategy consists of two major elements: creating advertising *messages* and selecting advertising *media.* In the past, companies often viewed media planning as secondary to the message-creation

Advertising strategy
The strategy by which the company accomplishes its advertising objectives. It consists of two major elements: creating advertising messages and selecting advertising media.

process. After the creative department created good advertisements, the media department then selected and purchased the best media for carrying those advertisements to the desired target audiences. This often caused friction between creatives and media planners.

Today, however, soaring media costs, more-focused target marketing strategies, and the blizzard of new online, mobile, and social media have promoted the importance of the media-planning function. The decision about which media to use for an ad campaign—television, newspapers, magazines, video, a Web site, or online social media, mobile devices, or e-mail—is now sometimes more critical than the creative elements of the campaign. Also, brand content and messages are now often co-created through interactions with and among consumers. As a result, more and more advertisers are orchestrating a closer harmony between their messages and the media that deliver them. As discussed in the previous chapter, the goal is to create and manage brand content across a full range of media, whether they are paid, owned, earned, or shared.

Creating the Advertising Message and Brand Content

No matter how big the budget, advertising can succeed only if it gains attention, engages consumers, and communicates well. Good advertising messages and content are especially important in today's costly and cluttered advertising environment.

In 1950, the average U.S. household received only three network television channels and a handful of major national magazines. Today, the average household receives about 180 channels, and consumers have more than 20,000 magazines from which to choose.[8] Add in the countless radio stations and a continuous barrage of catalogs, direct mail, out-of-home media, e-mail, and online, mobile, and social media exposures, and consumers are being bombarded with ads and brand content at home, work, and all points in between. For example, Americans are exposed to a cumulative 5.3 trillion online ad impressions each year and a daily diet of 400 million tweets, 144,000 hours of uploaded YouTube video, and 4.75 billion pieces of shared content on Facebook.[9]

Breaking through the Clutter. If all this clutter bothers some consumers, it also causes huge headaches for marketers. Take the situation facing network television advertisers. They pay an average of $354,000 to produce a single 30-second commercial. Then, each time they show it, they pay an average of $122,000 for 30 seconds of advertising time during a popular primetime program. They pay even more if it's an especially popular program, such as *Sunday Night Football* ($594,000), *American Idol* ($355,000), *The Big Bang Theory* ($317,000), or a mega-event such as the Super Bowl (averaging $4 million per 30 seconds!). Then their ads are sandwiched in with a clutter of other commercials, announcements, and network promotions, totaling as much as 20 minutes of nonprogram material per primetime hour, with long commercial breaks coming every six minutes on average. Such clutter in television and other ad media has created an increasingly hostile advertising environment.[10]

● **Advertising clutter: Today's consumers, armed with an arsenal of weapons, can choose what they watch and don't watch. Increasingly, they are choosing not to watch ads.**
iStockphoto.com

Until recently, television viewers were pretty much a captive audience for advertisers. But today's digital wizardry has given consumers a rich new set of information and entertainment choices. With the growth in cable and satellite TV, the Internet, video streaming, tablets, and smartphones, today's viewers have many more options.

Digital technology has also armed consumers with an arsenal of weapons for choosing what they watch or don't watch. ● Increasingly, thanks to the growth of DVR systems, consumers are choosing *not* to watch ads. Half of American TV households now have DVRs, and two-thirds of DVR owners use the device to skip commercials. One ad agency executive calls these DVR systems "electronic weedwhackers" when it comes to commercials. At the same time, video downloads and streaming are exploding, letting viewers watch entertainment on their own time—with or without commercials.[11]

Thus, advertisers can no longer force-feed the same old cookie-cutter messages and content to captive consumers through traditional media. Just to gain and hold attention, today's content must be better planned, more imaginative, more entertaining, and more emotionally engaging. Simply interrupting or disrupting consumers no longer works. Unless ads provide content that is interesting, useful, or entertaining, many consumers will simply skip by them.

Madison & Vine
A term that has come to represent the merging of advertising and entertainment in an effort to break through the clutter and create new avenues for reaching customers with more engaging messages.

Merging Advertising and Entertainment. To break through the clutter, many marketers have subscribed to a new merging of advertising and entertainment, dubbed "**Madison & Vine**." You've probably heard of Madison Avenue, the New York City street that houses the headquarters of many of the nation's largest advertising agencies. You may also have heard of Hollywood & Vine, the intersection of Hollywood Avenue and Vine Street in Hollywood, California, long the symbolic heart of the U.S. entertainment industry. Now, Madison Avenue and Hollywood & Vine have come together to form a new intersection—Madison & Vine—that represents the merging of advertising and entertainment in an effort to create new avenues for reaching consumers with more engaging messages.

This merging of advertising and entertainment takes one of two forms: advertainment or branded entertainment. The aim of *advertainment* is to make ads themselves so entertaining, or so useful, that people *want* to watch them. There's no chance that you'd watch ads on purpose, you say? Think again. For example, the Super Bowl has become an annual advertainment showcase. Tens of millions of people tune in to the Super Bowl each year, as much to watch the entertaining ads as to see the game. And ads posted online before and after the big game draw tens of millions of views.

These days, it's not unusual to see an entertaining ad or other brand content on YouTube before you see it on TV. And you might well seek it out at a friend's suggestion rather than having it forced on you by the advertiser. Moreover, beyond making their regular ads more engaging, advertisers are also creating new content forms that look less like ads and more like short films or shows. A range of new brand messaging platforms—from Webisodes and blogs to online videos and apps—now blur the line between ads and entertainment.

For example, as part of its long-running, highly successful Campaign for Real Beauty, Unilever's Dove brand created a thought-provoking three-minute video, called "Dove Real Beauty Sketches," about how women view themselves. The video compares images of women drawn by an FBI-trained sketch artist based on their self-descriptions versus strangers' descriptions. Side-by-side comparisons show that the stranger-described images are invariably more accurate and more flattering, creating strong reactions from the women. The tagline concludes, "You're more beautiful than you think." Although the award-winning video was never shown on TV, it drew more than 163 million global YouTube views within just two months, making it the most-watched video ever.[12]

Branded entertainment (or *brand integrations*) involves making the brand an inseparable part of some other form of entertainment. The most common form of branded entertainment is product placements—embedding brands as props within other programming. It might be a brief glimpse of Starbucks' coffee products on *Morning Joe* on MSNBC or of Microsoft's Surface tablet and Bing search engine in episodes of *Elementary* or *Arrow*. It might be scenes from *Captain America: The Winter Soldier* in which our superhero rides a new Harley-Davidson Street 750. Or the product placement might be scripted into an episode. For example, an entire episode of *New Girl* featured a new Ford Escape, including a not-so-subtle sequence in which one of the main characters demonstrates the SUV's foot-activated liftgate feature.[13]

Originally created with TV in mind, branded entertainment has spread quickly into other sectors of the entertainment industry. For example, it is widely used in movies. In fact, 2013's top 39 films contained 325 identifiable brand placements—*Pain and Gain* alone had 39 placements.[14] If you look carefully, you'll also see product placements in video games, comic books, Broadway musicals, and even pop music. For example, in *Call of Duty: Modern Warfare 3*, a Jeep Wrangler is prominently featured. Chrysler even sold a *Call of Duty: MW3* limited edition Jeep Wrangler.

● The highly acclaimed film *The LEGO Movie* was pretty much a 100-minute product placement for iconic LEGO construction bricks. According to one writer, "The audience happily sits through a cinematic sales pitch . . . that shows off the immense versatility of the product while

● **Branded entertainment: The highly acclaimed film *The LEGO Movie* was pretty much a 100-minute product placement for iconic LEGO construction bricks, what one writer calls "product-placement perfection."**

placing it in a deeply personal context. The majority of the film is a breathtaking display of what LEGO bricks are capable of as creative tools, but the personal element is what really elevates this film to product-placement perfection."[15]

Many companies are even producing their own branded entertainment. For example, Ford created "Random Acts of Fusion," a Web-only show that followed TV celebrities Joel McHale and Ryan Seacrest as they hosted video contests and free food festivals across America, letting people interact with the latest-model Ford Fusion as they went. The show increased traffic to the Ford Fusion Web site by 20 percent.

Similarly, IKEA has produced several Web-only series. The latest is the "IKEA Home Tour," which follows five IKEA employees on a yearlong road trip to provide families with home makeovers using merchandise from local IKEA stores. In keeping with the retailer's longtime practice of showing diversity in its ads and marketing, the employees visit many nontraditional families, such as a male couple in the Bronx planning to be married. "Consumers no longer want just a 30-second commercial," says an IKEA marketer. "They want to know who a company is, what it believes, and what its personality is."[16]

So, Madison & Vine is now the meeting place for the advertising and entertainment industries. The goal is for brand messages and content to become a part of the entertainment rather than interrupting it. As advertising agency JWT puts it, "We believe advertising needs to stop *interrupting* what people are interested in and *be* what people are interested in." However, advertisers must be careful that the new intersection itself doesn't become too congested. With all the new ad formats and product placements, Madison & Vine threatens to create even more of the very clutter that it was designed to break through. At that point, consumers might decide to take yet a different route.

Message and Content Strategy. The first step in creating effective advertising content is to plan a *message strategy*—the general message that will be communicated to consumers. The purpose of advertising is to get consumers to engage with or react to the product or company in a certain way. People will engage and react only if they believe they will benefit from doing so. Thus, developing an effective message strategy begins with identifying customer *benefits* that can be used as advertising appeals. Ideally, the message strategy will follow directly from the company's broader positioning and customer value-creation strategies.

Creative concept
The compelling "big idea" that will bring an advertising message strategy to life in a distinctive and memorable way.

Message strategy statements tend to be plain, straightforward outlines of benefits and positioning points that the advertiser wants to stress. The advertiser must next develop a compelling **creative concept**—or *big idea*—that will bring the message strategy to life in a distinctive and memorable way. At this stage, simple message ideas become great ad campaigns. Usually, a copywriter and an art director will team up to generate many creative concepts, hoping that one of these concepts will turn out to be the big idea. The creative concept may emerge as a visualization, a phrase, or a combination of the two.

The creative concept will guide the choice of specific appeals to be used in an advertising campaign. *Advertising appeals* should have three characteristics. First, they should be *meaningful*, pointing out benefits that make the product more desirable or interesting to consumers. Second, appeals must be *believable*. Consumers must believe that the product or service will deliver the promised benefits.

However, the most meaningful and believable benefits may not be the best ones to feature. Appeals should also be *distinctive*. They should tell how the product is better than competing brands. For example, the most meaningful benefit of using a body wash or fragrance is that it makes you feel cleaner or smell better. But Axe's Anarchy brand for men and women sets itself apart by the extreme nature of the "Axe Effect" it promises to create—Axe Anarchy For Him + For Her will "Unleash the Chaos." Similarly, the most meaningful benefit of owning a wristwatch is that it keeps accurate time, yet few watch ads feature this benefit. Instead, watch advertisers might select any of a number of advertising themes. For years, Timex has been the affordable watch that "takes a licking and keeps on ticking." In contrast, Rolex ads talk about the brand's "obsession with perfection" and the fact that "Rolex has been the preeminent symbol of performance and prestige for more than a century."

Message Execution. The advertiser now must turn the big idea into an actual ad execution that will capture the target market's attention and interest. The creative team must find the best approach, style, tone, words, and format for executing the message. The message can be presented in various **execution styles**, such as the following:

Execution style
The approach, style, tone, words, and format used for executing an advertising message.

- *Slice of life.* This style shows one or more "typical" people using the product in a normal setting. For example, a Silk Soymilk "Rise and Shine" ad shows a young professional starting the day with a healthier breakfast and high hopes.

- *Lifestyle.* This style shows how a product fits in with a particular lifestyle. For example, an ad for Athleta active wear shows a woman in a complex yoga pose and states: "If your body is your temple, build it one piece at a time."
- *Fantasy.* This style creates a fantasy around the product or its use. For example, a Calvin Klein "Drive in to Fantasy" ad shows a woman floating blissfully above a surf-strewn beach at sunset in her Calvin Klein Nightwear.
- *Mood or image.* This style builds a mood or image around the product or service, such as beauty, love, intrigue, serenity, or pride. Few claims are made about the product or service except through suggestion. For example, Dodge Ram Truck's moving Super Bowl XLVII commercial—"To the Farmer in Us All"—added poignant pictures to radio-broadcast-legend Paul Harvey's "So God Made a Farmer" speech, pulling down the number-two spot in *USA Today's* Ad Meter ratings that year. Except for a few brief frames and a closing picture, the two-minute ad never directly mentioned or showed sponsor Dodge Ram Trucks. However, it associated the brand with strong emotions and basic American values.
- *Musical.* This style shows people or cartoon characters singing about the product. For example, the M&M's "Love Ballad" ad, part of the Better with M campaign, featured Red singing Meat Loaf's "I'd Do Anything for Love," showcasing his commitment to actress Naya Rivera. Red has second thoughts, however, when Rivera can't resist adding Red to some of her favorite treats, including cookies, cake, and ice cream. To all of that, Red answers with the lyric, "But I won't do that . . . or that . . . or that . . . or that."
- *Personality symbol.* This style creates a character that represents the product. The character might be animated (Mr. Clean, the GEICO Gecko, or the Michelin Man) or real (perky Progressive Insurance spokeswoman Flo, Allstate's Mayhem, Ronald McDonald).
- *Technical expertise.* This style shows the company's expertise in making the product. Thus, natural foods maker Kashi shows its buyers carefully selecting ingredients for its products, and Jim Koch of the Boston Beer Company tells about his many years of experience in brewing Samuel Adams beer.
- *Scientific evidence.* This style presents survey or scientific evidence that the brand is better or better liked than one or more other brands. For years, Crest toothpaste has used scientific evidence to convince buyers that Crest is better than other brands at fighting cavities.
- *Testimonial evidence or endorsement.* This style features a highly believable or likable source endorsing the product. It could be ordinary people saying how much they like a given product. For example, Whole Foods features a variety of real customers in its Values Matter marketing campaign. Or it might be a celebrity presenting the product, such as Beyoncé speaking for Pepsi.

The advertiser also must choose a *tone* for the ad. For example, P&G always uses a positive tone: Its ads say something very positive about its products. Other advertisers now use edgy humor to break through the commercial clutter. Bud Light commercials are famous for this.

The advertiser must use memorable and attention-getting *words* in the ad. For example, rather than claiming simply that its laundry detergent is "superconcentrated," Method asks customers, "Are you jug addicted?" The solution: "Our patent-pending formula that's so fricken' concentrated, 50 loads fits in a teeny bottle. . . . With our help, you can get off the jugs and get clean."

Finally, *format* elements make a difference in an ad's impact as well as in its cost. A small change in an ad's design can make a big difference in its effect. In a print ad, the *illustration* is the first thing the reader notices—it must be strong enough to draw attention. Next, the *headline* must effectively entice the right people to read the copy. Finally, the *copy*—the main block of text in the ad—must be simple but strong and convincing. Moreover, these three elements must effectively work *together* to engage customers and persuasively present customer value. However, novel formats can help an ad stand out from the clutter. For example, in one striking print ad from Volkswagen, the illustration does most of the work in catching relevant attention

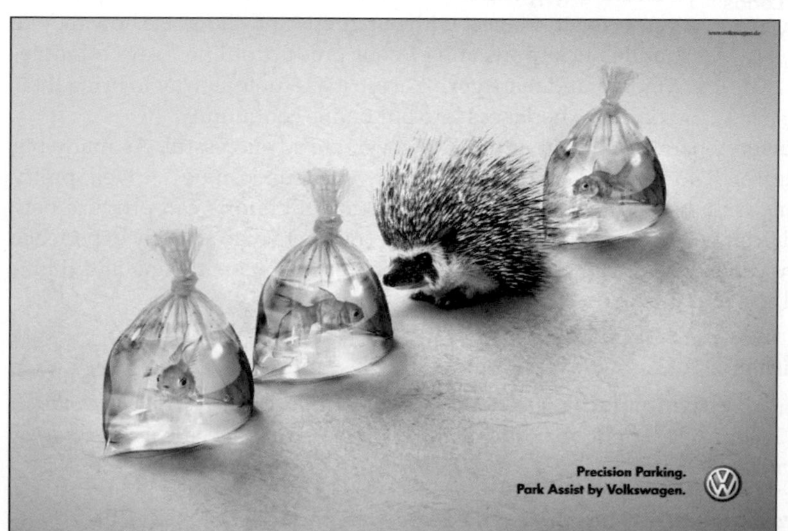

Novel formats can help an advertisement stand out. In this Volkswagen ad, the illustration does most of the work in illustrating the car maker's parking assist feature.

Used with permission of Volkswagen Aktiengesellschaft. Creative studio - The Operators for the car maker's precision parking assist feature. It shows a porcupine "parked" in a tight space between goldfish in water-filled plastic bags. The small-print headline says only "Precision Parking. Park Assist by Volkswagen." Enough said!

Consumer-Generated Content. Taking advantage of today's digital and social media technologies, many companies are now tapping consumers for marketing content, message ideas, or even actual ads and videos. Sometimes the results are outstanding; sometimes they are forgettable. If done well, however, user-generated content can incorporate the voice of the customer into brand messages and generate greater customer engagement.

Many brands invite consumers to submit ad message ideas, videos, and other brand content. Perhaps the best known consumer-generated content effort is the long-running annual "Crash the Super Bowl Challenge" held annually by PepsiCo's Doritos brand. Doritos invites consumers to create their own 30-second video ads, and winners receive large cash awards and have their ads run during the Super Bowl.

But brands across a wide range of industries—from automakers and fast-food chains to apparel brands and pet food marketers—are inviting customers to participate in generating marketing content. For example, Chevrolet held an Oscars Program Video Contest last year that produced 72 imaginative ad videos for its Chevy Cruze model. The winner—a delightfully quirky one-minute video called "Speed Chaser"—was shot in an open field for only $4,000. Similarly, Purina conducted a video contest on its YouTube page, inviting owners of everyday dogs to submit videos showing "How is your dog great?" Using a compilation of clips from more than 500 submitted videos, Purina created a 60-second "How I'm Great" commercial and aired it during the broadcast of the Westminster Kennel Club Dog Show. And to help boost digital and social media engagement, Taco Bell invited YouTube stars and influencers to create video content for its new Fiery Doritos Locos Tacos. Taco Bell ended up choosing 65 video ads to distribute online through Twitter feeds and social networks, and used one clever video—featuring a "3D Doritos Taco printer"—in subsequent paid online advertising.[17]

Consumer-generated content: Taco Bell boosted digital and social media coverage of the introduction of its Fiery Doritos Locos Tacos with consumer-generated videos distributed through Twitter feeds, social networks, and online advertising buys.

Taco Bell

Consumer-generated content can make customers an everyday part of the brand conversation. Yogawear company Lululemon recently launched its #TheSweatLife campaign, in which it invited customers to tweet or Instagram photos of themselves "getting their sweat on" in Lululemon gear. "Your perspiration is our inspiration," said the brand at its Web site. Within only a few months, the brand had received more than 7,000 photos, which it featured in a #TheSweatLife online gallery, quickly drawing more than 40,000 unique visitors. The user-generated content campaign created substantial customer engagement for Lululemon. "We created the program as a way to connect with our guests and showcase how they're authentically sweating in our product offline," says a Lululemon brand manager. "We see it as a unique way to bring their offline experiences into our online community."[18]

Not all consumer-generated content efforts, however, are so successful. As many big companies have learned, ads and other content made by amateurs can be . . . well, pretty amateurish. If done well, however, consumer-generated content efforts can produce new creative ideas and fresh perspectives on the brand from consumers who actually experience it. Such campaigns can boost consumer engagement and get customers talking and thinking about a brand and its value to them.

Selecting Advertising Media

Advertising media
The vehicles through which advertising messages are delivered to their intended audiences.

The major steps in **advertising media** selection are (1) determining *reach, frequency, impact,* and *engagement*; (2) choosing among major *media types*; (3) selecting specific *media vehicles*; and (4) choosing *media timing*.

Determining Reach, Frequency, Impact, and Engagement. To select media, the advertiser must determine the reach and frequency needed to achieve the advertising objectives. *Reach* is a measure of the *percentage* of people in the target market who are exposed to the ad campaign during a given period of time. For example, the advertiser might try to reach

70 percent of the target market during the first three months of the campaign. *Frequency* is a measure of how many *times* the average person in the target market is exposed to the message. For example, the advertiser might want an average exposure frequency of three.

But advertisers want to do more than just reach a given number of consumers a specific number of times. The advertiser also must determine the desired *media impact*—the *qualitative value* of message exposure through a given medium. For example, the same message in one magazine (say, *Time*) may be more believable than in another (say, the *National Enquirer*). For products that need to be demonstrated, messages on television or in an online video may have more impact than messages on radio because they use sight, motion, *and* sound. Products for which consumers provide input on design or features might be better promoted at an interactive Web site or social media page than in a direct mailing.

More generally, the advertiser wants to choose media that will *engage* consumers rather than simply reach them. In any medium, the relevance of ad content for its audience is often much more important than how many people it reaches. For example, Home Depot has learned that although it lacks the broad reach of local TV or print ads, a combination of mobile and online media can engage customers more deeply and personally. For example, it now runs ads on the Weather Channel's mobile app. When customers tap on the Home Depot banner ad, they're sent to the retailer's mobile Web site, which highlights products matching their local weather conditions and forecast. Expecting snow in your area? You'll likely see special deals on snow shovels and snow blowers. Such focused and engaging media placements nicely supplement Home Depot's broader advertising efforts.[19]

To engage consumers, Home Depot runs ads on Weather Channel's mobile app.

Provided by The Weather Channel

Although Nielsen is beginning to measure *media engagement* levels for some television, radio, and social media, such measures are still hard to find in most cases. Current media measures are things such as ratings, readership, listenership, and click-through rates. However, engagement happens inside the consumer. Notes one expert, "Just measuring the number of eyeballs in front of a television set is hard enough without trying to measure the intensity of those eyeballs doing the viewing."[20] Still, marketers need to know how customers connect with an ad and brand idea as a part of the broader brand relationship.

Engaged consumers are more likely to act upon brand messages and even share them with others. Thus, rather than simply tracking *consumer impressions* for a media placement—how many people see, hear, or read an ad—Coca-Cola now also tracks the *consumer expressions* that result, such as a comment, a "Like," uploading a photo or video, or sharing brand content on social networks. Today's empowered consumers often generate more messages about a brand than a company can.

For example, Coca-Cola estimates that on YouTube there are about 146 million views of content related to Coca-Cola. However, only about 26 million of those are of content that Coca-Cola created. The other 120 million are of content created by engaged consumers. "We can't match the volume of our consumers' output," says Coca-Cola's chief marketing officer, "but we can spark it with the right type [and placement] of content." To that end, many Coca-Cola marketing campaigns are aimed at generating expressions rather than just impressions. For example, the brand's recent "Ahh Effect" campaign called for teens to share the "ahh moments" they experience while drinking Coke at a www.AHH.com Web site and via social media using the hashtag #ThisisAHH. It then featured the user-generated personal expressions in "This is AHH" commercials on youth-oriented TV channels.[21]

Choosing among Major Media Types. As summarized in **Table 15.2**, the major media types are television, digital and social media, newspapers, direct mail, magazines, radio, and outdoor. Each medium has its advantages and its limitations. Media planners want to choose media that will effectively and efficiently present the advertising message to target customers. Thus, they must consider each medium's impact, message effectiveness, and cost. As discussed in the previous chapter, it's typically not a question of which one medium to use. Rather, the advertiser selects a mix of media and blends them into a fully integrated marketing communications campaign.

The mix of media must be reexamined regularly. For a long time, television and magazines dominated the media mixes of national advertisers, with other media often neglected. However, as mass-media costs rise, audiences shrink, and exciting new digital and social media emerge, many advertisers are finding new ways to reach consumers. They are supplementing the traditional mass media with more-specialized and highly targeted digital media that cost less, target more effectively, and engage consumers more fully. Today's

Table 15.2 | Profiles of Major Media Types

Medium	Advantages	Limitations
Television	Good mass-marketing coverage; low cost per exposure; combines sight, sound, and motion; appealing to the senses	High absolute costs; high clutter; fleeting exposure; less audience selectivity
Digital and social media	High selectivity; low cost; immediacy; engagement capabilities	Potentially low impact; high audience control of content and exposure
Newspapers	Flexibility; timeliness; good local market coverage; broad acceptability; high believability	Short life; poor reproduction quality; small pass-along audience
Direct mail	High audience selectivity; flexibility; no ad competition within the same medium; allows personalization	Relatively high cost per exposure; "junk mail" image
Magazines	High geographic and demographic selectivity; credibility and prestige; high-quality reproduction; long life and good pass-along readership	Long ad purchase lead time; high cost; no guarantee of position
Radio	Good local acceptance; high geographic and demographic selectivity; low cost	Audio only; fleeting exposure; low attention ("the half-heard" medium); fragmented audiences
Outdoor	Flexibility; high repeat exposure; low cost; low message competition; good positional selectivity	Little audience selectivity; creative limitations

marketers want to assemble a full mix of *paid, owned, earned, and shared media* that create and deliver engaging brand content to target consumers.

In addition to the explosion of online, mobile, and social media, cable and satellite television systems are thriving. Such systems allow narrow programming formats, such as all sports, all news, nutrition, arts, home improvement and gardening, cooking, travel, history, finance, and others that target select groups. Comcast and other cable operators are even testing systems that will let them target specific types of ads to TVs in specific neighborhoods or individually to specific types of customers. For example, ads for a Spanish-language channel would run in only Hispanic neighborhoods, or only pet owners would see ads from pet food companies. Advertisers can take advantage of such *narrowcasting* to "rifle in" on special market segments rather than use the "shotgun" approach offered by network broadcasting.

Finally, in their efforts to find less costly and more highly targeted ways to reach consumers, advertisers have discovered a dazzling collection of *alternative media*. These days, no matter where you go or what you do, you will probably run into some new form of advertising.

Marketers have discovered a dazzling array of alternative media, like this heated Caribou Coffee bus shelter.

Caribou Coffee

> Tiny billboards attached to shopping carts urge you to buy Pampers while ads roll by on the store's checkout conveyor touting your local Chevy dealer. Step outside and there goes a city trash truck sporting an ad for Glad trash bags or a school bus displaying a Little Caesar's pizza ad. A nearby fire hydrant is emblazoned with advertising for KFC's "fiery" chicken wings. You escape to the ballpark, only to find billboard-size video screens running Budweiser ads while a blimp with an electronic message board circles lazily overhead. In mid-winter, you wait in a city bus shelter that looks like an oven—with heat coming from the coils—shouting out Caribou Coffee's line-up of hot breakfast sandwiches.
>
> These days, you're likely to find ads—well—anywhere. Taxi cabs sport electronic messaging signs tied to GPS location sensors that can pitch local stores and restaurants wherever they roam. Ad space is being sold on parking-lot tickets, airline

boarding passes, subway turnstiles, highway toll booth gates, golf scorecards, ATMs, municipal garbage cans, and even police cars, doctors' examining tables, and church bulletins. One company even sells space on toilet paper furnished free to restaurants, stadiums, and malls—the paper carries advertiser logos, coupons, and codes you can scan with your smartphone to download digital coupons or link to advertisers' social media pages. Now that's a captive audience.

Such alternative media seem a bit far-fetched, and they sometimes irritate consumers who resent it all as "ad nauseam." But for many marketers, these media can save money and provide a way to hit selected consumers where they live, shop, work, and play.

Another important trend affecting media selection is the rapid growth in the number of *media multitaskers*, people who absorb more than one medium at a time. For example, it's not uncommon to find someone watching TV with a smartphone in hand, tweeting, snapchatting with friends, and chasing down product information on Google. One recent survey found that a whopping 88 percent of tablet owners and 86 percent of smartphone owners use the devices while watching TV. Although some of this multitasking is related to TV viewing—such as looking up related product and program information—most multitasking involves tasks unrelated to the shows being watched. Marketers need to take such media interactions into account when selecting the types of media they will use.[22]

Selecting Specific Media Vehicles. Media planners must also choose the best media vehicles—specific media within each general media type. For example, television vehicles include *Modern Family* and *ABC World News Tonight*. Magazine vehicles include *Time*, *Real Simple*, and *ESPN The Magazine*. Online and mobile vehicles include Twitter, Facebook, Pinterest, and YouTube.

Media planners must compute the cost per 1,000 persons reached by a vehicle. For example, if a full-page, four-color advertisement in the U.S. national edition of *Forbes* costs \$148,220 and *Forbes's* readership is 900,000 people, the cost of reaching each group of 1,000 persons is about \$164. The same advertisement in *Bloomberg Businessweek's* Northeast U.S. regional edition may cost only \$48,100 but reach only 155,000 people—at a cost per 1,000 of about \$310.[23] The media planner ranks each magazine by cost per 1,000 and favors those magazines with the lower cost per 1,000 for reaching target consumers. In the previous case, if a marketer is targeting Northeast business managers, *BusinessWeek* might be the more cost-effective buy, even at a higher cost per thousand.

Media planners must also consider the costs of producing ads for different media. Whereas newspaper ads may cost very little to produce, flashy television ads can be very costly. Many online and social media ads cost little to produce, but costs can climb when producing made-for-the-Web video and ad series.

In selecting specific media vehicles, media planners must balance media costs against several media effectiveness factors. First, the planner should evaluate the media vehicle's audience quality. For a Huggies disposable diapers advertisement, for example, *Parents* magazine would have a high exposure value; *Maxim* would have a low exposure value. Second, the media planner should consider audience engagement. Readers of *Vogue*, for example, typically pay more attention to ads than do *Time* readers. Third, the planner should assess the vehicle's editorial quality. *Time* and the *Wall Street Journal* are more believable and prestigious than *Star* or the *National Enquirer*.

Deciding on Media Timing. An advertiser must also decide how to schedule the advertising over the course of a year. Suppose sales of a product peak in December and drop in March (for winter outdoor gear, for instance). The firm can vary its advertising to follow the seasonal pattern, oppose the seasonal pattern, or be the same all year. Most firms do some seasonal advertising. For example, Mars currently runs M&M's special ads for almost every holiday and "season," from Easter, Fourth of July, and Halloween to the Super Bowl season and the Oscar season. The Picture People, the national chain of portrait studios, advertises more heavily before major holidays, such as Christmas, Easter, Valentine's Day, and Halloween. Some marketers do *only* seasonal advertising: For instance, P&G advertises its Vicks NyQuil only during the cold and flu season.

Finally, the advertiser must choose the pattern of the ads. *Continuity* means scheduling ads evenly within a given period. *Pulsing* means scheduling ads unevenly over a given time period. Thus, 52 ads could either be scheduled at one per week during the year or pulsed in several bursts. The idea behind pulsing is to advertise heavily for a short period to build awareness that carries over to the next advertising period. Those who favor pulsing

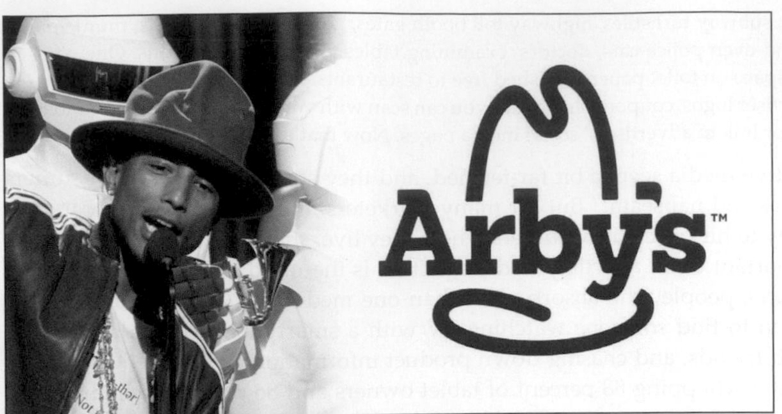

Media timing: Today's social media let advertisers respond to events in real time. Arby's "Hey @Pharrell, can we have our hat back?" tweet during the Grammy Awards earned the brand more than 75,000 retweets and 40,000 favorites.

WireImage/Arby's Restaurant Group, Inc.

feel that it can be used to achieve the same impact as a steady schedule but at a much lower cost. However, some media planners believe that although pulsing achieves minimal awareness, it sacrifices depth of advertising communications.

Today's online and social media let advertisers create ads that respond to events in real time. For example, Lexus recently introduced a new model through live streaming from the North American International Auto Show via Facebook's News Feed. Some 100,000 people watched the introduction live in only the first 10 minutes; another 600,000 viewed it online within the next few days. Oreos reacted in a timely way to a power outage during Super Bowl XLVII with an outage-related "You can still dunk in the dark" tweet ad. The fast-reaction ad was retweeted and favorited thousands of times in only 15 minutes. Similarly, Arby's created big buzz during the last year's Grammy Awards with a real-time tweet responding to Pharrell Williams' infamous Vivienne Westwood hat, which looks a bit like the hat in the familiar Arby's logo. The tweet "Hey @Pharrell, can we have our hat back?" earned more than 75,000 retweets and 40,000 favorites.[24]

Evaluating Advertising Effectiveness and the Return on Advertising Investment

Return on advertising investment
The net return on advertising investment divided by the costs of the advertising investment.

Measuring advertising effectiveness and the **return on advertising investment** has become a hot issue for most companies. Even in a recovering economy with marketing budgets again on the rise, like consumers, advertisers are still pinching their pennies and spending conservatively. That leaves top management at many companies asking their marketing managers, "How do we know that we're spending the right amount on advertising?" and "What return are we getting on our advertising investment?"

Advertisers should regularly evaluate two types of advertising results: the communication effects and the sales and profit effects. Measuring the *communication effects* of an ad or ad campaign tells whether the ads and media are communicating the ad message well. Individual ads can be tested before or after they are run. Before an ad is placed, the advertiser can show it to consumers, ask how they like it, and measure message recall or attitude changes resulting from it. After an ad is run, the advertiser can measure how the ad affected consumer recall or product awareness, engagement, knowledge, and preference. Pre- and post-evaluations of communication effects can be made for entire advertising campaigns as well.

Advertisers have gotten pretty good at measuring the communication effects of their ads and ad campaigns. However, *sales and profit* effects of advertising are often much harder to measure. For example, what sales and profits are produced by an ad campaign that increases brand awareness by 20 percent and brand preference by 10 percent? Sales and profits are affected by many factors other than advertising—such as product features, price, and availability.

One way to measure the sales and profit effects of advertising is to compare past sales and profits with past advertising expenditures. Another way is through experiments. For example, to test the effects of different advertising spending levels, Coca-Cola could vary the amount it spends on advertising in different market areas and measure the differences in the resulting sales and profit levels. More complex experiments could be designed to include other variables, such as differences in the ads or media used.

However, because so many factors affect advertising effectiveness, some controllable and others not, measuring the results of advertising spending remains an inexact science. For example, dozens of advertisers spend lavishly on high-profile Super Bowl ads each year. Although they sense that the returns are worth the sizable investment, few could actually measure or prove it (see Real Marketing 15.1). Managers often must rely on large doses of judgment along with quantitative analysis when assessing advertising performance.

Real Marketing 15.1

The Super Bowl: The Mother of All Advertising Events—But Is It Worth It?

The Super Bowl is the mother of all advertising events. Each year, dozens of blue chip advertisers showcase some of their best work to huge audiences around the world. But all this doesn't come cheap. Last year, major advertisers plunked down an average of $4 million per 30-second spot—that's $133,333 per second! Throw in ad production costs—which can run millions more per ad—and running even a single Super Bowl ad becomes a super-expensive proposition.

So each year, up pops the big debate: Is Super Bowl advertising worth all that money? Super Bowl stalwarts such as Anheuser-Busch, Doritos, Coca-Cola, and GM must think it's a good investment—they come back year after year. But for every big brand that invests in the Super Bowl, there are lots of others that just don't think the returns justify the costs.

The naysayers make some pretty good arguments. Super Bowl advertising is outrageously expensive. And, beyond the costs, the competition for attention during the Super Bowl is fierce. Every single ad represents the best efforts of a major marketer trying to design a knock-your-socks-off spectacular. Many advertisers feel they can get more for their dollar in venues that aren't so crowded with bigger-than-life commercials.

Still, the Super Bowl has much to offer advertisers. It plays to a huge and receptive audience. Super Bowl XLVIII drew more than 112 million U.S. viewers, making it the most-watched television event in history. What's more, during a typical Super Bowl, the ads draw as much or more viewership than the game. As a result, according to one study, the ROI for one Super Bowl ad can equal that of as many as 250 regular TV ads.

Perhaps more important, more and more these days, a Super Bowl ad itself is only the centerpiece of something much, much bigger. Long before the game begins, and long after it ends, consumers, ad critics, media pundits, and advertisers are previewing, reviewing, discussing, rating, and rehashing the commercials. "What used to be a one-day event, with some postgame water-cooler chat, is now an eight- to 13-week experience," says one Super Bowl marketer.

In this digital, mobile, and social media age, rather than surprising viewers with their blockbuster ads during the game, most sponsors now flood online and social media channels weeks in advance with teasers or even entire ads. Weeks and days before the Super Bowl XLVIII kickoff, ads posted by Budweiser, Doritos, Hyundai, Axe, Soda Stream, Chrysler, and others had already grabbed tens of millions of online views. Rather than stealing from a blockbuster ad, the previews seem to make them even more effective on game day. According to one study, 60 percent of the most-shared Super Bowl spots of all time were introduced before the game was broadcast. And on average, commercials uploaded to YouTube before the game generated 3.4 times more views than commercials released on game day.

Consider Anheuser-Busch's pregame activities for Super Bowl XLVIII. The company released its Budweiser "Puppy Love" ad—a heartwarming tale featuring a Golden Retriever puppy and a Clydesdale who became inseparable buddies—on YouTube four days before the game. Before releasing the ad, Budweiser was generating some 8,300 brand mentions across social media channels. The day following the "Puppy Love" prerelease, that shot up seven-fold to more than 56,000 mentions, more than 30 times more mentions than competitor Coors on that same day. By two days before the big game, "Puppy Love" had already garnered 27 million YouTube views. Perhaps because of the previews, during the game itself, the endearing ad became the runaway leader in almost every major Super Bowl ad rating.

Super Bowl advertisers are also working harder these days to create ads that engage consumers interactively during the game itself. More than half of this year's Super Bowl ads incorporated hashtags, and many ads prominently mentioned Facebook, Twitter, YouTube, and other social media. All those digital nods paid off. Google reports that 39 percent of Super Bowl viewers used a mobile device during the game in response to an ad. The number of searches for brands advertised during the Super Bowl spurted 200 percent on desktops, 970 percent on tablets, and 2,700 percent on smartphones compared to searches before the game.

Finally, for most Super Bowl advertisers, long after the game ends, the marketing content machine is still cranking. Next-day "water cooler" discussions about Super Bowl ads have been going on for decades. But digital, mobile, and social media have taken post-game buzz into the stratosphere. For days or even weeks following the game, online social channels hum with ad views and reviews, likes, shares, and comments. Becoming a part of all that online conversation and sharing can substantially extend a company's return on the game-day investment.

PepsiCo's Doritos brand begins its Super Bowl campaign each year a full four months prior to the event with its "Crash the Super Bowl" contest. Doritos invites consumers to submit their

The Doritos Crash the Super Bowl contest and ads generate substantial consumer engagement before, during, and after the big game, extending the brand's return on its hefty Super Bowl advertising investment.

own 30-second commercials and, based on fan votes, runs the best ones during the game. The contest and ads ensure several months of heavy consumer involvement. Now in its eighth year, "Crash the Super Bowl" has produced numerous top-place finishers in the *USA Today* Ad Meter rankings, earning each winner a $1 million cash prize. Last year's contest attracted 5,400 entries from 46 countries. The winner, "Time Machine"—a witty ad about a man who humors a small kid by taking a ride in his cardboard box time machine, only to be hoodwinked out of his bag of Doritos—placed fourth in the Ad Meter rankings. The homemade commercial cost $200 to make and took just eight hours to shoot. The runner-up ad, "Cowboy Kid"—a chuckler in which a kid dressed as a cowboy rides his huge dog and lassos a bag of Doritos out of his snarky big brother's hands, placed second in the ratings. Both ads created buzz well beyond the actual game-day broadcast.

Befitting the big game's "big-stage" status, many Super Bowl ads take on significance well beyond the brands they pitch. An example is Coca-Cola's Super Bowl XLVIII commercial, "It's Beautiful," a 60-second ad celebrating America's diversity. Set to the song "America the Beautiful," sung in seven different languages by a diverse set of young female vocalists, the inspirational ad features people and locations representing the nation's varied ethnic, racial, and religious makeup. "It's Beautiful" sparked a firestorm of debate. Detractors objected to the patriotic song being sung in anything but English; defenders applauded Coca-Cola's inclusiveness. In all, the provocative ad generated strong, mostly positive buzz for Coca-Cola. It ranked among the top three Super Bowl ads that year in terms of brand advocacy, sustaining audiences, and emotional engagement, and went on to become the game's most viral ad, edging out even fan favorite "Puppy Love."

So—back to the original question: Is Super Bowl advertising really worth the huge investment? The Super Bowl is certainly not for every brand. But for the right brands, and the brands that do it right, the answer is a resounding "yes." It's not just about running an ad or two during the big game. Instead, it's about consumers by the millions watching, streaming, sharing, commenting, debating, and buzzing about ads and brands before the game, in the moment, and after the main event. For the Super Bowl, says one marketing executive, "We are fundamentally playing a different game. [It's] no longer about 30 seconds [but] about a month long, really, really meaningful program." Says another Super Bowl regular: "Not only does the broadcast itself bring great value, but if you just look at the explosion in the social-media value and digital value in recent years, it's a terrific return on investment."

Sources: Stuart Elliott, "Super Bowl Ads Get Their Own Pregame Show," *New York Times*, January 17, 2014; Glenn Davis, "Inside the Numbers: Which Brands' Lived Up To Pregame Buzz?", *USA Today*, February 4,2014; "How Marketers Can Bring Their A-Game to the Super Bowl," *Advertising Age,* November 4, 2013, http://adage.com/print/291177; Veronica Maria Jarski, "Which Brand Really Won the Super Bowl Ad War?" *MarketingProfs*, March 15, 2014, www.marketingprofs.com/chirp/2014/24658/which-brand; "Pepsi Alters Super Bowl Strategy, Takes Masterbrand Approach," *Advertising Age,* January 24, 2014, http://adage.com/print/291271; Katie Kindelan, "Doritos 'Crash the SuperBowl' Champ Wins $1 Million," *ABC News,* February 3, 2014, http://abcnews.go.com/blogs/headlines/2014/ 02/doritos-crash-the-super-bowl-champ-wins-1-million/; and "2014 *USA Today* Ad Meter," http://admeter.usatoday.com/, accessed March 2014.

Other Advertising Considerations

In developing advertising strategies and programs, the company must address two additional questions. First, how will the company organize its advertising function—who will perform which advertising tasks? Second, how will the company adapt its advertising strategies and programs to the complexities of international markets?

Organizing for Advertising

Different companies organize in different ways to handle advertising. In small companies, advertising might be handled by someone in the sales department. Large companies have advertising departments whose job it is to set the advertising budget, work with the ad agency, and handle other advertising not done by the agency. However, most large companies use outside advertising agencies because they offer several advantages.

Advertising agency
A marketing services firm that assists companies in planning, preparing, implementing, and evaluating all or portions of their advertising programs.

How does an **advertising agency** work? Advertising agencies originated in the mid- to late 1800s from salespeople and brokers who worked for the media and received a commission for selling advertising space to companies. As time passed, the salespeople began to help customers prepare their ads. Eventually, they formed agencies and grew closer to the advertisers than to the media.

Today's agencies employ specialists who can often perform advertising tasks better than the company's own staff can. Agencies also bring an outside point of view to solving the company's problems, along with lots of experience from working with different clients and situations. So, today, even companies with strong advertising departments of their own use advertising agencies.

Some ad agencies are huge; the largest U.S. agency, Y&R, has annual gross U.S. revenues of $1.69 billion. In recent years, many agencies have grown by gobbling up other agencies, thus creating huge agency holding companies. The largest of these megagroups, WPP, includes several large advertising, PR, and promotion agencies, with combined worldwide revenues of more than $17 billion.[25]

Most large advertising agencies have the staff and resources to handle all phases of an advertising campaign for their clients, from creating a marketing plan to developing ad campaigns and preparing, placing, and evaluating ads and other brand content. Large brands commonly employ several agencies that handle everything from mass-media advertising campaigns to shopper marketing and social media content.

International Advertising Decisions

International advertisers face many complexities not encountered by domestic advertisers. The most basic issue concerns the degree to which global advertising should be adapted to the unique characteristics of various country markets.

Some advertisers have attempted to support their global brands with highly standardized worldwide advertising, with campaigns that work as well in Bangkok as they do in Baltimore. For example, McDonald's unifies its creative elements and brand presentation under the familiar "i'm lovin' it" theme in all its 100-plus markets worldwide. Visa coordinates its $500 million worldwide advertising efforts for its debit and credit cards under the "Everywhere you want to be" creative platform, which works as well in Korea as it does in the United States or Brazil.[26] And Snickers runs similar versions of its "You're not you when you're hungry" ads in 80 different countries, from the United States and the United Kingdom to Mexico, Australia, and even Russia. No matter what the country, the ads strike a common human emotion that everyone can relate to—people get out of sorts and do uncharacteristic things when they need nutrition. A Snickers bar can help them get back to being their real selves. Snickers let's local markets make adjustments for local languages and personalities. Otherwise, the ads are similar worldwide.[27]

In recent years, the increased popularity of online marketing and social media sharing has boosted the need for advertising standardization for global brands. Most big marketing and advertising campaigns include a large online presence. Connected consumers can now zip easily across borders via the Internet and social media, making it difficult for advertisers to roll out adapted campaigns in a controlled, orderly fashion. As a result, at the very least, most global consumer brands coordinate their Web sites internationally. For example, check out the McDonald's Web sites from Germany to Jordan to China. You'll find the golden arches, the "i'm lovin' it" logo and jingle, a Big Mac equivalent, and maybe even Ronald McDonald himself.

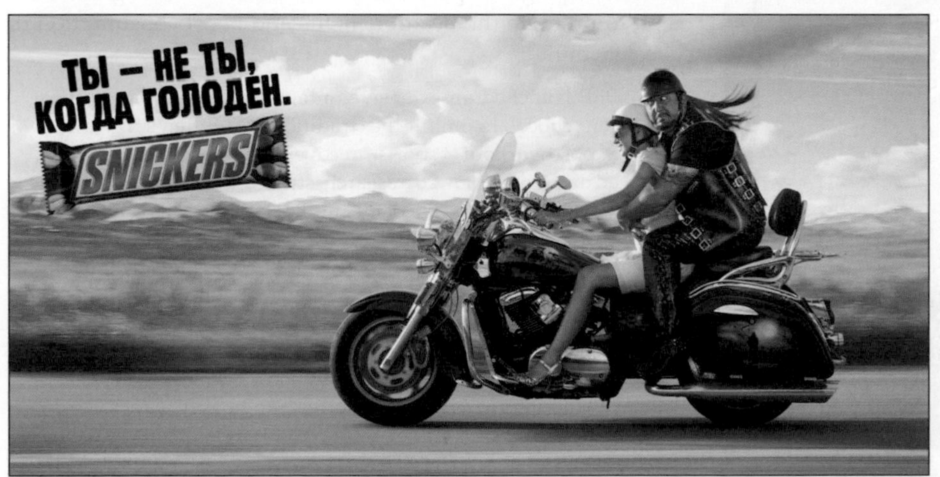

Snickers runs similar versions of its "You're not you when you're hungry" ads in 80 different countries, here Russia, making only minor adjustments for local languages and personalities.

SNICKERS® is a registered trademark of Mars, Incorporated. The trademark is used with permission. Mars, Incorporated is not associated with Pearson Education, Inc. The image of the MARS bar is printed with permission of Mars, Incorporated.

Standardization produces many benefits—lower advertising costs, greater global advertising coordination, and a more consistent worldwide image. But it also has drawbacks. Most important, it ignores the fact that country markets differ greatly in their cultures, demographics, and economic conditions. Thus, most international advertisers "think globally but act locally." They develop global advertising *strategies* that make their worldwide efforts more efficient and consistent. Then they adapt their advertising *programs* to make them more responsive to consumer needs and expectations within local markets. For example, although Visa employs its "Everywhere you want to be" theme globally, ads in specific locales employ local language and inspiring local imagery that make the theme relevant to the local markets in which they appear.

Global advertisers face several special problems. For instance, advertising media costs and availability differ vastly from country to country. Countries also differ in the extent to which they regulate advertising practices. Many countries have extensive systems of laws restricting how much a company can spend on advertising, the media used, the nature of advertising claims, and other aspects of the advertising program. Such restrictions often require advertisers to adapt their campaigns from country to country.

Public relations (PR)
Building good relations with the company's various publics by obtaining favorable publicity; building up a good corporate image; and handling or heading off unfavorable rumors, stories, and events.

Thus, although advertisers may develop global strategies to guide their overall advertising efforts, specific advertising programs must usually be adapted to meet local cultures and customs, media characteristics, and regulations.

Author Comment Not long ago, public relations was considered a marketing stepchild because of its limited marketing use. That situation is changing fast, however, as more marketers recognize PR's brand-building, customer engagement, and social power.

Public Relations

Another major mass-promotion tool, **public relations**, consists of activities designed to engage and build good relations with the company's various publics. PR departments may perform any or all of the following functions:[28]

- *Press relations or press agency.* Creating and placing newsworthy information in the news media to attract attention to a person, product, or service.
- *Product publicity.* Publicizing specific products.
- *Public affairs.* Building and maintaining national or local community relationships.
- *Lobbying.* Building and maintaining relationships with legislators and government officials to influence legislation and regulation.
- *Investor relations.* Maintaining relationships with shareholders and others in the financial community.
- *Development.* Working with donors or members of nonprofit organizations to gain financial or volunteer support.

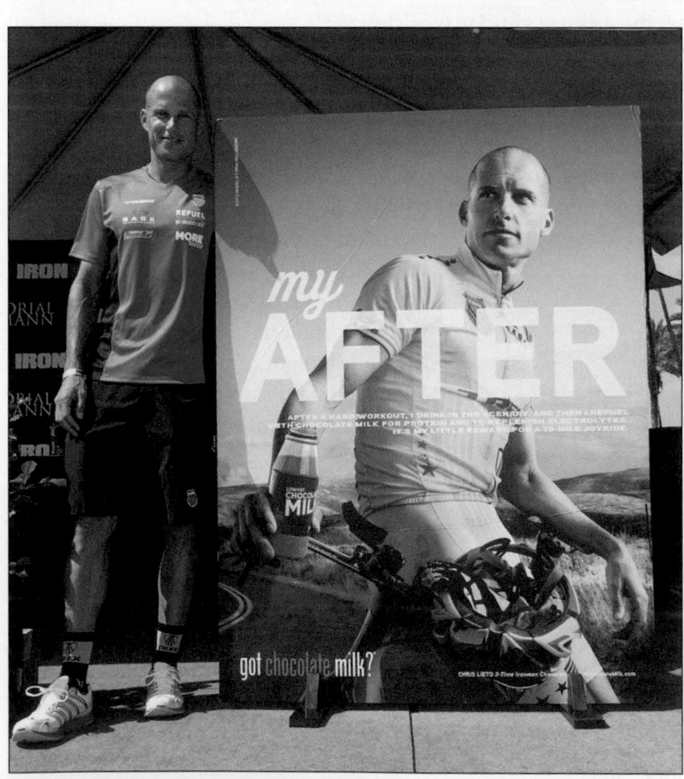

MilkPEP's "Built With Chocolate Milk" public relations campaign is repositioning chocolate milk as a sports recovery "after" beverage for both everyday and well-known adults, here Ironman World Champion Chris Lieto.

Bob Levey / Stringer

Public relations is used to promote products, people, places, ideas, activities, organizations, and even nations. Companies use PR to build good relations with consumers, investors, the media, and their communities. Trade associations have used PR to rebuild interest in commodities, such as eggs, apples, potatoes, onions, and even chocolate milk. For example, the Milk Processor Education Program (MilkPEP), known for its successful "Got Milk?" campaign in previous years, created a strong PR campaign to promote the health benefits and boost consumption of chocolate milk:[29]

> MilkPEP launched an extensive, integrated PR campaign to reposition chocolate milk—the traditional children's favorite—as a post-workout, sports recovery beverage for adults. Backed by more than 20 research studies that support the refueling benefits of chocolate milk, MilkPEP's "Built With Chocolate Milk" campaign enlists important influencers—such as athletes, sports nutritionists, fitness bloggers, and health researchers—to help change perceptions of chocolate milk from just a kid's drink to a legitimate sports drink, one that's "Trusted by Athletes. Backed by Science." Ads and social media content feature both everyday and well-known athletes, such as 12-time swimming medalist Dara Torres, pro hockey's Zach Parise, Ironman World Champions Chris Lieto and Mirinda Carfrae, and NBA basketball star Carmelo Anthony. For example, MilkPEP sponsored Pittsburgh Steelers football player Hines Ward to train and compete in the Ironman. The chocolate milk team followed Hines through workouts and meetings with dieticians, showing the science behind chocolate milk as a recovery drink, then posted videos and other accounts on YouTube, Twitter, and Facebook. Hines's experience with chocolate milk inspired both fans and fellow athletes to try the beverage. Beyond working

with professional athletes, MilkPEP also participates in hundreds of local events across the country, such as California's Big Sur Marathon, passing out free chocolate milk at finish lines. Thanks to strong PR, chocolate milk is now making a comeback, with 6 percent to 12 percent sales increases among targeted adults.

The Role and Impact of PR

Public relations can have a strong impact on public awareness at a much lower cost than advertising can. When using public relations, the company does not pay for the space or time in the media. Rather, it pays for a staff to develop and circulate information and manage events. If the company develops an interesting story or event, it could be picked up by several different media and have the same effect as advertising that would cost millions of dollars. What's more, public relations has the power to engage consumers and make them a part of the brand story and its telling (see Real Marketing 15.2).

PR results can sometimes be spectacular. Consider the launch of Apple's iPad:[30]

> Apple's iPad was one of the most successful new-product launches in history. The funny thing: Whereas most big product launches are accompanied by huge prelaunch advertising campaigns, Apple pulled this one off with no advertising. None at all. Instead, it simply fed the PR fire. It built buzz months in advance by distributing iPads for early reviews, feeding the offline and online press with tempting tidbits, and offering fans an early online peek at thousands of new iPad apps that would be available. At launch time, it fanned the flames with a cameo on the TV sitcom *Modern Family*, a flurry of launch-day appearances on TV talk shows, and other launch-day events. In the process, through PR alone, the iPad launch generated unbounded consumer excitement, a media frenzy, and long lines outside retail stores on launch day. Apple sold more than 300,000 of the sleek gadgets on the first day alone and more than two million in the first two months—even as demand outstripped supply. Apple repeated the feat a year later with the equally successful launch of iPad 2, which sold close to one million devices the weekend of its launch.

Despite its potential strengths, public relations is occasionally described as a marketing stepchild because of its sometimes limited and scattered use. The PR department is often located at corporate headquarters or handled by a third-party agency. Its staff is so busy dealing with various publics—stockholders, employees, legislators, and the press—that PR programs to support product marketing objectives may be ignored. Moreover, marketing managers and PR practitioners do not always speak the same language. Whereas many PR practitioners see their jobs as simply communicating, marketing managers tend to be much more interested in how advertising and PR affect brand building, sales and profits, and customer engagement and relationships.

This situation is changing, however. Although public relations still captures only a small portion of the overall marketing budgets of many firms, PR can be a powerful brand-building tool. Especially in this digital age, the lines between advertising and PR are becoming more and more blurred. For example, are brand Web sites, blogs, brand videos, and social media activities advertising or PR efforts? All are both. And as the use of earned and shared digital content grows rapidly, PR may play a bigger role in brand content management. More than any other department, PR has always been responsible for creating relevant marketing content that draws consumers to a brand rather than pushing messages out. "Knowing where influence and conversations are to be found is PR's stock in trade," says one expert. "PR pros are an organization's master storytellers. In a word, they *do* content."[31] The point is that PR should work hand in hand with advertising within an integrated marketing communications program to help build customer engagement and relationships.

Major Public Relations Tools

Public relations uses several tools. One of the major tools is *news*. PR professionals find or create favorable news about the company and its products or people. Sometimes news stories occur naturally; sometimes the PR person can suggest events or activities that would create news. Another common PR tool is *special events*, ranging from news conferences and speeches, brand tours, and sponsorships to laser light shows, multimedia presentations, or educational programs designed to reach and interest target publics.

Real Marketing 15.2

Public Relations and Customer Engagement at Coca-Cola: From Impressions to Expressions to Transactions

Coca-Cola aims to do much more with public relations than just create passive "impressions." It's looking to create customer engagement and inspire customer "expressions." According to Coca-Cola's chief marketing officer, Joe Tripodi, the PR goal is to develop "strongly sharable pieces of communication information that generate huge numbers of impressions online—and then, crucially, lead to expressions from consumers, who join the story and extend it, and then finally to transactions." That is, Coca-Cola uses PR to engage consumers and start customer conversations that will inspire consumers themselves to extend the brand's theme of open happiness and optimism.

Consider Coca-Cola's recent "Hug Me" campaign, in which the company installed a "happiness" vending machine overnight at a university in Singapore. The machine had a solid red front and trademark wavy white stripe, but it contained no Coca-Cola logo, no coin slot, and no soda selection buttons. Only the words "Hug Me" were visible in large white letters printed in Coca-Cola's famous script. With hidden cameras rolling, Coca-Cola captured the quizzical reactions of passersby as they first scratched their heads, then slowly approached the machine, and, finally, with smiles on their faces, gave it a big hug. Responding to that simple act of happiness, the machine magically dispensed a cold can of Coca-Cola, free of charge.

Coca-Cola's "Hug Me" video shows one person after another hugging the machine, receiving a Coke, and sharing their delight with others. Coca-Cola placed the video online, then stepped back and let the media and consumers carry the story forward. Within only one week's time, the video generated 112 million impressions. Given the low costs of the free Cokes and producing the video, the "Hug Me" campaign resulted in an amazingly low cost per impression. But even more valuable were the extensive customer expressions that followed, such as "Liking" the video and forwarding it to others. "The Coca Cola Hug Machine is a simple idea to spread some happiness," says a Coca-Cola marketer. "Our strategy is to deliver doses of happiness in an unexpected, innovative way . . . and happiness is contagious."

The "Hug Me" campaign was only the most recent in a long line of similar conversation-starting PR tactics by Coca-Cola. One Valentine's Day, the company placed a modified vending machine in the middle of a busy shopping mall that dispensed free Cokes to folks who confirmed their "couple" status with a hug or a kiss. A few years ago, another Coca-Cola Happiness machine placed at a university dispensed everything from free Cokes to popcorn, pizza, flowers, handshakes, and Polaroid photos. Making periodic "jackpot" sounds, the machine dispensed dozens of Cokes and a long plank layered with colorful cupcakes. These unexpected actions not only prompted smiles and cheers, but recipients could hardly wait to share their bounty and the story with anyone and everyone, extending Coke's happiness positioning.

Coca-Cola has fielded many other PR campaigns that employ its "impressions-expressions-transactions" model to inspire brand conversations. In its "Project Connect" campaign, the company printed 150 common first names on Coke bottles, an exploit that had consumers by the hundreds of thousands rifling through Coca-Cola displays in retail stores looking for their names.

Coca-Cola's long-running Arctic Home campaign employs the power of publicity and shared media to create engagement by connecting the company's brands to a culturally relevant cause. In that campaign, Coca-Cola has partnered with the World Wildlife Fund (WWF) to protect the habitat of polar bears—a cause that fits perfectly with Coke's longstanding use of digitally produced polar bears as spokes-critters in its ads. The Arctic Home campaign goes well beyond clever seasonal ads by integrating PR efforts with virtually every aspect of promotion and marketing. The campaign includes a dedicated Web site, a smartphone app, a pledge of $3 million to the WWF, advertisements and online videos featuring footage from the IMAX film *To the Arctic 3D*, and attention-grabbing white Coke cans highlighting the plight of polar bears. In its first year, Arctic Home produced an astounding 1.3 billion impressions, which in turn inspired untold customer engagement and expressions.

Coca-Cola's "BHAG," or "big hairy audacious goal," is not just to hold its market share in the soft drink category, where sales have been flat for years, but to double its business by the end of the decade. Public relations and the social media will play a central role in achieving this goal by making

The power of PR: Coca-Cola's "Hug Me" campaign created 112 million impressions in only one week's time. More important, it created countless customer expressions that extended the brand's theme of happiness and optimism.

customers a part of the brand story and turning them into an army of brand advocates who will carry the Coca-Cola Open Happiness message forward. "It's not just about pushing stuff out as we've historically done," says CMO Tripodi. "We have to create experiences that perhaps are had only by a few but are compelling enough to fuel conversations with many."

Sources: Tim Nudd, "Coca-Cola Joins the Revolution in a World Where the Mob Rules," *Adweek*, June 19, 2012, www.adweek.com/print/141217; "WWF and The Coca-Cola Company Team Up to Protect Polar Bears," http://worldwildlife.org/projects/wwf-and-the-coca-cola-company-team-up-to-protect-polar-bears, accessed June 2014; Natalie Zmuda, "Coca-Cola Gets Real with Polar Bears," *Advertising Age*, October 25, 2011, http://adage.com/print/230632/; Anthony Wing Kosner, "Hug Me: Coca-Cola Introduces Gesture Based Marketing in Singapore," *Forbes*, April 11, 2012, www.forbes.com/sites/anthonykosner/2012/04/11/hug-me-coca-cola-introduces-gesture-based-marketing-in-singapore/; "Cannes Lions 2012: Five-Points to a Great Marketing Strategy," afaqs.com, June 20, 2012, www.afaqs.com/news/story/34444; and www.youtube.com/watch?feature=endscreen&NR=1&v=-A-7H4aOhq0 and www.youtube.com/watch?v=D3j_pB3STsQ, accessed September 2014.

Public relations people also prepare *written materials* to reach and influence their target markets. These materials include annual reports, brochures, articles, and company newsletters and magazines. *Audiovisual materials*, such as DVDs and online videos, are being used increasingly as communication tools. *Corporate identity materials* can also help create a corporate identity that the public immediately recognizes. Logos, stationery, brochures, signs, business forms, business cards, buildings, uniforms, and company cars and trucks all become marketing tools when they are attractive, distinctive, and memorable. Finally, companies can improve public goodwill by contributing money and time to *public service activities*.

As previously discussed, the Web and social media are also important PR channels. Web sites, blogs, and social media such as YouTube, Facebook, Pinterest, Storify, and Twitter are providing new ways to reach and engage people. As noted, storytelling and engagement are core PR strengths, and that plays well into the use of online and social media.

As with the other promotion tools, in considering when and how to use product public relations, management should set PR objectives, choose the PR messages and vehicles, implement the PR plan, and evaluate the results. The firm's PR should be blended smoothly with other promotion activities within the company's overall integrated marketing communications effort.

15 Reviewing the Concepts

OBJECTIVES REVIEW AND KEY TERMS

Objectives Review

Companies must do more than make good products; they have to engage consumers, inform them persuasively about product benefits, and carefully position products in consumers' minds. To do this, they must master *advertising* and *public relations*.

OBJECTIVE 1 Define the role of advertising in the promotion mix. *(pp 474–475)*

Advertising—the use of paid media by a seller to inform, persuade, and remind buyers about its products or its organization—is an important promotion tool for engaging customers and communicating the value that marketers create for customers. American marketers spend more than $170 billion each year on advertising, and worldwide spending exceeds $518 billion. Advertising takes many forms and has many uses. Although advertising is employed mostly by business firms, a wide range of not-for-profit organizations, professionals, and social agencies also employ advertising to promote their causes to various target publics. *PR*—gaining favorable publicity and creating a favorable company image—is the least used of the major promotion tools, although it has great potential for building consumer awareness and preference.

Describe the major decisions involved in developing an advertising program. *(pp 475–490)*

Advertising decision making involves making decisions about the advertising objectives, budget, messages and media, and evaluation of the results. Advertisers should set clear target, task, and timing *objectives*, whether the aim is to inform, engage, persuade, or remind buyers. Advertising's goal is to move consumers through the buyer-readiness stages discussed in Chapter 14. Some advertising is designed to move people to immediate action. However, many of the ads you see today focus on building or strengthening long-term customer engagement and relationships. The advertising *budget* depends on many factors. No matter what method is used, setting the advertising budget is no easy task.

Advertising strategy consists of two major elements: creating advertising *messages and content* and selecting advertising *media*. The *message decision* calls for planning a message strategy and executing it effectively. Good messages and other content are especially important in today's costly and cluttered advertising environment. Just to gain and hold attention, today's messages must be better planned, more imaginative, more entertaining, and more rewarding to consumers. In fact, many marketers are now subscribing to a new merging of advertising and entertainment, dubbed *Madison & Vine*. The *media decision* involves defining reach, frequency, impact, and engagement goals; choosing major media types; selecting media vehicles; and choosing media timing. Message and media decisions must be closely coordinated for maximum campaign effectiveness.

Finally, *evaluation* calls for evaluating the communication and sales effects of advertising before, during, and after ads are placed. Advertising accountability has become a hot issue for most companies. Increasingly, top management is asking: "What return are we getting on our advertising investment?" and "How do we know that we're spending the right amount?" Other important advertising issues involve *organizing* for advertising and dealing with the complexities of international advertising.

OBJECTIVE 3 Define the role of public relations in the promotion mix. *(pp 490–491)*

Public relations, or *PR*—gaining favorable publicity and creating a favorable company image—is the least used of the major promotion tools, although it has great potential for building consumer awareness and preference.

PR is used to promote products, people, places, ideas, activities, organizations, and even nations. Companies use PR to build good relationships with consumers, investors, the media, and their communities. PR can have a strong impact on public awareness at a much lower cost than advertising can, and PR results can sometimes be spectacular. Although PR still captures only a small portion of the overall marketing budgets of many firms, it is playing an increasingly important brand-building role. In the digital, mobile, and social media age, the lines between advertising and PR are becoming more and more blurred.

OBJECTIVE 4 Explain how companies use PR to communicate with their publics. *(pp 491–493)*

Companies use PR to communicate with their publics by setting PR objectives, choosing PR messages and vehicles, implementing the PR plan, and evaluating PR results. To accomplish these goals, PR professionals use several tools, such as news and special events. They also prepare written, audiovisual, *and* corporate identity materials and contribute money and time to public service activities. The Internet has also become an increasingly important PR channel, as Web sites, blogs, and social media are providing interesting new ways to reach more people.

MyMarketingLab

Go to **mymktlab.com** to complete the problems marked with this icon .

Key Terms

OBJECTIVE 1

Advertising (p 474)

OBJECTIVE 2

Advertising objective (p 475)
Advertising budget (p 477)
Advertising strategy (p 477)
Madison & Vine (p 479)
Creative concept (p 480)
Execution style (p 480)
Advertising media (p 482)
Return on advertising investment (p 486)
Advertising agency (p 488)

OBJECTIVE 3

Public relations (PR) (p 490)

DISCUSSION AND CRITICAL THINKING

Discussion Questions

15-1 Describe the major elements of a firm's PR strategy. (AACSB: Communication)

15-2 What is the first step in creating effective advertising content? (AACSB: Communication)

15-3 Why has measuring advertising effectiveness become so important? What types of advertising results do marketers measure and what are the issues related to this assessment? (AACSB: Communication)

15-4 How are public relations handled by businesses in your country? (AACSB: Communication)

15-5 Discuss the tools used by public relations professionals. Is public relations free promotion for a company? (AACSB: Communication)

Critical Thinking Exercises

15-6 Imagine you have been tasked with setting the advertising budget for two brands. The first one is a new brand struggling to gain a market share, as few consumers have heard of it or tried it. The second brand is more mature and established. How would you set the budgets and how might market share concerns have an impact on your decision? (AACSB: Communication; Reflective Thinking)

15-7 According to a recently released study, mascots create more social media buzz than do celebrity endorsers. For example, in the study, the Pillsbury Doughboy scored 10 (highest on the scale) and LeBron James scored 1. In a small group, find an example of another company using a mascot to create social media buzz and suggest ways the company can create even more buzz. How is social media buzz measured? (AACSB: Communication; Use of IT; Reflective Thinking)

15-8 Many countries now have award ceremonies celebrating excellence in marketing. Research such events in your own country. What does the field of public relations encompass? Write a report on one of the award winners focusing on marketing-related activities. (AACSB: Communication; Use of IT; Reflective Thinking)

MINICASES AND APPLICATIONS

Online, Mobile, and Social Media Marketing **Facebook Audience Network**

Facebook has 1.23 billion monthly users, and a large majority of users typically visit the site daily on a mobile device. What started as an online social network allowing people to connect with each other has transformed into a behemoth media mogul that promises to be a game-changer in mobile advertising. Facebook announced its new mobile ad platform called Audience Network to deliver targeted mobile ads for advertisers. While there are other mobile ad platforms (Google is the dominant player), Facebook has a treasure trove of data that is useful for advertisers. Google is strong in search data, but Facebook is part of our lives. Facebook has been placing ads on its site for advertisers, but now Facebook will be pushing those ads to third-party apps. This is a win-win-win situation for advertisers, app developers, and Facebook because advertisers get their mobile ads to people based on very personal information, app developers get ad revenue, and Facebook gets a cut of the ad revenue for placing the ad. And it's no small cut—in just the last quarter of 2013, Facebook earned $1.3 billion in mobile ad revenue. That's 60 percent of Facebook's overall ad revenue.

15-9 Compare and contrast Facebook's, Google's, and Twitter's ad networks. Which is most effective for advertisers? (AACSB: Communication; Reflective Thinking)

15-10 Mobile advertising is one of the fastest growing sectors of digital advertising, but how is mobile advertising effectiveness measured? Research this issue and create a report of your findings. (AACSB: Communication; Reflective Thinking)

Marketing Ethics **Lie to Me**

The UK public relations industry is worth an estimated $12 billion per year. Some $9 billion is spent in-house by business organizations and the remaining $3 billion is spent on hiring freelance public relations specialists. A review of the public relations industry in the UK revealed a fascinating mix of operations and options. For the most part, the larger PR agencies are concentrated in London. These tended to be big-budget-oriented, extremely professional, large agencies with a host of blue-chip clients. There are also a large number of "micro" markets that are handled by PR specialists. These agencies have specialized knowledge of a product type, country, or sector. They are the "go-to" agencies in specialized situations; it would also seem to be the case that the bigger agencies have them subcontract when necessary. Outside of London, Manchester has the largest number of agencies with the greatest income. There are another 17 cities in the UK that have at least one dedicated PR agency with a range of clients. In the regional markets and the less densely populated areas of the UK there is greater fragmentation and a larger number of freelance PR specialists. These freelancers often work as a fairly small group and are not classified as agencies. PR as a part of the overall market effort seems alive and well in the UK.

15-11 Investigate the public relations industry in your own country. Is there a regulating organization? Are the agencies large or small? What is the spending on public relations? How does this compare to the UK? (AACSB: Communication; Reflective Thinking)

15-12 Suppose public relations is only necessary when something has gone wrong; why do most companies opt for a permanent PR cover? (AACSB: Communication; Use of IT; Reflective Thinking)

Marketing by the Numbers Dubai City Guide

Cyber Gear's Dubai City Guide has been active online since 1996. It has become a vital source of news and information for Dubai residents and visitors. With a wide range of stories covering news, city events, promotions, sales, art events, movie timings, and other features, it is constantly updated. The Web site is well organized and attractive, and reflects the vibrant nature of Dubai itself. Many tourists visit the site before coming to Dubai, and the guide has in excess of 80,000 subscribers and attracts over a million visitors per month. The site is largely funded by advertisers, and Cyber Gear has created a system by which advertisers can choose pages that best fit their target audiences. The site is very open about its visitor statistics, which is understandable given the fact that it faces a huge amount of competition from other advertising outlets and opportunities. The following statistics on the Web traffic for the site as of October 2010 are available at www.dubaicityguide.com/m/main/advertise-with-us-1.asp#vital.

A common measure of advertising efficiency is cost per thousand impressions (CPM). The following table outlines the typical CPM rates for advertising on the Web site:

Standard banner	$25 CPM
Leaderboard banner	$40 CPM
Skyscraper banner	$35 CPM
Space banner	$50 CPM

15-13 If a standard banner reaches 670,000 impressions, what would be the cost to the advertiser? (AACSB: Communication; Analytical Reasoning)

15-14 Calculate the total cost for an e-mail campaign to subscribers based on the cost of $150 CPM. (AACSB: Communication; Analytical Reasoning; Reflective Thinking)

Video Case E*TRADE

Super Bowl XXXIV, the first of the new millennium, was known as the Dot-com Bowl because of the glut of Internet companies that plopped down an average of $2.2 million per 30-second spot ad. Today, most of the companies that defined the dot-com glory days are gone. But one darling of the dot-com era, E*TRADE, remains among the few survivors. Although E*TRADE has experienced challenges since the turn of the century, it has also turned profits. Advertising on the big game hasn't worked out well for everyone. But for E*TRADE, Super Bowl ads have been part of a larger advertising effort that played a role in its survival. Although E*TRADE has altered its marketing mix strategies to adapt to changes in the marketing environment, it has continued to invest in the Super Bowl as an advertising medium. In this video segment, E*TRADE reports on its advertising strategy as well as the advantages and disadvantages of Super Bowl advertising.

After viewing the video featuring E*TRADE, answer the following questions:

15-15 What has been the role of advertising at E*TRADE?

15-16 What factors have played a role in E*TRADE's decision to advertise on the Super Bowl?

15-17 Analyze E*TRADE's most recent Super Bowl ads. Is E*TRADE still getting its money's worth from Super Bowl advertising? Explain.

Company Case Allstate: Bringing Mayhem to the Auto Insurance Advertising Wars

In the spring of 1950, the teenage daughter of Allstate general sales manager Davis Ellis was stricken with hepatitis shortly before she was to graduate from high school. The worried executive arrived home from work one evening just as his wife returned from the hospital where their daughter was admitted. As he met her at the front door, his wife reported, "The hospital said not to worry . . . we're in good hands with the doctor."

Later that year, Ellis became part of a team charged with developing the first major national advertising campaign for the Allstate Insurance Company. As the team discussed the message they wanted the brand to convey, Ellis recalled his wife's "we're in good hands" remark and how good it made him feel. The phrase projected security, reassurance, and responsibility, exactly the traits the team wanted customers to associate with Allstate. Thus was born the slogan, "You're in Good Hands with Allstate."

By the early 2000s, a study by Northwestern University found that the long-standing Allstate catchphrase was the most recognized slogan in the United States. For years, Allstate held the position as the second-largest personal lines insurer, trailing only State Farm. In 2003, Allstate hired actor Dennis Haysbert as the brand's spokesperson. After starring in dozens of Allstate commercials—each culminating with the question, "Are you in good hands?—Haysbert's deep voice became a comforting familiarity to television viewers. Today, the 'Good Hands' slogan is the oldest surviving slogan for a paid campaign.

An Advertising Shakeup

Although Allstate's advertising served it well for decades, by the late 1990s, the company had fallen into the same routine as the rest of its industry. Big auto insurance companies were spending modestly on sleepy ad campaigns featuring touchy-feely, reassuring messages such as Allstate's "You're in good hands," or State Farm's "Like a good neighbor." In an industry characterized by low budgets and even lower-key ads, no brand's marketing stood out.

However, the advertising serenity ended with the first appearance of the now-iconic GEICO Gecko in 1999, backed by a big budget and pitching direct sales and low prices. That single GEICO ad campaign sparked a frenzy of ad spending and creativity in the insurance industry that quickly escalated into a full-scale advertising war. Once-conservative car insurance ads became creative showstoppers, as edgy and creative as ads found in any industry. Here are a few highlights:

- *GEICO.* GEICO got the auto insurance advertising wars rolling when it was acquired by billionaire Warren Buffett's Berkshire Hathaway Inc. in 1996 and given a blank check to aggressively increase market share. That led to an onslaught of advertising, the likes of which the auto insurance industry had never seen. A string of creative GEICO campaigns featured everything from civilized cavemen to cash with googly eyes. But it was the GEICO Gecko that had the biggest impact. With his signature English accent, the Gecko made GEICO's simple message clear—"15 minutes can save you 15 percent or more on car insurance." More than any other industry spokesperson, the Gecko lent personality and pizzazz to the previously sleepy insurance industry and its staid brands.
- *Progressive.* Following GEICO's lead, in 2008 Progressive created its own endearing personality—perky sales clerk Flo. Progressive created the ever-upbeat, ruby-lipped Flo to help convince consumers who are already in the market that they can get an even better price deal from Progressive. Flo helped put Progressive hot on the heels of rising GEICO as the fourth largest auto insurer. Flo assists people when they are ready to shop. Progressive later introduced complementary campaigns featuring the Messenger—the mustachioed, leather-jacket-wearing stranger—and Brad—the easy-going, self-assured man with an absurdly funny sense of self-esteem who refers to himself only in the third person. Like the GEICO Gecko, Flo, the Messenger, and Brad pitch price savings as their primary appeal.
- *State Farm.* As GEICO and Progressive shook up the industry with their direct, low-price, high-profile selling models, conventional agent-based auto insurers were forced to respond. Ninety-year-old State Farm, the long-time industry leader, was hardly a stranger to advertising. Like Allstate, State Farm had a long-standing, widely recognized slogan—"Like a good neighbor, State Farm is there"—a jingle written by pop music icon Barry Manilow in 1971. Sensing the threat from the rising newcomers, State Farm fought back vigorously with a new campaign centered on its enduring jingle. In its "magic jingle" campaign, State Farm agents magically appear when summoned with the jingle by young drivers in trouble—including the likes of LeBron James. The campaign's goal—to convince consumers that they still need the services of one of State Farm's 18,000 agents. To help make the point more forcefully, State Farm doubled its ad budget.

'Good Hands' Meets Mayhem

Amid this surge in competition and advertising creativity, Allstate struggled just to hold its own, let alone to grow. Entering 2010, even with Haysbert's presence as company pitchman, Allstate had lost market share for two years running. The brand needed its own over-the-top personality. So Allstate brought mayhem to life—literally. With the new creepy Mayhem character played by actor Dean Winters, Allstate created a villainous counterpart to Haysbert's soothing hero. The campaign's goal: to convince consumers that there is more to buying car insurance than just price. Put more bluntly, says an ad agency executive involved with the campaign, "We wanted to kick Flo's ass."

Mayhem portrays all of the unlikely events that can lead to a major auto insurance claim. As a deer, he jumps into the path of a moving car at night, "because that's what we deer do." As a torrential downpour, he loves leaky sunroofs. As a malfunctioning GPS, he sends a driver swerving into another car. As snow, he weighs down the roof of a garage until it collapses, smashing the car within. Each quirky ad ends with the statement and question, "If you have cut-rate insurance, you could be paying for this yourself. Are you in good hands?"

Through such clever ads, Allstate's creative and award-winning "Mayhem. It's Everywhere." campaign has put a contemporary, attention-grabbing twist on the company's long-standing "You're in good hands with Allstate" slogan, helping to position the brand as a superior alternative to price-oriented competitors. Even with its long-standing "Good Hands" campaign, Allstate needed something unconventional. In fact, mayhem didn't just describe the Allstate campaign—it characterized the entire world of auto insurance advertising.

The Mayhem campaign quickly won many top ad industry awards. But perhaps a bigger indication of the campaign's impact is the extent to which the character has become ingrained in the pop culture. Although Mayhem has only about a third of Flo's 5.4 million Facebook fans, he commands an engagement score nearly eight times that of Progressive's perky spokeswoman. And when the character's creator recently saw a Mayhem-costumed trick-or-treater walking down her street, she called it "a career highlight that gave her chills."

More than just popular, Mayhem is right on message. At the end of each ad, he warns, "If you've got cut-rate insurance, you could be paying for this yourself." Then a reassuring Haysbert provides the solution: "Are you in good hands?" he asks. "Get Allstate. You can save money and be better protected from Mayhem." This "worth-paying-a-little-more" message puts Allstate back at the top in terms of customer value.

Mayhem Redux

Allstate's ads were not only creative, they were effective. After a few years of Mayhem ads complementing Haysbert's Good Hands ads, Allstate's unaided brand awareness of 74 percent trailed State Farm's by only a slight margin, despite State Farm's 60 percent greater ad spending. And for a time, the Mayhem campaign halted Allstate's market share slide. According to Allstate CEO Thomas Wilson, "It's working. If you look at our quotes and our new business, it's way up." All this prompted Allstate to extend the campaign, including the introduction of Mayhem's Hispanic cousin, Mala Suerte (bad luck), aimed at Hispanic consumers.

In extending the campaign, Allstate took Mayhem to the next level, giving the character his own Twitter account. Seemingly late to the Twitter party, Allstate executives indicated that the delay was intentional. "We've been very careful about not overdoing Mayhem and not overexposing [him]," said Jennifer Egeland, Allstate's director of advertising. "[We wanted] the right idea for launching him in the Twitter space."

The right idea was to conform to Mayhem's persona. At the beginning of the most recent football season, Mayhem polled followers about what he should portray in the next ad—a charcoal grill or a cheap bungee cord. Consumers voted for the cord. Mayhem disobeyed, tweeting: "Too bad I'm a tailgate grill. Who's got a light?" He followed that up with Vine videos of a car set on fire from a grill mishap. Allstate then released two new Mayhem ads—"Tailgate Grill Fire" and "Cheap Bungee Cord," making everyone happy. Similar antics ensued for the 2014 March Madness kickoff of the NCAA playoffs, helping drive more than 61,000 followers to the @Mayhem Twitter account.

With all this activity and public response, Allstate thought it had a surefire weapon for maintaining its market position. But the all-out auto insurance advertising war illustrates just how critical it is to stay one step ahead of the competition. For the most recent year, Allstate increased its ad budget to $887 million, outdoing even market leader State Farm's $802 million effort. However, both companies were eclipsed by GEICO's eye-popping $1.1 billion advertising spend. Today, no less than 11 car insurance brands are running national TV advertising campaigns. Combined, the auto insurers now spend more than $6 billion each year to get their messages out. That makes things confusing for consumers, who struggle under the deluge of clever ads for the respective brands.

The intense competition, big budgets, and focus on consumer advertising has kept industry market share dynamic. In fact, as last year's numbers rolled in, GEICO had moved to the number two spot behind State Farm with $18.57 billion in earned premiums, in a virtual dead heat with Allstate's $18.45 billion take. That represented a 3 percent increase for Allstate, which had continued to grow in recent years. But GEICO's growth has been consistently stronger, increasing 11 percent year-over-year. With that development, Allstate was left to reconsider the value it was getting out of its advertising investments, and just how it might slow GEICO down and retake its number two market position.

Questions for Discussion

15-18 Why has Allstate's "good hands" slogan withstood the test of time to become advertising's longest-running slogan?

15-19 Analyze Mayhem ads based on the process of creating an advertising message as outlined in the text (for Mayhem ads, check out www.allstate.com/mayhem-is-everywhere.aspx).

15-20 Discuss issues of selecting advertising media for the Mayhem campaign. How might this process differ from that of campaigns for other companies?

15-21 Based on the information in this case, how might Allstate measure the effectiveness of the Mayhem campaign?

15-22 Has the Mayhem campaign been effective? Support your answer.

Sources: Based on information found in Steve Daniels, "GEICO Overtakes Allstate as No. 2 Auto Insurer," *Advertising Age*, March 3, 2014, http://adage.com/print/291947; E. J. Schultz, "Inside Allstate's Strategy to Start Mayhem on Twitter," *Advertising Age*, October 15, 2013, http://adage.com/print/244690; Anthony Crup, "Allstate's Marketing Boss Talks Up 'March Mayhem'," *Ad Week*, March 25, 2014, www.adweek.com/print/156471; E. J. Schultz, "Cheat Sheet: Facts and Figures Behind the Faces in Those Car Insurance Ads," *Advertising Age*, February 21, 2011, http://adage.com/print/148986/; and advertisements and other information accessed at www.allstatenewsroom.com and www.allstate.com/mayhem-is-everywhere.aspx, June 2014.

MyMarketingLab

Go to **mymktlab.com** for the following Assisted-graded writing questions:

15-23 Discuss the characteristics advertising appeals should possess to be effective. (AACSB: Communication)

15-24 Brands are now starring in movies, television shows, video games, and books. Form a small group and monitor primetime television programming across a network or cable channel for one week. Identify the brands shown or mentioned in an episode of a program. What product categories seem to be more prevalent? How were the brands presented? Write a report on what you find. (AACSB: Communication; Reflective Thinking)

References

1. Quotes and other information from Scott Davis, "When GEICO Accelerated Past Allstate," *Forbes,* March 10, 2014, www.forbes.com/sites/scottdavis/2014/03/10/when-geico-accelerated-past-allstate/; E. J. Schultz, "Muscling Past Mayhem: GEICO Rides Giant Ad Budget Past Allstate," *Advertising Age,* July 8, 2013, www.adage.com/print/242980; Julie Campbell, "Insurance Industry Social Media Engagement Strategy Performances Ranked by Unmetric," *Live Insurance News,* February 1, 2013, www.liveinsurancenews.com/insurance-industry-social/8519578/; "25 Biggest Megabrands," *Advertising Age*, July 8, 2013, p. 15; Michele Miller, "'Hump Day'" GEICO Commercial: Creators Dish on Ad's Success, Its Development," *CBS News,* September 18, 2013, www.cbsnews.com/news/hump-day-geico-commercial-creators-dish-on-ads-success-its-development/; and www.geico.com, accessed September 2014.

2. Alexandra Bruell, "Global Spending Predicted to Hit $518B This Year," *Advertising Age,* April 29, 2013, p. 10; "US Digital Advertising & Marketing," *eMarketer*, www.emarketer.com/coverage/advertisingmarketing, accessed March 2014; Kristina Monllos, "Retail, Automotive Biggest Spenders in 2013," *Adweek,* March 25, 2014, www.adweek.com/print/156524; and "100 Leading National Advertisers 2014, *Advertising Age,* June 23, 2014, pp. 16–18.

3. See Alexandra Bruell, "Government Agencies Gird for Cuts Due to Sequestration," *Advertising Age*, March 4, 2013, http://adage.com/print/240132/; and "CDC Anti-Smoking Campaign Launched," March 29, 2013, www.wjla.com/articles/2013/03/cdc-anti-smoking-campaign-launched-86867.html.

4. "Walmart Gets Boost from Local-Price-Comparison Ads," *Advertising Age,* June 25, 2013, www.adage.com/print/242755; and Bruce Horovitz, "Taco Bell Still Giving Ronald McDonald Grief," *USA Today,* April 3, 2014.

5. "Take the Bing It On Challenge," September 6, 2012, www.bing.com/blogs/site_blogs/b/search/archive/2012/09/06/challenge-announce.aspx; www.bingiton.com, accessed June 2014; Alex Kantrowitz, "Microsoft's Google Bashing Is Having an Impact," *Advertising Age,* October 14, 2013, p. 24; and www.scroggled.com/Home, accessed September 2014.

6. "Competitors Take Issue with Walmart Ads," *The City Wire,* January 4, 2014, www.thecitywire.com/node/25852#.UzsgiPldV8F.

7. See Jean Halliday, "Thinking Big Takes Audi from Obscure to Awesome," *Advertising Age*, February 2, 2009, http://adage.com/print/134234; Chad Thomas and Andreas Cremer, "Audi Feels a Need for Speed in the U.S.," *Bloomberg Businessweek*, November 22, 2010, p. 1; and Kyle Stock, "Audi Swipes BMW's Luxury

Crown. Keeping It Will Be Harder," *Bloomberg BusinessWeek,* March 11, 2014, www.businessweek.com/articles/2014-03-11/where-audi-will-win-or-lose-the-luxury-car-race.

8. Justin Bachman, "The Ugly Numbers Behind Unbundled Cable," *Bloomberg Businessweek*, December 6, 2013, www.businessweek.com/articles/2013-12-06/the-ugly-numbers-behind-unbundled-cable-tv; and Thad McIlroy, "The Future of Magazines," *The Future of Publishing*, July 10, 2013, http://thefutureofpublishing.com/industries/the-future-of-magazines/.

9. Kelsey Libert and Kristen Tynski, "Research: The Emotions that Make Marketing Campaigns Go Viral," HBR Blog Network, October 24, 2013, http://blogs.hbr.org/2013/10/research-the-emotions that-make-marketing-campaigns-go-viral/.

10. "Results of 4A's 2011 Television Production Cost Survey," January 22, 2013, www.aaaa.org/news/bulletins/pages/tvprod_01222013.aspx; Sam Thielman, "The New Hour Is 43 Minutes Long," *Adweek,* June 24, 2013, p. 12; "Jeanine Poggi, "TV Ad Prices," *Advertising Age*, October 20, 2013, http://adage.com/print/244832; and "Who Bought What in Super Bowl XLVIII," *Advertising Age*, February 3, 2014, http://adage.com/print/244024.

11. Caleb Garling, "How Television Advertising Deals with DVRs Destroying Their Business," *SFGate,* December 27, 2013, http://blog.sfgate.com/techchron/2013/12/27/dvr-advertisements/; and "No Hardware, No Problem: VOD Lets Users Time-Shift with Ease," September 9, 2013, www.nielsen.com/us/en/newswire/2013/no-hardware--no-problem--vod-lets-users-time-shift-with-ease.html.

12. "Real Beauty Shines Through: Dove Wins Titanium Grand Prix, 163 Million Views on YouTube," *Google: Think Insights,* June2013, www.thinkwithgoogle.com/case-studies/dove-real-beauty-sketches.html; Nina Bahadur, "Dove 'Real Beauty' Campaign Turns 10: How a Brand Tried to Change the Conversation about Female Beauty," *Huffington Post,* February 6, 2014, www.huffingtonpost.com/2014/01/21/dove-real-beauty-campaign-turns-10_n_4575940.tml; and www.youtube.com/watch?v=XpaOjMXyJGk, accessed June 2014.

13. See Danny Sullivan, "Product Placement: The TV Ads Consumers Can't Skip or Hop," *Marketing Land,* May 28, 2013, http://marketingland.com/product-placement-tv-ads-45729; and Jonathan Welsh, "Can 'Captain America' Help Harley-Davidson Sell Motorcycles?" *Wall Street Journal,* April 1, 2014, http://blogs.wsj.com/speakeasy/2014/04/01/can-captain-america-help-harley-davidson-sell-motorcycles/.

14. Abe Sauer, "The Envelope, Please: The 2014 Brandcameo Product Placement Awards," *BrandChannel*, February 27, 2014, www.brandchannel.com/home/post/2014/02/27/140227-2014-Brandcameo-Product-Placement-Awards.aspx#continue.

15. "Why *The Lego Movie* Is the Perfect Piece of Product Placement," *A.V. Club,* February 11, 2014, http://www.avclub.com/article/why-the lego-movie-is-the-perfect-piece-of-product-201102.

16. "Ford Introduces All-New Fusion with Groundbreaking Transmedia Campaign," *Marketing Weekly News*, July 14, 2012, p. 277; and Stuart Elliott, "A Home Fixup Campaign for the Web," *New York Times,* April 2, 2014, p. B6.

17. For these and other examples, see David Gianatasio, "Ad of the Day: Cute, Quirky Chevy Commercial on the Oscars Was Made for $4,000," *Adweek,* March 3, 2014, www.adweek.com/print/156071; "Purina Pro Plan Debuts New Consumer-Generated Ad during Westminster Kennel Club Dog Show," *PRNewswire,* February 11, 2013; and "Taco Bell Commissions User-Generated YouTube Ads to Promote New Fiery Doritos Locos Taco," *Viral Gains,* www.viralgains.com/2013/08/taco-bell-commissions-user-generated-youtube-ads-promote-fiery-doritos-locos-taco/, accessed September 2014.

18. Quotes and other information from Lauren Drell, "User Generated Content: Lessons from 4 Killer Ad Campaigns," *American Express Open Forum,* January 28, 2013, www.openforum.com/articles/lessons-from-4-killer-ugc-campaigns/; and http://thesweatlife.lululemon.com/, accessed June 2014.

19. Antony Young, "Get Beyond the 30-Second Ad: In a World of Many Platforms, It's a Must," *Advertising Age,* April 12, 2013, http://adage.com/article/cmo-strategy/30-ad-a/240857/; and "The Weather Channel's Innovative Mobile Advertising," April 4, 2013, http://talkingnewmedia.blogspot.com/2013/04/the-weather-channels-innovative-mobile.html.

20. Brian Steinberg, "Viewer-Engagement Rankings Signal Change for TV Industry," *Advertising Age*, May 10, 2010, p. 12. For more on measuring engagement, see Kirby Thornton, "Neilsen Engages Twitter for TV Insights," *Media Is Power,* March 21, 2013, www.mediaispower.com/nielsen-engages-twitter-for-tv-insights/#sthash.yOJpbk51.ggCAZYJ5.dpbs; and "New Data Correlates Social Engagement with Traditional Radio Ratings," *PR Newswire,* April 10, 2013, www.prnewswire.com/news-releases/202264391.html.

21. Joe Tripoti, "Coca-Cola Marketing Shifts from Impressions to Expressions," April 27, 2011, http://blogs.hbr.org/cs/2011/04/coca-colas_marketing_shift_fro.html; Devon Glenn, "Coca-Cola on Social Content: 'Expressions Are More Valuable than Impressions,'" *Social Times,* September 11, 2012, http://socialtimes.com/coca-cola-on-social-content-expressions-are-more-valuable-than-impressions_b104547; and Anna Rudenko, "Coca-Cola USA Prompting Youngsters to Contribute Their "Ahh' Moments," *POPSOP,* March 24, 2014, http://popsop.com/2014/03/coca-cola-usa-prompting-youngsters-to-contribute-their-ahh-coke-moments/.

22. For these and other multitasking stats, See "Nielsen: Most Tablet/Smartphone Users Watch TV at Same Time," *Electronista*, April 5, 2012, www.electronista.com/articles/12/04/05/simultaneous.use.prevalent.in.us.market/; Lucia Moses, "Second-Screen Effect," *Adweek,* April 1, 2013, pp. 16–17; and "TiVo Social Media and Multitasking Survey," *Yahoo! Finance,* January 23, 2013, http://finance.yahoo.com/news/tivo-social-media-multitasking-survey-120600364.html.

23. *Forbes* and *Bloomberg Businessweek* cost and circulation data found online at www.bloombergmedia.com/magazine/businessweek/rates/ and www.forbesmedia.com/forbes-magazine-rates/, accessed September 2014.

24. For these and other examples, see Christopher Heine, "Lexus Nabs 100K Video Views on Facebook—in 10 Minutes," *Adweek,* January 23, 2013, www.adweek.com/news/technology/print/146726; Matt McGee, "Oreo, Audi, and Walgreens Newsjack Super Bowl 'Blackout Bowl,'" *Marketing Land,* February 3, 2013, http://marketingland.com/oreo-audi-walgreens-market-quickly-during-super-bowl-blackout-32407; and "Arby's Slayed the Grammys with This Tweet about Pharrell Williams' Hat," *Adweek*, January 27, 2014, www.adweek.com/print/155237.

25. Information on advertising agency revenues from "Agency Report," *Advertising Age,* April 28, 2014, pp. 8+.

26. Stuart Elliott, "Visa Trims Slogan to Expand Meaning," *New York Times,* January 13, 2014, p. B6.

27. See E. J. Schultz, "Behind the Snickers Campaign that Launched a Global Comeback," *Advertising Age,* October 4, 2013, http://adage.com/print/244593; and http://adsoftheworld.com/media/outdoor/snickers_runningandhttp://cargocollective.com/mirceaandronescu/SNICKERS-OOH, accessed September 2014.

28. Based on Glen Broom and Bey-Ling Sha, *Cutlip & Center's Effective Public Relations*, 11th ed. (Upper Saddle River, NJ: Prentice Hall, 2013), Chapter 1.

29. See Mark Fidelman, "8 of the Best Influencer Marketing Campaigns from 8 Hot Agencies," *Forbes,* August 6, 2013, www.forbes.com/sites/markfidelman/2013/08/06/8-of-the-best-influencer-marketing-campaigns-from-the-8-hottest-agencies; Melissa Malcolm, "Success Is Built with Chocolate Milk," *Dairy Foods,* February 2014, pp. 15–17; Polly Elmore, "Promoting Chocolate Milk as an Energy Drink," *PR Works,* February 3, 2014, http://prwrks.com/promoting-chocolate-milk-as-an-energy-drink; and http://gotchocolatemilk.com, accessed September 2014.

30. See Geoffrey Fowler and Ben Worthen, "Buzz Powers iPad Launch," *Wall Street Journal*, April 2, 2010; "Apple iPad Sales Top 2 Million since Launch," *Tribune-Review* (Pittsburgh), June 2, 2010; "PR Pros Must Be Apple's iPad as a True Game-Changer," *PRweek*, May 2010, p. 23; and "Apple Launches New iPad," March 7, 2012, www.apple.com/pr/library/2012/03/07Apple-Launches-New-iPad.html.

31. Sarah Skerik, "An Emerging PR Trend: Content PR Strategy and Tactics," *PR Newswire,* January 15, 2013, http://blog.prnewswire.com/2013/01/15/an-emerging-pr-trend-content-pr-strategy-tactics/.

16 Personal Selling and Sales Promotion

Chapter Preview

In the previous two chapters, you learned about engaging customers and communicating customer value through integrated marketing communications (IMC) and two elements of the promotion mix: advertising and public relations. In this chapter, we examine two more IMC elements: personal selling and sales promotion. Personal selling is the interpersonal arm of marketing communications, in which the sales force engages customers and prospects to build relationships and make sales. Sales promotion consists of short-term incentives to encourage the purchase or sale of a product or service. Although this chapter presents personal selling and sales promotion as separate tools, they must be carefully integrated with the other elements of the promotion mix.

First, let's look at a real-life sales force. When you think of salespeople, perhaps you think of pushy retail sales clerks, "yell and sell" TV pitchmen, or the stereotypical glad-handing "used-car salesman." But such stereotypes simply don't fit the reality of most of today's salespeople—sales professionals who succeed not by taking advantage of customers but by listening to their needs and helping to forge solutions. For most companies, personal selling plays an important role in building profitable customer relationships. Consider Procter & Gamble, whose customer-focused sales force has long been considered one of the nation's finest.

PROCTER & GAMBLE: It's Not Sales, It's "Customer Business Development"

For decades, Procter & Gamble has been at the top of almost every expert's A-list of outstanding marketing companies. The experts point to P&G's stable of top-selling consumer brands, or to the fact that year in and year out P&G is the world's largest advertiser. Consumers seem to agree. You'll find at least one of P&G's blockbuster brands in 99 percent of all American households; in many homes, you'll find a dozen or more familiar P&G products. But P&G is also highly respected for something else—its top-notch, customer-focused sales force.

P&G's sales force has long been an American icon for personal selling at its very best. When it comes to selecting, training, and managing salespeople, P&G sets the gold standard. The company employs a massive sales force of more than 5,000 salespeople worldwide. At P&G, however, they rarely call it "sales." Instead, it's "Customer Business Development" (CBD). And P&G sales reps aren't "salespeople"; they're "CBD managers" or "CBD account executives." All this might seem like just so much "corp-speak," but at P&G the distinction goes to the very core of how selling works.

P&G understands that if its customers don't do well, neither will the company. To grow its own business, therefore, P&G must first grow the business of the retailers that sell its brands to final consumers. And at P&G, the primary responsibility for helping customer companies grow falls to the sales force. In P&G's own words, "CBD is more than mere 'selling'—it's a P&G-specific approach which enables us to grow our business by working as a 'strategic partner' (as opposed to just a supplier) with those who ultimately sell our products to consumers." Says one CBD manager, "We depend on them as much as they depend on us." By partnering with each other, P&G and its customers create "win-win" relationships that help both to prosper.

Most P&G customers are huge and complex businesses—such as Walgreens, Walmart, or Dollar General—with thousands of stores and billions of dollars in revenues. Working with and selling to such customers can be a very complex undertaking, more than any single salesperson or sales team could accomplish. Instead, P&G assigns a full CBD team to every large

P&G's sales force has long been an American icon for selling at its very best. But at P&G they rarely call it "sales." Instead, it's called "Customer Business Development."

customer account. Each CBD team contains not only salespeople but also a full complement of specialists in every aspect of selling P&G's consumer brands at the retail level.

P&G Customer Business Development managers know that to grow P&G's business, they must first help their retail partners to sell P&G's brands.

Jin Lee/Getty Images USA, Inc.

CBD teams vary in size depending on the customer. For example, P&G's largest customer, Walmart, which accounts for an amazing 20 percent of the company's sales, commands a 350-person CBD team. By contrast, the P&G Dollar General team consists of about 30 people. Regardless of size, every CBD team constitutes a complete, multifunctional customer service unit. Each team includes a CBD manager and several CBD account executives (each responsible for a specific P&G product category), supported by specialists in marketing strategy, product development, operations, information systems, logistics, finance, and human resources.

To deal effectively with large accounts, P&G salespeople must be smart, well trained, and strategically grounded. They deal daily with high-level retail category buyers who may purchase hundreds of millions of dollars' worth of P&G and competing brands annually. It takes a lot more than a friendly smile and a firm handshake to interact with such buyers. Yet, individual P&G salespeople can't know everything, and thanks to the CBD sales structure, they don't have to. Instead, as members of a full CBD team, P&G salespeople have at hand all the resources they need to resolve even the most challenging customer problems. "I have everything I need right here," says a household care account executive. "If my customer needs help from us with in-store promotions, I can go right down the hall and talk with someone on my team in marketing about doing some kind of promotional deal. It's that simple."

Customer Business Development involves partnering with customers to jointly identify strategies that create shopper value and satisfaction and drive profitable sales at the store level. When it comes to profitably moving Tide, Pampers, Gillette, or other P&G brands off store shelves and into consumers' shopping carts, P&G reps and their teams often know more than the retail buyers they advise. In fact, P&G's retail partners often rely on CBD teams to help them manage not only the P&G brands on their shelves but also entire product categories, including competing brands.

Wait a minute. Does it make sense to let P&G advise on the stocking and placement of competitors' brands as well as its own? Would a P&G CBD rep ever tell a retail buyer to stock fewer P&G products and more of a competing brand? Believe it or not, it happens all the time. The CBD team's primary goal is to help the customer win in each product category. Sometimes, analysis shows that the best solution for the customer is "more of the other guy's product." For P&G, that's okay. It knows that creating the best situation for the retailer ultimately pulls in more customer traffic, which in turn will likely lead to increased sales for other P&G products in the same category. Because most of P&G's brands are market-share leaders, it stands to benefit more from the increased traffic than competitors do. Again, what's good for the customer is good for P&G—it's a win-win situation.

Honest and open dealings also help to build long-term customer relationships. P&G salespeople become trusted advisors to their retailer-partners, a status they work hard to maintain. "It took me four years to build the trust I now have with my buyer," says a veteran CBD account executive. "If I talk her into buying P&G products that she can't sell or out-of-stocking competing brands that she should be selling, I could lose that trust in a heartbeat."

Finally, collaboration is usually a two-way street—P&G gives and customers give back in return. "We'll help customers run a set of commercials or do some merchandising events, but there's usually a return-on-investment," explains another CBD manager. "Maybe it's helping us with distribution of a new product or increasing space for fabric care. We're very willing if the effort creates value for us as well as for the customer and the final consumer."

According to P&G, "Customer Business Development is selling and a whole lot more. It's a P&G-specific approach [that lets us] grow business by working as a 'strategic partner' with our accounts, focusing on mutually beneficial business-building opportunities. All customers want to improve their business; it's [our] role to help them identify the biggest opportunities."

Thus, P&G salespeople aren't the stereotypical glad-handers that some people have come to expect when they think of selling. P&G's "salespeople"—its CBD managers—are talented, well-educated, well-trained sales professionals who do all they can to help customers succeed. They know that good selling involves working with customers to solve their problems for mutual gain. They know that if customers succeed, they succeed.[1]

Objective Outline

OBJECTIVE 1	**Discuss the role of a company's salespeople in creating value for customers and building customer relationships.** Personal Selling (pp 502–504)
OBJECTIVE 2	**Identify and explain the six major sales force management steps.** Managing the Sales Force (pp 504–515)
OBJECTIVE 3	**Discuss the personal selling process, distinguishing between transaction-oriented marketing and relationship marketing.** The Personal Selling Process (pp 515–518)
OBJECTIVE 4	**Explain how sales promotion campaigns are developed and implemented.** Sales Promotion (pp 518–525)

In this chapter, we examine two more promotion mix tools: *personal selling* and *sales promotion*. Personal selling consists of interpersonal interactions with customers and prospects to make sales and maintain customer relationships. Sales promotion involves using short-term incentives to encourage customer purchasing, reseller support, and sales force efforts.

Author Comment | Personal selling is the interpersonal arm of the promotion mix. A company's sales force creates and communicates customer value by personally engaging customers and building customer relationships.

Personal Selling

Robert Louis Stevenson once noted, "Everyone lives by selling something." Companies around the world use sales forces to sell products and services to business customers and final consumers. But sales forces are also found in many other kinds of organizations. For example, colleges use recruiters to attract new students, and churches use membership committees to attract new members. Museums and fine arts organizations use fundraisers to contact donors and raise money. Even governments use sales forces. The U.S. Postal Service, for instance, uses a sales force to sell Express Mail and other shipping and mailing solutions to corporate customers. In the first part of this chapter, we examine personal selling's role in the organization, sales force management decisions, and the personal selling process.

The Nature of Personal Selling

Personal selling
Personal presentations by the firm's sales force for the purpose of engaging customers, making sales, and building customer relationships.

Personal selling is one of the oldest professions in the world. The people who do the selling go by many names, including salespeople, sales representatives, agents, district managers, account executives, sales consultants, and sales engineers.

People hold many stereotypes of salespeople—including some unfavorable ones. *Salesman* may bring to mind the image of Dwight Schrute, the opinionated Dunder Mifflin paper salesman from the old TV show *The Office*, who lacks both common sense and social skills. Or they may think of the real-life "yell-and-sell" TV pitchmen, who hawk everything from the Flex Seal to the FOCUS T25 Workout and the Ove Glove in infomercials. However, the majority of salespeople are a far cry from these unfortunate stereotypes.

As the opening P&G story shows, most salespeople are well-educated and well-trained professionals who add value for customers and maintain long-term customer relationships. They listen to their customers, assess customer needs, and organize the company's efforts to solve customer problems. The best salespeople are the ones who work closely with customers for mutual gain. Consider Boeing, the aerospace giant competing in the rough-and-tumble worldwide commercial aircraft market. It takes more than fast talk and a warm smile to sell expensive airplanes:

Professional selling: It takes more than fast talk and a warm smile to sell expensive airplanes. Boeing's real challenge is to win business by building partnerships—day-in, day-out, year-in, year-out—with its customers.
Boeing

> Selling high-tech aircraft at $150 million or more a copy is complex and challenging. A single big sale to an airline, airfreight carrier, government, and military customer can easily run into billions of dollars. Boeing salespeople head up an extensive team of company specialists—sales and service technicians, financial analysts, planners, engineers—all dedicated to finding ways to satisfy a large customer's needs. On the customer side, buying a batch of jetliners involves dozens or even hundreds of decision-makers from all levels of the buying organization, and layer upon layer of subtle and not-so-subtle buying influences. The selling process is nerve-rackingly slow—it can take two or three years from the first sales presentation to the day the sale is announced. After getting the order, salespeople then must stay in almost constant touch to keep track of the account's equipment needs and to make certain the customer stays satisfied. The real challenge is to win buyers' business by building day-in, day-out, year-in, year-out partnerships with them based on superior products and close collaboration.

Salesperson
An individual who represents a company to customers by performing one or more of the following activities: prospecting, communicating, selling, servicing, information gathering, and relationship building.

The term **salesperson** covers a wide range of positions. At one extreme, a salesperson might be largely an *order taker*, such as the department store salesperson standing behind the counter. At the other extreme are *order getters*, whose positions demand *creative selling*, *social selling*, and *relationship building* for products and services ranging from appliances, industrial equipment, and airplanes to insurance and IT services. In this chapter, we focus on the more creative types of selling and the process of building and managing an effective sales force.

The Role of the Sales Force

Personal selling is the interpersonal arm of the promotion mix. Advertising consists largely of nonpersonal communication with large groups of consumers. By contrast, personal selling involves interpersonal interactions and engagement between salespeople and individual customers—whether face to face, by phone, via e-mail or Twitter, through video or online conferences, or by other means. Personal selling can be more effective than advertising in more complex selling situations. Salespeople can probe customers to learn more about their problems and then adjust the marketing offer and presentation to fit each customer's special needs.

The role of personal selling varies from company to company. Some firms have no salespeople at all—for example, companies that sell only online, or companies that sell through manufacturers' reps, sales agents, or brokers. In most firms, however, the sales force plays a major role. In companies that sell business products and services, such as IBM, DuPont, or Boeing, salespeople work directly with customers. In consumer product companies such as P&G or Nike, the sales force plays an important behind-the-scenes role. It works with wholesalers and retailers to gain their support and help them be more effective in selling the company's products to final buyers.

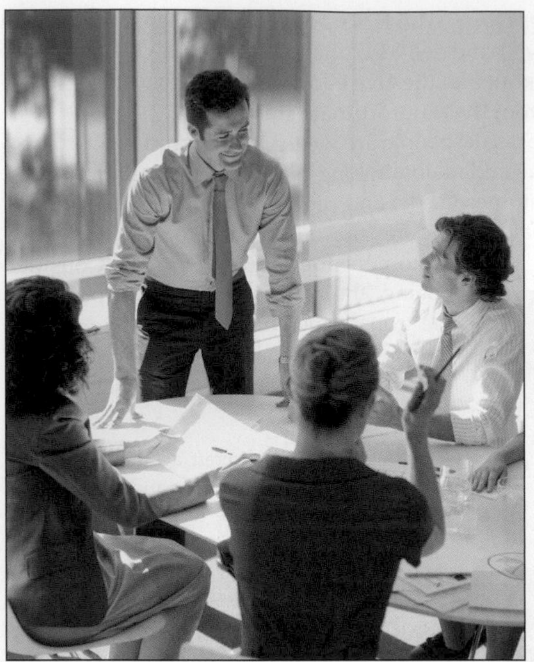

Salespeople link the company with its customers. To many customers, the salesperson is the company.

Digital Vision

Linking the Company with Its Customers

The sales force serves as a critical link between a company and its customers. In many cases, salespeople serve two masters—the seller and the buyer. First, they *represent the company to customers*. They find and develop new customers and communicate information about the company's products and services. They sell products by approaching and engaging customers, presenting their offerings, answering objections, negotiating prices and terms, closing sales, servicing accounts, and maintaining account relationships.

At the same time, salespeople *represent customers to the company*, acting inside the firm as "champions" of customers' interests and managing the buyer–seller relationship. Salespeople relay customer concerns about company products and actions back inside to those who can handle them. They learn about customer needs and work with other marketing and nonmarketing people in the company to develop greater customer value.

In fact, to many customers, the salesperson *is* the company—the only tangible manifestation of the company that they see. Hence, customers may become loyal to salespeople as well as to the companies and products they represent. This concept of *salesperson-owned loyalty* lends even more importance to the salesperson's customer-relationship-building abilities. Strong relationships with the salesperson will result in strong relationships with the company and its products. Conversely, poor salesperson relationships will probably result in poor company and product relationships.

Given its role in linking the company with its customers, the sales force must be strongly customer-solutions focused. In fact, such a customer-solutions focus is a must not only for the sales force but also for the entire organization.

Coordinating Marketing and Sales

Ideally, the sales force and other marketing functions (marketing planners, brand managers, marketing content managers, and researchers) should work together closely to jointly create value for customers. Unfortunately, however, some companies still treat sales and marketing as separate functions. When this happens, the separate sales and marketing groups may not get along well. When things go wrong, marketers blame the sales force for its poor execution of what they see as an otherwise splendid strategy. In turn, the sales team blames the marketers for being out of touch with what's really going on with customers. Neither group fully values the other's contributions. However, if not repaired, such disconnects between marketing and sales can damage customer relationships and company performance.

A company can take several actions to help bring its marketing and sales functions closer together. At the most basic level, it can increase communications between the two groups by arranging joint meetings and spelling out communication channels. It can create opportunities for salespeople and marketers to work together. Brand managers and researchers can tag along on sales calls or sit in on sales planning sessions. In turn, salespeople can sit in on marketing planning sessions and share their firsthand customer knowledge.

A company can also create joint objectives and reward systems for sales and marketing teams or appoint marketing–sales liaisons—people from marketing who "live with the sales force" and help coordinate marketing and sales force programs and efforts. Finally, it can appoint a high-level marketing executive to oversee both marketing and sales. Such a person can help infuse marketing and sales with the common goal of creating value for customers to capture value in return.[2]

Sales force management
Analyzing, planning, implementing, and controlling sales force activities.

Author Comment | Here's another definition of sales force management: "planning, organizing, leading, and controlling personal contact programs designed to achieve profitable customer relationships." Once again, the goal of every marketing activity is to create customer value, engage customers, and build customer relationships.

Managing the Sales Force

We define **sales force management** as analyzing, planning, implementing, and controlling sales force activities. It includes designing sales force strategy and structure, as well as recruiting, selecting, training, compensating, supervising, and evaluating the firm's salespeople. These major sales force management decisions are shown in **Figure 16.1** and discussed in the following sections.

FIGURE | 16.1
Major Steps in Sales Force Management

Designing sales force strategy and structure → Recruiting and selecting salespeople → Training salespeople → Compensating salespeople → Supervising salespeople → Evaluating salespeople

The goal of this process? You guessed it! The company wants to build a skilled and motivated sales team that will help to create customer value, engage customers, and build strong customer relationships.

Designing the Sales Force Strategy and Structure

Marketing managers face several sales force strategy and design questions. How should salespeople and their tasks be structured? How big should the sales force be? Should salespeople sell alone or work in teams with other people in the company? Should they sell in the field, by phone, or using online and social media? We address these issues next.

The Sales Force Structure

A company can divide sales responsibilities along any of several lines. The structure decision is simple if the company sells only one product line to one industry with customers in many locations. In that case the company would use a *territorial sales force structure*. However, if the company sells many products to many types of customers, it might need a *product sales force structure*, a *customer sales force structure*, or a combination of the two.

Territorial sales force structure
A sales force organization that assigns each salesperson to an exclusive geographic territory in which that salesperson sells the company's full line.

Product sales force structure
A sales force organization in which salespeople specialize in selling only a portion of the company's products or lines.

Customer (or market) sales force structure
A sales force organization in which salespeople specialize in selling only to certain customers or industries.

In the **territorial sales force structure**, each salesperson is assigned to an exclusive geographic area and sells the company's full line of products or services to all customers in that territory. This organization clearly defines each salesperson's job and fixes accountability. It also increases the salesperson's desire to build local customer relationships that, in turn, improve selling effectiveness. Finally, because each salesperson travels within a limited geographic area, travel expenses are relatively small. A territorial sales organization is often supported by many levels of sales management positions. For example, individual territory sales reps may report to area managers, who in turn report to regional managers who report to a director of sales.

If a company has numerous and complex products, it can adopt a **product sales force structure**, in which the sales force specializes along product lines. For example, GE employs different sales forces within different product and service divisions of its major businesses. Within GE Infrastructure, for instance, the company has separate sales forces for aviation, energy, transportation, and water processing products and technologies. No single salesperson can become expert in all of these product categories, so product specialization is required. Similarly, GE Healthcare employs different sales forces for diagnostic imaging, life sciences, and integrated IT products and services. In all, a company as large and complex as GE might have dozens of separate sales forces serving its diverse product and service portfolio.

Using a **customer** (or **market**) **sales force structure**, a company organizes its sales force along customer or industry lines. Separate sales forces may be set up for different industries, serving current customers versus finding new ones, and serving major accounts versus regular accounts. Organizing the sales force around customers can help a company build closer relationships with important customers. Many companies even have special sales forces to handle the needs of individual large customers. For example, appliance maker Whirlpool assigns individual teams of salespeople to big retail customers such as Sears, Lowe's, Best Buy, and Home Depot. Each Whirlpool sales team aligns with the large customer's buying team.[3]

Sales force structure: Whirlpool specializes its sales force by customer and by territory for each key customer group.
Paul Sancya/Associated Press

When a company sells a wide variety of products to many types of customers over a broad geographic area, it often employs a *complex sales force structure*, which combines several types of organization. Salespeople can be specialized by customer and territory; product and territory; product and customer; or territory, product, and customer. For example, Whirlpool specializes its sales force by customer (with different sales teams for Sears, Lowe's, Best Buy, Home Depot, and smaller independent retailers) *and* by territory for each key customer group (territory representatives, territory managers, regional managers, and so on). No single structure is best for all companies and situations. Each company should select a sales force structure that best serves the needs of its customers and fits its overall marketing strategy.

Sales Force Size

Once the company has set its structure, it is ready to consider *sales force size*. Sales forces may range in size from only a few salespeople to tens of thousands. Some sales forces are huge—for example, in the United States, PepsiCo employs 36,000 salespeople; American Express, 23,400; GE, 16,400; and Cisco Systems, 14,000.[4] Salespeople constitute one of the company's most productive—and most expensive—assets. Therefore, increasing their numbers will increase both sales and costs.

Many companies use some form of *workload approach* to set sales force size. Using this approach, a company first groups accounts into different classes according to size, account status, or other factors related to the amount of effort required to maintain the account. It then determines the number of salespeople needed to call on each class of accounts the desired number of times.

The company might think as follows: Suppose we have 1,000 A-level accounts and 2,000 B-level accounts. A-level accounts require 36 calls per year, and B-level accounts require 12 calls per year. In this case, the sales force's *workload*—the number of calls it must make per year—is 60,000 calls $[(1{,}000 \times 36) + (2{,}000 \times 12) = 36{,}000 + 24{,}000 = 60{,}000]$. Suppose our average salesperson can make 1,000 calls a year. Thus, we need 60 salespeople $(60{,}000 \div 1{,}000)$.

Other Sales Force Strategy and Structure Issues

Sales management must also determine who will be involved in the selling effort and how various sales and sales-support people will work together.

Outside sales force (or field sales force)
Salespeople who travel to call on customers in the field.

Inside sales force
Salespeople who conduct business from their offices via telephone, online and social media interactions, or visits from prospective buyers.

Outside and Inside Sales Forces. A company may have an **outside sales force** (or **field sales force**), an **inside sales force**, or both. Outside salespeople travel to call on customers in the field. In contrast, inside salespeople conduct business from their offices via telephone, online and social media interactions, or visits from buyers. The use of inside sales has grown in recent years as a result of increased outside selling costs and the surge in online, mobile, and social media technologies.

Some inside salespeople provide support for the outside sales force, freeing them to spend more time selling to major accounts and finding new prospects. For example, *technical sales-support people* provide technical information and answers to customers' questions. *Sales assistants* provide research and administrative backup for outside salespeople. They track down sales leads, call ahead and confirm appointments, follow up on deliveries, and answer customers' questions when outside salespeople cannot be reached. Using such combinations of inside and outside salespeople can help serve important customers better. The inside rep provides daily access and support, whereas the outside rep provides face-to-face collaboration and relationship building.

Other inside salespeople do more than just provide support. *Telemarketers* and *online sellers* use the phone, Internet, and social media to find new leads, learn about customers and their business, or sell and service accounts directly. Telemarketing and online selling can be very effective, less costly ways to sell to smaller, harder-to-reach customers. Depending on the complexity of the product and customer, for example, a telemarketer can make from 20 to 33 decision-maker contacts a day, compared to the average of 4 that an outside salesperson can make. In addition, whereas an average business-to-business (B-to-B) field sales call can average close to $600, a routine industrial telemarketing or online contact might average only $20 to $30.[5]

Although the federal government's Do Not Call Registry put a dent in telephone sales to consumers, telemarketing remains a vital tool for most B-to-B marketers. For some smaller companies, telephone and online selling may be the primary sales approaches. However, most of the larger companies also use these tactics extensively, either to sell directly to small and midsize customers or to assist their sales forces in selling to larger ones.

In addition to costs savings, in today's digital, mobile, and social media environments, many buyers are more receptive to—or even prefer—phone and online contact versus the high level of face-to-face contact once required. Many customers are more inclined to gather information online—one study showed that a typical buyer reports contacting a sales rep only after independently completing about 60 percent of the buying process. Then, they routinely use the phone, online meetings, and social media interactions to engage sellers and close deals. "With virtual meeting software such as GoToMeeting.com and WebEx, communications tools such as Skype, and social media sites such as Twitter, Facebook, and LinkedIn, it's become easier to sell with few if any face-to-face meetings," says an inside sales consultant.[6]

As a result of these trends, telephone and online selling are growing much faster than in-person selling. One study also notes the emergence of the "hybrid sales rep," a modern cross between a field sales rep and an inside rep, who often works from a remote location. Some 41 percent of outside sales activity is now done over the phone or a mobile device, from either a home office, a company office, or on the go.[7]

For many types of products and selling situations, phone or online selling can be as effective as a personal sales call:[8]

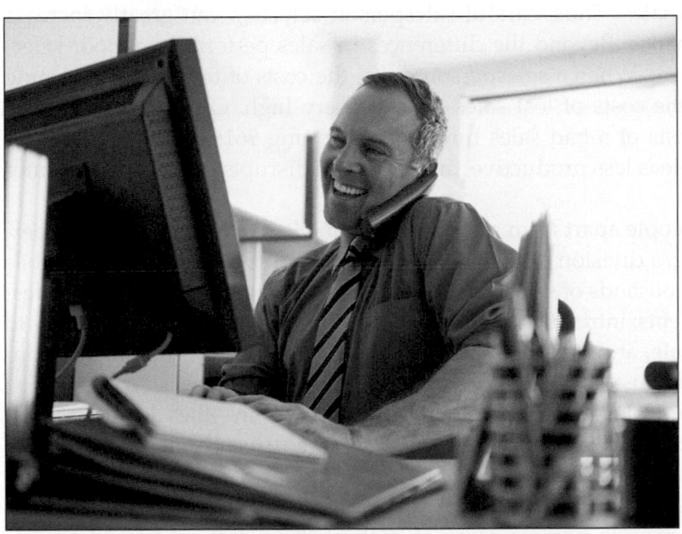

For many types of selling situations, phone or Web selling can be as effective as a personal sales call. At Climax Portable Machine Tools, phone reps build surprisingly strong and personal customer relationships.

Climax Portable Machining and Welding Systems, which manufactures portable maintenance tools for the metal cutting industry, has proven that telephone and online marketing can save money and still lavish attention on buyers. Under the old system, Climax sales engineers spent one-third of their time on the road, training distributor salespeople and accompanying them on calls. They could make about four contacts a day. Now, each of five sales engineers on Climax's inside sales team calls about 30 prospects a day, following up on leads generated by ads, e-mails, and the company's Facebook, Twitter, YouTube, and other social-media sites. Because it takes about five calls to close a sale, the sales engineers update a prospect's profile after each contact, noting the degree of commitment, requirements, next call date, and personal comments. "If anyone mentions he's going on a fishing trip, our sales engineer enters that in the sales information system and uses it to personalize the next call," says Climax's president, noting that this is one way to engage customers and build good relations.

Another is that the first contact with a prospect includes the sales engineer's business card with his or her picture on it. Climax's customer sales system also gives inside reps instant access to customer information entered by the outside sales force and service people. Armed with all the information, inside reps can build surprisingly strong and personal customer relationships. Of course, it takes more than friendliness to sell $15,000 machine tools without face-to-face contact (special orders may run $200,000), but the telephone and online approach works well. When Climax customers were asked, "Do you see the sales engineer often enough?" the response was overwhelmingly positive. Obviously, many people didn't realize that the only contact they had with Climax had been on the phone or Internet.

Team selling
Using teams of people from sales, marketing, engineering, finance, technical support, and even upper management to service large, complex accounts.

Team Selling. As products become more complex, and as customers grow larger and more demanding, a single salesperson simply can't handle all of a large customer's needs. Instead, most companies now use **team selling** to service large, complex accounts. Sales teams can unearth problems, solutions, and sales opportunities that no individual salesperson could. Such teams might include experts from any area or level of the selling firm—sales, marketing, technical and support services, research and development (R&D), engineering, operations, finance, and others.

In many cases, the move to team selling mirrors similar changes in customers' buying organizations. Many large customer companies have implemented team-based purchasing, requiring marketers to employ equivalent team-based selling. When dealing with large, complex accounts, one salesperson can't be an expert in everything the customer needs. Instead, selling is done by strategic account teams, quarterbacked by senior account managers or customer business managers.

Some companies, such as IBM, Xerox, and P&G, have used teams for a long time. As we discuss in the chapter-opening story, P&G sales reps are organized into Customer Business

Development (CBD) teams. Each CBD team is assigned to a major P&G customer, such as Walmart, Safeway, or CVS Pharmacy. The CBD organization places the focus on serving the complete needs of each major customer. It lets P&G "grow business by working as a 'strategic partner' with our accounts," not just as a supplier.[9]

Team selling does have some pitfalls, however. For example, salespeople are by nature competitive and have often been trained and rewarded for outstanding individual performance. Salespeople who are used to having customers all to themselves may have trouble learning to work with and trust others on a team. In addition, selling teams can confuse or overwhelm customers who are used to working with only one salesperson. Finally, difficulties in evaluating individual contributions to the team-selling effort can create some sticky compensation issues.

Recruiting and Selecting Salespeople

At the heart of any successful sales force operation is the recruitment and selection of good salespeople. The performance difference between an average salesperson and a top salesperson can be substantial. In a typical sales force, the top 30 percent of the salespeople might bring in 60 percent of the sales. Thus, careful salesperson selection can greatly increase overall sales force performance. Beyond the differences in sales performance, poor selection results in costly turnover. When a salesperson quits, the costs of finding and training a new salesperson—plus the costs of lost sales—can be very high. One sales consulting firm calculates the total costs of a bad sales hire at a whopping $616,000.[10] Also, a sales force with many new people is less productive, and turnover disrupts important customer relationships.

What sets great salespeople apart from all the rest? In an effort to profile top sales performers, Gallup Consulting, a division of the well-known Gallup polling organization, has interviewed hundreds of thousands of salespeople. Its research suggests that the best salespeople possess four key talents: intrinsic motivation, a disciplined work style, the ability to close a sale, and, perhaps most important, the ability to build relationships with customers.[11]

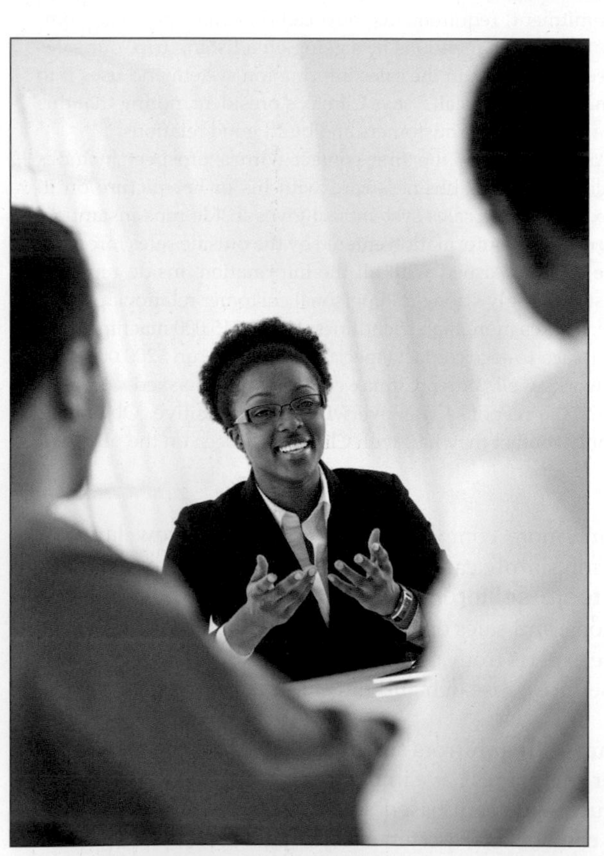

Great salespeople: The best salespeople possess intrinsic motivation, a disciplined work style, the ability to close a sale, and, perhaps most important, the ability to build relationships with customers.

Super salespeople are motivated from within—they have an unrelenting drive to excel. Some salespeople are driven by money, a desire for recognition, or the satisfaction of competing and winning. Others are driven by the desire to provide service and build relationships. The best salespeople possess some of each of these motivations. However, another analysis found that the best salespeople are driven by a strong sense of purpose: "The salespeople who sold with noble purpose, who truly want to make a difference to customers, consistently outsold the salespeople focused on sales goals and money." Selling with such a sense of customer-related purpose is not only more successful, it's also more profitable and more satisfying to salespeople.[12]

Super salespeople also have a disciplined work style. They lay out detailed, organized plans and then follow through in a timely way. But motivation and discipline mean little unless they result in closing more sales and building better customer relationships. Super salespeople build the skills and knowledge they need to get the job done. Perhaps most important, top salespeople are excellent customer problem solvers and relationship builders. They understand their customers' needs. Talk to sales executives and they'll describe top performers in these terms: good listeners, empathetic, patient, caring, and responsive. Top performers can put themselves on the buyer's side of the desk and see the world through their customers' eyes. They don't want just to be liked; they want to add value for their customers.

That said, there is no one right way to sell. Each successful salesperson uses a different approach, one that best applies his or her unique strengths and talents. For example, some salespeople enjoy the thrill of a harder sell in confronting challenges and winning people over. Others might apply "softer" talents to reach the same goal. "The key is for sales reps to understand and nurture their innate talents so they can develop their own personal approach and win business *their* way," says a selling expert.[13]

When recruiting, a company should analyze the sales job itself and the characteristics of its most successful salespeople to identify the traits needed by a successful salesperson in their industry. Then it must recruit the right salespeople. The human resources department looks for applicants by getting names from current salespeople, using employment agencies, searching the Internet and online social media, posting ads and notices on its Web site and industry media, and working through college placement services. Another source is to attract top salespeople from other companies. Proven salespeople need less training and can be productive immediately.

Recruiting will attract many applicants from which the company must select the best. The selection procedure can vary from a single informal interview to lengthy testing and interviewing. Many companies give formal tests to sales applicants. Tests typically measure sales aptitude, analytical and organizational skills, personality traits, and other characteristics. But test scores provide only one piece of information in a set that includes personal characteristics, references, past employment history, and interviewer reactions.

Training Salespeople

New salespeople may spend anywhere from a few weeks or months to a year or more in training. After the initial training ends, most companies provide continuing sales training via seminars, sales meetings, and Internet e-learning throughout the salesperson's career. According to one source, American firms spent nearly $20 billion on sales training last year. Although training can be expensive, it can also yield dramatic returns. For instance, one recent study showed that sales training conducted by ADP, an administrative services firm, resulted in a return on investment of nearly 340 percent in only 90 days.[14]

Training programs have several goals. First, salespeople need to know about customers and how to build relationships with them. Therefore, the training program must teach them about different types of customers and their needs, buying motives, and buying habits. It must also teach them how to sell effectively and train them in the basics of the selling process. Salespeople also need to know and identify with the company, its products, and its competitors. Therefore, an effective training program teaches them about the company's objectives, organization, products, and the strategies of major competitors.

Today, many companies are adding digital e-learning to their sales training programs. Online training may range from simple text- and video-based product training and Internet-based sales exercises that build sales skills to sophisticated simulations that re-create the dynamics of real-life sales calls. One of the most basic forms is virtual instructor-led training (VILT). Using this method, a small group of salespeople at remote locations logs on to an online conferencing site, where a sales instructor leads training sessions using online video, audio, and interactive learning tools.

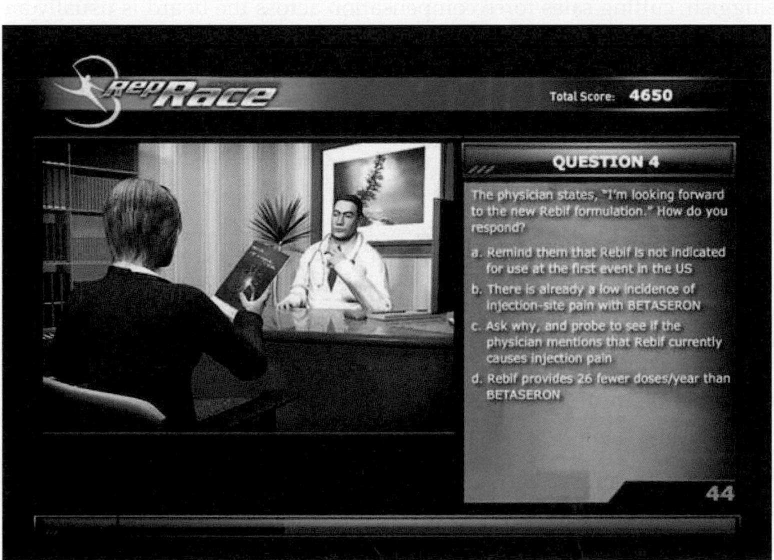

E-training can make sales training more efficient—and more fun. Bayer HealthCare Pharmaceuticals' role-playing video game—Rep Race—helped improve sales rep effectiveness by 20 percent.

Concentric Pharma Advertising

Training online instead of on-site can cut travel and other training costs, and it takes up less of a salesperson's selling time. It also makes on-demand training available to salespeople, letting them train as little or as much as needed, whenever and wherever needed. Although most e-learning is Web-based, many companies now offer on-demand training from anywhere via almost any mobile digital device.

Many companies are now using imaginative and sophisticated e-learning techniques to make sales training more efficient—and sometimes even more fun. For example, Bayer HealthCare Pharmaceuticals worked with Concentric Pharma Advertising, a health care marketing agency, to create a role-playing simulation video game to train its sales force on a new drug marketing program:[15]

> Most people don't usually associate fast-paced rock music and flashy graphics with online sales training tools. But Concentric Pharma Advertising's innovative role-playing video game—Rep Race: The Battle for Office Supremacy—has all that and a lot more. Rep Race gives Bayer sales reps far more entertainment than the staid old multiple-choice skills tests it replaces.

The game was created to help breathe new life into a mature Bayer product—Betaseron, an 18-year-old multiple sclerosis (MS) therapy treatment. The aim was to find a fresh, more active way to help Bayer sales reps apply the in-depth information they learned about Betaseron to actual selling and objections-handling situations. Bayer also wanted to increase rep engagement through interactive learning and feedback through real-time results. Bayer reps liked Rep Race from the start. According to Bayer, when the game was first launched, reps played it as many as 30 times. In addition to its educational and motivational value, Rep Race allowed Bayer to measure sales reps' individual and collective performance. In the end, Bayer calculated that the Rep Race simulation helped improve the Betaseron sales team's effectiveness by 20 percent.

Compensating Salespeople

To attract good salespeople, a company must have an appealing compensation plan. Compensation consists of four elements: a fixed amount, a variable amount, expenses, and fringe benefits. The fixed amount, usually a salary, gives the salesperson some stable income. The variable amount, which might be commissions or bonuses based on sales performance, rewards the salesperson for greater effort and success.

Management must determine what *mix* of these compensation elements makes the most sense for each sales job. Different combinations of fixed and variable compensation give rise to four basic types of compensation plans: straight salary, straight commission, salary plus bonus, and salary plus commission. According to one study of sales force compensation, 18 percent of companies pay straight salary, 19 percent pay straight commission, and 63 percent pay a combination of salary plus incentives. Another study showed that the average salesperson's pay consists of about 67 percent salary and 33 percent incentive pay.[16]

A sales force compensation plan can both motivate salespeople and direct their activities. Compensation should direct salespeople toward activities that are consistent with the overall sales force and marketing objectives. For example, if the strategy is to acquire new business, grow rapidly, and gain market share, the compensation plan might include a larger commission component, coupled with a new-account bonus to encourage high sales performance and new account development. In contrast, if the goal is to maximize current account profitability, the compensation plan might contain a larger base-salary component with additional incentives for current account sales or customer satisfaction.

In fact, more and more companies are moving away from high-commission plans that may drive salespeople to make short-term grabs for business. They worry that a salesperson who is pushing too hard to close a deal may ruin the customer relationship. Instead, companies are designing compensation plans that reward salespeople for building customer relationships and growing the long-run value of each customer.

When times get tough economically, some companies are tempted to cut costs by reducing sales compensation. However, although some cost-cutting measures make sense when business is sluggish, cutting sales force compensation across the board is usually an action of last resort. Top salespeople are always in demand, and paying them less might mean losing them at a time when they are most needed. Thus, short-changing key salespeople can result in short-changing important customer relationships. If the company must reduce its compensation expenses, rather than making across-the-board cuts, companies should continue to pay top performers well while turning loose low performers.

Supervising and Motivating Salespeople

New salespeople need more than a territory, compensation, and training—they need supervision and motivation. The goal of *supervision* is to help salespeople "work smart" by doing the right things in the right ways. The goal of *motivation* is to encourage salespeople to "work hard" and energetically toward sales force goals. If salespeople work smart and work hard, they will realize their full potential—to their own and the company's benefit.

Supervising Salespeople

Companies vary in how closely they supervise their salespeople. Many help salespeople identify target customers and set call objectives. Some may also specify how much time the sales force should spend prospecting for new accounts and set other time management priorities. One tool is the weekly, monthly, or annual *call plan* that shows which customers and prospects to call on and which activities to carry out. Another tool is *time-and-duty analysis.* In addition to time spent selling, the salesperson spends time traveling, waiting, taking breaks, and doing administrative chores.

FIGURE | 16.2
How Salespeople Spend Their Time
Source: "2014 Sales Performance Optimization Study," *CSO Insights*, www.csoinsights.com. Used with permission.

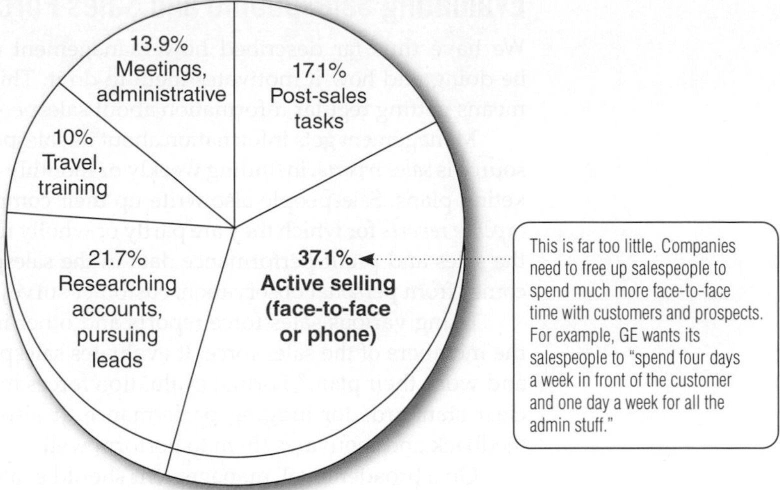
13.9%
Meetings,
administrative
17.1%
Post-sales
tasks
10%
Travel,
training
21.7%
Researching
accounts,
pursuing
leads
37.1%
Active selling
(face-to-face
or phone)
This is far too little. Companies need to free up salespeople to spend much more face-to-face time with customers and prospects. For example, GE wants its salespeople to "spend four days a week in front of the customer and one day a week for all the admin stuff."

Figure 16.2 shows how salespeople spend their time. On average, active selling time accounts for only 37 percent of total working time.[17] Companies are always looking for ways to save time—simplifying administrative duties, developing better sales-call and routing plans, supplying more and better customer information, and using phone, e-mail, online, or mobile conferencing instead of traveling.

Many firms have adopted *sales force automation systems*: computerized, digitized sales force operations that let salespeople work more effectively anytime, anywhere. Companies now routinely equip their salespeople with laptops or tablets, smartphones, wireless connections, videoconferencing technologies, and customer-contact and relationship management software. Armed with these technologies, salespeople can more effectively and efficiently profile customers and prospects, analyze and forecast sales, engage customers, make presentations, prepare sales and expense reports, and manage account relationships. The result is better time management, improved customer service, lower sales costs, and higher sales performance. In all, technology has reshaped the ways in which salespeople carry out their duties and engage customers.

Motivating Salespeople

Beyond directing salespeople, sales managers must also motivate them. Some salespeople will do their best without any special urging from management. To them, selling may be the most fascinating job in the world. But selling can also be frustrating. Salespeople often work alone, and they must sometimes travel away from home. They may also face aggressive competing salespeople and difficult customers. Therefore, salespeople often need special encouragement to do their best.

Management can boost sales force morale and performance through its organizational climate, sales quotas, and positive incentives. *Organizational climate* describes the feeling that salespeople have about their opportunities, value, and rewards for a good performance. Some companies treat salespeople as if they are not very important, so performance suffers accordingly. Other companies treat their salespeople as valued contributors and allow virtually unlimited opportunity for income and promotion. Not surprisingly, these companies enjoy higher sales force performance and less turnover.

Sales quota
A standard that states the amount a salesperson should sell and how sales should be divided among the company's products.

Many companies motivate their salespeople by setting **sales quotas**—standards stating the amount they should sell and how sales should be divided among the company's products. Compensation is often related to how well salespeople meet their quotas. Companies also use various *positive incentives* to increase the sales force effort. *Sales meetings* provide social occasions, breaks from the routine, chances to meet and talk with "company brass," and opportunities to air feelings and identify with a larger group. Companies also sponsor *sales contests* to spur the sales force to make a selling effort above and beyond what is normally expected. Other incentives include honors, merchandise and cash awards, trips, and profit-sharing plans.

Evaluating Salespeople and Sales Force Performance

We have thus far described how management communicates what salespeople should be doing and how it motivates them to do it. This process requires good feedback, which means getting regular information about salespeople to evaluate their performance.

Management gets information about its salespeople in several ways. The most important source is *sales reports*, including weekly or monthly work plans and longer-term territory marketing plans. Salespeople also write up their completed activities on *call reports* and turn in *expense reports* for which they are partly or wholly reimbursed. The company can also monitor the sales and profit performance data in the salesperson's territory. Additional information comes from personal observation, customer surveys, and talks with other salespeople.

Using various sales force reports and other information, sales management evaluates the members of the sales force. It evaluates salespeople on their ability to "plan their work and work their plan." Formal evaluation forces management to develop and communicate clear standards for judging performance. It also provides salespeople with constructive feedback and motivates them to perform well.

On a broader level, management should evaluate the performance of the sales force as a whole. Is the sales force accomplishing its customer relationship, sales, and profit objectives? Is it working well with other areas of the marketing and company organization? Are sales force costs in line with outcomes? As with other marketing activities, the company wants to measure its *return on sales investment*.

Author Comment Like just about everything else these days, digital technologies have impacted selling big time. Today's sales forces are mastering the use of online, mobile, and social media tools to engage business customers, build relationships, and make sales.

Social Selling: Online, Mobile, and Social Media Tools

Social selling
Using online, mobile, and social media to engage customers, build stronger customer relationships, and augment sales performance.

The fastest-growing sales trend is the explosion in **social selling**—the use of online, mobile, and social media to engage customers, build stronger customer relationships, and augment sales performance. New digital sales force technologies are creating exciting new avenues for connecting with and engaging customers in the digital and social media age. Some analysts even predict that the Internet will mean the death of person-to-person selling, as salespeople are ultimately replaced by Web sites, online social media, mobile apps, video and conferencing technologies, and other tools that allow direct customer contact. "Don't believe it," says one sales expert (see Real Marketing 16.1).[18] Used properly, online and social media technologies won't make salespeople obsolete; they will make salespeople more productive and effective.

The new digital technologies are providing salespeople with powerful tools for identifying and learning about prospects, engaging customers, creating customer value, closing sales, and nurturing customer relationships. Social selling technologies can produce big organizational benefits for sales forces. They help conserve salespeople's valuable time, save travel dollars, and give salespeople new vehicles for selling and servicing accounts.

Social selling hasn't really changed the fundamentals of selling. Sales forces have always taken the primary responsibility for reaching out to and engaging customers and managing customer relationships. Now, more of that is being done digitally. However, online and social media are dramatically changing the customer buying process. As a result, they are also changing the selling process. In today's digital world, many customers no longer rely as much as they once did on information and assistance provided by salespeople. Instead, they carry out more of the buying process on their own—especially the early stages. Increasingly, they use online and social media resources to analyze their own problems, research solutions, get advice from colleagues, and rank buying options before ever speaking to a salesperson. A recent study of business buyers found that 92 percent of buyers start their searches online and that, on average, buyers completed nearly 60 percent of the buying process before contacting a supplier.[19]

Thus, today's customers have much more control over the sales process than they had in the days when brochures, pricing, and product advice were only available from a sales rep. Customers can now browse corporate Web sites, blogs, and YouTube videos to identify and qualify sellers. They can hobnob with other buyers on social media such as LinkedIn, Google+, Twitter, or Facebook to share experiences, identify solutions, and evaluate products they are considering. As a result, if and when salespeople do enter the buying process, customers often know almost as much about a company's products as the salespeople do. "It's not just that buyers start the sales process without you," says an analyst, "they typically complete most of the purchase journey before having any contact with sales. And by that point they are far more informed about your business than you are about theirs."[20]

Real Marketing 16.1

B-to-B Salespeople: In This Digital and Social Media Age, Who Needs Them Anymore?

It's hard to imagine a world without salespeople. But according to some analysts, there will be a lot fewer of them a decade from now. With the explosion of the Internet, mobile devices, social media, and other technologies that link customers directly with companies, they reason, who needs face-to-face selling anymore? According to the doubters, salespeople are rapidly being replaced by Web sites, e-mail, blogs, mobile apps, video sharing, virtual trade shows, social media such as LinkedIn and Facebook, and a host of other digital-age interaction tools.

Research firm Gartner predicts that by 2020, 85 percent of all interactions between businesses will be executed without human intervention, requiring fewer salespeople. Of the 18 million salespeople now employed in the United States, the firm says, there will be only about 4 million left. "The world no longer needs salespeople," one doomsayer boldly proclaims. "Sales is a dying profession and soon will be as outmoded as oil lamps and the rotary phone." Says another, "If we don't find and fill a need faster than a computer, we won't be needed."

So, is business-to-business selling really dying? Will the Internet, mobile technologies, and social media replace the age-old art of selling face to face? To answer these questions, *SellingPower* magazine called together a panel of sales experts and asked them to weigh in on the future of B-to-B sales. The panel members agreed that technology is radically transforming the selling profession. Today's revolutionary changes in how people communicate are affecting every aspect of business, and selling is no exception.

But is B-to-B selling dead in this Internet age? Don't believe it, says the *SellingPower* panel. Technology, the Internet, and social media won't soon be replacing person-to-person buying and selling. Selling has changed, agrees the panel, and the technology can greatly enhance the selling process. But it can't replace many of the functions that salespeople perform. "The Internet can take orders and disseminate content, but what it can't do is discover customer needs," says one panelist. "It can't build relationships, and it can't prospect on its own." Adds another panelist, "Someone must define the company's value proposition and unique message and communicate it to the market, and that person is the sales rep."

What is dying, however, is what one panelist calls the account-maintenance role—the order taker who stops by the customer's office on Friday and says, "Hey, got anything for me?" Such salespeople are not creating value and can easily be replaced by automation. However, salespeople who excel at new customer acquisition, relationship management, and account growth with existing customers will always be in high demand.

There's no doubt about it—technology is transforming the profession of selling. Instead of relying on salespeople for basic information and education, customers can now do much of their own prepurchase research via Web sites, online searches, social media contacts, and other venues. Many customers now start the sales process online and do their homework about problems, competing products, and suppliers before the first sales meeting ever takes place. They don't need basic information or product education; they need solutions and new insights. So today's salespeople need "to move into the discovery and relationship-building phase, uncovering pain points and focusing on the prospect's business," says a panelist.

Rather than replacing salespeople, however, technology is augmenting them. Today's salespeople aren't really doing anything fundamentally new. They've always done customer research and social networking. Today, however, they are doing it on steroids, using a new kit of high-tech digital tools and applications.

For example, many companies are moving rapidly into online-community-based selling. Case in point: Enterprise-software company SAP, which five years ago set up EcoHub, its own online, community-powered social media and mobile marketplace consisting of customers, SAP software experts, partners, and almost anyone else who wanted to join. The EcoHub community grew quickly to more than 2 million users in 200 countries, extending across a broad online spectrum—a dedicated Web site, mobile apps, Twitter channels, LinkedIn groups, Facebook and Google+ pages, YouTube channels, and more. EcoHub grew to more than 600 "solution storefronts," where visitors could "discover, evaluate, and buy" software solutions and services from SAP and its partners. EcoHub also let users

Online selling tools, such as SAP's EcoHub and SAP Store online community-based marketplaces, can help to build customer engagement and generate buying interest and sales. But rather than replacing salespeople, such efforts extend their reach and effectiveness.

rate and share the solutions and advice they got from other community members.

SAP was surprised to learn that what it had originally seen as a place for customers to discuss issues, problems, and solutions turned into a significant point of sale. The information, give-and-take discussions, and conversations at the site drew in customers, even for big-ticket sales of $20–$30 million or more. In fact, EcoHub has now evolved into SAP Store, a gigantic SAP marketplace where customers can engage with SAP, its partners, and each other to share information, post comments and reviews, discover problems, and evaluate and buy SAP solutions.

However, although the SAP Store draws in new potential customers and takes them through many of the initial stages of product discovery and evaluation, it doesn't replace SAP's or its partners' salespeople. Instead, it extends their reach and effectiveness. Its real value is the flood of sales leads it creates for the SAP and partner sales forces. Once prospective customers have discovered, discussed, and evaluated SAP solutions online, SAP invites them to initiate contact, request a proposal, or start the negotiation process. That's where the person-to-person selling begins.

All this suggests that B-to-B selling isn't dying, it's just changing. The tools and techniques may be different as sales forces leverage and adapt to selling in the digital and social media age. But the panelists agree strongly that B-to-B marketers will never be able to do without strong sales teams. Salespeople who can discover customer needs, solve customer problems, and build relationships will be needed and successful, regardless of what else changes. Especially for those big-ticket B-to-B sales, "all the new technology may make it easier to sell by building strong ties to customers even before the first sit-down, but when the signature hits the dotted line, there will be a sales rep there."

Sources: Based on information from Lain Chroust Ehmann, "Sales Up!" *SellingPower*, January/February 2011, p. 40; Gerhared Gschwandtner, "How Many Salespeople Will Be Left by 2020?" *SellingPower,* May/June 2011, p. 7; Neil Baron, "Death of Sales People?" *Fast Company,* August 17, 2013, www.fastcompany.com/3020103/death-of-the-sales-people; "Getting Started with SAP EcoHub," http://ecohub.sap.com/getting-started, accessed November 2013; "SAP EcoHub to the SAP Store: The Evolution of the Online Channel at SAP," *YouTube,* www.youtube.com/watch?v=WADFf6k34V8, accessed June 2014; and https://store.sap.com/ and https://scn.sap.com, accessed September 2014.

In response to this new digital buying environment, sellers are reorienting their selling processes around the new customer buying process. They are "going where customers are"—social media, Web forums, online communities, blogs—in order to engage customers earlier. They are engaging customers not just where and when they are buying, but also where and when they are learning about and evaluating what they will buy.

Salespeople now routinely use digital tools that monitor customer social media exchanges to spot trends, identify prospects, and learn what customers would like to buy, how they feel about a vendor, and what it would take to make a sale. They generate lists of prospective customers from online databases and social networking sites, such as InsideView, Hoovers, and LinkedIn. They create dialogs when prospective customers visit their Web and social media sites through live chats with the sales team. They use Internet conferencing tools such as WebEx, Zoom, GoToMeeting, or TelePresence to talk live with customers about products and services. They provide videos and other information on their YouTube channels and Facebook pages.

Social selling: GE complements its sales force efforts through a wide variety of social media that engage business customers, connect them with GE salespeople, and promote customer purchasing and relationships. "We want to get our sales team 100 percent digitized."

GE

Today's sales forces are also ramping up their own use of social media to engage customers throughout the buying process. A recent survey of business-to-business marketers found that, although they have recently cut back on traditional media and event spending, 68 percent are investing more in social media, ranging from proprietary online customer communities to Webinars and social media and mobile applications. Consider industrial and consumer products giant GE:[21]

GE complements its sales force efforts through a wide variety of digital and social media that inform and engage business customers, connect them with GE salespeople, and promote customer purchasing and relationships. For example, GE's various divisions—from GE Aviation to GE Healthcare and GE Energy—offer dozens of industry-specific Web sites, containing thousands of individual site areas and tens of thousands of pages that provide B-to-B customers with purchasing solutions, product overviews, detailed technical information, online videos and Webinars, live chats, and real-time customer support. GE also builds brand awareness and helps its sales force engage business customers deeply through a comprehensive presence in major social media, such as Facebook, Twitter, LinkedIn, Google+, Salesforce.com, and even Instagram, Pinterest, and Vine. "We have a core belief that business is social," says GE's chief marketing officer. "If you're in business you need social because it's going to get you closer to your customers. We want to get our sales team 100 percent digitized."

Ultimately, social selling technologies are helping to make sales forces more efficient, cost-effective, and productive. The technologies help salespeople do what good salespeople have always done—build customer relationships by solving customer problems—but do it better, faster, and cheaper.

However, social selling also has some drawbacks. For starters, it's not cheap. In addition, such systems can intimidate low-tech salespeople or clients. Even more, there are some things you just can't present or teach via the Internet—things that require personal interactions. For these reasons, some high-tech experts recommend that sales executives use online and social media technologies to spot opportunities, provide information, maintain customer contact, and make preliminary client sales presentations but resort to old-fashioned, face-to-face meetings when the time draws near to close a big deal.

Author Comment So far, we've examined how sales management develops and implements overall sales force strategies and programs. In this section, we'll look at how individual salespeople and sales teams sell to customers and build relationships with them.

The Personal Selling Process

We now turn from designing and managing a sales force to the personal selling process. The **selling process** consists of several steps that salespeople must master. These steps focus on the goal of getting new customers and obtaining orders from them. However, most salespeople spend much of their time maintaining existing accounts and building long-term customer relationships. We will discuss the relationship aspect of the personal selling process in a later section.

Selling process
The steps that salespeople follow when selling, which include prospecting and qualifying, preapproach, approach, presentation and demonstration, handling objections, closing, and follow-up.

Steps in the Selling Process

As shown in **Figure 16.3**, the selling process consists of seven steps: prospecting and qualifying, preapproach, approach, presentation and demonstration, handling objections, closing, and follow-up.

Prospecting
The sales step in which a salesperson or company identifies qualified potential customers.

Prospecting and Qualifying

The first step in the selling process is **prospecting**—identifying qualified potential customers. Approaching the right customers is crucial to selling success. Salespeople don't want to call on just any potential customers. They want to call on those who are most likely to appreciate and respond to the company's value proposition—those the company can serve well and profitably.

A salesperson must often approach many prospects to get only a few sales. Although the company supplies some leads, salespeople need skill in finding their own. The best

FIGURE | 16.3
Steps in the Selling Process

As shown here, these steps are transaction-oriented—aimed at closing a specific sale with the customer...

...but remember that in the long run, a single sale is only one element of a long-term customer relationship. So the selling process steps must be understood in the broader context of maintaining profitable customer relationships.

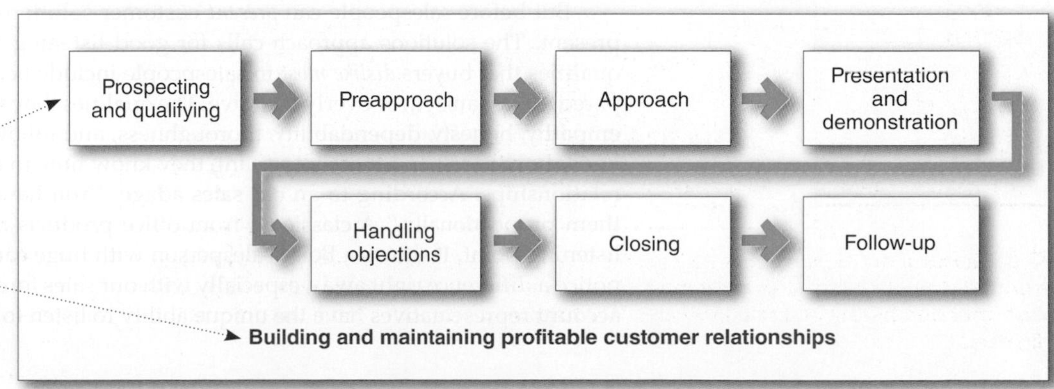

source is referrals. Salespeople can ask current customers for referrals and cultivate other referral sources, such as suppliers, dealers, noncompeting salespeople, and online or social media contacts. They can also search for prospects in directories or on the Internet and track down leads using the telephone, e-mail, and social media. Or, as a last resort, they can drop in unannounced on various offices (a practice known as *cold calling*).

Salespeople also need to know how to *qualify* leads—that is, how to identify the good ones and screen out the poor ones. Prospects can be qualified by looking at their financial ability, volume of business, special needs, location, and possibilities for growth.

Preapproach

Preapproach
The sales step in which a salesperson learns as much as possible about a prospective customer before making a sales call.

Before calling on a prospect, the salesperson should learn as much as possible about the organization (what it needs, who is involved in the buying) and its buyers (their characteristics and buying styles). This step is known as **preapproach**. A successful sale begins long before the salesperson makes initial contact with a prospect. Preapproach begins with good research and preparation. The salesperson can consult standard industry and online sources, acquaintances, and others to learn about the company. He or she can scour the prospect's Web and social media sites for information about its products, buyers, and buying processes. Then the salesperson must apply the research gathered to develop a customer strategy.

The salesperson should set *call objectives*, which may be to qualify the prospect, gather information, or make an immediate sale. Another task is to determine the best approach, which might be a personal visit, a phone call, an e-mail, or a text or tweet. The ideal timing should be considered carefully because many prospects are busiest at certain times of the day or week. Finally, the salesperson should give thought to an overall sales strategy for the account.

Approach

Approach
The sales step in which a salesperson meets the customer for the first time.

During the **approach** step, the salesperson should know how to meet and greet the buyer and get the relationship off to a good start. The approach might take place offline or online, in-person or via digital conferencing or social media. This step involves the salesperson's appearance, opening lines, and follow-up remarks. The opening lines should be positive to build goodwill from the outset. This opening might be followed by some key questions to learn more about the customer's needs or by showing a display or sample to attract the buyer's attention and curiosity. As in all stages of the selling process, listening to the customer is crucial.

Presentation and Demonstration

Presentation
The sales step in which a salesperson tells the "value story" to the buyer, showing how the company's offer solves the customer's problems.

During the **presentation** step of the selling process, the salesperson tells the "value story" to the buyer, showing how the company's offer solves the customer's problems. The *customer-solution approach* fits better with today's relationship marketing focus than does a hard sell or glad-handing approach.

The goal should be to show how the company's products and services fit the customer's needs. Buyers today want insights and solutions, not smiles; results, not razzle-dazzle. Moreover, they don't want just products. More than ever in today's economic climate, buyers want to know how those products will add value to their businesses. They want salespeople who listen to their concerns, understand their needs, and respond with the right products and services.

But before salespeople can *present* customer solutions, they must *develop* solutions to present. The solutions approach calls for good listening and problem-solving skills. The qualities that buyers *dislike most* in salespeople include being pushy, late, deceitful, unprepared, disorganized, or overly talkative. The qualities they *value most* include good listening, empathy, honesty, dependability, thoroughness, and follow-through. ● Great salespeople know how to sell, but more important, they know how to listen and build strong customer relationships. According to an old sales adage, "You have two ears and one mouth. Use them proportionally." A classic ad from office products maker Boise Cascade makes the listening point. It shows a Boise salesperson with huge ears drawn on. "With Boise, you'll notice a difference right away, especially with our sales force," says the ad. "At Boise . . . our account representatives have the unique ability to listen to your needs."

Great salespeople know how to sell, but more important, they know how to listen and build strong customer relationships.

Tony Garcia/Getty Images

Finally, salespeople must also plan their presentation methods. Good interpersonal communication skills count when it comes to engaging customers and making effective sales presentations. However, the current media-rich and cluttered communications environment presents many new challenges for sales presenters. Today's information-overloaded customers demand richer presentation experiences. For their part, presenters now face multiple distractions during presentations from mobile phones, text messages, and other digital competition. As a result, salespeople must deliver their messages in more engaging and compelling ways.

Thus, today's salespeople are employing advanced presentation technologies that allow for full multimedia presentations to only one or a few people. The venerable old sales presentation flip chart has been replaced with tablet computers, sophisticated presentation software, online presentation technologies, interactive whiteboards, and digital projectors.

Handling Objections

Customers almost always have objections during the presentation or when asked to place an order. The objections can be either logical or psychological, and they are often unspoken. In **handling objections**, the salesperson should use a positive approach, seek out hidden objections, ask the buyer to clarify any objections, take objections as opportunities to provide more information, and turn the objections into reasons for buying. Every salesperson needs training in the skills of handling objections.

Handling objections
The sales step in which a salesperson seeks out, clarifies, and overcomes any customer objections to buying.

Closing
The sales step in which a salesperson asks the customer for an order.

Follow-up
The sales step in which a salesperson follows up after the sale to ensure customer satisfaction and repeat business.

Closing

After handling the prospect's objections, the salesperson next tries to close the sale. However, some salespeople do not get around to **closing** or don't handle it well. They may lack confidence, feel guilty about asking for the order, or fail to recognize the right moment to close the sale. Salespeople should know how to recognize closing signals from the buyer, including physical actions, comments, and questions. For example, the customer might sit forward and nod approvingly or ask about prices and credit terms.

Salespeople can use any of several closing techniques. They can ask for the order, review points of agreement, offer to help write up the order, ask whether the buyer wants this model or that one, or note that the buyer will lose out if the order is not placed now. The salesperson may offer the buyer special reasons to close, such as a lower price, an extra quantity at no charge, or additional services.

Follow-Up

The last step in the selling process—**follow-up**—is necessary if the salesperson wants to ensure customer satisfaction and repeat business. Right after closing, the salesperson should complete any details on delivery time, purchase terms, and other matters. The salesperson then should schedule a follow-up call after the buyer receives the initial order to make sure proper installation, instruction, and servicing occur. This visit would reveal any problems, assure the buyer of the salesperson's interest, and reduce any buyer concerns that might have arisen since the sale.

Personal Selling and Managing Customer Relationships

The steps in the just-described selling process are *transaction oriented*—their aim is to help salespeople close a specific sale with a customer. But in most cases, the company is not simply seeking a sale. Rather, it wants to engage the customer over the long haul in a mutually profitable *relationship*. The sales force usually plays an important role in customer relationship building. Thus, as shown in Figure 16.3, the selling process must be understood in the context of building and maintaining profitable customer relationships. Moreover, as discussed in a previous section, today's buyers are increasingly moving through the early stages of the buying process themselves, before ever engaging sellers. Salespeople must adapt their selling process to match the new buying process. That means discovering and engaging customers on a relationship basis rather than a transaction basis.

Successful sales organizations recognize that winning and keeping accounts requires more than making good products and directing the sales force to close lots of sales. If the company wishes only to close sales and capture short-term business, it can do this by simply slashing its prices to meet or beat those of competitors. Instead, most companies want their salespeople to practice *value selling*—demonstrating and delivering superior customer value and capturing a return on that value that is fair for both the customer and the company. For example, as we discovered in the chapter-opening story, companies like P&G understand that they aren't just selling products to and through their retailer customers. They are partnering with these retail accounts to create more value for final consumers to their mutual benefit. P&G knows that it can succeed only if its retail partners succeed.

Value selling: Sales management's challenge is to transform salespeople from customer advocates for price cuts into company advocates for value.
© almagami/123rf.com

Unfortunately, in the heat of closing sales, salespeople too often take the easy way out by cutting prices rather than selling value. Sales management's challenge is to transform salespeople from customer advocates for price cuts into company advocates for value. Here's how Rockwell Automation sells value and relationships rather than price:[22]

> Under pressure from Walmart to lower its prices, a condiment producer asked several competing supplier representatives—including Rockwell Automation sales rep Jeff Policicchio—to help it find ways to reduce its operating costs. After spending a day in the customer's plant, Policicchio quickly put his finger on the major problem: Production was suffering because of down time due to poorly performing pumps on the customer's 32 large condiment tanks. Quickly gathering cost and usage data, Policicchio used his Rockwell Automation laptop value-assessment tool to develop an effective solution for the customer's pump problem.
>
> The next day, as he and competing reps presented their cost-reduction proposals to plant management, Policicchio offered the following value proposition: "With this Rockwell Automation pump solution, through less downtime, reduced administrative costs in procurement, and lower spending on repair parts, your company will save at least $16,268 per pump—on up to 32 pumps—relative to our best competitor's solution." Compared with competitors' proposals, Policicchio's solution carried a higher initial price. However, no competing rep offered more than fuzzy promises about possible cost savings. Most simply lowered their prices.
>
> Impressed by Policicchio's value proposition—despite its higher initial price—the plant managers opted to buy and try one Rockwell Automation pump. When the pump performed even better than predicted, the customer ordered all of the remaining pumps. By demonstrating tangible value rather than simply selling on price, Policicchio not only landed the initial sale but also earned a loyal future customer.

Thus, value selling requires listening to customers, understanding their needs, and carefully coordinating the whole company's efforts to create lasting relationships based on customer value.

Sales promotion
Short-term incentives to encourage the purchase or sale of a product or a service.

Author Comment | Sales promotion is the most short-term of the promotion mix tools. Whereas advertising or personal selling says "buy," sales promotions say "buy now."

Sales Promotion

Personal selling and advertising often work closely with another promotion tool, sales promotion. **Sales promotion** consists of short-term incentives to encourage the purchase or sales of a product or service. Whereas advertising offers reasons to buy a product or service, sales promotion offers reasons to buy *now*.

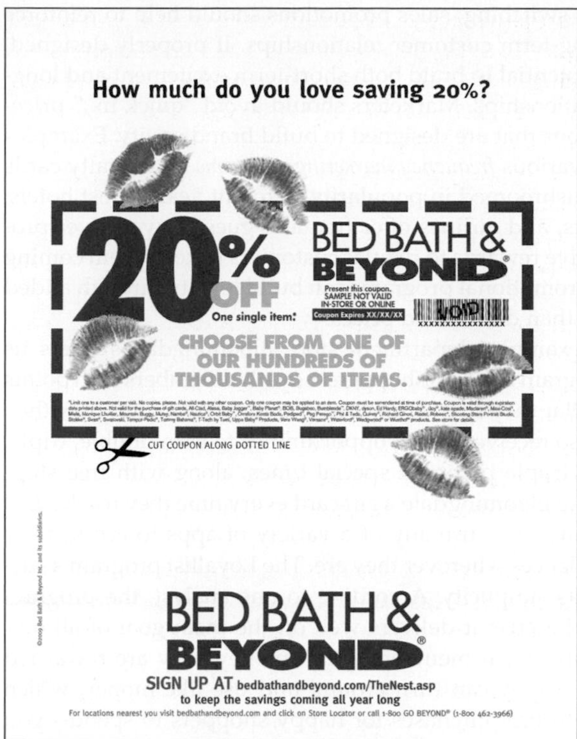

How much do you love saving 20%?
20% OFF
One single item!
BED BATH & BEYOND
Present this coupon. SAMPLE NOT VALID IN-STORE OR ONLINE
Coupon Expires XX/XX/XX
CHOOSE FROM ONE OF OUR HUNDREDS OF THOUSANDS OF ITEMS.
CUT COUPON ALONG DOTTED LINE
BED BATH & BEYOND
SIGN UP AT bedbathandbeyond.com/TheNest.asp
to keep the savings coming all year long

Sales promotions are found everywhere. For example, your favorite magazine is loaded with offers like this one that promote a strong and immediate response.

Bed Bath & Beyond Inc.

Examples of sales promotions are found everywhere. A freestanding insert in the Sunday newspaper contains a coupon offering $1 off Meow Mix Tender Centers food for your cat. A Bed Bath & Beyond ad in your favorite magazine offers 20 percent off on any single item. The end-of-the-aisle display in the local supermarket tempts impulse buyers with a wall of Coca-Cola cases—four 12-packs for $12. Buy a new Samsung laptop and get a free memory upgrade. A hardware store chain receives a 10 percent discount on selected Stihl power lawn and garden tools if it agrees to advertise them in local newspapers. Sales promotion includes a wide variety of promotion tools designed to stimulate earlier or stronger market response.

The Rapid Growth of Sales Promotion

Sales promotion tools are used by most organizations, including manufacturers, distributors, retailers, and not-for-profit institutions. They are targeted toward final buyers (*consumer promotions*), retailers and wholesalers (*trade promotions*), business customers (*business promotions*), and members of the sales force (*sales force promotions*). Today, in the average consumer packaged-goods company, sales promotion accounts for 60 percent of all marketing budgets.[23]

Several factors have contributed to the rapid growth of sales promotion, particularly in consumer markets. First, inside the company, product managers face greater pressures to increase current sales, and they view promotion as an effective short-run sales tool. Second, externally, the company faces more competition, and competing brands are less differentiated. Increasingly, competitors are using sales promotion to help differentiate their offers. Third, advertising efficiency has declined because of rising costs, media clutter, and legal restraints. Finally, consumers have become more deal oriented. In the current economy, consumers are demanding lower prices and better deals. Sales promotions can help attract today's more thrift-oriented consumers.

The growing use of sales promotion has resulted in *promotion clutter*, which is similar to advertising clutter. With so many products being sold on deal these days, a given promotion runs the risk of being lost in a sea of other promotions, weakening its ability to trigger an immediate purchase. Manufacturers are now searching for ways to rise above the clutter, such as offering larger coupon values, creating more dramatic point-of-purchase displays, or delivering promotions through new digital media—such as the Internet or mobile phones. According to one study, 88 percent of retailers now see digital promotions—such as mobile coupons, shopper e-mails, and online deals—as an important part of their shopper marketing efforts.[24]

In developing a sales promotion program, a company must first set sales promotion objectives and then select the best tools for accomplishing these objectives.

Sales Promotion Objectives

Sales promotion objectives vary widely. Sellers may use *consumer promotions* to urge short-term customer buying or boost customer brand involvement. Objectives for *trade promotions* include getting retailers to carry new items and more inventory, buy ahead, or promote the company's products and give them more shelf space. *Business promotions* are used to generate business leads, stimulate purchases, reward customers, and motivate salespeople. For the sales force, objectives include getting more sales force support for current or new products and getting salespeople to sign up new accounts.

Sales promotions are usually used together with advertising, personal selling, direct marketing, or other promotion mix tools. Consumer promotions must usually be advertised and can add excitement and pulling power to ads and other marketing content. Trade and business sales promotions support the firm's personal selling process.

When the economy tightens and sales lag, it's tempting to offer deep promotional discounts to spur consumer spending. In general, however, rather than creating only short-term sales or temporary brand switching, sales promotions should help to reinforce the product's position and build long-term customer relationships. If properly designed, every sales promotion tool has the potential to build both short-term excitement and long-term consumer engagement and relationships. Marketers should avoid "quick fix," price-only promotions in favor of promotions that are designed to build brand equity. Examples include the various *frequency marketing programs* and loyalty cards that have mushroomed in popularity in recent years. Most hotels, supermarkets, and airlines offer frequent-guest/buyer/flyer programs that give rewards to regular customers to keep them coming back. Such promotional programs can build loyalty through added value rather than discounted prices.

Customer loyalty programs: Bloomingdale's Loyallist program works well because of its simplicity. "Become a Loyallist," says the company. "It's better on the list."
Bloomingdale's, Inc.

For example, department store Bloomingdale's offers its Loyallist program for loyal shoppers. Loyallist members earn points for every dollar they spend, in-store or online, no matter how they pay. They also receive special opportunities to earn double, triple, or even quadruple points at special times, along with free shipping and a $25 Bloomingdale's gift card every time they reach 5,000 points. Loyalists can use any of a variety of apps to access their cards and balances wherever they are. The Loyallist program's success lies in its simplicity. According to one analyst, the program "is winning because it delivers well on the main goal of all loyalty programs: when members spend money, they are rewarded by points that they can turn around and use like money, which incentivizes future purchases for happy shoppers to spend—you guessed it—more money."[25]

Major Sales Promotion Tools

Many tools can be used to accomplish sales promotion objectives. Descriptions of the main consumer, trade, and business promotion tools follow.

Consumer Promotions

Consumer promotions
Sales promotion tools used to boost short-term customer buying and engagement or enhance long-term customer relationships.

Consumer promotions include a wide range of tools—from samples, coupons, refunds, premiums, and point-of-purchase displays to contests, sweepstakes, and event sponsorships.

Samples are offers of a trial amount of a product. Sampling is the most effective—but most expensive—way to introduce a new product or create new excitement for an existing one. Some samples are free; for others, the company charges a small amount to offset its cost. The sample might be sent by mail, handed out in a store or at a kiosk, attached to another product, or featured in an ad, e-mail, or mobile offer. Samples are sometimes combined into sample packs, which can then be used to promote other products and services. Sampling can be a powerful promotional tool. For example, a bevy of big-name food marketers—from Papa John's Pizza and Pizza Hut to Campbell Soup and PepsiCo—descended upon Super Bowl XLVIII-related events in New York and New Jersey, handing out free samples. Pizza Hut handed out more than 10,000 slices of its hand-tossed pizza. "It's a massive opportunity to sample our new product," said a Pizza Hut marketer.

Coupons are certificates that save buyers money when they purchase specified products. Most consumers love coupons. U.S. consumer packaged goods companies distributed 315 billion coupons with an average face value of $1.62 last year. Consumers redeemed more than 2.8 billion of them for a total savings of about $3.5 billion.[26] Coupons can promote early trial of a new brand or stimulate sales of a mature brand. However, to combat the increase in coupon clutter, most major consumer goods companies are issuing fewer coupons and targeting them more carefully.

Marketers are also cultivating new outlets for distributing coupons, such as supermarket shelf dispensers, electronic point-of-sale coupon printers, and online and mobile coupon programs. Digital coupons represent today's fastest-growing coupon segment. Digital coupons can be individually targeted and personalized in ways that print coupons can't. Digital coupons accounted for nearly 9 percent of all coupons redeemed last year; about 7 percent were printed from a computer at home, and about 3 percent were redeemed via smartphone or other mobile devices. According to one study, more than half of all U.S.

adults redeemed a digital coupon last year, and nearly 20 percent of adults used a mobile coupon phone, up more than 40 percent from the prior year.[27]

As mobile phones become appendages that many people can't live without, businesses are increasingly eyeing them as prime real estate for coupons, offers, and other marketing messages. For example, drugstore chain Walgreens makes coupons available to its customers through several mobile channels:[28]

> Using the Walgreens smartphone app, customers can instantly download coupons ranging in value from 50 cents to $5, good toward anything from health and beauty products to everyday essentials such as diapers. The coupons are conveniently scannable—no clipping or printing required. Customers simply pull up the coupons on the Walgreens app and cashiers scan them straight from the customer's phone. Walgreens also tweets mobile coupons to customers who check in to any of its 8,100 stores nationwide using check-in apps such as Foursquare, Yelp, or Shopkick. Walgreens has mobile scanning capabilities available at all of its stores, giving it the nation's largest retail mobile coupon program. "Through our mobile application, no matter where people are, they can find an easy way to save next time they come to Walgreens," says the company's president of e-commerce.

Mobile coupons: Drugstore chain Walgreens makes coupons available to its customers through several mobile channels.

Walgreens Digital Marketing & Emerging Media Team. Rich Lesperance, Director.

Rebates (or *cash refunds*) are like coupons except that the price reduction occurs after the purchase rather than at the retail outlet. The customer sends proof of purchase to the manufacturer, which then refunds part of the purchase price by mail. For example, Toro ran a clever preseason promotion on some of its snowblower models, offering a rebate if the snowfall in the buyer's market area turned out to be below average. Competitors were not able to match this offer on such short notice, and the promotion was very successful.

Price packs (also called *cents-off deals*) offer consumers savings off the regular price of a product. The producer marks the reduced prices directly on the label or package. Price packs can be single packages sold at a reduced price (such as two for the price of one) or two related products banded together (such as a toothbrush and toothpaste). Price packs are very effective—even more so than coupons—in stimulating short-term sales.

Premiums are goods offered either free or at low cost as an incentive to buy a product, ranging from toys included with kids' products to phone cards and DVDs. A premium may come inside the package (in-pack), outside the package (on-pack), or through the mail. For example, over the years, McDonald's has offered a variety of premiums in its Happy Meals—from *Madagascar* characters to Beanie Babies and LEGO hologram drink cups. Customers can visit www.happymeal.com to play games and watch commercials associated with the current Happy Meal sponsor.[29]

Advertising specialties, also called *promotional products*, are useful articles imprinted with an advertiser's name, logo, or message that are given as gifts to consumers. Typical items include T-shirts and other apparel, pens, coffee mugs, calendars, key rings, mouse pads, tote bags, coolers, golf balls, and caps. U.S. marketers spent nearly $18.5 billion on advertising specialties last year. Such items can be very effective. The "best of them stick around for months, subtly burning a brand name into a user's brain," notes a promotional products expert.[30]

Point-of-purchase (POP) promotions include displays and demonstrations that take place at the point of sale. Think of your last visit to the local Kroger, Costco, CVS, or Bed Bath & Beyond. Chances are good that you were tripping over aisle displays, promotional signs, "shelf talkers," or demonstrators offering free tastes of featured food products. Unfortunately, many retailers do not like to handle the hundreds of displays, signs, and posters they receive from manufacturers each year. Manufacturers have therefore responded by offering better POP materials, offering to set them up, and tying them in with television, print, or online messages.

Contests, sweepstakes, and *games* give consumers the chance to win something, such as cash, trips, or goods, by luck or through extra effort. A *contest* calls for consumers to submit an entry—a jingle, guess, suggestion—to be judged by a panel that will select the best entries. A *sweepstakes* calls for consumers to submit their names for a drawing. A *game* presents consumers with something—bingo numbers, missing letters—every time they buy, which may or may not help them win a prize.

All kinds of companies use sweepstakes and contests to create brand attention and boost consumer involvement. For example, Google's "Doodle 4 Google" contest invites kids to design a Google logo, based on the theme "If I could invent one thing to make the world a better place . . .," with prizes ranging from T-shirts and tablet computers to a $30,000 college scholarship. The "OXO I Do Sweepstakes" invites soon-to-be-married couples to "Like" OXO's Facebook page and earn a chance to win $500 toward their Amazon wedding registry. Enter the Coleman Camping Kit Giveaway and you win a gear prize pack worth more than $1,000. And if your recipe wins the annual Pillsbury Bake-Off, you could take home a $1 million prize.

Event marketing (or event sponsorships)
Creating a brand-marketing event or serving as a sole or participating sponsor of events created by others.

Finally, marketers can promote their brands through **event marketing** (or **event sponsorships**). They can create their own brand-marketing events or serve as sole or participating sponsors of events created by others. The events might include anything from mobile brand tours to festivals, reunions, marathons, concerts, or other sponsored gatherings. Event marketing is huge, and it may be the fastest-growing area of promotion. Effective event marketing links events and sponsorships to a brand's value proposition. And with the social sharing power of today's digital media, even local events can have far-reaching impact. For example, P&G's recent "Everyday Effect" takeover event in Manhattan illustrates how companies are now blending old-school promotional techniques with new-school social sharing technologies to enhance the impact of both (see Real Marketing 16.2).

All kinds of brands now hold events. One week, it might be the National Football League (NFL) filling the southern tip of Times Square with NFL players to promote new NFL jersey designs. The next week, it's a mob of Russian models on the northern triangle of Times Square (called Duffy Square), using it as a fashion runway for Maybelline. But according to one business reporter, energy drink maker Red Bull is the "mother of all event marketers":[31]

> Event pioneer Red Bull holds hundreds of events each year in dozens of sports around the world. Each event features off-the-grid experiences designed to bring the high-octane world of Red Bull to its community of enthusiasts. The brand even hosts a "Holy S**t" tab on its Web site, featuring videos of everything from 27-meter ocean cliff dives at its Cliff Diving Series event in Grimstad, Norway, to dare-devil freeskiing feats at its Red Bull Cold Rush event in the Colorado mountain peaks, to absolutely breathtaking wing suit flights at Red Bull events staged in exotic locations from Monterrey, Mexico, to Hunan Province, China. The Red Bull Final Descent series is a mountain biking challenge that pushes riders to the brink and back, over some of the most technically challenging terrain in North America. Red Bull events draw large crowds and plenty of media coverage. But it's about more than just the events—it's about customer engagement. It's about creating face-to-face experiences in which customers can actually feel the excitement and live the brand. "It's about deepening and enhancing relationships," says one analyst.

Event marketing: Red Bull hosts hundreds of events each year in dozens of sports around the world, designed to bring the high-octane world of Red Bull to its community of enthusiasts.
REUTERS/Max Rossi

Trade Promotions

Trade promotions
Sales promotion tools used to persuade resellers to carry a brand, give it shelf space, and promote it in advertising

Manufacturers direct more sales promotion dollars toward retailers and wholesalers (79 percent of all promotions dollars) than to final consumers (21 percent).[32] **Trade promotions** can persuade resellers to carry a brand, give it shelf space, promote it in advertising, and push it to consumers. Shelf space is so scarce these days that manufacturers often have to offer price-offs, allowances, buy-back guarantees, or free goods to retailers and wholesalers to get products on the shelf and, once there, to keep them on it.

Manufacturers use several trade promotion tools. Many of the tools used for consumer promotions—contests, premiums, displays—can also be used as trade promotions. Or the manufacturer may offer a straight *discount* off the list price on each case purchased during a stated period of time (also called a *price-off, off-invoice*, or *off-list*). Manufacturers also may offer an *allowance* (usually so much off per case) in return for the retailer's agreement to feature the manufacturer's products in some way. For example, an advertising allowance compensates retailers for advertising the product, whereas a display allowance compensates them for using special displays.

Manufacturers may offer *free goods*, which are extra cases of merchandise, to resellers who buy a certain quantity or who feature a certain flavor or size. They may also offer *push money*—cash or gifts to dealers or their sales forces to "push" the manufacturer's goods. Manufacturers may give retailers free *specialty advertising items* that carry the company's name, such as pens, calendars, memo pads, flashlights, and tote bags.

Real Marketing 16.2

P&G's "Everyday Effect" Event: A Great Marriage between Old-School Promotions and New-School Social Sharing

It was a hot, sunny June day in Manhattan, and pedestrians bustled along at 33rd Street and 7th Avenue near Madison Square Garden. But on this day, something special happened. In the middle of the sidewalk stood a glass shower stall, emblazoned with colorful Old Spice signage, causing even normally jaded New York City passersby to take notice. An Old Spice brand rep handed out samples of Old Spice bar soap and extended an unusual invitation—jump in the shower and give it a try. Surprisingly, many people accepted, including a well-dressed executive who lathered up while still in his finely tailored business suit.

Just another sales promotion gimmick? Not this time. The Old Spice Constant Shower was just one small piece of a live mega-promotion—P&G's "Everyday Effect" event—in which brand representatives and celebrities handed out more than 50,000 samples of 25 different P&G brands at multiple Manhattan locations in a single day. With street teams and exhibits all over town, the Everyday Effect takeover extravaganza was by far the biggest "consumer experience" event in P&G's 175-year history.

Visitors to the Gillette Man Cave "experience box" in Washington Square Park were pampered with free shaves and visits from actor Laz Alonso and New York Jets center Nick Mangold. At the CoverGirl Beauty box near Times Square, *Fast and Furious* actress Jordana Brewster helped with free beauty and nail touch-ups. The Iam's Loving Home box at Riverside Park on the Upper West Side featured *Dancing with the Stars* heartthrob Val Chmerkovskiy posing for photos with pets and handing out Iam's product samples. And in Harlem, P&G's "My Black Is Beautiful" reps served up beauty tips and free mini-makeovers. All day long, brand ambassadors, as well as characters such as the Charmin Bears, fanned out across city streets giving out product samples, high-value coupons, advice, and even special P&G pedicab rides. They dispensed Scope mouthwash samples to coffee drinkers, Febreze car vent clips to taxi drivers, and personal care products to barber shops and salons.

By itself, the massive Manhattan giveaway produced substantial benefits for P&G in terms of brand trial and experience. "Simply getting someone to try a product remains the holy grail for consumer-goods companies," says one analyst. The event also reinforced P&G's broader, ongoing Everyday Effect campaign showcasing the effects of its products on the lives of real people. "We're making a deliberate effort to demonstrate to consumers how our brands improve their everyday life in small yet meaningful ways," says P&G's North American group president. "That's what we call the P&G 'Everyday Effect.'"

However, some experts question whether the returns on such a massive—and expensive—local event could ever justify the investment. Beyond the costs of product samples, P&G had to rent pricey Manhattan real estate, employ hundreds of reps, erect expensive facilities and props, provide incentives for celebrities, and put a sizable security detail in place to keep things orderly.

But the impact of the Everyday Effect event went far beyond the city limits of New York City. What made the event extra special was the skillful way that P&G used social media channels to turbocharge consumer engagement, not just in Manhattan, but around the nation and world. Throughout the day, video of live events was streamed across P&G brand and social media sites. Nearly every element of the event was hashtagged, and visitors to event sites were given incentives to upload photos to their personal feeds. Followers of PGEveryday on Twitter and Facebook had opportunities to win Visa and Amazon gift cards. Participating celebrities not only helped draw coverage from more than 100 media outlets, they also reached out personally to their own fans through Twitter, Facebook, Instagram, and other social media.

"We chose New York as the world's largest stage," says a P&G brand executive. "At the end of the day, [we wanted to reach] as many New Yorkers as possible [but also] touch consumers we couldn't physically reach that day." Mission accomplished. By evening, the Everyday Effect event had scored some impressive social sharing results. The opt-in rate at the PGEveryday.com coupon and sampling site jumped 20 percent; the engagement rate for visitors to the PGEveryday Facebook page soared 151 percent. And the social media were abuzz with pictures and posts of the day's happenings. #EverydayEffect became the day's number-two trending topic

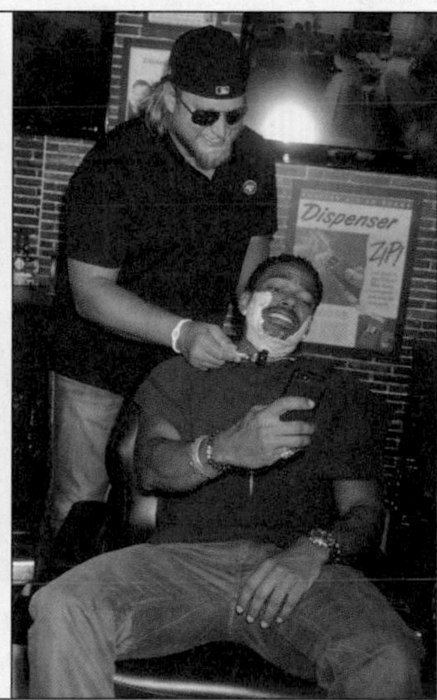

P&G's star-studded Everyday Effect event blended old-school live event marketing with new-school social sharing. Visitors to the Gillette Man Cave box were pampered with free shaves and visits from actor Laz Alonso and New York Jets center Nick Mangold. At the CoverGirl Beauty box, actress Jordana Brewster helped with free beauty and nail touch-ups. Such celebrities helped draw substantial social and traditional media coverage.

Everett Collection/Newscom (left). Dennis Van Tine/ABACAUSA.COM/Newscom (right).

on Twitter, behind only celebrity chef Paula Deen's fall from grace that day.

P&G's Everyday Effect event is an example of how companies these days are blending old-school promotion techniques, such as samples and pop-ups, with new-school social sharing technologies to enhance the impact of both. Increasingly, the two promotional approaches form an important symbiotic relationship: A live event creates special face-to-face brand engagements that generate needed social media content. In turn, the social media help amplify and extend the event's impact.

"On the one hand, social is extending the reach of events to intensify their impact beyond those in attendance," says one event marketing expert. "On the other, events are becoming crucial content sources for brands' Facebook, Twitter, and Instagram feeds." Says another expert, "Social media in isolation is sort of like a long distance relationship; the human contact piece is missing." In contrast, an "experiential [event], as a deep engagement thing, can be very satisfying but you can't get scale behind it." His conclusion: "Together they're a great marriage."

Sources: Stuart Feil, "All the World Is a Stage," *Adweek*, July 22, 2013, www.adweek.com/print/151231; Kyle Stock, "The Logic Behind P&G's Old-School Manhattan Giveaway," *Businessweek*, June 19, 2013, www.businessweek.com/articles/2013-06-19/the-logic-behind-p-and-gs-old-school-manhattan-giveaway; Barry Silverstein, "P&G Hosts Massive Everyday Effect Giveaway Event in New York City," *Brand Channel*, June 19, 2013, www.brandchannel.com/home/post/2013/06/19/PG-Everyday-Effect-Event-061913.aspx; and "Tweeting the #EverydayEffect," www.pgeveryday.com, accessed June 2014; and "Everyday Effect," *P&G Newsroom*, http://news.pg.com/category/tags/everyday-effect, accessed September 2014.

Business Promotions

Business promotions
Sales promotion tools used to generate business leads, stimulate purchases, reward customers, and motivate salespeople.

Companies spend billions of dollars each year on promotion geared toward industrial customers. **Business promotions** are used to generate business leads, stimulate purchases, reward customers, and motivate salespeople. Business promotions include many of the same tools used for consumer or trade promotions. Here, we focus on two additional major business promotion tools: conventions and trade shows and sales contests.

Many companies and trade associations organize *conventions and trade shows* to promote their products. Firms selling to the industry show their products at the trade show. Vendors at these shows receive many benefits, such as opportunities to find new sales leads, contact customers, introduce new products, meet new customers, sell more to present customers, and educate customers with publications and audiovisual materials. Trade shows also help companies reach many prospects that are not reached through their sales forces.

Some trade shows are huge. At this year's Bauma mining and construction equipment trade show in Munich, Germany, more than 3,400 exhibitors from 57 countries presented their latest product innovations to over 530,000 attendees from more than 200 countries.
Messe München

Some trade shows are huge. For example, at this year's International Consumer Electronics Show, 3,200 exhibitors attracted some 152,000 professional visitors. Even more impressive, at the Bauma mining and construction equipment trade show in Munich, Germany, more than 3,400 exhibitors from 57 countries presented their latest product innovations to over 530,000 attendees from more than 200 countries. Total exhibition space equaled about 6.1 million square feet (more than 127 football fields).[33]

A *sales contest* is a contest for salespeople or dealers to motivate them to increase their sales performance over a given period. Sales contests motivate and recognize good company performers, who may receive trips, cash prizes, or other gifts. Some companies award points for performance, which the receiver can turn in for any of a variety of prizes. Sales contests work best when they are tied to measurable and achievable sales objectives (such as finding new accounts, reviving old accounts, or increasing account profitability).

Developing the Sales Promotion Program

Beyond selecting the types of promotions to use, marketers must make several other decisions in designing the full sales promotion program. First, they must determine the *size of the incentive*. A certain minimum incentive is necessary if the promotion is to succeed;

a larger incentive will produce more sales response. The marketer also must set *conditions for participation*. Incentives might be offered to everyone or only to select groups.

Marketers must determine how to *promote and distribute the promotion* program itself. For example, a $2-off coupon could be given out in a package, in an advertisement, at the store, via the Internet, or in a mobile download. Each distribution method involves a different level of reach and cost. Increasingly, marketers are blending several media into a total campaign concept. The *length of the promotion* is also important. If the sales promotion period is too short, many prospects (who may not be buying during that time) will miss it. If the promotion runs too long, the deal will lose some of its "act now" force.

Evaluation is also very important. Marketers should work to measure the returns on their sales promotion investments, just as they should seek to assess the returns on other marketing activities. The most common evaluation method is to compare sales before, during, and after a promotion. Marketers should ask: Did the promotion attract new customers or more purchasing from current customers? Can we hold onto these new customers and purchases? Will the long-run customer relationship and sales gains from the promotion justify its costs?

Clearly, sales promotion plays an important role in the total promotion mix. To use it well, the marketer must define the sales promotion objectives, select the best tools, design the sales promotion program, implement the program, and evaluate the results. Moreover, sales promotion must be coordinated carefully with other promotion mix elements within the overall IMC program.

16 Reviewing the Concepts

OBJECTIVES REVIEW AND KEY TERMS

Objectives Review

This chapter is the third of four chapters covering the final marketing mix element—promotion. The previous two chapters dealt with overall integrated marketing communications and with advertising and public relations. This chapter investigated personal selling and sales promotion. Personal selling is the interpersonal arm of the communications mix. Sales promotion consists of short-term incentives to encourage the purchase or sale of a product or service.

Discuss the role of a company's salespeople in creating value for customers and building customer relationships. *(pp 502–504)*

Most companies use salespeople, and many companies assign them an important role in the marketing mix. For companies selling business products, the firm's sales force works directly with customers. Often, the sales force is the customer's only direct contact with the company and therefore may be viewed by customers as representing the company itself. In contrast, for consumer product companies that sell through intermediaries, consumers usually do not meet salespeople or even know about them. The sales force works behind the scenes, dealing with wholesalers and retailers to obtain their support and helping them become more effective in selling the firm's products.

As an element of the promotion mix, the sales force is very effective in achieving certain marketing objectives and carrying out such activities as prospecting, communicating, selling and servicing, and information gathering. But with companies becoming more market oriented, a customer-focused sales force also works to produce both customer satisfaction and company profit. The sales force plays a key role in engaging customers and developing and managing profitable customer relationships.

OBJECTIVE 2 **Identify and explain the six major sales force management steps.** *(pp 504–515)*

High sales force costs necessitate an effective sales management process consisting of six steps: designing sales force strategy and structure, recruiting and selecting, training, compensating, supervising, and evaluating salespeople and sales force performance.

In designing a sales force, sales management must address various issues, including what type of sales force structure will work best (territorial, product, customer, or complex structure), sales force size, who will be involved in selling, and how various salespeople and sales-support people will work together (inside or outside sales forces and team selling).

Salespeople must be recruited and selected carefully. In recruiting salespeople, a company may look to the job duties and the characteristics of its most successful salespeople to suggest the traits it wants in new salespeople. It must then look for applicants through recommendations of current salespeople, ads, and the Internet and social media, as well as college recruitment/placement centers. After the selection process is complete, training programs familiarize new salespeople not only with the art of selling but also with the company's history, its products and policies, and the characteristics of its customers and competitors.

The sales force compensation system helps to reward, motivate, and direct salespeople. In addition to compensation, all salespeople need supervision, and many need continuous encouragement because they must make many decisions and face many frustrations. Periodically, the company must evaluate their performance to help them do a better job. In evaluating salespeople, the company relies on information gathered from sales reports, personal observations, customer surveys, and conversations with other salespeople.

The fastest-growing sales trend is the explosion in social selling—using online, mobile, and social media in selling. The new digital technologies are providing salespeople with powerful tools for identifying and learning about prospects, engaging customers, creating customer value, closing sales, and nurturing customer relationships. Many of today's customers no longer rely as much on assistance provided by salespeople. Instead, increasingly, they use online and social media resources to analyze their own problems, research solutions, get advice from colleagues, and rank buying options before ever speaking to a salesperson. In response, sellers are reorienting their selling processes around the new customer buying process. They are using social media, Web forums, online communities, blogs, and other digital tools to engage customers earlier and more fully. Ultimately, online and social media technologies are helping to make sales forces more efficient, cost effective, and productive.

OBJECTIVE 3 Discuss the personal selling process, distinguishing between transaction-oriented marketing and relationship marketing. *(pp 515–518)*

Selling involves a seven-step process: prospecting and qualifying, preapproach, approach, presentation and demonstration, handling objections, closing, and follow-up. These steps help marketers close a specific sale and, as such, are transaction oriented. However, a seller's dealings with customers should be guided by the larger concept of relationship marketing. The company's sales force should help to orchestrate a whole-company effort to develop profitable long-term relationships with key customers based on superior customer value and satisfaction.

OBJECTIVE 4 Explain how sales promotion campaigns are developed and implemented. *(pp 518–525)*

Sales promotion campaigns call for setting sales promotion objectives (in general, sales promotions should be *consumer relationship building*); selecting tools; and developing and implementing the sales promotion program by using *consumer promotion tools* (from coupons, refunds, premiums, and point-of-purchase promotions to contests, sweepstakes, and events), *trade promotion tools* (from discounts and allowances to free goods and push money), and *business promotion tools* (conventions, trade shows, and sales contests), as well as determining such things as the size of the incentive, the conditions for participation, how to promote and distribute the promotion package, and the length of the promotion. After this process is completed, the company must evaluate its sales promotion results.

MyMarketingLab

Go to **mymktlab.com** to complete the problems marked with this icon .

Key Terms

OBJECTIVE 1

Personal selling (p 502)
Salesperson (p 503)

OBJECTIVE 2

Sales force management (p 504)
Territorial sales force structure (p 505)
Product sales force structure (p 505)
Customer (or market) sales force structure (p 505)
Outside sales force (or field sales force) (p 506)
Inside sales force (p 506)
Team selling (p 507)
Sales quota (p 511)
Social selling (p 512)

OBJECTIVE 3

Selling process (p 515)
Prospecting (p 515)
Preapproach (p 516)
Approach (p 516)
Presentation (p 516)
Handling objections (p 517)
Closing (p 517)
Follow-up (p 517)

OBJECTIVE 4

Sales promotion (p 518)
Consumer promotions (p 520)
Event marketing (or event sponsorships) (p 522)
Trade promotions (p 522)
Business promotions (p 524)

DISCUSSION AND CRITICAL THINKING

Discussion Questions

16-1 How can the sales force be a part of the promotion mix, and what is its key set of roles? (AACSB: Communication; Reflective Thinking)

16-2 What are the six effective steps of sales management processes necessitated by high sales force costs? (AACSB: Communication; Reflective Thinking)

16-3 Discuss how online, mobile, and social media tools are changing the selling function. (AACSB: Communication; Reflective Thinking)

16-4 Define *sales promotion* and discuss its objectives. (AACSB: Communication)

16-5 Discuss why a business may need to develop and use different types of consumer promotion tools. Identify and describe these tools. (AACSB: Communication)

Critical Thinking Exercises

16-6 What procedure do businesses in your country usually follow for selecting the right candidate for sales roles? Candidate selection techniques can vary; is there a common approach? (AACSB: Communication; Use of IT; Reflective Thinking)

16-7 How are sales dealt with in your country? Are the majority of them handled face to face, or is there a growing trend toward distance selling in the form of telephone sales and other methods? (AACSB: Communication; Reflective Thinking)

16-8 Think about a time when you were targeted by a sales promotion. How did the marketer distribute the sales promotion? What was the purpose of the sales promotion, and was it effective? (AACSB: Communications; Reflective Thinking)

MINICASES AND APPLICATIONS

Online, Mobile, and Social Media Marketing Sales Promotions

Sales promotion has always been an effective tool for influencing behavior and providing a means for measuring effectiveness. Marketers can measure how many buyers redeem a coupon, enter a contest, receive a premium, or buy bonus packs. But now, new technologies are taking sales promotion to a new level—generating consumer engagement. When AMC Theaters wanted to encourage movie goers to watch a movie on Sunday, typically a slow day for AMC, it offered a coupon for $1.00 popcorn and fountain drinks on Facebook for the week prior to a specific Sunday and encouraged respondents to invite their friends to claim a coupon as well. The result? More than 200,000 takers in six days and almost 50,000 of them driving their friends to AMC's fan page as well. Similarly, when Edible Arrangements wanted to acquire fans for its Facebook page and increase awareness for the company, it offered free boxes of chocolate covered fruit to consumers who entered and "Liked" the page. When the company quickly ran out of free samples, it changed the offer to a coupon and experienced double-digit growth as tens of thousands of customers flooded the stores to redeem the coupon—all in less than a week. When Nintendo Wii wanted to raise awareness and generate excitement for its NBA Jam game, it used an essay contest of "jamisms," with voting done in a bracket style like the NBA playoffs. In addition to the 3,000 entries, the contest generated buzz and thousands of impressions and new Facebook fans.

16-9 Businesses large and small are using online, social media, and mobile marketing to influence buyer behavior and generate customer engagement. Research tips for offering an online promotion. What should marketers consider when designing and launching online sales promotions? (AACSB: Communication; Use of IT; Reflective Thinking)

16-10 Design a sales promotion campaign using online, social media, and mobile marketing for a small business or organization in your community. Develop a presentation to pitch your campaign to the business or organization and incorporate what you've learned about the selling process. (AACSB: Communication; Reflective Thinking)

Marketing Ethics Drug Dealing

The pharmaceutical industry is innovating at a dizzying pace, but it is getting more difficult for pharmaceutical sales reps to reach doctors to inform them of new or improved products. One option is to host educational seminars. However, many educational seminars are held at lavish restaurants or destinations underwritten by pharmaceutical companies, and doctors providing the education are paid consulting and speaking fees to the tune of more than $2 billion since 2009. In some cases, speakers are given scripts developed by the pharmaceutical company, leading to the criticism that this is company-scripted marketing and the distinguished speaker is merely a "paid parrot" selling drugs for the company. Critics also claim that such promotion results in needlessly increased prescriptions for expensive drugs that are no better than generic alternatives. Many drug makers are reducing expenditures for such product promotions because of the Physician Payment Sunshine Act, a provision of the Affordable Care Act of 2010. *Pro Publica* has a "Dollars for Docs" searchable database, and by late 2014, as part of the Sunshine Act, a searchable government Web site will be available to the public to shed light on pharmaceutical sales practices.

16-11 Do you believe it is wrong for pharmaceutical companies to explain the benefits of their products to physicians this way? Suggest other alternatives for reaching doctors to inform them of the benefits of a company's products. (AACSB: Communication; Ethical Reasoning; Reflective Thinking)

16-12 Learn about the Physician Payment Sunshine Act. Search *Pro Publica's* "Dollars for Docs" database (http://projects.propublica.org/docdollars/) for local physicians to see if they have received payments from pharmaceutical companies. If the government's Web site is available, compare your findings with that of *Pro Publica's* database. Write a report on what you found. (AACSB: Communication; Use of IT; Reflective Thinking)

Marketing by the Numbers Salesforce Analysis

Wheels, Inc. is a manufacturer of bicycles sold through retail bicycle shops in the southeastern United States. The company has two salespeople who do more than just sell the products—they manage relationships with the bicycle shops to enable them to better meet consumers' needs. The company's sales reps visit the shops several times per year, often for hours at a time. The owner of Wheels is considering expanding to the rest of the country and would like to have distribution through 1,000 bicycle shops. To do so, however, the company would have to hire more salespeople. Each salesperson earns $40,000 plus 2 percent commission on all sales. Another alternative is to use the services of sales agents instead of its own salesforce. Sales agents would be paid 5 percent of sales.

16-13 Refer to Appendix 2 to answer this question. Determine the number of salespeople Wheels needs if it has 1,000 bicycle shop accounts that need to be called on four times per year. Each sales call lasts approximately 2.5 hours, and each sales rep has approximately 1,250 hours per year to devote to customers. (AACSB: Communication; Analytical Reasoning)

16-14 At what level of sales would it be more cost efficient for Wheels to use sales agents compared to its own sales force? To determine this, consider the fixed and variable costs for each alternative. What are the pros and cons of using a company's own sales force over independent sales agents? (AACSB: Communication; Analytical Reasoning; Reflective Thinking)

Video Case MedTronic

Many companies sell products that most customers can literally live without. But the devices that MedTronic sells are a matter of life and death. Patient well-being depends upon the insulin delivery devices, implantable defibrillators, and cardiac pacemakers designed and manufactured by MedTronic. In some markets, seven out of eight medical devices in use are MedTronic devices.

But what happens when you know you have a product that will help a given customer in terms of cost, time, and end-user well-being, but you can't get a foot in the door to communicate that information? This video demonstrates how MedTronic sales representatives maintain a customer-centered approach to the personal selling process as a means for effectively communicating MedTronic's product benefits.

After viewing the video featuring MedTronic, answer the following questions:

16-15 How is the sales force at MedTronic structured?

16-16 Identify the selling process for MedTronic. Give an example of each step.

16-17 Is MedTronic effective at building long-term customer relationships through its sales force? If so, how? If not, what could be improved?

Company Case SunGard: Building Sustained Growth by Selling the SunGard Way

If asked what company topped the most recent *Selling Power* magazine list of 50 Best Companies to Sell For, you'd probably guess IBM, P&G, or maybe Xerox, companies long known for their outstanding sales forces. But number one on this year's list is a company you probably know less about—software and technology services company SunGard.

What makes SunGard such a good place to work as a salesperson? For starters, SunGard has strong name recognition and a solid reputation in its industry. SunGard has long provided excellent compensation and training to its salespeople. And the company has consistently delivered strong customer growth and retention. However, although SunGard has long been good in these areas, what has made it outstanding and put it at the top of *Selling Powers* list is a recent complete transformation of SunGard's sales force model.

Pioneering a New Industry

In the late 1970s, the computer services division of the Sun Oil Company (today Sunoco) pioneered a service now considered indispensable by virtually every company in the world. Sun and 20 other Philadelphia-area companies entered an agreement to act as backups for each others' data systems. To create the needed capacity, the group developed a designated disaster recovery backup center. But when member companies were slow to pay their shares of the expenses, Sun Oil took over the backup operation and began selling computer services. In 1983, Sun Oil spun off the computer division and SunGard was born.

Since then, with the help of a few acquisitions, SunGard has grown steadily. It's now one of the world's leading software and technology services companies, with $4 billion in annual revenues. SunGard now provides processing solutions for the financial services industry, K–12 education, and public sector organizations. It serves 16,000 customers in more than 70 countries. As a business-to-business service provider, that requires a substantial sales force.

Good, But Not Great

When Russell Fradin took over as the CEO of SunGard in 2011, business was good. But the company faced some issues of concern. For starters, the Internet increasingly provided SunGard clients and potential clients with the information they needed to solve their own problems. For both its private and public sector businesses, compliance with government regulations was also increasing. And increasing of globalization made it more and more challenging for SunGard's sales reps to meet client needs. SunGard was not alone in dealing with these issues. But that just added to the pressure—any company finding effective ways to meet these challenges would gain considerable strategic advantage.

SunGard also faced plenty of internal issues. The company sold multiple product lines, and Fradin felt that the SunGard sales force wasn't achieving its potential in terms of selling the optimal mix of products. The company's thousands of sales reps spent most of their time and effort on selling licensed software, rather than developing broader solutions to customer problems. Moreover, with multiple divisions and product lines and a fragmented go-to-market approach, SunGard often had multiple sales reps pursuing the same clients, sapping productivity and even driving some customers away.

Based on these assessments, Fradin asked himself, "How can SunGard make its sales force—one of the company's biggest and most important investments—perform more effectively?" SunGard had decent systems in place for recruiting, hiring, and training its salespeople. And SunGard's sales executives did a reasonable job of making incremental changes. But Fradin felt that the company needed to do more in order to improve its growth and performance. If more drastic changes weren't made, the mounting challenges would likely limit future sales and profits. To Fradin's thinking, SunGard needed a complete sales force transformation.

According to a report by global sales consulting firm ZA Associates, companies that move sales force effectiveness from good to excellent by virtue of a sales force transformation can increase profitable growth by as much as 20 percent. But that kind of transformation would require a major effort, many months to plan and execute, and even longer to take hold. It would demand nothing less than a total commitment from everyone in the organization—those at the lowest rung on the corporate ladder up to senior management and executives. It would also require that everyone have a clear vision of the benefits, for both themselves and for the organization as a whole. Disruptions from implementing such a sweeping change would likely mean losing at least good people and clients. It might also result in a short-term dip in performance before the benefits begin to kick in.

Setting Transformation in Motion

In early 2012, Fradin hired Jim Neve and Ken Powell to head up SunGard's global sales efforts. The two-person team had worked together on other successful large-scale sales force transformations, and they planned to carry out the same process at SunGard. "We needed to maximize our channels, sell the broadest set of solutions possible, and go to market in a coordinated manner," said Powell. "We needed to build a sustainable growth engine."

Neve and Powell branded the sales force transformation initiative as "Selling the SunGard Way." More than just a fancy title, "Selling the SunGard Way" was a philosophy defined by specific goals and characteristics. First and foremost, the transformation would shift the basic sales approach from selling based on meeting customer needs to selling based on insight. SunGard reps needed to thoroughly understand the client buying decision process, anticipate needs before even customers themselves were aware of them, and tailor the client relationship to meet shifting concerns. Focusing on product functionality and price just wouldn't cut it anymore. And sales interactions would need to draw from technology and services across all SunGard business units, not just within specific divisions or product lines. In order to achieve these skills, SunGard's sales personnel would need greater knowledge and expertise of the full line of company products as well as the nature of each client's business.

After thoroughly surveying the needs of SunGard sales associates, Neve and Powell drafted a detailed transformation plan. Sales reps needed better training, detailed competitive analyses, and more effective sales campaigns. They needed better data, fewer administrative tasks, and a simplified interface for "Salesforce"—SunGard's main CRM sales management tool. To achieve such goals, Neve and Powell set out to overhaul SunGard's core sales functions, including recruiting, training, managing, and compensating sales force personnel.

This transformation would take time and effort, and it would cost millions. But by the time the plan was revealed, there was support throughout the company. "The whole organization gravitated toward change," said Powell. "[Everyone] knew it had to happen." To help cover costs, the company shifted budgets, reallocating funds from ineffective programs to the transformation project.

On the recruiting front, SunGard adopted a new talent-assessment tool that defined ideal job profiles and evaluated skills and performance patterns of potential hires. The company also hired a team of sales-development managers who were charged with increasing the productivity of first-year sales reps. Their job was to make sure that new sales reps received all the training and exposure necessary to understand the company's structure, strategic plans, products, and sales tools. That relieved front-line sales managers of these tasks, letting them focus more on selling. Sales-development manager compensation hinged on the performance of first-year sales reps.

For existing sales personnel, SunGard revised procedures, metrics, training, and tools to make them consistent across the organization. It also made major revision to its Salesforce CRM and sales management tool, with an eye toward providing salespeople with all the information they needed for every aspect of the sales process. The important tool now provided easy and immediate access to content such as case studies, customer information, and market data. Additional tools were made available to guide people through the necessary steps for more effectively closing a sale.

But to improve effectiveness for both new and existing sales personnel, SunGard needed to make even more changes in how performance was measured and tracked. For example, prior to the transformation, the company tracked incentives and commissions manually, and they were not readily accessible by relevant stakeholders. Under the new scheme, metrics such as individual goals and forecasts, as well as how often sales were made or lost, became part of an automated system, accessible by sales reps and managers via mobile interface at any time. They could even run "what-if" scenarios to determine potential earnings of different situations. This capability motivated sales reps by increasing accountability and promoting a competitive spirit.

From Transformation to Results

As the new sales structure and tools took root, it wasn't long before they began to bear fruit. "There was a tremendous product suite that had yet to capture its full market share," says Todd Albright, who joined SunGard as senior vice president of sales for the Americas after the transformation was underway. That market share will soon be achieved. "There were tremendous assets locked up at SunGard," Neve summarizes. "We put a road map in place to unlock those assets, translating them into new sales and revenue growth."

With its billion-dollar sales plan now in place, SunGard is on target. As one example, consider the productivity improvements for first-year reps. Prior to the transformation, about 75 percent of new reps booked their first sale before the end of their first year at an average of around $400,000. Through the new policies, that sales productivity will soon double, adding an incremental $30 to $40 million to annual sales.

If boosting sales force effectiveness was easy, every company would achieve optimal sales force productivity. SunGard was willing to pay the price. Implementation of the transformation just completed its first year. As expected, SunGard revenues contracted slightly, down about 16 percent from the previous year. However, profits rose by nearly 35 percent, thanks in part to reduced costs from more efficient operations.

Importantly, SunGard's sales force is now much more coordinated and collaborative. It's better trained and equipped to sell based on insight. Its products and services are bundled across product lines rather than within lines. And reps are developing partnerships with customers, assisting them in streamlining operations, accelerating growth, and complying with regulations. By transforming its sales force to "Selling the SunGard Way," SunGard is on a path to sustainable, organic growth for years to come.

Questions for Discussion

16-18 Compare SunGard's sales force structure before and after the transformation.

16-19 What are the positive and negative aspects of SunGard's new sales force structure?

16-20 How would the challenges faced by SunGard have impacted sales productivity had the company not initiated its transformational plan?

16-21 Identify specific ways SunGard's transformational plan addresses the different steps of managing the sales force.

16-22 Will "Selling the SunGard Way" really work? Why or why not?

Sources: Henry Canaday, "Selling the New SunGard Way," *Selling Power*, www.sellingpower.com/content/article/?a=10217/selling-the-new-sungard-way&page=1, accessed June 2014; "50 Best Companies to Sell For," *Selling Power*, www.sellingpower.com/2013/50-best-companies-to-sell-for/, accessed June 2014; Andris Zoltners, PK Sinha, and Sally Lorimer, "Improving Your Sales Force: Fine-tune or Transform?" *Harvard Business Review*, November 13, 2012, http://blogs.hbr.org/2012/11/improving-your-sales-force-fin/; and information from www.sungard.com/about-us and www.sungard.com/financials, accessed June 2014.

MyMarketingLab

Go to **mymktlab.com** for the following Assisted-graded writing questions:

16-23 Describe the roles a salesperson and the sales force perform in marketing. (AACSB: Communication; Reflective Thinking)

16-24 Interview a salesperson. Is this salesperson an order taker or an order getter? How much training did he or she receive to perform the sales job? Write a report of what you learned. (AACSB: Communication; Reflective Thinking)

References

1. Based on information from numerous P&G managers; with information from "500 Largest Sales Forces in America," *Selling Power,* September 2013, pp. 34, 40; Cassandra Jowett, "Schulich Grand Finds Her Calling in Customer Business Development at P&G," *TalentEgg,* January 8, 2013, http://talentegg.ca/incubator/2013/01/08/schulich-grad-finds-calling-customer-business-development-pg/; "Then and Now: Going to Great Lengths to Get P&G Products into the Hands of Consumers," *P&G Corporate Newsroom,* February 13, 2013, http://news.pg.com/blog/company-strategy/then-and-now-going-great-lengths-get-pg-products-hands-consumers; and http://we.experiencepg.com/home/customer_business_development_cbd_sales.html, accessed September 2014.
2. See Philip Kotler, Neil Rackham, and Suj Krishnaswamy, "Ending the War between Sales and Marketing," *Harvard Business Review*, July–August 2006, pp. 68–78; Elizabeth A. Sullivan, "The Ties That Bind," *Marketing News*, May 15, 2010; Allan Mayer, "Improving the Relationships between Sales and Marketing," *OneAccord,* May 30, 2012, www.oneaccordpartners.com/blog/bid/132539/; Philip Kotler and Kevin Lane Keller, *Marketing Management,* 14th ed. (Upper Saddle River, NJ: Prentice Hall, 2012), p. 554; and "Marketing Said, Sales Said," *Sales & Marketing Management,* September 9, 2013, www.salesandmarketing.com/content/marketing-said-sales-said.
3. See Henry Canaday, "In Transition," *Selling Power,* May 13, 2011, www.sellingpower.com/content/article/?a=9462/in-transition.
4. "Selling Power 500: The Largest Sales Force in America," *Selling Power,* July/August/September 2013, p. 32.
5. See discussions in Mike Ishmael, "The Cost of a Sales Call," October 22, 2012, http://4dsales.com/the-cost-of-a-sales-call/; Jeff Green, "The New Willy Loman Survives by Staying Home," *Bloomberg Businessweek,* January 14–January 20, pp. 16–17; and "What Is the Real Cost of a B2B Sales Call?" www.marketing-playbook.com/sales-marketing-strategy/what-is-the-real-cost-of-a-b2b-sales-call, accessed September 2014.
6. Jeff Green, "The New Willy Loman Survives by Staying Home," *Bloomberg Businessweek,* January 14, 2013, pp. 16–17; and Dave Stein, "The Evolution of Social Selling," *Sales & Marketing Management,* May/June 2013, p. 14.
7. Quote and facts from Jim Domanski, "Special Report: The 2012 B@B Tele-Sales Trend Report," www.salesopedia.com/downloads/2012%20B2B%20Tele-Sales%20Trend%20Special%20Reportl.pdf, accessed July 2013.

8. See "Case Study: Climax Portable Machine Tools," www.selltis.com/productCaseStudiesClimaxPortableMachineTools.aspx; and www.climaxportable.com, accessed September 2014.

9. "Customer Business Development," http://we.experiencepg.com/home/customer_business_development_cbd_sales.html, accessed September 2014.

10. Scott Fuhr, "Good Hiring Makes Good Cents," *Selling Power,* July/August/September 2012, pp. 20–21.

11. For this and more information and discussion, see www.gallupaustralia.com.au/consulting/118729/sales-force-effectiveness.aspx, accessed July 2012; Lynette Ryals and Iain Davies, "Do You Really Know Who Your Best Salespeople Are?" *Harvard Business Review*, December 2010, pp. 34–35; "The 10 Skills of Super' Salespeople," www.businesspartnerships.ca/articles/the_10_skills_of_super_salespeople.phtml, accessed July 2012; "Profile of a Super Seller," *Selling Power,* October/November/December 2012, pp. 12–13; and Gerhard Gschwandtner, "Love and Aggression," *Selling Power,* April/May/June 2013, pp. 37–39.

12. See Steve Denning, "The One Thing the Greatest Salespeople All Have," *Forbes,* November 29, 2013, www.forbes.com/sites/stevedenning/2012/11/29/the-one-thing-the-greatest-salespeople-all-have/.

13. Barbara Hendricks, "Strengths-Based Selling," February 8, 2011, www.gallup.com/press/146246/Strengths-Based-Selling.aspx.

14. Corporate Visions, Inc., "ADP Case Study," http://corporatevisions.com/v5/documents/secure_downloads/CVI_caseStudy_ADP.pdf, accessed June 2014; and Henry Canaday, "The Transformation of Enterprise Sales Training," *Selling Power,* https://wwwimages2.adobe.com/content/dam/Adobe/en/products/adobeconnect/pdfs/elearning/transformation-of-enterprise-sales-training.pdf, accessed September 2014.

15. Based on information found in Sara Donnelly, "Staying in the Game," *Pharmaceutical Executive*, May 2008, pp. 158–159; Bayer Healthcare Pharmaceuticals, Inc., "Improving Sales Force Effectiveness: Bayer's Experiment with New Technology," 2008, www.icmrindia.org/casestudies/catalogue/Marketing/MKTG200.htm; Tanya Lewis, "Concentric," *Medical Marketing and Media*, July 2008, p. 59, www.hydraframe.com/mobile/project_repracе.htm, accessed July 2012; Andrew Tolve, "Pharma Sales: How Simulation Can Help Reps Sell," *Eye for Pharma,* March 28, 2012, http://social.eyeforpharma.com/sales/pharma-sales-how-simulation-can-help-reps-sell; and Krishna Depura, "Online Sales Training for Busy Sales Representatives," *MindTickle,* www.mindtickle.com/blog/online-sales-training-for-busy-sales-representative/#more-1474, accessed June 2014.

16. For this and more discussion, see Joseph Kornak, "07 Compensation Survey: What's It All Worth?" *Sales & Marketing Management*, May 2007, pp. 28–39; Ken Sundheim, "How Sales Professionals Are Paid," *SellingProf,* www.sellingprof.com/leadership/how-sales-professionals-are-paid, accessed June 2014; and Alexander Group, "2014 Sales Compensation Trends Survey Results," January 2014, www.alexandergroup.com/resources/survey-findings.

17. See Louis Columbus, "Top-Five Focus Areas for Improving Sales Effectiveness Initiatives," *Accenture*, 2013, www.accenture.com/SiteCollectionDocuments/PDF/Accenture-Top-Five-Improvements-Sales-Effectiveness.pdf; and "2014 Sales Performance Optimization Study," CSO Insights, www.csoinsights.com/Publications/.

18. Lain Chroust Ehmann, "Sales Up!" *Selling Power*, January/February 2011, p. 40. Also see Scott Gillum, "The Disappearing Sales Process," *Forbes,* January 7, 2013, www.forbes.com/sites/gyro/2013/01/07/the-disappearing-sales-process/; and Matt Dixon and Steve Richard, "Solution Selling Is Dead: Why 2013 Is the Year of B2B Insight Selling," *Openview*, http://labs.openviewpartners.com/solution-selling-is-dead-2013-year-of-b2b-insight-selling/.

19. See "The Digital Evolution in B2B Marketing," Marketing Leaderships Council, December 2, 2012, p. 3; Scott Gillum, "The Disappearing Sales Process," *Forbes,* January 7, 2013, www.forbes.com/sites/gyro/2013/01/07/the-disappearing-sales-process/; and Alice Myerhoff, "How Selling Has Gone Social in the Last 15 Years," *Salesforce Blog,* March 13, 2014, http://blogs.salesforce.com/company/2014/03/social-selling-15-years-gp.html.

20. See "Barbara Giamanco and Kent Gregoire, "Tweet Me, Friend Me, Make Me Buy," *Harvard Business Review,* July–August 2012, pp. 88–94; and John Bottom, "Research: Are B2B Buyers Using Social Media?" *Slideshare,* September 10, 2013, www.slideshare.net/basebot/b2b-buyer-behaviour.

21. See "GE's Social Story," www.salesforcemarketingcloud.com/resources/videos/ges-social-story/, accessed June 2014; David Moth, "How General Electric Uses Facebook, Twitter, Pinterest and Google+," *Velocify,* May 2013, https://econsultancy.com/blog/62684-how-general-electric-uses-facebook-twitter-pinterest-and-google; and "GE Social Media," www.ge.com/news/social, accessed September 2014.

22. Example based on information from James C. Anderson, Nirmalya Kumar, and James A. Narus, "Become a Value Merchant," *Sales & Marketing Management*, May 6, 2008, pp. 20–23; and "Business Market Value Merchants," *Marketing Management*, March/April 2008, pp. 31+. For more discussion and examples, see Heather Baldwin, "Deeper Value Delivery," *Selling Power*, September/October 2010, p. 16; and Thomas P. Reilly, "Value-Added Selling Is Smart," *Selling Power,* June 27, 2012, www.sellingpower.com/content/article.php?a=8917.

23. Kantar Retail, *Making Connections: Trade Promotion Integration across the Marketing Landscape* (Wilton, CT: Kantar Retail, July 2012), p. 5.

24. Kantar Retail, *Making Connections: Trade Promotion Integration across the Marketing Landscape,* p. 6.

25. See "Top 10 Retail Loyalty Programs," *BigDoor,* http://bigdoor.com/blog/2013/12/11/top-10-retail-loyalty-programs/, accessed June 2014; and www.bloomingdales.com/loyallist?cm_sp=FOOTER-_-BOTTOM_NAV-_-LOYALLIST, accessed June 2014.

26. NCH Marketing Services, "NCH Annual Topline U.S. CPG Coupon Facts Report for Year-End 2013," February 2014, https://www2.nchmarketing.com/ResourceCenter/assets/0/22/28/76/226/457/0bddc7b288724aac83e8215e9a16f854.pdf.

27. See NCH Marketing Services, "NCH Annual Topline U.S. CPG Coupon Facts Report for Year-End 2013," "Majority of US Internet Users Will Redeem Digital Coupons in 2013," *eMarketer*, October 21, 2013, www.emarketer.com/Article/Majority-of-US-Internet-Users-Will-Redeem-Digital-Coupons-2013/1010313; and "Mobile Spurs Digital Coupon User Growth," *eMarketer,* January 31, 2014, www.emarketer.com/Article/Mobile-Spurs-Digital-Coupon-User-Growth/1009639.

28. Based on information from "Walgreens Brings Mobile Couponing and Exclusive Offers to Smartphone Users Beginning Black Friday," November 17, 2011, http://news.walgreens.com/article_display.cfm?article_id=5504; Kunar Patel, "At Walgreens, a Mobile Check-In Acts Like a Circular," *Advertising Age,* February 8, 2012, http://adage.com/print/232584/; and www.walgreens.com/topic/apps/learn_about_mobile_browser_app.jsp, accessed September 2014.

29. See www.happymeal.com/en_US/, accessed June 2014.

30. See "PPAI Reports Positive Results, U.S. Promotional Products Industry's Annual Sales Volume Increases to $18.5 Billion," *PPAI News,* July 8, 2013, www.ppai.org/press/documents/ppai%20reports%20positive%20results%20u.s.%20promotional%20products%20industrys%20annual%20sales%20volume%20increases%20to%2018.5%20bil.pdf.

31. Based on information found in Patrick Hanlon, "Face Slams: Event Marketing Takes Off," *Forbes,* May 9, 2012, www.forbes.com/sites/patrickhanlon/2012/05/09/face-slams-event-marketing-takes-off/; and www.redbull.com/us/en/events and www.redbull.com/cs/Satellite/en_INT/RedBull/HolyShit/011242745950125, accessed June 2014. The referenced wing suit flying video can be found at http://player.vimeo.com/video/31481531?autoplay=1.

32. Kantar Retail, *Making Connections: Trade Promotion Integration across the Marketing Landscape*, p. 10.

33. See "2013 CES Attendee Audit Summary Results," www.cesweb.org/CES/media/2014/landing%20pages/why%20attend%20ces/2013-CES-Audit_FINAL.pdf, accessed June 2014; "Bauma 2013 Records Highest Ever Attendance," *Construction Week,* April 22, 2013, www.constructionweekonline.com/article-22027-bauma-2013-records-highest-ever-attendance/#.UZPTULXYdyl; and "Bauma 2013 Equipment Show Sees Record Attendance of 530,000," *CMBOL*, April 23, 2013, www.cmbol.com/news/detail/2013/04/2013042314194724.shtm.

PART 1: Defining Marketing and the Marketing Process (Chapters 1–2)
PART 2: Understanding the Marketplace and Customer Value (Chapters 3–6)
PART 3: Designing a Customer Value-Driven Strategy and Mix (Chapters 7–17)
PART 4: Extending Marketing (Chapters 18–20)

17 Direct, Online, Social Media, and Mobile Marketing

Chapter Preview

In the previous three chapters, you learned about engaging consumers and communicating customer value through integrated marketing communication, and about four elements of the marketing communications mix: advertising, publicity, personal selling, and sales promotion. In this chapter, we examine direct marketing and its fastest-growing form, digital marketing (online, social media, and mobile marketing). Today, spurred by the surge in Internet usage and buying, as well as rapid advances in digital technologies—from smartphones, tablets, and other digital devices to the spate of online mobile and social media—direct marketing has undergone a dramatic transformation. As you read this chapter, remember that although direct and digital marketing are presented as separate tools, they must be carefully integrated with each other and with other elements of the promotion and marketing mixes.

Let's start by looking at Facebook, a company that markets *only* directly and digitally. The giant online social media network promises to become one of the world's most powerful and profitable digital marketers. Yet, as a money-making marketing company, Facebook is just getting started.

FACEBOOK: Going Online, Social, and Mobile—and Making Money Doing It

The world has rapidly gone online, social, and mobile. And no company is more online, social, and mobile than Facebook. The world's largest social network has a deep and daily impact on the lives of more than a billion members around the world. But despite Facebook's massive size and growth, it continues to grapple with a crucial question: How can it profitably tap the marketing potential of its massive online community to make money without driving off its legions of loyal users?

Facebook is humongous. In little more than a decade, it has acquired some 1.3 billion active monthly users—one-seventh of the world's population. More than a billion members now access Facebook on mobile devices, and some 757 million visit the site daily. Collectively, the Facebook community uploads 350 million photos, "Likes" 4.5 billion items, and shares 4.75 billion pieces of content daily.

With that many eyeballs glued to one virtual space for that much time, Facebook has tremendous impact and influence. Facebook's power comes not just from its size and omnipresence; rather, it lies in the deep social connections with and among users. Facebook's mission is "to give people the power to share and make the world more open and connected." It's a place where friends and family meet, share their stories, display their photos, and chronicle their lives. Hordes of people have made Facebook their digital home 24/7.

By wielding all that influence, Facebook has the potential to become one of the world's most powerful and profitable online marketers. Yet the burgeoning social network is only now beginning to tap its financial potential. Initially, CEO Mark Zuckerberg and the network's other idealistic young cofounders focused on building a user base and gave little thought to making money. In fact, without any help from Facebook, companies themselves were first to discover the social medium's commercial value. Most brands—small and large—built their own Facebook pages, gaining free access to the gigantic community's social-sharing potential.

As it has matured, however, Facebook has come to realize that it must make its own marketing moves. It is now developing a growing portfolio of products that will let it connect everyone in the world and make money doing it. The social network's first and best bet for converting the value of its massive user

Despite Facebook's staggering size and growth, it continues to grapple with a crucial question: How can it profitably tap the marketing potential of its massive online community without driving off loyal users?

base into real dollars is online advertising. In fact, during the past three years, as Facebook's revenues nearly quadrupled from $2 billion to $7.9 billion, advertising accounted for nearly 90 percent of those revenues.

Many online marketers make money through advertising. But Facebook has two unique advantages—unprecedented user data and deep user engagement. Facebook maintains one of the richest collections of user profile data in the world. So ads on Facebook can be carefully targeted, based on user location, gender, age, likes and interests, relationship status, workplace, and education. But Facebook ads do far more than simply capture the right eyeballs. They are "engagement ads" that take advantage of the network's social-sharing power to move people to action. Facebook ads blend in with regular user activities, and users can interact with ads by leaving comments, making recommendations, clicking the "Like" button, or following a link to a brand-sponsored Facebook page.

To realize its staggering marketing potential, Facebook is developing a growing portfolio of products and apps that will let it connect everyone in the world and make money doing it.

© epa european pressphoto agency b.v./Alamy

Facebook's appeal to both users and advertisers hinges on its ability to target specific kinds of content to well-defined user segments. However, Facebook's former "all things to all people" approach left many users, especially younger ones, visiting Facebook less and shifting time to more specialized competing social networks. To meet that growing threat, Facebook is now pursuing a multi-app strategy of providing "something for any and every individual." According to Zuckerberg, "Our vision for Facebook is to create a set of products that help you share any kind of content you want with any audience you want."

Facebook's first move under this new multi-app strategy was to pay a stunning $1 billion to acquire Instagram, the surging photo-sharing app. Although Facebook already had its own photo-sharing features, the Instagram acquisition brought a younger, 27-million-strong user base into the Facebook fold. And rather than incorporating Instagram as just another Facebook feature, Facebook has maintained Instagram as an independent brand, with its own personality and user base. Instagram and Facebook customers can choose their desired level of integration, including Instagram membership without a Facebook account. "The fact that Instagram is connected to other services beyond Facebook is an important part of the experience," says Zuckerberg.

Not long after the Instagram acquisition, in its quest to add unique new products and user segments, Facebook announced the creation of Creative Labs, a Facebook division charged with developing single-purpose mobile apps. It also unveiled the new division's first product—Paper, a mobile app that provides easy and personalized access to Facebook's News Feed. Although the core Facebook mobile app already provides access to this content, Paper lets users organize the feed by themes, interests, and sources, serving it all up in a fullscreen, distraction-free layout.

On the heels of the Paper launch came another stunning Facebook mega-acquisition. Dwarfing its Instagram deal, Facebook paid a shocking $19 billion for standalone messaging app WhatsApp. Facebook's own Messenger had already grown quickly to 200 million users. But similar to Instagram, WhatsApp immediately gave Facebook something it could not easily build on its own—an independent brand with more than 450 million registered international users, many of whom were not on Facebook. Most recently, Facebook acquired fitness and activity tracking app Moves, which will also continue to operate as a standalone brand.

By developing and acquiring such new products and apps, Facebook is doing what it does best—growing its membership and giving its diverse users more ways and reasons to connect and engage. Facebook's fuller portfolio lets users meet their individual needs within the broadening framework of the Facebook family. In turn, more and more-targetable users who spend increased time on the network create more opportunities for Facebook to attract advertising revenues.

Will increased advertising and commercialization alienate loyal Facebook users? Not if it's done right. Recent studies show that online users readily accept—even welcome—well-targeted online advertising and marketing. Tasteful and appropriately targeted offers can enhance rather than detract from the Facebook user experience. Moreover, although Facebook's founders initially opposed running ads or other marketing, worried that marketing might damage Facebook's free (and commercial-free) sharing culture, they've now come to realize that if Facebook doesn't make money, it can't continue to serve its members.

Whatever its future, Facebook seems to have barely scratched the surface. Its new multi-app, multi-segment strategy, combined with its massive, closely knit social structure, gives Facebook staggering potential. Carolyn Everson, Facebook's vice president of global sales, sums up Facebook's growth potential this way: "I'm not sure the marketing community understands our story yet. We evolve so quickly. We have a saying here: 'We are one percent done with our mission.'"[1]

Objective Outline

OBJECTIVE 1	**Define *direct and digital marketing* and discuss their rapid growth and benefits to customers and companies.** Direct and Digital Marketing (p 534–536)
OBJECTIVE 2	**Identify and discuss the major forms of direct and digital marketing.** Forms of Direct and Digital Marketing (p 536–538) Digital and Social Media (p 538)
OBJECTIVE 3	**Explain how companies have responded to the Internet and the digital age with various online marketing strategies.** Marketing, the Internet, and the Digital Age (p 539–540) Online Marketing (pp 540–544)
OBJECTIVE 4	**Discuss how companies use social media and mobile marketing to engage consumers and create brand community.** Social Media Marketing (pp 544–547) Mobile Marketing (pp 547–550)
OBJECTIVE 5	**Identify and discuss the traditional direct marketing forms and overview public policy and ethical issues presented by direct marketing.** Traditional Direct Marketing Forms (pp 550–554) Public Policy Issues in Direct and Digital Marketing (pp 554–557)

Many of the marketing and promotion tools that we've examined in previous chapters were developed in the context of *mass marketing*: targeting broad markets with standardized messages and offers distributed through intermediaries. Today, however, with the trend toward narrower targeting and the surge in digital and social media technologies, many companies are adopting *direct marketing*, either as a primary marketing approach or as a supplement to other approaches. In this section, we explore the exploding world of direct marketing and its fastest-growing form—digital marketing using online, social media, and mobile marketing channels.

Author Comment | For most companies, direct and digital marketing are supplemental channels or media. But for many other companies today—such as Amazon, GEICO, or Facebook—direct marketing is a complete way of doing business.

Direct and Digital Marketing

Direct and digital marketing involve engaging directly with carefully targeted individual consumers and customer communities to both obtain an immediate response and build

Direct and digital marketing
Engaging directly with carefully targeted individual consumers and customer communities to both obtain an immediate response and build lasting customer relationships.

lasting customer relationships. Companies use direct marketing to tailor their offers and content to the needs and interests of narrowly defined segments or individual buyers. In this way, they build customer engagement, brand community, and sales.

For example, Amazon.com interacts directly with customers via its Web site or mobile app to help them discover and buy almost anything and everything online. Similarly, GEICO interacts directly with customers—by telephone, through its Web site or phone app, or on its Facebook, Twitter, and YouTube pages—to build individual brand relationships, give insurance quotes, sell policies, or service customer accounts.

The New Direct Marketing Model

Early direct marketers—catalog companies, direct mailers, and telemarketers—gathered customer names and sold goods mainly by mail and telephone. Today, however, spurred by the surge in Internet usage and buying, and by rapid advances in digital technologies—from smartphones, tablets, and other digital devices to the spate of online social and mobile media—direct marketing has undergone a dramatic transformation.

In previous chapters, we discussed direct marketing as direct distribution—as marketing channels that contain no intermediaries. We also included direct and digital marketing elements of the promotion mix—as an approach for engaging consumers directly and creating brand community. In actuality, direct marketing is both of these things and much more.

Most companies still use direct marketing as a supplementary channel or medium. Thus, most department stores, such as Sears or Macy's, sell the majority of their merchandise off their store shelves, but they also sell through direct mail, online catalogs, and social media pages. Pepsi's Mountain Dew brand markets heavily through mass-media advertising and its retail partners' channels. However, it also supplements these channels with direct marketing. It uses its several brand Web sites and a long list of social media to engage its customer community in everything from designing their own Mountain Dew lifestyle pages to co-creating advertising campaigns and deciding which limited-edition flavors should be launched or retired. Through such direct interactions, Mountain Dew has created one of the most passionately loyal fan bases of any brand. By one estimate, simply letting fans pick flavors has generated $200 million in incremental revenues per year for Mountain Dew.[2]

However, for many companies today, direct and digital marketing are more than just supplementary channels or advertising media—they constitute a complete model for doing business. Firms employing this direct model use it as the only approach. Companies such as Facebook, Amazon, Google, eBay, Netflix, GEICO, and Priceline.com have successfully built their entire approach to the marketplace around direct and digital marketing. ● For example, Priceline.com, the online travel company, sells its services exclusively through online, mobile, and social media channels. Priceline.com and other online travel agency competitors such as Expedia and Orbitz, have pretty much driven traditional offline travel agencies to extinction.[3]

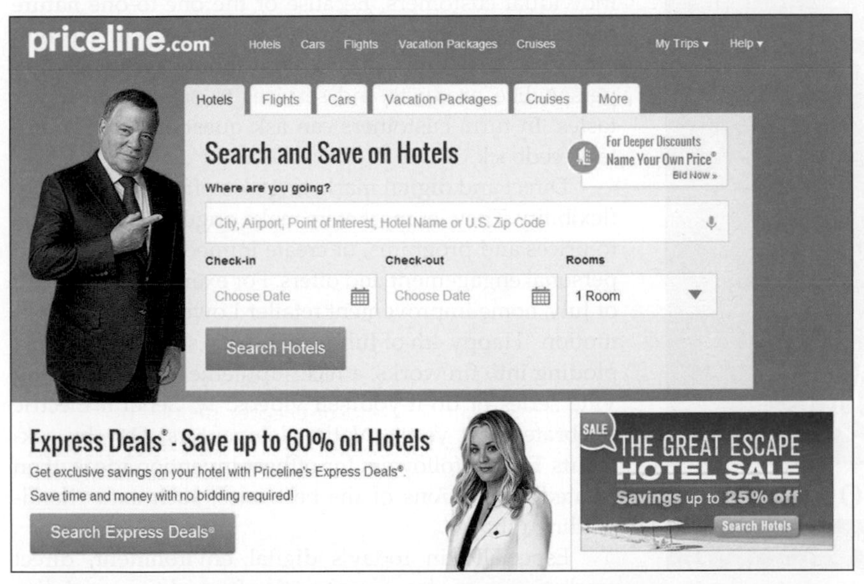

● **The new direct marketing model: Online travel agency Priceline.com sells its services exclusively through online, mobile, and social media channels. Along with other online competitors, Priceline.com has pretty much driven traditional offline travel agencies into extinction.**

priceline.com

Rapid Growth of Direct and Digital Marketing

Direct and digital marketing have become the fastest-growing form of marketing. According to the Direct Marketing Association (DMA), U.S. companies spent almost $133 billion on direct and digital marketing last year. As a result, direct-marketing-driven sales now amount to more than $2 trillion, accounting for 13 percent of the U.S. economy. The DMA estimates that direct marketing sales will grow 4.9 percent annually through 2016, compared with a projected 4.1 percent annual growth for total U.S. sales.[4]

Direct marketing continues to become more Internet-based, and digital direct marketing is claiming a surging share of marketing spending and sales. For example, U.S. marketers spent an estimated $43 billion on digital advertising alone last year, an amount expected to increase more than 14 percent this year. These efforts generated more than $260 billion in online consumer spending. Total digital advertising spending—including online display and search advertising, video, social media, mobile, e-mail, and other—now accounts for the second-largest share of media spending, behind only television. Over the next four years, digital marketing expenditures and digitally driven sales are expected to grow at a blistering 9 percent a year.[5]

Benefits of Direct and Digital Marketing to Buyers and Sellers

For buyers, direct and digital marketing are convenient, easy, and private. They give buyers anywhere, anytime access to an almost unlimited assortment of goods and a wealth of product and buying information. For example, on its Web site and mobile app, Amazon .com offers more information than most of us can digest, ranging from top-10 product lists, extensive product descriptions, and expert and user product reviews to recommendations based on customers' previous searches and purchases. Through direct marketing, buyers can interact with sellers by phone or on the seller's Web site or app to create exactly the configuration of information, products, or services they want and then order them on the spot. Finally, for consumers who want it, digital marketing through online, mobile, and social media provides a sense of brand engagement and community—a place to share brand information and experiences with other brand fans.

For sellers, direct marketing often provides a low-cost, efficient, speedy alternative for reaching their markets. Today's direct marketers can target small groups or individual customers. Because of the one-to-one nature of direct marketing, companies can interact with customers by phone or online, learn more about their needs, and personalize products and services to specific customer tastes. In turn, customers can ask questions and volunteer feedback.

Direct and digital marketing also offer sellers greater flexibility. They let marketers make ongoing adjustments to prices and programs, or create immediate, timely, and personal engagement and offers. For example, last Fourth of July, home improvement retailer Lowe's issued a stop-motion "Happy 4th of July" Vine video showing tools exploding into fireworks, a nice supplement to its ongoing Vine series of do-it-yourself videos. General Electric celebrated last year's National Inventors' Day by asking its Twitter followers for offbeat invention ideas, then created illustrations of the best ones, such as a "hand-holding robot."

Especially in today's digital environment, direct marketing provides opportunities for *real-time marketing* that links brands to important moments and trending events in customers' lives (see Real Marketing 17.1). It is a powerful tool for moving customers through the buying process and for building customer engagement, community, and personalized relationships.

Direct and digital marketing lets brands create immediate and timely customer engagement, as when GE celebrated last year's National Inventors' Day by asking Twitter followers for offbeat invention ideas, then created illustrations of the best ones.

GE

Author Comment | Direct marketing is rich in tools, from traditional favorites such as direct mail and catalogs to dazzling new digital tools—online, mobile, and social media.

Forms of Direct and Digital Marketing

The major forms of direct and digital marketing are shown in **Figure 17.1**. Traditional direct marketing tools include face-to-face selling, direct-mail marketing, catalog marketing, telemarketing, direct-response television marketing, and kiosk marketing. In recent

Real Marketing 17.1

Real-Time Marketing: Engaging Consumers in the Moment

A funny thing happened during Super Bowl XLVII in New Orleans. Early in the third quarter, the lights in the Mercedes-Benz Superdome suddenly went out. As 71,000 attendees and 106 million viewers restlessly bided their time and scratched their heads, engineers worked feverishly for a full 34 minutes to repair the power outage and bring the lights back on. But whereas the blackout was a disaster for Superdome management and CBS Sports, and an annoyance for players and fans, at least one marketer saw it as an opportunity. Shortly after the blackout began, Nabisco's Oreo brand tweeted out a simple message: "Power out? No problem. You can still dunk in the dark."

That now-famous single tweet, conceived and approved within just minutes, grabbed more attention for Oreo than the brand's extravagant first-quarter "cream versus cookie" spot. Within an hour, the "dunk in the dark" message was retweeted nearly 16,000 times and racked up more than 20,000 Facebook likes, resulting in tens of millions of favorable exposures. In the following days, Oreo received tons of media coverage, hailing it as "The Brand that Won the Blackout Bowl." Those were pretty impressive results for a one-off joke by a cookie maker.

Oreo's successful Super Bowl one-liner triggered a surge in real-time marketing. Brands of all kinds are now trying to create their own "Oreo moments" by aligning marketing content with real-world events and trending topics through timely tweets, videos, blog entries, and social media posts. Done right, real-time marketing can engage consumers in the moment and make a brand more relevant. Done poorly, however, it can come off as little more than an awkward or inappropriate interruption. According to one observer, "Like Mother Goose's girl with the curl on her forehead, real-time marketing can be very, very good—but when it's bad, it's horrid."

Too often, brands simply toss standalone, last-minute ads or messages into social channels, "hoping to catch lightning in a bottle." But hastily prepared or self-serving real-time messages can easily backfire, painting the brand as opportunistic or out of touch. For example, when Hurricane Sandy devastated America's east coast, retailer American Apparel blasted out an e-mail proclaiming a "Hurricane Sandy Sale" ("In case you're bored during the storm, 20% off everything for the next 36 hours"). As might be expected, the Twittersphere lit up with disgust at the retailer's opportunistic pitch, and the company's sentiment scores dropped from 67 to 7 overnight.

Isolated minute-by-minute marketing strikes rarely succeed. Instead, to be consistently successful, real-time marketing must be part of a broader, carefully conceived strategy that makes the brand itself an engaging and relevant part of consumers' lives. According to one marketing strategist, brands must "evolve their entire plan to marketing in a real-time world." Today's smartphone-wielding, social media-saturated customers "are no longer just second-screen *viewing*—they are second-screen *living*." Smart brands build agile, ongoing real-time marketing programs that listen in on the social space and respond with relevant marketing content that blends smoothly with the dynamics of customers' real-time social sharing.

For example, although the Oreo "dunk in the dark" tweet might have seemed off-the-cuff, it was only the latest in a long series of real-time marketing efforts designed to make Oreo a part of consumers' daily conversations. In the months preceding the Super Bowl, Oreo had successfully carried out its "Daily Twist" campaign. Each day for 100 days, the brand posted consumer-inspired Oreo cookie art tied to a relevant event. There was a Mars Rover Landing Oreo (an open-face cookie with tire tracks through its red crème filling), a Shin Shin Oreo (a tribute to the Tokyo Zoo's newly born Panda cub), an Elvis Week Oreo (with an Oreo profile of The King of Rock 'n Roll), and a Shark Week Oreo (with a jagged bite taken out of it, of course). Among other results of the groundbreaking Daily Twist campaign, Oreo saw a four-fold increase in Facebook shares and watched its Instagram following shoot from 2,200 to more than 85,000.

Starbucks, a social media powerhouse with nearly 37 million Facebook fans and 6 million Twitter followers, has long and systematically used real-time marketing to link the brand and what it stands for to current events important to its customers. For example, after Winter Storm Nemo hit the Northeastern United States with heavy snowfall and hurricane-force winds in early 2013, Starbucks Twitter and Facebook promotions offered free coffee to customers in affected areas. "We wanted to make a grand [and timely] gesture," said a Starbucks digital marketer.

On an even grander stage, in the fall of 2013, shortly after bipartisan bickering in Washington resulted in a partial shutdown of the U.S. federal government—furloughing hundreds of thousands of federal employees, closing national parks, reducing many public health services, and much more—Starbucks

Real-time marketing: Oreo's spectacularly successful "You can still dunk in the dark" tweet triggered a surge in real-time marketing, as brands of all kinds are now trying to create their own "Oreo moments" by aligning marketing content with real-world events and trending topics.

launched a #ComeTogether campaign. It began with tweets and Facebook postings by CEO Howard Schultz asking "How can we #cometogether to take care of each other?" and announcing that Starbucks would give a free tall brewed coffee to anyone kind enough to #payitforward and buy the next person in line their favorite beverage. That effort had customers flocking to Starbucks, and tweeting messages like this one: "Bought coffee for the stranger in front of me @Starbucks. Got mine for free. Feels good to #payitforward."

In the next phase of the #ComeTogether campaign, Starbucks distributed a petition via e-mail, social media, and national newspapers urging government officials to reopen government, pay national debts on time, and pass a long-term budget deal. In a single 24-hour period, Starbucks issued two tweets, a Facebook post, an Instagram video, and an e-mail urging customers to sign copies of the petition and bring them to their local Starbucks. Within a day of sending the first tweet, the company had collected more than 1 million signed petitions; only five days later, it tweeted a photo showing an apron-clad Starbucks team member delivering nearly 2 million petitions to the Capitol Building. In all, the #ComeTogether campaign engaged the Starbucks brand community in positive conversations and actions over an important real-time issue.

Whether connected to a social cause, a trending topic or event, a consumer's personal situation, or something else, the essential concept behind successful real-time marketing is pretty simple. Find or create ongoing connections between the brand and what's happening and important in consumers' lives, then engage consumers genuinely in the moment. One marketing executive suggests that real-time marketers should equate the practice to "meeting somebody in a social gathering—you don't accost them, instead you try to find a commonality of interest."

Sources: Georgia Wells, "Real-Time Marketing in a Real-Time World," *Wall Street Journal*, March 24, 2014, p. R3; Rachel VanArsdale, "Starbucks Real-Time Marketing Asks America to Come Together," October 17, 2013, http://themrsite.com/blog/2013/10/starbucks-real-time-marketing-asks-america-to-come-together//; Jeff Dachis, "Stop Whining about Real-Time Marketing," *Advertising Age*, October 10, 2013, http://adage.com/print/ /244665; Christopher Heine, "Ads in Real Time, All the Time," *Adweek*, February 18, 2013, p. 9; Lucia Moses, "Real-Time Marketing," *Adweek*, October 14, 2013, p. 17; Tim Nudd, "Real-Time Rules: Eight Opportunities for Marketing in the Moment, and the Brands that Got It Right," *Adweek*, September 9, 2013, pp. 22–25; and www.360i.com/work/oreo-daily-twist/, accessed September 2014.

years, however, a dazzling new set of digital direct marketing tools has burst onto the marketing scene, including online marketing (Web sites, online ads and promotions, e-mail, online videos, and blogs), social media marketing, and mobile marketing. We'll begin by examining the new direct digital and social media marketing tools that have received so much attention lately. Then, we'll look at the still heavily used and very important traditional direct marketing tools. As always, however, it's important to remember that all of these tools—both the new digital and the more traditional forms—must be blended into a fully integrated marketing communications program.

Author Comment | Direct digital and social media are surging and grabbing all the headlines these days, so we'll start with them. But the traditional direct marketing tools are still heavily used. We'll dig into them later in the chapter.

Digital and Social Media Marketing

As noted earlier, **digital and social media marketing** is the fastest-growing form of direct marketing. It uses digital marketing tools such as Web sites, online video, e-mail, blogs, social media, mobile ads and apps, and other digital platforms to directly engage consumers anywhere, anytime via their computers, smartphones, tablets, Internet-ready TVs, and other digital devices. The widespread use of the Internet and digital technologies is having a dramatic impact on both buyers and the marketers who serve them.

Digital and social media marketing
Using digital marketing tools such as Web sites, social media, mobile apps and ads, online video, e-mail, and blogs that engage consumers anywhere, anytime via their digital devices.

Marketing, the Internet, and the Digital Age

Much of the world's business today is carried out over digital networks that connect people and companies. These days, people connect digitally with information, brands, and each other at almost any time and from almost anywhere. The digital age has fundamentally changed customers' notions of convenience, speed, price, product information, service, and brand interactions. As a result, it has given marketers a whole new way to create customer value, engage customers, and build customer relationships.

Digital usage and impact continues to grow steadily. More than 85 percent of all U.S. adults use the Internet, and the average U.S. Internet user spends more than five hours a day using digital media. Moreover, more than 60 percent of smartphone owners access the Internet via their devices. In fact, Americans now use their smartphone and tablet apps more than their PCs to go online. Worldwide, 40 percent of the population has Internet

FIGURE | 17.1
Forms of Direct and Digital Marketing

We'll begin with the exciting new digital forms of direct marketing. But remember that the traditional forms are still heavily used, and that the new and old must be integrated for maximum impact.

Digital and social media marketing
Online marketing
(Web sites, online advertising, e-mail, online videos, blogs)
Social media marketing
Mobile marketing

Traditional direct marketing
Face-to-face selling
Direct-mail marketing
Catalog marketing
Telemarketing
Direct-response TV marketing
Kiosk marketing

access. And 22 percent have access to the mobile Internet, a number that's expected to double over the next five years as mobile becomes an ever-more-popular way to get online.[6]

As a result, more than half of all U.S. households now regularly shop online, and digital buying continues to grow at a healthy double-digit rate. U.S. online retail sales were an estimated $225 billion last year and are expected to grow 10 percent each year to $370 billion by 2017 as consumers shift their spending from physical to digital stores. Perhaps even more important, it's estimated that nearly half of all U.S. retail sales were either transacted directly online or influenced by Internet research.[7] And a growing number of consumers armed with smartphones and tablets use them as they shop in stores to find better deals and score price-matching offers.

To reach this burgeoning market, most companies now market online. Some companies operate *only* online. They include a wide array of firms, from *e-tailers* such as Amazon.com and Expedia.com that sell products and services directly to final buyers via the Internet to *search engines and portals* (such as Google, Yahoo!, and Bing), *transaction sites* (eBay, Craigslist), *content sites* (the *New York Times* on the Web, ESPN.com, and *Encyclopædia Britannica*), and *online social media* (Facebook, YouTube, Pinterest, Instragram, Twitter, and Flickr).

Multichannel marketing
Marketing both through stores and other traditional offline channels and through digital, online, social media, and mobile channels.

Today, however, it's hard to find a company that doesn't have a substantial online presence. Even companies that have traditionally operated offline have now created their own online sales, marketing, and brand community channels. In fact, **multichannel marketing** companies are having more online success than their online-only competitors. A recent ranking of the world's 10 largest online retail sites contained only three online-only retailers (Amazon.com, which was ranked number one, Netflix, and CDW). All the others were multichannel retailers.[8]

For example, number two on the list of online retail sites is Staples, the $23 billion office supply retailer. Staples operates more than 2,000 superstores worldwide. But you might be surprised to learn that almost half of Staples' sales are generated online, from its Web site and mobile app; its presence on social media such as Facebook, Google+, Twitter, YouTube, and LinkedIn; and its own Staples.com community.[9]

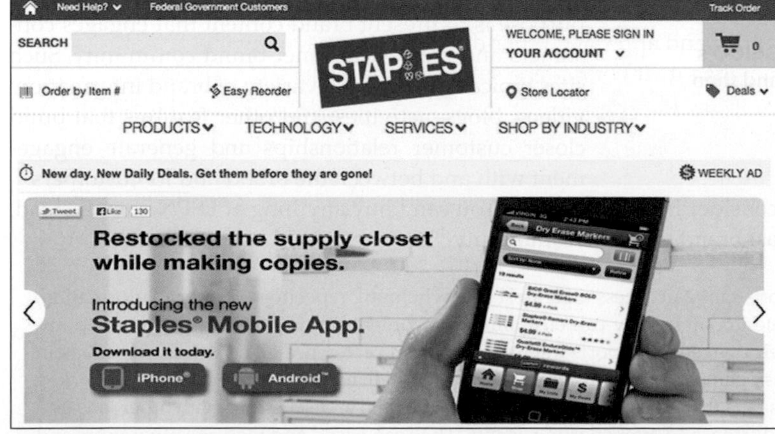

Multichannel marketing: More than 43 percent of Staples' sales come from its online marketing operations, including its Web site and mobile app, its presence on social media, and its own Staples.com community.
Courtesy of Staples the Office Superstore, LLC & Staples, Inc.

Selling online lets Staples build deeper, more personalized relationships with customers large and small. A large customer, such as GE or P&G, can create lists of approved office products at discount prices and then let company departments or even individuals do their own online and mobile purchasing. This reduces ordering costs, cuts through the red tape, and speeds up the ordering process for customers. At the same time, it encourages companies to use Staples as a sole source for office supplies. Even the smallest companies and individual consumers find 24/7 online ordering via the Web, Staples mobile app, or social media sites easier and more efficient.

In addition, Staples' online, mobile, and social media efforts complement store sales by engaging customers, enlarging product assortments, offering hot deals, and helping customers find a local store and check stock and prices. In return, local stores promote online buying through in-store kiosks. If customers don't find what they need on the shelves, they can quickly order it via the kiosk. Thus, Staples backs its "make more happen" positioning by offering a full range of contact points and delivery modes—online, social media, mobile, catalogs, phone, and in the store. No online-only or store-only seller can match that kind of call, click, or visit convenience and support. "We're offering more products, more ways to buy, and more great value," summarizes Staples' vice president of global marketing.

Direct digital and social media marketing takes any of the several forms shown in Figure 17.1. These forms include online marketing, social media marketing, and mobile marketing. We discuss each in turn, starting with online marketing.

Online Marketing

Online marketing
Marketing via the Internet using company Web sites, online ads and promotions, e-mail, online video, and blogs.

Online marketing refers to marketing via the Internet using company Web sites, online advertising and promotions, e-mail marketing, online video, and blogs. Social media and mobile marketing also take place online and must be closely coordinated with other forms of digital marketing. However, because of their special characteristics, we discuss the fast-growing social media and mobile marketing approaches in separate sections.

Web Sites and Branded Web Communities

For most companies, the first step in conducting online marketing is to create a Web site. Web sites vary greatly in purpose and content. Some Web sites are primarily **marketing Web sites**, designed to engage customers and move them closer to a direct purchase or other marketing outcome.

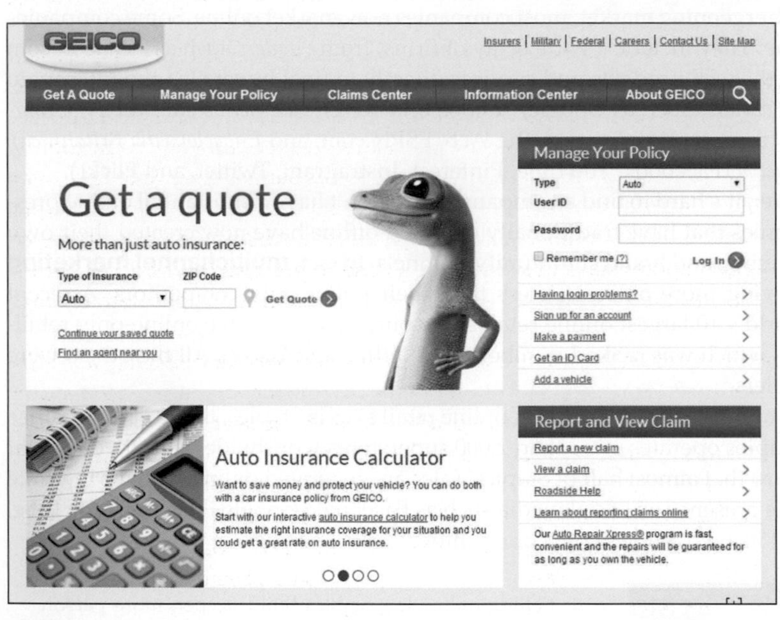

Marketing Web sites: Once a potential customer clicks in, GEICO's Web site wastes no time trying to turn the inquiry into a sale, and then into a long-term relationship.
GEICO

For example, GEICO operates a marketing Web site at www.geico.com. Once a potential customer clicks in, GEICO wastes no time trying to turn the inquiry into a sale, and then into a long-term relationship. A bold headline urges potential customers to "Get a quote," and the site provides all the information and tools needed to do just that, complete with an auto insurance calculator to help buyers estimate the right insurance coverage, rates, and savings. The straightforward site also makes it easy for current customers to manage their accounts and policies, add or replace vehicles, and make and view claims, all under the watchful eye of the familiar GEICO Gecko. Customers can also use GEICO's mobile app to access the brand's mobile Web site, where they can pay bills, get account and coverage information, view their ID cards, and even watch the latest GEICO ads and chat with Lily, their GEICO insurance voice assistant.

In contrast, **branded community Web sites** don't try to sell anything at all. Instead, their primary purpose is to present brand content that engages consumers and creates customer-brand community. Such sites typically offer a rich variety of brand information, videos, blogs, activities, and other features that build closer customer relationships and generate engagement with and between the brand and its customers.

For example, consider ESPN's Web site. You can't buy anything at ESPN.com. Instead, the site creates a vast branded sports community:[10]

Marketing Web site
A Web site that engages consumers to move them closer to a direct purchase or other marketing outcome.

Branded community Web site
A Web site that presents brand content that engages consumers and creates customer community around a brand.

At ESPN.com, sports fans can access an almost overwhelming repository of sports information, statistics, and game updates. They can customize site content by sport, team, players, and authors to match their own special sports interests and team preferences. The site engages fans in contests and fantasy games (everything from fantasy football, baseball, and basketball to hockey and poker). Sports fans from around the world can participate in discussions with other fans and celebrities before, during, and after sporting events. They can friend and message other users and post comments on message boards and blogs. By downloading various widgets and apps, fans can customize their ESPN experience and carry it with them wherever they go. In all, ESPN's Web site creates a virtual brand community without walls, a must-have experience that keeps fans coming back again and again.

Creating a Web site is one thing; getting people to *visit* the site is another. To attract visitors, companies aggressively promote their Web sites in offline print and broadcast advertising and through ads and links on other sites. But today's Web users are quick to abandon any Web site that doesn't measure up. The key is to create enough engaging and valued content to get consumers to come to the site, stick around, and come back again.

At the very least, a Web site should be easy to use and visually appealing. Ultimately, however, Web sites must also be *useful*. When it comes to online browsing and shopping, most people prefer substance over style and function over flash. For example, ESPN's site isn't all that flashy, and it's pretty heavily packed and congested. But it connects customers quickly and effectively to all the sports information and involvement they are seeking. Thus, effective Web sites contain deep and useful information, interactive tools that help find and evaluate content of interest, links to other related sites, changing promotional offers, and entertaining features that lend relevant excitement.

Online advertising
Advertising that appears while consumers are browsing online, including display ads, search-related ads, online classifieds, and other forms.

E-mail marketing
Sending highly targeted, highly personalized, relationship-building marketing messages via e-mail.

Online Advertising

As consumers spend more and more time online, companies are shifting more of their marketing dollars to **online advertising** to build brand sales or attract visitors to their Internet, mobile, and social media sites. Online advertising has become a major promotional medium. The main forms of online advertising are display ads and search-related ads. Together, display and search-related ads account for the largest portion of firms' digital marketing budgets, capturing 30 percent of all digital marketing spending.[11]

Online display ads might appear anywhere on an Internet user's screen and are often related to the information being viewed. For instance, while browsing vacation packages on Travelocity.com, you might encounter a display ad offering a free upgrade on a rental car from Enterprise Rent-A-Car. Online display ads have come a long way in recent years in terms of attracting and holding consumer attention. Today's *rich media* ads incorporate animation, video, sound, and interactivity. ● For example, while browsing sports-related content on your computer or phone, you might see a bright orange Gatorade G Series banner emerge to take over your screen. Your favorite football player then bursts through the banner before the action settles on a stationary click-through display ad showing how some of the world's biggest sports stars use Gatorade Prime to pre-fuel their bodies before games. The action-packed "takeover" ad takes only a few seconds but delivers major impact.[12]

● **Online display advertising: Gatorade's online "takeover" ad lasts only a few seconds but delivers major impact.**

The largest form of online advertising is *search-related ads* (or *contextual advertising*), which accounted for nearly half of all online advertising spending last year. In search advertising, text- and image-based ads and links appear atop or alongside search engine results on sites such as Google, Yahoo!, and Bing. For example, search Google for "LCD TVs." At the top and side of the resulting search list, you'll see inconspicuous ads for 10 or more advertisers, ranging from Samsung and Panasonic to Best Buy, Amazon.com, Walmart.com, Crutchfield, and CDW. Ninety-six percent of Google's $50 billion in revenues last year came from ad sales. Search is an always-on kind of medium, and the results are easily measured.[13]

A search advertiser buys search terms from the search site and pays only if consumers click through to its site. For instance, type "Coke" or "Coca-Cola" or even just "soft drinks" or "rewards" into your search engine and almost without fail "My Coke Rewards" comes up as one of the top options, perhaps along with a display ad and link to Coca-Cola's official Google+ page. This is no coincidence. Coca-Cola supports its popular online loyalty program largely through search buys. The soft drink giant started first with traditional TV and print advertising but quickly learned that search was the most effective way to bring consumers to its www.mycokerewards.com Web site to register. Now, any of dozens of purchased search terms will return mycokerewards.com at or near the top of the search list.

E-Mail Marketing

E-mail marketing remains an important and growing digital marketing tool. "Social media is the hot new thing," says one observer, "but e-mail is still the king."[14] By one estimate, 91 percent of all U.S. consumers use e-mail every day. What's more, e-mail is no longer limited to PCs and workstations; 65 percent of all e-mails are now opened

E-mail marketing: Today's e-mails are colorful, inviting, personalized, and interactive, like the CVS Pharmacy "Prepare for the Scare" e-mail coupon offer.

CVS Caremark Corporation

on mobile devices. Not surprisingly, then, a recent study found that e-mail is 40 times more effective at capturing customers than Facebook and Twitter combined. Marketers sent an estimated more than 838 *billion* e-mails last year. Despite all the e-mail clutter, thanks to its low costs, e-mail marketing still brings one of the highest marketing returns on investment. According to the Direct Marketing Association, marketers get a return of $44.25 on every $1 they spend on e-mail. U.S. companies spent $2 billion on e-mail marketing last year, up from only $243 million 11 years earlier.[15]

When used properly, e-mail can be the ultimate direct marketing medium. Most blue-chip marketers use it regularly and with great success. E-mail lets these marketers send highly targeted, tightly personalized, relationship-building messages. And today's e-mails are anything but the staid, text-only messages of the past. Instead, they are colorful, inviting, personalized, and interactive. For example, one recent CVS Pharmacy e-mail, sent to the chain's ExtraCare Rewards Program members prior to Halloween, contained a colorful, attention-getting coupon offering 30 percent off an in-store purchase. Clicking the "Get Coupon" button gave customers a choice of printing the coupon or simply having it zapped onto their loyalty cards for later automatic redemption. The CVS "Prepare for the Scare" e-mail also contained a "View myWeekly Ad" button, by which ExtraCare members could link through to a Web page loaded with personalized deals based on things they buy most. Thus, the much-viewed e-mail promoted both immediate store visits and customer loyalty.

But there's a dark side to the growing use of e-mail marketing. The explosion of **spam**—unsolicited, unwanted commercial e-mail messages that clog up our e-mail boxes—has produced consumer irritation and frustration. According to one research company, spam now accounts for 70 percent of all e-mail sent worldwide.[16] E-mail marketers walk a fine line between adding value for consumers and being intrusive and annoying.

Spam
Unsolicited, unwanted commercial e-mail messages.

To address these concerns, most legitimate marketers now practice *permission-based e-mail marketing*, sending e-mail pitches only to customers who "opt in." Many companies use configurable e-mail systems that let customers choose what they want to get. Amazon.com targets opt-in customers with a limited number of helpful "we thought you'd like to know" messages based on their expressed preferences and previous purchases. Few customers object, and many actually welcome such promotional messages. Amazon.com benefits through higher return rates and by avoiding alienating customers with e-mails they don't want.

Online Videos

Another form of online marketing is posting digital video content on brand Web sites or social media sites such as YouTube, Facebook, and others. Some videos are made for the Web and social media. Such videos range from "how-to" instructional videos and public relations (PR) pieces to brand promotions and brand-related entertainment. Other videos are ads that a company makes primarily for TV and other media but posts online before or after an advertising campaign to extend their reach and impact.

Good online videos can engage consumers by the millions. The online video audience is soaring, with over 60 percent of the U.S. population now streaming video.[17] Marketers hope that some of their videos will go viral. **Viral marketing**, the digital version of word-of-mouth marketing, involves creating videos, ads, and other marketing content that is so infectious that customers will seek them out or pass them along to their friends. Because customers find and pass along the message or promotion, viral marketing can be very inexpensive. And when video or other information comes from a friend, the recipient is much more likely to view or read it.

Viral marketing
The digital version of word-of-mouth marketing: videos, ads, and other marketing content that is so infectious that customers will seek it out or pass it along to friends.

All kinds of videos can go viral, producing engagement and positive exposure for a brand. For example, in one simple but honest McDonald's video, the director of marketing at McDonald's Canada answers an online viewer's question about why McDonald's products look better in ads than in real life by conducting a behind-the-scenes tour of how a McDonald's ad is made. The award-winning 3½-minute video pulled almost 15 million views and 15,000 shares, earning the company praise for its honesty and transparency. As another example, in association with the 2012 London Olympics and 2014 Sochi Winter

Viral marketing: Kmart's TV ad-like video featuring shoppers of all ages exclaiming "ship my pants" (try saying that out loud) pulled in nearly 8 million YouTube views and 38,000 Facebook likes in only one week.

Image courtesy of Sears Brands, LLC and © 2013 Sears Brands, LLC

Olympics, P&G produced heart-warming two-minute "Proud Sponsors of Moms" videos thanking the moms who helped the athletes reach Olympic heights. Those videos garnered tens of millions of views and shares. They also formed the basis for TV ads shown during the events.[18]

At the other extreme, to promote its Shop Your Way rewards program with its free shipping benefit, Kmart posted a TV ad-like video featuring shoppers of all ages exclaiming "ship my pants" (try saying that out loud). "Ship my pants? Right here?" says one surprised shopper. "I just shipped my pants, and it's very convenient," says another. The humorous video wasn't initially aired on TV. But after it pulled in nearly 8 million YouTube views and 38,000 Facebook likes in only one week, Kmart ran the commercial on selected TV channels.[19]

Evian, called by one reporter "the master of online video," has long reaped huge viral video rewards. Evian's first viral success, a 2009 "Roller Skating Babies" ad video playing off the brand's "Live Young" positioning, became the most-viewed ad of all time—but that was then. The sequel, titled "Amazing Baby & Me," which showed adults breakdancing with baby-fied reflections of themselves in city store windows, did even better. It became the most-watched YouTube video of 2013, pulling down an amazing 139 million (and counting) views in more than 80 countries, and generating over 120,000 tweets, more than 1 million shares, and over 289,000 Facebook comments. Less than a year later, the babies were back in another Evian ad video, "Amazing Baby & Me 2," in which Spiderman suddenly encounters a baby version of himself for a dance-off in the streets of New York City. By mid-year, that Evian ad video was well on its way to becoming the most-watched YouTube video of 2014. "Our job is to tell a great brand story which creates desire," says the digital director of Danone, Evian's parent company. "Digital formats amplify that story by allowing enthusiasm and excitement to spread."[20]

However, marketers usually have little control over where their viral messages end up. They can seed content online, but that does little good unless the message itself strikes a chord with consumers. Says one creative director, "You hope that the creative is at a high enough mark where the seeds grow into mighty oaks. If they don't like it, it ain't gonna move. If they like it, it'll move a little bit; and if they love it, it's gonna move like a fast-burning fire through the Hollywood hills."[21]

Blogs and Other Online Forums

Blogs
Online journals where people and companies post their thoughts and other content, usually related to narrowly defined topics.

Brands also conduct online marketing through various digital forums that appeal to specific special-interest groups. **Blogs** (or Web logs) are online journals where people and companies post their thoughts and other content, usually related to narrowly defined topics. Blogs can be about anything, from politics or baseball to haiku, car repair, brands, or the latest television series. According to one study, there are now more than 31 million blogs in the United States. Many bloggers use social networks such as Twitter, Facebook, and Instagram to promote their blogs, giving them huge reach. Such numbers can give blogs—especially those with large and devoted followings—substantial influence.[22]

Most marketers are now tapping into the blogosphere with brand-related blogs that reach their customer communities. For example, on the Netflix Blog, members of the Netflix team (themselves rabid movie fans) tell about the latest Netflix features, share tricks for getting the most out of the Netflix experience, and collect feedback from subscribers. The Disney Parks Blog is a place to learn about and discuss all things Disney, including a Behind the Scenes area with posts about dance rehearsals, sneak peeks at new construction sites, interviews with employees, and more. Whole Foods Market's Whole Story Blog features videos, images, and posts about healthy eating, recipes, and

Most marketers are now tapping into the blogosphere as a medium for reaching their customer communities. For example, The Sharpie Blog shares all the amazing stuff people do with Sharpie markers.

Sharpie®

what's happening inside the store. Clorox's Dr. Laundry Blog discusses everything from laundry basics to removing melted crayon from children's clothes, and The Sharpie Blog shares "all the amazing stuff" that people do with Sharpie markers.

Dell has a dozen or more blogs that facilitate "a direct exchange with Dell customers about the technology that connects us all." The blogs include Direct2Dell (the official Dell corporate blog), Dell TechCenter (information technology brought into focus), DellShares (insights for investor relations), Healthcare (about the health-care technology that connects us all), and Education (insights on using technology to enhance teaching, learning, and educational administration). Dell also has a very active and successful YouTube presence that it calls DellVlog, with more than 7,000 videos and more than 52 million video views. Dell bloggers often embed these YouTube videos into blog posts.[23]

Beyond their own brand blogs, many marketers use third-party blogs to help get their messages out. For example, McDonald's systematically reaches out to key "mommy bloggers," those who influence the nation's homemakers, who in turn influence their families' eating-out choices:[24]

> McDonald's recently hosted 15 bloggers on an all-expenses-paid tour of its headquarters in Oak Brook, Illinois. The bloggers toured the facilities (including the company's test kitchens), met McDonald's USA president, and had their pictures taken with Ronald at a nearby Ronald McDonald House. McDonald's knows that these mommy bloggers are very important. They have loyal followings and talk a lot about McDonald's in their blogs. So McDonald's is turning the bloggers into believers by giving them a behind-the-scenes view. McDonald's doesn't try to tell the bloggers what to say in their posts about the visit. It simply asks them to write one honest recap of their trip. However, the resulting posts (each acknowledging the blogger's connection with McDonald's) were mostly very positive. Thanks to this and many other such efforts, mommy bloggers around the country are now more informed about and connected with McDonald's. "I know they have smoothies and they have yogurt and they have other things that my kids would want," says one prominent blogger. "I really couldn't tell you what Burger King's doing right now," she adds. "I have no idea."

As a marketing tool, blogs offer some advantages. They can offer a fresh, original, personal, and cheap way to enter into consumer online and social media conversations. However, the blogosphere is cluttered and difficult to control. And although companies can sometimes leverage blogs to engage customers in meaningful relationships, blogs remain largely a consumer-controlled medium. Whether or not they actively participate in the blogs, companies should monitor and listen to them. Marketers can use insights from consumer online conversations to improve their marketing programs.

Social media
Independent and commercial online communities where people congregate, socialize, and exchange views and information.

Author Comment | As in about every other area of our lives, social media and mobile technologies have taken the marketing world by storm. They offer some amazing marketing possibilities. But truth be told, many marketers are still sweating over how to use them most effectively.

Social Media Marketing

As we've discussed throughout the text so far, the surge in Internet usage and digital technologies and devices has spawned a dazzling array of online **social media** and digital communities. Countless independent and commercial social networks have arisen that give consumers online places to congregate, socialize, and exchange views and information. These days, it seems, almost everyone is buddying up on Facebook or Google+, checking in with Twitter, tuning into the day's hottest videos at YouTube, pinning images on social scrapbooking site Pinterest, or sharing photos with Instagram and Snapchat. And, of course, wherever consumers congregate, marketers will surely follow. Most marketers are now riding the huge social media wave. According to one survey, nearly 90 percent of U.S. companies now use social media networks as part of their marketing mixes.[25]

Using Social Media

Marketers can engage in social media in two ways: They can use existing social media or they can set up their own. Using existing social media seems the easiest. Thus, most brands—large and small—have set up shop on a host of social media sites. Check the Web sites of brands ranging from Coca-Cola and Nike to Victoria's Secret or even the NFL's San Francisco 49ers and you'll find links to each brand's Facebook, Google+, Twitter, YouTube, Flickr, Instagram, or other social media pages. Such social media can create substantial brand communities. For example, the 49ers have 2.9 million Facebook fans; Coca-Cola has an eye-popping 80 million fans.

Some of the major social networks are huge. More than 1.2 billion people access Facebook every month, 3.4 times the combined populations of the United States and Canada. Similarly, Twitter has more than 645 million registered users, and more than 1 billion unique users visit YouTube monthly, watching more than 6 billion hours of video. The list goes on: Google+ has 400 million active users, LinkedIn 240 million, and Pinterest 70 million.[26]

Although these large social media networks grab most of the headlines, countless niche social media have also emerged. Niche online social networks cater to the needs of smaller communities of like-minded people, making them ideal vehicles for marketers who want to target special interest groups. There's at least one social media network for just about every interest, hobby, or group. Kaboodle.com is for shopaholics, whereas moms share advice and commiseration at CafeMom.com. GoFISHn, a Facebook community of 4,000 anglers, features maps that pinpoint where fish are biting and a photo gallery where members can show off their catches. FarmersOnly.com provides online dating for down-to-earth "country folks" who enjoy "blue skies, living free and at peace in wide open spaces, raising animals, and appreciating nature"—"because city folks just don't get it." At Birdpost.com, avid bird watchers can keep an online list of birds they've seen and share bird sightings with other members using modern satellite maps. And myTransponder.com is a Facebook community where pilots find work, students locate flight instructors, and trade-specific advertisers hone in on a hard-to-reach audience of more than 2,000 people who love aviation.[27]

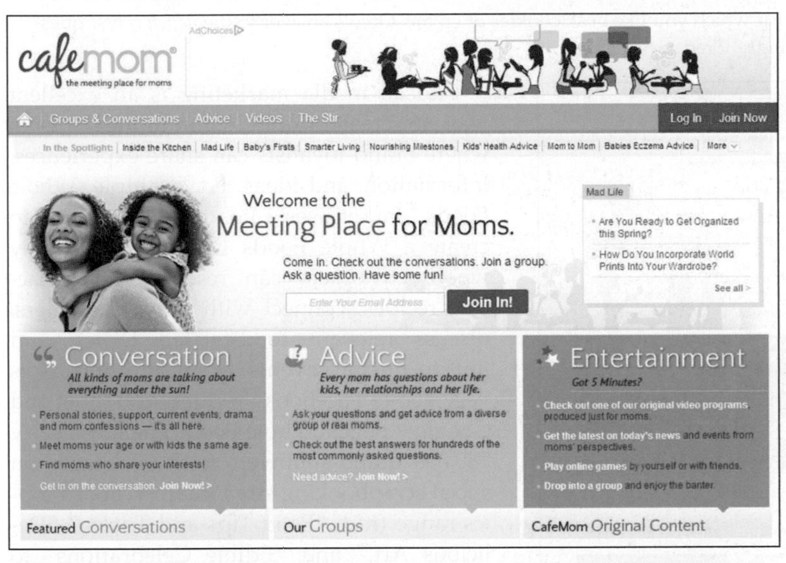

Countless niche social media have emerged, catering to needs of smaller communities of like-minded people. CafeMom is a "Meeting Place for Moms," where they can share conversations, advice, and entertainment.

CafeMom.com

Beyond these independent social media, many companies have created their own online brand communities. For example, in Nike's Nike+ running community—consisting of more than 20 million runners who together have logged more than 1 billion running miles worldwide—members join together online to upload, track, and compare their performances. Due to its success, Nike has expanded Nike+ to both basketball and general training, each with its own unique community site, app, and corresponding products.[28]

Social Media Marketing Advantages and Challenges

Using social media presents both advantages and challenges. On the plus side, social media are *targeted* and *personal*—they allow marketers to create and share tailored brand content with individual consumers and customer communities. Social media are *interactive*, making them ideal for starting and participating in customer conversations and listening to customer feedback. For example, Volvo uses its #Swedespeak Tweetchat platform as a kind of digital focus group to engage customers and obtain immediate input on everything from product features to creating ads. The regular Twitter chats are "creating good conversations," says Volvo's head marketer. "People enjoy being part of [the process]."[29]

Social media are also *immediate* and *timely*. They can be used to reach customers anytime, anywhere with timely and relevant marketing content regarding brand happenings and activities. As discussed earlier in the chapter, the rapid growth in social media usage has caused a surge in *real-time marketing*, allowing marketers to create and join consumer conversations around situations and events as they occur. Marketers can now watch what's trending and create content to match.

Social media can be very *cost effective*. Although creating and administering social media content can be costly, many social media are free or inexpensive to use. Thus, returns on social media investments are often high compared with those of expensive traditional media such as television or print. The low cost of social media puts them within easy reach of even small businesses and brands that can't afford the high costs of big-budget marketing campaigns.

Perhaps the biggest advantage of social media is their *engagement and social sharing capabilities*. Social media are especially well suited to creating customer engagement and community—for getting customers involved with the brand and with each other. More than any other channels, social media can involve customers in shaping and sharing brand content and experiences. Consider the recent Oreo Cookies vs. Crème Instagram campaign:[30]

> The two-month Oreo Cookies vs. Crème campaign began with a Super Bowl XLVII ad called "Whisper Fight," in which two men argued in a library over which part of an Oreo cookie they like best—the cookies or the crème. The ad invited consumers to take sides by posting photos they love on social scrapbooking site Instagram with the hashtag #cookiethis or #cremethis. Oreo then selected a number of the photos and worked with artists to create sculptures of the photos made of either cookies or crème. The campaign really got people buzzing about what they like best about Oreos. Prior to the Super Bowl airing, Oreo had about 2,200 Instagram followers. Immediately following the game, that number had jumped to about 22,000 followers and is now up to more than 142,000. The contest yielded nearly 32,000 fan submissions and 122 sculptures. More than just launching an Instagram page, Oreo launched "an engagement experience," says an Oreo brand manager. Oreo wrapped up the campaign with a series of short, funny online videos accessed by submitting votes for which you like best: cookies or crème. Oreo's answer to the *which is best* question? Not surprisingly, Oreo says it's both.

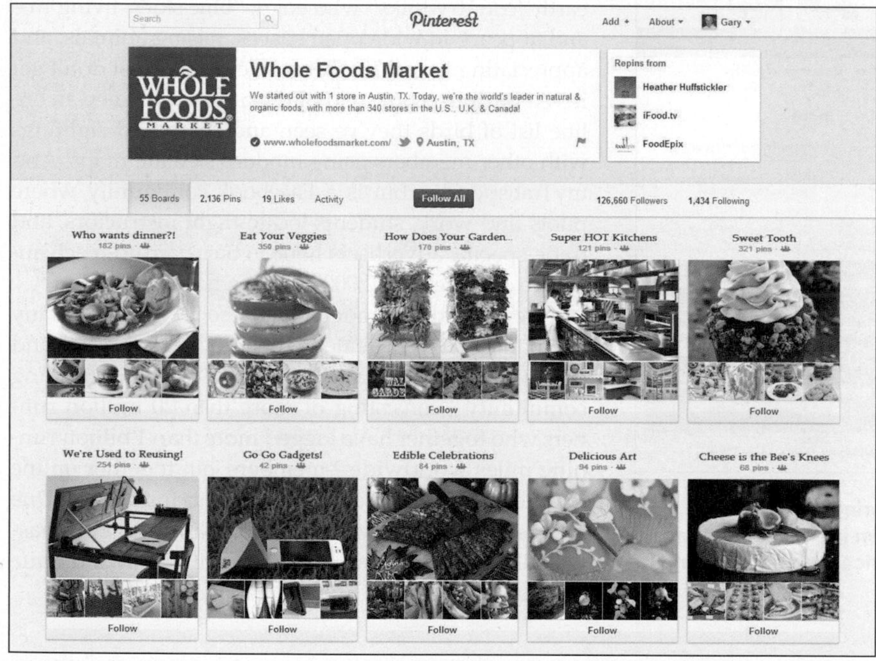

Whole Foods Market uses a host of social media to create a Whole Foods lifestyle community. For example, it engages nearly 120,000 brand followers with 46 boards on social scrapbooking site Pinterest.

Courtesy of Whole Foods Market. "Whole Foods Market" is a registered trademark of Whole Foods Market IP, L.P.

Social media marketing is an excellent way to create brand communities, places where brand loyalists can share experiences, information, and ideas. For example, Whole Foods Market uses a host of social media to create a Whole Foods lifestyle community where customers can research foods, access recipes, connect with other customers, discuss relevant food-related topics, and link to in-store events. In addition to its very active Facebook, Twitter, YouTube, and Google+ pages, Whole Foods engages nearly 180,000 brand followers with 59 boards on social scrapbooking site Pinterest. Board topics range from "Food Tips and Tricks," "Delicious Art," and "Edible Celebrations" to Super HOT Kitchens, which is loaded with pictures of captivating kitchens. Whole Foods isn't in the kitchen remodeling business, but cooking and kitchens are a big part of the Whole Foods customer lifestyle.[31]

Social media marketing also presents challenges. First, many companies are still experimenting with how to use them effectively, and results are hard to measure. Second, such social networks are largely user controlled. The company's goal in using social media is to make the brand a part of consumers' conversations and their lives. However, marketers can't simply muscle their way into consumers' digital interactions—they need to earn the right to be there. Rather than intruding, marketers must become a valued part of the online experience by developing a steady flow of engaging content.

Because consumers have so much control over social media content, even the seemingly most harmless social media campaign can backfire. For example, Frito-Lay recently launched a Do Us a Flavor contest, in which it asked people to come up with new potato chip flavors, submit them to its Web or Facebook site, and design bag art for their creations. Many consumers took the contest (and the $1 million grand prize) seriously, submitting flavors that people would truly want to eat. However, others hijacked the contest by submitting sometimes hilarious but completely bogus flavors, ranging from Crunchy Frog and Blue Cheese, Toothpaste and Orange Juice, 7th Grade Locker Room, and Bandaid in a Public Pool to Anthrax Ripple and "90% Air and Like 4 Chips." Unfortunately, for each submission, no matter how bogus, the Web site responded cheerfully with a colorful rendition of the bag and flavor name, along with a message like the following: "7th Grade Locker Room? That does sound yummy as a chip! Keep those tasty ideas coming for your next chance to win $1 million." With social media, "you're going into the consumer's backyard. This is their place," warns one social marketer. "Social media is a pressure cooker," says another. "The hundreds of thousands, or millions, of people out there are going to take your idea, and they're going to try to shred it or tear it apart and find what's weak or stupid in it."[32]

Integrated Social Media Marketing

Using social media might be as simple as posting some messages and promotions on a brand's Facebook or Twitter pages or creating brand buzz with videos or images on YouTube or Pinterest. However, most large companies are now designing full-scale social media efforts that blend with and support other elements of a brand's marketing strategy and tactics. More than making scattered efforts and chasing "Likes" and tweets, companies that use social media successfully are integrating a broad range of diverse media to create brand-related social sharing, engagement, and customer community.

Managing a brand's social media efforts can be a major undertaking. For example, Starbucks, one of the most successful social media marketers, manages 51 Facebook pages (including 43 in other countries); 31 Twitter handles (19 of them international); 22 Instagram names (14 international); plus Google+, Pinterest, YouTube, and Foursquare accounts. Managing and integrating all that social media content is challenging, but the results are worth the investment. Customers can engage with Starbucks digitally without ever setting foot in a store—and engage they do. With more than 36 million fans on its main U.S. page alone, Starbucks is the sixth-largest brand on Facebook. It ranks fifth on Twitter with 88.5 million followers.

But more than just creating online engagement and community, Starbucks' social media presence also drives customer into its stores. For example, in its first big social media promotion four years ago, Starbucks offered a free pastry with a morning drink purchase. A million people showed up. Its more recent "Tweet-a-Coffee" promotion, which let customers give a $5 gift card to a friend by putting both #tweetacoffee and the friend's handle in a tweet, resulted in $180,000 in purchases within little more than one month. Social media "are not just about engaging and telling a story and connecting," says Starbucks' head of global digital marketing. "They can have a material impact on the business."[33]

Mobile Marketing

Mobile marketing
Marketing messages, promotions, and other content delivered to on-the-go consumers through mobile phones, smartphones, tablets, and other mobile devices.

Mobile marketing features marketing messages, promotions, and other marketing content delivered to on-the-go consumers through their mobile devices. Marketers use mobile marketing to engage customers anywhere, anytime during the buying and relationship-building processes. The widespread adoption of mobile devices and the surge in mobile Web traffic have made mobile marketing a must for most brands.

With the recent proliferation of mobile phones, smartphones, and tablets, mobile device penetration is now greater than 100 percent in the United States (many people possess more than one mobile device). Almost 40 percent of U.S. households are currently mobile-only households with no landline phone. More than 65 percent of people in the United States own a smartphone, and over 60 percent of smartphone users use it to access the mobile Internet. They not only browse the mobile Internet but are also avid mobile app users. The mobile apps market has exploded globally: There are more than 2 million apps available and the average smartphone has 25 apps installed on it.[34]

Most people love their phones and rely heavily on them. According to one study, nearly 90 percent of consumers who own smartphones, tablets, computers, and TVs would give up all of those other screens before giving up their phones. On average, Americans check their phones 150 times a day—once every six-and-one-half minutes—and spend 58 minutes a day on their smartphones talking, texting, and visiting Web sites. Thus, although TV is still a big part of people's lives, mobile is rapidly becoming their "first screen." Away from home, it's their only screen.[35]

For consumers, a smartphone or tablet can be a handy shopping companion. It can provide on-the-go product information, price comparisons, advice and reviews from other consumers, and access to instant deals and digital coupons. Not surprisingly, then, mobile devices provide a rich platform for engaging consumers more deeply as they move through the buying process with tools ranging from mobile ads, coupons, and texts to apps and mobile Web sites.

Mobile advertising spending in the United States is surging; it more than doubled last year alone and is expected to double again by 2014. Almost every major marketer—from P&G and Macy's to your local bank or supermarket to nonprofits such as the ASPCA—is now integrating mobile marketing into its direct marketing programs. Such efforts can produce very positive outcomes. For example, 49 percent of mobile users search for more information after seeing a mobile ad.[36]

Companies use mobile marketing to stimulate immediate buying, make shopping easier, enrich the brand experience, or all of these. It lets marketers provide consumers with information, incentives, and choices at the moment they are expressing an interest or when they are in a position to make a buying choice. For example, McDonald's uses mobile marketing to promote new menu items, announce special promotions, and drive immediate traffic at its restaurants. One recent interactive ad on Pandora's mobile app read "Taste buds. Any size soft drink or sweet tea for $1. Tap to visit site." A tap on the mobile ad took customers to a mobile site promoting McDonald's ongoing summer promotion. Another McDonald's mobile campaign used a word scrabble game to entice customers to try the fast feeder's dollar menu items. Such efforts create both customer engagement and store traffic. Using a game "inside a mobile campaign is all about finding and maintaining engagement," says a McDonald's marketer.[37]

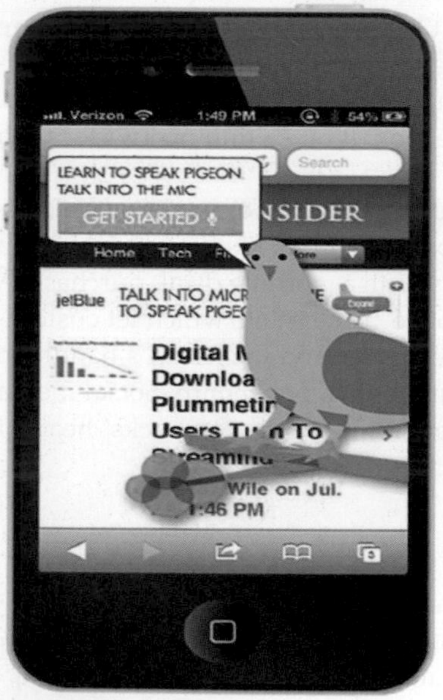

Today's rich-media mobile ads can create substantial engagement and impact. For example, JetBlue recently created a voice-activated mobile ad that interacts with customers and talks back. It starts with a JetBlue mobile banner ad that says, "Click here to learn how to speak pigeon." A click expands the ad, which then instructs users by voice to repeat words on the screen, such as "coo, coo, coo." When they've completed two full sentences in pigeon, users receive a virtual medal and the option to play again. Hitting "Learn more" takes users to the JetBlue Landing Perch, where they can explore and send messages to friends via digital carrier pigeons. The mobile ad is part of JetBlue's "Air on the Side of Humanity" campaign, which features pigeons—the ultimate frequent fliers. Rather than making direct sales pitches, the voice ad aims simply to enrich the JetBlue experience. The airline hopes people will "watch the ads, play with the pigeons, and remember us when they want to book tickets," says JetBlue's advertising manager.[38]

Mobile marketing: Today's rich media mobile ads can create substantial engagement. This voice-activated JetBlue mobile ad interacts with customers and talks back.

JetBlue Airways

Retailers can use mobile marketing to enrich the customer's shopping experience at the same time that they stimulate buying. For example, Macy's built its recent "Brasil: A Magical Journey" promotion around a popular and imaginative smartphone app. The campaign featured apparel from Brazilian designers and in-store experiences celebrating Brazilian culture. By using their smartphones to scan codes throughout the store, shoppers could learn about featured fashions and experience Brazilian culture through virtual tours, such as a trip to the Amazon, a visit to Rio de Janeiro during Carnival, or attending a Brazilian soccer match. "Mobile ads aim for 'of-the-moment' targeting, anywhere and everywhere," says one expert, whether it's at the time of a mobile search or in a store during the purchase decision.[39]

Many marketers have created their own mobile online sites, optimized for specific phones and mobile service providers. Others have created useful or entertaining mobile apps to engage customers with their brands and help them shop (see Real Marketing 17.2). For example, Clorox offers a myStain app that targets young moms with useful on-the-go stain removal solutions. Schwab offers "Schwab to Go," a mobile app that lets customers get up-to-the-minute investment news, monitor their accounts, and make trades at any time from any location. And Starbucks' mobile app lets customers use their phones as a Starbucks card to make fast and easy purchases.

As with other forms of direct marketing, however, companies must use mobile marketing responsibly or risk angering already ad-weary consumers. Most people don't want to be interrupted regularly by advertising, so marketers must be smart about how they engage people on mobiles. The key is to provide genuinely useful information and offers that will make consumers want to engage. And many marketers target mobile ads on an opt-in-only basis.

Real Marketing 17.2

Mobile Marketing: Smartphones Are Changing How People Live—and How They Buy

Armed only with a smartphone or other mobile device, you can learn, do, or buy almost anything these days, from anywhere, and at any time. Zipcar's app lets you find and reserve a Zipcar, honk the horn (so you can find it in a crowd), and even lock and unlock the doors—all from your phone. Tide's Stain Brain app helps you find ways to remove stains while out and about, and a Charmin-sponsored Sit or Squat app directs you to nearby public restrooms. REI's The Snow Report app gives you ski slope information for locations throughout the United States and Canada, such as snow conditions and the number of open lifts. The app even helps you share resort information with friends via Twitter and Facebook, and it links you to "Shop REI" for times "when you decide you can't live without a new set of K2 skis or a two-man Hubba Hubba tent." And with MasterCard's PayPass app, you can pay instantly and securely with your phone at any participating retailer—just "tap, pay, and be on your way."

Welcome to the world of mobile marketing. Today's smartphones and other mobile devices are changing how people live, becoming indispensable hubs for communication, information, and entertainment. They are also revolutionizing the way people shop and buy, giving marketers new opportunities to engage customers in more effective and satisfying ways.

Marketers are responding to the huge growth in mobile access and use. Mobile ad spending jumped 105 percent last year and is expected to triple in the next three years. And the mobile app market has outright exploded. Just five years ago, Apple's App Store had a then-astounding 10,000 apps. But by last year, Apple's App Store and Android's Google Play had topped one million apps each. Mobile has become today's brave new marketing frontier, especially for brands courting younger consumers. Mobile devices are very personal, ever-present, and always on. That makes them an ideal medium for obtaining quick responses to individualized, time-sensitive offers,

Some marketers are still just warming up to mobile, and most are still learning how to use it effectively. Successful mobile marketing goes beyond just giving people a coupon and a link to buy. Instead, it enhances brand engagement and creates a "frictionless" buying experience. For example, with Amazon's mobile app—thanks to "1-click" purchasing, Prime membership, and other features—customers located anywhere, anytime can have products delivered to practically any location in less than 24 hours with nothing more than a smartphone, a simple search or scan, and the click of a button.

Consumers have come to expect such frictionless mobile buying experiences from marketing giants like Amazon. But with recent rapid advances in mobile capabilities, from location-based technologies to mobile payment systems, more and more companies are becoming the Amazons of their industries. Consider mobile app-based car dispatch service Uber.

> For anyone who travels or grabs a cab regularly, Uber is the next-best thing to *Star Trek's* "Beam me up Scotty." Imagine finding yourself in a strange city, late at night, having just bid farewell to some new friends who introduced you to the city's hottest nightclub. Alone at the curb late on a rainy Saturday night, you're suddenly aware that you don't know exactly where you are, and there's not an unoccupied cab within hailing distance. No problem. You open your Uber app and with a few swipes, everything is arranged. Uber summons the nearest available cab, tells it where you're located (thanks to your phone's GPS), and even gives the driver a description of you based on your preset preferences. Within moments, a cab picks you up, and when it drops you off at your hotel, you just get out and walk away. The cab company bills Uber, freeing you from the hassle of fumbling for cash or a credit card and waiting to sign a receipt.

Mobile marketing can do much more than simply ease the buying process. It can also take ads, coupons, and other promotions to new levels. Mobile marketers can personalize promotions and weave them into relevant everyday customer experiences. For example, Kiip, a mobile reward network, specializes in helping brands provide customers with just the right reward at just the right time based on their everyday activities. The agency started by embedding its technology into video game apps such as Zombie Farm and Mega Jump. Gamers who reach a new game level or meet some other goal get a coupon to one of their favorite retailers, such as American Apparel.

Kiip now boasts a network of 2,500 apps and 60 million users across games, fitness, productivity, music, and cooking categories. Its client list includes the likes of McDonald's, Pepsi, Unilever, P&G, and American Express. For fitness apps like MapMyRun and productivity apps like Any.do, Kiip ties rewards to real-life achievements. When users cross things off their to-do lists or achieve a running goal, they get a reward from a relevant brand. For example, P&G's Secret deodorant recently rewarded female MapMyRun users with free song downloads for their workout playlists. And snack giant Mondelēz rewarded

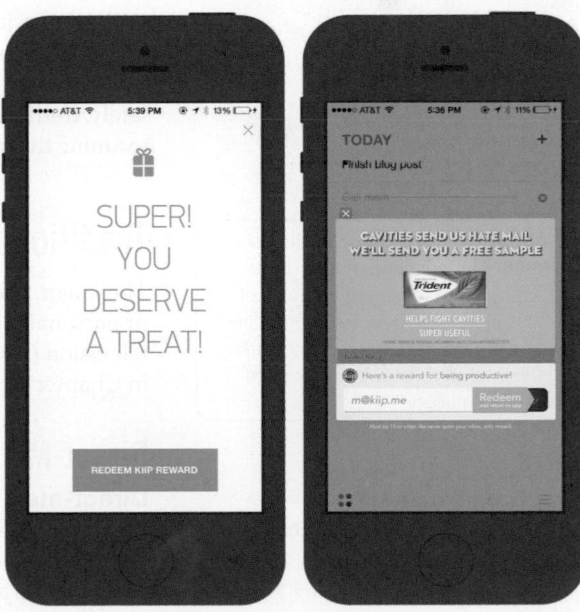

Mobile marketing: Mobile promotions agency Kiip helps client brands link mobile offers to relevant customer experiences and positive moments. "We want to capitalize on happiness," says Kiip's CEO. "Everything's better when you're happy."

Kiip, Inc.

Any.do users with free packs of Trident when they set new personal records.

Kiip helps marketers reach targeted users at positive moments with rewards relevant to their doings and accomplishments. Readers who finish a certain number of pages in a reading app receive a free magazine subscription. People using a couple's app to stay in touch receive credits toward a purchase from 1-800-Flowers. Kiip is even working with connected-car company Mojio, whose 4G telematic device plugs into a car's diagnostic port, tracks information about the car's status, and keeps the owner connected to favorite people, places, and things. Through Mojio, Kiip helps clients—from insurance companies and car repair shops to parking meter and garage operators—provide rewards tied to specific driver locations and behaviors.

Unlike typical banner ads, pop-ups, or e-mails, Kiip offers enhance a user's regular activities rather than interrupting them. According to Kiip's founder and CEO, Kiip "is less about real-time marketing and more about real-time-needs addressing." In fact, he asserts, Kiip isn't really in the mobile ad business at all—it's in the happiness business. "We want to capitalize on happiness," he says. "Everything's better when you're happy." Mobile timeliness, relevance, and happiness pay off in terms of consumer response. Users redeem Kiip's mobile promotions at a 22-percent clip, compared to the 0.3 percent for typical app ad engagement. Kiip's offers also increase mobile app revisits by 30 percent and more than double average app length-of-use.

Many consumers are initially skeptical about mobile marketing. But they often change their minds if mobile offers deliver useful brand and shopping information, entertaining content, or timely coupons and discounted prices. Most mobile efforts target only consumers who voluntarily opt in or download apps. In the increasingly cluttered mobile marketing space, customers just won't do that unless they see real value in it. The challenge for marketers: Develop valued mobile offers, ads, and apps that make customers come calling.

Sources: David Murphy, "It's All about the Experience," *Mobile Marketing*, April 24, 2014, http://mobilemarketingmagazine.com/gc-testbirds-april14; Lindsay Harrison, "Kiip: For Making Mobile Ads that People Want," *Fast Company*, February 11, 2013, www.fastcompany.com/most-innovative-companies/2013/kiip; Christina Chaey, "How Kiip Ties Brand Rewards to Game and Life Achievements to Make Mobile Ads Engaging," *Fastcocreate*, July 23, 2012, www.fastcocreate.com/1681287; Aaron Strout, "Frictionless Mobile Commerce: Five Examples of Companies that Are Leading," *Marketing Land*, May 1, 2014, http://marketingland.com/frictionless-commerce-5-examples-companies-leading-81351; Neil Undgerleider, "Advertisers Are about to Enter Your Connected Car," *Fast Company*, April 11, 2014, www.fastcompany.com/3028744/most-innovative-companies/advertisers-are-about-to-enter-your-connected-car; and www.kiip.com/me, access September 2014.

In all, digital direct marketing—online, social media, and mobile marketing—offers both great promise and many challenges for the future. Its most ardent apostles still envision a time when the Internet and digital marketing will replace magazines, newspapers, and even stores as sources for information, engagement, and buying. Most marketers, however, hold a more realistic view. For most companies, digital and social media marketing will remain just one important approach to the marketplace that works alongside other approaches in a fully integrated marketing mix.

Although the fast-growing digital marketing tools have grabbed most of the headlines lately, traditional direct marketing tools are very much alive and still heavily used. We now examine the traditional direct marketing approaches shown on the right side of Figure 17.1.

Author Comment | Again, although online, social media, and mobile direct marketing seem to be getting much of the attention these days, traditional direct media still carry a lot of the direct marketing freight. Just think about your often overstuffed mailbox.

Traditional Direct Marketing Forms

The major traditional forms of direct marketing—as shown in Figure 17.1—are face-to-face or personal selling, direct-mail marketing, catalog marketing, telemarketing, direct-response television (DRTV) marketing, and kiosk marketing. We examined personal selling in depth in Chapter 16. Here, we look into the other forms of traditional direct marketing.

Direct-Mail Marketing

Direct-mail marketing
Marketing that occurs by sending an offer, announcement, reminder, or other item directly to a person at a particular address.

Direct-mail marketing involves sending an offer, announcement, reminder, or other item to a person at a particular address. Using highly selective mailing lists, direct marketers send out millions of mail pieces each year—letters, catalogs, ads, brochures, samples, videos, and other "salespeople with wings." U.S. marketers spent an estimated more than $45 billion on direct mail last year (including both catalog and noncatalog mail), which accounted for 30 percent of all direct marketing spending and generated 31 percent of all direct marketing sales. According to the DMA, every dollar spent on direct mail generates $12.57 in sales.[40]

Direct mail is well suited to direct, one-to-one communication. It permits high target-market selectivity, can be personalized, is flexible, and allows the easy measurement of results. Although direct mail costs more per thousand people reached than mass media such as television or magazines, the people it reaches are much better prospects. Direct mail has proved successful in promoting all kinds of products, from books, insurance, travel, gift items, gourmet foods, clothing, and other consumer goods to industrial products of all kinds. Charities also use direct mail heavily to raise billions of dollars each year.

Some analysts predict a decline in the use of traditional forms of direct mail in the coming years, as marketers switch to newer digital forms, such as e-mail and online marketing, social media marketing, and mobile marketing. The newer digital direct marketing approaches deliver messages at incredible speeds and lower costs compared to the U.S. Post Office's "snail mail" pace.

However, even though new digital forms of direct marketing are bursting onto the scene, traditional direct mail is still heavily used by most marketers. Mail marketing offers some distinct advantages over digital forms. It provides something tangible for people to hold and keep and it can be used to send samples. "Mail makes it real," says one analyst. It "creates an emotional connection with customers that digital cannot. They hold it, view it, and engage with it in a manner entirely different from their [digital] experiences." In contrast, e-mail and other digital forms are easily filtered or trashed. "[With] spam filters and spam folders to keep our messaging away from consumers' inboxes," says a direct marketer, "sometimes you have to lick a few stamps."[41]

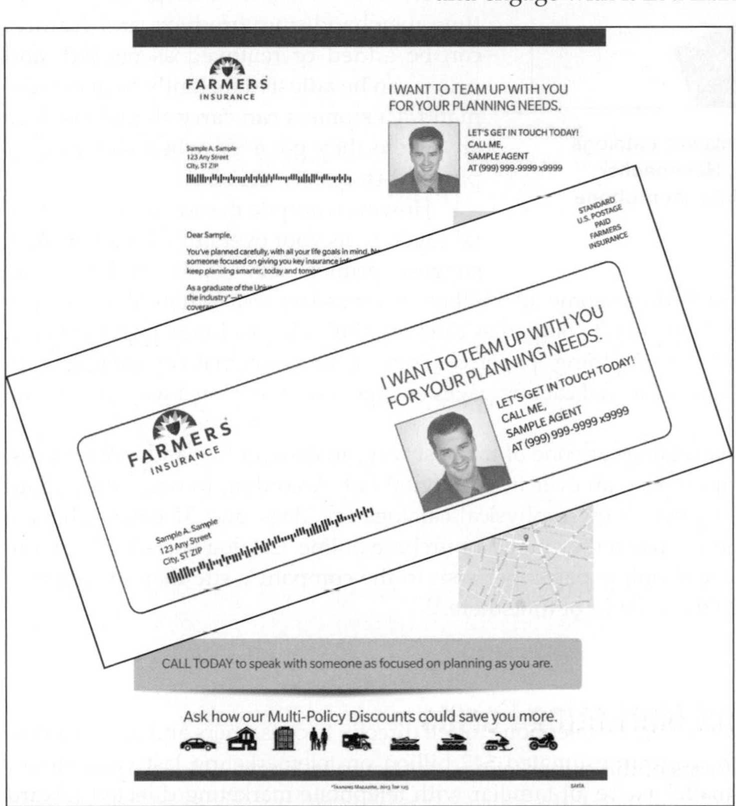

Direct mail marketing: Insurance companies like Farmers Insurance rely heavily on TV advertising to establish broad customer awareness. However, they also use lots of good old direct mail to communicate with consumers in a more direct and personalized way.

Farmers Insurance

Traditional direct mail can be an effective component of a broader integrated marketing campaign. For example, most large insurance companies rely heavily on TV advertising to establish broad customer awareness and positioning. However, the insurance companies also use lots of good old direct mail to break through the glut of insurance advertising on TV. Whereas TV advertising talks to broad audiences, direct mail communicates in a more direct and personal way. "Mail is a channel that allows all of us to find the consumer with a very targeted, very specific message that you can't do in broadcast," says Bill Fournell, head of agency marketing for Farmers Insurance. And "most people are still amenable to getting marketing communications in their mailbox, which is why I think direct mail will grow."[42]

Direct mail may be resented as *junk mail* if sent to people who have no interest in it. For this reason, smart marketers are targeting their direct mail carefully so as not to waste their money and recipients' time. They are designing permission-based programs that send direct mail only to those who want to receive it.

Catalog Marketing

Catalog marketing
Direct marketing through print, video, or digital catalogs that are mailed to select customers, made available in stores, or presented online.

Advances in technology, along with the move toward personalized, one-to-one marketing, have resulted in exciting changes in **catalog marketing**. *Catalog Age* magazine used to define a *catalog* as "a printed, bound piece of at least eight pages, selling multiple products, and offering a direct ordering mechanism." Today, this definition is sadly out of date.

With the stampede to the Internet and digital marketing, more and more catalogs are going digital. A variety of online-only catalogers have emerged, and most print catalogers have added Web-based catalogs and smartphone catalog shopping apps to their marketing mixes.

Digital catalogs: Apps such as Catalog Spree put a mall full of classic catalogs from retailers such as Macy's, Best Buy, Anthropologie, L.L. Bean, Hammacher Schlemmer, or Coldwater Creek only a swipe of the finger away on a smartphone or tablet.

Catalog Spree, the #1 catalog shopping app for the iPad and iPhone. www.catalogspree.com

For example, apps such as Catalog Spree put a mall full of classic catalogs from retailers such as Macy's, Anthropologie, L.L. Bean, Hammacher Schlemmer, Coldwater Creek, or West Elm only a swipe of the finger away on a smartphone or tablet. And days before the latest Lands' End catalog arrives in the mail, customers can access it digitally at landsend.com, at social media outlets such as Facebook, or via the Lands' End mobile app. With Lands' End Mobile, says the company, "You're carrying every item we carry."[43]

Digital catalogs eliminate printing and mailing costs. And whereas space is limited in a print catalog, online catalogs can offer an almost unlimited amount of merchandise. They also offer a broader assortment of presentation formats, including search and video. Finally, online catalogs allow real-time merchandising; products and features can be added or removed as needed, and prices can be adjusted instantly to match demand. Customers can carry digital catalogs anywhere they go, even when shopping at physical stores.

However, despite the advantages of digital catalogs, as your overstuffed mailbox may suggest, printed catalogs are still thriving. U.S. direct marketers mailed out some 12.5 billion catalogs last year—more than 100 per American household.[44] Why aren't companies ditching their old-fashioned paper catalogs in this new digital era? For one thing, paper catalogs create emotional connections with customers. Somehow, turning actual catalog pages engages consumers in a way that digital images simply can't.

In addition, printed catalogs are one of the best ways to drive online and mobile sales, making them more important than ever in the digital era. According to one study, about 58 percent of online shoppers browse physical catalogs for ideas, and 31 percent have a retailer's catalog with them when they make a purchase online. Catalog users look at more than double the number of online pages per visit to the company's site than the average visitor and spend twice the amount of time there.[45]

Telemarketing

Telemarketing
Using the telephone to sell directly to customers.

Telemarketing involves using the telephone to sell directly to consumers and business customers. U.S. marketers spent an estimated $42 billion on telemarketing last year, almost as much as on direct mail.[46] We're all familiar with telephone marketing directed toward consumers, but business-to-business (B-to-B) marketers also use telemarketing extensively. Marketers use *outbound* telephone marketing to sell directly to consumers and businesses. They also use *inbound* toll-free numbers to receive orders from television and print ads, direct mail, or catalogs.

Properly designed and targeted telemarketing provides many benefits, including purchasing convenience and increased product and service information. However, the explosion in unsolicited outbound telephone marketing over the years annoyed many consumers, who objected to the almost daily "junk phone calls." In 2003, U.S. lawmakers responded with the National Do Not Call Registry, which is managed by the Federal Trade Commission (FTC). The legislation bans most telemarketing calls to registered phone numbers (although people can still receive calls from nonprofit groups, politicians, and companies with which they have recently done business). Consumers responded enthusiastically. To date, more than 221 million home and mobile phone numbers have been registered at www.donotcall.gov or by calling 888-382-1222.[47] Businesses that break do-not-call laws can be fined up to $16,000 per violation. As a result, the program has been very successful.

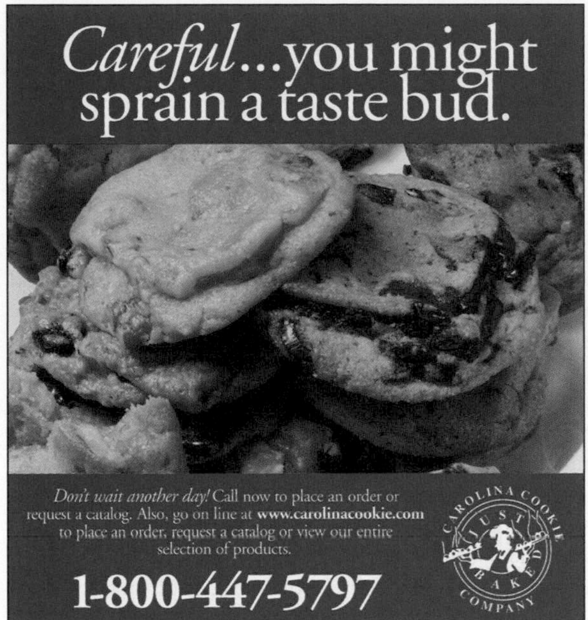

Careful...you might sprain a taste bud.
Don't wait another day! Call now to place an order or request a catalog. Also, go on line at www.carolinacookie.com to place an order, request a catalog or view our entire selection of products.
1-800-447-5797
CAROLINA COOKIE
JUST BAKED
COMPANY

Marketers use inbound toll-free 800 numbers to receive orders from television and print ads, direct mail, or catalogs. Here, the Carolina Cookie Company urges, "Don't wait another day. Call now to place an order or request a catalog."

Carolina Cookie Company

Do-not-call legislation has hurt parts of the consumer telemarketing industry. However, two major forms of telemarketing—inbound consumer telemarketing and outbound B-to-B telemarketing—remain strong and growing. Telemarketing also remains a major fundraising tool for nonprofit and political groups. Interestingly, do-not-call regulations appear to be helping some direct marketers more than it's hurting them. Rather than making unwanted calls, many of these marketers are developing "opt-in" calling systems, in which they provide useful information and offers to customers who have invited the company to contact them by phone or e-mail. The opt-in model provides better returns for marketers than the formerly invasive one.

Direct-Response Television Marketing

Direct-response television (DRTV) marketing takes one of two major forms: direct-response television advertising and interactive TV (iTV) advertising. Using *direct-response television advertising*, direct marketers air television spots, often 60 or 120 seconds in length, which persuasively describe a product and give customers a toll-free number or an online site for ordering. It also includes full 30-minute or longer advertising programs, called *infomercials*, for a single product.

Direct-response television (DRTV) marketing
Direct marketing via television, including direct-response television advertising (or infomercials) and interactive television (iTV) advertising.

Successful direct-response television advertising campaigns can ring up big sales. For example, little-known infomercial maker Guthy-Renker has helped propel its Proactiv Solution acne treatment and other "transformational" products into power brands that pull in $1.8 billion in sales annually to 5 million active customers (compare that to only about $150 million in annual drugstore sales of acne products in the United States). Guthy-Renker now combines DRTV with social media campaigns using Facebook, Pinterest, Google+, Twitter, and YouTube to create a powerful integrated direct marketing channel that builds consumer involvement and buying.[48]

DRTV ads are often associated with somewhat loud or questionable pitches for cleaners, stain removers, kitchen gadgets, and nifty ways to stay in shape without working very hard at it. For example, over the past few years yell-and-sell TV pitchmen like Anthony Sullivan (Swivel Sweeper, Awesome Auger) and Vince Offer (ShamWow, SlapChop) have racked up billions of dollars in sales of "As Seen on TV" products. Brands like OxiClean, ShamWow, and the Snuggie (a blanket with sleeves) have become DRTV cult classics. And direct marketer Beachbody brings in more than $32 million annually via an army of workout videos—from P90X and T-25 to Insanity and Hip Hop Abs—that it advertises on TV using before and after stories, clips of the workout, and words of encouragement from the creators.

In recent years, however, a number of large companies—from P&G, Disney, Revlon, and Apple to Toyota, Coca-Cola, Anheuser-Busch, and even the U.S. Navy—have begun using infomercials to sell their wares, refer customers to retailers, recruit members, or attract buyers to their online, mobile, and social media sites.

A more recent form of direct-response television marketing is *interactive TV (iTV)*, which lets viewers interact with television programming and advertising. Thanks to technologies such as interactive cable systems, Internet-ready smart TVs, and smartphones and tablets, consumers can now use their TV remotes, phones, or other devices to obtain more information or make purchases directly from TV ads. For example, fashion retailer H&M recently ran ads that let viewers with certain Samsung smart TVs use their remotes to interact directly with the commercials. A small pop-up menu, shown as the ads ran, offered product information, the ability to send that information to another device, and the option to buy directly.[49]

Also, increasingly, as the lines continue to blur between TV screens and other video screens, interactive ads and infomercials are appearing not just on TV, but also on mobile, online, and social media platforms, adding even more TV-like interactive direct marketing venues. For example, Target recently placed dozens of products from its new home collection in an episode of the TBS comedy series *Cougar Town*, which was also simulcast online at ShopCougarTown.com. When the products appeared on the television screen, viewers were encouraged to purchase them on their phones or other screens. Thus, when viewers watching the show saw, say, a lamp they liked, they could click on a red plus sign flashing on the product in the online version, which took them to Target.com where they could buy it. "It's a combination of being a product integration that's really integrated into the story line of the script, being on a major network, and with a unique shopping experience," concludes Target's marketing vice president.[50]

Kiosk Marketing

As consumers become more and more comfortable with digital and touchscreen technologies, many companies are placing information and ordering machines—called *kiosks* (good old-fashioned vending machines but so much more)—in stores, airports, hotels, college campuses, and other locations. Kiosks are everywhere these days, from self-service hotel and airline check-in devices, to unmanned product and information kiosks in malls, to in-store ordering devices that let you order merchandise not carried in the store. "Vending machines, which not long ago had mechanical levers and coin trays, now possess brains," says one analyst. Many modern "smart kiosks" are now wireless-enabled. And some machines can even use facial recognition software that lets them guess gender and age and make product recommendations based on that data.[51]

In-store Kodak, Fuji, and HP kiosks let customers transfer pictures from memory cards, mobile phones, and other digital storage devices; edit them; and make high-quality color prints. Seattle's Best kiosks in grocery, drug, and mass merchandise stores grind and brew fresh coffee beans and serve coffee, mochas, and lattes to on-the-go customers around the clock. Redbox operates more than 35,000 DVD rental kiosks in McDonald's, Walmart, Walgreens, CVS, Family Dollar, and other retail outlets—customers make their selections on a touchscreen, then swipe a credit or debit card to rent DVDs for less than $2 a day.

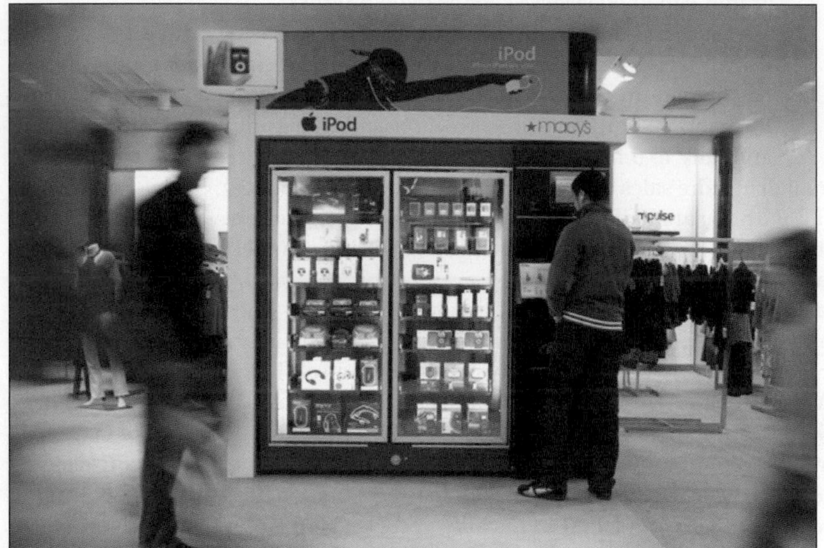

Kiosk marketing: ZoomShop kiosks around the country automatically dispense an assortment of popular consumer electronics products. This ZoomShop is located in a Macy's store and features Apple products, among others.
ZoomSystems

ZoomSystems creates small, free-standing kiosks called ZoomShops for retailers ranging from Apple, Sephora, and The Body Shop to Macy's and Best Buy. For example, 100 Best Buy Express ZoomShop kiosks across the country—conveniently located in airports, busy malls, military bases, and resorts—automatically dispense an assortment of portable media players, digital cameras, gaming consoles, headphones, phone chargers, travel gadgets, and other popular products. According to ZoomSystems, today's automated retailing "offers [consumers] the convenience of online shopping with the immediate gratification of traditional retail."[52]

Author Comment | Although we mostly benefit from direct and digital marketing, like most other things in life, they have a dark side as well. Marketers and customers alike must guard against irritating or harmful direct and digital marketing practices.

Public Policy Issues in Direct and Digital Marketing

Direct marketers and their customers usually enjoy mutually rewarding relationships. Occasionally, however, a darker side emerges. The aggressive and sometimes shady tactics of a few direct marketers can bother or harm consumers, giving the entire industry a black eye. Abuses range from simple excesses that irritate consumers to instances of unfair practices or even outright deception and fraud. The direct marketing industry has also faced growing privacy concerns, and online marketers must deal with Internet and mobile security issues.

Irritation, Unfairness, Deception, and Fraud

Direct marketing excesses sometimes annoy or offend consumers. For example, most of us dislike direct-response TV commercials that are too loud, long, and insistent. Our mailboxes fill up with unwanted junk mail, our e-mailboxes bulge with unwanted spam, and our computer, phone, and tablet screens flash with unwanted online or mobile display ads, pop-ups, or pop-unders.

Beyond irritating consumers, some direct marketers have been accused of taking unfair advantage of impulsive or less-sophisticated buyers. Television shopping channels, enticing Web sites, and program-long infomercials targeting television-addicted shoppers seem to be the worst culprits. They feature smooth-talking hosts, elaborately staged demonstrations, claims of drastic price reductions, "while they last" time limitations, and unequaled ease of purchase to inflame buyers who have low sales resistance.

Internet fraud has multiplied in recent years. The FBI's Internet Crime Complaint Center provides consumers with a convenient way to alert authorities to suspected violations.

FBI

Fraudulent schemes, such as investment scams or phony collections for charity, have also multiplied in recent years. *Internet fraud*, including identity theft and financial scams, has become a serious problem. According to the Internet Crime Complaint Center, since 2005, Internet scam complaints have more than tripled to almost 300,000 per year. The monetary loss of scam complaints exceeds $500 million per year.[53]

One common form of Internet fraud is *phishing*, a type of identity theft that uses deceptive e-mails and fraudulent online sites to fool users into divulging their personal data. For example, consumers may receive an e-mail, supposedly from their bank or credit card company, saying that their account's security has been compromised. The sender asks them to log on to a provided Web address and confirm their account number, password, and perhaps even their social security number. If they follow the instructions, users are actually turning this sensitive information over to scam artists. Although many consumers are now aware of such schemes, phishing can be extremely costly to those caught in the net. It also damages the brand identities of legitimate online marketers who have worked to build user confidence in Web, e-mail, and other digital transactions.

Many consumers also worry about *online and digital security*. They fear that unscrupulous snoopers will eavesdrop on their online transactions and social media postings, picking up personal information or intercepting credit and debit card numbers. Although online shopping has grown rapidly, one study showed that 67 percent of participants were still concerned about identity theft.[54]

Another Internet marketing concern is that of *access by vulnerable or unauthorized groups*. For example, marketers of adult-oriented materials and sites have found it difficult to restrict access by minors. Although Facebook allows no children under age 13 to have a profile, an estimated 40 percent of under-18 Facebook users are actually under 13. Facebook removes 200,000 underage accounts every day. And it's not just Facebook. Young users are logging onto social media such as Formspring, tweeting their locations to the Web, and making friends with strangers on Disney and other game sites. Concerned state and national lawmakers are currently debating bills that would help better protect children online. Unfortunately, this requires the development of technology solutions, and as Facebook puts it, "That's not so easy."[55]

Consumer Privacy

Invasion of privacy is perhaps the toughest public policy issue now confronting the direct marketing industry. Consumers often benefit from database marketing; they receive more offers that are closely matched to their interests. However, many critics worry that marketers may know *too* much about consumers' lives and that they may use this knowledge to take unfair advantage of consumers. At some point, they claim, the extensive use of databases intrudes on consumer privacy. Consumers, too, worry about their privacy. Although they are now much more willing to share personal information and preferences with marketers via digital and social media, they are still nervous about it. In one recent survey, some three-quarters of consumers agreed with the statement, "No one should ever be allowed to have access to my personal data or Web behavior." Another showed that 92 percent of U.S. Internet users worry about their privacy online.[56]

These days, it seems that almost every time consumers post something on social media or send a tweet, visit a Web site, enter a sweepstakes, apply for a credit card, or order products by phone or online, their names are entered into some company's already bulging database. Using sophisticated computer technologies, direct marketers can mine these databases to "microtarget" their selling efforts. Most marketers have become highly skilled at collecting and analyzing detailed consumer information both online and offline. Even the experts are sometimes surprised by how much marketers can learn. Consider this account by one *Advertising Age* reporter:[57]

> I'm no neophyte when it comes to targeting—not only do I work at *Ad Age*, but I cover direct marketing. Yet even I was taken aback when, as an experiment, we asked the database-marketing company to come up with a demographic and psychographic profile of me. Was it ever spot-on. Using only publicly available information, it concluded my date of birth, home phone number, and political-party affiliation. It gleamed that I was a college graduate, that I was married, and that one of my parents had passed away. It found that I have several bank, credit, and retail cards at "low-end" department stores. It knew not just how long I've lived at my house but how much it cost, how much it was worth, the type of mortgage that's on it, and—within a really close ballpark guess—how much is left to pay on it. It estimated my household income—again nearly perfectly—and determined that I am of British descent.
>
> But that was just the beginning. The company also nailed my psychographic profile. It correctly placed me into various groupings such as: someone who relies more on their own opinions than the recommendations of others when making a purchase; someone who is turned off by loud and aggressive advertising; someone who is family-oriented and has an interest in music, running, sports, computers, and is an avid concert-goer; someone who is never far from an Internet connection, generally used to peruse sports and general news updates; and someone who sees health as a core value. Scary? Certainly.

Some consumers and policy makers worry that the ready availability of information may leave consumers open to abuse. For example, they ask, should online sellers be allowed to plant cookies in the browsers of consumers who visit their sites and use tracking information to target ads and other marketing efforts? Should credit card companies be allowed to make data on their millions of cardholders worldwide available to merchants who accept their cards? Or is it right for states to sell the names and addresses of driver's license holders, along with height, weight, and gender information, allowing apparel retailers to target tall or overweight people with special clothing offers?

A Need for Action

To curb direct marketing excesses, various government agencies are investigating not only do-not-call lists but also do-not-mail lists, do-not-track online lists, and Can Spam legislation. In response to online privacy and security concerns, the federal government has considered numerous legislative actions to regulate how online, social media, and mobile operators obtain and use consumer information. For example, Congress is drafting legislation that would give consumers more control over how online information is used. In addition, the FTC is taking a more active role in policing online privacy.

All of these concerns call for strong actions by marketers to monitor and prevent privacy abuses before legislators step in to do it for them. For example, to head off increased government regulation, six advertiser groups—the American Association of Advertising Agencies, the American Advertising Federation, the Association of National Advertisers, the Direct Marketing Association, the Interactive Advertising Bureau, and the Network Advertising Initiative—recently issued a set of online advertising principles through the Digital Advertising Alliance. Among other measures, the self-regulatory principles call for online marketers to provide transparency and choice to consumers if Web viewing data is collected or used for targeting interest-based advertising. The ad industry has agreed on an *advertising option icon*—a little "i" inside a triangle—that it will add to behaviorally targeted online ads to tell consumers why they are seeing a particular ad and allowing them to opt out.[58]

Consumer privacy: The ad industry has agreed on an *advertising option icon* that will tell consumers why they are seeing a particular ad and allow them to opt out.

Digital Advertising Alliance

Of special concern are the privacy rights of children. In 2000, Congress passed the Children's Online Privacy Protection Act (COPPA), which requires online operators targeting children to post privacy policies on their sites. They must also notify parents about any information they're gathering and obtain parental consent before collecting personal information from children under age 13. With the subsequent advent of online social media, mobile phones, and other digital technologies, Congress in 2013 extended COPPA to include "identifiers such as cookies that track a child's activity online, as well as geolocation information, photos, videos, and audio recordings." The main concern is the amount of data mined by third parties from social media as well as social media's own hazy privacy policies.[59]

Many companies have responded to consumer privacy and security concerns with actions of their own. Still others are taking an industry-wide approach. For example, TRUSTe, a nonprofit self-regulatory organization, works with many large corporate sponsors, including Microsoft, Yahoo!, AT&T, Facebook, Disney, and Apple, to audit privacy and security measures and help consumers navigate the Internet safely. According to the company's Web site, "TRUSTe believes that an environment of mutual trust and openness will help make and keep the Internet a free, comfortable, and richly diverse community for everyone." To reassure consumers, the company lends its TRUSTe privacy seal to Web sites, mobile apps, e-mail marketing, and other online and social media channels that meet its privacy and security standards.[60]

The direct marketing industry as a whole is also addressing public policy issues. For example, in an effort to build consumer confidence in shopping direct, the Direct Marketing Association—the largest association for businesses practicing direct, database, and interactive marketing, including nearly half of the *Fortune* 100 companies—launched a "Privacy Promise to American Consumers." The Privacy Promise requires that all DMA members adhere to a carefully developed set of consumer privacy rules. Members must agree to notify customers when any personal information is rented, sold, or exchanged with others. They must also honor consumer requests to opt out of receiving further solicitations or having their contact information transferred to other marketers. Finally, they must abide by the DMA's Preference Service by removing the names of consumers who do not wish to receive mail, phone, or e-mail offers.[61]

Direct marketers know that, if left untended, such direct marketing abuses will lead to increasingly negative consumer attitudes, lower response and engagement rates, and calls for more restrictive state and federal legislation. Most direct marketers want the same things that consumers want: honest and well-designed marketing offers targeted only toward consumers who will appreciate and respond to them. Direct marketing is just too expensive to waste on consumers who don't want it.

17 Reviewing the Concepts

OBJECTIVES REVIEW AND KEY TERMS

Objectives Review

This chapter is the last of four chapters covering the final marketing mix element—promotion. The previous chapters dealt with advertising, public relations, personal selling, and sales promotion. This one investigates the burgeoning field of direct and digital marketing, including online, social media, and mobile marketing.

Define *direct and digital marketing* and discuss their rapid growth and benefits to customers and companies. *(pp 534–536)*

Direct and digital marketing involve engaging directly with carefully targeted individual consumers and customer communities to both obtain an immediate response and build lasting customer relationships. Companies use direct marketing to tailor their offers and content to the needs and interests of narrowly defined segments or individual buyers to build direct customer engagement, brand community, and sales. Today, spurred by the surge in Internet usage and buying, and by rapid advances in digital technologies—from smartphones, tablets, and other digital devices to the spate of online social and mobile media—direct marketing has undergone a dramatic transformation.

For buyers, direct and digital marketing are convenient, easy to use, and private. They give buyers anywhere, anytime access to an almost unlimited assortment of products and buying information. Direct marketing is also immediate and interactive, allowing buyers to create exactly the configuration of information, products, or services they desire and then order them on the spot. Finally, for consumers who want it, digital marketing through online, mobile, and social media provides a sense of brand engagement and community—a place to share bran information and experiences with other brand fans. For s ers, direct and digital marketing are powerful tools for ing customer engagement and close, personalized, in customer relationships. They also offer greater flexib marketers make ongoing adjustments to prices a or make immediate, timely, and personal a and offers.

OBJECTIVE 2 Identify and discuss the major forms of direct and digital marketing. *(pp 536–538)*

The main forms of direct and digital marketing include traditional direct marketing tools and the new direct digital marketing tools. Traditional direct approaches are face-to-face personal selling, direct-mail marketing, catalog marketing, telemarketing, DRTV marketing, and kiosk marketing. These traditional tools are still heavily used and very important in most firm's direct marketing efforts. In recent years, however, a dazzling new set of direct digital marketing tools has burst onto the marketing scene, including online marketing (Web sites, online ads and promotions, e-mail, online videos, and blogs), social media marketing, and mobile marketing. The chapter first discusses the fast-growing new digital direct marketing tools and then examines the traditional tools.

OBJECTIVE 3 Explain how companies have responded to the Internet and the digital age with various online marketing strategies. *(pp 539–544)*

The Internet and digital age have fundamentally changed customers' notions of convenience, speed, price, product information, service, and brand interactions. As a result, they have given marketers a whole new way to create customer value, engage customers, and build customer relationships. The Internet now influences a staggering 50 percent of total sales—including sales transacted online plus those made in stores but encouraged by online research. To reach this burgeoning market, most companies now market online.

Online marketing takes several forms, including company Web sites, online advertising and promotions, e-mail marketing, online video, and blogs. Social media and mobile marketing also take place online. But because of their special characteristics, we discuss these fast-growing digital marketing approaches in separate sections. For most companies, the first step in conducting online marketing is to create a Web site. The key to a successful Web site is to create enough value and engagement to get consumers to come to the site, stick around, and come back again.

Online advertising has become a major promotional medium. The main forms of online advertising are display ads and search-related ads. E-mail marketing is also an important form of digital marketing. Used properly, e-mail lets marketers send highly targeted, tightly personalized, relationship-building messages. Another important form of online marketing is posting digital video content on brand Web sites or social media. Marketers hope that some of their videos will go viral, engaging consumers by the millions. Finally, companies can use blogs as effective means of reaching customer communities. They can create their own blogs and advertise on existing blogs or influence content there.

Discuss how companies use social ...ile marketing to ...ners and create brand ... *544–550)*

...ependent and commercial social ...nsumers online places to congre... ...views and information. Most mar... ...e social media wave. Brands can ...ey can set up their own. Using ex... ...easiest. Thus, most brands—large and small—have set up shop on a host of social media sites. Some of the major social networks are huge; other niche social media cater to the needs of smaller communities of like-minded people. Beyond these independent social media, many companies have created their own online brand communities. More than making just scattered efforts and chasing "Likes" and tweets, most companies are integrating a broad range of diverse media to create brand-related social sharing, engagement, and customer community.

Using social media presents both advantages and challenges. On the plus side, social media are targeted and personal, interactive, immediate and timely, and cost effective. Perhaps the biggest advantage is their engagement and social sharing capabilities, making them ideal for creating customer community. On the down side, consumers' control over social media content make social media difficult to control.

Mobile marketing features marketing messages, promotions, and other content delivered to on-the-go consumers through their mobile devices. Marketers use mobile marketing to engage customers anywhere, anytime during the buying and relationship-building processes. The widespread adoption of mobile devices and the surge in mobile Web traffic have made mobile marketing a must for most brands, and almost every major marketer is now integrating mobile marketing into its direct marketing programs. Many marketers have created their own mobile online sites. Others have created useful or entertaining mobile apps to engage customers with their brands and help them shop.

OBJECTIVE 5 Identify and discuss the traditional direct marketing forms and overview the public policy and ethical issues presented by direct marketing. *(pp 550–557)*

Although the fast-growing digital marketing tools have grabbed most of the headlines lately, traditional direct marketing tools are very much alive and still heavily used. The major forms are face-to-face or personal selling, direct-mail marketing, catalog marketing, telemarketing, direct-response television (DRTV) marketing, and kiosk marketing.

Direct-mail marketing consists of the company sending an offer, announcement, reminder, or other item to a person at a specific address. Some marketers rely on catalog marketing—selling through catalogs mailed to a select list of customers, made available in stores, or accessed online. Telemarketing consists of using the telephone to sell directly to consumers. DRTV marketing has two forms: direct-response advertising (or infomercials) and interactive television (iTV) marketing. Kiosks are information and ordering machines that direct marketers place in stores, airports, hotels, and other locations.

Direct marketers and their customers usually enjoy mutually rewarding relationships. Sometimes, however, direct marketing presents a darker side. The aggressive and sometimes shady tactics of a few direct marketers can bother or harm consumers, giving the entire industry a black eye. Abuses range from simple excesses that irritate consumers to instances of unfair practices or even outright deception and fraud. The direct marketing industry has also faced growing concerns about invasion-of-privacy and Internet security issues. Such concerns call for strong action by marketers and public policy makers to curb direct marketing abuses. In the end, most direct marketers want the same things that consumers want: honest and well-designed marketing offers targeted only toward consumers who will appreciate and respond to them.

MyMarketingLab

Go to **mymktlab.com** to complete the problems marked with this icon .

Key Terms

OBJECTIVE 1

Direct and digital marketing (p 534)

OBJECTIVE 2

Digital and social media marketing (p 538)

OBJECTIVE 3

Multichannel marketing (p 539)
Onlinc markcting (p 540)
Marketing Web site (p 540)
Branded community Web site (p 540)
Online advertising (p 541)
E-mail marketing (p 541)
Spam (p 542)
Viral marketing (p 542)
Blogs (p 543)

OBJECTIVE 4

Social media (p 544)
Mobile marketing (p 547)

OBJECTIVE 5

Direct-mail marketing (p 550)
Catalog marketing (p 551)
Telemarketing (p 552)
Direct-response television (DRTV) marketing (p 553)

DISCUSSION AND CRITICAL THINKNG

Discussion Questions

17-1 List and briefly describe the various forms of traditional direct marketing approaches. (AACSB: Communication)

17-2 Compare and contrast a marketing Web site and a branded community Web site. (AACSB: Communication)

17-3 How can companies make effective use of blogs? (AACSB: Communication)

17-4 Discuss the advantages and challenges of social media marketing. (AACSB: Communication)

17-5 What types of direct marketing are used in your country? (AACSB: Communication)

Critical Thinking Exercises

17-6 Choose a product or service that is unique to your own country or region. Design and deliver a DRTV short sales piece to promote it and create sales. (AACSB: Communication; Reflective Thinking)

17-7 Review the FTC's guidelines on disclosure in online, social media, and mobile advertisements at www.ftc.gov/os/2013/03/130312dotcomdisclosures.pdf. Will the FTC's requirements regarding ads and endorsers make Twitter less effective as an advertising medium? (AACSB: Communication; Use of IT; Reflective Thinking)

17-8 Investigate the spread of Internet-based fraud in your country or region. Have there been instances of Internet fraud by marketers in your country? Discuss two such instances of fraud you have come across in recent times. (AACSB: Communication; Use of IT; Reflective Thinking)

MINICASES AND APPLICATIONS

Online, Mobile, and Social Media Marketing On the Move

By 2016, the value of mobile advertising in the Middle East will have grown at a rate of 37 percent to $2.8 billion. This is just a part of the spectacular growth rates in digital marketing across the whole region. Still ahead of the rest of the region is Saudi Arabia, with 36 percent of mobile Internet users taking notice of mobile advertising. UAE and Egypt are in a tie for second place with 32 percent. Across the region, around 60 percent of all mobile Internet users read mobile advertising sent to them; this compares very favorably with just 10 percent stating that they either never read it or do not get sent any advertising. The opportunities for businesses, big and small, local and multinational, are enormous. Mobile advertising budgets for tablets and smartphones are set to increase at a rate of at least 40 to 50 percent; this is the biggest segment of the digital market. Since 2013, over 57percent of all companies across the region have upped the amount of money they splurge on digital advertising. These figures are set against a very promising backdrop of global growth in mobile marketing. This rests on the fact that of the 4.55 billion people who own a mobile phone, over 1.75 billion of them have smartphones. In many countries, smartphones are far more common than older basic models. Inevitably, this means a new focus for marketers.

17-9 What local businesses in your community are using online, social media, and/or mobile marketing? Interview the owner or manager of one of the businesses to learn how he or she uses these marketing activities and how satisfied he or she is with the activities. (AACSB: Communication; Reflective Thinking)

17-10 Mobile marketing can be confusing for a small business owner. Develop a presentation to present to small business owners that describes mobile marketing, its advantages and disadvantages, and examples of how small businesses are using mobile marketing. (AACSB: Communication; Reflective Thinking)

Marketing Ethics Tracking in "Meat Space"

By now, you know about behavioral targeting—marketers tracking consumers' online behavior in cyberspace to send them targeted advertising. Krux Digital reports that the average visit to a Web page generated 56 instances of data collection, a five-fold increase in just one year. An investigation by the *Wall Street Journal* found that the 50 most popular U.S. Web sites installed more than 3,000 tracking files on the computer used in the study. The total was even higher—4,123 tracking files—for the top 50 sites that are popular with children and teens. Many sites installed more than 100 tracking tools each during the tests. Tracking tools include files placed on users' computers and on Web sites. Marketers use this information to target online advertisements. But now, wearable and mobile devices allow marketers to track consumer movements in the physical world. The term *meat space* refers to the physical world in which our bodies move and do things, and marketers are using information obtained from wearable and mobile devices to personalize offers while consumers move around their space. For example, Disney's Magic Bands and mobile app allow users to unlock hotel room doors, enter parks, use FastPasses, and reserve, order, and pay for food. But the real magic for Disney is the ability to track everything the user does as he or she moves around the "meat space." Since users willingly give their names and birthdates when ordering Magic Bands, Goofy just might walk up to your child to say, "Happy birthday, Billy!"

17-11 Debate whether or not it is ethical to track consumers' physical movements, especially children's. (AACSB: Communication; Ethical Reasoning)

17-12 Discuss other ways marketers can track consumers in meat space. (AACSB: Communication; Reflective Thinking)

Marketing by the Numbers Mobile Advertising

Consumers spend a quarter of their media-viewing time on mobile, but advertisers devote 1 percent of their media budgets to mobile devices. Although mobile advertising makes up a small percentage of online advertising, it is one of the fastest-growing advertising channels. One source reported more than 100 percent growth in mobile advertising between 2012 and 2013. But one obstacle is measuring return on investment in mobile. A study of chief marketing officers by *eMarketer* found that 41 percent of those investing in mobile advertising indicated that success of their mobile ad spending was "inconsistent" or "not sure."

17-13 How much is spent on mobile marketing and what is the growth rate of expenditures in this medium? Compare those expenditures to spending in other advertising media. (AACSB: Communication; Analytical Reasoning; Reflective Thinking)

17-14 How are marketers measuring the return on investment in mobile advertising? Develop a presentation suggesting metrics that marketers should use to measure the effectiveness of mobile advertising. (AACSB: Communication; Use of IT; Reflective Thinking)

Video Case Home Shopping Network

Long ago, television shopping was associated with low-quality commercials broadcast in the wee hours of the morning selling obscure merchandise. But Home Shopping Network (HSN) has played an instrumental role in making television shopping a legitimate outlet. Around-the-clock top-quality programming featuring name-brand merchandise is now the norm.

But just like any retailer, HSN has had its share of challenges. This video illustrates how HSN has focused on the principles of direct marketing in order to overcome challenges and form strong customer relationships. As market conditions continue to shift, HSN explores new ways to form and strengthen direct relationships with customers.

After viewing the video featuring HSN, answer the following questions:

17-15 Explain the different ways that HSN engages in direct marketing.

17-16 What advantages does HSN have, specifically over brick-and-mortar retailers?

17-17 Make recommendations for how HSN could make better use of its role as a direct marketer.

Company Case Pinterest: Revolutionizing the Web—Again

Ben Silbermann runs ragged. And it isn't because the 31-year-old husband is up before dawn every morning with his infant son. It has a lot more to do with the fact that he is the founder and CEO of Pinterest, the latest "hottest Web site on the planet." In less than two years, Pinterest reached the milestone of 10 million unique monthly visitors—faster than any other online site in history. At that time, it was driving more traffic than Google+, YouTube, and LinkedIn combined. A year later, it reached 50 million unique monthly visitors. So far, 70 million members have created 750 million Pinterest boards and have pinned 30 billion items. Pinterest is growing so fast that trying to quantify its success with such numbers seems pointless.

Rather, the impact of this brash young start-up can be observed in more substantial ways. In fact, Pinterest seems to have accomplished the unlikely achievement of revolutionizing the Web—something that seems to happen only every few years. Like Amazon, Google, Facebook, and others before it, Pinterest has put businesses and other online sites everywhere on notice that they'd better orient themselves around its platform or be left behind. And like other Internet revolutionists before it, Pinterest's impact has caused even the online giants to stop and take notice. Indeed, Pinterest is changing Web design. It is also changing e-commerce. And it looks as though Pinterest has solved one of the Internet's biggest problems—discovery.

The Discovery Problem

At first blush, Pinterest may seem like any other social media site, full of people sharing images and commenting on them. Silbermann's big idea for Pinterest came as he and college buddy Paul Sciarra struggled to make a business out of their first product, a shopping app called Tote. Although Tote failed to take off, it revealed a pent-up need among Internet users. Tote users didn't buy things (kind of a necessity for a shopping app). But they did e-mail themselves pictures of products to view later.

Silbermann—a lifetime collector of "stuff"—could identify with that. As a boy, he had a particular fascination with collecting bugs. "I really liked insects," he says. "All kinds: flies, grasshoppers, weevils." He spent his youth collecting, pinning, drying, tagging—creating his own private museum of natural history. So when Silbermann and Sciarra met Pinterest's third co-founder, Evan Sharp, the idea of digital collections—of books, clothes, or even insects—as a powerful medium for self-expression began to take shape.

As the three began working on developing Pinterest, something about all-things-Internet bothered Silbermann. Despite the seemingly infinite possibilities for exploration, expression, and creation, he felt that the Internet was organized in a way that boxed people in. For starters, the nature of "search" in any online context may seem to promote discovery, but it actually stunts it. For example, Google depends on finely tuned queries in order to yield useful results. Try to find something when you're not quite sure what you want—say, "nice Father's Day gift" or even "very special Father's Day gift"—and Google isn't really much help. The bottom line is, if you try talking to Google as you would talk to a friend or a department store clerk, it won't know where to begin.

The belief that discovery is a problem on the Internet isn't original to Silbermann. In fact, it's an issue that many digital designers have struggled with since the launch of the Web but no one has been able to solve fully. Take Amazon, for example. As successful as Amazon is, its entire structure mirrors every other e-commerce site—a detailed system of menus and categories. To browse for something, users must work within this structure while at the same time being pulled in dozens of different directions by suggested items and competing products.

"You spend three hours buying a $20 toaster," says Barry Schwartz, psychology professor and author of *The Paradox of Choice*. "Amazon and Google pretty much stink at browsing," echoes Leland Rechis, director of product experience at Etsy. But Amazon and Google are not alone. The entire Internet is structured as a series of ever-more-specific menus, inconsistent with how the human mind works. Such structure inhibits the types of free-associative leaps that happen naturally as people walk through shopping malls, meander through a museum, or even drive down the street.

As Silbermann and his co-founders worked to sketch out Pinterest, the three were also intent on eliminating another limiting characteristic of online design. Other social networks are organized around "feeds"—lines of text or images organized by time. This setup lets users browse multiple images at once. The Pinterest team wanted to change this. "We were really excited about bringing something that wasn't immediate and real time, something that wasn't a chronological feed," says Sharp. They pictured a grid of images, rather than the directories, time stamps, and pagination commonly imposed by the Web. The goal for Pinterest was to create an interface that would feel more like visiting a store or a museum.

As Pinterest took shape, its creators never questioned that it was to be a social network at its core. What set Pinterest apart in yet another way was Silbermann's ability to look outside the tunnel-vision of other social media entrepreneurship. Although the current social Web is frequented by millions, most users are observers, not creators. Thus, they take part on only one level. Not everyone is a photographer, a filmmaker, or a broadcaster. "Most people don't have anything witty to say on Twitter or anything gripping to put on Facebook, but a lot of them are really interesting people," Silbermann says. "They have awesome taste in books or furniture or design, but there was no way to share that."

Something Completely Different

The Pinterest team's focus on solving some of the most limiting characteristics of the Internet bore fruit. When Pinterest launched in March 2010, it was widely hailed as one of the most visually stunning online sites ever. Silbermann, Sciarra, and Sharp worked through 50 versions of the site, painstakingly tweaking and perfecting column widths, layouts, and ways of presenting pictures. "From the beginning, we were aware that if we were going to get somebody to spend all this time putting together a collection, at the very least, the collection had to be beautiful," Silbermann says. Pinterest's grid is a key element of its design—interlocking images of fixed width and varying heights that rearrange every time a new image is pinned, meaning users rarely see the same home page twice.

Pinterest also bucked conventional online design in other ways. At a time when "gamification" was hot, Pinterest displayed no elements of competition. There is no leader board or any other means of identifying the most popular pinners. Pinterest also did away with page views—the predominate metric for illustrating growth and momentum. Rather, Pinterest's "infinite scroll" automatically loads more images as the user expands the browser or scrolls downward. With almost no time spent clicking or waiting for pages to load, this feature has proven addictive for many.

"When you open up Pinterest," Silbermann says, "you should feel like you've walked into a building full of stuff that only you are interested in. Everything should feel handpicked for you." Silbermann and his cohorts have obviously succeeded. Page after page, Pinterest gives the feel of a collection designed by an individual to reflect her or his needs, ambitions, and desires. It's as if each person is saying, "Here are the beautiful things that make me who I am—or who I want to be." There is no single theme to a pinboard. Pinterest is a place where young women plan their weddings, individuals create the ultimate wish list of food dishes, and couples assemble furniture sets for their new homes. Unlike other social networks, every Pinterest home page is an ever-changing collage that reflects the sum of each user's choices.

Because Pinterest's design has departed from Internet convention in so many ways, it's only natural that its growth dynamics would also break from previous trends. Most successful social services spread through early adopters on the nation's coasts, then break through to the masses. But Pinterest's growth has been scattered throughout the heartland, driven by such unlikely cohorts as the "bloggernacle" of tech-savvy young Mormons. Additionally, nearly 83 percent of Pinterest's users are women, most between the ages of 25 and 54—another demographic not normally associated with fast-growing social media sites.

Hope for Monetization

But perhaps the biggest splash that Pinterest has made in the online pool is its huge influence on consumer purchasing. Although many dot-coms have made profits by online sales, the digital world in general still struggles with turning eyeballs into dollars. Even Facebook, although it turns a profit, prompts relatively few of its one-billion-plus members to open their wallets.

But something about the combination of Pinterest's elegant design and smart social dynamics has users shopping like mad. A Pinterest user following an image back to its source and then buying an item spends an average of $180. For Facebook users, it's only $80. And for Twitter, it's only $70. But Pinterest is having a much greater impact than those numbers indicate. Although Pinterest is still far from the top in terms of members and unique visits, when it comes to e-commerce referrals, Pinterest is the market leader, driving 40 percent of traffic and edging out social media dominator Facebook by 1 percent. Even more impressive, Pinterest traffic converts to a sale 22 percent more often than Facebook traffic.

Companies are jumping on this opportunity. Initially, brands could drive traffic to their own Pinterest or external sites by paying opinion leaders to pin images of their products. For example, companies pay 31-year-old Satsuki Shibuya, a designer with more than a million followers, between $150 and $1,200 per image. This method works well because, with Pinterest's authentic feel, it's almost impossible to tell the difference between paid pins and unpaid pins—something that can't be said of other online sites.

But recently, Pinterest has entered the world of advertising with promoted pins and is poised to make a big online advertising push. More than a dozen marketers have signed up with a $1 million to $2 million commitment, including Kraft, General Mills, Nestle, Gap, and Expedia. "Our target is 25- to 54-year-old women, and Pinterest is a perfect fit," says Deanie Elsner, chief marketing officer for Kraft Foods. For Kraft, Pinterest has already been an effective way to connect with the younger half of that demographic that is typically harder to reach. "It lets them be the hero," she said, referring to Kraft's practice of publishing recipes on its Pinterest site.

It's little wonder then that so many other social media sites have taken note of Pinterest. Numerous copycat sites (such as Fancy and Polyvore) have mimicked Pinterest's look and feel, right down to the font selections. The influence of Pinterest's design is also notable on sites such as Lady Gaga's social network LittleMonsters.com and the question-and-answer site Quora. Even Facebook's move to its current Timeline format is notably Pinterest-like.

Despite all the ways that Pinterest has departed from the typical path of social media development, it has largely stayed the course in terms of making money. That is, it spent the first few years building its network and honing its site. This year, the company will begin generating revenue. Silbermann and friends are still tossing other ideas around. In addition to advertising, Pinterest could also adopt a referral fee model, retaining a percentage of the sale of every item sold as the result of a pin. Pinterest has been valued at $5 billion and has had no trouble raising all the venture capital that it needs, despite having yet to earn any money. "There was never a doubt in our minds that we could make a s**tload of money," says a former Pinterest employee. Apparently, investors feel the same way.

Questions for Discussion

17-18 Analyze the forces in the marketing environment that have contributed to Pinterest's explosion in popularity.

17-19 Why has Pinterest demonstrated such a high influence on consumers' decisions to purchase products?

17-20 Discuss ways that companies can use Pinterest to build their own brands and generate sales.

17-21 What threats does Pinterest face in the future? Give recommendations for dealing with those threats.

Sources: Based on information from Jillian D'Onfro, "Here's Exactly Why Pinterest Is Worth Its $5 Billion Valuation," *Businessinsider*, May 17, 2014, www.businessinsider.com/why-pinterest-is-worth-5-billion-2014-5; Cotton Delo, "Pinterest Launches First Paid Ads with Kraft, Gap and Others," *Advertising Age*, May 12, 2014, www.adage.com/print/293142; Max Chafkin, "Can Ben Silbermann Turn Pinterest into the World's Greatest Shopfront?", *Fast Company*, October 2012, pp. 90–96; and Kimberly Warner-Cohen, "Pinterest Beats Facebook, Twitter in Online Shopping," *Wall St. Cheat Sheet*, April 9, 2014, http://wallstcheatsheet.com/technology/pinterest-beats-facebook-twitter-in-online-shopping.html/?a=viewall.

MyMarketingLab

Go to **mymktlab.com** for the following Assisted-graded writing questions:

17-22 What public policy issues are related to direct and digital marketing? (AACSB: Communication; Reflective Thinking)

17-23 What mobile applications currently exist and what's on the horizon? How many of these applications do you or someone you know use? In the increasingly cluttered mobile apps market, what distinguishes successful apps from less successful ones? (AACSB: Communication; Reflective Thinking)

References

1. Based on information from Sarah Kessler, "With Paper, Facebook Stops Trying to Be Everything for Everyone," *Fast Company,* January 30, 2014, www.fastcompany.com/3025762/with-paper-facebook-stops-trying-to-be-everything-for-everyone; Josh Constine, "Zuck Says Ads Aren't the Way to Monetize Messaging," *Techcrunch,* February 19, 2014, http://techcrunch.com/2014/02/19/whatsapp-will-monetize-later/; Shayndi Raice and Spencer E. Ante, "Insta-Rich: $1 Billion for Instagram," *Wall Street Journal,* April 10, 2012, http://online.wsj.com/news/articles/SB10001424052702303815404577333840377381670; "Facebook's Sales Chief: Madison Avenue Doesn't Understand Us Yet," *Advertising Age,* April 29, 2011, www.adage.com/print/227314/; Craig Smith, "By the Numbers: 105 Amazing Facebook User Statistics," *Digital Marketing Ramblings,* March 13, 2014, http://expandedramblings.com/index.php/by-the-numbers-17-amazing-facebook-stats/#.U2F1gtxH38u; and www.facebook.com, www.instagram.com, and www.whatsapp.com, accessed September 2014.
2. ComBlu, "The State of Online Branded Communities," http://comblu.com/downloads/ComBlu_StateOfOnlineCommunities_2012.pdf, accessed November 2012; "The Strangest Mountain Dew Flavors Ever Made," *Huffington Post,* April 2, 2014, www.huffingtonpost.com/the-daily-meal/the-strangest-mountain-de_b_5076837.html; and www.mountaindew.com, accessed September 2014.
3. See "Priceline Profit Tops Estimates as Bookings Rise," *Reuters,* February 20, 2014, www.reuters.com/article/2014/02/21/us-priceline-results-idUSBREA1J26X20140221; and http://ir.pricelinegroup.com/financials.cfm, accessed September 2014.
4. For these and other direct marketing statistics in this section, see Direct Marketing Association, *The DMA Statistical Fact Book 2014*, 36th ed., April 2014; and a wealth of other information at www.thedma.org, accessed September 2014.
5. Ginger Conion, "Outlook 2014: Marketing Spending to Rise," *Direct Marketing News*, January 10, 2014, www.dmnews.com/outlook-2014-marketing-spending-to-rise/article/328925/; Thad Reuter, "U.S. e-Commerce to Grow to 13% in 2013," *Internet Retailer*, March 13, 2013, https://www.internetretailer.com/2013/03/13/us-e-commerce-grow-13-2013; Sucharita Mulpuru, "US Online Retail Forecast, 2012 to 2017," March 13, 2013, www.forrester.com/US+Online+Retail+Forecast+2012+To+2017/fulltext/-/E-RES93281?objectid=RES93281; "Marketing Fact Pack 2014," *Advertising Age,* December 30, 2013, p. 14; and "Monthly and Annual Retail Trade," U.S. Census Bureau, www.census.gov/retail, accessed September 2014.
6. See Pew Research Center's Internet & American Life Project, "Internet User Demographics," www.pewinternet.org/data-trend/internet-use/latest-stats/, accessed June 2014; "Digital Set to Surpass TV in Time Spent with US Media," *eMarketer*, August 1, 2013, www.emarketer.com/Article/Digital-Set-Surpass-TV-Time-Spent-with-US-Media/1010096; "ITU Release Latest Tech Figures & Global Rankings," October 7, 2013, www.itu.int/net/pressoffice/press_releases/2013/41.aspx#.Uumujvad6cC; John Heggestuen, "One in Every 5 People in the World Own a Smartphone, One in Every 17 Own a Tablet," *Business Insider*, December 15, 2013, www.businessinsider.com/smartphone-and-tablet-penetration-2013-10; and James O'Tolle, "Mobile Apps Overtake PC Internet Usage in U.S., *CNN Money,* February 28, 2014, http://money.cnn.com/2014/02/28/technology/mobile/mobile-apps-internet//.
7. See Natash Lomas, "Forrester: U.S. Online Retail Sales to Rise to $370BN by 2017 (10% CAGR) as Ecommerce Motors on with Help from Tablets and Phones," *TechCrunch,* March 13, 2013, http://techcrunch.com/2013/03/13/forrester-2012-2017-ecommerce-forecast/; and "60% of U.S. Retail Sales Will Involve the Web by 2017," *Internet Retailer*, October 30, 2013, www.internetretailer.com/2013/10/30/60-us-retail-sales-will-involve-web-2017.
8. See "Internet Retailer: Top 500 Guide," www.top500guide.com/top-500/the-top-500-list, accessed September 2014.
9. See Paul Davidson, "Staples Closing 225 Stores, Strengthens Online Focus," *USA Today*, March 7, 2014, www.usatoday.com/story/money/business/2014/03/06/staples-closings/6114525/; "Staples Aims to Change Image with New Slogan," *Boston Globe,* January 3, 2014; and annual reports and other information found at www.staples.com, accessed September 2014.
10. See ComBlu, "The State of Online Branded Communities," http://comblu.com/downloads/ComBlu_StateOfOnlineCommunities_2012.pdf, November 2012, p. 19; "Why Join an Online Brand Community?" *Marketing Charts,* October 17, 2013, www.marketingcharts.com/wp/online/why-join-an-online-brand-community-37429/; and www.espn.com, accessed September 2014.
11. Ginger Conlon, "Outlook 2014: Marketing Spending to Rise," *Direct Marketing News*, January 10, 2014, www.dmnews.com/outlook-2014-marketing-spending-to-rise/article/328925.
12. See "IAC Internet Advertising Competition: Best Rich Media Online Ad," www.iacaward.org/iac/winners_detail.asp?yr=all&award_level=best&medium=Rich%20media%20Online%20Ad; and "Gatorade—Prime Rich Media Takeover," www.iacaward.org/iac/winner.asp?eid=10379, both accessed July 2014.
13. Ginger Conlon, "Outlook 2014: Marketing Spending to Rise"; and Google annual reports, http://investor.google.com/proxy.html, accessed September 2014.
14. "Social Media Is the Hot New Thing, but Email Is Still the King," *Advertising Age,* September 30, 2013, p. 18.
15. See Nora Aufreiter et al., "Why Marketers Keep Sending You Emails," January 2014, www.mckinsey.com/Insights/Marketing_Sales/Why_marketers_should_keep_sending_you_emails; Niti Shah, "18 Email Marketing Stats That'll Make You Better at Your Job," *HubSpot*, December 5, 2013, http://blog.hubspot.com/marketing/email-marketing-stats-list; and Amy Gesenhues, "Report: Marketing Emails Opened on Mobile Devices Jumped 61% to 65% in Q4 2013," January 23, 2014, http://marketingland.com/report-65-of-marketing-emails-were-opened-on-mobile-devices-in-q4-2013-71387.
16. Larry Bennett, "Worldwide Spam Rate Falls 2.5 Percent but New Tactics Emerge," *ZDNet*, January 23, 2014, www.zdnet.com/worldwide-spam-rate-falls-2-5-percent-but-new-tactics-emerge-7000025517/.
17. Linda Moses, "Online Video Ads Have Higher Impact than TV Ads," *Adweek,* May 1, 2013, www.adweek.com/print/148982; and "comScore Releases December 2013 U.S. Online Video Rankings," January 10, 2014, www.comscore.com/Insights/Press_Releases/2014/1/comScore_Releases_December_2013_US_Online_Video_Rankings.
18. For these and other examples, see "Samsung, Wieden & Kennedy Rule Ad Age's 2013 Viral Video Awards," *Advertising Age,* April 16, 2013, http://adage.com/article/240900/; and Alexander Coolidge, "P&G Aims for Moms' Heart with Latest 'Thank You' Ad," *USA Today,* January 8, 2014, www.usatoday.com/story/money/business/2014/01/08/pg-olympics-thank-you-ad/4380229/.
19. Laura Heller, "'Ship My Pants': Kmart's Unexpected Viral Hit," *Forbes,* April 15, 2013, www.forbes.com/sites/lauraheller/2013/04/15/ship-my-pants-kmarts-unexpected-viral-hit/; Ron Dicker, "Kmart Makes Merry Mischief Again with 'Ship My Pants,' Dickens Style," *Huffington Post,* December 13, 2013, www.huffingtonpost.com/2013/12/13/kmart-ship-my-pants-dickens-christmas-carol_n_4440133.html; and www.youtube.com/watch?v=I03UmJbK0lA, accessed September 2014.
20. "Evian: Masters of Online Video," *The Guardian,* www.theguardian.com/media-network/ebuzzing-partner-zone/evian-online-video-advertising-baby-me, accessed June 2014; and Emma Bazilian, "Ad of the Day: Evian Spins a Familiar Web with a Dancing Baby Spider-Man," *Adweek,* April 3, 2014, www.adweek.com/news/advertising-branding/ad-day-evian-spins-familiar-web-dancing-baby-spider-man-156755.
21. Troy Dreier, "The Force Was Strong with This One," *Streaming Media Magazine*, April/May 2011, pp. 66–68; also see Thales Teixeira, "The New Science of Viral Ads," *Harvard Business Review,* March 2012, pp. 25–28; and Hilary Masell Oswald, "The Biology of a Marketplace Sensation," *Marketing News,* September 2013, pp. 31–35.

22. "State of the Blogging World in 2012," *New Media Expo Blog*, July 25, 2012, www.blogworld.com/2012/07/25/state-of-the-blogging-world-in-2012; and "The Blogconomy: Blogging Statistics," *Social Media Today,* August 28, 2013, http://socialmediatoday.com/mikevelocity/1698201/blogging-stats-2013-infographic.

23. See http://en.community.dell.com/dell-blogs/default.aspx and www.youtube.com/user/DellVlog, accessed September 2014.

24. Based on information found in Keith O'Brien, "How McDonald's Came Back Bigger Than Ever," *New York Times,* May 6, 2012, p. MM44.

25. Stuart Feil, "How to Win Friends and Influence People," *Adweek,* September 10, 2013, pp. S1–S2.

26. http://newsroom.fb.com/company-info; www.youtube.com/yt/press/statistics.html; and www.statisticbrain.com/twitter-statistics/, accessed September 2014.

27. For these and other examples, see www.kaboodle.com, www.farmersonly.com, www.birdpost.com, and www.cafemom.com, all accessed September 2014.

28. See http://nikeinc.com/news/nike-coach-feature-motivates-runners-with-customized-training-plans and www.nikeplus.com, accessed June 2013.

29. Karl Greenberg, "Volvo Uses Twitter Chat for Digital Focus Groups," *Marketing Daily,* May 29, 2013, www.mediapost.com/publications/article/201309/#axzz2UsMXTPXB.

30. Based on information found at Tim Nudd, "Online Test Just Wants to Make You Happy," *Adweek,* March 18, 2013, www.adweek.com/adfreak/oreo-wraps-cookie-vs-creme-campaign-dozens-goofy-videos-148017; and Lisa Lacy, "Oreo to Fans: Cookie or Crème?" *ClickZ,* February 7, 2013, www.clickz.com/clickz/news/2241725/oreo-to-fans-cookie-or-creme.

31. See http://pinterest.com/wholefoods/, accessed September 2014.

32. Example and quotes from "Meme Watch: Lay's 'Do Us a Flavor' Crowdsourcing Hilariously Backfires," *Uproxx,* February 5, 2014, http://uproxx.com/gammasquad/2014/02/best-of-lays-do-us-a-flavor-parodies/?showall=true; Michael Bourne, "Sailing of 14 Social Cs," *Mullen Advertising*, February, 13, 2012, www.mullen.com/sailing-the-14-social-cs/; and Jenna Mullins, "The Submissions for New Lay's Chip Flavors Are Getting Out of Control (but We Love It)," *EOnline,* February 6, 2014, www.eonline.com/news/508137/the-submissions-for-new-lays-chip-flavors-are-getting-out-of-control-but-we-love-it.

33. Melissa Allison, "Re-Creating the Coffee Klatch Online," *Raleigh News & Observer,"* May 6, 2013, p. 1D; Todd Wassermann, *MAshable,* December 13, 2013, http://mashable.com/2013/12/05/starbuckss-tweet-a-coffee-180000/; and www.facebook.com/Starbucks and https://twitter.com/Starbucks, accessed September 2014.

34. Facts in this paragraph are from "Wireless Quick Facts," www.ctia.org/your-wireless-life/how-wireless-works/wireless-quick-facts, accessed June 2014; Tara Siegel Bernard, "Weighing the Need for Landline in a Cellphone World," *New York Times*, January 17, 2014, www.nytimes.com/2014/01/18/your-money/weighing-the-need-for-a-landline-in-a-cellphone-world.html?_r=0; "Smartphone Penetration Tops 65% of the US Mobile Market in Q4 2013," *MarketingCharts*, February 5, 2014, www.marketingcharts.com/wp/online/smartphone-penetration-tops-65-of-the-us-mobile-market-in-q4-2013-39595/; Pew Research Center's Internet & American Life Project, "Cell Phone Activities," www.pewinternet.org/data-trend/mobile/cell-phone-activities/, accessed June 2014; and Zoe Fox, "The Average Smartphone User Downloads 25 Apps," *Mashable*, September 5, 2013, http://mashable.com/2013/09/05/most-apps-download-countries/.

35. Jonathan Nelson, "Voice: One Screen to Rule Them All," *Adweek,* February 13, 2013, p. 15; Stephen Willard, "Study: People Check Their Cell Phones Every Six Minutes, 150 Times a Day," *Elite Daily,* February 11, 2013, http://elitedaily.com/news/world/study-people-check-cell-phones-minutes-150-times-day/; and John Fetto, "Americans Spend 58 Minutes a Day on Their Smartphones," *Experian,* May 28, 2013, www.experian.com/blogs/marketing-forward/2013/05/28/americans-spend-58-minutes-a-day-on-their-smartphones/.

36. "IAB Internet Advertising Revenue Report," April 2013, www.iab.net/media/file/IAB_Internet_Advertising_Revenue_Report_FY_2012_rev.pdf; "The Mobile Movement," accessed at www.thinkwithgoogle.com/insights/emea/library/studies/the-mobile-movement, May 2013; and "Mobile Advertising Fast Facts," *Advertising Age,* April 04, 2014, pp. 20+.

37. See Lauren Johnson, "McDonald's Beefs Up Advertising Strategy with Mobile Game," *Mobile Marketer,* March 28, 2013, www.mobilemarketer.com/cms/news/advertising/12447.html; and Rimma Kats, "McDonald's Beefs up Mobile Efforts via Targeted Campaign," *Mobile Marketing,* August 16, 2013, www.mobilemarketer.com/cms/news/advertising/13553.html.

38. See Judith Acquino, "JetBlue Voice-Activated Ad Teaches People to Speak 'Pigeon,'" *Ad Exchanger,"* September 26, 2013, www.adexchanger.com/online-advertising/jetblue-voice-activated-ads-teach-people-to-speak-pigeon/; and Lauren Johnson, "Top 10 Mobile Advertising Campaigns of 2013," December 24, 2013, www.mobilemarketer.com/cms/news/advertising/16847.html.

39. "Location, Location, Location," *Adweek,* February 13, 2012, pp. M9–M11. For the Macy's and other examples, see Michael Applebaum, "Mobile Magnetism," *Adweek,* June 24, 2012, p. S7.

40. See "Stats & Facts: Direct Marketing," *CMO Council,* www.cmo-council.org/facts-stats-categories.php?view=all&category=direct-marketing, access September 2014.

41. Julie Liesse, "When Times Are Hard, Mail Works," *Advertising Age*, March 30, 2009, p. 14; Paul Vogel, "Marketers Are Rediscovering the Value of Mail," *Deliver Magazine*, January 11, 2011, www.delivermagazine.com/2011/01/marketers-are-rediscovering-the-value-of-mail/; Laurie Beasley, "Why Direct Mail Still Yields the Lowest Cost-Per-Lead and Highest Conversion Rate," *Online Marketing Insights,* June 13, 2013, www.onlinemarketinginstitute.org/blog/2013/06/why-direct-mail-still-yields-the-lowest-cost-per-lead-and-highest-conversion-rate/; and Lois Geller, "If Direct Mail Is Dying, It's Sure Taking Its Time About It," *Forbes,* December 4, 2013, www.forbes.com/sites/loisgeller/2013/12/04/if-direct-mail-is-dying-its-sure-taking-its-time-about-it/.

42. Bruce Britt, "Marketing Leaders Discuss the Resurgence of Direct Mail," *Deliver Magazine,* January 18, 2011, www.delivermagazine.com/2011/01/marketing-leaders-discuss-resurgence-of-direct-mail/; also see Alex Palmer, "Insurance Marketers Leverage Targeted Marketing," *Direct Marketing,* February 1, 2012, www.dmnews.com/insurance-marketers-leverage-targeted-marketing/article/225127/.

43. See www.landsend.com/mobile/index.html and http://catalog-spree.com/, accessed September 2014.

44. Allison Schiff, "Catalogs Are Part of a Balanced Marketing Diet," *Direct Marketing,* March 11, 2013, www.dmnews.com/catalogs-are-part-of-a-balanced-marketing-diet/article/283668/.

45. Kurt Solomon, "Is the Catalog Dead?" November 5, 2013, www.kurtsalmon.com/US/vertical-insight/Is-the-Catalog-Dead-?vertical=Retail&id=936&language=en-us#.UzTUVV5dCcC.

46. "Data-Driven Marketing's Growth Accelerates," *Direct Marketing News,* http://media.dmnews.com/images/2014/01/10/direct_and_digital_529467.jpg, accessed June 2014.

47. See Alan Farnham, "Fighting Telemarketers: When Do-Not-Call List Fails, These Strategies Work," *ABC News,* January 21, 2014, http://abcnews.go.com/Business/best-ways-turn-tables-telemarketers/story?id=21534413; and www.donotcall.gov, accessed July 2014.

48. See Rachel Brown, "Perry, Fischer, Lavigne Tapped for Proactiv," *WWD*, January 13, 2010, p. 3; Rahul Parikh, "Proactiv's Celebrity Shell Game," Salon.com, February 28, 2011, www.salon.com/2011/02/28/proactiv_celebrity_sham; "Guthy-Renker Honored with Nine Era Moxie Awards for Year's Best Direct Marketing Campaigns," *Marketing Weekly News*, October 19, 2013, p. 145; and www.proactiv.com, accessed September 2014.

49. Jeanine Poggi, "H&M Super Bowl Ad Lets You Buy Beckham Bodywear by Remote Control," *Advertising Age,* January 6, 2014, www.adage.com/print/290915.

50. See "Cougar Town Episode Doubles as a Half-Hour Long Target Ad," *psfk,* March 2014, www.psfk.com/2014/03/cougar-town-target-ad.html#!Eo1Q8; and Andrew Adam Newman, "Like That Vase on TV? Click Your Phone to Buy It," *New York Times,* March 18, 2014, p. B6.

51. Stephanie Rosenbloom, "The New Touch-Face of Vending Machines," *New York Times*, May 25, 2010, www.nytimes.com/2010/05/26/business/26vending.html; "Automating Retail Success," www.businessweek.com/adsections/2011/pdf/111114_Verizon3.pdf; accessed July 2012; and "The Kiosk and Self-Service Top Five," *Kiosk Marketplace,* April 17, 2013, www.kioskmarketplace.com/article/211559/.

52. "Best Buy: Consumer Electronics Retailing on the Go," www.zoomsystems.com/our-partners/partner-portfolio/; and www.zoomsystems.com/about-us/company-overview/, accessed September 2014.

53. See Internet Crime Complaint Center, www.ic3.gov, accessed June 2014.

54. See "Many Consumers Fear Identity Theft Yet Still Engage in Risky Behavior," *PRNewswire*, October 21, 2013, www.prnewswire.com/news-releases/many-consumers-fear-identity-theft-yet-still-engage-in-risky-behavior-228595151.html.

55. See Susan Dominus, "Underage on Facebook," *MSN Living*, March 15, 2012; http://living.msn.com/family-parenting/underage-on-facebook-5; Josh Wolford, "Facebook Still Has a Big Problem with Underage Users, and They Know It," *WebProNews*, January 24, 2013, www.webpronews.com/facebook-still-has-a-big-problem-with-underage-users-and-they-know-it-2013-01.

56. See Hadley Malcolm, "Millennials Don't Worry about Online Privacy," *USA Today,* April 21, 2013; and "2014 TRUSTe US Consumer Confidence Index," *TRUSTe,* www.truste.com/us-consumer-confidence-index-2014/.

57. Based on information from Michael Bush, "My Life, Seen through the Eyes of Marketers," *Advertising Age,* April 26, 2010, http://adage.com/print/143479.

58. See "Facebook to Make Targeted Ads More Transparent for Users," *Advertising Age,* February 4, 2013, http://adage.com/article/239564/; and www.aboutads.info/, accessed September 2014.

59. See Richard Byrne Reilly, "Feds to Mobile Marketers: Stop Targeting Kids, or Else," *Venture Beat,* March 27, 2014, http://venturebeat.com/2014/03/27/feds-to-mobile-marketers-stop-targeting-kids-or-else-exclusive/; and www.business.ftc.gov/privacy-and-security/childrens-privacy, accessed September 2014.

60. Information on TRUSTe at www.truste.com, accessed September 2014.

61. Information on the DMA Privacy Promise at www.the-dma.org/cgi/dispissue?article=129 and www.dmaconsumers.org/privacy.html, accessed September 2014.

18 Creating Competitive Advantage

Chapter Preview

In previous chapters, you explored the basics of marketing. You learned that the aim of marketing is to engage customers and to create value *for* them in order to capture value *from* them in return. Good marketing companies win, keep, and grow customers by understanding customer needs, designing customer-driven marketing strategies, constructing value-delivering marketing programs, engaging customers, and building customer and marketing partner relationships. In the final three chapters, we'll extend this concept to three special areas: creating competitive advantage, global marketing, and social and environmental marketing sustainability.

To start, let's dig into the competitive strategy of SodaStream, a relatively small brand competing among the giants of the carbonated-beverage industry. Rather than competing head-on with the likes of Coca-Cola and PepsiCo, SodaStream prospers by dominating its own special home-carbonation niche, positioning itself as a smarter alternative to bottled and canned beverages.

SODASTREAM: Putting New Fizz in Carbonated Beverages

The carbonated-beverage market is dominated by huge competitors. Together Coca-Cola and PepsiCo capture a whopping 67 percent share of the $28 billion market. Number three Dr Pepper Snapple Group (with brands such as Dr Pepper, 7-Up, A&W, Canada Dry, and Crush) captures another 21 percent. These giants are investing vast sums in new products and marketing to expand their positions even further. So there's precious little left over for smaller competitors or new brands.

However, one small start-up brand—SodaStream—is putting new fizz into carbonated beverages. How does this small brand survive among the giants? Through smart competitive strategy. SodaStream doesn't compete head-on against the likes of Coca-Cola and Pepsi. Instead, it has carved out its own special market niche. Unlike Coke and Pepsi, SodaStream doesn't actually sell carbonated beverages and waters. Instead, it sells a line of home soda makers that let consumers make their own.

SodaStream isn't just surviving, it's thriving. Although still comparatively tiny—about $600 million in annual sales versus Coca-Cola's $48 billion and PepsiCo's $65 billion—SodaStream is growing fast and profitably. Its sales have quadrupled in just the past four years, even as the bottled carbonated-beverage market has declined 1 to 2 percent per year. In its niche, as the world leader in home-carbonation systems, SodaStream—not Coca-Cola or Pepsi—dominates.

Rather than taking on Coca-Cola and Pepsi directly, nicher SodaStream positions itself as a sensible, responsible alternative to the bottled and canned beverages of its supersized competitors. Its tagline: "SodaStream: Smart. Simple. Bubbles." SodaStream's countertop drink makers are simple and convenient to use. Powered by a pressurized carbon dioxide canister, a SodaStream transforms ordinary tap water into fresh carbonated beverages in only a few seconds, with no heavy bottles to lug around, store, or recycle. Empty canisters can be returned to the store and swapped for full ones. Compared with bottled and canned soft drinks and sparkling water, the SodaStream system is also economical. Using a SodaStream can produce the equivalent of an 8-pack of 12-ounce bottles at a 50-percent-lower cost than buying the product at the store.

Using a SodaStream is empowering, even fun. SodaStream invites customers to be creative and "set the bubbles free." The

Diminutive SodaStream faces carbonated-beverage competitors 80 to 100 times its size. But thanks to smart competitive strategy, SodaStream prospers in the shadows of the soft drink giants. In its fast-growing home-carbonation niche, SodaStream—not Coca-Cola or PepsiCo—dominates.

home carbonation system lets users customize their beverages in terms of flavor and amount of fizz. SodaStream offers more than 100 different SodaStream flavor syrups. The SodaStream appliances and bottles themselves offer a measure of self-expression. The devices come in eight different modern designs intended to spiff up countertops, even a penguin-shaped model and two models that carbonate water in glass carafes. Bottles come in a variety of designs, including bottles for holiday seasons and special occasions (expect customizable SodaStream bottles soon). Match that, Coke and Pepsi!

But wait, there's more. The carbonated beverages made at home with SodaStream are generally better for you. SodaStream flavor mixes contain no high-fructose corn syrup and about a third of the carbs and calories of store-bought brands. And many SodaStream users mix in fruit juices, or even just a splash of lemon or lime, making concoctions that are healthier than off-the-shelf sodas. Finally, SodaStream is more ecofriendly than bottled or canned sodas. It largely eliminates the energy consumption and harmful emissions associated with making, filling, transporting, and recycling plastic bottles and aluminum cans. The carbon footprint for beverages produced using the SodaStream system is 80 percent lower than for store-bought bottled beverages. According to the company, one reusable SodaStream bottle ends up replacing more than 10,000 conventional ones.

All of these consumer benefits create big opportunities for SodaStream and the home-carbonation niche that it dominates. And the brand is moving aggressively to grow its niche through innovation, product development, and marketing. For example, in line with recent beverage trends, SodaStream has developed Xstream Energy mixes (a line of flavors made to "revitalize your mind and body"), SodaStream Isotonic (a sports drink mix designed to "help replace lost fluids and boost your performance"), and SodaStream Sparkling Natural (100% free of artificial flavors, colorings, sweeteners, and preservatives).

SodaStream has also partnered with Kraft, Campbell, and Ocean Spray to develop new syrups for some of America's favorite drink flavors—from Country Time, Crystal Light, and Kool-Aid to V8 juice and Ocean Spray Cranberry. Beyond just adding new flavors and appliance designs, SodaStream recently partnered with Samsung to make a new Samsung Sparkling Refrigerator, with a SodaStream-powered still or sparkling water dispenser in the door.

As another key aspect of its competitive strategy, SodaStream is rapidly bubbling into new markets and channels. For example, five years ago, SodaStream products were sold in only 300 U.S. stores. Last year, that number increased to 15,000 stores (more than 60,000 worldwide), including big hitters such as Walmart; Target, Macy's, Kohl's, Costco, Williams-Sonoma, Amazon, and Bed Bath & Beyond. Because SodaStream sells an appliance rather than bottled beverages, it avoids the intense competition for shelf space on crowded beverage aisles. In fact, one of SodaStream's biggest challenges in new markets is just keeping shelves stocked. Its products fly off the shelves and sell-outs are common.

Rather than tackling its giant competitors head-on, nicher SodaStream positions itself as a sensible, responsible alternative to store-bought beverages. It promises "Smart. Simple. Bubbles."
Courtesy of SodaStream

As a result, SodaStream's U.S. sales increased 75 percent last year. And the brand still has plenty of room to grow. Its home soda makers have penetrated only 1 percent of U.S. homes, compared with 10 percent or more in many more-established European markets. In Sweden, an eye-popping 25 percent of homes carbonate their own beverages with SodaStream drink makers. That translates into big potential in less-mature markets.

Finally, whereas SodaStream avoids head-on competition with the beverage big shots in store aisles, it takes them on directly in edgy comparative ads. For example, in one ad designed for Super Bowl XLVII, SodaStream showed exploding Coke and Pepsi bottles, underscoring the environmental pitch that SodaStream could "save 500 million bottles on game day alone if you let the bubbles set you free." Under pressure from Coca-Cola and PepsiCo (two of the Super Bowl's biggest sponsors), CBS rejected the ad—SodaStream ran a revised version without the direct comparisons. However, the original comparative ad racked up 5 million online views. Again, in SodaStream's Super bowl XLVIII ad, Fox made the brand remove its ad-ending line, "Sorry, Coke and Pepsi." So for the end-of-the-year holiday season, SodaStream took its edgy comparative health and ecology messages to social media. For example, it took a swipe at Coke by posting renderings on Pinterest

Objective Outline

OBJECTIVE 1	**Discuss the need to understand competitors as well as customers through competitor analysis.** Competitor Analysis (pp 569–575)
OBJECTIVE 2	**Explain the fundamentals of competitive marketing strategies based on creating value for customers.** Competitive Strategies (pp 575–585)
OBJECTIVE 3	**Illustrate the need for balancing customer and competitor orientations in becoming a truly market-centered organization.** Balancing Customer and Competitor Orientations (pp 585–586)

of a slimmer, healthier Santa dressed in green. Tweets with the hashtag #GreenSanta also chronicled the Jolly Old Elf's transformation using SodaStream while cutting back on bottled brands.

Thus, SodaStream's future sparkles like a tall glass for its homemade bubbly. Worldwide last year, 7 million active SodaStream households made some 4.5 billion "can-equivalents" of SodaStream beverages. And the brand has just begun to pop the top on this market. Although it faces competitors 80 to 100 times its size, in its profitable home-carbonation niche, SodaStream goes largely unchallenged. Through smart competitive strategy, SodaStream prospers in the shadows of the carbonated-beverage giants.[1]

Today's companies face their toughest competition ever. In previous chapters, we argued that to succeed in today's fiercely competitive marketplace, companies must move from a product-and-selling philosophy to a customer-and-marketing philosophy.

This chapter spells out in more detail how companies can go about outperforming competitors to win, keep, and grow customers. To win in today's marketplace, companies must become adept not only in managing products but also in managing customer relationships in the face of determined competition and a difficult marketing environment. Understanding customers is crucial, but it's not enough. Building profitable customer relationships and gaining **competitive advantage** requires delivering more value and satisfaction to target customers than competitors do. Customers will see competitive advantages as customer advantages, giving the company an edge over its competitors.

Competitive advantage
An advantage over competitors gained by offering consumers greater value.

Competitor analysis
Identifying key competitors; assessing their objectives, strategies, strengths and weaknesses, and reaction patterns; and selecting which competitors to attack or avoid.

Competitive marketing strategies
Strategies that strongly position the company against competitors and give it the greatest possible competitive advantage.

In this chapter, we examine competitive marketing strategies—how companies analyze their competitors and develop successful, customer-value-based strategies for engaging customers and building profitable customer relationships. The first step is **competitor analysis**, the process of identifying, assessing, and selecting key competitors. The second step is developing **competitive marketing strategies** that strongly position the company against competitors and give the company the strongest possible strategic advantage.

Author Comment | Creating competitive advantage begins with a thorough understanding of competitors' strategies. But before a company can analyze its competitors, it must first identify them—a task that's not as simple as it seems.

Competitor Analysis

To plan effective marketing strategies, a company needs to find out all it can about its competitors. It must constantly compare its marketing strategies, products, prices, channels, and promotions with those of close competitors. In this way, the company can find areas of potential competitive advantage and disadvantage. As shown in **Figure 18.1**, competitor analysis involves first identifying and assessing competitors and then selecting which competitors to attack or avoid.

Identifying Competitors

Normally, identifying competitors would seem to be a simple task. At the narrowest level, a company can define its competitors as other companies offering similar products and services to the same customers at similar prices. Thus, Abercrombie & Fitch might see the Gap as a major competitor, but not Nordstrom or Target. The Ritz-Carlton might see the Four Seasons hotels as a major competitor, but not Holiday Inn, the Hampton Inn, or any of the thousands of bed-and-breakfasts that dot the nation.

However, companies actually face a much wider range of competitors. The company might define its competitors as all firms with the same product or class of products. Thus, the Ritz-Carlton would see itself as competing against all other hotels. Even more broadly, competitors might include all companies making products that supply the same service. Here the Ritz-Carlton would see itself competing not only against other hotels but also against anyone who supplies rooms for busy travelers. Finally, and still more broadly, competitors might include all companies that compete for the same consumer dollars. Here the Ritz-Carlton would see itself competing with travel and leisure products and services, from cruises and summer homes to vacations abroad.

Identifying latent competitors: By the time traditional video-rental retailer Blockbuster recognized and reacted to unforeseen competitors such as Netflix, Redbox, and digital video streaming services, it was too late.

Theodore Wood/Polaris/Newscom

Companies must avoid "competitor myopia." A company is more likely to be "buried" by its latent competitors than its current ones. For example, Kodak didn't lose out to competing film makers such as Fuji; it fell to the makers of digital cameras that use no film at all (see Real Marketing 18.1). And once-blazing-hot video-rental superstore Blockbuster didn't go bankrupt at the hands of other traditional brick-and-mortar retailers. It fell victim first to unexpected competitors such as direct marketer Netflix and kiosk marketer Redbox, and then to a host of new digital video streaming services and technologies. By the time Blockbuster recognized and reacted to these unforeseen competitors, it was too late.

Companies can identify their competitors from an *industry* point of view. They might see themselves as being in the oil industry, the pharmaceutical industry, or the beverage industry. A company must understand the competitive patterns in its industry if it hopes to be an effective player in that industry. Companies can also identify competitors from a *market* point of view. Here they define competitors as companies that are trying to satisfy the same customer need or build relationships with the same customer group.

From an industry point of view, Pepsi might see its competition as Coca-Cola and Dr Pepper Snapple Group (maker of Dr Pepper, 7 Up, A&W, Crush, and other brands). From a market point of view, however, the customer really wants "thirst quenching"—a need that can be satisfied by bottled water, energy drinks, fruit juice, iced tea, and many

FIGURE | 18.1
Steps in Analyzing Competitors

Identifying competitors isn't as easy as it seems. For example, Kodak saw other camera film makers as its major competitors. But its real competitors turned out to be the makers of digital cameras that used no film at all. Kodak fell behind in digital technologies and ended up declaring bankruptcy.

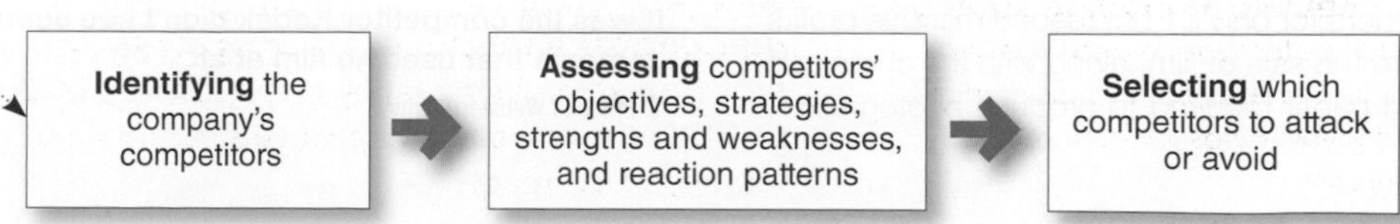

Real Marketing 18.1

Kodak: The Competitor It Didn't See Soon Enough—No Film

Kodak. That venerable brand name has been a household word for generations worldwide. For more than a century, people relied on Kodak for products to help them capture "Kodak moments"—important personal and family events to be shared and recorded for posterity. The Hollywood movie industry evolved around Kodak technology. In 1972, Paul Simon even had a number two hit single called "Kodachrome," a song that put into words the emotional role that Kodak products played in people's lives.

Today, however, Kodak is bankrupt, a company working its way through Chapter 11 reorganization. Once ranked among the bluest of blue chips, Kodak's shares are now penny stocks. The brand that once monopolized its industry, capturing 85 percent of all camera sales and 90 percent of a huge film market, now struggles to compete in any market at all. Once rolling in cash, for the last four years Kodak has been losing $43 million a month. And once employing more than 100,000 people worldwide, the company's mostly U.S. workforce has now dwindled to less than 10,000 workers.

How could such a storied brand fall so far so fast? Kodak fell victim to marketing and competitor myopia—focusing on a narrow set of current products and competitors rather than on underlying customer needs and emerging market dynamics. It wasn't competing film makers that brought Kodak down. It was the competitor Kodak didn't see soon enough—digital photography and cameras that used no film at all. All along, Kodak continued to make the very best film. But in an increasingly digital world, customers no longer needed film. Clinging to its legacy products, Kodak lagged behind competitors in making the shift to digital.

In 1880, George Eastman founded Kodak based on a method for dry-plate photography. In 1888, he introduced the Kodak camera, which used glass plates for capturing images. Looking to expand the market, Eastman next developed film and the innovative little Kodak Brownie film camera. He sold the camera for only $1 but reaped massive profits from the sale of film, along with the chemicals and paper required to produce photographs. Although Kodak also developed innovative imaging technologies for industries ranging from health care to publishing, throughout the twentieth century, cameras and film remained the company's massive cash cow.

Interestingly, way back in 1975, Kodak engineers invented the first digital camera—a toaster-sized image sensor that captured rough hues of black and white. However, failing to recognize the mass-market potential of digital photography, and fearing that digital technology would cannibalize its precious film business, Kodak shelved the digital project. Company managers simply could not envision a filmless world. So Kodak held fast to film and focused its innovation and competitive energies on making better film and out-innovating other film producers. When the company later realized its mistake, it was too late.

Blinded by its film fixation, Kodak failed to see emerging competitive trends associated with capturing and sharing images. Kodak's culture became bound up in its history and the nostalgia that accompanied it. "They were a company stuck in time," says one analyst. "Their history was so important to them—this rich century-old history when they made a lot of amazing things and a lot of money along the way. [Then,] their history [became] a liability."

By the time Kodak finally introduced a line of pocket-sized digital cameras in the late 1990s, the market was already crowded with digital products from Sony, Canon, and a dozen other camera makers. That was soon followed by a completely new category of competitors, as more and more people began pointing-and-clicking their phones and other mobile devices and sharing photos instantly via texting, e-mail, and online photo-sharing networks. Late to the digital game, Kodak became a relic of the past and an also-ran to a host of new-age digital competitors that hadn't even existed a decade or two earlier.

Somewhere along the way, swelled with success, once-mighty Kodak lost sight of founder George Eastman's visionary knack

Competitor myopia: It wasn't competing film makers that brought Kodak down. It was the competitor Kodak didn't see soon enough—digital photography and cameras that used no film at all.

© Finnbarr Webster/Alamy

for defining customer needs and competitor dynamics. According to one biographer, Eastman's legacy was not film; it was innovation. "George Eastman never looked back. He always looked forward to doing something better than what he had done, even if he had the best on the market at the time." If it had retained Eastman's philosophy, Kodak might well have been the market leader in digital technologies. We might all still be capturing "Kodak moments" on Kodak digital cameras and smartphones and sharing them on Kodak-run online sites and image-sharing social networks.

As Kodak emerges from bankruptcy, given the strength of the Kodak brand name, those things could still happen. But it's not likely. As a part of its bankruptcy plan, Kodak announced that it will stop making digital cameras (it has also discontinued its famous Kodachrome color film). Instead, it plans to license its name to other manufacturers that will make cameras under the Kodak brand. Some three-fourths of the company's revenues will now come from business segments, such as commercial digital printing and entertainment films. So, along with the company's fortunes, it looks as though the famed "Kodak moment" may have now passed into history.

Sources: Sam Gustin, "In Kodak Bankruptcy, Another Casualty of the Digital Revolution," *Time*, January 20, 2012, http://business.time.com/2012/01/20/in-kodak-bankruptcy-another-casualty-of-the-digital-revolution/; Ernest Scheyder, "Focus on Past Glory Kept Kodak from Digital Win," Reuters, January 19, 2012, www.reuters.com/article/2012/01/19/us-kodak-bankruptcy-idUSTRE80I1N020120119; Dawn McCarty and Beth Jink, "Kodak Files for Bankruptcy as Digital Era Spells End to Film," *Bloomberg Businessweek*, January 25, 2012, www.businessweek.com/news/2012-01-25/kodak-files-for-bankruptcy-as-digital-era-spells-end-to-film.html; Michael Hiltzik, "Kodak's Long Fade to Black," *Los Angeles Times*, December 4, 2011; "Kodak to Stop Making Digital Cameras," *Digital Photography Review*, February 9, 2012, www.dpreview.com/news/2012/02/09/Kodak_exits_camera_business; and "Kodak Transforms from Photo Pioneer to New Tech Company," *Baltimore Sun*, January 8, 2014, http://darkroom.baltimoresun.com/2014/01/kodak-transforms-from-photo-pioneer-to-new-tech-company-relists-on-new-york-stock-exchange/#1.

other fluids. Similarly, Google once defined its competitors as other search engine providers, such as Yahoo! or Microsoft's Bing. Now, Google takes a broader view of serving market needs for online and mobile access to the digital world. Under this market definition, Google squares off against once-unlikely competitors such as Apple, Samsung, Microsoft, and even Amazon and Facebook. In general, the market concept of competition opens the company's eyes to a broader set of actual and potential competitors.

Assessing Competitors

Having identified the main competitors, marketing management now asks: What are the competitors' objectives? What does each seek in the marketplace? What is each competitor's strategy? What are various competitors' strengths and weaknesses, and how will each react to actions the company might take?

Determining Competitors' Objectives

Each competitor has a mix of objectives. The company wants to know the relative importance that a competitor places on current profitability, market share growth, cash flow, technological leadership, service leadership, and other goals. Knowing a competitor's mix of objectives reveals whether the competitor is satisfied with its current situation and how it might react to different competitive actions. For example, a company that pursues low-cost leadership will react much more strongly to a competitor's cost-reducing manufacturing breakthrough than to the same competitor's increase in advertising.

A company also must monitor its competitors' objectives for various segments. If the company finds that a competitor has discovered a new segment, this might be an opportunity. If it finds that competitors plan new moves into segments now served by the company, it will be forewarned and, hopefully, forearmed.

Identifying Competitors' Strategies

Strategic group
A group of firms in an industry following the same or a similar strategy.

The more that one firm's strategy resembles another firm's strategy, the more the two firms compete. In most industries, the competitors can be sorted into groups that pursue different strategies. A **strategic group** is a group of firms in an industry following the same or a similar strategy in a given target market. For example, in the major appliance industry, GE and Whirlpool belong to the same strategic group. Each produces a full line of medium-price

Strategic groups: Viking belongs to the appliance industry strategic group offering a narrow line of higher-quality appliances supported by good service. "At Viking, it's more than just steel on the line," says this ad. "It's our pride."

Viking Range Corporation

appliances supported by good service. In contrast, Sub-Zero and Viking belong to a different strategic group. They produce a narrower line of higher-quality appliances, offer a higher level of service, and charge a premium price. "We're as passionate about building Viking products as chefs are about cooking with them," says Viking. "We innovate. We over-engineer. And then we use high-grade, heavy-duty materials to create the most powerful products available. At Viking, it's more than just steel on the line. It's our pride."[2]

Some important insights emerge from identifying strategic groups. For example, if a company enters a strategic group, the members of that group become its key competitors. Thus, if the company enters a group containing GE and Whirlpool, it can succeed only if it develops strategic advantages over these two companies.

Although competition is most intense within a strategic group, there is also rivalry among groups. First, some strategic groups may appeal to overlapping customer segments. For example, no matter what their strategy, all major appliance manufacturers will go after the apartment and homebuilders segment. Second, customers may not see much difference in the offers of different groups; they may see little difference in quality between GE and Whirlpool. Finally, members of one strategic group might expand into new strategy segments. Thus, GE's Monogram and Profile lines of appliances compete in the premium-quality, premium-price line with Viking and Sub-Zero.

The company needs to look at all the dimensions that identify strategic groups within the industry. It must understand how each competitor delivers value to its customers. It needs to know each competitor's product quality, features, and mix; customer services; pricing policy; distribution coverage; sales force strategy; and advertising, sales promotion, and online and social media programs. And it must study the details of each competitor's research and development (R&D), manufacturing, purchasing, financial, and other strategies.

Assessing Competitors' Strengths and Weaknesses

Marketers need to carefully assess each competitor's strengths and weaknesses to answer a critical question: What *can* our competitors do? As a first step, companies can gather data on each competitor's goals, strategies, and performance over the past few years. Admittedly, some of this information will be hard to obtain. For example, business-to-business (B-to-B) marketers find it hard to estimate competitors' market shares because they do not have the same syndicated data services that are available to consumer packaged-goods companies.

Companies normally learn about their competitors' strengths and weaknesses through secondary data, personal experience, and word of mouth. They can also conduct primary marketing research with customers, suppliers, and dealers. They can check competitors' online and social media sites. Or they can try **benchmarking** themselves against other firms, comparing the company's products and processes to those of competitors or leading firms in other industries to identify best practices and find ways to improve quality and performance. Benchmarking is a powerful tool for increasing a company's competitiveness.

Benchmarking
Comparing the company's products and processes to those of competitors or leading firms in other industries to identify best practices and find ways to improve quality and performance.

Estimating Competitors' Reactions

Next, the company wants to know: What *will* our competitors do? A competitor's objectives, strategies, and strengths and weaknesses go a long way toward explaining its likely actions. They also suggest its likely reactions to company moves, such as price cuts, promotion increases, or new-product introductions. In addition, each competitor has a certain philosophy of doing business, a certain internal culture and guiding beliefs. Marketing managers need a deep understanding of a competitor's mentality if they want to anticipate how that competitor will act or react.

Each competitor reacts differently. Some do not react quickly or strongly to a competitor's move. They may feel their customers are loyal, they may be slow in noticing the move,

Competitor reactions: In some industries, competitors live in relative harmony; in others, they are more openly combative. For example, in the U.S. wireless industry, T-Mobile, AT&T, and Verizon Wireless have attacked each other aggressively in comparative ads.

© T-Mobile USA, Inc. Used with permission.

or they may lack the funds to react. Some competitors react only to certain types of moves and not to others. Other competitors react swiftly and strongly to any action. Thus, P&G does not allow a competitor's new product to come easily into the market. Many firms avoid direct competition with P&G and look for easier prey, knowing that P&G will react fiercely if it is challenged. Knowing how major competitors react gives the company clues on how best to attack competitors or how best to defend its current positions.

In some industries, competitors live in relative harmony; in others, competitors are more openly combative. For example, competitors in the U.S. wireless industry have been at each other's throats for years. T-Mobile, AT&T, and Verizon Wireless have aggressively attacked each other in comparative ads. AT&T started the most recent round of attacks with full-page ads in the *New York Times*, *Wall Street Journal*, and *USA Today* telling "The truth about T-Mobile's network compared to AT&T—2X more dropped calls, 2X more failed calls, 50% slower download speeds." Understandably, T-Mobile responded with attack ads of its own. The first ad proclaimed: "If AT&T thought our network wasn't great, why did they try to buy it?" (referring to AT&T's failed attempt to buy T-Mobile two years earlier). "Someone is obviously worried." Later T-Mobile attack ads named both AT&T and Verizon directly and took them to task for everything from their phone upgrade policies to plan costs.[3] In some cases, such competitive exchanges can provide useful information to consumers. In other cases, they can reflect unfavorably on the entire industry.

Selecting Competitors to Attack and Avoid

A company has already largely selected its major competitors through prior decisions on customer targets, positioning, and its marketing mix strategy. Management now must decide which competitors to compete against most vigorously.

Strong or Weak Competitors

A company can focus on one of several classes of competitors. Most companies prefer to compete against weak competitors. This requires fewer resources and less time. But in the process, the firm may gain little. You could argue that a firm also should compete with strong competitors to sharpen its abilities. And sometimes, a company can't avoid its largest competitors, as in the case of T-Mobile, Verizon, and AT&T. But even strong competitors have some weaknesses, and succeeding against them often provides greater returns.

A useful tool for assessing competitor strengths and weaknesses is **customer value analysis**. The aim of customer value analysis is to determine the benefits that target customers value and how customers rate the relative value of various competitors' offers. In conducting a customer value analysis, the company first identifies the major attributes that customers value and the importance customers place on these attributes. Next, it assesses its performance against competitors on those valued attributes.

Customer value analysis
An analysis conducted to determine what benefits target customers value and how they rate the relative value of various competitors' offers.

The key to gaining competitive advantage is to examine how a company's offer compares to that of its major competitors in each customer segment. The company wants to find the place in the market where it meets customers' needs in a way rivals can't. If the company's offer delivers greater value than the competitor's offer on important attributes, it can charge a higher price and earn higher profits, or it can charge the same price and gain more market share. But if the company is seen as performing at a lower level than its major competitors on some important attributes, it must invest in strengthening those attributes or finding other important attributes where it can build a lead.

Close or Distant Competitors

Most companies will compete with close competitors—those that resemble them most—rather than distant competitors. Thus, Nike competes more against Adidas than against Timberland or Keen. And Target competes against Walmart rather than Neiman Marcus or Nordstrom.

At the same time, the company may want to avoid trying to "destroy" a close competitor. For example, in the late 1970s, then-market leader Bausch & Lomb moved aggressively against other soft contact lens manufacturers with great success. However, this forced weak competitors to sell out to larger firms such as Johnson & Johnson (J&J). As a result, Bausch & Lomb then faced much larger competitors—and it suffered the consequences. J&J acquired Vistakon, a small nicher with only $20 million in annual sales. Backed by J&J's deep pockets, the small but nimble Vistakon developed and introduced its innovative Acuvue disposable lenses. With Vistakon leading the way, J&J is now the dominant U.S. contact lens maker, with 42 percent market share, while Bausch & Lomb lags in fourth place with about a 10 percent market share. In this case, success in hurting a close rival brought in tougher competitors.[4]

Good or Bad Competitors

A company really needs and benefits from competitors. The existence of competitors results in several strategic benefits. Competitors may share the costs of market and product development and help legitimize new technologies. They may serve less-attractive segments or lead to more product differentiation. Finally, competitors may help increase total demand.

Good and bad competitors: Rather than spelling trouble for Amazon's Kindle, Apple's iPod introduction created a surge in tablet demand that benefited not only Amazon, but other tablet competitors such as Samsung, Microsoft, and Google.

Victor J. Blue/Bloomberg via Getty Images

For example, you might think that Apple's introduction of its stylish and trendy iPad tablet would have spelled trouble for Amazon's smaller, dowdier Kindle e-reader, which had been on the market for three years prior to the iPad's debut. Many analysts thought that Apple had created the "Kindle killer." However, as it turns out, the competing iPad created a stunning surge in tablet demand that benefited both companies. Kindle e-reader sales increased sharply with the iPad introduction, and new tablet demand spurred Amazon to introduce its own full line of Kindle tablets. As an added bonus, the surge in iPad usage increased Amazon's sales of e-books and other digital content, which can be read on the iPad using a free Kindle for iPad app.

Burgeoning tablet demand following the iPad introduction also opened the market to a host of new competitors, such as Samsung, Google, and Microsoft.[5]

However, a company may not view all its competitors as beneficial. An industry often contains *good competitors* and *bad competitors*. Good competitors play by the rules of the industry. Bad competitors, in contrast, break the rules. They try to buy share rather than earn it, take large risks, and play by their own rules.

For example, the nation's traditional newspapers face a lot of bad competitors these days. Digital services that overlap with traditional newspaper content are bad competitors because they offer for free real-time content that subscription-based newspapers printed once a day can't match. An example is the *Huffington Post*, the Pulitzer Prize-winning online newspaper started in 2005 by Arianna Huffington as an outlet for liberal commentary. The publication has since expanded and is now owned by AOL. The site offers news, blogs, and original content, and covers politics, business, entertainment, technology, popular media, lifestyle, culture, comedy, healthy living, women's interest, and local news. The ad-supported site is free to users, versus the subscription rates charged by traditional newspapers, and that's about as bad as a competitor can get. HuffingtonPost.com is currently the 20th most visited site in the United States.[6] Such unorthodox digital competitors have helped to drive many traditional newspapers into bankruptcy in recent years.

Finding Uncontested Market Spaces

Rather than competing head to head with established competitors, many companies seek out unoccupied positions in uncontested market spaces. They try to create products and services for which there are no direct competitors. Called a "blue-ocean strategy," the goal is to make competition irrelevant:[7]

> Companies have long engaged in head-to-head competition in search of profitable growth. They have fought for competitive advantage, battled over market share, and struggled for differentiation. Yet in today's overcrowded industries, competing head-on results in nothing but a bloody "red ocean" of rivals fighting over a shrinking profit pool. In their book *Blue Ocean Strategy*, two strategy professors contend that although most companies compete within such red oceans, the strategy isn't likely to create profitable growth in the future. Tomorrow's leading companies will succeed not by battling competitors but by creating "blue oceans" of uncontested market space.

Such strategic moves—termed value innovation—create powerful leaps in value for both the firm and its buyers, creating all new demand and rendering rivals obsolete. By creating and capturing blue oceans, companies can largely take rivals out of the picture.

Apple has long practiced this strategy, introducing product firsts such as the iPod, iTunes, iPhone, and iPad that created whole new categories. Similarly, Redbox reinvented the DVD-rental category via kiosks in convenient locations. And Southwest Airlines entered uncontested blue-ocean space (in this case, perhaps blue-sky space) in air travel as the first no frills, low-cost, direct point-to-point air carrier—it is now the nation's fourth largest airline.

Another example is GMCR's Keurig brand, which created an entirely new category in home coffee makers. Rather than competing against traditional coffee maker brands such as Hamilton Beach, Mr. Coffee, and Cuisinart that brew coffee by the pot, Keurig reinvented the process with innovative cup-at-a-time, pod-based coffee makers. The Keurig brewing system uses premeasured K-Cups that let customers brew any of 200 different coffee flavors one cup at a time, quickly and conveniently. "Brew the Love." says Keurig. Thanks to its blue-ocean strategy, Keurig has achieved annual sales of coffee makers and pods exceeding $4.4 billion, capturing a 40 percent dollar share of the market. Whereas other brands make money only from coffee maker sales, Keurig reaps 73 percent of its revenues from sales of K-Cup pods.[8]

Blue-ocean strategy: Keurig reinvented the home coffee brewing process with innovative cup-at-a-time pod-based coffee makers. "Brew the Love," says Keurig.

The KEURIG® trademarks and advertisements are used with permission from Keurig Green Mountain, Inc.

Designing a Competitive Intelligence System

We have described the main types of information that companies need about their competitors. This information must be collected, interpreted, distributed, and used. Gathering competitive intelligence can cost much money and time, so the company must design a cost-effective competitive intelligence system.

The competitive intelligence system first identifies the vital types of competitive information needed and the best sources of this information. Then, the system continuously collects information from the field (sales force, channels, suppliers, market research firms, Internet and social media sites, online monitoring, and trade associations) and published data (government publications, speeches, and online databases). Next the system checks the information for validity and reliability, interprets it, and organizes it in an appropriate way. Finally, it sends relevant information to decision makers and responds to inquiries from managers about competitors.

With this system, company managers receive timely intelligence about competitors in the form of reports and assessments, posted bulletins, newsletters, and e-mail and mobile alerts. Managers can also connect when they need to interpret a competitor's sudden move, know a competitor's weaknesses and strengths, or assess how a competitor will respond to a planned company move.

Author Comment | Now that we've identified competitors and know all about them, it's time to design a strategy for gaining competitive advantage.

Competitive Strategies

Having identified and evaluated its major competitors, a company now must design broad marketing strategies by which it can gain competitive advantage. But what broad competitive marketing strategies might the company use? Which ones are best for a particular company or for the company's different divisions and products?

Approaches to Marketing Strategy

No one strategy is best for all companies. Each company must determine what makes the most sense given its position in the industry and its objectives, opportunities, and resources. Even within a company, different strategies may be required for different businesses or products. Johnson & Johnson uses one marketing strategy for its leading brands in stable consumer markets, such as BAND-AID, Tylenol, Listerine, or J&J's baby products, and a different marketing strategy for its high-tech health-care businesses and products, such as Monocryl surgical sutures or NeuFlex finger joint implants.

Companies also differ in how they approach the strategy-planning process. Many large firms develop formal competitive marketing strategies and implement them religiously. However, other companies develop strategy in a less formal and orderly fashion. Some companies, such as Harley-Davidson, Red Bull, Virgin Atlantic Airways, and BMW's MINI unit, succeed by breaking many of the rules of marketing strategy. Such companies don't operate large marketing departments, conduct expensive marketing research, spell out elaborate competitive strategies, and spend huge sums on advertising. Instead, they sketch out strategies on the fly, stretch their limited resources, live close to their customers, and create more satisfying solutions to customer needs. They form buyer's clubs, use buzz marketing, and focus on winning customer loyalty. It seems that not all marketing must follow in the footsteps of marketing giants such as P&G, McDonald's, and Microsoft.

In fact, approaches to marketing strategy and practice often pass through three stages—entrepreneurial marketing, formulated marketing, and intrepreneurial marketing:

● Entrepreneurial marketing: Boston Beer Company founder Jim Koch first marketed his Samuel Adams beer by carrying bottles in a suitcase from bar to bar, telling his story, educating consumers, getting people to taste the beer, and persuading bartenders to carry it. The company is now the leading craft brewery in America.

Alexandra Schuler/dpa/picture-alliance/Newscom

- *Entrepreneurial marketing.* Most companies are started by individuals who live by their wits. They visualize an opportunity, construct flexible strategies on the backs of envelopes, and knock on every door to gain attention. ● Jim Koch, founder of Boston Beer Company, whose Samuel Adams Boston Lager beer has become the top-selling craft beer in America, started out in 1984 brewing a cherished family beer recipe in his kitchen. For marketing, Koch carried bottles of Samuel Adams in a suitcase from bar to bar, telling his story, educating consumers about brewing quality and ingredients, getting people to taste the beer, and persuading bartenders to carry it. For 10 years, he couldn't afford advertising; he sold his beer through direct selling and grassroots public relations. "It was all guerilla marketing," says Koch. "The big guys were so big, we had to do innovative things like that." Today, however, his business pulls in more than $628 million a year, making it the leader over more than 1,000 competitors in the craft brewery market.[9]
- *Formulated marketing.* As small companies achieve success, they inevitably move toward more-formulated marketing. They develop formal marketing strategies and adhere to them closely. Boston Beer now employs a large sales force and has a marketing department that carries out market research and plans strategy. Although Boston Beer is far less formal and sophisticated in its strategy than $40-billion mega-competitor Anheuser-Busch Inbev, it has adopted some of the tools used in professionally run marketing companies.
- *Intrepreneurial marketing.* Many large and mature companies get stuck in formulated marketing. They pore over the latest Nielsen numbers, scan market research reports, and try to fine-tune their competitive strategies and programs. These companies sometimes lose the marketing creativity and passion they had at the start. They now need to reestablish within their companies the entrepreneurial spirit and actions that made them successful in the first place. They need to encourage more marketing initiative and "intrepreneurship" at the local level.

Many companies build intrepreneurship into their core marketing operations. For example, IBM encourages employees at all levels to interact on their own with customers through blogs, social media, and other platforms. Google's Innovation Time-Off program encourages all of its engineers and developers to spend 20 percent of their time developing "cool and wacky" new-product ideas—blockbusters such as Google News, Gmail, and AdSense are just a few of the resulting products. And Facebook sponsors regular "hackathons," during which it encourages internal teams to come up with and present intrepreneurial ideas. One of the most important innovations in the company's history—the "Like button"—resulted from such a hackathon.[10]

The bottom line is that there are many approaches to developing effective competitive marketing strategies. There will be a constant tension between the formulated side of marketing and the creative side. It is easier to learn the formulated side of marketing, which has occupied most of our attention in this book. But we have also seen how marketing creativity and passion in the strategies of many of the companies studied—whether small or large, new or mature—have helped to build and maintain success in the marketplace. With this in mind, we now look at the broad competitive marketing strategies companies can use.

Basic Competitive Strategies

Three decades ago, Michael Porter suggested four basic competitive positioning strategies that companies can follow—three winning strategies and one losing one.[11] The three winning strategies are as follows:

- *Overall cost leadership.* Here the company works hard to achieve the lowest production and distribution costs. Low costs let the company price lower than its competitors and win a large market share. Walmart and JetBlue Airways are leading practitioners of this strategy.
- *Differentiation.* Here the company concentrates on creating a highly differentiated product line and marketing program so that it comes across as the class leader in the industry. Most customers would prefer to own this brand if its price is not too high. Nike and Caterpillar follow this strategy in apparel and heavy construction equipment, respectively.
- *Focus.* Here the company focuses its effort on serving a few market segments well rather than going after the whole market. For example, Ritz-Carlton focuses on the top 5 percent of corporate and leisure travelers. Bose concentrates on very high-quality electronics products that produce better sound. Hohner owns a stunning 85 percent of the harmonica market.

Companies that pursue a clear strategy—one of the above—will likely perform well. The firm that carries out that strategy best will make the most profits. But firms that do not pursue a clear strategy—*middle-of-the-roaders*—do the worst. Sears, Best Buy, and Holiday Inn encountered difficult times because they did not stand out as the lowest in cost, highest in perceived value, or best in serving some market segment. Middle-of-the-roaders try to be good on all strategic counts but end up being not very good at anything.

Two marketing consultants, Michael Treacy and Fred Wiersema, offer a more customer-centered classification of competitive marketing strategies.[12] They suggest that companies gain leadership positions by delivering superior value to their customers. Companies can pursue any of three strategies—called *value disciplines*—for delivering superior customer value:

- *Operational excellence.* The company provides superior value by leading its industry in price and convenience. It works to reduce costs and create a lean and efficient value delivery system. It serves customers who want reliable, good-quality products or services but want them cheaply and easily. Examples include Walmart, IKEA, Zara, and Southwest Airlines.
- *Customer intimacy.* The company provides superior value by precisely segmenting its markets and tailoring its products or services to exactly match the needs of targeted customers. It specializes in satisfying unique customer needs through a close relationship with and intimate knowledge of the customer. It empowers its people to respond quickly to customer needs. Customer-intimate companies serve customers who are willing to pay a premium to get precisely what they want. They will do almost anything to build long-term customer loyalty and to capture customer lifetime value. For example, Club Med, with its global network of summer and winter resorts, is focused upon delivering highly tailored holiday experiences to its guests (see Real Marketing 18.2). Other companies that practice customer intimacy include Lexus, Nordstrom, and Ritz-Carlton hotels.
- *Product leadership.* The company provides superior value by offering a continuous stream of leading-edge products or services. It aims to make its own and competing products obsolete. Product leaders are open to new ideas, relentlessly pursue new solutions, and work to get new products to market quickly. They serve customers who want state-of-the-art products and services, regardless of the costs in terms of price or inconvenience. One good example of a product leader is Apple:

> From the very beginning, Apple has churned out one cutting-edge product after another. It all started with the Apple Macintosh, the first personal computer ever to feature a graphic

Real Marketing 18.2 Club Med: Customer Intimacy to the Core

Imagine holidaying at a ski resort that was designed with the help of its future customers. Well that's what happened in December 2014 when Club Med added to its portfolio by opening another winter village, this time in Val Thorens in the French Alps. Opening another resort is hardly a remarkable feat for an established global resort chain, but this was Club Med's first ever crowd-sourced resort. Prior to finalizing the hotel, Club Med embarked on a social media campaign where its over 1 million Facebook followers could vote on aspects of the design—from the choice of the resort's name to the style of armchairs in the bar to whether the resort should include a rock-climbing wall and a snow track for mountain bikes.

Although these types of digital campaigns have now become commonplace to help launch consumer products, especially in the case of fast food and soft drinks, Club Med is the first to apply the strategy to a major hotel design. Although voters were limited to seven decisions with the choice of two predetermined options, this digital campaign does highlight Club Med's strategic approach to build on customer intimacy by creating loyal customer communities. According to Julien Lebreton, Club Med's digital strategy head, Club Med is essentially a community brand that can be leveraged using online and social networks. This digital connection enables Club Med to show that it listens to customers and is willing to incorporate their preferences into the design of new holiday facilities.

Club Med, short for Club Méditerranée, is a French-owned resort specialist that opened its first village in 1950 on the island of Majorca off the coast of Spain. The original point of difference for Club Med was its all-inclusive offering. Club Med credits itself as the inventor of the all-inclusive holiday, where meals, soft drinks and alcohol, most activities, child care, and entertainment are included in the upfront price. As the holiday is fully pre-paid, guests have the added flexibility of doing as much or as little as they like. This was Club Med's early form of its customer intimacy strategy in which its customers could easily structure their activity and food choices precisely according to their needs. Since that time, Club Med has expanded significantly, initially in Europe but it now operates in most continents and currently has around 80 resorts throughout the world. The resorts are classified as either "summer" (in hot locations, such as Thailand and Mexico) or "winter" (for snow skiing). Club Med's broad range of holiday offerings has increased its ability to meet the needs of its customers by having different themed and structured resorts.

Although the choice of locations and resort designs, along with the flexibility of the all-inclusive offering, enable the tailoring of a holiday to the precise needs of customers, it is the guest–staff relationship that makes Club Med truly customer intimate. Club Med portrays itself as a "club" where the guests are seen as "members" and referred to as G M (*Gentil Membre* in French, meaning "kind and friendly members"). And it usually refers to its resorts as "villages," which is designed to communicate a sense of a small, friendly, and multicultural community. Part of this is achieved by employing staff from a wide range of nationalities who often speak several languages. This helps ensure that each holiday experience meets the cultural and social needs of every guest. The villages are designed to facilitate engagement and a friendly relationship between customers and the key staff, known as G O (*Gentil Organisateur* in French, meaning "kind and friendly organizers"). It is this guest–staff relationship that is the centerpiece of Club Med's customer intimacy strategy. According to Club Med's job site, a staff member is the ambassador of the Club Med spirit and is responsible for representing Club Med's key values, which include kindness, responsibility, and multiculturalism.

Each member of the resort staff is usually assigned a sports activity, such as tennis, sailing, yoga, snorkeling, dance lessons, trapeze, or even being the in-residence comic relief. This is an unusual feature for a hotel chain, and increases the cost of operation. But the guest–staff relationship enables Club Med to differentiate itself in a competitive marketplace and allows it to execute its customer intimacy strategy by tailoring the Club Med experience to its members' needs on a day-to-day basis. This tailoring of the experience is delivered because one of the key responsibilities of the staff is to be friendly and interact with the guests, even joining them for lunch or dinner on occasions. Through this short-term relationship, the staff members get a sense of the needs and preferences of the guests and

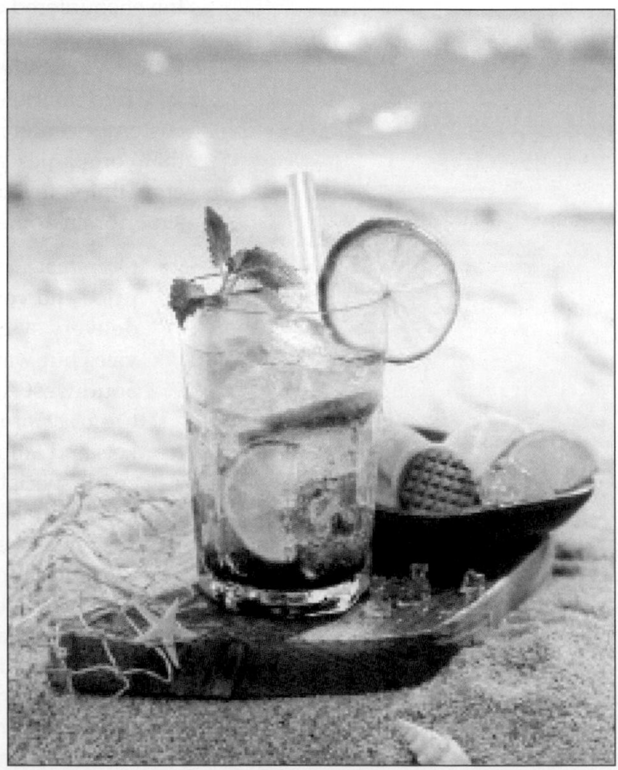

Customer intimacy: Club Med's deeply customer-focused philosophy is perhaps best summed up by its values—kindness, responsibility, and multiculturalism.

© foodandmore/123RF

are able to involve them in the activities and events planned for that day.

But all these inclusions and the personalized attention from the activity-based staff comes at a cost, which means that Club Med needs to charge higher rates than other hotels in order to maintain its profit margin. This creates a perception problem with first-time Club Med customers who see the high rates as a sign of "five-star" hotel quality; many resorts are, in fact, rated only as three- to four-star resorts. Therefore, it becomes critical to manage the customer's expectations and to promote its competitive advantage of offering a tailored holiday experience with a preset budget. In order to improve its offering to affluent travelers with high expectations, Club Med is in the process of opening more high-quality resorts, while exiting from its villages with lower standards. Its current focus is on expansion in China, where Club Med is planning to open five resorts by 2015, and it is also optimistic about expansion in other growing economies such as Brazil and Russia. As a result of such expectations of growth, at the end of 2014, Club Med was the subject of a bidding war between a Chinese investment consortium and a joint venture between an Italian investor and a U.S. private equity firm. This takeover battle has valued Club Med at 875 million euros, which goes to demonstrate the value of a well-executed customer intimacy strategy.

Sources: www.clubmed-corporate.com/?cat=219;www.clubmedjobs.com.au/100-jobs-be-discovered/working-village/organisation-our-villages; Nadia Cameron, "Club Med Ramps up Social Channel Investment with Snow Resort Crowdsourcing Campaign," CMO, March 4, 2014, www.cmo.com.au/article/539620/club_med_ramps_up_social_channel_investment _snow_resort_crowdsourcing_campaign; "Brands Embracing Co-Creativity," CMO Magazine, June 2014, www.fifthquadrant.com.au/fifthquadrant/media/CMOmagazine_June2014.pdf; Adam Thomson, "Bonomi and KKR in Last-Ditch Club Med Bid," *Financial Times*, November 11, 2014, www.ft.com/intl/cms/s/0/2dd2040c-69c8-11e4-9f65-00144feabdc0.html#axzz3LGP80B9l; and Matthew Parsons, "The Resort That Social Media Built: Two Innovative Travel Campaigns," TTG Digital, March 28, 2014, www.ttgdigital.com/toolkit/technology/the-resort-that-social-media-built-two-innovative-travel-campaigns/4690953.article, accessed November 2014.

Product leadership: Apple churns out one cutting-edge product after another, often creating whole new product categories. Apple's diehard fans have anointed the brand "the keeper of all things cool."

© Michael Nagle/Liaison/Getty Images

user interface and mouse. The innovative Mac changed the computer industry forever, gained an enthusiastic throng of brand fans, and began a chain of events that would establish Apple as one of the world's premier product leaders. Apple's product leadership results from understanding what makes its customer tick, then creating ahead-of-the-curve products that put customers at the front of the crowd.

Many tech companies make products that just occupy space and do work. By contrast, Apple has a genius for sparking consumer imaginations and creating "life-feels-good" products that customers want—usually before consumers themselves even know what they want. The result has been one Apple-led revolution after another. Groundbreaking Apple products such as the iPod, iTunes, iPhone, and iPad have all created whole new categories where none previously existed. Such product leadership has produced a consumer love affair with Apple. Diehard fans and gadget geeks around the world have long anointed Apple "the keeper of all things cool." In turn, the consumer love affair with Apple has produced stunning sales and profit results over the years.

Some companies successfully pursue more than one value discipline at the same time. For example, FedEx excels at both operational excellence and customer intimacy. However, such companies are rare; few firms can be the best at more than one of these disciplines. By trying to be *good at all* value disciplines, a company usually ends up being *best at none*.

Thus, most excellent companies focus on and excel at a single value discipline, while meeting industry standards on the other two. Such companies design their entire value delivery network to single-mindedly support the chosen discipline. For example, Walmart knows that customer intimacy and product leadership are important.

Compared with other discounters, it offers good customer service and an excellent product assortment. Still, it purposely offers less customer service and less product depth than does Nordstrom or Williams-Sonoma, which pursue customer intimacy. Instead, Walmart focuses obsessively on operational excellence—on reducing costs and streamlining its order-to-delivery process to make it convenient for customers to buy just the right products at the lowest prices.

By the same token, Ritz-Carlton wants to be efficient and employ the latest technologies. But what really sets the luxury hotel chain apart is its customer intimacy. The Ritz-Carlton creates custom-designed experiences to coddle its customers—to fulfill even the unexpressed desires of its very demanding clientele.

Classifying competitive strategies as value disciplines is appealing. It defines marketing strategy in terms of the single-minded pursuit of delivering superior value to customers. Each value discipline defines a specific way to build lasting customer relationships.

Competitive Positions

Firms competing in a given target market, at any point in time, differ in their objectives and resources. Some firms are large; others are small. Some have many resources; others are strapped for funds. Some are mature and established; others new and fresh. Some strive for rapid market share growth; others for long-term profits. And these firms occupy different competitive positions in the target market.

We now examine competitive strategies based on the roles firms play in the target market—leader, challenger, follower, or nicher. Suppose that an industry contains the firms shown in **Figure 18.2**. As you can see, 40 percent of the market is in the hands of the **market leader**, the firm with the largest market share. Another 30 percent is in the hands of **market challengers**, runner-up firms that are fighting hard to increase their market share. Another 20 percent is in the hands of **market followers**, other runner-up firms that want to hold their share without rocking the boat. The remaining 10 percent is in the hands of **market nichers**, firms that serve small segments not being pursued by other firms.

Market leader
The firm in an industry with the largest market share.

Market challenger
A runner-up firm that is fighting hard to increase its market share in an industry.

Market follower
A runner-up firm that wants to hold its share in an industry without rocking the boat.

Market nicher
A firm that serves small segments that the other firms in an industry overlook or ignore.

Table 18.1 shows specific marketing strategies that are available to market leaders, challengers, followers, and nichers.[13] Remember, however, that these classifications often do not apply to a whole company but only to its position in a specific industry. Large companies such as GE, Microsoft, Google, P&G, or Disney might be leaders in some markets and nichers in others. For example, Amazon leads the online retailing market but challenges Apple and Samsung in smartphones and tablets. P&G leads in many segments, such as laundry detergents and shampoo, but it challenges Unilever in hand soaps and Kimberly-Clark in facial tissues. Such companies often use different strategies for different business units or products, depending on the competitive situations of each.

Market Leader Strategies

Most industries contain an acknowledged market leader. The leader has the largest market share and usually leads the other firms in price changes, new-product introductions, distribution coverage, and promotion spending. The leader may or may not be admired or respected, but other firms concede its dominance. Competitors focus on the leader as a company to challenge, imitate, or avoid. Some of the best-known market leaders are Walmart (retailing), Amazon (online retailing), McDonald's (fast food), Verizon (wireless), Coca-Cola (beverages), Caterpillar (earth-moving equipment), Nike (athletic footwear and apparel), Facebook (social media), and Google (Internet search).

A leader's life is not easy. It must maintain a constant watch. Other firms keep challenging its strengths or trying to take advantage of its weaknesses. The market leader can easily miss a turn in the market and plunge into second or third place. A product innovation may

FIGURE | 18.2
Competitive Market Positions and Roles

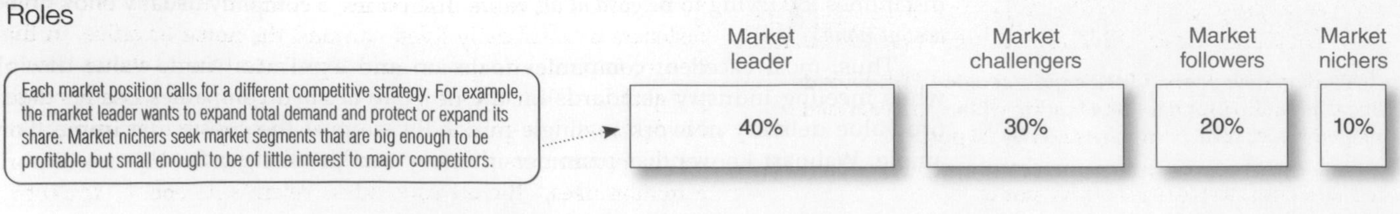

Each market position calls for a different competitive strategy. For example, the market leader wants to expand total demand and protect or expand its share. Market nichers seek market segments that are big enough to be profitable but small enough to be of little interest to major competitors.

Market leader	Market challengers	Market followers	Market nichers
40%	30%	20%	10%

Table 18.1 Strategies for Market Leaders, Challengers, Followers, and Nichers

Market Leader Strategies	Market Challenger Strategies	Market Follower Strategies	Market Nicher Strategies
Expand total market	Full frontal attack	Follow closely	By customer, market, quality-price, service
Protect market share	Indirect attack	Follow at a distance	
Expand market share			Multiple niching

come along and hurt the leader (as when Netflix's direct marketing and video streaming unseated then-market leader Blockbuster or when Apple developed the iPod and iTunes and took the market lead from Sony's Walkman portable audio devices). The leader might grow arrogant or complacent and misjudge the competition (as when Sears lost its lead to Walmart). Or the leader might look old-fashioned against new and peppier rivals (as when Abercrombie & Fitch lost ground to stylish or lower-cost brands such as H&M, Urban Outfitters, and American Eagle).

To remain number one, leading firms can take any of three actions. First, they can find ways to expand total demand. Second, they can protect their current market share through good defensive and offensive actions. Third, they can try to expand their market share further, even if market size remains constant.

Expanding Total Demand

The leading firm normally gains the most when the total market expands. If Americans eat more fast food, McDonald's stands to gain the most because it holds more than three times the fast-food market share of its nearest competitors, Subway and Burger King. If McDonald's can convince more Americans that fast food is the best eating-out choice in these economic times, it will benefit more than its competitors.

Market leaders can expand the market by developing new users, new uses, and more usage of its products. They usually can find *new users* or untapped market segments in many places. For example, traditionally boy-focused LEGOs—Europe's biggest toymaker—now successfully targets girls:[14]

> Three years ago, 90 percent of LEGOs were purchased for boys. However, the brand's sales to girls tripled in 2012 with the introduction of LEGO Friends, a girl-specific line featuring five cute little dolls with fetching names and background stories. Based on extensive research into differences between how boys and girls play, the LEGO Friends line features pastel color bricks and construction sets that encourage girls to build everything from Olivia's House or Emma's Pet Salon to Andrea's City Park Café. LEGO Friends has become one of the most successful lines in LEGO history, helping to boost the company's sales in 2012 by 25 percent and profits by 35 percent, even as other toy companies struggled.

Finding new users: LEGO's girl-specific LEGO Friends line tripled the brand's sales to girls within one year and helped boost total company sales by 25 percent.

Marketers can also expand markets by discovering and promoting *new uses* for the product. For example, since its founding, Velcro Industries has been finding all kinds of "creative ways to connect this to that." But its recent "A Million Uses" ad, video, and social media marketing campaign aims to increase product usage by showcasing all the amazing ways that consumers can use Velcro hook-and-loop fasteners in their daily lives—around the home or office, in the garden, or for craft and do-it-yourself projects. One ad shows how a gadget geek uses Velcro One-Wrap ties to organize all those wires behind his desk, while a gardener uses them to hold orchids upright and an outdoorsman uses them to bundle fishing rods. "It's one wrap with a million uses," the ad concludes. Velcro's Facebook, YouTube, and

Pinterest sites are also loaded with imaginative new uses, such as a guide on Pinterest for making Velcro jewelry.[15]

Finally, market leaders can encourage *more usage* by convincing people to use the product more often or use more per occasion. For example, Campbell's urges people to eat soup and other Campbell's products more often by running ads containing new recipes. At the Campbell's Kitchen Web site (www.campbellskitchen.com), visitors can search for or exchange recipes, create their own personal recipe box, learn ways to eat healthier, and sign up for a daily or weekly Meal Mail program. At the Campbell's Facebook and Twitter sites, consumers can join in on Campbell's Kitchen Community conversations.

Protecting Market Share

While trying to expand total market size, the leading firm also must protect its current business against competitors' attacks. Walmart must constantly guard against Target and Costco; Caterpillar against Komatsu; Apple's iPad and iPhone against Samsung; and McDonald's against Wendy's and Burger King.

What can the market leader do to protect its position? First, it must prevent or fix weaknesses that provide opportunities for competitors. It must always fulfill its value promise and work tirelessly to engage valued customers in strong relationships. Its prices must remain consistent with the value that customers see in the brand. The leader should "plug holes" so that competitors do not jump in.

But the best defense is a good offense, and the best response is *continuous innovation*. The market leader refuses to be content with the way things are and leads the industry in new products, customer services, distribution effectiveness, promotion, and cost cutting. It keeps increasing its competitive effectiveness and value to customers. And when attacked by challengers, the market leader reacts decisively. For example, in the $2.2 billion alkaline battery market, P&G's market-leading Duracell brand has been relentless in its offense against challengers such as Energizer.[16]

Protecting market share: Thanks to relentless innovation and brand-building, market leader Duracell is surging while challengers like Energizer have languished.

Duracell

The alkaline battery market has been in a bit of a decline in recent years with the growth in smartphones, tablets, MP3 players and other consumer electronics that run on rechargeable batteries. But thanks to relentless innovation and brand-building, market leader Duracell is surging while challengers like Energizer have languished. For example, Duracell recently introduced the super-premium Duracell Quantum line, "the best alkaline battery ever built," with innovative DURALOCK technology that helps preserve power in storage for up to 10 years. The brand also expanded its product mix with the Duracell Powermat wireless charging system for mobile devices.

To defend its market-leading position, P&G backs the brand with aggressive partnership-building and promotion. For example, it recently muscled Energizer out of Sam's Club, and it remains the official battery brand of the NFL. Duracell's "Trusted Everywhere" marketing campaign builds emotional connections through ads featuring firefighters and other first responders. And the brand has built a substantial digital and social media presence—it has 6.1 million Facebook "Likes" (Energizer has 168,000). Thus, despite the market's woes, Duracell has seen eye-popping recent growth. It now holds a 46 percent share of the U.S. alkaline battery market. Much of Duracell's recent success has come at the expense of challenger Energizer. "The Energizer bunny may still be going," says one analyst, "but he doesn't have quite the same spring in his step lately."

Expanding Market Share

Market leaders also can grow by increasing their market shares further. In many markets, small market share increases mean very large sales increases. For example, in the U.S. shampoo market, a 1 percent increase in market share is worth $70 million in annual sales; in carbonated soft drinks, $1.25 billion![17]

Studies have shown that, on average, profitability rises with increasing market share. Because of these findings, many companies have sought expanded market shares to improve profitability. GE, for example, declared that it wants to be at least number one or two in each of its markets or else get out. GE shed its computer, air-conditioning, small appliances, and television businesses because it could not achieve top-dog position in those industries.

However, some studies have found that many industries contain one or a few highly profitable large firms, several profitable and more focused firms, and a large number of medium-sized firms with poorer profit performance. It appears that profitability increases as a business gains share relative to competitors in its *served market*. For example, Lexus holds only a small share of the total car market, but it earns a high profit because it is a leading brand in the luxury-performance car segment. And it has achieved this high share in its served market because it does other things right, such as producing high-quality products, creating outstanding service experiences, and building close customer relationships.

Companies must not think, however, that gaining increased market share will automatically improve profitability. Much depends on their strategy for gaining increased share. There are many high-share companies with low profitability and many low-share companies with high profitability. The cost of buying higher market share may far exceed the returns. Higher shares tend to produce higher profits only when unit costs fall with increased market share or when the company offers a superior-quality product and charges a premium price that more than covers the cost of offering higher quality.

Market Challenger Strategies

Firms that are second, third, or lower in an industry are sometimes quite large, such as PepsiCo, Ford, Lowe's, Hertz, and AT&T. These runner-up firms can adopt one of two competitive strategies: They can challenge the market leader and other competitors in an aggressive bid for more market share (market challengers), or they can play along with competitors and not rock the boat (market followers).

A market challenger must first define which competitors to challenge and its strategic objective. The challenger can attack the market leader, a high-risk but potentially high-gain strategy. Its goal might be to take over market leadership. Or the challenger's objective may simply be to wrest more market share.

Although it might seem that the market leader has the most going for it, challengers often have what some strategists call a "second-mover advantage." The challenger observes what has made the market leader successful and improves on it. For example, Home Depot invented the home-improvement superstore. However, after observing Home Depot's success, number two Lowe's, with its brighter stores, wider aisles, and arguably more helpful salespeople, has positioned itself as the friendly alternative to Big Bad Orange. Over the past decade, follower Lowe's has substantially closed the gap in sales and market share with Home Depot.

In fact, challengers often become market leaders by imitating and improving on the ideas of pioneering processors. For example, McDonald's first imitated and then mastered the fast-food system first pioneered by White Castle. And founder Sam Walton admitted that Walmart borrowed most of its practices from discount pioneer Sol Price's FedMart and Price Club chains and then perfected them to become today's dominant retailer.

Alternatively, the challenger can avoid the leader and instead challenge firms its own size or smaller local and regional firms. These smaller firms may be underfinanced and not serving their customers well. Several of the major beer companies grew to their present size not by challenging large competitors but by gobbling up small local or regional competitors. For example, SABMiller became the world's number two brewer by acquiring brands such as Miller, Molson, Coors, and dozens of others. If the challenger goes after a small local company, its objective may be to put that company out of business. The important point remains: The challenger must choose its opponents carefully and have a clearly defined and attainable objective.

How can the market challenger best attack the chosen competitor and achieve its strategic objectives? It may launch a full *frontal attack*, matching the competitor's product, advertising, price, and distribution efforts. It attacks the competitor's strengths rather than its weaknesses. The outcome depends on who has the greater strength and endurance. PepsiCo challenges Coca-Cola in this way, and Ford challenges Toyota frontally.

If the market challenger has fewer resources than the competitor, however, a frontal attack makes little sense. Thus, many new market entrants avoid frontal attacks, knowing that market leaders can head them off with ad blitzes, price wars, and other retaliations. Rather than challenging head-on, the challenger can make an *indirect attack* on the competitor's weaknesses or on gaps in the competitor's market coverage. It can carve out toeholds using tactics that established leaders have trouble responding to or choose to ignore.

For example, SodaStream challenges the soft drink market leaders in this way. And consider how challenger Red Bull entered the U.S. soft drink market in the late 1990s against

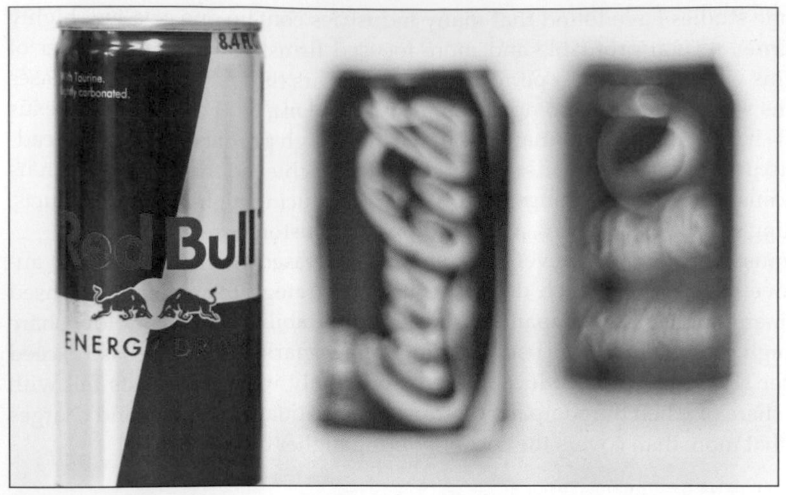

When it entered the U.S. market, rather than attacking market leaders Coca-Cola and Pepsi directly, Red Bull used indirect, unconventional marketing approaches.

Lindsey Hoover – Impact Photo

market leaders Coca-Cola and PepsiCo.[18] Red Bull tackled the leaders indirectly by selling a high-priced niche product in nontraditional distribution points. It began by selling Red Bull via unconventional outlets that were under the radar of the market leaders, such as nightclubs and bars where young revelers gulped down their caffeine fix so they could go all night. Once it had built a core customer base, the brand expanded into more traditional outlets. "Red Bull used the pull of high margins to elbow its way into the corner store, where it now sits in refrigerated bins within arm's length of Coke and Pepsi," says an analyst. Finally, Red Bull used a collection of guerilla marketing tactics rather than the high-cost traditional media used by the market leaders. The indirect approach worked for Red Bull. Despite rapidly intensifying competition in the United States, Red Bull captures a 43 percent share of the energy drink market.

Market Follower Strategies

Not all runner-up companies want to challenge the market leader. The leader never takes challenges lightly. If the challenger's lure is lower prices, improved service, or additional product features, the market leader can quickly match these to defuse the attack. The leader probably has more staying power in an all-out battle for customers. For example, a few years ago, when Kmart launched its renewed low-price "bluelight special" campaign, directly challenging Walmart's everyday low prices, it started a price war that it couldn't win. Walmart had little trouble fending off Kmart's challenge, leaving Kmart worse off for the attempt. Thus, many firms prefer to follow rather than challenge the market leader.

A follower can gain many advantages. The market leader often bears the huge expenses of developing new products and markets, expanding distribution, and educating the market. By contrast, as with challengers, the market follower can learn from the market leader's experience. It can copy or improve on the leader's products and programs, usually with much less investment. Although the follower will probably not overtake the leader, it often can be as profitable.

Following is not the same as being passive or a carbon copy of the market leader. A follower must know how to hold current customers and win a fair share of new ones. It must find the right balance between following closely enough to win customers from the market leader and following at enough of a distance to avoid retaliation. Each follower tries to bring distinctive advantages to its target market—location, services, financing. A follower is often a major target of attack by challengers. Therefore, the market follower must keep its manufacturing costs and prices low or its product quality and services high. It must also enter new markets as they open up.

Market Nicher Strategies

Almost every industry includes firms that specialize in serving market niches. Instead of pursuing the whole market or even large segments, these firms target subsegments. Nichers are often smaller firms with limited resources. But smaller divisions of larger firms also may pursue niching strategies. Firms with low shares of the total market can be highly successful and profitable through smart niching.

Why is niching profitable? The main reason is that the market nicher ends up knowing the target customer group so well that it meets their needs better than other firms that casually sell to that niche. As a result, the nicher can charge a substantial markup over costs because of the added value. Whereas the mass marketer achieves high volume, the nicher achieves high margins.

Nichers try to find one or more market niches that are safe and profitable. An ideal market niche is big enough to be profitable and has growth potential. It is one that the firm can serve effectively. Perhaps most important, the niche is of little interest to major competitors.

And the firm can build the skills and customer goodwill to defend itself against a major competitor as the niche grows and becomes more attractive.

The key idea in niching is specialization. Nichers thrive by meeting in depth the special needs of well-targeted customer groups. For example, when it comes to online dating sites, general sites such as eHarmony.com and Match.com get the most notice. But recently, there's been an explosion of niche dating sites that focus on the narrower preferences of small but well-defined audiences:[19]

> PURRsonals.com pairs cat lovers; SeaCaptainDate.com helps lovers of the ocean "find your first mate." Faith-focused ChristianMingle.com will help "Find God's match for you"; and TallFriends.com brings tall people nose to nose (there's even a choice for people taller than 6'11"!). If that's not nichie enough for you, maybe you need a super-nicher such as GlutenfreeSingles.com, with 4,000 love-seeking wheat-free users. Atlasphere.com offers 16,000 profiles of diehard "objectivists," people who REALLY love *Atlas Shrugged* author Ayn Rand and the philosophy of life suggested by her books. Laid back 420Dating.com is for "mellow" people who smoke marijuana—"Why toke alone?" asks the site. If you get caught, Meet-an-Inmate.com matches inhabitants of penal institutions with pen pals. There's even a dating site for mustache wearers and people who love them (StachePassions.com).
>
> Although some of these niche sites seem a bit extreme, they can be ideal for people who think they know precisely what kind of person they want. For example, FarmersOnly.com serves 100,000 country-folk members seeking like-minded mates with rural persuasions. Farmers Only founder Jerry Miller started the dating site after noticing that the isolated and demanding farming lifestyle makes it hard to find understanding partners. He cites an example in which a country girl and her city boyfriend discussed marriage. Their relationship went to seed when she said that she wanted to raise horses; he said they could keep the horses in the garage. At that point, says Miller, "She knew they were not compatible." Hence the dating service's popular tagline: FarmersOnly.com, because "City folks just don't get it."

Market nichers: FarmersOnly.com pairs country folk with like-minded others, because "City folks just don't get it."

FarmersOnly Media Inc.

A market nicher can specialize along any of several market, customer, product, or marketing mix lines. For example, it can specialize in serving one type of *end user*, as when a law firm specializes in the criminal, civil, or business law markets. The nicher can specialize in serving a given *customer-size* group. Many nichers specialize in serving small and midsize customers who are neglected by the majors.

Some nichers focus on one or a few *specific customers*, selling their entire output to a single company, such as Walmart or GM. Still other nichers specialize by *geographic market*, selling only in a certain locality, region, or area of the world. *Quality-price* nichers operate at the low or high end of the market. For example, HP specializes in the high-quality, high-price end of the hand-calculator market. Finally, *service nichers* offer services not available from other firms. For example, LendingTree provides online lending and realty services, connecting homebuyers and sellers with national networks of mortgage lenders and realtors who compete for the customer's business. "When lenders compete," it proclaims, "you win."

Niching carries some major risks. For example, the market niche may dry up, or it might grow to the point that it attracts larger competitors. That is why many companies practice *multiple niching*. By developing two or more niches, a company increases its chances for survival. Even some large firms prefer a multiple niche strategy to serving the total market. For example, as discussed in Chapter 7, apparel maker VF Corporation markets more than 30 lifestyle brands in niche markets ranging from jeanswear, sportswear, and contemporary styles to outdoor gear and imagewear (workwear). For example, VF's Vans unit creates footwear, apparel, and accessories for skate-, surf-, and snowboarders. Its 7 for All Mankind brand offers premium denim and accessories sold in boutiques and high-end department stores. In contrast, the company's Red Kap, Bulwark, and Chef Designs workwear brands provide an array of uniforms and protective apparel for businesses and public agencies, whether it's outfitting a police force or a chef's crew. Together, these separate niche brands combine to make VF a $10.8-billion apparel powerhouse.[20]

Balancing Customer and Competitor Orientations

Whether a company is the market leader, challenger, follower, or nicher, it must watch its competitors closely and find the competitive marketing strategy that positions it most effectively. And it must continually adapt its strategies to the fast-changing competitive

FIGURE | 18.3
Evolving Company Orientations

		Customer-centered: No	Customer-centered: Yes
Competitor-centered	No	Product orientation	Customer orientation
	Yes	Competitor orientation	Market orientation

Market-centered companies understand both customers and competitors. They build profitable customer relationships by delivering more customer value than competitors do.

environment. This question now arises: Can the company spend *too* much time and energy tracking competitors, damaging its customer orientation? The answer is yes. A company can become so competitor centered that it loses its even more important focus on maintaining profitable customer relationships.

Competitor-centered company
A company whose moves are mainly based on competitors' actions and reactions.

A **competitor-centered company** is one that spends most of its time tracking competitors' moves and market shares and trying to find strategies to counter them. This approach has some pluses and minuses. On the positive side, the company develops a fighter orientation, watches for weaknesses in its own position, and searches out competitors' weaknesses. On the negative side, the company becomes too reactive. Rather than carrying out its own customer relationship strategy, it bases its own moves on competitors' moves. As a result, it may end up simply matching or extending industry practices rather than seeking innovative new ways to create more value for customers.

Customer-centered company
A company that focuses on customer developments in designing its marketing strategies and delivering superior value to its target customers.

A **customer-centered company**, by contrast, focuses more on customer developments in designing its strategies. Clearly, the customer-centered company is in a better position to identify new opportunities and set long-run strategies that make sense. By watching customer needs evolve, it can decide what customer groups and what emerging needs are the most important to serve. Then it can concentrate its resources on delivering superior value to target customers.

Market-centered company
A company that pays balanced attention to both customers and competitors in designing its marketing strategies.

In practice, today's companies must be **market-centered companies**, watching both their customers and their competitors. But they must not let competitor watching blind them to customer focusing.

Figure 18.3 shows that companies might have any of four orientations. First, they might be product oriented, paying little attention to either customers or competitors. Next, they might be customer oriented, paying attention to customers. In the third orientation, when a company starts to pay attention to competitors, it becomes competitor oriented. Today, however, companies need to be market oriented, paying balanced attention to both customers and competitors. Rather than simply watching competitors and trying to beat them on current ways of doing business, they need to watch customers and find innovative ways to build profitable customer relationships by delivering more customer value than competitors do.

18 Reviewing the Concepts

OBJECTIVES REVIEW AND KEY TERMS

Objectives Review

Today's companies face their toughest competition ever. Understanding customers is an important first step in developing strong customer relationships, but it's not enough. To gain competitive advantage, companies must use this understanding to design market offers that deliver more value than the offers of competitors seeking to win over the same customers. This chapter examines how firms analyze their competitors and design effective competitive marketing strategies.

OBJECTIVE 1 **Discuss the need to understand competitors as well as customers through competitor analysis.** *(pp 569–575)*

To prepare an effective marketing strategy, a company must consider its competitors as well as its customers. Building profitable customer relationships requires satisfying target consumer needs *better than competitors do*. A company must continuously analyze competitors and develop *competitive marketing strategies* that position it effectively against competitors and give it the strongest possible *competitive advantage*.

Competitor analysis first involves identifying the company's major competitors, using both an industry-based and a market-based analysis. The company then gathers information on competitors' objectives, strategies, strengths and weaknesses, and reaction patterns. With this information in hand, it can select competitors to attack or avoid. Competitive intelligence must be collected, interpreted, and distributed continuously. Company marketing managers should be able to obtain full and reliable information about any competitor affecting their decisions.

Explain the fundamentals of competitive marketing strategies based on creating value for customers. *(pp 575–585)*

Which competitive marketing strategy makes the most sense depends on the company's industry and on whether it is the market leader, challenger, follower, or nicher. The *market leader* has to mount strategies to expand the total market, protect market share, and expand market share. A *market challenger* is a firm that tries aggressively to expand its market share by attacking the leader, other runner-up companies, or smaller firms in the industry. The challenger can select from a variety of direct or indirect attack strategies.

A *market follower* is a runner-up firm that chooses not to rock the boat, usually from fear that it stands to lose more than it might gain. But the follower is not without a strategy and seeks to use its particular skills to gain market growth. Some followers enjoy a higher rate of return than the leaders in their industry. A *market nicher* is a smaller firm that is unlikely to attract the attention of larger firms. Market nichers often become specialists in some end use, customer size category, specific customer group, geographic area, or service.

OBJECTIVE 3 **Illustrate the need for balancing customer and competitor orientations in becoming a truly market-centered organization.** *(pp 585–586)*

A competitive orientation is important in today's markets, but companies should not overdo their focus on competitors. Companies are more likely to be hurt by emerging consumer needs and new competitors than by existing competitors. *Market-centered companies* that balance customer and competitor considerations are practicing a true market orientation.

MyMarketingLab

Go to **mymktlab.com** to complete the problems marked with this icon .

Key Terms

OBJECTIVE 1

Competitive advantage (p 568)
Competitor analysis (p 568)
Competitive marketing strategies (p 568)
Strategic group (p 571)
Benchmarking (p 572)
Customer value analysis (p 573)

OBJECTIVE 2

Market leader (p 580)
Market challenger (p 580)
Market follower (p 580)
Market nicher (p 580)

OBJECTIVE 3

Competitor-centered company (p 586)
Customer-centered company (p 586)
Market-centered company (p 586)

DISCUSSION AND CRITICAL THINKING

Discussion Questions

18-1 Briefly describe the activities involved when conducting a competitor analysis. (AACSB: Communication)

18-2 How does a company go about obtaining competitive intelligence, and what does the company do with it? (AACSB: Communication)

18-3 Describe the characteristics and likely actions of a market follower. Are they successful? (AACSB: Communication)

18-4 Describe the strategies market nichers can adopt and explain why nichers might have an advantage over market leaders. (AACSB: Communication)

18-5 Compare and contrast competitor-centered, customer-centered, and market-centered companies. Which orientation is best? (AACSB: Communication; Reflective Thinking)

Critical Thinking Exercises

18-6 Companies pursuing a blue ocean strategy attempt to find uncontested market spaces. Apple, Redbox, Southwest Airlines, and Keurig were described in the chapter as examples of companies pursuing and succeeding with such a strategy. Describe another example of a company that is successfully pursuing a blue ocean strategy. (AACSB: Communication; Reflective Thinking)

18-7 Form a small group and conduct a customer value analysis for competing companies in an industry of your choice. Who are the strong and weak competitors? For the strong competitors, what are their vulnerabilities? (AACSB: Communication; Reflective Thinking)

18-8 One source of competitive information is product teardowns. Information such as a bill of materials (BOM)—a listing of all the elements of a product and their costs—can be very useful. Find an example of a product teardown with cost information and discuss the value of that information for competitors. (AACSB: Communication; Reflective Thinking)

MINICASES AND APPLICATIONS

Online, Mobile, and Social Media Marketing I'll Eat My Hat

According to the online resource www.veravo.com, there is a fascinating insight into the minds of UAE Internet users. The service tracked the top 20 Google Adwords that appear before, after, or alongside the regular list. Advertisers pay when their advertisements are clicked. The advertiser creates an account with Google and sets the maximum bid it is willing to pay per click. The position of the advertisement is worked out as a combination of the pay-per-click bid and the quality of the "landing page." In effect, the position is auctioned off by Google. As a result, advertisers will fight over the top spot by outbidding one another. The most expensive Adword was found to be *fedora*, referring to the hat of the same name and worth an incredible $17.40 per click. At $8.62 was the phrase *hair transplant in dubai*. Running about equal in terms of cost per click were *Gucci, blonde hair,* and *liposuction*. Also valued in excess of $7 were *rhinoplasty, breast augmentation, Dubai investments, laser hair removal, diamond sizes,* and, perhaps most bizarre, the U.S. professional wrestler Daniel Bryan. As a snapshot of the obsessions of a nation, Google Adwords is not a strictly scientific measure, but it does give a very different insight into what is hot and what is not in the search engine world.

18-9 What do you think the identified Adwords tell us about the UAE? Are the words really representative of the interests of the country's population? (AACSB: Communication; Reflective Thinking)

18-10 Globally, Google Adwords is worth 68 percent of Google's income. Google is making over $120 million a day. What are the advantages and disadvantages of Adwords? (AACSB: Communication; Reflective Thinking)

Marketing Ethics Corporate Spying against Nonprofits

Many corporations now have a chief corporate security officer to assess and mitigate all sorts of threats facing the organization. Threats come from many sources—competitors, governments, and consumer groups. Competitors and foreign government organizations employ sophisticated means to conduct corporate espionage. In fact, the U.S. Department of Justice recently charged five Chinese military officers with economic espionage, claiming they stole valuable trade secrets from several U.S. companies. But corporate espionage tables are turned when it comes to dealing with the threat posed by consumer groups, such as Greenpeace and Moveon.org. It has come to light that several large corporations are using espionage tactics to infiltrate consumer groups posing a threat to their businesses. For example, Mary Lou Sapone, also known as Mary McFate, appeared to be a prominent volunteer for many nonprofit groups, even running for a seat on the board of directors of one gun-control group. In reality, she was not a moral do-gooder but was, in fact, a consultant at private security firm Beckett Brown International (BBI). In Greenpeace's lawsuit against Dow Chemical, one of BBI's clients, she was described as an "experienced infiltrator of nonprofits" and has been paid by corporations to spy on nonprofit citizen organizations for many years. Walmart, Kraft, Chevron, Coca-Cola, McDonald's, and even the U.S. Chamber of Commerce have been linked to this type of espionage.

✪ **18-11** Discuss examples of companies using espionage tactics to gather information from nonprofit organizations. Is it ethical to obtain information this way? (AACSB: Communication; Ethical Reasoning; Reflective Thinking)

18-12 Learn about the Economic Espionage Act of 1996. Are companies violating this law when employing espionage tactics to gather information on nonprofit organizations? (AACSB: Communication; Reflective Thinking)

Marketing by the Numbers Market Share

Bottled water is a hot industry with sales of $11.8 billion in the United States. Big players in this industry include Nestlé, PepsiCo, and Coca-Cola. Nestlé is the market leader with four brands among the top 10 leading brands. Nestlé's Pure Life brand was the top-selling brand with sales of $1.18 billion, but the company's other brands make up an additional $1.6 billion, giving the company total overall sales of almost $3 billion. Nestlé saw an opportunity in this market and launched a new brand called Resource, targeted to affluent women. Resource is fortified with electrolytes and is promoted as "more than hydration, it's total electrolytenment." Nestlé is attempting to take market share away from Glacéau's Vitaminwater and Smartwater. If Resource attains just 3 percent market share, it will be among the top 10 selling brands.

18-13 Refer to Appendix 2, Marketing by the Numbers, and calculate Nestlé's Pure Life and the company's overall market share in the bottled water industry. (AACSB: Communication; Analytical Reasoning)

18-14 How much revenue does one market share point represent in this industry? Assuming total market sales remain the same, what sales must Resource attain to be among the top 10 selling brands? (AACSB: Communication; Reflective Thinking)

Video Case Umpqua Bank

The retail banking industry has become very competitive. And with a few powerhouses that dominate the market, how is a small bank to thrive? By differentiating itself through a competitive advantage that the big guys can't touch.

That's exactly what Umpqua has done. One step inside a branch of this Oregon-based community bank and it is immediately apparent that this is not your typical Christmas club savings account/free toaster bank. Umpqua has created a business model that has transformed banking from retail drudgery to a holistic experience. Umpqua has created an environment where people just love to hang out. It not only has its own music download service featuring local artists, it even has its own blend of coffee.

But under all these bells and whistles lies the core of what makes Umpqua so different: a rigorous service culture where every branch and each employee gets measured on how well they serve customers. That's why every customer feels like he or she gets the help and attention needed from employees.

After viewing the video featuring Umpqua Bank, answer the following questions about creating competitive advantage:

18-15 With what companies does Umpqua compete?

18-16 What is Umpqua's competitive advantage?

18-17 Do you think that Umpqua will be able to maintain this advantage in the long run? Why or why not?

Company Case L.L.Bean: A Customer-Centric Icon Focuses Inward

What happens when a company achieves perfection in executing its competitive advantage? If it's L.L.Bean, it moves on to something else. For decades, in addition to producing high-quality merchandise and innovative designs, the direct marketing apparel retailer has won the hearts of customers everywhere with service that exceeds industry standards. Putting customers first has resulted in consistent growth that today has L.L.Bean selling more than $1.5 billion worth of clothing worldwide.

But after more than 100 years of focusing externally to provide outstanding customer experiences, the catalog retailer from Maine is now changing its ways. Under a new strategic initiative, L.L.Bean is also focusing internally, looking to achieve greater efficiency through operational improvements. After years of strong performance, the new moves beg the question—can a company focus internally on itself without losing its external focus on the customer?

The Customer Is in the DNA

Like many successful businesses, L.L.Bean was born of humble circumstances. In 1911, Maine resident Leon Leonwood (L.L.) Bean returned from a hunting trip with cold, damp feet and a revolutionary idea. He went to a local cobbler and commissioned a pair of boots the likes of which the world had never seen. Bean's design called for leather uppers to be stitched to rubber work boots. He called it the Maine Hunting Shoe, a boot that was both comfortable and functional, allowing for extensive treks in the Maine woods in all kinds of weather. That boot not only launched a company, it forever changed outdoor footwear.

Working out of the basement of his brother's apparel shop, Bean went into business. He obtained a list of non-resident Maine hunting license holders and mailed out a three-page promotional flyer making a persuasive claim: "You cannot expect success hunting deer or moose if your feet are not properly dressed. The Maine Hunting Shoe is designed by a hunter who has tramped the Maine woods for the last 18 years. We guarantee them to give perfect satisfaction in every way."

The direct marketing effort worked. The first 100 orders flowed in quickly and were promptly filled. However, shoe design was flawed, and 90 of those first 100 pairs were returned after the leather tops separated from the rubber bottoms. Remaining true to his promise, Bean refunded the money for all 90 pairs, almost going out of business in the process. But it was that commitment to keeping customers satisfied at any cost that launched a very successful company. That core value laid a foundation for quality merchandise and exceptional customer service.

Bean believed that if he did right by his customers, not only would they remain loyal, they would promote the company to others. Thus, L.L.Bean has progressively set customer service standards that seem all but impossible to maintain. At the core is the famous L.L.Bean 100 percent satisfaction guarantee. "Our products are guaranteed to give 100 percent satisfaction in every way. Return anything purchased from us at any time if it proves otherwise. We do not want you to have anything from L.L.Bean that is not completely satisfactory." As one customer points out, the 100 percent satisfaction guarantee isn't just an empty promise. "Several years ago we purchased a lamp from L.L.Bean. We had the lamp for two or three years when the paint started to chip off. We asked them if we could get it repaired. They sent us a new lamp." This is not an isolated experience—customer testimonials are replete with such accounts.

As Bean's business transitioned to the digital space over the print catalog, the company remained focused on providing the best customer experience possible. In addition to its satisfaction guarantee, L.L.Bean offers free shipping without a minimum purchase. And even though the company's Web and mobile interfaces are up and running 24 hours a day, seven days a week, its well-staffed call center is also open 24/7 if a customer wishes to speak to a representative in person. "Last night I had to correct an online order," reports one exuberant customer. "I dialed customer service and put the phone down, thinking I'd have to wait forever until I got to a person, it being Christmas Season and all. I was wrong. A woman picked up my call immediately, and our conversation was five minutes long."

Over the past few years, L.L.Bean has won numerous customer service awards, including the number one ranking from ForeSee's Brand Satisfaction survey, the number one outdoor outfitter by Forrester, number 14 on Stores.org's Favorite 50 Retailers, and number two on Prosper's most recent Customer Service Champions. According to CEO Chris McCormick, there's no magic involved in providing great service. "A lot of people have fancy things to say about customer service," he says. "But it's just a day-in, day-out, ongoing, never-ending, persevering, compassionate kind of activity." In other words, it's a long game with no shortcuts.

Because L.L.Bean sells directly to customers, it has always been in a position to gather customer data. Maintaining a customer database has enabled L.L.Bean to do more than just give good service or respond to customer concerns with a "customer is always right" mentality. It has allowed L.L.Bean to become intimately acquainted with its customers, providing service that is tailored to each individual. And as the company has grown in its ability to analyze an ever-growing quantity of customer data, it has continued to find new ways to provide such tailored service.

Sustaining Competitive Advantage

For a long time, exceptional customer service was enough to give L.L.Bean a competitive advantage. But more retailers—both traditional and online—are becoming known for the same types of service policies that L.L.Bean has practiced for years. Zappos reps will talk to you for as long as you wish, providing free shipping for both purchases and returns. Amazon has forged new ground by selling almost every type of good imaginable at competitive prices with superior personalized service that is unsurpassed on such a mass level. And what is number two Customer Service Champion L.L.Bean to do when number three is Lands' End? Although Lands' End targets a somewhat different type of customer, there is certainly overlap with L.L.Bean's clientele. A competency is only a competitive advantage if other companies can't match it.

This increasingly competitive retail market has caused L.L.Bean to reevaluate its strategic initiatives. Although the company built itself by primarily focusing outward on customer service, it is now enhancing that with an inward focus on improving company processes. In an effort to become more efficient, L.L.Bean is making a major investment in its systems infrastructure. "The systems we're implementing are about operational excellence," says Terry Sutton, L.L.Bean's vice president of business transformation. "As a direct marketer, we know a lot about customers. In the past we've fixed problems reactively to keep customers happy. We have known for a long time that we needed to be operationally excellent."

At first glance, it might seem that L.L.Bean's redirected focus is unwarranted. After all, the direct retailer is coming off a record year for profits and four straight years of revenue growth. By the end of the last fiscal year, the company was struggling just to fill orders, having sold a record 400,000 pairs of its iconic hunting boots—now a popular item on college campuses. L.L.Bean's board was so happy with recent financial results, it authorized an 8 percent bonus for all full-time employees, the biggest since 2005. "L.L.Bean has performed very well in a marketplace that continued to struggle with economic uncertainty, political distractions, and shaky consumer confidence," said CEO McCormick.

But L.L.Bean management is not content to remain content. Having moved conservatively for the past five years, the company is now poised to become more aggressive. It plans to accelerate growth and grab market share. It also plans to improve operational efficiency. So far, the company has made substantial investments toward improving its Web site as well as making various internal processes more efficient. Such investments will only increase in the coming year as McCormick has pledged an additional $100 million capital investment—the company's largest ever for a single year—in the Web operation, retail expansion, and business systems.

Looking forward, it is clear that L.L.Bean intends to keep serving customers the same way the company has for over 100 years. That component is in the company's DNA. But the direct outfitter is also clearly dedicated to forging new strengths by making internal process improvements to the company's operations. Some analysts might question whether a corporate customer intimacy culture focused on serving customers can add an operational excellence focus on more efficient internal processes. By increasing operational excellence, what will be the cost to L.L.Bean's founding core strength of providing exceptional customer service?

Questions for Discussion

18-18 How would you classify L.L.Bean in terms of competitive position? Why?

18-19 Is L.L.Bean a market-centered company? Support your answer.

18-20 Evaluate L.L.Bean according to Treacy and Wiersema's value disciplines.

18-21 Can L.L.Bean continue to maintain its customer focus while simultaneously focusing inward on operational efficiency? What is the relationship between the two?

18-22 In the face of L.L.Bean's changing competitive environment, what other recommendations would you make to the company?

Sources: Pam Goodfellow, "Amazon.com, L.L.Bean, Lands' End Named Customer Service Champions," *Forbes*, May 6, 2014, www.forbes.com/sites/prospernow/2014/05/06/amazon-com-l-l-bean-lands-end-named-customer-service-champions-by-consumers/; Brad Power, "Customer Intimacy, Meet Operational Excellence," *Harvard Business Review*, September 6, 2013, http://blogs.hbr.org/2013/09/customer-intimacy-meet-operati/; David Sharp, "L.L.Bean Has Record Year, Plans $100M in Spending," *Associated Press*, March 7, 2014, www.bigstory.ap.org/article/ll-bean-has-record-year-plans-100m-spending; Gregory Ciotti, "Lessons in Customer Service from the World's Most Beloved Companies," www.helpscout.net, accessed October 9, 2013; and additional information and quotes from www.yelp.com/biz/ll-bean-inc-freeport-2 and www.llbean.com/customerService/aboutLLBean/company_information.html?nav=s1-ln, September 2014.

MyMarketingLab

Go to **mymktlab.com** for the following Assisted-graded writing questions:

18-23 Explain the difference between a good and a bad competitor. (AACSB: Communication; Reflective Thinking)

18-24 Discuss the similarities and differences between Michael Porter's competitive strategies and the Tracy and Wiersema "value disciplines." Which classification of competitive strategies has more appeal for marketers and why? (AACSB: Communication; Reflective Thinking)

References

1. Based on information from Natalie Zmuda and Jeanine Poggi, "SodaStream Plots 'Edgy' Return to Super Bowl," *Advertising Age*, November 1, 2013, http://adage.com/print/245079/; Rick Aristotle Munarriz, "SodaStream Takes a Snarky Swipe at Coke with Green Santa Campaign," *Daily Finance,* December 13, 2013, www.dailyfinance.com/on/sodastream-snarky-green-santa-viral-ad-campaign-coke/; Nadav Shemer, "SodaStream: For Making DIY Carbonation Sexy," *Fast Company,* February 11, 2013, www.fastcompany.com/most-innovative-companies/2013/sodastream; Jayson Derrick, "SodaStream: Tremendous Growth Prospects and Potential Buy Out Target," Seekingalpha.com, September 9, 2013, seekingalpha.com/article/1681552; Bruce Horovitz, "SodaStream's Super Bowl Ad Gets Rejected—Again," *USA Today,* January 25, 2014; "SodaStream Investor Presentation," http://sodastream.investorroom.com/sodastreamoverview, accessed February 2014; and www.sodastream.com, accessed September 2014.
2. See www.vikingrange.com/consumer/category/products/3-year-signature-warranty, accessed October 2014.
3. David Beren, "T-Mobile's New Print Attack Ad Hits AT&T, Verizon Again,, and Again," *TmoNews,* July 24, 2014, www.tmonews.com/2013/07/t-mobiles-new-print-attack-ad-hits-att-verizon-again-and-again/; "Here's T-Mobile's Awesome Response to AT&T's Attack Ads," *9TO5 Mac,* March 6, 2013, http://9to5mac.com/2013/03/06/heres-t-mobiles-awesome-response-to-atts-attack-ads/; and Jacob Siegal, "T-Mobile's AT&T Attack Ads May Have Gone Too Far," *Yahoo! News,* September 17, 2013, http://news.yahoo.com/t-mobile-t-attack-ads-may-gone-too-204009101.html.
4. See "Contact Lenses 2013," *Contact Lens Spectrum,* January 1, 2014, www.clspectrum.com/articleviewer.aspx?articleID=107853; and "Bausch & Lomb," www.wikinvest.com/wiki/Bausch_&_Lomb, accessed September 2014.
5. See Casey Johnston, "Kindle Fire Nabs 33% of Android Tablet Market, Nexus 7 just 8%," *ars technica,* January 8, 2013, http://arstechnica.com/gadgets/2013/01/kindle-fire-nabs-33-of-android-tablet-market-nexus-7-just-8/; and Jim Edwards, "Samsung Is Stealing Apple's iPad Share," *Business Insider,* October 21, 2013, www.businessinsider.com/samsung-is-stealing-apples-ipad-market-share-2013-10.
6. "Alexa Top Sites in the U.S.," www.alexa.com/topsites/countries/US, accessed January 2014.
7. Adapted from information found in W. Chan Kim and Renée Mauborgne, "Blue Ocean Strategy: How to Create Uncontested Market Space and Make Competition Irrelevant," www.blueoceanstrategy.com/pre/downloads/BlueOceanStrategySummary.pdf, accessed March 2014; also see Kim and Mauborgne, *Blue Ocean Strategy: How to Create Uncontested Market Space and Make Competition Irrelevant* (Boston: Harvard Business Press, 2005). For other discussion, see "Blue Ocean Strategy," www.blueoceanstrategy.com/, accessed September 2014.
8. See Eddie Yoon and Linda Deeken, "Why It Pays to Be a Category Creator," *Harvard Business Review,* March 2013, pp. 21–24; and http://investor.gmcr.com/financials.cfm and www.keurig.com/, accessed September 2014.
9. See Dinah Eng, "Samuel Adams's Beer Revolution," *Fortune,* April 8, 2013, pp. 23–26; and www.bostonbeer.com/phoenix.zhtml?c=69432&p=irol-overview and www.ab-inbev.com/go/investors/financial_information/our_key_figures.cfm, accessed September 2014.
10. For these and other examples, see Dan Schwabel, "Why Companies Want You to Become an Intrapreneur," *Forbes,* September 9, 2013, www.forbes.com/sites/danschawbel/2013/09/09/why-companies-want-you-to-become-an-intrapreneur/.
11. Michael E. Porter, *Competitive Strategy: Techniques for Analyzing Industries and Competitors* (New York: Free Press, 1980), Chapter 2; and Porter, "What Is Strategy?" *Harvard Business Review*, November–December 1996, pp. 61–78. Also see Stefan Stern, "May the Force Be with You and Your Plans for 2008," *Financial Times*, January 8, 2008, p. 14; and "Porter's Generic Strategies," www.quickmba.com/strategy/generic.shtml, accessed October 2014.
12. See Michael Treacy and Fred Wiersema, "Customer Intimacy and Other Value Disciplines," *Harvard Business Review*, January–February 1993, pp. 84–93; Treacy and Wiersema, *The Discipline of Market Leaders: Choose Your Customers, Narrow Your Focus, Dominate Your Market* (New York: Perseus Press, 1997); and Wiersema, *Double-Digit Growth: How Great Companies Achieve It—No Matter What* (New York: Portfolio, 2003). Also see Elaine Cascio, "Fast, Cheap, or Good—Pick Two," *Inter@ction Solutions,* January/February 2012, p. 8; Jürgen Kai-Uwe Brock and Josephine Yu Zhou, "Customer Intimacy," *Journal of Business and Industrial Marketing,* 2012, pp. 370–383; and Joe Weinman, "How Customer Intimacy Is Evolving to Collective Intimacy, Thanks to Big Data," *Forbes,* June 4, 2013, www.forbes.com/sites/joeweinman/2013/06/04/how-customer-intimacy-is-evolving-to-collective-intimacy-thanks-to-big-data/.
13. For more discussion, see Philip Kotler and Kevin Lane Keller, *Marketing Management*, 14th ed. (Upper Saddle River, NJ: Prentice Hall, 2012), Chapter 11.
14. Robert Klara, "New Kid with the Block," *Adweek,* April 15, 2013, pp. 30–31; Neda Ulaby, "Girls' Legos Are a hit, But Why Do Girls Need Special Legos?" *NPR,* June 29, 2013, www.npr.org/blogs/monkeysee/2013/06/28/196605763; Christian Wienberf, "Lego Profit Soars 35% as Toy Bricks for Girls Drive Sales Growth," *BloombergBusinessweek,* February 21, 2013, www.businessweek.com/news/2013-02-21/lego-profit-soars-35-percent-as-toy-bricks-for-girls-drive-sales-growth; and http://friends.lego.com/en-us/products, accessed January 2014.
15. See "Velcro Industries Launches Integrated Marketing Campaign to Promote VELCRO Brand One-Wrap Ties," *BusinessWire,* May 28, 2013, www.businesswire.com/news/home/20130528005147/en/; Rupal Parekh, "Can Marketing Push Make Velcro Stick?" *Advertising Age,* June 3, 2013, p. 8; and www.velcro.com and www.pinterest.com/velcrobrand/, accessed September 2014.
16. "Duracell vs. Energizer—One Charges Up, One Sputters," *Advertising Age,* November 6, 2013, www.adage.com/print/245108; "Best Global Brands of 2013: Duracell," *Interbrand,* www.interbrand.com/en/best-global-brands/2013/Duracell; and www.facebook.com/duracell and www.facebook.com/duracell, accessed September 2014.
17. See "Shampoo, Conditioners and Styling Products—US—April 2013," http://store.mintel.com/shampoo-conditioners-and-styling-products-us-april-2013; and "Soft Drink Industry: Market Research Reports, Statistics and Analysis," www.reportlinker.com/ci02018/Soft-Drink.html, accessed September 2014.
18. Example based on information from David J. Bryce and Jeffrey H. Dyer, "Strategies to Crack Well-Guarded Markets," *Harvard Business Review*, May 2007, pp. 84–91; with information from Teressa Iezzi, "For Showing What It Really Means to Transform Yourself into a Media Brand," *Fast Company*, www.fastcompany.com/most-innovative-companies/2012/red-bull-media-house, accessed August 2012; and "The Top 15 Energy Drink Brands," *caffeineinformer,* www.caffeineinformer.com/the-15-top-energy-drink-brands, accessed March 2014.
19. See Angela Chen, "The Rise of Niche Online Dating Sites," *Wall Street Journal,* October 15, 2013, http://online.wsj.com/news/articles/SB10001424052702304561004579137441269527948; Laura T. Coffey, "From Farmers to Salad Toppings: 26 Weirdly Niche Dating Sites," *USA Today,* August 5, 2013, www.today.com/health/farmers-salad-toppings-26-weirdly-niche-dating-sites-6C10843053; and www.farmersonly.com, accessed September 2014.
20. Information from www.vfc.com, accessed September 2014.

19 The Global Marketplace

Chapter Preview

You've now learned the fundamentals of how companies develop competitive marketing strategies to engage customers, create customer value, and build lasting customer relationships. In this chapter, we extend these fundamentals to global marketing. Although we discussed global topics in each previous chapter—it's difficult to find an area of marketing that doesn't contain at least some international elements—here we'll focus on special considerations that companies face when they market their brands globally. Advances in communication, transportation, and digital technologies have made the world a much smaller place. Today, almost every firm, large or small, faces international marketing issues. In this chapter, we will examine six major decisions marketers make in going global.

To start our exploration of global marketing, let's look at Coca-Cola, a truly global operation. You'll find a Coca-Cola product within arm's length of almost anyone, anywhere in the world. With 3,500 products and 17 billion-dollar brands, the company sells "moments of happiness" more than 1.9 billion times a day in more than 200 countries. Like many companies, Coca-Cola's greatest growth opportunities lie in international markets. Here, we examine the company's odyssey into Africa.

COCA-COLA IN AFRICA: "Everything Is Right There to Have It Happen."

Coca-Cola is one of the world's truly iconic brands—a $47-billion global powerhouse. It puts Coke products within "an arm's length" of 98 percent of the world's population. Already the world's number-one soft drink maker, Coca-Cola is in the middle of a 12-year plan to double its global system revenues by 2020. But achieving such growth won't be easy. The major problem: Soft drink sales growth has lost its fizz in North America and Europe, two of Coca-Cola's largest and most profitable markets. In fact, the U.S. soft drink market has shrunk for five straight years. With sales stagnating in its mature markets, Coca-Cola must look elsewhere to meet its ambitious growth goals.

In recent years, Coca-Cola has sought growth primarily in developing global markets such as China and India, which boast large emerging middle classes but relatively low per capita consumption of Coke. However, both China and India are now crowded with competitors and notoriously difficult for outsiders to navigate. So while Coca-Cola will continue to compete heavily in those countries, it has set its sights on an even more promising long-term growth opportunity—Africa.

Many Western companies view Africa as an untamed final frontier—a kind of no man's land plagued by poverty, political corruption and instability, unreliable transportation, and shortages of fresh water and other essential resources. But Coca-Cola sees plenty of opportunity in Africa to justify the risks. According to one source, 6 of the world's 10 fastest-growing markets are in Africa. The continent has a growing population of more than 1 billion people and a just-emerging middle class. The number of African households earning at least $5,000—the income level where families begin to spend at least half their income on non-food items—has tripled over the past 30 years to more than a third of the population. "You've got an incredibly young population, a dynamic population," says Coca-Cola CEO Muhtar Kent, "[and] huge disposable income. I mean $1.6 trillion of GDP, which is bigger than Russia, bigger than India."

Coca-Cola is no stranger to Africa. It has operated there since 1929, and it's the only multinational that offers its products in every African country. The company has a dominant 29 percent market share in Africa and the Middle East, as compared with Pepsi's 15 percent share. Coca-Cola's sparkling beverage revenues in Africa and the Middle East grew by 6 percent last year, compared with a 2 percent decline in North America and 1 percent decline in Europe.

With its home markets losing their fizz, Coca-Cola is looking for growth in emerging markets such as Africa. But in Africa, "Coke is, in a sense, sticking its hand into a bees' nest to get some honey."

But there's still plenty of room for Coca-Cola to grow in Africa. For example, annual per capita consumption of Coke in Kenya is just 40 servings, compared with more developed countries like Mexico, where consumption runs at an eye-popping 728 servings per year. So the stage is set for Coca-Cola on the African continent, not just for its flagship Coke brand but also for its large stable of other soft drinks, waters, and juices. Whereas the beverage giant invested $6 billion in the African market over the past decade, it plans to invest twice that amount during the next 10 years—an effort that includes bottling plants, distribution networks, retailer support, and an Africa-wide promotional campaign called "One Billion Reasons to Believe in Africa."

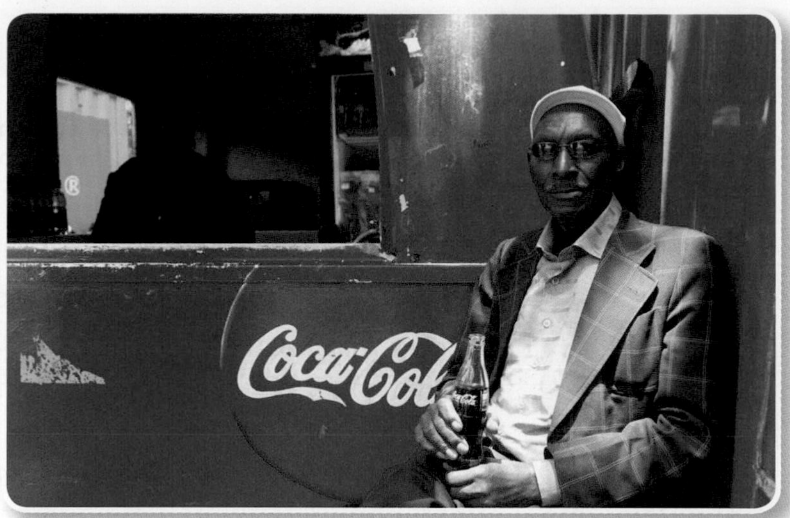

With sales stagnating in its mature markets, Coca-Cola is looking to emerging markets—such as Africa—to meet its ambitious growth goals. Its African distribution network is rudimentary but effective.

Getty Images

Marketing in Africa is a very different proposition from marketing in more developed regions. "Africa . . . is not Atlanta," observes one analyst, "and Coke is, in a sense, sticking its hand into a bees' nest to get some honey." To grow its sales in Africa, beyond just marketing through traditional channels in larger African cities, Coca-Cola is now invading smaller communities with more grassroots tactics. "[Just] being in a country is very easy; you can go and set up a depot in every capital city," says CEO Kent. But in Africa, "that's not what we're about. There's nowhere in Africa that we don't go. We go to every town, every village, every community, every township." In Africa, every small shop in every back alley has become important, as Coca-Cola launches what another analyst describes as "a street-by-street campaign to win drinkers . . . not yet used to guzzling Coke by the gallon."

For example, take the Mamakamau Shop in Uthiru, a poor community outside Nairobi, Kenya. Piles of trash burn outside the shop and sewage trickles by in an open trench. Besides Coca-Cola products, the shop—known as a duka—also carries everything from mattresses to plastic buckets, all in a room about the size of a small bedroom. Still, proprietor Mamakamau Kingori has earned Coca-Cola's "Gold" vendor status, its highest level, for selling about 72 cola products a day, priced at 30 Kenyan shillings (37 U.S. cents) for a 500-milliliter bottle. Most customers drink the soda in the store while sitting on overturned red crates—they can't afford to pay the bottle deposit. Coca-Cola's Kenyan bottler will reuse the glass bottles up to 70 times.

To earn her "Gold" status, Kingori follows carefully prescribed selling techniques. She uses a red, Coke-provided, refrigerated cooler by the front entrance, protected by a blue cage. Like other mom-and-pop stores in her area, she keeps the cooler fully stocked with Coke on top, Fanta in the middle, and large bottles on the bottom. Inside the store, she posts red menu signs provided by Coca-Cola that push combo meals, such as a 300-milliliter Coke and a ndazi, a type of local donut, for 25 Kenyan shillings.

In Kabira, another poor Nairobi neighborhood, the crowded streets are lined with shops painted Coke red. The local bottler hires an artist to paint the shops with logos and Swahili phrases like "Burudika na Coke Baridi," meaning "enjoy Coke cold." In countless communities across Africa, whether it's the dukas in Nairobi or tuck shops in Johannesburg, South Africa, small stores play a big role in helping Coca-Cola grow.

Such shops are supplied by a rudimentary but effective network of Coca-Cola distributors. For example, in downtown Nairobi, men in red lab coats load hand-pulled trolleys with 22 to 40 crates of Coke and other soft drinks from Rosinje Distributors, one of 3,200 Micro Distribution Centers (MDCs) that Coca-Cola operates in Africa. These centers are the spine of Coca-Cola's African distribution network. For example, the Nairobi plant ships Coke, Fanta, Stoney Ginger Beer, and other Coca-Cola brands to almost 400 area MDCs. From there, crews hustle the products—sometimes a case at a time carried on their heads—to local shops and beverage kiosks. Because of the poor roads crowded with traffic, moving drinks by hand is often the best method. The MDCs help Coca-Cola to get its products into remote areas, making them available as people develop a taste for soft drinks and have the income to buy them.

Despite their elemental nature, Coca-Cola's marketing approaches in Africa are proving effective. The company's first rule is to get its products "cold and close." "If they don't have roads to move products long distances on trucks, we will use boats, canoes, or trolleys," says the president of Coca-Cola South Africa. For example, in Nigeria's Makako district—a maze of stilt houses on the Lagos lagoon—women criss-cross the waterways selling Coca-Cola directly from canoes to residents.

There's little doubt that Coca-Cola's increased commitment to Africa will be key to its achieving its global goals. As CEO Muhtar Kent concludes: "Africa is the untold story and could be the big story of the next decade, like India and China were this past decade. . . . Everything is right there to have it happen."[1]

Objective Outline

In the past, U.S. companies paid little attention to international trade. If they could pick up some extra sales via exports, that was fine. But the big market was at home, and it teemed with opportunities. The home market was also much safer. Managers did not need to learn other languages, deal with strange and changing currencies, face political and legal uncertainties, or adapt their products to different customer needs and expectations. Today, however, the situation is much different. Organizations of all kinds, from Coca-Cola and Nike to Google, MTV, and even the NBA, have gone global.

Author Comment The rapidly changing global environment provides both opportunities and threats. It's difficult to find a marketer today that isn't affected in some way by global developments.

Global Marketing Today

The world is shrinking rapidly with the advent of faster digital communication, transportation, and financial flows. Products developed in one country— McDonald's hamburgers, Netflix video service, Samsung electronics, Zara fashions, Caterpillar construction equipment, German BMWs, Facebook social networking—have found enthusiastic acceptance in other countries. It would not be surprising to hear about a German businessman wearing an Italian suit meeting an English friend at a Japanese restaurant who later returns home to drink Russian vodka while watching *American Idol* on TV and checking Facebook posts from friends around the world.

International trade has boomed over the past three decades. Since 1990, the number of multinational corporations in the world has more than doubled to more than 63,000. Some of these multinationals are true giants. In fact, of the largest 150 economies in the world, only 77 are countries. The remaining 73 are multinational corporations. Walmart, the world's largest company (based on a weighted average of sales, profits, assets, and market

Many American companies have now made the world their market. Nearly 60 percent of Apple's sales come from outside the Americas.

AFP/Getty Images

value), has annual revenues greater than the gross domestic product (GDP) of all but the world's 25 largest countries.[2] Despite a dip in world trade caused by the recent worldwide recession, the world trade of products and services last year was valued at more than $18.8 trillion, about 31.8 percent of GDP worldwide.[3]

Many U.S. companies have long been successful at international marketing: Coca-Cola, McDonald's, Starbucks, Nike, GE, IBM, Apple, Google, Colgate, Caterpillar, Boeing, and dozens of other American firms have made the world their market. In the United States, non-American brands such as Toyota, Nestlé, Samsung, IKEA, Canon, and Adidas have become household words. Other products and services that appear to be American are, in fact, produced or owned by foreign companies, such as Ben & Jerry's ice cream, Budweiser beer, 7-Eleven, GE and RCA televisions, Carnation milk, Universal Studios, and Motel 6. Michelin, the oh-so-French tire manufacturer, now does 35 percent of its business in North America; J&J, the maker of quintessentially all-American products such as BAND-AIDs and Johnson's Baby Shampoo, does nearly 55 percent of its business abroad. And America's own Caterpillar belongs more to the wider world, with 69 percent of its sales coming from outside the United States.[4]

But as global trade grows, global competition is also intensifying. Foreign firms are expanding aggressively into new international markets, and home markets are no longer as rich in opportunity. Few industries are currently safe from foreign competition. If companies delay taking steps toward internationalizing, they risk being shut out of growing markets in Western and Eastern Europe, China and the Pacific Rim, Russia, India, Brazil, and elsewhere. Firms that stay at home to play it safe might not only lose their chances to enter other markets but also risk losing their home markets. Domestic companies that never thought about foreign competitors suddenly find these competitors in their own backyards.

Ironically, although the need for companies to go abroad is greater today than in the past, so are the risks. Companies that go global may face highly unstable governments and currencies, restrictive government policies and regulations, and high trade barriers. The recently dampened global economic environment has also created big global challenges. In addition, corruption is an increasing problem; officials in several countries often award business not to the best bidder but to the highest briber.

Global firm

A firm that, by operating in more than one country, gains R&D, production, marketing, and financial advantages in its costs and reputation that are not available to purely domestic competitors.

A **global firm** is one that, by operating in more than one country, gains marketing, production, research and development (R&D), and financial advantages that are not available to purely domestic competitors. Because the global company sees the world as one market, it minimizes the importance of national boundaries and develops global brands. The global company raises capital, obtains materials and components, and manufactures and markets its goods wherever it can do the best job.

For example, U.S.-based Otis Elevator, the world's largest elevator maker, is headquartered in Farmington, Connecticut. However, it offers products in more than 200 countries and achieves 83 percent of its sales from outside the United States. It gets elevator door systems from France, small geared parts from Spain, electronics from Germany, and special motor drives from Japan. It operates manufacturing facilities in the Americas, Europe, and Asia, and engineering and test centers in the United States, Austria, Brazil, China, Czech Republic, France, Germany, India, Italy, Japan, Korea, and Spain. In turn, Otis Elevator is a wholly owned subsidiary of global commercial and aerospace giant United Technologies Corporation.[5] Many of today's global corporations—both large and small—have become truly borderless.

This does not mean, however, that every firm must operate in a dozen countries to succeed. Smaller firms can practice global niching. But the world is becoming smaller, and every company operating in a global industry—whether large or small—must assess and establish its place in world markets.

FIGURE | 19.1
Major International Marketing Decisions

It's a big and beautiful but threatening world out there for marketers! Most large American firms have made the world their market. For example, once all-American McDonald's now captures nearly 69 percent of its sales from outside the United States.

The rapid move toward globalization means that all companies will have to answer some basic questions: What market position should we try to establish in our country, in our economic region, and globally? Who will our global competitors be and what are their strategies and resources? Where should we produce or source our products? What strategic alliances should we form with other firms around the world?

As shown in **Figure 19.1**, a company faces six major decisions in international marketing. We discuss each decision in detail in this chapter.

Author Comment As if operating within a company's own borders wasn't difficult enough, going global adds many layers of complexities. For example, Coca-Cola markets its products in hundreds of countries around the globe. It must understand the varying trade, economic, cultural, and political environments in each market.

Looking at the Global Marketing Environment

Before deciding whether to operate internationally, a company must understand the international marketing environment. That environment has changed a great deal in recent decades, creating both new opportunities and new problems.

The International Trade System

U.S. companies looking abroad must start by understanding the international *trade system*. When selling to another country, a firm may face restrictions on trade between nations. Governments may charge *tariffs* or *duties*, taxes on certain imported products designed to raise revenue or protect domestic firms. Tariffs and duties are often used to force favorable trade behaviors from other nations.

For example, the European Union (EU) recently placed import duties on Chinese solar panels after determining that Chinese companies were selling the panels in EU countries at under-market prices. To retaliate, the very next day, the Chinese government placed duties on EU wine exports to China. The duties targeted the wines of Spain, France, and Italy but spared Germany, which had taken China's side in the solar panel dispute. The disputes were resolved when Chinese solar panel producers agreed to a minimum price in Europe and Europe agreed to help China develop its own wine industry in return for promoting European wines there.[6]

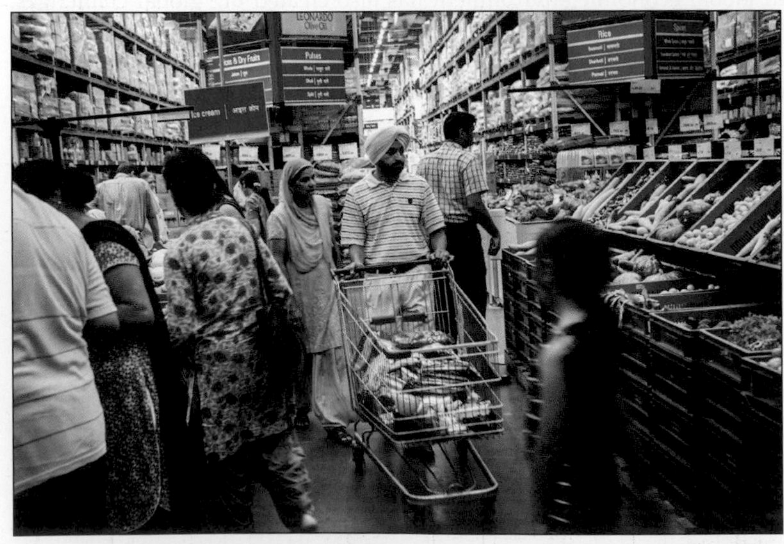
Nontariff trade barriers: Because of nontariff obstacles, Walmart recently suspended its once-ambitious plans to expand into India's huge but fragmented retail market.
Bloomberg via Getty Images

Countries may set *quotas*, limits on the amount of foreign imports that they will accept in certain product categories. The purpose of a quota is to conserve on foreign exchange and protect local industry and employment. Firms may also encounter *exchange controls*, which limit the amount of foreign exchange and the exchange rate against other currencies.

A company also may face *nontariff trade barriers*, such as biases against its bids, restrictive product standards, or excessive host-country regulations or enforcement. For example, Walmart recently suspended its once-ambitious plans to expand into India's huge but fragmented retail market by opening hundreds of Walmart superstores there. Beyond difficult market conditions, such as spotty electricity and poor roads, India is notorious for throwing up nontariff obstacles to protect the nation's own predominately mom-and-pop retailers, which control 96 percent of India's $500 billion in retail sales. One such obstacle is a government regulation requiring foreign retailers in India to buy 30 percent of the merchandise they sell from local small businesses. Such a requirement is nearly impossible for Walmart, because small suppliers can't produce the quantities of goods needed by the giant retailer. Further, India's few large domestic retailers are not bound by the same rule, making it difficult for Walmart to compete profitably. Walmart is now looking for a domestic partner that can help it crack the mammoth Indian market.[7]

At the same time, certain other forces can *help* trade between nations. Examples include the World Trade Organization (WTO) and various regional free trade agreements.

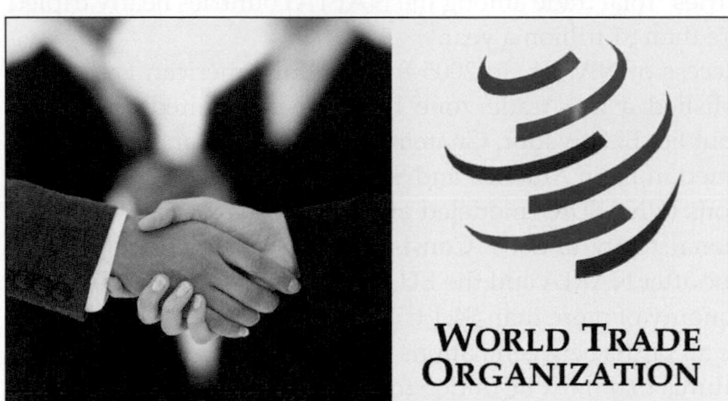

The WTO promotes trade by reducing tariffs and other international trade barriers. It also imposes international trade sanctions and mediates global trade disputes.

(left) Corbis Images; (right) Donald Stampfli/Associated Press

The World Trade Organization

The General Agreement on Tariffs and Trade (GATT), established in 1947 and modified in 1994, was designed to promote world trade by reducing tariffs and other international trade barriers. It established the World Trade Organization (WTO), which replaced GATT in 1995 and now oversees the original GATT provisions. WTO and GATT member nations (currently numbering 159) have met in eight rounds of negotiations to reassess trade barriers and establish new rules for international trade. The WTO also imposes international trade sanctions and mediates global trade disputes. Its actions have been productive. The first seven rounds of negotiations reduced the average worldwide tariffs on manufactured goods from 45 percent to just 5 percent.[8]

The most recently completed negotiations, dubbed the Uruguay Round, dragged on for seven long years before concluding in 1994. The benefits of the Uruguay Round will be felt for many years, as the accord promoted long-term global trade growth, reduced the world's remaining merchandise tariffs by 30 percent, extended the WTO to cover trade in agriculture and a wide range of services, and toughened the international protection of copyrights, patents, trademarks, and other intellectual property. A new round of global WTO trade talks, the Doha Round, began in Doha, Qatar, in late 2001 and was set to conclude in 2005; however, the discussions still continued through 2014.[9]

Regional Free Trade Zones

Economic community
A group of nations organized to work toward common goals in the regulation of international trade.

Certain countries have formed *free trade zones* or **economic communities**. These are groups of nations organized to work toward common goals in the regulation of international trade. One such community is the *European Union (EU)*. Formed in 1957, the EU set out to create a single European market by reducing barriers to the free flow of products, services, finances, and labor among member countries and developing policies on trade with nonmember nations. Today, the EU represents one of the world's largest single markets. Currently, it has 28 member countries containing more than half a billion consumers and accounting for almost 20 percent of the world's exports.[10] The EU offers tremendous trade opportunities for U.S. and other non-European firms.

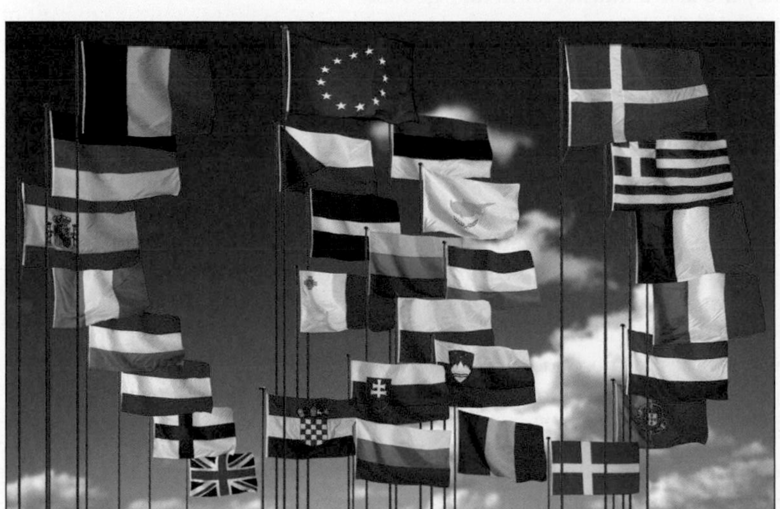

Economic communities: The European Union represents one of the world's single largest markets. Its current member countries contain more than half a billion consumers and account for 20 percent of the world's exports.

Over the past decade and a half, 18 EU member nations have taken a significant step toward unification by adopting the euro as a common currency. Widespread adoption of the euro has decreased much of the currency risk associated with doing business in Europe, making member countries with previously weak currencies more attractive markets. However, the adoption of a common currency has also caused problems as European economic powers such as Germany and France have had to step in recently to prop up weaker economies such as those of Greece, Portugal, and Cyprus. This recent "euro crisis" has led some analysts to predict the possible break-up of the euro zone as it is now set up.[11]

It is unlikely that the EU will ever go against 2,000 years of tradition and become the "United States of Europe." A community with more than two-dozen different languages and cultures will always have difficulty coming together and acting as a single entity. Still, with a combined annual GDP of more than $16 trillion, the EU has become a potent economic force.[12]

In 1994, the *North American Free Trade Agreement (NAFTA)* established a free trade zone among the United States, Mexico, and Canada. The agreement created a single market of 470 million people who produce and consume $19.5 trillion worth of goods and services annually. Over the past 20 years, NAFTA has eliminated trade barriers and investment restrictions among the three countries. Total trade among the NAFTA countries nearly tripled from $288 billion in 1993 to more than $1 trillion a year.[13]

Following the apparent success of NAFTA, in 2005 the Central American Free Trade Agreement (CAFTA-DR) established a free trade zone between the United States and Costa Rica, the Dominican Republic, El Salvador, Guatemala, Honduras, and Nicaragua. Other free trade areas have formed in Latin America and South America. For example, the Union of South American Nations (UNASUR), modeled after the EU, was formed in 2004 and formalized by a constitutional treaty in 2008. Consisting of 12 countries, UNASUR makes up the largest trading bloc after NAFTA and the EU, with a population of more than 387 million and a combined economy of more than $4.1 trillion. Similar to NAFTA and the EU, UNASUR aims to eliminate all tariffs between nations by 2019.[14]

Each nation has unique features that must be understood. A nation's readiness for different products and services and its attractiveness as a market to foreign firms depend on its economic, political-legal, and cultural environments.

Economic Environment

The international marketer must study each country's economy. Two economic factors reflect the country's attractiveness as a market: its industrial structure and its income distribution.

The country's *industrial structure* shapes its product and service needs, income levels, and employment levels. The four types of industrial structures are as follows:

- *Subsistence economies.* In a subsistence economy, the vast majority of people engage in simple agriculture. They consume most of their output and barter the rest for simple goods and services. These economies offer few market opportunities. Many African countries fall into this category.
- *Raw material exporting economies.* These economies are rich in one or more natural resources but poor in other ways. Much of their revenue comes from exporting these resources. Some examples are Chile (tin and copper) and the Democratic Republic of the Congo (copper, cobalt, and coffee). These countries are good markets for large equipment, tools and supplies, and trucks. If there are many foreign residents and a wealthy upper class, they are also a market for luxury goods.
- *Emerging economies (industrializing economies).* In an emerging economy, fast growth in manufacturing results in rapid overall economic growth. Examples include the BRIC countries—Brazil, Russia, India, and China. As manufacturing increases, the country needs more imports of raw textile materials, steel, and heavy machinery, and fewer imports of finished textiles, paper products, and automobiles. Industrialization typically creates a new rich class and a growing middle class, both demanding new types of imported goods. As more developed markets stagnate and become increasingly competitive, many marketers are now targeting growth opportunities in emerging markets.
- *Industrial economies.* Industrial economies are major exporters of manufactured goods, services, and investment funds. They trade goods among themselves and also export them to other types of economies for raw materials and semifinished goods. The varied manufacturing activities of these industrial nations and their large middle class make them rich markets for all sorts of goods. Examples include the United States, Japan, and Norway.

The second economic factor is the country's *income distribution*. Industrialized nations may have low-, medium-, and high-income households. In contrast, countries with subsistence economies consist mostly of households with very low family incomes. Still other countries may have households with either very low or very high incomes. Even poor or emerging economies may be attractive markets for all kinds of goods. These days, companies in a wide range of industries—from cars to computers to food—are increasingly targeting even low- and middle-income consumers in emerging economies.

For example, consider Brazil, now the world's sixth-largest economy. Thanks to historically low unemployment, rising wages, and an influx of foreign direct investment, Brazil's consumer markets are soaring. Brazil's exploding middle class has grown by 40 million in just the past five years. Until recently, marketers have typically targeted consumers in Brazil's wealthiest, most-populated, and easiest-to-reach areas, such as Sao Paulo, Brazil's richest state. However, as competition stiffens in more accessible and affluent regions, companies are now turning their attention to middle- and lower-income consumers in other areas of the country.

Brazil's northeast region is its poorest, and many residents there lack access to basics such as roads and running water. With more mouths to feed in every household, northeastern Brazilian consumers are also sticklers for low prices. But as it happens, northeast Brazil is also the region with the greatest growth in household income. So marketers are finding innovative ways to meet the distribution challenges in regions like the northeast to capture the growing potential there. Consider Nestlé:[15]

To tap the potential in less developed regions of Brazil, Nestlé developed its "Ate Voce" ("Reaching You") program, by which its reps go door-to-door with push carts—a method residents find very appealing—selling "kits" full of dairy products, cookies, yogurt, and desserts. More than just selling products, these Nestlé vendors are trained to serve as nutrition consultants, helping customers to develop healthier diets. ● To serve consumers in northeast Brazil's Amazon River basin, which lacks a solid network of roads and highways, Nestlé has even launched a floating supermarket that takes goods directly to consumers. Setting sail from Belem, Brazil's biggest city along the Amazon, the boat serves 1.5 million consumers in 27 riverside towns with 300 different Nestlé products. It spends one day at each stop. Customers can check the floating store's schedule at nestleatevoce.com.br, call a toll-free number, or text for more information and plan their shopping accordingly. This and other innovative Ate Voce marketing initiatives are paying off for Nestlé. "Demand for our products has more than doubled in the north and northeast compared to other Brazilian regions," says Nestlé's marketing manager in Brazil.

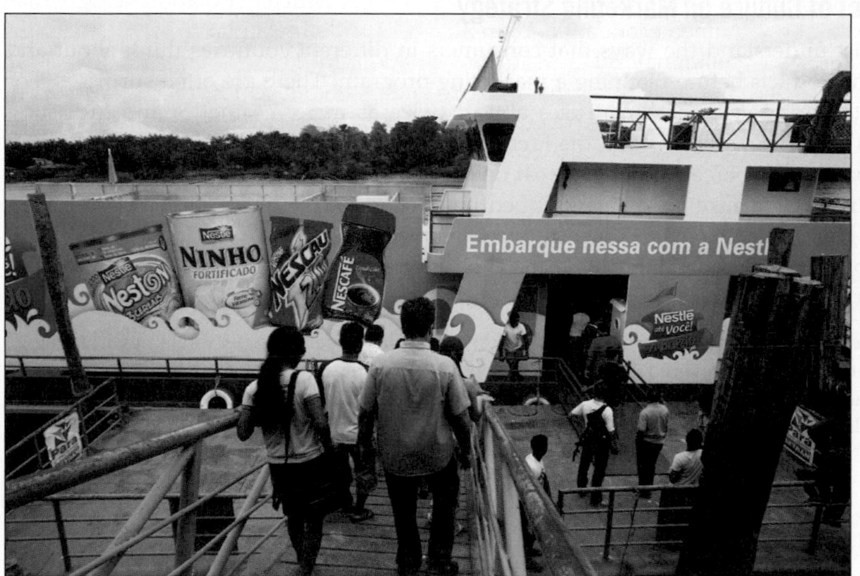

● **Marketing in emerging markets: To tap the growing potential in Brazil's less developed regions, Nestlé's "Ate Voce" ("Reaching You") program includes innovative distribution approaches, such as this floating supermarket that serves customers in the country's Amazon River basin.**

Bloomberg via Getty Images

Political-Legal Environment

Nations differ greatly in their political-legal environments. In considering whether to do business in a given country, a company should consider factors such as the country's attitudes toward international buying, government bureaucracy, political stability, and monetary regulations.

Some nations are very receptive to foreign firms; others are less accommodating. For example, India has tended to bother foreign businesses with import quotas, currency restrictions, and other limitations that make operating there a challenge. In contrast, neighboring Asian countries, such as Singapore and Thailand, court foreign investors and shower them with incentives and favorable operating conditions. Political and regulatory stability is another issue. For example, Russia is consumed by corruption and governmental red tape, which the government finds difficult to control, increasing the risk of doing business there. Although most international marketers still find the Russian market attractive, the corrupt climate will affect how they handle business and financial matters.[16]

Companies must also consider a country's monetary regulations. Sellers want to take their profits in a currency of value to them. Ideally, the buyer can pay in the seller's currency or in other world currencies. Short of this, sellers might accept a blocked currency—one whose removal from the country is restricted by the buyer's government—if they can buy other goods in that country that they need or can sell elsewhere for a needed currency. In addition to currency limits, a changing exchange rate also creates high risks for the seller.

Most international trade involves cash transactions. Yet many nations have too little hard currency to pay for their purchases from other countries. They may want to pay with other items instead of cash. *Barter* involves the direct exchange of goods or services. For example, Venezuela regularly barters oil, which it produces in surplus quantities, for food on the international market—rice from Guyana; coffee from El Salvador; sugar, coffee, meat, and more from Nicaragua; and beans and pasta from the Dominican Republic. Venezuela has even struck a deal to supply oil to Cuba in exchange for Cuban doctors and medical care for Venezuelans.[17]

Cultural Environment

Each country has its own folkways, norms, and taboos. When designing global marketing strategies, companies must understand how culture affects consumer reactions in each of its world markets. In turn, they must also understand how their strategies affect local cultures.

The Impact of Culture on Marketing Strategy

Sellers must understand the ways that consumers in different countries think about and use certain products before planning a marketing program. There are often surprises. For example, the average French man uses almost twice as many cosmetics and grooming aids as his wife. The Germans and the French eat more packaged, branded spaghetti than Italians do. Some 49 percent of Chinese eat on the way to work. Most American women let down their hair and take off makeup at bedtime, whereas 15 percent of Chinese women style their hair at bedtime and 11 percent put *on* makeup.[18]

Companies that ignore cultural norms and differences can make some very expensive and embarrassing mistakes. Here are two examples:

> Nike inadvertently offended Chinese officials when it ran an ad featuring LeBron James crushing a number of culturally revered Chinese figures in a kung fu-themed television ad. The Chinese government found that the ad violated regulations to uphold national dignity and respect the "motherland's culture" and yanked the multimillion-dollar campaign. With egg on its face, Nike released a formal apology. Burger King made a similar mistake when it created in-store ads in Spain showing Hindu goddess Lakshmi atop a ham sandwich with the caption "a snack that is sacred." Cultural and religious groups worldwide objected strenuously—Hindus are vegetarian. Burger King apologized and pulled the ads.[19]

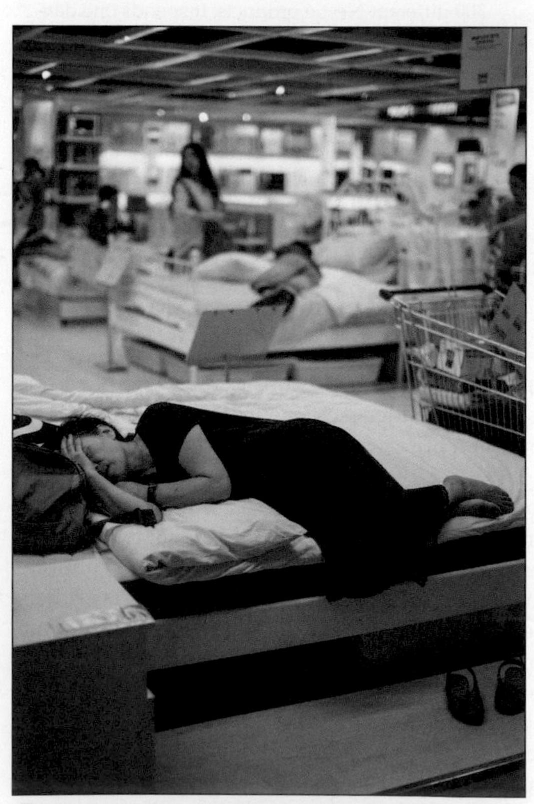

The impact of culture on marketing strategy: IKEA customers in China want a lot more from its stores than just affordable Scandinavian-design furniture.

© ZUMA Press, Inc./Alamy

Business norms and behaviors also vary from country to country. For example, American executives like to get right down to business and engage in fast and tough face-to-face bargaining. However, Japanese and other Asian businesspeople often find this behavior offensive. They prefer to start with polite conversation, and they rarely say no in face-to-face conversations. As another example, firm handshakes are a common and expected greeting in most Western countries; in some Middle Eastern countries, however, handshakes might be refused if offered. Microsoft founder Bill Gates once set off a flurry of international controversy when he shook the hand of South Korea's president with his right hand while keeping his left hand in his pocket, something that Koreans consider highly disrespectful. In some countries, when being entertained at a meal, not finishing all the food implies that it was somehow substandard. In other countries, in contrast, wolfing down every last bite might be taken as a mild insult, suggesting that the host didn't supply enough quantity.[20] American business executives need to understand these kinds of cultural nuances before conducting business in another country.

By the same token, companies that understand cultural nuances can use them to their advantage in the global markets. For example, furniture retailer IKEA's stores are a big draw for up-and-coming Chinese consumers. But IKEA has learned that customers in China want a lot more from its stores then just affordable Scandinavian-designed furniture:[21]

> In Chinese, IKEA is known as Yi Jia. Translated, it means "comfortable home," a concept taken literally by the millions of consumers who visit one of IKEA's 15 huge Chinese stores each year. "Customers come on family outings, hop into display beds and nap, pose for snapshots with the décor, and hang out for hours to enjoy

the air conditioning and free soda refills," notes one observer. On a typical Saturday afternoon, for example, display beds and other furniture in a huge Chinese IKEA store are occupied, with customers of all ages lounging or even fast asleep. One Chinese IKEA has even hosted several weddings. IKEA managers encourage such behavior, figuring that familiarity with the store will result in later purchasing when shoppers' incomes eventually rise to match their aspirations. "Maybe if you've been visiting IKEA, eating meatballs, hot dogs, or ice cream for 10 years, then maybe you will consider IKEA when you get yourself a sofa," says the company's Asia-Pacific president. Thanks to such cultural understandings, IKEA already captures about 7 percent of the surging Chinese home-furnishings market, and its sales in China increased 17 percent last year. What do Chinese consumers think of Swedish meatballs? "They love them," says IKEA China's marketing director.

Thus, understanding cultural traditions, preferences, and behaviors can help companies not only avoid embarrassing mistakes but also take advantage of cross-cultural opportunities.

The Impact of Marketing Strategy on Cultures

Whereas marketers worry about the impact of global cultures on their marketing strategies, others may worry about the impact of marketing strategies on global cultures. For example, social critics contend that large American multinationals, such as McDonald's, Coca-Cola, Starbucks, Nike, Google, Disney, and Facebook, aren't just globalizing their brands; they are Americanizing the world's cultures. Other elements of American culture have become pervasive worldwide. For instance, more people now study English in China than speak it in the United States. Of the 10 most watched TV shows in the world, 7 are American. If you assemble businesspeople from Brazil, Germany, and China, they'll likely transact in English. And the thing that binds the world's teens together in a kind of global community, notes one observer, "is American culture—the music, the Hollywood fare, the electronic games, Google, Facebook, American consumer brands. The . . . rest of the world is becoming [evermore] like us—in ways good and bad."[22]

"Today, globalization often wears Mickey Mouse ears, eats Big Macs, drinks Coke or Pepsi, and does its computing with Windows," says Thomas Friedman in his book *The Lexus and the Olive Tree: Understanding Globalization*. "Some Chinese kids' first English word [is] Mickey," notes another writer.[23]

Critics worry that, under such "McDomination," countries around the globe are losing their individual cultural identities. Teens in Turkey watch MTV, connect with others globally through Facebook, and ask their parents for more Westernized clothes and other symbols of American pop culture and values. Grandmothers in small European villas no longer spend each morning visiting local meat, bread, and produce markets to gather the ingredients for dinner. Instead, they now shop at Walmart Supercenters. Women in Saudi Arabia see American films, question their societal roles, and shop at any of the country's growing number of Victoria's Secret boutiques. In China, most people never drank coffee before Starbucks entered the market. Now Chinese consumers rush to Starbucks stores "because it's a symbol of a new kind of lifestyle." ● Similarly, in China, where McDonald's operates more than 80 restaurants in Beijing alone, nearly half of all children identify the chain as a domestic brand.

● **The impact of marketing strategy on culture: Nearly half of all children in China identify McDonald's as a domestic brand.**

Tomoko Kunihiro

Such concerns have sometimes led to a backlash against American globalization. Well-known U.S. brands have become the targets of boycotts and protests in some international markets. As symbols of American capitalism, companies such as Coca-Cola, McDonald's, Nike, and KFC have been singled out by antiglobalization protestors in hot spots around the world, especially when anti-American sentiment peaks.

Despite such problems, defenders of globalization argue that concerns of Americanization and the potential damage to American brands are overblown. U.S. brands are doing very well internationally. In the most recent Millward Brown BrandZ brand value survey of global consumer brands, 20 of the top 25 global brands were American owned, including megabrands such as Google, Apple, IBM, Microsoft, McDonald's, Coca-Cola, GE, Amazon .com, and Walmart.[24]

Many iconic American brands are soaring globally. For example, Chinese consumers appear to have an insatiable appetite for Apple iPhones and iPads. When Apple introduced its latest iPhone model in China recently, demand was so heavy that the company had to abandon sales in some Beijing stores to avert the threat of rioting by mobs of eager consumers. Similarly, many international markets covet American fast food. For instance, on the day that KFC introduced its outrageous Double Down sandwich—bacon, melted cheese, and a "secret sauce" between two deep-fried chicken patties—in one of its restaurants in Japan, fans formed long lines and slept on the sidewalks outside to get a taste. "It was like the iPhone," says the CMO of KFC International, "people [were] crazy." The U.S. limited-time item generated substantial online buzz and has since become a runaway success worldwide, from Canada to Australia, the Philippines, and Malaysia.[25]

More fundamentally, the cultural exchange goes both ways: America gets as well as gives cultural influence. True, Hollywood dominates the global movie market, but British TV originated the programming that was Americanized into such hits as *House of Cards*, *American Idol*, and *Dancing with the Stars*. Although Chinese and Russian youth are donning NBA superstar jerseys, the increasing popularity of soccer in America has deep international roots.

Even American childhood has been increasingly influenced by European and Asian cultural imports. Most kids know all about imports such as Hello Kitty, the Bakugan Battle Brawler, or any of a host of Nintendo or Sega game characters. And J. K. Rowling's so-very-British Harry Potter books shaped the thinking of a generation of American youngsters, not to mention the millions of American oldsters who fell under their spell as well. For the moment, English remains the dominant language of the Internet, and having Web and mobile access often means that third-world youth have greater exposure to American popular culture. Yet these same technologies let Eastern European students studying in the United States hear Webcast news and music from Poland, Romania, or Belarus.

Thus, globalization is a two-way street. If globalization has Mickey Mouse ears, it is also talking on a Samsung smartphone, buying furniture at IKEA, driving a Toyota Camry, and watching a British-inspired show on a Panasonic plasma TV.

Deciding Whether to Go Global

Not all companies need to venture into international markets to survive. For example, most local businesses need to market well only in their local marketplaces. Operating domestically is easier and safer. Managers don't need to learn another country's language and laws. They don't have to deal with unstable currencies, face political and legal uncertainties, or redesign their products to suit different customer expectations. However, companies that operate in global industries, where their strategic positions in specific markets are affected strongly by their overall global positions, must compete on a regional or worldwide basis to succeed.

Any of several factors might draw a company into the international arena. For example, global competitors might attack the company's home market by offering better products or lower prices. The company might want to counterattack these competitors in their home markets to tie up their resources. The company's customers might be expanding abroad and require international servicing. Or, most likely, international markets might simply provide better opportunities for growth. For example, as we discovered in the story at the start of the chapter, Coca-Cola has emphasized international growth in recent years to offset stagnant or declining U.S. soft drink sales. Today, non-U.S. sales account for 60 percent of Coca-Cola's total revenues and 81 percent of its earnings, and the company is making major pushes into 90 emerging markets, such as China, India, and the entire African continent.[26]

Before going abroad, the company must weigh several risks and answer many questions about its ability to operate globally. Can the company learn to understand the preferences and buyer behavior of consumers in other countries? Can it offer competitively attractive products? Will it be able to adapt to other countries' business cultures and deal effectively with foreign nationals? Do the company's managers have the necessary international experience? Has management considered the impact of regulations and the political environments of other countries?

Deciding Which Markets to Enter

Before going abroad, the company should try to define its international *marketing objectives and policies*. It should decide what *volume* of foreign sales it wants. Most companies start small when they go abroad. Some plan to stay small, seeing international sales as a small part of their business. Other companies have bigger plans, however, seeing international business as equal to—or even more important than—their domestic business.

The company also needs to choose in *how many* countries it wants to market. Companies must be careful not to spread themselves too thin or expand beyond their capabilities by operating in too many countries too soon. Next, the company needs to decide on the *types* of countries to enter. A country's attractiveness depends on the product, geographical factors, income and population, political climate, and other considerations. In recent years, many major new markets have emerged, offering both substantial opportunities and daunting challenges.

After listing possible international markets, the company must carefully evaluate each one. It must consider many factors. ● For example, Netflix's decision to expand into European markets such as Germany, France, Italy, and Spain seems like a no-brainer. Netflix needs to grow its subscriber base to cover rapidly rising content costs, and Europe offers huge opportunities. Western Europe boasts 134 million broadband homes, compared with 88 million in the United States. The as-yet-largely-untapped European video-services market is expected to grow by 67 percent to more than $1.1 billion by 2017. Netflix has already entered the U.K and the Nordic nations, and is the leading video service in Sweden after only two years.[27]

● **Entering new global markets: Netflix's decision to expand into new European markets seems like a no-brainer. But despite its huge market potential, Europe presents Netflix with some formidable challenges.**

However, as Netflix considers expanding into new European markets, it must ask some important questions. Can it compete effectively on a country-by-country basis with local competitors? Can it master the varied cultural and buying differences of European consumers? Will it be able to meet environmental and regulatory hurdles in each country? For example, Netflix's expansion has been slow and difficult in Latin America, where e-commerce is less established.

In entering new European markets, Netflix will face many challenges. For example, Europe is now crowded with formidable competitors. More than a dozen local Netflix-like rivals have sprung up there during the past few years—services such as Snap in Germany, Infinity in Italy, and CanalPlay in France have been busy locking in subscribers and content rights. And Amazon.com's Lovefilm is already the leading streaming service in Germany.

Content is another major consideration. Although Netflix is building its own portfolio of international content rights, European competitors already own exclusive in-country rights to many popular U.S. and non-U.S. shows. Netflix may also encounter local regulatory obstacles. Regulations in France, for instance, restrict services like Netflix from airing films until three years after they open nationally in theaters, and video services there are usually required to invest in film production in the country. Despite these challenges, however, Netflix CEO Reed Hastings seems unfazed. "We can still build a very successful business [in these new markets]," he says. Wherever Netflix goes, "I think the key is having unique content, a great reputation, a good value proposition," things at which Netflix excels.

Table 19.1 | Indicators of Market Potential

Demographic Characteristics	Sociocultural Factors
Education Population size and growth Population age composition	Consumer lifestyles, beliefs, and values Business norms and approaches Cultural and social norms Languages
Geographic Characteristics	**Political and Legal Factors**
Climate Country size Population density—urban, rural Transportation structure and market accessibility	National priorities Political stability Government attitudes toward global trade Government bureaucracy Monetary and trade regulations
Economic Factors	
GDP size and growth Income distribution Industrial infrastructure Natural resources Financial and human resources	

Possible global markets should be ranked on several factors, including market size, market growth, the cost of doing business, competitive advantage, and risk level. The goal is to determine the potential of each market, using indicators such as those shown in **Table 19.1**. Then the marketer must decide which markets offer the greatest long-run return on investment.

Author Comment | A company has many options for entering an international market, from simply exporting its products to working jointly with foreign companies to setting up its own foreign-based operations.

Deciding How to Enter the Market

Once a company has decided to sell in a foreign country, it must determine the best mode of entry. Its choices are *exporting*, *joint venturing*, and *direct investment*. **Figure 19.2** shows the three market entry strategies, along with the options each one offers. As the figure shows, each succeeding strategy involves more commitment and risk but also more control and potential profits.

Exporting
Entering foreign markets by selling goods produced in the company's home country, often with little modification.

Exporting

The simplest way to enter a foreign market is through **exporting**. The company may passively export its surpluses from time to time, or it may make an active commitment to

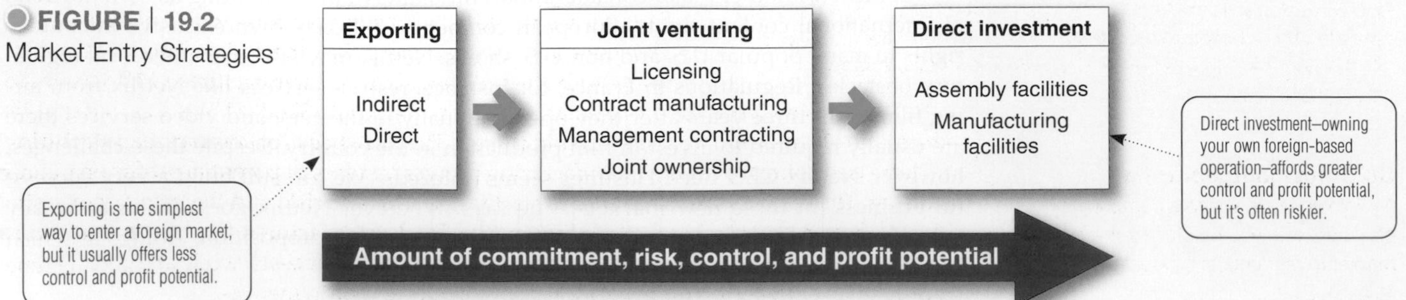

FIGURE | 19.2 Market Entry Strategies

expand exports to a particular market. In either case, the company produces all its goods in its home country. It may or may not modify them for the export market. Exporting involves the least change in the company's product lines, organization, investments, or mission.

Companies typically start with *indirect exporting*, working through independent international marketing intermediaries. Indirect exporting involves less investment because the firm does not require an overseas marketing organization or network. It also involves less risk. International marketing intermediaries bring know-how and services to the relationship, so the seller normally makes fewer mistakes. Sellers may eventually move into *direct exporting*, whereby they handle their own exports. The investment and risk are somewhat greater in this strategy, but so is the potential return.

Joint Venturing

Joint venturing
Entering foreign markets by joining with foreign companies to produce or market a product or service.

A second method of entering a foreign market is by **joint venturing**—joining with foreign companies to produce or market products or services. Joint venturing differs from exporting in that the company joins with a host country partner to sell or market abroad. It differs from direct investment in that an association is formed with someone in the foreign country. There are four types of joint ventures: *licensing*, *contract manufacturing*, *management contracting*, and *joint ownership*.

Licensing

Licensing
Entering foreign markets through developing an agreement with a licensee in the foreign market.

Licensing is a simple way for a manufacturer to enter international marketing. The company enters into an agreement with a licensee in the foreign market. For a fee or royalty payments, the licensee buys the right to use the company's manufacturing process, trademark, patent, trade secret, or other item of value. The company thus gains entry into a foreign market at little risk; at the same time, the licensee gains production expertise or a well-known product or name without having to start from scratch.

In Japan, Budweiser beer flows from Kirin breweries, and Mizkan produces Sunkist lemon juice, drinks, and dessert items. ● Tokyo Disney Resort is owned and operated by Oriental Land Company under license from The Walt Disney Company. The 45-year license gives Disney licensing fees plus a percentage of admissions and food and merchandise sales. And Coca-Cola markets internationally by licensing bottlers around the world and supplying them with the syrup needed to produce the product. Its global bottling partners range from the Coca-Cola Bottling Company of Saudi Arabia to Europe-based Coca-Cola Hellenic, which bottles and markets 136 Coca-Cola brands to 585 million people in 28 countries, from Italy and Greece to Nigeria and Russia.[28]

● **International licensing: The Tokyo Disney Resort is owned and operated by Oriental Land Company (a Japanese development company) under license from The Walt Disney Company.**
© David Harding / Alamy

Licensing has potential disadvantages, however. The firm has less control over the licensee than it would over its own operations. Furthermore, if the licensee is very successful, the firm has given up these profits, and if and when the contract ends, it may find it has created a competitor.

Contract Manufacturing

Contract manufacturing
A joint venture in which a company contracts with manufacturers in a foreign market to produce its product or provide its service.

Another option is **contract manufacturing**, in which the company makes agreements with manufacturers in the foreign market to produce its product or provide its service. For example, P&G serves 650 million consumers across India with the help of nine contract manufacturing sites there. And Volkswagen contracts with Russia's largest auto manufacturer, GAZ Group, to make Volkswagen Jettas for the Russian market, as well as its Škoda (VW's Czech Republic subsidiary) Octavia and Yeti models sold there.[29] The drawbacks of contract manufacturing are decreased control over the manufacturing process and loss of potential profits on manufacturing. The benefits are the chance to start faster, with less risk, and the later opportunity either to form a partnership with or buy out the local manufacturer. Contract manufacturing can also reduce plant investment, transportation, and tariff costs, while at the same time helping to meet the host country's local manufacturing requirements.

Management Contracting

Management contracting
A joint venture in which the domestic firm supplies the management know-how to a foreign company that supplies the capital; the domestic firm exports management services rather than products.

Under **management contracting**, the domestic firm provides the management know-how to a foreign company that supplies the capital. In other words, the domestic firm exports management services rather than products. Hilton uses this arrangement in managing hotels around the world. For example, the hotel chain operates DoubleTree by Hilton hotels in countries ranging from the UK and Italy to Peru and Costa Rica, to China, Russia, and Tanzania. The properties are locally owned, but Hilton manages the hotels with its world-renowned hospitality expertise.[30]

Management contracting is a low-risk method of getting into a foreign market, and it yields income from the beginning. The arrangement is even more attractive if the contracting firm has an option to buy some share in the managed company later on. The arrangement is not sensible, however, if the company can put its scarce management talent to better uses or if it can make greater profits by undertaking the whole venture. Management contracting also prevents the company from setting up its own operations for a period of time.

Joint Ownership

Joint ownership
A cooperative venture in which a company creates a local business with investors in a foreign market, who share ownership and control.

Joint ownership ventures consist of one company joining forces with foreign investors to create a local business in which they share possession and control. A company may buy an interest in a local firm, or the two parties may form a new business venture. Joint ownership may be needed for economic or political reasons. For example, the firm may lack the financial, physical, or managerial resources to undertake the venture alone. Alternatively, a foreign government may require joint ownership as a condition for entry.

Often, companies form joint ownership ventures to merge their complementary strengths in developing a global marketing opportunity. For example, Chrysler's parent company, Fiat, recently formed a 50/50 joint venture with Chinese state-run Guangzhou Automobile Group (GAC) to produce Jeep vehicles in China. Jeep was one of the first Western auto brands sold in China, and the brand is well recognized and popular there. However, all of the Jeeps sold in China have been imported from the United States and subject to steep 25 percent import tariffs, driving Jeep prices to sky-high levels. For example, before the joint venture, a top-of-the-line Jeep Grand Cherokee sold for as much as $205,000 in China, more than triple its U.S. price. Under the joint venture, once approved, Chrysler and GAC will partner to produce Jeeps in China, avoiding tariffs, reducing production costs, and allowing competitive Jeep prices in the world's largest automotive market.[31]

Joint ownership has certain drawbacks, however. The partners may disagree over investment, marketing, or other policies. Whereas many U.S. firms like to reinvest earnings for growth, local firms often prefer to take out these earnings; whereas U.S. firms emphasize the role of marketing, local investors may rely on selling.

Direct investment
Entering a foreign market by developing foreign-based assembly or manufacturing facilities.

Direct Investment

The biggest involvement in a foreign market comes through **direct investment**—the development of foreign-based assembly or manufacturing facilities. For example, Ford has made more than $4 billion in direct investments in several Asian countries, including India, China, and Thailand. It built its second facility in India, a $1 billion state-of-the-art manufacturing and engineering plant that will produce 240,000 cars a year, helping to satisfy Ford's burgeoning demand in India and other Asian and African markets. Similarly, Honda and Toyota have made substantial direct manufacturing investments in North America. For example, 90 percent of the Honda and Acura models sold in the United States are made in North America. "Our fundamental philosophy is to produce where we sell," says a Honda executive.[32]

Direct investment: Ford has made major direct investments in several countries such as India, China, and Thailand to help satisfy Ford's burgeoning demand in Asian markets.
AFP/Getty Images

Standardized global marketing
An international marketing strategy that basically uses the same marketing strategy and mix in all of the company's international markets.

Adapted global marketing
An international marketing approach that adjusts the marketing strategy and mix elements to each international target market, which creates more costs but hopefully produces a larger market share and return.

If a company has gained experience in exporting and if the foreign market is large enough, foreign production facilities offer many advantages. The firm may have lower costs in the form of cheaper labor or raw materials, foreign government investment incentives, and freight savings. The firm may also improve its image in the host country because it creates jobs. Generally, a firm develops a deeper relationship with the government, customers, local suppliers, and distributors, allowing it to adapt its products to the local market better. Finally, the firm keeps full control over the investment and therefore can develop manufacturing and marketing policies that serve its long-term international objectives.

The main disadvantage of direct investment is that the firm faces many risks, such as restricted or devalued currencies, falling markets, or government changes. In some cases, a firm has no choice but to accept these risks if it wants to operate in the host country.

Author Comment The major global marketing decision usually boils down to this: How much, if at all, should a company adapt its marketing strategy and programs to local markets? How might the answer differ for Boeing versus McDonald's?

Deciding on the Global Marketing Program

Companies that operate in one or more foreign markets must decide how much, if at all, to adapt their marketing strategies and programs to local conditions. At one extreme are global companies that use **standardized global marketing**, essentially using the same marketing strategy approaches and marketing mix worldwide. At the other extreme is **adapted global marketing**. In this case, the producer adjusts the marketing strategy and mix elements to each target market, resulting in more costs but hopefully producing a larger market share and return.

The question of whether to adapt or standardize the marketing strategy and program has been much debated over the years. On the one hand, some global marketers believe that technology is making the world a smaller place, and consumer needs around the world are becoming more similar. This paves the way for global brands and standardized global marketing. Global branding and standardization, in turn, result in greater brand power and reduced costs from economies of scale.

Think globally, act locally: Starbucks' outstanding success in China results from building on its global brand identity and values while at the same time adapting its brand strategy to the unique characteristics of Chinese consumers.
© Chris Willson / Alamy

On the other hand, the marketing concept holds that marketing programs will be more engaging if tailored to the unique needs of each targeted customer group. If this concept applies within a country, it should apply even more across international markets. Despite global convergence, consumers in different countries still have widely varied cultural backgrounds. They still differ significantly in their needs and wants, spending power, product preferences, and shopping patterns. Because these differences are hard to change, most marketers today adapt their products, prices, channels, and promotions to fit consumer desires in each country.

However, global standardization is not an all-or-nothing proposition. It's a matter of degree. Most international marketers suggest that companies should "think globally but act locally." They should seek a balance between standardization and adaptation, leveraging global brand recognition but adapting their marketing, products, and operations to specific markets. For example, cosmetics giant L'Oréal and its brands are truly global. But the company's outstanding international success comes from achieving a global-local balance that adapts and differentiates brands to make them responsive to local needs while integrating them across world markets to optimize their global impact (see Real Marketing 19.1).

Collectively, local brands still account for the overwhelming majority of consumer purchases. Most consumers, wherever they live, lead very local lives. So a global brand must engage consumers at a local level, respecting the culture and becoming a part of it. Starbucks operates this way. The company's overall brand strategy provides global strategic direction. Then regional or local units focus on adapting the strategy and brand to specific local markets. For example, when Starbucks entered China in 1998, given the strong Chinese tea-drinking culture, few observers expected success. But Starbucks quickly proved the doubters wrong:[33]

> Starbucks' success in China results from building on its global brand identity and values while at the same time adapting its brand strategy to the unique characteristics of Chinese consumers. Rather than forcing U.S. products on the Chinese,

Real Marketing 19.1

L'Oréal: "The United Nations of Beauty"

How does a French company successfully market an American version of a Korean skin-beautifier under a French brand name in Australia? Ask L'Oréal, which sells more than $30 billion worth of cosmetics, hair care products, skin care concoctions, and fragrances each year in 150 countries, making it the world's biggest cosmetics marketer. L'Oréal sells its brands globally by understanding how they appeal to varied cultural nuances of beauty in specific local markets. Then it finds the best balance between standardizing its brands for global impact and adapting them to meet local needs and desires.

L'Oréal is as global as a company gets. With offices spread across 130 nations and more than half of its sales coming from markets outside Europe and North America, the company no longer has a clearly defined home market. L'Oréal's well-known brands originated in a half dozen or more different cultures, including French (L'Oréal Paris, Garnier, Lancôme), American (Maybelline, Kiehl's, SoftSheen-Carson, Ralph Lauren, Redkin), British (The Body Shop), Italian (Giorgio Armani), and Japanese (Shu Uemura). The master global marketer is the uncontested world leader in makeup, skin care, and hair coloring, and second only to P&G in hair care.

L'Oréal's global mastery starts with a corps of highly multicultural managers. The company is famous for building global brand teams around managers who have deep backgrounds in several cultures. L'Oréal managers around the world bring diverse cultural perspectives to their brands as if they were, say, German, or American, or Chinese—or all three at once. As explained by one Indian-American-French manager of a team that launched a men's skin care line in Southeast Asia: "I cannot think about things one way. I have a stock of references in different languages: English, Hindi, and French. I read books in three different languages, meet people from different countries, eat food from different [cultures], and so on."

For example, a French-Irish-Cambodian skin care manager noticed that, in Europe, face creams tended to be either "tinted" (considered makeup) or "lifting" (considered skin care). In Asia, however, many face creams combine both traits. Recognizing the growing popularity of Asian beauty trends in Europe, the manager and his team developed a tinted lifting cream for the French market, a product that proved highly successful.

L'Oréal digs deep to understand what beauty means to consumers in different parts of the world. It outspends all major competitors on R&D, painstakingly researching beauty and personal care behaviors unique to specific locales. L'Oréal has set up R&D centers all over the world, perfecting a local observation approach it calls "geocosmetics." This science is fueled with insights gained through everything from in-home visits to observations made in "bathroom laboratories" equipped with high-tech gadgetry. L'Oréal's research produces precise information about regional beauty and hygiene rituals, as well as about local conditions and constraints that affect the use of its products, such as humidity and temperature:

> How many minutes does a Chinese woman devote to her morning beauty routine? How do people wash their hair in Bangkok? How many brush strokes does a Japanese woman or a French woman use to apply mascara? These beauty rituals, repeated thousands of times, are inherently cultural. Passed on by tradition, influenced by climate and by local living conditions, they strive to achieve an ideal of perfection that is different from one country and from one continent to the next. They provide an incredibly rich source of information for L'Oréal. Behind these rituals, there are physiological realities: fine, straight, and short eyelashes cannot be made-up the same way as thick, curled, and long lashes.

L'Oréal uses such detailed insights to create products and positioning for brands in local markets. "Beauty is less and less one size fits all," says a L'Oréal executive in China. "You have to have an answer for very different needs." For example, more than 260 scientists now work in L'Oréal's Shanghai research center, tailoring products ranging from lipstick to herbal cleaners to cucumber toners for Chinese tastes.

At the same time that understanding the minute details of local customer behavior helps L'Oréal be responsive to specific market needs, it also lets the company achieve global scale by integrating brands across world cultures. For example, consider Elséve Total Reparação, a hair care line initially developed at L'Oréal's labs in Rio de Janeiro to address specific hair problems described by Brazilian

Global-local balance: Cosmetics and beauty care giant L'Oréal balances local brand responsiveness and global brand impact, making it "The United Nations of Beauty."

Getty Images

women. In Brazil, more than half of all women have long, dry, dull, and very curly hair, resulting from the humid Brazilian climate, exposure to the sun, frequent washing, and smoothing and straightening treatments. Elséve Total Reparação was an immediate hit in Brazil, and L'Oréal quickly rolled it out to other South American and Latin American markets. The company then tracked down other global locales with climate characteristics and hair care rituals similar to those faced by Brazilian women. Subsequently, L'Oréal launched the brand as Elséve Total Repair in numerous European, Indian, and other South East Asian markets, where consumers greeted it with similar enthusiasm.

Such adaptation often plays out across multiple L'Oréal brands—which takes us back to that Korean skin-beautifier sold under a French brand in Australia mentioned in the opening paragraph. Blemish Balm Cream (BB Cream) was originally created by L'Oréal dermatologists in Korea to soothe skin and hide minor blemishes. It quickly became a high-flying Korean brand. However, applying their deep knowledge of skin colors, treatments, and makeup worldwide, L'Oréal researchers developed a successful new-generation BB Cream adapted to conditions and skin colors in U.S. markets (where BB stands for "beauty balm") and launched it under the Maybelline New York brand. Still not finished, L'Oréal created yet another local version for Europe under the Garnier brand, which it also introduced in other world markets, including Australia.

L'Oréal doesn't just adapt its product formulations globally. It also adapts brand positioning and marketing to international needs and expectations. For example, nearly 20 years ago, the company bought stodgy American makeup producer Maybelline. To reinvigorate and globalize the brand, it moved the unit's headquarters from Tennessee to New York City and added "New York" to the label. The resulting urban, street-smart, Big Apple image played well with the midprice positioning of the workaday makeup brand globally. The makeover soon earned Maybelline a 20 percent market share in its category in Western Europe. The young urban positioning also hit the mark in Asia, where few women realized that the trendy "New York" Maybelline brand belonged to French cosmetics giant L'Oréal.

Thus, L'Oréal and its brands are truly global. But the company's international success comes from achieving a global-local balance that adapts and differentiates brands in local markets while optimizing their impact across global markets. L'Oréal is one of the few companies that have achieved both local brand responsiveness and global brand integration. When a former CEO once addressed a UNESCO conference, nobody batted an eyelid when he described L'Oréal as "The United Nations of Beauty."

Sources: Based on information from Hae-Jung Hong and Yves Doz, "L'Oréal Masters Multiculturalism," *Harvard Business Review*, June, 2013, pp. 114–119; Liza Lin, "L'Oréal Puts on a Happy Face in China," *Bloomberg Businessweek*, April 1–April 7, 2013, pp. 25–26; and www.lorealusa.com/Article.aspx?topcode=CorpTopic_RI_CustomerInnovation and www.lorealusa.com/research-innovation/when-the-diversity-of-types-of-beauty-inspires-science/stories-of-multicultural-innovations.aspx, accessed September, 2014.

Starbucks developed new flavors—such as green-tea-flavored coffee drinks—that appeal to local tastes. Rather than just charging U.S.-style premium prices in China, Starbucks boosted prices even higher, positioning the brand as a status symbol for the rapidly growing Chinese middle and upper classes. And rather than pushing take-out orders, which account for most of its U.S. revenues, Starbucks promoted dine-in services—making its stores the perfect meeting place for Chinese professionals and their friends. Whereas U.S. locations do about 70 percent of their business before 10 A.M., China stores do more than 70 percent of their business in the afternoon and evening. Under this adapted strategy, Starbucks China is thriving. China is now Starbucks' largest market outside of the United States, with more than 1,000 current stores and 1,600 stores in 70 cities planned by the end of 2015. "We're trying to build a different kind of company in China and are mindful of how we grow while maintaining the heart and soul of what Starbucks stands for," says the president of Starbucks China.

Product

Five strategies are used for adapting product and marketing communication strategies to a global market (see **Figure 19.3**).[31] We first discuss the three product strategies and then turn to the two communication strategies.

Straight product extension
Marketing a product in a foreign market without making any changes to the product.

Straight product extension means marketing a product in a foreign market without making any changes to the product. Top management tells its marketing people, "Take the product as is and find customers for it." The first step, however, should be to find out whether foreign consumers use that product and what form they prefer.

Straight extension has been successful in some cases and disastrous in others. Apple iPads, Gillette razors, Black & Decker tools, and even 7–Eleven Slurpees are all sold successfully in about the same form around the world. But when General Foods introduced its standard powdered JELL-O in the British market, it discovered that British consumers

FIGURE | 19.3
Five Global Product and Communications Strategies

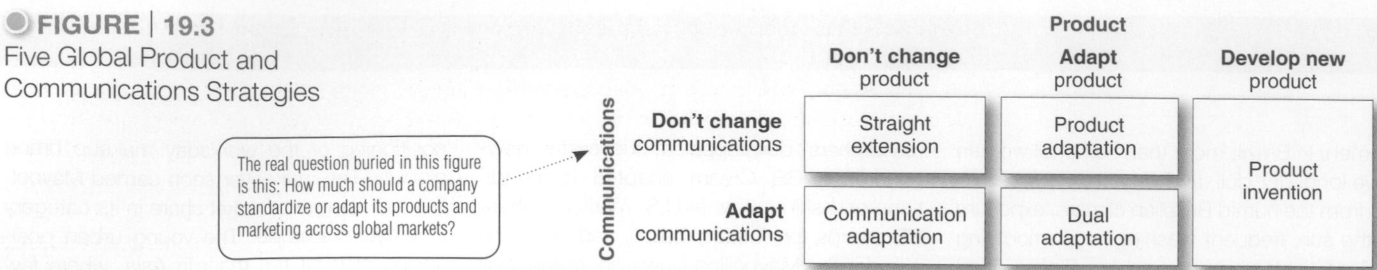

prefer a solid wafer or cake form. Likewise, Philips began to make a profit in Japan only after it reduced the size of its coffeemakers to fit into smaller Japanese kitchens and its shavers to fit smaller Japanese hands. And Panasonic's refrigerator sales in China surged 10-fold in a single year after it shaved the width of its appliances by 15 percent to fit smaller Chinese kitchens.[35] Straight extension is tempting because it involves no additional product development costs, manufacturing changes, or new promotion. But it can be costly in the long run if products fail to satisfy consumers in specific global markets.

Product adaptation
Adapting a product to meet local conditions or wants in foreign markets.

Product adaptation involves changing the product to meet local requirements, conditions, or wants. For example, McDonald's operates in 118 countries, with sometimes widely varying local food preferences. So although you'll find its signature burgers and fries in most locations around the world, the chain has added menu items that meet the unique taste buds of customers in local markets. McDonald's serves salmon burgers in Norway, mashed-potato burgers in China, shrimp burgers in Japan, a Samurai Pork Burger in Thailand, chicken porridge in Malaysia, and Spam and eggs in Hawaii. In a German McDonald's, you'll find the Nurnburger (three large bratwurst on a soft roll with lots of mustard, of course); in Israel, there's the McFalafel (chickpea fritters, tomatoes, cucumber, and cheese topped with tahini and wrapped in lafa). And menus in Turkey feature a chocolate orange fried pie (Brazil adds banana, Egypt taro, and Hawaii pineapple).

In many major global markets, McDonald's adapts more than just its menu. It also adjusts its restaurant design and operations. For example, McDonald's France has redefined itself as a French company that adapts to the needs and preferences of French consumers:[36]

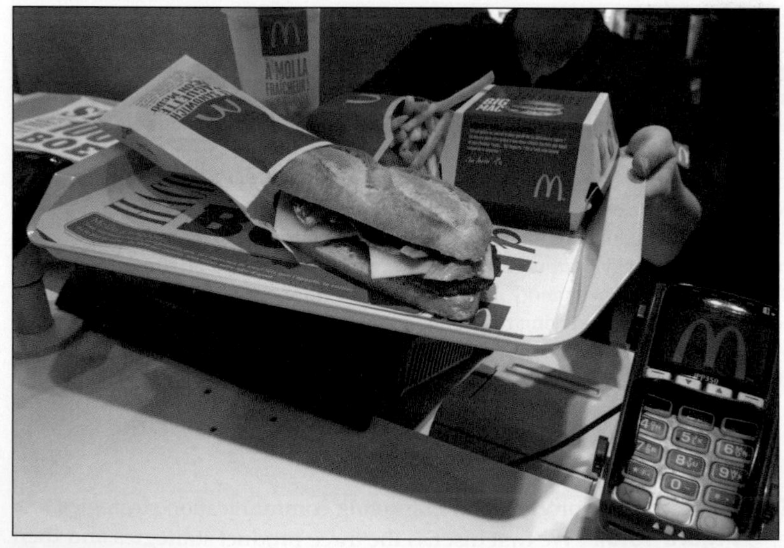

Think globally, act locally: By leveraging the power of its global brand but constantly adapting to the needs and preferences of French consumers and their culture, McDonald's has turned France into its second-most profitable world market.
ERIC PIERMONT/AFP/Getty Images/Newscom

"France—the land of haute cuisine, fine wine, and cheese—would be the last place you would expect to find a thriving [McDonald's]," opines one observer. Yet the fast-food giant has turned France into its second-most profitable world market. Although a McDonald's in Paris might at first seem a lot like one in Chicago, McDonald's has carefully adapted its French operations to the preferences of local customers. At the most basic level, although a majority of revenues still come from burgers and fries, McDonald's France has changed its menu to please the French palate. For instance, it offers up burgers with French cheeses such as chevre, cantel, and bleu, topped off with whole-grain French mustard sauce. And French consumers love baguettes, so McDonald's bakes them fresh in its restaurants and sells them in oh-so-French McBaguette sandwiches.

But perhaps the biggest difference isn't in the food, but in the design of the restaurants themselves, which have been adapted to suit French lifestyles. For example, French meal times tend to be longer, with more food consumed per sitting. So McDonald's has refined its restaurant interiors to create a comfortable, welcoming environment where customers want to linger and perhaps order an additional coffee or dessert. McDonald's even provides table-side service. As a result, the average French McDonald's customer spends about four times what an American customer spends per visit.

Product invention
Creating new products or services for foreign markets.

Product invention consists of creating something new to meet the needs of consumers in a given country. As markets have gone global, companies ranging from appliance manufacturers and carmakers to candy and soft drink producers have developed products that meet the special purchasing needs of low-income consumers in developing economies.

For example, Chinese appliance producer Haier developed sturdier washing machines for rural users in emerging markets, where it found that lighter-duty machines often became clogged with mud when farmers used them to clean vegetables as well as clothes. And solar lighting manufacturer d.light Solar has developed affordable solar-powered home lighting systems for the hundreds of millions of people in the developing world who don't have access to reliable power. d.light's hanging lamps and portable lanterns require no energy source other than the sun and can last up to 15 hours on one charge. The company has already reached 10 million users, is adding 1 million users per month, and plans to reach 100 million users by 2020.[37]

Promotion

Companies can either adopt the same communication strategy they use in the home market or change it for each local market. Consider advertising messages. Some global companies use a standardized advertising theme around the world. For example, Chevrolet recently swapped out its previous, American-focused "Chevy Runs Deep" positioning and advertising theme with a more global "Find New Roads" theme. The new theme is one "that works in all markets," says a GM marketing executive. "The theme has meaning in mature markets like the U.S. as well as emerging markets like Russia and India, where the potential for continued growth is the greatest." The time is right for a more globally consistent Chevy brand message. Chevrolet sells cars in more than 140 countries, and nearly two-thirds of its sales are now outside the United States, compared with only about one-third a decade ago.[38]

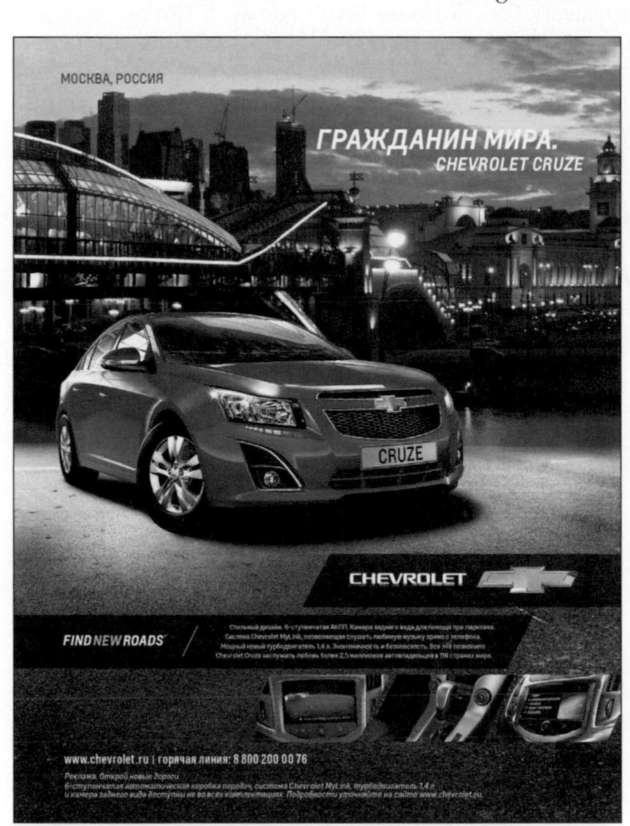

Communication standardization: With nearly two-thirds of its sales now outside the United States, Chevy recently switched to a new, more global "Find New Roads" positioning and advertising theme that has meaning in all markets worldwide, here Russia.

General Motors, LLC 2011

Of course, even in highly standardized communications campaigns, some adjustments might be required for language and cultural differences. For example, ads for Pepsi's youthful "Live for Now" campaign have a similar look worldwide but are adapted in different global markets to feature local consumers, languages, and events. Similarly, in Western markets, fast-casual clothing retailer H&M runs fashion ads with models showing liberal amounts of bare skin. But in the Middle East, where attitudes toward public nudity are more conservative, the retailer runs the same ads digitally adapted to better cover its models.

Global companies often have difficulty crossing the language barrier, with results ranging from mild embarrassment to outright failure. Seemingly innocuous brand names and advertising phrases can take on unintended or hidden meanings when translated into other languages. For example, Interbrand of London, the firm that created household names such as Prozac and Acura, recently developed a brand name "hall of shame" list, which contained these and other foreign brand names you're never likely to see inside the local Kroger supermarket: Krapp toilet paper (Denmark), Plopp chocolate (Scandinavia), Crapsy Fruit cereal (France), Poo curry powder (Argentina), and Pschitt lemonade (France). Similarly, advertising themes often lose—or gain—something in the translation. In Chinese, the KFC slogan "finger-lickin' good" came out as "eat your fingers off." And Motorola's Hellomoto ringtone sounds like "Hello, Fatty" in India.

Marketers must be watchful to avoid such mistakes, taking great care when localizing their brand names and messages to specific global markets. In important but culturally different markets such as China, finding just the right name can make or break a brand (see Real Marketing 19.2).

Communication adaptation
A global communication strategy of fully adapting advertising messages to local markets.

Rather than standardizing their advertising globally, other companies follow a strategy of **communication adaptation**, fully adapting their advertising messages to local markets. For example, in the United States and most Western countries, where running is accepted as a positive, healthful activity, Nike advertising focuses on products and personal performance. In China, however, running is viewed as a boring sport, or even

Real Marketing 19.2

Localizing Chinese Brand Names: Very Important but Notoriously Tricky

After a long day's work, an average upscale Beijinger can't wait to dash home, lace on a comfortable pair of Enduring and Persevering, pop the top on a refreshing can of Tasty Fun, then hop into his Dashing Speed and head to the local tavern for a frosty glass of Happiness Power with friends. Translation? In China, those are the brand-name meanings for Nike, Coca-Cola, Mercedes, and Heineken, respectively.

To Westerners, such names sound pretty silly, but to brands doing business in China, the world's biggest and fastest growing consumer market, they are no laughing matter. Perhaps more than anywhere else in the world, brand names in China take on deep significance. Finding just the right name can make or break a brand. "Often, a company's most important marketing decision in China is localizing its name," asserts one global branding analyst. "It's also a notoriously tricky one."

Ideally, to maintain global consistency, the Chinese name should sound similar to the original, while at the same time conveying the brand's benefits in meaningful symbolic terms. Nike's Chinese brand name, Nai ke, does this well. Not only does it sound the same when pronounced in Chinese, its "Enduring and Persevering" meaning powerfully encapsulates the "Just Do It" essence of the Nike brand the world over. Similarly, P&G's Tide is Taizi in China, which translates to "gets out the dirt," a perfect moniker for a tough-acting detergent. Coca-Cola's Chinese name—Ke kou ke le—dates all the way back to 1928. It not only sounds much like the English name, the Chinese symbols convey happiness in the mouth, a close fit to Coca-Cola's current "open happiness" positioning. Other names that wear well on Chinese ears while also conveying a brand's essence include Lay's snack foods—Le shi ("happy things"); Reebok—Rui bu ("quick steps"); and Colgate—Gau lu jie ("revealing superior cleanliness").

Chinese brand names can convey subtle meanings that might not be apparent to Western sensibilities. For example, "Dashing Speed" seems appropriate enough for an upscale automobile brand like Mercedes. So does BMW's name—Bao Ma—which translates to "Precious Horse." However, in China, "precious" has a feminine connotation, whereas "dashing speed" is more masculine. This works out well for both car makers, which target different genders among China's upper crust. For instance, BMW is a market leader among affluent Chinese women.

Some brand names translate naturally. For example, when Garnier introduced its Clear shampoo in China, it lucked out. The Chinese word for "clear"—Qing—is one of a select few Chinese words with unusually positive associations that are used in many brand names. Garnier added the word *yang*, which means "flying" or "scattering to the wind." According to the director of Garnier's brand consultancy, the Qing Yang brand name connotes "very light, healthy, and happy—think of hair in the air," just what the brand intends. Other universally positive Chinese words commonly found in brand names include "le" and "xi" (happy), "li" (strength or power), "ma" (horse), and "fu" (lucky). Thus, Kia sells one model in China named Qian li ma, or "thousand kilometer horse," suggesting unusual strength.

There was a time when Western companies entering China simply created a brand name that was phonetically similar to the domestic name, even if it had no meaning in the Chinese language. In fact, such obviously foreign looking and sounding names often communicated a sense of Western cache. For example, Cadillac went with *Ka di la ke*—a meaningless group of sounds that gave status to the luxury brand. And McDonald's got away with *Mai dang lao*, a term that sounds like the English version but whose characters translate into gibberish—"wheat," "should," and "labor." Other global companies with short names such as IBM or Gap simply expect consumers to learn their Western names.

Today, however, with so many foreign brands entering the crowded Chinese market, most companies expect more of their Chinese brand names. If Chinese consumers can't pronounce a name or don't know what it stands for, they are much less likely to buy it or talk about it with others, in person or in social media. Instead, with some work, companies can come up with names that will engage and inspire buyers. In China, it's not Subway, it's Sai bai wei—"better than 100 tastes." It's not Marriott but Wan Hao, or "10,000 wealthy elites."

However, finding the right names and characters can be a daunting challenge. Brand

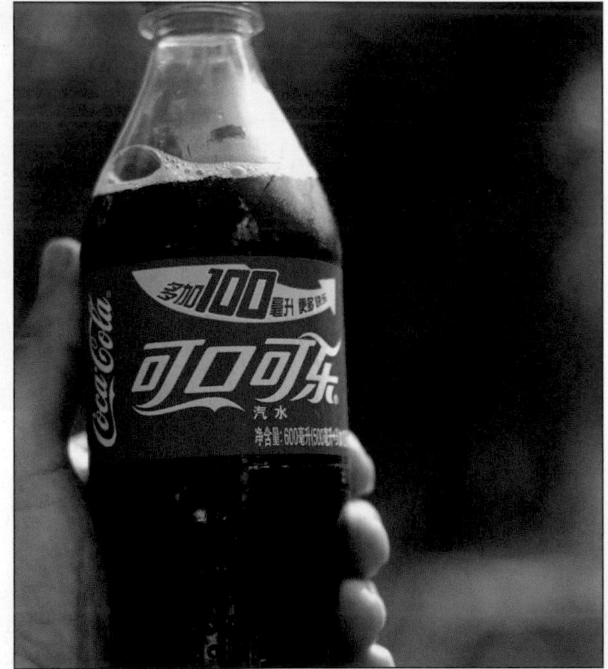

Brand names in China take on deep significance. Coca-Cola's Chinese name, when pronounced, sounds much like the English name, and the Chinese symbols convey "tasty fun" or "happiness in the mouth," a close fit to Coca-Cola's current worldwide "open happiness" positioning.

name development in China has become more of a science than an art, involving global branding consultants, computer software, linguistic analysis, and extensive consumer testing. Some global names require careful recrafting. For example, Microsoft had to rethink the introduction of its Bing search engine in China, where the most common translations of the character pronounced "bing" are words like "defect" or "virus," not good associations for a digital product. Microsoft changed the name of its product in China to Bi ying, which means "very certain to respond." Still, the brand is having difficulty shaking the resemblance to the original name.

Similarly, S.C. Johnson belatedly renamed its popular Mr. Muscle line of cleaners to Mr. Powerful (Weimeng xiansheng) in China, where Mr. Muscle had a less compelling second meaning—"Mr. Chicken Meat." And French automaker Peugeot thought it had a winning brand name with *Biao zhi*, only to learn too late that it was too close to *biaozi*, slang for prostitute. It's no surprise that the brand generated more off-color jokes than sales.

Sources: "Lost in Translation? Pick Your Chinese Brand Name Carefully," *Shanghalist*, March 28, 2014, http://shanghaiist.com/2014/03/28/hutong-school-pick-your-chinese-brand-name-carefully.php; Michael Wines, "Picking Brand Names in China Is a Business Itself," *New York Times*, November 12, 2011, p. A4; Carly Chalmers, "12 Amazing Translations of Chinese Brand Names," *todaytranslations*, August 27, 2013, www.todaytranslations.com/blog/12-amazing-translations-of-chinese-brand-names/; and Angela Doland, "Why Western Companies Like LinkedIn Need Chinese Brand Names," *Advertising Age*, March 5, 2014, adage.com/print/291960/.

a punishment—something rigorous and painful. It's not something that most people in Asia's polluted cities choose to do, especially on streets jammed with pedestrians, bicycles, cars, and even rickshaws. "The joke is that when there's a person running in the city (and it's often a Westerner), people turn to see who's chasing him," quips one observer.

However, China is the largest footwear market in the world, offering huge untapped potential for Nike. So, in China, rather than pushing products and performance, Nike's advertising focuses on just trying to get more Chinese to put on running shoes. Ads and social media feature ordinary people who choose to run on city streets, letting them relate their reasons in their own words. "I run to make the hidden visible," says one young woman. "I run to get lost," says another. Salad—a stressed-out office worker who lives and runs in Shanghai—relates: "The city is always noisy and busy. This adds even more pressure to my day. I guess for me, running is about shutting down the noise." To make running a more social activity, Nike also sponsors nighttime "Lunar Runs" in big cities like Beijing and marathons in Shanghai, featuring fitness instructors, live music, and celebrities to introduce Chinese students and young professionals to running as a fun and rewarding after-class or after-work activity. The goal is to get more people to at least give running a try. But changing basic perceptions of the sport won't be easy. "It's a very long road for us," says a Nike China marketer.[39]

Media also need to be adapted internationally because media availability and regulations vary from country to country. TV advertising time is very limited in Europe, for instance, ranging from four hours a day in France to none in Scandinavian countries. Advertisers must buy time months in advance, and they have little control over airtimes. However, mobile phone ads are much more widely accepted in Europe and Asia than in the United States. Magazines also vary in effectiveness. For example, magazines are a major medium in Italy but a minor one in Austria. Newspapers are national in the United Kingdom but only local in Spain.[40]

Price

Companies also face many considerations in setting their international prices. For example, how might Makita price its power tools globally? It could set a uniform price globally, but this amount would be too high of a price in poor countries and not high enough in rich ones. It could charge what consumers in each country would bear, but this strategy ignores differences in the actual costs from country to country. Finally, the company could use a standard markup of its costs everywhere, but this approach might price Makita out of the market in some countries where costs are high.

Regardless of how companies go about pricing their products, their foreign prices probably will be higher than their domestic prices for comparable products. An Apple iPad that sells for $399 in the United States goes for $546 in the United Kingdom. Why? Apple faces a *price escalation* problem. It must add the cost of transportation, tariffs, importer margin,

International pricing: Google's Motorola division developed the ultra-cheap Moto G smartphone intended primarily for emerging markets where consumers want low-cost phones.

AFP/Getty Images

wholesaler margin, and retailer margin to its factory price. Depending on these added costs, a product may have to sell for two to five times as much in another country to make the same profit.

To overcome this problem when selling to less-affluent consumers in developing countries, many companies make simpler or smaller versions of their products that can be sold at lower prices. Others have introduced new, more affordable brands for global markets. For example, Google's Motorola division developed the ultra-cheap Moto G smartphone. Although not a flashy, high-tech gadget, the full-function device sells for only $179 in the United States with no contract. Google first introduced the phone in Brazil, one of the largest and fastest-growing emerging markets, then in other parts of South America, the Middle East, India, and more of Asia. Intended primarily for emerging markets where consumers want low-cost phones, the Moto G may also sell well to cost-conscious consumers in major developed markets, such as the United States and Europe. Google's new phone puts pressure on Apple, which has focused on selling older models at reduced prices rather than developing cheaper models. "The last few years have been about selling the top-of-the-line smartphones," says one analyst. "The next few years should be about selling a lower-cost version and welcoming in vast new numbers of subscribers."[41]

Recent economic and technological forces have had an impact on global pricing. For example, the Internet is making global price differences more obvious. When firms sell their wares over the Internet, customers can see how much products sell for in different countries. They can even order a given product directly from the company location or dealer offering the lowest price. This is forcing companies toward more standardized international pricing.

Distribution Channels

Whole-channel view
Designing international channels that take into account the entire global supply chain and marketing channel, forging an effective global value delivery network.

An international company must take a **whole-channel view** of the problem of distributing products to final consumers. **Figure 19.4** shows the two major links between the seller and the final buyer. The first link, *channels between nations*, moves company products from points of production to the borders of countries within which they are sold. The second link, *channels within nations*, moves products from their market entry points to the final consumers. The whole-channel view takes into account the entire global supply chain and marketing channel. It recognizes that to compete well internationally, the company must effectively design and manage an entire *global value delivery network*.

Channels of distribution within countries vary greatly from nation to nation. There are large differences in the numbers and types of intermediaries serving each country market and in the transportation infrastructure serving these intermediaries. For example, whereas large-scale retail chains dominate the U.S. scene, most of the retailing in other countries is done by small, independent retailers. In India or Indonesia, millions of retailers operate tiny shops or sell in open markets.

Even in world markets containing similar types of sellers, retailing practices can vary widely. For example, you'll find plenty of Walmarts, Carrefours, Tescos, and other retail

FIGURE | 19.4
Whole-Channel Concept for International Marketing

Distribution channels can vary dramatically around the world. For example, in the U.S., Coca-Cola distributes products through sophisticated retail channels. In less-developed countries, it delivers Coke using everything from push carts to delivery donkeys

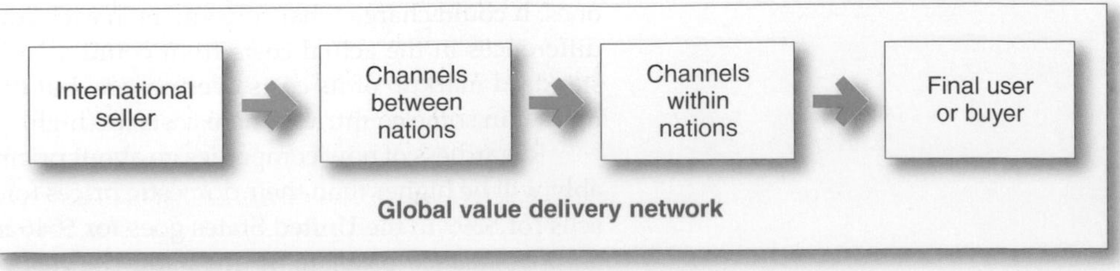

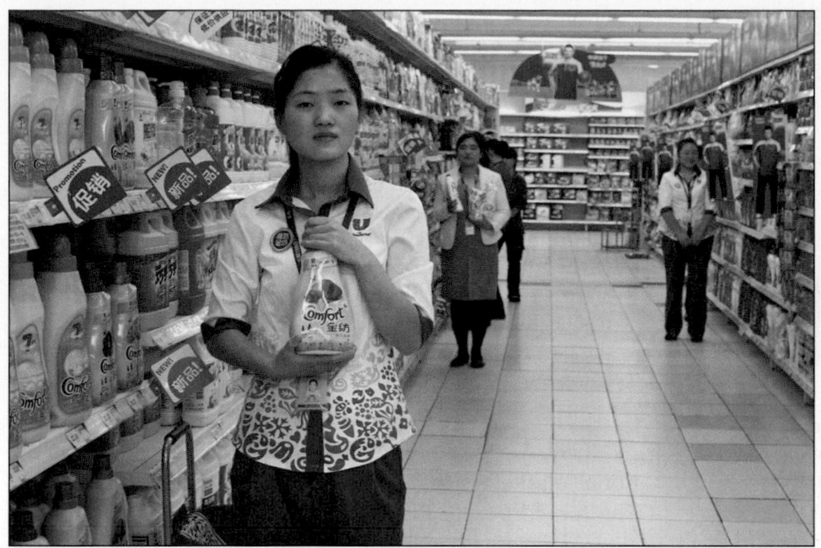

Distribution channels vary from nation to nation. Whereas consumer brands sold in Western superstores like Walmart or Target rely largely on self-service, these brands in China hire armies of uniformed, microphone-wearing, in-store promoters to dispense samples and pitch their products in person.

Darcy Holdorf Photography

superstores in major Chinese cities. But whereas consumer brands sold in such stores in Western markets rely largely on self-service, brands in China hire armies of uniformed in-store promoters—called "promoter girls" or "push girls"—to dispense samples and pitch their products person to person. In a Beijing Walmart, on any given weekend, you'll find 100 or more such promoters acquainting customers with products from Kraft, Unilever, P&G, Johnson & Johnson, and a slew of local competitors. "Chinese consumers know the brand name through media," says the director of a Chinese retail marketing service, "but they want to feel the product and get a detailed understanding before they make a purchase."[42]

Similarly, as we learned in the chapter-opening story about its ventures in Africa, Coca-Cola adapts its distribution methods to meet local challenges in global markets. For example, in Montevideo, Uruguay, where larger vehicles are challenged by traffic, parking, and pollution difficulties, Coca-Cola purchased 30 small, efficient, three-wheeled ZAP alternative transportation trucks. The little trucks average about one-fifth the fuel consumption and scoot around congested city streets with greater ease. In rural areas, Coca-Cola uses a manual delivery process. In China, an army of more than 10,000 Coca-Cola sales reps makes regular visits to small retailers, often on foot or bicycle. To reach the most isolated spots, the company even relies on teams of delivery donkeys. In Tanzania, 93 percent of Coca-Cola's products are manually delivered via pushcarts and bicycles.[43]

Author Comment | Many large companies, regardless of their "home country," now think of themselves as truly *global* organizations. They view the entire world as a single borderless market. For example, although headquartered in Chicago, Boeing is as comfortable selling planes to Lufthansa or Air China as to American Airlines.

Deciding on the Global Marketing Organization

Companies manage their international marketing activities in at least three different ways: Most companies first organize an export department, then create an international division, and finally become a global organization.

A firm normally gets into international marketing by simply shipping out its goods. If its international sales expand, the company will establish an *export department* with a sales manager and a few assistants. As sales increase, the export department can expand to include various marketing services so that it can actively go after business. If the firm moves into joint ventures or direct investment, the export department will no longer be adequate.

Many companies get involved in several international markets and ventures. A company may export to one country, license to another, have a joint ownership venture in a third, and own a subsidiary in a fourth. Sooner or later it will create *international divisions* or subsidiaries to handle all its international activity.

International divisions are organized in a variety of ways. An international division's corporate staff consists of marketing, manufacturing, research, finance, planning, and personnel specialists. It plans for and provides services to various operating units, which can be organized in one of three ways. They can be *geographical organizations*, with country managers who are responsible for salespeople, sales branches, distributors, and licensees in their respective countries. Or the operating units can be *world product groups*, each responsible for worldwide sales of different product groups. Finally, operating units can be *international subsidiaries*, each responsible for their own sales and profits.

Many firms have passed beyond the international division stage and are truly *global organizations*. For example, consider Reckitt Benckiser (RB), a $13.6-billion European producer of household, health, and personal care products and consumer goods with a stable full of familiar brands (Air Wick, Lysol, Woolite, Calgon, Mucinex, Clearasil, French's, and many others—see www.rb.com):[44]

RB products are sold in more than 200 markets across the world. Its top 400 managers represent 53 different nationalities. The company is headquartered in the United Kingdom and its CEO is Indian. Its U.S. business is run by a Dutchman, its Russian business by an Italian, and its Australian

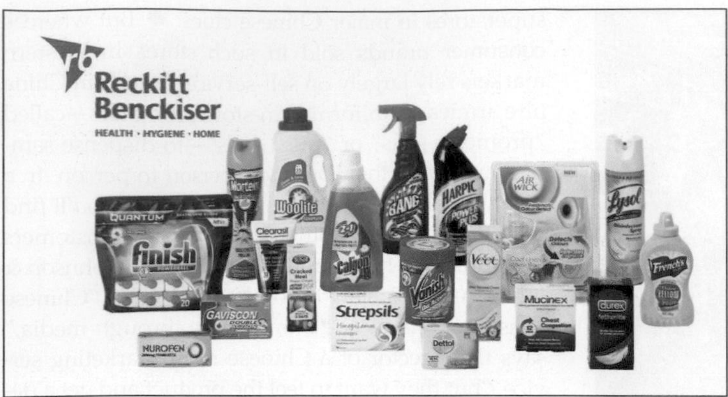

European household, health, and consumer goods producer Reckitt Benckiser has a truly global organization. "Most of our top managers . . . view themselves as global citizens rather than as citizens of any given nation."

Reckitt Benckiser plc

business by a Brazilian. "Most of our top managers . . . view themselves as global citizens rather than as citizens of any given nation," says RB's chief executive officer.

RB recently relocated several of its operations to put key marketers in key countries within their regions. For example, it recently moved its Latin American headquarters from Miami to Sao Paulo, Brazil. The company has spent the past decade building a culture of global mobility because it thinks that's one of the best ways to generate new ideas and create global entrepreneurs. And it has paid off. Products launched in the past three years—all the result of global cross-fertilization—account for 35–40 percent of net revenue. Over the past few years, even during the economic downturn, the company has outperformed its rivals—P&G, Unilever, and Colgate—in growth.

Global organizations don't think of themselves as national marketers that sell abroad but as global marketers. The top corporate management and staff plan worldwide manufacturing facilities, marketing policies, financial flows, and logistical systems. The global operating units report directly to the chief executive or the executive committee of the organization, not to the head of an international division. Executives are trained in worldwide operations, not just domestic *or* international operations. Global companies recruit management from many countries, buy components and supplies where they cost the least, and invest where the expected returns are greatest.

Today, major companies must become more global if they hope to compete. As foreign companies successfully invade their domestic markets, companies must move more aggressively into foreign markets. They will have to change from companies that treat their international operations as secondary to companies that view the entire world as a single borderless market.

19 Reviewing the Concepts

OBJECTIVES REVIEW AND KEY TERMS

Objectives Review

Companies today can no longer afford to pay attention only to their domestic market, regardless of its size. Many industries are global industries, and firms that operate globally achieve lower costs and higher brand awareness. At the same time, global marketing is risky because of variable exchange rates, unstable governments, tariffs and trade barriers, and several other factors. Given the potential gains and risks of international marketing, companies need a systematic way to make their global marketing decisions.

OBJECTIVE 1 Discuss how the international trade system and the economic, political-legal, and cultural environments affect a company's international marketing decisions. *(pp 594–604)*

A company must understand the *global marketing environment*, especially the international trade system. It should assess each foreign market's *economic*, *political-legal*, and *cultural characteristics*. The company can then decide whether it wants to go abroad and consider the potential risks and benefits. It must decide on the volume of international sales it wants, how many countries it wants to market in, and which specific markets it wants to enter. These decisions call for weighing the probable returns against the level of risk.

OBJECTIVE 2 Describe three key approaches to entering international markets. *(pp 604–607)*

The company must decide how to enter each chosen market—whether through *exporting*, *joint venturing*, or *direct investment*. Many companies start as exporters, move to joint ventures, and finally make a direct investment in foreign markets. In *exporting*, the company enters a foreign market by sending and selling products through international marketing intermediaries (indirect exporting) or the company's own department, branch, or sales representatives or agents (direct exporting). When establishing a *joint venture*, a company enters foreign markets by joining with foreign companies to produce or market a product or service. In *licensing*, the company enters a foreign market by contracting with a licensee in the foreign market and offering the right to use a manufacturing process, trademark, patent, trade secret, or other item of value for a fee or royalty.

Explain how companies adapt their marketing strategies and mixes for international markets. *(pp 607–615)*

Companies must also decide how much their marketing strategies and their products, promotion, price, and channels should be adapted for each foreign market. At one extreme, global companies use *standardized global marketing* worldwide. Others use *adapted global marketing*, in which they adjust the marketing strategy and mix to each target market, bearing more costs but hoping for a larger market share and return. However, global standardization is not an all-or-nothing proposition. It's a matter of degree. Most international marketers suggest that companies should "think globally but act locally"—that they should seek a balance between globally standardized strategies and locally adapted marketing mix tactics.

Identify the three major forms of international marketing organization. *(pp 615–616)*

The company must develop an effective organization for international marketing. Most firms start with an *export department* and graduate to an *international division*. A few become *global organizations*, with worldwide marketing planned and managed by the top officers of the company. Global organizations view the entire world as a single, borderless market.

MyMarketingLab

Go to **mymktlab.com** to complete the problems marked with this icon ✪.

Key Terms

OBJECTIVE 1

Global firm (p 595)
Economic community (p 597)

OBJECTIVE 2

Exporting (p 604)
Joint venturing (p 605)
Licensing (p 605)
Contract manufacturing (p 605)
Management contracting (p 606)
Joint ownership (p 606)
Direct investment (p 606)

OBJECTIVE 3

Standardized global marketing (p 607)
Adapted global marketing (p 607)
Straight product extension (p 609)
Product adaptation (p 610)
Product invention (p 610)
Communication adaptation (p 611)
Whole-channel view (p 614)

DISCUSSION AND CRITICAL THINKING

Discussion Questions

✪ **19-1** Explain what is meant by the term *global firm* and list the six major decisions involved in international marketing. (AACSB: Communication)

19-2 What options are open to a business once it has decided to enter an overseas market? (AACSB: Communication)

19-3 Explain what is meant by licensing as a means of entering a market. (AACSB: Communication)

✪ **19-4** What factors do companies consider when deciding on possible global markets to enter? (AACSB: Communication; Reflective Thinking)

19-5 How do businesses in your country manage their international marketing activities? Study two local companies and discuss their international marketing strategies. (AACSB: Communication)

Critical Thinking Exercises

✪ **19-6** Not all countries have open trading relationships with all other countries. Some apply restrictions to certain countries. Which countries are subject to restricted trade by your country? Is this a two-way restriction? (AACSB: Communication; Use of IT; Reflective Thinking)

19-7 What is a *free trade zone*? Give an example of a free trade zone and research how successful it has been. (AACSB: Communication; Reflective Thinking)

19-8 One way to analyze the cultural differences among countries is to conduct a Hofstede analysis. Visit http://geert-hofstede.com/ to learn what this analysis considers. Develop a presentation explaining how three countries of your choice differ from the United States. (AACSB: Communication; Use of IT; Reflective Thinking)

MINICASES AND APPLICATIONS

Online, Mobile, and Social Media Marketing Russian E-Commerce

Russia is emerging as the next big e-commerce frontier with a population of 143 million, 60 million of whom are Internet users. Although online sales currently make up less than 2 percent of retail sales in Russia, they are projected to increase to 5 percent—that's $36 billion—by 2015. That fact has caught the attention of global e-commerce firms such as the U.S. companies Amazon and eBay, as well as China's equivalent of Amazon, Alibaba. The leading local online retailer in Russia is Ozon Group, often referred to as "Russia's Amazon." Ozon's sales last year were close to $500 million, an almost 70 percent increase in just two years. There are obstacles to e-commerce in Russia, however. The majority of consumers do not have credit cards because many do not trust them to pay for purchases online or offline, making Russia a heavily cash-based marketplace. Delivery is another problem. To combat these barriers, Ozon developed its own courier system, and drivers not only collect cash payments, they even offer style advice on apparel orders when delivered. Russian consumers ordering items from international e-commerce sites such as Amazon may never receive their packages. In fact, officials at Moscow airport reported having 500 metric tons of unprocessed packages in one month alone. Seeing an opportunity for revenue, Russia's Customs Service is considering import duties on packages ordered from foreign Web sites.

19-9 What types of barriers are present in Russia that might slow the expansion of international e-commerce there? (AACSB: Communication; Reflective Thinking)

19-10 What types of barriers are present in Russia that might slow the expansion of international e-commerce there? (AACSB: Communication; Reflective Thinking)

19-11 Suggest the best ways companies such as eBay and Amazon can enter this market. (AACSB: Communication; Reflective Thinking)

Marketing Ethics Cleaning Up the Chinese Pharmaceutical Market

By 2020, the Chinese pharmaceutical market will be worth $1 trillion per year. Clearly, pharmaceutical businesses from around the world have recognized the potential of the market and at the same time existing Chinese businesses have realized the potential threats to their market share. In order to grab some market share and profit, some pharmaceutical companies have been less than honest in their dealings and have found themselves under intense scrutiny from China's National Development and Reform Commission (NDRC). The NDRC as of 2014 was investigating no less than 60 domestic and overseas companies for price fixing alone. There are allegations about bribes being paid to hospital doctors; in one case an overseas company is accused of paying out v$5 million to promote its eye lens implants. The relationships and business practices between Chinese institutions and overseas suppliers have brought out the differences between what is acceptable and ethical in China compared to some other countries to the forefront. The Chinese government is keen to stamp out corruption, but corruption is ingrained and persistent. China ranks 80th out of 176 countries on the Transparency International Index. This tracks corruption across a variety of business markets. In one corruption case, the corruption took place outside of the normal parameters of business dealings; the individuals did deals outside the company's systems. In this particular case, there was a 30 percent drop in sales as the company scaled back in order to ensure it had oversight of all aspects of business operations in China. If foreign companies are found to be giving out bribes by the NDRC, then it is not just a question of business as usual after paying the fine, as they must also repair their reputations.

19-12 Should pharmaceutical companies learn to adapt to paying bribes in China? Debate both sides of this issue. (AACSB: Communication; Ethical Reasoning)

19-13 Discuss whether multi-national companies have difficulties breaking into the market in your country. (AACSB: Communication; Reflective Thinking)

Marketing by the Numbers Attracting Alternative Markets

Some 18 million tourists visited Greece during 2014. This represents a figure approaching twice the population of Greece. Only 50 years ago, the country was attracting around 33,000 tourists a year. Tourism has wrought fundamental changes to Greece; it has had a massive social and financial impact on the country. Yet, Greece is one of those countries that struggle to manage and promote their tourism industry with a degree of professionalism and continuity. According to the Aristotle University in Thessaloniki, tourism in Greece peaked in 1990, at about the same time as tourism worldwide reached a peak. Over the years, Greece has welcomed tourists who have been interested in very different things, culminating in mass tourism, which has been in decline for the past decade. With a poor economic outlook, Greece needs to look for alternatives and seize on them quickly before its competitors do.

19-14 Develop a relevant demographic profile of a potential new market for a country like Greece that is looking to attract alternative tourist markets. (AACSB: Communication; Use of IT; Reflective Thinking)

19-15 For the market you selected, is this an attractive market for the Greek tourism sector? Refer to Appendix 2: Marketing by the Numbers to develop a market potential estimation of this market. (AACSB: Communication; Analytic Reasoning; Reflective Thinking)

Video Case The U.S. Film Industry

If you like movies, you've no doubt seen a foreign film at some point. But did you know that American films are some of the biggest and most anticipated foreign films in the world? In fact, foreign box office and DVD sales account for nearly 70 percent of all revenues for the U.S. film industry. With that much financial impact, foreign markets are playing a bigger and bigger role not only in the pricing, distribution, and promotion of U.S. films, but in the product itself.

This video illustrates the challenges faced by the U.S. film industry stemming from differences in the marketing environment throughout different international markets. The result is that this industry is now like any other export industry: The marketing mix must be adapted at an optimum level in order to meet the needs of global markets while still maintaining the benefits of standardization.

After viewing this video, answer the following questions about the U.S. film industry and the global marketplace:

19-16 Which part of the marketing environment seems to be having the greatest impact on U.S. films abroad?

19-17 Which of the five strategies for adapting products and promotion for the global market is most relevant to the U.S. film industry?

19-18 Is the U.S. film industry now dependent upon foreign markets for success? Compare the export of U.S. films to other U.S. exports.

Company Case IKEA: Making Life Better for the World's Many People

Walmart may be the biggest retailer in the world. But IKEA is the largest furniture retailer. Last year, more than 684 million shoppers flocked to the Scandinavian retailer's 303 huge stores in 26 countries, generating revenues of more than $36 billion. That's an average of more than $118 million per store per year, about two-and-a-half times the average sales of a Walmart store. From Beijing to Moscow to Middletown, Ohio, customers pour into IKEA's stores for simple, practical furniture at affordable prices. IKEA is big and getting bigger—its sales have doubled during the past decade. But it's also practical and methodical, growing by only 20 or so superstores each year.

Even these big numbers don't begin to illustrate the impact that IKEA has had on consumers all over the world. Far more than just a big furniture chain, IKEA has achieved global growth and success by connecting with consumers of all nationalities and cultures. IKEA has excelled as a curator of people's lifestyles. Consumers around the world shop at IKEA to signal that they have arrived, that they both have good taste and recognize value. In fact, without IKEA, many people in the world would have little access to affordable, contemporary products for their homes. IKEA's mission is to "create a better everyday life for the many people." It accomplishes this seemingly impossible mission by striking just the right balance between global brand standardization and catering to the local cultural differences in global markets.

A Standardized Global Brand

*In the 1940s, Ingvar Kamprad developed what became known as the "IKEA Concept." He was a native of Småland, Sweden, where the soil was poor and the people had a reputation for working hard, living frugally, and making the most of limited resources. The IKEA Concept reflects those characteristics—"offering a wide range of well-designed, functional home furnishing products at prices so low that as many people as possible will be able to afford them."

Some aspects of IKEA's products are consistent in all markets. For starters, its products are rooted in Swedish, contemporary design. The classic, simple lines of the IKEA design produce timeless products that few companies in any industry can match. For example, POANG—an upholstered chair based on a laminated, bentwood frame with only two front legs—was created in 1976 but remains one of the company's best-selling lines today. The same holds true for the BILLY bookcase. In fact, most of IKEA's best-selling products have been around for years. And that's how IKEA intends customers to enjoy them—for years.

Low price is another key common component of IKEA's products. The benchmark for every IKEA product is half the price of similar products from competitors. And with its relentless focus on cost-cutting, IKEA can keep the price of a product constant or even reduce it over time. Selling the same products in every market achieves scale, which also contributes to IKEA's low-cost structure. So does its "flat pack" approach—designing furniture so that it can be packed and sold in pieces and assembled by customers at home.

IKEA stores around the world also share a standard design. For starters, they're huge. At an average size of 300,000 square feet, the average IKEA store exceeds the size of the average Walmart Supercenter by 50 percent. These large stores let IKEA achieve another aspect of its global brand concept—a one-stop home shopping experience that includes furniture, appliances, and household goods for every room. Although such massive size may be overwhelming to some consumers, IKEA's stores are organized in three main sections. Its *showrooms* are set up in a series of rooms that not only show off each product, but also put products in an actual room context, giving customers ideas for how they might use the products in their homes. The *marketplace* section contains the small items—everything from desk lamps to kitchen utensils—also organized by area of the home. The *warehouse* allows customers to pull their own furniture items in flat-pack boxes and cart them out. One main thoroughfare weaves its way clockwise through the store from one area to the next, a design that encourages customers to see the store in its entirety. Parents can drop their children in the Småland play area and the entire family can eat in the three-meal-a-day restaurant or the snack bar, making it easy to hang around and shop for hours.

Listening, Understanding, and Adapting

Although most of IKEA's standardized formula works in every market, the company has learned that one size does not fit all when it comes to global customers. So IKEA tweaks its marketing mix in different markets to better meet local consumer needs. The retailer seeks constant feedback from customers in stores, and it visits thousands more each year though in-home visits, observing how consumers live and asking about their dreams and challenges.

When the first U.S. IKEA store opened in Philadelphia in 1985, the beds that it carried were the same as those offered in its other world markets. But Americans weren't buying them, and sales suffered. As IKEA opened more U.S. stores, it worked to figure out the American manner of sleeping. It learned that height, firmness, and maximum size are key bed characteristics sought by U.S. consumers. So, IKEA altered the composition of its mattresses and added king size beds to the mix. Then, it altered the presentation and promotion of these products so the concept was clear. Not surprisingly, its sleep product lines really took off.

A more recent change resulting from listening to consumers in the United States and certain other markets is offering more services. Whereas picking, pulling, hauling, and assembling still works for most people, for others it was all just too much trouble. IKEA now offers flat-rate pricing on pulling orders and home delivery. It even maintains a list of contractors in each market that customers can call on to assemble the items in their homes.

Some markets have required more changes. As IKEA has expanded into Asia, for example, it has learned that customer needs vary substantially from those in Europe and the United States. Take China, for example. With some of the largest cities in the world, China has no shortage of customers. But most of China's 1.3 billion people don't buy home furnishings. So IKEA focuses instead on China's exploding middle class—"the many people" in growing urban populations who are more educated and fall into a 25- to 35-year-old age range. For this reason, IKEA stores in China are located closer to city centers, rather than in the suburbs, and are located near light-rail transportation lines.

Some of the changes for IKEA China are based on the fundamental principle of stocking products that people in a given area will buy. In China, for example, people love a good, hard mattress, so IKEA sells mostly firmer ones there. Whereas IKEA stores in China carry the same number of products as those in other parts of the world—most of them from the standard IKEA range—in China the company also stocks rice cookers and chopsticks. And when IKEA stocked 250,000 placemats commemorating the year of the rooster, they sold out in just weeks.

In massive city centers such as Beijing and Shanghai, home ownership among the middle class has gone from nearly zero to about 70 percent in the past 15 years. Because virtually all new homeowners have little sense for how to furnish and decorate their homes, they are eager to learn from the West. However, not everything that works in more developed parts of the world works in China. For one thing, the average living space in China's crowded cities is much smaller than in Europe and the United States. An average Chinese family lives in a small apartment in a high-rise building, often with multigenerational family members. So in China, IKEA focuses on products geared toward saving space and organizing a household. And it helps consumers figure out how to live smart and organize in small living spaces.

Pricing in China is somewhat of a paradox. Chinese customers are attracted to IKEA's design and the comprehensive selection, so that's where IKEA puts its emphasis in terms of positioning. But at the same time, in emerging markets such as China, low prices are the norm, and IKEA must cut prices drastically to remain competitive. When it first opened its doors in China more than a decade ago, IKEA found that it was more expensive than local low-priced firms. Competitors began selling copies of IKEA's designs at a fraction of the price. Using its cost-cutting expertise, however, IKEA has reduced prices in China by more than 50 percent over the past 10 years. The classic Klippan sofa, for example, now costs only $160, a third of what it did a decade ago (the same sofa costs $470 in Sweden).

Another challenge in selling furniture in the world's most populated country is that there are significant differences across the country's many regions. For example, in some regions, apartments have smaller rooms. Thus, IKEA designs showrooms in those areas to reflect the smaller size. Apartment buildings throughout China have balconies. But in northern China, balconies are widely used for food storage, whereas in southern China, they double as laundries. IKEA showrooms in these regions reflect such differences and regional needs.

The Chinese market features another unusual characteristic—gawkers. IKEA stores in China boast more traffic than those in any other part of the world (the Beijing store pulls in 28,000 customers on a typical Saturday—a strong week's draw for a typical European IKEA). But the majority of visitors just hang out and look. Actually, many visitors are there just to enjoy the air conditioning, a cheap meal, and a place to relax in comfort. People often lounge for extended periods in showrooms as they would in their own living rooms. Some even pull back the covers on an IKEA bed, take off their shoes, and hunker down for a good nap. Whereas this kind of behavior would get customers booted out of IKEAs in other markets, management recognizes that with China's rapidly growing middle class, allowing such behavior is an investment in the future.

IKEA plans to expand its number of stores in China from 15 to 40 during the next six years. But IKEA's China operations are just one example of IKEA's strategy throughout the world. The company also plans to double its number of stores in the United States during the same period. And as IKEA continues to grow in existing markets, it is also eyeing new markets with vast, untapped potential, such as India, where it plans to open 25 stores. Having doubled sales in the past decade, IKEA plans to double them again by 2020. And that's based on the same methodical growth of 20 to 25 new stores per year. With its keen ability to understand the cultural differences of each market and to adapt its marketing accordingly, there seems to be little standing in IKEA's way.

Questions for Discussion

19-19 Does IKEA have a truly global strategy, or just a series of regional strategies? Explain.

19-20 Discuss IKEA's global strategy in terms of the five global product and communications strategies.

19-21 If IKEA can sell a sofa in China for $160, why doesn't it sell the product at that low price in all of its markets?

19-22 Can competitors easily duplicate IKEA's strategy? Why or why not?

19-23 Should IKEA expand more rapidly than 20 to 25 stores per year? Explain.

Sources: Based on information from www.ikea.com/ms/en_US/this-is-ikea/index.html, accessed September, 2014. Also see Anna Ringstrom, "IKEA Turns the Global Local for Asia Push," *Reuters*, March 6, 2013, www.reuters.com/article/2013/03/07/us-ikea-expansion-idUSBRE92606220130307; Pan Kwan Yuk, "IKEA in China: Turning Gawkers into Consumers," *Financial Times*, April 4, 2013, http://blogs.ft.com/beyond-brics/2013/04/04/ikea-in-china-turning-gawkers-into-consumers/?Authorised=false#axzz2VAi2u6c8; Jens Hansegard, "IKEA Taking China by Storm," *Wall Street Journal*, March 26, 2012, http://online.wsj.com/article/SB10001424052702304636404577293083481821536.html; and Jens Hansegard and Niclas Rolander, "IKEA's Focus Remains on Its Superstores," *Wall Street Journal*, January 29, 2014, p. B9.

MyMarketingLab

Go to **mymktlab.com** for the following Assisted-graded writing questions:

19-24 Discuss the strategies used for adapting products to a global market. Which strategy is best? (AACSB: Communication)

19-25 Name and describe the advantages and disadvantages of the different types of joint venturing when entering a foreign market. (AACSB: Communication; Reflective Thinking)

References

1. Based on information from Monica Mark, "Coca-Cola and Nestlé Target New Markets in Africa," *The Guardian*, May 4, 2012, www.guardian.co.uk/world/2012/may/04/coca-cola-nestle-markets-africa; Duane Stanford, "Africa: Coke's Last Frontier," *Bloomberg Businessweek,* November 1, 2010, pp. 54–61; Annaleigh Vallie, "Coke Turns 125 and Has Much Life Ahead," *Business Day,* May 16, 2011, www.businessday.co.za/articles/Content.aspx?id_142848; "Coca-Cola Makes Big Bets on Africa's Future," *Trefis*, May 25, 2012, www.trefis.com/stock/ko/articles/123022/coca-cola-makes-big-bets-on-africas-future/2012-05-25; "Deloitte on Africa," Deloitte, www.deloitte.com/assets/Dcom-SouthAfrica/Local%20Assets/Documents/rise_and_rise.pdf, accessed July 2013; Andrew Cave, "Glaxo and Unilever Take Note: How General Electric and Coca-Cola Are Winning an Africa," *Forbes,* April 2, 2014, www.forbes.com/sites/andrewcave/2014/04/02/glaxo-and-unilever-take-note-how-general-electric-and-coca-cola-are-winning-in-africa/; and Coca-Cola annual reports and other information from www.thecoca-colacompany.com, accessed June 2014.
2. Data from "*Fortune* 500," *Fortune*, June 2014, http://money.cnn.com/magazines/fortune/fortune500/; Christopher Stolarski, "The FDI Effect," Marquette University Research and Scholarship 2011, www.marquette.edu/research/documents/discover-2011-FDI-effect.pdf; and "List of Countries by GDP: List by the CIA World Factbook," Wikipedia, http://en.wikipedia.org/wiki/List_of_countries_by_GDP_(nominal), accessed September 2014.
3. "Modest Trade Growth Anticipated for 2014 and 2015 Following Two Year Slump," WTO Press Release, April 14, 2014, www.wto.org/english/news_e/pres14_e/pr721_e.htm.
4. Information from www.michelin.com/corporate, www.jnj.com, and www.caterpillar.com, accessed September 2014.
5. See www.otisworldwide.com/d1-about.html, www.otisworldwide.com/pdf/Otis_Fact_Sheet_2012_with_milestones.pdf; and UTC Annual Report, http://2013ar.utc.com/assets/pdfs/UTCAR13_Full-Report.pdf, accessed July 2014.
6. Rob Schmitz, "Trade Spat between China and EU Threatens Exports of Solar Panels, Wine," *Marketplace,* June 6, 2013, www.marketplace.org/topics/world/trade-spat-between-china-and-eu-threatens-exports-solar-panels-wine; Jonathan Stearns, "EU Nations Approve Pact with China on Solar-Panel Imports," *Bloomberg*, December 2, 2013, www.bloomberg.com/news/2013-12-02/u-nations-approve-pact-with-china-on-solar-panel-trade.html; and Ben Blanchard and Francesco Guarascio, "EU, China End Wine Dispute Ahead of Xi's European Tour," *Reuters*, March 21, 2014, www.reuters.com/article/idUSBREA2K0QE20140321.
7. Gardiner Harris, "Wal-Mart Drops Ambitious Expansion Plan for India," *New York Times*, October 10, 2013, p. B3; and Paul Ausick, "Walmart Still Struggles in India," *247wallst,* April 8, 2014, http://247wallst.com/retail/2014/04/08/walmart-still-struggles-in-india/.
8. "What Is the WTO?" www.wto.org/english/thewto_e/whatis_e/what_we_do_e.htm, accessed June 2014.
9. See "The Doha Round," www.wto.org/english/tratop_e/dda_e/dda_e.htm, accessed June 2014.
10. "The EU at a Glance," http://europa.eu/about-eu/index_en.htm; and "EU Statistics and Opinion Polls," http://europa.eu/documentation/statistics-polls/index_en.htm, accessed June 2014.
11. "Economic and Monetary Affairs," http://europa.eu/pol/emu/index_en.htm, accessed October 2013; Dan O'Brien, "Risk of Euro Break-Up Now Higher Than Ever Before," *The Irish Times*, April 5, 2013, www.irishtimes.com/business/economy/europe/risk-of-euro-break-up-now-higher-than-ever-before-1.1349443; Jack Ewing, "European Banks Feel Heat in Crimea Crisis, with Austria Bearing Brunt," *New York Times*, March 28, 2014, p. B6; and "European Union: The Euro," http://europa.eu/about-eu/basic-information/money/euro/, accessed June 2014.
12. CIA, *The World Factbook*, https://www.cia.gov/library/publications/the-world-factbook, accessed June 2014.
13. Statistics and other information from CIA, *The World Factbook*; and Harold Meyerson, "Free Trade and the Loss of U.S. Jobs,"

Washington Post, January 14, 2014, www.washingtonpost.com/opinions/harold-meyerson-free-trade-and-the-loss-of-us-jobs/2014/01/14/894f5750-7d59-11e3-93c1-0e888170b723_story.html.

14. See "Explainer: What Is UNASUR?" www.as-coa.org/articles/explainer-what-unasur, accessed November 2013; and http://en.wikipedia.org/wiki/Union_of_South_American_Nations, accessed September 2014.

15. See Kenneth Rapoza, "Brazil's 'Poor' Middle Class, and the Poor that No Longer Serve Them," *Forbes*, January 22, 2013, www.forbes.com/sites/kenrapoza/2013/01/22/brazils-poor-middle-class-and-the-poor-that-no-longer-serve-them/print/; Claudia Penteado, "Brazil's Northeast Goes from 'Land of Laziness' to Next China," *Advertising Age*, June 13, 2011, http://adage.com/print/228070/; Richard Wallace, "Middle-Classes on the Up: Why Brazil Is Growing," *IGD,* September 15, 2011, www.igd.com/our-expertise/Retail/retail-outlook/4713/Middle-classes-on-the-up-why-Brazil-is-growing/; and "German Retailers Won't Kick in Brazil," *German Retail Blog,* May 7, 2014, www.german-retail-blog.com/topic/past-blogs/German-retailers-wont-kick-in-Brazil-279.

16. See "2013 Investment Climate Statement—Russia," U.S. Bureau of Economic and Business Affairs, February 2013, www.state.gov/e/eb/rls/othr/ics/2013/204720.htm; and "Welcome to the U.S. Commercial Service in Russia," http://export.gov/russia/, accessed September 2014.

17. Laurent Belsie, "What Will Venezuela Do with Its Oil?" *Christian Science Monitor,* March 6, 2013, www.csmonitor.com/Environment/2013/0307/What-will-Venezuela-do-with-its-oil-Top-five-energy-challenges-after-Chavez/Oil-bartering; John Paul Rathbone, "Venezuela: In Search of a Solution," *Financial Times,* March 2, 2014, www.ft.com/intl/cms/s/2/45c3cae4-a049-11e3-8557-00144feab7de.html#axzz2xgjEix7Y; and International Reciprocal Trade Association, www.irta.com/index.php/about/modern-trade-barter, accessed September 2014.

18. For these and other examples, see Emma Hall, "Do You Know Your Rites? BBDO Does," *Advertising Age*, May 21, 2007, p. 22.

19. Jamie Bryan, "The Mintz Dynasty," *Fast Company*, April 2006, pp. 56–61; Viji Sundaram, "Offensive Durga Display Dropped," *India-West*, February 2006, p. A1; and Emily Bryson York and Rupal Parekh, "Burger King's MO: Offend, Earn Media, Apologize, Repeat," *Advertising Age*, July 8, 2009, http://adage.com/print?article_id=137801. For other examples, see Ruth Manuel-Logan, "Dunkin' Donuts Apologizes for 'Racist' Blackface Ad," *New One,* September 3, 2013, http://newsone.com/2709598/dunkin-donuts-charcoal/; and Chris Isidore, "Chevy Pulls Ad Offensive to Chinese," *CNNMoney,* May 1, 2013, money.cnn.com/2013/05/01/news/companies/offensive-chevy-ad/.

20. For these and other examples, see Bill Chappell, "Bill Gates' Handshake with South Korea's Park Sparks Debate," *NPR,* April 23, 2013, www.npr.org/blogs/thetwo-way/2013/04/23/178650537/bill-gates-handshake-with-south-koreas-park-sparks-debate; "Managing Quality Across the (Global) Organization, Its Stakeholders, Suppliers, and Customers," Chartered Quality Institute, www.thecqi.org/Knowledge-Hub/Knowledge-portal/Corporate-strategy/Managing-quality-globally, accessed September 2014.

21. Quotes and other information found in David Pierson, "Beijing Loves IKEA—but Not for Shopping," *Los Angeles Times,* August 25, 2009, http://articles.latimes.com/2009/aug/25/business/fi-china-ikea25; Michael Wei, "In IKEA's China Stores, Loitering Is Encouraged," *Bloomberg Businessweek,* November 1, 2010, pp. 22–23; and Pan Kwan Yuk, "IKEA in China: Turning Gawkers into Customers," *BeyondBrics*, April 4, 2013, http://blogs.ft.com/beyond-brics/2013/04/04/ikea-in-china-turning-gawkers-into-consumers/?#axzz2SobYFh98; and "A Wedding in Aisle 3? Why Ikea Encourages Chinese to Make Its Stores Their Own," *Advertising Age,* December 10, 2013, http://adage.com/print/245573/.

22. Andres Martinez, "The Next American Century," *Time*, March 22, 2010, p. 1.

23. Thomas L. Friedman, *The Lexus and the Olive Tree: Understanding Globalization* (New York: Anchor Books, 2000); and Michael Wei and Margaret Conley, "Global Brands: Some Chinese Kids' First Word: Mickey," *Bloomberg Businessweek,* June 19, 2011, pp. 24–25.

24. "BrandZ Top 100 Most Valuable Global Brands 2014," Millward Brown, www.millwardbrown.com/brandz/2014/Top100/Docs/2014_BrandZ_Top100_Chart.pdf.

25. See Kim-Mai Cutler, "Apple's Chinese iPhone Sales 'Mind-Boggling,' Bring China Revenues to $7.9 Billion," *Tech Crunch,* April 24, 2012, http://techcrunch.com/2012/04/24/apples-iphone-sales-in-china-are-up-by-fivefold-from-a-year-ago/; and Rachael Tepper, "Yum! Brands' International Product Strategy: How the Double Down Went Global," *Huffington Post*, March 11, 2013, http://www.huffingtonpost.com/2013/03/11/yum-brands-international-product-strategy_n_2814360.html.

26. Kimberly Warren-Cohen, "Coca-Cola Sees Market Growth in Non-Soda and Emerging Markets," *Wall Street Cheat Sheet,* April 16, 2014, http://wallstcheatsheet.com/business/coca-cola-sees-growth-in-non-soda-and-emerging-markets.html/?a=viewall; William J. Holstein, "How Coca-Cola Manages 90 Emerging Markets," *Strategy+Business*, November 7, 2011, www.strategy-business.com/article/00093?pg=all; "2013 Annual Report," www.coca-colacompany.com/our-company/company-reports; annual reports and other financial and review data from www.coca-colacompany.com/our-company/, accessed September 2014.

27. This Netflix example is based on information found in Sam Schechner, "Europe's Media Giants Prep for Netflix Landing," *Wall Street Journal,* January 29, 2014, http://online.wsj.com/news/articles/SB20001424052702303277704579348774128548520.

28. See www.olc.co.jp/en/ and www.coca-colahellenic.com/aboutus/, accessed September 2014.

29. See "Škoda and Volkswagen Group Russia: One year of Successful Production in Nizhny Novgorod," December 11, 2013, www.volkswagenag.com/content/vwcorp/info_center/en/news/2013/12/Nizhny_Novgorod.html; and www.pg.com/en_IN/company/pg-india.shtml, accessed September 2014.

30. See http://en.wikipedia.org/wiki/Doubletree, accessed September 2014.

31. Mike Ramsey and Christina Rogers, "Chrysler's Jeep Faces Uphill Climb in China," *Wall Street Journal,* May 10, 2013, p. B4; and "Fiat Said Near Deal to Start Jeep SUV Production in China," *Bloomberg,* December 4, 2013, www.bloomberg.com/news/2013-12-03/fiat-said-near-deal-to-make-jeeps-in-china-with-plant-compromise.html.

32. Aradhana Aravindan, "Ford Looks to Ride Emerging Market mini-SUV Boom in India," *Reuters*, June 17, 2013, www.reuters.com/article/idUSBRE95G0RJ20130617; Alan Ohnsman, "Major Auto Production at Toyota, Honda Boosts U.S. Economy," July 17, 2012, www.autonews.com; www.india.ford.com/about, accessed June 2014; and www.hondainamerica.com/manufacturing, accessed September 2014.

33. "A Tale of Two Countries: Starbucks in India and China," *Starbucks Newsroom,* March 27, 2014, http://news.starbucks.com/news/a-tale-of-two-countries-starbucks-growth-in-india-and-china; Anita Chong Beattie, "Can Starbucks Make China Love Joe?" *Advertising Age,* November 5, 2012, pp. 20–21; and "Starbucks Unveils Accelerated Global Growth Plans," http://investor.starbucks.com/mobile.view?c=99518&v=203&d=1&id=1764541, accessed September 2014.

34. See Warren J. Keegan and Mark C. Green, *Global Marketing*, 7th ed. (Upper Saddle River, NJ: Prentice Hall, 2013), pp. 303–308.

35. Toshiro Wakayama, Junjiro Shintaku, and Tomofumi Amano, "What Panasonic Learned in China," *Harvard Business Review,* December 2012, pp. 109–113.

36. Information on McDonald's menus and operations found in Lucy Fancourt, Bredesen Lewis, and Nicholas Majka, "Born in the USA, Made in France: How McDonald's Succeeds in the Land of Michelin Stars," Knowledge@Wharton, January 3, 2012, http://knowledge.wharton.upenn.edu/article.cfm?articleid=2906; Richard Vines and Caroline Connan, "McDonald's Wins Over French Chef with McBaguette Sandwich," *Bloomberg*, January 15, 2013, www.bloomberg.com/news/2013-01-15/mcdonald-s-wins-over-french-chef-with-mcbaguette-sandwich.html; and "McDonald's Food You Can't Get Here," *Chicago Tribune, www.chicagotribune.com/business/ct-biz-mcdonalds-food-around-the-world,0,5168632.photogallery*, accessed September 2014.

37. See Normandy Madden, "In China, Multinationals Forgo Adaptation for New-Brand Creation," *Advertising Age,* January 17, 2011, p. 10; Susan Adams, "The 10 Companies Considered 'Best for the World,'" *Forbes,* March 31, 2014, www.forbes.com/sites/susanadams/2014/03/31/10-companies-considered-best-for-the-world/; Meg Cichon, "Solar Making Big Strides to Power the Developing World," *Renewable Energy World,* May 7, 2014, www.renewableenergyworld.com/rea/news/article/2014/05/solar-making-big-strides-to-power-the-developing-world; and www.dlightdesign.com/, accessed September 2014.

38. Jeffrey N. Ross, "Chevrolet Will 'Find New Roads' as Brand Grows Globally: Aligns around the World behind Singular Vision," January 8, 2013, http://media.gm.com/media/us/en/gm/news.detail.html/content/Pages/news/us/en/2013/Jan/0107-find-new-roads.html; and Dale Buss, "Chevy Wins at Sochi by Giving Dimension to 'Find New Roads,'" *Forbes,* February 24, 2014, www.forbes.com/sites/dalebuss/2014/02/24/chevrolet-wins-at-sochi-as-find-new-roads-theme-gets-traction/.

39. "Nike Faces Ultimate Marketing Challenge in China: Make Running Cool," *Advertising Age,* October 31, 2011, pp. 1+; "Firms Help Spur a Running Craze in China," *China Sports News,* December 30, 2013, www.chinasportsbeat.com/2013/12/firms-help-spur-running-craze-in-china.html; and "Nike Faces Tough Competition in Europe and China," *Forbes,* March 4, 2014, www.forbes.com/sites/greatspeculations/2014/03/04/nike-faces-tough-competition-in-europe-and-china/.

40. See George E. Belch and Michael A. Belch, *Advertising and Promotion: An Integrated Marketing Communications Perspective*, 8th ed. (New York: McGraw Hill, 2011), Chapter 20; Shintero Okazaki and Charles R. Taylor, "What Is SMS Advertising and Why Do Multinationals Adopt It?" *Journal of Business Research*, January 2008, pp. 4–12; and Warren J. Keegan and Mark C. Green, *Global Marketing*, 7th ed. (Upper Saddle River, NJ: Prentice Hall, 2013), pp. 398–400.

41. Information and quote from Alistar Barr and Edward C. Baig, "Google Targets Low-End Smartphone Market with Moto G," *USA Today,* November 13, 2013, www.usatoday.com/story/tech/2013/11/13/google-motorola-moto-g/3516039/; and Brian X. Chen, "Motorola to Offer Moto G Smartphone Aimed at Emerging Markets," *New York Times,* November 14, 2013, p. B5.

42. Anita Chang Beattie, "Catching the Eye of a Chinese Shopper," *Advertising Age,* December 10, 2013, pp. 20–21.

43. See "Coca-Cola Rolls Out New Distribution Model with ZAP," ZAP, January 23, 2008, www.marketwired.com/press-release/coca-cola-rolls-out-new-distribution-model-with-zap-813288.htm; Jane Nelson, Eriko Ishikawa, and Alexis Geaneotes, "Developing Inclusive Business Models: A Review of Coca-Cola's Manual Distribution Centers in Ethiopia and Tanzania," Harvard Kennedy School, 2009, www.hks.harvard.edu/m-rcbg/CSRI/publications/other_10_MDC_report.pdf; and "How Coca-Cola's Distribution System Works," *Colalife,* December 19, 2010, www.colalife.org/2010/12/19/how-coca-colas-distribution-system-works. For some interesting photos of Coca-Cola distribution methods in third-world and emerging markets, see www.flickr.com/photos/73509998@N00/sets/72157594299144032, accessed September 2014.

44. Based on information found in Bart Becht, "Building a Company without Borders," *Harvard Business Review*, April 2010, pp. 103–106; "From Cincy to Singapore: Why P&G, Others Are Moving Key HQs," *Advertising Age,* June 10, 2012, http://adage.com/print/235288; G. A. Chester, "3 Things to Love about Reckitt Benckiser," *Daily Finance,* June 19, 2013, www.dailyfinance.com/2013/06/19/3-things-to-love-about-reckitt-benckiser/; and www.rb.com/Investors-media/Investor-information, accessed September 2014.

20 Social Responsibility and Ethics

Chapter Preview

In this final chapter, we'll examine the concept of sustainable marketing, meeting the needs of consumers, businesses, and society—now and in the future—through socially and environmentally responsible marketing actions. We'll start by defining sustainable marketing and then look at some common criticisms of marketing as it impacts individual consumers, as well as public actions that promote sustainable marketing. Finally, we'll see how companies themselves can benefit from proactively pursuing sustainable marketing practices that bring value to not only individual customers but also society as a whole. Sustainable marketing actions are more than just the right thing to do; they're also good for business.

First, let's look at an example of sustainable marketing in action at Patagonia, a company founded on a mission of inspiring business solutions to environmental problems. The company donates 1 percent of its revenue annually to environmental causes and adheres fiercely to a "Five Rs" mantra: "reduce, repair, reuse, recycle, and reimagine." But Patagonia recently took sustainability to a whole new level, telling its customers, "Don't buy our products."

PATAGONIA: "Conscious Consumption": Telling Consumers to Buy *Less*

Patagonia—the high-end outdoor clothing and gear company—was founded on a mission of using business to help save the planet. More than 40 years ago, mountain-climber entrepreneur Yvon Chouinard started the company with this enduring mission: "Build the best product, cause no unnecessary harm, use business to inspire and implement solutions to the environmental crisis." Now, Chouinard and Patagonia are taking that mission to new extremes. They're actually telling consumers "don't buy our products."

It started two years ago with a full-page *New York Times* ad on Black Friday, the day after Thanksgiving and busiest shopping day of the year, showing Patagonia's best-selling R2 jacket and pronouncing "Don't Buy This Jacket." Patagonia backed the ad with messaging in its retail stores, at its Web site and social media pages, and with additional ads at NYTimes.com. To top things off, Patagonia customers received a follow-up e-mail prior to Cyber Monday—the season's major online shopping day—reasserting the brand's buy less message. Here's part of what it said:

> Because Patagonia wants to be in business for a good long time—and leave a world inhabitable for our kids—we want to do the opposite of every other business today. We ask you to buy less and to reflect before you spend a dime on this jacket or anything else.
>
> The environmental cost of everything we make is astonishing. Consider the R2 Jacket shown, one of our best sellers. To make it required 135 liters of water, enough to meet the daily needs (three glasses a day) of 45 people. Its journey from its origin as 60% recycled polyester to our Reno warehouse generated nearly 20 pounds of carbon dioxide, 24 times the weight of the finished product. This jacket left behind, on its way to Reno, two-thirds its weight in waste. And this is a 60% recycled polyester jacket, knit and sewn to a high standard. But, as is true of all the things we can make and you can buy, this jacket comes with an environmental cost higher than its price.
>
> There is much to be done and plenty for us all to do. Don't buy what you don't need. Think twice before you buy anything. [Work with us] to reimagine a world where we take only what nature can replace.

A for-profit firm telling its customers to buy *less*? It sounds crazy. But that message is right on target with Patagonia's reason for being. Founder Chouinard contends that capitalism is on an unsustainable path. Today's companies and customers are

Patagonia was founded on a mission of using business to help save the planet. Recently, the company has taken its sustainability mission to new extremes, actually telling customers: "Don't buy our products."

wasting the world's resources by making and buying low-quality goods that they buy mindlessly and throw away too quickly. Instead, Chouinard and his company are calling for *conscious consumption*, asking customers to think before they buy and to stop consuming for consumption's sake.

Coming from Patagonia, a company that spends almost nothing on traditional advertising, the paradoxical "Don't Buy This Jacket" ad had tremendous impact. The Internet was soon ablaze with comments from online journalists, bloggers, and customers regarding the meaning and motivation behind Patagonia's message. Analysts speculated about whether the ad would help or harm sales—whether it would engage customers and build loyalty or be perceived as little more than a cheap marketing gimmick.

But to Patagonia, far from a marketing gimmick, the campaign expressed the brand's deeply held philosophy of sustainability. The purpose was to increase awareness of and participation in the Patagonia Common Threads Initiative, which urges customers to take a pledge to work together with the company to consume more responsibly. Common Threads rests on five Rs of joint action toward sustainability:

Reduce: **WE** make useful gear that lasts a long time. **YOU** don't buy what you don't need.

Repair: **WE** help you repair your Patagonia gear. **YOU** pledge to fix what's broken.

Reuse: **WE** help find a home for Patagonia gear you no longer need. **YOU** sell or pass it on.

Recycle: **WE** take back your Patagonia gear that is worn out. **YOU** pledge to keep your stuff out of the landfill and incinerator.

Reimagine: **TOGETHER** we reimagine a world where we take only what nature can replace.

So Patagonia's conscious consumption solution seems pretty simple. Making, buying, repairing, and reusing higher-quality goods results in less consumption, which in turn uses fewer resources and lowers costs for everyone. "Have a Patagonia ski parka with a rip in the arm?" asks one reporter. "Don't throw it away and buy a new one. Send it back, and the company will sew it up. Is your tent beyond repair? Send it back, and Patagonia will recycle the material." Patagonia has always been committed to the idea of quality as a cure for overconsumption. To that end, it makes durable products with timeless designs, products that customers can keep and use for a long time.

So on that Black Friday weekend, while other companies were inundating customers with promotions that encouraged them to "buy, buy, buy," Patagonia stood on its founding principles. It said, "Hey, look: Only purchase what you need," explains Rob BonDurant, vice president of marketing and communications at Patagonia. "The message, 'Don't buy this jacket,' is obviously super counterintuitive to what a for-profit company would say, especially on a day like Black Friday, but honestly

Sense-of-mission marketing: A for-profit company telling consumers to buy less sounds crazy. But it's right on target with Patagonia's conscious consumption mission, which urges consumers to buy only what they need and take only what the planet can replace.

Patagonia, Inc.

[it] is what we really were after, [communicating] this idea of evolving capitalism and conscious consumption that we wanted to effect."

Not just any company can pull off something like this—such a message can only work if it is real. Patagonia didn't just suddenly stick an ad in the *New York Times* on Black Friday. It had been sending—and living—this message for decades. Can other companies follow Patagonia's lead? "If it is [just] a marketing campaign, no," says BonDurant. "If it is a way they live their lives and do their business, absolutely. . . . The key to the whole effort [is]: Put your money where your mouth is," he says. "You can't just apply it to your messaging or to a particular window of time. It has to be done 24 hours a day, 365 days a year."

Pushing conscious consumption doesn't mean that Patagonia wants customers to stop buying its products. To the contrary, like other for-profit brands, Patagonia really does care about doing well on Black Friday and the rest of the holiday season. As a company that sells products mostly for cold-weather activities, Patagonia reaps a whopping 40 percent of its revenues during the final two months of the year. But to Patagonia, business is

Objective Outline

OBJECTIVE 1	**Define *sustainable marketing* and discuss its importance.** **Sustainable Marketing** (pp 627–628)
OBJECTIVE 2	**Identify the major social criticisms of marketing.** **Social Criticisms of Marketing** (pp 628–635)
OBJECTIVE 3	**Define *consumerism* and *environmentalism* and explain how they affect marketing strategies.** **Consumer Actions to Promote Sustainable Marketing** (pp 635–641)
OBJECTIVE 4	**Describe the principles of sustainable marketing.** **Business Actions Toward Sustainable Marketing** (pp 641–645)
OBJECTIVE 5	**Explain the role of ethics in marketing.** **Marketing Ethics** (pp 645–648) **The Sustainable Company** (p 648)

about more than making money. And according to BonDurant, the "Don't Buy This Jacket" campaign has more than paid for itself with the interest and involvement it created for the Common Threads Initiative. As an added bonus, however, the campaign has also boosted sales. During the first year of the campaign, Patagonia's sales surged by almost a third.

"It is not enough just to make good products anymore," says BonDurant. "There also has to be a message that people can buy into, that people feel they are a part of, that they can be solutions-based. That is what [Patagonia's "buy only what you need"] communication efforts are really all about." But what's good for customers and the planet is also good for Patagonia. Says founder Chouinard, "I know it sounds crazy, but every time I have made a decision that is best for the planet, I have made money. Our customers know that—and they want to be part of that environmental commitment."[1]

Responsible marketers discover what consumers want and respond with market offerings that create value for buyers and capture value in return. The *marketing concept* is a philosophy of customer value and mutual gain. Its practice leads the economy by an invisible hand to satisfy the many and changing needs of millions of consumers.

Not all marketers follow the marketing concept, however. In fact, some companies use questionable marketing practices that serve their own rather than consumers' interests. Moreover, even well-intentioned marketing actions that meet the current needs of some consumers may cause immediate or future harm to other consumers or the larger society. Responsible marketers must consider whether their actions are sustainable in the longer run.

FIGURE | 20.1
Sustainable Marketing

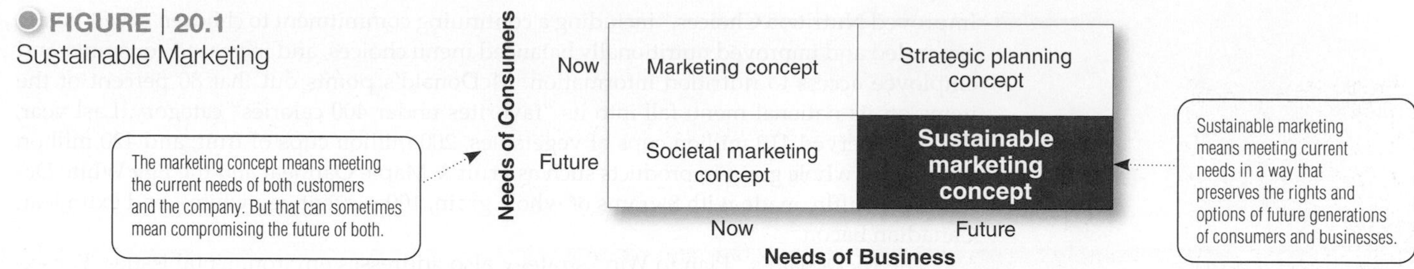
Needs of Consumers
Now
Future
Marketing concept
Strategic planning concept
Societal marketing concept
Sustainable marketing concept
Now
Future
Needs of Business
The marketing concept means meeting the current needs of both customers and the company. But that can sometimes mean compromising the future of both.
Sustainable marketing means meeting current needs in a way that preserves the rights and options of future generations of consumers and businesses.

This chapter examines sustainable marketing and the social and environmental effects of private marketing practices. First, we address the question: What is sustainable marketing and why is it important?

Author Comment | Marketers must think beyond immediate customer satisfaction and business performance toward sustainable strategies that preserve the world for future generations.

Sustainable Marketing

Sustainable marketing
Socially and environmentally responsible marketing that meets the present needs of consumers and businesses while also preserving or enhancing the ability of future generations to meet their needs.

Sustainable marketing calls for socially and environmentally responsible actions that meet the present needs of consumers and businesses while also preserving or enhancing the ability of future generations to meet their needs. **Figure 20.1** compares the sustainable marketing concept with marketing concepts we studied in earlier chapters.

The *marketing concept* recognizes that organizations thrive by determining the current needs and wants of target customers and fulfilling them more effectively and efficiently than competitors do. It focuses on meeting the company's short-term sales, growth, and profit needs by engaging customers and giving them what they want now. However, satisfying consumers' immediate needs and desires doesn't always serve the future best interests of either customers or the business.

For example, McDonald's early decisions to market tasty but fat- and salt-laden fast foods created immediate satisfaction for customers, as well as sales and profits for the company. However, critics assert that McDonald's and other fast-food chains contributed to a longer-term national obesity epidemic, damaging consumer health and burdening the national health system. In turn, many consumers began looking for healthier eating options, causing a slump in the sales and profits of the fast-food industry. Beyond issues of ethical behavior and social welfare, McDonald's was also criticized for the sizable environmental footprint of its vast global operations, everything from wasteful packaging and solid waste creation to inefficient energy use in its stores. Thus, McDonald's strategy was not sustainable in the long run in terms of either consumer or company benefit.

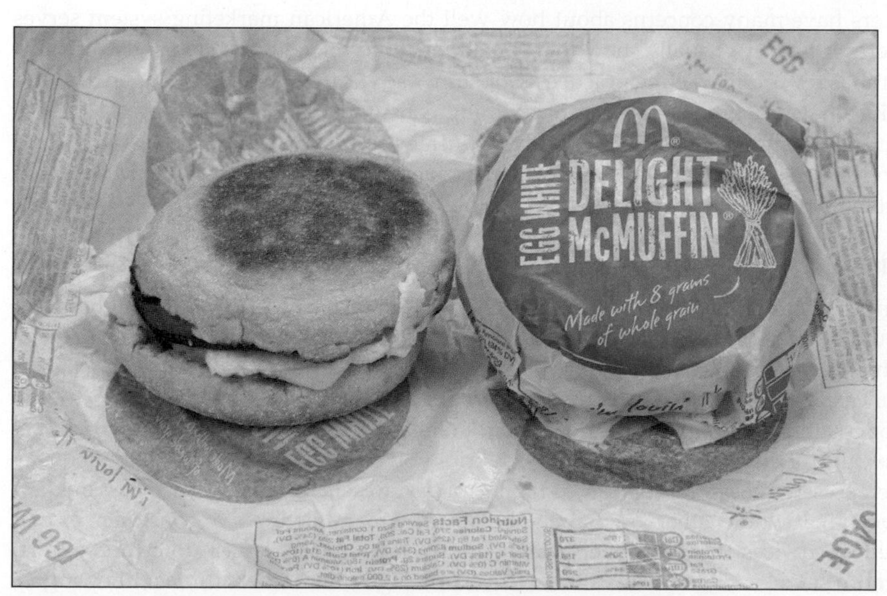
EGG WHITE DELIGHT McMUFFIN
Made with 8 grams of whole grain

Sustainable marketing: Under its "Plan to Win" strategy, McDonald's has created sustainable value for both customers and the company. Now, 80 percent of the chain's menu is under 400 calories, including this Egg White Delight McMuffin, which weighs in with 8 grams of whole grain against only 250 calories and 5 grams of fat.

Whereas the *societal marketing concept* identified in Figure 20.1 considers the future welfare of consumers and the *strategic planning concept* considers future company needs, the *sustainable marketing concept* considers both. Sustainable marketing calls for socially and environmentally responsible actions that meet both the immediate and future needs of customers and the company.

For example, McDonald's has responded to these challenges in recent years with a more sustainable "Plan to Win" strategy of diversifying into salads, fruits, grilled chicken, low-fat milk, and other healthy fare. The company also launched a major multifaceted education campaign—called "it's what i eat and what i do . . . i'm lovin' it"—to help consumers better understand the keys to living balanced, active lifestyles. And it recently announced a list of "Commitments to Offer

Improved Nutrition Choices," including a continuing commitment to children's well-being, expanded and improved nutritionally balanced menu choices, and increased consumer and employee access to nutrition information. McDonald's points out that 80 percent of the items on its national menu fall into its "favorites under 400 calories" category. Last year, the chain served 410 million cups of vegetables, 200 million cups of fruit, and 420 million servings of whole grain in products such as Fruit & Maple Oatmeal and the Egg White Delight McMuffin, made with 8 grams of whole grain, 100 percent egg whites, and extra lean Canadian bacon.[2]

The McDonald's "Plan to Win" strategy also addresses environmental issues. For example, it calls for food-supply sustainability, reduced and environmentally sustainable packaging, reuse and recycling, and more responsible store designs. McDonald's has even developed an environmental scorecard that rates its suppliers' performance in areas such as water use, energy use, and solid waste management.

McDonald's more sustainable strategy is benefiting the company as well as its customers. Since announcing its "Plan to Win" strategy, McDonald's sales have increased by more than 60 percent, and profits have almost tripled. Thus, McDonald's is well positioned for a sustainably profitable future.[3]

Truly sustainable marketing requires a smooth-functioning marketing system in which consumers, companies, public policy makers, and others work together to ensure socially and environmentally responsible marketing actions. Unfortunately, however, the marketing system doesn't always work smoothly. The following sections examine several sustainability questions: What are the most frequent social criticisms of marketing? What steps have private citizens taken to curb marketing ills? What steps have legislators and government agencies taken to promote sustainable marketing? What steps have enlightened companies taken to carry out socially responsible and ethical marketing that creates sustainable value for both individual customers and society as a whole?

Author Comment In most ways, we all benefit greatly from marketing activities. However, like most other human endeavors, marketing has its flaws. Here we present both sides of some of the most common criticisms of marketing.

Social Criticisms of Marketing

Marketing receives much criticism. Some of this criticism is justified; much is not. Social critics claim that certain marketing practices hurt individual consumers, society as a whole, and other business firms.

Marketing's Impact on Individual Consumers

Consumers have many concerns about how well the American marketing system serves their interests. Surveys usually show that consumers hold mixed or even slightly unfavorable attitudes toward marketing practices. Consumer advocates, government agencies, and other critics have accused marketing of harming consumers through high prices, deceptive practices, high-pressure selling, shoddy or unsafe products, planned obsolescence, and poor service to disadvantaged consumers. Such questionable marketing practices are not sustainable in terms of long-term consumer or business welfare.

High Prices

Many critics charge that the American marketing system causes prices to be higher than they would be under more "sensible" systems. Such high prices are hard to swallow, especially when the economy is tight. Critics point to three factors—*high costs of distribution*, *high advertising and promotion costs*, and *excessive markups*.

A long-standing charge is that greedy marketing channel members mark up prices beyond the value of their services. As a result, distribution costs too much, and consumers pay for these excessive costs in the form of higher prices. Resellers respond that intermediaries do work that would otherwise have to be done by manufacturers or consumers. Their prices reflect services that consumers want—more convenience, larger stores and assortments, more service, longer store hours, return privileges, and others. In fact, they argue, retail competition is so intense that margins are actually quite low. And discounters such as Walmart, Costco, and others pressure their competitors to operate efficiently and keep their prices down.

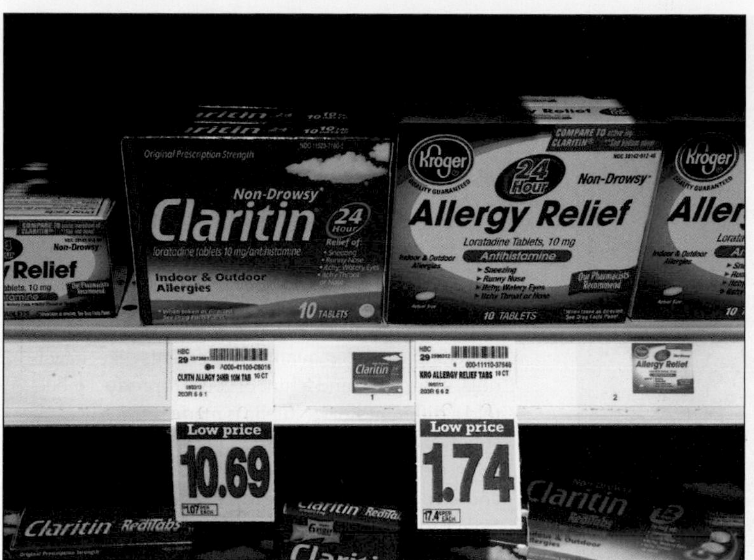

A heavily promoted national brand sells for much more than a virtually identical non-branded or store-branded product. Critics charge that promotion adds only psychological value to the product rather than functional value.

Keri Miksza

Modern marketing is also accused of pushing up prices to finance unneeded advertising, sales promotion, and packaging. For example, a heavily promoted national brand sells for much more than a virtually identical store-branded product. Critics charge that much of this promotion and packaging adds only psychological, not functional, value. Marketers respond that although advertising adds to product costs, it also adds value by informing potential buyers of the availability and merits of a brand. Brand name products may cost more, but branding assures buyers of consistent quality. Moreover, although consumers can usually buy functional versions of products at lower prices, they *want* and are willing to pay more for products that also provide psychological benefits—that make them feel wealthy, attractive, or special.

Critics also charge that some companies mark up goods excessively. They point to the drug industry, where a pill costing five cents to make may cost the consumer $2 to buy, and to the high charges for auto repairs and other services. Marketers respond that most businesses try to price fairly to consumers because they want to build customer relationships and repeat business. Also, they assert, consumers often don't understand the reasons for high markups. For example, pharmaceutical markups help cover the costs of making and distributing existing medicines, plus the high costs of developing and testing new medicines. As pharmaceuticals company GlaxoSmithKline has stated in its ads, "Today's medicines finance tomorrow's miracles."

Deceptive Practices

Marketers are sometimes accused of deceptive practices that lead consumers to believe they will get more value than they actually do. Deceptive practices fall into three groups: promotion, packaging, and pricing. *Deceptive promotion* includes practices such as misrepresenting the product's features or performance or luring customers to the store for a bargain that is out of stock. *Deceptive packaging* includes exaggerating package contents through subtle design, using misleading labeling, or describing size in misleading terms.

Deceptive pricing includes practices such as falsely advertising "factory" or "wholesale" prices or a large price reduction from a phony high retail list price. For example, Overstock.com was recently fined $6.8 million by a California court as a result of a fraudulent pricing lawsuit filed by the attorneys general of eight California counties. The suit charged that the online giant routinely advertised its prices as lower than fabricated "list prices." It recites one example in which Overstock sold a patio set for $449 while claiming that the list price was $999. When the item was delivered, the customer found that it had a Walmart sticker stating a price of $247.[4]

Deceptive practices have led to legislation and other consumer protection actions. For example, in 1938 Congress enacted the Wheeler-Lea Act, which gave the Federal Trade Commission (FTC) power to regulate "unfair or deceptive acts or practices." The FTC has since published several guidelines listing deceptive practices. Despite regulations, however, some critics argue that deceptive claims are still common, even for well-known brands. For example, the FTC recently upheld charges that POM Wonderful made false and unsupported health claims for its pomegranate juice and supplements. It also slapped Nissan's hands for a misleading TV ad showing a Nissan Frontier pickup truck dramatically pushing a stranded dune buggy up a steep sand dune—both vehicles were dragged by cables that viewers couldn't see. And Skechers recently paid $55 million in consumer refunds to resolve allegations by the FTC and attorneys general in 44 states that it made false advertising claims that its rocker-bottom Shape-ups and other toning shoes would help customers tone muscles and lose weight.[5]

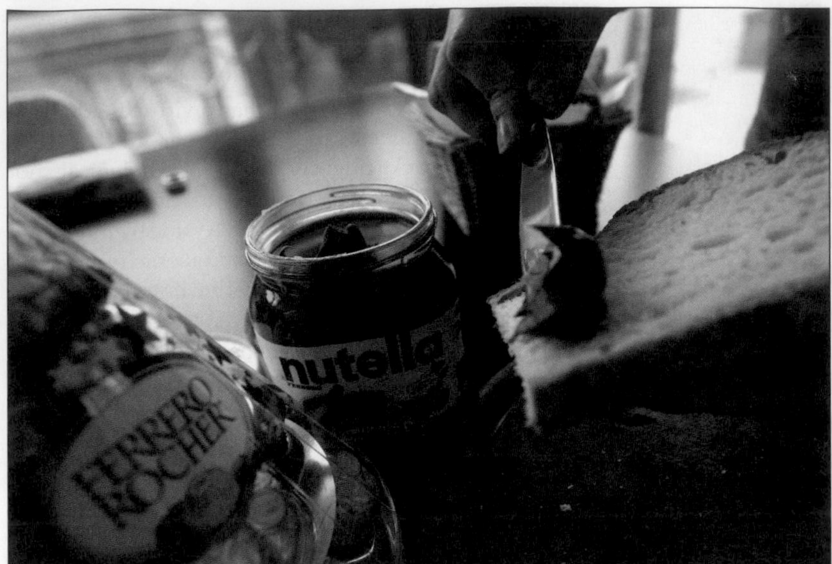

Deceptive practices: Ferrero recently settled a class action suit claiming that ads for its popular, gooey-good Nutella chocolate hazelnut spread made deceptive claims that the product was "healthy" and "part of a balanced meal."

REUTERS/Stefano Rellandini

Confections and candy maker Ferrero recently paid out $3 million to settle a class action suit claiming that ads for its popular Nutella chocolate hazelnut spread made deceptive claims that the product was "healthy" and "part of a balanced meal."[6]

> It all began when a California mom filed a deceptive advertising claim after realizing that the Nutella she'd been feeding her 4-year-old daughter at breakfast was actually little short of the next best thing to a candy bar. While TV ads talked about Nutella's "simple, quality ingredients like hazelnuts, skim milk, and a hint of cocoa," product labels told a different story. Nutella is made primarily from sugar and palm oil. Each 2-tablespoon serving of the gooey-good spread contains 21 grams of sugar and 200 calories, with half of those calories coming from 11 grams of fat. Nutella ads never mentioned the sugar or fat. In addition to the $3-million deceptive advertising settlement, Ferrero has agreed to change its advertising and nutritional labels.

The toughest problem often is defining what is "deceptive." For instance, an advertiser's claim that its chewing gum will "rock your world" isn't intended to be taken literally. Instead, the advertiser might claim, it is "puffery"—innocent exaggeration for effect. However, others claim that puffery and alluring imagery can harm consumers in subtle ways. Think about the popular and long-running MasterCard Priceless commercials that once painted pictures of consumers fulfilling their priceless dreams despite the costs. The ads suggested that your credit card could make it happen. But critics charge that such imagery by credit card companies encouraged a spend-now-pay-later attitude that caused many consumers to *over*use their cards.

Marketers argue that most companies avoid deceptive practices. Because such practices harm a company's business in the long run, they simply aren't sustainable. Profitable customer relationships are built on a foundation of value and trust. If consumers do not get what they expect, they will switch to more reliable products. In addition, consumers usually protect themselves from deception. Most consumers recognize a marketer's selling intent and are careful when they buy, sometimes even to the point of not believing completely true product claims.

High-Pressure Selling

Salespeople are sometimes accused of high-pressure selling that persuades people to buy goods they had no thought of buying. It is often said that insurance, real estate, and used cars are *sold*, not *bought*. Salespeople are trained to deliver smooth, canned talks to entice purchases. They sell hard because sales contests promise big prizes to those who sell the most. Similarly, TV infomercial pitchmen use "yell and sell" presentations that create a sense of consumer urgency that only those with strong willpower can resist.

But in most cases, marketers have little to gain from high-pressure selling. Although such tactics may work in one-time selling situations for short-term gain, most selling involves building long-term relationships with valued customers. High-pressure or deceptive selling can seriously damage such relationships. For example, imagine a P&G account manager trying to pressure a Walmart buyer or an IBM salesperson trying to browbeat an information technology manager at GE. It simply wouldn't work.

Shoddy, Harmful, or Unsafe Products

Another criticism concerns poor product quality or function. One complaint is that, too often, products and services are not made well or do not perform well. A second complaint concerns product safety. Product safety has been a problem for several reasons, including company indifference, increased product complexity, and poor quality control. A third complaint is that many products deliver little benefit, or may even be harmful.

Harmful products: NYC Health asks, "Are you pouring on the pounds?" Is the soft drink industry being irresponsible by promoting overindulgence or is it simply serving the wants of customers by offering products that ping consumer taste buds while letting consumers make their own consumption choices?

New York Department of Health and Mental Hygiene

For example, think about the soft drink industry. Many critics blame the plentiful supply of sugar-laden, high-calorie soft drinks for the nation's rapidly growing obesity epidemic. Studies show that more than two-thirds of American adults are either obese or overweight. In addition, one-third of American children are obese.[7] This national weight issue continues despite repeated medical studies showing that excess weight brings increased risks for heart disease, diabetes, and other maladies, even cancer. The critics are quick to fault what they see as greedy beverage marketers cashing in on vulnerable consumers, turning us into a nation of Big Gulpers. New York City's mayor even tried to pass a ban on soft drinks 16 ounces and larger, and the New York City Department of Health and Mental Hygiene (NYC Health) has fielded a "Pouring on the Pounds" ad campaign highlighting the risks of drinking too many sugary drinks for both children and adults.[8]

Is the soft drink industry being socially irresponsible by aggressively promoting overindulgence to ill-informed or unwary consumers? Or is it simply serving the wants of customers by offering products that ping consumer taste buds while letting consumers make their own consumption choices? Is it the industry's job to police public tastes? As in many matters of social responsibility, what's right and wrong may be a matter of opinion. Whereas some analysts criticize the industry, others suggest that responsibility lies with consumers. "Soft drinks have unfairly become the whipping boy of most anti-obesity campaigns," suggests one business reporter. "Maybe friends shouldn't give friends Big Gulps, but to my knowledge, no one's ever been forced to buy and drink one. There's an element of personal responsibility and control that [needs to be addressed]."[9]

Most manufacturers *want* to produce quality goods. After all, the way a company deals with product quality and safety problems can damage or help its reputation. Companies selling poor-quality or unsafe products risk damaging conflicts with consumer groups and regulators. Unsafe products can result in product liability suits and large awards for damages. More fundamentally, consumers who are unhappy with a firm's products may avoid future purchases and talk other consumers into doing the same. In today's social media and online review environment, word of poor quality can spread like wildfire. Thus, quality missteps are not consistent with sustainable marketing. Today's marketers know that good quality results in customer value and satisfaction, which in turn creates sustainable customer relationships.

Planned Obsolescence

Critics also have charged that some companies practice *planned obsolescence*, causing their products to become obsolete before they actually should need replacement. They accuse some producers of using materials and components that will break, wear, rust, or rot sooner than they should. And if the products themselves don't wear out fast enough, other companies are charged with *perceived obsolescence*—continually changing consumer concepts of acceptable styles to encourage more and earlier buying. An obvious example is the fast-fashion industry with its constantly changing clothing fashions, which some critics claim creates a wasteful disposable clothing culture. "Too many garments end up in landfill sites," bemoans one designer. "They are deemed aesthetically redundant and get discarded at the end of the season when there are often years of wear left."[10]

Still others are accused of introducing planned streams of new products that make older models obsolete, turning consumers into "serial replacers." Critics claim that this occurs in the consumer electronics industries. If you're like most people, you probably have a drawer full of yesterday's hottest technological gadgets—from mobile phones and cameras to iPods and flash drives—now reduced to the status of fossils. It seems that anything more than a year or two old is hopelessly out of date. For example, early iPods had nonremovable batteries that failed in about 18 months, so that they had to be replaced. It wasn't until unhappy owners filed a class action suit that Apple started offering replacement batteries.

Also, rapid new product launches—as many as three in one 18-month period—made older iPod models obsolete.[11]

Marketers respond that consumers *like* style changes; they get tired of the old goods and want a new look in fashion. Or they *want* the latest high-tech innovations, even if older models still work. No one has to buy a new product, and if too few people like it, it will simply fail. Finally, most companies do not design their products to break down earlier because they do not want to lose customers to other brands. Instead, they seek constant improvement to ensure that products will consistently meet or exceed customer expectations.

Much of the so-called planned obsolescence is the working of the competitive and technological forces in a free society—forces that lead to ever-improving goods and services. For example, if Apple produced a new iPhone or iPad that would last 10 years, few consumers would want it. Instead, buyers want the latest technological innovations. "Obsolescence isn't something companies are forcing on us," confirms one analyst. "It's progress, and it's something we pretty much demand. As usual, the market gives us exactly what we want."[12]

Poor Service to Disadvantaged Consumers

Finally, the American marketing system has been accused of poorly serving disadvantaged consumers. For example, critics claim that the urban poor often have to shop in smaller stores that carry inferior goods and charge higher prices. The presence of large national chain stores in low-income neighborhoods would help to keep prices down. However, the critics accuse major chain retailers of *redlining*, drawing a red line around disadvantaged neighborhoods and avoiding placing stores there.

For example, the nation's poor areas have 30 percent fewer supermarkets than affluent areas do. As a result, many low-income consumers find themselves in *food deserts*, which are awash with small markets offering frozen pizzas, Cheetos, Moon Pies, and Cokes, but where fruits and vegetables or fresh fish and chicken are out of reach. Currently, some 23.5 million Americans—including 6.5 million children—live in low-income areas that lack stores selling affordable and nutritious foods. What's more, 2.3 million households have no access to a car but live more than a mile from a supermarket, forcing them to shop at convenience stores where expensive processed food is the only dietary choice. In turn, the lack of access to healthy, affordable fresh foods has a negative impact on the health of underserved consumers in these areas. Many national chains, such as Walmart, Walgreens, SuperValu, and even Whole Foods Market, have recently agreed to open or expand more stores that bring nutritious and fresh foods to underserved communities. For example, Whole Foods has recently been opening stores in disadvantaged parts of cities such as Detroit, Chicago, and New Orleans, "trying to serve the needs of communities that others ignore completely."[13]

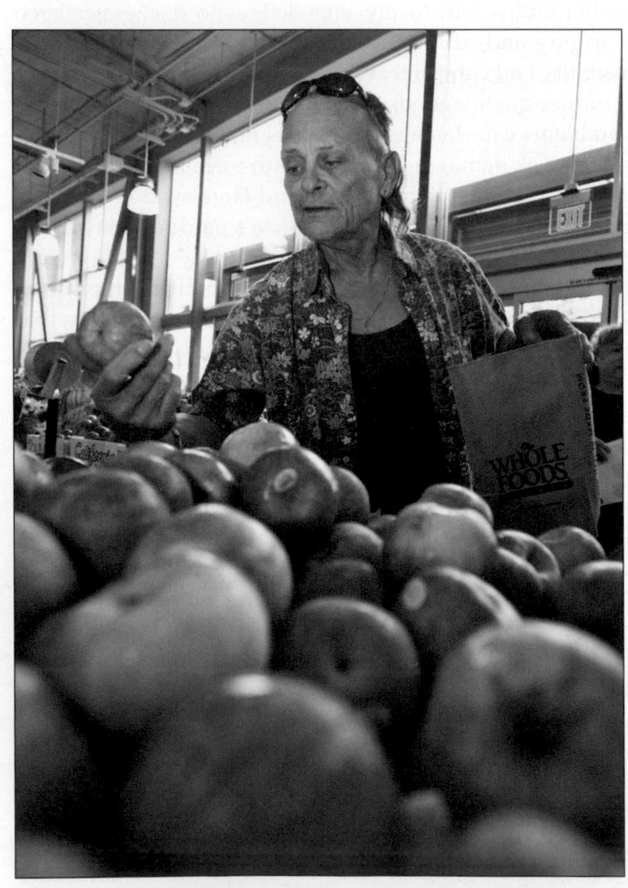

Serving underserved consumers: To combat "food deserts," many national food chains, such as Whole Foods Market, are opening stores in underserved communities ignored by other sellers.

© ZUMA Press, Inc / Alamy

Clearly, better marketing systems must be built to service disadvantaged consumers. In fact, many marketers profitably target such consumers with legitimate goods and services that create real value. In cases in which marketers do not step in to fill the void, the government likely will. For example, the FTC has taken action against sellers that advertise false values, wrongfully deny services, or charge disadvantaged customers too much.

Marketing's Impact on Society as a Whole

The American marketing system has been accused of adding to several "evils" in American society at large, such as creating too much materialism, too few social goods, and a glut of cultural pollution.

False Wants and Too Much Materialism

Critics have charged that the marketing system urges too much interest in material possessions, and that America's love affair with worldly possessions is not sustainable. Too often, people are judged by what they *own* rather than by who they *are*. The critics do not view this interest in material things as a natural state of mind but rather as a matter of false wants created by marketing. Marketers, they claim, stimulate people's desires for goods and create materialistic models

What does
More Fun
Less Stuff
mean to you?
Tell us at:
newdream.org/less-stuff
MORE FUN!
LESS stuff
more of what matters

Materialism: A marketing campaign by the Center for a New American Dream urges people to reject "buy more" messages and instead say "More fun! Less stuff!"

Center for the New American Dream

of the good life. Thus, marketers have created an endless cycle of mass consumption based on a distorted interpretation of the "American Dream."

In this view, marketing's purpose is to promote consumption, and the inevitable outcome of successful marketing is unsustainable *over*consumption. According to the critics, more is not always better. Some critics have taken their concerns straight to the public. For example, consumer activist Annie Leonard founded *The Story of Stuff* project with a 20-minute online video about the social and environmental consequences of America's love affair with stuff—"How our obsession with stuff is trashing the planet, our communities, and our health." The video has been viewed more than 40 million times online, in schools, and in community centers around the world.[14]

Similarly, the Center for a New American Dream is a nonprofit organization founded on a mission to "help Americans to reduce and shift their consumption to improve quality of life, protect the environment, and promote social justice." Through educational videos and marketing campaigns such as "More fun! Less stuff!," the organization works with individuals, institutions, communities, and businesses to help conserve natural resources, counter the commercialization of culture, and promote positive changes in the way goods are produced and consumed.[15]

Marketers respond that such criticisms overstate the power of business to create needs. They claim people have strong defenses against advertising and other marketing tools. Marketers are most effective when they appeal to existing wants rather than when they attempt to create new ones. Furthermore, people seek information when making important purchases and often do not rely on single sources. Even minor purchases that may be affected by advertising messages lead to repeat purchases only if the product delivers the promised customer value. Finally, the high failure rate of new products shows that companies are not able to control demand.

On a deeper level, our wants and values are influenced not only by marketers but also by family, peer groups, religion, cultural background, and education. If Americans are highly materialistic, these values arose out of basic socialization processes that go much deeper than business and marketing could produce alone.

Moreover, consumption patterns and attitudes are also subject to larger forces, such as the economy. As discussed in Chapter 1, the recent Great Recession put a damper on materialism and conspicuous spending. Additionally, today's consumers are more supportive of environmental and social sustainability efforts by companies. As a result, instead of encouraging today's more sensible and conscientious consumers to overspend their means or spend wastefully, most marketers are working to help them find greater value with less and to share their material prosperity with the less fortunate.

An example is the "Shwopping" movement started by British retailing giant Marks & Spencer, by which it urges customers to exchange an old item of clothing, even if it's not from M&S, each time they buy something new. Shwopped items go to Oxfam International, a nonprofit organization that resells, recycles, or forwards them to raise money and help people around the world overcome poverty. "We hope to collect as many clothes as we sell and change the way we all shop forever," says Marks & Spencer.[16]

Too Few Social Goods

Business has been accused of overselling private goods at the expense of public goods. As private goods increase, they require more public services that are usually not forthcoming. For example, an increase in automobile ownership (private good) requires more highways, traffic control, parking spaces, and police services (public goods). The overselling of private goods results in social costs. For cars, some of the social costs include traffic congestion, gasoline shortages, and air pollution. For example, American travelers lose, on average, 38 hours a year in traffic jams, costing the United States more than $120 billion a year—$820 per commuter. In the process, they waste 2.9 billion gallons of fuel and emit millions of tons of greenhouse gases.[17]

A way must be found to restore a balance between private and public goods. One option is to make producers bear the full social costs of their operations. For example, the government is requiring automobile manufacturers to build cars with more efficient engines and better pollution-control systems. Automakers will then raise their prices to cover the extra costs. If buyers find the price of some car models too high, however, these models will disappear. Demand will then move to those producers that can support the sum of the private and social costs.

A second option is to make consumers pay the social costs. For example, many cities around the world are now charging congestion tolls in an effort to reduce traffic congestion. To decrease rush hour traffic on the Bay Bridge between Oakland and San Francisco, California, the Metropolitan Transportation Commission charges a $6 toll during peak commute hours versus $4 at other times. The charge reduced the flow of drivers during peak hours, cutting the average 32-minute wait time some bridges approach in half.[18]

Cultural Pollution

Critics charge the marketing system with creating *cultural pollution*. They feel our senses are being constantly assaulted by marketing and advertising. Commercials interrupt serious programs; pages of ads obscure magazines; billboards mar beautiful scenery; spam fills our e-mailboxes; flashing display ads intrude on our online and mobile screens. What's more, the critics claim, these interruptions continually pollute people's minds with messages of materialism, sex, power, or status. Some critics call for sweeping changes.

Cultural pollution: People's senses are sometimes assaulted by a clutter of commercial messages and noise.

Christian Science Monitor/Getty Images

Marketers answer the charges of commercial noise with these arguments: First, they hope that their ads primarily reach the target audience. But because of mass-communication channels, some ads are bound to reach people who have no interest in the product and are therefore bored or annoyed. People who buy magazines they like or who opt in to e-mail, social media, or mobile marketing programs rarely complain about the ads because they involve products and services of interest.

Second, because of ads, many television, radio, online, and social media sites are free to users. Ads also help keep down the costs of magazines and newspapers. Many people think viewing ads is a small price to pay for these benefits. In addition, consumers find many television commercials entertaining and seek them out; for example, ad viewership during the Super Bowl usually equals or exceeds game viewership. Finally, today's consumers have alternatives. For example, they can zip or zap TV commercials on recorded programs or avoid them altogether on many paid cable, satellite, and online channels. Thus, to hold consumer attention, advertisers are making their ads more entertaining and informative.

Marketing's Impact on Other Businesses

Critics also charge that a company's marketing practices can harm other companies and reduce competition. They identify three problems: acquisitions of competitors, marketing practices that create barriers to entry, and unfair competitive marketing practices.

Critics claim that firms are harmed and competition is reduced when companies expand by acquiring competitors rather than by developing their own new products. The large number of acquisitions and the rapid pace of industry consolidation over the past several decades have caused concern that vigorous young competitors will be absorbed, thereby reducing competition. In virtually every major industry—retailing, entertainment, financial services, utilities, transportation, automobiles, telecommunications, health care—the number of major competitors is shrinking.

Acquisition is a complex subject. In some cases, acquisitions can be good for society. The acquiring company may gain economies of scale that lead to lower costs and lower prices. In addition, a well-managed company may take over a poorly managed company and improve its efficiency. An industry that was not very competitive might become more competitive after the acquisition. But acquisitions can also be harmful, and therefore are closely regulated by the government.

Critics have also charged that marketing practices bar new companies from entering an industry. Large marketing companies can use patents and heavy promotion spending or tie up suppliers or dealers to keep out or drive out competitors. Those concerned with antitrust regulation recognize that some barriers are the natural result of the economic advantages of doing business on a large scale. Existing and new laws can challenge other barriers. For example, some critics have proposed a progressive tax on advertising spending to reduce the role of selling costs as a major barrier to entry.

Finally, some firms have, in fact, used unfair competitive marketing practices with the intention of hurting or destroying other firms. They may set their prices below costs, threaten to cut off business with suppliers, or discourage the buying of a competitor's products. Although various laws work to prevent such predatory competition, it is often difficult to prove that the intent or action was really predatory.

In recent years, Walmart has been accused of using predatory pricing in selected market areas to drive smaller, mom-and-pop retailers out of business. Walmart has become a lightning rod for protests by citizens in dozens of towns who worry that the megaretailer's unfair practices will choke out local businesses. However, whereas critics charge that Walmart's actions are predatory, others assert that its actions are just the healthy competition of a more-efficient company against less-efficient ones.

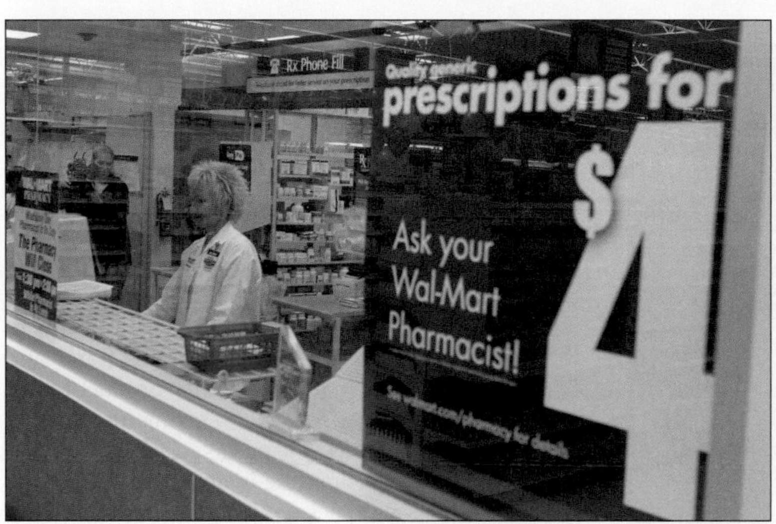

● **Walmart prescription pricing: Is it predatory pricing or is it just good business?**

Associated Press

For instance, ● when Walmart began a program to sell generic drugs at $4 a prescription, local pharmacists complained of predatory pricing. They charged that at those low prices, Walmart must be selling under cost to drive them out of business. But Walmart claimed that, given its substantial buying power and efficient operations, it could make a profit at those prices. The $4 pricing program, the retailer claimed, was not aimed at putting competitors out of business. Rather, it was simply a good competitive move that served customers better and brought more of them in the door. Moreover, Walmart's program drove down prescription prices at the pharmacies of other supermarkets and discount stores, such as Kroger and Target. Currently, more than 300 prescription drugs are available for $4 at the various chains, and Walmart claims that the program has saved its customers more than $4.8 billion.[19]

Author Comment | Sustainable marketing isn't something that only businesses and governments can do. Through consumerism and environmentalism, consumers themselves can play an important role.

Consumer Actions to Promote Sustainable Marketing

Sustainable marketing calls for more responsible actions by both businesses and consumers. Because some people view businesses as the cause of many economic and social ills, grassroots movements have arisen from time to time to keep businesses in line. Two major movements have been *consumerism* and *environmentalism*.

Consumerism

Consumerism
An organized movement of citizens and government agencies designed to improve the rights and power of buyers in relation to sellers.

Consumerism is an organized movement of citizens and government agencies to improve the rights and power of buyers in relation to sellers. Traditional *sellers' rights* include the following:

- The right to introduce any product in any size and style, provided it is not hazardous to personal health or safety, or, if it is, to include proper warnings and controls
- The right to charge any price for the product, provided no discrimination exists among similar kinds of buyers
- The right to spend any amount to promote the product, provided it is not defined as unfair competition
- The right to use any product message, provided it is not misleading or dishonest in content or execution
- The right to use buying incentive programs, provided they are not unfair or misleading

Traditional *buyers' rights* include the following:

- The right not to buy a product that is offered for sale
- The right to expect the product to be safe
- The right to expect the product to perform as claimed

In comparing these rights, many believe that the balance of power lies on the seller's side. True, the buyer can refuse to buy. But critics feel that the buyer has too little information, education, and protection to make wise decisions when facing sophisticated sellers. Consumer advocates call for the following additional consumer rights:

- The right to be well informed about important aspects of the product
- The right to be protected against questionable products and marketing practices
- The right to influence products and marketing practices in ways that will improve "quality of life"
- The right to consume now in a way that will preserve the world for future generations of consumers

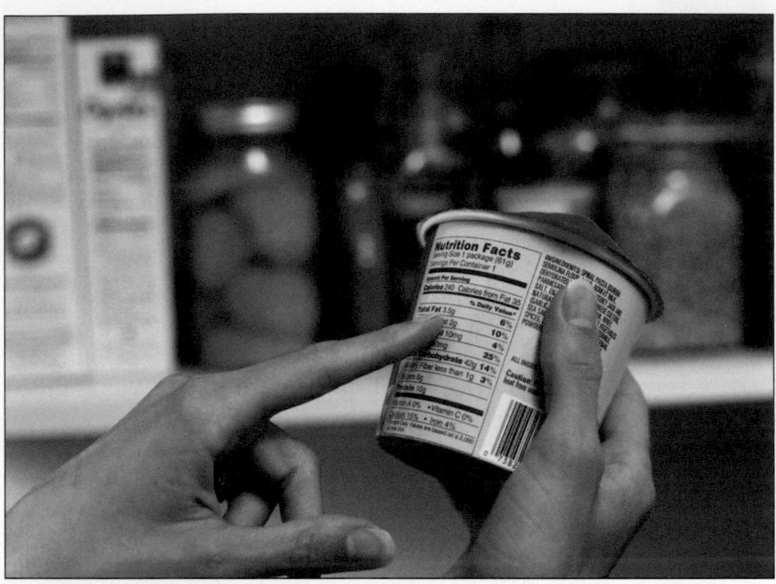

Consumer desire for more information led to package labels with useful facts, from ingredients and nutrition facts to recycling and country of origin information.

Ryan McVay

Each proposed right has led to more specific proposals by consumerists and consumer protection actions by the government. The right to be informed includes the right to know the true interest on a loan (truth in lending), the true cost per unit of a brand (unit pricing), the ingredients in a product (ingredient labeling), the nutritional value of foods (nutritional labeling), product freshness (open dating), and the true benefits of a product (truth in advertising). Proposals related to consumer protection include strengthening consumer rights in cases of business fraud and financial protection, requiring greater product safety, ensuring information privacy, and giving more power to government agencies. Proposals relating to quality of life include controlling the ingredients that go into certain products and packaging and reducing the level of advertising "noise." Proposals for preserving the world for future consumption include promoting the use of sustainable ingredients, recycling and reducing solid wastes, and managing energy consumption.

Sustainable marketing applies not only to businesses and governments but also to consumers. Consumers have not only the *right* but also the *responsibility* to protect themselves instead of leaving this function to the government or someone else. Consumers who believe they got a bad deal have several remedies available, including contacting the company; making their case through the media or social media; contacting federal, state, or local agencies; and going to small-claims courts. Consumers should also make good consumption choices, rewarding companies that act responsibly while punishing those that don't. Ultimately, the move from irresponsible consumption to sustainable consumption is in the hands of consumers.

Environmentalism

Environmentalism
An organized movement of concerned citizens, businesses, and government agencies designed to protect and improve people's current and future living environment.

Whereas consumerists consider whether the marketing system is efficiently serving consumer wants, environmentalists are concerned with marketing's effects on the environment and the environmental costs of serving consumer needs and wants. **Environmentalism** is an organized movement of concerned citizens, businesses, and government agencies designed to protect and improve people's current and future living environment.

Environmentalists are not against marketing and consumption; they simply want people and organizations to operate with more care for the environment. They call for doing away with what sustainability advocate and Unilever CEO Paul Polman calls "mindless consumption." According to Polman, "the road to well-being doesn't go via reduced consumption. It has to be done via more responsible consumption."[20] The marketing system's goal, environmentalists assert, should not be to maximize consumption, consumer choice, or consumer satisfaction but rather to maximize life quality. Life quality means not only the quantity and quality of consumer goods and services but also the quality of the environment, now and for future generations.

Environmentalism is concerned with damage to the ecosystem caused by global warming, resource depletion, toxic and solid wastes, litter, the availability of fresh water, and

FIGURE | 20.2
Environmental Sustainability and Sustainable Value

Source: Based on Stuart L. Hart, "Sustainable Value," www.stuartlhart.com/sustainablevalue.html, July 2014.

	Today: Greening	Tomorrow: Beyond Greening
Internal	**Pollution prevention** Eliminating or reducing waste before it is created	**New clean technology** Developing new sets of environmental skills and capabilities
External	**Product stewardship** Minimizing environmental impact throughout the entire product life cycle	**Sustainability vision** Developing a strategic framework for creating sustainable value

This framework addresses more than just natural environmental challenges. It also points to opportunities for creating sustainable value for markets and the firm through environmentally sustainable strategies and practices.

other problems. Other issues include the loss of recreational areas and the increase in health problems caused by bad air, polluted water, and chemically treated food.

Over the past several decades, such concerns have resulted in federal and state laws and regulations governing industrial commercial practices impacting the environment. Some companies have strongly resented and resisted such environmental regulations, claiming that they are too costly and have made their industries less competitive. These companies responded to consumer environmental concerns by doing only what was required to avert new regulations or keep environmentalists quiet.

Environmental sustainability
A management approach that involves developing strategies that both sustain the environment and produce profits for the company.

In recent years, however, most companies have accepted responsibility for doing no harm to the environment. They are shifting from protest to prevention and from regulation to responsibility. More and more companies are now adopting policies of **environmental sustainability**. Simply put, environmental sustainability is about generating profits while helping to save the planet. Today's enlightened companies are taking action not because someone is forcing them to or to reap short-run profits but because it's the right thing to do—because it's for their customers' well-being, the company's well-being, and the planet's environmental future. For example, consumer products giant Unilever has successfully built its core mission around environmental sustainability—its aim is to "make sustainable living commonplace" (see Real Marketing 20.1).

Figure 20.2 shows a grid that companies can use to gauge their progress toward environmental sustainability. It includes both internal and external *greening* activities that will pay off for the firm and environment in the short run, and *beyond greening* activities that will pay off in the longer term. At the most basic level, a company can practice *pollution prevention*. This involves more than pollution control—cleaning up waste after it has been created. Pollution prevention means eliminating or minimizing waste *before* it is created. Companies emphasizing prevention have responded with internal green marketing programs—designing and developing ecologically safer products, recyclable and biodegradable packaging, better pollution controls, and more energy-efficient operations.

For example, Nike makes shoes out of "environmentally preferred materials," recycles old sneakers, and educates young people about conservation, reuse, and recycling. Its revolutionary woven Flyknit shoes are lightweight, comfortable, and durable but produce 66 percent less material waste in production—the material wasted making each pair of Flyknits weighs only as much as a sheet of paper.

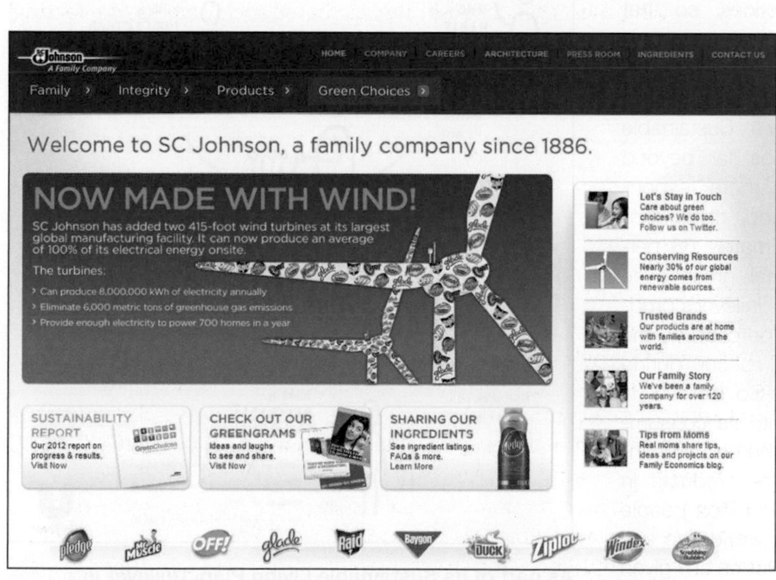

Environmental sustainability: Among other sustainability efforts, SC Johnson obtains 100 percent of its electricity at its largest global manufacturing facility from renewable sources. Its products are "Now Made with Wind."

Image courtesy of SC Johnson

SC Johnson—maker of familiar household brands ranging from Windex, Pledge, Shout, and Scrubbing Bubbles to Ziploc, Off, and Raid—sells concentrated versions of all of its household cleaners in recyclable bottles, helping eliminate empty trigger bottles from entering landfills. The company currently obtains 100 percent of the electricity used at its largest global manufacturing facility from renewable sources. And by rating the environmental impact of product ingredients, it has cut millions of pounds of volatile organic compounds (VOCs) from its products. For example,

Real Marketing 20.1

Sustainability at Unilever: Creating a Better Future Every Day

When Paul Polman took over as CEO of Unilever a few years ago, the foods, home, and personal care products company was a slumbering giant. Despite its stable of star-studded brands—including the likes of Dove, Axe, Noxzema, Sunsilk, OMO, Hellmann's, Knorr, Lipton, and Ben & Jerry's—Unilever had experienced a decade of stagnant sales and profits. The company needed renewed energy and purpose. "To drag the world back to sanity, we need to know why we are here," said Polman.

To answer the "why are we here" question and find a more energizing mission, Polman looked beyond the usual corporate goals of growing sales, profits, and shareholder value. Instead, he asserted, growth results from accomplishing a broader social and environmental mission. Unilever exists "for consumers, not shareholders," he said. "If we are in sync with consumer needs and the environment in which we operate, and take responsibility for our [societal impact], then the shareholder will also be rewarded."

Evaluating and working on sustainability impact is nothing new at Unilever. Prior to Polman taking the reins, the company already had multiple programs in place to manage the impact of its products and operations. But the existing programs and results—while good—simply didn't go far enough for Polman. So in late 2010 Unilever launched its Sustainable Living Plan—an aggressive long-term plan that takes capitalism to the next level. Under the plan, the company set out to "create a better future every day for people around the world: the people who work for us, those we do business with, the billions of people who use our products, and future generations whose quality of life depends on the way we protect the environment today." According to Polman, Unilever's long-run *commercial* success depends on how well it manages the *social* and *environmental* impact of its actions.

The Sustainable Living Plan sets out three major social and environmental objectives to be accomplished by 2020: "(1) To help more than one billion people take action to improve their health and well-being; (2) to halve the environmental footprint of the making and use of our products; and (3) to enhance the livelihoods of millions of people as we grow our business."

The Sustainable Living Plan pulls together all of the work Unilever had already been doing and sets ambitious new sustainability goals. These goals span the entire value chain, from how the company sources raw materials to how consumers use and dispose of its products. "Our aim is to make our activities more sustainable and also encourage our customers, suppliers, and others to do the same," says the company.

On the "upstream supply side," more than half of Unilever's raw materials come from agriculture, so the company is helping suppliers develop sustainable farming practices that meet its own high expectations for environmental and social impact. Unilever assesses suppliers against two sets of standards. The first is the Unilever Supplier Code, which calls for socially responsible actions regarding human rights, labor practices, product safety, and care for the environment. Second, specifically for agricultural suppliers, the Unilever Sustainable Agriculture Code details Unilever's expectations for sustainable agriculture practices, so that it and its suppliers "can commit to the sustainability journey together."

But Unilever's Sustainable Living Plan goes far beyond simply creating more responsible supply and distribution chains. Approximately 68 percent of the total greenhouse gas footprint of Unilever's products, and 50 percent of the water footprint, occur during consumer use. So Unilever is also working with its consumers to improve the environmental impact of its products in use. Around two billion people in 190 markets worldwide use a Unilever product on any given day. Therefore, small everyday consumer actions can add up to a big difference. Unilever sums it up with this equation: "Unilever brands × small everyday actions × billions of consumers = big difference."

For example, almost one-third of households worldwide use Unilever laundry products to do their washing—approximately 125 billion washes every year. Therefore, under its Sustainable Living Plan, Unilever is both creating more eco-friendly laundry products and motivating consumers to improve their laundry habits.

Around the world, for instance, Unilever is encouraging consumers to wash clothes at lower temperatures and use the correct dosage of detergent. Unilever products such as OMO and Persil Small & Mighty concentrated laundry detergents use less packaging, making them cheaper and less polluting to transport. More important, they've been reformulated to wash

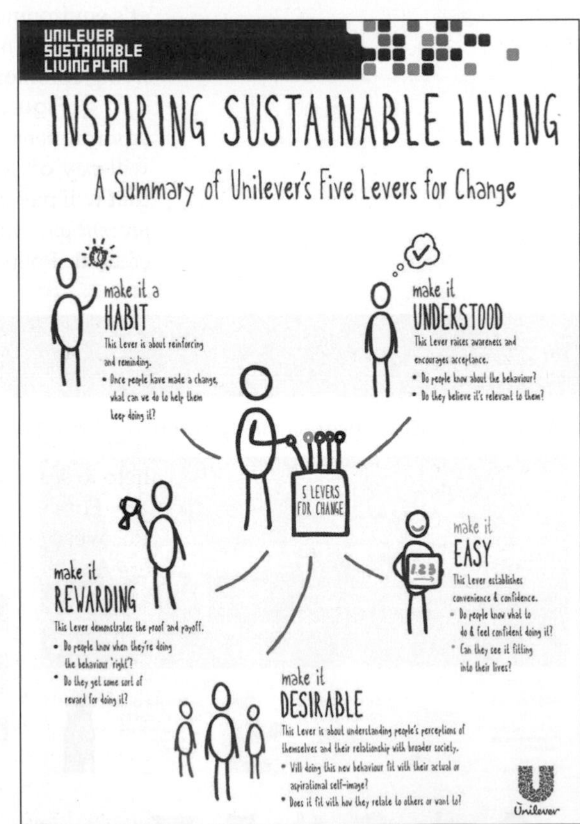

As part of its Sustainable Living Plan, Unilever is working with its more than 2 billion customers worldwide to improve the social and environmental impact of its products in use. "Small actions. Big difference."

efficiently at lower temperatures, using less energy and water. Unilever estimates these changes have achieved a 15 percent reduction in greenhouse gas emissions. Another Unilever product, Comfort One Rinse fabric conditioner, was created for hand washing clothes in developing and emerging markets where water is often in short supply. The innovative product requires only one bucket of water for rinsing rather than three, saving consumers time, effort, and 30 liters of water per wash.

Such energy and water savings don't show up on Unilever's income statement, but they will be extremely important to the people and the planet. "Ultimately," says the company, "we will only succeed if we inspire people around the world to take small, everyday actions that can add up to a big difference for the world." To meet this objective, Unilever has identified "Five Levers for Change"—things that its marketers can do to inspire people to adopt specific sustainable behaviors. The model helps marketers identify the barriers and triggers for change. The levers for change are: make it understood, make it easy, make it desirable, make it rewarding, and make it a habit.

Will Unilever's Sustainable Living Plan produce results for the company? So far, so good. Unilever is making excellent progress on its overall mission of "making sustainable living commonplace" and on its 68 aggressive Sustainable Living Plan goals. The company has already achieved 11 specific targets, is right on pace with 51 more, and is making good progress on the other six. And despite volatility in its global markets, Unilever's sales and profits continue to grow.

The sustainability plan is not just the right thing to do for people and the environment, claims Polman, it's also right for Unilever. The quest for sustainability saves money by reducing energy use and minimizing waste. It fuels innovation, resulting in new products and new consumer benefits. And it creates new market opportunities: More than half of Unilever's sales are from developing countries, the very places that face the greatest sustainability challenges.

In all, Polman predicts, the sustainability plan will help Unilever double in size, while also creating a better future for billions of people without increasing the environmental footprint. "We do not believe there is a conflict between sustainability and profitable growth," he concludes. "The daily act of making and selling consumer goods drives economic and social progress. There are billions of people around the world who deserve the better quality of life that everyday products like soap, shampoo, and tea can provide. Sustainable living is not a pipedream. It can be done, and there is very little downside."

Sources: Based on quotes and other information from Andrew Saunders, "Paul Polman of Unilever," *Management Today*, March 2011, pp. 42–47; Adi Ignatius, "Captain Planet," *Harvard Business Review*, June 2012, pp. 2–8; Holly Ellyatt, "Unilever Profit Beats, Shares Jump," *CNBC*, January 21, 2014, www.cnbc.com/id/101349908; "Making Progress, Driving Change," www.unilever.com/images/slp_Unilever-Sustainable-Living-Plan-2013_tcm13-388693.pdf, accessed July 2014; and www.unilever.com/sustainable-living-2014/ and www.unilever.com/images/Unilever_AR13_tcm13-383757.pdf, accessed September 2014.

by simple reformulating of its Windex glass cleaner, SC Johnson cut 1.8 million pounds of VOCs while giving the product 30 percent more cleaning power. SC Johnson boasts that since 1886, it has been "committed to working every day to do what's right for people, the planet, and generations to come."[21]

At the next level, companies can practice *product stewardship*—minimizing not only pollution from production and product design but also all environmental impacts throughout the full product life cycle, while at the same time reducing costs. Many companies have adopted *design for environment (DFE)* and *cradle-to-cradle* practices. This involves thinking ahead to design products that are easier to recover, reuse, recycle, or safely return to nature after usage, thus becoming part of the ecological cycle. DFE and cradle-to-cradle practices not only help to sustain the environment, but they can also be highly profitable for the company.

For example, more than a decade ago, IBM started a business—IBM Global Asset Recovery Services—designed to reuse and recycle parts from returned mainframe computers and other equipment. Last year, IBM processed more than 42.1 million pounds of end-of-life products and product waste worldwide, stripping down old equipment to recover chips and valuable metals. Since 2002 it has processed more than 981 million pounds of machines, parts, and material. IBM Global Asset Recovery Services finds uses for more than 99 percent of what it takes in, sending less than 1 percent to landfills and incineration facilities. What started out as an environmental effort has now grown into a multibillion-dollar IBM business that profitably recycles electronic equipment at 22 sites worldwide.[22]

Today's *greening* activities focus on improving what companies already do to protect the environment. The *beyond greening* activities identified in Figure 20.2 look to the future. First, internally, companies can plan for *new clean technology*. Many organizations that have made good sustainability headway are still limited by existing technologies. To create fully sustainable strategies, they will need to develop innovative new technologies.

For example, by 2020, Coca-Cola has committed to reclaiming and recycling the equivalent of all the packaging it uses around the world. It has also pledged to dramatically reduce its overall environmental footprint. To accomplish these goals, the company invests heavily in new clean technologies that address a host of environmental issues, such as recycling, resource usage, and distribution:[23]

> First, to attack the solid waste problem caused by its plastic bottles, Coca-Cola invested heavily to build the world's largest state-of-the-art plastic-bottle-to-bottle recycling plant. As a more permanent solution, Coke is researching and testing new bottles made from aluminum, corn, or bioplastics. It has been steadily replacing its PET plastic bottles with PlantBottle packaging, which incorporates 30 percent plant-based materials. The company is also designing more eco-friendly distribution alternatives. Currently, some 10 million vending machines and refrigerated coolers gobble up energy and use potent greenhouse gases called hydrofluorocarbons (HFCs) to keep Cokes cold. To eliminate them, the company invested $40 million in research and began installing sleek new HFC-free coolers that use 30 to 40 percent less energy—so far one million have been installed. Coca-Cola also aims to become "water neutral" by researching ways to help its bottlers add back all the fresh water they extract during the production of Coca-Cola beverages.

Finally, companies can develop a *sustainability vision*, which serves as a guide to the future. It shows how the company's products and services, processes, and policies must evolve and what new technologies must be developed to get there. This vision of sustainability provides a framework for pollution control, product stewardship, and new environmental technology for the company and others to follow. It addresses not just challenges in the natural environment but also strategic opportunities for using environmental strategies to create sustainable value for the firm and its markets.

Most companies today focus on the upper-left quadrant of the grid in Figure 20.2, investing most heavily in pollution prevention. Some forward-looking companies practice product stewardship and are developing new environmental technologies. However, emphasizing only one or two quadrants in the environmental sustainability grid can be shortsighted. Investing only in the left half of the grid puts a company in a good position today but leaves it vulnerable in the future. In contrast, a heavy emphasis on the right half suggests that a company has good environmental vision but lacks the skills needed to implement it. Thus, companies should work at developing all four dimensions of environmental sustainability.

Walmart, for example, is doing just that. ● Through its own environmental sustainability actions and its impact on the actions of suppliers, Walmart has emerged in recent years as the world's super "eco-nanny":[24]

> When it comes to sustainability, perhaps no company in the world is doing more good these days than Walmart. That's right—big, bad Walmart. The giant retailer is now one of the world's biggest crusaders for the cause of saving the world for future generations. For starters, Walmart is rolling out new high-efficiency stores, each one saving more energy than the last. These stores use wind turbines to generate energy, high-output linear fluorescent lighting to reduce what energy stores do use, and native landscaping to cut down on watering and fertilizer. Store heating systems burn recovered cooking oil from the deli fryers and motor oil from the Tire and Lube Express centers. All organic waste, including produce, meats, and paper, is hauled off to a company that turns it into mulch for the garden.
>
> Walmart is not only greening up its own operations but also laying down the eco-law to its vast network of 100,000 suppliers to get them to do the same. It recently announced plans to cut some 20 million metric tons of greenhouse gas emissions from its supply chain within five years—equivalent to removing more than 3.8 million cars from the road for a year. To get this done, Walmart is asking its huge corps of suppliers to examine the carbon life cycles of their products and rethink how they source, manufacture, package, and transport these goods. It has developed the Walmart Sustainability Index program, which helps suppliers understand, monitor, and enhance the sustainability of its products and the supply chain. With its immense buying power, Walmart can humble even the mightiest supplier. When imposing its environmental demands on suppliers, Walmart has even more clout than government regulators. Whereas the EPA can only level nominal fines, Walmart can threaten a substantial chunk of a supplier's business.

● **For Walmart, sustainability is about more than just doing the right thing. Above all, it's makes good business sense—"driving out hidden costs, conserving our natural resources for future generations, and providing sustainable and affordable products for our customers so they can save money and live better."**

AP Images/PRNewsFoto/Walmart; Bebay/iStockphoto.

For Walmart, leading the eco-charge is about more than just doing the right thing. Above all, it also makes good business sense. More efficient operations and less wasteful products are not only good for the environment but also save Walmart money. Lower costs, in turn, let Walmart do more of what it has always done best—save customers money.

Public Actions to Regulate Marketing

Citizen concerns about marketing practices will usually lead to public attention and legislative proposals. Many of the laws that affect marketing were identified in Chapter 3. The task is to translate these laws into a language that marketing executives understand as they make decisions about competitive relations, products, price, promotion, and distribution channels. **Figure 20.3** illustrates the major legal issues facing marketing management.

Author Comment | In the end, marketers themselves must take responsibility for sustainable marketing. That means operating in a responsible and ethical way to bring both immediate and future value to customers.

Business Actions toward Sustainable Marketing

At first, many companies opposed consumerism, environmentalism, and other elements of sustainable marketing. They thought the criticisms were either unfair or unimportant. But by now, most companies have grown to embrace sustainability principles as a way to create both immediate and future customer value and strengthen customer relationships.

Sustainable Marketing Principles

Under the sustainable marketing concept, a company's marketing should support the best long-run performance of the marketing system. It should be guided by five sustainable marketing principles: *consumer-oriented marketing, customer value marketing, innovative marketing, sense-of-mission marketing,* and *societal marketing.*

Consumer-Oriented Marketing

Consumer-oriented marketing
A company should view and organize its marketing activities from the consumer's point of view.

Consumer-oriented marketing means that the company should view and organize its marketing activities from the consumer's point of view. It should work hard to sense, serve, and satisfy the needs of a defined group of customers—both now and in the future. The good marketing companies that we've discussed throughout this text have had this in common: an all-consuming passion for delivering superior value to carefully chosen customers. Only by seeing the world through its customers' eyes can the company build sustainable and profitable customer relationships.

Customer Value Marketing

Customer value marketing
A company should put most of its resources into customer value-building marketing investments.

According to the principle of **customer value marketing**, the company should put most of its resources into customer value-building marketing investments. Many things marketers

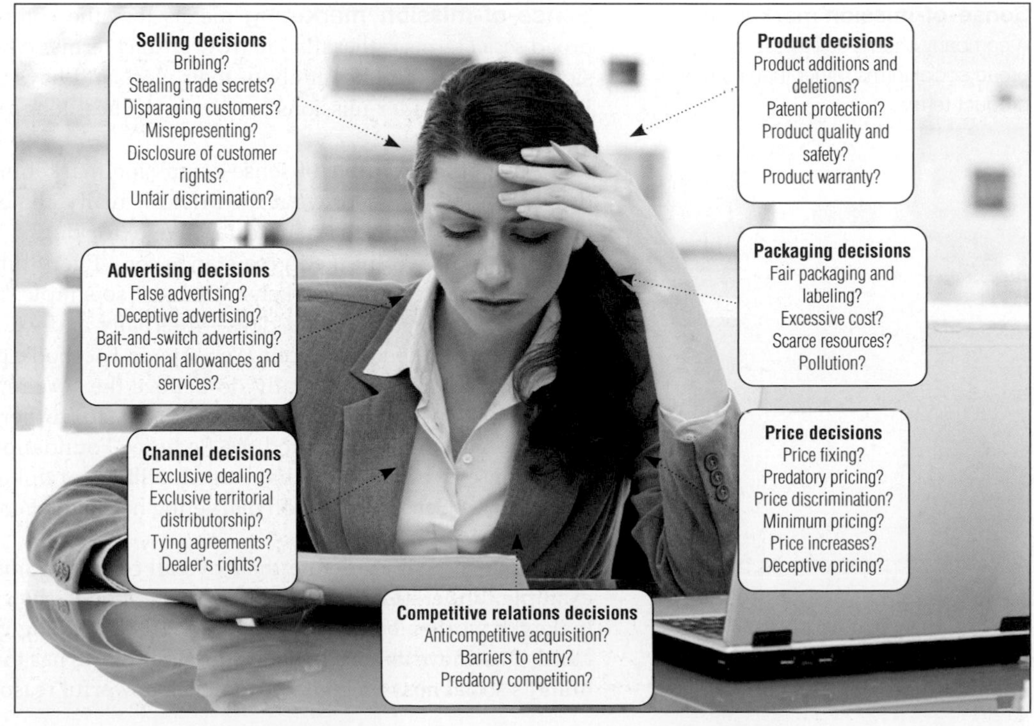

Selling decisions
Bribing?
Stealing trade secrets?
Disparaging customers?
Misrepresenting?
Disclosure of customer rights?
Unfair discrimination?
Product decisions
Product additions and deletions?
Patent protection?
Product quality and safety?
Product warranty?
Advertising decisions
False advertising?
Deceptive advertising?
Bait-and-switch advertising?
Promotional allowances and services?
Packaging decisions
Fair packaging and labeling?
Excessive cost?
Scarce resources?
Pollution?
Channel decisions
Exclusive dealing?
Exclusive territorial distributorship?
Tying agreements?
Dealer's rights?
Price decisions
Price fixing?
Predatory pricing?
Price discrimination?
Minimum pricing?
Price increases?
Deceptive pricing?
Competitive relations decisions
Anticompetitive acquisition?
Barriers to entry?
Predatory competition?

FIGURE | 20.3
Major Marketing Decision Areas That May Be Called into Question under the Law
Source: (photo) wavebreakmedia ltd/Shutterstock.com.

do—one-shot sales promotions, cosmetic product changes, direct-response advertising—may raise sales in the short run but add less *value* than would actual improvements in the product's quality, features, or convenience. Enlightened marketing calls for building long-run consumer engagement, loyalty, and relationships by continually improving the value consumers receive from the firm's market offering. By creating value *for* consumers, the company can capture value *from* consumers in return.

Innovative marketing
A company should seek real product and marketing improvements.

Innovative Marketing

The principle of **innovative marketing** requires that the company continuously seek real product and marketing improvements. The company that overlooks new and better ways to do things will eventually lose customers to another company that has found a better way. Think back to the Nike story in Chapter 2:[25]

Innovative marketing: New products, such as the Nike FuelBand and Flyknit Racer, along with its innovative social media marketing efforts, recently earned Nike the title as Fast Company's number one most innovative marketer.
Rodrigo Reyes Marin/AFLO/Newscom

For nearly 50 years, through innovative marketing, Nike has built the ever-present swoosh into one of the world's best-known brand symbols. When sales languished in the late 1990s and new competitors made gains, Nike knew it had to reinvent itself via product and marketing innovation. "One of my fears is being this big, slow, constipated, bureaucratic company that's happy with its success," says Nike CEO Mark Parker. Instead, over the past few years, a hungry Nike has unleashed a number of highly successful new products. For example, with the new Nike Flyknit Racer, Nike has now reinvented the very way that shoes are manufactured. The featherweight Flyknit feels more like a sock with a sole. Woven not sewn, the Flyknit is super comfortable and durable, more affordable to make, and more environmentally friendly than traditional sneakers. Top off Nike's new products with a heavy investment in social media content and Nike remains the world's largest sports apparel company, an impressive 25 percent larger than closest rival adidas. Both *Forbes* and *Fast Company* recently anointed Nike as the world's number one most innovative company.

Sense-of-mission marketing
A company should define its mission in broad social terms rather than narrow product terms.

Sense-of-Mission Marketing

Sense-of-mission marketing means that the company should define its mission in broad *social* terms rather than narrow *product* terms. When a company defines a social mission, employees feel better about their work and have a clearer sense of direction. Brands linked with broader missions can serve the best long-run interests of both the brand and consumers.

As another example of sense-of-mission marketing, the Pedigree brand makes good dog food, but that's not what the brand is really all about. Instead, seven years ago, the brand came up with the manifesto, "We're for dogs." That statement is a perfect encapsulation of everything Pedigree stands for. "Everything that we do is because we love dogs," says a Pedigree marketer. "It's just so simple." This mission-focused positioning drives everything the brand does—internally and externally. One look at a Pedigree ad or a visit to the pedigree.com Web site or Facebook page confirms that the people behind the Pedigree brand really do believe the "We're for dogs" mission. Associates are even encouraged to take their dogs to work. To further fulfill the "We're for dogs" brand promise, the company created the Pedigree Foundation, which, along with the Pedigree Adoption Drive campaign, has raised millions of dollars for helping "shelter dogs" find good homes. Sense-of-mission marketing has made Pedigree the world's number-one dog food brand.[26]

Some companies define their overall corporate missions in broad societal terms. For example, under TOMS' buy-one-give-one model, the company seeks both profits and to make the world a better place. Thus, at TOMS, "doing good" and "doing well" go hand in hand. To achieve its social-change mission, TOMS has to make money. At the same time, the brand's social mission gives customers a powerful reason to buy (see Real Marketing 20.2).

Real Marketing 20.2

TOMS: "*Be* the Change You Want to See in the World"

If the world were a village of 100 people, 14 of the 100 would be illiterate, 20 would be malnourished, 23 would drink polluted water, 25 would have no shelter, 33 would have no electricity, and 40 would have no shoes. Less than a decade ago, these stark facts, especially the last one, struck Blake Mycoskie up close and personally as he visited Argentina to learn how to play polo, practice his tango, and do some community service work. While there, the sight of barefooted children, too poor to have shoes, stunned him.

So Mycoskie launched TOMS Shoes with $300,000 of his own money. The founding concept was this: For every pair of TOMS shoes that customers bought, the company would donate another pair of shoes to a child in need around the world. Mycoskie had previously started five successful strictly for-profit businesses. "But I was ready to do something more meaningful," says Mycoskie. "I always knew I wanted to help others. Now, it was time to do something that wasn't just for profit." Mycoskie remembered Mahatma Gandhi's saying: "*Be* the change you want to see in the world."

"Doing good" is an important part of TOMS' mission. But so is "doing well"—the company is very much a for-profit venture. At TOMS, the two missions go hand in hand. Beyond being socially admirable, the buy-one-give-one-away concept is also a good business proposition. To achieve social change, TOMS has to make money—lots of it. At the same time, the social mission gives customers a powerful reason to buy.

With all these "do good" and "do well" goals swirling in his head, Mycoskie returned home from his Argentina trip, hired an intern, and set about making 250 pairs of shoes in the loft of his Santa Monica, California, home. Stuffing the shoes into three duffel bags, he made the fledgling company's first of many "Shoe Drop" tours, returning to the Argentine village and giving one pair of shoes to each child. Mycoskie arrived back home to find an article about his project on the front page of the *Los Angeles Times* Calendar section. TOMS had been in business for only two weeks, but by that very afternoon, he had orders for 2,200 pairs of shoes on his Web site.

True to the company's one-for-one promise, Mycoskie undertook a second TOMS Shoe Drop tour. Consistent with his new title, "Chief Shoe Giver of TOMS Shoes," he led 15 employees and volunteers back to Argentina, where they went from school to school, village to village, and gave away another 10,000 pairs of shoes. "We [didn't] just drop the shoes off, as the name might imply," says Mycoskie. "We [placed] the shoes on each child's feet so that we [could] establish a connection, which is such an important part of our brand. We want to give the children the feeling of love, and warmth, and experience. But *we* also get those feelings as we give the shoes."

Today, TOMS Shoes is, in fact, both "doing good" *and* "doing well." TOMS has given away more than 10 million pairs of shoes in 59 countries. Under its one-for-one model, that means TOMS has also *sold* more than 10 million pairs of shoes, ringing up an estimated $300 million in annual revenues. Retailers such as Nordstroms, Neiman-Marcus, Urban Outfitters, Amazon.com, and even Whole Foods Market now offer TOMS shoes in locations across America. And the company just keeps growing. "Within the next 18 to 24 months, we expect we'll have given away 10 million more," says an optimistic Mycoskie. "I had no idea it would ever get this big."

TOMS' rapid growth is the result of purchases by caring customers who then tell the TOMS story to their friends. Although strongly represented on Facebook, Twitter, Pinterest, Instagram, YouTube, and other social media, TOMS spends almost nothing on traditional advertising and promotion. Instead, loyal TOMS disciples promote the brand with evangelical zeal. "Ultimately, it is our customers who drive our success," says Mycoskie. "Giving not only makes you feel good, but it actually is a very good business strategy, especially in this day and age. Your customers become your marketers."

Riding this success, TOMS and Mycoskie are now looking for even more ways to make the world a better place. Beyond the one-for-one shoes program (The Gift of Shoes), TOMS has already expanded its lines to include TOMS-branded eyewear and coffee. For each pair of TOMS glasses purchased, the company donates a free pair (The Gift of Sight); for each bag of TOMS coffee bought, the company donates a week of clean water to a person in need (The Gift of Water).

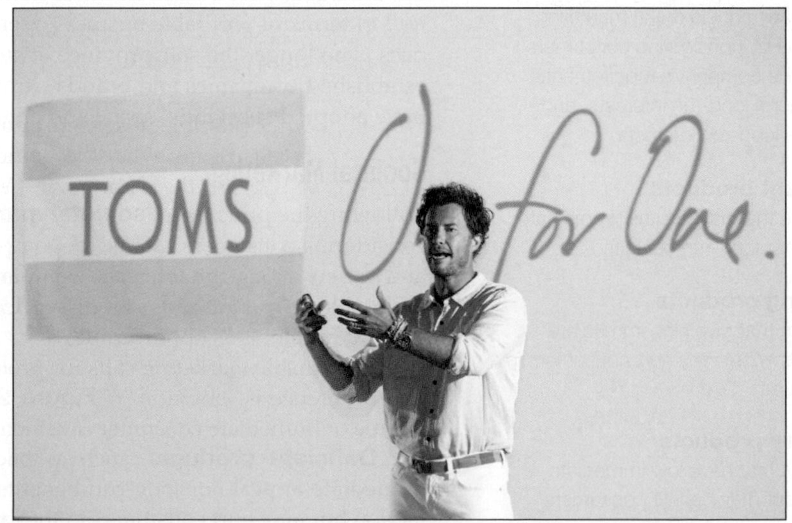

Founder Blake Mycoskie launched TOMS on a "one for one" model and a mission that seeks both company profits and to make the world a better place. At TOMS, "doing well" and "doing good" go hand in hand.

In fact, Mycoskie asserts, TOMS isn't just a shoe seller anymore—the company has even detached the word "Shoes" from its brand. Instead, he envisions TOMS as a lifestyle brand that sells many different products and uses the proceeds to fund social initiatives. "I want to show people that one-for-one is not just for the lifestyle-fashion space," Mycoskie says. "It can even be for everyday products."

How far might TOMS expand? Mycoskie isn't telling yet, but in addition to trademarking the term "One for One" for the shoe, eyewear, and coffee categories, TOMS has also sought to extend that trademark to a host of other beverages, from beer and mineral water to fruit drinks. And TOMS' parent company, Mycoskie LLC, has registered more than 200 Internet domain names, including tomswine.com, tomscreditcard.com, tickettogive.com, and tomsmortgage.com. Mycoskie even envisions a chain of TOMS café-stores where people can not only buy TOMS shoes, glasses, or a bag of whole bean coffee, they can order a coffee beverage Starbucks style.

All this sounds pretty far-reaching. But, Mycoskie explains, TOMS' target customers are already seeking ways to consume responsibly. They're shopping at farmers markets, buying organic food and clothing, giving up their birthdays to raise money for charity, and buying TOMS shoes. Through expansion, TOMS is "taking them along this path where they can integrate giving," says Mycoskie. Customers who buy TOMS products are buying into doing something positive with their consumer dollars. Confirms the head of retail marketing for TOMS, "We're about empowering people, inspiring people, helping them to see the life they could live differently."

More than affecting how consumers buy and see life, TOMS is also out to change the way companies do business. "I believe what we're doing is affecting the way businesses will be built for hundreds of years to come," says Mycoskie grandly. If the number of copycats is any indication, that change is already underway. Dozens of companies have now adopted the one-for-one model pioneered by TOMS, from Warby Parker (eyewear), KNO Clothing (clothes for the homeless), and LSTN (headphones for hearing restoration) to One World Futbol (soccer balls), Smile Squared (toothbrushes), Soapbox Soaps (bars of soap), and Open Happiness (baby outfits and blankets—"one to love, one to give").

"My thinking was that TOMS would show that entrepreneurs no longer had to choose between earning money or making a difference in the world," says Mycoskie. "Business and charity or public service don't have to be mutually exclusive. In fact, when they come together, they can be very powerful."

Sources: Stephanie Strom, "Turning Coffee into Water to Expand Business Model," *New York Times*, March 12, 2014, B3; Stacy Perman, "Making a Do-Gooder's Business Model Work," *BusinessWeek Online*, January 26, 2009, www.businessweek.com/smallbiz/content/jan2009/sb20090123_ 264702.htm; Cotton Timberlake, "Compassionate Consumerism Draws Copycats," *Businessweek*, August 2, 2012, www.businessweek.com/articles/2012-08-02/compassionate-consumerism-draws-copycats; Jeff Chu and Jessica Weiss, "The Cobbler's Conundrum," *Fast Company*, July/August 2013, pp. 98–112; Christopher Marquis and Andrew Park, "Inside the Buy-One Give-One Model," *Stanford Social Innovation Review*, Winter 2014, pp. 28–33; and www.toms.com/about-toms#companyInfo and www.toms.com/one-for-one-en, accessed September 2014.

However, having a *double bottom line* of values and profits isn't easy. Over the years, brands such as Ben & Jerry's, Timberland, The Body Shop, and Burt's Bees—all known and respected for putting "principles before profits"—have at times struggled with less-than-stellar financial returns. In recent years, however, a new generation of social entrepreneurs has emerged, well-trained business managers who know that to *do good*, they must first *do well* in terms of profitable business operations. Moreover, today, socially responsible business is no longer the sole province of small, socially conscious entrepreneurs. Many large, established companies and brands—from Walmart and Nike to Starbucks and PepsiCo—have adopted substantial social and environmental responsibility missions.

Societal marketing
A company should make marketing decisions by considering consumers' wants, the company's requirements, consumers' long-run interests, and society's long-run interests.

Deficient products
Products that have neither immediate appeal nor long-run benefits.

Pleasing products
Products that give high immediate satisfaction but may hurt consumers in the long run.

Salutary products
Products that have low immediate appeal but may benefit consumers in the long run.

Desirable products
Products that give both high immediate satisfaction and high long-run benefits.

Societal Marketing

Following the principle of **societal marketing**, a company makes marketing decisions by considering consumers' wants, the company's requirements, consumers' long-run interests, and society's long-run interests. Companies should be aware that neglecting consumer and societal long-run interests is a disservice to consumers and society. Alert companies view societal problems as opportunities.

Sustainable marketing calls for products that are not only pleasing but also beneficial. The difference is shown in **Figure 20.4**. Products can be classified according to their degree of immediate consumer satisfaction and long-run consumer benefit.

Deficient products, such as bad-tasting and ineffective medicine, have neither immediate appeal nor long-run benefits. **Pleasing products** give high immediate satisfaction but may hurt consumers in the long run. Examples include cigarettes and junk food. **Salutary products** have low immediate appeal but may benefit consumers in the long run, for instance, bicycle helmets or some insurance products. **Desirable products** give both high immediate satisfaction and high long-run benefits, such as a tasty *and* nutritious breakfast food.

vapur

Desirable products: Vapur Anti-Bottles' reusable, collapsible water bottles are highly functional and also more convenient, stylish, and environmentally friendly than either the disposable plastic bottles or rigid water bottles they replace.

Examples of desirable products abound. For example, Vapur makes a line of reusable, lightweight, collapsible water bottles that are highly functional and also more convenient, stylish, and environmentally friendly than either the disposable plastic bottles or rigid water bottles they replace. When full, pliable Vapur Anti-Bottles can be easily stuffed in pockets or backpacks; when empty, they can be rolled, folded, or flattened and easily tucked away. At the same time, the bottles require less energy to make and transport than rigid bottles, and unlike disposable plastic bottles, they don't clog landfills or require recycling. Vapur also donates portions of its sales to organizations such as Leave No Trace and The Conservation Alliance, and its Drops of Hope program annually donates thousands of Vapur bottles to charitable organizations around the world.[27]

Companies should try to turn all of their products into desirable products. The challenge posed by pleasing products is that they sell very well but may end up hurting the consumer. The product opportunity, therefore, is to add long-run benefits without reducing the product's pleasing qualities. The challenge posed by salutary products is to add some pleasing qualities so that they will become more desirable in consumers' minds.

For example, PepsiCo hired a team of "idealistic scientists," headed by a former director of the World Health Organization, to help the company create attractive new healthy product options while "making the bad stuff less bad." PepsiCo wants healthy products to be a $30 billion business for the company by 2020. The group of physicians, PhDs, and other health advocates, under the direction of PepsiCo's vice president for global health policy, looks for healthier ingredients that can go into multiple products as well as reductions of sugar, salt, and fat while maintaining the same flavor in its familiar products. For example, in 2011 Frito-Lay cut the salt in all of its potato chips by 25 percent. And, to help cut calories, it uses a zero-calorie sweetener, Pure Via, in its Tropicana Trop50 orange juice and Gatorade G2 brands. By 2012, PepsiCo's nutrition business revenue represented 20 percent of its annual net revenue, and 49 percent of its U.S. beverage volume came from juices, low- or zero-calorie drinks, and active hydration beverages.[28]

Marketing Ethics

Good ethics are a cornerstone of sustainable marketing. In the long run, unethical marketing harms customers and society as a whole. Further, it eventually damages a company's reputation and effectiveness, jeopardizing its very survival. Thus, the sustainable marketing goals of long-term consumer and business welfare can be achieved only through ethical marketing conduct.

Conscientious marketers face many moral dilemmas. The best thing to do is often unclear. Because not all managers have fine moral sensitivity, companies need to develop *corporate marketing ethics policies*—broad guidelines that everyone in the organization must follow. These policies should cover distributor relations, advertising standards, customer service, pricing, product development, and general ethical standards.

The finest guidelines cannot resolve all the difficult ethical situations the marketer faces. **Table 20.1** lists some difficult ethical issues marketers could face during their careers. If marketers choose immediate-sales-producing actions in all of these cases, their

FIGURE | 20.4
Societal Classification of Products

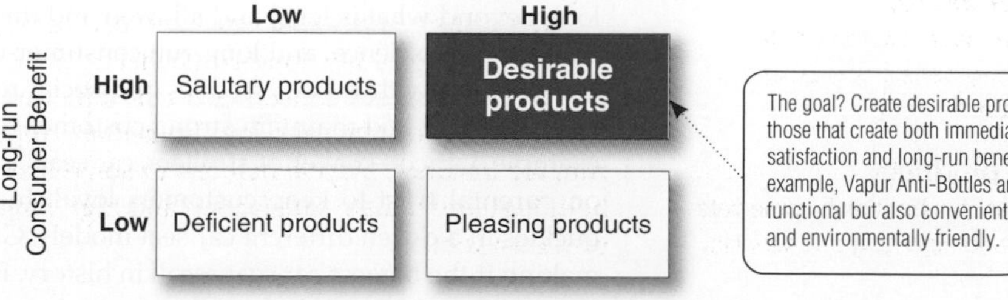
Immediate Satisfaction
Low
High
Long-run Consumer Benefit
High
Low
Salutary products
Desirable products
Deficient products
Pleasing products
The goal? Create desirable products–those that create both immediate customer satisfaction and long-run benefit. For example, Vapur Anti-Bottles are highly functional but also convenient, stylish, and environmentally friendly.

Table 20.1 | Some Morally Difficult Situations in Marketing

1. Your R&D department has slightly changed one of your company's products. It is not really "new and improved," but you know that putting this statement on the package and in advertising will increase sales. What would you do?
2. You have been asked to add a stripped-down model to your line that could be advertised to pull customers into the store. The product won't be very good, but salespeople will be able to switch buyers who come into the store up to higher-priced units. You are asked to give the green light for the stripped-down version. What would you do?
3. You are thinking of hiring a product manager who has just left a competitor's company. She would be more than happy to tell you all the competitor's plans for the coming year. What would you do?
4. One of your top dealers in an important territory recently has had family troubles, and his sales have slipped. It looks like it will take him a while to straighten out his family troubles. Meanwhile, you are losing many sales. Legally, on performance grounds, you can terminate the dealer's franchise and replace him. What would you do?
5. You have a chance to win a big account in another country that will mean a lot to you and your company. The purchasing agent hints that a "gift" would influence the decision. Such gifts are common in that country, and some of your competitors will probably make one. What would you do?
6. You have heard that a competitor has a new product feature that will make a big difference in sales. The competitor will demonstrate the feature in a private dealer meeting at the annual trade show. You can easily send a snooper to this meeting to learn about the new feature. What would you do?
7. You have to choose between three advertising campaigns outlined by your agency. The first (a) is a soft-sell, honest, straight-information campaign. The second (b) uses sex-loaded emotional appeals and exaggerates the product's benefits. The third (c) involves a noisy, somewhat irritating commercial that is sure to gain audience attention. Pretests show that the campaigns are effective in the following order: c, b, and a. What would you do?
8. You are interviewing a capable female applicant for a job as salesperson. She is better qualified than the men who have been interviewed. Nevertheless, you know that in your industry some important customers prefer dealing with men, and you will lose some sales if you hire her. What would you do?

marketing behavior might well be described as immoral or even amoral. If they refuse to go along with *any* of the actions, they might be ineffective as marketing managers and unhappy because of the constant moral tension. Managers need a set of principles that will help them figure out the moral importance of each situation and decide how far they can go in good conscience.

But *what* principle should guide companies and marketing managers on issues of ethics and social responsibility? One philosophy is that the free market and the legal system should decide such issues. Under this principle, companies and their managers are not responsible for making moral judgments. Companies can in good conscience do whatever the market and legal systems allow.

However, history provides an endless list of examples of company actions that were legal but highly irresponsible. A second philosophy puts responsibility not on the system but in the hands of individual companies and managers. This more enlightened philosophy suggests that a company should have a social conscience. Companies and managers should apply high standards of ethics and morality when making corporate decisions, regardless of "what the system allows."

Each company and marketing manager must work out a philosophy of socially responsible and ethical behavior. Under the societal marketing concept, each manager must look beyond what is legal and allowed and develop standards based on personal integrity, corporate conscience, and long-run consumer welfare.

Dealing with issues of ethics and social responsibility in an open and forthright way helps to build and maintain strong customer relationships based on honesty and trust. For example, Graco—maker of strollers, car seats, and other children's products—relies heavily on parental trust to keep customers loyal. In early 2014, after receiving reports of stuck buckles in a dozen different car seat models, Graco quickly recalled some 3.8 million units, making it the biggest car seat recall in history. But the company didn't stop with the official recall. Instead, it swiftly launched a proactive campaign to alert parents of the problem, answer their questions, and give them detailed advice on what steps to take. Graco went live and interactive with specific information on the Graco Blog, YouTube, Twitter, Facebook, and a dedicated Web page. For example, customers who messaged Graco's Twitter account received prompt responses from Graco's twitterers about whether their car seat buckles were part of the recall, plus useful, one-on-one information about how to order and install repair kits. Graco's swift and responsible actions in this and other recall cases have drawn praise from both public policy advocates and customers. "I will ALWAYS continue to use Graco products," tweeted one customer, "thanks to the way this was handled."[29]

As with environmentalism, the issue of ethics presents special challenges for international marketers. Business standards and practices vary a great deal from one country to the next. For example, bribes and kickbacks are illegal for U.S. firms, and various treaties against bribery and corruption have been signed and ratified by more than 60 countries. Yet these are still standard business practices in many countries. The World Bank estimates that bribes totaling more than $1 trillion per year are paid out worldwide. One study showed that the most flagrant bribe-paying firms were from Indonesia, Mexico, China, and Russia. Other countries where corruption is common include Sierra Leone, Kenya, and Yemen. The least corrupt were companies from Australia, Denmark, Finland, and Japan.[30] The question arises as to whether a company must lower its ethical standards to compete effectively in countries with lower standards. The answer is no. Companies should make a commitment to a common set of shared standards worldwide.

Many industrial and professional associations have suggested codes of ethics, and many companies are now adopting their own codes. For example, the American Marketing Association, an international association of marketing managers and scholars, developed a code of ethics that calls on marketers to adopt the following ethical norms:[31]

- *Do no harm.* This means consciously avoiding harmful actions or omissions by embodying high ethical standards and adhering to all applicable laws and regulations in the choices we make.
- *Foster trust in the marketing system.* This means striving for good faith and fair dealing so as to contribute toward the efficacy of the exchange process as well as avoiding deception in product design, pricing, communication, and delivery or distribution.
- *Embrace ethical values.* This means building relationships and enhancing consumer confidence in the integrity of marketing by affirming these core values: honesty, responsibility, fairness, respect, transparency, and citizenship.

Companies are also developing programs to teach managers about important ethical issues and help them find the proper responses. They hold ethics workshops and seminars and create ethics committees. Furthermore, most major U.S. companies have appointed high-level ethics officers to champion ethical issues and help resolve ethics problems and concerns facing employees. And most companies have established their own codes of ethical conduct.

Google is a good example. Its official Google Code of Conduct is the mechanism by which the company puts its well-known "Don't be evil" motto into practice. The detailed code's core message is simple: Google employees (know inside as "Googlers") must earn users' faith and trust by holding themselves to the highest possible standards of ethical business conduct. The Google Code of Conduct is "about providing our users unbiased access to information, focusing on their needs, and giving them the best products and services that we can. But it's also about doing the right thing more generally—following the law, acting honorably, and treating each other with respect."

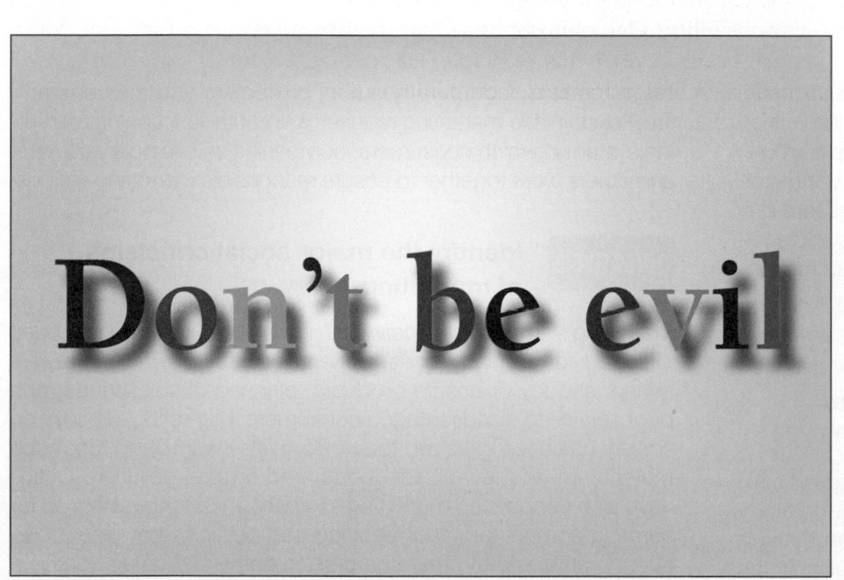

Marketing ethics: Google's Code of Conduct is the mechanism by which the company puts its well-known "Don't be evil" motto into practice.

Google requires all Googlers—from board members to the newest employee—to take personal responsibility for practicing both the spirit and letter of the code and encouraging other Googlers to do the same. It urges employees to report violations to their managers, to human resources representatives, or using an Ethics & Compliance hotline. "If you have a question or ever think that one of your fellow Googlers or the company as a whole may be falling short of our commitment, don't be silent," states the code. "We want—and need—to hear from you."[32]

Still, written codes and ethics programs do not ensure ethical behavior. Ethics and social responsibility require a total corporate commitment. They must be a component of the overall corporate culture. As the Google Code of Conduct concludes: "It's impossible to spell out every possible ethical scenario we might face. Instead, we rely on one another's good judgment to uphold a high standard of integrity for ourselves and our company. Remember . . . don't be evil. If you see something that isn't right, speak up!"

The Sustainable Company

At the foundation of marketing is the belief that companies that fulfill the needs and wants of customers will thrive. Companies that fail to meet customer needs or that intentionally or unintentionally harm customers, others in society, or future generations will decline.

Says one observer, "Sustainability is an emerging business megatrend, like electrification and mass production, that will profoundly affect companies' competitiveness and even their survival." Says another, "increasingly, companies and leaders will be assessed not only on immediate results but also on . . . the ultimate effects their actions have on societal wellbeing. This trend has been coming in small ways for years but now is surging. So pick up your recycled cup of fair-trade coffee, and get ready."[33]

Sustainable companies are those that create value for customers through socially, environmentally, and ethically responsible actions. Sustainable marketing goes beyond caring for the needs and wants of today's customers. It means having concern for tomorrow's customers in assuring the survival and success of the business, shareholders, employees, and the broader world in which they all live. It means pursuing the mission of a triple bottom line: people, planet, profits. Sustainable marketing provides the context in which companies can build profitable customer relationships by creating value *for* customers in order to capture value *from* customers in return—now and in the future.

20 Reviewing the Concepts

OBJECTIVES REVIEW AND KEY TERMS

Objectives Review

In this chapter, we addressed many of the important *sustainable marketing* concepts related to marketing's sweeping impact on individual consumers, other businesses, and society as a whole. Sustainable marketing requires socially, environmentally, and ethically responsible actions that bring value to not only present-day consumers and businesses but also future generations and society as a whole. Sustainable companies are those that act responsibly to create value for customers in order to capture value from customers in return—now and in the future.

OBJECTIVE 1 Define *sustainable marketing* and discuss its importance. *(pp 627–628)*

Sustainable marketing calls for meeting the present needs of consumers and businesses while preserving or enhancing the ability of future generations to meet their needs. Whereas the marketing concept recognizes that companies thrive by fulfilling the day-to-day needs of customers, sustainable marketing calls for socially and environmentally responsible actions that meet both the immediate and future needs of customers and the company. Truly sustainable marketing requires a smooth-functioning marketing system in which consumers, companies, public policy makers, and others work together to ensure responsible marketing actions.

OBJECTIVE 2 Identify the major social criticisms of marketing. *(pp 628–635)*

Marketing's *impact on individual consumer welfare* has been criticized for its high prices, deceptive practices, high-pressure selling, shoddy or unsafe products, planned obsolescence, and poor service to disadvantaged consumers. Marketing's *impact on society* has been criticized for creating false wants and too much materialism, too few social goods, and cultural pollution. Critics have also denounced marketing's *impact on other businesses* for harming competitors and reducing competition through acquisitions, practices that create barriers to entry, and unfair competitive marketing practices. Some of these concerns are justified; some are not.

OBJECTIVE 3 Define *consumerism* and *environmentalism* and explain how they affect marketing strategies. (pp 635–641)

Concerns about the marketing system have led to citizen action movements. *Consumerism* is an organized social movement intended to strengthen the rights and power of consumers relative to sellers. Alert marketers view it as an opportunity to serve consumers better by providing more consumer information, education, and protection. *Environmentalism* is an organized social movement seeking to minimize the harm done to the environment and quality of life by marketing practices. Most companies are now accepting responsibility for doing no environmental harm. They are adopting policies of *environmental sustainability*—developing strategies that both sustain the environment and produce profits for the company. Both consumerism and environmentalism are important components of sustainable marketing.

OBJECTIVE 4 Describe the principles of sustainable marketing. (pp 641–645)

Many companies originally resisted these social movements and laws, but most now recognize a need for positive consumer information, education, and protection. Under the sustainable marketing concept, a company's marketing should support the best long-run performance of the marketing system. It should be guided by five sustainable marketing principles: *consumer-oriented marketing*, *customer value marketing*, *innovative marketing*, *sense-of-mission marketing*, and *societal marketing*.

OBJECTIVE 5 Explain the role of ethics in marketing. (pp 645–648)

Increasingly, companies are responding to the need to provide company policies and guidelines to help their managers deal with questions of *marketing ethics*. Of course, even the best guidelines cannot resolve all the difficult ethical decisions that individuals and firms must make. But there are some principles from which marketers can choose. One principle states that the free market and the legal system should decide such issues. A second and more enlightened principle puts responsibility not on the system but in the hands of individual companies and managers. Each firm and marketing manager must work out a philosophy of socially responsible and ethical behavior. Under the sustainable marketing concept, managers must look beyond what is legal and allowable and develop standards based on personal integrity, corporate conscience, and long-term consumer welfare.

MyMarketingLab

Go to **mymktlab.com** to complete the problems marked with this icon .

Key Terms

OBJECTIVE 1

Sustainable marketing (p 627)

OBJECTIVE 3

Consumerism (p 635)
Environmentalism (p 636)
Environmental sustainability (p 637)

OBJECTIVE 4

Consumer-oriented marketing (p 641)
Customer value marketing (p 641)
Innovative marketing (p 642)
Sense-of-mission marketing (p 642)
Societal marketing (p 644)
Deficient products (p 644)
Pleasing products (p 644)
Salutary products (p 644)
Desirable products (p 644)

DISCUSSION AND CRITICAL THINKING

Discussion Questions

20-1 What is sustainable marketing? Explain how the sustainable marketing concept differs from the marketing concept and the societal marketing concept. (AACSB: Communication)

20-2 What is planned obsolescence? How do marketers respond to this criticism? (AACSB: Communication; Reflective Thinking)

20-3 How can marketing be criticized in terms of its negative impact on competitors and competition? (AACSB: Communication)

20-4 What is environmentalism? Why is this a starting point in terms of sustainability for businesses? (AACSB: Communication)

20-5 What are the five sustainable marketing principles, and how should companies be guided by them in their activities? (AACSB: Communication)

Critical Thinking Exercises

20-6 The chapter discusses McDonald's responses to social responsibility criticisms. Find other examples of how marketers have responded to social criticisms of their products or marketing practices. (AACSB: Communication; Reflective Thinking)

20-7 Deceptive advertising hurts consumers and competitors alike, and the Federal Trade Commission has stepped up efforts to combat this practice. Discuss a recent example of deceptive advertising investigated by the FTC and one investigated by the self-regulatory body, the National Advertising Division (NAD). (AACSB: Communication; Use of IT; Reflective Thinking)

20-8 In a small group, discuss each of the morally difficult situations in marketing presented in Table 20.1. Which ethics philosophy is guiding your decision in each situation? (AACSB: Communication; Ethical Reasoning)

MINICASES AND APPLICATIONS

Online, Mobile, and Social Media Marketing Teens and Social Media

Facebook recently announced that it will let teens' posts become public. Before the change, Facebook would only allow 13- to 17-year-old users' posts to be seen by their "friends" and "friends of friends." Now, however, their posts can be seen by anyone on the network if the teen chooses to make their posts "public." Twitter, another social medium gaining popularity with teens, has always let users, including teens, share tweets publicly. But because of Facebook's vast reach, privacy advocates are very concerned about this latest development, particularly when it comes to children's safety. Online predators and bullying are real safety issues facing youth. Other criticisms of Facebook's decision boil down to money—some argue that this is just about monetizing kids. Facebook will be able to offer a younger demographic to advertisers wanting to reach them. Facebook defends its actions, saying the change in policy is due to teenagers wanting the ability to post publicly, primarily for fundraising and promoting extracurricular activities such as sports and other school student organizations. Facebook has added precautions, such as a pop-up warning before teens can post publicly and making "seen only by friends" as the default that must be changed if the teen desires posts to be public.

20-9 Do you think Facebook is acting responsibly or merely trying to monetize kids as critics claim? (AACSB: Communication; Ethical Reasoning)

20-10 Come up with creative ways marketers can reach this demographic on Facebook without alienating their parents. (AACSB: Communication; Reflective Thinking)

Marketing Ethics Pricey Deal?

Kmart recently introduced a new Lease-to-Own program targeted to low-income consumers and is taking some heat over it. Rent-to-own is not new—chains such as Aaron's and Rent-A-Center have been around for years—but it is new that a mainstream retailer is moving into this market. Kmart's parent corporation, Sears Holdings Corporation, launched a similar program, and according to a company executive, it is satisfying the unmet needs of new customers. Some critics say that it is just encouraging instant gratification and exploiting disadvantaged consumers. These types of customers don't qualify for credit and don't have enough cash to purchase desired products outright, such as televisions and other big ticket items. However, a $300 TV purchased through Kmart's program ends up costing consumers $415 if purchased at the end of the lease. If customers just make minimum payments over the course of the lease, one expert calculated, that it is equivalent to charging a 117 percent annual interest rate. Sears' spokespeople defend their service as being better for consumers compared to other rent-to-own options because the retailer does not mark up the price of the product beyond the normal retail markup and limits the lease period to 18 months, whereas other national rental chains' prices are much higher and leases can run two to four years.

20-11 Are Sears and Kmart exploiting disadvantaged consumers? Explain why or why not. (AACSB: Communication; Ethical Reasoning)

20-12 Low-income consumers often don't have bank accounts and credit cards. Describe how some financial institutions are trying to meet the needs of these "unbanked" consumers. (AACSB: Communication; Reflective Thinking)

Marketing by the Numbers The Cost of Sustainability

Kroger, the country's leading grocery-only chain, added a line of private label organic and natural foods call Simple Truth to its stores. If you've priced organic foods, you know they are more expensive. For example, a dozen conventionally farmed Grade-A eggs at Kroger costs consumers $1.70, whereas Simple Truth eggs are priced at $3.50 per dozen. One study found that, overall, the average price of organic foods is 85 percent more than conventional foods. However, if prices get too high, consumers will not purchase the organic options. One element of sustainability is organic farming, which costs much more than conventional farming, and those higher costs are passed on to consumers. Suppose that a conventional egg farmer's average fixed costs per year for conventionally farmed eggs are $1 million per year, but an organic egg farmer's fixed costs are three times that amount. The organic farmer's variable costs of $1.80 per dozen are twice as much as a conventional farmer's variable costs. Refer to Appendix 2, Marketing by the Numbers, to answer the following questions.

20-13 Most large egg farmers sell eggs directly to retailers. Using Kroger's prices, what is the farmer's price per dozen to the retailer for conventional and organic eggs if Kroger's margin is 20 percent based on its retail price? (AACSB: Communication; Analytical Reasoning)

20-14 How many dozen eggs does a conventional farmer need to sell to break even? How many does an organic farmer need to sell to break even? (AACSB: Communication; Analytical Reasoning)

Video Case Life is good

Most companies these days are trying to figure out how they can be more socially responsible in the manufacturing and marketing of the goods and services they produce. But few companies produce goods and services with the primary purpose of making the world a better place. Life is good is one of those companies. Most people are familiar with the cheerful logo on Life is good products. But few are aware of what the company does with its profits behind the scenes.

This video focuses on Life is good Playmakers, a nonprofit organization dedicated to helping children overcome life-threatening challenges. From the time Life is good started selling T-shirts in the early 1990s, its founders supported Playmakers. The relationship between the two organizations progressively became stronger, ultimately leading Life is good to make Playmakers an official branch of the company.

After viewing the video featuring Life is good, answer the following questions:

20-15 Give as many examples as you can of how Life is good defies the common social criticisms of marketing.

20-16 Discuss how Life is good practices sustainable marketing principles.

20-17 With all its efforts to do *good*, can Life is good continue to do *well*? Explain.

Company Case Warby Parker: Eyewear with a Purpose

As young brothers in rural India, Toti and Omprakash Tewtia did everything together. They started a farming business together, and raised their families together. Between the two of them, they have 15 children. Now grandfathers, the Tewtia brothers have three generations living in their home, kids running about, playing and laughing. It's a lively scene.

As they grew old together, their vision began to decline. When the highlight of your day is reading to your grandchildren, this is more than just an inconvenience. Story time would end in headaches, and then stopped altogether when the brothers couldn't see well enough to read.

Poor vision was taking a toll on their business as well. For years, they had cultivated the land in their village, but the last crop had been lost. How on earth could career farmers, who have been working the land since childhood, have allowed this to happen? They couldn't see the insects that were ravaging their fields. Without proper glasses, their livelihood was put in jeopardy.

The Tewtia brothers live far away from an optical shop or an eye doctor. Although they had both been able to get reading glasses many years ago, they haven't been able to find new glasses as their prescriptions changed. All that changed when the folks from Warby Parker showed up. "We knew a good opportunity had come to us when we saw them drive into our village."

Now proudly sporting his new glasses, Toti looks in the mirror and sees a much younger man. "These glasses have taken me back to my young time!" Story time is again a nightly tradition for their grandkids. And with a healthy crop ready to harvest, they're on top of their game.

The story of the Tewtia brothers is the story of cause-related marketing based on one-to-one giving—a hot concept that has really taken off in the past decade. It's also the story of Warby Parker—one of the hottest start-ups in the fashion industry.

Doing Well by Selling Cheap

It all started when four classmates at the University of Pennsylvania's Wharton School hatched a winning plan. One day, they realized that they were all complaining about how ridiculously expensive prescription eyeglasses are. "We each had [the same] experience: Walking to an optical shop, getting super excited about a pair of glasses, and walking out feeling like we got punched in the stomach," relates Neil Blumenthal, one of the four co-founders of Warby Parker. "We thought, there's got to be a better way here."

That's when the four business school students started doing some research to answer a simple question: Why are prescription eyeglasses so expensive? They discovered a few key reasons. For starters, although there are many eyeglass retailers, the majority of the industry is owned and controlled by one company. The Luxottica Group of Italy owns brands such as Oakley and Ray-Ban and retail chains such as LensCrafters, Pearle Vision, and Sunglass Hut. Luxottica's stranglehold on the eyeglass industry keeps prices high. The team also discovered that all those fancy fashion brands (such as Armani, Ralph Lauren, Gucci) emblazoned on eyewear frames don't actually make the glasses. The brands are licensed to manufacturers (most of them owned by Luxottica) and get a fat cut just for lending their brand names.

So Blumenthal and his buddies set out to create a business plan that would bypass the standard manufacturers and channels and reinvent how you buy eyewear. The core focus of their strategy was price, with style taking a close second. "The markups in this industry are insane," notes Blumenthal, pointing out that most glasses are sold for at least three times their wholesale price. To come in at a low price, Warby Parker developed its own line of fashionable frames in-house, contracted the manufacturing, and opened up an online storefront to sell it all directly to customers. The price point: $95, including anti-glare polycarbonate lenses. That's one-third to one-sixth the price charged by major retailers. And Warby Parker sports some of the most fashionable designs around, all made from the same high-quality materials that the market leaders use.

Warby Parker opened its online shop in 2010. With almost no competitors selling glasses online, Warby Parker had a chance to really stand out. It made buying easy for customers with features such as virtual "try-ons," recommendations based on the shapes of a customer's face, home try-ons of up to five frames, and free shipping for purchases and returns. Thanks to some PR features in *GQ* and *Vogue*, the young start-up was inundated with purchases and requests for home try-ons. In fact, it had so many requests that it ran out of inventory and had a waitlist of 20,000 customers.

Without the brickspace to welcome would-be customers, co-founder David Gilboa had an idea. "We said, 'well, the store's my apartment. Come on over.'" So Gilboa and his buddies were soon hosting people from all over Philadelphia, the company's home base. With glasses laid out on the dining-room table, customers flowed in by the dozens, even hundreds. That experience really helped to solidify the company's ability to connect with customers and develop the type of customer service akin to customer service champs such as Amazon.com.

When Making a Profit Isn't Enough

Although the company's founders started with the objective of selling fashionable eyeglasses on the cheap, they quickly realized that they wanted to do more. They wanted to make a difference in people's lives on a more fundamental level. They found what they were seeking in a "one-for-one" concept pioneered by do-gooder company TOMS. For every pair of shoes TOMS sells, it donates a pair to a child in need, a child who otherwise would not have access to shoes. The Warby Parker crew quickly went to work figuring out if they could do something similar with eyewear.

They learned that almost one billion people worldwide lack access to glasses. Without good vision, people like the Tewtia brothers are not able to work or learn to their full potential. With demand established, Warby Parker looked into the feasibility of providing the supply. Although in business for only a short time, the company was not only breaking even at the $95 price point, it was making a nice margin. In fact, there were more than enough profits to cover the costs of donating a pair of glasses for every pair sold. By partnering with nonprofit organizations such as VisionSpring, Warby Parker could minimize the costs of finding people in need, determining their prescriptions, and distributing glasses to them.

What started as an afterthought quickly became Warby Parker's reason for doing business and one of its key selling points. The company calls it "buy a pair, give a pair" and has positioned the Warby Parker brand around the concept of doing good for others while getting really great products at prices much lower than customers might normally pay. "We believe that everyone has the right to see," states the Warby Parker Web site, noting that getting the correct glasses can add 20 percent to someone's income by increasing productivity and performance.

Warby Parker's one-for-one model is a bit different from the TOMS approach of taking its products out and delivering them to needy people in third-world countries. Instead, from the start, Warby Parker has worked closely with organizations such as VisionSpring to pioneer a new five-step plan:

1. *Buy.* Customers purchase a new pair of Warby Parker glasses.
2. *Give.* Warby Parker provides funding and/or glasses to nonprofit partners like VisionSpring.
3. *Train.* Warby Parker's nonprofit partners provide glasses and training to low-income entrepreneurs (especially women) in developing countries to start their own businesses selling glasses.
4. *Sell.* Local entrepreneurs sell affordable glasses, earning a livelihood while serving individuals in their communities who otherwise would not have access to glasses.
5. *Buy.* Individuals who previously couldn't afford glasses are able to purchase and wear the glasses they need to learn and work.

This model not only makes affordable glasses available to people who normally couldn't get them, it also provides jobs, creates businesses that stimulate local economies by continually providing a much-needed product, and empowers customers to make their own choices, avoiding the culture of dependence that accompanies most foreign assistance.

In three years, Warby Parker has been responsible for distributing more than 500,000 pairs of glasses throughout South America, South Asia, Africa, and even the United States. Warby Parker's model has touched the lives of people like Parmesh, a skilled carpenter in India whose business declined along with his eyesight. When VisionSpring rolled into his village, where there were no eye doctors, he signed up for a free eye exam and purchased a pair of glasses. Not only can he see better, but as he tells it, "I feel successful in these glasses. I think people respect me for the way I look in them." His business is once again booming.

Warby Parker's model is built around a snowball concept—helping one person has an impact on other people, who help even more people, and so on. Take the case of Juana, a 30-year-old mother who lives in Sololá, a mountainside village in Guatemala. From an early age, Juana was on her own and learned how to work hard and take care of herself. Recently, she received training from Community Enterprise Solutions, a nonprofit organization that helps distribute eyewear to people whose livelihoods have been compromised by poor vision. Now, in her tiny but well-organized and clean space, she offers free eye exams and sells eyeglasses, right alongside efficient wood stoves and water filters.

On the home front, Warby Parker is making it easier than ever for people of means to help others make a better life for themselves. The firm is rolling out its own Warby Parker stores and showrooms (a dozen so far)—third-place style outlets that are designed for hanging out as much as they are for trying on and buying glasses. So not only can shoppers try out glasses online or at home, they can do so in person at a growing number of brick-and-mortar showrooms.

Given the company's quick early success, it has no shortage of investors willing to provide the funds needed for expansion. The young company has become a model for merging online and real-world commerce. In fact, Warby Parker has become a reference point for dot.com success. Not long ago, Warby Parker was "the Netflix of eyeglasses." Not anymore. Today, e-commerce start-ups commonly brand themselves as "the Warby Parker of [fill in the blank]." This year, the company's fast growth earned it the number 17 spot on *Fast Company's* "50 Most Innovative Companies" list.

The aspirations of other start-ups extend beyond the financial aspects of e-commerce success. Plenty of companies now operate on a one-for-one business model—companies that have applied this model to clothing (Polarbearicana), socks and footwear (ToeSox), water purification products (Bottle Bright), soap (Hand In Hand), and pet beds (AlphaPooch), to name just a few. But among these do-good companies, Warby Parker is setting the bar very high. It not only gives a pair of glasses for every one purchased, its products are also cheaper—much cheaper—than competing goods, the opposite of most one-for-one operations. And Warby Parker's one-for-one model sets a standard not just for giving products away, but for genuinely empowering people to help themselves while helping others. With all this and comfortable profits to boot, it's more than rose-colored glasses making Warby Parker's future look bright.

Questions for Discussion

20-18 Discuss Warby Parker's business model in terms of the basic concept of sustainable marketing.

20-19 Give as many examples as you can for how Warby Parker defies the common social criticisms of marketing.

20-20 Of the five sustainable marketing principles discussed in the text, which one best describes Warby Parker's approach?

20-21 Analyze Warby Parker's business according to the Societal Classification of Products (Figure 20.4).

20-22 Would Warby Parker be more or less financially successful if it were not so focused on social responsibility? Explain.

Sources: Based on information from www.warbyparker.com and http://shopwithmeaning.org/warby-parker-glasses-stylish-buy-one-give-one-eyewear/, accessed June 2014. Also see Jason Feifer, "Warby Parker: For Being the Warby Parker of Warby Parkers," *Fast Company*, February 10, 2014, www.fastcompany.com/most-innovative-companies/2014/warby-parker; Drake Baer, "Why Warby Parker Invited 20,000 Customers to Their Apartment," *Fast Company*, May 10, 2013, www.fastcompany.com/3009501/bottom-line/why-warby-parker-invited-20000-customers-to-their-apartment.

MyMarketingLab

Go to **mymktlab.com** for the following Assisted-graded writing questions:

20-23 How can marketing practices create barriers to entry that potentially harm other firms? Are these barriers helpful or harmful to consumers? (AACSB: Communication; Reflective Thinking)

20-24 In a small group, discuss each of the morally difficult situations in marketing presented in Table 20.1. Which ethics philosophy is guiding your decision in each situation? (AACSB: Communication; Ethical Reasoning)

References

1. Based on information from Katherine Ling, "Walking the Talk," *Marketing News*, March 15, 2012, p. 24; Brain Dumaine, "Built to Last," *Fortune*, August 13, 2012, p. 16; Kyle Stock, "Patagonia's 'Buy Less' Plea Spurs More Buying," *Bloomberg Businessweek*, August 28, 2013, www.businessweek.com/printer/articles/147326-patagonias-buy-less-plea-spurs-more-buying; and www.patagonia.com/email/11/112811.html, www.patagonia.com/us/common-threads?src=112811_mt1, and www.patagonia.com/us/environmentalism, accessed September 2014.
2. See "McDonald's USA Continues Journey to Provide Guests with Nutrition-Minded Menu Offerings and Calorie Information," September 26, 2013, http://news.mcdonalds.com/US/news-stories/McDonalds-USA-2013-Nutrition-Progress-Report; "McDonald's USA Nutrition Journey," September 2013, http://news.mcdonalds.com/getattachment/06344ba3-94c0-4171-90ad-35f304142151, http://news.mcdonalds.com/getattachment/52eccdd6-baba-4d43-bbcf-d6c3166edd63, and www.mcdonalds.com/us/en/food/meal_bundles/favoritesunder400.html, accessed September 2014.
3. McDonald's financial information and other facts from www.aboutmcdonalds.com/mcd/investors.html and www.aboutmcdonalds.com/mcd, accessed September 2014.
4. Tony T Liu, "Overstock.com Receives $6.8 Million Fine for False Advertising," *Orange Country Business Attorney Blog,* February 11, 2014, www.orangecountybusinessattorneyblog.com/2014/02/11/overstock-com-receives-6-8-million-fine-false-advertising/.
5. See "Challenging Deceptive Advertising and Marketing," www.ftc.gov/reports/annual-report-standard/ftc-2013/challenging-deceptive-advertising-and-marketing, accessed November 2013; and Katy Bachman, "FTC Says 'No Way' to Nissan Frontier-Pushing Dune Buggy Ad," *Adweek,* January 23, 2014, www.adweek.com/print/155151.
6. Based on information from Ted Burnham, "Nutella Maker May Settle Deceptive Ad Lawsuit for $3 Million," NPR, April 26, 2012, www.npr.org/blogs/thesalt/2012/04/26/151454929/nutella-maker-may-settle-deceptive-ad-lawsuit-for-3-million; and https://nutellaclass-actionsettlement.com/, accessed July 2013.
7. See "Overweight and Obesity in the U.S.," *FRAC,* http://frac.org/initiatives/hunger-and-obesity/obesity-in-the-us/, accessed July 2014; and "Overweight and Obesity," Centers for Disease Control and Prevention, www.cdc.gov/obesity/data/index.html, accessed September 2014.
8. See Chris Dolmetsch, "New York Big-Soda Ban Rejected by State's Highest Court," *Bloomberg Businessweek,* June 26, 2014, www.businessweek.com/news/2014-06-26/new-york-big-soda-ban-rejected-by-state-s-highest-court; and "Pouring on the Pounds Ad Campaign," *NYC Health,* www.nyc.gov/html/doh/html/living/sugarydrink-media.shtml, accessed September 2014.
9. Elena Ferretti, "Soft Drinks Are the Whipping Boy of Anti-Obesity Campaigns," Fox News, June 1, 2012, www.foxnews.com/leisure/2012/06/01/soda-ban/. Also see Stephanie Strom, "In Ads, Coke

Confronts Soda's Link to Obesity," *New York Times*, January 14, 2013; and Natalie Zmuda and others, "Coca-Cola Would Like to Teach the World to Move," *Advertising Age*, September 11, 2013, http://adage.com/print/244077.

10. Brian Clark Howard, "Planned Obsolescence: 8 Products Designed to Fail," *Popular Mechanics*, www.popularmechanics.com/technology/planned-obsolescence-460210#slide-5, accessed September 2014.

11. See "Law Targets Obsolete Products," April 22, 2013, *The Connexion*, www.connexionfrance.com/Planned-obsolescence-obsolete-products-iPod-washing-machine-printers-14655-view-article.html.

12. Rob Walker, "Replacement Therapy," *Atlantic Monthly*, September 2011, p. 38.

13. See Spence Cooper, "National Food Chains Join First Lady to Reach 'Food Deserts,'" *Friends Eat*, July 25, 2011, http://blog.friendseat.com/michelle-obama-program-reaches-food-deserts; "Whole Foods Takes the High, Low (Priced) Roads," *Adweek*, June 3, 2013, pp. 10–11; Matt Lerner, "Do You Live in a Food Desert?" *Walk Score*, March 26, 2014, http://blog.walkscore.com/2014/03/best-and-worst-u-s-food-deserts/; and U.S. Department of Agriculture, "Creating Access to Healthy, Affordable Food," http://apps.ams.usda.gov/fooddeserts, accessed September 2014.

14. See "The Story of Stuff," www.storyofstuff.com, accessed September 2014.

15. See www.newdream.org/, www.newdream.org/about/mission, and www.newdream.org/blog/more-fun-less-stuff-photos, accessed July 2014.

16. See www.marksandspencer.com/s/plan-a-shwopping, accessed September 2014.

17. See Texas Transportation Institute, "Inconsistent Traffic Conditions Forcing Texas Commuters to Allow Even More Extra Time," http://d2dtl5nnlpfr0r.cloudfront.net/tti.tamu.edu/documents/tti-umr.pdf, accessed September 2014.

18. See Michael Cabanatuan, "Tolls Thin Traffic in Bay Bridge Carpool Lanes," *San Francisco Chronicle*, November 7, 2011, www.sfgate.com/news/article/Tolls-thin-traffic-in-Bay-Bridge-carpool-lanes-2323670.php#photo-1829296; and http://bata.mtc.ca.gov/tolls/schedule.htm, accessed September 2014.

19. See "Walmart Launches National Advertising Campaign to Show 'The Real Walmart,'" May 4, 2013, http://news.walmart.com/news-archive/2013/05/04/walmart-launches-national-advertising-campaign-to-show-the-real-walmart; and www.walmart.com/cp/PI-4-Prescriptions/1078664, accessed September 2014.

20. See Philip Kotler, "Reinventing Marketing to Manage the Environmental Imperative," *Journal of Marketing*, July 2011, pp. 132–135; and Kai Ryssdal, "Unilever CEO: For Sustainable Business, Go against 'Mindless Consumption,'" *Marketplace*, June 11, 2013, www.marketplace.org/topics/sustainability/consumed/unilever-ceo-paul-polman-sustainble-business.

21. See Matt Townsend, "Is Nike's Flyknit the Swoosh of the Future?" *Bloomberg Businessweek*, March 19, 2012, pp. 31–32; and "SC Johnson Integrity," www.scjohnson.com/en/commitment/overview.aspx, accessed September 2014.

22. See Alan S. Brown, "The Many Shades of Green," *Mechanical Engineering*, January 2009, http://memagazine.asme.org/Articles/2009/January/Many_Shades_Green.cfm; and www-03.ibm.com/financing/us/recovery/, accessed September 2014.

23. Based on information from Simon Houpt, "Beyond the Bottle: Coke Trumpets Its Green Initiatives," *The Globe and Mail (Toronto)*, January 13, 2011; Marc Gunther, "Coca-Cola's Green Crusader," *Fortune*, April 28, 2008, p. 150; "Coca-Cola Installs 1 Millionth HFC-Free Cooler Globally, Preventing 5.25MM Metric Tons of CO2," January 22, 2014, www.coca-colacompany.com/press-center/press-releases/coca-cola-installs-1-millionth-hfc-free-cooler-globally-preventing-525mm-metrics-tons-of-co2; "Position Statement on Climate Protection," January 1, 2012, www.coca-colacompany.com/stories/position-statement-on-climate-protection; and www.coca-cola.com/content-store/en_US/SC/PlantBottle/, accessed September 2014.

24. Based on information from "Walmart Convenes Key Partners at First-ever Sustainable Product Expo to Accelerate Supply Chain Innovation," April 29, 2014, http://news.walmart.com/news-archive/2014/04/29/walmart-convenes-key-partners-at-first-ever-sustainable-product-expo-to-accelerate-supply-chain-innovation; "Walmart," *Fast Company*, March 2010, p. 66; Jack Neff, "Why Walmart Has More Green Clout Than Anyone," *Advertising Age*, October 15, 2007, p. 1; Denise Lee Yohn, "A Big, Green, Reluctant Hug for Retailing's 800-lb. Gorilla," *Brandweek*, May 5, 2008, p. 61; "Green Logistics the Walmart Way," *Inbound Logistics*, June 2013, www.inboundlogistics.com/cms/article/green-logistics-the-walmart-way/; and http://walmartstores.com/sustainability/ and www.walmartsustainabilityhub.com/, accessed September 2014.

25. See Austin Carr, "Nike: The No. 1 Most Innovative Company of 2013," *Fast Company*, March 2013, www.fastcompany.com/most-innovative-companies/2013/nike; and Haydn Shaughnessy, "The World's Most Innovative Companies, A New View," *Forbes*, January 13, 2014, www.forbes.com/sites/haydnshaughnessy/2014/01/13/a-new-way-of-looking-at-the-worlds-most-innovative-companies/.

26. Information from Eleftheria Parpis, "Must Love Dogs," *Adweek*, February 18, 2008, www.adweek.com; and www.pedigree.com and www.mars.com/global/brands/petcare.aspx accessed September 2014.

27. See http://vapur.us/about-vapur and http://vapur.us/cause, accessed September 2014. Vapur® and Anti-Bottle® are registered trademarks of Vapur, Inc.

28. Nanette Byrnes, "Pepsi Brings in the Health Police," *Bloomberg Businessweek*, January 25, 2010, pp. 50–51; Mike Esterl, "You Put What in This Chip?" *Wall Street Journal*, March 24, 2011, p. D1; and www.pepsico.com/Purpose/Human-Sustainability/Product-Choices, accessed September 2014.

29. Example based on information from "5 Things Parents Should Know about Graco's Car Seat Recall," *Consumer Reports*, April 17, 2014, www.consumerreports.org/cro/news/2014/02/5-things-parents-should-know-about-graco-s-car-seat-recall/index.htm; and Jayne O'Donnell, "Millions of Graco Child (but Not Infant) Seats Recalled," *USA Today*, February 11, 2014, www.usatoday.com/story/money/business/2014/02/11/graco-recall/5396939/.

30. See Transparency International, "Bribe Payers Index 2011," http://bpi.transparency.org/bpi2011; and "Global Corruption Barometer 2013," www.transparency.org/gcb2013. Also see Michael Montgomery, "The Cost of Corruption," American RadioWorks, http://americanradioworks.publicradio.org/features/corruption/, accessed September 2014.

31. See www.marketingpower.com/AboutAMA/Pages/Statement%20of%20Ethics.aspx, accessed September 2014.

32. See http://investor.google.com/corporate/code-of-conduct.html#toc-VIII, accessed September 2014.

33. David A. Lubin and Daniel C. Esty, "The Sustainability Imperative," *Harvard Business Review*, May 2010, pp. 41–50; and Roasbeth Moss Kanter, "It's Time to Take Full Responsibility," *Harvard Business Review*, October 2010, p. 42.

APPENDIX 1 MARKETING PLAN

The Marketing Plan: An Introduction

As a marketer, you will need a good marketing plan to provide direction and focus for your brand, product, or company. With a detailed plan, any business will be better prepared to launch a new product or build sales for existing products. Nonprofit organizations also use marketing plans to guide their fundraising and outreach efforts. Even government agencies put together marketing plans for initiatives such as building public awareness of proper nutrition and stimulating area tourism.

The Purpose and Content of a Marketing Plan

Unlike a business plan, which offers a broad overview of the entire organization's mission, objectives, strategy, and resource allocation, a marketing plan has a more limited scope. It serves to document how the organization's strategic objectives will be achieved through specific marketing strategies and tactics, with the customer as the starting point. It is also linked to the plans of other departments within the organization. Suppose, for example, a marketing plan calls for selling 200,000 units annually. The production department must gear up to make that many units, the finance department must arrange funding to cover the expenses, the human resources department must be ready to hire and train staff, and so on. Without the appropriate level of organizational support and resources, no marketing plan can succeed.

Although the exact length and layout will vary from company to company, a marketing plan usually contains the sections described in Chapter 2. Smaller businesses may create shorter or less formal marketing plans, whereas corporations frequently require highly structured marketing plans. To guide implementation effectively, every part of the plan must be described in considerable detail. Sometimes a company will post its marketing plans on an intranet site, which allows managers and employees in different locations to consult specific sections and collaborate on additions or changes.

The Role of Research

Marketing plans are not created in a vacuum. To develop successful strategies and action programs, marketers need up-to-date information about the environment, the competition, and the market segments to be served. Often, analysis of internal data is the starting point for assessing the current marketing situation, supplemented by marketing intelligence and research investigating the overall market, the competition, key issues, and threats and opportunities. As the plan is put into effect, marketers use a variety of research techniques to measure progress toward objectives and identify areas for improvement if results fall short of projections.

Finally, marketing research helps marketers learn more about their customers' requirements, expectations, perceptions, and satisfaction levels. This deeper understanding provides a foundation for building competitive advantage through well-informed segmenting, targeting, differentiating, and positioning decisions. Thus, the marketing plan should outline what marketing research will be conducted and how the findings will be applied.

The Role of Relationships

The marketing plan shows how the company will establish and maintain profitable customer relationships. In the process, however, it also shapes a number of internal and external relationships. First, it affects how marketing personnel work with each other and with other departments to deliver value and satisfy customers. Second, it affects how the company works with suppliers, distributors, and strategic alliance partners to achieve the objectives listed in the plan. Third, it influences the company's dealings with other stakeholders, including government regulators, the media, and the community at large. All of these relationships are important to the organization's success, so they should be considered when a marketing plan is being developed.

From Marketing Plan to Marketing Action

Companies generally create yearly marketing plans, although some plans cover a longer period. Marketers start planning well in advance of the implementation date to allow time for marketing research, thorough analysis, management review, and coordination between departments. Then, after each action program begins, marketers monitor ongoing results, compare them with projections, analyze any differences, and take corrective steps as needed. Some marketers also prepare contingency plans for implementation if certain conditions emerge. Because of inevitable and sometimes unpredictable environmental changes, marketers must be ready to update and adapt marketing plans at any time.

For effective implementation and control, the marketing plan should define how progress toward objectives will be measured. Managers typically use budgets, schedules, and performance standards for monitoring and evaluating results. With budgets, they can compare planned expenditures with actual expenditures for a given week, month, or other period. Schedules allow management to see when tasks were supposed to be completed—and when they were actually completed. Performance standards track the outcomes of marketing programs to see whether the company is moving toward its objectives. Some examples of performance standards are market share, sales volume, product profitability, and customer satisfaction.

Sample Marketing Plan: Chill Beverage Company

Executive Summary

The Chill Beverage Company is preparing to launch a new line of vitamin-enhanced water called NutriWater. Although the bottled water market is maturing, the vitamin-enhanced water category is still growing. NutriWater will be positioned by the slogan "Expect more"—indicating that the brand offers more in the way of desirable product features and benefits at a competitive price. Chill Beverage is taking advantage of its existing experience and brand equity among its loyal current customer base of Millennials who consume its Chill Soda soft drink. NutriWater will target similar Millennials who are maturing and looking for an alternative to soft drinks and high-calorie sugared beverages.

The primary marketing objective is to achieve first-year U.S. sales of $35 million, roughly 2 percent of the enhanced water market. Based on this market share goal, the company expects to sell more than 20 million units the first year and break even in the final period of the year.

Current Marketing Situation

Founded in 2005, the Chill Beverage Company found success primarily by distributing niche and emerging products in the beverage industry. Its Chill Soda soft drink brand hit the market with six unique flavors in glass bottles. A few years later, the Chill Soda brand introduced an energy drink as well as a line of natural juice drinks. The company now markets dozens of Chill Soda flavors, many unique to the brand. Chill Beverage has grown its business every year since it was founded. In the most recent year, it achieved $185 million in revenue and net profits of $14.5 million. As part of its future growth strategy, Chill Beverage is currently preparing to enter a new beverage category with a line of vitamin-enhanced waters.

As a beverage category, bottled water experienced tremendous growth during the 1990s and 2000s. Currently, the average person in the United States consumes more than 31 gallons of bottled water every year, a number that has increased 20-fold in just 30 years. Bottled water consumption is second only to soft drink consumption, ahead of milk, beer, and coffee. Although bottled water growth has tapered off somewhat in recent years, it is still moderately strong at 3 to 4 percent growth annually. Most other beverage categories have experienced declines. In the most recent year, 10.1 billion gallons of bottled water were sold in the United States with a value of approximately $12.3 billion.

Competition is more intense now than ever as demand slows, industry consolidation continues, and new types of bottled water emerge. The U.S. market is dominated by three global corporations. With a portfolio of 12 brands (including Poland Spring, Nestlé Pure Life, and Arrowhead), Nestlé leads the market for "plain" bottled water. However, when all subcategories of bottled water are included (enhanced water, flavored water, and so on), Coca-Cola leads the U.S. market with a 22.9 percent share. Nestlé markets only plain waters but is number two at 21.5 percent of the total bottled water market. PepsiCo is third with 16.2 percent of the market. To demonstrate the strength of the vitamin-enhanced water segment, Coca-Cola's Vitaminwater is the fourth-largest bottled water brand, behind plain water brands Nestlé Pure Life, Coca-Cola's Dasani, and Pepsi's Aquafina.

To break into this market, dominated by huge global corporations and littered with dozens of other small players, Chill Beverage must carefully target specific segments with features and benefits valued by those segments.

Market Description

The bottled water market consists of many different types of water. Varieties of plain water include spring, purified, mineral, and distilled. Although these different types of water are sold as consumer products, they also serve as the core ingredient for other types of bottled waters including enhanced water, flavored water, sparkling water, or any combination of those categories.

Although some consumers may not perceive much of a difference between brands, others are drawn to specific product features and benefits provided by different brands. For example, some consumers may perceive spring water as healthier than other types of water. Some may look for water that is optimized for hydration. Others seek additional nutritional benefits claimed by bottlers that enhance their brands with vitamins, minerals, herbs, and other additives. Still other consumers make selections based on flavor. The industry as a whole has positioned bottled water of all kinds as a low-calorie, healthy alternative to soft drinks, sports drinks, energy drinks, and other types of beverages.

Bottled water brands also distinguish themselves by size and type of container, multipacks, and refrigeration at point-of-sale. Chill Beverage's market for NutriWater consists of consumers of single-serving-sized bottled beverages who are looking for a healthy yet flavorful alternative. "Healthy" in this context means both low-calorie and enhanced nutritional content. This market includes traditional soft drink consumers who want to improve their health as well as non-soft drink consumers who want an option other than plain bottled water. Specific segments that Chill Beverage will target during the first year include athletes, the health conscious, the socially responsible, and Millennials who favor independent corporations. The Chill Soda brand has established a strong base of loyal customers, primarily among Millennials. This generational segment is becoming a prime target as it matures and seeks alternatives to full-calorie soft drinks. **Table A1.1** shows how NutriWater addresses the needs of targeted consumer segments.

Product Review

Chill Beverage's new line of vitamin-enhanced water—called NutriWater—offers the following features:

- Six new-age flavors: Peach Mango, Berry Pomegranate, Kiwi Dragonfruit, Mandarin Orange, Blueberry Grape, and Key Lime.
- Single-serving size, 20-ounce, PET recyclable bottles.
- Formulated for wellness, replenishment, and optimum energy.
- Full Recommended Daily Allowance (RDA) of essential vitamins and minerals (including electrolytes).
- Higher vitamin concentration—vitamin levels are two to ten times higher than market-leading products, with more vitamins and minerals than any other brand.
- Additional vitamins—vitamins include A, E, and B2, as well as folic acid—none of which are contained in the market-leading products.
- All natural—no artificial flavors, colors, or preservatives.
- Sweetened with pure cane sugar and Stevia, a natural zero-calorie sweetener.
- Twenty-five cents from each purchase will be donated to Vitamin Angels, a nonprofit organization with a mission to prevent vitamin deficiency in at-risk children.

Competitive Review

As sales of bottled waters entered a strong growth phase in the 1990s, the category began to expand. In addition to the various types of plain water, new categories emerged. These

Table A1.1 | Segment Needs and Corresponding Features/Benefits of NutriWater

Targeted Segment	Customer Need	Corresponding Features/Benefits
Athletes	• Hydration and replenishment of essential minerals • Energy to maximize performance	• Electrolytes and carbohydrates • B vitamins, carbohydrates
Health conscious	• Maintain optimum weight • Optimize nutrition levels • Avoid harmful chemicals and additives • Desire to consume a tastier beverage than water	• Half the calories of fully sugared beverages • Higher levels of vitamins A, B, C, E, Zinc, chromium, and folic acid than other products; vitamins unavailable in other products • All natural ingredients • Six new-age flavors
Socially conscious	• Support causes that help solve world's social problems	• 25 cent donation from each purchase to Vitamin Angels
Millennials	• Aversion to mass-media advertising/ technologically savvy • Counter-culture attitude • Diet enhancement due to fast-paced lifestyle	• Less-invasive online and social networking promotional tactics • Small, privately held company • Full RDA levels of essential vitamins and minerals

included flavored waters—such as Aquafina's Flavorsplash—as well as enhanced waters. Enhanced waters emerged to bridge the gap between soft drinks and waters, appealing to people who knew they should drink more water and less soft drinks but still wanted flavor. Development of brands for this product variation has occurred primarily in start-up and boutique beverage companies. In the 2000s, major beverage corporations acquired the most successful smaller brands, providing the bigger firms with a solid market position in this category and diversification in bottled waters in general. Currently, enhanced water sales account for approximately 18 percent of the total bottled water market.

The fragmentation of this category, combined with domination by the market leaders, has created a severely competitive environment. Although there is indirect competition posed by all types of bottled waters and even other types of beverages (soft drinks, energy drinks, juices, teas), this competitive analysis focuses on direct competition from enhanced water brands. For the purposes of this analysis, enhanced water is bottled water with additives that are intended to provide health and wellness benefits. The most common additives include vitamins, minerals (including electrolytes), and herbs. Most commonly, enhanced waters are sweetened, flavored, and colored. This definition distinguishes enhanced water from sports drinks that have the primary purpose of maximizing hydration by replenishing electrolytes.

Enhanced water brands are typically sweetened with a combination of some kind of sugar and a zero-calorie sweetener, resulting in about half the sugar content, carbohydrates, and calories of regular soft drinks and other sweetened beverages. The types of sweeteners used create a point of differentiation. Many brands, including the market leaders, sell both regular and zero-calorie varieties.

Pricing for this product is consistent across brands and varies by type of retail outlet, with convenience stores typically charging more than grocery stores. The price for a 20-ounce bottle ranges from $1.00 to $1.89, with some niche brands costing slightly more. Key competitors to Chill Beverage's NutriWater line include the following:

- *Vitaminwater.* Created in 2000 as a new product for Energy Brands' Glacéau, which was also the developer of Smartwater (distilled water with electrolytes). Coca-Cola purchased Energy Brands for $4.1 billion in 2007. Vitaminwater is sold in regular and zero-calorie versions. With 15 bottled varieties as well as availability in fountain form and drops, Vitaminwater offers more options than any brand on the market. Whereas Vitaminwater varieties are distinguished by flavor, they are named according to functional benefits such as Stur-D (healthy bones), Defense (strengthens immune system), Focus (mental clarity), and Restore (post workout recovery). The brand's current slogan is "Hydration for every occasion—morning, noon, and night." Vitaminwater is vapor distilled, de-ionized, and/or filtered and is sweetened with crystalline fructose (corn syrup) and erythritol all-natural sweetener. Together with Smartwater, Vitaminwater exceeds $1.1 billion in annual sales and commands 61 percent of the enhanced waters market.

- *SoBe Lifewater.* PepsiCo bought SoBe in 2000. SoBe introduced Lifewater in 2008 with a hit Super Bowl ad as an answer to Coca-Cola's Vitaminwater. The Lifewater line includes 15 regular and zero-calorie varieties. Each bottle of Lifewater is designated by flavor and one of six different functional categories: Electrolytes, Lean Machine, B-Energy, C-Boost, Antioxidants, and Pure. Each variety is infused with a formulation of vitamins, minerals, and herbs designed to provide the claimed benefit. The most recent line—Pure—contains only water, a hint of flavor, and electrolytes. Sweetened with a combination of sugar and erythritol, Lifewater makes the claim to be "all natural." It contains no artificial flavors or colors. However, some analysts debate the "natural" designation for erythritol. Lifewater is sold in 20-ounce PET bottles and multipacks as well as 1-liter PET bottles. With more than $200 million in annual revenues, Lifewater is the number two enhanced water brand.
- *Propel Zero.* Gatorade created Propel in 2000, just one year prior to PepsiCo's purchase of this leading sports drink marketer. Originally marketed and labeled as "fitness water," it is now available only as Propel Zero. Although the fitness water designation has been dropped, Propel Zero still leans toward that positioning with the label stating "REPLENISH + ENERGIZE + PROTECT." Propel Zero comes in seven flavors, each containing the same blend of B vitamins, vitamin C, vitamin E, antioxidants, and electrolytes. It is sweetened with sucralose. Propel Zero is available in a wider variety of sizes, with 16.9-, 20-, and 24-ounce PET bottles and multipacks. Propel Zero is also marketed in powder form and as a liquid enhancer to be added to bottled water. With $181 million in revenues, Propel Zero is the number three enhanced water brand with a 10 percent share of the enhanced waters market.
- *RESCUE Water.* The Arizona Beverage Company is best known as the number one producer of ready-to-drink bottled teas. However, it also bottles a variety of other beverages including smoothies, sports drinks, energy drinks, and juice blends. Its newest brand is RESCUE Water, introduced to the U.S. market in 2010. It sets itself apart from other enhanced waters with green tea extract added to a blend of vitamins and minerals. This provides a significant point of differentiation for those desiring green tea, but rules the brand out for the majority of customers who do not want it. It comes in five flavors, each with its own functional benefit. RESCUE Water touts other points of distinction as well, including branded Twinlab vitamins, all-natural ingredients, and a high-tech plastic bottle that resembles glass and maximizes freshness. Its Blueberry Coconut Hydrate variety contains real coconut water, an emerging alternative beverage category. Although RESCUE Water sales and market share figures are not yet known because of the product's newness, the Arizona Beverage Company is a multibillion dollar corporation with a long history of successful new product introductions.
- *Niche brands.* The market for enhanced waters includes at least four companies that market their wares on a small scale through independent retailers: Assure, Ex Aqua Vitamins, Ayala Herbal Water, and Skinny Water. Some brands feature exotic additives and/or artistic glass bottles.

Despite the strong competition, NutriWater believes it can create a relevant brand image and gain recognition among the targeted segments. The brand offers strong points of differentiation with higher and unique vitamin content, all-natural ingredients, and support for a relevant social cause. With other strategic assets, Chill Beverage is confident that it can establish a competitive advantage that will allow NutriWater to grow in the market. **Table A1.2** shows a sample of competing products.

Channels and Logistics Review

The purchase of Vitaminwater by Coca-Cola left a huge hole in the independent distributor system. NutriWater will be distributed through an independent distributor to a network of retailers in the United States. This strategy will avoid some of the head-on competition

Table A1.2 | Sample of Competitive Products

Competitor	Brand	Features
Coca-Cola	Vitaminwater	Regular and zero-calorie versions; 15 varieties; each flavor provides a different function based on blend of vitamins and minerals; vapor distilled, de-ionized, and/or filtered; sweetened with crystalline fructose and erythritol; 20-ounce single-serve or multi-pack, fountain, and drops.
PepsiCo	SoBe Lifewater	Regular and zero-calorie versions; 15 varieties; six different functional categories; vitamins, minerals, and herbs; Pure—mildly flavored, unsweetened water; sweetened with sugar and erythritol; "all natural"; 20-ounce single-serve and multi-packs as well as 1-liter bottles.
PepsiCo	Propel Zero	Zero-calorie only; seven flavors; fitness positioning based on "REPLENISH + ENERGIZE + PROTECT"; B vitamins, vitamin C, vitamin E, antioxidants, and electrolytes; sweetened with sucralose; 16.9-ounce, 20-ounce, and 24-ounce PET bottles and multipacks; powdered packets; liquid enhancer.
Arizona Beverage	RESCUE Water	Full calorie only; five flavors, each with its own blend of vitamins and minerals; green tea extract (caffeine included); only brand with coconut water; Twinlab branded vitamins; high-tech plastic bottle.

for shelf space with the Coca-Cola and PepsiCo brands and will also directly target likely NutriWater customers. As with the rollout of the core Chill Soda brand, this strategy will focus on placing coolers in retail locations that will exclusively hold NutriWater. These retailers include:

- *Grocery chains.* Regional grocery chains such as HyVee in the Midwest, Wegman's in the East, and WinCo in the West.
- *Health and natural food stores.* Chains such as Whole Foods, as well as local health food co-ops.
- *Fitness centers.* National fitness center chains such as 24 Hour Fitness, Gold's Gym, and other regional chains.

As the brand gains acceptance, channels will expand into larger grocery chains, convenience stores, and unique locations relevant to the target customer segment.

Strengths, Weaknesses, Opportunities, and Threat Analysis

NutriWater has several powerful strengths on which to build, but its major weakness is lack of brand awareness and image. Major opportunities include a growing market and consumer trends targeted by NutriWater's product traits. Threats include barriers to entry posed by limited retail space, as well as image issues for the bottled water industry. **Table A1.3** summarizes NutriWater's main strengths, weaknesses, opportunities, and threats.

Strengths

NutriWater can rely on the following important strengths:

1. *Superior quality.* NutriWater boasts the highest levels of added vitamins of any enhanced water, including full RDA levels of many vitamins. It is all natural with no artificial flavors, colors, or preservatives. It is sweetened with both pure cane sugar and the natural zero-calorie sweetener, Stevia.
2. *Expertise in alternative beverage marketing.* The Chill Soda brand went from nothing to a successful and rapidly growing soft drink brand with fiercely loyal customers in a matter of only one decade. This success was achieved by starting small and focusing on gaps in the marketplace.

Table A1.3 | NutriWater's Strengths, Weaknesses, Opportunities, and Threats

Strengths	Weaknesses
• Superior quality • Expertise in alternative beverage marketing • Social responsibility • Antiestablishment image	• Lack of brand awareness • Limited budget
Opportunities	**Threats**
• Growing market • Gap in the distribution network • Health trends • Antiestablishment image	• Limited shelf space • Image of enhanced waters • Environmental issues

3. *Social responsibility.* Every customer will have the added benefit of helping malnourished children throughout the world. Although the price of NutriWater is in line with other competitors, low promotional costs allow for the substantial charitable donation of 25 cents per bottle while maintaining profitability.
4. *Antiestablishment image.* The big brands have decent products and strong distribution relationships. But they also carry the image of the large, corporate establishments. Chill Beverage has achieved success with an underdog image while remaining privately held. Vitaminwater and SoBe were built on this same image, but both are now owned by major multinational corporations.

Weaknesses

1. *Lack of brand awareness.* As an entirely new brand, NutriWater will enter the market with limited or no brand awareness. The affiliation with Chill Soda will be kept at a minimum in order to prevent associations between NutriWater and soft drinks. This issue will be addressed through promotion and distribution strategies.
2. *Limited budget.* As a smaller company, Chill Beverage has much smaller funds available for promotional and research activities.

Opportunities

1. *Growing market.* Although growth in the overall market for bottled water has slowed to some extent, its current rate of growth in the 3 percent range is relatively strong among beverage categories. Of the top six beverage categories, soft drinks, beer, milk, and fruit drinks experienced declines. The growth for coffee was less than 1 percent. More important than the growth of bottled waters in general, the enhanced water category is experiencing growth in the high single and low double digits.
2. *Gap in the distribution network.* The market leaders distribute directly to retailers. This gives them an advantage in large national chains. However, no major enhanced water brands are currently being sold through independent distributors.
3. *Health trends.* Weight and nutrition continue to be issues for consumers in the United States. The country has the highest obesity rate for developed countries at 34 percent, with well over 60 percent of the population officially "overweight." Those numbers continue to rise. Additionally, Americans get 21 percent of their daily calories from beverages, a number that has tripled in the last three decades. Consumers still desire flavored beverages but look for lower calorie alternatives.
4. *Antiestablishment image.* Millennials (born between 1977 and 2000) maintain a higher aversion to mass marketing messages and global corporations than do Gen Xers and Baby Boomers.

Threats

1. *Limited shelf space.* Whereas competition is generally a threat for any type of product, competition in retail beverages is particularly high because of limited retail space. Carrying a new beverage product requires retailers to reduce shelf or cooler space already occupied by other brands.
2. *Image of enhanced waters.* The image of enhanced waters is currently in question as Coca-Cola recently fought a class-action lawsuit accusing it of violating FDA regulations by promoting the health benefits of Vitaminwater. The lawsuit exposed the number one bottled water brand as basically sugar water with minimal nutritional value.
3. *Environmental issues.* Environmental groups continue to educate the public on the environmental costs of bottled water, including landfill waste, carbon emissions from production and transportation, and harmful effects of chemicals in plastics.

Objectives and Issues

Chill Beverage has set aggressive but achievable objectives for NutriWater for the first and second years of market entry.

First-Year Objectives

During the initial year on the market, Chill Beverage aims for NutriWater to achieve a 2 percent share of the enhanced water market, or approximately $35 million in sales, with break-even achieved in the final period of the year. With an average retail price of $1.69, that equates with a sales goal of 20,710,059 bottles.

Second-Year Objectives

During the second year, Chill Beverage will unveil additional NutriWater flavors, including zero-calorie varieties. The second-year objective is to double sales from the first year, to $70 million.

Issues

In launching this new brand, the main issue is the ability to establish brand awareness and a meaningful brand image based on positioning that is relevant to target customer segments. Chill Beverage will invest in nontraditional means of promotion to accomplish these goals and to spark word-of-mouth. Establishing distributor and retailer relationships will also be critical in order to make the product available and provide point-of-purchase communications. Brand awareness and knowledge will be measured in order to adjust marketing efforts as necessary.

Marketing Strategy

NutriWater's marketing strategy will involve developing a "more for the same" positioning based on extra benefits for the price. The brand will also establish channel differentiation, as it will be available in locations where major competing brands are not. The primary target segment is Millennials. This segment is comprised of tweens (ages 10 to 12), teens (13 to 18), and young adults (19 to 33). NutriWater will focus specifically on the young adult market. Subsets of this generational segment include athletes, the health conscious, and the socially responsible.

Positioning

NutriWater will be positioned on an "Expect more" value proposition. This will allow for differentiating the brand based on product features (expect more vitamin content and all natural ingredients), desirable benefits (expect greater nutritional benefits), and values (do more for a social cause). Marketing will focus on conveying that NutriWater is more than just a beverage: It gives customers much more for their money in a variety of ways.

Product Strategy

NutriWater will be sold with all the features described in the Product Review section. As awareness takes hold and retail availability increases, more varieties will be made available.

A zero-calorie version will be added to the product line, providing a solid fit with the health benefits sought by consumers. Chill Beverage's considerable experience in brand-building will be applied as an integral part of the product strategy for NutriWater. All aspects of the marketing mix will be consistent with the brand.

Pricing

There is little price variation in the enhanced waters category, particularly among leading brands. For this reason, NutriWater will follow a competition-based pricing strategy. Given that NutriWater claims superior quality, it must be careful not to position itself as a lower-cost alternative. Manufacturers do not quote list prices on this type of beverage, and prices vary considerably based on type of retail outlet and whether or not the product is refrigerated. Regular prices for single 20-ounce bottles of competing products are as low as $1.00 in discount-retailer stores and as high as $1.89 in convenience stores. Because NutriWater will not be targeting discount retailers and convenience stores initially, this will allow Chill Beverage to set prices at the average to higher end of the range for similar products in the same outlets. For grocery chains, this should be approximately $1.49 per bottle, with that price rising to $1.89 at health food stores and fitness centers, where prices tend to be higher.

Distribution Strategy

Based on the information in the Channels and Logistics Review, NutriWater will employ a selective distribution strategy with well-known regional grocers, health and natural food stores, and fitness centers. This distribution strategy will be executed through a network of independent beverage distributors, as there are no other major brands of enhanced water following this strategy. Chill Beverage gained success for its core Chill Soda soft drink line using this method. It also placed coolers with the brand logo in truly unique venues such as skate, surf, and snowboarding shops; tattoo and piercing parlors; fashion stores; and music stores—places that would expose the brand to target customers. Then, the soft drink brand expanded by getting contracts with retailers such as Panera, Barnes & Noble, Target, and Starbucks. This same approach will be taken with NutriWater by starting small, then expanding into larger chains. NutriWater will not target all the same stores used originally by Chill Soda, as many of those outlets were unique to the positioning and target customer for the Chill Soda soft drink brand.

Marketing Communication Strategy

As with the core Chill Soda brand, the marketing communication strategy for NutriWater will not follow a strategy based on traditional mass-communication advertising. Initially, there will be no broadcast or print advertising. Promotional resources for NutriWater will focus on three areas:

- *Online and mobile marketing.* The typical target customer for NutriWater spends more time online than with traditional media channels. A core component for this strategy will be building Web and mobile brand sites and driving traffic to those sites by creating a presence on social networks, including Facebook, Google+, and Twitter. The NutriWater brand will also incorporate location-based services by Foursquare and Facebook to help drive traffic to retail locations. A mobile phone ad campaign will provide additional support to the online efforts.
- *Trade promotions.* Like the core Chill Soda brand, NutriWater's success will rely on relationships with retailers to create product availability. Primary incentives to retailers will include point-of-purchase displays, branded coolers, and volume incentives and contests. This push marketing strategy will combine with the other pull strategies.
- *Event marketing.* NutriWater will deploy teams in brand-labeled RVs to distribute product samples at events such as skiing and snowboarding competitions, golf tournaments, and concerts.

Marketing Research

To remain consistent with the online promotional approach, as well as using research methods that will effectively reach target customers, Chill Beverage will monitor online discussions via services such as Radian6. In this manner, the company will gauge customer perceptions of the brand, the products, and general satisfaction. For future development of the product and new distribution outlets, crowdsourcing methods will be utilized.

Action Programs

NutriWater will be introduced in February. The following are summaries of action programs that will be used during the first six months of the year to achieve the stated objectives.

January. Chill Beverage representatives will work with both independent distributors and retailers to educate them on the trade promotional campaign, incentives, and advantages for selling NutriWater. Representatives will also ensure that distributors and retailers are educated on product features and benefits as well as instructions for displaying point-of-purchase materials and coolers. The brand Web site and other sites such as Facebook will present teaser information about the product as well as availability dates and locations. Buzz will be enhanced by providing product samples to selected product reviewers, opinion leaders, influential bloggers, and celebrities.

February. On the date of availability, product coolers and point-of-purchase displays will be placed in retail locations. The full brand Web site and social network campaign will launch with full efforts on Facebook, Google+, and Twitter. This campaign will drive the "Expect more" slogan, as well as illustrate the ways that NutriWater delivers more than expected on product features, desirable benefits, and values by donating to Vitamin Angels and the social cause of battling vitamin deficiency in children.

March. To enhance the online and social marketing campaign, location-based services Foursquare and Facebook Places will be employed to drive traffic to retailers. Point-of-purchase displays and signage will be updated to support these efforts and to continue supporting retailers. The message of this campaign will focus on all aspects of "Expect more."

April. A mobile phone ad campaign will provide additional support, driving Web traffic to the brand Web site and social network sites, as well as driving traffic to retailers.

May. A trade sales contest will offer additional incentives and prizes to the distributors and retailers that sell the most NutriWater during a four-week period.

June. An event marketing campaign will mobilize a team of NutriWater representatives in NutriWater RVs to concerts and sports events. This will provide additional visibility for the brand as well as giving customers and potential customers the opportunity to sample products.

Budgets

Chill Beverage has set a first-year retail sales goal of $35 million with a projected average retail price of $1.69 per unit for a total of 20,710,059 units sold. With an average wholesale price of 85 cents per unit, this provides revenues of $17.6 million. Chill Beverage expects to break even during the final period of the first year. A break-even analysis assumes per-unit wholesale revenue of 85 cents per unit, a variable cost per unit of 14 cents, and estimated first-year fixed costs of $12,500,000. Based on these assumptions, the break-even calculation is:

$$\frac{\$12{,}500{,}000}{\$0.85/\text{unit} - \$0.14/\text{unit}} = 17{,}605{,}634$$

Controls

Chill Beverage is planning tight control measures to closely monitor product quality, brand awareness, brand image, and customer satisfaction. This will enable the company to react quickly in correcting any problems that may occur. Other early warning signals that will be monitored for signs of deviation from the plan include monthly sales (by segment and channel) and monthly expenses. Given the market's volatility, contingency plans are also in place to address fast-moving environmental changes such as shifting consumer preferences, new products, and new competition.

Sources: "Channel Check," *Bevnet*, June 2014, p. 18; "Channel Check," *Bevnet*, November/December 2013, p. 30; Chris Hogan, "Bottled Water Trends for 2014," *Food Manufacturing*, January/February 2014, p. 38; "Jeffrey Klineman, "Restoring an Icon," *Beverage Spectrum Magazine*, December 2010, pp. 16–18; Matt Casey, "Enhanced Options Divide a Category," *Beverage Spectrum Magazine*, December 2008, p. 74; and product and market information obtained from www.sobe.com, www.vitaminwater.com, www.nestle-waters.com, and www.drinkarizona.com, July 2014.

APPENDIX 2 MARKETING BY THE NUMBERS

Marketing managers are facing increased accountability for the financial implications of their actions. This appendix provides a basic introduction to measuring marketing financial performance. Such financial analysis guides marketers in making sound marketing decisions and in assessing the outcomes of those decisions.

The appendix is built around a hypothetical manufacturer of consumer electronics products—HD. The company is introducing a device that plays videos and television programming streamed over the Internet on multiple devices in a home, including high-definition televisions, tablets, and mobile phones. In this appendix, we will analyze the various decisions HD's marketing managers must make before and after the new-product launch.

The appendix is organized into *three sections*. The *first section* introduces pricing, break-even, and margin analysis assessments that will guide the introduction of HD's new product. The *second section* discusses demand estimates, the marketing budget, and marketing performance measures. It begins with a discussion of estimating market potential and company sales. It then introduces the marketing budget, as illustrated through a *pro forma* profit-and-loss statement followed by the actual profit-and-loss statement. Next, we discuss marketing performance measures, with a focus on helping marketing managers to better defend their decisions from a financial perspective. In the *third section,* we analyze the financial implications of various marketing tactics.

Each of the three sections ends with a set of quantitative exercises that provide you with an opportunity to apply the concepts you learned to situations beyond HD.

Pricing, Break-Even, and Margin Analysis

Pricing Considerations

Determining price is one of the most important marketing-mix decisions. The limiting factors are demand and costs. Demand factors, such as buyer-perceived value, set the price ceiling. The company's costs set the price floor. In between these two factors, marketers must consider competitors' prices and other factors such as reseller requirements, government regulations, and company objectives.

Most current competing Internet streaming products sell at retail prices between $100 and $500. We first consider HD's pricing decision from a cost perspective. Then, we consider consumer value, the competitive environment, and reseller requirements.

Determining Costs

Fixed costs
Costs that do not vary with production or sales level.

Variable costs
Costs that vary directly with the level of production.

Total costs
The sum of the fixed and variable costs for any given level of production.

Recall from Chapter 10 that there are different types of costs. **Fixed costs** do not vary with production or sales level and include costs such as rent, interest, depreciation, and clerical and management salaries. Regardless of the level of output, the company must pay these costs. Whereas total fixed costs remain constant as output increases, the fixed cost per unit (or average fixed cost) will decrease as output increases because the total fixed costs are spread across more units of output. **Variable costs** vary directly with the level of production and include costs related to the direct production of the product (such as costs of goods sold—COGS) and many of the marketing costs associated with selling it. Although these costs tend to be uniform for each unit produced, they are called variable because their total varies with the number of units produced. **Total costs** are the sum of the fixed and variable costs for any given level of production.

HD has invested $10 million in refurbishing an existing facility to manufacture the new video streaming product. Once production begins, the company estimates that it will incur fixed costs of $20 million per year. The variable cost to produce each device is estimated to be $125 and is expected to remain at that level for the output capacity of the facility.

Setting Price Based on Costs

Cost-plus pricing (or **markup pricing**)
A standard markup to the cost of the product.

HD starts with the cost-based approach to pricing discussed in Chapter 10. Recall that the simplest method, **cost-plus pricing** (or **markup pricing**), simply adds a standard markup to the cost of the product. To use this method, however, HD must specify expected unit sales so that total unit costs can be determined. Unit variable costs will remain constant regardless of the output, but *average unit fixed costs* will decrease as output increases.

To illustrate this method, suppose HD has fixed costs of $20 million, variable costs of $125 per unit, and expects unit sales of 1 million players. Thus, the cost per unit is given by:

$$\text{Unit cost} = \text{variable cost} + \frac{\text{fixed costs}}{\text{unit sales}} = \$125 + \frac{\$20{,}000{,}000}{1{,}000{,}000} = \$145$$

Relevant costs
Costs that will occur in the future and that will vary across the alternatives being considered.

Note that we do *not* include the initial investment of $10 million in the total fixed cost figure. It is not considered a fixed cost because it is not a *relevant* cost. **Relevant costs** are those that will occur in the future and that will vary across the alternatives being considered. HD's investment to refurbish the manufacturing facility was a one-time cost that will not reoccur in the future. Such past costs are *sunk costs* and should not be considered in future analyses.

Break-even price
The price at which total revenue equals total cost and profit is zero.

Also notice that if HD sells its product for $145, the price is equal to the total cost per unit. This is the **break-even price**—the price at which unit revenue (price) equals unit cost and profit is zero.

Suppose HD does not want to merely break even but rather wants to earn a 25% markup on sales. HD's markup price is:[1]

$$\text{Markup price} = \frac{\text{unit cost}}{(1 - \text{desired return on sales})} = \frac{\$145}{1 - .25} = \$193.33$$

This is the price at which HD would sell the product to resellers such as wholesalers or retailers to earn a 25% profit on sales.

Return on investment (ROI) pricing (or **target-return pricing**)
A cost-based pricing method that determines price based on a specified rate of return on investment.

Another approach HD could use is called **return on investment (ROI) pricing** (or **target-return pricing**). In this case, the company *would* consider the initial $10 million investment, but only to determine the dollar profit goal. Suppose the company wants a 30% return on its investment. The price necessary to satisfy this requirement can be determined by:

$$\text{ROI price} = \text{unit cost} + \frac{\text{ROI} \times \text{investment}}{\text{unit sales}} = \$145 + \frac{0.3 \times \$10{,}000{,}000}{1{,}000{,}000} = \$148$$

That is, if HD sells its product for $148, it will realize a 30% return on its initial investment of $10 million.

In these pricing calculations, unit cost is a function of the expected sales, which were estimated to be 1 million units. But what if actual sales were lower? Then the unit cost would be higher because the fixed costs would be spread over fewer units, and the realized percentage markup on sales or ROI would be lower. Alternatively, if sales are higher than the estimated 1 million units, unit cost would be lower than $145, so a lower price would produce the desired markup on sales or ROI. It's important to note that these cost-based pricing methods are *internally* focused and do not consider demand, competitors' prices, or reseller requirements. Because HD will be selling this product to consumers through wholesalers and retailers offering competing brands, the company must consider markup pricing from this perspective.

Setting Price Based on External Factors

Whereas costs determine the price floor, HD also must consider external factors when setting price. HD does not have the final say concerning the final price of its product to consumers—retailers do. So it must start with its suggested retail price and work back. In doing so, HD must consider the markups required by resellers that sell the product to consumers.

Markup
The difference between a company's selling price for a product and its cost to manufacture or purchase it.

In general, a dollar **markup** is the difference between a company's selling price for a product and its cost to manufacture or purchase it. For a retailer, then, the markup is the difference between the price it charges consumers and the cost the retailer must pay for the product. Thus, for any level of reseller:

$$\text{Dollar markup} = \text{selling price} - \text{cost}$$

Markups are usually expressed as a percentage, and there are two different ways to compute markups—on *cost* or on *selling price*:

$$\text{Markup percentage on cost} = \frac{\text{dollar markup}}{\text{cost}}$$

$$\text{Markup percentage on selling price} = \frac{\text{dollar markup}}{\text{selling price}}$$

To apply reseller margin analysis, HD must first set the suggested retail price and then work back to the price at which it must sell the product to a wholesaler. Suppose retailers expect a 30% margin and wholesalers want a 20% margin based on their respective selling prices. And suppose that HD sets a manufacturer's suggested retail price (MSRP) of $299.99 for its product.

HD selected the $299.99 MSRP because it is lower than most competitors' prices but is not so low that consumers might perceive it to be of poor quality. In addition, the company's research shows that it is below the threshold at which more consumers are willing to purchase the product. By using buyers' perceptions of value and not the seller's cost to determine the MSRP, HD is using **value-based pricing**. For simplicity, we will use an MSRP of $300 in further analyses.

Value-based pricing
Offering just the right combination of quality and good service at a fair price.

To determine the price HD will charge wholesalers, we must first subtract the retailer's margin from the retail price to determine the retailer's cost ($300 − ($300 × 0.30) = $210). The retailer's cost is the wholesaler's price, so HD next subtracts the wholesaler's margin ($210 − ($210 × 0.20) = $168). Thus, the **markup chain** representing the sequence of markups used by firms at each level in a channel for HD's new product is:

Markup chain
The sequence of markups used by firms at each level in a channel.

Suggested retail price:	$300
minus retail margin (30%):	– $90
Retailer's cost/wholesaler's price:	$210
minus wholesaler's margin (20%):	– $42
Wholesaler's cost/HD's price:	$168

By deducting the markups for each level in the markup chain, HD arrives at a price for the product to wholesalers of $168.

Break-Even and Margin Analysis

The previous analyses derived a value-based price of $168 for HD's product. Although this price is higher than the break-even price of $145 and covers costs, that price assumed a demand of 1 million units. But how many units and what level of dollar sales must HD achieve to break even at the $168 price? And what level of sales must be achieved to realize various profit goals? These questions can be answered through break-even and margin analysis.

Determining Break-Even Unit Volume and Dollar Sales

Based on an understanding of costs, consumer value, the competitive environment, and reseller requirements, HD has decided to set its price to wholesalers at $168. At that price, what sales level will be needed for HD to break even or make a profit on its product? **Break-even analysis** determines the unit volume and dollar sales needed to be profitable given a particular price and cost structure. At the break-even point, total revenue equals total costs and profit is zero. Above this point, the company will make a profit; below it, the company will lose money. HD can calculate break-even volume using the following formula:

Break-even analysis
Analysis to determine the unit volume and dollar sales needed to be profitable given a particular price and cost structure.

$$\text{Break-even volume} = \frac{\text{fixed costs}}{\text{price} - \text{unit variable cost}}$$

Unit contribution
The amount that each unit contributes to covering fixed costs—the difference between price and variable costs.

The denominator (price – unit variable cost) is called **unit contribution**. It represents the amount that each unit contributes to covering fixed costs. Break-even volume represents the level of output at which all (variable and fixed) costs are covered. In HD's case, break-even unit volume is:

$$\text{Break-even volume} = \frac{\text{fixed cost}}{\text{price} - \text{variable cost}} = \frac{\$20{,}000{,}000}{\$168 - \$125} = 465{,}116.2 \text{ units}$$

Thus, at the given cost and pricing structure, HD will break even at 465,117 units.

To determine the break-even dollar sales, simply multiply unit break-even volume by the selling price:

$$\text{BE sales} = \text{BE}_{\text{vol}} \times \text{price} = 465{,}117 \times \$168 = \$78{,}139{,}656$$

Contribution margin
The unit contribution divided by the selling price.

Another way to calculate dollar break-even sales is to use the percentage contribution margin (hereafter referred to as **contribution margin**), which is the unit contribution divided by the selling price:

$$\text{Contribution margin} = \frac{\text{price} - \text{variable cost}}{\text{price}} = \frac{\$168 - \$125}{\$168} = 0.256 \text{ or } 25.6\%$$

Then,

$$\text{Break-even sales} = \frac{\text{fixed costs}}{\text{contribution margin}} = \frac{\$20{,}000{,}000}{0.256} = \$78{,}125{,}000$$

Note that the difference between the two break-even sales calculations is due to rounding.

Such break-even analysis helps HD by showing the unit volume needed to cover costs. If production capacity cannot attain this level of output, then the company should not launch this product. However, the unit break-even volume is well within HD's capacity. Of course, the bigger question concerns whether HD can sell this volume at the $168 price. We'll address that issue a little later.

Understanding contribution margin is useful in other types of analyses as well, particularly if unit prices and unit variable costs are unknown or if a company (say, a retailer) sells many products at different prices and knows the percentage of total sales variable costs represent. Whereas unit contribution is the difference between unit price and unit variable costs, total contribution is the difference between total sales and total variable costs. The overall contribution margin can be calculated by:

$$\text{Contribution margin} = \frac{\text{total sales} - \text{total variable costs}}{\text{total sales}}$$

Regardless of the actual level of sales, if the company knows what percentage of sales is represented by variable costs, it can calculate contribution margin. For example, HD's unit variable cost is $125, or 74% of the selling price ($125 ÷ $168 = 0.74). That means for every $1 of sales revenue for HD, $0.74 represents variable costs, and the difference ($0.26) represents contribution to fixed costs. But even if the company doesn't know its unit price and unit variable cost, it can calculate the contribution margin from total sales and total variable costs or from knowledge of the total cost structure. It can set total sales equal to 100% regardless of the actual absolute amount and determine the contribution margin:

$$\text{Contribution margin} = \frac{100\% - 74\%}{100\%} = \frac{1 - 0.74}{1} = 1 - 0.74 = 0.26 \text{ or } 26\%$$

Note that this matches the percentage calculated from the unit price and unit variable cost information. This alternative calculation will be very useful later when analyzing various marketing decisions.

Determining "Break Even" for Profit Goals

Although it is useful to know the break-even point, most companies are more interested in making a profit. Assume HD would like to realize a $5 million profit in the first year. How many must it sell at the $168 price to cover fixed costs and produce this profit? To determine this, HD can simply add the profit figure to fixed costs and again divide by the unit contribution to determine unit sales:

$$\text{Unit volume} = \frac{\text{fixed cost} + \text{profit goal}}{\text{price} - \text{variable cost}} = \frac{\$20{,}000{,}000 + \$5{,}000{,}000}{\$168 - \$125} = 581{,}395.3 \text{ units}$$

Thus, to earn a $5 million profit, HD must sell 581,396 units. Multiply by the price to determine the dollar sales needed to achieve a $5 million profit:

$$\text{Dollar sales} = 581{,}396 \text{ units} \times \$168 = \$97{,}674{,}528$$

Or use the contribution margin:

$$\text{Sales} = \frac{\text{fixed cost} + \text{profit goal}}{\text{contribution margin}} = \frac{\$20{,}000{,}000 + \$5{,}000{,}000}{0.256} = \$97{,}656{,}250$$

Again, note that the difference between the two break-even sales calculations is due to rounding.

As we saw previously, a profit goal can also be stated as a return on investment goal. For example, recall that HD wants a 30% return on its $10 million investment. Thus, its absolute profit goal is $3 million ($10,000,000 × 0.30). This profit goal is treated the same way as in the previous example:[2]

$$\text{Unit volume} = \frac{\text{fixed cost} + \text{profit goal}}{\text{price} - \text{variable cost}} = \frac{\$20{,}000{,}000 + \$3{,}000{,}000}{\$168 - \$125} = 534{,}884 \text{ units}$$

$$\text{Dollar sales} = 534{,}884 \text{ units} \times \$168 = \$89{,}860{,}512$$

Or

$$\text{Dollar sales} = \frac{\text{fixed cost} + \text{profit goal}}{\text{contribution margin}} = \frac{\$20{,}000{,}000 + \$3{,}000{,}000}{0.256} = \$89{,}843{,}750$$

Finally, HD can express its profit goal as a percentage of sales, which we also saw in previous pricing analyses. Assume HD desires a 25% return on sales. To determine the unit and sales volume necessary to achieve this goal, the calculation is a little different from the previous two examples. In this case, we incorporate the profit goal into the unit contribution as an additional variable cost. Look at it this way: If 25% of each sale must go toward profits, that leaves only 75% of the selling price to cover fixed costs. Thus, the equation becomes:

$$\text{Unit volume} = \frac{\text{fixed cost}}{\text{price} - \text{variable cost} - (0.25 \times \text{price})} \text{ or } \frac{\text{fixed cost}}{(0.75 \times \text{price}) - \text{variable cost}}$$

So,

$$\text{Unit volume} = \frac{\$20{,}000{,}000}{(0.75 \times \$168) - \$125} = 20{,}000{,}000 \text{ units}$$

$$\text{Dollar sales necessary} = 20{,}000{,}000 \text{ units} \times \$168 = \$3{,}360{,}000{,}000$$

Thus, HD would need more than $3 billion in sales to realize a 25% return on sales given its current price and cost structure! Could it possibly achieve this level of sales? The major point is this: Although break-even analysis can be useful in determining the level of sales needed to cover costs or to achieve a stated profit goal, it does not tell the company whether it is *possible* to achieve that level of sales at the specified price. To address this issue, HD needs to estimate demand for this product.

Before moving on, however, let's stop here and practice applying the concepts covered so far. Now that you have seen pricing and break-even concepts in action as they relate to HD's new product, here are several exercises for you to apply what you have learned in other contexts.

Marketing by the Numbers Exercise Set One

Now that you've studied pricing, break-even, and margin analysis as they relate to HD's new-product launch, use the following exercises to apply these concepts in other contexts.

1.1. Elkins, a manufacturer of ice makers, realizes a cost of $250 for every unit it produces. Its total fixed costs equal $5 million. If the company manufactures 500,000 units, compute the following:

a. unit cost

b. markup price if the company desires a 10% return on sales

c. ROI price if the company desires a 25% return on an investment of $1 million

1.2. A gift shop owner purchases items to sell in her store. She purchases a chair for $125 and sells it for $275. Determine the following:
   a. dollar markup
   b. markup percentage on cost
   c. markup percentage on selling price

1.3. A consumer purchases a coffee maker from a retailer for $90. The retailer's markup is 30%, and the wholesaler's markup is 10%, both based on selling price. For what price does the manufacturer sell the product to the wholesaler?

1.4. A lawn mower manufacturer has a unit cost of $140 and wishes to achieve a margin of 30% based on selling price. If the manufacturer sells directly to a retailer who then adds a set margin of 40% based on selling price, determine the retail price charged to consumers.

1.5. Advanced Electronics manufactures DVDs and sells them directly to retailers, who typically sell them for $20. Retailers take a 40% margin based on the retail selling price. Advanced's cost information is as follows:

DVD package and disc	$2.50/DVD
Royalties	$2.25/DVD
Advertising and promotion	$500,000
Overhead	$200,000

Calculate the following:
   a. contribution per unit and contribution margin
   b. break-even volume in DVD units and dollars
   c. volume in DVD units and dollar sales necessary if Advanced's profit goal is 20% profit on sales
   d. net profit if 5 million DVDs are sold

Demand Estimates, the Marketing Budget, and Marketing Performance Measures

Market Potential and Sales Estimates

HD has now calculated the sales needed to break even and to attain various profit goals on its new product. However, the company needs more information regarding demand in order to assess the feasibility of attaining the needed sales levels. This information is also needed for production and other decisions. For example, production schedules need to be developed and marketing tactics need to be planned.

Total market demand
The total volume that would be bought by a defined consumer group in a defined geographic area in a defined time period in a defined marketing environment under a defined level and mix of industry marketing effort.

Market potential
The upper limit of market demand.

The **total market demand** for a product or service is the total volume that would be bought by a defined consumer group in a defined geographic area in a defined time period in a defined marketing environment under a defined level and mix of industry marketing effort. Total market demand is not a fixed number but a function of the stated conditions. For example, next year's total market demand for this type of product will depend on how much other producers spend on marketing their brands. It also depends on many environmental factors, such as government regulations, economic conditions, and the level of consumer confidence in a given market. The upper limit of market demand is called **market potential**.

One general but practical method that HD might use for estimating total market demand uses three variables: (1) the number of prospective buyers, (2) the quantity purchased by an average buyer per year, and (3) the price of an average unit. Using these numbers, HD can estimate total market demand as follows:

$$Q = n \times q \times p$$

where

Q = total market demand
n = number of buyers in the market
q = quantity purchased by an average buyer per year
p = price of an average unit

Chain ratio method
Estimating market demand by multiplying a base number by a chain of adjusting percentages.

A variation of this approach is the **chain ratio method**. This method involves multiplying a base number by a chain of adjusting percentages. For example, HD's product is designed to stream high-definition video on high-definition televisions as well as play other video content streamed from the Internet to multiple devices in a home. Thus, consumers who do not own a high-definition television will not likely purchase this player. Additionally, only households with broadband Internet access will be able to use the product. Finally, not all HDTV-owning Internet households will be willing and able to purchase this product. HD can estimate U.S. demand using a chain of calculations like the following:

Total number of U.S. households ×
The percentage of HDTV-owning U.S. households with broadband Internet access ×
The percentage of these households willing and able to buy this device

The U.S. Census Bureau estimates that there are approximately 115 million households in the United States.[3] HD's research indicates that 60% of U.S. households own at least one HDTV and have broadband Internet access. Finally, the company's research also revealed that 30% of households possess the discretionary income needed and are willing to buy a product such as this. Then, the total number of households willing and able to purchase this product is:

$$115 \text{ million households} \times 0.60 \times 0.30 = 20.7 \text{ million households}$$

Households only need to purchase one device because it can stream content to other devices throughout the household. Assuming the average retail price across all brands is $350 for this product, the estimate of total market demand is as follows:

$$20.7 \text{ million households} \times 1 \text{ device per household} \times \$350 = \$7{,}245{,}000{,}000$$

This simple chain of calculations gives HD only a rough estimate of potential demand. However, more detailed chains involving additional segments and other qualifying factors would yield more accurate and refined estimates. Still, these are only *estimates* of market potential. They rely heavily on assumptions regarding adjusting percentages, average quantity, and average price. Thus, HD must make certain that its assumptions are reasonable and defendable. As can be seen, the overall market potential in dollar sales can vary widely given the average price used. For this reason, HD will use unit sales potential to determine its sales estimate for next year. Market potential in terms of units is 20.7 million (20.7 million households × 1 device per household).

Assuming that HD forecasts it will have a 3.6% market share in the first year after launching this product, then it can forecast unit sales at 20.7 million units × 0.036 = 745,200 units. At a selling price of $168 per unit, this translates into sales of $125,193,600 (745,200 units × $168 per unit). For simplicity, further analyses will use forecasted sales of $125 million.

This unit volume estimate is well within HD's production capacity and exceeds not only the break-even estimate (465,117 units) calculated earlier, but also the volume necessary to realize a $5 million profit (581,396 units) or a 30% return on investment (534,884 units). However, this forecast falls well short of the volume necessary to realize a 25% return on sales (20 million units!) and may require that HD revise expectations.

To assess expected profits, we must now look at the budgeted expenses for launching this product. To do this, we will construct a pro forma profit-and-loss statement.

The Profit-and-Loss Statement and Marketing Budget

Pro forma (or **projected**) **profit-and-loss statement** (or **income statement** or **operating statement**)
A statement that shows projected revenues less budgeted expenses and estimates the projected net profit for an organization, product, or brand during a specific planning period, typically a year.

All marketing managers must account for the profit impact of their marketing strategies. A major tool for projecting such profit impact is a **pro forma** (or **projected**) **profit-and-loss statement** (also called an **income statement** or **operating statement**). A pro forma statement shows projected revenues less budgeted expenses and estimates the projected net profit for an organization, product, or brand during a specific planning period, typically a year. It includes direct product production costs, marketing expenses budgeted to attain a given sales forecast, and overhead expenses assigned to the organization or product. A profit-and-loss statement typically consists of several major components (see **Table A2.1**):

- *Net sales.* Gross sales revenue minus returns and allowances (for example, trade, cash, quantity, and promotion allowances). HD's net sales for 2015 are estimated to be $125 million, as determined in the previous analysis.
- *Cost of goods sold* (sometimes called *cost of sales*). The actual cost of the merchandise sold by a manufacturer or reseller. It includes the cost of inventory, purchases, and other costs associated with making the goods. HD's cost of goods sold is estimated to be 50% of net sales, or $62.5 million.

Table A2.1 | Pro Forma Profit-and-Loss Statement for the 12-Month Period Ended December 31, 2015

			% of Sales
Net Sales		$125,000,000	100
Cost of Goods Sold		62,500,000	50
Gross Margin		$62,500,000	50
Marketing Expenses			
Sales expenses	$17,500,000		
Promotion expenses	15,000,000		
Freight	12,500,000	45,000,000	36
General and Administrative Expenses			
Managerial salaries and expenses	$2,000,000		
Indirect overhead	3,000,000	5,000,000	4
Net Profit Before Income Tax		$12,500,000	10

- *Gross margin (or gross profit).* The difference between net sales and cost of goods sold. HD's gross margin is estimated to be $62.5 million.
- *Operating expenses.* The expenses incurred while doing business. These include all other expenses beyond the cost of goods sold that are necessary to conduct business. Operating expenses can be presented in total or broken down in detail. Here, HD's estimated operating expenses include *marketing expenses* and *general and administrative expenses.*

  Marketing expenses include sales expenses, promotion expenses, and distribution expenses. The new product will be sold through HD's sales force, so the company budgets $5 million for sales salaries. However, because sales representatives earn a 10% commission on sales, HD must also add a variable component to sales expenses of $12.5 million (10% of $125 million net sales), for a total budgeted sales expense of $17.5 million. HD sets its advertising and promotion to launch this product at $10 million. However, the company also budgets 4% of sales, or $5 million, for cooperative advertising allowances to retailers who promote HD's new product in their advertising. Thus, the total budgeted advertising and promotion expenses are $15 million ($10 million for advertising plus $5 million in co-op allowances). Finally, HD budgets 10% of net sales, or $12.5 million, for freight and delivery charges. In all, total marketing expenses are estimated to be $17.5 million + $15 million + $12.5 million = $45 million.

  General and administrative expenses are estimated at $5 million, broken down into $2 million for managerial salaries and expenses for the marketing function and $3 million of indirect overhead allocated to this product by the corporate accountants (such as depreciation, interest, maintenance, and insurance). Total expenses for the year, then, are estimated to be $50 million ($45 million marketing expenses + $5 million in general and administrative expenses).
- *Net profit before taxes.* Profit earned after all costs are deducted. HD's estimated net profit before taxes is $12.5 million.

In all, as Table A2.1 shows, HD expects to earn a profit on its new product of $12.5 million in 2015. Also note that the percentage of sales that each component of the profit-and-loss statement represents is given in the right-hand column. These percentages are determined by dividing the cost figure by net sales (that is, marketing expenses represent 36% of net sales determined by $45 million ÷ $125 million). As can be seen, HD projects a net profit return on sales of 10% in the first year after launching this product.

Marketing Performance Measures

Profit-and-loss statement (or income statement or operating statement)
A statement that shows actual revenues less expenses and net profit for an organization, product, or brand during a specific planning period, typically a year.

Now let's fast-forward a year. HD's product has been on the market for one year and management wants to assess its sales and profit performance. One way to assess this performance is to compute performance ratios derived from HD's **profit-and-loss statement** (or **income statement** or **operating statement**).

Whereas the pro forma profit-and-loss statement shows *projected* financial performance, the statement given in **Table A2.2** shows HD's *actual* financial performance based on actual sales, cost of goods sold, and expenses during the past year. By comparing the profit-and-loss statement from one period to the next, HD can gauge performance against goals, spot favorable or unfavorable trends, and take appropriate corrective action.

The profit-and-loss statement shows that HD lost $1 million rather than making the $12.5 million profit projected in the pro forma statement. Why? One obvious reason is that net sales fell $25 million short of estimated sales. Lower sales translated into lower variable costs associated with marketing the product. However, both fixed costs and the cost of goods sold as a percentage of sales exceeded expectations. Hence, the product's contribution margin was 21% rather than the estimated 26%. That is, variable costs represented 79% of sales (55% for cost of goods sold, 10% for sales commissions, 10% for freight, and 4% for co-op allowances). Recall that contribution margin can be calculated by subtracting that fraction from one ($1 - 0.79 = 0.21$). Total fixed costs were $22 million, $2 million more than estimated. Thus, the sales that HD needed to break even given this cost structure can be calculated as:

$$\text{Break-even sales} = \frac{\text{fixed costs}}{\text{contribution margin}} = \frac{\$22{,}000{,}000}{0.21} = \$104{,}761{,}905$$

If HD had achieved another $5 million in sales, it would have earned a profit.

Market share
Company sales divided by market sales.

Although HD's sales fell short of the forecasted sales, so did overall industry sales for this product. Overall industry sales were only $2.5 billion. That means that HD's **market share** was 4% ($100 million ÷ $2.5 billion = 0.04 = 4%), which was higher than forecasted. Thus, HD attained a higher-than-expected market share but the overall market sales were not as high as estimated.

Operating ratios
The ratios of selected operating statement items to net sales.

Analytic Ratios

The profit-and-loss statement provides the figures needed to compute some crucial **operating ratios**—the ratios of selected operating statement items to net sales. These

Table A2.2 | Profit-and-Loss Statement for the 12-Month Period Ended December 31, 2015

			% of Sales
Net Sales		$100,000,000	100
Cost of Goods Sold		55,000,000	55
Gross Margin		$45,000,000	45
Marketing Expenses			
Sales expenses	$15,000,000		
Promotion expenses	14,000,000		
Freight	10,000,000	39,000,000	39
General and Administrative Expenses			
Managerial salaries and expenses	$2,000,000		
Indirect overhead	5,000,000	7,000,000	7
Net Profit Before Income Tax		−$1,000,000	−1

ratios let marketers compare the firm's performance in one year to that in previous years (or with industry standards and competitors' performance in that year). The most commonly used operating ratios are the gross margin percentage, the net profit percentage, and the operating expense percentage. The inventory turnover rate and return on investment (ROI) are often used to measure managerial effectiveness and efficiency.

Gross margin percentage
The percentage of net sales remaining after cost of goods sold—calculated by dividing gross margin by net sales.

The **gross margin percentage** indicates the percentage of net sales remaining after cost of goods sold that can contribute to operating expenses and net profit before taxes. The higher this ratio, the more a firm has left to cover expenses and generate profit. HD's gross margin ratio was 45%:

$$\text{Gross margin percentage} = \frac{\text{gross margin}}{\text{net sales}} = \frac{\$45{,}000{,}000}{\$100{,}000{,}000} = 0.45 = 45\%$$

Note that this percentage is lower than estimated, and this ratio is seen easily in the percentage of sales column in Table A2.2. Stating items in the profit-and-loss statement as a percent of sales allows managers to quickly spot abnormal changes in costs over time. If there was previous history for this product and this ratio was declining, management should examine it more closely to determine why it has decreased (that is, because of a decrease in sales volume or price, an increase in costs, or a combination of these). In HD's case, net sales were $25 million lower than estimated, and cost of goods sold was higher than estimated (55% rather than the estimated 50%).

Net profit percentage
The percentage of each sales dollar going to profit—calculated by dividing net profits by net sales.

The **net profit percentage** shows the percentage of each sales dollar going to profit. It is calculated by dividing net profits by net sales:

$$\text{Net profit percentage} = \frac{\text{net profit}}{\text{net sales}} = \frac{-\$1{,}000{,}000}{\$100{,}000{,}000} = -0.01 = -1.0\%$$

This ratio is easily seen in the percent of sales column. HD's new product generated negative profits in the first year; this is not a good situation, given that before the product launch net profits before taxes were estimated at more than $12 million. Later in this appendix, we will discuss further analyses the marketing manager should conduct to defend the product.

Operating expense percentage
The portion of net sales going to operating expenses—calculated by dividing total expenses by net sales.

The **operating expense percentage** indicates the portion of net sales going to operating expenses. Operating expenses include marketing and other expenses not directly related to marketing the product, such as indirect overhead assigned to this product. It is calculated by:

$$\text{Operating expense percentage} = \frac{\text{total expenses}}{\text{net sales}} = \frac{\$46{,}000{,}000}{\$100{,}000{,}000} = 0.46 = 46\%$$

This ratio can also be quickly determined from the percent of sales column in the profit-and-loss statement by adding the percentages for marketing expenses and general and administrative expenses (39% + 7%). Thus, 46 cents of every sales dollar went for operations. Although HD wants this ratio to be as low as possible, and 46% is not an alarming amount, it is of concern if it is increasing over time or if a loss is realized.

Inventory turnover rate (or **stockturn rate**)
The number of times an inventory turns over or is sold during a specified time period (often one year)—calculated based on costs, selling price, or units.

Another useful ratio is the **inventory turnover rate** (also called **stockturn rate** for resellers). The inventory turnover rate is the number of times an inventory turns over or is sold during a specified time period (often one year). This rate tells how quickly a business is moving inventory through the organization. Higher rates indicate that lower investments in inventory are made, thus freeing up funds for other investments. It may be computed on a cost, selling price, or unit basis. The formula based on cost is:

$$\text{Inventory turnover rate} = \frac{\text{cost of goods sold}}{\text{average inventory at cost}}$$

Assuming HD's beginning and ending inventories were $30 million and $20 million, respectively, the inventory turnover rate is:

$$\text{Inventory turnover rate} = \frac{\$55{,}000{,}000}{(\$30{,}000{,}000 + \$20{,}000{,}000)/2} = \frac{\$55{,}000{,}000}{\$25{,}000{,}000} = 2.2$$

That is, HD's inventory turned over 2.2 times in 2015. Normally, the higher the turnover rate, the higher the management efficiency and company profitability. However, this rate should be compared to industry averages, competitors' rates, and past performance to determine if HD is doing well. A competitor with similar sales but a higher inventory turnover rate will have fewer resources tied up in inventory, allowing it to invest in other areas of the business.

Return on investment (ROI)
A measure of managerial effectiveness and efficiency—net profit before taxes divided by total investment.

Companies frequently use **return on investment (ROI)** to measure managerial effectiveness and efficiency. For HD, ROI is the ratio of net profits to total investment required to manufacture the new product. This investment includes capital investments in land, buildings, and equipment (here, the initial $10 million to refurbish the manufacturing facility) plus inventory costs (HD's average inventory totaled $25 million), for a total of $35 million. Thus, HD's ROI for this product is:

$$\text{Return on investment} = \frac{\text{net profit before taxes}}{\text{investment}} = \frac{-\$1{,}000{,}000}{\$35{,}000{,}000} = -.0286 = -2.86\%$$

ROI is often used to compare alternatives, and a positive ROI is desired. The alternative with the highest ROI is preferred to other alternatives. HD needs to be concerned with the ROI realized. One obvious way HD can increase ROI is to increase net profit by reducing expenses. Another way is to reduce its investment, perhaps by investing less in inventory and turning it over more frequently.

Marketing Profitability Metrics

Given the previous financial results, you may be thinking that HD should drop this new product. But what arguments can marketers make for keeping or dropping this product? The obvious arguments for dropping the product are that first-year sales were well below expected levels and the product lost money, resulting in a negative return on investment.

So what would happen if HD did drop this product? Surprisingly, if the company drops the product, the profits for the total organization will decrease by $4 million! How can that be? Marketing managers need to look closely at the numbers in the profit-and-loss statement to determine the *net marketing contribution* for this product. In HD's case, the net marketing contribution for the product is $4 million, and if the company drops this product, that contribution will disappear as well. Let's look more closely at this concept to illustrate how marketing managers can better assess and defend their marketing strategies and programs.

Net Marketing Contribution

Net marketing contribution (NMC)
A measure of marketing profitability that includes only components of profitability controlled by marketing.

Net marketing contribution (NMC), along with other marketing metrics derived from it, measures *marketing* profitability. It includes only components of profitability that are controlled by marketing. Whereas the previous calculation of net profit before taxes from the profit-and-loss statement includes operating expenses not under marketing's control, NMC does not. Referring back to HD's profit-and-loss statement given in Table A2.2, we can calculate net marketing contribution for the product as:

$$\begin{aligned}\text{NMC} &= \text{net sales} - \text{cost of goods sold} - \text{marketing expenses}\\ &= \$100\text{ million} - \$55\text{ million} - \$41\text{ million} = \$4\text{ million}\end{aligned}$$

The marketing expenses include sales expenses ($15 million), promotion expenses ($14 million), freight expenses ($10 million), and the managerial salaries and expenses of the marketing function ($2 million), which total $41 million.

Thus, the product actually contributed $4 million to HD's profits. It was the $5 million of indirect overhead allocated to this product that caused the negative profit. Further, the amount allocated was $2 million more than estimated in the pro forma profit-and-loss statement. Indeed, if only the estimated amount had been allocated, the product would have earned a *profit* of $1 million rather than losing $1 million. If HD drops the product, the $5 million in fixed overhead expenses will not disappear—it will simply have to be allocated elsewhere. However, the $4 million in net marketing contribution *will* disappear.

Marketing Return on Sales and Investment

To get an even deeper understanding of the profit impact of marketing strategy, we'll now examine two measures of marketing efficiency—*marketing return on sales* (marketing ROS) and *marketing return on investment* (marketing ROI).[4]

Marketing return on sales (or **marketing ROS**)
The percent of net sales attributable to the net marketing contribution—calculated by dividing net marketing contribution by net sales.

Marketing return on sales (or **marketing ROS**) shows the percent of net sales attributable to the net marketing contribution. For our product, ROS is:

$$\text{Marketing ROS} = \frac{\text{net marketing contribution}}{\text{net sales}} = \frac{\$4{,}000{,}000}{\$100{,}000{,}000} = 0.04 = 4\%$$

Thus, out of every $100 of sales, the product returns $4 to HD's bottom line. A high marketing ROS is desirable. But to assess whether this is a good level of performance, HD must compare this figure to previous marketing ROS levels for the product, the ROSs of other products in the company's portfolio, and the ROSs of competing products.

Marketing return on investment (or marketing ROI)
A measure of the marketing productivity of a marketing investment—calculated by dividing net marketing contribution by marketing expenses.

Marketing return on investment (or **marketing ROI**) measures the marketing productivity of a marketing investment. In HD's case, the marketing investment is represented by $41 million of the total expenses. Thus, marketing ROI is:

$$\text{Marketing ROI} = \frac{\text{net marketing contribution}}{\text{marketing expenses}} = \frac{\$4{,}000{,}000}{\$41{,}000{,}000} = 0.0976 = 9.76\%$$

As with marketing ROS, a high value is desirable, but this figure should be compared with previous levels for the given product and with the marketing ROIs of competitors' products. Note from this equation that marketing ROI could be greater than 100%. This can be achieved by attaining a higher net marketing contribution and/or a lower total marketing expense.

In this section, we estimated market potential and sales, developed profit-and-loss statements, and examined financial measures of performance. In the next section, we discuss methods for analyzing the impact of various marketing tactics. However, before moving on to those analyses, here's another set of quantitative exercises to help you apply what you've learned to other situations.

Marketing by the Numbers Exercise Set Two

2.1. Determine the market potential for a product that has 20 million prospective buyers who purchase an average of 2 items per year in which the price averages $50. How many units must a company sell if it desires a 10% share of this market?

2.2. Develop a profit-and-loss statement for the Westgate division of North Industries. This division manufactures light fixtures sold to consumers through home improvement and hardware stores. Cost of goods sold represents 40% of net sales. Marketing expenses include selling expenses, promotion expenses, and freight. Selling expenses include sales salaries totaling $3 million per year and sales commissions (5% of sales). The company spent $3 million on advertising last year, and freight costs were 10% of sales. Other costs include $2 million for managerial salaries and expenses for the marketing function and another $3 million for indirect overhead allocated to the division.

a. Develop the profit-and-loss statement if net sales were $20 million last year.
b. Develop the profit-and-loss statement if net sales were $40 million last year.
c. Calculate Westgate's break-even sales.

2.3. Using the profit-and-loss statement you developed in question 2.2b, and assuming that Westgate's beginning inventory was $11 million, ending inventory was $7 million, and total investment was $20 million including inventory, determine the following:

a. gross margin percentage
b. net profit percentage
c. operating expense percentage
d. inventory turnover rate
e. return on investment (ROI)
f. net marketing contribution
g. marketing return on sales (marketing ROS)
h. marketing return on investment (marketing ROI)
i. Is the Westgate division doing well? Explain your answer.

Financial Analysis of Marketing Tactics

Although the first-year profit performance for HD's new product was less than desired, management feels that this attractive market has excellent growth opportunities. Although the sales of HD's product were lower than initially projected, they were not unreasonable given the size of the current market. Thus, HD wants to explore new marketing tactics to help grow the market for this product and increase sales for the company.

For example, the company could increase advertising to promote more awareness of the new product and its category. It could add salespeople to secure greater product distribution. HD could decrease prices so that more consumers could afford its product. Finally, to expand the market, HD could introduce a lower-priced model in addition to the higher-priced original offering. Before pursuing any of these tactics, HD must analyze the financial implications of each.

Increase Advertising Expenditures

HD is considering boosting its advertising to make more people aware of the benefits of this device in general and of its own brand in particular. What if HD's marketers recommend increasing national advertising by 50% to $15 million (assume no change in the variable cooperative component of promotional expenditures)? This represents an increase in fixed costs of $5 million. What increase in sales will be needed to break even on this $5 million increase in fixed costs?

A quick way to answer this question is to divide the increase in fixed cost by the contribution margin, which we found in a previous analysis to be 21%:

$$\text{Increase in sales} = \frac{\text{increase in fixed cost}}{\text{contribution margin}} = \frac{\$5{,}000{,}000}{0.21} = \$23{,}809{,}524$$

Thus, a 50% increase in advertising expenditures must produce a sales increase of almost $24 million to just break even. That $24 million sales increase translates into an almost 1 percentage point increase in market share (1% of the $2.5 billion overall market equals $25 million). That is, to break even on the increased advertising expenditure, HD would have to increase its market share from 4% to 4.95% ($123,809,524 ÷ $2.5 billion = 0.0495 or 4.95% market share). All of this assumes that the total market will not grow, which might or might not be a reasonable assumption.

Increase Distribution Coverage

HD also wants to consider hiring more salespeople in order to call on new retailer accounts and increase distribution through more outlets. Even though HD sells directly to wholesalers, its sales representatives call on retail accounts to perform other functions in addition to selling, such as training retail salespeople. Currently, HD employs 60 sales reps who earn an average of $50,000 in salary plus 10% commission on sales. The product is currently sold to consumers through 1,875 retail outlets. Suppose HD wants to increase that number of outlets to 2,500, an increase of 625 retail outlets. How many additional salespeople will HD need, and what sales will be necessary to break even on the increased cost?

Workload method
An approach to determining sales force size based on the workload required and the time available for selling.

One method for determining what size sales force HD will need is the **workload method**. The workload method uses the following formula to determine the salesforce size:

$$NS = \frac{NC \times FC \times LC}{TA}$$

where

NS = number of salespeople
NC = number of customers
FC = average frequency of customer calls per customer
LC = average length of customer call
TA = time an average salesperson has available for selling per year

HD's sales reps typically call on accounts an average of 20 times per year for about 2 hours per call. Although each sales rep works 2,000 hours per year (50 weeks per year × 40 hours per week), they spent about 15 hours per week on nonselling activities such as administrative duties and travel. Thus, the average annual available selling time per sales rep per year is 1,250 hours (50 weeks × 25 hours per week). We can now calculate how many sales reps HD will need to cover the anticipated 2,500 retail outlets:

$$NS = \frac{2{,}500 \times 20 \times 2}{1{,}250} = 80 \text{ salespeople}$$

Therefore, HD will need to hire 20 more salespeople. The cost to hire these reps will be $1 million (20 salespeople × $50,000 salary per salesperson).

What increase in sales will be required to break even on this increase in fixed costs? The 10% commission is already accounted for in the contribution margin, so the contribution margin remains unchanged at 21%. Thus, the increase in sales needed to cover this increase in fixed costs can be calculated by:

$$\text{Increase in sales} = \frac{\text{increase in fixed cost}}{\text{contribution margin}} = \frac{\$1{,}000{,}000}{0.21} = \$4{,}761{,}905$$

That is, HD's sales must increase almost $5 million to break even on this tactic. So, how many new retail outlets will the company need to secure to achieve this sales increase? The average revenue generated per current outlet is $53,333 ($100 million in sales divided by 1,875 outlets). To achieve the nearly $5 million sales increase needed to break even, HD would need about 90 new outlets ($4,761,905 ÷ $53,333 = 89.3 outlets), or about 4.5 outlets per new rep. Given that current reps cover about 31 outlets apiece (1,875 outlets ÷ 60 reps), this seems very reasonable.

Decrease Price

HD is also considering lowering its price to increase sales revenue through increased volume. The company's research has shown that demand for most types of consumer electronics products is elastic—that is, the percentage increase in the quantity demanded is greater than the percentage decrease in price.

What increase in sales would be necessary to break even on a 10% decrease in price? That is, what increase in sales will be needed to maintain the total contribution that HD realized at the higher price? The current total contribution can be determined by multiplying the contribution margin by total sales:[5]

$$\text{Current total contribution} = \text{contribution margin} \times \text{sales} = .21 \times \$100 \text{ million} = \$21 \text{ million}$$

Price changes result in changes in unit contribution and contribution margin. Recall that the contribution margin of 21% was based on variable costs representing 79% of sales. Therefore, unit variable costs can be determined by multiplying the original price by this percentage: $168 × 0.79 = $132.72 per unit. If price is decreased by 10%, the new price is $151.20. However, variable costs do not change just because price decreased, so the contribution and contribution margin decrease as follows:

	Old	**New (reduced 10%)**
Price	$168	$151.20
– Unit variable cost	$132.72	$132.72
= Unit contribution	$35.28	$18.48
Contribution margin	$35.28/$168 = 0.21 or 21%	$18.48/$151.20 = 0.12 or 12%

So, a 10% reduction in price results in a decrease in the contribution margin from 21% to 12%.[6] To determine the sales level needed to break even on this price reduction, we calculate the level of sales that must be attained at the new contribution margin to achieve the original total contribution of $21 million:

$$\text{New contribution margin} \times \text{new sales level} = \text{original total contribution}$$

So,

$$\text{New sales level} = \frac{\text{original contribution}}{\text{new contribution margin}} = \frac{\$21{,}000{,}000}{0.12} = \$175{,}000{,}000$$

Thus, sales must increase by $75 million ($175 million – $100 million) just to break even on a 10% price reduction. This means that HD must increase market share to 7% ($175 million ÷ $2.5 billion) to achieve the current level of profits (assuming no increase in the total market sales). The marketing manager must assess whether or not this is a reasonable goal.

Extend the Product Line

Cannibalization
The situation in which one product sold by a company takes a portion of its sales from other company products.

As a final option, HD is considering extending its product line by offering a lower-priced model. Of course, the new, lower-priced product would steal some sales from the higher-priced model. This is called **cannibalization**—the situation in which one product sold by a company takes a portion of its sales from other company products. If the new product has a lower contribution than the original product, the company's total contribution will decrease on the cannibalized sales. However, if the new product can generate enough new volume, it is worth considering.

To assess cannibalization, HD must look at the incremental contribution gained by having both products available. Recall in the previous analysis that we determined unit variable costs were $132.72 and unit contribution was just over $35. Assuming costs remain the same next year, HD can expect to realize a contribution per unit of approximately $35 for every unit of the original product sold.

Assume that the first model offered by HD is called HD1 and the new, lower-priced model is called HD2. HD2 will retail for $250, and resellers will take the same markup percentages on price as they do with the higher-priced model. Therefore, HD2's price to wholesalers will be $140 as follows:

Retail price:	$250
minus retail margin (30%):	− $75
Retailer's cost/wholesaler's price:	$175
minus wholesaler's margin (20%):	− $35
Wholesaler's cost/HD's price	$140

If HD2's variable costs are estimated to be $120, then its contribution per unit will equal $20 ($140 − $120 = $20). That means for every unit that HD2 cannibalizes from HD1, HD will *lose* $15 in contribution toward fixed costs and profit (that is, $\text{contribution}_{HD2} - \text{contribution}_{HD1}$ = $20 − $35 = −$15). You might conclude that HD should not pursue this tactic because it appears as though the company will be worse off if it introduces the lower-priced model. However, if HD2 captures enough *additional* sales, HD will be better off even though some HD1 sales are cannibalized. The company must examine what will happen to *total* contribution, which requires estimates of unit volume for both products.

Originally, HD estimated that next year's sales of HD1 would be 600,000 units. However, with the introduction of HD2, it now estimates that 200,000 of those sales will be cannibalized by the new model. If HD sells only 200,000 units of the new HD2 model (all cannibalized from HD1), the company would lose $3 million in total contribution (200,000 units × −$15 per cannibalized unit = −$3 million)—not a good outcome. However, HD estimates that HD2 will generate the 200,000 of cannibalized sales plus an *additional* 500,000 unit sales. Thus, the contribution on these additional HD2 units will be $10 million (i.e., 500,000 units × $20 per unit = $10 million). The net effect is that HD will gain $7 million in total contribution by introducing HD2.

The following table compares HD's total contribution with and without the introduction of HD2:

	HD1 Only	**HD1 and HD2**
HD1 contribution	600,000 units × $35 = $21,000,000	400,000 units × $35 = $14,000,000
HD2 contribution	0	700,000 units × $20 = $14,000,000
Total contribution	$21,000,000	$28,000,000

The difference in the total contribution is a net gain of $7 million ($28 million − $21 million). Based on this analysis, HD should introduce the HD2 model because it results in a positive incremental contribution. However, if fixed costs will increase by more than $7 million as a result of adding this model, then the net effect will be negative and HD should not pursue this tactic.

Now that you have seen these marketing tactic analysis concepts in action as they relate to HD's new product, here are several exercises for you to apply what you have learned in this section in other contexts.

Marketing by the Numbers Exercise Set Three

3.1. Alliance, Inc. sells gas lamps to consumers through retail outlets. Total industry sales for Alliance's relevant market last year were $100 million, with Alliance's sales representing 5% of that total. Contribution margin is 25%. Alliance's sales force calls on retail outlets and each sales rep earns $50,000 per year plus 1% commission on all sales. Retailers receive a 40% margin on selling price and generate average revenue of $10,000 per outlet for Alliance.

a. The marketing manager has suggested increasing consumer advertising by $200,000. By how much would dollar sales need to increase to break even on this expenditure? What increase in overall market share does this represent?
b. Another suggestion is to hire two more sales representatives to gain new consumer retail accounts. How many new retail outlets would be necessary to break even on the increased cost of adding two sales reps?
c. A final suggestion is to make a 10% across-the-board price reduction. By how much would dollar sales need to increase to maintain Alliance's current contribution? (See endnote vi to calculate the new contribution margin.)
d. Which suggestion do you think Alliance should implement? Explain your recommendation.

3.2. PepsiCo sells its soft drinks in approximately 400,000 retail establishments, such as supermarkets, discount stores, and convenience stores. Sales representatives call on each retail account weekly, which means each account is called on by a sales rep 52 times per year. The average length of a sales call is 75 minutes (or 1.25 hours). An average salesperson works 2,000 hours per year (50 weeks per year × 40 hours per week), but each spends 10 hours a week on nonselling activities, such as administrative tasks and travel. How many salespeople does PepsiCo need?

3.3. Hair Zone manufactures a brand of hair-styling gel. It is considering adding a modified version of the product—a foam that provides stronger hold. Hair Zone's variable costs and prices to wholesalers are:

	Current Hair Gel	New Foam Product
Unit selling price	2.00	2.25
Unit variable costs	.85	1.25

Hair Zone expects to sell 1 million units of the new styling foam in the first year after introduction, but it expects that 60% of those sales will come from buyers who normally purchase Hair Zone's styling gel. Hair Zone estimates that it would sell 1.5 million units of the gel if it did not introduce the foam. If the fixed cost of launching the new foam will be $100,000 during the first year, should Hair Zone add the new product to its line? Why or why not?

References

1. This is derived by rearranging the following equation and solving for price: Percentage markup = (price − cost) ÷ price.

2. Again, using the basic profit equation, we set profit equal to ROI × I: ROI × I = (P × Q) − TFC − (Q × UVC). Solving for Q gives Q = (TFC + (ROI × I)) ÷ (P − UVC).

3. U.S. Census Bureau, http://quickfacts.census.gov/qfd/states/00000.html, Accessed June 13, 2014.

4. See Roger J. Best, *Market-Based Management*, 4th ed. (Upper Saddle River, NJ: Prentice Hall, 2005).

5. Total contribution can also be determined from the unit contribution and unit volume: Total contribution = unit contribution × unit sales. Total units sold in 2015 were 595,238 units, which can be determined by dividing total sales by price per unit ($100 million ÷ $168). Total contribution = $35.28 contribution per unit × 595,238 units = $20,999,996.64 (difference due to rounding).

6. Recall that the contribution margin of 21% was based on variable costs representing 79% of sales. Therefore, if we do not know price, we can set it equal to $1.00. If price equals $1.00, 79 cents represents variable costs and 21 cents represents unit contribution. If price is decreased by 10%, the new price is $0.90. However, variable costs do not change just because price decreased, so the unit contribution and contribution margin decrease as follows:

	Old	New (reduced 10%)
Price	$1.00	$0.90
− Unit variable cost	$0.79	$0.79
= Unit contribution	$0.21	$0.11
Contribution margin	$0.21/$1.00 = 0.21 or 21%	$0.11/$0.90 = 0.12 or 12%

APPENDIX 3 CAREERS IN MARKETING

You may have decided you want to pursue a marketing career because it offers constant challenge, stimulating problems, the opportunity to work with people, and excellent advancement opportunities. But you still may not know which part of marketing best suits you—marketing is a very broad field offering a wide variety of career options.

This appendix helps you discover what types of marketing jobs best match your special skills and interests, shows you how to conduct the kind of job search that will get you the position you want, describes marketing career paths open to you, and suggests other information resources.

Marketing Careers Today

The marketing field is booming, with nearly a third of all working Americans now employed in marketing-related positions. Marketing salaries may vary by company, position, and region, and salary figures change constantly. In general, entry-level marketing salaries usually are only slightly below those for engineering and chemistry, but equal or exceed starting salaries in economics, finance, accounting, general business, and the liberal arts. Moreover, if you succeed in an entry-level marketing position, it's likely that you will be promoted quickly to higher levels of responsibility and salary. In addition, because of the consumer and product knowledge you will gain in these jobs, marketing positions provide excellent training for the highest levels in an organization.

Overall Marketing Facts and Trends

In conducting your job search, consider the following facts and trends that are changing the world of marketing:

Focus on customers. More and more, companies are realizing that they win in the marketplace only by creating superior value for customers. To capture value from customers, they must first find new and better ways to solve customer problems and improve customer brand experiences. This increasing focus on the customer puts marketers at the forefront in many of today's companies. As the primary customer-facing function, marketing's mission is to get all company departments to "think customer."

Technology. Technology is changing the way marketers work. For example, Internet, mobile, and other digital technologies are rapidly changing the ways marketers interact with and service customers. They are also changing everything from the ways marketers create new products and advertise them to how marketers access information and recruit personnel. Whereas advertising firms have traditionally recruited "generalists" in account management, *generalist* has now taken on a whole new meaning—advertising account executives must now have both broad and specialized knowledge.

Diversity. The number of women and minorities in marketing continues to grow, and women and minorities also are advancing rapidly into marketing management. For example, women now outnumber men by nearly two to one as advertising account executives. As marketing becomes more global, the need for diversity in marketing positions will continue to increase, opening new opportunities.

Global. Companies such as Coca-Cola, McDonald's, Google, IBM, Walmart, and Procter & Gamble have become multinational, with manufacturing and marketing operations in hundreds of countries. Indeed, such companies often make more profit from sales outside the United States than from within. And it's not just the big companies that are involved in international marketing. Organizations of all sizes have moved into the global arena. Many new marketing opportunities and careers will be directly linked to the expanding global marketplace. The globalization of business also means that you will need more cultural, language, and people skills in the marketing world of the twenty-first century.

Not-for-profit organizations. Increasingly, colleges, arts organizations, libraries, hospitals, and other not-for-profit organizations are recognizing the need for effectively marketing their "products" and services to various publics. This awareness has led to new marketing positions—with these organizations hiring their own marketing directors and marketing vice presidents or using outside marketing specialists.

Looking for a Job in Today's Marketing World

To choose and find the right job, you will need to apply the marketing skills you've learned in this course, especially marketing analysis and planning. Follow these eight steps for marketing yourself: (1) Conduct a self-assessment and seek career counseling; (2) examine job descriptions; (3) explore the job market, follow up, and assess opportunities; (4) develop search strategies; (5) prepare résumés; (6) write a cover letter and assemble supporting documents; (7) interview for jobs; and (8) take a follow-up interview.

Conduct a Self-Assessment and Seek Career Counseling

If you're having difficulty deciding what kind of marketing position is the best fit for you, start out by doing some self-testing or seeking career counseling. Self-assessments require that you honestly and thoroughly evaluate your interests, strengths, and weaknesses. What do you do well (your best and favorite skills) and not so well? What are your favorite interests? What are your career goals? What makes you stand out from other job seekers?

The answers to such questions may suggest which marketing careers you should seek or avoid. For help in completing an effective self-assessment, look for the following books in your local bookstore: Shoya Zichy, *Career Match: Connecting Who You Are with What You Love to Do* (AMACOM Books, 2007) and Richard Bolles, *What Color Is Your Parachute? 2015* (Ten Speed Press, 2014; also see www.eparachute.com). Many online sites also offer self-assessment tools, such as the Keirsey Temperament Theory and the Temperament Sorter, a free but broad assessment available at Keirsey.com. For a more specific evaluation, CareerLeader.com offers a complete online business career self-assessment program designed by the Directors of MBA Career Development at Harvard Business School. You can use this for a fee.

For help in finding a career counselor to guide you in making a career assessment, Richard Bolles's *What Color Is Your Parachute? 2015* contains a useful state-by-state sampling. CareerLeader.com also offers personal career counseling. (Some counselors can help you in your actual job search, too.) You can also consult the career counseling, testing, and placement services at your college or university.

Examine Job Descriptions

After you have identified your skills, interests, and desires, you need to see which marketing positions are the best match for them. Two U.S. Labor Department publications available in your local library or online—the *Occupation Outlook Handbook* (www.bls.gov/ooh) and the *Dictionary of Occupational Titles* (www.occupationalinfo.org)—describe the duties involved in various occupations, the specific training and education needed, the availability of jobs in each field, possibilities for advancement, and probable earnings.

Your initial career shopping list should be broad and flexible. Look for different ways to achieve your objectives. For example, if you want a career in marketing management, consider the public as well as the private sector, and local and regional as well as national and international firms. Be open initially to exploring many options, then focus on specific industries and jobs, listing your basic goals as a way to guide your choices. Your list might include "a job in a start-up company, near a big city on the West Coast, doing new-product planning with a computer software firm."

Explore the Job Market and Assess Opportunities

At this stage, you need to look at the market and see what positions are actually available. You do not have to do this alone. Any of the following may assist you.

Career Development Centers

Your college's career development center and its Web site are excellent places to start. For example, the Web sites of the undergraduate career services center provide lists of career links that can help to focus your job search. Most schools also provide career coaches and career education courses. Also check the National Association of Colleges and Employers Web site (www.naceweb.org). It publishes a national forecast of hiring intentions of employers as they relate to new college graduates (search: "Job Outlook").

In addition, find out everything you can about the companies that interest you by consulting company Web sites, business magazine articles and online sites, annual reports, business reference books, faculty, career counselors, and others. Try to analyze the industry's and the company's future growth and profit potential, advancement opportunities, salary levels, entry positions, travel time, and other factors of significance to you.

Job Fairs

Career development centers often work with corporate recruiters to organize on-campus job fairs. You might also use the Internet to check on upcoming career fairs in your region. For example, visit National Career Fairs at www.nationalcareerfairs.com or Coast to Coast Career Fairs listings at www.coasttocoastcareerfairs.com.

Networking

Networking—asking for job leads from friends, family, people in your community, and career centers—is one of the best ways to find a marketing job. Studies estimate that 60 to 90 percent of jobs are found through networking. The idea is to spread your net wide, contacting anybody and everybody.

Internships

An internship is filled with many benefits, such as gaining experience in a specific field of interest and building up a network of contacts. The biggest benefit: the potential of being offered a job shortly before or soon after graduation. According to a recent survey by the National Association of Colleges and Employers, employers converted 51.2 percent of last year's interns into full-time hires. In addition, 63 percent of the seniors who had paid internship experience and applied for a job received at least one job offer. Conversely, only 35.2 percent of seniors without internship experience who applied for a job received an offer. In addition, survey results show that the median accepted salary offer for seniors with a paid internship was 40 percent higher than the median accepted salary offered to non-intern seniors.

Many company Internet sites have separate internship areas. For example, check out Internships.com, InternshipPrograms.com, MonsterCollege (college.monster.com/education), CampusCareerCenter.com, InternJobs.com, and GoAbroad.com (www.goabroad.com/intern-abroad). If you know of a company for which you wish to work, go to that company's corporate Web site, enter the human resources area, and check for internships. If none are listed, try e-mailing the human resources department, asking if internships are offered.

Job Hunting on the Internet

A constantly increasing number of sites on the Internet deal with job hunting. You can also use the Internet to make contacts with people who can help you gain information on and research companies that interest you. The Riley Guide offers a great introduction to what jobs are available (www.rileyguide.com). CareerBuilder.com and Monster.com are good general sites for seeking job listings. Other helpful sites are Disability.gov and HireDiversity.com, which contain information on opportunities for African Americans, Hispanic Americans, Asian Americans, and Native Americans.

Most companies have their own online sites on which they post job listings. This may be helpful if you have a specific and fairly limited number of companies that you are keeping your eye on for job opportunities. But if this is not the case, remember that to find out what interesting marketing jobs the companies themselves are posting, you may have to visit hundreds of corporate sites.

Professional Networking Sites

Many companies have now begun to take advantage of social networking sites to find talented applicants. From LinkedIn to Facebook to Google+, social networking has become professional networking. For example, companies ranging from P&G to BASF have career pages on LinkedIn (www.linkedin.com/company/procter-&-gamble/careers and www.linkedin.com/company/basf/careers) to find potential candidates for entry-level positions. And companies ranging from Walmart (www.facebook.com/walmartcareers) to

Marriott (www.facebook.com/marriottjobsandcareers) have career listings pages on Facebook in addition to LinkedIn. For job seekers, online professional networking offers more efficient job targeting and reduces associated costs as compared with traditional interaction methods such as traveling to job fairs and interviews, printing résumés, and other expenses.

However, although the Internet offers a wealth of resources for searching for the perfect job, be aware that it's a two-way street. Just as job seekers can search the Internet to find job opportunities, employers can search for information on job candidates. Jobs searches can sometimes be derailed by information mined by potential employers from online social networking sites that reveals unintended or embarrassing anecdotes and photos. Internet searches can sometimes also reveal inconsistencies and résumé inflation.

Develop Search Strategies

Once you've decided which companies you are interested in, you need to contact them. One of the best ways is through on-campus interviews. However, not every company you are interested in will visit your school. In such instances, you can write, e-mail, or phone the company directly or ask marketing professors or school alumni for contacts.

Prepare Résumés

A résumé is a concise yet comprehensive written summary of your qualifications, including your academic, personal, and professional achievements, that showcases why you are the best candidate for the job. Because an employer will spend on average only 15 to 20 seconds reviewing your résumé, you want to be sure that you prepare a good one.

In preparing your résumé, remember that all information on it must be accurate and complete. Résumés typically begin with the applicant's full name, telephone number, and mail and e-mail addresses. A simple and direct statement of career objectives generally appears next, followed by work history and academic data (including awards and internships), and then by personal activities and experiences applicable to the job sought.

The résumé sometimes ends with a list of references the employer may contact (at other times, references may be listed separately). If your work or internship experience is limited, nonexistent, or irrelevant, then it is a good idea to emphasize your academic and nonacademic achievements, showing skills related to those required for excellent job performance.

There are three main types of résumés. Reverse *chronological* résumés, which emphasize career growth, are organized in reverse chronological order, starting with your most recent job. They focus on job titles within organizations, describing the responsibilities and accomplishments for each job. *Functional* résumés focus less on job titles and work history and more on assets and achievements. This format works best if your job history is scanty or discontinuous. *Mixed*, or *combination*, résumés take from each of the other two formats. First, the skills used for a specific job are listed, then the job title is stated. This format works best for applicants whose past jobs are in other fields or seemingly unrelated to the position. For further explanation and examples of these types of résumés, see the Résumé Resource format page (www.resume-resource.com/format.html).

Many books can assist you in developing your résumé. A popular guide is Brenda Greene, *Get the Interview Every Time: Proven Résumé and Cover Letter Strategies from Fortune 500 Hiring Professionals* (Kaplan Publishing, 2009). Software programs, such as *Résumé-Maker* (www.ResumeMaker.com), provide hundreds of sample résumés and ready-to-use phrases while guiding you through the résumé preparation process. CareerOneStop (www.careeronestop.org/resumeguide/introduction.aspx) offers a step-by-step résumé tutorial, and Monster (career-advice.monster.com) offers résumé advice and writing services. Finally, you can even create your own personalized online résumé at sites such as optimalresume.com.

Online Résumés

The Internet is now a widely used job-search environment, so it's a good idea to have your résumé ready for the online environment. You can forward it to networking contacts or recruiting professionals through e-mail. You can also post it in online databases with the hope that employers and recruiters will find it.

Successful Internet-ready résumés require a different strategy than that for paper résumés. For instance, when companies search résumé banks, they search key words and industry buzz words that describe a skill or the core work required for each job, so nouns are much more important than verbs. Two good resources for preparing Internet-ready résumés are Susan Ireland's Résumé Site (susanireland.com/resume/online/email/) and the Riley Guide (www.rileyguide.com/eresume.html).

After you have written your Internet-ready résumé, you need to post it. The following sites may be good locations to start: Monster (www.monster.com), LinkedIn (www.linkedin.com/job/), and CareerBuilder.com (www.careerbuilder.com/JobSeeker/Resumes/PostResumeNew/PostYourResume.aspx). However, use caution when posting your résumé on various sites. In this era of identity theft, you need to select sites with care so as to protect your privacy. Limit access to your personal contact information, and don't use sites that offer to "blast" your résumé into cyberspace.

Résumé Tips

- Communicate your worth to potential employers in a concrete manner, citing examples whenever possible.
- Be concise and direct.
- Use active verbs to show you are a doer.
- Do not skimp on quality or use gimmicks. Spare no expense in presenting a professional résumé.
- Have someone critique your work. A single typo can eliminate you from being considered.
- Customize your résumé for specific employers. Emphasize your strengths as they pertain to your targeted job.
- Keep your résumé compact, usually one page.
- Format the text to be attractive, professional, and readable. Times New Roman is often the font of choice. Avoid too much "design" or gimmicky flourishes.

Write Cover Letter, Follow Up, and Assemble Supporting Documents

Cover Letter

You should include a cover letter informing the employer that a résumé is enclosed. But a cover letter does more than this. It also serves to summarize in one or two paragraphs the contents of the résumé and explains why you think you are the right person for the position. The goal is to persuade the employer to look at the more detailed résumé. A typical cover letter is organized as follows: (1) the name and position of the person you are contacting; (2) a statement identifying the position you are applying for, how you heard of the vacancy, and the reasons for your interest; (3) a summary of your qualifications for the job; (4) a description of what follow ups you intend to make, such as phoning in two weeks to see if the résumé has been received; and (5) an expression of gratitude for the opportunity of being a candidate for the job. CareerOneStop (www.careeronestop.org/ResumeGuide/Writeeffectivecoverletters.aspx) offers a step-by-step tutorial on how to create a cover letter, and Susan Ireland's Web site contains more than 50 cover letter samples (susanireland.com/letter/cover-letter-examples). Another popular guide is Kimberly Sarmiento's *Complete Guide to Writing Effective Résumé Cover Letters* (Atlantic Publishing, 2009).

Follow Up

Once you send your cover letter and résumé to prospective employers via the method they prefer—e-mail, their Web site, or regular mail—it's often a good idea to follow up. In today's market, job seekers can't afford to wait for interviews to find them. A quality résumé and an attractive cover letter are crucial, but a proper follow up may be the key to landing an interview. However, before you engage your potential employer, be sure to research the company. Knowing about the company and understanding its place in the industry will help you shine. When you place a call, send an e-mail, or mail a letter to a company contact, be sure to restate your interest in the position, check on the status of your résumé, and ask employers about any questions they may have.

Letters of Recommendation

Letters of recommendation are written references by professors, former and current employers, and others that testify to your character, skills, and abilities. Some companies may request letters of recommendation, to be submitted either with the résumé or at the interview. Even if letters of recommendation aren't requested, it's a good idea to bring them with you to the interview. A good reference letter tells why you would be an excellent candidate for the position. In choosing someone to write a letter of recommendation, be confident that the person will give you a good reference. In addition, do not assume the person knows everything about you or the position you are seeking. Rather, provide the person with your résumé and other relevant data. As a courtesy, allow the reference writer at least a month to complete the letter and enclose a stamped, addressed envelope with your materials.

In the packet containing your résumé, cover letter, and letters of recommendation, you may also want to attach other relevant documents that support your candidacy, such as academic transcripts, graphics, portfolios, and samples of writing.

Interview for Jobs

As the old saying goes, "The résumé gets you the interview; the interview gets you the job." The job interview offers you an opportunity to gather more information about the organization, while at the same time allowing the organization to gather more information about you. You'll want to present your best self. The interview process consists of three parts: before the interview, the interview itself, and after the interview. If you pass through these stages successfully, you will be called back for the follow-up interview.

Before the Interview

In preparing for your interview, do the following:

1. Understand that interviewers have diverse styles, including the "chitchat," let's-get-to-know-each-other style; the interrogation style of question after question; and the tough-probing "why, why, why" style, among others. So be ready for anything.
2. With a friend, practice being interviewed and then ask for a critique. Or videotape yourself in a practice interview so that you can critique your own performance. Your college placement service may also offer "mock" interviews to help you.
3. Prepare at least five good questions whose answers are not easily found in the company literature, such as "What is the future direction of the firm?" "How does the firm differentiate itself from competitors?" or "Do you have a new-media division?"
4. Anticipate possible interview questions, such as "Why do you want to work for this company?" or "Why should we hire you?" Prepare solid answers before the interview. Have a clear idea of why you are interested in joining the company and the industry to which it belongs.
5. Avoid back-to-back interviews—they can be exhausting, and it is unpredictable how long each will last.
6. Prepare relevant documents that support your candidacy, such as academic transcripts, letters of recommendation, graphics, portfolios, and samples of writing. Bring multiple copies to the interview.
7. Dress conservatively and professionally. Be neat and clean.
8. Arrive 10 minutes early to collect your thoughts and review the major points you intend to cover. Check your name on the interview schedule, noting the name of the interviewer and the room number. Be courteous and polite to office staff.
9. Approach the interview enthusiastically. Let your personality shine through.

During the Interview

During the interview, do the following:

1. Shake hands firmly in greeting the interviewer. Introduce yourself, using the same form of address that the interviewer uses. Focus on creating a good initial impression.
2. Keep your poise. Relax, smile when appropriate, and be upbeat throughout.
3. Maintain eye contact and good posture, and speak distinctly. Don't clasp your hands or fiddle with jewelry, hair, or clothing. Sit comfortably in your chair.
4. Along with the copies of relevant documents that support your candidacy, carry extra copies of your résumé with you.
5. Have your story down pat. Present your selling points. Answer questions directly. Avoid either one-word or too-wordy answers.
6. Let the interviewer take the initiative but don't be passive. Find an opportunity to direct the conversation to things about yourself that you want the interviewer to hear.
7. To end on a high note, make your most important point or ask your most pertinent question during the last part of the interview.
8. Don't hesitate to "close." You might say, "I'm very interested in the position and I have enjoyed this interview."

9. Obtain the interviewer's business card or address and phone number so that you can follow up later.

A tip for acing the interview: Before you open your mouth, find out *what it's like* to be a brand manager, sales representative, market researcher, advertising account executive, or other position for which you're interviewing. See if you can find a "mentor"—someone in a position similar to the one you're seeking, perhaps with another company. Talk with this mentor about the ins and outs of the job and industry.

After the Interview

After the interview, do the following:

1. Record the key points that arose. Be sure to note who is to follow up and when a decision can be expected.
2. Analyze the interview objectively, including the questions asked, the answers to them, your overall interview presentation, and the interviewer's responses to specific points.
3. Immediately send a thank-you letter or e-mail, mentioning any additional items and your willingness to supply further information.
4. If you do not hear from the employer within the specified time, call, e-mail, or write the interviewer to determine your status.

Follow-Up Interview

If your first interview takes place off-site, such as at your college or at a job fair, and if you are successful with that initial interview, you will be invited to visit the organization. The in-company interview will probably run from several hours to an entire day. The organization will examine your interest, maturity, enthusiasm, assertiveness, logic, and company and functional knowledge. You should ask questions about issues of importance to you. Find out about the working environment, job role, responsibilities, opportunities for advancement, current industrial issues, and the company's personality. The company wants to discover if you are the right person for the job, whereas you want to find out if it is the right job for you. The key is to determine if the right *fit* exists between you and the company.

Marketing Jobs

This section describes some of the key marketing positions.

Advertising

Advertising is one of the most exciting fields in marketing, offering a wide range of career opportunities.

Job Descriptions

Key advertising positions include copywriter, art director, production manager, account executive, account planner, and media planner/buyer.

- *Copywriters* write advertising copy and help find the concepts behind the written words and visual images of advertisements.
- *Art directors,* the other part of the creative team, help translate the copywriters' ideas into dramatic visuals called "layouts." Agency artists develop print layouts, package designs, television and video layouts (called "storyboards"), corporate logotypes, trademarks, and symbols. *Production managers* are responsible for physically creating ads, either in-house or by contracting through outside production houses.
- *Account development executives* research and understand clients' markets and customers and help develop marketing and advertising strategies to impact them.
- *Account executives* serve as liaisons between clients and agencies. They coordinate the planning, creation, production, and implementation of an advertising campaign for the account.
- *Account planners* serve as the voice of the consumer in the agency. They research consumers to understand their needs and motivations as a basis for developing effective ad campaigns.
- *Media planners (or buyers)* determine the best mix of television, radio, newspaper, magazine, digital, and other media for the advertising campaign.

Skills Needed, Career Paths, and Typical Salaries

Work in advertising requires strong people skills in order to interact closely with an often-difficult and demanding client base. In addition, advertising attracts people with strong skills in planning, problem solving, creativity, communication, initiative, leadership, and presentation. Advertising involves working under high levels of stress and pressure created by unrelenting deadlines. Advertisers frequently have to work long hours to meet deadlines for a presentation. But work achievements are very apparent, with the results of creative strategies observed by thousands or even millions of people.

Positions in advertising sometimes require an MBA. But most jobs only require a business, graphic arts, or liberal arts degree. Advertising positions often serve as gateways to higher-level management. Moreover, with large advertising agencies opening offices all over the world, there is the possibility of eventually working on global campaigns.

Starting advertising salaries are relatively low compared to those of some other marketing jobs because of strong competition for entry-level advertising jobs. Compensation will increase quickly as you move into account executive or other management positions. For more facts and figures, see the online pages of *Advertising Age*, a key ad industry publication (www.adage.com, click on the Jobs link) and the American Association of Advertising Agencies (www.aaaa.org).

Brand and Product Management

Brand and product managers plan, direct, and control business and marketing efforts for their products. They are involved with research and development, packaging, manufacturing, sales and distribution, advertising, promotion, market research, and business analysis and forecasting.

Job Descriptions

A company's brand management team consists of people in several positions:

- *Brand managers* guide the development of marketing strategies for a specific brand.
- *Assistant brand managers* are responsible for certain strategic components of the brand.
- *Product managers* oversee several brands within a product line or product group.
- *Product category managers* direct multiple product lines in the product category.
- *Market analysts* research the market and provide important strategic information to the project managers.
- *Project directors* are responsible for collecting market information on a marketing or product project.
- *Research directors* oversee the planning, gathering, and analyzing of all organizational research.

Skills Needed, Career Paths, and Typical Salaries

Brand and product management requires high problem-solving, analytical, presentation, communication, and leadership skills, as well as the ability to work well in a team. Product management requires long hours and involves the high pressure of running large projects. In consumer goods companies, the newcomer—who usually needs an MBA—joins a brand team as an assistant and learns the ropes by doing numerical analyses and assisting senior brand people. This person eventually heads the team and later moves on to manage a larger brand, then several brands.

Many industrial goods companies also have product managers. Product management is one of the best training grounds for future corporate officers. Product management also offers good opportunities to move into international marketing. Product managers command relatively high salaries. Because this job category encourages or requires a master's degree, starting pay tends to be higher than in other marketing categories such as advertising or retailing.

Sales and Sales Management

Sales and sales management opportunities exist in a wide range of profit and not-for-profit organizations and in product and service organizations, including financial, insurance, consulting, and government organizations.

Job Descriptions

Key jobs include consumer sales, industrial sales, national account managers, service support, sales trainers, and sales management

- *Consumer sales* involves selling consumer products and services through retailers.
- *Industrial sales* involves selling products and services to other businesses.

- *National account managers (NAMs)* oversee a few very large accounts.
- *Service support* personnel support salespeople during and after the sale of a product.
- *Sales trainers* train new hires and provide refresher training for all sales personnel.
- *Sales management* includes a sequence of positions ranging from district manager to vice president of sales.

Salespeople enjoy active professional lives, working outside the office and interacting with others. They manage their own time and activities. And successful salespeople can be very well paid. Competition for top jobs can be intense. Every sales job is different, but some positions involve extensive travel, long workdays, and working under pressure. You can also expect to be transferred more than once between company headquarters and regional offices. However, most companies are now working to bring good work–life balance to their salespeople and sales managers.

Skills Needed, Career Paths, and Typical Salaries

Selling is a people profession in which you will work with people every day, all day long. In addition to people skills, sales professionals need sales and communication skills. Most sales positions also require strong problem-solving, analytical, presentation, and leadership abilities, as well as creativity and initiative. Teamwork skills are increasingly important.

Career paths lead from salesperson to district, regional, and higher levels of sales management and, in many cases, to the top management of the firm. Today, most entry-level sales management positions require a college degree. Increasingly, people seeking selling jobs are acquiring sales experience in an internship capacity or from a part-time job before graduating. Sales positions are great springboards to leadership positions, with more CEOs starting in sales than in any other entry-level position. This might explain why competition for top sales jobs is intense.

Starting base salaries in sales may be moderate but compensation is often supplemented by significant commission, bonus, or other incentive plans. In addition, many sales jobs include a company car or car allowance. Successful salespeople are among most companies' highest paid employees.

Other Marketing Jobs

Retailing

Retailing provides an early opportunity to assume marketing responsibilities. Key jobs include store manager, regional manager, buyer, department manager, and salesperson. *Store managers* direct the management and operation of an individual store. *Regional managers* manage groups of stores across several states and report performance to headquarters. *Buyers* select and buy the merchandise that the store carries. The *department manager* acts as store manager of a department, such as clothing, but on the department level. The *salesperson* sells merchandise to retail customers. Retailing can involve relocation, but generally there is little travel, unless you are a buyer. Retailing requires high people and sales skills because retailers are constantly in contact with customers. Enthusiasm, willingness, and communication skills are very helpful for retailers, too.

Retailers work long hours, but their daily activities are often more structured than in some types of marketing positions. Starting salaries in retailing tend to be low, but pay increases as you move into management or a retailing specialty job.

Marketing Research

Marketing researchers interact with managers to define problems and identify the information needed to resolve them. They design research projects, prepare questionnaires and samples, analyze data, prepare reports, and present their findings and recommendations to management. They must understand statistics, consumer behavior, psychology, and sociology. As more and more marketing research goes digital, they must also understand the ins and outs of obtaining and managing online information. A master's degree helps. Career opportunities exist with manufacturers, retailers, some wholesalers, trade and industry associations, marketing research firms, advertising agencies, and governmental and private nonprofit agencies.

New Product Planning

People interested in new product planning can find opportunities in many types of organizations. They usually need a good background in marketing, marketing research, and sales forecasting; they need organizational skills to motivate and coordinate others; and they may need a technical background. Usually, these people work first in other marketing positions before joining the new product department.

Marketing Logistics (Physical Distribution)

Marketing logistics, or physical distribution, is a large and dynamic field, with many career opportunities. Major transportation carriers, manufacturers, wholesalers, and retailers all employ logistics specialists. Increasingly, marketing teams include logistics specialists, and marketing managers' career paths include marketing logistics assignments. Coursework in quantitative methods, finance, accounting, and marketing will provide you with the necessary skills for entering the field.

Public Relations

Most organizations have a public relations staff to anticipate problems with various publics, handle complaints, deal with media, and build the corporate image. People interested in public relations should be able to speak and write clearly and persuasively, and they should have a background in journalism, communications, or the liberal arts. The challenges in this job are highly varied and very people-oriented.

Not-for-Profit Services

The key jobs in not-for-profits include marketing director, director of development, event coordinator, publication specialist, and intern/volunteer. The *marketing director* is in charge of all marketing activities for the organization. The *director of development* organizes, manages, and directs the fundraising campaigns that keep a not-for-profit in existence. An *event coordinator* directs all aspects of fundraising events, from initial planning through implementation. The *publication specialist* oversees publications designed to promote awareness of the organization.

Although typically an unpaid position, the *intern/volunteer* performs various marketing functions, and this work can be an important step to gaining a full-time position. The not-for-profit sector is typically not for someone who is money-driven. Rather, most not-for-profits look for people with a strong sense of community spirit and the desire to help others. Therefore, starting pay is usually lower than in other marketing fields. However, the bigger the not-for-profit, the better your chance of rapidly increasing your income when moving into upper management.

Other Resources

Professional marketing associations and organizations are another source of information about careers. Marketers belong to many such societies. You may want to contact some of the following in your job search:

Advertising Women of New York, 28 West 44th Street, Suite 912, New York, NY 10036. (212) 221-7969 (www.awny.org)

American Advertising Federation, 1101 Vermont Avenue, NW, Washington, DC 20005. (202) 898-0089 (www.aaf.org)

American Marketing Association, 311 South Wacker Drive, Suite 5800, Chicago, IL 60606. (800) AMA-1150 (www.marketingpower.com)

The Association of Women in Communications, 3337 Duke Street, Alexandria, VA 22314. (703) 370-7436 (www.womcom.org)

Market Research Association, 1156 15th Street NW, Suite 302, Washington, DC 20005. (202) 800-2545 (www.marketingresearch.org)

National Association of Sales Professionals, 555 Friendly Street, Bloomfield Hills, MI 48341. (866) 365-1520 (www.nasp.com)

National Management Association, 2210 Arbor Boulevard, Dayton, OH 45439. (937) 294-0421 (www.nma1.org)

National Retail Federation, 1101 New York Ave NW, Washington, DC 20005. (800) 673-4692 (www.nrf.com)

Product Development and Management Association, 330 Wabash Avenue, Suite 2000, Chicago, IL 60611. (312) 321-5145 (www.pdma.org)

Public Relations Society of America, 33 Maiden Lane, Eleventh Floor, New York, NY 10038. (212) 460-1400 (www.prsa.org)

Sales and Marketing Executives International, PO Box 1390, Sumas, WA, 98295. (312) 893-0751 (www.smei.org)

GLOSSARY

Adapted global marketing An international marketing approach that adjusts the marketing strategy and mix elements to each international target market, which creates more costs but hopefully produces a larger market share and return.

Administered VMS A vertical marketing system that coordinates successive stages of production and distribution through the size and power of one of the parties.

Adoption process The mental process through which an individual passes from first hearing about an innovation to final adoption.

Advertising Any paid form of nonpersonal presentation and promotion of ideas, goods, or services by an identified sponsor.

Advertising agency A marketing services firm that assists companies in planning, preparing, implementing, and evaluating all or portions of their advertising programs.

Advertising budget The dollars and other resources allocated to a product or a company advertising program.

Advertising media The vehicles through which advertising messages are delivered to their intended audiences.

Advertising objective A specific communication *task* to be accomplished with a specific *target* audience during a specific period of *time*.

Advertising strategy The strategy by which the company accomplishes its advertising objectives. It consists of two major elements: creating advertising messages and selecting advertising media.

Affordable method Setting the promotion budget at the level management thinks the company can afford.

Agent A wholesaler who represents buyers or sellers on a relatively permanent basis, performs only a few functions, and does not take title to goods.

Age and life-cycle segmentation Dividing a market into different age and life-cycle groups.

Allowance Promotional money paid by manufacturers to retailers in return for an agreement to feature the manufacturer's products in some way.

Alternative evaluation The stage of the buyer decision process in which the consumer uses information to evaluate alternative brands in the choice set.

Approach The sales step in which a salesperson meets the customer for the first time.

Attitude A person's consistently favorable or unfavorable evaluations, feelings, and tendencies toward an object or idea.

Baby boomers The 78 million people born during the years following World War II and lasting until 1964.

Basing-point pricing A geographical pricing strategy in which the seller designates some city as a basing point and charges all customers the freight cost from that city to the customer.

Behavioral segmentation Dividing a market into segments based on consumer knowledge, attitudes, uses of a product, or responses to a product.

Behavioral targeting Using online consumer tracking data to target advertisements and marketing offers to specific consumers.

Belief A descriptive thought that a person holds about something.

Benchmarking Comparing the company's products and processes to those of competitors or leading firms in other industries to identify best practices and find ways to improve quality and performance.

Benefit segmentation Dividing the market into segments according to the different benefits that consumers seek from the product.

Big data The huge and complex data sets generated by today's sophisticated information generation, collection, storage, and analysis technologies.

Blogs Online journals where people and companies post their thoughts and other content, usually related to narrowly defined topics.

Brand A name, term, sign, symbol, or design, or a combination of these, that identifies the products or services of one seller or group of sellers and differentiates them from those of competitors.

Brand equity The differential effect that knowing the brand name has on customer response to the product or its marketing.

Brand extension Extending an existing brand name to new product categories.

Brand value The total financial value of a brand.

Branded community Web site A Web site that presents brand content that engages consumers and creates customer community around a brand.

Break-even analysis Analysis to determine the unit volume and dollar sales needed to be profitable given a particular price and cost structure.

Break-even price The price at which total revenue equals total cost and profit is zero.

Break-even pricing (target return pricing) Setting price to break even on the costs of making and marketing a product, or setting price to make a target return.

Broker A wholesaler who does not take title to goods and whose function is to bring buyers and sellers together and assist in negotiation.

Business analysis A review of the sales, costs, and profit projections for a new product to find out whether these factors satisfy the company's objectives.

Business buyer behavior The buying behavior of organizations that buy goods and services for use in the production of other products and services that are sold, rented, or supplied to others.

Business buying process The decision process by which business buyers determine which products and services their organizations need to purchase and then find, evaluate, and choose among alternative suppliers and brands.

Business portfolio The collection of businesses and products that make up the company.

Business promotions Sales promotion tools used to generate business leads, stimulate purchases, reward customers, and motivate salespeople.

Buyer-readiness stages The stages consumers normally pass through on their way to a purchase: awareness, knowledge, liking, preference, conviction, and, finally, the actual purchase.

Buyers People in an organization's buying center who make an actual purchase.

Buying center All the individuals and units that play a role in the purchase decision-making process.

Buzz marketing Cultivating opinion leaders and getting them to spread information about a product or a service to others in their communities.

By-product pricing Setting a price for by-products in order to make the main product's price more competitive.

Cannibalization The situation in which one product sold by a company takes a portion of its sales from other company products.

Captive-product pricing Setting a price for products that must be used along with a main product, such as blades for a razor and games for a video-game console.

Catalog marketing Direct marketing through print, video, or digital catalogs that are mailed to select customers, made available in stores, or presented online.

Category killer A giant specialty store that carries a very deep assortment of a particular line.

Causal research Marketing research to test hypotheses about cause-and-effect relationships.

Chain ratio method Estimating market demand by multiplying a base number by a chain of adjusting percentages.

Channel conflict Disagreements among marketing channel members on goals, roles, and rewards—who should do what and for what rewards.

Channel level A layer of intermediaries that performs some work in bringing the product and its ownership closer to the final buyer.

Closing The sales step in which a salesperson asks the customer for an order.

Co-branding The practice of using the established brand names of two different companies on the same product.

Cognitive dissonance Buyer discomfort caused by postpurchase conflict.

Commercialization Introducing a new product into the market.

Communication adaptation A global communication strategy of fully adapting advertising messages to local markets.

Competition-based pricing Setting prices based on competitors' strategies, prices, costs, and market offerings.

Competitive advantage An advantage over competitors gained by offering greater customer value, either by having lower prices or providing more benefits that justify higher prices.

Competitive marketing intelligence The systematic monitoring, collection, and analysis of publicly available information about consumers, competitors, and developments in the marketing environment.

Competitive marketing strategies Strategies that strongly position the company against competitors and give it the greatest possible competitive advantage.

Competitive-parity method Setting the promotion budget to match competitors' outlays.

Competitor analysis Identifying key competitors; assessing their objectives, strategies, strengths and weaknesses, and reaction patterns; and selecting which competitors to attack or avoid.

Competitor-centered company A company whose moves are mainly based on competitors' actions and reactions.

Complex buying behavior Consumer buying behavior in situations characterized by high consumer involvement in a purchase and significant perceived differences among brands.

Concentrated (niche) marketing A market-coverage strategy in which a firm goes after a large share of one or a few segments or niches.

Concept testing Testing new product concepts with a group of target consumers to find out if the concepts have strong consumer appeal.

Consumer buyer behavior The buying behavior of final consumers—individuals and households that buy goods and services for personal consumption.

Consumer market All the individuals and households that buy or acquire goods and services for personal consumption.

Consumer product A product bought by final consumers for personal consumption.

Consumer promotions Sales promotion tools used to boost short-term customer buying and engagement or enhance long-term customer relationships.

Consumer-generated marketing Brand exchanges created by consumers themselves—both invited and uninvited—by which consumers are playing an increasing role in shaping their own brand experiences and those of other consumers.

Consumer-oriented marketing A company should view and organize its marketing activities from the consumer's point of view.

Consumerism An organized movement of citizens and government agencies designed to improve the rights and power of buyers in relation to sellers.

Content marketing Creating, inspiring, and sharing brand messages and conversations with and among consumers across a fluid mix of paid, owned, earned, and shared channels.

Contract manufacturing A joint venture in which a company contracts with manufacturers in a foreign market to produce its product or provide its service.

Contractual VMS A vertical marketing system in which independent firms at different levels of production and distribution join together through contracts.

Contribution margin The unit contribution divided by the selling price.

Convenience product A consumer product that customers usually buy frequently, immediately, and with minimal comparison and buying effort.

Convenience store A small store, located near a residential area, that is open long hours seven days a week and carries a limited line of high-turnover convenience goods.

Conventional distribution channel A channel consisting of one or more independent producers, wholesalers, and retailers, each a separate business seeking to maximize its own profits, perhaps even at the expense of profits for the system as a whole.

Corporate chains Two or more outlets that are commonly owned and controlled.

Corporate VMS A vertical marketing system that combines successive stages of production and distribution under single ownership—channel leadership is established through common ownership.

Cost-based pricing Setting prices based on the costs of producing, distributing, and selling the product plus a fair rate of return for effort and risk.

Cost-plus pricing (markup pricing) Adding a standard markup to the cost of the product.

Creative concept The compelling "big idea" that will bring an advertising message strategy to life in a distinctive and memorable way.

Cross-cultural marketing Including ethnic themes and cross-cultural perspectives within a brand's mainstream marketing, appealing to consumer similarities across subcultural segments rather than differences.

Crowdsourcing Inviting broad communities of people—customers, employees, independent scientists and researchers, and even the public at large—into the new product innovation process.

Cultural environment Institutions and other forces that affect society's basic values, perceptions, preferences, and behaviors.

Culture The set of basic values, perceptions, wants, and behaviors learned by a member of society from family and other important institutions.

Customer (or **market**) **sales force structure** A sales force organization in which salespeople specialize in selling only to certain customers or industries.

Customer equity The total combined customer lifetime values of all of the company's customers.

Customer insights Fresh marketing information-based understandings of customers and the marketplace that become the basis for creating customer value, engagement, and relationships.

Customer lifetime value The value of the entire stream of purchases a customer makes over a lifetime of patronage.

Customer relationship management The overall process of building and maintaining profitable customer relationships by delivering superior customer value and satisfaction.

Customer relationship management (CRM) Managing detailed information about individual customers and carefully managing customer touch points to maximize customer loyalty.

Customer satisfaction The extent to which a product's perceived performance matches a buyer's expectations.

Customer value analysis An analysis conducted to determine what benefits target customers value and how they rate the relative value of various competitors' offers.

Customer value marketing A company should put most of its resources into customer value-building marketing investments.

Customer value-based pricing Setting price based on buyers' perceptions of value rather than on the seller's cost.

Customer-centered company A company that focuses on customer developments in designing its marketing strategies and delivering superior value to its target customers.

Customer-centered new product development New product development that focuses on finding new ways to solve customer problems and create more customer-satisfying experiences.

Customer-engagement marketing Making the brand a meaningful part of consumers' conversations and lives by fostering direct and continuous customer involvement in shaping brand conversations, experiences, and community.

Customer-perceived value The customer's evaluation of the difference between all the benefits and all the costs of a marketing offer relative to those of competing offers.

Deciders People in an organization's buying center who have formal or informal power to select or approve the final suppliers.

Decline stage The PLC stage in which a product's sales fade away.

Deficient products Products that have neither immediate appeal nor long-run benefits.

Demand curve A curve that shows the number of units the market will buy in a given time period, at different prices that might be charged.

Demands Human wants that are backed by buying power.

Demographic segmentation Dividing the market into segments based on variables such as age, life-cycle stage, gender, income, occupation, education, religion, ethnicity, and generation.

Demography The study of human populations in terms of size, density, location, age, gender, race, occupation, and other statistics.

Department store A retail store that carries a wide variety of product lines, each operated as a separate department managed by specialist buyers or merchandisers.

Derived demand Business demand that ultimately comes from (derives from) the demand for consumer goods.

Descriptive research Marketing research to better describe marketing problems, situations, or markets, such as the market potential for a product or the demographics and attitudes of consumers.

Desirable products Products that give both high immediate satisfaction and high long-run benefits.

Differentiated (segmented) marketing A market-coverage strategy in which a firm decides to target several market segments and designs separate offers for each.

Differentiation Actually differentiating the market offering to create superior customer value.

Digital and social media marketing Using digital marketing tools such as Web sites, social media, mobile apps and ads, online video, e-mail, and blogs that engage consumers anywhere, at any time, via their digital devices.

Direct and digital marketing Engaging directly with carefully targeted individual consumers and customer communities to both obtain an immediate response and build lasting customer relationships.

Direct investment Entering a foreign market by developing foreign-based assembly or manufacturing facilities.

Direct marketing channel A marketing channel that has no intermediary levels.

Direct-mail marketing Marketing that occurs by sending an offer, announcement, reminder, or other item directly to a person at a particular address.

Direct-response television (DRTV) marketing Direct marketing via television, including direct-response television advertising (or infomercials) and interactive television (iTV) advertising.

Discount A straight reduction in price on purchases during a stated period of time or of larger quantities.

Discount store A retail operation that sells standard merchandise at lower prices by accepting lower margins and selling at higher volume.

Disintermediation The cutting out of marketing channel intermediaries by product or service producers or the displacement of traditional resellers by radical new types of intermediaries.

Dissonance-reducing buying behavior Consumer buying behavior in situations characterized by high involvement but few perceived differences among brands.

Distribution center A large, highly automated warehouse designed to receive goods from various plants and suppliers, take orders, fill them efficiently, and deliver goods to customers as quickly as possible.

Diversification Company growth through starting up or acquiring businesses outside the company's current products and markets.

Dynamic pricing Adjusting prices continually to meet the characteristics and needs of individual customers and situations.

E-mail marketing Sending highly targeted, highly personalized, relationship-building marketing messages via e-mail.

E-procurement Purchasing through electronic connections between buyers and sellers—usually online.

Economic community A group of nations organized to work toward common goals in the regulation of international trade.

Economic environment Economic factors that affect consumer purchasing power and spending patterns.

Environmental sustainability A management approach that involves developing strategies that both sustain the environment and produce profits for the company.

Environmental sustainability Developing strategies and practices that create a world economy that the planet can support indefinitely.

Environmentalism An organized movement of concerned citizens, businesses, and government agencies designed to protect and improve people's current and future living environment.

Ethnographic research A form of observational research that involves sending trained observers to watch and interact with consumers in their "natural environments."

Event marketing (or **event sponsorships**) Creating a brand-marketing event or serving as a sole or participating sponsor of events created by others.

Exchange The act of obtaining a desired object from someone by offering something in return.

Exclusive distribution Giving a limited number of dealers the exclusive right to distribute the company's products in their territories.

Execution style The approach, style, tone, words, and format used for executing an advertising message.

Experience curve (learning curve) The drop in the average per-unit production cost that comes with accumulated production experience.

Experimental research Gathering primary data by selecting matched groups of subjects, giving them different treatments, controlling related factors, and checking for differences in group responses.

Exploratory research Marketing research to gather preliminary information that will help define problems and suggest hypotheses.

Exporting Entering foreign markets by selling goods produced in the company's home country, often with little modification.

Factory outlet An off-price retailing operation that is owned and operated by a manufacturer and normally carries the manufacturer's surplus, discontinued, or irregular goods.

Fad A temporary period of unusually high sales driven by consumer enthusiasm and immediate product or brand popularity.

Fashion A currently accepted or popular style in a given field.

Fixed costs (overhead) Costs that do not vary with production or sales level.

FOB-origin pricing A geographical pricing strategy in which goods are placed free on board a carrier; the customer pays the freight from the factory to the destination.

Focus group interviewing Personal interviewing that involves inviting 6 to 10 people to gather for a few hours with a trained interviewer to talk about a product, service, or organization. The interviewer "focuses" the group discussion on important issues.

Follow-up The sales step in which a salesperson follows up after the sale to ensure customer satisfaction and repeat business.

Franchise A contractual association between a manufacturer, wholesaler, or service organization (a franchisor) and independent businesspeople (franchisees) who buy the right to own and operate one or more units in the franchise system.

Franchise organization A contractual vertical marketing system in which a channel member, called a franchisor, links several stages in the production-distribution process.

Freight-absorption pricing A geographical pricing strategy in which the seller absorbs all or part of the freight charges in order to get the desired business.

Gatekeepers People in an organization's buying center who control the flow of information to others.

Gender segmentation Dividing a market into different segments based on gender.

General need description The stage in the business buying process in which a buyer describes the general characteristics and quantity of a needed item.

Generation X The 49 million people born between 1965 and 1976 in the "birth dearth" following the baby boom.

Generation Z People born after 2000 (although many analysts include people born after 1995) who make up the kids, tweens, and teens markets.

Geographic segmentation Dividing a market into different geographical units, such as nations, states, regions, counties, cities, or even neighborhoods.

Geographical pricing Setting prices for customers located in different parts of the country or world.

Global firm A firm that, by operating in more than one country, gains R&D, production, marketing, and financial advantages in its costs and reputation that are not available to purely domestic competitors.

Good-value pricing Offering just the right combination of quality and good service at a fair price.

Government market Governmental units—federal, state, and local—that purchase or rent goods and services for carrying out the main functions of government.

Gross margin percentage The percentage of net sales remaining after cost of goods sold—calculated by dividing gross margin by net sales.

Group Two or more people who interact to accomplish individual or mutual goals.

Growth stage The PLC stage in which a product's sales start climbing quickly.

Growth-share matrix A portfolio-planning method that evaluates a company's SBUs in terms of market growth rate and relative market share.

Habitual buying behavior Consumer buying behavior in situations characterized by low consumer involvement and few significant perceived brand differences.

Handling objections The sales step in which a salesperson seeks out, clarifies, and overcomes any customer objections to buying.

Horizontal marketing system A channel arrangement in which two or more companies at one level join together to follow a new marketing opportunity.

Idea generation The systematic search for new product ideas.

Idea screening Screening new product ideas to spot good ones and drop poor ones as soon as possible.

Income segmentation Dividing a market into different income segments.

Independent off-price retailer An off-price retailer that is independently owned and operated or a division of a larger retail corporation.

Indirect marketing channel A marketing channel containing one or more intermediary levels.

Individual marketing Tailoring products and marketing programs to the needs and preferences of individual customers.

Industrial product A product bought by individuals and organizations for further processing or for use in conducting a business.

Influencers People in an organization's buying center who affect the buying decision; they often help define specifications and also provide information for evaluating alternatives.

Information search The stage of the buyer decision process in which the consumer is motivated to search for more information.

Innovative marketing A company should seek real product and marketing improvements.

Inside sales force Salespeople who conduct business from their offices via telephone, online and social media interactions, or visits from prospective buyers.

Institutional market Schools, hospitals, nursing homes, prisons, and other institutions that provide goods and services to people in their care.

Integrated logistics management The logistics concept that emphasizes teamwork—both inside the company and among all the marketing channel organizations—to maximize the performance of the entire distribution system.

Integrated marketing communications (IMC) Carefully integrating and coordinating the company's many communications channels to deliver a clear, consistent, and compelling message about the organization and its products.

Intensive distribution Stocking the product in as many outlets as possible.

Interactive marketing Training service employees in the fine art of interacting with customers to satisfy their needs.

Intermarket (cross-market) segmentation Forming segments of consumers who have similar needs and buying behaviors even though they are located in different countries.

Internal databases Collections of consumer and market information obtained from data sources within the company network.

Internal marketing Orienting and motivating customer-contact employees and supporting service employees to work as a team to provide customer satisfaction.

Introduction stage The PLC stage in which a new product is first distributed and made available for purchase.

Inventory turnover rate (or stockturn rate) The number of times an inventory turns over or is sold during a specified time period (often one year)—calculated based on costs, selling price, or units.

Joint ownership A cooperative venture in which a company creates a local business with investors in a foreign market, who share ownership and control.

Joint venturing Entering foreign markets by joining with foreign companies to produce or market a product or service.

Learning Changes in an individual's behavior arising from experience.

Licensing Entering foreign markets through developing an agreement with a licensee in the foreign market.

Lifestyle A person's pattern of living as expressed in his or her activities, interests, and opinions.

Line extension Extending an existing brand name to new forms, colors, sizes, ingredients, or flavors of an existing product category.

Local marketing Tailoring brands and marketing to the needs and wants of local customer segments—cities, neighborhoods, and even specific stores.

Macroenvironment The larger societal forces that affect the microenvironment—demographic, economic, natural, technological, political, and cultural forces.

Madison & Vine A term that has come to represent the merging of advertising and entertainment in an effort to break through the clutter and create new avenues for reaching customers with more engaging messages.

Management contracting A joint venture in which the domestic firm supplies the management know-how to a foreign company that supplies the capital; the domestic firm exports management services rather than products.

Manufacturers' and retailers' branches and offices Wholesaling by sellers or buyers themselves rather than through independent wholesalers.

Market The set of all actual and potential buyers of a product or service.

Market challenger A runner-up firm that is fighting hard to increase its market share in an industry.

Market development Company growth by identifying and developing new market segments for current company products.

Market follower A runner-up firm that wants to hold its share in an industry without rocking the boat.

Market leader The firm in an industry with the largest market share.

Market nicher A firm that serves small segments that the other firms in an industry overlook or ignore.

Market offerings Some combination of products, services, information, or experiences offered to a market to satisfy a need or want.

Market penetration Company growth by increasing sales of current products to current market segments without changing the product.

Market potential The upper limit of market demand.

Market segment A group of consumers who respond in a similar way to a given set of marketing efforts.

Market segmentation Dividing a market into smaller segments of buyers with distinct needs, characteristics, or behaviors that might require separate marketing strategies or mixes.

Market share Company sales divided by market sales.

Market targeting (targeting) Evaluating each market segment's attractiveness and selecting one or more segments to enter.

Market-centered company A company that pays balanced attention to both customers and competitors in designing its marketing strategies.

Market-penetration pricing Setting a low price for a new product in order to attract a large number of buyers and a large market share.

Market-skimming pricing (price skimming) Setting a high price for a new product to skim maximum revenues layer by layer from the segments willing to pay the high price; the company makes fewer but more profitable sales.

Marketing The process by which companies create value for customers and build strong customer relationships in order to capture value from customers in return.

Marketing channel (distribution channel) A set of interdependent organizations that help make a product or service available for use or consumption by the consumer or business user.

Marketing channel design Designing effective marketing channels by analyzing customer needs, setting channel objectives, identifying major channel alternatives, and evaluating those alternatives.

Marketing channel management Selecting, managing, and motivating individual channel members and evaluating their performance over time.

Marketing concept A philosophy in which achieving organizational goals depends on knowing the needs and wants of target markets and delivering the desired satisfactions better than competitors do.

Marketing control Measuring and evaluating the results of marketing strategies and plans and taking corrective action to ensure that the objectives are achieved.

Marketing environment The actors and forces outside marketing that affect marketing management's ability to build and maintain successful relationships with target customers.

Marketing implementation Turning marketing strategies and plans into marketing actions to accomplish strategic marketing objectives.

Marketing information system (MIS) People and procedures dedicated to assessing information needs, developing the needed information, and helping decision makers to use the information to generate and validate actionable customer and market insights.

Marketing intermediaries Firms that help the company to promote, sell, and distribute its goods to final buyers.

Marketing logistics (physical distribution) Planning, implementing, and controlling the physical flow of materials, final goods, and related information from points of origin to points of consumption to meet customer requirements at a profit.

Marketing management The art and science of choosing target markets and building profitable relationships with them.

Marketing mix The set of tactical marketing tools—product, price, place, and promotion—that the firm blends to produce the response it wants in the target market.

Marketing myopia The mistake of paying more attention to the specific products a company offers than to the benefits and experiences produced by these products.

Marketing research The systematic design, collection, analysis, and reporting of data relevant to a specific marketing situation facing an organization.

Marketing return on investment (or marketing ROI) The net return from a marketing investment divided by the costs of the marketing investment.

Marketing return on sales (or marketing ROS) The percent of net sales attributable to the net marketing contribution—calculated by dividing net marketing contribution by net sales.

Marketing strategy The marketing logic by which the company hopes to create customer value and achieve profitable customer relationships.

Marketing strategy development Designing an initial marketing strategy for a new product based on the product concept.

Marketing Web site A Web site that engages consumers to move them closer to a direct purchase or other marketing outcome.

Markup The difference between a company's selling price for a product and its cost to manufacture or purchase it.

Markup chain The sequence of markups used by firms at each level in a channel.

Maturity stage The PLC stage in which a product's sales growth slows or levels off.

Merchant wholesaler An independently owned wholesale business that takes title to the merchandise it handles.

Microenvironment The actors close to the company that affect its ability to serve its customers—the company, suppliers, marketing intermediaries, customer markets, competitors, and publics.

Micromarketing Tailoring products and marketing programs to the needs and wants of specific individuals and local customer segments; it includes *local marketing* and *individual marketing*.

Millennials (or **Generation Y**) The 83 million children of the baby boomers born between 1977 and 2000.

Mission statement A statement of the organization's purpose—what it wants to accomplish in the larger environment.

Mobile marketing Marketing messages, promotions, and other content delivered to on-the-go consumers through mobile phones, smartphones, tablets, and other mobile devices.

Modified rebuy A business buying situation in which the buyer wants to modify product specifications, prices, terms, or suppliers.

Motive (drive) A need that is sufficiently pressing to direct the person to seek satisfaction of the need.

Multichannel distribution system A distribution system in which a single firm sets up two or more marketing channels to reach one or more customer segments.

Multichannel marketing Marketing both through stores and other traditional offline channels and through digital, online, social media, and mobile channels.

Multimodal transportation Combining two or more modes of transportation.

Natural environment The physical environment and the natural resources that are needed as inputs by marketers or that are affected by marketing activities.

Need recognition The first stage of the buyer decision process, in which the consumer recognizes a problem or need.

Needs States of felt deprivation.

Net marketing contribution (NMC) A measure of marketing profitability that includes only components of profitability controlled by marketing.

Net profit percentage The percentage of each sales dollar going to profit—calculated by dividing net profits by net sales.

New product A good, service, or idea that is perceived by some potential customers as new.

New product development The development of original products, product improvements, product modifications, and new brands through the firm's own product development efforts.

New task A business buying situation in which the buyer purchases a product or service for the first time.

Nonpersonal communication channels Media that carry messages without personal contact or feedback, including major media, atmospheres, and events.

Objective-and-task method Developing the promotion budget by (1) defining specific promotion objectives, (2) determining the tasks needed to achieve these objectives, and (3) estimating the costs of performing these tasks. The sum of these costs is the proposed promotion budget.

Observational research Gathering primary data by observing relevant people, actions, and situations.

Occasion segmentation Dividing the market into segments according to occasions when buyers get the idea to buy, actually make their purchase, or use the purchased item.

Off-price retailer A retailer that buys at less-than-regular wholesale prices and sells at less than retail.

Online advertising Advertising that appears while consumers are browsing online, including display ads, search-related ads, online classifieds, and other forms.

Online focus groups Gathering a small group of people online with a trained moderator to chat about a product, service, or organization and gain qualitative insights about consumer attitudes and behavior.

Online marketing Marketing via the Internet using company Web sites, online ads and promotions, e-mail, online video, and blogs.

Online marketing research Collecting primary data online through Internet surveys, online focus groups, Web-based experiments, or tracking of consumers' online behavior.

Online social networks Online social communities—blogs, social networking Web sites, and other online communities—where people socialize or exchange information and opinions.

Operating expense percentage The portion of net sales going to operating expenses—calculated by dividing total expenses by net sales.

Operating ratios The ratios of selected operating statement items to net sales.

Opinion leader A person within a reference group who, because of special skills, knowledge, personality, or other characteristics, exerts social influence on others.

Optional-product pricing The pricing of optional or accessory products along with a main product.

Order-routine specification The stage of the business buying process in which the buyer writes the final order with the chosen supplier(s), listing the technical specifications, quantity needed, expected time of delivery, return policies, and warranties.

Outside sales force (or field sales force) Salespeople who travel to call on customers in the field.

Packaging The activities of designing and producing the container or wrapper for a product.

Partner relationship management Working closely with partners in other company departments and outside the company to jointly bring greater value to customers.

Percentage-of-sales method Setting the promotion budget at a certain percentage of current or forecasted sales or as a percentage of the unit sales price.

Perception The process by which people select, organize, and interpret information to form a meaningful picture of the world.

Performance review The stage of the business buying process in which the buyer assesses the performance of the supplier and decides to continue, modify, or drop the arrangement.

Personal communication channels Channels through which two or more people communicate directly with each other, including face to face, on the phone, via mail or e-mail, or even through an Internet "chat."

Personality The unique psychological characteristics that distinguish a person or group.

Personal selling Personal presentation by the firm's sales force for the purpose of engaging customers, making sales, and building customer relationships.

Pleasing products Products that give high immediate satisfaction but may hurt consumers in the long run.

Political environment Laws, government agencies, and pressure groups that influence and limit various organizations and individuals in a given society.

Portfolio analysis The process by which management evaluates the products and businesses that make up the company.

Positioning Arranging for a market offering to occupy a clear, distinctive, and desirable place relative to competing products in the minds of target consumers.

Positioning statement A statement that summarizes company or brand positioning using this form: To (target segment and need) our (brand) is (concept) that (point of difference).

Postpurchase behavior The stage of the buyer decision process in which consumers take further action after purchase, based on their satisfaction or dissatisfaction.

Preapproach The sales step in which a salesperson learns as much as possible about a prospective customer before making a sales call.

Presentation The sales step in which a salesperson tells the "value story" to the buyer, showing how the company's offer solves the customer's problems.

Price The amount of money charged for a product or service, or the sum of the values that customers exchange for the benefits of having or using the product or service.

Price elasticity A measure of the sensitivity of demand to changes in price.

Primary data Information collected for the specific purpose at hand.

Pro forma (or **projected**) **profit-and-loss statement** (or **income statement** or **operating statement**) A statement that shows projected revenues less budgeted expenses and estimates the projected net profit for an organization, product, or brand during a specific planning period, typically a year.

Problem recognition The first stage of the business buying process in which someone in the company recognizes a problem or need that can be met by acquiring a good or a service.

Product Anything that can be offered to a market for attention, acquisition, use, or consumption that might satisfy a want or need.

Product adaptation Adapting a product to meet local conditions or wants in foreign markets.

Product bundle pricing Combining several products and offering the bundle at a reduced price.

Product concept A detailed version of the new product idea stated in meaningful consumer terms.

Product concept The idea that consumers will favor products that offer the most quality, performance, and features; therefore, the organization should devote its energy to making continuous product improvements.

Product development Company growth by offering modified or new products to current market segments.

Product development Developing the product concept into a physical product to ensure that the product idea can be turned into a workable market offering.

Product invention Creating new products or services for foreign markets.

Product life cycle (PLC) The course of a product's sales and profits over its lifetime.

Product line A group of products that are closely related because they function in a similar manner, are sold to the same customer groups, are marketed through the same types of outlets, or fall within given price ranges.

Product line pricing Setting the price steps between various products in a product line based on cost differences between the products, customer evaluations of different features, and competitors' prices.

Product mix (or **product portfolio**) The set of all product lines and items that a particular seller offers for sale.

Product position The way a product is defined by consumers on important attributes—the place the product occupies in consumers' minds relative to competing products.

Product quality The characteristics of a product or service that bear on its ability to satisfy stated or implied customer needs.

Product sales force structure A sales force organization in which salespeople specialize in selling only a portion of the company's products or lines.

Product specification The stage of the business buying process in which the buying organization decides on and specifies the best technical product characteristics for a needed item.

Product/market expansion grid A portfolio-planning tool for identifying company growth opportunities through market penetration, market development, product development, or diversification.

Production concept The idea that consumers will favor products that are available and highly affordable; therefore, the organization should focus on improving production and distribution efficiency.

Profit-and-loss statement (or **income statement** or **operating statement**) A statement that shows actual revenues less expenses and net profit for an organization, product, or brand during a specific planning period, typically a year.

Promotion mix (or **marketing communications mix**) The specific blend of promotion tools that the company uses to persuasively communicate customer value and build customer relationships.

Promotional pricing Temporarily pricing products below the list price, and sometimes even below cost, to increase short-run sales.

Proposal solicitation The stage of the business buying process in which the buyer invites qualified suppliers to submit proposals.

Prospecting The sales step in which a salesperson or company identifies qualified potential customers.

Psychographic segmentation Dividing a market into different segments based on social class, lifestyle, or personality characteristics.

Psychological pricing Pricing that considers the psychology of prices and not simply the economics; the price is used to say something about the product.

Public Any group that has an actual or potential interest in or impact on an organization's ability to achieve its objectives.

Public relations (PR) Building good relations with the company's various publics by obtaining favorable publicity, building up a good corporate image, and handling or heading off unfavorable rumors, stories, and events.

Public relations (PR) Building good relations with the company's various publics by obtaining favorable publicity; building up a good corporate image; and handling or heading off unfavorable rumors, stories, and events.

Pull strategy A promotion strategy that calls for spending a lot on consumer advertising and promotion to induce final consumers to buy the product, creating a demand vacuum that "pulls" the product through the channel.

Purchase decision The buyer's decision about which brand to purchase.

Push strategy A promotion strategy that calls for using the sales force and trade promotion to push the product through channels. The producer promotes the product to channel members who in turn promote it to final consumers.

Reference prices Prices that buyers carry in their minds and refer to when they look at a given product.

Relevant costs Costs that will occur in the future and that will vary across the alternatives being considered.

Retailer A business whose sales come *primarily* from retailing.

Retailing All the activities involved in selling goods or services directly to final consumers for their personal, nonbusiness use.

Return on advertising investment The net return on advertising investment divided by the costs of the advertising investment.

Return on investment (ROI) A measure of managerial effectiveness and efficiency—net profit before taxes divided by total investment.

Return on investment (ROI) pricing (or **target-return pricing**) A cost-based pricing method that determines price based on a specified rate of return on investment.

Sales force management Analyzing, planning, implementing, and controlling sales force activities.

Sales promotion Short-term incentives to encourage the purchase or sale of a product or a service.

Salesperson An individual who represents a company to customers by performing one or more of the following activities: prospecting, communicating, selling, servicing, information gathering, and relationship building.

Sales quota A standard that states the amount a salesperson should sell and how sales should be divided among the company's products.

Salutary products Products that have low immediate appeal but may benefit consumers in the long run.

Sample A segment of the population selected for marketing research to represent the population as a whole.

Secondary data Information that already exists somewhere, having been collected for another purpose.

Segmented pricing Selling a product or service at two or more prices, where the difference in prices is not based on differences in costs.

Selective distribution The use of more than one but fewer than all of the intermediaries that are willing to carry the company's products.

Selling concept The idea that consumers will not buy enough of the firm's products unless the firm undertakes a large-scale selling and promotion effort.

Selling process The steps that salespeople follow when selling, which include prospecting and qualifying, preapproach, approach, presentation and demonstration, handling objections, closing, and follow-up.

Sense-of-mission marketing A company should define its mission in broad social terms rather than narrow product terms.

Service An activity, benefit, or satisfaction offered for sale that is essentially intangible and does not result in the ownership of anything.

Service inseparability Services are produced and consumed at the same time and cannot be separated from their providers.

Service intangibility Services cannot be seen, tasted, felt, heard, or smelled before they are bought.

Service perishability Services cannot be stored for later sale or use.

Service profit chain The chain that links service firm profits with employee and customer satisfaction.

Service retailer A retailer whose product line is actually a service; examples include hotels, airlines, banks, colleges, and many others.

Service variability The quality of services may vary greatly depending on who provides them and when, where, and how they are provided.

Share of customer The portion of the customer's purchasing that a company gets in its product categories.

Shopper marketing Focusing the entire marketing process on turning shoppers into buyers as they approach the point of sale, whether during in-store, online, or mobile shopping.

Shopping center A group of retail businesses built on a site that is planned, developed, owned, and managed as a unit.

Shopping product A consumer product that the customer, in the process of selecting and purchasing, usually compares on such attributes as suitability, quality, price, and style.

Showrooming The shopping practice of coming into retail store showrooms to check out merchandise and prices but instead buying from an online-only rival, sometimes while in the store.

Social class Relatively permanent and ordered divisions in a society whose members share similar values, interests, and behaviors.

Social marketing The use of commercial marketing concepts and tools in programs designed to influence individuals' behavior to improve their well-being and that of society.

Social media Independent and commercial online communities where people congregate, socialize, and exchange views and information.

Social selling Using online, mobile, and social media to engage customers, build stronger customer relationships, and augment sales performance.

Societal marketing A company should make marketing decisions by considering consumers' wants, the company's requirements, consumers' long-run interests, and society's long-run interests.

Societal marketing concept The idea that a company's marketing decisions should consider consumers' wants, the company's requirements, consumers' long-run interests, and society's long-run interests.

Spam Unsolicited, unwanted commercial e-mail messages.

Specialty product A consumer product with unique characteristics or brand identification for which a significant group of buyers is willing to make a special purchase effort.

Specialty store A retail store that carries a narrow product line with a deep assortment within that line.

Standardized global marketing An international marketing strategy that basically uses the same marketing strategy and mix in all of the company's international markets.

Store brand (or **private brand**) A brand created and owned by a reseller of a product or service.

Straight product extension Marketing a product in a foreign market without making any changes to the product.

Straight rebuy A business buying situation in which the buyer routinely reorders something without any modifications.

Strategic group A group of firms in an industry following the same or a similar strategy.

Strategic planning The process of developing and maintaining a strategic fit between the organization's goals and capabilities and its changing marketing opportunities.

Style A basic and distinctive mode of expression.

Subculture A group of people with shared value systems based on common life experiences and situations.

Supermarket A large, low-cost, low-margin, high-volume, self-service store that carries a wide variety of grocery and household products.

Superstore A store much larger than a regular supermarket that offers a large assortment of routinely purchased food products, nonfood items, and services.

Supplier development Systematic development of networks of supplier-partners to ensure an appropriate and dependable supply of products and materials for use in making products or reselling them to others.

Supplier search The stage of the business buying process in which the buyer tries to find the best vendors.

Supplier selection The stage of the business buying process in which the buyer reviews proposals and selects a supplier or suppliers.

Supply chain management Managing upstream and downstream value-added flows of materials, final goods, and related information among suppliers, the company, resellers, and final consumers.

Survey research Gathering primary data by asking people questions about their knowledge, attitudes, preferences, and buying behavior.

Sustainable marketing Socially and environmentally responsible marketing that meets the present needs of consumers and businesses while also preserving or enhancing the ability of future generations to meet their needs.

SWOT analysis An overall evaluation of the company's strengths (S), weaknesses (W), opportunities (O), and threats (T).

Systems selling (or **solutions selling**) Buying a packaged solution to a problem from a single seller, thus avoiding all the separate decisions involved in a complex buying situation.

Target costing Pricing that starts with an ideal selling price, then targets costs that will ensure that the price is met.

Target market A set of buyers sharing common needs or characteristics that the company decides to serve.

Team selling Using teams of people from sales, marketing, engineering, finance, technical support, and even upper management to service large, complex accounts.

Team-based new product development New product development in which various company departments work closely together, overlapping the steps in the product development process to save time and increase effectiveness.

Technological environment Forces that create new technologies, creating new product and market opportunities.

Telemarketing Using the telephone to sell directly to customers.

Territorial sales force structure A sales force organization that assigns each salesperson to an exclusive geographic territory in which that salesperson sells the company's full line.

Test marketing The stage of new product development in which the product and its proposed marketing program are tested in realistic market settings.

Third-party logistics (3PL) provider An independent logistics provider that performs any or all of the functions required to get a client's product to market.

Total costs The sum of the fixed and variable costs for any given level of production.

Total market demand The total volume that would be bought by a defined consumer group in a defined geographic area in a defined time period in a defined marketing environment under a defined level and mix of industry marketing effort.

Trade promotions Sales promotion tools used to persuade resellers to carry a brand, give it shelf space, and promote it in advertising

Undifferentiated (mass) marketing A market-coverage strategy in which a firm decides to ignore market segment differences and go after the whole market with one offer.

Uniform-delivered pricing A geographical pricing strategy in which the company charges the same price plus freight to all customers, regardless of their location.

Unit contribution The amount that each unit contributes to covering fixed costs—the difference between price and variable costs.

Unsought product A consumer product that the consumer either does not know about or knows about but does not normally consider buying.

Users Members of the buying organization who will actually use the purchased product or service.

Value chain The series of internal departments that carry out value-creating activities to design, produce, market, deliver, and support a firm's products.

Value delivery network A network composed of the company, suppliers, distributors, and, ultimately, customers who partner with each other to improve the performance of the entire system in delivering customer value.

Value proposition The full positioning of a brand—the full mix of benefits on which it is positioned.

Value-added pricing Attaching value-added features and services to differentiate a company's offers and charging higher prices.

Value-based pricing Offering just the right combination of quality and good service at a fair price.

Variable costs Costs that vary directly with the level of production.

Variety-seeking buying behavior Consumer buying behavior in situations characterized by low consumer involvement but significant perceived brand differences.

Vertical marketing system (VMS) A channel structure in which producers, wholesalers, and retailers act as a unified system. One channel member owns the others, has contracts with them, or has so much power that they all cooperate.

Viral marketing The digital version of word-of-mouth marketing: videos, ads, and other marketing content that is so infectious that customers will seek it out or pass it along to friends.

Wants The form human needs take as they are shaped by culture and individual personality.

Warehouse club An off-price retailer that sells a limited selection of brand name grocery items, appliances, clothing, and other goods at deep discounts to members who pay annual membership fees.

Whole-channel view Designing international channels that take into account the entire global supply chain and marketing channel, forging an effective global value delivery network.

Wholesaler A firm engaged *primarily* in wholesaling activities.

Wholesaling All the activities involved in selling goods and services to those buying for resale or business use.

Word-of-mouth influence The impact of the personal words and recommendations of trusted friends, family, associates, and other consumers on buying behavior.

Workload method An approach to determining sales force size based on the workload required and the time available for selling.

Zone pricing A geographical pricing strategy in which the company sets up two or more zones. All customers within a zone pay the same total price; the more distant the zone, the higher the price.

INDEX

Name, Organization, Brand, Company Index

Note: A reference appearing in italic indicates a figure on that page. The letter n indicates the reference note number on the page containing the name listed

B

Subject Index

Note: Page numbers in italic indicate a photo or figure appears on that page.

N

T

[illegible] Improves Student Engagement Before, During, and After Class

[illegible]